Allez, viens!®

Your passport to proficiency

Sans frontières

Plan your itinerary for success

What's your **Destination?**

Communication!

Allez, viens! takes your classroom there.

It's even possible that **"What's next?"** will become your students' favorite question!

Communication and culture in context

The clear structure of each chapter makes it easy for students to present, practice, and apply language skills—all in the context of the location where the chapter takes place!

Grammar support and practice in every lesson

Allez, viens! builds a proven communicative approach on a solid foundation of grammar and vocabulary so students become proficient readers, writers, and speakers of French. With the Travaux pratiques de grammaire, Grammar Tutor, and the CD-ROM and DVD Tutors, students can practice the way they learn best.

Technology that takes you there

Bring the world into your classroom with integrated technology: CD-ROM, DVD, and Internet resources, including an Online Student Edition.

Assessment for state and national standards

To help you incorporate standardized test practice, the Standardized Assessment Tutor provides reading, writing, and math tests in French that target the skills students need. The Joie de lire Reader and Reading Strategies and Skills Handbook offer additional reading practice and reading skills development.

Easy lesson planning for all learning styles

Planning lessons has never been easier with a Lesson Planner with Differentiated Instruction, an editable One-Stop Planner® CD-ROM, and a Student Make-Up Assignments with Alternative Quizzes resource.

Travel a balanced program that's easy to navigate.

Le monde à votre portée!

Allez, viens!

Program components

Texts
- Student Edition
- Annotated Teacher's Edition

Middle School Program
- En avant! 1A Student Edition
- En route! 1B Student Edition
- 1A/1B Annotated Teacher's Edition
- Middle School Teaching Resources, including Middle School Lesson Plans
- Exploratory Guide

Planning and Presenting
- One-Stop Planner CD-ROM with ExamView® Test Generator
- Lesson Planner with Differentiated Instruction
- Student Make-Up Assignments with Alternative Quizzes
- Teaching Transparencies

Grammar
- Travaux pratiques de grammaire
- Grammar Tutor for Students of French

Reading and Writing
- Reading Strategies and Skills Handbook
- Joie de lire Reader
- Cahier d'activités

Listening and Speaking
- Audio CD Program
- Listening Activities
- Activities for Communication
- TPR Storytelling Book (Levels 1 and 2)

Assessment
- Testing Program
- Alternative Assessment Guide
- Student Make-Up Assignments with Alternative Quizzes
- Standardized Assessment Tutor

Technology
- One-Stop Planner CD-ROM with ExamView Test Generator
- Audio CD Program
- Interactive CD-ROM Tutor
- Video Program
- Video Guide
- DVD (Levels 1–3)
- Online Edition

Internet
- go.hrw.com
- www.hrw.com

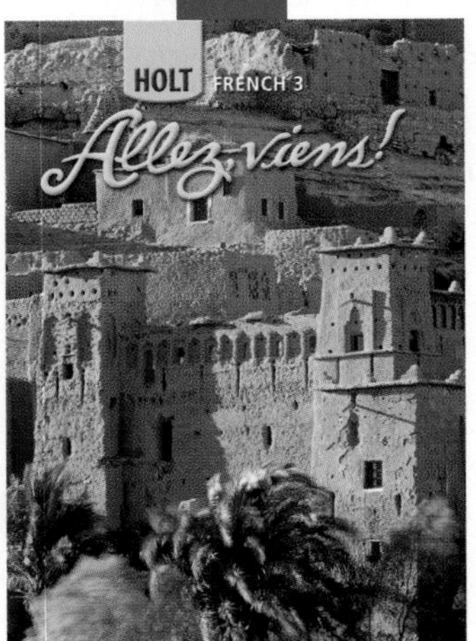

Destination: Communication

TEACHER'S EDITION

HOLT FRENCH 1

Allez, viens!

HOLT, RINEHART AND WINSTON
A Harcourt Education Company
Orlando • **Austin** • New York • San Diego • Toronto • London

Printed in the United States of America

ISBN 0-03-036946-0

1 2 3 4 5 6 7 8 9 048 09 08 07 06 05 04

ACKNOWLEDGMENTS

Photography Credits

Abbreviations used: (t) top, (c) center, (l) left, (r) right, (bkgd) background

Front Cover: © David Noton/Masterfile

Back Cover: © Peter Byron/PhotoEdit; (frame) © 2006 Image Farm, Inc.

Front Matter T9, HRW Photo/Sam Dudgeon; T29, Courtesy Neel Heisel; T43 (l), HRW Photo/Lance Schriner. Preliminary Chapter T74 (l), Kathy Willens/Wide World Photos, Inc.; (c), Gastaud/Sipa Press; (r), Sean Roberts/Everett Collection. Chapter 1, 15D, Robert Fried; 32, Courtesy Sarah Sherman; 40, Courtesy Pai Rosenthal. Chapter 2 45D (l), © Philippe Renault/Hémisphères; (r), Robert Fried; 55, Courtesy Van Ruckman; 67, Courtesy Sharon Telich. Chapter 3, 73D (l), SuperStock; (r), Robert Fried; 73E (both), HRW Photo/Edge Productions; 85, Courtesy Colleen Turpin; 96, Courtesy Paula Gill. Chapter 4, 105D (l), SuperStock; (r), Robert Fried; 116, Courtesy Todd Bowen; 129, Courtesy June Ricks. Chapter 5, 139D (l), © David R. Frazier Photolibrary; (r), HRW Photo/Victoria Smith; 139E (r) HRW Photo/Edge Productions; 139G, HRW Photo/Edge Productions; 156, Courtesy Jacqueline Donnelly; 162, Courtesy Colleen Webster. Chapter 6, 167D (l), SuperStock; (r), HRW Photo/Sam Dudgeon; 176, Courtesy James May. Chapter 7, 197D (l), Owen Franken/Stock Boston; (r), Robert Fried; 205, Courtesy Bernadette Takano; 219, Courtesy J. Eames. Chapter 8, 229C (l), HRW Photo/Sam Dudgeon; (r), HRW Photo/Eric Beggs; 229D (l), G. Huet/SuperStock; (r), Robert Fried; 249, Courtesy Lynn Payne; 253, Courtesy Beth Pierce. Chapter 9, 263D (l), © Laurent Giraudou/Hémisphères; (r), Robert Fried; 279, Courtesy Nicole Mitescu; 285, Courtesy Elaine Bind. Chapter 10, 291D (l), Superstock; (r), HRW Photo/Michelle Bridwell; 297, Courtesy Carol Chadwick; 316, Courtesy Paula Bernard. Chapter 11, 321D, HRW Photo/Sam Dudgeon; 329, Courtesy Laura Grable; 343, Courtesy Ricky Adamson. Chapter 12, 353D, Robert Fried; 371, Courtesy Melinda Marks; 377, Courtesy Tanya Stevenson.

Art Credits

All art, unless otherwise noted, by Holt, Rinehart & Winston.
Preliminary Chapter: T76-1, MapQuest.com. Chapter 2: 45H, Guy Maestracci. Chapter 7: 197H, Vincent Rio. Chapter 12: 353D, Edson Campos; 353G, Brian Stevens.

ACKNOWLEDGMENTS continued on page R64 which is an extension of the copyright page.

Allez viens! Level 1 Annotated Teacher's Edition

CONTRIBUTING WRITERS

Jennie Bowser Chao
Consultant
East Lansing, MI

Ms. Chao was the principal writer of the Level 1 *Annotated Teacher's Edition.*

Jayne Abrate
The University of Missouri
Rolla Campus
Rolla, MO

Dr. Abrate contributed teaching suggestions, notes, and background information for the Location Openers of the Level 1 *Annotated Teacher's Edition.*

Margaret Sellstrom
Consultant
Austin, TX

Ms. Sellstrom contributed answers to activities of the Level 1 *Annotated Teacher's Edition.*

TEACHER-TO-TEACHER CONTRIBUTORS

Sarah Sherman
Johnson Middle School
Walpole, MA

Pai Rosenthal
Rachel Carson Middle School
Herndon, VA

Van W. Ruckman
North High School
Evansville, IN

Sharon Telich
Westside Middle School
Omaha, NE

Colleen Turpin
Lionville Middle School
Downingtown, PA

Paula Gill
Bethel Middle School
Bethel, CT

Todd Bowen
Adlai E. Stevenson High School
Lincolnshire, IL

June Ricks
Fort Zumwalt West HS
O'Fallon, MO

Jacqueline King Donnelly
Holland High School
Holland, MI

Colleen Webster
Olathe North High School
Olathe, KS

James C. May
Rufus King High School
Milwaukee, WI

Dr. Susan Hayden
Aloha High School
Beaverton, OR

Bernadette Takano
Norman North High School
Norman, OK

Dr. J. Eames
Pulaski County High
Somerset, KY

Beth Pierce
Columbia High School
Columbia, MS

Lynn Payne
Hidden Valley High School
Roanoke, VA

Nicole Mitescu
Claremont High School
Claremont, CA

Elaine Bind
McDonogh School
Ownings Mills, MD

Carol Chadwick
Taipei American School
Taipei, Taiwan

Paula Bernard
Sandy Creek High School
Fayette County, GA

Ricky Adamson
Forrest City High School
Forrest City, AR

Laura Grable
Riverhead Middle School
Riverhead, NY

Melinda Marks
Grant Union High School
Sacramento, CA

Tanya Stevenson
Terrill Middle School
Scotch Plains, NJ

PROFESSIONAL ESSAYS

Bringing Standards into the Classroom
Paul Sandrock
Foreign Language Consultant
Department of Public Instruction
Madison, WI

Reading Strategies and Skills
Nancy A. Humbach
Miami University
Oxford, OH

Using Portfolios in the Language Classroom
Jo Anne S. Wilson
J. Wilson Associates
Glen Arbor, MI

Teaching Culture
Nancy A. Humbach
Miami University
Oxford, OH

Dorothea Bruschke
Parkway School District
Chesterfield, MO

Learning Styles and Multi-Modality Teaching
Mary B. McGehee
Louisiana State University
Baton Rouge, LA

To the Teacher

We have seen significant advances in modern language curriculum practices:

1. a redefinition of the objectives of foreign language study involving a commitment to the development of proficiency in the four skills and in cultural awareness;
2. a recognition of the need for longer sequences of study;
3. a new student-centered approach that redefines the role of the teacher as facilitator and encourages students to take a more active role in their learning;
4. the inclusion of students of all learning abilities.

The new Holt, Rinehart and Winston World Languages programs take into account not only these advances in the field of foreign language education but also the input of teachers and students around the country.

Principles and Practices

As nations become increasingly interdependent, the need for effective communication and sensitivity to other cultures becomes more important. Today's youth must be culturally and linguistically prepared to participate in a global society. At Holt, Rinehart and Winston, we believe that proficiency in more than one language is essential to meeting this need.

The primary goal of the Holt, Rinehart and Winston World Languages programs is to help students develop linguistic proficiency and cultural sensitivity. By interweaving language and culture, our programs seek to broaden students' communication skills while at the same time deepening their appreciation of other cultures.

We believe that all students can benefit from foreign language instruction. We recognize that not everyone learns at the same rate or in the same way; nevertheless, we believe that all students should have the opportunity to acquire language proficiency to a degree commensurate with their individual abilities.

Holt, Rinehart and Winston's World Languages programs are designed to accommodate all students by appealing to a variety of learning styles.

We believe that effective language programs should motivate students. Students deserve an answer to the question they often ask: "Why are we doing this?" They need to have goals that are interesting, practical, clearly stated, and attainable.

Holt, Rinehart and Winston's World Languages programs promote success. They present relevant content in manageable increments that encourage students to attain achievable functional objectives.

We believe that proficiency in another language is best nurtured by programs that encourage students to think critically and to take risks when expressing themselves in the language. We also recognize that students should strive for accuracy in communication. While it is imperative that students have a knowledge of the basic structures of the language, it is also important that they go beyond the simple manipulation of forms.

Holt, Rinehart and Winston's World Languages programs reflect a careful progression of activities that guide students from comprehensible input of authentic language through structured practice to creative, personalized expression. This progression, accompanied by consistent re-entry and spiraling of functions, vocabulary, and structures, provides students with the tools and the confidence to express themselves in their new language.

Finally, we believe that a complete program of language instruction should take into account the needs of teachers in today's increasingly demanding classrooms.

At Holt, Rinehart and Winston, we have designed programs that offer practical teacher support and provide resources to meet individual learning and teaching styles.

Annotated Teacher's Edition

Contents

Pacing and Planning

Traditional Schedule

Days of instruction: 180

Location Opener	2 days per Location Opener x 6 Location Openers	12 days
Chapter	13 days per chapter x 12 chapters	156 days
		168 days

If you are teaching on a traditional schedule, we suggest following the plan above and spending 13 days per chapter. A complete set of lesson plans in the interleaf provides detailed suggestions for each chapter. For more suggestions, see the **Lesson Planner with Differentiated Instruction.**

Chapitre 9 : Au téléphone
Suggested Lesson Plans *50-Minute Schedule*

Block Schedule

Blocks of instruction: 90

Location Opener	1/2 block per Location Opener x 6 Location Openers	3 blocks
Chapter	7 blocks per chapter x 12 chapters	84 blocks
		87 blocks

If you are teaching on a block schedule, we suggest following the plan above and spending seven blocks per chapter. A complete set of lesson plans in the interleaf provides detailed suggestions for each chapter. For more suggestions, see the **Lesson Planner with Differentiated Instruction.**

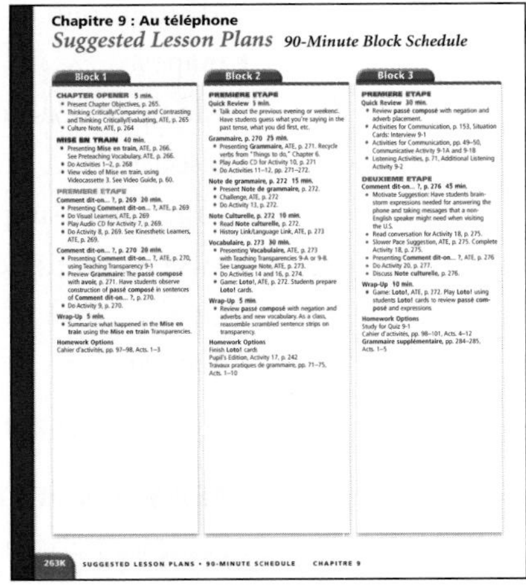
Chapitre 9 : Au téléphone
Suggested Lesson Plans *90-Minute Block Schedule*

Use the **One-Stop Planner CD-ROM with Test Generator** to aid in lesson planning and pacing.

- Editable lesson plans with direct links to teaching resources
- Printable worksheets from resource books
- Direct launches to the HRW Internet activities
- Video and audio segments
- Test Generator
- Clip Art for vocabulary items

Pacing Tips

At the beginning of each chapter, you will find a Pacing Tip to help you plan your lessons.

Articulation Across Levels

The following chart shows how topics are repeated across levels in ***Allez, viens!*** from the end of Level 1 to the beginning of Level 3.

- In each level, the last chapter is a review chapter.
- In Levels 2 and 3, the first two chapters review the previous level.

LEVEL 1

CHAPTER 12
Review of Level 1

- Contractions with **de** and **à**
- The partitive
- The **passé composé**
- Possessive adjectives
- Asking for and giving directions
- Asking for advice
- Expressing need
- Family vocabulary
- Inviting
- Making requests
- Making suggestions
- Making excuses
- Pointing out places; things

LEVEL 2

Review of Level 1

CHAPTER 1

- Adjective agreement
- **Avoir** and **être**
- **Choisir** and other **–ir** verbs
- The imperative
- The future with **aller**
- Asking for information
- Asking for and giving advice
- Asking for, making, and responding to suggestions
- Clothing and colors
- Describing yourself and others
- Expressing likes and dislikes
- Family vocabulary
- Relating a series of events
- Pronunciation: **liaison**

CHAPTER 2

- Using **tu** and **vous**
- Question formation
- Adjectives that precede the noun
- Contractions with **de** and **à**
- Prepositions of location
- Asking for and giving directions
- Asking how someone is feeling and telling how you are feeling
- Making suggestions
- Pointing out where things are
- Paying compliments
- Pronunciation: intonation

CHAPTER 12
Review of Level 2

- The **passé composé** and the **imparfait**
- Asking for and giving information
- Asking for and giving advice
- Clothing vocabulary
- Complaining
- Describing people and places
- Expressing discouragement and offering encouragement
- Giving directions
- Making and responding to suggestions
- Relating a series of events
- Sports and activities

LEVEL 3

Review of Level 2

CHAPTER 1

- The **passé composé** and the **imparfait**
- Definite, indefinite and partitive articles
- Question formation
- Describing what a place was like
- Exchanging information
- Expressing indecision
- Food vocabulary
- Inquiring; expressing enthusiasm and dissatisfaction
- Making recommendations
- Ordering and asking for details

CHAPTER 2

- The future with **aller**
- The imperative
- Pronouns and their placement
- Asking for and giving directions
- Asking about and telling where things are
- Expressing enthusiasm and boredom
- Expressing impatience
- Making, accepting, and refusing suggestions
- Reassuring someone

CHAPTER 12
Review of Level 3

- The future tense
- The subjunctive
- **Si** clauses
- Prepositions with countries
- Expressing anticipation
- Expressing certainty and doubt
- Expressing excitement and disappointment
- Greeting and introducing people
- Inquiring
- Making suppositions
- Offering encouragement

Allez, viens! French Level 1
Scope and Sequence

FUNCTIONS	GRAMMAR	VOCABULARY	CULTURE	RE-ENTRY
CHAPITRE PRELIMINAIRE Allez, viens!, *Pages xxvi–11*				
• Introducing yourself • Spelling • Counting • Understanding classroom instructions	• French alphabet • French accent marks	• French names • French numbers 0–20 • French classroom expressions	• The French-speaking world • Famous French-speaking people • The importance of learning French • French gestures for counting	
Poitiers — CHAPITRE 1 Faisons connaissance!, *Pages 16–45*				
• Greeting people and saying goodbye • Asking how people are; telling how you are • Asking someone's name and age and giving yours • Expressing likes, dislikes, and preferences about things • Expressing likes, dislikes, and preferences about activities	• **Ne...pas** • The definite articles **le, la, l',** and **les** • The connectors **et** and **mais** • Subject pronouns • **-er** verbs	• Things you like or don't like • Activities you like or don't like to do	• Greetings and goodbyes • Hand gestures • Leisure time activities	• Introductions • Numbers 0–20 • Expressing likes, dislikes, and preferences about things
Poitiers — CHAPITRE 2 Vive l'école!, *Pages 46–73*				
• Agreeing and disagreeing • Asking for and giving information • Telling when you have class • Asking for and expressing opinions	• Using **si** instead of **oui** to contradict a negative statement • The verb **avoir**	• School subjects • School-related words • Class times • Parts of the school day • Numbers 21–59	• The French educational system/**le bac** • **L'heure officielle** • Curriculum in French schools • The French grading system	• Greetings • The verb **aimer** • Numbers for telling time

Location	FUNCTIONS	GRAMMAR	VOCABULARY	CULTURE	RE-ENTRY
Poitiers	**CHAPITRE 3 Tout pour la rentrée,** ***Pages 74–101***				
	• Making and responding to requests • Asking others what they need and telling what you need • Telling what you'd like and what you'd like to do • Getting someone's attention • Asking for information • Expressing thanks	• The indefinite articles **un, une,** and **des** • The demonstrative adjectives **ce, cet, cette,** and **ces** • Adjective agreement and placement	• School supplies • Things you might buy for school and fun • Colors • Numbers 60–201	• Bagging your own purchases • Buying school supplies in French-speaking countries • French currency (euros)	• The verb **avoir** • Expressing likes and dislikes • Numbers
Québec	**CHAPITRE 4 Sports et passe-temps,** ***Pages 106–135***				
	• Telling how much you like or dislike something • Exchanging information • Making, accepting, and turning down suggestions	• Expressions with **faire** and **jouer** • Question formation • **De** after a negative verb • The verb **faire** • The pronoun **on** • Adverbs of frequency	• Sports and hobbies • Weather expressions • Months of the year • Time expressions • Seasons	• Old and new in Quebec City • Celsius and Fahrenheit • Sports in francophone countries • **Maison des jeunes et de la culture**	• Expressing likes and dislikes • The verb **aimer;** regular **-er** verbs • Agreeing and disagreeing
Paris	**CHAPITRE 5 On va au café?,** ***Pages 140–167***				
	• Making suggestions and excuses • Making a recommendation • Getting someone's attention • Ordering food and beverages • Inquiring about and expressing likes and dislikes • Paying the check	• The verb **prendre** • The imperative	• Foods and beverages	• Food served in a café • Waitpersons as professionals • **La litote** • Tipping	• Accepting and turning down a suggestion • Expressing likes and dislikes • Numbers 20–100

	FUNCTIONS	GRAMMAR	VOCABULARY	CULTURE	RE-ENTRY
Paris	**CHAPITRE 6 Amusons-nous!, *Pages 168–197***				
	• Making plans • Extending and responding to invitations • Arranging to meet someone	• Using **le** with days of the week • The verb **aller** and **aller** + infinitive • Contractions with **à** • The verb **vouloir** • Information questions	• Places to go • Things to do	• Going out • Dating in France • Conversational time	• Expressing likes and dislikes • Days of the week • Making, accepting, and turning down suggestions • Sports and hobbies • **L'heure officielle**
Paris	**CHAPITRE 7 La famille, *Pages 198–225***				
	• Identifying people • Introducing people • Describing and characterizing people • Asking for, giving, and refusing permission	• Possession with **de** • Possessive adjectives • Adjective agreement • The verb **être**	• Family members • Adjectives to describe and characterize people	• Family life • Pets in France	• Asking for and giving people's names and ages • Adjective agreement
Abidjan	**CHAPITRE 8 Au marché, *Pages 230–259***				
	• Expressing need • Making, accepting, and declining requests • Telling someone what to do • Offering, accepting, or refusing food	• The partitive articles • **Avoir besoin de** • The verb **pouvoir** • **De** with expressions of quantity • The pronoun **en**	• Food items • Expressions of quantity • Meals	• The Ivorian market • Shopping for groceries in francophone countries • The metric system • Foods of Côte d'Ivoire • Mealtimes in francophone countries	• Food vocabulary • Activities • The imperative
Arles	**CHAPITRE 9 Au téléphone, *Pages 264–291***				
	• Asking for and expressing opinions • Inquiring about and relating past events • Making and answering a telephone call • Sharing confidences and consoling others • Asking for and giving advice	• The **passé composé** with **avoir** • Placement of adverbs with the **passé composé** • The **-re** verb: **répondre** • The object pronouns **le, la, les, lui,** and **leur**	• Daily activities	• History of Arles • The French telephone system • Telephone habits of French-speaking teenagers	• Chores • Asking for, giving, and refusing permission • **Aller** + infinitive

	FUNCTIONS	GRAMMAR	VOCABULARY	CULTURE	RE-ENTRY
Arles	**CHAPITRE 10 Dans un magasin de vêtements,** ***Pages 292–321***				
	• Asking for and giving advice • Expressing need; inquiring • Asking for an opinion; paying a compliment; criticizing • Hesitating; making a decision	• The verbs **mettre** and **porter** • Adjectives used as nouns • The **-ir** verbs: **choisir** • The direct object pronouns **le, la,** and **les** • **C'est** versus **il/elle est**	• Articles of clothing	• Clothing sizes • Fashion in francophone countries • Responding to compliments	• The future with **aller** • Colors • Likes and dislikes
Arles	**CHAPITRE 11 Vive les vacances!,** ***Pages 322–349***				
	• Inquiring about and sharing future plans • Expressing indecision; expressing wishes • Asking for advice; making, accepting, and refusing suggestions • Reminding; reassuring • Seeing someone off • Asking for and expressing opinions • Inquiring about and relating past events	• The prepositions **à** and **en** • The **-ir** verbs: **partir**	• Vacation places and activities • Travel items	• **Colonies de vacances** • Vacations	• **Aller** + infinitive • Asking for advice • Clothing vocabulary • The imperative • Weather expressions • The **passé composé** • The verb **vouloir**
Fort-de-France	**CHAPITRE 12 En ville,** ***Pages 354–383***				
REVIEW CHAPTER	• Pointing out places and things • Making and responding to requests • Asking for advice • Making suggestions • Asking for and giving directions	• The pronoun **y** • Contractions with **de**	• Buildings • Things to do or buy in town • Means of transportation • Locations	• Store hours in France and Martinique • Making "small talk" in francophone countries • Getting a driver's license in francophone countries • **DOMs** and **TOMs** • Public areas downtown	• Contractions with **à** • The partitive • Contractions with **de** • Family vocabulary • Possessive adjectives • The **passé composé** • Expressing need • Making excuses • Inviting

Allez, viens! French Level 2
Scope and Sequence

	FUNCTIONS	GRAMMAR	VOCABULARY	CULTURE	RE-ENTRY
Environs de Paris	**CHAPITRE 1 Bon séjour!, *Pages 4–31***				
REVIEW CHAPTER	• Describing and characterizing yourself and others • Expressing likes, dislikes, and preferences • Asking for information • Asking for and giving advice • Asking for, making, and responding to suggestions • Relating a series of events	• The verbs **avoir** and **être** • Adjective agreement • The interrogative adjective **quel** • **Choisir** and other **-ir** verbs • The imperative • The future with **aller**	• Travel items	• Travel documents for foreign countries • Studying abroad • Ethnic restaurants	• Adjectives to characterize people • Regular **-er** verbs • Pronunciation: **liaison** • Family vocabulary • Clothing and colors • Weather expressions and seasons
Environs de Paris	**CHAPITRE 2 Bienvenue à Chartres!, *Pages 32–59***				
REVIEW CHAPTER	• Welcoming someone and responding to someone's welcome • Asking about how someone is feeling and telling how you're feeling • Pointing out where things are • Paying and responding to compliments • Asking for and giving directions	• Using **tu** and **vous** • Question formation • Adjectives that precede the noun • Contractions with **à**	• Furniture and rooms • Places in town	• Polite behavior for a guest • Teenagers' bedrooms in France • Paying and receiving compliments • **Notre-Dame de Chartres** • Houses in francophone countries	• Pronunciation: intonation • Prepositions of location • Contractions with **de** • Making suggestions
Environs de Paris	**CHAPITRE 3 Un repas à la française, *Pages 60–89***				
	• Making purchases • Asking for, offering, accepting, and refusing food • Paying and responding to compliments • Asking for and giving advice • Extending good wishes	• The object pronoun **en** • The partitive articles • The indirect object pronouns **lui** and **leur**	• Places to shop • Food items to buy • Meals • Gift items	• Neighborhood stores • Typical meals in the francophone world • Courses of a meal • The euro • Special occasions	• Giving prices • Expressions of quantity • Food vocabulary • The verbs **vouloir** and **pouvoir**

	FUNCTIONS	GRAMMAR	VOCABULARY	CULTURE	RE-ENTRY
Martinique	**CHAPITRE 4 Sous les tropiques,** ***Pages 94–123***				
	• Asking for information and describing a place • Asking for and making suggestions • Emphasizing likes and dislikes • Relating a series of events	• Recognizing reflexive verbs • The reflexive pronouns **se** and **me** • The relative pronouns **ce qui** and **ce que** • The present tense of reflexive verbs • Adverbs of frequency	• Places, flora, and fauna • Vacation activities • Daily activities	• **La ville de Saint-Pierre** • Places to visit in different regions • **Yoles rondes** • The **créole** language • **Carnaval** • Music and dance in Martinique	• **De** with adjectives and plural nouns • Connectors for sequencing events • Adverbs of frequency • Pronunciation: **e muet** • Sports vocabulary • Weather expressions
Touraine	**CHAPITRE 5 Quelle journée!,** ***Pages 128–155***				
	• Expressing concern for someone • Inquiring; expressing satisfaction and frustration • Sympathizing with and consoling someone • Giving reasons and making excuses • Congratulating and reprimanding someone	• The **passé composé** with **avoir** • Introduction to the **passé composé** with **être**	• School day vocabulary	• **Carnet de correspondance** • Meals at school • French grades and report cards • School life in francophone countries	• Connector words • Sports and leisure activities • Pronunciation: the nasal sound [ɛ̃] • Question words • Reflexive verbs
Touraine	**CHAPITRE 6 A nous les châteaux!,** ***Pages 156–183***				
	• Asking for opinions; expressing enthusiasm, indifference, and dissatisfaction • Expressing disbelief and doubt • Asking for and giving information	• The phrase **c'était** • The **passé composé** with **être** • Formal and informal phrasing of questions • The verb **ouvrir**	• Weekend activities • Verbs that use **être** in the **passé composé**	• Types of châteaux in France • Studying historical figures in school • Buses and trains in France	• Pronunciation: [y] versus [u] • The **passé composé** with **avoir** • Expressing satisfaction and frustration • Telling time

	FUNCTIONS	GRAMMAR	VOCABULARY	CULTURE	RE-ENTRY
Touraine	**CHAPITRE 7 En pleine forme, *Pages 184–213***				
	• Expressing concern for someone and complaining • Giving advice; accepting and rejecting advice • Expressing discouragement and offering encouragement • Justifying your recommendations; advising against something	• Reflexive verbs in the **passé composé** • The pronoun **en** with activities • The verb **devoir** • The verb **se nourrir**	• Health expressions • Parts of the body • Injuries • Staying fit • Good and bad eating habits	• Pharmacies in France • Figures of speech • Teenagers' exercise habits • Staying healthy • Mineral water	• Expressing doubt • Telling how often you do something • Pronunciation: the [r] sound • Sports activities
Côte d'Ivoire	**CHAPITRE 8 C'était comme ça, *Pages 218–247***				
	• Telling what or whom you miss; reassuring someone • Asking and telling what things were like • Reminiscing • Making and responding to suggestions	• The **imparfait** of **avoir** and **être** • Formation of the **imparfait** • **Si on** + the **imparfait**	• Describing places • Childhood activities • Things to see and buy in Côte d'Ivoire	• Village life in Côte d'Ivoire • Ethnic groups in West Africa • High school in Côte d'Ivoire • Félix Houphouët-Boigny • City versus country living • Abidjan	• Pronunciation: the [ɛ] sound • Adjectives of physical traits and personality • Chores • Places in a city
Provence	**CHAPITRE 9 Tu connais la nouvelle?, *Pages 252–279***				
	• Wondering what happened; offering possible explanations • Accepting and rejecting explanations • Breaking some news; showing interest • Beginning, continuing, and ending a story	• **Avoir l'air** + adjective • The **passé composé** vs. the **imparfait** • The **passé composé** and the **imparfait** with interrupted actions • Using **être en train de** and the **imparfait**	• Feelings • Personal happenings	• The **cours Mirabeau,** Aix-en-Provence • Friendship • **Histoires marseillaises**	• School-related mishaps • The **passé composé** of reflexive verbs • Accidents and injuries • The relative pronouns **ce qui** and **ce que** • Explanations and apologies

	FUNCTIONS	GRAMMAR	VOCABULARY	CULTURE	RE-ENTRY
Provence	**CHAPITRE 10 Je peux te parler?,** ***Pages 280–307***				
	• Sharing a confidence • Asking for and giving advice • Asking for and granting a favor; making excuses • Apologizing and accepting an apology; reproaching someone	• Object pronouns and their placement • Direct object pronouns with the **passé composé** • Object pronouns before an infinitive	• Apologetic actions • Party preparations	• Paul Cézanne • Roman ruins in Aix-en-Provence • **Provençale** cuisine • Talking about personal problems	• Accepting and refusing advice • Personal happenings • Pronunciation: the nasal sound [ã] • Making excuses
Provence	**CHAPITRE 11 Chacun ses goûts,** ***Pages 308–337***				
	• Identifying people and things • Asking for and giving information • Giving opinions • Summarizing	• The verb **connaître** • **C'est** versus **il/elle est** • The relative pronouns **qui** and **que**	• Songs and singers • Types of music • Types of movies • Types of books	• **La Fête de la musique** • Musical tastes • Movie theaters in France • The **Minitel**® and the Internet for French speakers	• Emphasizing likes and dislikes • Making and responding to suggestions
Québec	**CHAPITRE 12 A la belle étoile,** ***Pages 342–371***				
REVIEW CHAPTER	• Asking for and giving information; giving directions • Complaining; expressing discouragement and offering encouragement • Asking for and giving advice • Relating a series of events; describing people and places	• The verb **emporter** • The **passé composé** and the **imparfait**	• Animals • Outdoor activities • Camping equipment • Rules related to nature	• **Le parc de la Jacques-Cartier** • Ecology in Canada • Endangered animals • French-Canadian expressions	• Sports and activities • Clothing vocabulary • Making and responding to suggestions

Allez, viens! French Level 3

Scope and Sequence

	FUNCTIONS	GRAMMAR	VOCABULARY	CULTURE	RE-ENTRY
la France	**CHAPITRE 1 France, les régions,** ***Pages 4–31***				
REVIEW CHAPTER	• Renewing old acquaintances • Inquiring; expressing enthusiasm and dissatisfaction • Exchanging information • Asking and describing what a place was like • Expressing indecision • Making recommendations • Ordering and asking for details	• The **passé composé** • The **imparfait**	• French menu	• Traditional regional clothing • Regional specialties • Regional foods	• Sports and activities • Food vocabulary • Definite, indefinite, and partitive articles • Question formation
la Belgique	**CHAPITRE 2 Belgique, nous voilà!,** ***Pages 32–61***				
REVIEW CHAPTER	• Asking for and giving directions • Expressing impatience • Reassuring someone • Expressing enthusiasm and boredom • Asking and telling where things are	• The verb **conduire** • The imperative • Pronouns and their placement	• At the gas station • Adjectives	• Languages in Belgium • Favorite comic book characters • Overview of Belgium	• The future with **aller** • Making, accepting, and refusing suggestions
la Suisse	**CHAPITRE 3 Soyons responsables!,** ***Pages 62–91***				
	• Asking for, granting, and refusing permission • Expressing obligation • Forbidding • Reproaching • Justifying your actions and rejecting others' excuses	• The subjunctive • **Ne...pas** + infinitive	• Household chores • Personal responsibilities • Social responsibilities	• Swiss work ethic • Switzerland's neutrality • Overview of Switzerland • Environmental issues • **La minuterie**	• The verb **devoir** • Complaining • Chores • Negative expressions

	FUNCTIONS	GRAMMAR	VOCABULARY	CULTURE	RE-ENTRY
la France	**CHAPITRE 4 Des goûts et des couleurs, *Pages 92–121***				
	• Asking for and giving opinions • Asking which one(s) • Pointing out and identifying people and things • Paying and responding to compliments • Reassuring someone	• The interrogative and demonstrative pronouns • The causative **faire**	• Clothing and styles • Describing clothing and hairstyles • Hair and hairstyles	• French clothing stores • Fashion and personal style • French sense of fashion	• Clothing vocabulary • Adjectives referring to clothing • Family vocabulary • Chores
le Sénégal	**CHAPITRE 5 C'est notre avenir, *Pages 126–155***				
	• Asking about and expressing intentions • Expressing conditions and possibilities • Asking about future plans • Expressing wishes • Expressing indecision • Giving advice • Requesting information • Writing a formal letter	• The future • The conditional • Question formation with inversion	• Future choices and plans • Careers	• Careers and education in Senegal • Overview of Senegal • Planning for a career • Types of job training	• The subjunctive • Giving advice • The **passé composé** • The imperfect • Making a telephone call • Expressing likes and preferences
le Maroc	**CHAPITRE 6 Ma famille, mes copains et moi, *Pages 156–185***				
	• Making, accepting, and refusing suggestions • Making arrangements • Making and accepting apologies • Showing and responding to hospitality • Expressing and responding to thanks • Quarreling	• Reciprocal verbs • The past infinitive	• Family relationships	• Bargaining in North Africa • Values of francophone teenagers • Overview of Morocco • Hospitality in Morocco	• Reflexive verbs • Expressing thanks

	FUNCTIONS	GRAMMAR	VOCABULARY	CULTURE	RE-ENTRY
La République centrafricaine	**CHAPITRE 7 Un safari-photo, *Pages 186–215***				
	• Making suppositions • Expressing doubt and certainty • Asking for and giving advice • Expressing astonishment • Cautioning someone • Expressing fear • Reassuring someone • Expressing relief	• Structures and their complements • Using the subjunctive • Irregular subjunctive forms	• Rainforest and savannah • Packing for a safari • African animals	• Overview of the Central African Republic • Animal conservation in the Central African Republic • Stereotypical impressions of francophone regions	• The subjunctive • Travel items • The conditional
la Tunisie	**CHAPITRE 8 La Tunisie, pays de contrastes, *Pages 216–245***				
	• Asking someone to convey good wishes • Closing a letter • Expressing hopes or wishes • Giving advice • Complaining • Expressing annoyance • Making comparisons	• **Si** clauses • The comparative	• Traditional life • City life	• Overview of Tunisia • Traditional and modern life in Tunisia • Carthage • Modernization in francophone countries • Traditional and modern styles of dress in Tunisia	• The imperfect • Intonation • Adjective agreement • Describing a place
le Canada	**CHAPITRE 9 C'est l'fun!, *Pages 250–279***				
	• Agreeing and disagreeing • Expressing indifference • Making requests • Asking for and making judgments • Asking for and making recommendations • Asking about and summarizing a story	• Negative expressions • The expression **ne...que** • The relative pronouns **qui, que,** and **dont**	• Television programming • The television • Types of movies	• Multilingual broadcasting in Canada • Overview of Montreal • Favorite types of movies • The Canadian film industry	• Expressing opinions • Quarreling • Agreeing and disagreeing • Types of films • Summarizing a story • Continuing and ending a story • Relating a series of events • Relative pronouns

	FUNCTIONS	GRAMMAR	VOCABULARY	CULTURE	RE-ENTRY
la Guadeloupe	**CHAPITRE 10 Rencontres au soleil, *Pages 280–309***				
	• Bragging; flattering • Teasing • Breaking some news; showing interest • Expressing disbelief; telling a joke	• The superlative • The past perfect	• Sea life • Everyday life	• Climate and natural assets of Guadeloupe • Overview of Guadeloupe • **La Fête des Cuisinières** • Daily routines of francophone teenagers • Greetings in Guadeloupe	• Forms of the comparative • Reciprocal verbs • Adjective agreement • Breaking some news
la Louisiane	**CHAPITRE 11 Laissez les bons temps rouler!, *Pages 310–339***				
	• Asking for confirmation • Asking for and giving opinions • Agreeing and disagreeing • Asking for explanations • Making observations • Giving impressions		• Musical instruments • Kinds of music • Cajun food	• **Mardi Gras** and festivals in Louisiana • Cajun French • Cajun music • History of Louisiana • Parties and celebrations in francophone countries	• Renewing old acquaintances • Food vocabulary • Types of music • Agreeing and disagreeing • Asking for and giving opinions • Emphasizing likes • Making suggestions • Expressing opinions • The relative pronouns **ce qui** and **ce que**
Autour du monde	**CHAPITRE 12 Echanges sportifs et culturels, *Pages 340–367***				
REVIEW CHAPTER	• Expressing anticipation • Making suppositions • Expressing certainty and doubt • Inquiring • Expressing excitement and disappointment	• The future after **quand** and **dès que**	• Sports and equipment • Places of origin	• International sporting events in francophone countries • Stereotypes of people in francophone countries	• Sports vocabulary • Making suppositions • **Si** clauses • Expressing certainty and doubt • The future • Prepositions with countries • Greeting people • Introducing people • Asking someone's name and age and giving yours • Offering encouragement

Allez, viens! in the Middle Grades

Middle School Resources

The ***En avant!*** Level 1A and ***En route!*** Level 1B programs are based on the ***Allez, viens!*** series. ***En avant! & En route!*** address the unique needs and interests of young adolescents with a rich and highly diverse program that engages students' interest and promotes enthusiasm for learning at various stages of developement.

***En avant!* Level 1A** begins with a preliminary chapter, which introduces the students to the French-speaking world, and is followed by six chapters of instructional material to be covered in the first year of middle school.

En route!* Level 1B,** which is the second book of the middle school Pupil's Edition, begins with a review chapter the covers major functions, vocabulary, grammar, and cultural topics presented in ***En avant! Level 1A. This review chapter is followed by six instructional chapters.

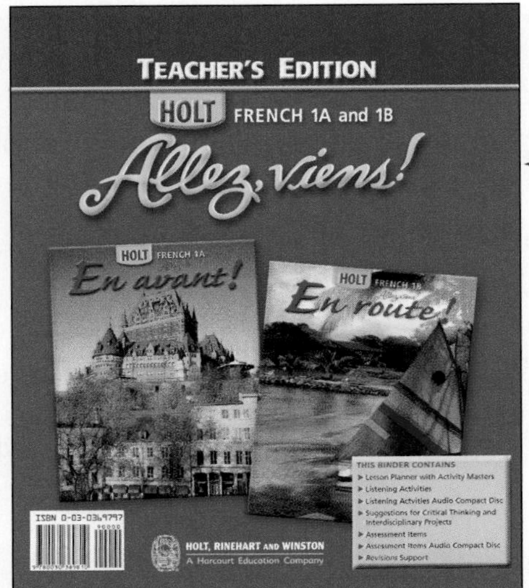

The ***Allez viens!* Level 1 Middle School Teaching Resources** binder was developed to address the needs of teachers and students who use ***En avant! & En route!*** in the middle grades. The materials in the binder are meant to complement the Levels 1A and 1B *Pupil's Edition* and ancillary materials, and provide additional material geared especially for middle school students.

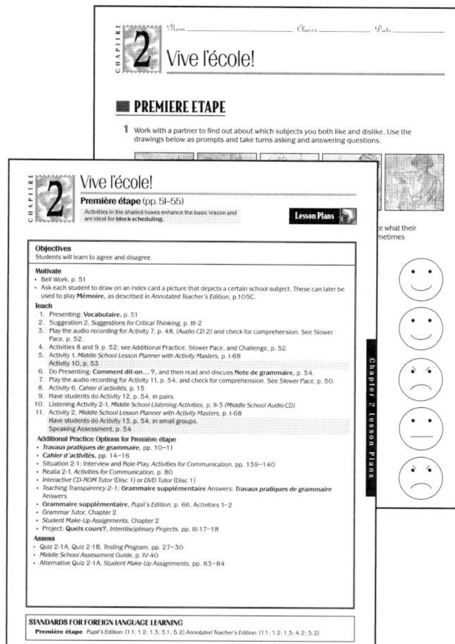

Vive l'école!

PREMIERE ETAPE

Vive l'école!

Première étape (pp. 51–55)

Lesson Plans

Objectives

Motivate

Teach

Additional Practice Options for Première étape

Assess

STANDARDS FOR FOREIGN LANGUAGE LEARNING

Within Middle School Teaching Resources you will find the following features.

The **Lesson Planner with Activity Masters** contains the same type of lesson plans as the high school program, except that it emphasizes those activities in the core program that are most suitable for younger learners. The four Activity Masters per chapter are unique to the middle school binder and contain both closed- and open-ended activities, many of which target the creative, hands-on, and visual learning styles prevalent in middle school students.

The **Middle School Listening Activities** are also designed with the middle school learner in mind and consist of both discrete and global listening practice. All recordings for the Middle School Listening Activities are on *Audio CD 1*, located in the front cover of the binder.

The **Suggestions for Critical Thinking** offer suggestions for extending the material beyond an informational level in order to increase comprehension of language and culture and develop higher-order thinking skills.

The **Interdisciplinary Projects** are suggestions for four-skills activities based on the chapter theme and content. They extend across disciplines and allow students to use knowledge and skills from other subject areas.

The **Middle School Assessment Guide** offers assessment possibilities that go beyond the pencil-paper tests that are provided in the Level 1 *Testing Program*. The *Assessment Guide* provides chapter-by-chapter suggestions for portfolio assessment, performance assessment, and CD-ROM assessment. In addition, speaking tests for each chapter and a midterm and final are provided.

The **Diagnostic Instrument** serves as a bridge between the first and second year of the middle school grades. This tool shows students where in the program to go (*Cahier d'activités, Travaux pratiques de grammaire,* or **Grammaire supplémentaire** in the *Pupil's Edition*) to practice certain grammar, vocabulary or functions that they learned in the first year.

The **Révisions Chapter** section contains Lesson Plans, Activity Masters, and Quizzes that are specifically coordinated with the *Révisions* chapter in the *Pupil's Edition*. These materials are designed with the middle school learner in mind, to address the needs of planning lessons, practicing, and assessing the material covered in the *Révisions* chapter.

Pupil's Edition

***Allez, viens!* offers an integrated approach to language learning. Presentation and practice of functional expressions, vocabulary, and grammar structures are interwoven with cultural information, language learning tips, and realia to facilitate both learning and teaching. The technology, audiovisual materials, and additional print resources are integrated throughout each chapter.**

Allez, viens! Level 1

Allez, viens! *Level 1* consists of a preliminary chapter that introduces students to French and the French-speaking world, followed by twelve instructional chapters. To facilitate articulation from one level to the next, Chapter 11 introduces minimal new material and Chapter 12 is a review chapter.

Following is a description of the various features in ***Allez, viens!*** and suggestions on how to use them in the classroom.

Starting Out...

Location Opener In ***Allez, viens!***, chapters are arranged by location. Each new location is introduced by four pages of colorful photos and information about the region.

Chapter Opener These two pages provide a visual introduction to the theme of the chapter and include a list of objectives students will be expected to achieve.

Setting The Scene...

Mise en train Language instruction begins with this comprehensible input that models language in a culturally authentic setting. Presented also on video and audio CD, the highly visual presentation allows students to practice their receptive skills and to begin to recognize some of the new functions and vocabulary they will encounter in the chapter. Following **Mise en train** is a series of activities to check comprehension.

Building Proficiency Step By Step...

Première, Deuxième, and **Troisième étape** are the core instructional sections where most language acquisition will take place. The communicative goals in each chapter center on the functional expressions presented in **Comment dit-on...?** boxes. These expressions are supported by material in the **Vocabulaire, Grammaire,** and **Note de grammaire** sections. Activities following the above features are designed to practice recognition or to provide closed-ended practice. Activities then progress from controlled to open-ended practice where students are able to express themselves in meaningful communication.

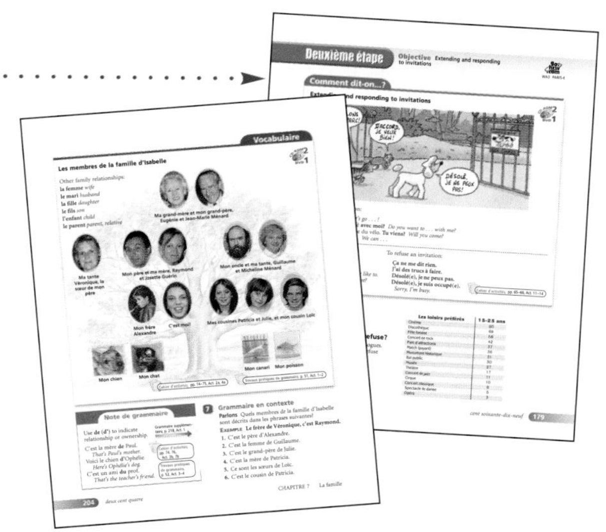

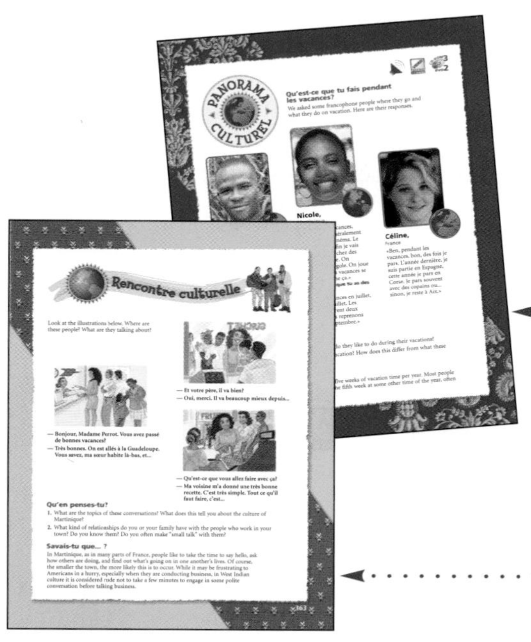

Discovering the People and the Culture...

There are also two major cultural features to help students develop an appreciation and understanding of the cultures of French-speaking countries.

Panorama Culturel presents interviews conducted throughout the French-speaking world on a topic related to the chapter theme. The interviews may be presented on video or done as a reading supplemented by the compact disc recording. Culminating activities on this page verify comprehension and encourage students to think critically about the target culture as well as their own.

Rencontre culturelle invites students to compare and contrast other cultures with their own.

Note culturelle

When you count on your fingers, which finger do you start with? The French way is to start counting with your thumb as number one, your index finger as two, and so on. How would you show four the French way? And eight?

Note culturelle helps students gain knowledge and understanding of other cultures.

Understanding Authentic Documents...

Lisons! presents reading strategies that help students understand authentic French documents and literature presented in each chapter. The accompanying prereading, reading, and postreading activities develop students' overall reading skills and challenge their critical thinking abilities.

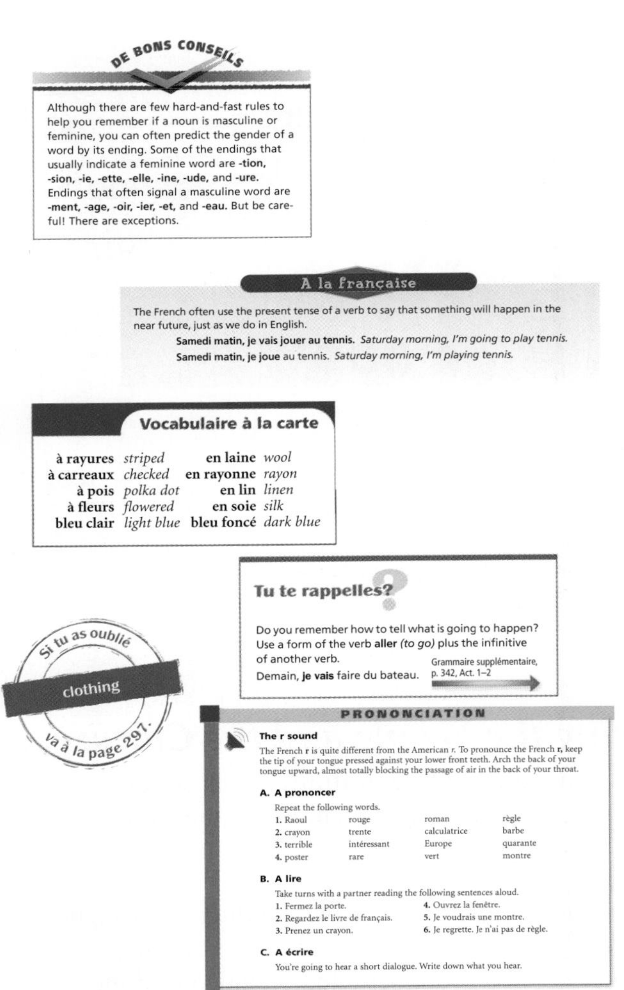

DE BONS CONSEILS

Although there are few hard-and-fast rules to help you remember if a noun is masculine or feminine, you can often predict the gender of a word by its ending. Some of the endings that usually indicate a feminine word are **-tion, -sion, -ie, -ette, -elle, -ine, -ude,** and **-ure.** Endings that often signal a masculine word are **-ment, -age, -oir, -ier, -et,** and **-eau.** But be careful! There are exceptions.

A la française

The French often use the present tense of a verb to say that something will happen in the near future, just as we do in English.

Samedi matin, je vais jouer au tennis. *Saturday morning, I'm going to play tennis.*
Samedi matin, je joue au tennis. *Saturday morning, I'm playing tennis.*

Vocabulaire à la carte

à rayures	*striped*	**en laine**	*wool*
à carreaux	*checked*	**en rayonne**	*rayon*
à pois	*polka dot*	**en lin**	*linen*
à fleurs	*flowered*	**en soie**	*silk*
bleu clair	*light blue*	**bleu foncé**	*dark blue*

Tu te rappelles?

Do you remember how to tell what is going to happen? Use a form of the verb **aller** *(to go)* plus the infinitive of another verb.

Demain, **je vais** faire du bateau.

Grammaire supplémentaire, p. 342, Act. 1–2

Si tu as oublié
clothing
va à la page 297.

PRONONCIATION

The r sound

The French **r** is quite different from the American *r*. To pronounce the French **r**, keep the tip of your tongue pressed against your lower front teeth. Arch the back of your tongue upward, almost totally blocking the passage of air in the back of your throat.

A. A prononcer

Repeat the following words.

1. Raoul	rouge	roman	règle
2. crayon	trente	calculatrice	barbe
3. terrible	intéressant	Europe	quarante
4. poster	rare	vert	montre

B. A lire

Take turns with a partner reading the following sentences aloud.

1. Fermez la porte.
2. Regardez le livre de français.
3. Prenez un crayon.
4. Ouvrez la fenêtre.
5. Je voudrais une montre.
6. Je regrette. Je n'ai pas de règle.

C. A écrire

You're going to hear a short dialogue. Write down what you hear.

Targeting Students' Needs...

In each **étape** several special features may be used to enhance language learning and cultural appreciation.

De bons conseils suggests effective ways for students to learn a foreign language.

A la française provides students with tips for speaking more natural-sounding French.

Vocabulaire à la carte presents optional vocabulary related to the chapter theme.

Tu te rappelles? is a re-entry feature that lists and briefly explains previously learned vocabulary, functions, and grammar that students might need to review at the moment.

Si tu as oublié is a handy page reference to either an earlier chapter where material was presented or to a reference section in the back of the book.

At the end of each **Troisième étape** is **Prononciation,** which explains certain sounds and spelling rules. In a dictation exercise, students hear and write sentences using the targeted sounds and letters.

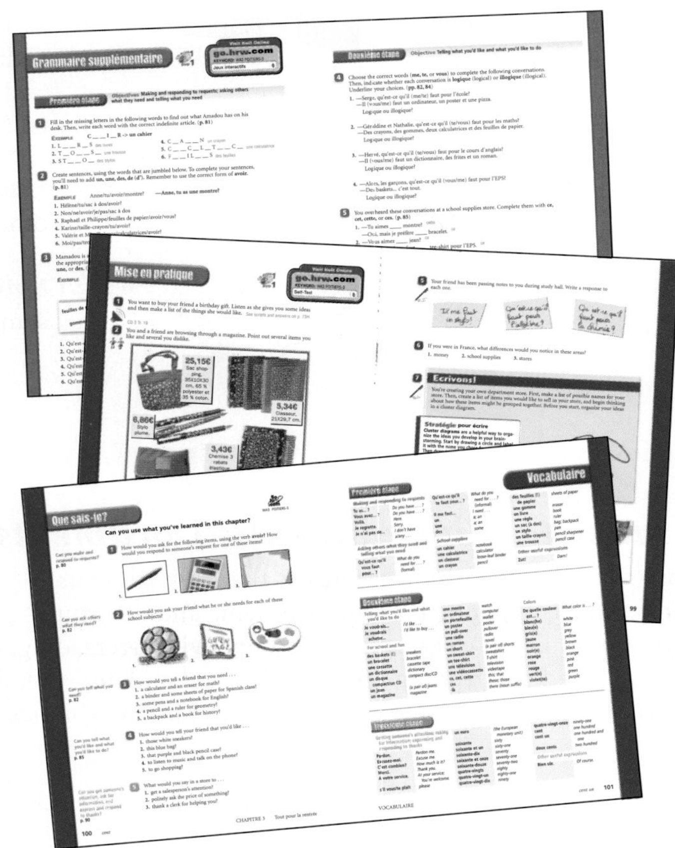

Wrapping It All Up...

Grammaire supplémentaire provides additional practice on the grammar concepts presented in the chapter.

Mise en pratique gives students the opportunity to review what they have learned and to apply their skills in new communicative contexts. Focusing on all four language skills as well as cultural awareness, the **Mise en pratique** can help you determine whether students are ready for the Chapter Test.

Ecrivons! helps students develop their writing skills by focusing on the writing process. Each **Ecrivons!** gives students a topic related to the theme and functions of the chapter.

Que sais-je? is a checklist that students can use on their own to see if they have achieved the goals stated on the Chapter Opener.

Vocabulaire presents the chapter vocabulary grouped by **étape** and arranged according to function or theme.

Technology Resources

Go.Online!

- The **Online Edition** presents the *Pupil's Edition* in an interactive format that allows students to listen to audio at point of use and to complete activities online.

  The *Enhanced Online Edition* features the full *Video Program* and a Student Notebook (**Cahier électronique**).

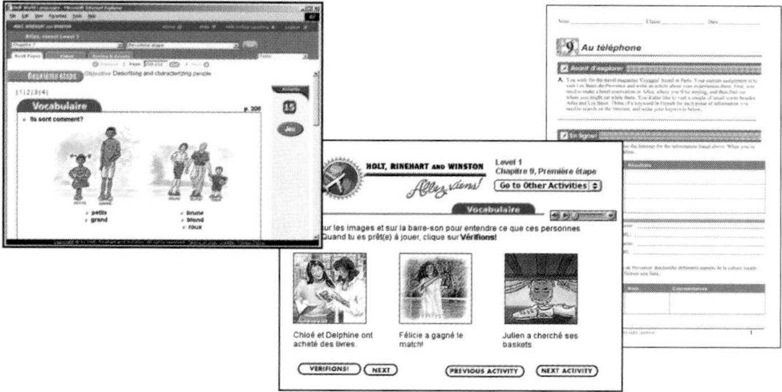

Keywords in the *Pupil's Edition* provide access to two types of online activities:

- **Jeux interactifs** are directly correlated to the instructional material in the textbook. They can be used as homework, extra practice, or assessment.
- **Activités Internet** provide students with selected Web sites in French-speaking countries and activities related to the chapter theme. A printable worksheet in PDF format includes pre-surfing, surfing, and post-surfing activities that guide students through their research.

Interactive CD-ROM Tutor

The *Interactive CD-ROM Tutor* offers:

- a variety of supporting activities correlated to the core curriculum of ***Allez, viens!*** and targeting all five skills
- a Teacher Management System (TMS) that allows teachers to view and assess students' work, manage passwords and records, track students' progress as they complete the activities, and activate English translations
- features such as a grammar reference section and a glossary to help students complete the activities

Video Program-DVD Tutor

The *Video Program* and *DVD Tutor* provide the following video support:

- **Location Opener** documentaries
- **Mise en train** and **Suite** dramatic episodes
- **Panorama Culturel** interviews on a variety of cultural topics
- **Vidéoclips** which present authentic footage from target cultures

The *Video Guide* contains background information, suggestions for presentation, and activities for all portions of the *Video Program*.

One-Stop Planner CD-ROM with ExamView Test Generator

The *One-Stop Planner CD-ROM* is a convenient tool to aid in lesson planning and pacing.

Easy navigation through menus or through lesson plans allows for a quick overview of available resources. For each chapter the *One-Stop Planner* includes:

- Editable lesson plans with direct links to teaching resources
- Printable worksheets from resource books
- Direct launches to the HRW Internet activities
- Video and audio segments
- Test Generator
- Clip Art for vocabulary items

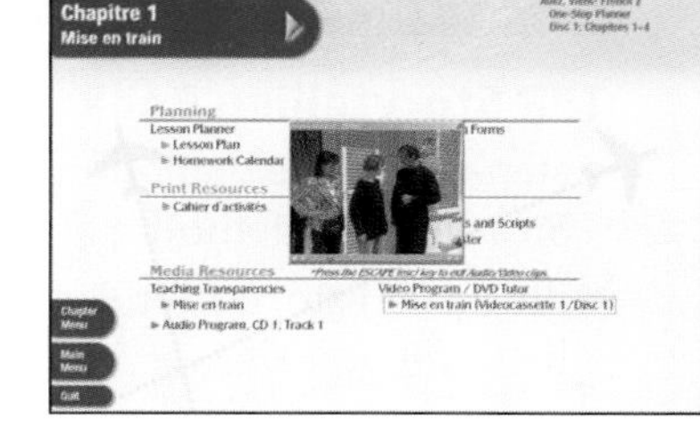

Ancillaries

The *Allez, viens!* French program offers a comprehensive ancillary package that addresses the concerns of today's teachers and is relevant to students' lives.

Lesson Planning

One-Stop Planner with Test Generator

- editable lesson plans
- printable worksheets from the resource books
- direct link to HRW Internet activities
- entire video and audio programs
- Test Generator
- Clip Art for vocabulary items

Lesson Planner with Differentiated Instruction

- complete lesson plans for every chapter
- block scheduling suggestions
- correlations to Standards for Foreign Language Learning
- a homework calendar
- chapter by chapter lesson plans for
- substitute teachers
- lesson plan forms for customizing lesson plans

Student Make-Up Assignments

- diagnostic information for students who are behind in their work
- copying masters for make-up assignments

Listening and Speaking

TPR Storytelling Book

- step-by-step explanation of the TPR Storytelling method
- illustrated stories for each **étape** with vocabulary lists and gestures
- teaching suggestions

Listening Activities

- print material associated with the *Audio Program*
- Student Response Forms for all *Pupil's Edition* listening activities
- Additional Listening Activities
- scripts, answers
- lyrics to each chapter's song

Audio Compact Discs

Listening activities for the *Pupil's Edition*, the Additional Listening Activities, and the *Testing Program*

Activities for Communication

- Communicative Activities for partner work based on an information gap
- Situation Cards to practice interviews and role-plays
- Realia: reproductions of authentic documents

Grammar

Travaux pratiques de grammaire

- re-presentations of major grammar points
- additional focused practice
- *Teacher's Edition* with overprinted answers

Grammar Tutor for Students of French

- presentations of grammar concepts in English
- re-presentations of French grammar concepts
- discovery and application activities

Reading and Writing

Reading Strategies and Skills Handbook

- explanations of reading strategies
- copying masters for application of strategies

Joie de lire 1

- readings on familiar topics
- cultural information
- additional vocabulary
- interesting and engaging activities

Cahier d'activités

- activities for practice
- *Teacher's Edition* with overprinted answers

Teaching Transparencies

Colorful transparencies that help present and practice vocabulary, grammar, culture, and a variety of communicative functions

Exploratory Guide

- lessons with activity masters
- vocabulary lists
- review and assessment options

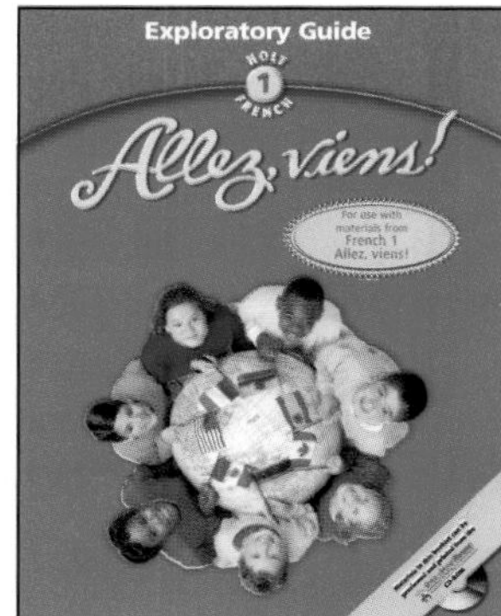

Assessment

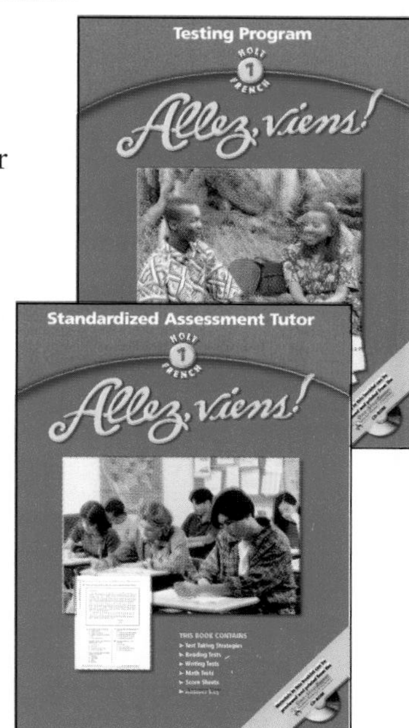

Testing Program

- Grammar and Vocabulary quizzes
- **Etape** quizzes that test the four skills
- Chapter Tests
- Speaking Tests
- Midterm and Final Exams
- Score sheets, scripts, answers

Alternative Assessment Guide

- Suggestions for oral and written Portfolio Assessment
- Performance Assessment
- CD-ROM Assessment
- rubrics, portfolio checklists, and evaluation forms

Student Make-Up Assignments

Alternative Grammar and Vocabulary quizzes for students who missed class and have to make up the quiz

Standardized Assessment Tutor

Reading, writing, and math tests in a standardized, multiple-choice format

Middle School

Middle School Teaching Resources

- material geared toward the middle school learner, (lesson plans, activity masters, critical thinking activities, interdisciplinary projects)
- an Assessment Guide with portfolio suggestions, performance and CD-ROM assessment
- Midterm and Final exam geared toward the younger learner
- two Middle School audio CDs

Annotated Teacher's Edition

Using the Chapter Interleaf

Each chapter of the *Allez, viens! Annotated Teacher's Edition* includes the following interleaf pages to help you plan, teach, and expand your lessons.

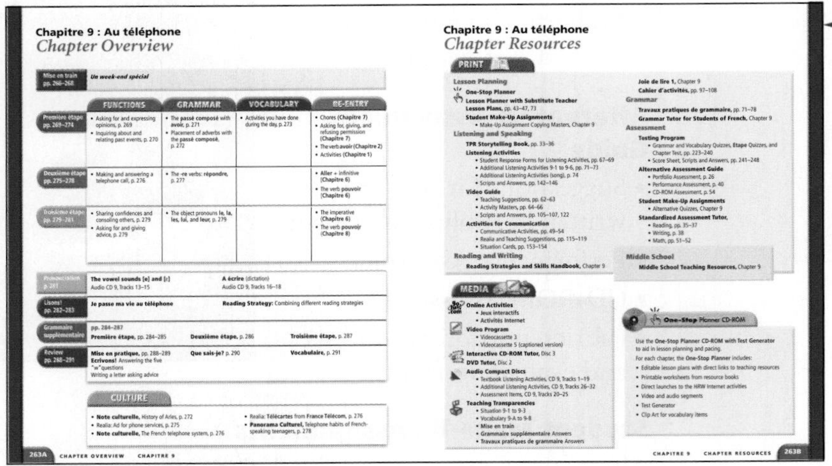
Chapitre 9 : Au téléphone
Chapter Overview

Chapitre 9 : Au téléphone
Chapter Resources

Chapter Overview

The Chapter Overview chart outlines at a glance the functions, grammar, vocabulary, re-entry, and culture featured in the chapter. You will also find a list of corresponding print and audiovisual resources organized by listening, speaking, reading, and writing skills, grammar, and assessment.

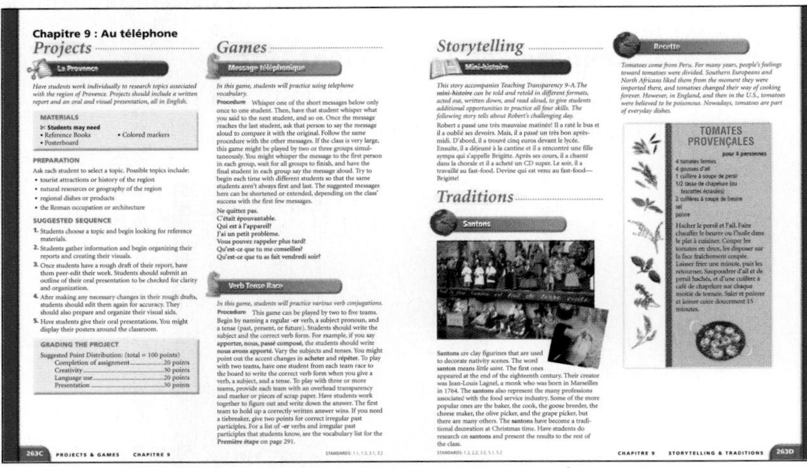
Chapitre 9 : Au téléphone
Projects

Games

Storytelling

Traditions

Projects/Games/ Storytelling/Traditions

Projects allow students to personalize and expand on the information from the chapter. Games reinforce the chapter content. In the Storytelling feature, you will find a story related to a *Teaching Transparency.* The Traditions feature concentrates on a unique aspect of the culture of the region. A recipe typical for the region accompanies this feature.

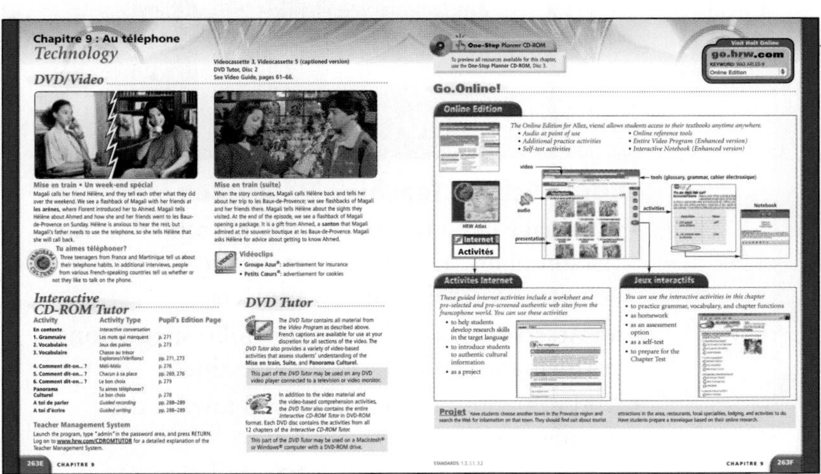
Chapitre 9 : Au téléphone
Technology

DVD/Video

Interactive CD-ROM Tutor

DVD Tutor

Go.Online!

Technology

These pages assist you in integrating technology into your lesson plans. The Technology page provides a detailed list of video, DVD, CD-ROM, and Internet resources for your lesson. You will also find an Internet research project in each chapter.

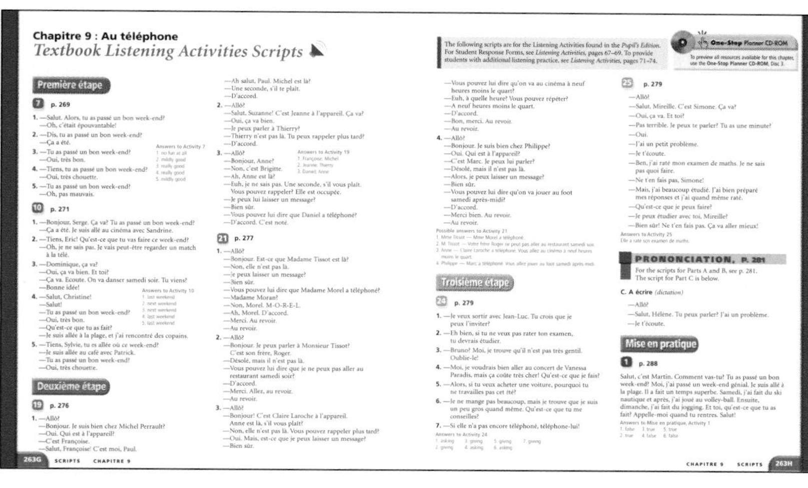

Chapitre 9 : Au téléphone
Textbook Listening Activities Scripts

Textbook Listening Activities Scripts

Textbook Listening Activities Scripts provide the scripts of the chapter listening activities for reference or for use in class. The answers to each activity are provided below each script for easy reference.

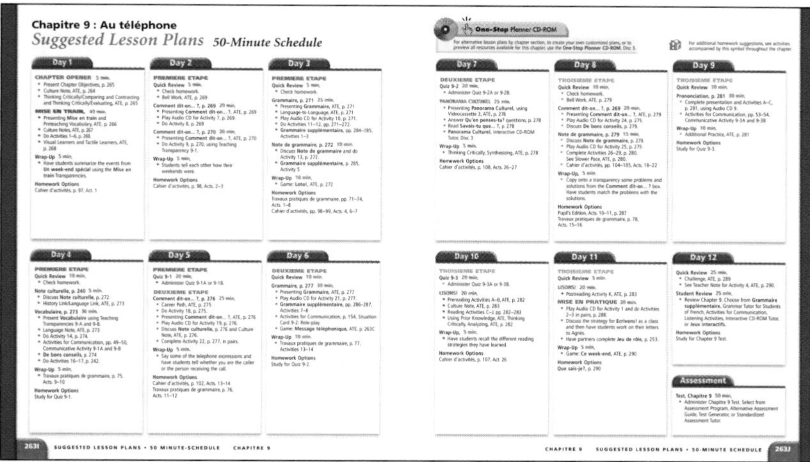

Chapitre 9 : Au téléphone
Suggested Lesson Plans *50-Minute Schedule*

Suggested Lesson Plans— 50-Minute Schedule

This lesson plan is used for classes with 50-minute schedules. Each lesson plan provides a logical sequence of instruction along with homework suggestions.

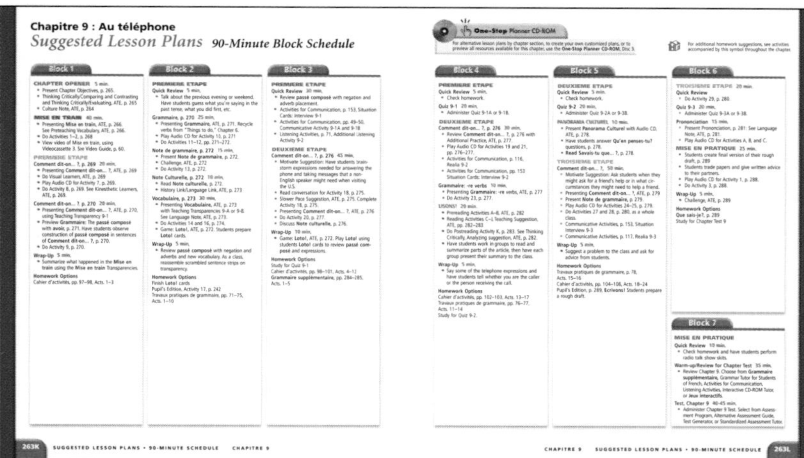

Chapitre 9 : Au téléphone
Suggested Lesson Plans *90-Minute Block Schedule*

Suggested Lesson Plans— 90-Minute Schedule

This lesson plan is used for classes with 90-minute schedules. Each lesson plan provides a logical sequence of instruction along with homework suggestions.

Using the Wrap-Around Teacher Text

Resource boxes provide a quick list of all the resources you can use for each chapter section.

Presenting boxes offer useful suggestions for presenting new material.

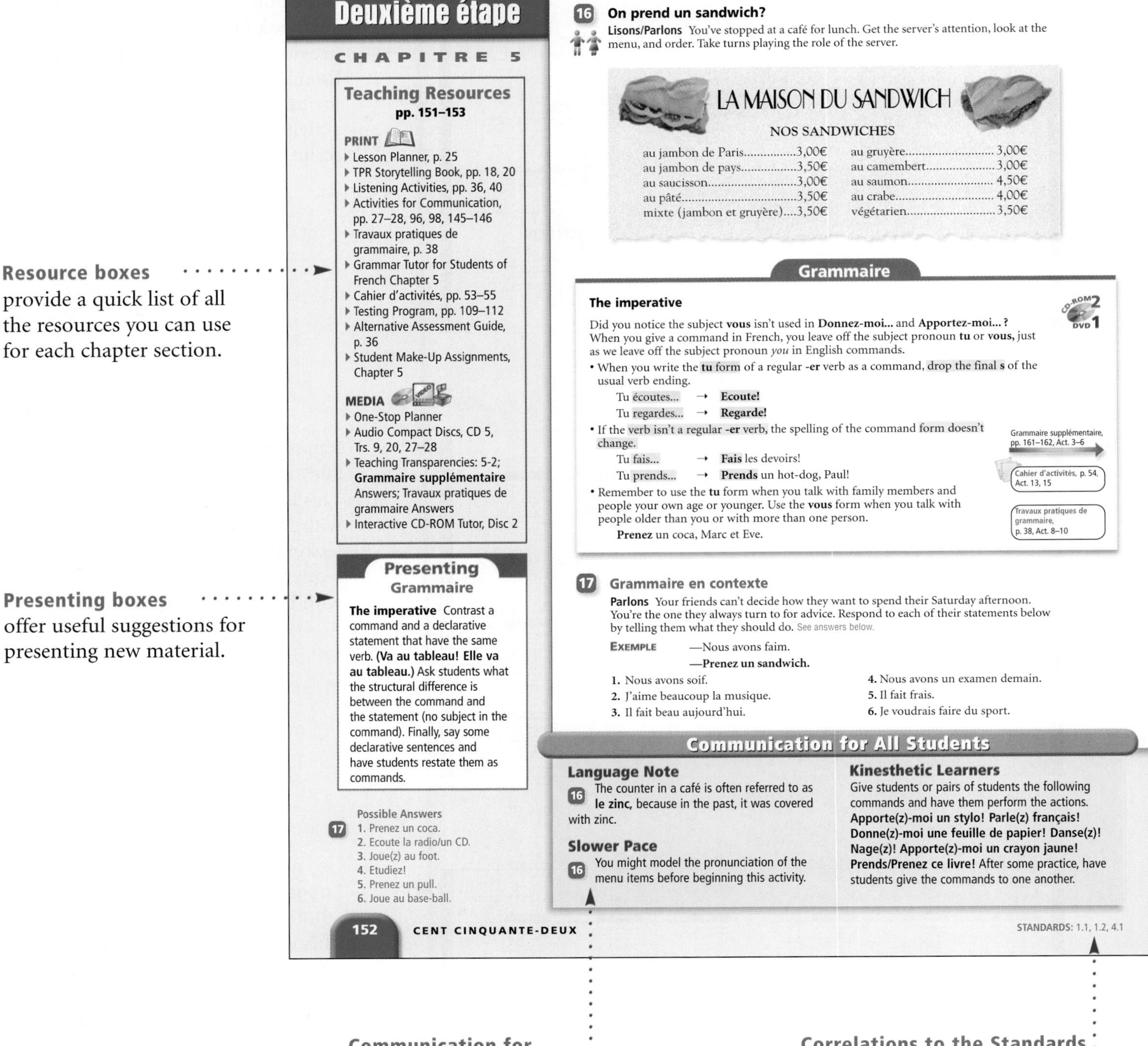

Deuxième étape

CHAPITRE 5

Teaching Resources
pp. 151–153

PRINT
- Lesson Planner, p. 25
- TPR Storytelling Book, pp. 18, 20
- Listening Activities, pp. 36, 40
- Activities for Communication, pp. 27–28, 96, 98, 145–146
- Travaux pratiques de grammaire, p. 38
- Grammar Tutor for Students of French Chapter 5
- Cahier d'activités, pp. 53–55
- Testing Program, pp. 109–112
- Alternative Assessment Guide, p. 36
- Student Make-Up Assignments, Chapter 5

MEDIA
- One-Stop Planner
- Audio Compact Discs, CD 5, Trs. 9, 20, 27–28
- Teaching Transparencies: 5-2; **Grammaire supplémentaire** Answers; Travaux pratiques de grammaire Answers
- Interactive CD-ROM Tutor, Disc 2

Presenting Grammaire

The imperative Contrast a command and a declarative statement that have the same verb. **(Va au tableau! Elle va au tableau.)** Ask students what the structural difference is between the command and the statement (no subject in the command). Finally, say some declarative sentences and have students restate them as commands.

Possible Answers

17
1. Prenez un coca.
2. Ecoute la radio/un CD.
3. Joue(z) au foot.
4. Etudiez!
5. Prenez un pull.
6. Joue au base-ball.

16 On prend un sandwich?

Lisons/Parlons You've stopped at a café for lunch. Get the server's attention, look at the menu, and order. Take turns playing the role of the server.

LA MAISON DU SANDWICH

NOS SANDWICHES

au jambon de Paris	3,00€	au gruyère	3,00€
au jambon de pays	3,50€	au camembert	3,00€
au saucisson	3,00€	au saumon	4,50€
au pâté	3,50€	au crabe	4,00€
mixte (jambon et gruyère)	3,50€	végétarien	3,50€

Grammaire

The imperative

CD-ROM 2 DVD 1

Did you notice the subject **vous** isn't used in **Donnez-moi...** and **Apportez-moi...?** When you give a command in French, you leave off the subject pronoun **tu** or **vous,** just as we leave off the subject pronoun *you* in English commands.

- When you write the **tu** form of a regular **-er** verb as a command, drop the final **s** of the usual verb ending.
  - Tu écoutes... → **Ecoute!**
  - Tu regardes... → **Regarde!**
- If the verb isn't a regular **-er** verb, the spelling of the command form doesn't change.
  - Tu fais... → **Fais** les devoirs!
  - Tu prends... → **Prends** un hot-dog, Paul!
- Remember to use the **tu** form when you talk with family members and people your own age or younger. Use the **vous** form when you talk with people older than you or with more than one person.
  - **Prenez** un coca, Marc et Eve.

Grammaire supplémentaire, pp. 161–162, Act. 3–6
Cahier d'activités, p. 54, Act. 13, 15
Travaux pratiques de grammaire, p. 38, Act. 8–10

17 Grammaire en contexte

Parlons Your friends can't decide how they want to spend their Saturday afternoon. You're the one they always turn to for advice. Respond to each of their statements below by telling them what they should do. See answers below.

EXEMPLE —Nous avons faim.
—Prenez un sandwich.

1. Nous avons soif.
2. J'aime beaucoup la musique.
3. Il fait beau aujourd'hui.
4. Nous avons un examen demain.
5. Il fait frais.
6. Je voudrais faire du sport.

Communication for All Students

Language Note

16 The counter in a café is often referred to as **le zinc,** because in the past, it was covered with zinc.

Slower Pace

16 You might model the pronunciation of the menu items before beginning this activity.

Kinesthetic Learners

Give students or pairs of students the following commands and have them perform the actions. **Apporte(z)-moi un stylo! Parle(z) français! Donne(z)-moi une feuille de papier! Danse(z)! Nage(z)! Apporte(z)-moi un crayon jaune! Prends/Prenez ce livre!** After some practice, have students give the commands to one another.

152 CENT CINQUANTE-DEUX

STANDARDS: 1.1, 1.2, 4.1

Communication for All Students
Under this head you will find helpful suggestions for students with different learning styles and abilities.

Correlations to the Standards for Foreign Language Learning are provided for your reference.

18 **Grammaire en contexte**

Parlons You don't know what to order at the café. The server makes some suggestions for you, but you don't like the suggestions. Take turns playing the server.

EXEMPLE —**Prenez un sandwich au fromage.**
—**Non, je n'aime pas le fromage.**
—**Alors, prenez un sandwich au jambon.**
—**Non, apportez-moi un hot-dog, s'il vous plaît.**

Note culturelle

In France, waiters and waitresses are considered professionals. In better restaurants, waiters and waitresses must not only be good servers but they must also be knowledgeable about food and wine. Even in simple restaurants or cafés, servers take great pride in their work. Contrary to what you may have seen in American movies, it is impolite to address a waiter as **Garçon.** It is more polite to say **Monsieur** to a waiter, and **Madame** or **Mademoiselle** to a waitress. It is expected that diners will take time to enjoy their food, so service in French restaurants may seem slow to Americans. It is not uncommon for a meal to last several hours.

19 **A la crêperie**

Lisons/Parlons You and some friends get together at a **crêperie.** Look at the menu and order. Take turns playing the server.

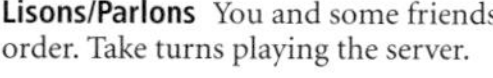

La Crêperie Normande

Crêpes salées :

Jambon - fromage	4,50€
Epinards - crème fraîche	4,50€
Champignons	5,00€

Crêpes sucrées :

Sucre	3,50€
Banane - Chantilly	4,50€
Chocolat	4,00€
Glace vanille - sauce noisette	5,00€

20 **Mon journal** 

Ecrivons Make a list of the foods and drinks you like to have when you go out with your friends. Then, mention several items you'd try if you were at a café in France.

Cultures and Communities

Culture Notes

19 • Crêpes are a specialty of Brittany **(Bretagne)**. Traditionally, they are served during **la fête de la chandeleur**, a Christian, religious holiday in February celebrating the presentation of Jesus in the temple. **Crêperies** usually serve both dessert and dinner **crêpes**, as well as sparkling apple cider.

• **Note culturelle** In some cafés, you will find pinball machines **(les flippers)**, table soccer **(le baby-foot)**, and video games **(les jeux vidéo)**. Video games may be located in a separate room at the back of the café. Decks of cards and checker games are also available in many cafés.

STANDARDS: 1.1, 1.3, 2.1, 3.1, 3.2, 4.2, 5.1

Deuxième étape

CHAPITRE 5

Language-to-Language
If you have students who speak Spanish, you might have them tell how informal commands in Spanish are similar to informal commands for **-er** verbs in French. (They both drop the final **-s.**) You might also stress that verbs in French that do not end in **-er** keep the final **-s** in informal commands, but in Spanish, the **-s** is dropped from all regular verbs.

Challenge
19 Have students give their reactions to some of the items **(J'aime beaucoup... , Nous n'aimons pas... , Je voudrais...).**

Mon journal
20 For an additional journal entry suggestion for Chapter 5, see *Cahier d'activités*, page 149.

Cooperative Learning
After students practice the vocabulary orally, have groups of four or five role-play a restaurant scene. One student is the server, one is the chef, and the others are the customers. The customers give their orders to the server, who writes them down. The server then goes to the chef and reads aloud the orders. The chef writes down the items, while repeating the orders aloud. Finally, the server "serves" the customers, restating each person's order.

Assess
- Testing Program, pp. 109–112
  Quiz 5-2A, Quiz 5-2B
  Audio CD 5, Tr. 20
- Student Make-Up Assignments, Chapter 5, Alternative Quiz
- Alternative Assessment Guide, p. 36

The Annotated Teacher's Edition Wrap-Around Text offers helpful suggestions and information at point-of-use. You will also find annos, cultural information, correlations to the Standards for Foreign Language Learning, and references to other ancillaries.

Assessment
At the end of every **étape** and again at the end of the chapter, you will find references to all the assessment material available for that section of the chapter.

Cultures and Communities
Under this head you will find helpful cultural information and suggestions that relate the content to students' families and communities.

Bringing Standards into the Classroom

by Paul Sandrock, Foreign Language Consultant, Wisconsin Department of Public Education

The core question that guided the development of the National Standards and their accompanying goals was simply: what matters in instruction?

Each proposed standard was evaluated. Did the standard target material that will have application beyond the classroom? Was the standard too specific or not specific enough? Teachers should be able to teach the standard and assess it in multiple ways. A standard needs to provide a target for instruction and learning throughout a student's K–12 education.

In the development of standards, foreign languages faced other unique challenges. The writers could not assume a K–12 sequence available to all students. In fact, unlike other disciplines, they could not guarantee that all students would experience even any common sequence.

From this context, the National Standards in Foreign Language Education Project's task force generated the five C's, five goals for learning languages: communication, cultures, connections, comparisons, and communities. First presented in 1995, the standards quickly became familiar to foreign language educators across the US, representing our professional consensus and capturing a broad view of the purposes for learning another language.

To implement the standards, however, requires a shift from emphasizing the means to focusing on the ends. It isn't a matter of grammar versus communication, but rather how much grammar is needed to communicate. Instead of teaching to a grammatical sequence, teaching decisions become based on what students need to know to achieve the communicative goal.

The Focus on Communication

The first standard redefined communication, making its purpose **interpersonal, interpretive,** and **presentational** communication. Teaching to the purpose of interpersonal communication takes us away from memorized dialogues to spontaneous, interactive conversation, where the message is most important and where meaning needs to be negotiated between the speakers. Interpretive communication is not an exercise in translation, but asks beginners to tell the gist of an authentic selection that is heard, read, or viewed, while increasingly advanced learners tell deeper and deeper levels of detail and can interpret based on their knowledge of the target culture. In the presentational mode of communication, the emphasis is on the audience, requiring the speaker or writer to adapt language to fit the situation and to allow for comprehension without any interactive negotiation of the meaning.

Standards challenge us to refocus many of the things we've been doing all along. The requirements of speaking and our expectation of how well students need to speak change when speaking is for a different purpose. This focus on the purpose of the communication changes the way we teach and test the skills of listening, speaking, reading, and writing.

Standards help us think about how to help students put the pieces of language to work in meaningful ways. Our stan-

Standards for Foreign Language Learning

Communication Communicate in Languages Other than English	**Standard 1.1** Students engage in conversations, provide and obtain information, express feelings and emotions, and exchange opinions. **Standard 1.2** Students understand and interpret written and spoken language on a variety of topics. **Standard 1.3** Students present information, concepts, and ideas to an audience of listeners or readers on a variety of topics.
Cultures Gain Knowledge and Understanding of Other Cultures	**Standard 2.1** Students demonstrate an understanding of the relationship between the practices and perspectives of the culture studied. **Standard 2.2** Students demonstrate an understanding of the relationship between the products and perspectives of the culture studied.
Connections Connect with Other Disciplines and Acquire Information	**Standard 3.1** Students reinforce and further their knowledge of other disciplines through the foreign language. **Standard 3.2** Students acquire information and recognize the distinctive viewpoints that are only available through the foreign language and its cultures.
Comparisons Develop Insight into the Nature of Language and Culture	**Standard 4.1** Students demonstrate understanding of the nature of language through comparisons of the language studied and their own. **Standard 4.2** Students demonstrate understanding of the concept of culture through comparisons of the cultures studied and their own.
Communities Participate in Multilingual Communities at Home and Around the World	**Standard 5.1** Students use the language both within and beyond the school setting. **Standard 5.2** Students show evidence of becoming life-long learners by using the language for personal enjoyment and enrichment.

dards answer *why* we are teaching various components of language, and we select *what* we teach in order to achieve those very standards.

The 5 C's

Originally the five C's were presented as five equal circles. During the years since the National Standards were printed, teachers implementing and using the standards to write curriculum, texts, and lesson plans have come to see that communication is at the core, surrounded by four C's that influence the context for teaching and assessing.

The four C's surrounding our core goal of **Communication** change our classrooms by bringing in real-life applications for the language learned:

- **Cultures:** Beyond art and literature, learning occurs in the context of the way of life, patterns of behavior, and contributions of the people speaking the language being taught.
- **Connections:** Beyond content limited to the culture of the people speaking the target language, teachers go out to other disciplines to find topics and ideas to form the context for language learning.
- **Comparisons:** Foreign language study is a great way for students to learn more about native language and universal principles of language and culture by comparing and contrasting their own to the target language and culture.
- **Communities:** This goal of the standards adds a broader motivation to the context for language learning. The teacher makes sure students use their new language beyond the class hour, seeking ways to experience the target culture.

Implementation at the Classroom Level: Assessment and Instruction

After the publication of the standards, states developed more specific performance standards that would provide evidence of the application of the national content standards. Standards provide the organizing principle for teaching and assessing. The standards-oriented teacher, when asked what she's teaching, cites the standard "students will sustain a conversation." With that clear goal in mind, she creates lessons to teach various strategies to ask for clarification and to practice asking follow-up questions that explore a topic in more depth.

Textbook writers and materials providers are responding to this shift. Standards provide our goals; the useful textbooks and materials give us an organization and a context. Standards provide the ends; textbooks and materials can help us practice the means. Textbooks can bring authentic materials into the classroom, real cultural examples that avoid stereotypes, and a broader exposure to the variety of people who speak the language being studied. Textbooks can model the kind of instruction that will lead students to successful demonstration of the knowledge and skill described in the standards.

To really know that standards are the focus, look at the assessment. If standards are the target, assessment won't consist only of evaluation of the means (grammatical structures and vocabulary) in isolation. If standards are the focus, teachers will assess students' use of the second language in context. The summative assessment of our target needs to go beyond the specific and include open-ended, personalized tasks. Regardless of how the students show what they can do, the teacher will be able to gauge each student's progress toward the goal.

Assessment is like a jigsaw puzzle. If we test students only on the means, we just keep collecting random puzzle pieces. We have to test, and students have to practice, putting the pieces together in meaningful and purposeful ways. In order to learn vocabulary that will help students "describe themselves," for example, students may have a quiz on Friday with an expectation of close to 100% accuracy. But if that is all we ever do with those ten words, they will quickly be gone from students' memory, and we will only have collected a puzzle piece from each student. It is absolutely essential to have students use those puzzle pieces to complete the puzzle to provide evidence of what they "can do" with the language.

During this period of implementing our standards, we've learned that the standards provide a global picture, the essence of our goals. But they are not curriculum, nor are they lesson plans. The standards influence how we teach, but do not dictate one content nor one methodology. How can we implement the standards in our classrooms? Think about the targets; think about how students will show achievement of those targets through our evaluation measures; then think about what we need to teach and how that will occur in our classrooms. Make it happen in your classroom to get the results we've always wanted: students who can communicate in a language other than English.

Allez, viens!

supports the Standards for Foreign Language Learning in the following ways:

THE PUPIL'S EDITION

- Encourages students to take responsibility for their learning by providing clearly defined objectives at the beginning of each chapter.
- Provides a variety of pair- and group-work activities to give students an opportunity to use the target language in a wide range of settings and contexts.
- Offers culture-related activities and poses questions that develop students' insight and encourage them to develop observational and analytical skills.

THE ANNOTATED TEACHER'S EDITION

- Provides a broad framework for developing a foreign language program and offers specific classroom suggestions for reaching students with various learning styles.
- Offers ideas for multicultural and multidisciplinary projects as well as community and family links that encourage students to gain access to information both at school and in the community.

THE ANCILLARY PROGRAM

- Provides students with on-location video footage of native speakers interacting in their own cultural and geographic context.
- Includes multiple options for practicing new skills and assessing performance, including situation cards, portfolio suggestions, speaking tests, and other alternatives.
- Familiarizes students with the types of tasks they will be expected to perform on exit exams.

Reading Strategies and Skills

by Nancy Humbach, Miami University

Reading is the most enduring of the language skills. Long after a student ceases to study the language, the ability to read will continue to provide a springboard to the renewal of the other skills. We must consider all the ways in which our students will read and address the skills needed for those tasks.

How can we accomplish this goal? How can we, as teachers, present materials, encourage students to read, and at the same time foster understanding and build the student's confidence and interest in reading?

Selection of Materials

Reading material in the foreign language classroom should be relevant to students' backgrounds and at an accessible level of difficulty, i.e., at a level of difficulty only slightly above the reading ability of the student.

Authentic materials are generally a good choice. They provide cultural context and linguistic authenticity seldom found in materials created for students, and the authentic nature of the language provides a window on a new world. The problem inherent in the selection of authentic materials at early levels is obvious: the level of difficulty is frequently beyond the skill of the student. At the same time, however, readers are inspired by the fact that they can understand materials designed to be read by native speakers.

Presenting a Selection/ Reading Strategies

We assume that students of a second language already have a reading knowledge in their first language and that many of the skills they learned in their "reading readiness" days will serve them well. Too often, however, students have forgotten such skills as activating background knowledge, skimming, scanning, and guessing content based on context clues. Helping students to reactivate these skills is part of helping them become better readers.

Teachers should not assume their students' ability to transfer a knowledge set from one reading to another. Students use these skills on a regular basis, but often do not even realize they are doing so. To help students become aware of these processes, they need to be given strategies for reading. These strategies offer students a framework for the higher-level skills they need to apply when reading. Strategies also address learners of different learning styles and needs.

Advance Organizers

One way to activate the student's background knowledge is through advance organizers. They also serve to address the student's initial frustrations at encountering an unfamiliar text.

Advance organizers call up pertinent background knowledge, feelings, and experiences that can serve to focus the attention of the entire group on a given topic. In addition, they provide for a sharing of information among the students. Background information that includes cultural references and cultural information can reactivate in students skills that will help them with a text and provide for them clues to the meaning of the material.

A good advance organizer will provide some information and guide students to think about the scenarios being presented. An advance organizer might include photographs, drawings, quotations, maps, or information about the area where the story takes place. It might also be posed as a question, for example, "What would you do if you found yourself in….?" Having students brainstorm in advance, either as a whole class or in small groups, allows them to construct a scenario which they can verify as they read.

Prereading Activities

Prereading activities remind students of how much they really know and can prepare students in a number of ways to experience the language with less frustration. While we know that we must choose a reading selection that is not far beyond students' experience and skill level, we also know that no group of students reads at the same level. In the interest of assisting students to become better language learners, we can provide them with opportunities to work with unfamiliar structures and vocabulary ahead of time.

Preparing students for a reading selection can include a number of strategies that may anticipate but not dwell on potential problems to be encountered by students. Various aspects of grammar, such as differences in the past tenses and the meanings conveyed, can also cause problems. Alerting students to some of the aspects of the language allows them to struggle less, understand more quickly, and enjoy a reading selection to a greater degree.

Grouping vocabulary by category or simply choosing a short list of critical words for a section of reading is helpful. Providing an entire list of vocabulary items at one time can be overwhelming. With a bit of organization, the task becomes manageable to the point where students begin to master words they will find repeated throughout the selection.

Having students skim for a particular piece of information or scan for words, phrases, indicators of place or time, and names, and then asking them to write a sentence or two about the gist of a paragraph or story, gives them a sense of independence and success before they begin to read.

Getting into the Assignment

Teachers can recount the times they have assigned a piece of reading for homework, only to find that few students even attempted the work. Therefore, many teachers choose to complete the reading in class. Homework assignments should then be structured to have the student return to the selection and complete a assignment that requires critical thinking and imagination.

During class, several techniques assist students in maintaining interest and attention to the task. By varying these techniques, the teacher can provide for a lively class, during which students realize they *are* able to read. Partners can read passages to each other or students can take turns reading in small groups. The teacher might pose a question to be answered during that reading. Groups might also begin to act out short scenes, reading only the dialogue. Students might read a description of a setting and then draw what they imagine it to be. Of course, some selections might be silent reading with a specific amount of time announced for completion.

Reading aloud for comprehension and reading aloud for pronunciation practice are two entirely unrelated tasks. We can all recall classes where someone read aloud to us from weary lecture notes. Active engagement of the readers, on the other hand, forces them to work for comprehension, for the development of thought processes, and for improvement of language skills.

Postreading Activities

It is important to provide students with an opportunity to expand the knowledge they have gained from the reading selection. Students should apply what they have learned to their own personal experiences. How we structure activities can provide students more opportunities to reflect on their reading and learn how much they have understood. We often consider a written test the best way to ensure comprehension; however, many other strategies allow students to keep oral skills active. These might include acting out impromptu scenes from the story and creating dialogues that do not exist in a story, but might be imagined, based on other information. Consider the possibility of debates, interviews, TV talk show formats, telephone dialogues, or a monologue in which the audience hears only one side of the conversation.

Written assignments are also valid assessment tools, allowing students to incorporate the vocabulary and structures they have learned in the reading. Students might be encouraged to write journal entries for a character, create a new ending, or retell the story from another point of view. Newspaper articles, advertisements, and other creations can also be a means of following up. Comparisons with other readings require students to keep active vocabulary and structures they have studied previously. Encourage students to read their creations aloud to a partner, to a group, or to the class.

Conclusion

Reading can be exciting. The combination of a good selection that is relevant and rates high on the interest scale, along with good preparation, guidance, and postreading activities that demonstrate to the students the level of success attained, can encourage them to continue to read. These assignments also allow for the incorporation of other aspects of language learning, and incorporate the Five C's of the National Standards. Communication and culture are obvious links, but so are connections (advance organizers, settings, and so on), comparisons (with other works in the heritage or target language), and communities (learning why a type of writing is important in a culture).

Allez, viens!

offers reading practice and develops reading skills and strategies in the following ways:

THE PUPIL'S EDITION

- Provides an extensive reading section in each chapter called **Lisons!** Each **Lisons!** section offers a strategy students apply to an authentic text, as well as activities to guide understanding and exploration of the text.

THE ANNOTATED TEACHER'S EDITION

- Provides teachers with additional activities and information in every **Lisons!** section. Additional suggestions are provided for Pre-reading, Reading, and Postreading activities.

THE ANCILLARY PROGRAM

- ***Joie de lire*** This component offers reading selections of various formats and difficulty levels. Each chapter has a prereading feature, a reading selection with comprehension questions, and two pages of activities.
- The *Reading Strategies and Skills Handbook* offers useful strategies that can be applied to reading selections in the *Pupil's Edition*, ***Joie de lire,*** or a selection of your choosing.
- The ***Cahier d'activités*** contains a reading selection tied to the chapter theme, and reading activities for each chapter in ***Allez, viens!***

Using Portfolios in the Language Classroom

by Jo Anne S. Wilson, J. Wilson Associates

Portfolios offer a more realistic and accurate way to assess the process of language teaching and learning.

The communicative, whole-language approach of today's language instruction requires assessment methods that parallel the teaching and learning strategies in the proficiency-oriented classroom. We know that language acquisition is a process. Portfolios are designed to assess the steps in that process.

What Is a Portfolio?

A portfolio is a purposeful, systematic collection of a student's work. A useful tool in developing a student profile, the portfolio shows the student's efforts, progress, and achievements for a given period of time. It may be used for periodic evaluation, as the basis for overall evaluation, or for placement. It may also be used to enhance or provide alternatives to traditional assessment measures, such as formal tests, quizzes, class participation, and homework.

Why Use Portfolios?

Portfolios benefit both students and teachers because they:

- **Are ongoing and systematic.** A portfolio reflects the real-world process of production, assessment, revision, and reassessment. It parallels the natural rhythm of learning.
- **Offer an incentive to learn.** Students have a vested interest in creating the portfolios, through which they can showcase their ongoing efforts and tangible achievements. Students select the works to be included and have a chance to revise, improve, evaluate, and explain the contents.
- **Are sensitive to individual needs.** Language learners bring varied abilities to the classroom and do not acquire skills in a uniformly neat and orderly fashion. The personalized, individualized assessment offered by portfolios responds to this diversity.
- **Provide documentation of language development.** The material in a portfolio is evidence of student progress in the language learning process. The contents of the portfolio make it easier to discuss their progress with the students as well as with parents and others.
- **Offer multiple sources of information.** A portfolio presents a way to collect and analyze information from multiple sources that reflects a student's efforts, progress, and achievements in the language.

Portfolio Components

The language portfolio should include both oral and written work, student self-evaluation, and teacher observation, usually in the form of brief, nonevaluative comments about various aspects of the student's performance.

The Oral Component

The oral component of a portfolio might be an audio- or videocassette. It may contain both rehearsed and extemporaneous monologues and conversations. For a rehearsed speaking activity, give a specific communicative task that students can personalize according to their individual interests (for example, ordering a favorite meal in a restaurant). If the speaking activity is extemporaneous, first acquaint students with possible topics for discussion or even the specific task they will be expected to perform. (For example, tell them they will be asked to discuss a picture showing a sports activity or a restaurant scene.)

The Written Component

Portfolios are excellent tools for incorporating process writing strategies into the language classroom. Documentation of various stages of the writing process—brainstorming, multiple drafts, and peer comments—may be included with the finished product.

Involve students in selecting writing tasks for the portfolio. At the beginning levels, the tasks might include some structured writing, such as labeling or listing. As students become more proficient, journals, letters, and other more complicated writing tasks are valuable ways for them to monitor their progress in using the written language.

Student Self-Evaluation

Students should be actively involved in critiquing and evaluating their portfolios and monitoring their own progress.

The process and procedure for student self-evaluation should be considered in planning the contents of the portfolio. Students should work with you and their peers to design the exact format. Self-evaluation encourages them to think about what they are learning (content), how they learn (process), why they are learning (purpose), and where they are going in their learning (goals).

Teacher Observation

Systematic, regular, and ongoing observations should be placed in the portfolio after they have been discussed with the student. These observations provide feedback on the student's progress in the language learning process.

Teacher observations should be based on an established set of criteria that has been developed earlier with input from the student. Observation techniques may include the following:

- Jotting notes in a journal to be discussed with the student and then placed in the portfolio
- Using a checklist of observable behaviors, such as the willingness to take risks when using the target language or staying on task during the lesson
- Making observations on adhesive notes that can be placed in folders
- Recording anecdotal comments, during or after class, using a cassette recorder.

Knowledge of the criteria you use in your observations gives students a framework for their performance.

Electronic Portfolios

Technology can provide help with managing student portfolios. Digital or computer-based portfolios offer a means of saving portfolios in an electronic format. Students can save text, drawings, photographs, graphics, audio or video recordings, or any combination of multimedia information. Teachers can create their own portfolio templates or consult one of the many commercial software programs available to create digital portfolios. Portfolios saved on videotapes or compact discs provide a convenient way to access and store students' work. By employing technology, this means of alternative assessment addresses the learning styles and abilities of individual students. Additionally, electronic portfolios can be shared among teachers, and parents have the ability to easily see the students' progress.

Logistically, the hypermedia equipment and software available for students' use determine what types of entries will be included in the portfolios. The teacher or a team of teachers and students may provide the computer support.

How Are Portfolios Evaluated?

The portfolio should reflect the process of student learning over a specific period of time. At the beginning of that time period, determine the criteria by which you will assess the final product and convey them to the students. Make this evaluation a collaborative effort by seeking students' input as you formulate these criteria and your instructional goals.

Students need to understand that evaluation based on a predetermined standard is but one phase of the assessment process; demonstrated effort and growth are just as important. As you consider correctness and accuracy in both oral and written work, also consider the organization, creativity, and improvement revealed by the student's portfolio over the time period. The portfolio provides a way to monitor the growth of a student's knowledge, skills, and attitudes and shows the student's efforts, progress, and achievements.

How to Implement Portfolios

Teacher-teacher collaboration is as important to the implementation of portfolios as teacher-student collaboration. Confer with your colleagues to determine, for example, what kinds of information you want to see in the student portfolio, how the information will be presented, the purpose of the portfolio, the intended purposes (grading, placement, or a combination of the two), and criteria for evaluating the portfolio. Conferring among colleagues helps foster a departmental cohesiveness and consistency that will ultimately benefit the students.

The Promise of Portfolios

The high degree of student involvement in developing portfolios and deciding how they will be used generally results in renewed student enthusiasm for learning and improved achievement. As students compare portfolio pieces done early in the year with work produced later, they can take pride in their progress as well as reassess their motivation and work habits.

Allez, viens!

supports the use of portfolios in the following ways:

THE PUPIL'S EDITION

- Includes numerous oral and written activities that can be easily adapted for student portfolios, such as **Mon journal, Ecrivons!,** and **Jeu de rôle.**

THE ANNOTATED TEACHER'S EDITION

- Suggests activities in the Portfolio Assessment feature that may serve as portfolio items.

THE ANCILLARY PROGRAM

- Includes criteria in the *Alternative Assessment Guide* for evaluating portfolios.
- Provides Speaking Tests in the *Testing Program* for each chapter that can be adapted for use as portfolio assessment items.
- Offers several oral and written scenarios on the *Interactive CD-ROM Tutor* that students can develop and include in their portfolios.

Teaching Culture

by Nancy A. Humbach, Miami University, and Dorothea Bruschke, Parkway School District

We must integrate culture and language in a way that encourages curiosity, stimulates analysis, and teaches students to hypothesize.

The teaching of culture has undergone some important and welcome changes in recent years. Instead of teaching the standard notions of cultures, language and regions, we now stress the teaching of analysis and the critical thinking skills required to evaluate a culture, by comparing it to one's own, but within its own setting. The setting includes the geography, climate, history, and influences of peoples who have interacted within that cultural group.

The National Standards for the Teaching of Foreign Languages suggests organizing the teaching of culture into three categories: products, practices, and perspectives. Through the presentation of these aspects of culture, students should gain the skill to analyze the culture, evaluate it within its context, compare it to their culture and develop the ability to function comfortably in that culture.

Skill and practice in the analysis of cultural phenomena equip students to enter a cultural situation, assess it, create strategies for dealing with it, and accepting it as a natural part of the people. The ultimate goal of this philosophy is to reduce the "we vs. they" approach to culture. If students are encouraged to accept and appreciate the diversity of other cultures, they will be more willing and better able to develop the risk-taking strategies necessary to learn a language and to interact with people of different cultures.

There are many ways to help students become culturally knowledgeable and to assist them in developing an awareness of differences and similarities between the target culture and their own. Two of these approaches involve critical thinking, that is, trying to find reasons for a certain behavior through observation and analysis, and putting individual observations into larger cultural patterns. We must integrate culture and language in a way that encourages curiosity, stimutates analysis, and teaches students to hypothesize.

First Approach: Questioning

The first approach involves questioning as the key strategy. At the earliest stages of language learning, students begin to learn ways to greet peers, elders, and strangers, as well as the use of **tu** and **vous.** Students need to consider questions such as: "How do French-speaking people greet each other? Are there different levels of formality? Who initiates a handshake? When is a handshake or kisses on the cheeks **(la bise)** appropriate?" Each of these questions leads students to think about the values that are expressed through word and gesture. They start to "feel" the other culture, and at the same time, understand how much of their own behavior is rooted in their cultural background.

Magazines, newspapers, advertisements, and television commercials are all excellent sources of cultural material. For example, browsing through a French magazine, one finds a number of advertisements for food items and bottled water. Could this indicate a great interest in eating and preparing healthy food? Reading advertisements can be followed up with viewing videos and films, or with interviewing native speakers or people who have lived in French-speaking countries about customs involving food selection and preparation. Students might want to find answers to questions such as: "How much time do French people spend shopping for and preparing a meal? How long does a typical meal **en famille** last? What types of food and beverages does it involve?" This type of questioning might lead students to discover different attitudes toward food and mealtimes.

An advertisement for a refrigerator or a picture of a French kitchen can provide an insight into practices of shopping for food. Students first need to think about the refrigerator at home, take an inventory of what is kept in it, and consider when and where their family shops. Next, students should look closely at a French refrigerator. What is its size? What could that mean? (Shopping takes place more often, stores are within walking distance, and people eat more fresh foods.)

Food wrappers and containers also provide good clues to cultural insight. For example, since bread is often purchased fresh from a **boulangerie,** it is usually carried in one's hand or tote bag, with no packaging at all. Since most people shop daily and carry their own groceries home, heavier items like sodas often come in bottles no larger than one and one-half liters.

Second Approach: Associating Words with Images

The second approach for developing cultural understanding involves forming associations of words with the cultural images they suggest. Language and culture are so closely related that one might actually say that language *is* culture. Most words, especially nouns, carry a cultural connotation. Knowing the literal equivalent of a word in another language is of little use to students in understanding this connotation. For example, **ami** cannot be translated simply as *friend,* **pain** as *bread,* or **rue** as *street.* The French word **pain,** for instance, carries with it the image of a small local bakery stocked with twenty or thirty different varieties of freshly-baked bread, all warm from a brick oven. At breakfast, bread is sliced, covered with butter and jam, and eaten as a **tartine;** it is eaten throughout the afternoon and evening meals, in particular as an accompaniment to the cheese course. In French-speaking countries, "bread" is more than a grocery item; it is an essential part of every meal.

When students have acquired some sense of the cultural connotation of words —not only through teachers' explanations but, more importantly, through observation of visual images—they start to discover the larger underlying cultural themes, or what is often called deep culture.

These larger cultural themes serve as organizing categories into which individual cultural phenomena fit to form a pattern. Students might discover, for example, that French speakers, because they live in much more crowded conditions, have a great need for privacy (cultural theme), as reflected in such phenomena as closed doors, fences or walls around property, and sheers on windows. Students might also discover that love of nature and the outdoors is an important cultural theme, as indicated by such phenomena as flower boxes and planters in public places—even on small traffic islands—well-kept public parks in every town, and people going for a walk or going hiking.

As we teach culture, students learn not only to recognize elements of the target culture but also of their American cultural heritage. They see how elements of culture reflect larger themes or patterns. Learning what constitutes American culture and how that information relates to other people throughout the world can be an exciting journey for a young person.

As language teachers, we are able to facilitate that journey into another culture and into our own, to find our similarities as well as our differences from others. We do not encourage value judgments about others and their culture, nor do we recommend adopting other ways. We simply say to students, "Other ways exist. They exist for many reasons, just as our ways exist due to what our ancestors have bequeathed us through history, traditions, values, and geography."

Allez, viens!

develops cultural understanding and awareness in the following ways:

THE PUPIL'S EDITION

- Informs students about French-speaking countries through photo essays, maps, almanac boxes, and **Notes culturelles** that invite comparison with the students' own cultural experiences.
- Engages students in analysis and comparison of live, personal interviews with native speakers in the **Panorama Culturel** sections.
- Uses the **Rencontre culturelle** section to expose students to cross-cultural situations that require observation, analysis, and problem-solving.
- Helps students integrate the language with its cultural connotations through a wealth of authentic art, documents, and literature.

THE ANNOTATED TEACHER'S EDITION

- Provides the teacher with additional culture, history, and language notes, background information on photos and almanac boxes, and multicultural links.
- Suggests problem-solving activities and critical thinking questions that allow students to hypothesize, analyze, and discover larger underlying cultural themes.

THE ANCILLARY PROGRAM

- Includes additional realia to develop cultural insight by serving as a catalyst for questioning and direct discovery.
- Offers activities that require students to compare and contrast cultures.
- Provides songs, short readings, and poems as well as many opportunities for students to experience regional variation and idioms in the video, audio, and CD-ROM programs.

Learning Styles and Multi-Modality Teaching

by Mary B. McGehee, Louisiana State University

Incorporating a greater variety of activities to accommodate the learning styles of all students can make the difference between struggle and pleasure in the foreign language classroom.

The larger and broader population of students who are enrolling in foreign language classes brings a new challenge to foreign language educators, calling forth an evolution in teaching methods to enhance learning for all our students. Educational experts now recognize that every student has a preferred sense for learning and retrieving information: visual, auditory, or kinesthetic. Incorporating a greater variety of activities to accommodate the learning styles of all students can make the difference between struggle and pleasure in the foreign language classroom.

Accommodating Different Learning Styles

A modified arrangement of the classroom is one way to provide more effective and enjoyable learning for all students. Rows of chairs and desks must give way at times to circles, semicircles, or small clusters. Students may be grouped in fours or in pairs for cooperative work or peer teaching. It is important to find a balance of arrangements, thereby providing the most comfort in varied situations.

Since visual, auditory, and kinesthetic learners will be in the class, and because every student's learning will be enhanced by a multi-sensory approach, lessons must be directed toward all three learning styles. Any language lesson content may be presented visually, aurally, or kinesthetically.

Visual presentations and practice may include the chalkboard, charts, posters, television, overhead projectors, books, magazines, picture diagrams, flash cards, bulletin boards, films, slides, or videos. Visual learners need to see what they are to learn. Lest the teacher think he or she will never have the time to prepare all those visuals, Dickel and Slak (1983) found that visual aids generated by students are more effective than ready-made ones.

Auditory presentations and practice may include stating aloud the requirements of the lesson, oral questions and answers, paired or group work on a progression of oral exercises from repetition to communication, tapes, CDs, dialogues, and role-playing. Jingles, catchy stories, and memory devices using songs and rhymes are good learning aids. Having students record themselves and then listen as they play back the cassette allows them to practice in the auditory mode.

Kinesthetic presentations entail the students' use of manipulatives, chart materials, gestures, signals, typing, songs, games, and role-playing. These lead the students to associate sentence constructions with meaningful movements.

A Sample Lesson Using Multi-Modality Teaching

A multi-sensory presentation on greetings might proceed as follows:

For Visual Learners

As the teacher begins oral presentation of greetings and introductions, he or she simultaneously shows the written forms on transparencies, with the formal expressions marked with an adult's hat, and the informal expressions marked with a baseball cap.

The teacher then distributes cards with the hat and cap symbols representing the formal and informal expressions. As the students hear taped mini-dialogues, they hold up the appropriate card to indicate whether the dialogues are formal or informal. On the next listening, the students repeat the sentences they hear.

For Auditory Learners

A longer taped dialogue follows, allowing the students to hear the new expressions a number of times. They write from dictation several sentences containing the new expressions. They may work in pairs, correcting each other's work as they "test" their own understanding of the lesson at hand. Finally, students respond to simple questions using the appropriate formal and informal responses cued by the cards they hold.

For Kinesthetic Learners

For additional kinesthetic input, members of the class come to the front of the room, each holding a hat or cap symbol. As the teacher calls out situations, the students play the roles, using gestures and props appropriate to the age group they are portraying. Non-cued, communicative role-playing with props further enables the students to "feel" the differences between formal and informal expressions.

Helping Students Learn How to Use Their Preferred Mode

Since we require all students to perform in all language skills, part of the assistance we must render is to help them develop strategies within their preferred learning modes to carry out an assignment in another mode. For example, visual students hear the teacher assign an oral exercise and visualize what they must do. They must see themselves carrying out the assignment, in effect watching themselves as if there were a movie going on in their heads. Only then can they also hear themselves saying the right things. Thus, this assignment will be much easier for the visual learners who have been taught this process, if they have not already figured it out for themselves. Likewise, true auditory students, confronted with a reading/writing assignment, must talk themselves through it, converting the entire process into sound as they plan and prepare their work. Kinesthetic students presented with a visual or auditory task must first break the assignment into tasks and then work their way through them.

Students who experience difficulty because of a strong preference for one mode of learning are often unaware of the degree of preference. In working with these students, I prefer the simple and direct assessment of learning styles offered by Richard Bandler and John Grinder in their book *Frogs into Princes,* which allows the teacher and student to quickly determine how the student learns. In an interview with the student, I follow the assessment with certain specific recommendations of techniques to make the student's study time more effective.

The following is an example of an art-based activity from *Allez,viens!*

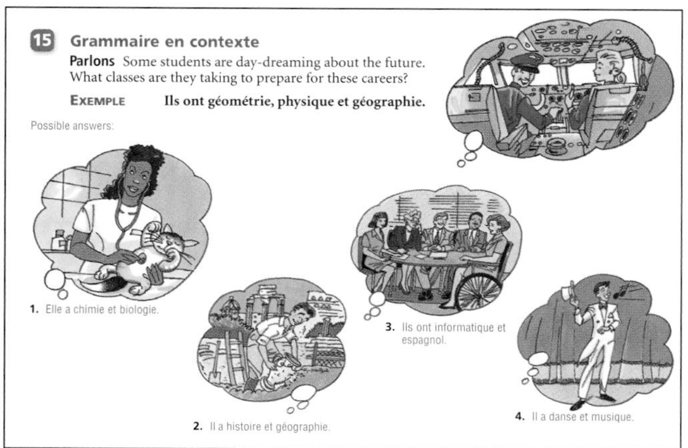

It is important to note here that teaching students to maximize their study does not require that the teacher give each student an individualized assignment. It does require that each student who needs it be taught how to prepare the assignment using his or her own talents and strengths. This communication between teacher and student, combined with teaching techniques that reinforce learning in all modes, can only maximize pleasure and success in learning a foreign language.

References

Dickel, M.J. and S. Slak. "Imaging Vividness and Memory for Verbal Material." *Journal of Mental Imagery* 7, i (1983):121–126.

Bandler, Richard, and John Grinder. *Frogs into Princes.* Real People Press, Moab, UT. 1978.

Allez, viens!

accommodates different learning styles in the following ways:

THE PUPIL'S EDITION

- Presents basic material in audio, video, print, and online formats.
- Includes role-playing activities and a variety of multi-modal activities, including an extensive listening strand and many art-based activities.

THE ANNOTATED TEACHER'S EDITION

- Provides suggested activities for visual, auditory, and kinesthetic learners as well as suggestions for slower-paced learning and challenge activities.
- Includes Total Physical Response activities.

THE ANCILLARY PROGRAM

- Provides additional reinforcement activities for a variety of learning styles.
- Presents a rich blend of audiovisual input through the video program, audio program, CD-ROM tutor, transparencies, and blackline masters.

Professional References

This section provides information about several resources that can enrich your French class. Included are addresses of government offices of francophone countries, pen pal organizations, subscription agencies, and many others. Since addresses change frequently, you may want to verify them before you send your requests. You may also want to refer to the HRW web site at http://www.hrw.com for current information.

CULTURAL AGENCIES

For historic and tourist information about France and francophone countries, contact:

French Cultural Services
972 Fifth Ave.
New York, NY 10021
(212) 439-1400

French Cultural Services
540 Bush St.
San Francisco, CA 94108
(415) 397-4330

TOURIST OFFICES

French Government Tourist Office
444 Madison Ave.
New York, NY 10022
(212) 838-7800

Délégation du Québec
53 State Street
Exchange Place Bldg., 19th floor
Boston, MA 02109
(617) 723-3366

Caribbean Tourism Association
20 E. 46th St., 4th floor
New York, NY 10017
(212) 682-0435

INTERCULTURAL EXCHANGE

American Field Service
198 Madison Ave.
New York, NY 10016
(212) 299-9000

CIEE Student Travel Services
205 East 42nd St.
New York, NY 10017
(212) 661-1414

PEN PAL ORGANIZATIONS

For the names of pen pal groups other than those listed below, contact your local chapter of AATF. There are fees involved, so be sure to write for information.

Student Letter Exchange
(League of Friendship)
211 Broadway, Suite 201
Lynbrook, NY 11563
(516) 887-8628

World Pen Pals
PO BOX 337
Saugerties, NY 12477
(914) 246-7828

PERIODICALS

Subscriptions to the following cultural materials are available directly from the publishers. See also the section on Subscription Services.

- ***Phosphore*** is a monthly magazine for high school students.
- ***Okapi*** is a bimonthly environmentally-oriented magazine for younger teenagers in France.
- ***Le Monde*** is the major daily newspaper in France.
- ***Le Figaro*** is an important newspaper in France. Daily or Saturday editions are available by subscription.
- ***Elle*** is a weekly fashion magazine for women.
- ***Paris Match*** is a general interest weekly magazine.
- ***Le Point*** is a current events weekly magazine.
- ***L'Express*** is a current events weekly magazine.

SUBSCRIPTION SERVICES

French-language magazines can be obtained through subscription agencies in the United States. The following companies are among the many that can provide your school with subscriptions.

EBSCO Subscription Services
5724 Hwy 280 E
Birmingham, AL 35242
(205) 991-6600

Continental Book Company
8000 Cooper Ave., Bldg. 29
Glendale, NY 11385
(718) 326-0560

PROFESSIONAL ORGANIZATIONS

The two major organizations for French teachers at the secondary-school level are:

The American Council on the Teaching of Foreign Languages (ACTFL)
6 Executive Blvd.
Upper Level
Yonkers, NY 10701
(914) 963-8830

The American Association of Teachers of French (AATF)
Mailcode 4510
Southern Illinois University
Carbondale, IL 61820

A Bibliography for the French Teacher

This bibliography is a compilation of several resources available for professional enrichment.

SELECTED AND ANNOTATED LIST OF READINGS

I. Methods and Approaches

Cohen, Andrew D. *Assessing Language Ability in the Classroom,* (2nd ed.). Boston, MA: Heinle, 1994.
- Assessment processes, oral interviews, role-playing situations, dictation, and portfolio assessment.

Hadley, Alice Omaggio. *Teaching Language in Context,* (2nd ed.). Boston, MA: Heinle, 1993.
- Overview of the proficiency movement and a survey of past language-teaching methods and approaches; application of the five skills in language education; includes sample activities, teaching summaries, and references.

Lafayette, R. (Ed.). *National Standards: A Catalyst for Reform.* Lincolnwood, IL: National Textbook Co., 1996.
- Outline and implications of the National Standards for the modern language classroom; addresses technology, teacher training, materials development, and the changing learning environment.

Lee, James F., and Bill VanPatten. *Making Communicative Language Teaching Happen.* New York: McGraw-Hill, 1995.
- Task-based approach to language education, includes activities and test sections to encourage communicative interaction in the classroom.

II. Second-Language Theory

Brown, H. Douglas. *Principles of Language Learning and Teaching* (3rd. ed.). Englewood Cliffs, NJ: Prentice Hall Regents, 1994.
- Addresses the cognitive, psychological, and sociocultural factors influencing the language-learning process; also includes theories of learning, styles and strategies, motivation, and culture; as well as assessment, error analysis, communicative competence, and theories of acquisition.

Ellis, Rod. *The Study of Second Language Acquisition.* Oxford: Oxford University Press, 1994.
- Provides an overview of second language acquisition: error analysis, acquisition orders, social factors, affective variables, individual differences, and the advantages and disadvantages of classroom instruction.

Krashen, Stephen. *The Power of Reading.* New York: McGraw, 1994.
- Updates Optimal Input Theory by incorporating the reading of authentic texts.

III. Technology-Enhanced instruction

Bush, Michael D., and Robert M. Terry, (Eds.), in conjunction with ACTFL. *Technology Enhanced Language Learning.* Lincolnwood, IL: National Textbook Co., 1997.
- Articles deal with the application of technology in the modern language classroom, including: computer-mediated communication, electronic discussions, hypermedia, the Internet, multimedia, videos, and the WWW.

Muyskens, Judith Ann. (Ed.). *New Ways of Learning and Teaching: Focus on Technology and Foreign Language Education.* Boston: Heinle and Heinle, 1997.
- Compilation of articles on the use of technology in the classroom; techniques for applying technology tools to the four skills and culture; also discusses implementation, teacher training, and language laboratories.

Steen, Douglas R., Mark R. Roddy, Derek Sheffield, and Michael Bryan Stout. *Teaching With the Internet: Putting Teachers before Technology.* Bellevue, WA: Resolution Business Press, Inc., 1995.
- Designed for K–12 teachers and based on educational theory, provides tips and strategies for using the Internet in and out of the classroom, cites specific case studies; topics include the Internet, e-mail, mailing lists, newsgroups, the WWW, creating a Web page, and other research services.

IV. Professional Journals

Calico
(Published by the Computer Assisted Language Instruction Consortium)
- Dedicated to the intersection of modern language learning and high technology. Research articles on videodiscs, using computer-assisted language learning, how-to articles, and courseware reviews.

The Foreign Language Annals
(Published by the American Council on the Teaching of Foreign Languages)
- Consists of research and how-to-teach articles.

The French Review
(Published by the American Association of Teachers of French)
- Articles on French-language literature.

The IALL Journal of Language Learning Technologies
(Published by the International Association for Learning Laboratories)
- Research articles as well as practical discussions pertaining to technology and language instruction.

The Modern Language Journal
- Primarily features research articles.

HOLT FRENCH 1

Allez, viens!

HOLT, RINEHART AND WINSTON

A Harcourt Education Company

Orlando • **Austin** • New York • San Diego • Toronto • London

VIDEO PRODUCTION
Video materials produced by Edge Productions, Inc., Aiken, S.C.

ACKNOWLEDGMENTS

PHOTOGRAPHY CREDITS

Abbreviations used: (t) top, (c) center, (b) bottom, (l) left, (r) right, (bkgd) background

Front Cover: © David Noton/Masterfile

Back Cover: © Peter Byron/PhotoEdit; (frame) © 2006 Image Farm, Inc.

Acknowledgements appear on page R64, which is an extension of the copyright page.

Printed in the United States of America

ISBN 0-03-036942-8

1 2 3 4 5 6 7 8 9 048 09 08 07 06 05 04

AUTHORS

John DeMado
Washington, CT

Mr. DeMado helped form the general philosophy of the French program and wrote activities to practice basic material, functions, grammar, and vocabulary.

Emmanuel Rongiéras d'Usseau
Le Kremlin-Bicêtre, France

Mr. Rongiéras d'Usseau contributed to the development of the scope and sequence, created the basic material and listening scripts, selected realia, and wrote activities.

CONTRIBUTING WRITERS

Jayne Abrate
The University of Missouri
Rolla Campus
Rolla, MO

Sally Adamson Taylor
Publishers Weekly
San Francisco, CA

Linda Bistodeau
Saint Mary's University
Halifax, Nova Scotia

Betty Peltier
Consultant
Batz-sur-Mer, France

REVIEWERS

Dominique Bach
Rio Linda Senior High School
Rio Linda, CA

Jeannette Caviness
Mount Tabor High School
Winston-Salem, NC

Jennie Bowser Chao
Consultant
Oak Park, IL

Pierre F. Cintas
Penn State University
Abington College
Abington, PA

Donna Clementi
Appleton West High School
Appleton, WI

Cathy Cramer
Homewood High School
Birmingham, AL

Robert H. Didsbury
Consultant
Raleigh, NC

Jennifer Jones
U.S. Peace Corps volunteer
Côte d'Ivoire 1991–1993
Austin, TX

Joan H. Manley
The University of Texas at El Paso
El Paso, TX

Jill Markert
Pflugerville High School
Pflugerville, TX

Inge McCoy
Southwest Texas State University
San Marcos, TX

Gail Montgomery
Foreign Language Program
Administrator
Greenwich, CT Public Schools

Agathe Norman
Consultant
Austin, TX

Audrey O'Keefe
Jordan High School
Los Angeles, CA

Sherry Parker
Selvidge Middle School
Ballwin, MO

Sherron N. Porter
Robert E. Lee High School
Baton Rouge, LA

Marc Prévost
Austin Community College
Austin, TX

Norbert Rouquet
Consultant
La Roche-sur-Yon, France

Michèle Shockey
Gunn High School
Palo Alto, CA

Ashley Shumaker
Central High School West
Tuscaloosa, AL

Antonia Stergiades
Washington High School
Massillon, OH

Frederic L. Toner
Texas Christian University
Fort Worth, TX

Jeannine Waters
Harrisonburg High School
Harrisonburg, VA

Jo Anne S. Wilson
Consultant
Glen Arbor, MI

FIELD TEST PARTICIPANTS

Marie Allison
New Hanover High School
Wilmington, NC

Gabrielle Applequist
Capital High School
Boise, ID

Jana Brinton
Bingham High School
Riverton, UT

Nancy J. Cook
Sam Houston High School
Lake Charles, LA

Rachael Gray
Williams High School
Plano, TX

Katherine Kohler
Nathan Hale Middle School
Norwalk, CT

Nancy Mirsky
Museum Junior High School
Yonkers, NY

Myrna S. Nie
Whetstone High School
Columbus, OH

Jacqueline Reid
Union High School
Tulsa, OK

Judith Ryser
San Marcos High School
San Marcos, TX

Erin Hahn Sass
Lincoln Southeast High School
Lincoln, NE

Linda Sherwin
Sandy Creek High School
Tyrone, GA

Norma Joplin Sivers
Arlington Heights High School
Fort Worth, TX

Lorabeth Stroup
Lovejoy High School
Lovejoy, GA

Robert Vizena
W.W. Lewis Middle School
Sulphur, LA

Gladys Wade
New Hanover High School
Wilmington, NC

Kathy White
Grimsley High School
Greensboro, NC

TO THE STUDENT

Some people have the opportunity to learn a new language by living in another country. Most of us, however, begin learning another language and getting acquainted with a foreign culture in a classroom with the help of a teacher, classmates, and a textbook. To use your book effectively, you need to know how it works.

Allez, viens! (*Come along!*) is organized to help you learn French and become familiar with the cultures of people who speak French. The Preliminary Chapter presents basic concepts in French and strategies for learning a new language. This chapter is followed by six Location Openers and twelve chapters.

Location Opener Six four-page photo essays called Location Openers introduce different French-speaking places. You can also see these locations on video, the *CD-ROM Tutor,* and the *DVD Tutor.*

Chapter Opener The Chapter Opener pages tell you the chapter theme and goals.

Mise en train *(Getting Started)* This illustrated story, which is also on video, shows you French-speaking people in real-life situations, using the language you'll learn in the chapter.

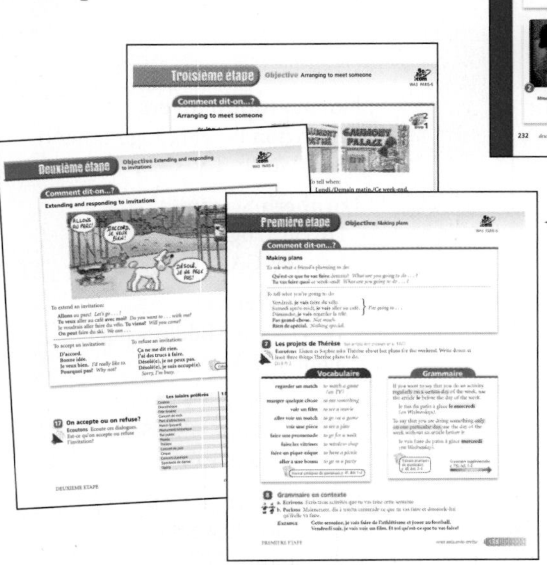

Première, Deuxième, and Troisième étape *(First, Second, Third Part)* After the **Mise en train**, the chapter is divided into three sections called **étapes**. Within the **étape,** are **Comment dit-on... ?** *(How Do You Say . . . ?)* boxes that contain the French expressions you'll need to communicate and **Vocabulaire** and **Grammaire/Note de grammaire** boxes that give you the French words and grammatical structures you'll need to know. Activities in each **étape** enable you to develop your skills in listening, reading, speaking, and writing.

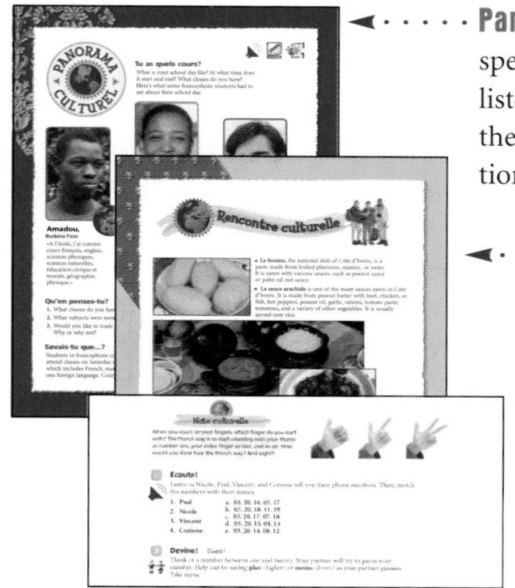

Panorama Culturel *(Cultural Panorama)* On this page are interviews with French-speaking people from around the world. You can watch these interviews on video or listen to them on audio CD. You can also watch them using the *CD-ROM Tutor* and the *DVD Tutor,* then check to see how well you understood by answering some questions about what the people say.

Rencontre culturelle *(Cultural Encounter)* This section, found in six of the chapters, gives you a firsthand encounter with some aspect of a French-speaking culture.

Note culturelle *(Culture Note)* In each chapter, there are notes with more information about the cultures of French-speaking people.

Lisons! *(Let's Read!)* The reading section follows the three **étapes**. The selections are related to the chapter themes and help you develop your reading skills in French.

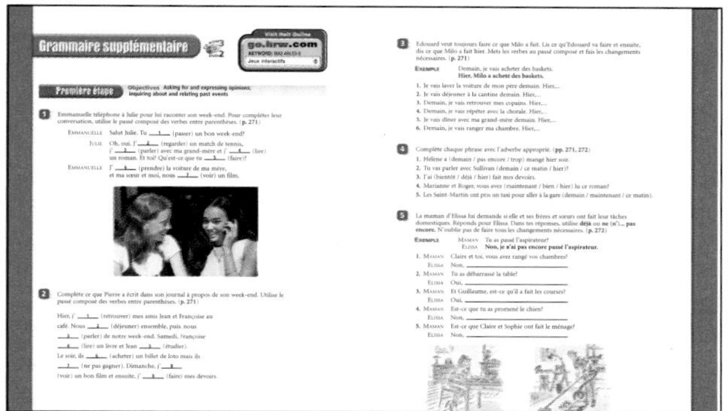

Grammaire supplémentaire *(Additional Grammar Practice)* This section begins the chapter review. You will find four pages of activities that provide additional practice on the grammar concepts you learned in the chapter.

Mise en pratique *(Review)* The activities on these pages practice what you've learned in the chapter and help you improve your listening, reading, and communication skills. You'll also review what you've learned about culture. A section called **Ecrivons**! *(Let's Write!)* in Chapters 3–12 will help develop your writing skills.

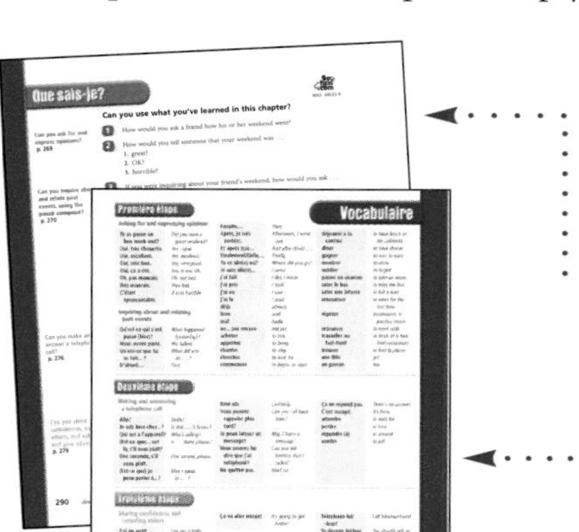

Que sais-je? *(Let's See if I Can . . .)* This page at the end of each chapter contains a series of questions and short activities to help you see if you've achieved the chapter goals.

Vocabulaire *(Vocabulary)* On the French-English vocabulary list on the last page of the chapter, the words are grouped by **étape**. These words and expressions will be on the quizzes and tests.

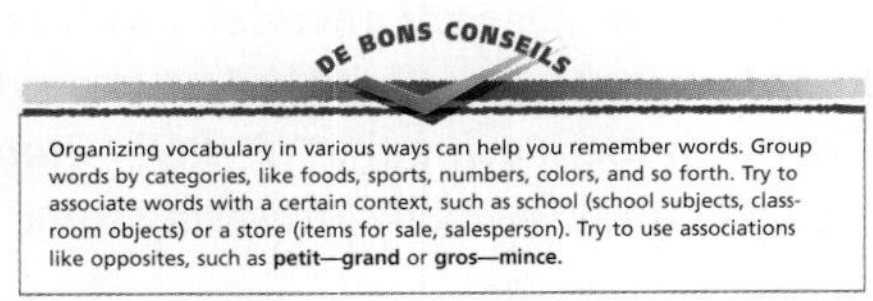
DE BONS CONSEILS

Organizing vocabulary in various ways can help you remember words. Group words by categories, like foods, sports, numbers, colors, and so forth. Try to associate words with a certain context, such as school (school subjects, classroom objects) or a store (items for sale, salesperson). Try to use associations like opposites, such as **petit—grand** or **gros—mince**.

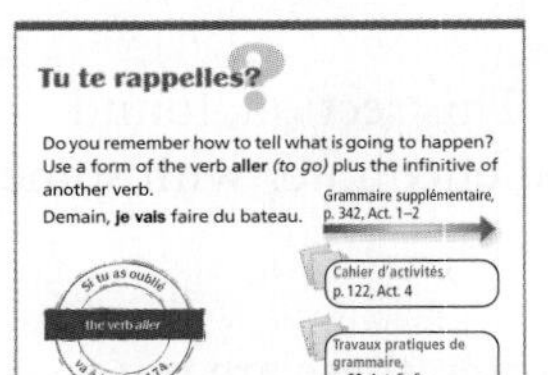
Tu te rappelles?

Do you remember how to tell what is going to happen? Use a form of the verb **aller** *(to go)* plus the infinitive of another verb.

Demain, **je vais** faire du bateau.

Grammaire supplémentaire, p. 342, Act. 1–2

Cahier d'activités, p. 122, Act. 4

Travaux pratiques de grammaire, p. 90, Act. 5–6

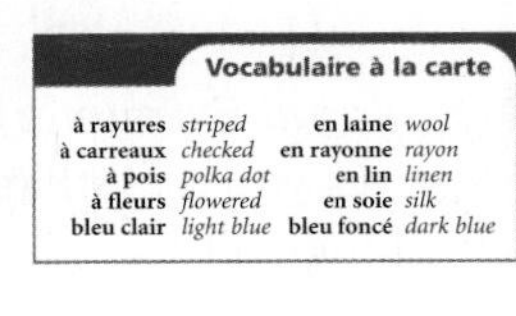
Vocabulaire à la carte

à rayures	*striped*	**en laine**	*wool*
à carreaux	*checked*	**en rayonne**	*rayon*
à pois	*polka dot*	**en lin**	*linen*
à fleurs	*flowered*	**en soie**	*silk*
bleu clair	*light blue*	**bleu foncé**	*dark blue*

A la française

The French often use the present tense of a verb to say that something will happen in the near future, just as we do in English.

Samedi matin, je vais jouer au tennis. *Saturday morning, I'm going to play tennis.*
Samedi matin, je joue au tennis. *Saturday morning, I'm playing tennis.*

You'll also find special features in each chapter that provide extra tips and reminders.

De bons conseils (*Helpful advice*) offers study hints to help you succeed in a foreign language class.

Tu te rappelles? (*Do you remember?*) and **Si tu as oublié** (*If you forgot*) remind you of expressions, grammar, and vocabulary you may have forgotten.

A la française (*The French way*) gives you additional expressions to add more color to your speech.

Vocabulaire à la carte (*Additional Vocabulary*) lists extra words you might find helpful. These words will not appear on the quizzes and tests unless your teacher chooses to include them.

You'll also find French-English and English-French vocabulary lists at the end of the book. The words you'll need to know for the quizzes and tests are in boldface type.

At the end of your book, you'll find more helpful material, such as:

- a summary of the expressions you'll learn in the **Comment dit-on... ?** boxes
- additional vocabulary words you might want to use
- a summary of the grammar you'll study
- a grammar index to help you find where structures are presented

Allez, viens! Come along on an exciting trip to new cultures and a new language!

Bon voyage!

Explanation of Icons in *Allez, viens!*

Throughout* Allez, viens!, *you'll see these symbols, or icons, next to activities and presentations. The following key will help you understand them.

Video/DVD Whenever this icon appears, you'll know there is a related segment in the *Allez, viens! Video* and *DVD* Programs.

Listening Activities

Pair Work/Group Work Activities

Writing Activities

Interactive Games and Activities Whenever this icon appears, you'll know there is a related activity on the *Allez, viens! Interactive CD-ROM Tutor* and on the *DVD Tutor*.

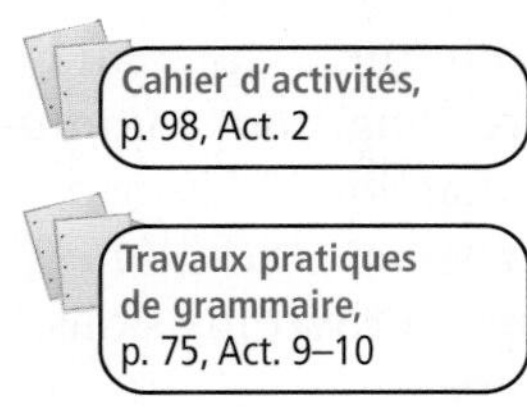

Practice Activities These icons tell you which activities from the *Cahier d'activités* and the *Travaux pratiques de grammaire* practice the material presented.

Grammaire supplémentaire, p. 286, Act. 15–16

Grammaire supplémentaire This reference tells you where you can find additional grammar practice in the review section of the chapter.

Internet Activities This icon provides the keyword you'll need to access related online activities at **go.hrw.com.**

Allez, viens! Contents

Come along—to a world of new experiences!

Allez, viens! offers you the opportunity to learn the language spoken by millions of people in countries in Europe, Africa, Asia, and around the world. Let's find out what those countries are.

CHAPITRE PRELIMINAIRE

ALLEZ, VIENS

à Poitiers!

LOCATION FOR CHAPITRES 1, 2, 3 12

CHAPITRE 1

Faisons connaissance! 16

Chapitre 2

Vive l'école! 46

Chapitre 3

Tout pour la rentrée 74

ALLEZ, VIENS

à Québec!

CHAPITRE 4

Sports et passe-temps 106

ALLEZ, VIENS

à Paris!

CHAPITRE 5

Chapitre 6

Amusons-nous! 168

CHAPITRE 7

La famille 198

ALLEZ, VIENS

à Abidjan!

CHAPITRE 8

Au marché.....230

ALLEZ, VIENS

en Arles!

Chapitre 10

Dans un magasin de vêtements 292

Chapitre 11

Vive les vacances! 322

ALLEZ, VIENS

à Fort-de-France!

CHAPITRE 12

En ville.....354

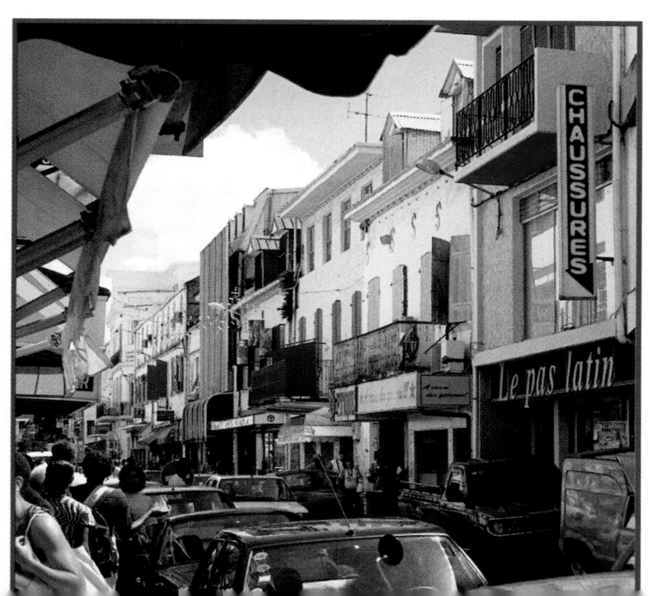

REFERENCE SECTION

Cultural References

Page numbers referring to material in the* Pupil's Edition *appear in regular type. When the material referenced is located in the* Annotated Teacher's Edition, *page numbers appear in boldface type.

RECIPES

RESTAURANTS AND CAFES

SCHOOL LIFE

SHOPPING

SPORTS

TELEPHONE

TIME AND TEMPERATURE

TRADITIONS

TRANSPORTATION

LA FRANCE

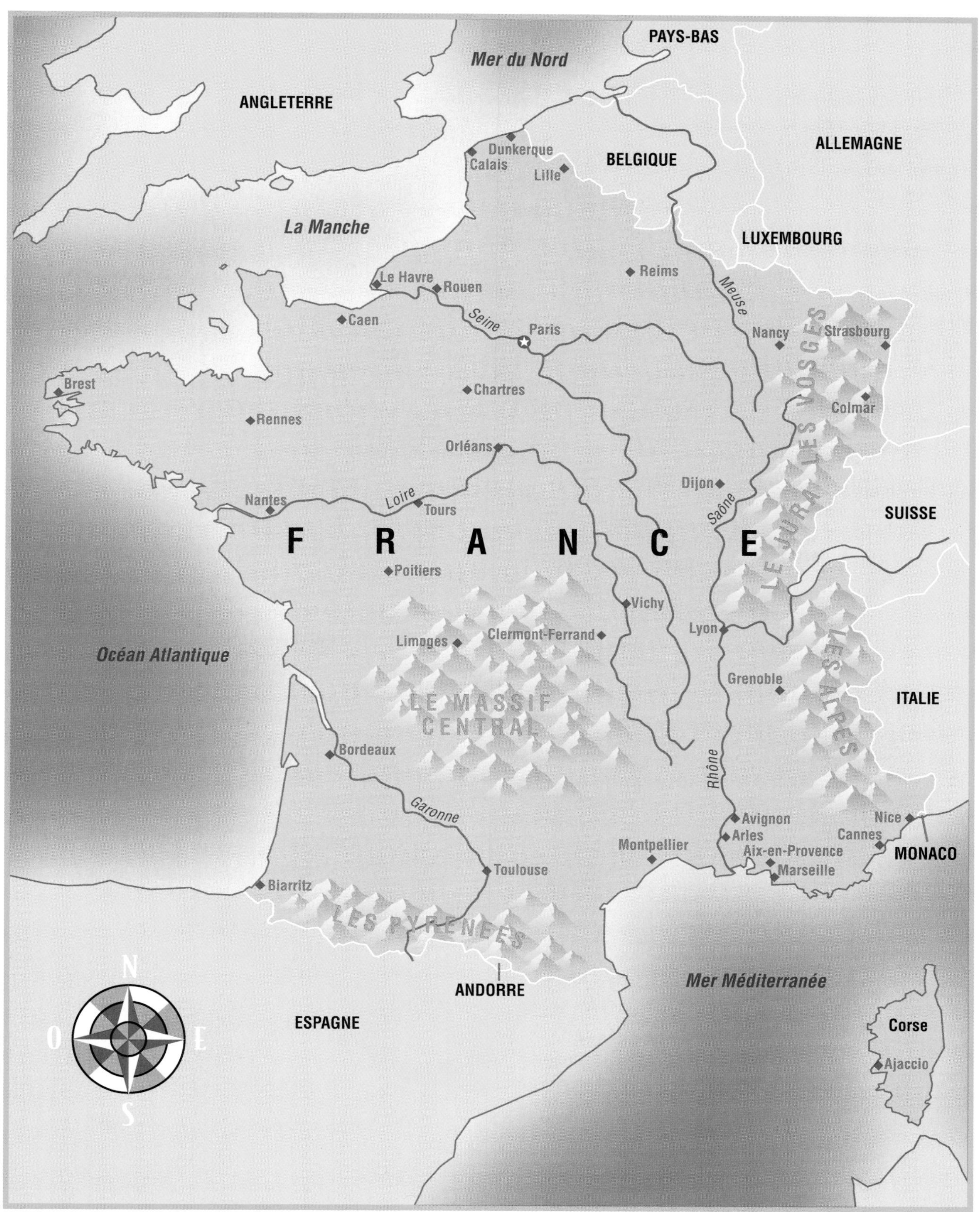

PAYS-BAS
Mer du Nord
ANGLETERRE
ALLEMAGNE
Dunkerque
Calais
BELGIQUE
Lille
La Manche
LUXEMBOURG
Reims
Le Havre
Rouen
Meuse
Caen
Seine
Paris
Nancy
Strasbourg
LES VOSGES
Brest
Chartres
Colmar
Rennes
Orléans
Dijon
Nantes
Loire
Tours
Saône
SUISSE
LE JURA
F R A N C E
Poitiers
Vichy
Lyon
Limoges
Clermont-Ferrand
Océan Atlantique
LES ALPES
Grenoble
ITALIE
LE MASSIF CENTRAL
Bordeaux
Rhône
Garonne
Avignon
Nice
Arles
Cannes
Montpellier
Aix-en-Provence
MONACO
Toulouse
Marseille
Biarritz
LES PYRÉNÉES
N
Mer Méditerranée
ANDORRE
O
E
ESPAGNE
Corse
Ajaccio
S

L'AFRIQUE FRANCOPHONE

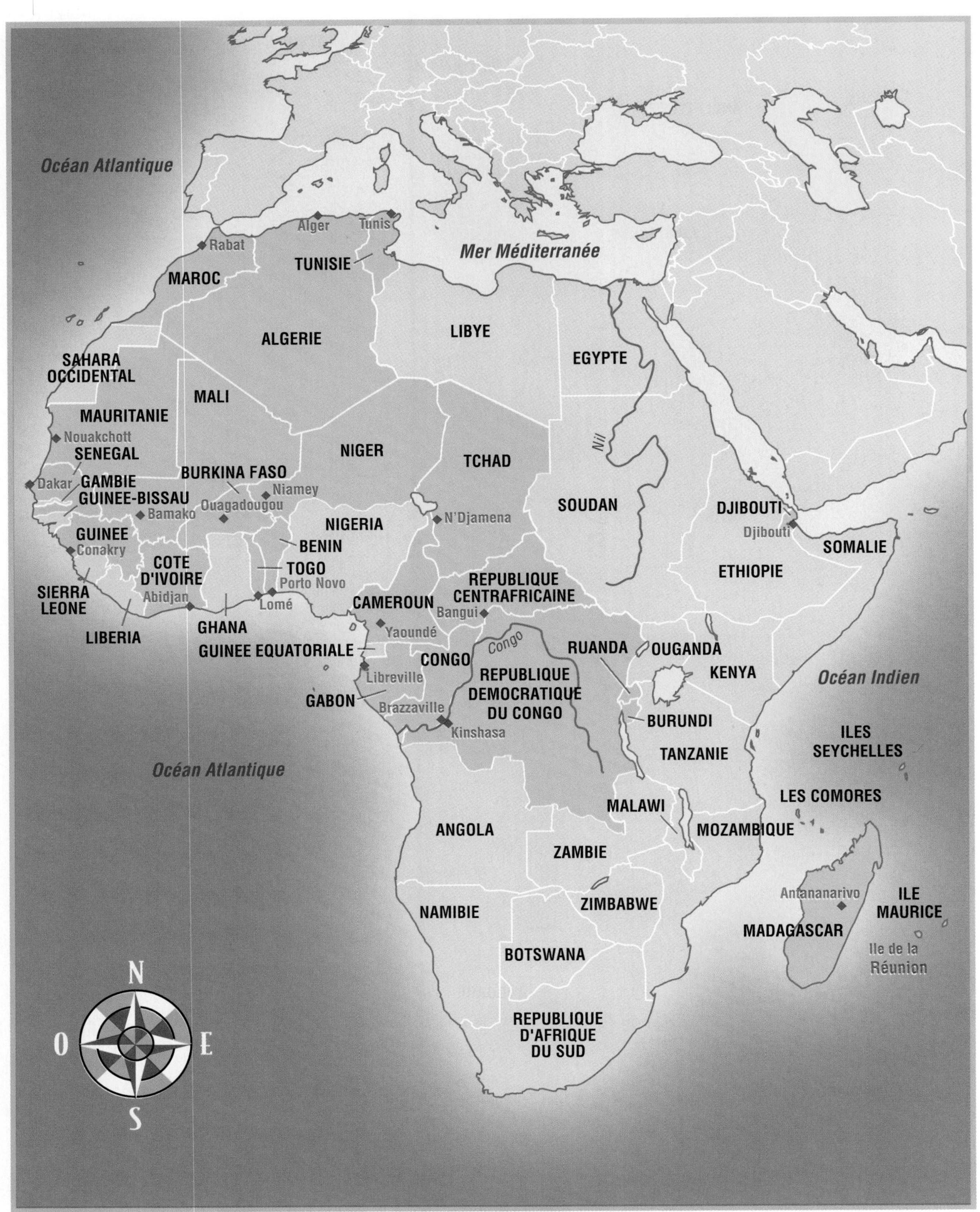

L'AMERIQUE FRANCOPHONE

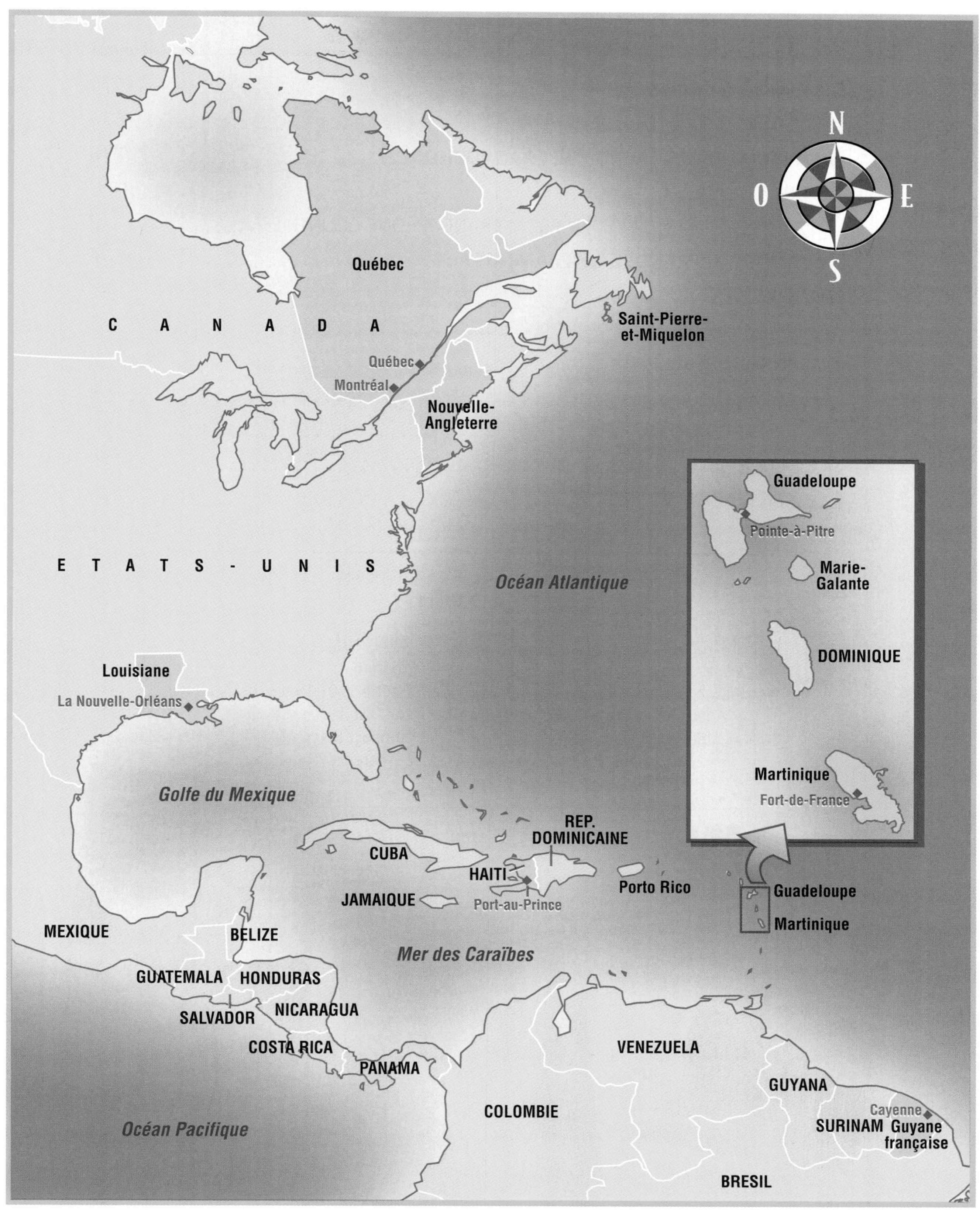

Chapitre Préliminaire : pp. T74–11

Chapter Overview

CONTENTS

Teaching Resources

pp. T76–11

PRINT 

- Lesson Planner, pp. 1–2
- Listening Activities, p. 2
- Video Guide, pp. 1–2, 87
- Cahier d'activités, pp. 1–2

MEDIA 

- Video Program Videocassette 1, 01:13–05:29
- DVD Tutor, Disc 1
- Audio Compact Discs, CD 1, Trs. 1–10
- Map Transparency 4

Chapitre Préliminaire : *Allez, viens!*

Textbook Listening Activities Scripts 

The following scripts are for the listening activities found in the *Pupil's Edition.* For Student Response Forms, see *Listening Activities,* page 2.

To preview all resources available for this chapter, use the **One-Stop Planner CD-ROM**, Disc 1.

Noms de filles/Noms de garçons, p. 5

For this script, see *Pupil's Edition.*

L'alphabet, p. 6

For this script, see *Pupil's Edition.*

p. 7

1. k–a–n–g–o–u–r–o–u
2. s–e–r–p–e–n–t
3. p–i–n–g–o–u–i–n
4. c–r–a–b–e
5. s–i–n–g–e
6. t–i–g–r–e

Answers to Activity 3
1. f
2. e
3. b
4. a
5. d
6. c

Les accents, p. 8

For this script, see *Pupil's Edition.*

p. 8

1. p–o–è–m–e
2. h–ô–p–i–t–a–l
3. a–m–é–r–i–c–a–i–n
4. c–a–n–o–ë
5. f–r–a–n–ç–a–i–s
6. s–é–v–è–r–e

Les chiffres de 0 à 20, p. 9

For this script, see *Pupil's Edition.*

p. 9

1. Moi, mon numéro de téléphone, c'est le zéro trois, vingt, quatorze, zéro huit, douze.
2. Téléphone-moi au zéro trois, vingt, seize, zéro cinq, dix-sept.
3. Mon numéro, c'est le zéro trois, vingt, dix-huit, onze, dix-neuf.
4. Voilà le numéro : zéro trois, vingt, quinze, zéro quatre, treize.

Answers to Activity 6
1. e
2. a
3. b
4. d

A l'école, p. 10

For this script, see *Pupil's Edition.*

p. 10

1. Allez au tableau!
2. Fermez la porte!
3. Regardez la carte!
4. Levez la main!
5. Ouvrez le livre!
6. Sortez une feuille de papier!
7. Levez-vous!

Answers to Activity 9
1. Lynn
2. Emilio
3. Brian
4. Alison
5. Paul
6. Dena
7. Evelyne

CHAPITRE PRELIMINAIRE

Teacher Note

The video for the Preliminary Chapter will introduce your students to some of the people they will see in the rest of *Allez, viens!* Some are actors in the **romans-photos** found in the **Mise en train** sections, and others are people interviewed for the **Panorama Culturel.** You may wish to play the video to preview the program and to give your students an introduction to the French language.

Language Note

The title of this French program, *Allez, viens!*, is a popular idiomatic expression meaning *Come along!*, *Come on!*, or *Let's go! Allez, viens!* is particularly appropriate as the title of this program because it is an invitation to each student of French to *Come along!* on an exciting trip to a new culture and a new language.

Visual Learners

You might want to use *Map Transparency 4* **(Le Monde francophone)** as you introduce students to the countries where French is spoken.

CHAPITRE PRELIMINAIRE

Allez, viens!

Bienvenue dans le monde francophone!

Welcome to the French-speaking world!

You know, of course, that French is spoken in France, but did you know that French is spoken by many people in North America? About one-third of Canadians speak French, mostly in Quebec province. In the United States, about 375,000 people in New England, whose ancestors immigrated from Canada, speak or understand French. French is also an official language in the state of Louisiana.

French is the official language of France's overseas possessions. These include the islands of Martinique and Guadeloupe in the Caribbean Sea, French Guiana in South America, the island of Réunion in the Indian Ocean, and several islands in the Pacific Ocean. French is also spoken in Haiti.

French is also widely used in over twenty African countries where it is an official language. Many people in West and Central African countries, such as Senegal, the Republic of Côte d'Ivoire, Mali, Niger, and Chad, speak French. In North Africa, French has played an important role in Algeria, Tunisia, and Morocco. Although Arabic is the official language of these North African countries, French is used in many schools across North Africa.

Take a minute to find France on the map. Several of the countries bordering France use French as an official language. It's the first or second language of many people in Belgium, Switzerland, Luxembourg, and Andorra, as well as in the principality of Monaco.

As you look at the map, what other places can you find where French is spoken? Can you imagine how French came to be spoken in these places?

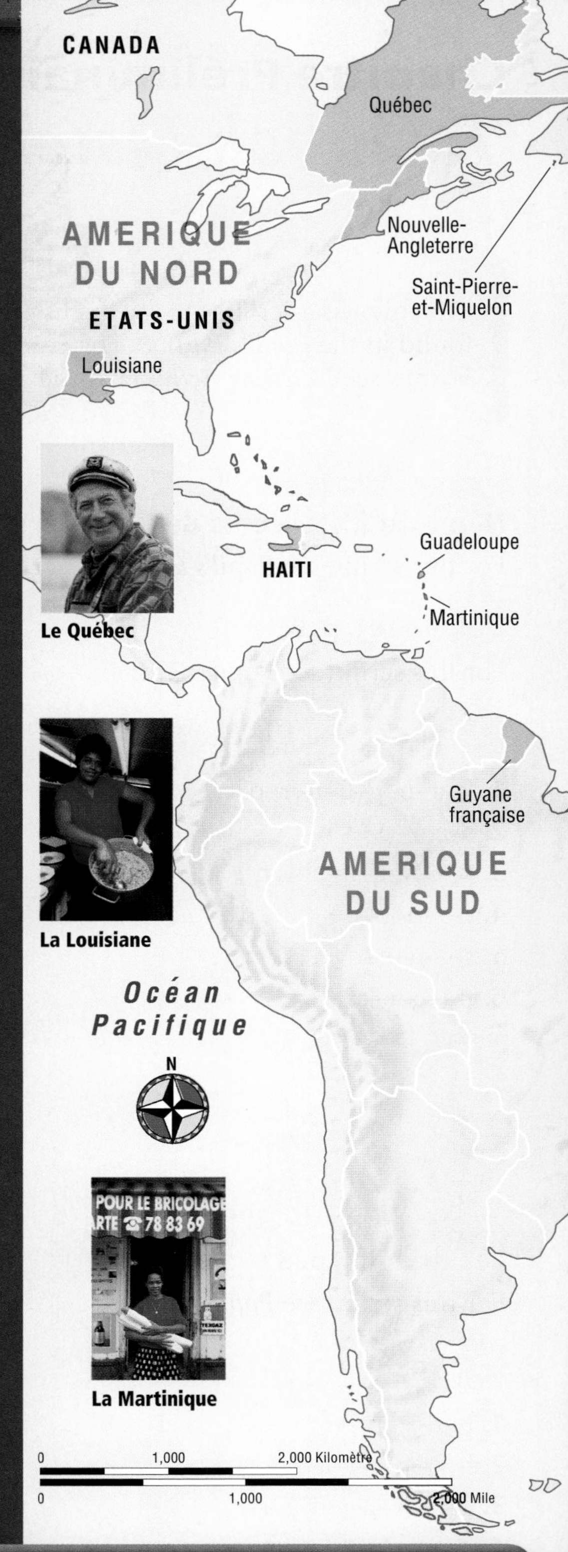

Connections and Comparisons

Geography Link

Ask students what comes to mind when they think of the French-speaking countries of the world. Besides France, do they know any other countries where French is spoken? Have them name cities in the United States with French names. (Des Moines, Beaumont, Pierre, Baton Rouge, Detroit, St. Louis, La Crosse)

History Link

Ask students if they have heard of the French explorers Marquette, Joliet, and La Salle. Marquette and Joliet explored the Wisconsin, Mississippi, and Illinois rivers, and La Salle explored the Ohio River, the Great Lakes, and the Mississippi River. Cartier and Champlain were explorers of Canada.

BELGIQUE
LUXEMBOURG
EUROPE
FRANCE
SUISSE
MONACO
TUNISIE
MAROC
ALGERIE
AFRIQUE
MAURITANIE
MALI
NIGER
SENEGAL
TCHAD
BURKINA FASO
GUINEE
BENIN
COTE D'IVOIRE
TOGO
DJIBOUTI
CAMEROUN
REPUBLIQUE CENTRAFRICAINE
GABON
CONGO
RUANDA
REPUBLIQUE DEMOCRATIQUE DU CONGO
BURUNDI
ILES SEYCHELLES
ILES COMORES
MADAGASCAR
ILE MAURICE
Ile de la Réunion
Océan Indien
Océan Atlantique
LAOS
VIET-NAM
CAMBODGE
Océan Pacifique
Polynésie-Française
Nouvelle-Calédonie
AUSTRALIE

Le Maroc

La France

La Côte d'Ivoire

Le Sénégal

Le Viêt-nam

CHAPITRE PRELIMINAIRE

Teacher Note

The scripts for the listening activities in the Preliminary Chapter are on page T75 and are recorded on *Audio CD 1*.

Building on Previous Skills

If they are available, show photos, slides, or short videos of the places mentioned. You might also start a discussion by asking students if they have any travel stories to share, if they would like to live or travel overseas, and if they have preconceived impressions of people in these places. Point out that even different regions of the United States can feel like foreign countries at times!

Presenting The Map

Ask students to look at the map of the French-speaking world on these two pages. Ask them where French is spoken and what ethnic groups are represented in these areas. Call out the names of some francophone countries and have students locate them on the map. Circulate to help students find the different countries or ask individual students to point to the places you mention on *Map Transparency 4* or on a large wall map.

History Link

France had overseas colonies until the 1960s and still maintains close ties with many of the countries. Algeria was the last to gain its independence in 1962.

Cultures and Communities

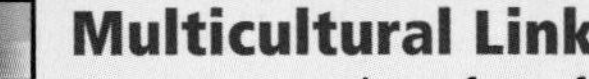

Culture Notes

- There are numerous mosques in France because of its large African Muslim population.
- Martinique and Guadeloupe are departments **(départements)** of France, so the people of these islands are French citizens and have French passports. They speak both French and Creole.

Multicultural Link

Numerous authors from francophone regions are quite popular in France: Maryse Condé (Guadeloupe), Tahar Ben Jelloun (Morocco), and Albert Camus (Algeria). Have students research various francophone authors and report their findings to the class.

STANDARDS: 2.2, 3.1

Tu les connais?

CHAPITRE PRELIMINAIRE

Background Information

1. **Isabelle Adjani** started a theater troupe with some friends at age 13, and at 15, she began her acting career at the **Comédie-Française,** a historic theater in Paris. While playing Agnès in Molière's *L'Ecole des femmes,* she continued to study for the **baccalauréat.** Her film portrayals have won her three **Césars,** the French equivalent of the Oscars.
2. **Jacques-Yves Cousteau** won over 20 film awards and produced numerous TV series and specials. His interest in inventing and ocean exploration manifested itself early, and at age 11, he made a patentable improvement on a marine crane. During World War II, he worked for the resistance movement. His voyages in his vessel *Calypso* began in 1951, and in 1959, he helped invent a mini-submarine that holds two people and photography equipment. He founded the Cousteau Society in 1973 to alert the public to pollution in the oceans.
3. **Léopold Senghor** served in the French parliament from 1946 to 1960, when he was elected president of Senegal. He founded the magazine *L'Etudiant noir* with Aimé Césaire. In the first issue in 1934, they presented the principles of **Négritude,** a literary movement that emphasized the Black experience. Senghor was a member of the **Institut de France.** In June of 1983, he was elected to the prestigious **Académie française.** In October 1996, a large celebration was held in Paris in honor of Senghor's ninetieth birthday.
4. **Marie Curie,** famous for giving radioactivity its name, was born in Poland and moved to Paris where she attended the Sorbonne. After discovering several radioactive elements, she and her husband finally isolated radium in 1902. She drove an ambulance and provided X-ray service to hospitals during World War I. She is the only person to win two Nobel prizes in science, but she was denied entrance into the French Academy by one vote because of her gender. She died of leukemia.

Tu les connais? ▪ *Do you know them?*

In science, politics, technology, and the arts, French-speaking people have made important contributions. How many of these people can you match with their descriptions?

A

B

C

1 **Isabelle Adjani (b. 1955)** A talented actress and producer, Isabelle Yasmine Adjani is well known for her award-winning roles in French films. In the 1980s, Adjani publicly acknowledged her Algerian heritage and began a personal campaign to raise consciousness about racism in France.

2 **Jacques Cousteau (1910-1997)** Jacques-Yves Cousteau first gained worldwide attention for his undersea expeditions as the commander of the Calypso and for inventing the aqualung. In order to record his explorations, he invented a process for filming underwater.

3 **Léopold Senghor (1906-2001)** A key advocate of Négritude, which asserts the values and the spirit of black African civilization, Senghor was a man of many talents. He was the first black African high school teacher in France. He was President of Senegal from 1960 to 1980. He was also the first black member of the **Académie Française.**

4 **Marie Curie (1867-1934)** Along with her husband Pierre, Marie Curie won a Nobel prize in physics for her study of radioactivity. Several years later, she also won an individual Nobel prize for chemistry. Marie Curie was the first woman to teach at the Sorbonne in Paris.

D

STANDARDS: 2.2

5 **Victor Hugo (1802-1885)** Novelist, poet, and political activist, Hugo led the Romantic Movement in French literature. In his most famous works, *Notre-Dame de Paris (The Hunchback of Notre Dame)* and *Les Misérables,* he sympathizes with the victims of poverty and condemns a corrupt political system.

6 **Zinedine Zidane (b. 1972)** Zinedine Zidane, one of the most well-known soccer players in France and Europe, has received numerous awards and recognition for his accomplishments in soccer. In 1998, he helped lead the National French Team to victory by scoring two important goals to win the World Soccer Championship. He also received the Golden Ball award and was elected Best Player of the World.

7 **Céline Dion (b. 1968)** A native of Quebec, Dion is an award-winning singer whose work includes hit songs in both English and French. In 1996, her album *Falling Into You* was awarded the Grammy® for Album of the Year and Best Pop Album. Dion also performed in the opening ceremonies of the 1996 Olympic Games in Atlanta, Georgia.

8 **Gérard Depardieu (b. 1948)** Gérard Depardieu is a popular actor, director, and producer, who has appeared in over 70 films. His performance in the 1990 movie *Green Card,* which won him a Golden Globe award, marked his American film debut.

F

G

E

H

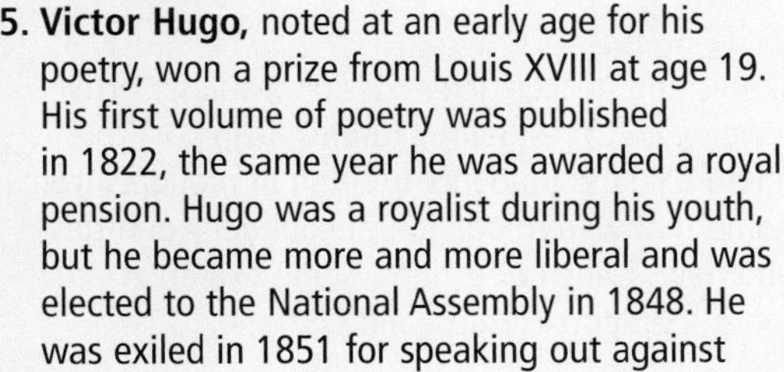

1C 2D 3G 4A 5B 6H 7E 8F

Tu les connais?

CHAPITRE PRELIMINAIRE

6. **Zinedine Zidane** started his career as a soccer player in the club of Cannes. He was first selected to play for the French National team, **"les bleus"**, in August 1994. From 1996 to 2001, he played for the **Juventus** from Turini. He won the World Cup in 1998 and the Euro Cup in 2000. In 2001, he transferred to **Real** from Madrid.
7. **Céline Dion** is from Charlemagne, a town 20 kilometers east of Montreal. The youngest of 14 children, Dion began her musical career at the age of 12. Raised in Quebec, a francophone region of Canada, she did not learn English until she was in her late teens. At the 1997 World Music Awards, she was named World's Overall Best-Selling Artist and World's Best-Selling Pop Artist.
8. **Gérard Depardieu**, one of six children of an illiterate sheet metal worker, had a rough childhood, which included arrests for petty theft and truancy. By his late teens, he was in jail and had become mute. A prison official sent him to a speech therapist who helped him discover acting. When he started his career, he had difficulty reading scripts, but was quickly noticed for his talent in an extremely wide range of roles. His films include *My Father the Hero, Danton* (about the French Revolution), *Jean de Florette, Le Retour de Martin Guerre* (remade in the United States as *Sommersby*), *Cyrano de Bergerac,* and *Tous les Matins du monde,* which also starred his son Guillaume.

5. **Victor Hugo,** noted at an early age for his poetry, won a prize from Louis XVIII at age 19. His first volume of poetry was published in 1822, the same year he was awarded a royal pension. Hugo was a royalist during his youth, but he became more and more liberal and was elected to the National Assembly in 1848. He was exiled in 1851 for speaking out against Napoleon III. Hugo's exile, spent mostly in the Channel Islands, lasted 19 years, during which time he continued to write. Because of his popularity during his lifetime, his 80th birthday was widely celebrated. His principal works include eight novels, nine plays, and 22 volumes of poetry.

Challenge

Ask students if they know of other famous French-speaking people. You might have students prepare oral reports on them.

CHAPITRE PRELIMINAIRE

Teacher Note

Some activities suggested in the *Teacher's Edition* ask students to contact various people, businesses, and organizations in the community. Before assigning these activities, it is advisable to request parental permission. In some cases, you may also want to obtain permission from the parties the students will be asked to contact.

Career Path

Ask students to discuss why French is necessary in business, travel, and other areas if "everyone speaks English." Ask them why it is different to read something in the language in which it was written rather than in translation. Ask if any of the professions listed on this page interest them and why. In addition, have students find classified ads for employment that either require or prefer knowledge of a foreign language. You might bring in a variety of ads from different newspapers for this activity.

Pourquoi apprendre le français?

Why learn French?

To expand your horizons

When you study a language, you learn much more than vocabulary and grammar. You learn about the people who speak the language and the influence they've had on our lives. Francophone (French-speaking) cultures continue to make notable contributions to many fields, including art, literature, movies, fashion, cuisine, science, and technology.

For travel

Someday you may live, travel, or be an exchange student in one of the more than 30 countries all over the world where French is spoken. You can imagine how much more meaningful your experience will be if you can talk to people in their own language.

For career opportunities

Being able to communicate in another language can be an advantage when you're looking for employment in almost any field. As a journalist, sportscaster, hotel receptionist, tour guide, travel agent, buyer for a large company, lawyer, engineer, economist, financial expert, flight attendant, diplomat, translator, teacher, writer, interpreter, publisher, or librarian, you may have the opportunity to use French in your work. Did you know that nearly 4,000 American companies have offices in France?

For fun!

Perhaps the best reason for studying French is for the fun of it. Studying another language is a challenge to your mind, and you'll get a great feeling of accomplishment the first time you have a conversation in French.

Connections and Comparisons

Thinking Critically

Observing Have students work in pairs or small groups to identify the careers shown in some of the photos and to think of products and brand names from francophone countries. Examples include Perrier® and Evian® mineral water, Le Lion (Food Lion®) supermarkets, Air France®, Peugeot® cars, Michelin® tires, Sea-Doo® jet skis, CCM® skates and hockey gear, Rossignol® skis, Cartier® jewelry, and Yves Saint-Laurent® fashions. You might also ask students to bring in products from home that were made in francophone countries and have French directions. Some examples are food, shampoo, clothes, and perfume.

STANDARDS: 2.2, 5.1

Qui suis-je? ▪ *Who am I?*

Here's how to introduce yourself to young people who speak French.

To ask someone's name:
Tu t'appelles comment?
To give your name:
Je m'appelle...

Note culturelle

French-speaking people use **tu** *(you)* when they talk to a friend, a family member, or a person their own age or younger. In Chapter 1, you'll learn how to address an adult using the more formal **vous.**

Here's a list of some popular French names for girls and boys. Can you find your name, or a name similar to yours?

CD 1 Trs. 1–2

Noms de filles

Dominique
Corinne
Stéphanie
Julie
Audrey
Emilie
Sabrina
Séverine
Virginie
Valérie
Lætitia
Karine
Aurélie
Christelle
Delphine
Nathalie
Laurence
Céline
Elodie
Sandrine
Claudine

Noms de garçons

Vincent
Bernard
Stéphane
Eric
Jean
Daniel
Philippe
Frédéric
Cédric
Nicolas
Michel
Olivier
Jérôme
Christophe
Mathieu
Christian
David
Laurent
Marc
Gilles
Etienne
Pierre

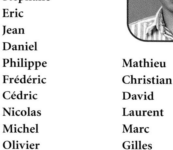

1 Présente-toi! *Introduce yourself!*

If you like, choose a French name for yourself. Introduce yourself to two or three students in the class, using your own name or your new French name. Ask them their names, too.

Cultures and Communities

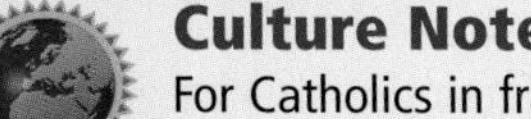

Culture Note

For Catholics in francophone countries, each day of the year commemorates a saint. French-speaking Catholics choose a personal saint when they are confirmed as members of the Church. They sometimes celebrate their saint's day **(la fête)** with a cake and cards as they do their own birthdays. People in France sometimes refer to well-known saints' days instead of saying the date; for example, **On se verra avant la Sainte-Catherine.** *(We'll see each other before November 25th.)* Ask students to try to guess which saints are commemorated on February 14 (**Saint-Valentin**) and March 17 (**Saint-Patrick**).

STANDARDS: 1.2, 1.3, 2.1, 5.1

Qui suis-je?

CHAPITRE PRELIMINAIRE

Language Arts Link

Ask students if the English language ever had an informal or intimate way of saying *you.* (The pronouns *thou* and *thee,* to address close friends and family, are still used by groups such as the Quakers.)

Presenting
Noms

You might want to have students make name cards for their desks; this will help you learn their names. They might want to choose a French name.

Teacher Notes

- Other French boys' names are Antoine, Emmanuel, François, Guillaume, and Julien.
- Additional French girls' names are Anne, Béatrice, Charlotte, Claire, Françoise, Hélène, Jeanne, Nicole, and Véronique.
- Some French African boys' names (from Côte d'Ivoire) are Koffi, Kouassi, Yapo, Séka, Alidou, Moussa, Kouamé, and Daba.
- Some French African girls' names (from Côte d'Ivoire) are Amenan, Aya, Awa, Ami, Fatoumata, Adjoua, Assika, Aminata, Djeneba, and Ahou.

Language-to-Language

Just as in English, some French names have a masculine and feminine form, which sometimes sound the same: Michel/Michèle, René(e), and Frédéric/Frédérique. Still other names are used for both boys and girls: Claude and Dominique.

L'alphabet

CHAPITRE PRELIMINAIRE

Motivating Activity

Ask students to suggest situations in which you use the alphabet. These situations might include taking or leaving phone messages, making reservations, understanding acronyms (FBI, FDA), and distinguishing between homonyms, such as *pear* and *pair*, or **mère** (*mother*) and **maire** *(mayor)*. You might use the "Alphabet Song" to help students learn the pronunciation of the letters.

Language Note

You might want to tell students that learning to pronounce the alphabet, especially the vowels, can help with their French pronunciation.

L'alphabet ▪ *The alphabet*

CD 1 Tr. 3

The French alphabet looks the same as the English alphabet. The difference is in pronunciation. Look at the letters and words below as your teacher pronounces them or as you listen to the audio recording. Which letters sound similar in English and French? Which ones have a different sound?

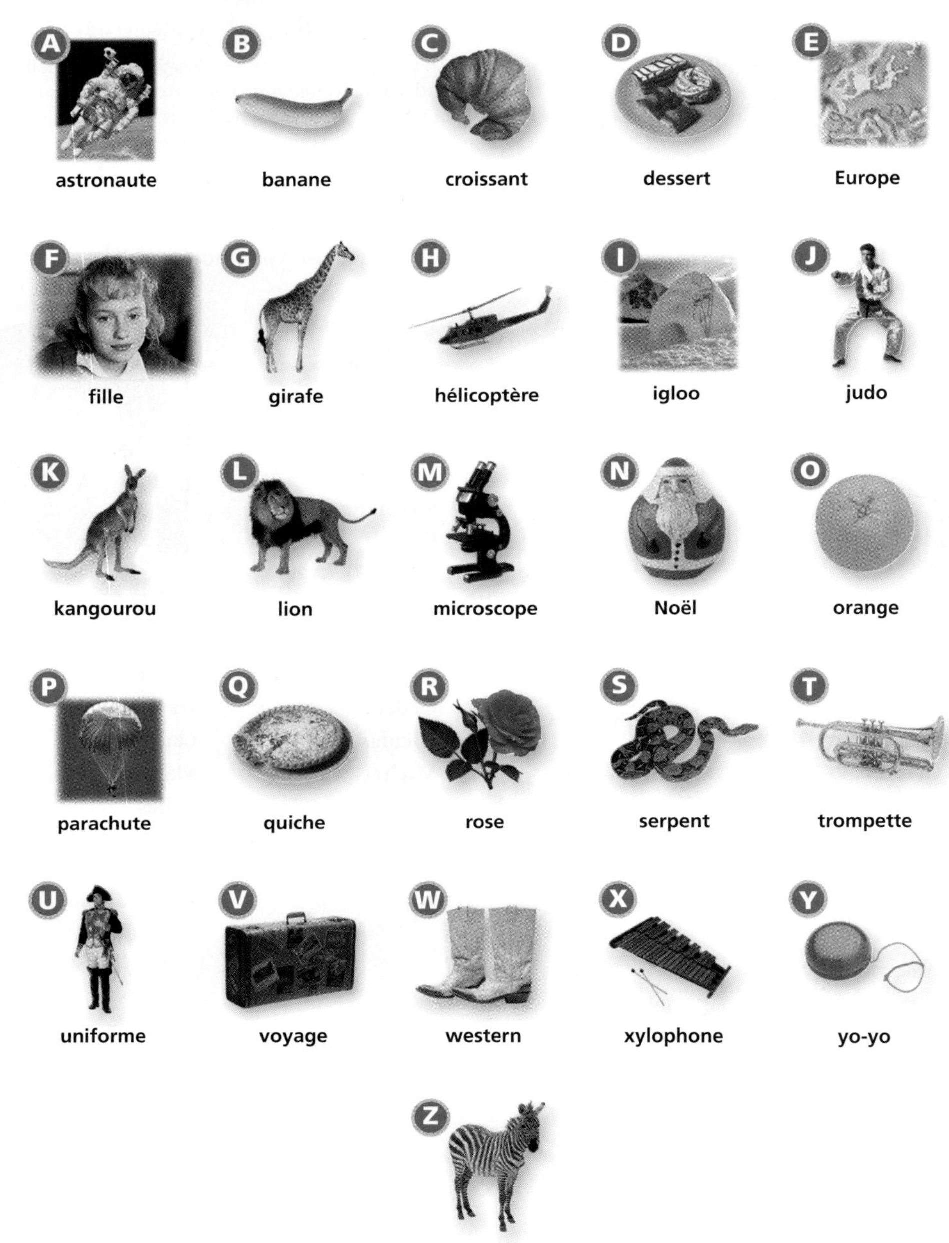

Communication for All Students

Additional Practice

- Ask students to spell their names, names of famous people and classroom objects that you have labeled.
- Write a short run-on message, interspersing extra letters throughout. Distribute copies. Then, dictate only the letters of your message. Have students circle each letter as they hear it to spell out your message. In the example below, dictate the boldfaced letters to spell out the message **J'adore le français.**

v y **j** n **a** w m p c **d** y l h **o**
r c u **e** b x **l** t **e** q g **f** z v y **r**
a m b **n** w **ç** h **a** g u **i** p **s** k

STANDARDS: 1.2, 4.1

Have you noticed that many French words look like English words? Words in different languages that look alike are called cognates. Although they're pronounced differently, cognates have the same meaning in French and English. You may not realize it, but you already know hundreds of French words.

Can you figure out what these words mean?

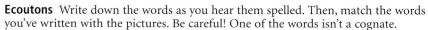

carotte chocolat adresse musique examen

2 Le dictionnaire

Scan the French-English vocabulary list in the back of your book to see if you can find ten cognates.

3 Les animaux See scripts on p. T91. 1. f 2. e 3. b 4. a 5. d 6. c

Ecoutons Write down the words as you hear them spelled. Then, match the words you've written with the pictures. Be careful! One of the words isn't a cognate.

CD 1 Tr. 4

a. crabe

b. pingouin

c. tigre

d. singe

e. serpent

f. kangourou

4 Tu t'appelles comment?

Can you spell your name, pronouncing the letters in French?

L'alphabet

CHAPITRE PRELIMINAIRE

Group Work

2 This activity might be done in groups, with one student in each group responsible for compiling the list. Set a time limit within which each group must find and write down ten cognates.

Additional Practice

3 Ask students to repeat the letters or have them try to pronounce the animals' names.

Challenge

4 If students have made name cards, you might collect them and redistribute them to different individuals. Each student should spell the name on the card and point out that particular student. As a variation, the student who hears his or her name spelled might say **C'est moi.**

Connections and Comparisons

Language-to-Language

2 Explain one of the sources of cognates. Both French and English have words with Latin roots; for example, *unitas* (Latin), **unité** (French), *unity* (English). You may also want to warn students about false cognates **(faux amis)**, words in two languages that look alike but have different meanings. **Librairie** and *library* look alike, but **librairie** is the French word for *bookstore.* The French word for *library* is **bibliothèque.** Other examples of false cognates are the French word **pain,** which means *bread,* not *pain;* **raisin,** which means *grape,* not *raisin;* and **sympathique,** which means *nice,* not *sympathetic.*

STANDARDS: 1.2, 4.1

Presenting
Les accents

Make an overhead transparency of several French words, some with accents and some without. Ask students if they notice any peculiarities. As they mention the accents, explain each one. Let them know that accents can sometimes change the meaning of a word, like **où** *(where)* and **ou** *(or)* or **sûr** *(sure)* and **sur** *(on).*

Les accents ▪ *Accent marks*

CD 1 Tr. 5

Have you noticed the marks over some of the letters in French words? These marks are called accents. They're very important to the spelling, the pronunciation, and even the meaning of French words.

The **accent aigu** (´) tells you to pronounce an *e* similar to the *a* in the English word *date:*	**éléphant** **Sénégal**
The **accent grave** (`) tells you to pronounce an *e* like the *e* in the English word *jet:*	**zèbre** **chèque**
However, an **accent grave** over an *a* or *u* doesn't change the sound of these letters:	**à** **où**
The **accent circonflexe** (ˆ) can appear over any vowel, and it doesn't change the sound of the letter:	**pâté** **forêt** **île** **hôtel** **flûte**
The **cédille** (¸) under a *c* tells you to pronounce the *c* like an *s:*	**français** **ça**
When two vowels appear next to each other, a **tréma** (¨) over the second one tells you to pronounce each vowel separately:	**Noël** **Haïti**
You usually will not see accents on capital letters.	**île** **Ile** **état** **Etats-Unis**

When you spell a word aloud, be sure to say the accents, as well as the letters.

Quelle est l'orthographe? *What is the spelling?* See scripts on p. T91.

CD 1 Tr. 6

Ecoutons Write down the words as you hear them spelled.

1. poème
2. hôpital
3. Américain
4. canoë
5. français
6. sévère

Communication for All Students

Language Note

Students will sometimes recognize English words in French words if they imagine an *s* after a circumflex: **forêt** *(forest),* **hôpital** *(hospital).* You may want to explain the need for a cedilla. A *c* followed by an *a, o,* or *u* is a hard *c* as in **carte,** unless it is written with a cedilla, in which case, it is a soft *c* as in **ça.**

Additional Practice

5 Five of these six words are cognates. Write the six words on the board and have students check their answers to this listening activity. Then, have students give the equivalent English words and practice pronouncing the French words.

STANDARDS: 1.2, 4.1

Les chiffres de 0 à 20 ▪ *Numbers from 0 to 20*

How many times a day do you use numbers? Giving someone a phone number, checking grades, and getting change at the store all involve numbers. Here are the French numbers from 0 to 20.

CD 1 Tr. 7

Vocabulaire

0 zéro	1 un	2 deux	3 trois	4 quatre	5 cinq	6 six
7 sept	8 huit	9 neuf	10 dix	11 onze	12 douze	13 treize
14 quatorze	15 quinze	16 seize	17 dix-sept	18 dix-huit	19 dix-neuf	20 vingt

Note culturelle

When you count on your fingers, which finger do you start with? The French way is to start counting with your thumb as number one, your index finger as two, and so on. How would you show four the French way? And eight?

6 Mon numéro de téléphone See scripts on p. T75.

Ecoutons Listen as Nicole, Paul, Vincent, and Corinne tell you their phone numbers. Then, match the numbers with their names.

CD 1 Tr. 8

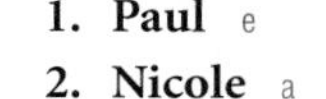

1. **Paul** e
2. **Nicole** a
3. **Vincent** b
4. **Corinne** d

a. 03. 20. 16. 05. 17
b. 03. 20. 18. 11. 19
c. 03. 20. 17. 07. 18
d. 03. 20. 15. 04. 13
e. 03. 20. 14. 08. 12

7 Devine! *Guess!*

Think of a number between one and twenty. Your partner will try to guess your number. Help out by saying **plus** *(higher)* or **moins** *(lower)* as your partner guesses. Take turns.

8 Plaques d'immatriculation *License plates*

Look at the license plates pictured below. Take turns with a partner reading aloud the numbers and letters you see.

1. 

2. 

3. 1872 LD 94
4. 

5. 2463 RP 13
6. 1869 AR01

Communication for All Students

Additional Practice

6 After this listening activity, have students pair off to practice reading the phone numbers aloud. They might also practice saying their own phone numbers in French.

Auditory Learners

Read pairs of numbers aloud and tell students to write down the smaller (or larger) number.

Slower Pace

Students may learn numbers more easily if they group them in short sequences; for example, 1–3, 4–6, 7–9, and then 1–9.

Les chiffres

CHAPITRE PRELIMINAIRE

Motivating Activity

Ask students to suggest why numbers are important. They might list flight numbers, time, temperature, phone numbers, train platform numbers, prices, dates, ages, TV channels, radio stations, and money changing. Point out that the spelling of numbers is also important for writing checks and other banking transactions.

Presenting Les chiffres

You might teach numbers using only numerals before students see the words. Call out the numbers that correspond to the age range of your students and ask them to raise their hands when they hear their age.

Math Link

Have students count backwards from 20 or forward by twos and threes. You could also have students identify the prime numbers **(les nombres premiers)** from 0 to 20. **(2, 3, 5, 7, 11, 13, 17, 19)**

Culture Note

You might tell students that phone numbers in France are preceded by a two-digit number similar to an area code in the United States, followed by four sets of two-digit numbers.

STANDARDS: 1.1, 1.2, 3.2, 4.2

A l'école

CHAPITRE PRELIMINAIRE

Presenting
A l'école

First, demonstrate the commands without English by using gestures and actions. Point out to students that many of the commands are also useful in settings other than the classroom.

Teacher Note

Here are some additional commands and/or statements you might want to give your students:

Effacez le tableau! *Erase the board.*
Ecrivez au tableau! *Write on the board.*
Est-ce que je peux aller aux toilettes? *May I go to the bathroom?*
Silence, s'il vous plaît! *Quiet, please.*
Comment dit-on... en français? *How do you say . . . in French?*
Regardez le tableau! *Look at the chalkboard.*
Ecrivez votre nom! *Write your name.*

A l'école ▪ *At school*

You should familiarize yourself with these common French instructions. You'll hear your teacher using them in class.

CD 1 Tr. 9

Ecoutez!	Listen!
Répétez!	Repeat!
Levez-vous!	Stand up!
Levez la main!	Raise your hand!
Asseyez-vous!	Sit down!
Ouvrez vos livres à la page... !	Open your books to page . . . !
Fermez la porte!	Close the door!
Sortez une feuille de papier!	Take out a sheet of paper!
Allez au tableau!	Go to the blackboard!
Regardez la carte!	Look at the map!

9 Les instructions See scripts on p. T91.

Ecoutons Listen to the teacher in this French class tell his students what to do. Then, decide which student is following each instruction.

CD 1 Tr. 10

1. Lynn
2. Emilio
3. Brian
4. Alison
5. Paul
6. Dena
7. Evelyne

Communication for All Students

Additional Practice

9 Have students look at the classroom illustration and tell whether the following statements are true or false.

1. **Alison lève la main.**
2. **Emilio ouvre la porte.**
3. **Evelyne se lève.**
4. **Amy ferme la porte.**
5. **Lynn est au tableau.**
6. **Brian regarde le professeur.**
7. **Mike répète le vocabulaire.**

Next, have students carry out the commands as you say them aloud. Students might then practice giving and following the commands in pairs or small groups.

STANDARDS: 1.2

Conseils pour apprendre le français

Tips for studying French

Listen

It's important to listen carefully to what is going on in class. Ask questions if you don't understand, even if you think your question is silly. Other people are probably wondering the same thing! You won't be able to understand everything you hear, but you will quickly realize that you don't need to! Don't get frustrated. You're actually absorbing the language even when you don't realize it.

Speak

Practice speaking French every day. Talking with your teachers and classmates is an easy and fun way to learn. Don't be afraid to take risks with the language. Your mistakes will help you identify problems and will show you important differences in the way English and French work.

Practice

Learning a new language is like learning to play a sport or an instrument. You can't spend one night practicing and then expect to play perfectly the next morning. You didn't learn English that way either! Short, daily study sessions are more effective than once-a-week cramming sessions. Also, try to practice with a friend or a classmate, since language is all about communication.

Expand

Increase your contact with French outside of class in every way you can. You might find French-language programs on TV, on the radio, or at the video store, or even someone living near you who speaks French. Magazines, French newspapers, and the Internet are other great sources for French-language material. Don't be afraid to read, watch, or listen! You don't need to understand every word. You can get a lot out of a story or an article by concentrating on the words you recognize and doing a little intelligent guesswork.

Organize

As you learn French, your memory is going to get a workout, so it's important to be organized and efficient. Throughout the textbook you'll see tips (**De bons conseils**) that will help you study smart. For starters, try looking for cognates when you read. Cognates are words that look similar and have the same meaning in French and English, such as **chocolat** and *chocolate*, **musique** and *music*. Once you recognize which words are cognates, you can then spend more of your time studying the words that are completely unfamiliar.

Connect

Some English and French words have common roots in Latin, so your knowledge of English can give you clues about the meaning of many French words. Look for an English connection when you need to guess unfamiliar words. You may also find that learning French will help you in English class!

Have fun!

Above all, remember to have fun!
The more you try, the more you'll learn.
Bonne chance! *(Good luck!)*

Cultures and Communities

Multicultural Link

Give homework assignments that provide opportunities for students to experience the French language in authentic situations. For example, many video stores carry movies in French from different francophone countries, that students can watch for extra credit. They should report to the class what the movie was about and how much of the French they understood.

Community Link

You may want to establish telephone partners with students from another school to encourage your students to use French outside of the class. This will also allow you to give assignments for oral practice.

Auditory Learners

For additional listening, introduce students occasionally to popular French songs and accompanying lyrics.

Teaching Suggestion

If you have access to magazines, newspapers, or any other realia from French-speaking countries, make them available to your students. This will provide them with additional authentic input. Look on p. T46 for useful addresses where you can obtain such information.

Location Opener

CHAPTERS 1, 2, 3

Teaching Resources
pp. 12–15

PRINT  
- Lesson Planner, p. 3
- Video Guide, pp. 3–4

MEDIA 
- One-Stop Planner
- Video Program
  Videocassette 1, 05:47–07:38
- DVD Tutor, Disc 1
- Interactive CD-ROM Tutor, Disc 1
- Map Transparency 1

 go.hrw.com
WA3 POITIERS

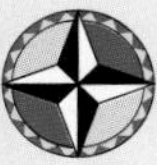

Using the Almanac and Map

Terms in the Almanac
- **Le Palais de Justice** is a courthouse built in the nineteenth century around the remains of the palais des Ducs d'Aquitaine.
- **Le musée Sainte-Croix,** located on the site of the Abbaye Sainte-Croix, houses a fine arts collection and an archeological museum.
- **L'Hypogée des Dunes,** an underground chapel from the seventh century, is built over an ancient Roman cemetery.
- **Saint Hilaire** was the first bishop of Poitiers.
- **Aliénor d'Aquitaine** (1122–1204) was Duchess of Aquitaine. Among her nine children with Henry II of England were Richard the Lionhearted and John Lackland, the English king who was forced to sign the Magna Carta in 1215.

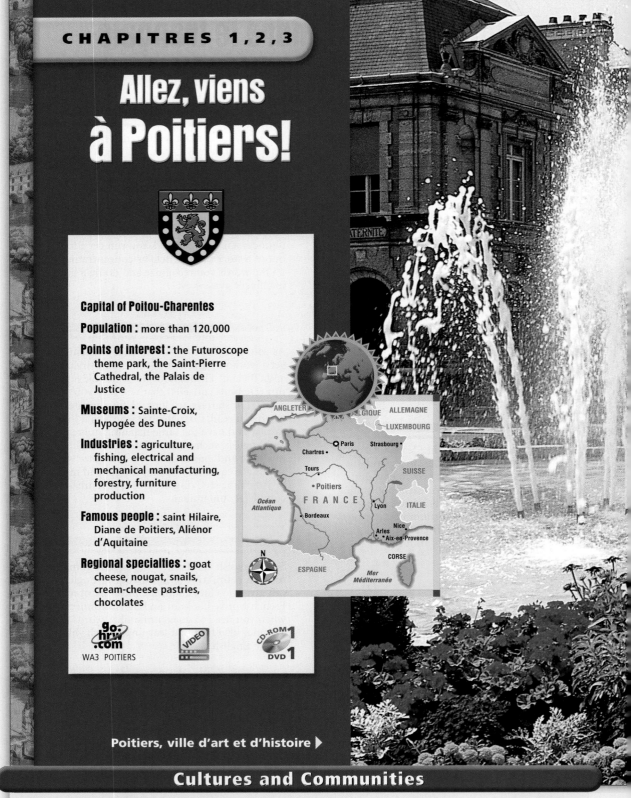

CHAPITRES 1,2,3

Allez, viens à Poitiers!

Capital of Poitou-Charentes

Population : more than 120,000

Points of interest : the Futuroscope theme park, the Saint-Pierre Cathedral, the Palais de Justice

Museums : Sainte-Croix, Hypogée des Dunes

Industries : agriculture, fishing, electrical and mechanical manufacturing, forestry, furniture production

Famous people : saint Hilaire, Diane de Poitiers, Aliénor d'Aquitaine

Regional specialties : goat cheese, nougat, snails, cream-cheese pastries, chocolates

ANGLETERRE
BELGIQUE
ALLEMAGNE
LUXEMBOURG
Paris
Chartres
Strasbourg
Tours
SUISSE
Poitiers
FRANCE
Océan Atlantique
Lyon
ITALIE
Bordeaux
Nice
Arles
Aix-en-Provence
CORSE
ESPAGNE
Mer Méditerranée
N

go.hrw.com WA3 POITIERS
VIDEO
CD-ROM 1 DVD 1

Poitiers, ville d'art et d'histoire ▶

Cultures and Communities

Background Information
Poitiers, often called **Ville d'art et d'histoire** and **Ville de tous les âges,** is an ancient city. It is the capital of Poitou-Charentes, one of the 22 regions into which France is now divided. In 56 B.C., the town came under Roman control, which lasted for several centuries. A famous battle occurred near Poitiers in 732 when Charles Martel, grandfather of Charlemagne, defeated the invading Saracens, Muslims who had crossed from North Africa into Spain and settled there. In the twelfth century, Poitiers was the city from which **Aliénor d'Aquitaine,** and later her son Richard I the Lionhearted **(Richard Cœur de Lion),** ruled the provinces of Aquitaine and Poitou.

STANDARDS: 2.2, 3.1

Connections and Comparisons

History Link

Have students research and report on the many fascinating historical figures from this region, such as **Aliénor d'Aquitaine, Henri II,** Richard the Lionhearted, and others. Have them make a timeline of the events of the eleventh and twelfth centuries that occurred in Aquitaine and Poitou.

Literature Link

Henry II of England, the husband of **Aliénor d'Aquitaine,** was responsible for the assassination of Sir Thomas Becket, Archbishop of Canterbury. Their story was the basis for T. S. Eliot's play *Murder in the Cathedral* and Jean Anouilh's play *Becket.*

Map Activities

- Have students name the bodies of water and the countries surrounding France.
- Have students locate the island of Corsica **(Corse)** in the Mediterranean Sea. Corsica is part of France and is located about 115 miles east-southeast of the city of Nice.

Photo Flash!

La place Aristide Bruant
The beautiful square shown on pages 12 and 13 was named after Aristide Bruant, a popular singer-songwriter **(chansonnier),** who sang his own songs in various cafés near Montmartre in Paris. Aristide Bruant was immortalized in the works of painter Henri de Toulouse-Lautrec. He lived from 1851 to 1925.

Building on Previous Skills

Have students tell what they know about France: the people, culture, food, cities, tourist attractions, and so on. Then, have them compare their impressions with the photos of Poitiers on pages 12–15.

Language Notes

- The earliest inhabitants of the region were the **Pictaves,** or **Pictons,** a Gallic tribe of sailors and tradesmen. Their name is a possible origin of the name of the region, Poitou, and of the city, Poitiers.
- You might give students the French equivalents of the regional specialties listed in the almanac: *goat cheese* **(chabichou),** *nougat* **(nougâtines),** *snails* **(escargots),** *cream-cheese pastry* **(tourteau fromager),** and *chocolates* **(marguerites).**

Location Opener

CHAPTERS 1, 2, 3

Using the Photo Essay

1 Two other impressive attractions of **le Futuroscope** are the "Showscan," which produces a realistic image at 60 frames per second, and the "Dynamic Simulator," which has moving seats that are synchronized with the action on the screen.

3 **La Pierre Levée** This monument was a popular gathering place for students in the sixteenth century when the author François Rabelais was a frequent visitor to Poitiers.

Culture Note

3 Dolmens are enormous stone structures, somewhat like tables, with a large stone placed horizontally on other stones standing vertically. About 150 are found in the Poitou region. Menhirs are tall, freestanding stones. Both dolmens and menhirs date from between 5000 and 2000 B.C.

Architecture Link

4 The **gothique angevin** style of the **cathédrale Saint-Pierre** marked a transition from Roman to Gothic architecture. Roman architecture was characterized by rounded arches, heavy, solid walls, few windows, and dark interiors. In contrast, the development of **arcs-boutants** *(flying buttresses),* which supported the weight of the roof, permitted higher walls and large numbers of **vitraux** *(stained-glass windows).* Gothic architecture was characterized by the pointed **arc brisé** *(Gothic arch).*

Poitiers

Poitiers is famous for its art and history. It was here in 732 A.D. that Charles Martel defeated the Saracens in the Battle of Poitiers. Home to an important university and attractions such as a futuristic park devoted to cinematic technology, Poitiers is also a very modern city.

Visit Holt Online
go.hrw.com
KEYWORD: WA3 POITIERS
Activités Internet

1 **Le Futuroscope**
People of all ages enjoy this popular futuristic theme park filled with cinematic exhibits. Of particular interest are the 360-degree theater and the **Kinémax** with its 600-square-meter screen.

2 **L' Hôtel de ville**
In most French cities you will find the **Hôtel de ville,** which houses the government administration offices.

Connections and Comparisons

History Link

2 The French flag flying over the **Hôtel de ville** is known as **le tricolore** because of its three colors: blue, white, and red **(bleu, blanc et rouge).** The tricolor flag first appeared shortly after the French Revolution in 1789. Ask students if they know the nickname of the flag of the United States (the Star-Spangled Banner).

History/Architecture Link

3 Ask students if they know of other huge stone structures in the world that were built in ancient times (the pyramids in Egypt, Mexico, and South America, and the stone structures on Easter Island and at Stonehenge in England). Ask students to imagine how these structures were built without modern machinery.

STANDARDS: 2.1, 3.1

3 La Pierre Levée
This kind of prehistoric monument, called a dolmen, is constructed of upright stones supporting a horizontal stone. Found especially in Britain and France, dolmens are believed to be tombs. This one dates from about 3000 B.C.

4 La cathédrale Saint-Pierre
Construction of this Gothic cathedral of incredible height was begun at the end of the twelfth century. Its elaborate façade has three gabled portals like this one and a rose window.

In chapters 1, 2, and 3,

you will meet some students who live in Poitiers. Once among the biggest cities in France (in the sixteenth century), Poitiers is now a mid-size city, a university town full of young people. It is known for its pleasant atmosphere and Romanesque churches.

5 Le centre-ville
The heart of French cities and towns is called **le centre-ville.** In Poitiers, it is the bustling center of town where people gather in cafés and frequent the many shops.

6 Les marchés
At least once a week, French towns usually have an outdoor market such as this **marché aux fleurs.**

Cultures and Communities

Culture Notes

4 On most cathedrals, the sculptures over the central door **(le portail)** depict the Last Judgment. God is surrounded by St. Peter, Mary, angels, or other holy figures. Below are the souls condemned to Purgatory, and at the very bottom are those in Hell. The figures in the four arches over the door include apostles, prophets, and saints.

5 Since most train stations in France are located in the **centre-ville,** train travel is very convenient, and people generally do not need their cars for travel outside the metropolitan area or even within the city itself.

Location Opener

CHAPTERS 1, 2, 3

5 Le centre-ville Because Poitiers is an ancient city, the oldest streets are very narrow and unsuitable for automobile traffic. Some have been converted to pedestrian shopping areas where traffic is not allowed.

Thinking Critically

5 Observing Ask students if there are any particular features they notice about the buildings in this photo.

6 Le marché aux fleurs The French are generally very fond of flowers and gardening, and flower markets are a common sight throughout France. French gardens **(les jardins à la française)** are defined by their sculpted shrubs and plants laid out in intricate, symmetrical designs.

Thinking Critically

6 Observing Call students' attention to the flowers and gardens in the photographs on pages 12–15. Would they find similar decorations around American buildings or towns?

6 Drawing Inferences Ask students for the name of the café at the end of the street in this photo. Tell them that **la gargouille** means *gargoyle* and ask why this name was chosen for the café and where they think this area might be located (possibly near a church or cathedral — see Art Link). Finally, ask students what they think a **glacier** is (*ice cream shop*).

Art Link

Les gargouilles, or *gargoyles,* are decorative sculptures on cathedrals and churches. They serve to drain off rainwater and are often carved in the form of grotesque animals and monsters.

Chapitre 1 : Faisons connaissance!
Chapter Overview

Mise en train pp. 18–20	***Salut, les copains!***

	FUNCTIONS	GRAMMAR	VOCABULARY	RE-ENTRY
Première étape pp. 22–25	• Greeting people and saying goodbye, p. 22 • Asking how people are and telling how you are, p. 23 • Asking someone's name and giving yours, p. 24 • Asking someone's age and giving yours, p. 25			• Introductions **(Chapitre Préliminaire)** • Numbers 0–20 **(Chapitre Préliminaire)**
Deuxième étape pp. 26–29	• Expressing likes, dislikes, and preferences about things, p. 26	• **ne... pas,** p. 26 • The definite articles **le, la, l', les,** and the gender of nouns, p. 28	• Things you like or dislike, p. 27	
Troisième étape pp. 31–35	• Expressing likes, dislikes, and preferences about activities, p. 32	• Subject pronouns and **-er** verbs, p. 33	• Activities you like or dislike, p. 31	

Prononciation p. 35	**Intonation** Audio CD 1, Tracks 25–26	**A écrire** (dictation) Audio CD 1, Tracks 27–29	
Lisons! pp. 36–37	**Petites Annonces**	**Reading Strategy:** Using titles, subtitles, illustrations, and captions	
Grammaire supplémentaire	**pp. 38–41** **Première étape,** p. 38	**Deuxième étape,** p. 39	**Troisième étape,** pp. 40–41
Review pp. 42–45	**Mise en pratique,** pp. 42–43	**Que sais-je?** p. 44	**Vocabulaire,** p. 45

CULTURE

- **Rencontre culturelle,** Greetings and goodbyes, p. 21
- **Note culturelle,** Gestures, p. 23
- Realia: French movie ad for *Casablanca,* p. 26
- **Panorama Culturel,** Leisure-time activities, p. 30

Chapitre 1 : Faisons connaissance!

Chapter Resources

Lesson Planning

One-Stop Planner

Lesson Planner with Differentiated Instruction, pp. 3–7, 65

Student Make-Up Assignments

- Make-Up Assignment Copying Masters, Chapter 1

Listening and Speaking

TPR Storytelling Book, pp. 1–4

Listening Activities

- Student Response Forms for Listening Activities, pp. 3–5
- Additional Listening Activities 1-1 to 1-6, pp. 7–9
- Additional Listening Activities (song), p. 10
- Scripts and Answers, pp. 102–106

Video Guide

- Teaching Suggestions, pp. 6–7
- Activity Masters, pp. 8–10
- Scripts and Answers, pp. 88–90, 118

Activities for Communication

- Communicative Activities, pp. 1–6
- Realia and Teaching Suggestions, pp. 75–79
- Situation Cards, pp. 137–138

Reading and Writing

Reading Strategies and Skills Handbook, Chapter 1

Joie de lire 1, Chapter 1

Cahier d'activités, pp. 3–12

Grammar

Travaux pratiques de grammaire, pp. 1–9

Grammar Tutor for Students of French, Chapter 1

Assessment

Testing Program

- Grammar and Vocabulary Quizzes, **Etape** Quizzes, and Chapter Test, pp. 1–18
- Score Sheet, Scripts and Answers, pp. 19–26

Alternative Assessment Guide

- Portfolio Assessment, p. 18
- Performance Assessment, p. 32
- CD-ROM Assessment, p. 46

Student Make-Up Assignments

- Alternative Quizzes, Chapter 1

Standardized Assessment Tutor

- Reading, pp. 1–3
- Writing, p. 4
- Math, pp. 25–26

Middle School

Middle School Teaching Resources, Chapter 1

MEDIA

Online Activities

- **Jeux interactifs**
- **Activités Internet**

Video Program

- Videocassette 1
- Videocassette 5 (captioned version)

Interactive CD-ROM Tutor, Disc 1

DVD Tutor, Disc 1

Audio Compact Discs

- Textbook Listening Activities, CD 1, Tracks 11–30
- Additional Listening Activities, CD 1, Tracks 37–43
- Assessment Items, CD 1, Tracks 31–36

Teaching Transparencies

- Situation 1-1 to 1-3
- Vocabulary 1-A to 1-D
- **Mise en train**
- **Grammaire supplémentaire** Answers
- **Travaux pratiques de grammaire** Answers

One-Stop Planner CD-ROM

Use the **One-Stop Planner CD-ROM with Test Generator** to aid in lesson planning and pacing.

For each chapter, the **One-Stop Planner** includes:

- Editable lesson plans with direct links to teaching resources
- Printable worksheets from resource books
- Direct launches to the HRW Internet activities
- Video and audio segments
- Test Generator
- Clip Art for vocabulary items

Chapitre 1 : Faisons connaissance!

Projects

Moi!

Students make a collage, like those in the ***Mise en train,*** *showing their favorite and least favorite activities.*

MATERIALS

Students may need

- Magazines
- Glue or tape
- Colored pens and markers
- Construction paper or posterboard

SUGGESTED SEQUENCE

1. Working individually, students start by making a list of activities they can name in French that they like and don't like to do.
2. Students plan how to present their likes and dislikes visually.
3. Students find pictures in magazines or make their own drawings that illustrate their likes and dislikes and start writing what they want to say in French. Students should mount their illustrations around the text on a large sheet of construction paper or posterboard.
4. Students write their text on a sheet of paper and give it to another student to edit.
5. Finally, students write the final version of the text and arrange the final placement of the illustrations.

Students might show their projects to a family member or a friend who is not taking French to see if they have made themselves understood. As students present their projects to the class, have them cover the French text on their project and tell their classmates in French about their likes and dislikes as they show their pictures.

GRADING THE PROJECT

Suggested Point Distribution: (total = 100 points)

Content	20 points
Oral presentation	20 points
Presentation/appearance	20 points
Language use	20 points
Creativity	20 points

Games

Introductions

In this game, students will practice giving their name and age.

Before you begin the game, you might want to put the following incomplete sentences on the board or on a transparency. Explain that you use **Il/Elle a...** to give another person's age.

Je m'appelle...	**Il/Elle s'appelle...**
J'ai...ans.	**Il/Elle a...ans.**

This game can be played by the whole class or by two or three large groups. Student A begins by giving his or her name and age in French. Student B must repeat A's name and age and then give his or her own name and age. Student C must repeat the names and ages of A and B and then give his or her own name and age, and so on. The game continues until a student makes a mistake. At this point, the game can start over, beginning with the student who made the mistake or with the following student.

Jacques a dit

In this game, students will practice giving commands.

As you begin the game, tell students that they must carry out the commands that are preceded by **Jacques a dit...** If you don't say **Jacques a dit...**, students who carry out the command are eliminated from the game. Before you start, you may want to demonstrate gestures students might use to carry out the commands: cupping a hand behind the ear in response to **Ecoutez!** or pretending to carry bags or pay for purchases in response to **Faites les magasins!** Students who are eliminated from the game can stay involved by acting as monitors or by writing down the commands that are used.

Here are some commands you might use:

Dansez!	**Faites le ménage!**
Parlez au téléphone!	**Dormez!**
Lisez!	**Regardez la télévision!**
Voyagez!	**Etudiez!**
Ecoutez de la musique!	**Faites du sport!**
Faites les magasins!	**Faites du vélo!**
Nagez!	

You might use the commands from the Preliminary Chapter.

Storytelling

Mini-histoire

This story accompanies Teaching Transparency 1-3. The ***mini-histoire*** *can be told and retold in different formats, acted out, written down, and read aloud, to give students additional opportunities to practice all four skills. The following story describes a typical afternoon at Thierry's house.*

En général, Mme Delanoë préfère faire le ménage. Thierry aime faire du sport, surtout jouer au football. Marthe aime étudier l'anglais. Thérèse aime sortir avec ses copains et faire les magasins. Antoine adore parler au téléphone. Dominique aime écouter de la musique et étudier les maths, mais elle aime surtout faire du sport. Pas Claudine, elle aime dormir!

Traditions

Fromages de Poitou-Charentes

The region of Poitou-Charentes is well-known for its cereal crops and its livestock, especially its goats. Back in 8th century A.D., when the Saracens were defeated by Charles Martel in Poitiers, they retreated to the Poitou countryside to breed goats. Since then, goat cheeses have been one of the major assets of the region. Nowadays, of the 300 million litres of goat's milk produced in France each year, 75% is processed in Poitou-Charentes alone, most of it in the **département des Deux-Sèvres** in the south of the region. Among a wide variety of goat cheeses found in Poitou, perhaps the most famous is a small, cone-shaped cheese called **chabichou,** produced in Deux-Sèvres. Its name comes from the Arabic **chebli,** meaning *goat cheese.* With time, the word changed to **chabi,** now referring to goat cheeses from the Poitou-Charentes and Touraine regions. The word **chabichou** has also become a nickname for the people of Poitou. The **chabichou** is a soft cheese with a rather pronounced flavor. It can be eaten fresh, as early as three weeks after its manufacture. As a hands-on project, you might ask your students to go to the biggest supermarket in their area to look for French goat cheeses. Have them read the labels, find out what regions the cheeses come from, and report their findings to the class. As an alternative project, have students search the Internet to find out how cheese is made and ask for volunteers to present their results to the class.

Recette

*There are more than 500 types of cheeses made in France. Each region has its own goat cheese, and each artisan has his or her own recipe for making cheese. The taste of the goat cheese (**chèvre**) depends on the breed of the goat, what it eats, and the shape of the cheese. Some typical shapes of goat cheese are the **bûche,** the **brique,** the **pavé,** and the **galette.***

SALADE DE CHEVRE CHAUD

pour 4 personnes

une salade
4 petits fromages de chèvre
toasts
vinaigrette

Mettre le fromage de chèvre sur des toasts. Préchauffer le four à 350° F. Mettre les toasts et le fromage de chèvre dans le four pendant 5 à 10 minutes. Servir les toasts et le fromage de chèvre sur un lit de salade.

Vinaigrette

Mélanger 8 cuillères d'huile d'olive, 2 cuillères de vinaigre, du sel et du poivre. Verser sur la salade au moment de servir.

Chapitre 1 : Faisons connaissance!

Technology

Videocassette 1, Videocassette 5 (captioned version)
DVD Tutor, Disc 1
See Video Guide, pp. 5–10.

DVD/Video

Mise en train • Salut, les copains!

In this segment of the video, Claire introduces herself and welcomes us to the city of Poitiers. Next, teenagers from around the French-speaking world say hello and introduce themselves. They each talk about the things they like and what they like to do. We then return to Claire, who is joined by some of her friends in Poitiers. They also introduce themselves.

Salut, les copains! (suite)

Marc arrives at school on his bicycle and sees M. Balland, the math teacher. They greet each other and ask how things are going. Then, Claire arrives and introduces Ann, an American exchange student. M. Balland leaves, and Jérôme arrives on his moped, which breaks down. Later that day, Claire, Ann, Marc, and Jérôme go to a café. Marc, Jérôme, and Claire pay for Ann's part of the check to welcome her to Poitiers.

Qu'est-ce que tu aimes faire après l'école?

Several teenagers from different French-speaking countries tell us what they like to do when they have some free time.

Vidéoclips

- **Crunch®**: advertisement for chocolate
- **Tornado®**: advertisement for vacuum cleaner

Interactive CD-ROM Tutor

Activity	Activity Type	Pupil's Edition Page
En contexte	*Interactive conversation*	
1. Comment dit-on... ?	Chacun à sa place	pp. 22–23
2. Comment dit-on... ?	Méli-mélo	pp. 22–23
3. Vocabulaire	Le bon choix	pp. 9, 25
4. Vocabulaire	Jeu des paires	p. 27
5. Vocabulaire	Chasse au trésor Explorons!/Vérifions!	p. 31
6. Grammaire	Les mots qui manquent	pp. 28, 33
Panorama Culturel	Qu'est-ce que tu aimes faire après l'école? Le bon choix	p. 30
A toi de parler	*Guided recording*	pp. 42–43
A toi d'écrire	*Guided writing*	pp. 42–43

Teacher Management System

Launch the program, type "admin" in the password area and press RETURN. Log on to **www.hrw.com/CDROMTUTOR** for a detailed explanation of the Teacher Management System.

DVD Tutor

The *DVD Tutor* contains all material from the *Video Program* as described above. French captions are available for use at your discretion for all sections of the video. The *DVD Tutor* also provides a variety of video-based activities that assess students' understanding of the **Mise en train, Suite,** and **Panorama Culturel.**

This part of the *DVD Tutor* may be used on any DVD video player connected to a television or video monitor.

In addition to the video material and the video-based comprehension activities, the *DVD Tutor* also contains the entire *Interactive CD-ROM Tutor* in DVD-ROM format. Each DVD disc contains the activities from all 12 chapters of the *Interactive CD-ROM Tutor.*

This part of the *DVD Tutor* may be used on a Macintosh® or Windows® computer with a DVD-ROM drive.

To preview all resources available for this chapter, use the **One-Stop Planner CD-ROM,** Disc 1.

Visit Holt Online
go.hrw.com
KEYWORD: WA3 POITIERS-1
Online Edition

Go.Online!

Online Edition

The Online Edition for Allez, viens! *allows students access to their textbooks anytime anywhere.*

- *Audio at point of use*
- *Additional practice activities*
- *Self-test activities*
- *Online reference tools*
- *Entire Video Program (Enhanced version)*
- *Interactive Notebook (Enhanced version)*

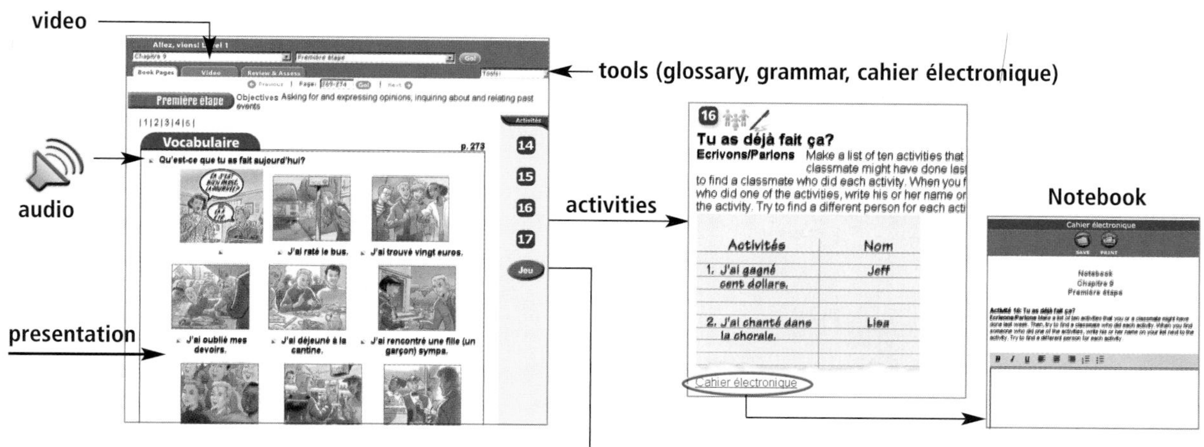

Activités Internet

These guided internet activities include a worksheet and pre-selected and pre-screened authentic web sites from the francophone world. You can use these activities

- to help students develop research skills in the target language
- to introduce students to authentic cultural information
- as a project

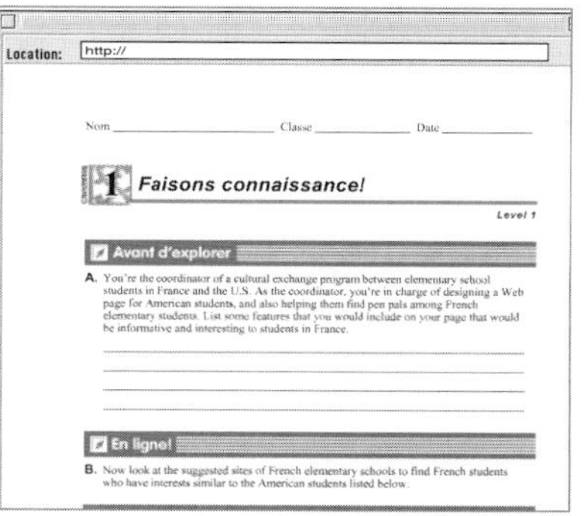

Jeux interactifs

You can use the interactive activities in this chapter

- to practice grammar, vocabulary, and chapter functions
- as homework
- as an assessment option
- as a self-test
- to prepare for the Chapter Test

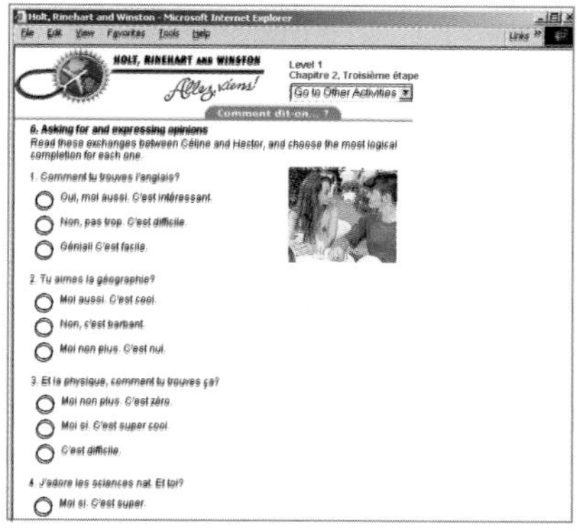

Projet Have students do a Web search for places in Poitiers where they can do their favorite activities. Based on their likes, they might find movie theaters with film listings, places where they can practice sports, or listings of musical performances. Have students identify the event they would like to attend and find out how much it would cost them. Have students document their sources by noting the names and URLs of all the sites they consulted.

Chapitre 1 : Faisons connaissance!

Textbook Listening Activities Scripts

Première étape

6 p. 22

1. — Bonjour, Philippe!
— Bonjour, Elodie!

2. — Au revoir, Mlle Latour!
— Au revoir, Paul!

3. — Salut, Julien.
— Salut. Au revoir.

4. — Tchao, Sophie!
— A tout à l'heure, Christelle!

5. — Salut, Gilles.
— Bonjour, M. Dupont.

Answers to Activity 6

1. hello
2. goodbye
3. goodbye
4. goodbye
5. hello

9 p. 23

1. — Alors, Valérie, ça va?
— Super!

2. — Tiens, salut, Jean-Michel. Comment ça va?
— Oh, ça va.

3. — Et toi, Anne?
— Moi, ça va très bien!

4. — Bonjour, Marie. Ça va?
— Pas terrible!

5. — Et toi, Karim?
— Pas mal.

Answers to Activity 9

1. good
2. fair
3. good
4. bad
5. fair

12 p. 24

1. Il s'appelle Michel.
2. Elle s'appelle Corinne.
3. Elle, elle s'appelle Danielle.
4. Il s'appelle Mathieu.
5. Lui, il s'appelle Stéphane.
6. Elle s'appelle Laurence.

Answers to Activity 12

1. garçon
2. fille
3. fille
4. garçon
5. garçon
6. fille

13 p. 25

Il s'appelle comment?
Comment s'appelle-t-il?
Il aime les concerts!
Il s'appelle Robert.
Elle s'appelle comment?
Comment s'appelle-t-elle?
Elle est très sympa!
Elle s'appelle Linda.
Comment s'appelle-t-il?
Il s'appelle comment?
Le garçon blond là-bas.
Il s'appelle Thomas!
Comment s'appelle-t-elle?
Elle s'appelle comment?
Elle aime faire du ski.
Elle s'appelle Julie!
Comment t'appelles-tu?
Tu t'appelles comment?
Moi, je m'appelle Jean.
Voilà! J'me présente!

Answers to Activity 13

Robert, Linda, Thomas, Julie, Jean

15 p. 25

1. Salut! Je m'appelle Bruno. J'ai quinze ans.
2. Bonjour! Je m'appelle Véronique. J'ai dix-sept ans.
3. Salut! Ça va? Je m'appelle Laurent. J'ai seize ans.
4. Salut! Je m'appelle Céline. J'ai treize ans.

Answers to Activity 15

1. Bruno–15
2. Véronique–17
3. Laurent–16
4. Céline–13

The following scripts are for the Listening Activities found in the *Pupil's Edition.* For Student Response Forms, see *Listening Activities,* pages 3–5. To provide students with additional listening practice, see *Listening Activities,* pages 7–10.

To preview all resources available for this chapter, use the **One-stop Planner CD-ROM**, Disc 1.

Deuxième étape

18 p. 26

PAUL Claude, c'est bien pour un garçon, mais je n'aime pas ça pour une fille. Claudette, Claudine ou...

SOPHIE Oh, je n'aime pas Claudette!

PAUL O.K., O.K. Pour une fille, j'adore Sandrine.

SOPHIE Oui, Sandrine, c'est adorable. J'aime bien Sandrine aussi, mais j'aime mieux Lætitia. C'est original, non?

PAUL Lætitia Dubois? Hum? Possible, mais j'aime mieux Sandrine.

Answers to Activity 18a

Paul prefers Sandrine. Sophie prefers Lætitia.

20 p. 28

1. C'est Pierre. Moi, j'adore le ski.
2. Salut. C'est Monique. Moi, j'aime les hamburgers.
3. C'est Robert. Moi, j'aime les concerts.
4. Bonjour! C'est Suzanne. Moi, je n'aime pas la glace.
5. C'est Paul. J'aime la plage.
6. C'est Emilie. Moi, j'aime les amis.

Answers to Activity 20

a. Paul
b. Suzanne
c. Emilie
d. Monique
e. Robert
f. Pierre

Troisième étape

24 p. 32

1. J'aime parler au téléphone.
2. J'aime étudier.
3. J'aime danser.
4. J'aime faire le ménage.
5. J'aime dormir.
6. J'aime regarder la télé.

Answers to Activity 24

1. Nicolas
2. Danielle
3. Solange
4. Hervé
5. Olivier
6. Stéphanie

PRONONCIATION, P. 35

For the script for Part A , see p. 35.
The scripts for Parts B and C are below.

B. A écouter

1. Tu t'appelles Nicole? question
2. Moi, je m'appelle Marie. statement
3. Elle aime les maths. statement
4. Nous aimons les escargots et les frites. statement
5. Ça va? question

C. A écrire *(dictation)*

1. — Pierre, tu aimes regarder la télé?
   — Oui, mais j'aime mieux sortir avec les copains.
2. — Salut, Sylvie. Ça va?
   — Très bien. Et toi?
   — Ça va.

Mise en pratique

2 p. 42

Bonjour, c'est Sandrine Dupont à l'appareil, de l'O.I.C. J'ai des détails sur votre correspondant. C'est un garçon, Robert Perrault. Il a quinze ans et il est parisien. Il aime faire du sport, écouter de la musique et sortir avec les copains. Par contre, il n'aime pas danser. Voilà, j'espère que ça va. Pour plus de détails, téléphonez au zéro un, dix-sept, treize, quinze, zéro neuf.

Answers to Mise en pratique, Activity 2

Name–Robert Perrault
Age–15
Phone number–01.17.13.15.09
Likes–sports, listening to music, and going out with friends
Dislikes–dancing

Chapitre 1 : Faisons connaissance!

50-Minute Lesson Plans

Day 1

CHAPTER OPENER 5 min.
- Present Chapter Objectives, p. 17
- Thinking Critically, p. 17

MISE EN TRAIN 40 min.
- Motivating Activity: Ask students what information they gave the last time they introduced themselves.
- Presenting **Mise en train** and Preteaching Vocabulary, ATE, pp. 18–19
- Activities 1–5, p. 20
- Presenting **Rencontre culturelle,** ATE, p. 21
- Culture Notes, ATE, p. 21

Wrap-Up 5 min.
- Use Chapter 1 **Mise en train** Transparencies to summarize what happened in the **Mise en train.**

Homework Options
Cahier d'activités, p. 3, Acts. 1–2

Day 2

PREMIERE ETAPE
Quick Review 5 min.
- Check homework.
- Bell Work, ATE, p. 22

Comment dit-on... ?, p. 22 20 min.
- Presenting **Comment dit-on... ?,** ATE, p. 22
- Play Audio CD for Activity 6, p. 22
- Do Activities 7–8, p. 22.

Comment dit-on... ?, p. 23 20 min.
- Presenting **Comment dit-on... ?,** ATE, p. 23
- Play Audio CD for Activity 9, p. 23.
- Discuss **Note culturelle,** p. 23, and Culture Note, ATE, p. 23.
- Do Activity 10, p. 24.

Wrap-Up 5 min.
- Tell students to imagine they are in different situations ("You received an 'A+' on a math test.") and have them respond in French to the question **Ça va? (Super!).**

Homework Options
Cahier d'activités p. 4, Acts. 3–4
Travaux pratiques de grammaire, pp. 1–2, Acts. 1–3

Day 3

PREMIERE ETAPE
Quick Review 5 min.
- Check homework.
- Have pairs of students prepare and present Activity 11, p. 24.

Comment dit-on... ?, p. 24 30 min.
- Presenting **Comment dit-on... ?,** ATE, p. 24
- Play Audio CD for Activities 12–13, pp. 24–25, and discuss Culture Note, ATE, p. 25.
- Activity 14, p. 25
- Building on Previous Skills, ATE, p. 25

Wrap-Up 15 min.
- Group Work, ATE, p. 24

Homework Options
Have students create name tags by gluing a small photo to an index card (or drawing a self-portrait) and writing **Je m'appelle** ___ plus their real name or a French name they have chosen.

Day 4

PREMIERE ETAPE
Quick Review 10 min.
- Have students introduce themselves to the class and present their name tags.

Comment dit-on... ?, p. 25 25 min.
- Presenting **Comment dit-on... ?,** ATE, p. 25
- Language Note, ATE, p. 25
- Play Audio CD for Activity 15, p. 25
- Do Activity 16, p. 25.
- Cahier d'activités, pp. 5–6, Acts. 5–7

Wrap-Up 15 min.
Travaux pratiques de grammaire, p. 2, Acts. 4–6

Homework Options
Study for **Première étape** quiz.

Day 5

PREMIERE ETAPE
Quiz 1-1 20 min.
- Administer Quiz 1-1A or Quiz 1-1B.

DEUXIEME ETAPE
Comment dit-on... ?, p. 26 10 min.
- Presenting **Comment dit-on... ?,** ATE, p. 26

Note de grammaire, p. 26 5 min.
- Discuss **Note de grammaire,** p. 26.
- Play Audio CD for Activity 18, p. 26.

Vocabulaire, p. 27 10 min.
- Present **Vocabulaire** using Teaching Transparencies 1-A and 1-B.
- Language Notes, ATE, p. 27, and Culture Note, ATE, p. 27
- Play Audio CD for Activity 20, p. 28.

Wrap-Up 5 min.
- Visual Learners, ATE, p. 27

Homework Options
Cahier d'activités, p. 7, Acts. 8–9
Travaux pratiques de grammaire, pp. 3–4, Acts. 7–11

Day 6

DEUXIEME ETAPE
Quick Review 10 min.
- Check homework.

Grammaire, p. 28 30 min.
- Presenting **Grammaire,** ATE, p. 28
- Do Activity 21, p. 29.
- Discuss **De bons conseils,** p. 29, and **A la française,** p. 29.
- **Grammaire supplémentaire,** p. 39, Acts. 3–4.
- Cahier d'activités, pp. 7–8, Acts. 10–13

Wrap-Up 10 min.
- Travaux pratiques de grammaire, p. 5, Acts. 12–14

Homework Options
Study for **Deuxième étape** quiz.

For alternative lesson plans by chapter section, to create your own customized plans, or to preview all resources available for this chapter, use the **One-Stop Planner CD-ROM**, Disc 1.

For additional homework suggestions, see activities accompanied by this symbol throughout the chapter.

Day 7

DEUXIEME ETAPE

Quiz 1-2 20 min.
- Administer Quiz 1-2A or Quiz 1-2B.

TROISIEME ETAPE
- Motivating Activity: Ask students to tell in English what activities they like to do after school or during their free time.

Vocabulaire, p. 31 15 min.
- Presenting **Vocabulaire,** ATE, p. 31

PANORAMA CULTUREL 10 min.
- Presenting **Panorama Culturel,** ATE, p. 30, view Videocassette 1, first three interviews only.
- Read and discuss **Qu'en penses-tu?** and **Savais-tu que?,** p. 30.

Wrap-Up 5 min.
- Make statements stating the likes mentioned in the **Panorama Culturel** and have students tell which interviewee would make the statement.

Homework Options
Cahier d'activités, p. 12, Acts. 22–23

Day 8

TROISIEME ETAPE

Quick Review 10 min.
- Check homework.
- Bell Work, ATE, p. 31

Vocabulaire, p. 31 20 min.
- Review **Vocabulaire** using Teaching Transparencies 1-C and 1-D.
- Additional Practice, ATE, p. 31
- Play Audio CD for Activity 24, p. 32.

Comment dit-on... ?, p. 32 15 min.
- Presenting **Comment dit-on... ?,** ATE, p. 32
- Do Activity 25, p. 32.
- Additional Listening Activities 1-5 and 1-6, Listening Activities, p. 9

Wrap-Up 5 min.
- Have students complete the chart suggested in the first part of the Teacher to Teacher Suggestion.

Homework Options
Travaux pratiques de grammaire, pp. 6–7, Acts. 15–17

Day 9

TROISIEME ETAPE

Quick Review 10 min.
- Check homework.
- Review: Have students tell a partner one activity they like and one they dislike. Have students report the information they learned from their partners back to the class.

Grammaire, p. 33 15 min.
- Presenting **Grammaire,** ATE, p. 33
- Do Acts. 26–29, pp. 33–35.
- Travaux pratiques de grammaire, pp. 7–9, Acts. 18–24

Prononciation, p. 281 15 min.
- Play Audio CD for Activities A–C, p. 35.

Wrap-Up 10 min.
- Have students do Situation 1-3: Role-play, Activities for Communication, p. 138.

Homework Options
Study for **Troisième étape** quiz.

Day 10

TROISIEME ETAPE

Quiz 1-3 20 min.
- Administer Quiz 1-3A or Quiz 1-3B.

LISONS! 25 min.
- Prereading Activities A–C, ATE, p. 36
- Reading Activities D–F, ATE, pp. 36–37
- Postreading Activities G–H, ATE, p. 37

Wrap-Up 5 min.
- Thinking Critically, ATE, p. 36

Homework Options
Cahier d'activités, p. 11, Acts. 20–21

Day 11

LISONS!

Quick Review 15 min.
- Have students do the Challenge Activity, p. 34, and share their descriptions with the class.
- Multicultural Link, p. 37

MISE EN PRATIQUE 30 min.
- Do Activities 1 and 2, p. 42, as a class, and Activity 3, p. 42, in pairs.
- Have students do Activities 4 and 5, p. 43, individually. See Portfolio suggestion, ATE, p. 43. Have students exchange their rough drafts and give written advice to their partners.
- Have partners complete **Jeu de rôle,** p. 43.

Wrap-Up 5 min.
- Discuss Career Path, ATE, p. 42.

Homework Options
Que sais-je?, p. 44
Finish Activity 5, p. 43

Day 12

MISE EN PRATIQUE

Quick Review 15 min.
- Check homework and collect letters (Activity 5, p. 43).
- Have students play game, ATE, p. 45.

Chapter Review 35 min.
- Review Chapter 1. Choose from **Grammaire supplémentaire,** Grammar Tutor for Students of French, Activities for Communication, Listening Activities, Interactive CD-ROM Tutor, or **Jeux interactifs.**

Homework Options
Study for Chapter 1 Test.

Assessment

Test, Chapter 1 50 min.
- Administer Chapter 1 Test. Select from Testing Program, Alternative Assessment Guide, Test Generator, or Standardized Assessment Tutor.

Chapitre 1 : Faisons connaissance!
90-Minute Lesson Plans

Block 1

CHAPTER OPENER **5 min.**
- Present Chapter Objectives, p. 17

MISE EN TRAIN **40 min.**
- Presenting **Mise en train,** ATE, pp. 18–19
- Do Activity 1, p. 20.
- Use Map Transparency 4 and 4a (Overlay) to locate countries where teenagers are from.
- View video of **Mise en train,** Videocassette 1, Video Guide, p. 5. Post-Viewing Activity, Video Guide, p. 8
- **Rencontre culturelle,** p. 21

PREMIERE ETAPE

Comment dit-on... ?, p. 22 **15 min.**
- Presenting **Comment dit-on... ?,** ATE, p. 22
- Play Audio CD for Activity 6, p. 22.
- Activity 7, p. 22, Kinesthetic Learners, ATE, p. 22

Comment dit-on... ?, p. 23 **25 min.**
- Presenting **Comment dit-on... ?,** ATE, p. 23
- **Note culturelle,** p. 23
- Play Audio CD for Activity 9, p. 23. See Teaching Suggestion, ATE, p. 23.
- Do Activity 10, p. 24.

Wrap-Up **5 min.**
- Use Chapter 1 **Mise en train** Transparencies to summarize what happened in the **Mise en train.**

Homework Options
Pupil's Edition, Activity 8, p. 22
Cahier d'activités, p. 4, Acts. 3–4
Travaux pratiques de grammaire, p. 1, Act. 1

Block 2

PREMIERE ETAPE

Quick Review **5 min.**
- Have each student greet 3 peers and ask them how they feel.

Comment dit-on... ?, p. 24 **30 min.**
- Presenting **Comment dit-on... ?,** ATE, p. 24
- Play Audio CD for Activity 15, p. 25.
- Game: **Introductions,** ATE, p. 15C
- Communicative Activity 1-1A and 1-1B, Activities for Communication, pp. 1–2

DEUXIEME ETAPE

Comment dit-on... ?, p. 26 **30 min.**
- Presenting **Comment dit-on... ?,** ATE, p. 26
- **Note de grammaire,** p. 26.
- Play Audio CD for Activity 18, p. 26.
- Do Activity 19, p. 26.

Vocabulaire, p. 27 **20 min.**
- Presenting **Vocabulaire,** ATE, p. 27. Thinking Critically, ATE, p. 27
- Play Audio CD for Activity 20, p. 28.
- Use Additional Practice, ATE, p. 26, have students generate a list of what they like and dislike. Then have them share it with the rest of the group.

Wrap-Up **5 min.**
- Hold pictures of vocabulary items p. 27. Ask students **Qu'est-ce que c'est?**

Homework Options
Study for **Première étape** quiz.
Travaux pratiques de grammaire, pp. 1–3, Acts. 2–8
Cahier d'activités, pp. 7–8, Acts. 9 and 12
Pupil's Edition, Activity 1, p. 25

Block 3

PREMIERE ETAPE

Quick Review **10 min.**
- Situation Card 1-1: Interview, Activities for Communication, p. 137

Quiz 1-1 **20 min.**
- Administer Quiz 1-1A or 1-1B.

DEUXIEME ETAPE

Quick Review **5 min.**
- Communicative Activity 1-2A and 1-2B, Activities for Communication, pp. 3–4

Grammaire: the definite articles, p. 28 **35 min.**
- Presenting **Grammaire,** p. 28
- Do Activity 21, p. 29.
- **Grammaire supplémentaire,** pp. 38–39, Activities 2–3
- Game 4, Interactive CD-ROM Tutor (Disc 1)

PANORAMA CULTUREL **15 min.**
- View **Panorama Culturel**, Videocassette 1, (first 3 interviews only), p. 30
- Have students answer **Qu'en penses-tu?** questions, p. 30.
- Read **Savais-tu que…?**, p. 30

Wrap-Up **5 min.**
- Students tell the class what they like and dislike, using **et** and **mais.** (Activity 23, p. 29 as a speaking activity)

Homework Options
Study for **Deuxième étape** quiz.
Travaux pratiques de grammaire, pp. 4–5, Acts. 9–14

For alternative lesson plans by chapter section, to create your own customized plans, or to preview all resources available for this chapter, use the **One-Stop Planner CD-ROM**, Disc 1.

For additional homework suggestions, see activities accompanied by this symbol throughout the chapter.

Block 4

DEUXIEME ETAPE

Quick Review 10 min.

Quiz 1-2 20 min.
- Administer Quiz 1-2A or 1-2B.

TROISIEME ETAPE

Vocabulaire, p. 31 35 min.
- **Vocabulaire,** p. 31. Use Teaching Transparencies 1-C and 1-D to introduce the vocabulary, then have the students ask each other what they like and dislike.
- Play Audio CD for Activity 24, p. 32.
- Game: **Jacques a dit,** ATE, p. 15C

Comment dit-on... ?, p. 32 15 min.
- Presenting **Comment dit-on... ?,** ATE, p. 32
- Do Activity 25, p. 32.

Wrap-Up 10 min.
- Hold up pictures of vocabulary items p. 31. Ask students: **Qu'est-ce qu'il/elle aime?**

Homework Options

Cahier d'activités, p. 10, Acts. 18–19
Travaux pratiques de grammaire, pp. 6–7, Acts. 15–17

Block 5

TROISIEME ETAPE

Quick Review 10 min.
- Situation Card Interview 1-2, Activities for Communication, p. 137

Grammaire: Subject pronouns and –er verbs, p. 33 35 min.
- Presenting **Grammaire: Subject pronouns and –er verbs,** ATE, p. 33.
- Activity 26, p. 33 and Additional Practice, ATE, p. 33
- Do Activity 27, p. 34.
- **Grammaire supplémentaire,** pp. 39–40, Acts. 5–8

Prononciation 15 min.
- Present **Prononciation**, p. 35. Language Note, ATE, p. 35
- Play Audio CD for Activities A–C, p. 35.

LISONS! 20 min.
- Prereading Activities A–C, ATE, p. 36
- Reading Activities D–F, ATE, pp. 36–37
- Postreading Activities G–H, Community Link, ATE, p. 37
- Have students work in groups. Have each group summarize one ad from the text, and present their summary to the class.
- Thinking Critically, ATE, p. 36
- Multicultural Link, ATE, p. 37

Wrap-Up 10 min.
- Communicative Activity 1-3A and 1-3B Activities for Communication, pp. 5–6

Homework Options

Study for **Troisième étape** quiz.
Travaux pratiques de grammaire, pp. 8–9, Acts. 19–24

Block 6

TROISIEME ETAPE

Quick Review 10 min.

Quiz 1-3 20 min.
- Administer Quiz 1-3A or 1-3B.

MISE EN PRATIQUE 40 min.
- Activities 1 and 4, pp. 42–43
- Activity 5, p. 43: Students write a rough draft, and then trade papers and give written advice to their partners. See Portfolio suggestion, ATE, p. 43

Wrap-Up 20 min.
- Role Play 1-3, Activities for Communication, p. 138: 10 min. for students to prepare; 10 min. to present skits to the class.

Homework Options

Que sais-je?, p. 40
Finish letter for Activity 5, p. 43.
Study for Chapter 1 Test.

Block 7

MISE EN PRATIQUE

Quick Review 5 min.
- Check homework and collect letters (Activity 5, p. 43).

Chapter Review 35 min.
- Review Chapter 1. Choose from **Grammaire supplémentaire,** Grammar Tutor for Students of French, Activities for Communication, Listening Activities, Interactive CD-ROM Tutor, or **Jeux interactifs**

Test, Chapter 1 50 min.
- Administer Chapter 1 Test. Select from Testing Program, Alternative Assessment Guide, Test Generator, or Standardized Assessment Tutor.

CHAPITRE 1

One-Stop Planner CD-ROM

For resource information, see the **One-Stop Planner,** Disc 1.

Pacing Tips

All three **étapes** in this chapter are more or less balanced in terms of new content to be covered. The **Deuxième étape** and **Troisième étape** introduce new vocabulary and grammar, so you might keep that in mind while planning your lessons. For Lesson Plans and timing suggestions, see pages 15I–15L.

Meeting the Standards

Communication

- Greeting people and saying goodbye, p. 22
- Asking how people are and telling how you are, p. 23
- Asking someone's name and giving yours, p. 24
- Asking someone's age and giving yours, p. 25
- Expressing likes, dislikes, and preferences about things, p. 26
- Expressing likes, dislikes, and preferences about activities, p. 32

Cultures

- Rencontre culturelle, p. 21
- Culture Note, pp. 16, 21, 23, 25, 27, 34
- Note culturelle, p. 23
- Panorama Culturel, p. 30

Connections

- Sports Link, p. 30

Comparisons

- Multicultural Link, pp. 16, 34
- Thinking Critically, p. 27

Communities

- Family Link, p. 21
- De l'école au travail, p. 35
- Community Link, p. 37
- Career Path, p. 42

Cultures and Communities

Culture Note

French people might seem a little distant when you meet them for the first time. They typically don't say hello to people they don't know, as Americans sometimes do. French people aren't as likely as Americans are to make eye contact with people they don't know in public settings. However, once you know a French person, he/she will be as friendly and warm as any of your American friends.

Multicultural Link

Have students research greetings used by people of other cultures, such as the Japanese and the Inuits.

CHAPITRE 1

Faisons connaissance!

Objectives

In this chapter you will learn to

Première étape

- greet people and say goodbye
- ask how people are and tell how you are
- ask someone's name and age and give yours

Deuxième étape

- express likes, dislikes, and preferences about things

Troisième étape

- express likes, dislikes, and preferences about activities

Visit Holt Online
go.hrw.com
KEYWORD: WA3 POITIERS-1
Online Edition

◀ **Salut! Ça va?**

Connections and Comparisons

Thinking Critically

Observing Ask students to observe how the French teenagers in the photo are greeting each other. Do American teenagers greet each other the same way? For homework, ask students to observe at least three different people greeting someone else, describe the individuals and the actions they observed, and tell whether any of these actions would be inappropriate with other people.

Thinking Critically

Analyzing Ask students the following questions. What do you say to someone you've just met? What differences would there be between meeting someone your own age and introducing yourself to an adult? Why?

Chapter Opener

CHAPITRE 1

Focusing on Outcomes

- Have students suggest as many English expressions as possible to say hello and goodbye. When would they use each expression? What gestures (if any) do they use with these greetings (a handshake, a kiss, a hug)?
- Have students brainstorm what they would write about if they were introducing themselves in a letter to a pen pal.

NOTE: The self-check activities in **Que sais-je?** on page 44 help students assess their achievement of the objectives.

STANDARDS: 4.2

Mise en train

CHAPITRE 1

Teaching Resources
pp. 18–20

PRINT 
- Lesson Planner, p. 3
- Video Guide, pp. 6, 8
- Cahier d'activités, p. 3

MEDIA 
- One-Stop Planner
- Video Program
  Mise en train
  Videocassette 1, 07:39–12:43
  Videocassette 5 (captioned version), 00:46–05:49
  Suite
  Videocassette 1, 12:46–16:05
  Videocassette 5 (captioned version), 05:55–09:11
- DVD Tutor, Disc 1
- Audio Compact Discs, CD 1, Trs. 11–12
- **Mise en train** Transparencies

Presenting Mise en train

Have students look at the questions in Activity 1 on page 20 before you play the video, so that they will have an idea of what they will see and hear. Then, show *Map Transparency 4* **(Le Monde francophone)** on the overhead projector, or use a wall map if you have one. Ask students to locate the places on the map where the teenagers say they live. You might also use the Preteaching Vocabulary suggestions below.

Mise en train Transparencies

The **roman-photo** is an abridged version of the video episode.

MISE EN TRAIN ▪ *Salut, les copains!*

CD 1 Trs. 11–12

Stratégie pour comprendre
What can you tell about these teenagers just by looking at their photos? Look for hints about where they live, how old they are, and what they like to do.

1 **Claire**
Bonjour! Ça va? Je m'appelle Claire. J'ai 15 ans. Je suis française, de Poitiers. J'adore le cinéma. Mais j'aime aussi danser, lire, voyager et écouter de la musique.

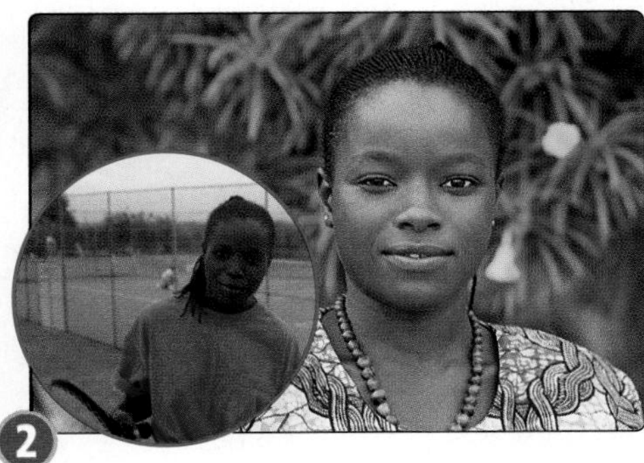

2 **Djeneba**
Salut! Je m'appelle Djeneba. J'ai 16 ans. Je suis ivoirienne. J'aime étudier, mais j'aime mieux faire du sport. C'est super cool!

3 **Ahmed**
Salut! Je m'appelle Ahmed. Je suis marocain. J'aime tous les sports, surtout le football. J'aime aussi faire du vélo.

4 **Thuy**
Salut! Ça va? Je m'appelle Thuy. J'ai 14 ans. Je suis vietnamienne. J'aime faire les magasins. En général, je n'aime pas la télévision. J'aime mieux aller au cinéma.

Preteaching Vocabulary

Recognizing Cognates

The **Mise en train** contains several words that students will be able to recognize as cognates. Have students find as many cognates as they can as each francophone teenager introduces himself or herself, and list the cognates on the board. Then, based on the list, have students guess what these French-speaking teenagers might like or dislike.

1. **adore, cinéma**
2. **super, cool**
3. **sports**
4. **général, télévision**
5. **musique, voyager**
7. **téléphone**
8. **ski**

STANDARDS: 1.2

5

Didier
Salut! Je m'appelle Didier. J'ai 13 ans. Je suis belge. J'aime écouter de la musique. J'aime aussi les vacances. J'aime surtout voyager!

6

Stéphane
Bonjour! Je m'appelle Stéphane. J'ai 15 ans et je suis martiniquais. J'aime la plage, la mer, le soleil, la musique et j'aime aussi nager. J'aime surtout danser.

7

André
Tiens, bonjour! Comment ça va? Je m'appelle André. J'ai 17 ans et je suis suisse. Je parle français et allemand. J'aime beaucoup la télévision. J'aime aussi parler au téléphone avec mes copains.

8

Emilie
Bonjour! Je m'appelle Emilie. J'ai 16 ans. Je suis québécoise. J'adore faire du sport, surtout du ski et du patin. J'aime bien aussi faire de l'équitation.

Cahier d'activités, p. 3, Act. 1–2

Teaching Suggestion

Have students identify any statements made by the teenagers that also apply to them.

Salut, les copains! (suite)

You may choose to continue with ***Salut, les copains! (suite)*** at this time or wait until later in the chapter. In the second part of the video, Marc arrives at school and greets his math teacher. Then Claire arrives and introduces Ann to her friends and teacher. Later that day, Claire and her friends take Ann to a café and pay for her part of the check to welcome her to Poitiers.

Using the Captioned Video/DVD

If students have difficulty understanding French spoken at a normal speed, use Videocassette 5 to allow students to see the French captions for ***Salut, les copains!*** and ***Salut, les copains! (suite).*** Hearing the language and watching the story will reduce anxiety about the new language and facilitate comprehension. The reinforcement of seeing the written vocabulary words as they watch the gestures and actions will help prepare students to do the comprehension activities on page 20.
NOTE: The *DVD Tutor* contains captions for all sections of the *Video Program.*

STANDARDS: 1.2

Mise en train

CHAPITRE 1

Slower Pace

2 Have students find the cognates in the activity and write them down. Have them find the name of the person in each sentence in ***Salut, les copains!*** They should then find the name(s) of the activity(-ies) in that person's remarks and decide whether the information in both the true-false statement and the basic text are the same.

Auditory Learners

3 Play the video of ***Salut, les copains!*** Have students call out when they identify each of these functions. Then, stop the video and have students repeat the French expressions.

These activities check for comprehension only. Students should not yet be expected to produce language modeled in **Mise en train.**

1 Tu as compris? *Did you understand?*

Answer the following questions about the teenagers you've just met. Look back at ***Salut, les copains!*** if you have to. Don't be afraid to guess. See answers below.

1. What are these teenagers talking about?
2. What information do they give you in the first few lines of their introductions?
3. What are some of the things they like?
4. Which of them have interests in common?

2 Vrai ou faux? *True or false?*

According to ***Salut, les copains!***, are the following statements true (**vrai**) or false (**faux**)?

1. André aime parler au téléphone. vrai
2. Ahmed n'aime pas le sport. faux
3. Stéphane aime écouter de la musique. vrai
4. Claire aime voyager et danser. vrai
5. Didier n'aime pas voyager. faux
6. Emilie aime faire de l'équitation. vrai
7. Thuy aime la télévision. faux
8. Djeneba n'aime pas faire du sport. faux

3 Cherche les expressions *Look for the expressions*

Look back at ***Salut, les copains!*** How do the teenagers . . .

1. say hello? Bonjour./Salut.
2. give their name? Je m'appelle...
3. give their age? J'ai... ans.
4. say they like something? J'aime...

J'ai... ans. J'aime... Je suis...
Bonjour. Salut. Je m'appelle...

4 Qui est-ce? *Who is it?*

Can you identify the teenagers in ***Salut, les copains!*** from these descriptions?

1. Elle est québécoise. Emilie
2. Il parle allemand. André
3. Il a quinze ans. Stéphane
4. Il aime voyager. Didier
5. Elle adore le ski. Emilie
6. Elle n'aime pas la télévision. Thuy
7. Il adore le football. Ahmed
8. Elle aime étudier. Djeneba

5 Et maintenant, à toi *And now, it's your turn*

Which of the students in ***Salut, les copains!*** would you most like to meet? Why? Jot down your thoughts and share them with a classmate.

Possible answers

1
1. names, ages, interests, and nationalities
2. name, age, nationality, what they like to do
3. music, dancing, sports, movies, reading, traveling, shopping, television
4. Claire and Thuy — movies; Djeneba, Ahmed, and Emilie — sports; Claire, Didier, and Stéphane — music; Claire and Didier — traveling

Comprehension Check

Additional Practice

2 Have students work individually or in pairs to write three or four additional true-false statements based on ***Salut, les copains!*** Students might exchange papers and mark their answers, or you might call on individuals to read one of their statements and have other students respond.

Challenge

4 After the students have completed Activity 4, have them reread ***Salut, les copains!*** and write one more distinguishing characteristic of each person.

STANDARDS: 1.2

Rencontre culturelle

Look at what the people in these photos are doing.

—Salut, Mireille!
—Salut, Lucien!

—Bonjour, Maman!
—Bonjour, mon chou!

—Salut, Lucien!
—Salut, Jean-Philippe!

—Salut, Agnès!
—Tchao, Mireille!

—Bonjour, Monsieur Balland.
—Bonjour, Marc.

—Au revoir, Monsieur Legrand.
—Au revoir, Isabelle.

Qu'en penses-tu? *What do you think?* See answers below.

1. How do these teenagers greet adults? Other teenagers? What gestures do they use?
2. How do they say goodbye? What gestures do they use?
3. Is this similar to the way you greet people and say goodbye in the United States?

Savais-tu que...? *Did you know . . . ?*

In France, girls kiss both girls and boys on the cheek when they meet or say goodbye. The number of kisses varies from two to four depending on the region. Boys shake hands with one another. Teenagers may kiss adults who are family members or friends of the family, but they shake hands when they greet other adults.

To address adults who aren't family members, teenagers generally use the titles **madame, mademoiselle,** or **monsieur. Mme, Mlle,** and **M.** are the written abbreviations of these titles.

Cultures and Communities

Culture Notes

- In France, people say **Bonjour** only the first time they see someone on a given day. If they see that person again during the same day, they might just say **Ça va?**
- In African countries, greetings are very important. People shake hands when meeting or saying goodbye. However, women usually don't shake hands. In French-speaking countries, it is the norm for people to kiss each other on the cheeks, as it is in France.
- In Djoula, the market language of Côte d'Ivoire, greeting one another is truly an art form. There are separate greetings for men, women, a person who is working, a person you haven't seen in a long time, and a person who is going to the market.

STANDARDS: 2.1, 3.2, 4.2

Presenting Rencontre culturelle

Have volunteers read or act out the dialogues. You might play the role of the adult. Then, ask the questions in **Qu'en penses-tu?** or have groups work together to answer them.

Language Note

You might want to point out the difference in punctuation in the abbreviations **Mme, Mlle,** and **M.** When an abbreviation ends with the same letter as the word it abbreviates, there is no period at the end.

Family Link

Have students teach a member of their family to greet someone in French, to introduce himself or herself, and to spell his or her name. Ask students if it was easy to teach this information and if their family members learned quickly. How would their family members feel about kissing others on the cheek everytime they meet? When assigning Family Link activities, keep in mind that some students and their families may consider family matters private.

Answers

1. Adults: Bonjour, Maman! Bonjour, Monsieur Balland.
   Teenagers: Salut!
   Gestures—adults: kiss (relatives); handshake
   Gestures—teenagers: kiss; handshake
2. Adults: Au revoir, Monsieur Legrand.
   Teenagers: Salut! Tchao! Gestures—adults: handshake Gestures—teenagers: kiss

CHAPITRE 1

Teaching Resources
pp. 22–25

PRINT 

- Lesson Planner, p. 4
- TPR Storytelling Book, pp. 1, 4
- Listening Activities, pp. 3–4, 7
- Activities for Communication, pp. 1–2, 75, 78, 137–138
- Travaux pratiques de grammaire, pp. 1–2
- Grammar Tutor for Students of French, Chapter 1
- Cahier d'activités, pp. 4–6
- Testing Program, pp. 1–4
- Alternative Assessment Guide, p. 32
- Student Make-Up Assignments, Chapter 1

MEDIA

- One-Stop Planner
- Audio Compact Discs, CD 1, Trs. 13–17, 31, 37–38
- Teaching Transparencies: 1-1; **Grammaire supplémentaire** Answers; Travaux pratiques de grammaire Answers
- Interactive CD-ROM Tutor, Disc 1

Bell Work
Write several numbers between 0 and 20 at random on the board. Have students write the words for these numbers. Then, have them correct their papers by turning to page 9 in the Preliminary Chapter.

Presenting
Comment dit-on... ?

Say these expressions, using appropriate gestures. Have students repeat after you and imitate your gestures.

Première étape

Objectives Greeting people and saying goodbye; asking how people are and telling how you are; asking someone's name and age and giving yours

WA3 POITIERS-1

Comment dit-on...?

Greeting people and saying goodbye

To anyone:

Bonjour. *Hello.*

Au revoir. *Goodbye.*
A tout à l'heure. *See you later.*
A bientôt. *See you soon.*
A demain. *See you tomorrow.*

To someone your own age or younger:

Salut. *Hi.*

Salut. *Bye.*
Tchao. *Bye.*

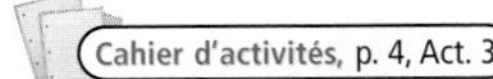

6 Bonjour ou Au revoir? See scripts and answers on p. 15G.

Ecoutons Imagine you overhear the following short conversations on the street in Poitiers. Listen carefully and decide whether the speakers are saying hello or goodbye.

CD 1 Tr. 13

7 Comment le dire? *How should you say it?*

Parlons How would you say hello to these people in French?

Mme Leblanc
Bonjour!

M. Diab
Bonjour!

Nadia
Salut!

Eric
Salut!

Mme Desrochers
Bonjour!

8 Comment répondre? *How should you answer?*

Parlons How would you respond to the greeting from each of the following people?

1. Bonjour!

2. Au revoir!/A tout à l'heure!/A bientôt!/A demain!

3. Au revoir!/A tout à l'heure!/A bientôt!/Salut!/Tchao!

4. Salut!

Communication for All Students

Language Note
Explain to students that **A tout à l'heure** is used to say goodbye only when you will see the person later the same day. To say *See you later* in a more general way, young people now use the expression **A plus!**, short for **A plus tard.** Tell students that they should pronounce the "s" in **A plus.**

Kinesthetic Learners
Have students practice saying the expressions while making the corresponding gestures.

Challenge
8 Have students draw or cut out pictures of people greeting each other or saying goodbye. Have them add captions or speech bubbles in French.

Comment dit-on...?

Asking how people are and telling how you are

To ask how your friend is:
Comment ça va? or **Ça va?**

To tell how you are:

Super! *Great!*
Très bien. *Very well.*

Ça va. *Fine.*
Comme ci comme ça. *So-so.*
Pas mal. *Not bad.*
Bof! *(expression of indifference)*

Pas terrible. *Not so great.*

To keep a conversation going:
Et toi? *And you?*

Cahier d'activités, p. 4, Act. 4

Travaux pratiques de grammaire, p. 1, Act. 1

A la française

To ask an adult how he or she is, you can say:
Comment allez-vous?
To keep a conversation with an adult going, you can say:
Et vous?
You'll learn more about using **vous** later in this chapter.

9 **Comment ça va?** See scripts and answers on p. 15G.

CD 1
Tr. 14

Ecoutons You're going to hear a student ask Valérie, Jean-Michel, Anne, Marie, and Karim how they're feeling. Are they feeling good, fair, or bad?

Note culturelle

Gestures are an important part of communication. They often speak louder than words. Can you match the gestures with these expressions?

a. Super!
b. Comme ci comme ça.
c. Pas terrible!

When you say **super,** use a thumbs-up gesture. When you say **comme ci comme ça,** hold your hand in front of you, palm down, and rock it from side to side. When you say **pas terrible,** shrug your shoulders and frown.

1. c

2. b

3. a

Communication for All Students

Visual Learners

Have students add the functional expressions to their notebooks. You might want to illustrate the intonation pattern by drawing on the board or on a transparency lines that curve upward above **Et toi?** and **Ça va?**

Kinesthetic Learners

Have students pair off and practice the expressions, using the appropriate gestures. One student gives an expression, and his or her partner makes the appropriate gesture.

Presenting Comment dit-on... ?

Draw the three faces to represent the expressions in **Comment dit-on... ?** on a transparency and number them. Say the expressions in the box aloud in random order and ask students to call out or write down the number of the face that corresponds to the expression.

Culture Note

The gesture for **comme ci comme ça** can also show uncertainty. For example, if someone says that the bus will arrive at eight o'clock while making this gesture, then it means that the bus will arrive around eight, more or less.

STANDARDS: 1.2, 2.1, 3.2

Teaching Resources
pp. 22–25

PRINT

- Lesson Planner, p. 4
- TPR Storytelling Book, pp. 1, 4
- Listening Activities, pp. 3–4, 7
- Activities for Communication, pp. 1–2, 75, 78, 137–138
- Travaux pratiques de grammaire, pp. 1–2
- Grammar Tutor for Students of French, Chapter 1
- Cahier d'activités, pp. 4–6
- Testing Program, pp. 1–4
- Alternative Assessment Guide, p. 32
- Student Make-Up Assignments, Chapter 1

MEDIA 

- One-Stop Planner
- Audio Compact Discs, CD 1, Trs. 13–17, 31, 37–38
- Teaching Transparencies: 1-1; **Grammaire supplémentaire** Answers; Travaux pratiques de grammaire Answers
- Interactive CD-ROM Tutor, Disc 1

Presenting
Comment dit-on... ?

Give your name and ask several individuals theirs. Students should recall these expressions using **je** and **tu** from the Preliminary Chapter. Have students practice asking and giving their names. Point to boys and girls in the class, naming them. Occasionally, give a wrong name. Ask students to correct you, saying **Non, il/elle s'appelle...**

Answers

10 Bonjour,... !
Salut,... ! Ça va?
Super! Et toi?
Très bien.
Bon. Alors, à tout à l'heure!
Tchao.

10 Méli-mélo! *Mishmash!*

Ecrivons/Parlons Work with a classmate to rewrite the conversation in the correct order, using your own names. Then, act it out with your partner. Remember to use the appropriate gestures. See answers below.

Très bien. Super! Et toi? Tchao. Salut,... ! Ça va? Bonjour,... ! Bon. Alors, à tout à l'heure!

11 Et ton voisin (ta voisine)? *And your neighbor?*

Parlons Create a conversation with a partner. Be sure to greet your partner, ask how he or she is feeling, respond to any questions your partner asks you, and say goodbye. Don't forget to include the gestures you learned in the **Note culturelle** on page 23.

Comment dit-on...?

Asking someone's name and giving yours

—Tu t'appelles comment?
—Je m'appelle Magali.

To ask someone his or her name:
Tu t'appelles comment?

To give your name:
Je m'appelle...

Travaux pratiques de grammaire, p. 2, Act. 5

To ask someone else's name:
Il/Elle s'appelle comment? *What is his/her name?*

To give someone else's name:
Il/Elle s'appelle... *His/Her name is . . .*

12 Il ou elle? See scripts and answers on p. 15G.

Ecoutons Listen as some French teenagers tell you about their friends. Are they talking about a boy (**un garçon**) or a girl (**une fille**)?

CD 1 Tr. 15

Communication for All Students

Slower Pace

12 Before doing this listening activity, ask students to say **il** or **elle** as you point to different students. Then, hold up pictures of people, asking **C'est un garçon?** or **C'est une fille?** Remind students that some French girls' and boys' names sound the same, such as Dominique, Michel/Michèle, and Claude.

Group Work

Teams of 3–5 students create short dialogues like the one in Activity 10. Have students write lines on separate strips of paper. Teams mix up their strips of paper and exchange them. Team members work together to arrange the slips of paper in the correct order. Then, each team reads its dialogue aloud in order, one student at a time.

Il s'appelle comment?

See scripts and answers on p. 15G.

CD 1 Tr. 16

Ecoutons You're going to hear a song called ***S'appeler rap.*** Which of the following names are mentioned in the song?

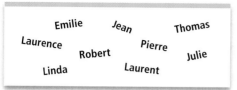

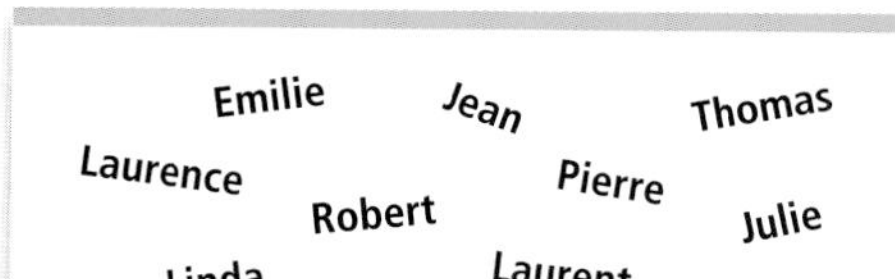

14 Je te présente... *Let me introduce . . .*

Parlons Select a French name for yourself from the list of names on page 5, or ask your teacher to suggest others. Then, say hello to a classmate, introduce yourself, and ask his or her name. Now, introduce your partner to the rest of the class, using **il s'appelle** or **elle s'appelle.**

Comment dit-on...?

Asking someone's age and giving yours

CD-ROM 1 DVD 1

To find out someone's age:	To give your age:
Tu as quel âge?	**J'ai** douze **ans.**
	treize
	quatorze
	quinze
	seize
	dix-sept
	dix-huit

Grammaire supplémentaire, p. 38, Act. 1–2

Travaux pratiques de grammaire, pp. 1–2, Act. 2–4, 6

Je me présente...

See scripts and answers on p. 15G.

Ecoutons Listen as Bruno, Véronique, Laurent, and Céline introduce themselves to you. Write down each student's age.

CD 1 Tr. 17

16 Faisons connaissance! *Let's get to know one another!*

Parlons Create a conversation with two other classmates. Introduce yourself, ask your partners' names and ages, and ask how they are.

Mon journal *My journal*

Ecrivons A good way to learn French is to use it to express your own thoughts and feelings. From time to time, you'll be asked to write about yourself in French in a journal. As your first journal entry, identify yourself, giving your name, your age, and anything else important to you that you've learned how to say in French.

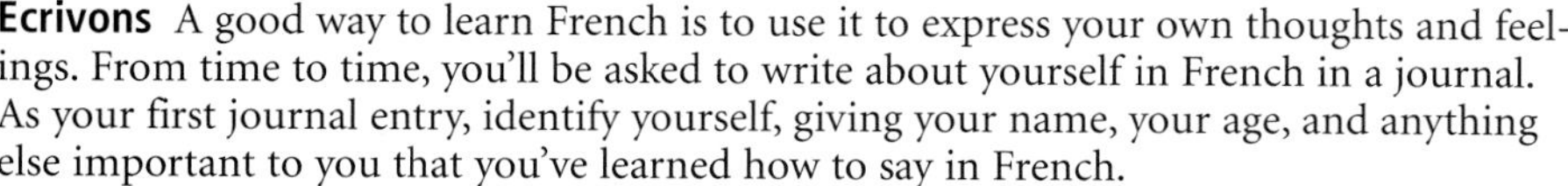

Cultures and Communities

Culture Note

Next to Activity 13 is a photo of the popular French rapper known as MC Solaar. A native of Senegal, Claude M'Barali created his stage name from the English abbreviation for *Master of Ceremonies* and the French word for sun, **le soleil.** In his music, which is a combination of jazz, funk, and soul, MC Solaar advocates peace and tries to serve as a voice for young people. MC Solaar has created many tongue twisters to describe his philosophy; one example is **Ma tactique attaque tous tes tics avec tact.** *(My tactics attack all your tics with tact.)* Among his most popular albums are ***Qui sème le vent récolte le tempo*** *(He Who Sows the Wind Reaps the Tempo)* and ***Prose combat.***

Première étape

CHAPITRE 1

Building on Previous Skills

14 Review the alphabet from the Preliminary Chapter. Have partners practice spelling their names after introducing each other.

Presenting Comment dit-on... ?

Review the numbers 1–20. Then, write **âge** on the board and ask the students what they think it means. Now, write **14 ans** and ask what they think **ans** means. Tell the students we get the words *annual* and *anniversary* from the same root. Next, have students pair off and practice the question and response several times.

Language Note

You might want to tell your students that, in everyday speech, they might give a short answer when asked their age: **Quatorze ans.**

Assess

- Testing Program, pp. 1–4 Quiz 1-1A, Quiz 1-1B Audio CD 1, Tr. 31
- Student Make-Up Assignments, Chapter 1, Alternative Quiz
- Alternative Assessment Guide, p. 32

STANDARDS: 1.3, 3.1, 5.2

Deuxième étape

CHAPITRE 1

Teaching Resources
pp. 26–29

PRINT
- Lesson Planner, p. 5
- TPR Storytelling Book, pp. 2, 4
- Listening Activities, pp. 4–5, 8
- Activities for Communication, pp. 3–4, 76, 78–79, 137–138
- Travaux pratiques de grammaire, pp. 3–5
- Grammar Tutor for Students of French, Chapter 1
- Cahier d'activités, pp. 7–8
- Testing Program, pp. 5–8
- Alternative Assessment Guide, p. 32
- Student Make-Up Assignments, Chapter 1

MEDIA
- One-Stop Planner
- Audio Compact Discs, CD 1, Trs. 18–19, 32, 39–40
- Teaching Transparencies: 1-2, 1-A, 1-B; **Grammaire supplémentaire** Answers; Travaux pratiques de grammaire Answers
- Interactive CD-ROM Tutor, Disc 1

Bell Work
Have students write the answers to the following questions: **Ça va? Tu t'appelles comment? Tu as quel âge?**

Presenting
Comment dit-on... ?

Gather pictures of various things you like and dislike; some may be those in **Comment dit-on...?** Tell the class in French which ones you like, which you really like, which you prefer, and which you dislike, using the expressions in **Comment dit-on... ?** Then, ask students in French if they like or dislike the same things. They might just answer **Oui** or **Non** at first.

Deuxième étape

Objective Expressing likes, dislikes, and preferences about things

WA3 POITIERS-1

Comment dit-on...?

Expressing likes, dislikes, and preferences about things

To ask if someone likes something:

Tu aimes les hamburgers?
Tu aimes le vélo **ou** le ski? *Do you like . . . or . . . ?*

To say that you dislike something:

Je n'aime pas les hamburgers.

To say that you like something:

J'adore le chocolat.
J'aime bien le sport.
J'aime les hamburgers.

To say that you prefer something:

J'aime les frites, **mais j'aime mieux** le chocolat. *I like . . . , but I prefer . . .*
Je préfère le français.

Note de grammaire

J'aime la pizza.
Je n'aime pas la pizza.

Look at the sentences in the illustrations to the left. Can you figure out when to use **ne (n')... pas?**

You put **ne (n')... pas** around the verb **aime** to make the sentence negative. Notice the contraction **n'** before the vowel.

J'aime le sport.
Je **n'**aime **pas** le sport.

Travaux pratiques de grammaire, p. 3, Act. 7–8

Grammaire supplémentaire, p. 39, Act. 3

See scripts and answers on p. 15H.

18 Grammaire en contexte

CD 1 Tr. 18

a. Ecoutons Listen to Paul and Sophie Dubois discuss names for their baby girl. Which of the names does Paul prefer? And Sophie?

Claude — Sandrine — Claudette — Lætitia — Claudine

b. Parlons Do you agree with Paul and Sophie's choices? With a partner, discuss whether you like or dislike the names Paul and Sophie mention. What's your favorite French girl's name? And your favorite French boy's name? You might refer to the list of names on page 5.

EXEMPLE — **Tu aimes... ?**
— **Oui, mais je n'aime pas...**

19 Quel film? *Which movie?*

Parlons With two of your classmates, decide on a movie you all like.

EXEMPLE — **J'aime *The Truman Show!* Et toi?**
— **Moi, je n'aime pas *The Truman Show.* Tu aimes *Chicken Run*®?**
— **Oui, j'aime *Chicken Run,* mais j'aime mieux *Wallace and Gromit!***

CASABLANCA RE
1942. 1h40. Film d'aventures américain en noir et blanc de Michael Curtiz avec Humphrey Bogart, Ingrid Bergman, Paul Henreid, Conrad Veidt, Claude Rains.
Casablanca à l'heure de Vichy. Un réfugié américain retrouve une femme follement aimée et fuit la persécution nazie. Une distribution étincelante et une mise en scène efficace.
• V.O. Saint Lambert 96

Communication for All Students

Visual Learners
Students might draw smiling, neutral, and unhappy faces and write sentences about what they like and dislike under the appropriate faces.

Additional Practice
19 Students might also discuss music groups or sports teams, in addition to movies.

Vocabulaire

CD-ROM 1
DVD 1

les amis (m.)

le cinéma

le ski

le football

le magasin

la plage

le vélo

la glace

l'école (f.)

le français

les frites (f.)

le chocolat

l'anglais (m.)

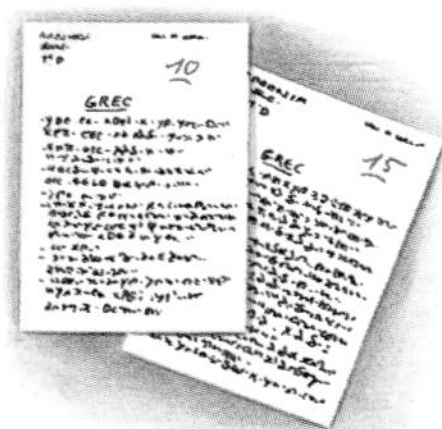
les examens (m.)

DECEMBRE						
L	M	M	J	V	S	D
		1	2	3	4	5
6	7	8	9	10	11	12
13	14	15	16	17	18	19
20	21	22	23	24	25	26
27	28	29	30	31		

les vacances (f.)

les escargots (m.)

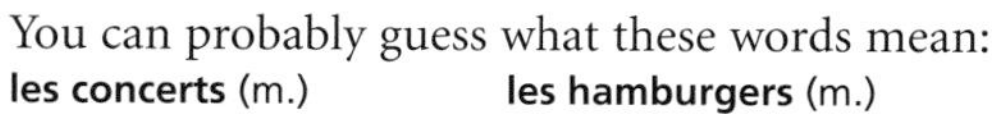
You can probably guess what these words mean:

les concerts (m.) **les hamburgers** (m.) **les maths** (f.) **la pizza** **le sport**

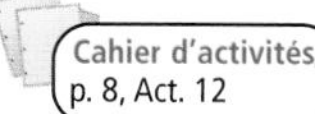
Cahier d'activités, p. 8, Act. 12

Travaux pratiques de grammaire, p. 4, Act. 9–11

Deuxième étape

CHAPITRE 1

Presenting Vocabulaire

Have students scan the vocabulary for cognates **(cinéma, ski, examens, vacances, chocolat).** Make sure they are also aware of the **faux amis (magasins, football, glace).** Have students make flashcards of this vocabulary with the French on one side and drawings or magazine pictures on the other.

Visual Learners

Bring in magazine illustrations of the vocabulary items. Ask students **Qu'est-ce que c'est?** as you hold up each illustration. Ask individual students whether they like the item, using **Tu aimes... ?** Then, have partners practice asking each other.

Culture Note

As students learn the words **plage** and **vélo,** they may be interested in learning about the beaches of the Riviera **(la Côte d'Azur),** or about the Tour de France, the famous bicycle race that covers more than 4,000 km (2,500 miles).

Connections and Comparisons

Thinking Critically

Comparing and Contrasting You might tell students that **examen** rarely translates as *exam* in English. **Examen** usually refers to comprehensive tests such as the **CAP (certificat d'aptitude professionnelle)** or the **baccalauréat** (at the end of **lycée**) that French students take at the end of a school cycle. Depending on the type of **examen** a student takes, he or she can obtain a professional certification or be admitted into specialized schools or universities. In French elementary and secondary schools, students are tested through **contrôles** or **interros (interrogations écrites** and **interrogations orales).** Ask students about comprehensive tests that American high school students have to take.

Deuxième étape

CHAPITRE 1

Teaching Resources
pp. 26–29

PRINT

- Lesson Planner, p. 5
- TPR Storytelling Book, pp. 2, 4
- Listening Activities, pp. 4–5, 8
- Activities for Communication, pp. 3–4, 76, 78–79, 137–138
- Travaux pratiques de grammaire, pp. 3–5
- Grammar Tutor for Students of French, Chapter 1
- Cahier d'activités, pp. 7–8
- Testing Program, pp. 5–8
- Alternative Assessment Guide, p. 32
- Student Make-Up Assignments, Chapter 1

MEDIA 

- One-Stop Planner
- Audio Compact Discs, CD 1, Trs. 18–19, 32, 39–40
- Teaching Transparencies: 1-2, 1-A, 1-B; **Grammaire supplémentaire** Answers; Travaux pratiques de grammaire Answers
- Interactive CD-ROM Tutor, Disc 1

Challenge

20 Ask students to check their answers with a partner by telling what each teenager likes or dislikes.

Presenting Grammaire

The definite article Many languages have several ways of saying *the.* Explain that French has four different articles that depend on the type of noun they're used with (masculine, feminine, an initial vowel sound, and plural). Have students repeat the articles and nouns after you. Hold up vocabulary flashcards and have students identify each item, using the correct article.

20 **Moi, j'aime...** See scripts and answers on p. 15H.

CD 1
Tr. 19

Ecoutons Listen as several French teenagers call in to a radio talk-show poll of their likes and dislikes. Match their names with the pictures that illustrate the activities they like or dislike.

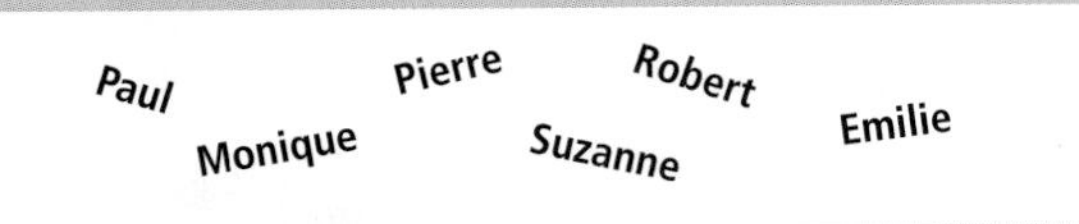

a.

b.

c.

d.

e.

f.

Grammaire

The definite articles *le, la, l',* and *les*

There are four ways to say *the* in French: **le, la, l',** and **les.** These words are called *definite articles.* Look at the articles and nouns below. Can you tell when to use **les?** When to use **l'?**

le français	la glace	l'école	les escargots
le football	la pizza	l'anglais	les magasins

- As you may have guessed, you always use **les** before plural nouns.
- Before a singular noun, you use **l'** if the noun begins with a vowel sound, **le** if the noun is masculine, or **la** if the noun is feminine. How do you know which nouns are masculine and which are feminine? While it is usually true that nouns that refer to males are masculine (**le garçon** *the boy*) and those that refer to females are feminine (**la fille** *the girl*), there are no hard-and-fast rules for other nouns. You'll just have to learn the definite article that goes with each one.

Grammaire supplémentaire, p. 39, Act. 4–5

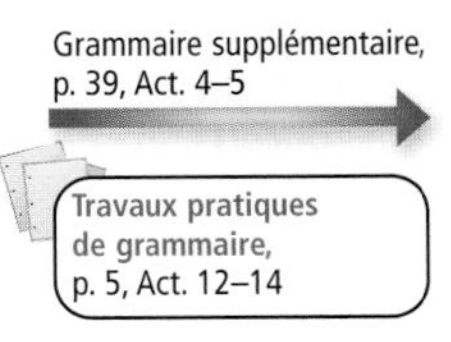

Travaux pratiques de grammaire, p. 5, Act. 12–14

Communication for All Students

Slower Pace

20 Before they hear the recording, students might look back at the **Vocabulaire** on page 27 to find the words for the things shown in the pictures and practice them orally with a partner. After correcting their answers, students might write the letters of the pictures in the order of their own preference and compare their list with a partner's.

Auditory Learners

Read aloud some sentences that contain nouns and articles from the **Vocabulaire** on page 27, some singular, some plural. Have students hold up one hand if the noun they hear is singular and both hands if it's plural. For example, if you say **J'aime la pizza,** they would raise one hand; if you say **J'aime les escargots,** they would raise both hands.

STANDARDS: 1.2, 4.1

21 Grammaire en contexte

Lisons/Parlons Lucie and Gilbert are talking about the things they like. With a partner, complete their conversation according to the pictures.

la plage

LUCIE Moi, j'aime bien [la plage]. Et toi?

les copains

le cinéma

GILBERT Moi, j'aime mieux [le cinéma]. J'aime bien aussi sortir avec [les copains].

J'adore le sport aussi. Et toi, tu aimes le sport?

le vélo

le ski

LUCIE Oui, j'adore [le vélo] et j'aime bien [le ski] aussi.

22 Grammaire en contexte

Ecrivons/Parlons Choose six things from the vocabulary on page 27. Next, write down which of those things you like and which you dislike. Then, with a partner, try to guess each other's likes and dislikes by asking **Tu aimes... ?**

A la française

Two common words you can use to connect your ideas are **et** *(and)* and **mais** *(but)*. Here's how you can use them to combine sentences.

J'aime les hamburgers. J'aime le chocolat.
J'aime les hamburgers **et** le chocolat.

J'aime le français. Je n'aime pas les maths.
J'aime le français **mais** je n'aime pas les maths.

De bons conseils

How can you remember if a noun is masculine or feminine? Here are a few hints. Choose the one that works best for you.

- Practice saying each noun aloud with **le** or **la** in front of it. (NOTE: This won't help with nouns that begin with vowels!)
- Write the feminine nouns in one column and the masculine nouns in another. You might even write the feminine nouns in one color and the masculine nouns in a second color.
- Make flash cards of the nouns, writing the feminine and masculine nouns in different colors.

23 Mon journal

Ecrivons In your journal, write down some of your likes and dislikes. Use **et** and **mais** to connect your sentences. You might want to illustrate your journal entry.

Communication for All Students

Visual/Auditory Learners

To review vocabulary, put pictures or drawings of the vocabulary on the board or on a transparency and number them. Then, say the French words for the pictures in random order. Students should call out the numbers of the corresponding pictures in French. Finally, call out the numbers of the pictures and have students say the corresponding French words.

Challenge

22 After students have completed Activity 22 orally, have them read **A la française**. Then, have them use the information they got from their partner to write a short paragraph about his or her likes and dislikes. Tell them to use **et** and **mais** to connect their sentences.

STANDARDS: 1.1, 1.3

Deuxième étape

CHAPITRE 1

Teacher Note

When giving assignments that entail the disclosure of personal information, keep in mind that some students and their families may consider these matters private. In some cases, you may want to give an alternate assignment in which students may substitute fictitious information.

Writing Assessment

23 Have students exchange journal entries with a partner to peer-edit each other's work. You may wish to use the following rubric in assessing this or other writing activities.

Writing Rubric	Points			
	4	3	2	1
Content (Complete–Incomplete)				
Comprehensibility (Comprehensible–Incomprehensible)				
Accuracy (Accurate–Seldom accurate)				
Organization (Well organized–Poorly organized)				
Effort (Excellent–Minimal)				

18–20: A 14–15: C Under
16–17: B 12–13: D 12: F

Mon journal

23 For an additional journal entry suggestion for Chapter 1, see *Cahier d'activités,* page 145.

Assess

- Testing Program, pp. 5–8
  Quiz 1-2A, Quiz 1-2B
  Audio CD 1, Tr. 32
- Student Make-Up Assignments, Chapter 1, Alternative Quiz
- Alternative Assessment Guide, p. 32

CHAPITRE 1

Teaching Resources
p. 30

PRINT 
- Video Guide, pp. 7, 8-9
- Cahier d'activités, p. 12

MEDIA 
- One-Stop Planner
- Video Program
  Videocassette 1, 16:08–18:07
- DVD Tutor, Disc 1
- Audio Compact Discs, CD 1, Trs. 20–23
- Interactive CD-ROM Tutor, Disc 1

Presenting Panorama Culturel

First, have students view the video. Next, ask simple yes-no questions based on the video or have students tell in English what they have understood about these people. Then, ask them the following **Questions** and have them answer the questions in **Qu'en penses-tu?** This might be done in small groups or as a writing assignment.

Questions

1. **Qu'est-ce que Gabrielle aime faire?** (Elle aime lire, écouter de la musique, parler et discuter avec des amis.)
2. **Est-ce que Fabienne aime la plage? Où est-ce qu'elle aime aussi aller?** (Oui. Elle aime aussi aller au cinéma.)
3. **Qu'est-ce que Caroline aime faire après l'école?** (Elle aime regarder la télévision, aller à la piscine ou lire des livres.)

Answer
1. They all like to read.

CD-ROM 1 DVD 1

Qu'est-ce que tu aimes faire après l'école?

What do you like to do when you have free time? Do you think teenagers in French-speaking countries like to do the same things? Here's what some students had to say about their favorite leisure-time activities.

Gabrielle,
Québec

«J'aime lire. J'aime écouter de la musique. J'aime parler... discuter avec mes amis.» Tr. 21

Fabienne,
Martinique

«Alors, quand j'ai du temps libre, j'aime aller au cinéma, aller à la plage, lire et puis voilà, c'est tout.» Tr. 22

Caroline,
France

«Après l'école, j'aime regarder la télévision, aller à la piscine ou lire des livres.» Tr. 23

Qu'en penses-tu?

1. What do all three of these people have in common? See answer below.
2. What interests do you and your friends share with these people?
3. What do these people do that you don't like to do?
4. Which of these people would you most like to meet? Why?

Savais-tu que...?

In general, French-speaking teenagers enjoy the same kinds of activities you do. However, some activities do tend to be especially popular in certain areas, such as badminton and hockey in Canada, dancing and soccer in West Africa, and soccer and cycling in France. In many francophone countries, students have a great deal of homework, so they do not have very much leisure time after school. Of course, people are individuals, so their tastes vary. In French, you might say **Chacun ses goûts!** *(To each his own!).*

Connections and Comparisons

Sports Link

- Just as differents sports and activities are popular in different regions, so are they different across time. A sport or activity that was popular twenty or thirty years ago may no longer be popular. Have students interview their parents or their parents' friends from other countries about the sports and activities that they liked to practice when they were teenagers.
- When one speaks of football in France, one is generally talking about soccer. Tell students they must say **le football américain** if they mean *football.* Soccer is very popular in most French-speaking countries. Have students research the origin of the sport and how it developed.

STANDARDS: 2.1, 3.2, 4.2

Troisième étape

Objective Expressing likes, dislikes, and preferences about activities

WA3 POITIERS-1

Vocabulaire

CD-ROM 1
DVD 1

Stéphanie adore **regarder la télé.**

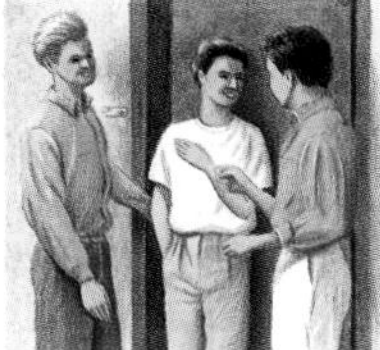

Etienne aime **sortir avec les copains.**

Nicolas aime **parler au téléphone.**

Olivier aime **dormir.**

Danielle aime **étudier.**

Sylvie aime bien **faire du sport.**

Michèle aime **faire les magasins.**

Hervé aime **faire le ménage.**

Raymond aime **faire de l'équitation.**

Serge aime **voyager.**

Eric aime **écouter de la musique.**

Laurence aime bien **nager.**

Solange adore **danser.**

Annie aime **lire.**

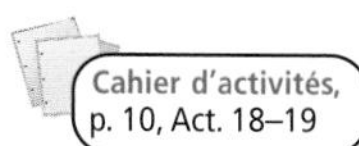

Cahier d'activités, p. 10, Act. 18–19

Travaux pratiques de grammaire, pp. 6–7, Act. 15–17

Communication for All Students

Additional Practice

Have students categorize the activities in the **Vocabulaire** into those they can do indoors or outdoors, or into those they like to do during the day or in the evening.

Kinesthetic Learners

Give commands using the activities in the **Vocabulaire: Regarde(z) la télé! Fais/Faites de l'équitation! Nage(z)!** Have students mime the activities to show that they understand.

Troisième étape

CHAPITRE 1

Teaching Resources
pp. 31–35

PRINT

- Lesson Planner, p. 6
- TPR Storytelling Book, pp. 3, 4
- Listening Activities, pp. 5, 9
- Activities for Communication, pp. 5–6, 77, 79, 137–138
- Travaux pratiques de grammaire, pp. 6–9
- Grammar Tutor for Students of French, Chapter 1
- Cahier d'activités, pp. 9–10
- Testing Program, pp. 9–12
- Alternative Assessment Guide, p. 32
- Student Make-Up Assignments, Chapter 1

MEDIA 

- One-Stop Planner
- Audio Compact Discs, CD 1, Trs. 24, 33, 41–42
- Teaching Transparencies: 1-3, 1-C, 1-D; **Grammaire supplémentaire** Answers; Travaux pratiques de grammaire Answers
- Interactive CD-ROM Tutor, Disc 1

Bell Work!

Ask students to write sentences telling two things they like and two things they dislike.

Presenting Vocabulaire

To present this vocabulary, you might want to show pictures of the activities or mime the activities yourself, while saying aloud what you like to do. **(J'aime écouter de la musique.)** After students have repeated the expressions, have volunteers tell what they like to do. Then, have students work in small groups, with each student miming an activity while the others try to guess what it is.

Teaching Resources
pp. 31–35

PRINT 

- Lesson Planner, p. 6
- TPR Storytelling Book, pp. 3, 4
- Listening Activities, pp. 5, 9
- Activities for Communication, pp. 5–6, 77, 79, 137–138
- Travaux pratiques de grammaire, pp. 6–9
- Grammar Tutor for Students of French, Chapter 1
- Cahier d'activités, pp. 9–10
- Testing Program, pp. 9–12
- Alternative Assessment Guide, p. 32
- Student Make-Up Assignments, Chapter 1

MEDIA 

- One-Stop Planner
- Audio Compact Discs, CD 1, Trs. 24, 33, 41–42
- Teaching Transparencies: 1-3, 1-C, 1-D; **Grammaire supplémentaire** Answers; Travaux pratiques de grammaire Answers
- Interactive CD-ROM Tutor, Disc 1

Presenting Comment dit-on...?

Act out the activities or refer to the pictures in the **Vocabulaire** on page 31, and ask **Qui aime...?**, completing the question with the activity. Have individuals raise their hands and answer **Moi, et j'aime aussi...** if they want to add another activity that they like. Point out that the verbs following the forms of **aimer** are in the infinitive form. You might explain to your students that the *infinitive* is the *to* form of a verb and that **-er**, **-re**, and **-ir** are typical infinitive endings of French verbs.

24 Mon activité préférée See scripts and answers on p. 15H.

CD 1
Tr. 24

Ecoutons You're going to hear six students tell you what they like to do. For each statement you hear, decide which of the students pictured on page 31 is speaking.

Comment dit-on...?

CD-ROM 1 DVD 1

Expressing likes, dislikes, and preferences about activities

To ask if someone likes an activity:

Tu aimes voyager?

To tell what you like to do:

J'aime voyager.
J'adore danser.
J'aime bien dormir.

To tell what you don't like to do:

Je n'aime pas aller aux concerts.

To tell what you prefer to do:

J'aime mieux regarder la télévision.
Je préfère lire.

Cahier d'activités, p. 9, Act. 16

25 Sondage *Poll*

a. **Lisons** Complete the following poll.

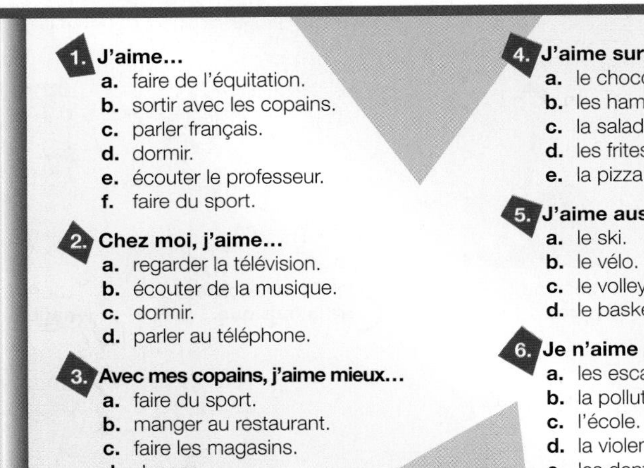

1. **J'aime...**
   a. faire de l'équitation.
   b. sortir avec les copains.
   c. parler français.
   d. dormir.
   e. écouter le professeur.
   f. faire du sport.
2. **Chez moi, j'aime...**
   a. regarder la télévision.
   b. écouter de la musique.
   c. dormir.
   d. parler au téléphone.
3. **Avec mes copains, j'aime mieux...**
   a. faire du sport.
   b. manger au restaurant.
   c. faire les magasins.
   d. danser.
   e. nager.
   f. aller au cinéma.
4. **J'aime surtout...**
   a. le chocolat.
   b. les hamburgers.
   c. la salade.
   d. les frites.
   e. la pizza.
5. **J'aime aussi...**
   a. le ski.
   b. le vélo.
   c. le volley.
   d. le basket-ball.
6. **Je n'aime pas...**
   a. les escargots.
   b. la pollution.
   c. l'école.
   d. la violence.
   e. les dentistes.
   f. les examens.

b. **Parlons** Compare your responses to the poll with those of a classmate. Which interests do you have in common?

Teacher to Teacher

Sarah Sherman
Johnson Middle School
Walpole, MA

Sarah suggests the following as an extension to Activity 25.

"After they complete the poll, I have students design their own **"sondage"** using vocabulary from the chapter. I hand each student a chart with three columns. In the top row, they fill in the heads **"j'aime," "je n'aime pas"** and **"je déteste"**. In the column under each head, students fill in vocabulary they learned in the chapter. After they have completed their charts, students circulate around the room, asking each other how they feel about the items on their list. Afterward, the class discusses the results to see what items were most popular in each category."

STANDARDS: 1.2, 5.2

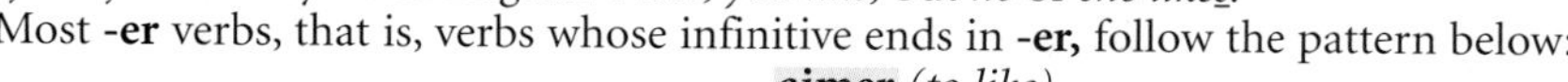

Grammaire

Subject pronouns and *-er* verbs

CD-ROM 1 DVD 1

The verb **aimer** has different forms. In French, the verb forms change according to the subjects just as they do in English: *I like, you like,* but *he* or *she likes.*

Most **-er** verbs, that is, verbs whose infinitive ends in **-er,** follow the pattern below:

aimer *(to like)*

J' aime	Nous aim**ons**
Tu aim**es**	Vous aim**ez**
Il/Elle aime	Ils/Elles aim**ent**

- The forms **aime, aimes,** and **aiment** sound the same.
- The subject pronouns in French are **je/j'** *(I),* **tu** *(you),* **il** *(he* or *it),* **elle** *(she* or *it),* **nous** *(we),* **vous** *(you),* **ils** *(they),* and **elles** *(they).*
- Notice that there are two pronouns for *they.* Use **elles** to refer to a group of females. Use **ils** to refer to a group of males or a group of males and females.
- **Tu** and **vous** both mean *you.* Use **vous** when you talk to more than one person or to an adult who is not a family member. Use **tu** when you talk to a friend, family member, or someone your own age.
- Noun subjects take the same verb forms as their pronouns.

Philippe aime la salade.	**Sophie et Julie aiment** faire du sport.
Il aime la salade.	**Elles aiment** faire du sport.

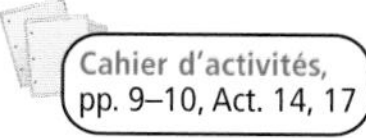
Cahier d'activités, pp. 9–10, Act. 14, 17

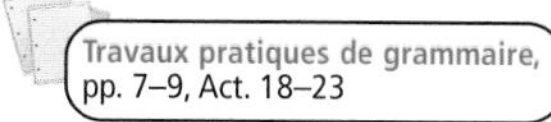
Travaux pratiques de grammaire, pp. 7–9, Act. 18–23

Grammaire supplémentaire, pp. 40–41, Act. 6–10

26 Grammaire en contexte

a. Parlons Would you use **tu** or **vous** to greet the following people? How would you ask them if they like a certain thing or activity?

Mes amis
Vous aimez... ?

Mlle Normand
Vous aimez... ?

Flore et Loïc
Vous aimez... ?

Lucie
Tu aimes... ?

b. Parlons Now complete the following phrases to tell what these people like, according to the illustrations above. Answers may vary.

1. Mes amis... aiment le cinéma.
2. Mlle Normand... aime voyager.
3. Flore et moi, nous... aimons faire du sport.
4. Moi, je m'appelle Lucie. J'... aime étudier.

Presenting Grammaire

Subject pronouns and *-er* verbs Introduce this section by reviewing subject pronouns. Ask students to recall any subject pronouns they have learned in French. Supply the ones they don't know, without using English, by pointing to individuals and groups as you say the pronouns in French: **nous, ils, elles...** Then, have students look at the **Grammaire** and repeat the pronouns and verb forms after you. You might want to discuss **liaison** and **élision** at this time. See **Prononciation** on page 63 for information on **liaison.**

Challenge

26 To extend this activity, have students pair off. Call out two names of people pictured here: Lucie and Mlle Normand, for example. Partners should assume the identity of these people and create a brief dialogue between them, using **tu** or **vous** appropriately.

Communication for All Students

Game

Grammaire This would be a good time for students to play a variation of the game **Introductions** on page 15C, using the verb **aimer.** Student A might start by saying **"J'aime faire les magasins."** Student B repeats that and then adds his or her own preferred activity. The game continues until a student makes a mistake, at which point the game could start all over again, beginning with the student who made the mistake or with the following student.

Additional Practice

26 You might want to hold up pictures of people of various ages, asking **tu ou vous?**

STANDARDS: 4.1

Troisième étape

CHAPITRE 1

Teaching Resources
pp. 31–35

PRINT 
- Lesson Planner, p. 6
- TPR Storytelling Book, pp. 3, 4
- Listening Activities, pp. 5, 9
- Activities for Communication, pp. 5–6, 77, 79, 137–138
- Travaux pratiques de grammaire, pp. 6–9
- Grammar Tutor for Students of French, Chapter 1
- Cahier d'activités, pp. 9–10
- Testing Program, pp. 9–12
- Alternative Assessment Guide, p. 32
- Student Make-Up Assignments, Chapter 1

MEDIA
- One-Stop Planner
- Audio Compact Discs, CD 1, Trs. 24, 33, 41–42
- Teaching Transparencies: 1-3, 1-C, 1-D; **Grammaire supplémentaire** Answers; Travaux pratiques de grammaire Answers
- Interactive CD-ROM Tutor, Disc 1

Additional Practice
27 Students might pair off and ask and tell each other whether they like or dislike the activities shown. Remind them to use the connectors **et** and **mais.**

Challenge
Have students write a short description of a friend, family member, or famous personality, naming that person's favorite activities.

Additional Practice
Show *Teaching Transparency 1-3* and have students tell what the people in each room like to do.

27 **Grammaire en contexte**

Parlons Your French pen pal wants to know what your friends like to do. Use the following photographs as cues.

Julio
Il aime lire.

Robert
Il aime voyager.

Mark, David et Thomas
Ils aiment nager.

Agnès
Elle aime faire les magasins.

Marie
Elle aime faire de l'équitation.

Eric
Il aime parler au téléphone.

Karen
Elle aime écouter de la musique.

Pamela
Elle aime dormir.

Emily et Raymond
Ils aiment danser.

28 **Les vedettes!** *Celebrities!*

a. **Ecrivons** Make a list of three public figures (movie stars, musicians, athletes, and so on) you admire. Write down one or two things you think each person might like to do.

EXEMPLE **Shaquille O'Neal aime faire du sport, surtout *(especially)* du basket-ball!**

b. **Parlons** Now, get together with a classmate. Tell your partner what one of the celebrities you've chosen likes to do. Use **il** or **elle** instead of the person's name. Your partner will try to identify the celebrity. Take turns.

Cultures and Communities

Culture Note
27 You might want to point out the train in the second photo. Train travel is very common in France, owing to an efficient and inexpensive railway system.

Multicultural Link
28 You might want to refer students to the famous French-speaking people described in **Tu les connais?** on pages 2 and 3 of the Preliminary Chapter.

STANDARDS: 1.1, 1.3

29 De l'école au travail

Parlons During your summer vacation you're working as a reporter for a French newspaper. Your new assignment for the paper is to do a survey about what is popular with young people right now. Interview your classmates, making sure to ask them a variety of questions in French about what foods they like, how they feel about school, and what activities they like and dislike.

30 Mon journal

Ecrivons Expand your previous journal entry by adding the activities you like and dislike. Tell which activities you and your friends like to do together. Find or draw pictures to illustrate the activities.

PRONONCIATION

Intonation

See scripts and answers on p. 15H.

CD 1
Trs. 25–29

As you speak, your voice rises and falls. This is called *intonation.*

A. A prononcer

In French, your voice rises at the end of each group of words within a statement and falls at the end of a statement. Repeat each of the following phrases:

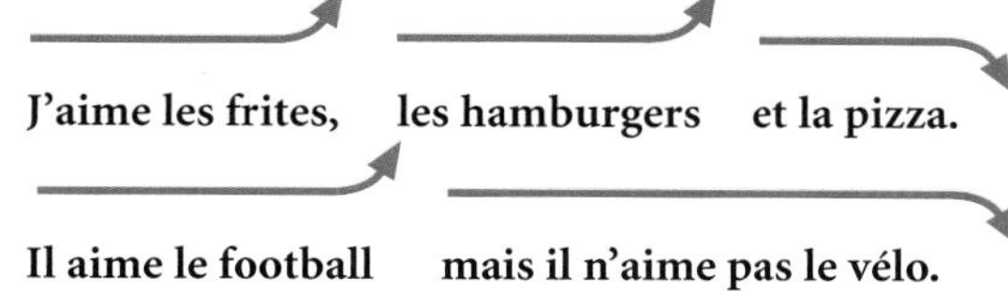

J'aime les frites,
les hamburgers
et la pizza.
Il aime le football
mais il n'aime pas le vélo.

If you want to change a statement into a question, raise your voice at the end of the sentence. Repeat these questions.

Tu aimes l'anglais?

Tu t'appelles Julie?

B. A écouter

Decide whether each of the following is a statement or a question.

C. A écrire

You're going to hear two short dialogues. Write down what the people say.

Communication for All Students

Visual Learners

29 Have students organize the information they gathered from the survey in the form of a pie graph. They should use three separate pie graphs to present the results of the three categories of questions: food, school, and activities. Then, have students discuss the results as a class.

Challenge

Prononciation After students have finished the activities, you might have them make up their own statements and questions about likes and dislikes, and have them practice the intonation in pairs or small groups. Pairs or groups could then volunteer to recite their statements and questions in front of the class, using the proper intonation.

STANDARDS: 1.1, 1.3, 3.1, 5.1

Troisième étape

Mon journal

30 For an additional journal entry suggestion for Chapter 1, see *Cahier d'activités,* page 145.

Language Note

Prononciation You might tell students that the rising intonation indicates a yes-no question, rather than a question that seeks information.

Teaching Suggestion

Have students read the **Mise en train** again, silently or aloud in small groups. They might copy some of the text into their notebooks, underlining functional expressions, circling activities or things, and highlighting **ne... pas** or other structures. This will help them to review functions, vocabulary, and grammar.

Assess

- Testing Program, pp. 9–12
  Quiz 1-3A, Quiz 1-3B
  Audio CD 1, Tr. 33
- Student Make-Up Assignments
  Chapter 1, Alternative Quiz
- Alternative Assessment Guide, p. 32

Teaching Resources
pp. 36–37

PRINT 

- Lesson Planner, p. 7
- Cahier d'activités, p. 11
- Reading Strategies and Skills Handbook, Chapter 1
- Joie de lire 1, Chapter 1
- Standardized Assessment Tutor, Chapter 1

MEDIA 

- One-Stop Planner

Prereading
Activities A–C

Connecting through your Experience
Ask students if they have pen pals or friends they write to, why people want pen pals, and when writing is better than phoning. You might pass around any ads for pen pals you may have found. See page T46 for addresses.

Reading
Activities D–F

Monitoring Comprehension
To check for understanding, ask simple questions about the pen pals. **(Il/Elle s'appelle comment? Qui aime la musique?)**

Answers

B. *Possible answers:* correspondre, réponse, lettres, musique, science-fiction, fan, âge, adresse, photo d'identité

D. Aime faire les boutiques—Hugues Vallet/Laurence Simon
Aime les animaux—Christiane Saulnier
Parle français et espagnol—Karim Marzouk
Aime la musique et le cinéma—Amélie Perrin
Aime le rap et la techno—Mireille Lacombe

Petites Annonces

Stratégie pour lire
You can often figure out what a reading selection is about simply by looking at the titles, subtitles, illustrations, and captions.

A. Look at the pictures and titles of this article from a French magazine. What do you think the article is about? pen pals

B. Do you remember what you've learned about cognates? Can you find at least five cognates in this article? See answers below.

C. What do you think **Petites Annonces** means? classified ads

D. Which of the pen pals would you choose if you were searching for the following? See answers below.
Quelqu'un qui *(someone who)…*

aime faire les boutiques
aime les animaux
parle français et espagnol
aime la musique et le cinéma
aime le rap et la techno

Petites Annonces

Christiane Saulnier
Marseille
Si vous aimez la télévision, les animaux et les vacances, qu'est-ce que vous attendez pour m'écrire et m'envoyer votre photo! Je voudrais correspondre avec des filles ou des garçons de 13 à 16 ans. J'attends votre réponse avec impatience!

Karim Marzouk
Tunis, Tunisie
J'adorerais recevoir des lettres de personnes habitant le monde entier; j'adore voyager, écouter de la musique, aller au concert et lire sur la plage. J'aime bien les langues et je parle aussi l'arabe et l'espagnol. A bientôt.

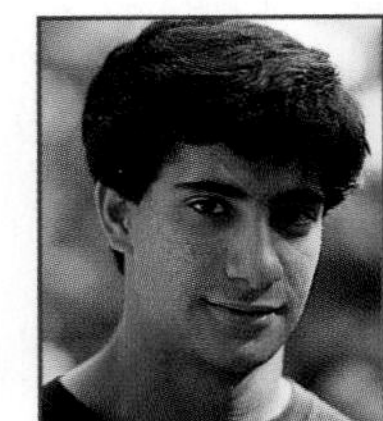

Mireille Lacombe
Nantes
J'ai 15 ans et je voudrais bien correspondre avec des filles et des garçons de 13 à 17 ans. J'aime le rap et surtout la techno. Je fais aussi de l'équitation. Ecrivez-moi vite et je promets de vous répondre (photos S.V.P.)!

Didier Kouassi
Abidjan, Côte d'Ivoire
La techno me fait délirer et je suis aussi très sportif. Je cherche des correspondants filles ou garçons entre 15 et 17 ans. N'hésitez pas à m'écrire!

Communication for All Students

Thinking Critically
Analyzing Ask students to group the pen pals by interest. Then, ask them to choose the pen pal(s) they would most like to correspond with.

Challenge
Have students prepare a videotape of themselves that they might send to a pen pal agency. They should introduce themselves, talk about their likes and dislikes and also give details on what they are looking for in a pen pal. Students can either exchange their videotape with students from another French class or include it in their portfolio.

STANDARDS: 1.2, 3.1, 4.1, 5.2

★ COPAINS ★ COPINES ★

Laurence Simon
Le Marin, Martinique
J'ai 16 ans, je suis dingue de sport, j'aime les soirs de fête entre copains. Le week-end, j'aime faire les magasins. Alors, si vous me ressemblez, dépêchez-vous de m'écrire. Réponse assurée à 100%!

Etienne Hubert
Poitiers
Je suis blond aux yeux bleus, assez grand, timide mais très sympa. J'aime sortir et j'aime lire la science-fiction. Je cherche des amis entre 14 et 16 ans. Répondez vite!

Hugues Vallet
La Rochelle
Je voudrais correspondre avec des filles et des garçons de 16 à 18 ans. J'aime sortir, délirer et faire les boutiques. Je suis fan de Vanessa Paradis et de Julia Roberts. Alors, j'attends vos lettres!

Amélie Perrin
Périgord
Je voudrais correspondre avec des jeunes de 14 à 17 ans qui aiment faire la fête, écouter de la musique et aller au cinéma. Moi, j'étudie la danse et la photographie. Ecrivez-moi et je me ferai une joie de vous répondre.

Vous voulez correspondre avec des gens sympas? Écrivez votre petite annonce en précisant vos nom, prénom, âge et adresse, et en y joignant une photo d'identité.

E. Several of your friends are looking for pen pals. Based on their wishes, find a good match for each of them in **Petites Annonces.**

1. My pen pal should like sports. Didier Kouassi, Laurence Simon
2. I'd like to hear from someone who likes going out. Etienne Hubert, Hugues Vallet
3. I'm looking for a pen pal who likes to go to the movies. Amélie Perrin
4. It would be great to have a pen pal who enjoys shopping. Laurence Simon, Hugues Vallet
5. I'd like to hear from someone from Africa. Karim Marzouk, Didier Kouassi
6. I'd like a pen pal who likes to travel. Karim Marzouk

F. If you want to place an ad for a pen pal, what should you do? See answers below.

G. One of your classmates is looking for a pen pal. Make a short list of questions that will help you identify which pen pal has the most in common with your classmate. Then, interview your classmate, compare his or her answers with the ads included in **Petites Annonces,** and decide which pen pal would be the best match. Find out if your classmate agrees with your decision.

H. Jot down a few things you might like to include in your own letter requesting a pen pal. Using your notes, write your own request for a pen pal like the ones you read in **Petites Annonces.**

Cahier d'activités, p. 11, Act. 20–21

Postreading
Activities G-H

Community Link
French exchange students in your community or advanced students of French are possible pen pals. You might have classes exchange letters. It might be fun for students to assume a pen name **(nom de plume)** so that they are corresponding with a mystery pen pal. Later in the year, you can arrange a soirée where the correspondents finally meet. Have students introduce themselves in French to each other.

Cultures and Communities

Multicultural Link
Ask students the following: What can be gained from corresponding with someone from another culture? Are you already familiar with other cultures? Is there any culture in particular that interests you? Have you traveled to other regions in the United States? What, if anything, seemed strange or different to you? If your region has several ethnic groups, how do they interact? Are there any students from other cultures at your school? Students might interview them to find out what was difficult for them when they came to this country (being careful, of course, to respect their privacy). You might discuss with students appropriate ways to begin their interviews with foreign students.

Answers
F. Send your name, age, photo, and address to the magazine.

STANDARDS: 1.2, 1.3, 3.1, 4.1, 5.1, 5.2

Grammaire supplémentaire

CHAPITRE 1

For **Grammaire supplémentaire** Answer Transparencies, see the *Teaching Transparencies* binder.

Answers

1
1. 19 dix-neuf
2. 17 dix-sept
3. 13 treize
4. 20 vingt
5. 16 seize
6. 12 douze

2
1. Je m'appelle Bernard. J'ai dix ans.
2. Je m'appelle Aurélie. J'ai huit ans.
3. Je m'appelle Ousmane. J'ai sept ans.
4. Je m'appelle Cédric. J'ai quinze ans.
5. Je m'appelle Lætitia. J'ai quatre ans.
6. Je m'appelle Lisette. J'ai onze ans.

Grammaire supplémentaire

Première étape

Objectives Greeting people and saying goodbye; asking how people are and telling how you are; asking someone's name and age and giving yours

1 Can you find the pattern in these phone numbers? Figure out which number completes each pattern. Then, write out the number in French. (**pp. 9, 25**)

Exemple 02. **11**. 20. 29. 38; **onze**

1. 05. 12. ______ . 26. 33; ______
2. 03. 10. ______ . 24. 31; ______
3. 01. ______ . 25. 37. 49;______
4. 05. ______ . 35. 50. 65; ______
5. 04. 10. ______ . 22. 28; ______
6. 02. ______ . 22. 32. 42; ______

2 These French speakers are telling you their name and age. The age of each speaker corresponds to the number of letters in his or her place of origin. Make two statements for each speaker by following the example below. (**pp. 9, 24, 25**)

Exemple Pierre/France
Je m'appelle Pierre. J'ai six ans.

1. Bernard/Martinique
2. Aurélie/Belgique
3. Ousmane/Sénégal
4. Cédric/Guyane française
5. Lætitia/Mali
6. Lisette/Burkina Faso

Grammar Resources for Chapter 1

The **Grammaire supplémentaire** activities are designed as supplemental activities for the grammatical concepts presented in the chapter. You might use them as additional practice, for review, or for assessment.

For more grammar presentations, review, and practice, refer to the following:

- Travaux pratiques de grammaire
- Grammar Tutor for Students of French
- Grammar Summary on pp. R15-R28
- Cahier d'activités
- Grammar and Vocabulary quizzes (Testing Program)
- Test Generator
- Interactive CD-ROM Tutor
- DVD Tutor
- **Jeux interactifs** at go.hrw.com

Deuxième étape

Objective Expressing likes, dislikes, and preferences about things

3 Complete the following sentences, using the correct form of **aimer** and **ne (n')... pas** when appropriate. (**p. 26**)

Exemple — Tu adores la plage, mais tu **n'aimes pas** la piscine.

1. Moi, j'aime bien la musique classique, mais je/j' _____ le rock.
2. Tu n'aimes pas le sport, mais tu _____ le vélo.
3. J'adore la glace, mais je/j' _____ le chocolat.
4. J'aime bien l'école, mais je/j' _____ les examens.
5. Tu aimes les concerts, mais tu _____ le cinéma.
6. Tu n'aimes pas les hamburgers, mais tu _____ les frites.
7. J'aime la télé, mais je/j' _____ le cinéma.
8. Tu n'aimes pas l'anglais, mais tu _____ le français.

4 Complete Gabrielle's journal entry with the appropriate definite articles **le, la, l'**, or **les.** (**p. 28**)

J'aime __1__ école. J'aime bien __2__ anglais et __3__ français, mais je n'aime pas __4__ examens. J'adore __5__ sport et __6__ plage. J'aime __7__ football et __8__ vélo aussi.

5 Use the following cues to create four questions and four answers. Remember to add the appropriate definite articles: **le, la, l'**, or **les.** (**p. 28**)

Exemple salade/Eric/tu/aimes? aime/j'/hamburgers/aussi *(also)*
Eric, tu aimes la salade? **Oui, et j'aime aussi les hamburgers.**

1. tu/aimes/frites/Marianne?
   aime/j'/pizza/aussi
   —Oui, et...
2. tu/ne/pas/maths/aimes/Isabelle?
   français/aussi/aime/j'
   —Si *(yes)*, et...
3. aimes/escargots/Nathalie/tu?
   j'/aussi/aime/chocolat
   —Oui, et...
4. tu/aimes/ne/pas/magasins?
   plage/j'/aussi/aime
   —Si, et...

Communication for All Students

Game

Mémoire This game is played like the one described on p. 105C. It practices both numbers and the verb **aimer.** You need a set of 8 flashcards with the subject pronouns **(j', tu, il, elle, nous, vous, ils,** and **elles)** and another set with the conjugated forms of the verb **aimer.** Number all the cards on the reverse side, and tape them face down on the board. Then, have students take turns calling two numbers to try to match the pronoun with the correct verb form.

Grammaire supplémentaire

CHAPITRE 1

Answers

3
1. n'aime pas
2. aimes
3. n'aime pas
4. n'aime pas
5. n'aimes pas
6. aimes
7. n'aime pas
8. aimes

4
1. l'
2. l'
3. le
4. les
5. le
6. la
7. le
8. le

5
1. –Marianne, tu aimes les frites?
   ...j'aime aussi la pizza.
2. –Isabelle, tu n'aimes pas les maths?
   ...j'aime aussi le français.
3. –Nathalie, tu aimes les escargots?
   ...j'aime aussi le chocolat.
4. –Tu n'aimes pas les magasins?
   ...j'aime aussi la plage.

STANDARDS: 1.2, 1.3, 3.1

Grammaire supplémentaire

CHAPITRE 1

For **Grammaire supplémentaire** Answer Transparencies, see the *Teaching Transparencies* binder.

Grammaire supplémentaire

WA3 POITIERS-1

Troisième étape

Objective **Expressing likes, dislikes, and preferences about activities**

6 Séverine is looking for a pen pal. Complete her ad with the appropriate forms of the verbs in parentheses. (**p. 33**)

J'ai 16 ans. Je/J' __1__ (adorer) faire du sport. Je/J' __2__ (aimer) aussi sortir avec les copains. Nous __3__ (aimer) bien aller au cinéma, mais nous __4__ (préférer) aller danser. Parfois, nous __5__ (écouter) de la musique. Nous __6__ (adorer) le rap, surtout MC Solaar; il __7__ (danser) très bien. Nous __8__ (aimer) aussi les fast-foods. Si vous __9__ (aimer) le sport, écrivez-moi! A bientôt!

7 Etienne and Solange don't have much in common. Complete their conversation with the appropriate forms of the verbs in parentheses. (**p. 33**)

ETIENNE Dis, Solange, tu __1__ (aimer) faire du vélo?

SOLANGE Non, je n' __2__ (aimer) pas le sport, mais j' __3__ (adorer) danser.

ETIENNE Moi, je ne __4__ (danser) pas, mais j' __5__ (écouter) souvent la radio.

SOLANGE Ah oui? Tu __6__ (écouter) quel type de musique?

ETIENNE Moi, j' __7__ (adorer) le rap. Mes copains __8__ (aimer) aller à des concerts de rap, mais moi, j' __9__ (aimer) mieux regarder des vidéo-clips à la télé. Et toi, tu __10__ (regarder) la télé?

SOLANGE Moi, non. J' __11__ (aimer) mieux aller au cinéma.

8 There are many things these students like to do, but what do they prefer to do? Complete these conversations with the appropriate subject pronouns. (**p. 33**)

EXEMPLE —Pierre aime les frites. —Oui, mais **il** aime mieux les escargots.

1. —Lucie et Marie aiment regarder la télé.
   —Oui, mais _____ préfèrent aller au cinéma.
2. —Hugo et toi, vous aimez parler au téléphone?
   —Oui, mais _____ préférons sortir avec les copains.
3. —Olivier et Lise aiment faire les magasins.
   —Oui, mais _____ aiment mieux faire du sport.
4. —Aurélie aime lire.
   —Oui, mais _____ aime mieux dormir.
5. —Christelle et moi, nous aimons le volley.
   —Oui, mais _____ préférez le basket-ball, non?

Answers

6
1. adore
2. aime
3. aimons
4. préférons
5. écoutons
6. adorons
7. danse
8. aimons
9. aimez

7
1. aimes
2. aime
3. adore
4. danse
5. écoute
6. écoutes
7. adore
8. aiment
9. aime
10. regardes
11. aime

8
1. elles
2. nous
3. ils
4. elle
5. vous

Teacher to Teacher

Pai Rosenthal
Rachel Carson Middle School
Herndon, VA

Pai's students have fun practicing "avoir" and the conjugation of –er verbs.

"Give each group of 4–5 students a stuffed animal. Call out an **–er** verb. One student throws the animal to another while calling out a pronoun (in random order). The catcher repeats the pronoun, adds the proper conjugation and quickly tosses the animal to another player. Play continues until teacher calls stop. Call on the student who has the stuffed animal to recite the whole conjugation. As a challenge, you might have students make a sentence using that verb."

STANDARDS: 1.2

Grammaire supplémentaire

CHAPITRE 1

9 Given their likes and dislikes, what do the following students probably do on weekends? Complete each sentence, using a personal pronoun and the correct form of the appropriate verb. (**p. 33**)

EXEMPLE Hervé et moi, nous aimons danser.
Le week-end, nous dansons.

1. Mary aime bien parler français avec sa copine.
   Le week-end, ...
2. Jules et Loïc aiment regarder des matches de football.
   Le week-end, ...
3. Moi, j'adore écouter de la musique.
   Le week-end, ...
4. Sylvie et Marianne aiment bien nager.
   Le week-end, ...
5. Stéphane et toi, vous aimez parler au téléphone.
   Le week-end, ...
6. Toi, tu adores danser.
   Le week-end, ...

10 Complete the following sentences, using the correct form of **aimer** and **ne (n')... pas** when appropriate. (**pp. 26, 33**)

EXEMPLE —Jean adore la plage, mais il **n'aime pas** la piscine.
—Julio n'aime pas voyager, mais il **aime** lire.

1. Jean aime bien les frites, mais il ______ les escargots.
2. Stéphanie n'aime pas les discothèques, mais elle ______ danser.
3. Victor adore écouter la radio, mais il ______ regarder la télé.
4. Yvette aime bien parler au téléphone, mais elle ______ étudier.
5. José aime sortir avec ses copains, mais il ______ le cinéma.
6. Agnès n'aime pas faire le ménage, mais elle ______ faire les magasins.

Review and Assess

You may wish to assign the **Grammaire supplémentaire** activities as additional practice or homework after presenting material throughout the chapter. Assign Activities 1–2 after **Comment dit-on… ?** (p. 25), Activity 3 after **Note de grammaire** (p. 26), Activities 4–5 after **Grammaire** (p. 28), Activities 6–10 after **Grammaire** (p. 33). To prepare students for the **Etape** Quizzes and Chapter Test, we suggest doing the **Grammaire supplémentaire** activities in the following order. Have students complete Activities 1–2 before taking Quizzes 1-1A or 1-1B; Activities 3–5 before Quizzes 1-2A or 1-2B; and Activities 6–10 before Quizzes 1-3A or 1-3B.

Answers

9
1. ...elle parle français avec sa copine.
2. ...ils regardent des matches de football.
3. ...j'écoute de la musique.
4. ...elles nagent.
5. ...vous parlez au téléphone.
6. ...tu danses.

10
1. n'aime pas
2. aime
3. n'aime pas
4. n'aime pas
5. n'aime pas
6. aime

STANDARDS: 1.2

Mise en pratique

CHAPITRE 1

The **Mise en pratique** reviews and integrates all four skills and culture in preparation for the Chapter Test.

Teaching Resources
pp. 42–43

PRINT 

- Lesson Planner, p. 7
- Listening Activities, p. 5
- Video Guide, pp. 7, 10
- Grammar Tutor for Students of French, Chapter 1
- Standardized Assessment Tutor, Chapter 1

MEDIA

- One-Stop Planner
- Video Program Videocassette 1, 18:08–19:25
- DVD Tutor, Disc 1
- Audio Compact Discs, CD 1, Tr. 30
- Interactive CD-ROM Tutor, Disc 1

Portfolio

3 **Oral** This activity is appropriate for students' oral portfolios. For portfolio suggestions, see *Alternative Assessment Guide,* page 18.

Career Path

Have students imagine that they are employed by an organization like the **Organisation internationale de correspondants.** How would their knowledge of French and English help them with their job? With whom would they most likely be working? Have students think of similar jobs that would require knowledge of a foreign language (coordinator of an exchange program, working for a college study abroad office).

Mise en pratique

Visit Holt Online
go.hrw.com
KEYWORD: WA3 POITIERS-1
Self-Test

1 Do the following photos represent French culture, American culture, or both?

1.

2.

3.

4.

5.

2 **L'Organisation internationale de correspondants (l'O.I.C.),** a pen-pal organization you wrote to, has left a phone message on your answering machine. Listen carefully to the message and write down your pen pal's name, age, phone number, likes, and dislikes.

3 Tell a classmate, in French, about your new pen pal.

Apply and Assess

Kinesthetic Learners

1 You might ask groups to prepare and act out two scenes that contrast French and American greetings.

Challenge

2 You might have students pretend to call the O.I.C. and leave information about themselves on the organization's answering machine. Students might make an audiocassette, which could be used as an oral portfolio entry.

STANDARDS: 1.1, 1.2, 4.2

4 You've received your first letter from Robert Perrault. Read it twice—the first time for general understanding, the second time for details. Then, answer the questions below in English.

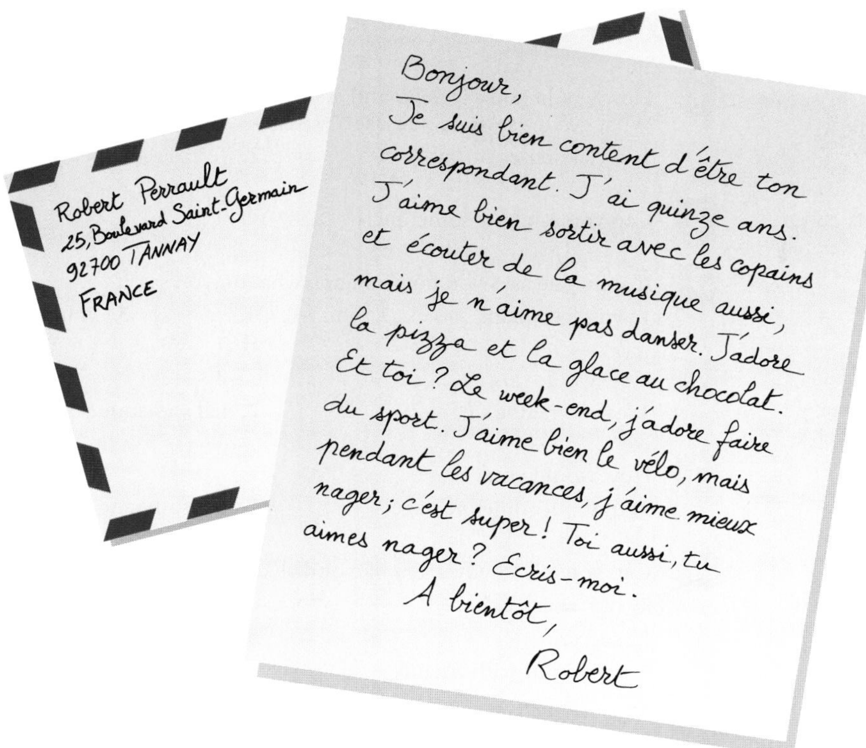

Robert Perrault
25, Boulevard Saint-Germain
92700 TANNAY
FRANCE

Bonjour,
Je suis bien content d'être ton correspondant. J'ai quinze ans. J'aime bien sortir avec les copains et écouter de la musique aussi, mais je n'aime pas danser. J'adore la pizza et la glace au chocolat. Et toi ? Le week-end, j'adore faire du sport. J'aime bien le vélo, mais pendant les vacances, j'aime mieux nager ; c'est super ! Toi aussi, tu aimes nager ? Écris-moi.
À bientôt,
Robert

1. How old is Robert? 15
2. What sports does he like? biking, swimming
3. What foods does he like? pizza, chocolate ice cream
4. What doesn't he like to do? dance

5 Now, answer Robert's letter. Begin your reply with **Cher Robert.** Be sure to . . .

- introduce yourself.
- ask how he's doing.
- tell about your likes and dislikes.
- ask him about other likes and dislikes he might have.
- answer his questions to you.
- say goodbye.

6 **Jeu de rôle**

A French exchange student has just arrived at your school. How would you find out his or her name? Age? Likes and dislikes? Act out the scene with a partner. Take turns playing the role of the French student.

Mise en pratique

CHAPITRE 1

Portfolio

5 **Written** You may want to ask students to write their letters on stationery and keep them in their portfolios. Students might also record their letter as if they were going to send an audiocassette to Robert. They might want to include their favorite song or get members of their family to say **Bonjour!** Have students write a script for the recording. For portfolio suggestions, see *Alternative Assessment Guide,* page 18.

Apply and Assess

Teaching Suggestion

5 Remind students to use Robert's letter as a model for their own.

Visual Learners

Have students draw a picture of a person that represents what activities or things he or she likes and dislikes. Then, have them exchange their picture with another student. Students should take turns guessing what the person in their partner's picture likes or dislikes. This activity can also be done in small groups.

Que sais-je?

CHAPITRE 1

Teaching Resources
p. 44

PRINT 
- Grammar Tutor for Students of French, Chapter 1

MEDIA
- Interactive CD-ROM Tutor, Disc 1
- Online self-test

go.hrw.com
WA3 POITIERS-1

Teacher Note
This page is intended to help students prepare for the Chapter Test. It is a brief checklist of the major points covered in the chapter. The students should be reminded that this is only a checklist and does not necessarily include everything that will appear on the test.

Que sais-je?

WA3 POITIERS-1

Can you use what you've learned in this chapter?

Can you greet people and say goodbye? p. 22

1 How would you say hello and goodbye to the following people? What gestures would you use? See answers below.
1. a classmate
2. your French teacher

Can you ask how people are and tell how you are? p. 23

2 Can you ask how someone is? Ça va?/Comment ça va?

3 If someone asks you how you are, what do you say if . . .
1. you feel great? Super!
2. you feel OK? Pas mal.
3. you don't feel well? Pas terrible.

Can you ask someone's name and age and give yours? pp. 24–25

4 How would you . . .
1. ask someone's name? Tu t'appelles comment?
2. tell someone your name? Je m'appelle...

5 How would you . . .
1. find out someone's age? Tu as quel âge?
2. tell someone how old you are? J'ai... ans.

Can you express likes, dislikes, and preferences about things? p. 26

6 Can you tell whether you like or dislike the following? See answers below.
1. horseback riding
2. soccer
3. going out with friends
4. shopping
5. the movies

Can you express likes, dislikes, and preferences about activities? p. 32

7 Can you ask a friend in French if he or she likes . . . See answers below.

a.

b.

c.

d.

e.

8 Can you tell in French what these people like, dislike, or prefer?
1. Robert never studies. Robert n'aime pas étudier.
2. Emilie thinks reading is the greatest. Emilie adore lire.
3. Hervé prefers pizza. Hervé préfère la pizza.
4. Nathalie never goes to the beach. Nathalie n'aime pas la plage.
5. Nicole is always biking or playing soccer. Nicole aime le vélo et le football.

Answers

1
1. Hello—bonjour, salut; Goodbye—au revoir, salut, tchao, à bientôt, à tout à l'heure; boys shake hands with other boys and use the **bise** with girls, and girls use the **bise** with both boys and girls
2. Hello—bonjour; Goodbye—au revoir, à demain, à bientôt, à tout à l'heure; hand wave/no specific gesture

Possible answers:

6
1. J'aime faire de l'équitation.
2. Je n'aime pas le football.
3. J'aime mieux sortir avec les copains.
4. Je n'aime pas faire les magasins.
5. J'aime le cinéma.

7
a. Tu aimes étudier?
b. Tu aimes regarder la télévision?
c. Tu aimes danser?
d. Tu aimes le ski?
e. Tu aimes dormir?

Review and Assess

Game
Tic Tac Toe Divide the class into two teams, one representing X, the other O. Contestants choose a square, and you ask them a question from **Que sais-je?** If they answer correctly, they win the square they chose. If their answer is incorrect, the other team may choose the same or another square. The team that wins three squares in a row wins the game.

Additional Practice
7 To review the **vous** form, have students ask pairs of students if they like what is pictured here.

Vocabulaire

Vocabulaire

CHAPITRE 1

Première étape

Greeting people and saying goodbye

Bonjour!	*Hello!*
Salut!	*Hi!* or *Goodbye!*
Au revoir!	*Goodbye!*
A tout à l'heure!	*See you later!*
A bientôt.	*See you soon.*
A demain.	*See you tomorrow.*
Tchao!	*Bye!*
madame (Mme)	*ma'am; Mrs.*
mademoiselle (Mlle)	*miss; Miss*
monsieur (M.)	*sir; Mr.*

Asking how people are and telling how you are

(Comment) ça va?	*How's it going?*
Ça va.	*Fine.*
Super!	*Great!*
Très bien.	*Very well.*
Comme ci comme ça.	*So-so.*
Bof!	*(expression of indifference)*
Pas mal.	*Not bad.*
Pas terrible.	*Not so great.*
Et toi?	*And you?*

Asking someone's name and giving yours

Tu t'appelles comment?	*What's your name?*
Je m'appelle...	*My name is . . .*
Il/Elle s'appelle comment?	*What's his/her name?*
Il/Elle s'appelle...	*His/Her name is . . .*

Asking someone's age and giving yours

Tu as quel âge?	*How old are you?*
J'ai... ans.	*I am . . . years old.*
douze	*twelve*
treize	*thirteen*
quatorze	*fourteen*
quinze	*fifteen*
seize	*sixteen*
dix-sept	*seventeen*
dix-huit	*eighteen*

Deuxième étape

Expressing likes, dislikes, and preferences about things

j'aime (bien)...	*I (really) like . . .*
Je n'aime pas...	*I don't like . . .*
J'aime mieux...	*I prefer . . .*
Je préfère...	*I prefer . . .*
J'adore...	*I adore . . .*
Tu aimes... ?	*Do you like . . . ?*
les amis (m.)	*friends*
l'anglais (m.)	*English*
le chocolat	*chocolate*
le cinéma	*the movies*
les concerts (m.)	*concerts*
l'école (f.)	*school*
les escargots (m.)	*snails*
les examens (m.)	*tests*
le football	*soccer*
le français	*French*
les frites (f.)	*French fries*
la glace	*ice cream*
les hamburgers (m.)	*hamburgers*
les magasins (m.)	*stores*
les maths (f.)	*math*
la pizza	*pizza*
la plage	*beach*
le ski	*skiing*
le sport	*sports*
les vacances (f.)	*vacation*
le vélo	*biking*

Other useful expressions

et	*and*
mais	*but*
non	*no*
oui	*yes*
ou	*or*

Troisième étape

Expressing likes, dislikes, and preferences about activities

aimer	*to like*
danser	*to dance*
dormir	*to sleep*
écouter de la musique	*to listen to music*
étudier	*to study*
faire de l'équitation	*to go horseback riding*
faire les magasins	*to go shopping*
faire le ménage	*to do housework*
faire du sport	*to play sports*
lire	*to read*
nager	*to swim*
parler au téléphone	*to talk on the phone*
regarder la télé	*to watch TV*
sortir avec les copains	*to go out with friends*
voyager	*to travel*

Other useful expressions

aussi	*also*
surtout	*especially*

For subject pronouns, see page 33.

Review and Assess

Visual Learners

You might want to use the *Teaching Transparencies* for Chapter 1 to review functional expressions and vocabulary.

Game

Dessiner, c'est gagner Divide the class into teams. A volunteer from one team goes to the board. Show the student a vocabulary word or expression by pointing it out in the book or by using a flashcard. The student has 30 seconds to illustrate the word for his or her team, who must say the correct French word or expression within the time limit. Teams alternate turns.

Chapter 1 Assessment

- **Testing Program**
  Chapter Test, pp. 13–18

  Audio Compact Discs, CD 1, Trs. 34–36
  Speaking Test, p. 343
- **Alternative Assessment Guide**
  Performance Assessment, p. 32
  Portfolio Assessment, p. 18
  CD-ROM Assessment, p. 46
- **Interactive CD-ROM Tutor, Disc 1**
  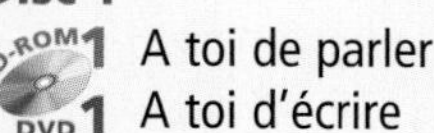
  1 A toi de parler
  1 A toi d'écrire
- **Standardized Assessment Tutor**
  Chapter 1
- **One-Stop Planner, Disc 1**
  Test Generator
  Chapter 1

STANDARDS: 1.1

Chapitre 2 : Vive l'école!

Chapter Overview

Mise en train pp. 48–50	***La rentrée***

	FUNCTIONS	GRAMMAR	VOCABULARY	RE-ENTRY
Première étape pp. 51–54	• Agreeing and disagreeing, p. 54	• Using **si** instead of **oui** to contradict a negative statement, p. 54	• School subjects, p. 51	• Greetings **(Chapitre 1)** • The verb **aimer (Chapitre 1)** • The definite articles **le, la, l'**, and **les (Chapitre 1)** • Subject pronouns **(Chapitre 1)**
Deuxième étape pp. 55–59	• Asking for and giving information, p. 55 • Telling when you have class, p. 58	• The verb **avoir**, p. 55	• Time of day, p. 55 • Class schedules, p. 56 • Numbers 21-59, p. 57	• Numbers for telling time **(Chapitre 1)** • Subject pronouns **(Chapitre 1)**
Troisième étape pp. 61–63	• Asking for and expressing opinions, p. 61			• The verb **aimer (Chapitre 1)** • Expressing likes, dislikes, and preferences about things **(Chapitre 1)**

Prononciation p. 63	**Liaison** Audio CD 2, Tracks 12–14	**A écrire** (dictation) Audio CD 2, Tracks 15–17	
Lisons! pp. 64–65	**Sondage : Les lycéens ont-ils le moral?**	**Reading Strategy** Using visual clues to determine meaning	
Grammaire supplémentaire	**pp. 66–69** **Première étape,** p. 66	**Deuxième étape,** pp. 66–68	**Troisième étape,** p. 69
Review pp. 70–73	**Mise en pratique,** pp. 70–71	**Que sais-je?** p. 72	**Vocabulaire,** p. 73

CULTURE

- **Note culturelle,** The French educational system/**Le bac,** p. 53
- Realia: **Baccalauréat,** p. 53
- Realia: French class schedule, p. 56
- **Note culturelle,** 24-hour time, p. 58
- **Panorama Culturel,** Curriculum in francophone schools, p. 60
- **Note culturelle,** The French grading system, p. 61

Chapitre 2 : Vive l'école!

Chapter Resources

Visit Holt Online
go.hrw.com
KEYWORD: WA3 POITIERS-2
Online Edition

Lesson Planning

One-Stop Planner

Lesson Planner with Differentiated Instruction, pp. 8–12, 66

Student Make-Up Assignments
- Make-Up Assignment Copying Masters, Chapter 2

Listening and Speaking

TPR Storytelling Book, pp. 5–8

Listening Activities
- Student Response Forms for Listening Activities, pp. 11–13
- Additional Listening Activities 2-1 to 2-6, pp. 15–17
- Additional Listening Activities (song), p. 18
- Scripts and Answers, pp. 107–111

Video Guide
- Teaching Suggestions, pp. 12–13
- Activity Masters, pp. 14–16
- Scripts and Answers, pp. 90–92, 118

Activities for Communication
- Communicative Activities, pp. 7–12
- Realia and Teaching Suggestions, pp. 80–84
- Situation Cards, pp. 139–140

Reading and Writing

Reading Strategies and Skills Handbook, Chapter 2

Joie de lire 1, Chapter 2

Cahier d'activités, pp. 13–24

Grammar

Travaux pratiques de grammaire, pp. 10–16

Grammar Tutor for Students of French, Chapter 2

Assessment

Testing Program
- Grammar and Vocabulary Quizzes, **Etape** Quizzes, and Chapter Test, pp. 27–44
- Score Sheet, Scripts and Answers, pp. 45–52

Alternative Assessment Guide
- Portfolio Assessment, p. 19
- Performance Assessment, p. 33
- CD-ROM Assessment, p. 47

Student Make-Up Assignments
- Alternative Quizzes, Chapter 2

Standardized Assessment Tutor
- Reading, pp. 5–7
- Writing, p. 8
- Math, pp. 25–26

Middle School

Middle School Teaching Resources, Chapter 2

Online Activities
- **Jeux interactifs**
- **Activités Internet**

Video Program
- Videocassette 1
- Videocassette 5 (captioned version)

Interactive CD-ROM Tutor, Disc 1

DVD Tutor, Disc 1

Audio Compact Discs
- Textbook Listening Activities, CD 2, Tracks 1–18
- Additional Listening Activities, CD 2, Tracks 25–31
- Assessment Items, CD 2, Tracks 19–24

Teaching Transparencies
- Situation 2-1 to 2-3
- Vocabulary 2-A and 2-B
- **Mise en train**
- **Grammaire supplémentaire** Answers
- **Travaux pratiques de grammaire** Answers

Use the **One-Stop Planner CD-ROM with Test Generator** to aid in lesson planning and pacing.

For each chapter, the **One-Stop Planner** includes:
- Editable lesson plans with direct links to teaching resources
- Printable worksheets from resource books
- Direct launches to the HRW Internet activities
- Video and audio segments
- Test Generator
- Clip Art for vocabulary items

Chapitre 2 : Vive l'école!

Projects

Mon avenir

Students will make posters that show pictures of themselves and illustrate their career goals and the steps toward these goals. See the Teacher Note on page 56 for French names of professions.

MATERIALS

Students may need

- Large pieces of plain or construction paper
- Scissors
- Pens or crayons
- Glue
- Magazines

PREPARATION

Students make a short list in French or English of several careers that interest them. They then add the names of several school subjects that are helpful for each career.

SUGGESTED SEQUENCE

1. **First Draft** Students pick their top career choice, which they will represent in a dream bubble above their picture. Next, to illustrate themselves, their goals, and the steps toward their goals, students might draw or cut out pictures from magazines. They might want to sketch a layout before they assemble the final poster.
2. **Final Draft** Students paste their illustrations on the poster and then label the pictures of their career choice with the names of the subjects necessary to prepare for that career. The posters might be displayed in the classroom.

GRADING THE PROJECT

Suggested Point Distribution: (total = 100 points)

Completion of assignment	40 points
Presentation (spelling, neatness, organization)	40 points
Creativity	20 points

TEACHER NOTE

The posters might be included in students' portfolios along with the notes they made about career possibilities and the subjects required for each.

Games

Loto

In this game, students will practice telling time using the 24-hour system.

Have students make a grid, five squares across and five squares down. They should write **libre** in the center square. Have them fill in the squares by drawing clocks that show times on the hour, quarter past the hour, quarter to the hour, or half past the hour. Call out various times, using the 24-hour system. Students should make a small pencil mark in the corner of the appropriate square when their clock shows the time called. A student who marks a complete row of clocks horizontally, vertically, or diagonally wins, provided that he or she is able to say the times in each square correctly. After erasing the pencil marks, students are ready for another game.

Variation Instead of clocks, students fill in their **Loto** grids with numbers from 20–59. Call out numbers or easy addition or subtraction problems. Students make a small pencil mark in the corner of the appropriate square when their number is called or the solution to the problem is given. Ask students who win to write additional problems while the rest of the class continues to play. They might then call out the problems they've written.

Dessin animé

In this game, students will practice the names of school subjects in French.

Form two or more teams and have one player from one team go to the board. Whisper to the player the name of a subject in French. In 60 seconds or less, the student must make a drawing to represent that subject; letters and symbols are not allowed. The first team to correctly guess the French word for the subject wins a point. The turn then passes to another team. This game might also be played in small groups with individuals competing against one another. In this situation, students can choose subjects from the vocabulary list at the end of the chapter and draw them on paper or on transparencies.

Variation You might want to have students act out the subjects instead of drawing them.

STANDARDS: 1.3, 5.2

Storytelling

Mini-histoire

This story accompanies Teaching Transparency 2-3. The ***mini-histoire*** *can be told and retold in different formats, acted out, written down, and read aloud, to give students additional opportunities to practice all four skills. In the following story, Mathieu tells about his favorite school subjects.*

En général, j'aime le mardi matin. J'ai informatique à huit heures. C'est super intéressant! J'aime surfer le Web, et surtout, j'aime lire et regarder les sites sportifs sur Internet. J'aime aussi mon cours d'arts plastiques. J'ai arts plastiques le jeudi après le déjeuner. Le prof s'appelle Maurice Gentilhomme, et il est super cool. J'aime aussi mon cours de musique. C'est passionnant.

Traditions

Marais poitevins

To the southwest of Poitiers lie the Poitevin marshes. These marshes have been partially drained over a period of centuries, but a large area still remains. The picturesque area of the marshes nearest Poitiers is often referred to as **la Venise verte.** It is so named because the traditional means of transportation in the area is by flat-bottom boat along the series of winding canals lined by forests, trees such as poplars and weeping willows, and green fields where cattle graze. Tourists can appreciate the bucolic poetry of "Green Venice" by taking a cruise on a **plate,** one of the flat-bottom boats. These cruises are the best way to view the waterlilies and lovely villages of whitewashed houses clustered atop dams and small islands.

Recette

The ***Quiche Lorraine*** *is said to have been created in the sixteenth century in Nancy, France. The original recipe contained only eggs, smoked bacon, and butter, and the crust was made out of bread. Cheese was added later on to the recipe. A quiche can be prepared with a variety of ingredients, including spinach and salmon. Usually, French people eat quiche as an appetizer, or sometimes as a main dish with a salad. It is also a favorite lunch dish. Cafés and restaurants serve a single serving of quiche to people for lunch. Quiches fall under the fast food category for the French.*

QUICHE LORRAINE

pour 6 personnes

Pâte brisée

2 tasses de farine
une pincée de sel
1 cuillère à soupe de sucre
1/2 tasse de beurre froid
3 cuillères à soupe d'eau
(ou aller au supermarché acheter la pâte toute faite)

Garniture

5 œufs
2 tasses de crème fraîche
1 tranche épaisse de jambon coupée en cubes
au choix ajouter des champignons coupés et du fromage râpé

Pâte brisée

Mettre la farine, le sucre et le sel dans un bol. Couper le beurre en petits morceaux. Mélanger le beurre et la farine avec les doigts. Ajouter l'eau petit à petit. Faire une boule avec la pâte. Laisser reposer pendant 30 minutes.

Garniture

Dans un bol, mélanger les œufs et la crème fraîche. Ajouter le jambon (les champignons et le fromage).

Rouler la pâte et la mettre dans le moule. Ajouter la garniture. Mettre dans le four à 375° F pendant 45 minutes.

STANDARDS: 1.3, 3.2

Technology

Videocassette 1, Videocassette 5 (captioned version)
DVD Tutor, Disc 1
See Video Guide, pp. 11–16.

DVD/Video

Mise en train • La rentrée

In this segment of the video, Claire and Ann meet Delphine on the way to school. They talk about their classes and whether or not they like them. Delphine is worried that she will be late, so she leaves. As Claire and Ann approach the school, they meet Marc and Jérôme. The four of them compare their schedules and express opinions about their classes. They discover they all have gym at the same time. Jérôme realizes he forgot his sneakers.

Tu as quels cours?

Several teenagers from different French-speaking countries tell us about a typical school day and the classes they have.

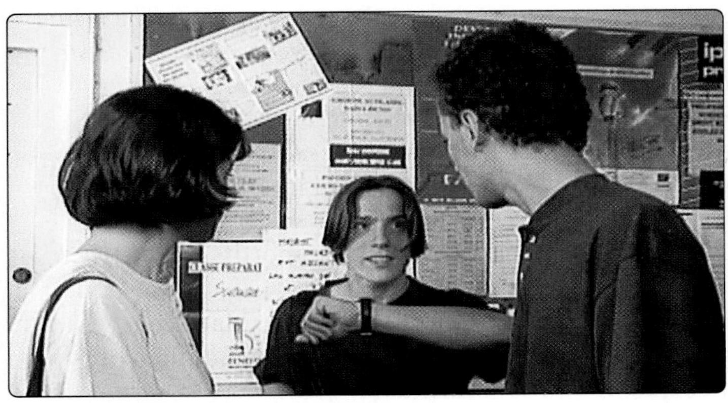

La rentrée (suite)

The story continues later in the school day. Marc meets Jérôme after the last class of the morning. Marc tells him how he likes his math class. Jérôme is preoccupied with his sneakers and decides to go home during lunch to get them. He rides through the streets of Poitiers, rushing to get back to school in time. He returns, shoes in hand, only to find that gym class has been canceled! The teacher is sick, and they have study hall. Jérôme can't believe he went to all that trouble for nothing.

Vidéoclip

- ***Tout ce que j'ai, tout ce que j'aime*** : music video by Pierre Flynn

Interactive CD-ROM Tutor

Activity	Activity Type	Pupil's Edition Page
En contexte	*Interactive conversation*	
1. Vocabulaire	Jeu des paires	p. 51
2. Grammaire	Les mots qui manquent	p. 55
3. Vocabulaire	Le bon choix	pp. 55–56
4. Comment dit-on... ?	Jeu des paires	pp. 56–58
5. Comment dit-on... ?	Chacun à sa place	pp. 54, 61
6. Comment dit-on... ?	Méli-mélo	pp. 56, 61
Panorama Culturel	Tu as quels cours? Le bon choix	p. 60
A toi de parler	*Guided recording*	pp. 70–71
A toi d'écrire	*Guided writing*	pp. 70–71

Teacher Management System

Launch the program, type "admin" in the password area and press RETURN. Log on to **www.hrw.com/CDROMTUTOR** for a detailed explanation of the Teacher Management System.

DVD Tutor

The *DVD Tutor* contains all material from the *Video Program* as described above. French captions are available for use at your discretion for all sections of the video. The *DVD Tutor* also provides a variety of video-based activities that assess students' understanding of the **Mise en train, Suite,** and **Panorama Culturel.**

This part of the *DVD Tutor* may be used on any DVD video player connected to a television or video monitor.

In addition to the video material and the video-based comprehension activities, the *DVD Tutor* also contains the entire *Interactive CD-ROM Tutor* in DVD-ROM format. Each DVD disc contains the activities from all 12 chapters of the *Interactive CD-ROM Tutor.*

This part of the *DVD Tutor* may be used on a Macintosh® or Windows® computer with a DVD-ROM drive.

To preview all resources available for this chapter, use the **One-Stop Planner CD-ROM,** Disc 1.

Visit Holt Online
go.hrw.com
KEYWORD: WA3 POITIERS-2
Online Edition

Go.Online!

Online Edition

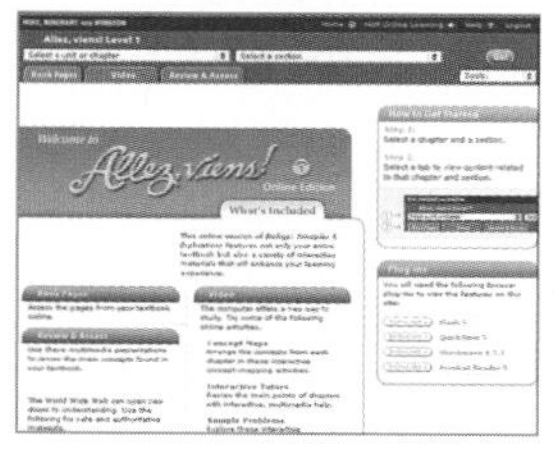

The Online Edition for Allez, viens! *allows students access to their textbooks anytime anywhere.*

- *Audio at point of use*
- *Additional practice activities*
- *Self-test activities*
- *Online reference tools*
- *Entire Video Program (Enhanced version)*
- *Interactive Notebook (Enhanced version)*

HRW Atlas

video

audio

presentation

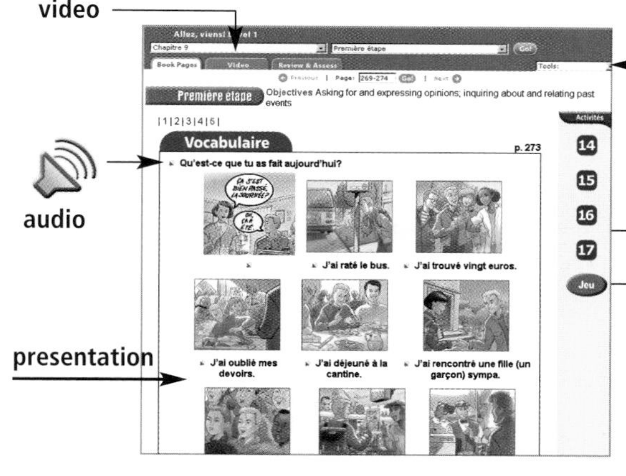

tools (glossary, grammar, cahier électronique)

activities

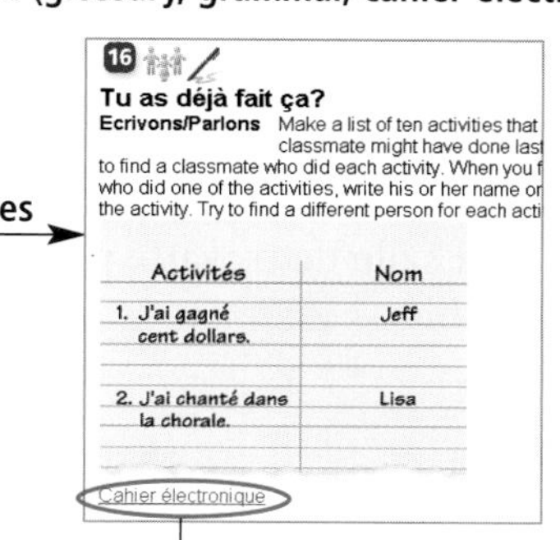

Notebook

Activités Internet

These guided internet activities include a worksheet and pre-selected and pre-screened authentic web sites from the francophone world. You can use these activities

- to help students develop research skills in the target language
- to introduce students to authentic cultural information
- as a project

Jeux interactifs

You can use the interactive activities in this chapter

- to practice grammar, vocabulary, and chapter functions
- as homework
- as an assessment option
- as a self-test
- to prepare for the Chapter Test

Projet Have students do a Web search for high schools in Poitiers and choose one they would like to attend if they were part of an exchange program. Have them explain why they chose that particular high school. Then, have them document their sources by noting the names and URLs of all the sites they consulted.

Chapitre 2 : Vive l'école!

Textbook Listening Activities Scripts 

Première étape

7 p. 52

1. CELINE Mais non! C'est de l'espagnol!
AURELIE Zut!
2. AURELIE Alors, qu'est-ce que c'est?
CELINE C'est un cours d'arts plastiques.
3. CELINE C'est ici, le français?
AURELIE Non. C'est la salle d'informatique.
4. AURELIE Voilà! Enfin. C'est le français.
CELINE Mais non! C'est de l'histoire!
5. CELINE Oh là là! Ce n'est pas ici non plus.
AURELIE Et là, qu'est-ce que c'est?
CELINE C'est la salle de travaux pratiques de chimie.

Answers to Activity 7
1. L'espagnol — 022
2. Les arts plastiques — 023
3. L'informatique — 323
4. L'histoire — 223
5. Les travaux pratiques de chimie — 222

11 p. 54

HELENE Salut, Gérard. Tu as physique maintenant?
GERARD Euh, oui.
HELENE Tu aimes ça?
GERARD Non, pas trop.
HELENE Moi, si! J'aime bien la physique!
GERARD Et toi, tu as quoi maintenant?
HELENE J'ai géométrie. J'adore!
GERARD Moi aussi! C'est super intéressant, mais j'aime mieux l'informatique.

Answers to Activity 11
Agree — la géométrie
Disagree — la physique.

Deuxième étape

18 p. 57

1. Salut, Stéphanie. C'est Frédéric. Tu as quoi le lundi matin? Moi, le lundi, j'ai allemand, français, sport et sciences nat.
2. Salut, Stéphanie. C'est Nadine. Tu as quoi le jeudi? Le matin, j'ai maths, sciences nat et allemand. L'après-midi, j'ai français, géographie et musique. Et toi?
3. Salut! Ça va? Ici Georges. Tu as quoi le mercredi? Moi, j'ai maths, anglais, français et histoire/géo.

Answers to Activity 18
Frédéric — same
Nadine — different
Georges — same

20 p. 58

ANNE Salut, Jérôme. Tu as quoi maintenant?
JEROME C'est huit heures? Alors, j'ai anglais!
ANNE Et tu as espagnol à quelle heure?
JEROME Euh... quatorze heures quinze.
ANNE Moi, j'ai histoire à quatorze heures quinze. Et toi, tu as histoire à quelle heure?
JEROME J'ai histoire à neuf heures et après, j'ai maths à dix heures vingt. La récré, c'est à dix heures. J'aime ça!

Answers to Activity 20
Anglais—8h00
Espagnol—14h15
Histoire—9h00
Maths—10h20

The following scripts are for the listening activities found in the *Pupil's Edition*. For Student Response Forms, see *Listening Activities*, pages 11–13. To provide students with additional listening practice, see *Listening Activities*, pages 15–18.

One-Stop Planner CD-ROM

To preview all resources available for this chapter, use the **One-Stop Planner CD-ROM**, Disc 1.

Troisième étape

24 p. 61

ERIC Dis, tu as sciences nat avec moi ce matin?

AURELIE Oui. Comment tu trouves ça, les sciences nat?

ERIC C'est génial!

AURELIE Et on a aussi géographie cet aprèm, n'est-ce pas? Ça te plaît, la géo?

ERIC Oui. C'est super! Tu n'aimes pas, toi?

AURELIE Non, pas trop. Mais j'adore l'allemand. C'est cool.

ERIC L'allemand? Mais c'est nul, l'allemand! J'aime mieux l'anglais. C'est plus intéressant.

AURELIE Mais c'est plus difficile.

Answers to Activity 24

Eric aime les sciences nat, la géographie et l'anglais.
Eric n'aime pas l'allemand.
Aurélie aime l'allemand.
Aurélie n'aime pas la géographie.

PRONONCIATION, P. 63

For the scripts for Parts A and B, see p. 63. The script for Part C is below.

C. A écrire *(dictation)*

1. — Nous aimons l'informatique. C'est cool.
   — Moi, j'aime mieux les arts plastiques.
2. — Ils ont quoi mardi?
   — Ils ont anglais et physique.

Mise en pratique

1 p. 70

Le lycée aux Etats-Unis, c'est bizarre! On a chimie tous les matins à neuf heures cinq! Et on a sport, mais à quatorze heures quarante-six! Pourquoi «quarante-six»? On a latin à onze heures trente. Ça, c'est normal. Mais on a informatique l'après-midi à treize heures cinquante-deux! Je ne comprends pas l'emploi du temps américain!

Answers to Mise en pratique, Activity 1

André thinks that his schedule is strange because some classes don't start exactly on the hour or half hour.
Chimie — 9h05
Sport — 14h46 (2:46 P.M.)
Latin — 11h30
Informatique — 13h52 (1:52 P.M.)

Chapitre 2 : Vive l'école!

50-Minute Lesson Plans

Day 1

CHAPTER OPENER 5 min.
- Present Chapter Objectives, p. 47
- Culture Note, ATE, p. 46
- Thinking Critically suggestions, ATE, p. 47

MISE EN TRAIN 40 min.
- Presenting **Mise en train** and Preteaching Vocabulary, ATE, pp. 48–49
- Thinking Critically, ATE, p. 49
- Do Activities 1–6, p. 50.

Wrap-Up 5 min.
- Write a chart with the headings **Nul** and **Cool** on the chalkboard. Say different school subjects and have students vote on whether each subject belongs under **Nul** or **Cool.**

Homework Options
Cahier d'activités, p. 13, Act. 1

Day 2

PREMIERE ETAPE
Quick Review 5 min.
- Check homework.
- Bell Work, ATE, p. 51

Vocabulaire, p. 51 25 min.
- Present **Vocabulaire,** p. 51, using Teaching Transparency 2-A.
- Teacher Note, ATE, p. 51
- Play Audio CD for Activity 7, p. 52.
- Do Activities 8–9, p. 52.

Note culturelle, p. 53 15 min.
- Discuss **Note culturelle,** p. 53
- Thinking Critically, ATE, p. 53, and Culture Notes, p. 53
- Do Language-to-Language, ATE, p. 53 and then do Activity 10, p. 53.

Wrap-Up 5 min.
- Additional Practice, ATE, p. 53

Homework Options
Cahier d'activités pp. 14–15, Acts. 2–5
Travaux pratiques de grammaire, pp. 10–11, Acts. 1–4

Day 3

PREMIERE ETAPE
Quick Review 5 min.
- Check homework.
- Play the Game: **Dessin animé,** ATE, p. 45C.

Comment dit-on... ?, p. 54 10 min.
- Presenting **Comment dit-on... ?,** ATE, p. 54

Note de grammaire, p. 54 20 min.
- Discuss **Note de grammaire**, p. 54.
- Play Audio CD for Activity 11, p. 54.
- Do Activities 11–13, p. 54.
- **Grammaire supplémentaire**, p. 66, Activities 1–2
- Cahier d'activités pp. 15–16, Acts. 6–9

Wrap-Up 15 min.
- Express opinions stating whether a course is easy or hard, interesting or boring and take a poll of the students' opinions.

Homework Options
Study for **Première étape** quiz.

Day 4

PREMIERE ETAPE
Quiz 2-1 20 min.
- Administer Quiz 2-1A, Quiz 2-1B.

DEUXIEME ETAPE
Comment dit-on... ?/ Vocabulaire, p. 55 10 min.
- Presenting **Comment dit-on... ?/ Vocabulaire,** ATE, p. 55
- Do Activity 14, p. 55.

Grammaire, p. 55 15 min.
- Presenting **Grammaire**, ATE, p. 55
- Activity 15, p. 56, and Teacher Note, ATE, p. 56
- **Grammaire supplémentaire,** p. 66, Activity 3

Wrap-Up 5 min.
- Travaux pratiques de grammaire, p. 12, Act. 6

Homework Options
Cahier d'activités p. 17, Act. 12
Travaux pratiques de grammaire, pp. 12–13, Acts. 7–9

Day 5

DEUXIEME ETAPE
Quick Review 10 min.
- Check homework.
- Bell Work, ATE, p. 55

Vocabulaire, p. 56 30 min.
- Presenting **Vocabulaire,** ATE, p. 56
- Culture Note, p. 57
- Do Activities 16–17, p. 57.
- Additional Practice, ATE, p. 57
- Travaux pratiques de grammaire, p. 13, Act. 10

Wrap-Up 10 min.
- Have each student name his or her favorite TV show, then give the day of the week the show is on in French.

Homework Options
Travaux pratiques de grammaire, p. 14, Acts. 11–12

Day 6

DEUXIEME ETAPE
Quick Review 10 min.
- Check homework.

Vocabulaire, p. 57 30 min.
- Presenting **Vocabulaire,** ATE, p. 57
- Do Activity 19, p. 58.
- Math Link, ATE, p. 57

Wrap-Up 10 min.
- Find photos of celebrities and research their ages (no age higher than 59). Show the photos to students and have them guess each celebrity's age in French.

Homework Options
Cahier d'activités, p. 17, Act. 11
Travaux pratiques de grammaire, pp. 14–15, Acts. 13–14

For alternative lesson plans by chapter section, to create your own customized plans, or to preview all resources available for this chapter, use the **One-Stop Planner CD-ROM**, Disc 1.

For additional homework suggestions, see activities accompanied by this symbol throughout the chapter.

Day 7

DEUXIEME ETAPE

Quick Review 10 min.
- Check homework.
- Additional Practice, ATE, p. 58

Comment dit-on... ?, p. 58 30 min.
- Presenting **Comment dit-on... ?,** ATE, p. 58
- Discuss **Note culturelle**, p. 58.
- Do Activities 21–22, p. 59.
- Cahier d'activités, pp. 17–18, Acts. 10, 13–14

Wrap-Up 10 min.
- Game: **Loto!**, ATE, p. 45C

Homework Options
Study for **Deuxième étape** quiz.

Day 8

DEUXIEME ETAPE

Quiz 2-2 20 min.
- Administer Quiz 2-2A or Quiz 2-2B.

PANORAMA CULTUREL 25 min.
- Present **Panorama Culturel** using Videocassette 1, p. 60.
- Do **Qu'en penses-tu?** and **Savais-tu que…?,** p. 60
- Thinking Critically, ATE, p. 60
- **Panorama Culturel,** Interactive CD-ROM Tutor (Disc 1)

Wrap-Up 5 min.
- Have students tell what their ideal class schedule would be like.

Homework Options
Cahier d'activités, p. 24, Acts. 25–27

Day 9

TROISIEME ETAPE

Quick Review 10 min.
- Check homework.
- Bell Work, ATE, p. 61

Comment dit-on... ?, p. 61 15 min.
- Presenting **Comment dit-on... ?,** ATE, p. 61
- Auditory Learners, ATE, p. 61
- Discuss **Note culturelle,** ATE, p. 61.
- Play Audio CD for Act. 24, p. 61.
- Do Activity 25, and Activity 27 or 28, pp. 62–63.

Prononciation, p. 63 15 min.
- Play audio CD for Activities A–C, p. 63.

Wrap-Up 10 min.
- Communicative Activity 2-3, Activities for Communication, pp. 11–12

Homework Options
Study for **Troisième étape** quiz.

Day 10

TROISIEME ETAPE

Quiz 20 min.
- Administer Quiz 2-3A or Quiz 2-3B.

LISONS! 25 min.
- Prereading Activities A–C, ATE, p. 64
- Thinking Critically, ATE, p. 64
- Reading Activities D–G, ATE, p. 65

Wrap-Up 5 min.
- Postreading Activity H, ATE, p. 65

Homework Options
Cahier d'activités, p. 23, Acts. 23–24

Day 11

LISONS!

Quick Review 15 min.
- Situation Card 2-3: Role-play, Activities for Communication p. 140

MISE EN PRATIQUE 30 min.
- Play Audio CD for Act. 1, p. 70.
- Do Activities 2 and 5, pp. 70–71, as a class, and Activity 3, p. 70, in small groups.
- Have students do Activity 6, p. 71, individually.
- Have partners complete **Jeu de rôle,** p. 71.

Wrap-Up 5 min.
- Discuss Career Path, ATE, p. 71.

Homework Options
Que sais-je?, p. 72

Day 12

MISE EN PRATIQUE

Quick Review 15 min.
- Auditory Learners, ATE, p. 71
- Have students play Game: **Tic Tac Toe,** ATE, p. 73.

Chapter Review 35 min.
- Review Chapter 2. Choose from **Grammaire supplémentaire,** Grammar Tutor for Students of French, Activities for Communication, Listening Activities, Interactive CD-ROM Tutor, or **Jeux interactifs.**

Homework Options
Study for Chapter 2 Test.

Assessment

Test, Chapter 2 40–45 min.
- Administer Chapter 2 Test. Select from Testing Program, Alternative Assessment Guide, Test Generator, or Standardized Assessment Tutor.

Chapitre 2 : Vive l'école!

90-Minute Lesson Plans

Block 1

CHAPTER OPENER 5 min.

- Present Chapter Objectives, p. 47
- Culture Note, ATE, p. 46
- Focusing on Outcomes, ATE, p. 47
- Thinking Critically suggestions, ATE, p. 47

MISE EN TRAIN 40 min.

- Presenting **Mise en train,** ATE, p. 48. See Preteaching Vocabulary ATE, p. 48.
- Do Activity 1, p. 50.
- View video of **Mise en train,** Videocassette 1, Video Guide, p. 11. Video Guide Activity Master, p. 14

PREMIERE ETAPE

Vocabulaire, p. 51 25 min.

- Bell Work, ATE, p. 51
- Presenting **Vocabulaire,** ATE, p. 51 or Teaching Transparencies 2-1 and 2-A
- Play Audio CD for Activity 7, p. 52.
- Do Activity 9, p. 52. Have students write answers on blackboard, use answers to review **–er** verb conjugations.

Note culturelle, p. 53 15 min.

- **Note culturelle,** p. 53, Culture Notes and Thinking Critically, ATE, p. 53
- Do Activity 10, p. 53 and Language-to-Language, ATE, p. 53.

Wrap-Up 5 min.

- Use the **Mise en train** transparencies to summarize what happened in the **Mise en train.**

Homework Options

Cahier d'activités, pp. 14–15, Acts. 3–5
Travaux pratiques de grammaire, p. 10, Acts. 1–2

Block 2

PREMIERE ETAPE

Quick Review 10 min.

- Challenge, ATE, p. 52

Comment dit-on... ?, p. 54 40 min.

- Presenting **Comment dit-on... ?,** p. 54
- Play Audio CD for Activity 11, p. 54.
- **Note de grammaire,** p. 54
- Do Activity 12, p. 54.
- **Grammaire supplémentaire** p. 66, Activities 1–2
- Have partners prepare and act out a conversation between a student and a school counselor, in which they discuss the student's interests and the subjects he or she likes and dislikes. (10 min. to prepare skits, 5 min. to present)

DEUXIEME ETAPE

Comment dit-on... ?, p. 55 10 min.

- Bell Work, ATE, p. 55
- Presenting **Comment dit-on... ?,** ATE, p. 55 using Teaching Transparency 2-2

Vocabulaire, p. 55 15 min.

- Presenting **Vocabulaire,** ATE, p. 55.
- Do Activity 14, p. 55.

Wrap-Up 15 min.

- Realia 2-1, Activities for Communication, p. 80

Homework Options

Study for **Première étape** quiz.
Travaux pratiques de grammaire, p. 11, Acts. 3–5
Cahier d'activités, pp. 15–16, Acts. 6–9

Block 3

PREMIERE ETAPE

Quick Review 10 min.

Quiz 2-1 20 min.

- Administer Quiz 2-1A or 2-1B.

DEUXIEME ETAPE

Quick Review 5 min.

- Ask students questions such as: **Tu as quels cours aujourd'hui?**

Grammaire: avoir, p. 55 30 min.

- Presenting **Grammaire: avoir,** ATE, p. 55
- Do Activity 15, p. 56.
- **Grammaire supplémentaire,** p. 66, Activity 3
- Game 2, Interactive CD-ROM Tutor

Vocabulaire, p. 56 20 min.

- Presenting **Vocabulaire,** ATE, p. 56 using questions from Activity 16, p. 57
- Culture Note and Additional Practice, ATE, p. 57
- Do Activity 17, p. 57.
- Play Audio CD for Activity 18, p. 57.

Wrap-Up 5 min.

- Review the days of the week in French.

Homework Options

Cahier d'activités, p. 17, Act. 12
Travaux pratiques de grammaire, pp. 12–14 Acts. 6–12

For alternative lesson plans by chapter section, to create your own customized plans, or to preview all resources available for this chapter, use the **One-Stop Planner CD-ROM**, Disc 1.

For additional homework suggestions, see activities accompanied by this symbol throughout the chapter.

Block 4

DEUXIEME ETAPE

Quick Review 5 min.
- Review numbers 0–20

Vocabulaire, p. 57 20 min.
- Presenting **Vocabulaire,** ATE, p. 57
- Do Activity 19, p. 58.
- Play Game: **Loto** variation, ATE, p. 45C

Comment dit-on... ?, p. 58 35 min.
- Presenting **Comment dit-on... ?,** ATE, p. 58
- Play Audio CD for Activity 20, p. 58.
- **Note culturelle,** ATE, p. 58
- Do Activities 21 and 22, p. 59.
- **Role-play 2-2,** Activities for Communication, p. 140

PANORAMA CULTUREL 20 min.
- Present **Panorama Culturel,** p. 60
- View **Panorama Culturel** video (first 3 interviews only), Videocassette 1.
- Have students answer **Qu'en penses-tu?** questions, p. 60.
- Read **Savais-tu que?,** p. 60.

Wrap-Up 5 min.
- Communicative Activity 2-2A and 2-2B Activities for Communication, pp. 9–10

Homework Options

Study for **Deuxième étape** quiz.
Cahier d'activités, pp. 18–19, Acts. 13–16
Travaux pratiques de grammaire , pp. 14–15, Acts. 13–17
Grammaire supplémentaire, Act. 4, p. 67

Block 5

DEUXIEME ETAPE

Quick Review 10 min.

Quiz 2-2 20 min.
- Administer Quiz 2-2A or 2-3B.

TROISIEME ETAPE

Comment dit–on...?, p. 61 25 min.
- Motivating Suggestion: Call out numbers in French. Have students write them down as numerals and as words.
- Presenting **Comment dit-on... ?,** ATE, p. 61
- Auditory Learners, ATE, p. 61
- Play Audio for Activity 24, p. 61 and **Note culturelle,** ATE, p. 61
- **Grammaire supplémentaire,** p. 68, Activity 5
- Do Activity 28, p. 63.

Prononciation 15 min.
- Presenting **Prononciation**, ATE, p. 63. Language Note, ATE, p. 63
- Do Activities A, B, and C.

Wrap-Up 20 min.
- Role Play 2-3, Activities for Communication, p. 80

Homework Options

Study for **Troisième étape** quiz.
Travaux pratiques de grammaire, p. 16, Acts. 18–20
Cahier d'activités, pp. 20–22, Acts. 17–22

Block 6

TROISIEME ETAPE

Quick Review 10 min.
- Communicative Activity 2-3A and 2-3B, Activities for Communication, pp. 11–12

Quiz 2-3 20 min.
- Administer Quiz 2-3A or 2-3B

LISONS! 20 min.
- Prereading Activities A–C, ATE, p. 64
- Reading Activities D–G, ATE, pp. 64–65
- Postreading Activity H, ATE, p. 65

MISE EN PRATIQUE 35 min.
- Play Audio CD for Activity 1, p. 70.
- Do Activities 2, 4 and 5, pp. 70–71.
- **Jeu de rôle,** p. 71 (10 min. to prepare skit, 10 min. to present to class)

Wrap-Up 5 min.
- Express opinions stating whether a course is easy or hard, interesting or boring and take a poll of the students' opinions.

Homework Options

Que sais-je?, p. 72
Study for Chapter 2 Test.

Block 7

MISE EN PRATIQUE

Quick Review 5 min.
- Auditory Learners, ATE, p. 71

Chapter Review 35 min.
- Review Chapter 2. Choose from **Grammaire supplémentaire,** Grammar Tutor for Students of French, Activities for Communication, Listening Activities, Interactive CD-ROM Tutor, or **Jeux interactifs.**

Test, Chapter 2 50 min.
- Administer Chapter 2 Test. Select from Testing Program, Alternative Assessment Guide, Test Generator, or Standardized Assessment Tutor.

Chapter Opener

CHAPITRE 2

One-Stop Planner CD-ROM

For resource information, see the **One-Stop Planner,** Disc 1.

Pacing Tips

The **Deuxième étape** presents a lot of functional phrases and vocabulary. The verb **avoir** is also presented in this **étape.** The **Troisième étape** is the lightest, so you might keep that in mind while planning your lessons. For Lesson Plans and timing suggestions, see pages 45I–45L.

Meeting the Standards

Communication

- Agreeing and disagreeing, p. 54
- Asking for and giving information, p. 55
- Telling when you have class, p. 58
- Asking for and expressing opinions, p. 61

Cultures

- Culture Note, pp. 46, 53, 57
- Note culturelle, p. 53
- Note culturelle, p. 58
- Panorama Culturel, p. 60
- Note culturelle, p. 61

Connections

- Math Link, p. 57

Comparisons

- Thinking Critically: Comparing and Contrasting, p. 49
- Thinking Critically: Comparing and Contrasting, p. 53
- Thinking Critically: Analyzing, p. 60
- Thinking Critically: Synthesizing, p. 60

Communities

- De l'école au travail, p. 63
- Career Path, p. 71

Cultures and Communities

Culture Note

The school in the photo is the **Lycée Henry IV,** originally a monastery built by Clovis in 502. Many additions were made to the original construction in following centuries. During the French Revolution, the building became national property, and in 1796, it was alloted to public education. The school was named **Ecole centrale du Panthéon.** Under Napoléon, this school became the first **lycée** in France. It was first renamed as **Lycée Corneille** and then **Lycée Napoléon**. The school's current name dates from the late 18th century. In 1998, the building was classified as a national historic monument. This **lycée** is one of the most prestigious schools in France.

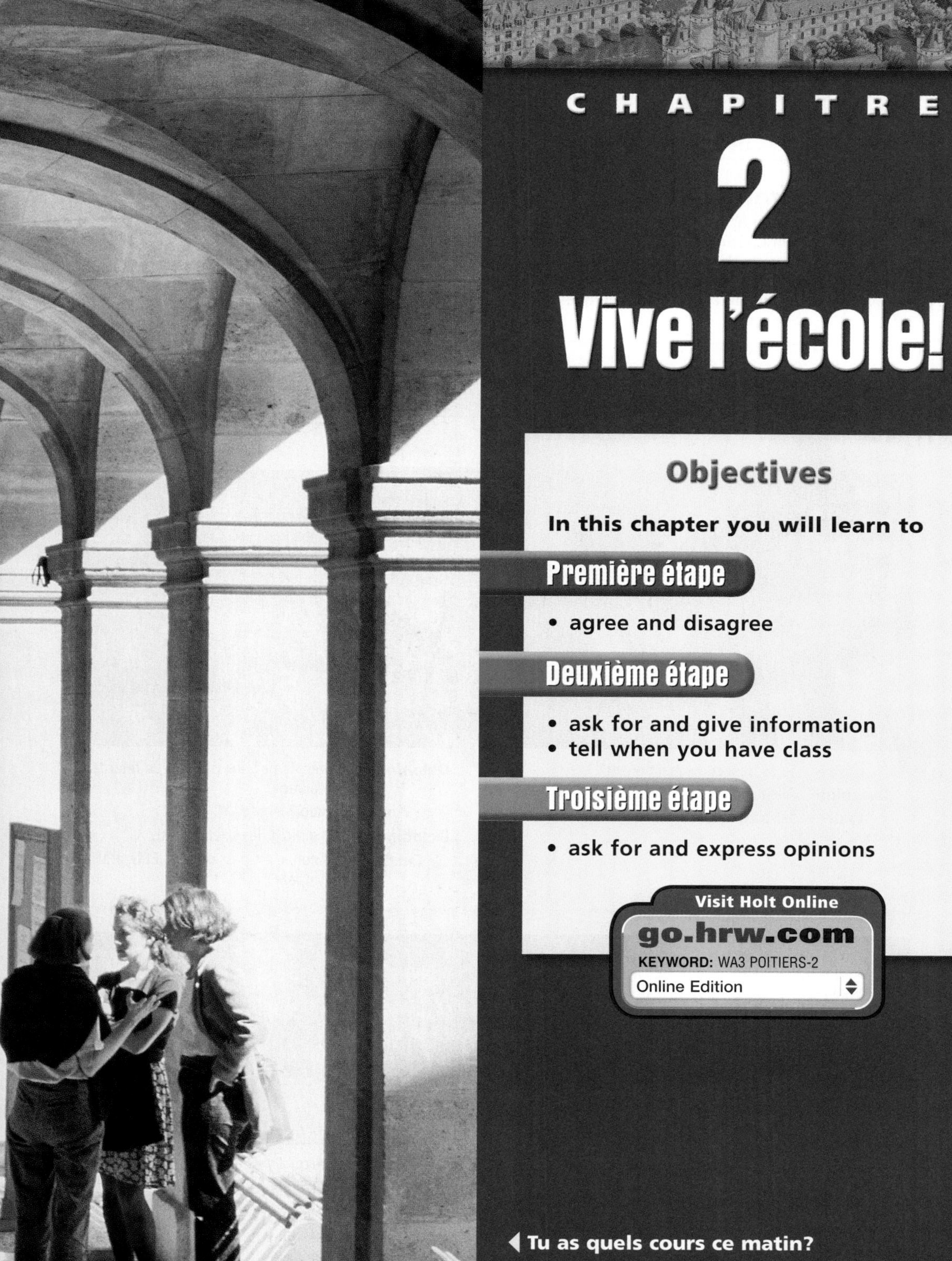

CHAPITRE

2

Vive l'école!

Objectives

In this chapter you will learn to

Première étape

- agree and disagree

Deuxième étape

- ask for and give information
- tell when you have class

Troisième étape

- ask for and express opinions

Visit Holt Online
go.hrw.com
KEYWORD: WA3 POITIERS-2
Online Edition

◀ **Tu as quels cours ce matin?**

Chapter Opener

CHAPITRE 2

Focusing on Outcomes

Call students' attention to the chapter objectives. Ask small groups to brainstorm expressions in English they might use to accomplish the chapter objectives. For example, to express opinions, they might list *boring, fun, OK,* and *interesting.* NOTE: The self-check activities in **Que sais-je?** on page 72 help students assess their achievement of the objectives.

Teacher Note

In this chapter, students will ask about time **(à quelle heure?)**, days of the week **(quel(s) jour(s)?)**, school subjects **(quel(s) cours?)**, and opinions **(comment tu trouves...?)**. Other interrogative expressions will be presented later.

Connections and Comparisons

Thinking Critically

Comparing and Contrasting French students entering the **collège (en sixième)** must take a foreign language. Most **baccalauréat** exams require two foreign languages. Ask students why there might be more emphasis on foreign languages in French schools than in American schools.

Thinking Critically

Analyzing In France, high school class schedules are different from those of most American students. For example, some students may have two consecutive hours of the same class, or they may have two non-consecutive hours of the same class in one day. Have students discuss the advantages or disadvantages of organizing a school day in this manner.

STANDARDS: 4.2

Mise en train

CHAPITRE 2

Teaching Resources
pp. 48–50

PRINT 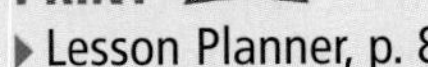

- Lesson Planner, p. 8
- Video Guide, pp. 12, 14
- Cahier d'activités, p. 13

MEDIA 

- One-Stop Planner
- Video Program
  Mise en train
  Videocassette 1, 19:40–23:26
  Videocassette 5 (captioned version), 09:17–13:03
  Suite
  Videocassette 1, 23:28–27:08
  Videocassette 5 (captioned version), 13:06–16:46
- DVD Tutor, Disc 1
- Audio Compact Discs, CD 2, Trs. 1–2
- **Mise en train** Transparencies

Presenting
Mise en train

Before you play the video, have students answer the questions at the top of this page. You might also use the Preteaching Vocabulary suggestions below. After students view the video, ask the questions in Activity 1 on page 50 to check comprehension.

Mise en train Transparencies

The **roman-photo** is an abridged version of the video episode.

MISE EN TRAIN ▪ *La rentrée*

CD 2
Trs. 1–2

DVD VIDEO

Stratégie pour comprendre
Make a list of the cognates you hear or see from La rentrée. Do these words have a common theme? Based on your list of cognates, what do you think these teenagers are talking about? Can you guess where they are?

Les jeunes de Poitiers :

Claire

Delphine

Jérôme

Marc

et du Texas :

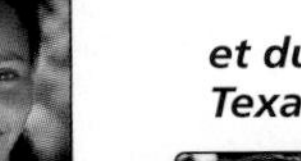
Ann

C'est la première semaine de cours...

1
Claire : Tu as quel cours maintenant?
Delphine : Allemand. J'adore. Et toi, tu as quoi?
Claire : Sciences nat.

2
Delphine : Ecoutez, Je ne veux pas être en retard. Bon courage!
Ann : Pourquoi?
Delphine : C'est difficile, les sciences nat.
Claire : Mais non, c'est passionnant. Et le prof est sympa.

3
Claire : Alors, les garçons, ça boume?
Jérôme : Super.
Marc : Bof. Pas terrible.

4
Claire : Qu'est-ce qu'il y a?
Marc : Oh rien. J'ai maths.
Ann : Tu n'aimes pas les maths?
Marc : Non, c'est nul.

Preteaching Vocabulary

Recognizing Cognates
Before presenting the material, ask students to look at the **Mise en train** to find the names of subjects they may be taking. Ask them if they can find any cognates other than school subjects.

1 sciences
3 super
5 sport
6 géographie
2 courage
4 maths
5 cool

STANDARDS: 1.2

5
Ann : Moi, j'adore. C'est super intéressant.
Marc : J'aime mieux le sport. C'est plus cool.

6
Claire : Et après, tu as quoi?
Marc : Après les maths, j'ai géographie.

7
Ann : Et toi, Jérôme, tu as quoi maintenant?
Jérôme : Euh, je ne sais pas très bien.
Claire : Tu n'as pas allemand?
Jérôme : Si, tu as raison.

8
Ann : Tu aimes l'allemand, toi?
Jérôme : Oui, mais j'aime encore mieux l'espagnol. C'est plus facile pour moi.
Ann : Tu étudies aussi l'espagnol?
Jérôme : Oui. Et l'anglais aussi.

9
Claire : Dis, tu as sport cet aprèm?
Marc : Oui, à quatorze heures.
Ann : Génial! Nous aussi!
Jérôme : Alors, on a tous sport cet aprèm.

10
Ann : Il est quelle heure?
Claire : Huit heures! Vite. Allons-y! On est en retard!
Marc : Eh bien, Jérôme? Qu'est-ce qu'il y a?
Jérôme : Je n'ai pas mes baskets.

Cahier d'activités, p. 13, Act. 1

Using the Captioned Video/DVD

If students have difficulty understanding French spoken at a normal speed, use Videocassette 5 to allow students to see the French captions for ***La rentrée*** and ***La rentrée (suite).*** Hearing the language and watching the story will reduce anxiety about the new language and facilitate comprehension. The reinforcement of seeing the written vocabulary words as they watch the gestures and actions will help prepare students to do the comprehension activities on page 50. NOTE: The *DVD Tutor* contains captions for all sections of the *Video Program.*

Mise en train

CHAPITRE 2

Thinking Critically

Comparing and Contrasting
Ask students to examine the photos for similarities and differences between their school experience and schools in France. Students might consider the subjects offered, how students arrive at school, and how students dress.

Teaching Suggestion

Have students give the meanings for the following abbreviations:
nat = naturelles
maths = mathématiques
baskets = chaussures de basket-ball
aprèm = après-midi
géo = géographie
Ask students to list as many examples as they can of abbreviations of school subjects used in English. Some examples are *PE* or *phys ed* (physical education), *math* (mathematics), *psych* (psychology), *home ec* (home economics), *trig* (trigonometry), *ag* (agriculture), and *bio* (biology).

La rentrée (suite)

You may choose to continue with ***La rentrée (suite)*** at this time or wait until later in the chapter. In the second part of the video, Marc meets Jérôme after the last class of the morning. Jérôme is preoccupied with his sneakers and decides to go home during lunch to get them. He rushes home and back only to find that gym class has been canceled because the teacher is sick. Jérôme can't believe that he went to all that trouble for nothing.

STANDARDS: 1.2, 4.2

Mise en train

CHAPITRE 2

Challenge

2 Have students correct the false statements.

Teaching Suggestion

5 Have students identify the numbers of the frames in the **Mise en train** that support their answers.

These activities check for comprehension only. Students should not yet be expected to produce language modeled in **Mise en train.**

1 Tu as compris?

Réponds aux questions suivantes sur ***La rentrée.***

1. What are the students discussing? their schedules
2. What do you think the title ***La rentrée*** means? back to school
3. What class do they all have together? gym class
4. Why are they in a hurry at the end of the conversation? They are late for class.
5. What is Jérôme worried about? He forgot his shoes for P.E.

2 Vrai ou faux?

1. Ann est américaine. vrai
2. Jérôme n'aime pas l'espagnol. faux
3. Ann et Marc n'aiment pas les maths. faux
4. Jérôme a allemand. vrai
5. Marc n'a pas sport cet aprèm. faux

3 Cherche les expressions

See answers below.

In ***La rentrée,*** what do the students say to . . .

1. ask what class someone has?
2. tell why they like a class?
3. tell why they don't like a class?
4. tell which class they prefer?
5. ask what time it is?

C'est difficile. | C'est nul. | Il est quelle heure? | C'est super intéressant. | J'aime encore mieux... | C'est plus cool. | Tu as quel cours? | Tu as quoi? | Le prof est sympa. | J'aime mieux... | C'est passionnant.

4 Ils aiment ou pas?

Do these students like or dislike the subjects or teachers they're talking about?

1. «Les sciences nat, c'est passionnant.» like
2. «Les maths, c'est nul.» dislike
3. «C'est super intéressant, les maths.» like
4. «Le prof est sympa.» like

5 Qu'est-ce qui manque?

Choose the correct words from the box to complete these sentences based on ***La rentrée.***

1. Après maths, Marc a _____. géographie
2. Jérôme a _____. allemand
3. Jérôme aime mieux _____ que l'allemand. l'espagnol
4. On a tous sport à _____ heures. quatorze
5. On est en retard! Il est _____ heures. huit

géographie | allemand | quatorze | huit | l'espagnol

6 Et maintenant, à toi

Which students in ***La rentrée*** share your own likes or dislikes about school subjects?

Comprehension Check

Building on Previous Skills

4 Have students answer each item in French, either orally or in writing, using the expressions they learned in Chapter 1 to express likes and dislikes. **(Il/Elle aime les maths. Il/Elle n'aime pas les sciences nat.)** Then, have them give their own opinions of each subject.

Challenge

Ask students to find a synonym in the **Mise en train** for the greeting **Ça va? (Ça boume?)** Have them try to guess the meaning of Jérôme's statement **Si, tu as raison.**

Answers

3
1. Tu as quoi? Tu as quels cours?
2. C'est passionnant. Le prof est sympa. C'est super intéressant. C'est plus cool.
3. C'est difficile. C'est nul.
4. J'aime mieux... ; J'aime encore mieux...
5. Il est quelle heure?

Objective Agreeing and disagreeing

WA3 POITIERS-2

Vocabulaire

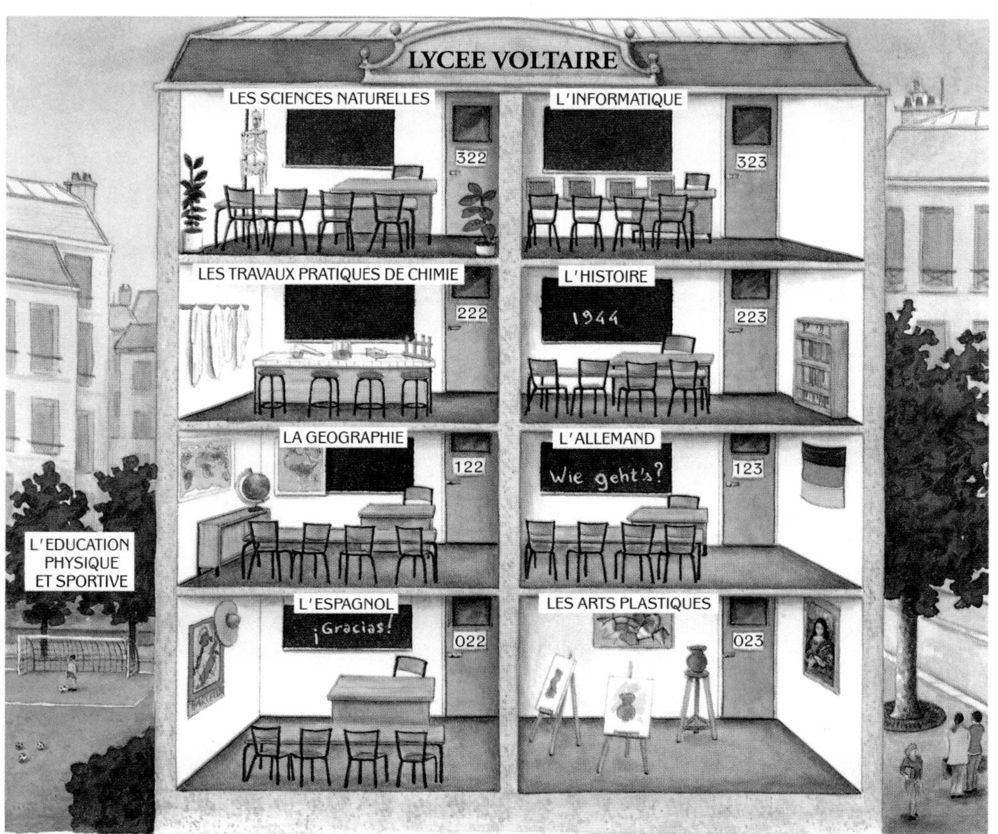

l'algèbre (f.) *algebra*
la biologie *biology*
la chimie *chemistry*
la géométrie *geometry*
la physique *physics*
la chorale *choir*
le cours de développement personnel et social (DPS) *health*
la danse *dance*
le latin *Latin*
la musique *music*
le cours *course, school subject*
les devoirs (m.) *homework*
l'élève (m./f.) *student*
le professeur *teacher*

*You can abbreviate **Education Physique et Sportive** as **EPS.** In conversation, students often say **le sport** instead of **EPS.**

Cahier d'activités, pp. 14–16, Act. 2–5, 7

Travaux pratiques de grammaire, pp. 10–11, Act. 1–4

Communication for All Students

Building on Previous Skills

Re-enter **l'anglais, les maths,** and **le français** from Chapter 1 by asking students how they feel about each of these classes. **(Tu aimes mieux l'anglais ou les maths?)**

Teacher Note

You might want to tell students that **sciences naturelles** is sometimes referred to as **biologie-géologie** or **sciences de la vie et de la terre (SVT).** This area of study includes both lectures and a lab.

Teaching Resources
pp. 51–54

PRINT

- Lesson Planner, p. 9
- TPR Storytelling Book, pp. 5, 8
- Listening Activities, pp. 11, 15
- Activities for Communication, pp. 7–8, 80, 83, 139–140
- Travaux pratiques de grammaire, pp. 10–11
- Grammar Tutor for Students of French, Chapter 2
- Cahier d'activités, pp. 14–16
- Testing Program, pp. 27–30
- Alternative Assessment Guide, p. 33
- Student Make-Up Assignments, Chapter 2

MEDIA

- One-Stop Planner
- Audio Compact Discs, CD 2, Trs. 3–4, 19, 25–26
- Teaching Transparencies: 2-1, 2-A; **Grammaire supplémentaire** Answers; Travaux pratiques de grammaire Answers
- Interactive CD-ROM Tutor, Disc 1

Bell Work

Have students write sentences telling three things they like to do and three things they don't like to do.

Presenting Vocabulaire

Begin by asking **Qui aime la biologie?** Continue asking about other subjects. Write the following categories on the board **les sciences, les langues, l'éducation civique** *(government),* **les maths, les cours facultatifs** *(electives),* and **les cours obligatoires** *(required courses).* Then, give the name of a subject and ask **Quelle catégorie?** Write the subject under the proper category.

STANDARDS: 1.1, 1.3

Teaching Resources
pp. 51–54

PRINT

- Lesson Planner, p. 9
- TPR Storytelling Book, pp. 5, 8
- Listening Activities, pp. 11, 15
- Activities for Communication, pp. 7–8, 80, 83, 139–140
- Travaux pratiques de grammaire, pp. 10–11
- Grammar Tutor for Students of French, Chapter 2
- Cahier d'activités, pp. 14–16
- Testing Program, pp. 27–30
- Alternative Assessment Guide, p. 33
- Student Make-Up Assignments, Chapter 2

MEDIA  

- One-Stop Planner
- Audio Compact Discs, CD 2, Trs. 3–4, 19, 25–26
- Teaching Transparencies: 2-1, 2-A; **Grammaire supplémentaire** Answers; Travaux pratiques de grammaire Answers
- Interactive CD-ROM Tutor, Disc 1

Slower Pace

7 Before students hear the recording, have them locate and give the numbers of each classroom.

Additional Practice

8 Students might pair off and ask each other questions based on the pictures: **Qui aime le français?**

Slower Pace

8 Before doing this activity, ask students to imagine what they think the interests of the two students might be.

7 C'est où? See scripts and answers on p. 45G.

CD 2 Tr. 3

Ecoutons On the first day of school, Céline and Aurélie are looking for their French class. As you listen to their conversation, look at the drawing of the school on page 51 and write the numbers of the classrooms they're looking into.

8 Ils aiment quels cours?

Parlons Name three subjects Nicole and Gérard probably like, according to their interests.

Nicole

l'algèbre, la chimie, les mathématiques

Gérard

la géographie, l'histoire, le français

9 C'est qui?

Parlons Tell your partner what subject one of these students likes, without naming the person. Your partner will try to guess the person's name. Take turns until you've identified all of the students.

EXEMPLE — **Il aime le français.**
— **C'est Michel.**

Michel

Julien

Il aime le sport.

Nathalie

Elle aime la chorale.

Virginie

Elle aime la danse.

Guillaume

Il aime la géographie.

Franck

Il aime l'anglais.

Karine

Elle aime la chimie.

Communication for All Students

Challenge

8 You might have students draw their own pictures illustrating their interests. Then, have partners exchange papers and tell what subjects their classmate likes.

Kinesthetic/Visual Learners

9 Give various items (a compass, a Spanish dictionary) to different students. Have students use facial expressions to indicate whether they like or dislike the subject associated with the item. Have the class tell what each student likes and dislikes. **(Joël aime les maths. Jennifer n'aime pas l'espagnol.)**

Study at regular intervals. It's best to learn language in small chunks and to review frequently. Cramming will not usually work for French. Study at least a little bit every day, whether you have an assignment or not. The more often you review words and structures, the easier it will be for you to understand and participate in class.

Note culturelle

In France and other countries that follow the French educational system, the grade levels are numbered in descending order. When students begin junior high **(le collège)** at about 10 or 11 years of age, they enter the grade called **sixième.** Then they go into **cinquième, quatrième,** and **troisième.** The grade levels at the high school **(le lycée)** are called **seconde, première,** and **terminale.**

Le baccalauréat, or **le bac,** is a national exam taken at the end of study at a **lycée.** Not all students take the **bac,** but those who plan to go on to a university must pass it. It's an extremely difficult oral and written test that covers all major subjects. Students spend the final year of the **lycée, la terminale,** preparing for this exam. There are three major categories of **baccalauréat** exams: **le bac général, le bac technologique,** and **le bac professionnel.** Each category is divided into a more specialized series of exams, depending upon a student's chosen field of study. For example, a student specializing in literature would take the **bac général littéraire,** or simply **le bac L.**

Baccalauréat : Les hauts et les bas

Taux de réussite par série (en %).

Examen et série	Total
Bac Général	
Littéraire (L)	76,5
Economique et social (ES)	76
Sciences (S)	76,3
Bac Technologique	
Sciences et technologies industrielles (STI)	73,4
Sciences et technologies de laboratoire (STL)	79,7
Sciences médico-sociales (SMS)	81
Sciences et technologies tertiaires (STT)	80,6
Bac Professionnel	
Industriel	74,3
Tertiaire	81
Hôtellerie	79,5

Cahier d'activités, p. 24, Act. 25

10 Mon journal

Ecrivons Make a list of your favorite school subjects in your journal. If you were taking these subjects in France, which **bac** do you think you would take?

EXEMPLE **Je passerais le bac...**

Connections and Comparisons

Thinking Critically

Comparing and Contrasting Have students compare passing the **baccalauréat** with graduating from high school in the United States. How does the Scholastic Assessment Test (SAT) or the American College Test (ACT) compare with the **baccalauréat?**

Language-to-Language

Tell students that **passer** can be a false cognate. **Passer un examen** means *to take an exam.* To say *I passed the bac,* you would say **J'ai réussi au bac.**

Culture Notes

- There are many types of **baccalauréat** exams in France. Each one tests students on a number of subjects that are weighted differently according to the student's major. For example, a student who is majoring in literature needs to score higher in literature, philosophy, and languages than in math in order to pass. Students who don't score high enough must try to get a better grade by taking oral exams. If students fail, they must repeat their last year at the **lycée (terminale)** before retaking the **baccalauréat.** Students who don't have their **baccalauréat** need to pass a college entrance exam called **l'ESEU (Examen spécial d'entrée à l'université)** in order to be admitted to college.
- Children may enter **l'école maternelle** as early as two years of age. These schools are subsidized by the government and are strictly monitored. Some families have in-home child care, which is also licensed and monitored by the government.

Additional Practice

10 Have students work in pairs and write sentences in their journals about the subjects their partner likes. **(Les cours préférés de... sont...)**

Mon journal

10 You might ask students to write about their most difficult subjects and their favorite ones. Give them these sentence starters: **Pour moi, les cours les plus difficiles sont...** and **Mes cours préférés sont...** For an additional journal entry suggestion for Chapter 2, see *Cahier d'activités,* page 146.

STANDARDS: 1.3, 2.1, 2.2, 3.1, 3.2, 4.2

Première étape

CHAPITRE 2

Presenting Comment dit-on... ?

Read the text of the illustrations to students, using appropriate intonation and facial gestures. Ask them to guess whether each character likes or dislikes the subjects. Have students tell you what subjects they like. Agree with some and disagree with others. Then, tell them what you like and elicit their responses. You might have students form groups of three and role-play the mini-dialogues in the illustrations, changing the names of the subjects to reflect their own feelings.

Speaking Assessment

13 You may wish to use the following rubric to assess their performance.

Speaking Rubric	Points			
	4	3	2	1
Content (Complete–Incomplete)				
Comprehension (Total–Little)				
Comprehensibility (Comprehensible–Incomprehensible)				
Accuracy (Accurate–Seldom accurate)				
Fluency (Fluent–Not fluent)				

18–20: A 14–15: C Under
16–17: B 12–13: D 12: F

Assess

- Testing Program, pp. 27–30 Quiz 2-1A, Quiz 2-1B Audio CD 2, Tr. 19
- Student Make-Up Assignments, Chapter 2, Alternative Quiz
- Alternative Assessment Guide, p. 33

Comment dit-on...?

Agreeing and disagreeing

To agree:

Oui, beaucoup. *Yes, very much.*
Moi aussi. *Me too.*
Moi non plus. *Neither do I.*

To disagree:

Moi, non. *I don't.*
Non, pas trop. *No, not too much.*
Moi, si. *I do.*
Pas moi. *Not me.*

Cahier d'activités, p. 15, Act. 6

Note de grammaire

Use **si** instead of **oui** to contradict a negative statement or question.
— Tu **n'**aimes **pas** la biologie?
— Mais **si!** J'adore la bio!

Grammaire supplémentaire, p. 66, Act. 1–2

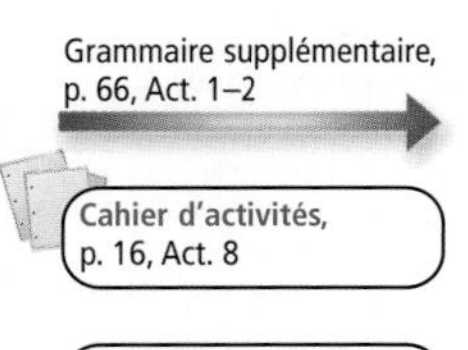

Cahier d'activités, p. 16, Act. 8

Travaux pratiques de grammaire, p. 11, Act. 5

11 Grammaire en contexte

See scripts and answers on p. 45G.

CD 2 Tr. 4

Ecoutons Listen as Hélène and Gérard talk about the subjects they like and dislike. Which one do they agree on? Which one do they disagree on?

12 Grammaire en contexte

Parlons Ask your partner's opinion about several subjects and then agree or disagree. Take turns.

Exemple — **Tu aimes les arts plastiques?**
— **Non, pas trop.**
— **Moi, si.**

13 Ça te plaît?

Parlons Get together with two classmates. Find at least two things or activities that you all like. Then, tell the rest of the class what you agree on.

Exemple Eleve 1 — **J'aime les hamburgers. Et toi?**
Eleve 2 — **Oui, beaucoup.**
Eleve 3 — **Moi aussi.**
Eleve 1 — **Nous aimons tous les hamburgers.**

le cinéma
le foot
les concerts
la pizza
faire du sport
écouter de la musique
faire les magasins
la glace
le ski

Communication for All Students

Slower Pace

11 Distribute a list of school subjects. Have students listen to the dialogue and circle the subjects they hear mentioned. After you give the correct subjects, tell students to listen again to decide whether Hélène and Gérard like or dislike these courses.

Challenge

13 Ask the group reporter to differentiate among the students when giving the final report: **Pierre et moi, nous aimons la glace, mais Marie n'aime pas ça. Elle aime mieux la pizza.**

STANDARDS: 1.1, 1.2, 1.3, 5.1, 5.2

Deuxième étape

Objectives Asking for and giving information; telling when you have class

WA3 POITIERS-2

Comment dit-on...?

Asking for and giving information

To ask about someone's classes:

Tu as quels cours aujourd'hui?
What classes do you have . . . ?
Tu as quoi le matin?
What do you have . . . ?
Vous avez espagnol l'après-midi?
Do you have . . . ?

To tell what classes you have:

J'ai arts plastiques et physique.
I have . . .
J'ai algèbre, DPS et sport.

Oui, et **nous avons** aussi géo.
. . . we have . . .

Vocabulaire

le matin	*in the morning*
l'après-midi (m.)	*in the afternoon*
aujourd'hui	*today*
demain	*tomorrow*
maintenant	*now*

Travaux pratiques de grammaire, p. 12, Act. 6

14 On a quoi?

a. **Parlons** Find out what subjects your partner has in the morning and in the afternoon.

EXEMPLE — **Tu as quoi le matin (l'après-midi)?**
— **Bio, algèbre et chorale. Et toi?**
— **Moi, j'ai algèbre, chimie, chorale et DPS.**

b. **Parlons** Now, tell the rest of the class which subjects you and your partner have in common.

EXEMPLE **Marc et moi, nous avons algèbre et chorale.**

Grammaire

The verb *avoir*

Avoir is an irregular verb. That means it doesn't follow the pattern of the **-er** verbs you learned in Chapter 1.

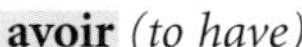

avoir *(to have)*

J'	**ai**	Nous	**avons**
Tu	**as**	Vous	**avez**
Il/Elle/On	**a**	Ils/Elles	**ont**

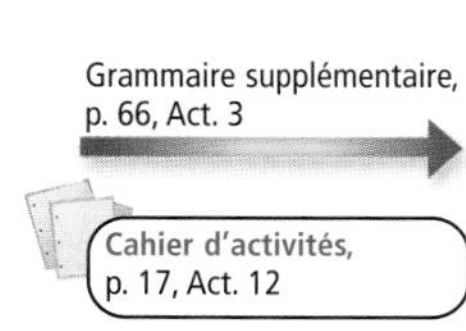

Grammaire supplémentaire, p. 66, Act. 3

Cahier d'activités, p. 17, Act. 12

Travaux pratiques de grammaire, pp. 12–13, Act. 7–9

As you saw in Chapter 1, you often use an article (**le, la, l',** or **les**) before a noun. When you're telling which school subjects you have, however, you don't use an article.

Elle a chimie maintenant.
Vous avez quoi le matin?

Teacher to Teacher

Van W. Ruckman
North High School
Evansville, IN

Van uses this activity in his classroom to practice the verb *avoir*.

"I made sets of matching memory cards of objects representing different school subjects (a computer for **informatique**, test tubes for **chimie**, a Spanish-English dictionary for **espagnol**, and so on). I distribute the cards and have my students play **Va à la pêche.** The students circulate and ask each other, for example: **"Tu as chimie?"** I stress that students must answer with a full sentence: **"Oui, j'ai chimie."** or **"Non, va à la pêche!"** Students continue asking the questions until they find a match for their card. Students have fun using **avoir** and it's a great review of the vocabulary from the previous **étape.**"

Deuxième étape

CHAPITRE 2

Teaching Resources pp. 55–59

PRINT

- Lesson Planner, p. 10
- TPR Storytelling Book, pp. 6, 8
- Listening Activities, pp. 12, 16
- Activities for Communication, pp. 9–10, 81, 83–84, 139–140
- Travaux pratiques de grammaire, pp. 12–15
- Grammar Tutor for Students of French, Chapter 2
- Cahier d'activités, pp. 17–19
- Testing Program, pp. 31–34
- Alternative Assessment Guide, p. 33
- Student Make-Up Assignments, Chapter 2

MEDIA

- One-Stop Planner
- Audio Compact Discs, CD 2, Trs. 5–6, 20, 27–28
- Teaching Transparencies: 2-2, 2-B; **Grammaire supplémentaire** Answers; Travaux pratiques de grammaire Answers
- Interactive CD-ROM Tutor, Disc 1

Bell Work

Write on the board **Tu aimes l'algèbre?** and **J'aime l'anglais.** Have students answer the question and respond to the statement, agreeing or disagreeing with each one.

Presenting Comment dit-on... ?, Vocabulaire

Teach **le matin, l'après-midi,** and **aujourd'hui** by using a clock or calendar.

Grammaire

Write the paradigm of **avoir** on the board or on a transparency. Then, erase the forms at random and have students say them aloud from memory.

STANDARDS: 1.1

Deuxième étape

CHAPITRE 2

Teaching Resources
pp. 55–59

PRINT

- Lesson Planner, p. 10
- TPR Storytelling Book, pp. 6, 8
- Listening Activities, pp. 12, 16
- Activities for Communication, pp. 9–10, 81, 83–84, 139–140
- Travaux pratiques de grammaire, pp. 12–15
- Grammar Tutor for Students of French, Chapter 2
- Cahier d'activités, pp. 17–19
- Testing Program, pp. 31–34
- Alternative Assessment Guide, p. 33
- Student Make-Up Assignments, Chapter 2

MEDIA

- One-Stop Planner
- Audio Compact Discs, CD 2, Trs. 5–6, 20, 27–28
- Teaching Transparencies: 2-2, 2-B; **Grammaire supplémentaire** Answers; Travaux pratiques de grammaire Answers
- Interactive CD-ROM Tutor, Disc 1

Presenting Vocabulaire

Start by presenting the days of the week. Ask students **Quel jour est-ce aujourd'hui?** Next, call out a certain day and time **(le mardi matin, à 10h15)** and have students call out the class that Stéphanie has then. You might also say the name of a subject and have students tell the day(s) that Stéphanie has that subject. Practice the days of the week by naming one and having students name the following day or the preceding day. To elicit quick responses, you might point forward for the following day and backwards for the preceding day.

15 Grammaire en contexte

Parlons Some students are day-dreaming about the future. What classes are they taking to prepare for these careers?

EXEMPLE **Ils ont géométrie, physique et géographie.**

Possible answers:

1. Elle a chimie et biologie.

2. Il a histoire et géographie.

3. Ils ont informatique et espagnol.

4. Il a danse et musique.

Vocabulaire

Voilà l'emploi du temps de Stéphanie Lambert.

EMPLOI DU TEMPS — **NOM:** Stéphanie Lambert — **CLASSE:** 3e

		LUNDI	MARDI	MERCREDI	JEUDI	VENDREDI	SAMEDI	DIMANCHE
MATIN	**8h00**	Allemand	Arts plastiques	Mathématiques	Mathématiques	Français		
	9h00	Français	Arts plastiques	Anglais	Sciences nat	Français	Anglais	L
	10h00	**Récréation**	**Récréation**	**Récréation**	**Récréation**	**Récréation**	TP physique	
	10h15	EPS	Allemand	Français	EPS	Sciences nat	TP physique	I
	11h15	Sciences nat	**Etude**	Histoire/Géo	**Etude**	Arts plastiques	**[Sortie]**	
	12h15	**Déjeuner**	**Déjeuner**	**[Sortie]**	**Déjeuner**	**Déjeuner**	**APRES-MIDI**	B
APRES-MIDI	**14h00**	Histoire/Géo	Mathématiques	**APRES-MIDI**	Histoire/Géo	Allemand	**LIBRE**	
	15h00	Anglais	Physique/Chimie	**LIBRE**	Physique/Chimie	Mathématiques		R
	16h00	**Récréation**	**[Sortie]**		**Récréation**	**[Sortie]**		
	16h15	Mathématiques			Arts plastiques			E
	17h15	**[Sortie]**			**[Sortie]**			

Cahier d'activités, pp. 18–19, Act. 14–15

Travaux pratiques de grammaire, pp. 13–14, Act. 10–12

Grammaire supplémentaire, p. 67, Act. 4

Communication for All Students

Teacher Note

15 Professions will be presented later, but students might want to know the names of the professions pictured here: **le/la pilote, le/la vétérinaire, l'archéologue, la femme (l'homme) d'affaires, le danseur (la danseuse), le chanteur (la chanteuse).**

Group Work

15 Students might do this activity in groups, with each person naming a subject suggested by each illustration. Each student might then name another profession, in English or French, and ask group members to name appropriate subjects. You might want to give students the French names for other professions.

16 Tu comprends?

Lisons/Parlons Answer the following questions about Stéphanie Lambert's schedule on page 56.

1. Can you find and copy the words in the schedule that refer to days of the week? lundi, mardi, mercredi, jeudi, vendredi, samedi, dimanche
2. **Déjeuner** and **Récréation** don't refer to school subjects. What do you think they mean? lunch and break
3. What do you think **14h00** means? 2:00 P.M.
4. If **étudier** means *to study,* what do you think **Etude** means? study hall
5. You know that **sortir** means *to go out.* What do you think **Sortie** means? school is out (literally: exit)
6. Can you list two differences between Stéphanie's schedule and yours? She goes to school on Saturdays and gets out early on Wednesdays.

17 L'emploi du temps de Stéphanie

Lisons/Ecrivons Stéphanie is telling a friend about her schedule. Complete her statements according to her schedule on page 56.

Le __1__ matin, j'ai allemand, français, EPS et sciences nat. Je n'aime pas trop les sciences. J'ai histoire-géo le __2__, le __3__ et le __4__. J'adore l'histoire! Et le mercredi __5__, je n'ai pas cours. Normalement, j'ai __6__ à 10h00, mais le __7__, j'ai travaux pratiques de physique à 10h00. Je n'ai pas cours le __8__.

1. lundi 2. lundi 3. mercredi 4. jeudi 5. après-midi 6. récréation 7. samedi 8. dimanche

18 Elles ont quels cours? See scripts and answers on p. 45G.

CD 2, Tr. 5

Ecoutons Look at Stéphanie's schedule as you listen to three of her friends call her on the phone. They're going to tell her what subjects they have on a certain day of the week. Do they have the same subjects as Stéphanie on that day?

Vocabulaire

You've already learned the numbers 0–20. Here are the numbers 21–59 in French.

21	22	23	24	25
vingt et un(e)	vingt-deux	vingt-trois	vingt-quatre	vingt-cinq
26	27	28	29	30
vingt-six	vingt-sept	vingt-huit	vingt-neuf	trente
31	32	40	41	42
trente et un(e)	trente-deux	quarante	quarante et un(e)	quarante-deux
50	51	52	59	
cinquante	cinquante et un(e)	cinquante-deux	cinquante-neuf	

Cahier d'activités, p. 17, Act. 11

Travaux pratiques de grammaire, pp. 14–15, Act. 13–14

Connections and Comparisons

Math Link

Divide the class into two or more teams. Ask each student to write an addition or subtraction problem on a piece of paper, making sure that the numbers used in the problem and the answer are not more than 59. Collect the papers and ask a contestant from each team to go to the board. For the first round, read aloud one of the problems. The first contestant to write the correct answer in numerals wins a point for his or her team. For the second round, contestants must write out the numbers in words in order to win a point. You will need to teach the words **plus/et** *(plus),* **moins** *(minus),* and **font** *(equals).* **(Deux et deux font quatre. Quatre moins deux font deux.)**

Culture Note

In France and many other countries, the first day of the week is Monday, not Sunday, as it is in the United States.

Additional Practice

16 Ask how many times a week Stéphanie has various classes, how many different classes she has, and what **TP de physique** means **(travaux pratiques de physique,** *physics lab).*

Slower Pace

18 Have students form small groups. Play the recording, stopping it after each speaker. Have students in each group write down the subjects each speaker has that day.

Additional Practice

18 After students have done this activity, you might want to give a typed copy of the script for the first, second, or third speaker to small groups of students. Then, have them write sentences using **aussi** and the connectors **et** and **mais** to compare and contrast the speaker's schedule with Stéphanie's.

Presenting Vocabulaire

Review the numbers 1–20. Then, before students open their books, start with the number **vingt** and have students count after you from 20–29. Point out that 21 is different from 22 through 29. Teach the word **trente** and ask students to count from 31–39 based on what they have just learned about the 20s. Repeat this process with **quarante** and **cinquante**.

STANDARDS: 1.2, 3.1, 3.2, 4.2

Teaching Resources
pp. 55–59

PRINT
- Lesson Planner, p. 10
- TPR Storytelling Book, pp. 6, 8
- Listening Activities, pp. 12, 16
- Activities for Communication, pp. 9–10, 81, 83–84, 139–140
- Travaux pratiques de grammaire, pp. 12–15
- Grammar Tutor for Students of French, Chapter 2
- Cahier d'activités, pp. 17–19
- Testing Program, pp. 31–34
- Alternative Assessment Guide, p. 33
- Student Make-Up Assignments, Chapter 2

MEDIA 

- One-Stop Planner
- Audio Compact Discs, CD 2, Trs. 5–6, 20, 27–28
- Teaching Transparencies: 2-2, 2-B; **Grammaire supplémentaire** Answers; Travaux pratiques de grammaire Answers
- Interactive CD-ROM Tutor, Disc 1

Presenting
Comment dit-on... ?

Use a clock to teach official time. Explain that if you add 12 to every hour after noon, you will have the correct 24-hour time. (1 + 12 = 13) Then, say a time and have students give the official time in French. This could be a game played with teams of 3–4. Have each team make a clock. When you call out a time, each team holds up its clock to show the time. A point is awarded for the correct time. Then, write other times on the board or on a transparency. Ask students to state the times in French, according to the 24-hour system.

19 Tu connais les nombres?

1. **Parlons** Say these numbers in French.
   a. 25 **b.** 37 **c.** 46 **d.** 53

   1. a. vingt-cinq b. trente-sept c. quarante-six d. cinquante-trois

2. **Ecrivons** Write the numerals for these numbers.
   a. vingt-huit (28) **b.** trente-quatre (34) **c.** quarante et un (41) **d.** cinquante-cinq (55)

Comment dit-on...?

Telling when you have class

CD-ROM 1 DVD 1

To find out at what time someone has a certain class:
Tu as maths **à quelle heure?**

To tell at what time you have a certain class:
J'ai maths **à neuf heures.**

huit heures

dix heures quinze

sept heures vingt

quinze heures trente

seize heures quarante-cinq

Cahier d'activités, p. 18, Act. 13

Travaux pratiques de grammaire, p. 15, Act. 15–17

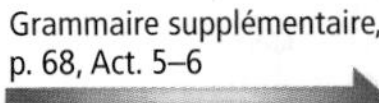
Grammaire supplémentaire, p. 68, Act. 5–6

20 A quelle heure? See scripts and answers on p. 45G.

CD 2 Tr. 6

Ecoutons Listen as Jérôme answers Anne's questions about his schedule. At what time does he have these classes: **anglais, espagnol, histoire,** and **maths?**

Note culturelle

Although in familiar conversation people may use the 12-hour system to give the time, they use the 24-hour system **(l'heure officielle)** to give schedules for transportation, schools, stores, and movies. For example, the school day generally begins at 8h00 **(huit heures)** and continues until 17h00 **(dix-sept heures)** or 18h00 **(dix-huit heures)** with a break from 12h00 **(douze heures)** to 14h00 **(quatorze heures).** You will learn about the 12-hour system in Chapter 6.

A la française

In casual conversation, you might try using the abbreviated forms of words just as French teenagers do. For example, **la récréation** can be abbreviated to **la récré.** Do you recall the abbreviated forms of the words listed to the right? If not, look for them in ***La rentrée*** or in Stéphanie's schedule.

les sciences naturelles
la géographie
l'éducation physique et sportive
l'après-midi
les mathématiques
le professeur

Communication for All Students

Additional Practice

Have students write six-digit locker combinations grouped in three double digits (not greater than 59) on small pieces of paper. Then, ask them to work in pairs, with one partner reading aloud the numbers in double digits, and the other writing them down.

Kinesthetic Learners

Have each student make a clock face with movable hands, using a paper plate and brads or pipe cleaners. Have students pair off. One student mimes a daily action, such as brushing one's teeth. The partner tells at what time that action might normally take place and shows the time on his or her clock.

21 Une journée chargée See answers below.

Parlons Claudine is busy today. What does she have at each of the times listed?

EXEMPLE **A huit heures, elle a géographie.**

8h00

1. 9h35

2. 11h50

3. 14h05

4. 16h20

22 Nos emplois du temps

a. **Ecrivons/Parlons** You and your partner prepare blank schedules showing only the times classes meet at your school. Take turns asking at what time you each have the classes listed here. Fill in each other's schedule, writing the subjects next to the appropriate times.

EXEMPLE **— Tu as histoire à quelle heure?**
— A onze heures trente.

b. **Parlons/Ecrivons** Now complete the schedules by asking what subjects you each have at the remaining times.

EXEMPLE **— Tu as quoi à treize heures?**

français histoire sport
maths sciences anglais

23 Mon journal 

Ecrivons Make a list of your classes in your journal. Include the days and times they meet and the names of your teachers.

Communication for All Students

Challenge

21 You might have students add what they are doing at the times shown in the pictures, according to their own schedules. Have pairs of students describe their schedules to each other, including days and times. You might also play the variation of **Loto** as described on page 45C.

Additional Practice

21 Have students imagine the rest of Claudine's day. What does she do after school? Students must choose at least three activities and tell at what time she does them. You might want to refer your students to the list of expressions on page 31.

Deuxième étape

CHAPITRE 2

Language Note

Point out that **heure** is used in both the question and the answer, but that the spelling is plural after all numbers beyond one. The question is always in the singular, however. **(Il est quelle heure?)**

Block Scheduling

22 Students on block schedules may want to know the following terms when they talk about their schedules: **tous les deux jours** *(every other day)* and **deux/trois fois par semaine** *(two/three times a week).*

Portfolio

22 **Oral** Students might want to include this conversation in their oral portfolios. For portfolio suggestions, see *Alternative Assessment Guide,* page 19.

Mon journal

23 For an additional journal entry suggestion for Chapter 2, see *Cahier d' activités,* page 146.

Assess

- Testing Program, pp. 31–34 Quiz 2-2A, Quiz 2-2B Audio CD 2, Tr. 20
- Student Make-Up Assignments, Chapter 2, Alternative Quiz
- Alternative Assessment Guide, p. 33

Answers

21
1. A neuf heures trente-cinq, elle a maths.
2. A onze heures cinquante, elle a récréation.
3. A quatorze heures cinq, elle a espagnol.
4. A seize heures vingt, elle a biologie/sciences naturelles.

CHAPITRE 2

Teaching Resources
p. 60

PRINT 
- Video Guide, pp. 13, 14–15
- Cahier d'activités, p. 24

MEDIA
- One-Stop Planner
- Video Program
  Videocassette 1, 27:12–30:54
- DVD Tutor, Disc 1
- Audio Compact Discs, CD 2, Trs. 7–10
- Interactive CD-ROM Tutor, Disc 1

Presenting
Panorama Culturel

Ask students what courses they are required to take and what courses they think French-speaking students might be required to take. Play the video, and then ask if there were any unfamiliar courses mentioned. You might use the **Questions** below to check comprehension.

Questions

1. **Qu'est-ce qu'Amadou a comme cours?** (français, anglais, sciences physiques, sciences naturelles, éducation civique et morale, géographie, physique)
2. **Qu'est-ce que Yannick étudie comme matière principale?** (économie)
3. **Quelles langues est-ce que Yannick étudie?** (anglais, portugais, français)
4. **A quelle heure est-ce que Yannick a l'interclasse?** (de midi à deux heures)

Tu as quels cours?

What is your school day like? At what time does it start and end? What classes do you have? Here's what some francophone students had to say about their school day.

Amadou,
Burkina Faso

«A l'école, j'ai comme cours français, anglais, sciences physiques, sciences naturelles, éducation civique et morale, les épreuves physiques.» Tr. 8

Yannick,
Martinique

«Comme je suis en première S, j'ai de l'économie. Je fais de l'anglais, du portugais, du français, de l'éducation physique, de l'histoire, de la géographie et des maths.»

Tu peux décrire ton emploi du temps?

«Je commence à huit heures. Je termine à midi. J'ai l'interclasse de midi à deux heures et [j'ai cours] de deux heures à dix-sept heures.» Tr. 9

Patrice,
Québec

«Comme cours, j'ai le français, l'anglais, les maths. J'ai aussi éducation physique. J'ai l'art plastique, l'informatique... beaucoup de matières comme ça.» Tr. 10

Qu'en penses-tu?

1. What classes do you have in common with these students?
2. What subjects were mentioned that aren't taught at your school?
3. Would you like to trade schedules with any of these students? Why or why not?

Savais-tu que...?

Students in francophone countries commonly have Wednesday afternoons free and attend classes on Saturday mornings. In general, they follow the same core curriculum, which includes French, math, science, history, geography, physical education, and at least one foreign language. Courses like industrial arts and band are not often taught.

Connections and Comparisons

Thinking Critically

Analyzing Have students compare the subjects they are taking with those the interviewees are taking and make lists of the ones they don't have in common. Have them give advantages and disadvantages of the courses that the interviewees are taking, such as Portuguese or geography, as well as those of American courses, such as band and home economics.

Thinking Critically

Synthesizing Have students research the educational systems in francophone countries, such as Canada and Côte d'Ivoire, and make a list of the best aspects of each system. Using their notes, they should create the ideal school system.

STANDARDS: 2.1, 3.2, 4.2

Objective Asking for and expressing opinions

WA3 POITIERS-2

Comment dit-on...?

Asking for and expressing opinions

To ask someone's opinion:
Comment tu trouves ça?
Comment tu trouves le cours de biologie?

To express a favorable opinion:

C'est... *It's . . .*
facile. *easy.*
génial. *great.*
super. *super.*
cool. *cool.*
intéressant. *interesting.*
passionnant. *fascinating.*

To express indifference:

C'est pas mal. *It's not bad.*
Ça va. *It's OK.*

To express an unfavorable opinion:

C'est... *It's . . .*
difficile. *hard.*
pas terrible. *not so great.*
pas super. *not so hot.*
zéro. *a waste of time.*
nul. *useless.*
barbant. *boring.*

Cahier d'activités, pp. 20–21, Act. 17–19

Travaux pratiques de grammaire, p. 16, Act. 18–20

Grammaire supplémentaire, p. 69, Act. 8–9

A la française

In informal conversation, French speakers will often leave out the **ne** in a negative sentence.

J'aime pas les hamburgers, moi.
C'est pas super, la géo.

In writing, you should include the **ne** in negative sentences.

Grammaire supplémentaire, p. 69, Act. 7

24 Quel cours aiment-ils? See scripts and answers on p. 45H.

CD 2 Tr. 11

Ecoutons Listen as Aurélie and Eric talk about their subjects. Which ones does Eric like? Which doesn't he like? And Aurélie?

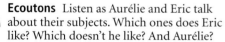

les sciences nat
la géo
l'anglais
l'allemand
l'histoire
les maths
l'espagnol

Note culturelle

The French system of grading is based on a scale of 0–20. A score of less than 10 isn't a passing grade. Students are usually pleased with a score of 10 or higher. They must work very hard to receive a 17 or an 18, and it's very rare to earn a 19 or a 20.

Communication for All Students

Auditory Learners

Call out the words **cinéma, télévision, concert,** and **école** and have students react to each word with an appropriate French expression of opinion.

Slower Pace

24 Distribute a list of the subjects mentioned in the script. Tell students to listen for the subjects the speakers don't like and circle them. Play the recording again. This time, students are to identify the speakers who don't like the subjects they have circled and write the speakers' names next to the subjects.

Troisième étape

Teaching Resources pp. 61–63

PRINT

- Lesson Planner, p. 11
- TPR Storytelling Book, pp. 7, 8
- Listening Activities, pp. 13, 17
- Activities for Communication, pp. 11–12, 82, 84, 139–140
- Travaux pratiques de grammaire, p. 16
- Grammar Tutor for Students of French, Chapter 2
- Cahier d'activités, pp. 20–22
- Testing Program, pp. 35–38
- Alternative Assessment Guide, p. 33
- Student Make-Up Assignments, Chapter 2

MEDIA

- One-Stop Planner
- Audio Compact Discs, CD 2, Trs. 11, 21, 29–30
- Teaching Transparencies: 2-3; **Grammaire supplémentaire** Answers; Travaux pratiques de grammaire Answers
- Interactive CD-ROM Tutor, Disc 1

Bell Work

Ask students to write down their daily class schedules, showing official times and the subjects in French.

Presenting Comment dit-on... ?

Use appropriate facial expressions and gestures as you present the new vocabulary. Have students repeat the words after you. Then, make the facial expressions and gestures and have students try to recall the appropriate words.

STANDARDS: 2.1, 3.2, 4.2

Troisième étape

CHAPITRE 2

Teaching Resources
pp. 61–63

PRINT

- Lesson Planner, p. 11
- TPR Storytelling Book, pp. 7, 8
- Listening Activities, pp. 13, 17
- Activities for Communication, pp. 11–12, 82, 84, 139–140
- Travaux pratiques de grammaire, p. 16
- Grammar Tutor for Students of French, Chapter 2
- Cahier d'activités, pp. 20–22
- Testing Program, pp. 35–38
- Alternative Assessment Guide, p. 33
- Student Make-Up Assignments, Chapter 2

MEDIA 

- One-Stop Planner
- Audio Compact Discs, CD 2, Trs. 11, 21, 29–30
- Teaching Transparencies: 2-3; **Grammaire supplémentaire** Answers; Travaux pratiques de grammaire Answers
- Interactive CD-ROM Tutor, Disc 1

Portfolio

26 **Written** Students should have a classmate edit their work before they hand it in. You might have students place their letter in their written portfolio. For portfolio suggestions, see *Alternative Assessment Guide,* page 19.

25 Qu'est-ce qu'on dit?

Parlons What do you think these students are saying? Possible answers:

1. L'histoire, c'est... nul.

2. La géométrie, c'est... pas terrible.

3. L'algèbre, c'est... facile.

4. La biologie, c'est... intéressant.

5. L'espagnol, c'est... difficile.

6. Les arts plastiques, c'est... génial.

26 La vie scolaire

Lisons/Ecrivons Read this letter that your new pen pal Laurent wrote to you after his first day of class. Then, write your reply.

Salut !
Ça va au lycée ? Tu aimes les cours ? Moi, mes cours sont pas mal. J'adore les maths, c'est facile. Mais la physique, c'est barbant. Et la bio, c'est difficile. Et toi ? Tu aimes les sciences ? Pas moi. J'aime mieux les langues. C'est génial, et c'est plus intéressant. J'ai sport l'après-midi. J'aime bien ; c'est cool. Et toi ? Tu as sport aussi ? Ça te plaît ?
A bientôt,
Laurent

27 Comment tu trouves?

Parlons With your partner, discuss how you feel about your classes.

Exemple — **Tu as maths?**
— **Oui, à neuf heures.**
— **Comment tu trouves ça?**
— **C'est super!**

Communication for All Students

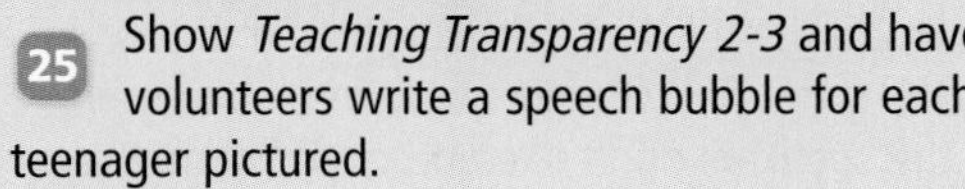

Additional Practice

25 Show *Teaching Transparency 2-3* and have volunteers write a speech bubble for each teenager pictured.

Challenge

25 Ask students to imagine themselves in the classes pictured here and to give their own opinions, beginning with **A mon avis,...**

Additional Practice

26 After students have read Laurent's letter, check their comprehension with true-false statements: **Laurent aime les maths (T); Laurent adore les langues (T); Il n'aime pas le sport (F); Il aime beaucoup les sciences (F); Il adore la physique (F).**

STANDARDS: 1.1, 1.2, 1.3, 3.1, 5.1

28  

De l'école au travail

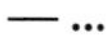

Parlons/Ecrivons You work part-time as an office aide for the school board. You've been asked to interview some French exchange students to get their opinion on the American school system. Create a conversation in which you interview the exchange student, your partner, about his or her classes. Ask questions about his or her class schedule and level of difficulty of each class. Then, switch roles. Be sure to take notes during the interview to provide to the school board.

EXEMPLE — **Tu as quels cours le matin?**

— ...

— **Comment tu trouves ça?**

PRONONCIATION

CD 2
Trs. 12–17

Liaison See scripts and answers on p. 45H.

In French you don't usually pronounce consonants at the end of a word, such as the **s** in **les** and the **t** in **c'est.** But you do pronounce some final consonants if the following word begins with a vowel sound. This linking of the final consonant of one word with the beginning vowel of the next word is called **liaison.**

les examens	**C'est intéressant.**	**vous avez**	**deux élèves**
z	t	z	z

A. A prononcer

Repeat the following phrases and sentences.

les maths / les escargots
nous n'aimons pas / nous aimons
C'est super. / C'est intéressant.
les profs / les élèves

B. A lire

Take turns with a partner reading the following sentences aloud. Make all necessary liaisons.

1. Ils ont maths.
2. Elles ont histoire.
3. Elles aiment l'espagnol.
4. Elle a deux examens lundi.
5. Vous avez cours le samedi?
6. Nous aimons les arts plastiques.

C. A écrire

You're going to hear two short dialogues. Write down what you hear.

Troisième étape

CHAPITRE 2

Presenting Prononciation

Ask students to suggest examples of liaison they've already learned (between **ils/elles** and the forms of **aimer, écouter,** and **avoir**). Write their suggestions on the board. Then, draw the liaison links between each set of words and have students repeat them. Have them deduce the rule for making liaison.

Language Note

Make sure students make a z sound, not an s sound, when making liaison with phrases like **les élèves** and **ils ont.**

Assess

- Testing Program, pp. 35–38
  Quiz 2-3A, Quiz 2-3B
  Audio CD 2, Tr. 21
- Student Make-Up Assignments, Chapter 2, Alternative Quiz
- Alternative Assessment Guide, p. 33

Communication for All Students

Challenge

28 Have students write down their classmates' answers about their favorite and least favorite classes. Collect the papers and have volunteers make a list of the top two or three choices in each category.

Additional Practice

Prononciation When students have completed the dictation in Part C, have them indicate on their paper where liaison occurs by linking the appropriate words with a pencil mark.

STANDARDS: 1.1, 4.1, 5.2

Lisons!

CHAPITRE 2

Teaching Resources
pp. 64–65

PRINT 

- Lesson Planner, p. 12
- Cahier d'activités, p. 23
- Reading Strategies and Skills Handbook, Chapter 2
- Joie de lire 1, Chapter 2
- Standardized Assessment Tutor, Chapter 2

MEDIA 

- One-Stop Planner

Prereading
Activities A–C

Establishing a Purpose for Reading
Bring in newspapers or textbooks that contain graphs and ask what information they convey. Discuss the advantages of graphs over written explanations.

Reading
Activities D–G

Teaching Suggestion
Have students read the graphs carefully and then do Activities D through G.

Answers

C. Distants – distant, aloof
Respectueux – respectful, considerate
Compétents – competent
Absents – absent

Lisons!

SONDAGE
Les lycéens ont-ils le moral?

Stratégie pour lire
You'll find photos, drawings, charts, and other visual clues when you read newspapers, magazines, and even your textbooks! These illustrations will usually give you an idea of what you're going to read before you begin.

A. First, look at the illustrations. Based on what you see, do you think you're going to read . . .
1. price lists?
2. math exercises?
3. results from a survey?
4. ads from a sales catalogue?

B. Now, scan the titles and texts. Based on the titles and the drawings, do you think these articles are about . . .
1. teenagers' favorite pastimes?
2. grades given to students on exams?
3. students' attitudes toward school?
4. prices at several stores?

C. Here are some cognates from the graph entitled **Profs.** What do you think these words mean in English? See answers below.

distants respectueux compétents absents

SONDAGE
Les lycéens ont-ils le moral?

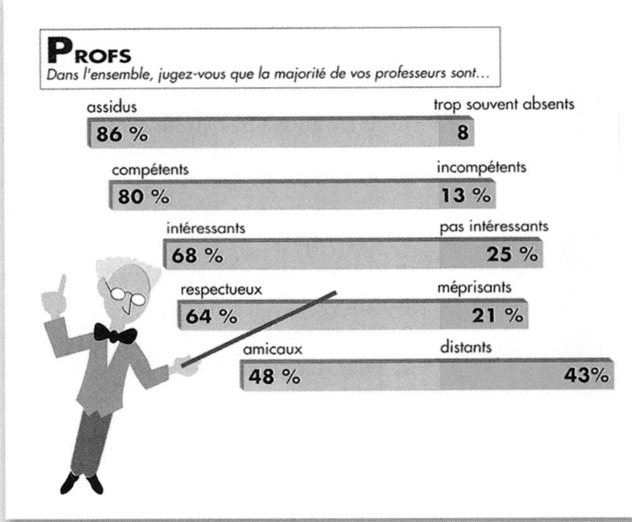

Communication for All Students

Challenge
A. B. You might ask students to support the choices they made in these activities.

Thinking Critically
C. Analyzing Have students compile a list of questions they might include in a survey about student attitudes toward school and their teachers.

Building on Previous Skills
Have students read the title boxes and pick out the cognates. Next, have them determine what information is displayed in each graph and in what way. They might do this in small groups.

STANDARDS: 1.2, 2.1, 3.1, 3.2, 4.1, 4.2

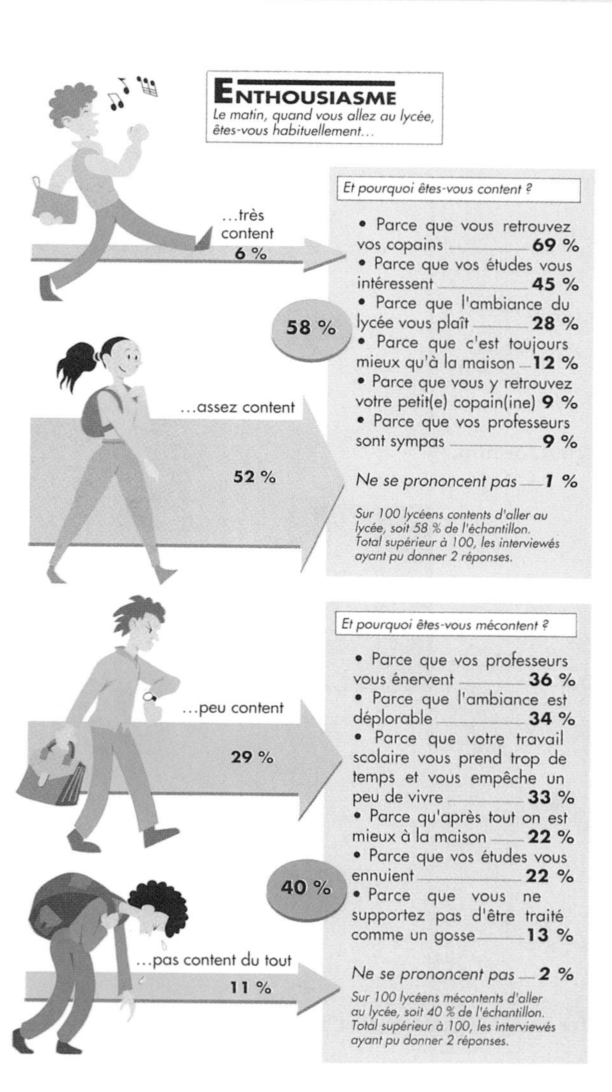

ENTHOUSIASME
Le matin, quand vous allez au lycée, êtes-vous habituellement...
...très content
6 %
Et pourquoi êtes-vous content ?
• Parce que vous retrouvez vos copains 69 %
• Parce que vos études vous intéressent 45 %
• Parce que l'ambiance du lycée vous plaît 28 %
• Parce que c'est toujours mieux qu'à la maison 12 %
• Parce que vous y retrouvez votre petit(e) copain(ine) 9 %
• Parce que vos professeurs sont sympas 9 %
Ne se prononcent pas 1 %
Sur 100 lycéens contents d'aller au lycée, soit 58 % de l'échantillon. Total supérieur à 100, les interviewés ayant pu donner 2 réponses.
58 %
...assez content
52 %
...peu content
29 %
Et pourquoi êtes-vous mécontent ?
• Parce que vos professeurs vous énervent 36 %
• Parce que l'ambiance est déplorable 34 %
• Parce que votre travail scolaire vous prend trop de temps et vous empêche un peu de vivre 33 %
• Parce qu'après tout on est mieux à la maison 22 %
• Parce que vos études vous ennuient 22 %
• Parce que vous ne supportez pas d'être traité comme un gosse 13 %
Ne se prononcent pas 2 %
Sur 100 lycéens mécontents d'aller au lycée, soit 40 % de l'échantillon. Total supérieur à 100, les interviewés ayant pu donner 2 réponses.
40 %
...pas content du tout
11 %

D. Knowing that the words at each end of the bar on the graph are opposites, what do you think the following words mean?
1. **assidus** regular, constant
2. **incompétents** incompetent
3. **pas intéressants** uninteresting
4. **méprisants** disdainful
5. **amicaux** friendly

E. According to the graph, . . .
1. do French students generally have a positive or negative image of their teachers?
2. how do most of the students feel about their teachers?
3. what do the students criticize the most? See answers below.

F. Look at the drawings for **Enthousiasme.** What do you think the following categories mean in English? Which category is the best? Which is the worst? See answers below.

peu content	très content
pas content du tout	assez content

G. According to the percentages, do most of the students have a positive or a negative attitude when they go to the **lycée?** positive

H. Conduct the same surveys in your class and compile the results. How do the attitudes of your classmates compare with those of the French **lycéens?**

Cahier d'activités, p. 23, Act. 23–24

Lisons!

CHAPITRE 2

Postreading
Activity H

Using Text Organizers
H. You might have students present the results of their survey in a colorful graph.

Communication for All Students

Group Work
Discuss the results of the class survey. Ask students to work in groups of 3 or 4 to come up with suggestions on improving student and teacher attitudes and behavior. After comparing the results with those in **Lisons!**, have students suggest reasons why the results of the two surveys are similar or different. Ask students to share their reasons with the rest of the class.

Challenge
Ask students to give you examples of the ways in which students behave that would support the statements in the **Lisons!** Also ask them for examples of teacher behavior that would illustrate the different categories.

Answers

E. 1. positive
2. They think they are diligent, competent, interesting, respectful, and friendly.
3. They criticize them for being distant.

F. Très content – *very happy (best)*
Assez content – *somewhat happy*
Peu content – *not very happy*
Pas content du tout – *not happy at all (worst)*

STANDARDS: 1.2, 1.3, 2.1, 3.1, 3.2, 4.1, 4.2, 5.2

Grammaire supplémentaire

CHAPITRE 2

For **Grammaire supplémentaire** Answer Transparencies, see the *Teaching Transparencies* binder.

Answers

1
1. Si
2. Oui
3. Oui
4. Si
5. Oui
6. Si

2
1. Oui
2. Si
3. Non
4. Si
5. Oui
6. Oui

3
1. as
2. ai
3. ai
4. a
5. a
6. a
7. avons

Grammaire supplémentaire

Première étape

Objective Agreeing and disagreeing

1 Would you answer **si** or **oui** to each of the following questions? (**p. 54**)

1. Hervé n'aime pas faire le ménage?
2. Vous aimez le cours de physique?
3. Tu aimes écouter de la musique?
4. Annick et Ahmed n'aiment pas le prof de français?
5. Jean-Paul aime la chorale?
6. Olivia n'aime pas faire du sport?

2 Complete the following conversations, using **si, oui,** or **non,** as appropriate. (**p. 54**)

1. —Tu aimes les sciences naturelles?
   — _____, j'adore!
2. —Marc n'aime pas parler au téléphone?
   — _____, il aime bien parler avec ses copains.
3. —Ils aiment la physique?
   — _____, ils n'aiment pas les cours de science.
4. —Tu n'aimes pas le ski?
   — _____, j'aime bien le sport en général.
5. —Tu aimes faire de l'équitation?
   — _____, mais je préfère lire et regarder la télévision.
6. —Nicole aime les concerts?
   — _____, elle adore la musique.

Deuxième étape

Objectives Asking for and giving information; telling when you have class

3 Complete the conversation below with the correct forms of the verb **avoir.** (**p. 55**)

—Céline, tu __1__ quels cours aujourd'hui?
—Le matin, j' __2__ sciences nat et français. L'après-midi, j' __3__ histoire et géométrie.
—Et Vincent, il __4__ quels cours?
—Il __5__ chimie et espagnol le matin, et l'après-midi, il __6__ informatique.
—Le mardi et le jeudi matin, nous __7__ travaux pratiques de chimie.

Grammar Resources for Chapter 2

The **Grammaire supplémentaire** activities were designed as supplemental activities for the grammatical concepts presented in the chapter. You might use them as additional practice, for review, or for assessment.

For more grammar presentations, review and practice, refer to the following:

- Travaux pratiques de grammaire
- Grammar Tutor for Students of French
- Grammar Summary on pp. R15–R28
- Cahier d'activités
- Grammar and Vocabulary quizzes (Testing Program)
- Test Generator
- Interactive CD-ROM Tutor
- DVD Tutor
- **Jeux interactifs** at go.hrw.com

STANDARDS: 1.2

4 Using the information from Marc's and Ingrid's schedules, answer the questions that follow. (**pp. 55, 56**)

EXEMPLE —Marc a français le mardi?
—Non, il n'a pas français le mardi.

EMPLOI DU TEMPS **NOM:** Marc Champlain

		LUNDI	MARDI	MERCREDI	JEUDI	VENDREDI	SAMEDI	DIMANCHE
MATIN	8h00	Arts plastiques	Allemand	Français	Sciences nat	Mathématiques		
	9h00	Sciences nat	Histoire/Géo	EPS	Allemand	Physique	Mathématiques	L
	10h00	Récréation	Récréation	Récréation	Récréation	Récréation	TP Physique	
	10h15	Allemand	Physique	Anglais	Mathématiques	Français	TP Physique	I
	11h15	Mathématiques	Etude	Histoire/Géo	Etude	Français	[Sortie]	
	12h15	Déjeuner	Déjeuner	[Sortie]	Déjeuner	Déjeuner	APRES-MIDI	B
APRES-MIDI	14h00	Anglais	Mathématiques	APRES-MIDI	Arts plastiques	Arts plastiques	LIBRE	
	15h00	EPS	Chimie	LIBRE	Arts plastiques	Anglais		R
	16h00	Récréation	[Sortie]		Récréation	[Sortie]		
	16h15	Histoire/Géo			Chimie			E
	17h15	[Sortie]			[Sortie]			

EMPLOI DU TEMPS **NOM:** Ingrid Valmont

		LUNDI	MARDI	MERCREDI	JEUDI	VENDREDI	SAMEDI	DIMANCHE
MATIN	8h00	Arts plastiques	Français	Anglais	Français	Géométrie		
	9h00	DPS	Géométrie	EPS	Français	Géométrie	Anglais	L
	10h00	Récréation	Récréation	Récréation	Récréation	Récréation	TP Biologie	
	10h15	Espagnol	Sciences nat	Espagnol	Biologie	Sciences nat	TP Biologie	I
	11h15	Géométrie	Etude	Histoire/Géo	Etude	Espagnol	[Sortie]	
	12h15	Déjeuner	Déjeuner	[Sortie]	Déjeuner	Déjeuner	APRES-MIDI	B
APRES-MIDI	14h00	Anglais	Biologie	APRES-MIDI	Arts plastiques	Arts plastiques	LIBRE	
	15h00	Biologie	EPS	LIBRE	Arts plastiques	Français		R
	16h00	Récréation	[Sortie]		Récréation	[Sortie]		
	16h15	Histoire/Géo			Géométrie			E
	17h15	[Sortie]			[Sortie]			

1. Ingrid n'a pas biologie le lundi?
2. Marc a anglais le mercredi?
3. Ingrid a espagnol le jeudi?
4. Ingrid et Marc n'ont pas arts plastiques le lundi?
5. Marc et Ingrid ont EPS le lundi?
6. Ingrid a histoire le mercredi?
7. Marc a allemand le samedi?
8. Marc et Ingrid ont français le samedi?
9. Ingrid et Marc ont l'après-midi libre le samedi?
10. Marc n'a pas mathématiques le vendredi?

Teacher to Teacher

Sharon Telich
Westside Middle School
Omaha, NE

Here is Sharon's idea to reinforce the concept of *Si* versus *Oui*.

"Have each student prepare two flashcards, one with **Si** written on it and the other with **Oui.** Make a list of questions that would be answered "yes" by most of the class. Personalize the questions by using students' names whenever possible. As you read each question aloud, the students must answer "yes" by holding up a card that says **Oui** or **Si.** After surveying the class for all the answers, have one student give the survey results."

Answers

4
1. Si, elle a biologie le lundi.
2. Oui, il a anglais le mercredi.
3. Non, elle n'a pas espagnol le jeudi.
4. Si, ils ont arts plastiques le lundi.
5. Marc a EPS le lundi, mais Ingrid n'a pas EPS le lundi.
6. Oui, elle a histoire le mercredi.
7. Non, il n'a pas allemand le samedi.
8. Non, ils n'ont pas français le samedi.
9. Oui, ils ont l'après-midi libre le samedi.
10. Si, il a mathématiques le vendredi.

Grammaire supplémentaire

CHAPITRE 2

For **Grammaire supplémentaire** Answer Transparencies, see the *Teaching Transparencies* binder.

Grammaire supplémentaire

WA3 POITIERS-2

5 Mathieu and some of his friends are discussing their school schedules. Complete each of the following sentences with the correct form of the verb **avoir.** Then, write out the time given in parentheses. (**pp. 55, 58**)

EXEMPLE Sylvie _____ latin à (9h30). Sylvie **a** latin à **neuf heures trente.**

1. J' _____ sciences nat à (8h45).
2. Anne et moi, nous _____ EPS à (13h50).
3. Mathieu et Jeanne, vous _____ latin à (11h20), non?
4. Séverine, tu _____ quoi à (15h30)?
5. Chad et Mireille _____ maths à (16h15).
6. André et Hélène _____ français à (9h45).
7. Jean, Alain et moi, nous _____ récréation à (14h25).

6 Unscramble each of these sentences, using the correct form of **avoir.** Then, match each clock with the sentence that mentions the corresponding time. (**pp. 55, 58**)

a.

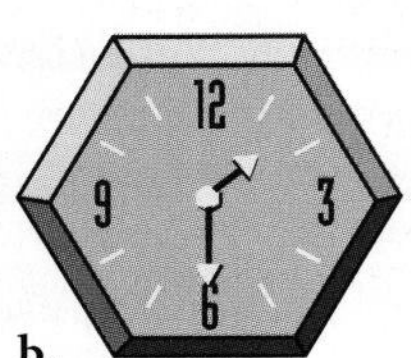
b.

c.

d.

e.

f.

g.

1. avoir / huit / mathématiques / heures / à / j'
2. DPS / quinze / à / heures / avoir / neuf / nous
3. quarante / chimie / avoir / à / heures / dix / Audrey
4. treize / Florent / à / Bernard / quarante-cinq / géographie / et / avoir / heures
5. avoir / et / quatorze / Sophie / à / moi, / nous / heures / français / vingt
6. plastiques / heures / à / trente / arts / avoir / treize / tu
7. heures / à / vous / seize / EPS / avoir / vingt-cinq

Communication for All Students

Additional Practice

6 Have students use the times shown on the different clocks to write a complete sentence describing a class they have at each time or an activity they do at that time on a specific day.

Challenge

7 Have students work in groups of two or three to create mini-dialogues, using the statements in Activity 7. Students might want to change some of the personal pronouns to fit their dialogues (for example, replace the **ils** in the 3rd item with **je**). Once they have finished, have them act out their conversations in front of the class.

Answers

5
1. ai, huit heures quarante-cinq
2. avons, treize heures cinquante
3. avez, onze heures vingt
4. as, quinze heures trente
5. ont, seize heures quinze
6. ont, neuf heures quarante-cinq
7. avons, quatorze heures vingt-cinq

6
1. J'ai mathématiques à huit heures. g
2. Nous avons DPS à neuf heures quinze. a
3. Audrey a chimie à dix heures quarante. f
4. Florent et Bernard ont géographie à treize heures quarante-cinq. d
5. Sophie et moi, nous avons français à quatorze heures vingt. e
6. Tu as arts plastiques à treize heures trente. b
7. Vous avez EPS à seize heures vingt-cinq. c

STANDARDS: 1.2

Troisième étape

Objective Asking for and expressing opinions

Grammaire supplémentaire

CHAPITRE 2

7 Rewrite these informal remarks and questions in formal French. (**pp. 26, 61**)

1. «C'est pas super, l'algèbre.»
2. «Elle aime pas la chimie?»
3. «Ils aiment pas les devoirs.»
4. «Mais non! L'anglais, c'est pas difficile!»
5. «Tu aimes pas la géographie?»

8 David and Olivia are discussing their schedules and their classes. Complete their conversation with either the correct form of the verb in parentheses or the word or phrase that expresses their opinion. (**pp. 33, 55, 61**)

—Olivia, tu __1__ (avoir) quels cours le lundi matin?
—J' __2__ (avoir) histoire, maths et français. Et toi, tu __3__ (avoir) quels cours?
—Florent et moi, nous __4__ (avoir) chimie, allemand et anglais.
—Vous __5__ (aimer) la chimie?
—Florent n' __6__ (aimer) pas ça. Mais moi, j' __7__ (adorer) la chimie. C'est __8__ (passionnant/pas super)!
—Ah bon! Florent __9__ (avoir) biologie le mardi. Il __10__ (adorer) ça. Et toi, tu __11__ (aimer) ça, la biologie?
—Moi, non. C'est __12__ (pas mal/nul).

9 Some friends are talking about their courses and school schedules. Complete each sentence with the correct verb form. Then, select the word from the box that most logically tells how each person feels about his or her course. (**pp. 33, 55, 61**)

—J' __1__ (avoir) maths à huit heures. Je __2__ (ne pas aimer). Je __3__ (préférer) dormir. Les maths, c'est __4__.
—J' __5__ (adorer) nager. J' __6__ (avoir) natation à quatre heures de l'après-midi. C'est __7__.
—J' __8__ (aimer) lire. J' __9__ (avoir) français à neuf heures vingt. C'est __10__.
—J' __11__ (avoir) chimie à dix heures cinquante. J' __12__ (ne pas aimer) étudier, et je __13__ (ne pas aimer) la chimie. C'est __14__.
—J' __15__ (avoir) anglais à deux heures vingt-cinq. J' __16__ (aimer bien) la littérature. C'est __17__!

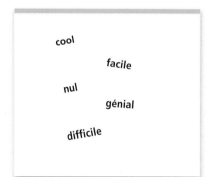

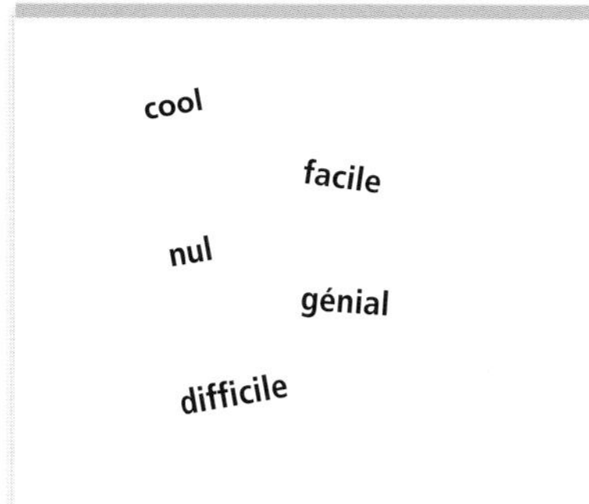

Review and Assess

You may wish to assign the **Grammaire supplémentaire** activities as additional practice or homework after presenting material throughout the chapter. Assign Activities 1–2 after **Note de grammaire** (p. 54), Activity 3 after **Grammaire** (p. 55), Activity 4 after **Vocabulaire** (p. 56), Activities 5–6 after **Comment dit-on... ?** (p. 58), Activity 7 after **A la française** (p. 61), Activities 8–9 after **Comment dit-on... ?** (p. 61). To prepare students for the **Etape** Quizzes and Chapter Test, we suggest doing the **Grammaire supplémentaire** activities in the following order. Have students complete Activities 1–2 before taking Quizzes 2-1A or 2-1B; Activities 3–6 before Quizzes 2-2A or 2-2B; and Activities 7–9 before Quizzes 2-3A or 2-3B.

Answers

7
1. Ce n'est pas super, l'algèbre.
2. Elle n'aime pas la chimie?
3. Ils n'aiment pas les devoirs.
4. Mais non! L'anglais, ce n'est pas difficile!
5. Tu n'aimes pas la géographie?

8
1. as
2. ai
3. as
4. avons
5. aimez
6. aime
7. adore
8. passionnant
9. a
10. adore
11. aimes
12. nul

9
1. ai
2. n'aime pas
3. préfère
4. nul
5. adore
6. ai
7. génial
8. aime
9. ai
10. facile
11. ai
12. n'aime pas
13. n'aime pas
14. difficile
15. ai
16. aime bien
17. cool

STANDARDS: 1.1, 1.2, 1.3

Mise en pratique

CHAPITRE 2

The **Mise en pratique** reviews and integrates all four skills and culture in preparation for the Chapter Test.

Teaching Resources
pp. 70–71

PRINT 

- Lesson Planner, p. 12
- Listening Activities, p. 13
- Video Guide, pp. 13, 16
- Grammar Tutor for Students of French, Chapter 2
- Standardized Assessment Tutor, Chapter 2

MEDIA

- One-Stop Planner
- Video Program Videocassette 1, 30:55–36:50
- DVD Tutor, Disc 1
- Audio Compact Discs, CD 2, Tr. 18
- Interactive CD-ROM Tutor, Disc 1

Visual Learners

1 Students might benefit from seeing the typed script after hearing it once. You might have students circle the subjects and times.

Auditory Learners

2 Make a list of true/false statements about the schedule: **Eliane a EPS à 10h le lundi.** (false) Read the statements to the students and ask them to tell you whether they are true or false.

Answers

2
1. anglais, français, EPS et sciences nat
2. histoire/géographie, physique et français
3. histoire – mercredi à 8h00, jeudi à 14h00
   anglais – lundi à 8h00, mercredi à 9h00, vendredi à 15h00, samedi à 9h00
   maths – lundi à 16h15, mardi à 10h15 et à 14h00, jeudi à 8h00

Mise en pratique

1 Listen as André, a French exchange student, tells you how he feels about his American schedule. What is his reaction to his schedule in general? At what times does he have the following subjects: **chimie, sport, latin, informatique?** See scripts and answers on p. 45H.

CD 2 Tr. 18

2 Answer these questions according to Eliane's schedule. See answers below.

1. Eliane a quoi le lundi matin?
2. Elle a quels cours le jeudi après-midi?
3. Quels jours et à quelle heure est-ce qu'elle a histoire? Anglais? Maths?

EMPLOI DU TEMPS — **NOM:** Eliane Soulard — **CLASSE:** 3e

		LUNDI	MARDI	MERCREDI	JEUDI	VENDREDI	SAMEDI	DIMANCHE
MATIN	8h00	Anglais	Arts plastiques	Histoire/Géo	Mathématiques	Musique		L
	9h00	Français	Musique	Anglais	Sciences nat	Arts plastiques	Anglais	
	10h00	Récréation	Récréation	Récréation	Récréation	Récréation	TP physique	I
	10h15	EPS	Mathématiques	Sciences nat	EPS	Sciences nat	TP physique	
	11h15	Sciences nat	Etude	Arts plastiques	Etude	Français	[Sortie]	B
	12h15	**Déjeuner**	**Déjeuner**	**[Sortie]**	**Déjeuner**	**Déjeuner**	**APRES-MIDI**	
APRES-MIDI	14h00	Arts plastiques	Mathématiques	**APRES-MIDI**	Histoire/Géo	Physique	**LIBRE**	R
	15h00	Musique	Physique	**LIBRE**	Physique	Anglais		
	16h00	Récréation	[Sortie]		Récréation	[Sortie]		E
	16h15	Mathématiques			Français			
	17h15	[Sortie]			[Sortie]			

3 Tell three classmates whether or not you like Eliane's schedule and why. Then, ask them if they like it.

EXEMPLE **J'aime l'emploi du temps d'Eliane. Elle a étude et arts plastiques. C'est cool! Et vous?**

4 How does an American class schedule compare with Eliane's? With a partner, make a list of similarities and differences.

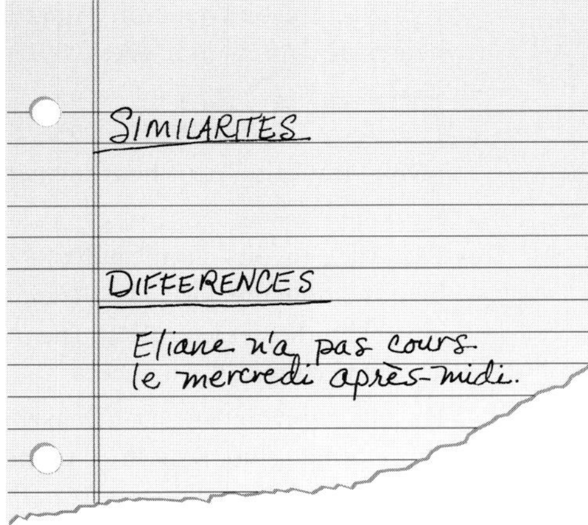

SIMILARITES
DIFFERENCES
Eliane n'a pas cours le mercredi après-midi.

Apply and Assess

Group Work

3 Have students work in groups of four. One student in each group might be selected to report the number of votes for and against Eliane's schedule and to explain why the group feels the way it does.

Additional Practice

4 You might extend this activity to include a comparison of the grading system in French and American high schools. Have students refer back to the **Note culturelle** on page 61 for an explanation of the French grading scale.

STANDARDS: 1.2, 1.3, 4.2

5 Answer these questions according to Eliane's report card. See answers below.

1. What are Eliane's best subjects?
2. What would she probably say about French class? Music class? Science class?

BULLETIN TRIMESTRIEL

Année scolaire : 2002 - 2003

NOM et Prénom: Soulard Eliane   Classe de: 3e

MATIERES D'ENSEIGNEMENT	Moyenne de l'élève	OBSERVATIONS
Français	5	Montre peu d'enthousiasme
Anglais	8	Assez mauvais travail!
Mathématiques	18	Très bonne élève!
Histoire-Géographie	11	Travail moyen
Sciences naturelles	17	Elève sérieuse
Education physique	12	Un peu paresseuse
Physique-Chimie	18	Très douée pour la physique
Arts plastiques	14	Bon travail.
Musique	13	Fait des efforts.

Ce bulletin doit être conservé précieusement par les parents.
Il n'en sera pas délivré de duplicata.

6 Create your ideal schedule showing subjects, days, and times. Write it down in the form of a French **emploi du temps.**

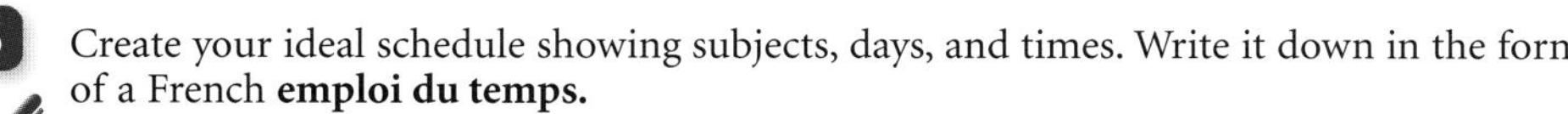

7 **Jeu de rôle**

Create a conversation with two classmates. Talk about . . .

a. the subjects you like best and your opinion of them.

b. the subjects you don't like and your opinion of them.

c. whether or not you agree with your classmates' likes and dislikes.

Mise en pratique

CHAPITRE 2

Building on Previous Skills

5 Have students find cognates in the teacher's comments to help them understand the meaning.

Challenge

5 Have students make their own French report card. They should give themselves the grades they think they deserve in each subject using the French grading system.

Career Path

Many college students pursuing degrees in foreign language spend a year teaching English abroad. Ask students if they can think of other careers that might require people to teach English in a foreign country (Peace Corps). If students were to spend a year teaching English in a French **lycée,** what information from this chapter will help them? What else would they need to learn?

Apply and Assess

Auditory Learners

6 Have partners dictate their ideal schedules to each other and write down the classes and times as they hear them. Then, have them exchange the schedules to check each other's work.

Answers

5
1. mathématiques, physique-chimie, sciences naturelles
2. Possible answers: Le français, c'est barbant/c'est difficile/c'est nul/c'est zéro.
   La musique, c'est pas mal/c'est intéressant.
   Les sciences nat, c'est cool/c'est facile/c'est génial/c'est intéressant/c'est passionnant.

STANDARDS: 1.1, 1.2, 1.3, 5.1

Que sais-je?

CHAPITRE 2

Teaching Resources
p. 72

PRINT 
- Grammar Tutor for Students of French, Chapter 2

MEDIA 
- Interactive CD-ROM Tutor, Disc 1
- Online self-test

go.hrw.com
WA3 POITIERS-2

Teacher Note
This page is intended to help students prepare for the Chapter Test. It is a brief checklist of the major points covered in the chapter. The students should be reminded that this is only a checklist and does not necessarily include everything that will appear on the test.

Answers

3
1. Tu as français et chorale.
2. Paul a physique.
3. Nous avons sport.
4. Francine et Séverine ont espagnol.

4
1. Tu as géométrie à quelle heure?
2. Tu as informatique à quelle heure?
3. Tu as arts plastiques à quelle heure?

5
1. J'ai sport à neuf heures quinze.
2. J'ai allemand à onze heures quarante-cinq.
3. J'ai DPS à quinze heures cinquante.

6
1. C'est passionnant!
2. C'est pas terrible.
3. C'est barbant.

Que sais-je?

WA3 POITIERS-2

Can you use what you've learned in this chapter?

Can you agree and disagree? p. 54

1 How would you agree if your friend said the following? How would you disagree with your friend?
1. J'adore l'histoire! *agree* — Moi aussi! *disagree* — Moi, non.
2. J'aime les sciences nat. Et toi? *agree* — Oui, beaucoup! *disagree* — Non, pas trop.
3. Je n'aime pas le français. *agree* — Moi non plus. *disagree* — Moi, si!

Can you ask for and give information? p. 55

2 How would you ask . . .
1. what subjects your friend has in the morning? Tu as quoi le matin?
2. what subjects your friend has in the afternoon? Tu as quoi l'après-midi?
3. what subjects your friend has on Tuesdays? Tu as quoi le mardi?
4. if your friend has music class? Tu as musique?
5. if your friend has English today? Tu as anglais aujourd'hui?

3 How would you say in French that the following students have these classes, using the verb **avoir?** See answers below.
1. you / French and choir
2. Paul / physics
3. we / gym
4. Francine and Séverine / Spanish

Can you tell when you have class? p. 58

4 How would you ask your friend at what time he or she has these classes? See answers below.

1.

2.

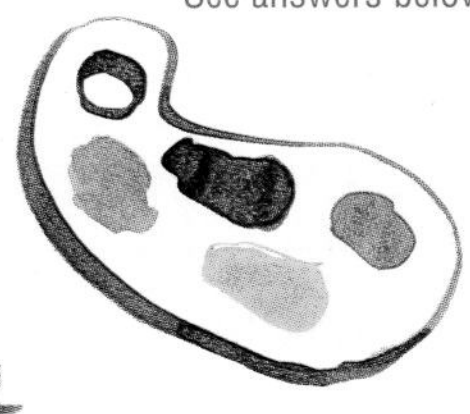
3.

5 How would you tell your friend that you have the following classes at the times given? See answers below.

1. 9h15

2. 11h45

3. 15h50

Can you ask for and express opinions? p. 61

6 How would you tell your friend that your geography class is . . . See answers below.
1. fascinating?
2. not so great?
3. boring?

Review and Assess

Challenge
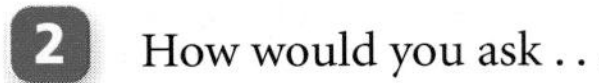
1 Have students work in groups of four to tell how they feel about their classes. As each student talks about his or her classes, the rest of the group should agree or disagree with his or her opinion.

Additional Practice
6 Have students come up with as many phrases as possible to express each reaction to the geography class.

STANDARDS: 1.1, 1.2

Première étape

School subjects

l'algèbre (f.)	*algebra*
l'allemand (m.)	*German*
les arts (m.) **plastiques**	*art class*
la biologie	*biology*
la chimie	*chemistry*
la chorale	*choir*
le cours de développement personnel et social (DPS)	*health*
la danse	*dance*
l'éducation (f.) **physique et sportive (EPS)**	*physical education*
l'espagnol (m.)	*Spanish*
la géographie	*geography*
la géométrie	*geometry*
l'histoire (f.)	*history*
l'informatique (f.)	*computer science*
le latin	*Latin*
la musique	*music*
la physique	*physics*
les sciences (f.) **naturelles**	*natural science*
le sport	*gym*
les travaux (m.) **pratiques**	*lab*

School-related words

le cours	*course*
les devoirs (m.)	*homework*
l'élève (m./f.)	*student*
le professeur (le prof)	*teacher*

Agreeing and disagreeing

Oui, beaucoup.	*Yes, very much.*
Moi aussi.	*Me too.*
Moi, non.	*I don't.*
Non, pas trop.	*No, not too much.*
Moi non plus.	*Neither do I.*
Moi, si.	*I do.*
Pas moi.	*Not me.*

Deuxième étape

Asking for and giving information

Tu as quels cours... ?	*What classes do you have . . . ?*
Tu as quoi... ?	*What do you have . . . ?*
J'ai...	*I have . . .*
Vous avez... ?	*Do you have . . . ?*
Nous avons...	*We have . . .*
avoir	*to have*

Telling when you have class

Tu as... à quelle heure?	*At what time do you have . . . ?*
à... heures	*at . . . o'clock*
à... heures quinze	*at . . . fifteen*
à... heures trente	*at . . . thirty*
à... heures quarante-cinq	*at . . . forty-five*
aujourd'hui	*today*
demain	*tomorrow*
maintenant	*now*
le matin	*in the morning*
l'après-midi (m.)	*in the afternoon*
le lundi	*on Mondays*
le mardi	*on Tuesdays*
le mercredi	*on Wednesdays*
le jeudi	*on Thursdays*
le vendredi	*on Fridays*
le samedi	*on Saturdays*
le dimanche	*on Sundays*

Parts of the school day

la récréation	*break*
l'étude (f.)	*study hall*
le déjeuner	*lunch*
la sortie	*dismissal*
l'après-midi libre	*afternoon off*

Numbers

See page 57 for the numbers 21 through 59

Troisième étape

Asking for and expressing opinions

Comment tu trouves ça?	*What do you think of that/it?*
Comment tu trouves... ?	*What do you think of . . . ?*
Ça va.	*It's OK.*
C'est...	*It's . . .*
super.	*super.*
cool.	*cool.*
facile.	*easy.*
génial.	*great.*
intéressant.	*interesting.*
passionnant.	*fascinating.*
pas mal.	*not bad.*
barbant.	*boring*
difficile.	*difficult.*
nul.	*useless.*
pas super.	*not so hot.*
pas terrible.	*not so great.*
zéro.	*a waste of time.*

Vocabulaire

CHAPITRE 2

Teaching Suggestion

You might want to have students list the feminine nouns together and the masculine nouns together in their notebooks. Ask them also to note any similarities within each group. For example, many of the feminine nouns end in **-ie.**

Review and Assess

Game

Tic Tac Toe Divide the class into two teams and draw a grid on the board or on a transparency. In each square, write one of the chapter functions or vocabulary categories in English: agreeing, disagreeing, telling time, school subjects, expressing positive and negative opinions, the numbers 20–59, days of the week, and so on. Call out a French expression or sentence. If the contestant chooses the category your remark represents, the team symbol goes in the square. If not, a player from the other team may try. You can also reverse the procedure by supplying French expressions in the grid and calling out the categories in English.

Chapter 2 Assessment

- **Testing Program**
  Chapter Test, pp. 39–44
   Audio Compact Discs, CD 2, Trs. 22–24
  Speaking Test, p. 343
- **Alternative Assessment Guide**
  Performance Assessment, p. 33
  Portfolio Assessment, p. 19
  CD-ROM Assessment, p. 47
- **Interactive CD-ROM Tutor, Disc 1**
  CD-ROM 1 A toi de parler
  DVD 1 A toi d'écrire
- **Standardized Assessment Tutor**
  Chapter 2
- **One-Stop Planner, Disc 1**
   Test Generator
  Chapter 2

STANDARDS: 1.1, 1.2

Chapitre 3 : Tout pour la rentrée

Chapter Overview

Mise en train pp. 76–78	***Pas question!***

	FUNCTIONS	GRAMMAR	VOCABULARY	RE-ENTRY
Première étape pp. 79–82	• Making and responding to requests, p. 80 • Asking others what they need and telling what you need, p. 82	• The indefinite articles **un, une,** and **des,** p. 81	• School supplies, p. 79	• The verb **avoir (Chapitre 2)** • Using **ne... pas (Chapitre 1)**
Deuxième étape pp. 84–87	• Telling what you'd like and what you'd like to do, p. 85	• The demonstrative adjectives **ce, cet, cette,** and **ces,** p. 85 • Adjective agreement and placement, p. 87	• Additional items for school, p. 84 • Colors, p. 86	• Expressing likes and dislikes **(Chapitre 1)** • Activities **(Chapitre 1)** • The verb **avoir (Chapitre 2)**
Troisième étape pp. 88–91	• Getting someone's attention, asking for information, and expressing and responding to thanks, p. 90		• Numbers 60–201, p. 88	• Numbers 0–59 **(Chapitres 1–2)**

Prononciation p. 91	The **r** sound Audio CD 3, Tracks 13–15	**A écrire** (dictation) Audio CD 3, Tracks 16–18	
Lisons! pp. 92–93	**Univers: Tout pour la rentrée**	**Reading Strategy:** Scanning for specific information	
Grammaire supplémentaire	**pp. 94–97** **Première étape,** p. 94	**Deuxième étape,** pp. 95–96	**Troisième étape,** p. 97
Review pp. 98–101	**Mise en pratique,** pp. 98–99 **Ecrivons!** Cluster diagrams Creating a department store	**Que sais-je?** p. 100	**Vocabulaire,** p. 101

CULTURE

- **Note culturelle,** Bagging your own purchases, p. 80
- **Panorama Culturel,** Buying school supplies in French-speaking countries, p. 83
- **Note culturelle,** The Euro, p. 88
- **Note culturelle,** Writing prices in French, p. 90

Chapitre 3 : Tout pour la rentrée

Chapter Resources

Visit Holt Online
go.hrw.com
KEYWORD: WA3 POITIERS-3
Online Edition

Lesson Planning

One-Stop Planner

Lesson Planner with Differentiated Instruction, pp. 13–17, 67

Student Make-Up Assignments
- Make-Up Assignment Copying Masters, Chapter 3

Listening and Speaking

TPR Storytelling Book, pp. 9–12

Listening Activities
- Student Response Forms for Listening Activities, pp. 19–21
- Additional Listening Activities 3-1 to 3-6, pp. 23–25
- Additional Listening Activities (songs), p. 26
- Scripts and Answers, pp. 112–116

Video Guide
- Teaching Suggestions, pp. 18–19
- Activity Masters, pp. 20–22
- Scripts and Answers, pp. 92–94, 119

Activities for Communication
- Communicative Activities, pp. 13–18
- Realia and Teaching Suggestions, pp. 85–89
- Situation Cards, pp. 141–142

Reading and Writing

Reading Strategies and Skills Handbook, Chapter 3

Joie de lire 1, Chapter 3

Cahier d'activités, pp. 25–36

Grammar

Travaux pratiques de grammaire, pp. 17–24

Grammar Tutor for Students of French, Chapter 3

Assessment

Testing Program
- Grammar and Vocabulary Quizzes, **Etape** Quizzes, and Chapter Test, pp. 53–70
- Score Sheet, Scripts and Answers, pp. 71–78

Alternative Assessment Guide
- Portfolio Assessment, p. 20
- Performance Assessment, p. 34
- CD-ROM Assessment, p. 48

Student Make-Up Assignments
- Alternative Quizzes, Chapter 3

Standardized Assessment Tutor
- Reading, pp. 9–11
- Writing, p. 12
- Math, pp. 25–26

Middle School

Middle School Teaching Resources, Chapter 3

MEDIA

Online Activities
- **Jeux interactifs**
- **Activités Internet**

Video Program
- Videocassette 1
- Videocassette 5 (captioned version)

Interactive CD-ROM Tutor, Disc 1

DVD Tutor, Disc 1

Audio Compact Discs
- Textbook Listening Activities, CD 3, Tracks 1–19
- Additional Listening Activities, CD 3, Tracks 26–33
- Assessment Items, CD 3, Tracks 20–25

Teaching Transparencies
- Situation 3-1 to 3-3
- Vocabulary 3-A to 3-D
- **Mise en train**
- **Grammaire supplémentaire** Answers
- **Travaux pratiques de grammaire** Answers

One-Stop Planner CD-ROM

Use the **One-Stop Planner CD-ROM with Test Generator** to aid in lesson planning and pacing.

For each chapter, the **One-Stop Planner** includes:
- Editable lesson plans with direct links to teaching resources
- Printable worksheets from resource books
- Direct launches to the HRW Internet activities
- Video and audio segments
- Test Generator
- Clip Art for vocabulary items

Projects

La publicité

Students will create advertisements for their own stores, either by creating an illustrated catalog or by preparing and performing a television or radio commercial. This project can be done individually, in pairs, or in groups.

MATERIALS

Students may need

- Paper, Scissors
- Magazines
- Colored pens and pencils
- Glue or tape

PREPARATION

Have students determine the type of store or the products they want to advertise. They should make a list of their products, looking up any words they might need, and assign a price to each item.

SUGGESTED SEQUENCE

1. **First Draft** Have students choose the format for their advertisement, either a catalog or a commercial.

   If they choose to make a catalog, they will need to find or create illustrations for their products and design an attractive layout.

   If students choose to create a commercial, they should start writing the script. Encourage students to find visual aids to get their message across.
2. **Peer-editing** Those students who create commercials should now rehearse them.

   Those students doing catalogs should ask for feedback from the commercial writers regarding the descriptions and prices of the items as well as the layout.
3. **Final Draft** Students doing commercials should correct any mistakes pointed out in peer-editing, gather all their visual aids, and present the commercial to the class.

   Students making catalogs should revise their projects according to the feedback from their classmates and display them around the classroom.

GRADING THE PROJECT

Suggested Point Distribution: (total = 100 points)

Completion of assignment ....20 points
Language use ....20 points
Presentation..............................30 points
Content ....30 points

Games

Go Fish

In this game, students will practice vocabulary for school supplies.

Procedure This game should be prepared ahead of time. Draw or glue pictures of school supplies onto index cards. You will need four cards of each item for a complete deck and a complete deck for each pair or group playing the game. Deal each player five cards and place the remaining cards face down on the table. Then, players should remove all matching pairs from their hands and set them aside. The dealer begins by asking a player for a card. (**Stan, tu as un stylo?**) If the player has the card, he or she must give it to the person who asks for it, who then sets the pair aside and takes another turn. If the player doesn't have the card, the person requesting the card must draw one from the pile, and the next player takes a turn. The game ends when one player puts down or gives away the last card. All players count their pairs, and the player with the most pairs wins.

Je vois quelque chose (I Spy)

This game will help students review colors and classroom vocabulary.

Procedure Have students think of an item in the classroom. It must be visible, and it should be an item that students can name in French. Ask a volunteer to tell only the color of his or her item. (**Je vois quelque chose de bleu, de blanc...**) Other students then try to guess what the item is. (**C'est un stylo?**) You might want to set a one-minute time limit for each item. You might even limit the number of guesses to keep a fast pace. The student who guesses correctly then tells the color of his or her item. If one student guesses correctly more than once, he or she may choose another student to continue the game. If no one guesses correctly, the student should name the item and choose another student to continue.

STANDARDS: 1.3

Storytelling

Mini-histoire

This story accompanies Teaching Transparency 3-3. The ***mini-histoire*** *can be told and retold in different formats, acted out, written down, and read aloud, to give students additional opportunities to practice all four skills. In the following story, Patrick and Mathieu are at a school-supplies store. Patrick is telling Mathieu what he needs for the beginning of school.*

Pour la rentrée, il me faut un classeur rouge, des gommes, et une trousse noire. Il me faut aussi un pull-over gris, un jean noir, des shorts rouges et des tee-shirts blancs pour le cours d'EPS. Je voudrais acheter aussi un portefeuille noir, un dictionnaire et des sweat-shirts. J'aimerais aussi des baskets, mais je n'aime pas ces baskets.

Traditions

Langues

The **langue d'oïl** and **langue d'oc** (**Occitan**) were languages spoken in the northern and southern parts of France respectively for over 1,000 years. The names of the languages were derived from the manner in which the people said "**oui**" in the two regions. Although the language spoken in the Poitou region was the **langue d'oïl,** a lot of areas in the region were influenced by and adopted the Occitan language and culture. Guillaume IX, Count of Poitiers and Duke of Aquitaine and Gascogne, was a lyric poet who composed songs in Occitan. During the twelfth century, Poitiers became an important center for culture and civilization. It was here, under the patronage of Guillaume IX, that **troubadour** literature flourished. Roving **troubadours** performed poems and told stories of courtly love written in **Provençal,** a version of Occitan. In the latter part of the nineteenth century, the language experienced a renaissance when Frédéric Mistral and other poets from Provence formed a literary school to safeguard the region's language. Mistral won the Nobel Prize for Literature in 1904 for his poetry. Thousands of people still speak **Provençal,** especially the older generations of rural areas. There has also been a recent revival in the use of the language in folk music and local literature. Have students search the Internet using the key words "Provençal" or "Occitan" to create a glossary of some common Provençal words.

Recette

Touraine and Anjou, two regions situated in the heartland of the Loire Valley, are well-known for their castles. These regions, abundant in fruits and vegetables, are also famous for the ***Belle angevine*** *pears, used in many popular desserts. Fruit* ***gratins*** *like the* ***gratin de poires*** *are easy desserts to make. They only require fruit and a batter that resembles the batter used to make* ***crêpes.*** *To make this recipe, students may wish to look for "Anjou pears" at the supermarket.*

GRATIN DE POIRES

pour 6 personnes

- 8 poires
- 2 tasses de lait
- 1 tasse de farine
- 1/2 tasse de sucre
- 1 cuillère à soupe de beurre
- 4 cuillères à soupe d'amandes pilées
- 1 sachet de sucre vanillé ou une cuillère d'extrait de vanille

Dans un bol, mélanger la farine, le sucre, le sucre vanillé et le lait.

Eplucher et couper les poires en lamelles. Beurrer un plat qui va au four. Mettre les poires dans le plat. Verser la pâte sur les poires. Mettre au four à 375° F pendant 30 minutes. Servir tiède.

Chapitre 3 : Tout pour la rentrée
Technology

DVD/Video

Videocassette 1, Videocassette 5 (captioned version)
DVD Tutor, Disc 1
See Video Guide, pp. 17–22.

Mise en train • Pas question!

In this segment of the video, Julie and her mother, Mme Pelletier, are shopping for school supplies. Julie's mother asks a saleswoman for help. They pick out a pencil case, colored pencils, a calculator, and other school supplies. Julie sees a schoolbag that she really likes, but it's too expensive. Mme Pelletier wants to buy a less expensive bag. Julie says she would rather go without a bag than have one she doesn't like.

Qu'est-ce qu'il te faut comme fournitures scolaires?

Several teenagers from different French-speaking countries tell us what school supplies they bought or they need for the first day of school.

Pas question! (suite)

The story continues the next day as Julie and Sarah are leaving for school. Her mother shows her a bag in a catalog. Julie tries to order it through the Internet, but it is out of stock. She goes back to the store she went to with her mother and finds the same bag that her mother had wanted her to buy, but in a different color. She buys the bag as well as two T-shirts. Mme Pelletier is surprised to see that Julie bought the inexpensive bag after all.

Vidéoclips

- **Waterman®:** advertisement for pens
- **France Télécom®:** advertisement for French telephone company

Interactive CD-ROM Tutor

Activity	Activity Type	Pupil's Edition Page
En contexte	*Interactive conversation*	
1. Vocabulaire	Jeu des paires	p. 79
2. Grammaire	Le bon choix	p. 81
3. Vocabulaire	Chasse au trésor Explorons! Vérifions!	p. 84
4. Grammaire	Méli-mélo	p. 87
5. Grammaire	Les mots qui manquent	pp. 85, 87
6. Vocabulaire	Le bon choix	p. 88
Panorama Culturel	Qu'est-ce qu'il te faut comme fournitures scolaires? Le bon choix	p. 83
A toi de parler	*Guided recording*	pp. 98–99
A toi d'écrire	*Guided writing*	pp. 98–99

Teacher Management System

Launch the program, type "admin" in the password area and press RETURN. Log on to **www.hrw.com/CDROMTUTOR** for a detailed explanation of the Teacher Management System.

DVD Tutor

The *DVD Tutor* contains all material from the *Video Program* as described above. French captions are available for use at your discretion for all sections of the video. The *DVD Tutor* also provides a variety of video-based activities that assess students' understanding of the **Mise en train, Suite,** and **Panorama Culturel.**

This part of the *DVD Tutor* may be used on any DVD video player connected to a television or video monitor.

In addition to the video material and the video-based comprehension activities, the *DVD Tutor* also contains the entire *Interactive CD-ROM Tutor* in DVD-ROM format. Each DVD disc contains the activities from all 12 chapters of the *Interactive CD-ROM Tutor.*

This part of the *DVD Tutor* may be used on a Macintosh® or Windows® computer with a DVD-ROM drive.

To preview all resources available for this chapter, use the **One-Stop Planner CD-ROM,** Disc 1.

Go.Online!

Online Edition

The Online Edition for Allez, viens! *allows students access to their textbooks anytime anywhere.*

- *Audio at point of use*
- *Additional practice activities*
- *Self-test activities*
- *Online reference tools*
- *Entire Video Program (Enhanced version)*
- *Interactive Notebook (Enhanced version)*

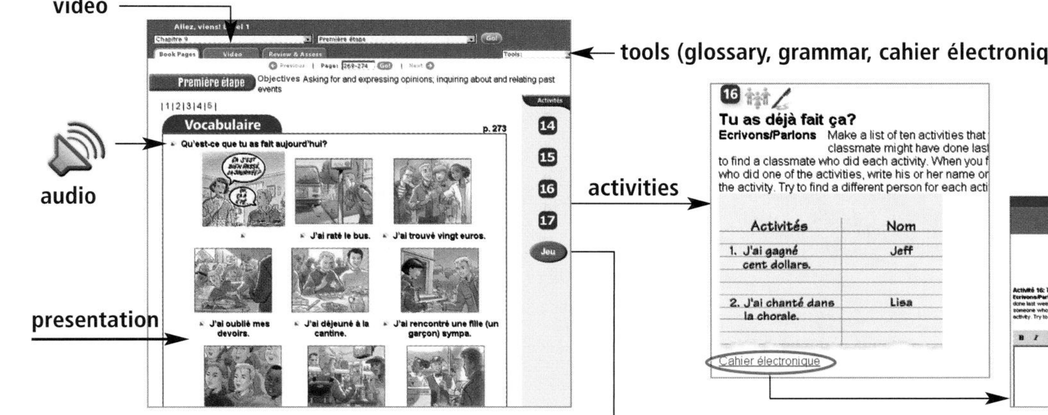

Notebook

HRW Atlas

Internet Activités

Activités Internet

These guided internet activities include a worksheet and pre-selected and pre-screened authentic web sites from the francophone world. You can use these activities

- to help students develop research skills in the target language
- to introduce students to authentic cultural information
- as a project

Jeux interactifs

You can use the interactive activities in this chapter

- to practice grammar, vocabulary, and chapter functions
- as homework
- as an assessment option
- as a self-test
- to prepare for the Chapter Test

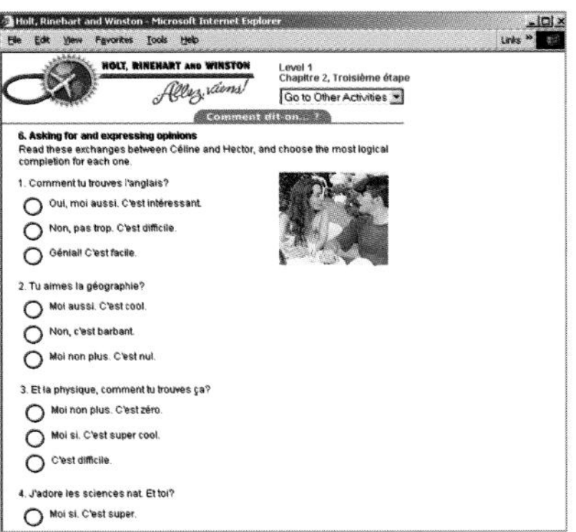

Projet Have students do a Web search to find stores in Poitiers where they can buy electronic items such as computers, televisions, and video recorders, and to find the store with the best selection. Then, have them prepare a sales brochure for that particular store with the information they gathered. Have students document their sources by noting the names and URLs of all the sites they consulted.

Chapitre 3 : Tout pour la rentrée

Textbook Listening Activities Scripts 

Première étape

6 p. 79

1. HAFAIDH Qu'est-ce qu'il y a dans mon sac? Voilà le cahier de français. J'ai aussi des stylos et des crayons dans ma trousse et une gomme.

2. KARINE Bon, qu'est-ce qu'il y a dans mon sac? Je ne peux rien trouver! Tiens, voilà le cahier de français. Il y a, bien sûr, des feuilles de papier et ma trousse avec un crayon et des stylos dedans. Ah, voilà la règle pour les maths.

Answers to Activity 6

a. neither
b. Karine
c. Hafaïdh

9 p. 81

1. — Jacqueline, tu as une feuille de papier?
— Ben, oui. Voilà.

2. — Ali, tu as un crayon?
— Non, mais j'ai un stylo.

3. — Paul, tu as un crayon?
— Oui. Le voilà.

4. — Xavier, tu as une calculatrice?
— Je regrette. Je n'ai pas de calculatrice.

Answers to Activity 9

1. c
2. a
3. b
4. e

Deuxième étape

14 p. 84

1. Je voudrais un jean.
2. Moi, j'aime faire du sport. Je voudrais des baskets.
3. Je voudrais acheter un portefeuille.
4. J'aime beaucoup la musique. Je voudrais un disque compact.
5. J'adore lire. Je voudrais acheter un roman.

Answers to Activity 14

1. Dorothée
2. Odile
3. M. Prévost
4. Stéphane
5. Denis

15 p. 85

Euh..., je voudrais aller à la plage ce week-end, il me faut un short et un tee-shirt. Alors, pour l'école je voudrais des baskets et un dictionnaire. Je voudrais aussi acheter une montre parce que je suis toujours en retard. Enfin, j'adore écouter de la musique, donc je voudrais une radio.

Answers to Activity 15

un short, un tee-shirt, des baskets, un dictionnaire, une montre et une radio

The following scripts are for the listening activities found in the *Pupil's Edition.* For Student Response Forms, see *Listening Activities,* pages 19–21. To provide students with additional listening practice, see *Listening Activities,* pages 23–26.

One-Stop Planner CD-ROM

To preview all resources available for this chapter, use the **One-Stop Planner CD-ROM**, Disc 1.

Troisième étape

23 p. 88

1. Vous écoutez quatre-vingt-dix-neuf FM, le rock des Lillois!
2. Génial, phénoménal et amical, c'est canal B sur quatre-vingt-quatorze mégahertz de plaisir.
3. Quatre-vingt-neuf virgule cinq pour swinguer dans les chaumières.
4. Qui m'aime? Moi, FM cent deux virgule trois. La station des copains.

Answers to Activity 23
1. a 2. e 3. c 4. d

27 p. 90

1. — Bonjour. C'est combien, ce classeur?
   — Quatre euros cinquante.
   — Merci beaucoup.
2. — C'est dix euros trente-neuf, cette calculatrice?
   — Oui.
   — Merci.
   — A votre service.
3. — Pardon, madame. C'est combien, ce cahier?
   — Trois euros quinze.
   — Merci, madame.
4. — Une règle, c'est combien?
   — Deux euros quarante.
   — Merci.
   — A votre service.
5. — Pardon, madame.
   — Oui.
   — Vous avez des trousses?
   — Oui. Ces trousses-là font six euros trente-six.
   — Eh bien, ce n'est pas cher.
6. — C'est combien, ce livre?
   — Sept euros soixante-dix-sept.
   — Merci, madame.

Answers to Activity 27
1. classeur — 4, 50€
2. calculatrice — 10, 39€
3. cahier — 3, 15€
4. règle — 2, 40€
5. trousse — 6, 36€
6. livre — 7, 77€

PRONONCIATION, P. 91

For the scripts for Parts A and B, see p. 91.
The script for Part C is below.

C. A écrire *(dictation)*
— Pardon, monsieur.
— Oui?
— Je voudrais un crayon rouge et une trousse rose.
— Cinq euros soixante-dix-huit, s'il vous plaît.

Mise en pratique

1 p. 98

J'aime beaucoup faire du sport. Il me faut des baskets.
J'adore écouter de la musique. Je voudrais des cassettes.
Je n'ai pas de dictionnaire pour le cours d'espagnol.
Je voudrais une calculatrice pour le cours d'algèbre.

Answers to Mise en pratique, Activity 1
des baskets, des cassettes, un dictionnaire et une calculatrice

Chapitre 3 : Tout pour la rentrée
50-Minute Lesson Plans

Day 1

CHAPTER OPENER 5 min.
- Motivating Activity: Ask students the following questions: What do you shop for before the beginning of the school year? Are you taking classes that require special supplies? Ask students to list items they need versus items they want.
- Photo Flash!, ATE, p. 74
- Present Chapter Objectives, p. 75, using Focusing on Outcomes, ATE, p. 75.

MISE EN TRAIN 40 min.
- Thinking Critically, ATE, p. 74
- Presenting **Mise en train** and Preteaching Vocabulary, ATE, p. 76
- Do Activities 1–5, p. 78.

Wrap-Up 5 min.
- Cooperative Learning, ATE, p. 77

Homework Options
Cahier d'activités, p. 25, Act. 1

Day 2

PREMIERE ETAPE
Quick Review 10 min.
- Check homework.
- Bell Work, ATE, p. 79

Vocabulaire, p. 79 30 min.
- Presenting **Vocabulaire,** ATE, p. 79, using Teaching Transparency 3-A
- Auditory/Kinesthetic Learners, ATE, p. 79
- Play Audio CD for Activity 6, p. 79.
- Do Activity 7, p. 80.
- Discuss **Note culturelle,** ATE, p. 80, and the questions in Thinking Critically: Drawing Inferences, ATE, p. 80.
- **Note culturelle,** p. 80
- Cahier d'activités, p. 26, Acts. 2–3

Wrap-Up 10 min.
- Do Activity 8, p. 80, in small groups or as a class.

Homework Options
Travaux pratiques de grammaire, pp. 17–18, Acts. 1–3

Day 3

PREMIERE ETAPE
Quick Review 10 min.
- Check homework
- Motivate: Ask students to list the twelve school supplies they learned the previous day. Review the French words for the items.

Comment dit-on. . .?, p. 80 10 min.
- Presenting **Comment dit-on... ?,** ATE, p. 80
- Thinking Critically: Analyzing, ATE, p. 80

Grammaire, p. 81 20 min.
- Presenting **Grammaire,** ATE, p. 81
- Play Audio CD for Activity 9, p. 81.
- Do Activity 10, p. 81.
- Travaux pratiques de grammaire, pp. 18–19, Acts. 4–7

Wrap-Up 10 min.
- Play Game: Go fish, ATE, p. 73C.

Homework Options
Grammaire supplémentaire, p. 94, Acts. 1–2
Cahier d'activités, p. 27, Act. 4

Day 4

PREMIERE ETAPE
Quick Review 5 min.
- Check homework.

Comment dit-on... ?, p. 82 35 min.
- Presenting **Comment dit-on... ?,** ATE, p. 82
- Do Activities 11–12, p. 82.
- Cahier d'activités, p. 28, Acts. 5–6

Wrap-Up 10 min.
Display ten school supplies on a table and allow students a minute to look at them. Cover the objects and have students write down as many objects as they can.

Homework Options
Study for **Première étape** quiz.

Day 5

PREMIERE ETAPE
Quiz 3-1 20 min.
- Administer Quiz 3-1A or Quiz 3-1B.

PANORAMA CULTUREL 25 min.
- Present **Panorama Culturel** using Videocassette 1, p. 83.
- Discuss **Qu'en penses-tu?,** p. 83.
- **Panorama Culturel,** Interactive CD-ROM Tutor (Disc 1)
- Culture Notes, ATE, p. 83

Wrap-Up 5 min.
- Discuss with students the kind of school uniform they would like to wear if uniforms became their school's policy.

Homework Options
Cahier d'activités, p. 36, Acts. 21–22

Day 6

DEUXIEME ETAPE
Quick Review 10 min.
- Check homework and do Bell Work, ATE p. 84.

Vocabulaire, p. 84 10 min.
- Presenting **Vocabulaire,** p. 84, ATE, using Teaching Transparencies 3-B and 3-C
- Tactile/Kinesthetic Learners, ATE, p. 84
- Play Audio CD for Activity 14, p. 84.

Comment dit-on... ?, p. 85 10 min.
- Presenting **Comment dit-on... ?,** ATE, p. 85
- Play Audio CD for Activity 15, p. 85.
- Do Activity 16, p. 85.

Grammaire, p. 85 10 min.
- Presenting **Grammaire,** ATE, p. 85.
- Do Activities 19–20, p. 86.
- **Grammaire supplémentaire,** pp. 94–95, Activities 3–4

Wrap-Up 10 min.
- Do Activity 16, p. 85.

Homework Options
Cahier d'activités, p. 29, Acts. 7–8
Travaux pratiques de grammaire, p. 21, Acts. 10–11

For alternative lesson plans by chapter section, to create your own customized plans, or to preview all resources available for this chapter, use the **One-Stop Planner CD-ROM**, Disc 1.

For additional homework suggestions, see activities accompanied by this symbol throughout the chapter.

Day 7

DEUXIEME ETAPE

Quick Review 10 min.
- Check homework.
- Bring new school supplies and supplies that show a little wear and tear. Students will tell which they like using **ce, cet, cette,** and **ces.**

Vocabulaire, p. 86 15 min.
- Presenting **Vocabulaire,** ATE, p. 86
- Additional Practice, ATE, p. 86
- Do Activity 21, p. 87.

Grammaire, p. 87 20 min.
- Presenting **Grammaire,** ATE, p. 87
- Communicative Activity 3-2, Activities for Communication, pp. 15–16
- Travaux pratiques de grammaire, pp. 22–23, Acts. 12–15

Wrap-Up 5 min.
- Game: **Je vois quelque chose**, ATE, p. 73C

Homework Options
Study for **Deuxième étape** quiz.

Day 8

DEUXIEME ETAPE

Quiz 3-2 20 min.
- Have students complete Quiz 3-2A or Quiz 3-2B.

TROISIEME ETAPE

Vocabulaire, p. 88 15 min.
- Presenting **Vocabulaire,** ATE, p. 88
- Play Audio CD for Activity 23, p. 88.
- Cahier d'activités, p. 32, Acts. 15–16

Note culturelle, p. 88 10 min.
- Discuss **Note culturelle,** p. 88, and Culture Notes, ATE, p. 89.
- Do Activities 24–25, p. 89.

Wrap-Up 5 min.
- Bring in a jar of jelly beans. Have students guess the number of jelly beans in the jar in French and the price in euros.

Homework Options
Cahier d'activités, p. 33, Act. 17
Travaux pratiques de grammaire, p. 24, Acts. 16–18

Day 9

TROISIEME ETAPE

Quick Review 10 min.
- Check homework.

Comment dit-on... ?, p. 90 15 min.
- Presenting **Comment dit-on... ?,** ATE, p. 90
- Culture Note, ATE, p. 90
- Discuss **Note culturelle,** p. 90.
- Play Audio CD for Activity 27, p. 90.
- Do Activity 28 and Career Path, ATE, p. 90.

Prononciation, p. 91 15 min.
- Play Audio CD for Activities A–C, p. 91.

Wrap-Up 10 min.
- Situation Card 3-3: Role-play, Activities for Communication, p. 142

Homework Options
Study for **Troisième étape** quiz.

Day 10

TROISIEME ETAPE

Quiz 3-3 20 min.
- Administer Quiz 3-3A or Quiz 3-3B.

LISONS! 25 min.
- Thinking Critically, ATE, p. 92
- Prereading Activities A–B, ATE, p. 92
- Reading Activities C–J, ATE, pp. 92–93
- Postreading Activity K, ATE, p. 93
- Thinking Critically suggestions, ATE, p. 93

Wrap-Up 5 min.
- Show various school supplies and give a price in euros. Have students compare the prices to those in the **Lisons!** and tell if the prices are too high, too low, or about right.

Homework Options
Cahier d'activités, p. 35, Act. 20

Day 11

MISE EN PRATIQUE 30 min.

Quick Review 10 min.
- Communicative Activity 3-3A and 3-3B, Activities for Communication, pp. 17–18
- Play Audio CD for Activity 1, p. 98.
- Do Activities 2–3 and 5–6, pp. 98–99.
- Additional Practice, ATE, p. 98
- **Ecrivons!**, p. 99

Wrap-Up 10 min.
- Have partners exchange papers for peer-editing and feedback.

Homework Options
Que sais-je?, p. 100

Day 12

MISE EN PRATIQUE

Quick Review 15 min.
- Check homework and do **Jeu de rôle,** p. 99.

Chapter Review 35 min.
- Review Chapter 3. Choose from **Grammaire supplémentaire,** Grammar Tutor for Students of French, Activities for Communication, Listening Activities, Interactive CD-ROM Tutor, or **Jeux interactifs.**

Homework Options
Study for Chapter 3 Test.

Assessment

Test, Chapter 3 40–45 min.
- Administer Chapter 3 Test. Select from Testing Program, Alternative Assessment Guide, Test Generator, or Standardized Assessment Tutor.

Chapitre 3 : Tout pour la rentrée

90-Minute Lesson Plans

Block 1

CHAPTER OPENER 5 min.
- Present Chapter Objectives, p. 75
- Motivating Activity: Ask students questions such as: At the beginning of the school year, do you go shopping for school supplies? Clothes? Do you need extra or special supplies for some of your classes? How much do school supplies cost? Do you have to buy books for certain classes?

MISE EN TRAIN 45 min.
- Presenting **Mise en train,** ATE, p. 76
- Preteaching Vocabulary, ATE, p. 76
- Cooperative Learning, ATE, p. 77
- Language-to-Language, ATE, p. 77
- View video of **Mise en train,** Videocassette 1, Video Guide, p. 17. Do Video Guide Activities 1–3, p. 20. Pause video for all numbers and ask students what number they just heard.

PREMIERE ETAPE

Vocabulaire, p. 79 25 min.
- Presenting **Vocabulaire,** ATE, p. 79
- Auditory/Kinesthetic Learners, ATE, p. 79
- Play Audio CD For Activity 6, p. 79.
- Do Activity 7, p. 80, in writing. Then recycle **ne...pas** by calling on students to give the missing items in complete sentences.
- **Note culturelle,** p. 80 and Thinking Critically: Analyzing, ATE, p. 80

Comment dit-on... ?, p. 80 10 min.
- Presenting **Comment dit-on... ?,** ATE, p. 80, Thinking Critically: Drawing Inferences, ATE, p. 80

Wrap-Up 5 min.
- Have students summarize what happened in the **Mise en train** using Chapter 3 **Mise en train** Transparencies.

Homework Options

Travaux pratiques de grammaire, p. 17, Act. 1

Block 2

PREMIERE ETAPE

Quick Review 5 min.
- Pull school supplies out of a bag. For each item, ask **Qu'est-ce que c'est?**

Grammaire, p. 81 25 min.
- Presenting **Grammaire,** ATE, p. 81
- Play Audio for Activity 9, p. 81. See Culture Note, ATE, p. 81.
- Activity 2 **Grammaire supplémentaire,** p. 94
- Do Activity 10, p. 81. See Challenge, ATE, p. 81.

Comment dit-on... ?, p. 82 20 min.
- Presenting **Comment dit-on...?,** ATE, p. 82
- Language Note, ATE, p. 82 and **Vocabulaire à la carte,** p. 82.
- Do Activity 11, p. 82.
- Additional Listening Activity 3-1 and 3-2, Listening Activities, p. 23

PANORAMA CULTUREL 15 min.
- Present **Panorama Culturel,** p. 83.
- View **Panorama Culturel** Videocassette 1 (first 3 interviews only)
- Have students answer **Qu'en penses-tu?** questions, p. 83.
- Read **Savais-tu que?,** p. 83.

DEUXIEME ETAPE

Vocabulaire, p. 84 20 min.
- Presenting **Vocabulaire,** ATE, p. 84
- Tactile/Kinesthetic Learners, ATE, p. 84
- Play Audio CD for Activity 14, p. 84. See Challenge suggestion, ATE, p. 84.

Wrap-Up 5 min.
- Display ten school supplies on a table and allow students a minute to look at them. Cover the objects and have students write down as many objects as they can.

Homework Options

Study for **Première étape** quiz.
Travaux pratiques de grammaire, pp. 18–19, Acts. 2–7
Cahier d'activités, pp. 27–28, Act. 4, part b only, 5–6

Block 3

PREMIERE ETAPE

Quick Review 10 min.
- Situation Card 3-1: Interview, Activities for Communication, p. 4

Quiz 3-1 20 min.
- Administer Quiz 3-1A or 3-1B.

DEUXIEME ETAPE

Quick Review 5 min.
- Communicative Activity 3-1A and 3-1B, Activities for Communication, pp. 13–14

Comment dit–on...?, p. 85 10 min.
- Presenting **Comment dit-on...?,** ATE, p. 85
- Play Audio CD for Activity 15, p. 85.
- Do Activity 16, p. 85.
- Do Activity 17, p. 85, orally.

Grammaire, p. 85 25 min.
- Presenting **Grammaire,** ATE, p. 85
- Do Activity 19, p. 86. When going over answers, ask why for each answer.
- **Grammaire supplémentaire**, pp. 94–95, Activities 3–4
- Do Activity 20, p. 86.

Vocabulaire, p. 86 5 min.
- Show markers to present each color.
- Show markers again and ask: **C'est quelle couleur?**
- Do Activity 21, p. 87.

Grammaire, p. 87 10 min.
- Presenting **Grammaire,** ATE, p. 87

Wrap-Up 5 min.
- Show items and ask **Qu'est-ce que c'est?** Sample answer: **C'est un stylo noir.**

Homework Options

Cahier d'activités, pp. 29–30, Acts. 7–10
Travaux pratiques de grammaire, pp. 20–21, Acts. 8–11

For alternative lesson plans by chapter section, to create your own customized plans, or to preview all resources available for this chapter, use the **One-Stop Planner CD-ROM**, Disc 1.

For additional homework suggestions, see activities accompanied by this symbol throughout the chapter.

Block 4

DEUXIEME ETAPE

Quick Review 10 min.
- Cahier d'activités, p. 31, Activity 13: Teacher reads the descriptions, students draw the answers by dressing a stick figure.

Grammaire, p. 87, con't 15 min.
- **Grammaire supplémentaire,** pp. 95–96, Activities 5–6
- Situation Card 3-2: Interview, Activities for Communication, p. 142

TROISIEME ETAPE

Vocabulaire, p. 88 45 min.
- Motivating Activity: Have students count from 0 to 59
- Presenting **Vocabulaire,** ATE, p. 88
- Play Audio CD for Activity 23, p. 88. See Teaching Suggestion, ATE, p. 88.
- **Note culturelle,** p. 88, Culture Notes, ATE, p. 89
- Do Activity 24, p. 89.
- Do Activity 25, p. 89. See Math Link, ATE, p. 89.
- Play Game:, **Loto,** ATE, p. 45C, only use numbers from 60 to 99.

Wrap-Up 20 min.
- TPRS Book p. 10: make copies deleting the **mini-histoire.** Have students re-create the story then act it out. (10 minutes to prepare, 10 minutes to present to class)

Homework Options

Study for **Deuxième étape** quiz.

Cahier d'activités, p. 30, Act. 12, p. 32, Acts. 15–16

Travaux pratiques de grammaire, pp. 22–23, Acts. 12–15

Block 5

DEUXIEME ETAPE

Quick Review 10 min.

Quiz 3-2 20 min.
- Administer Quiz 3-2A or 3-2B.

TROISIEME ETAPE

Quick Review 5 min.
- Call out numbers, students write the numerals and the word for each.

Comment dit–on...?, p. 90 15 min.
- Presenting **Comment dit-on... ?,** ATE, p. 90
- Culture Note, ATE, p. 90
- Play Audio CD for Activity 27, p. 90.
- **Note culturelle,** p. 90
- **Grammaire supplémentaire**, p. 96, Activities 7–8
- Do Activity 28, p. 90.

Prononciation 15 min.
- Present **Prononciation**, p. 91.
- Play Audio CD for Activities A, B, and C.

LISONS! 20 min.
- Prereading Activities A–B, ATE, p. 92
- Reading Activities C–J, ATE, pp. 92–93
- Postreading Activity K, ATE, p. 93

Wrap-Up 5 min.
- Challenge, ATE, p. 88

Homework Options

Study for **Troisième étape** quiz.

Travaux pratiques de grammaire, p. 24, Acts. 16–18

Cahier d'activités, pp. 33–34, Acts. 17–19

Block 6

TROISIEME ETAPE

Quick Review 10 min.

Quiz 3-3 20 min.
- Administer Quiz 3-3A or 3-3B.

MISE EN PRATIQUE 40 min.
- Play Audio CD for Activity 1, p. 98.
- Do Activities, 3, 4, and 6, pp. 98–99.
- Do Activity 7 **Ecrivons!**, p. 99.

Wrap-Up 20 min.
- Situation Card 3-3: Role Play 3-3, Activities for Communication, p. 142 (10 minutes to prepare, 10 minutes to present to class)

Homework Options

Que sais-je?, p. 100

Study for Chapter 3 Test.

Block 7

MISE EN PRATIQUE

Chapter Review 40 min.
- Check homework and do **Jeu de rôle,** p. 99.
- Review Chapter 3. Choose from **Grammaire supplémentaire,** Grammar Tutor for Students of French, Activities for Communication, Listening Activities, Interactive CD-ROM Tutor, or **Jeux interactifs.**

Test, Chapter 3 50 min.
- Administer Chapter 3 Test. Select from Testing Program, Alternative Assessment Guide, Test Generator, or Standardized Assessment Tutor.

Chapter Opener

CHAPITRE 3

One-Stop Planner CD-ROM

For resource information, see the **One-Stop Planner,** Disc 1.

Pacing Tips

Keep in mind when planning your lessons that the **Deuxième étape** presents a lot of new vocabulary and grammar. The demonstrative adjectives and adjective agreement and placement are covered in the **Deuxième étape.** The **Troisième étape** is the lightest. For Lesson Plans and timing suggestions, see pages 73I–73L.

Meeting the Standards

Communication

- Making and responding to requests, p. 80
- Asking others what they need and telling what you need, p. 82
- Telling what you'd like and what you'd like to do, p. 85
- Getting someone's attention, p. 90
- Asking for information, p. 90
- Expressing and responding to thanks, p. 90

Cultures

- Note culturelle, pp. 80, 88, 90
- Multicultural Link, p. 81
- Culture Notes, pp. 75, 81, 83, 89
- Panorama Culturel, p. 83

Connections

- Math Link, p. 89
- Science Link, p. 86

Comparisons

- Thinking Critically: Drawing Inferences, p. 80
- Thinking Critically: Comparing and Contrasting, p. 93

Communities

- Career Path, p. 90
- De l'école au travail, p. 91

Connections and Comparisons

Photo Flash!

The French teenager and her mother in the photo are trying to decide whether to buy a **calculatrice** *(calculator)* or a **calculatrice-traductrice** *(calculator-translator),* which is a calculator and an electronic dictionary in one. Do students in the United States commonly use a **calculatrice-traductrice?**

Thinking Critically

Analyzing Ask students if they shop with friends, a family member, or alone. Have them think of possible difficulties that might arise while shopping with a parent.

CHAPITRE 3

Tout pour la rentrée

Objectives

In this chapter you will learn to

Première étape

- make and respond to requests
- ask others what they need and tell what you need

Deuxième étape

- tell what you'd like and what you'd like to do

Troisième étape

- get someone's attention
- ask for information
- express and respond to thanks

Visit Holt Online
go.hrw.com
KEYWORD: WA3 POITIERS-3
Online Edition

C'EST LA RENTRÉE

◀ C'est combien, cette calculatrice?

Chapter Opener

CHAPITRE 3

Focusing on Outcomes

Call students' attention to the chapter objectives. Ask small groups to brainstorm expressions in English they might use to accomplish the chapter objectives. For example, to express what they'd like to do, they might suggest *I'd like to . . . , I feel like . . . , I want to . . . ,* and so on. NOTE: The self-check activities in **Que sais-je?** on page 100 help students assess their achievement of the objectives.

Teacher Note

Students will learn **je voudrais** in this chapter; the present tense forms of **vouloir** are presented later.

Cultures and Communities

Culture Notes

- There are usually no lockers in French schools, so students must have a sturdy bookbag in which to carry their supplies from class to class.
- In France, the fountain pen is still a very popular writing instrument. Most students also use pencil cases.

STANDARDS: 2.2

Mise en train

CHAPITRE 3

Teaching Resources
pp. 76–78

PRINT 

- Lesson Planner, p. 13
- Video Guide, pp. 18, 20
- Cahier d'activités, p. 25

MEDIA

- One-Stop Planner
- Video Program

  Mise en train
  Videocassette 1, 37:07–41:56
  Videocassette 5 (captioned version), 16:51–21:41

  Suite
  Videocassette 1, 41:59–46:20
  Videocassette 5 (captioned version), 21:44–26:06
- DVD Tutor, Disc 1
- Audio Compact Discs, CD 3, Trs. 1–2
- **Mise en train** Transparencies

Presenting Mise en train

Before you play the video, have students read the questions in Activity 1 on page 78. Tell them to look for the answers as they view the episode. You might also ask them to guess the moods of Julie and her mother and what the problem might be.

Mise en train Transparencies

The **roman-photo** is an abridged version of the video episode.

MISE EN TRAIN ▪ *Pas question!*

CD 3
Trs. 1–2

Stratégie pour comprendre

Where are Julie and Mme Pelletier? What could they be shopping for? Use the context of the setting to guess the meanings of the words you don't know.

Madame Pelletier

Julie

La vendeuse

1
Mme Pelletier : Alors, qu'est-ce qu'il te faut?
Julie : Eh bien, des crayons, des stylos, une gomme, une calculatrice, un pot de colle...

2
Mme Pelletier : Pardon, mademoiselle, vous avez des trousses, s'il vous plaît?
La vendeuse : Oui, bien sûr. Là, à côté des cahiers.

3
Julie : Et voilà une boîte de crayons de couleur.
Mme Pelletier : C'est combien?
Julie : Trois cinquante.

4
Julie : Regarde, Maman, une calculatrice-traductrice. C'est chouette!
Mme Pelletier : Oui. C'est pour les maths ou pour l'anglais?
Julie : Euh, il me faut une calculatrice pour les maths. Mais une calculatrice-traductrice, c'est pratique pour l'anglais.

Preteaching Vocabulary

Guessing words from context

Have students guess what the title ***Pas question!*** means. Then, have students discuss what could happen when a teenager goes shopping with a parent. Using this as a context, have students look at the photos and find words in each frame that tell them what the focus of the conversation is.

Have students guess the meaning of the following words based on the context: ❶ **pot de colle** ❷ **cahiers** ❸ **boîte de crayons** ❽ **sac.** Have them suggest reasons for Julie's bad mood at the end.

STANDARDS: 1.2

5 **Mme Pelletier :** C'est combien, mademoiselle?
La vendeuse : 80 euros.

6 **Mme Pelletier :** 80 euros! Oh là là! C'est pas possible!

7 **Mme Pelletier :** Et cette calculatrice-là?
La vendeuse : 20 euros.
Mme Pelletier : Bien. Alors, cette calculatrice.

8 **Julie :** Eh, Maman, regarde ce sac vert. Il est super!
Mme Pelletier : Oui. Pas mal. Mais cher. 33 euros!

9 **Mme Pelletier :** Moi, j'aime mieux ce sac-là, à 12 euros.
Julie : Non! Il est horrible!
Mme Pelletier : Pourquoi?
Julie : Je n'aime pas ce rouge.

10 **Mme Pelletier :** Moi, je n'achète pas un sac à 33 euros.
Julie : Alors, j'aime mieux aller à l'école sans sac!

Cahier d'activités, p. 25, Act. 1

Using the Captioned Video/DVD

Students who have difficulty understanding French spoken at a normal speed may benefit from seeing the captioned version of ***Pas question!*** In order to reduce anxiety about the new language and to facilitate comprehension, use Videocassette 5 to allow students to see the French captions for ***Pas question!*** and ***Pas question! (suite)***. You might suggest that students watch the captioned video first without sound. Seeing written words that they may recognize and associating them with gestures and actions, without interference from the spoken words, will increase their comprehension and boost their confidence, thus preparing them to watch the video with sound and to do the comprehension activities on page 78.

Mise en train

CHAPITRE 3

Language-to-Language

You might point out the connection between the word **colle** *(glue)* and the word **collage,** which is also used in English (illustrations glued together to make a picture).

Cooperative Learning

Have students calculate in dollars the prices of the items in the story. Form groups of four: a recorder, a reader to call out prices in euros, a money-changer to calculate the dollar price, and a checker to review the calculations. Students will need a copy of the latest money exchange rates, which can be found in the newspaper.

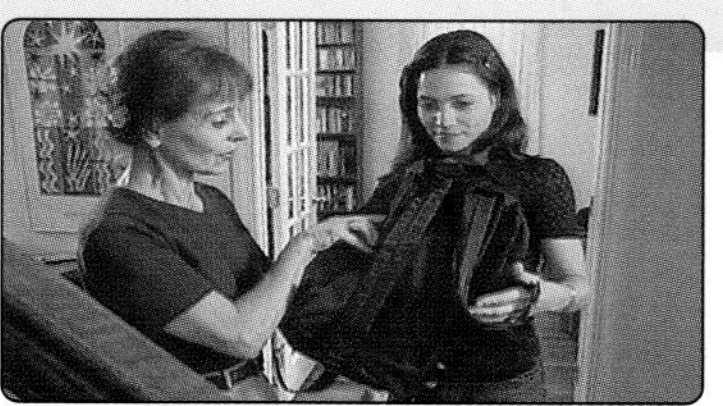

Pas question! (suite)

You may choose to continue with ***Pas question! (suite)*** at this time or wait until later in the chapter. The story continues the next day as Julie and Sarah are leaving for school. Julie is carrying her school supplies in her arms and drops everything. Her mother suggests that she order a bag through the Internet. Julie tries to order it but it is out of stock. She goes back to the store she went to with her mother, and buys the same bag in a different color. She also buys two T-shirts, one of them as a gift for her mother. Mme Pelletier is surprised that Julie bought the inexpensive bag after all.

Mise en train

CHAPITRE 3

Slower Pace

2 Students might work in pairs to find the answers. To check their answers, you might have students repeat each sentence, replacing **elle** with either Julie or Mme Pelletier.

Teaching Suggestion

5 You might suggest several possible endings to the story:
a. Julie va à l'école sans sac.
b. Mme Pelletier achète le sac à 33€.
c. Mme Pelletier achète le sac à 12€.
You might write these on a transparency and have the class vote on an ending for the story.

These activities check for comprehension only. Students should not yet be expected to produce language modeled in **Mise en train.**

1 Tu as compris?

Réponds aux questions suivantes d'après l'épisode de ***Pas question!***

1. What is the relationship between Julie and Mme Pelletier? How do you know? daughter and mother; Julie calls her **Maman.**
2. Where are they? in a store
3. What are they doing there? buying school supplies
4. Why does Julie need a calculator? for math class
5. What is Mme Pelletier's main concern? saving money
6. What do you think of Julie's decision at the end of ***Pas question!***?

2 Julie ou sa mère?

Dans les phrases suivantes, on parle de Julie ou de Mme Pelletier?

1. Elle aime la calculatrice à 80 €. Julie
2. Elle voudrait une calculatrice-traductrice. Julie
3. Elle aime mieux le sac à 12 €. Mme Pelletier
4. Elle aime mieux le sac vert. Julie
5. Elle va aller à l'école sans sac. Julie
6. Elle n'achète pas un sac à 33 €. Mme Pelletier

3 Cherche les expressions

Can you find an expression in ***Pas question!*** to . . .

1. ask what someone needs? See answers below.
2. tell what you need?
3. get a salesperson's attention?
4. ask the price of something?
5. say you like or prefer something?
6. say you don't like something?

Il est horrible!
C'est combien?
Il me faut...
J'aime mieux...
Il est super!
Pardon, mademoiselle...
Qu'est-ce qu'il te faut?

4 Mets en ordre

Mets les phrases suivantes dans un ordre chronologique, d'après l'épisode de ***Pas question!***

1. Mme Pelletier asks the price of a calculator. 4
2. Mme Pelletier asks a salesperson if she has any pencil cases. 2
3. Julie says she will go to school without a bag. 6
4. Mme Pelletier asks Julie what she needs for school. 1
5. Mme Pelletier asks the price of a box of colored pencils. 3
6. Julie points out a bag she likes. 5

5 Et maintenant, à toi

What do you think will happen next in the story? Discuss your ideas with a partner.

Comprehension Check

Slower Pace

3 Before students watch the video, have them match the functions and the expressions in the box. Then, play the video and have students raise their hand when they hear these expressions.

Additional Practice

Quote at random the characters in the video and have students identify the speakers.

Challenge

After the students have watched the video, show some school supplies to the class and ask the students if those items were mentioned in the video.

Answers

3
1. Qu'est-ce qu'il te faut?
2. Il me faut...
3. Pardon, mademoiselle...
4. C'est combien?
5. Il est super!/J'aime mieux...
6. Il est horrible!

STANDARDS: 1.2

Première étape

Objectives Making and responding to requests; asking others what they need and telling what you need

WA3 POITIERS-3

Vocabulaire

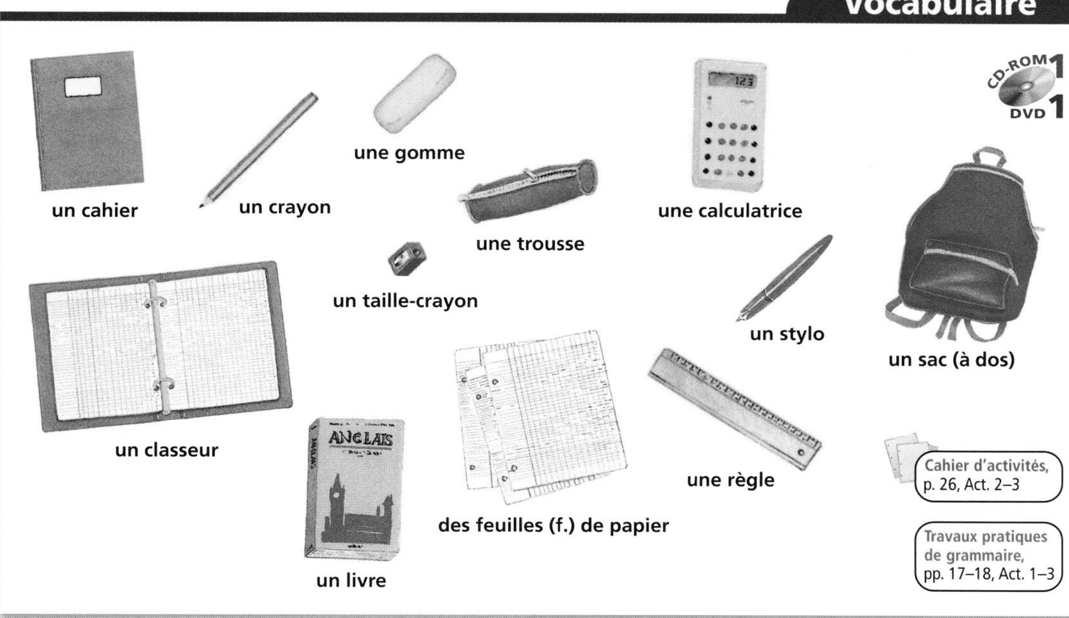

Make flashcards to learn new words. On one side of a card, write the French word you want to learn. If the word is a noun, include an article **(le, la, les)** to help you remember the gender. On the other side, paste or draw a picture to illustrate the meaning of the word. Then, ask a classmate to show you the picture while you try to name the object, or use the cards to test yourself.

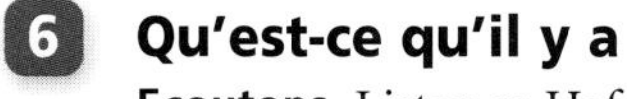

6 Qu'est-ce qu'il y a dans mon sac? See scripts and answers on p. 73G.

Ecoutons Listen as Hafaïdh and Karine check the contents of their bookbags. Then, look at the pictures and decide which bag belongs to each of them.

CD 3 Tr. 3

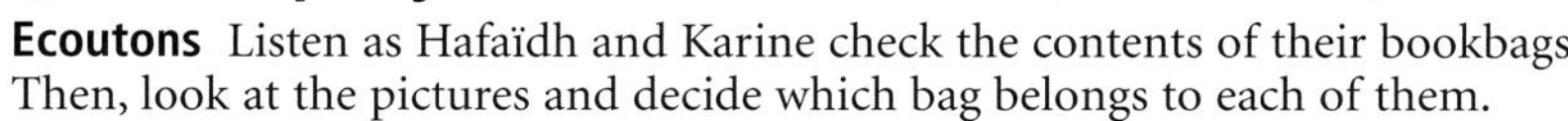

a. 

b. 

c. 

Communication for All Students

Auditory/Kinesthetic Learners

After presenting all the words, ask **Qui a un(e)... ?** Have students hold up the object you named and say **Moi. J'ai un(e)...**

Slower Pace

6 Before playing the recording, have students identify the items in each bookbag.

Auditory Learners

6 Describe the contents of each bookbag and have students give the letter of the corresponding photo.

Première étape

CHAPITRE 3

Teaching Resources
pp. 79–82

PRINT

- Lesson Planner, p. 14
- TPR Storytelling Book, pp. 9, 12
- Listening Activities, pp. 19, 23
- Activities for Communication, pp. 13–14, 85, 88, 141–142
- Travaux pratiques de grammaire, pp. 17–19
- Grammar Tutor for Students of French, Chapter 3
- Cahier d'activités, pp. 26–28
- Testing Program, pp. 53–56
- Alternative Assessment Guide, p. 34
- Student Make-Up Assignments, Chapter 3

MEDIA

- One-Stop Planner
- Audio Compact Discs, CD 3, Trs. 3–4, 20, 26–27
- Teaching Transparencies: 3-1, 3-A; **Grammaire supplémentaire** Answers; Travaux pratiques de grammaire Answers
- Interactive CD-ROM Tutor, Disc 1

Bell Work

Have students list all the classes they have this semester and tell whether they like them or not.

Presenting Vocabulaire

Before students see the French words, gather the objects pictured. Hold them up as you say the French words, having students repeat after you. Then, say the French words for various items and have students try to identify them by pointing to the correct item.

Teaching Resources
pp. 79–82

PRINT 

- Lesson Planner, p. 14
- TPR Storytelling Book, pp. 9, 12
- Listening Activities, pp. 19, 23
- Activities for Communication, pp. 13–14, 85, 88, 141–142
- Travaux pratiques de grammaire, pp. 17–19
- Grammar Tutor for Students of French, Chapter 3
- Cahier d'activités, pp. 26–28
- Testing Program, pp. 53–56
- Alternative Assessment Guide, p. 34
- Student Make-Up Assignments, Chapter 3

MEDIA 

- One-Stop Planner
- Audio Compact Discs, CD 3, Trs. 3–4, 20, 26–27
- Teaching Transparencies: 3-1, 3-A; **Grammaire supplémentaire** Answers; Travaux pratiques de grammaire Answers
- Interactive CD-ROM Tutor, Disc 1

Presenting
Comment dit-on... ?

Circulate among the students, asking for certain items. **(Tu as une règle?)** Prompt the responses **Voilà** and **Non, je regrette.** Then, have students practice the same exchange with a partner. Next, have students ask you for certain things, saying **Vous avez... ?** Have them ask a partner for two things they need.

7 Objets trouvés

Lisons/Ecrivons When Paulette gets home from the store, she realizes that she forgot to put some of her school supplies into her bag. Look at the receipt showing what she bought and make a list, in French, of the missing items.

See answers below.

Exemple **Elle n'a pas le...**

VEN 13-05-03 3004
047CA BELLIOT Stéphanie

GOMME CAOUTCH.	0,50
CRAYONS GRAH.	0,79
REGLE GRADUEE	3,85
CAH. BROUILLON	1,53
COPIES DBLES PF GC	1,38
CLASSEUR 17X22	4,64
TROUSSE	7,23
SOUS/TOTAL	19,92
TOTAL	19,92
REÇU	50,00
RENDU	30,08

00617 7 ARTC 16:36TM

Note culturelle

In large stores in France, customers are expected to place their items on the conveyer belt and then remove and bag them as well. Most stores provide small plastic sacks, but many shoppers bring their own basket **(un panier)** or net bag **(un filet).** Since space is limited in small stores and boutiques, browsing inside these stores is not as common. In some cases, items and their prices are placed in window displays. Most people window-shop until they are ready to make a purchase. A sign that reads **Entrée libre** indicates that browsers are welcome.

8 Devine!

Parlons/Ecrivons Write down the name of one of the objects from the **Vocabulaire** on page 79. Don't let the other members of your group know what you've chosen. They will then take turns guessing which object you chose.

Exemple **—C'est un taille-crayon?**
—Oui, c'est ça. *or* **Non, ce n'est pas ça.**

Comment dit-on...?

Making and responding to requests

To ask someone for something:

Tu as un stylo?
Vous avez un crayon?

To respond:

Oui. **Voilà.** *Here.*
Non. **Je regrette. Je n'ai pas de** crayons.
Sorry. I don't have any . . .

Cahier d'activités, p. 27, Act. 4b

—Tu as une calculatrice, Paul?
—J'ai un stylo, un crayon, une règle et des feuilles de papier, mais je n'ai pas de calculatrice!

Connections and Comparisons

Thinking Critically

Drawing Inferences Ask students whether they should use **tu** or **vous** with a classmate and with a salesperson. Ask students what they think the reaction would be if they used the wrong pronoun (surprised, offended). You might give comparable examples in English (calling people by their first name when you don't know them very well).

Thinking Critically

Analyzing Have students consider these questions: What are the advantages and disadvantages of having to bag your own purchases? Of having shoppers bring their own bags? Do American stores encourage shoppers to bring their own bags? Why or why not?

Answers

7 Elle n'a pas le classeur. Elle n'a pas le cahier.
Elle n'a pas la gomme. Elle n'a pas la règle. Elle n'a pas les copies.

STANDARDS: 1.3, 2.1, 3.1, 3.2, 4.2

Grammaire

The indefinite articles *un, une,* and *des*

The articles **un** and **une** both mean *a* or *an.* Use **un** with masculine nouns and **une** with feminine nouns. Use **des** *(some)* with plural nouns. Notice that **un, une,** and **des** change to **de** after **ne... pas.**

J'ai **un** crayon, mais je n'ai pas **de** papier.

Nous avons **des** règles, mais nous n'avons pas **de** stylo.

CD-ROM 1 DVD 1

Grammaire supplémentaire, p. 94, Act. 1–2

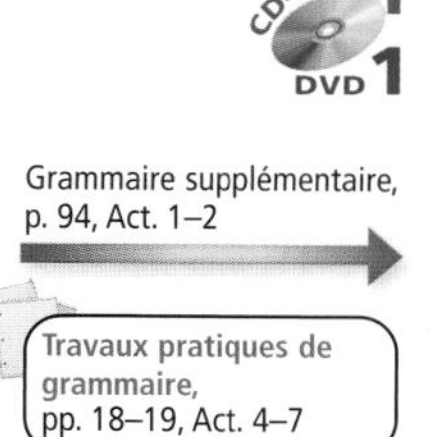

Travaux pratiques de grammaire, pp. 18–19, Act. 4–7

9 **Grammaire en contexte** See scripts and answers on p. 73G.

CD 3 Tr. 4

Ecoutons Listen as Nadine asks her friends for some school supplies. Match her friends' responses to the appropriate pictures.

a.

b.

c.

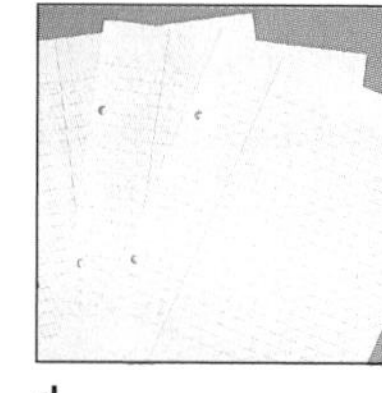
d.

e.

10 **Grammaire en contexte**

Parlons With a partner, take turns pointing out the differences you notice between Christophe's desk and Annick's.

EXEMPLE **Regarde! Christophe a une gomme, mais Annick n'a pas de gomme.**

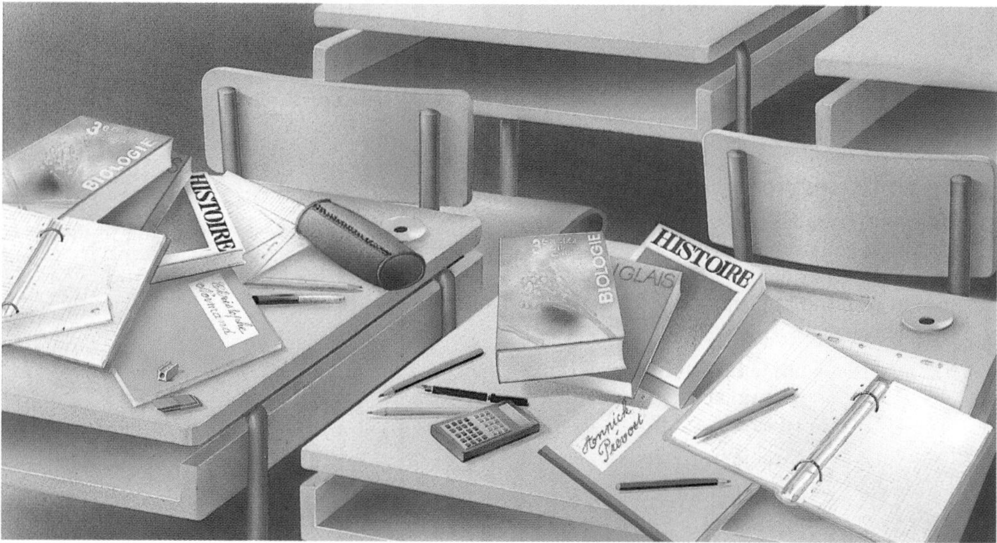

Communication for All Students

Additional Practice

9 Have partners make a list of 3 or 4 items and ask each other if they have these items. Then, have individuals tell which items their partners have and don't have.

Challenge

10 As a variation, form small groups or teams for a competition. Set a time limit within which groups must write down all of the items they see on one of the desks in the illustration.

Presenting Grammaire

The indefinite articles Hold up an object that is a masculine noun in French, such as a pencil, and have students tell you what you have. **(Vous avez un crayon.)** Repeat with a feminine noun **(Vous avez une gomme.)** and with several other objects. **(Vous avez des crayons et des gommes.)** Put the items away, show your empty hands, and have students tell you that you don't have these objects. **(Vous n'avez pas de...)** Then, have students make a chart in their notebooks with two columns and four rows. Down the left-hand side of the chart, they should write *masculine, feminine, vowel sound,* and *plural.* They should label the columns *Definite articles* and *Indefinite articles.* Have students fill in the chart with **le, la, l', les, un, une,** and **des,** and keep it for later use.

Teacher Note

Demonstrative adjectives can be added to the chart when they are presented later in this chapter.

Culture Note

French notebook paper is usually graph paper rather than lined. It is sold either as **copies simples** *(single-page sheets)* or **copies doubles,** which are two-page sheets used for **rédactions** or **interros écrites.**

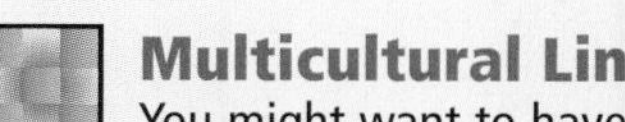

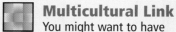

Multicultural Link

You might want to have students compile a list of school supplies and other items they need for school. Have them look for two or three of the items at home with labels and/or instructions in different languages.

Première étape

CHAPITRE 3

Presenting Comment dit-on... ?

Have pairs of students role-play the short dialogue in the illustration, substituting other courses and objects. Students might want to know the negative **Il ne me faut pas de...**

Additional Vocabulary

You might want to give students the names of other items they might like to know in French: **un surligneur** *(highlighter);* **la craie** *(chalk);* and **un cahier de textes** *(memo book or personal calendar for young people).*

Assess

- Testing Program, pp. 53–56 Quiz 3-1A, Quiz 3-1B Audio CD 3, Tr. 20
- Student Make-Up Assignments, Chapter 3, Alternative Quiz
- Alternative Assessment Guide, p. 34

Comment dit-on...?

Asking others what they need and telling what you need

To ask what someone needs:

Qu'est-ce qu'il te faut pour les maths?
What do you need for . . . ? (informal)
Qu'est-ce qu'il vous faut pour la géo?
What do you need for . . . ? (formal)

To tell what you need:

Il me faut un stylo et un classeur.

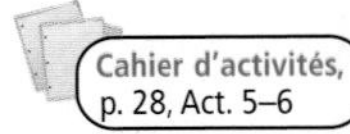

Cahier d'activités, p. 28, Act. 5–6

Grammaire supplémentaire, p. 94, Act. 3

Alors, qu'est-ce qu'il te faut pour l'anglais?
Euh, il me faut un classeur et un sac aussi.

Vocabulaire à la carte

Here are some additional words you can use to talk about your school supplies.

un compas	*a compass*
des crayons (m.) **de couleur**	*some colored pencils*
un feutre	*a marker*
du liquide (m.) **correcteur**	*some correction fluid*
du ruban (m.) **adhésif**	*some transparent tape*
une tenue de gymnastique	*a gym uniform*

11 Qu'est-ce qu'il te faut?

Ecrivons/Parlons Make a list of your school subjects. Exchange lists with a partner. Then, take turns asking each other what you need for various classes.

EXEMPLE — **Qu'est-ce qu'il te faut pour les maths?**
— **Il me faut une calculatrice et un crayon.**

12 Aide-mémoire

Ecrivons Write a note to remind yourself of the school supplies you need to buy for two or three of your classes.

13 Un petit service

Parlons You're late for class, and you've forgotten your supplies. Ask a friend if he or she has what you need. Your friend should respond appropriately. Then, change roles.

EXEMPLE — **Oh là là! J'ai histoire! Il me faut un stylo et un cahier. Tu as un stylo?**
— **Non, je regrette.**
— **Zut!**

Pour le français il me faut...

Communication for All Students

Language Note

Vocabulaire à la carte Make sure students don't pronounce the **s** at the end of **compas. Feutre** also means *felt,* as in *felt-tip pen.*

Challenge

Ask students to imagine situations other than shopping for school supplies when they might use the expressions in **Comment dit-on... ?** (at a pharmacy, library, or post office, and when cooking).

Qu'est-ce qu'il te faut comme fournitures scolaires?

We asked some francophone students what supplies they bought for the opening of school, **la rentrée.** Here's what they had to say.

Séverine,
Martinique

«Alors, donc pour l'école j'ai acheté un nouveau sac à dos, des livres pour étudier, des vêtements, entre autres des jeans, des chaussures, bien sûr et puis bon, des tee-shirts, des jupes, des robes.» Tr. 6

Onélia,
France

«Il faut des classeurs, des cahiers, des crayons, des règles, des instruments de géométrie, [une] calculatrice pour les mathématiques, des feuilles... C'est tout.» Tr. 7

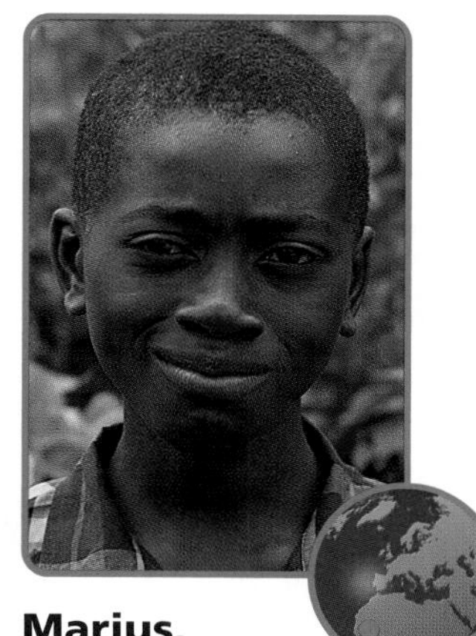

Marius,
Côte d'Ivoire

«Pour l'école, il faut des règles, des bics, des stylos, des cahiers, des livres et la tenue.» Tr. 8

Qu'en penses-tu? Answers may vary.

1. What school supplies did you have to purchase for the school year?
2. What other items do you usually buy at the beginning of a school year?
3. What did these students buy that is usually provided by schools in the United States? textbooks
4. What are the advantages and disadvantages of each system?

Savais-tu que...?

In French-speaking countries, students usually buy their own textbooks and even maintain their own grade book, **un livret scolaire.** Some schools require students to purchase school uniforms. A store that specializes in school supplies, textbooks, and paper products is called **une librairie-papeterie.**

Cultures and Communities

Culture Notes

- You might tell students that Ivorian students wear school uniforms. In high school, the boys wear khaki shirts and pants, while the girls wear blue skirts and white blouses.
- In France, there are several types of report cards. A **carnet de correspondence** is a small notebook in which students write down their grades every day. A **relevé de notes** is a report of the student's grades for the month, with the teacher's comments. A **bulletin trimestriel** is sent to the parents three times a year at the end of each trimester. It reports the average of the grades for the trimester plus the grades of the final exam. At the end of each year, the grades of the three **bulletins** are recorded in the **livret scolaire.**

CHAPITRE 3

Teaching Resources
p. 83

PRINT
- Video Guide, pp. 19, 21
- Cahier d'activités, p. 36

MEDIA
- One-Stop Planner
- Video Program Videocassette 1, 46:25–48:29
- DVD Tutor, Disc 1
- Audio Compact Discs, CD 3, Trs. 5–8
- Interactive CD-ROM Tutor, Disc 1

Presenting Panorama Culturel

As students view the video or listen to the recording, have them jot down the items mentioned by the interviewees. Then, in pairs have them take turns reading the interviews aloud. Next, ask students the **Questions** to check comprehension. Finally, have them discuss the questions in **Qu'en penses-tu?** as a class.

Questions

1. **Qu'est-ce que Séverine a acheté comme vêtements pour l'école?** (des jeans, des chaussures, des tee-shirts, des jupes et des robes)
2. **Onélia a besoin de quelles fournitures scolaires?** (des classeurs, des cahiers, des crayons, des règles, des instruments de géométrie, une calculatrice et des feuilles) **Pour quel cours?** (les maths, la géométrie)
3. **Qu'est-ce que Marius a acheté pour l'école?** (des règles, des bics, des stylos, des cahiers, des livres et la tenue)

Teaching Resources
pp. 84–87

PRINT

- Lesson Planner, p. 15
- TPR Storytelling Book, pp. 10, 12
- Listening Activities, pp. 20, 24
- Activities for Communication, pp. 15–16, 86, 88, 141–142
- Travaux pratiques de grammaire, pp. 20–23
- Grammar Tutor for Students of French, Chapter 3
- Cahier d'activités, pp. 29–31
- Testing Program, pp. 57–60
- Alternative Assessment Guide, p. 34
- Student Make-Up Assignments, Chapter 3

MEDIA 

- One-Stop Planner
- Audio Compact Discs, CD 3, Trs. 9–10, 21, 28–29
- Teaching Transparencies: 3-2, 3-B, 3-C, 3-D; **Grammaire supplémentaire** Answers; Travaux pratiques de grammaire Answers
- Interactive CD-ROM Tutor, Disc 1

Bell Work

Have students make a list of five things they have with them for class and anything they did not bring. They might begin with **Aujourd'hui, j'ai...** and **Je n'ai pas de...**

Presenting Vocabulaire

Say the cognates at the bottom of the **Vocabulaire** and have students guess their English equivalents. Then, present the other words **(baskets, ordinateur, montre, portefeuille,** and **roman)** by showing the actual items, drawing them on the board, or showing pictures of them.

Deuxième étape

Objective Telling what you'd like and what you'd like to do

WA3 POITIERS-3

Vocabulaire

Qu'est-ce qu'on va acheter?

CD-ROM 1 DVD 1

Hervé regarde **un short.**

Odile regarde **des baskets.**

Denis regarde **un roman.**

Stéphane regarde **un disque compact/un CD.**

Dorothée regarde **un jean.**

Mme Roussel regarde **un ordinateur.**

M. Beauvois regarde **une montre.**

M. Prévost regarde **un portefeuille.**

You can probably figure out what these words mean:

un bracelet	**un magazine**	**une radio**	**une télévision**
une cassette	**un poster**	**un sweat-shirt**	**une vidéocassette**
un dictionnaire	**un pull-over**	**un tee-shirt**	

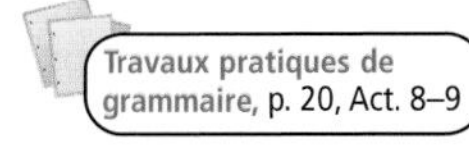
Travaux pratiques de grammaire, p. 20, Act. 8–9

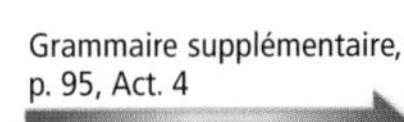
Grammaire supplémentaire, p. 95, Act. 4

14 Le shopping See scripts and answers on p. 73G.

Ecoutons Several shoppers in the **Vocabulaire** are going to tell you what they would like to buy. As you listen to each speaker, look at the illustrations above and identify the person. Write down his or her name.

CD 3 Tr. 9

Communication for All Students

Building on Previous Skills

To review previously learned vocabulary, have students tell why they think the people in the **Vocabulaire** are looking at the objects. **(Hervé aime faire les magasins. Denis aime lire. Stéphane adore la musique.)**

Tactile/Kinesthetic Learners

Name an item in the classroom and have students point to it or pick it up from among items you have displayed on a table.

Challenge

14 Have students write down the item each person would like to buy as well as the person's name.

Comment dit-on...?

Telling what you'd like and what you'd like to do

Je voudrais un sac. *I'd like . . .*
Je voudrais acheter un tee-shirt. *I'd like to buy . . .*

15 Les achats See scripts and answers on p. 73G.

Ecoutons Georges has just won a gift certificate from his favorite department store. Listen as he tells you what he would like to buy and make a list of his choices.

CD 3 Tr. 10

16 Vive le week-end!

Parlons What would you like to do this weekend? Find three classmates who want to do the same thing.

Exemple —**Je voudrais sortir avec des copains. Et toi?**
—**Moi aussi.** *or* **Moi, je voudrais faire du sport.**

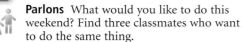

faire les magasins · faire le ménage · danser · dormir · écouter de la musique · parler au téléphone · faire du sport · regarder la télévision · étudier · nager · sortir avec des copains

17 Un cadeau

Ecrivons Make a list of what you would like to buy for . . .

1. a friend who likes horror movies and books.
2. a friend who loves sports.
3. someone who's always late for class.
4. a friend who loves music.
5. someone who loves French.
6. your best friend.

18 Mon journal

Ecrivons You earned 100 dollars this summer. Write down three or four items you'd like to buy for yourself.

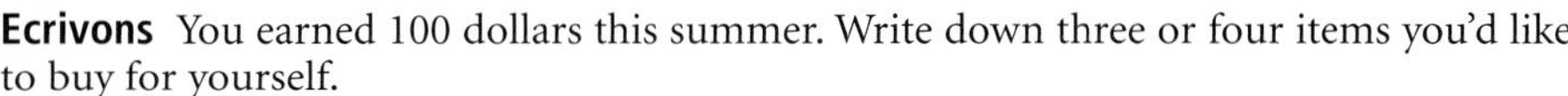

Grammaire

The demonstrative adjectives *ce, cet, cette,* and *ces*

Ce, cet, and **cette** mean *this* or *that.* **Ces** means *these* or *those.*

	Singular	*Plural*
Masculine before a consonant sound	**ce** stylo	**ces** stylos
Masculine before a vowel sound	**cet** examen	**ces** examens
Feminine	**cette** école	**ces** écoles

When you want to specify *that* as opposed to *this*, add **-là** *(there)* to the end of the noun.

—J'aime **ce sac.**
—Moi, j'aime mieux **ce sac-là.**

Grammaire supplémentaire, pp. 95–96, Act. 5–6

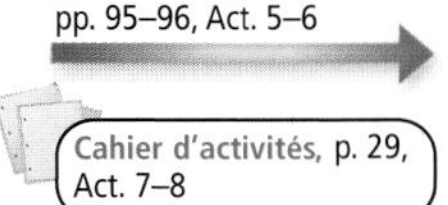

Cahier d'activités, p. 29, Act. 7–8

Travaux pratiques de grammaire, p. 21, Act. 10–11

Teacher to Teacher

Colleen Turpin
Lionville Middle School
Downingtown, PA

Colleen's students use color to learn demonstrative adjectives.

"To practice the demonstrative adjectives **ce, cet, cette,** and **ces**, I have students write each one on a color-coded index card: blue and green for masculine singular and plural forms, pink and yellow for feminine singular and plural forms. I call out the names of objects or show pictures of objects, and students hold up the appropriate card. Color-coded cards can be used any time gender needs to be practiced."

Presenting Comment dit-on... ?

After modeling the function, hold up various items or illustrations of items or activities and have individual students say what they would like or what they would like to do.

Language Notes

- French teenagers often use the abbreviation **CD** for **disque compact.**
- Tell students that the infinitive form of a verb is used after **Je voudrais.** You might also tell them that this is a polite way to express a desire.

Presenting Grammaire

The demonstrative adjectives Show students two of the same item and ask them which one they would choose. For example, hold up two different pens and ask **Tu aimes mieux quel stylo?** Students should answer **Ce stylo-là** as they point to the one they choose. Tell students that forms of *this* and *that* are called demonstrative adjectives because they point out or distinguish one or more things among many.

Teacher Note

Tell students that to specify *this* as opposed to *that,* they can add **-ci** to the end of the first noun. **(Moi, je préfère ce sac-ci, mais je n'aime pas ce sac-là.)** The suffix **-ci** is no longer very common in spoken French.

Teaching Suggestion

Grammaire Review definite and indefinite articles. If you had students make the suggested chart of articles (see Presenting on page 81), have them add **ce, cet, cette,** and **ces** to it now.

Deuxième étape

CHAPITRE 3

Teaching Resources
pp. 84–87

PRINT

- Lesson Planner, p. 15
- TPR Storytelling Book, pp. 10, 12
- Listening Activities, pp. 20, 24
- Activities for Communication, pp. 15–16, 86, 88, 141–142
- Travaux pratiques de grammaire, pp. 20–23
- Grammar Tutor for Students of French, Chapter 3
- Cahier d'activités, pp. 29–31
- Testing Program, pp. 57–60
- Alternative Assessment Guide, p. 34
- Student Make-Up Assignments, Chapter 3

MEDIA 

- One-Stop Planner
- Audio Compact Discs, CD 3, Trs. 9–10, 21, 28–29
- Teaching Transparencies: 3-2, 3-B, 3-C, 3-D; **Grammaire supplémentaire** Answers; Travaux pratiques de grammaire Answers
- Interactive CD-ROM Tutor, Disc 1

Presenting Vocabulaire

Say each color as you point out items of that color. Then, name three colors in a row and challenge a volunteer to point to items of those colors in the order in which the colors were mentioned. Ask students if they see any similarities or associations with English. Then, ask students to give the colors of the sky, a Valentine, fall, Halloween, and the French flag.

Science Link

Have students arrange the colors according to the spectrum they learned about in science or art class.

19 Grammaire en contexte

Lisons Claire is shopping for a gift for her mother. The salesperson is making suggestions. Choose the correct articles to complete their conversation.

LE VENDEUR Vous aimez (ce/cette) montre, mademoiselle?
CLAIRE Oui, mais ma mère a déjà (un/une) montre.
LE VENDEUR Et (ces/ce) roman?
CLAIRE Non, elle n'aime pas lire.
LE VENDEUR Elle aime (la /l') musique?
CLAIRE Oui. Elle adore le jazz.
LE VENDEUR (Cet/Cette) cassette de Wynton Marsalis, peut-être?
CLAIRE C'est une bonne idée.

20 Grammaire en contexte

Parlons Take turns with a partner asking and answering questions about the items below.

EXEMPLE — **Tu aimes ce sac?**
— **Non. J'aime mieux ce sac-là.**

Moi aussi. Non. Non, je n'aime pas ça.
Oui, mais j'aime mieux... Oui, j'adore!
J'aime bien. Moi non plus.

1. 
2. 
3. 
4. 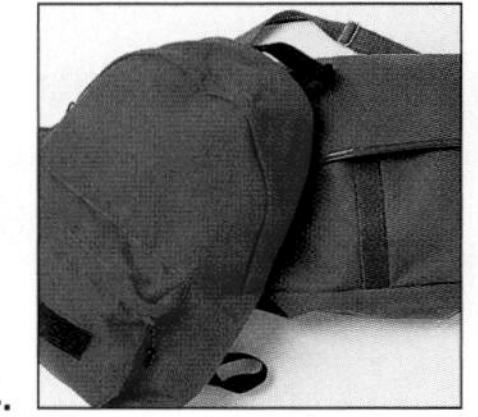

Vocabulaire

De quelle couleur est...

le sac?	la trousse?
ROUGE	ROUGE
ORANGE	ORANGE
JAUNE	JAUNE
VERT	VERTE
BLEU	BLEUE
VIOLET	VIOLETTE

Cahier d'activités, pp. 29–30, Act. 9–10

Travaux pratiques de grammaire, p. 22, Act. 12

Communication for All Students

Slower Pace

19 Have students determine the gender and number of the noun in each sentence before they choose the correct article or adjective.

Additional Practice

You might want to hold up various items and ask about the color: **C'est bleu ou rouge?** Have individuals or the entire class respond. For more of a challenge, ask **C'est de quelle couleur?**

STANDARDS: 1.1, 3.1, 5.1

21 Vrai ou faux?

Parlons Regarde l'image et dis si les phrases suivantes sont vraies ou fausses.

1. Claire a un sac jaune. vrai
2. Claire et Thierry ont des tee-shirts bleus. faux
3. Claire a un short marron. faux
4. Thierry a des baskets bleues. faux
5. Thierry a un classeur rouge. vrai
6. Claire et Thierry ont des shorts noirs. faux

Grammaire

Adjective agreement and placement

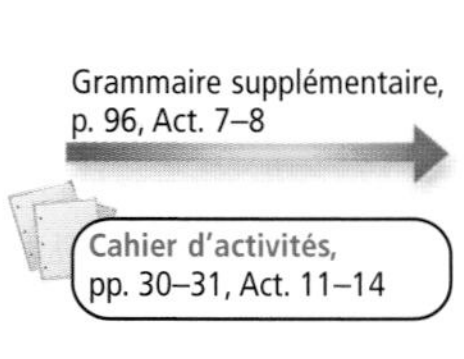

Did you notice in the **Vocabulaire** on page 86 that the spelling of some colors changes according to the nouns they describe?

	Singular	*Plural*
Masculine	le classeur vert	les classeurs vert**s**
Feminine	la gomme vert**e**	les gommes vert**es**

- Usually, you add an **e** to make an adjective feminine; however, when an adjective ends in an unaccented **e,** you don't have to add another **e: le classeur rouge, la gomme rouge.**
- Some adjectives don't follow this pattern: **blanc, blanche; violet, violette.**
- Usually, you add an **s** to make an adjective plural; however, when an adjective ends in an **s,** you don't have to add another **s: les crayons gris.**
- Some adjectives don't change form. Two examples are **orange** and **marron.**
- Colors and many other adjectives are placed after the nouns they describe.

Grammaire supplémentaire, p. 96, Act. 7–8

Cahier d'activités, pp. 30–31, Act. 11–14

Travaux pratiques de grammaire, pp. 22–23, Act. 13–15

22 Grammaire en contexte

Ecrivons/Parlons Create a list of six objects. Ask your classmates if they have the items on your list. When you find someone who does, find out what color each item is and write the person's name next to the appropriate item.

un tee-shirt · une montre · un short · un stylo · un pull-over · des baskets · une trousse · un portefeuille

Deuxième étape

CHAPITRE 3

Presenting Grammaire

Adjective agreement and placement Have students deduce how the feminine forms of colors are formed by studying the **Vocabulaire** on page 86. Then, ask students how they think the spelling of the colors would change if they described several things. Show various combinations of school supplies in certain colors (two red binders, one green pencil, three white rulers) and have volunteers write the French equivalents on the board **(les classeurs rouges, le crayon vert, les règles blanches).**

Assess

- Testing Program, pp. 57–60 Quiz 3-2A, Quiz 3-2B Audio CD 3, Tr. 21
- Student Make-Up Assignments, Chapter 3, Alternative Quiz
- Alternative Assessment Guide, p. 34

Communication for All Students

Visual Learners

21 First, ask students to identify in French the clothes in the illustration.

Slower Pace

22 Review the colors in French before starting this activity. You might say **Cette personne a des baskets noires** and have students call out the name of the person in class wearing those sneakers.

Game

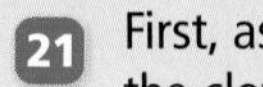

Play the game **Je vois quelque chose** on page 73C to practice vocabulary and colors. Extend it to refer to people: **Je vois quelqu'un qui a des baskets blanches.** You might also re-enter previously learned vocabulary: **Je vois quelqu'un qui a une calculatrice noire.**

Teaching Resources
pp. 88–91

PRINT 
- Lesson Planner, p. 16
- TPR Storytelling Book, pp. 11, 12
- Listening Activities, pp. 21, 25
- Activities for Communication, pp. 17–18, 87, 89, 141–142
- Travaux pratiques de grammaire, p. 24
- Grammar Tutor for Students of French, Chapter 3
- Cahier d'activités, pp. 32–34
- Testing Program, pp. 61–64
- Alternative Assessment Guide, p. 34
- Student Make-Up Assignments, Chapter 3

MEDIA
- One-Stop Planner
- Audio Compact Discs, CD 3, Trs. 11–12, 22, 30–31
- Teaching Transparencies: 3-3; **Grammaire supplémentaire** Answers; Travaux pratiques de grammaire Answers
- Interactive CD-ROM Tutor, Disc 1

Bell Work
Have students make a list of three things they would like or would like to do.

Presenting Vocabulaire
Ask students to count aloud from 60–69. Next, write **soixante-dix** on the board and ask students what number it represents. Then, ask students to guess how to count from 71–79. Do the same with **quatre-vingts** and with **quatre-vingt-dix.** Finally, write **cent** and ask students to suggest English words that have the same root *(century, cent, centennial).* Have students count by hundreds from 200–900.

Troisième étape

Objectives Getting someone's attention; asking for information; expressing and responding to thanks

WA3 POITIERS-3

Vocabulaire

60	70	71	72	80	81
soixante	soixante-dix	soixante et onze	soixante-douze	quatre-vingts	quatre-vingt-un
90	91	100	101	200	201
quatre-vingt-dix	quatre-vingt-onze	cent	cent un	deux cents	deux cent un

CD-ROM 1 DVD 1

Cahier d'activités, pp. 32–33, Act. 15–17
Travaux pratiques de grammaire, p. 24, Act. 16–18
Grammaire supplémentaire, p. 97, Act. 9

23 **Le top des radios** See scripts and answers on p. 73H.

Ecoutons Listen to four French disc jockeys announce the dial frequencies of their radio stations. Then, match the frequencies to the station logos.

CD 3 Tr. 11

RADIOS ROCK

RCV 99 MHZ (LILLE)
a.

100.3 MHZ
b.

C'ROCK 89.5 MHZ (VIENNE)
c.

OUÏ FM 102.3 MHZ (PARIS)
d.

94 MHz
e.

After a transition of three years, France changed its currency in 2002. It phased out its own French **franc** to replace it with the currency shared by most of the countries of Western Europe, the **euro.** That means that if you are traveling in Europe, you could use the same money in Spain, France, and Germany without having to convert to local currencies. Euro bills come in denominations of 5, 10, 20, 50, 100, 200, and 500 euros. Euro coins, called **cents** come in denominations of 1, 2, 5, 10, 20, and 50. There are one hundred cents in each euro. Belgium and Luxembourg are among the European countries that have adopted the euro.

Communication for All Students

Additional Practice
23 After this activity, ask students to say the frequency and call letters of their favorite radio stations. **(Moi, j'écoute KVMJ 95.5 FM.)** You might take a poll to see which three stations are the most popular.

Challenge
Read aloud some addition and subtraction problems for students to solve. You might have students work individually, in pairs, or in small groups. You will need to teach the words **et/plus** *(plus)* and **moins** *(minus).* Ask volunteers to write the problems and answers on the board and read them aloud.

STANDARDS: 1.2, 2.2, 3.2

Ça fait combien?

Parlons/Ecrivons How much money is shown in each illustration? Give the totals in French.

1. soixante et un euros trente cents (61,30 €)

2. cent vingt-quatre euros cinquante cents (124,50 €)

C'est combien?

Lisons Look at the drawing of the store display below. How much money does each of these customers spend in **Papier Plume?**

1. Alain achète deux stylos et une trousse. neuf euros soixante-sept (9,67 €)
2. Geneviève achète un classeur, un dictionnaire et un cahier. quarante et un euros quatre-vingt-quinze (41,95 €)
3. Paul achète six crayons et un taille-crayon. un euro trente-six (1,36 €)
4. Marcel achète une règle, une gomme et un stylo. quatre euros quatre-vingt-dix (4,90 €)
5. Sarah achète deux cahiers et un dictionnaire. trente-neuf euros douze (39,12 €)
6. Cécile achète une règle et une calculatrice. dix-neuf euros soixante et un (19,61 €)

Cultures and Communities

Culture Notes

- Euro bills increase in size according to the value of the bill. Euro bills are illustrated with architectural elements and bridges. As for euro coins, one side features a common European theme, and the other side contains a national symbol surrounded by the European Union's twelve stars.
- Francophone Swiss and Belgians say **septante** and **nonante** for 70 and 90. For 80, the Belgians say **quatre-vingts,** while some Swiss people say **octante.**

Auditory Learners

25 For listening comprehension, make some true–false statements as students look at the illustration. **(La trousse coûte 5€. (faux) Les règles coûtent 2,25€. (vrai))**

Reteaching

25 **School supplies, numbers**
Write on the board the prices of several items in euros:

un crayon = 0,11€
un cahier = 1,65€
une trousse = 5,37€
six stylos = 12,90€

Say the names of the items and their prices and have students repeat them. Then, write several more items on the board and have individual students suggest prices for them. Next, have students work in pairs, with one student naming items and prices at random, and the other student calculating the total cost and the change due from a **100€** bill.

Language Notes

- Ask students to suggest slang terms we use in English to refer to money (dough, bucks). You might give them some other terms in French for money. Money in slang is **le fric.**
- Some idiomatic expressions with numbers include **couper les cheveux en quatre** *(to split hairs),* **voir trente-six chandelles** *(to see stars),* **faire les cent pas** *(to pace up and down).*

Math Link

Using the present exchange rate, have students calculate the cost in dollars of some of the school supplies in the ad in Activity 25. Ask students whether supplies seem to cost more, less, or about the same in France as in the U.S. (Generally, school supplies are a little more expensive in France.)

Teaching Resources
pp. 88–91

PRINT

- Lesson Planner, p. 16
- TPR Storytelling Book, pp. 11, 12
- Listening Activities, pp. 21, 25
- Activities for Communication, pp. 17–18, 87, 89, 141–142
- Travaux pratiques de grammaire, p. 24
- Grammar Tutor for Students of French, Chapter 3
- Cahier d'activités, pp. 32–34
- Testing Program, pp. 61–64
- Alternative Assessment Guide, p. 34
- Student Make-Up Assignments, Chapter 3

MEDIA 

- One-Stop Planner
- Audio Compact Discs, CD 3, Trs. 11–12, 22, 30–31
- Teaching Transparencies: 3-3; **Grammaire supplémentaire** Answers; Travaux pratiques de grammaire Answers
- Interactive CD-ROM Tutor, Disc 1

Mon journal

26 For an additional journal entry suggestion for Chapter 3, see *Cahier d'activités,* page 147. You might also refer students to additional school supplies listed in the Additional Vocabulary on page R12.

Presenting
Comment dit-on... ?

Ask students to look first at the illustrations. Then, have them read the two dialogues and infer which functions the girl is expressing in each (1st: asking how much something costs; 2nd: expressing thanks). After introducing the expressions, have students role-play the dialogues, changing the item and price.

26 Mon journal

Ecrivons Do you budget your money? Make a list of the items you've bought in the last month and the approximate price of each in euros. To convert American prices to euros, look up the current exchange rate in the newspaper or on the Web.

Comment dit-on...?

Getting someone's attention; asking for information; expressing and responding to thanks

To get someone's attention:

Pardon, monsieur/madame/mademoiselle.

Excusez-moi, monsieur/madame/mademoiselle.

To ask how much something costs:

C'est combien, s'il vous plaît? *How much is it, please?*

To express and respond to thanks:

Merci. *Thanks*
A votre service. *You're welcome.*

Grammaire supplémentaire, p. 97, Act. 10–11

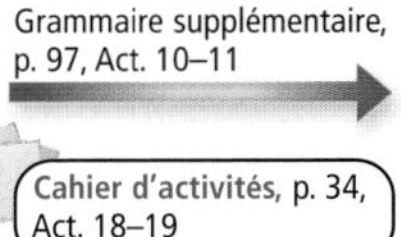

Cahier d'activités, p. 34, Act. 18–19

27 C'est combien? See scripts and answers on p. 73H.

CD 3 Tr. 12

Ecoutons/Ecrivons In a department store in France, you overhear shoppers asking salespeople for the prices of various items. As you listen to the conversations, write down the items mentioned and their prices.

Note culturelle

Prices expressed in euros can be said in two ways in French: either **quarante-cinq euros cinquante** or **quarante-cinq cinquante (45,50).** Notice that prices are written in French with a comma where a decimal point would be used in American prices.

28 Jeu de rôle

Parlons You're buying school supplies in a French **librairie-papeterie.** For each item you want, get the salesperson's attention and ask how much the item costs. The salesperson will give you the price. Act out this scene with a partner. Then, change roles.

EXEMPLE — **Excusez-moi, madame. C'est combien, cette trousse bleue?**
— **C'est six euros.**
— **Merci.**

Cultures and Communities

Career Path

26 Have students work in pairs to think of careers that would involve foreign currencies, such as the **euro.** Ask them how a knowledge of French could benefit them in these careers. You may want to have students do research on the Internet for ideas.

Culture Note

Explain to students that although **A votre service** means *you're welcome/at your service,* it is used only in certain situations. The expression will be used by people who work in service-oriented businesses, such as restaurants and shops, but not in casual conversation.

STANDARDS: 1.1, 1.2, 1.3, 2.1, 3.2, 4.2, 5.1, 5.2

De l'école au travail

Parlons You have a job with an international distributor of magazines selling subscriptions over the telephone to French-speaking customers. With a partner, take turns playing the roles of customer and salesperson, using the advertisement to discuss the prices of subscriptions in French.

Abonnez-vous à :

FEMME A LA MODE	(12 numéros) France 35 €
DECOUVERTE SCIENTIFIQUE	(22 numéros) France 75 €
L'AFRIQUE DE NOS JOURS	(12 numéros) France 40 €, Europe 40 €, Dom-Tom 40 €, Afrique 45 €
TELE-TUBE	(52 numéros) France et Dom-Tom 90 €, USA $140, Canada $180, Autres pays 130 €
LA VOIX DU MONDE	(52 numéros) France 110 €
LES GRANDS MOUVEMENTS DE L'ECONOMIE	(12 numéros) France 25 €
LA VIE SPORTIVE	(12 numéros) France 20 €

PRONONCIATION

CD 3 Trs. 13–18

The r sound See scripts and answers on p. 73H.

The French **r** is quite different from the American *r.* To pronounce the French **r,** keep the tip of your tongue pressed against your lower front teeth. Arch the back of your tongue upward, almost totally blocking the passage of air in the back of your throat.

A. A prononcer

Repeat the following words.

1. Raoul	rouge	roman	règle
2. crayon	trente	calculatrice	barbe
3. terrible	intéressant	Europe	quarante
4. poster	rare	vert	montre

B. A lire

Take turns with a partner reading the following sentences aloud.

1. Fermez la porte.
2. Regardez le livre de français.
3. Prenez un crayon.
4. Ouvrez la fenêtre.
5. Je voudrais une montre.
6. Je regrette. Je n'ai pas de règle.

C. A écrire

You're going to hear a short dialogue. Write down what you hear.

Communication for All Students

Slower Pace

29 Ask individuals to name the different magazines and the prices shown here. Ask them what kinds of magazines they think these are.

Teaching Suggestion

Prononciation To make the French **r** sound, have students practice the correct position of the tongue by pronouncing the French word **garage.** At first, they may simply say **gara,** since the two consonants are produced in the back of the throat. Then, have them say the whole word **garage.**

Troisième étape

Teacher Note

For descriptions of French-language periodicals and subscription information, see page T46.

Speaking Assessment

29 You may wish to have students present their conversation to the rest of the class. Explain the assessment mode before they act out their scenes. You may wish to evaluate their performance using the following rubric.

Speaking Rubric	Points			
	4	3	2	1
Content (Complete–Incomplete)				
Comprehension (Total–Little)				
Comprehension (Comprehensible–Incomprehensible)				
Accuracy (Accurate–Seldom accurate)				
Fluency (Fluent–Not fluent)				

18–20: A
16–17: B
14–15: C
12–13: D
Under 12: F

Assess

- Testing Program, pp. 61–64 Quiz 3-3A, Quiz 3-3B Audio CD 3, Tr. 22
- Student Make-Up Assignments, Chapter 3, Alternative Quiz
- Alternative Assessment Guide, p. 34

STANDARDS: 1.1, 1.2, 4.1, 5.1

Lisons!

CHAPITRE 3

Teaching Resources
pp. 92–93

PRINT 
- Lesson Planner, p. 17
- Cahier d'activités, p. 35
- Reading Strategies and Skills Handbook, Chapter 3
- Joie de lire 1, Chapter 3
- Standardized Assessment Tutor, Chapter 3

MEDIA 
- One-Stop Planner

Prereading
Activities A–B

Using Context Clues
Have students identify the type of reading they are faced with so that they will know what type of information to look for. Ask them for words or phrases that give clues as to what the ad is about.

Reading
Activities C–J

Visual/Auditory Learners
You might want to read the selection aloud or have partners read it to each other.

Answers
C. *Price:* 6,37€, 4,18€, 0,68€, 0,95€ 2,15€, 4,92€, 5,76€, 0,63€ 2,55€, 0,44€, 3,83€, 2,18€, 0,80€
Size: 30 cm., 30 mm., 19 mm. × 33 m., 24 × 32 cm., 0,50 × 2 m.
Quantity: 12 pastilles, 8 chiffres, 4 opérations
D. for three
E. école; *for school use*
F. *Most expensive*—ensemble d'ardoise
Least expensive—ruban adhésif transparent

Lisons!

UNIVERS : TOUT POUR LA RENTRÉE

Stratégie pour lire
When you read material like this, you are generally looking for specific information—prices, colors, or sizes, for example. When that is your purpose, you don't have to read or understand every word. You can simply scan the material until you find what you are looking for.

A. At what time of year would you expect to see an advertisement like this? fall

B. When you buy school supplies, what is most important to you? Color? Price? Brand name?

C. Working with a partner, scan the ad for information about price, size, and quantity. Make a list of the words you find in the text that fit each of these categories.

D. What do you think **les 3** means?

E. The word **écolier** is used to describe the notebook. Do you recognize a word you've learned before in this word? What do you think **écolier** means?

F. What is the most expensive item? The least expensive? See answers below.

C. See answers below.
D. See answer below.
E. See answers below.

UNIVERS
TOUT POUR LA RENTREE
VENEZ VOIR NOS PRIX REMARQUABLES!

ENSEMBLE D'ARDOISE: ardoise naturelle, éponge, crayon.
6,37€

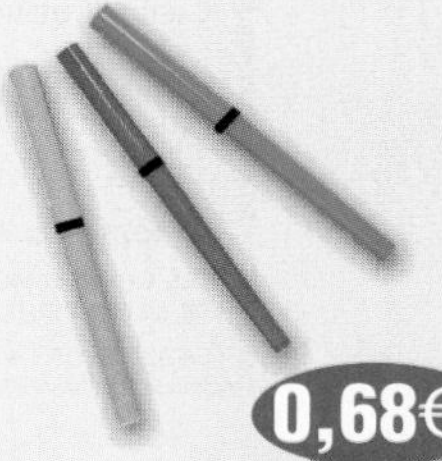

0,68€
SURLIGNEUR FLUORESCENT divers coloris

4,18€
STYLO PLUME

REGLE Graduation millimétrique, 30cm.
0,95€

2,15€
COMPAS POINTE FIXE

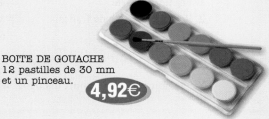

BOITE DE GOUACHE 12 pastilles de 30 mm et un pinceau.
4,92€

Connections and Comparisons

Motivating Activity
There are several large discount store chains in France, such as **Monoprix, Prisunic, Nouvelles Galeries,** and **Tati,** where you can buy school supplies. Have students name some discount store chains in the U.S. where school supplies are available.

Thinking Critically
Analyzing Ask students where they go shopping for school supplies and why they go there. Next, ask students to imagine they are going to school in another country. Ask them how they would find the supplies and clothes they want.

5,76€
CALCULATRICE
8 chiffres, 4 opérations,
fonctions : mémoire, %,
√. Garantie 1 an.

2,18€
CHEMISE
à rabat et élastique,
dim. 24 X 32 cm,
différents coloris.

0,80€
ROULEAU PROTEGE-LIVRES
en polypropylène, différents coloris
et transparent, dim. 0,50 X 2 m.
0,50 x 2m

G. What item(s) in this ad might each of these people ask for? See answers below.
1. a secretary
2. an architect
3. an artist

H. Do you think these are good prices? How can you tell? See answers below.

I. What do you think these cognates mean? See answers below.

adhésif	coloris
éponge	transparent

J. There are probably some items in this advertisement that you don't normally buy for school. Match the French words for these items with the English definitions. Look at the text and the pictures if you need help.

1. rouleau protège-livres d
2. ardoise a
3. gouache e
4. colle b
5. stylo plume c

a. a writing slate
b. glue
c. fountain pen
d. a roll of plastic material used to protect books
e. paint

K. If you had 10 € to spend on school supplies, which items in the ad would you buy? Remember, you need supplies for all of your classes.

Cahier d'activités, p. 35, Act. 20

Postreading
Activity K

Thinking Critically
Observing After your students have looked at the ad, ask them to make a list of items that are missing in this ad that they might have expected to find (a computer), and a list of items they were perhaps surprised to see (**une ardoise**).

Connections and Comparisons

Thinking Critically
Comparing and Contrasting Have students compare the items in the ad to the one(s) they usually see. Do the items shown seem similar to those used by American students? How do they differ in price or appearance? Which supplies would high school students use?

Thinking Critically
Analyzing Have students examine the ad and determine why they think it is effective or ineffective.

Answers

G. *Possible answers:*
1. *Secretary:* stylo plume, surligneur
2. *Architect:* feutres à dessin, compas, règle
3. *Artist:* gouache, feutres à dessin

H. The ad claims that the prices are remarkable.

I. adhésif: *adhesive*
éponge: *sponge*
coloris: *colors*
transparent: *transparent*

STANDARDS: 1.2, 3.1, 4.2

Grammaire supplémentaire

CHAPITRE 3

For **Grammaire supplémentaire** Answer Transparencies, see the *Teaching Transparencies* binder.

Grammaire supplémentaire

Première étape

Objectives Making and responding to requests; asking others what they need and telling what you need

1 Fill in the missing letters in the following words to find out what Amadou has on his desk. Then, write each word with the correct indefinite article. (**p. 81**)

Exemple C __ __ I __ R -> **un cahier**

1. L __ __ R __ S des livres
2. T __ O __ __ S __ une trousse
3. S T __ __ O __ des stylos
4. C __ A __ __ N un crayon
5. C __ __ C __ L __ T __ __ C __ une calculatrice
6. F __ __ I L __ __ S des feuilles

2 Create sentences, using the words that are jumbled below. To complete your sentences, you'll need to add **un, une, des, de (d')**. Remember to use the correct form of **avoir.** (**p. 81**)

Exemple Anne/tu/avoir/montre? **—Anne, tu as une montre?**

1. Hélène/tu/sac à dos/avoir?
2. Non/ne/avoir/je/pas/sac à dos
3. Raphaël et Philippe/feuilles de papier/avoir/vous?
4. Karine/taille-crayon/tu/avoir?
5. Valérie et Mireille/vous/calculatrices/avoir?
6. Moi/pas/trousse/je/avoir/ne

3 Mamadou is asking you what you need to bring to school. Answer his questions, using the appropriate words from the box. Use each noun only once and remember to add **un, une,** or **des.** (**pp. 81, 82**)

Exemple —Qu'est-ce qu'il te faut pour le sport?
—Il me faut un tee-shirt.

feuilles de papier, calculatrice, règle, livre, gomme, cahier, crayon

1. Qu'est-ce qu'il te faut pour la géométrie?
2. Qu'est-ce qu'il te faut pour l'anglais?
3. Qu'est-ce qu'il te faut pour l'algèbre?
4. Qu'est-ce qu'il te faut pour les arts plastiques?
5. Qu'est-ce qu'il te faut pour l'histoire?
6. Qu'est-ce qu'il te faut pour la chimie?

Alors, qu'est-ce qu'il te faut pour l'anglais?
Euh, il me faut un classeur et un sac aussi.

Answers

1
1. des livres
2. une trousse
3. des stylos
4. un crayon
5. une calculatrice
6. des feuilles

2
1. Hélène, tu as un sac à dos?
2. Non, je n'ai pas de sac à dos.
3. Raphaël et Philippe, vous avez des feuilles de papier?
4. Karine, tu as un taille-crayon?
5. Valérie et Mireille, vous avez des calculatrices?
6. Moi, je n'ai pas de trousse.

3 *Possible answers*
1. Il me faut une règle.
2. Il me faut des feuilles de papier.
3. Il me faut une calculatrice.
4. Il me faut une gomme et un crayon.
5. Il me faut un livre.
6. Il me faut un cahier.

Grammar Resources for Chapter 3

The **Grammaire supplémentaire** activities were designed as supplemental activities for the grammatical concepts presented in the chapter. You might use them as additional practice, for review, or for assessment.

For more grammar presentations, review, and practice, refer to the following:
- Travaux pratiques de grammaire
- Grammar Tutor for Students of French
- Grammar Summary on pp. R15–R28
- Cahier d'activités
- Grammar and Vocabulary quizzes (Testing Program)
- Test Generator
- Interactive CD-ROM Tutor
- DVD Tutor
- **Jeux interactifs** at **go.hrw.com**

STANDARDS: 1.2

Grammaire supplémentaire

CHAPITRE 3

Deuxième étape

Objective Telling what you'd like and what you'd like to do

4 Choose the correct words (**me, te,** or **vous**) to complete the following conversations. Then, indicate whether each conversation is **logique** (logical) or **illogique** (illogical). Underline your choices. (**pp. 82, 84**)

1. —Serge, qu'est-ce qu'il (me/te) faut pour l'école?
   —Il (vous/me) faut un ordinateur, un poster et une pizza.
   Logique ou illogique?

2. —Géraldine et Nathalie, qu'est-ce qu'il (te/vous) faut pour les maths?
   —Des crayons, des gommes, deux calculatrices et des feuilles de papier.
   Logique ou illogique?

3. —Hervé, qu'est-ce qu'il (te/vous) faut pour le cours d'anglais?
   —Il (vous/me) faut un dictionnaire, des frites et un roman.
   Logique ou illogique?

4. —Alors, les garçons, qu'est-ce qu'il (vous/me) faut pour l'EPS?
   —Des baskets... c'est tout.
   Logique ou illogique?

5 You overheard these conversations at a school supplies store. Complete them with **ce, cet, cette,** or **ces.** (**p. 85**)

1. —Tu aimes ____ montre? cette
   —Oui, mais je préfère ____ bracelet. ce
2. —Vous aimez ____ jean? ce
   —Oui, mais il me faut ____ tee-shirt pour l'EPS. ce
3. —Je voudrais acheter ____ ordinateur. cet
   —Moi aussi, mais il te faut ____ calculatrice pour les maths. cette
4. —Comment tu trouves ____ baskets? ces
   —Super! J'aime ____ short aussi. ce
5. —Je voudrais acheter ____ cassette. cette
   —Moi, je préfère acheter ____ disque compact. ce
6. —Il me faut ____ feuilles de papier. ces
   —Moi aussi. Il me faut ____ règle aussi. cette

Communication for All Students

Visual Learners

Display ten school supplies on a tray or table and allow students one minute to look at them. Then, cover the objects and have students write down as many objects as they can remember. You might give a prize or extra credit to the student who remembers the most objects and give credit for completion to the others.

Additional Practice

To review the demonstrative adjectives, bring some school supplies to class. As you hold up an item or items, have students call out the correct demonstrative adjective (**ce, cette, cet,** or **ces**).

Answers

4
1. te; me; illogique
2. vous; logique
3. te; me; illogique
4. vous; logique

5
1. cette, ce
2. ce, ce
3. cet, cette
4. ces, ce
5. cette, ce
6. ces, cette

STANDARDS: 1.1, 1.2

Grammaire supplémentaire

CHAPITRE 3

For **Grammaire supplémentaire** Answer Transparencies, see the *Teaching Transparencies* binder.

Answers

6 *Possible answers:*
1. b; Je voudrais sortir avec ces amis.
2. f; Je voudrais regarder cette vidéocassette.
3. a; Je voudrais lire ces magazines.
4. c; Je voudrais avoir ces cours.
5. d; Je voudrais acheter cette calculatrice.
6. e; Je voudrais écouter ce disque compact.

7
1. Je voudrais des trousses marron.
2. Je voudrais des calculatrices blanches.
3. Je voudrais des stylos rouges.
4. Je voudrais une règle verte.
5. Je voudrais un sac noir.
6. Je voudrais des cahiers gris.
7. Je voudrais une gomme violette.

8
1. Il me faut une calculatrice grise.
2. Il me faut des baskets noires.
3. Il me faut des feuilles blanches.
4. Il me faut deux règles jaunes.
5. Il me faut une trousse marron.

Grammaire supplémentaire

WA3 POITIERS-3

6 Match a verb from column A with a noun from column B, using each word only once. Then, write six logical sentences telling what you would like to do, using **je voudrais,** and **ce, cet, cette,** or **ces.** (**p. 85**)

EXEMPLE étudier roman **Je voudrais étudier ce roman.**

A	B
1. sortir avec	**a.** magazines
2. regarder	**b.** amis
3. lire	**c.** cours (m. pl.)
4. avoir	**d.** calculatrice
5. acheter	**e.** disque compact
6. écouter	**f.** vidéocassette

7 Unscramble the colors. Then, use them to describe the items you would like to have. Remember to add the appropriate endings to the colors if necessary. (**p. 87**)

EXEMPLE LEBU/des tee-shirts **Je voudrais des tee-shirts bleus.**

1. RARONM/des trousses
2. NLCAB/des calculatrices
3. ORUEG/des stylos
4. ETVR/une règle
5. RNIO/un sac
6. RIGS/des cahiers
7. OLEVIT/une gomme

8 You're telling the salesperson what school supplies you need to buy. Rewrite each sentence to include the given adjective in its correct form and position. (**p. 87**)

1. Il me faut une calculatrice. (gris)
2. Il me faut des baskets. (noir)
3. Il me faut des feuilles. (blanc)
4. Il me faut deux règles. (jaune)
5. Il me faut une trousse. (marron)

Teacher to Teacher

Paula Gill
Bethel Middle School
Bethel, CT

Paula's students roll the die to review vocabulary and grammar.

"I use this activity to practice the forms of the verb **aimer,** school supplies, and the demonstrative adjectives.

Students work in pairs. Each pair has a deck of pictures of the school supplies and a wooden cube on which I have written six subject pronouns in French. Students take turns rolling the die and making affirmative and negative sentences, using the subject pronoun that comes up, the correct form of **aimer,** and the noun. **(Examples: Nous n'aimons pas cette calculatrice. Elle aime ce poster.)**"

STANDARDS: 1.2

Troisième étape

Objectives Getting someone's attention; asking for information; expressing and responding to thanks

9 Murielle needs to buy a calculator, two tee-shirts, three pencils, a dictionary, and a pair of sneakers for school. First, write out the total amount she will spend for each of these items. Remember that she is buying more than one of some of the items. Then, write out the total amount of all her purchases. (**p. 88**)

1. Une calculatrice—25,98 €: ______
2. Un tee-shirt—13,86 €: ______
3. Un crayon—1,80 €: ______
4. Un dictionnaire—35,76 €: ______
5. Des baskets—58,63 €: ______

Total : ______

10 Complete this conversation with the appropriate form of the words in parentheses. (**pp. 81, 85, 87, 90**)

JULIE Excusez-moi, madame. C'est combien, __1__ (ce/cet/cette) montre __2__ (gris)?

LA VENDEUSE Vingt euros, mademoiselle. Elle vous plaît?

JULIE Oui, beaucoup. J'aime aussi __3__ (ce/cet/cette) télévision __4__ (blanc). Et vous avez __5__ (des/de/d') calculatrices __6__ (violet)?

LA VENDEUSE Non. Je regrette, mademoiselle. Je n'ai pas __7__ (des/de/d') calculatrices.

11 Ask how much the following items cost, using **ce, cet, cette,** or **ces,** and the appropriate form of the adjectives. (**pp. 85, 87, 90**)

EXEMPLE trousse/bleu **C'est combien, cette trousse bleue?**

1. crayons/noir
2. montre/violet
3. télévision/gris
4. classeurs/orange
5. bracelet/rose

- une calculatrice ✓
- un dictionnaire ✓
- des gommes ✓
- des cahiers ✓
- une règle ✓
- des crayons ✓
- une montre ✗

Review and Assess

You may wish to assign the **Grammaire supplémentaire** activities as additional practice or homework after presenting material throughout the chapter. Assign Activities 1–2 after **Grammaire** (p. 81), Activity 3 after **Comment dit-on... ?** (p. 82), Activity 4 after **Vocabulaire** (p. 84), Activities 5–6 after **Grammaire** (p. 85), Activities 7–8 after **Grammaire** (p. 87), Activity 9 after **Vocabulaire** (p. 88), Activities 10–11 after **Comment dit-on… ?** (p. 90). To prepare students for the **Etape** Quizzes and Chapter Test, we suggest doing the **Grammaire supplémentaire** activities in the following order. Have students complete Activities 1–3 before taking Quizzes 3-1A or 3-1B; Activities 4–8 before Quizzes 3-2A or 3-2B; and Activities 9–11 before Quizzes 3-3A or 3-3B.

Grammaire supplémentaire

CHAPITRE 3

Answers

9
1. Vingt-cinq euros quatre-vingt-dix-huit
2. Treize euros quatre-vingt-six
3. Un euro quatre-vingts
4. Trente-cinq euros soixante-seize
5. Cinquante-huit euros soixante-trois

Total : Cent trente-six euros trois

10
1. cette
2. grise
3. cette
4. blanche
5. des
6. violettes
7. de

11
1. C'est combien, ces crayons noirs?
2. C'est combien, cette montre violette?
3. C'est combien, cette télévision grise?
4. C'est combien, ces classeurs orange?
5. C'est combien, ce bracelet rose?

Mise en pratique

CHAPITRE 3

The **Mise en pratique** reviews and integrates all four skills and culture in preparation for the Chapter Test.

Teaching Resources
pp. 98–99

PRINT 

- Lesson Planner, p. 17
- Listening Activities, p. 21
- Video Guide, pp. 19, 22
- Grammar Tutor for Students of French, Chapter 3
- Standardized Assessment Tutor, Chapter 3

MEDIA  

- One-Stop Planner
- Video Program Videocassette 1, 48:31–50:29
- DVD Tutor, Disc 1
- Audio Compact Discs, CD 3, Tr. 19
- Interactive CD-ROM Tutor, Disc 1

Building on Previous Skills

2 Encourage students to use the expressions of agreement and disagreement they learned in Chapter 2: **Moi aussi, Moi non plus, Moi si,** and so forth.

Portfolio

3 **Written** This activity is appropriate for students' written portfolios. For portfolio suggestions, see page 20 of the *Alternative Assessment Guide.*

4 **Oral** This activity might be included in students' oral portfolios and/or performed for the class. For portfolio suggestions, see page 20 of the *Alternative Assessment Guide.*

Mise en pratique

CD-ROM 1
DVD 1

1 You want to buy your friend a birthday gift. Listen as she gives you some ideas and then make a list of the things she would like. See scripts and answers on p. 73H.

CD 3 Tr. 19

2 You and a friend are browsing through a magazine. Point out several items you like and several you dislike.

25,15€
Sac shopping, 35X10X30 cm, 65 % polyester et 35 % coton.
5,34€
Classeur, 21X29,7 cm.
6,86€
Stylo plume.
3,43€
Chemise 3 rabats élastique, 24X32 cm.
29,73€
Sac à dos, 65 % polyester et 35 % coton.
9,07€
Portefeuille, 65 % polyester et 35 % coton.

3 Make a list in French of two or three of the items pictured above that you'd like to buy. Include the colors and prices of the items you choose.

4 Tell your partner about the items you've chosen in Activity 3. Give as much detail as you can, including the color and price.

Apply and Assess

Challenge

1 Have students listen to the recording again. This time they should note the reasons why the speaker would like each gift.

Additional Practice

2 Have students use the advertisement to do a "chain" activity to practice telling what they would like and the vocabulary for colors and objects. One student could begin by saying **Je voudrais un classeur vert.** The next student might say **Marc voudrait un classeur vert et moi, je voudrais un stylo bleu,** and so on.

STANDARDS: 1.1, 1.2

5 Your friend has been passing notes to you during study hall. Write a response to each one.

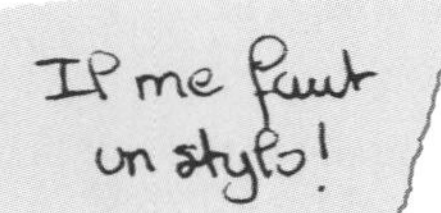
Il me faut
un stylo!

Qu'est-ce qu'il
faut pour
l'algèbre?

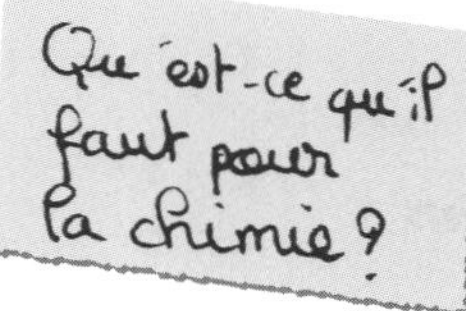
Qu'est-ce qu'il
faut pour
la chimie?

6 If you were in France, what differences would you notice in these areas?

1. money **2.** school supplies **3.** stores See answers below.

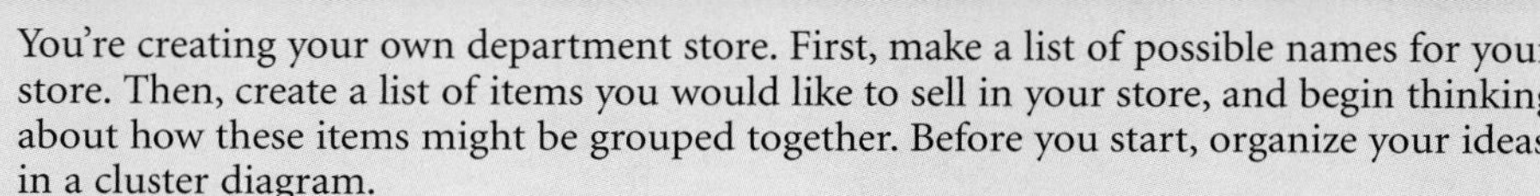

7 ## Ecrivons!

You're creating your own department store. First, make a list of possible names for your store. Then, create a list of items you would like to sell in your store, and begin thinking about how these items might be grouped together. Before you start, organize your ideas in a cluster diagram.

Stratégie pour écrire

Cluster diagrams are a helpful way to organize the ideas you develop in your brainstorming. Start by drawing a circle and label it with the name you chose for your store. Then draw two or three other circles, each connected to the first circle. In each of the new circles you draw, write the name of an item you plan to sell. Add more circles as you need them. Connect your circles with lines to group similar items together as they might be organized in a department store.

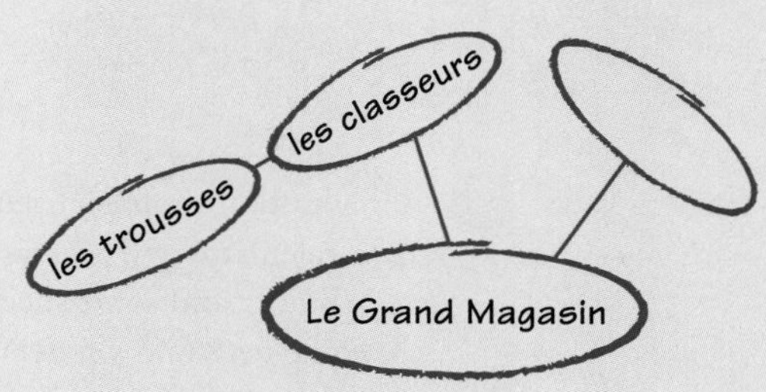
les classeurs
les trousses
Le Grand Magasin

8 ## Jeu de rôle

Visit the "store" your partner created and decide on something you'd like to buy. Your partner will play the role of the salesperson. Get the salesperson's attention, tell what you want, ask the price(s), pay for your purchase(s), thank the salesperson, and say goodbye. Your partner should respond appropriately. Then, change roles, using the store you created. Remember to use **madame, monsieur,** or **mademoiselle,** and **vous.**

Mise en pratique

CHAPITRE 3

Challenge

5 Extend this activity by asking students to write notes of their own to one another, exchange them, and write replies.

Apply and Assess

Process Writing

Beginning with this chapter, students will have the opportunity to develop their writing skills with the **Ecrivons!** feature. This feature will be presented in each chapter in the **Mise en pratique** review section, before the **Jeu de rôle.** The **Ecrivons!** feature gives students a writing strategy to apply to their assignment. For this chapter, when students have finished their first draft, have them exchange papers for peer-editing and feedback. Help them create a checklist of things to look for as they edit their partner's paper. In subsequent chapters, students will learn to use all the steps of the writing process. For rubrics and evaluation guidelines for written assignments, see pages 6–9 of the *Alternative Assessment Guide.*

Possible Answers

6
1. French money has more coins.
2. Notebook paper looks like graph paper.
3. One is expected to bag one's own purchases.

STANDARDS: 1.1, 1.3, 3.1, 5.1, 5.2

Que sais-je?

CHAPITRE 3

Teaching Resources
p. 100

PRINT 
- Grammar Tutor for Students of French, Chapter 3

MEDIA 
- Interactive CD-ROM Tutor, Disc 1
- Online self-test

go.hrw.com
WA3 POITIERS-3

Teacher Note
This page is intended to help students prepare for the Chapter Test. It is a brief checklist of the major points covered in the chapter. Students should be reminded that this is only a checklist and does not necessarily include everything that will appear on the test.

Answers

1
1. Vous avez/Tu as un stylo?
2. Vous avez/Tu as une calculatrice?
3. Vous avez/Tu as des feuilles de papier?

Possible responses
Non, je regrette; Non, je n'ai pas de... ; Oui, voilà.

2
1. Qu'est-ce qu'il te faut pour le sport?
2. Qu'est-ce qu'il te faut pour l'allemand?
3. Qu'est-ce qu'il te faut pour les arts plastiques?

3
1. Il me faut une calculatrice et une gomme pour les maths.
2. Il me faut un classeur et des feuilles pour l'espagnol.
3. Il me faut des stylos et un cahier pour l'anglais.
4. Il me faut un crayon et une règle pour la géométrie.
5. Il me faut un sac et un livre pour l'histoire.

4
1. Je voudrais ces baskets blanches.
2. Je voudrais ce sac bleu.
3. Je voudrais cette trousse violette et noire.
4. Je voudrais écouter de la musique et parler au téléphone.
5. Je voudrais faire les magasins.

Que sais-je?

WA3 POITIERS-3

Can you use what you've learned in this chapter?

Can you make and respond to requests? p. 80

1 How would you ask for the following items, using the verb **avoir?** How would you respond to someone's request for one of these items? See answers below.

1. 
2. 
3. 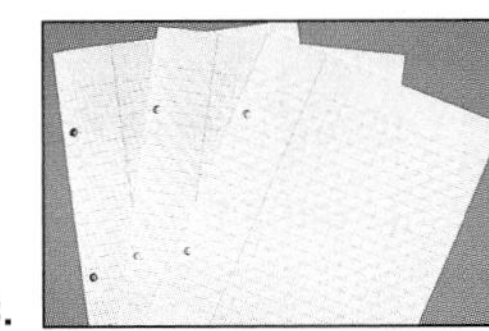

Can you ask others what they need? p. 82

2 How would you ask your friend what he or she needs for each of these school subjects? See answers below.

1. 
2. 

3. 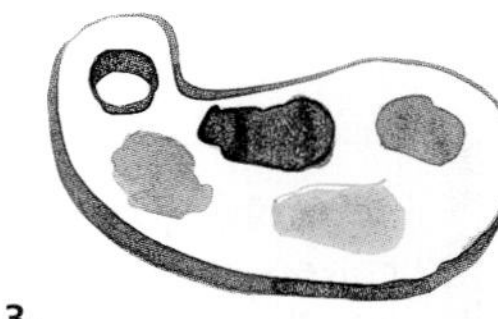

Can you tell what you need? p. 82

3 How would you tell a friend that you need . . . See answers below.
1. a calculator and an eraser for math?
2. a binder and some sheets of paper for Spanish class?
3. some pens and a notebook for English?
4. a pencil and a ruler for geometry?
5. a backpack and a book for history?

Can you tell what you'd like and what you'd like to do? p. 85

4 How would you tell your friend that you'd like . . . See answers below.
1. those white sneakers?
2. this blue bag?
3. that purple and black pencil case?
4. to listen to music and talk on the phone?
5. to go shopping?

Can you get someone's attention, ask for information, and express and respond to thanks? p. 90

5 What would you say in a store to . . .
1. get a salesperson's attention? Pardon, madame/mademoiselle/monsieur...
2. politely ask the price of something? C'est combien, s'il vous plaît?
3. thank a clerk for helping you? Merci.

Review and Assess

Teaching Suggestion
In pairs, have students ask and respond to each of the questions in Activities 1–5.

Challenge
3 Encourage students to use the responses to this activity to create a conversation between two friends shopping for school supplies.

STANDARDS: 1.1

Vocabulaire

Première étape

Making and responding to requests

Tu as... ?	*Do you have . . . ?*
Vous avez... ?	*Do you have . . . ?*
Voilà.	*Here.*
Je regrette.	*Sorry.*
Je n'ai pas de...	*I don't have a/any . . .*

Asking others what they need and telling what you need

Qu'est-ce qu'il vous faut pour... ?	*What do you need for . . . ?* (formal)
Qu'est-ce qu'il te faut pour... ?	*What do you need for . . . ?* (informal)
Il me faut...	*I need . . .*
un	*a; an*
une	*a; an*
des	*some*

School supplies

un cahier	*notebook*
une calculatrice	*calculator*
un classeur	*loose-leaf binder*
un crayon	*pencil*
des feuilles (f.) **de papier**	*sheets of paper*
une gomme	*eraser*
un livre	*book*
une règle	*ruler*
un sac (à dos)	*bag; backpack*
un stylo	*pen*
un taille-crayon	*pencil sharpener*
une trousse	*pencil case*

Other useful expressions

Zut!	*Darn!*

Deuxième étape

Telling what you'd like and what you'd like to do

Je voudrais...	*I'd like . . .*
Je voudrais acheter...	*I'd like to buy . . .*

For school and fun

des baskets (f.)	*sneakers*
un bracelet	*bracelet*
une cassette	*cassette tape*
un dictionnaire	*dictionary*
un disque compact/un CD	*compact disc/CD*
un jean	*(a pair of) jeans*
un magazine	*magazine*
une montre	*watch*
un ordinateur	*computer*
un portefeuille	*wallet*
un poster	*poster*
un pull-over	*pullover*
une radio	*radio*
un roman	*novel*
un short	*(a pair of) shorts*
un sweat-shirt	*sweatshirt*
un tee-shirt	*T-shirt*
une télévision	*television*
une vidéocassette	*videotape*
ce, cet, cette	*this; that*
ces	*these; those*
-là	*there (noun suffix)*

Colors

De quelle couleur est... ?	*What color is . . . ?*
blanc(he)	*white*
bleu(e)	*blue*
gris(e)	*grey*
jaune	*yellow*
marron	*brown*
noir(e)	*black*
orange	*orange*
rose	*pink*
rouge	*red*
vert(e)	*green*
violet(te)	*purple*

Troisième étape

Getting someone's attention; asking for information; expressing and responding to thanks

Pardon.	*Pardon me.*
Excusez-moi.	*Excuse me.*
C'est combien?	*How much is it?*
Merci.	*Thank you.*
A votre service.	*At your service; You're welcome.*
s'il vous/te plaît	*please*
un euro	*(the European monetary unit)*
soixante	*sixty*
soixante et un	*sixty-one*
soixante-dix	*seventy*
soixante et onze	*seventy-one*
soixante-douze	*seventy-two*
quatre-vingts	*eighty*
quatre-vingt-un	*eighty-one*
quatre-vingt-dix	*ninety*
quatre-vingt-onze	*ninety-one*
cent	*one hundred*
cent un	*one hundred and one*
deux cents	*two hundred*

Other useful expressions

Bien sûr.	*Of course.*

Vocabulaire

CHAPITRE 3

Building on Previous Skills

Encourage students to try to remember words by association. For example, **un portefeuille** carries **(porte)** little pieces of paper **(feuilles),** such as euro notes.

Chapter 3 Assessment

- **Testing Program**
  Chapter Test, pp. 65–70
   Audio Compact Discs, CD 3, Trs. 23–25
  Speaking Test, p. 344
- **Alternative Assessment Guide**
  Performance Assessment, p. 34
  Portfolio Assessment, p. 20
  CD-ROM Assessment, p. 48
- **Interactive CD-ROM Tutor, Disc 1**
  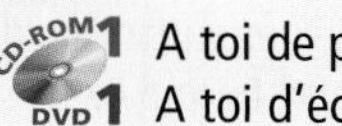 CD-ROM 1 A toi de parler
  DVD 1 A toi d'écrire
- **Standardized Assessment Tutor**
  Chapter 3
- **One-Stop Planner, Disc 1**
  Test Generator
  Chapter 3

Review and Assess

Game

Catégories Bring in a foam ball. Call out a category based on the chapter vocabulary (things you write with, things you wear, things you listen to, things you use to organize). As you name the category, toss the ball to a student. The student should say a related vocabulary word and toss the ball to another student, who should name a different item from that category. When a student cannot come up with a word, he or she is out of the game. The winners are the last ones remaining. You decide when a category has been exhausted. At that time, change the category and have all students resume play.

STANDARDS: 1.1

Location Opener

CHAPTER 4

Teaching Resources
pp. 102–105

PRINT 

- Lesson Planner, p. 18
- Video Guide, pp. 23–24

MEDIA 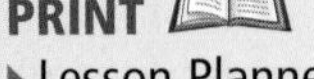

- One-Stop Planner
- Video Program
  Videocassette 2, 01:21-03:24
- DVD Tutor, Disc 1
- Interactive CD-ROM Tutor, Disc 1
- Map Transparency 3

go.hrw.com
WA3 QUEBEC CITY

Using the Almanac and Map

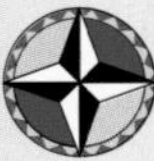

Terms in the Almanac

- **Le château Frontenac,** named for the comte de Frontenac, governor of **la Nouvelle-France** in the late seventeenth century, was built on a site that once served as a residence for colonial governors. The building is now a luxury hotel.
- **L'université Laval,** formerly the Quebec Seminary, founded in 1852, is the oldest French-language university in North America.
- **Le mont Sainte-Anne,** located 40 kilometers east of Quebec City, is famous for its ski slopes.
- **Québec Expérience** is a multimedia, 3-D, sound and light presentation, spotlighting the Amerindian, French, and English influences in Quebec City's history.
- **Le marquis de Montcalm** commanded the French troops during the French and Indian War.

CHAPITRE 4

Allez, viens à Québec!

Capitale de la province du Québec

Population : plus de 600.000

Points d'intérêt : le château Frontenac, l'université Laval, la terrasse Dufferin, le musée du Québec, les fortifications de Québec, les chutes Montmorency, le mont Sainte-Anne, Québec Expérience

Québécois célèbres : Samuel de Champlain, François de Montmorency-Laval, le marquis de Montcalm

Ressources et industries : dérivés du bois, du cuir et de l'érable; tourisme

Spécialités : ragoût de boulettes, tourtière, cretons, soupe aux pois, tarte au sucre, tarte à la ferlouche

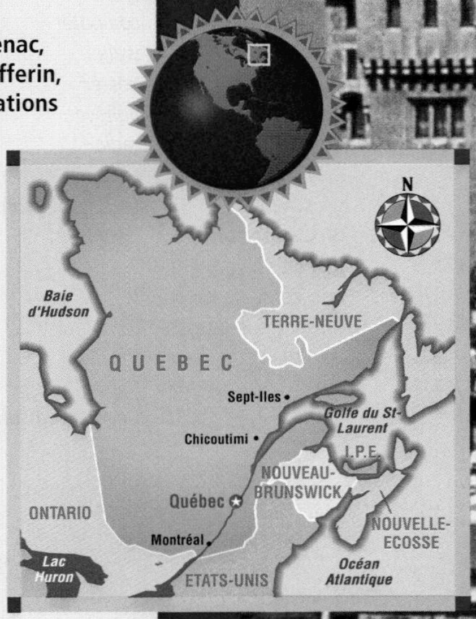

Baie d'Hudson
QUEBEC
TERRE-NEUVE
Sept-Iles
Golfe du St-Laurent
Chicoutimi
I.P.E.
NOUVEAU-BRUNSWICK
Québec
ONTARIO
Montréal
NOUVELLE-ECOSSE
Lac Huron
ETATS-UNIS
Océan Atlantique

go.hrw.com WA3 QUEBEC CITY

VIDEO

CD-ROM 1 DVD 1

Le château Frontenac

Cultures and Communities

Background Information

La Nouvelle-France, claimed for the French by the explorer Jacques Cartier in 1534, was ceded to the British by the Treaty of Paris in 1763 at the end of the Seven Years' War (known in North America as the French and Indian War). Quebec City, one of the oldest cities in North America, was founded in 1608 by Samuel de Champlain. It is known for its old-world charm, narrow streets, beautiful parks, and numerous cafés. The name **Québec** comes from the Algonquian word **Kébec**, meaning *narrowing of the river* (referring to its strategic location where the St. Lawrence River narrows). Quebec City has been the capital of the province of Quebec since 1791.

STANDARDS: 2.2, 3.1, 5.1

Location Opener

CHAPTER 4

Map Activity

The vast majority of place names in Quebec are derived from geographic features, Amerindian words, or saints' names. Have students look at the map and identify a place in each category **(Sept-Iles, Chicoutimi, Golfe du St-Laurent).**

Teacher Notes

You might want to tell your students about these Canadian specialties.

- **dérivés de l'érable:** Canada is known for its maple products. A favorite treat of children, **tire,** is formed by pouring maple syrup on snow where it congeals to form a sort of caramel.
- **ragoût de boulettes:** pork stew with meatballs, eaten on special occasions
- **tourtière:** a meat pie usually eaten at Christmastime
- **cretons:** similar to **pâté,** made from ground pork
- **tarte au sucre:** a sugar pie made with brown sugar or sometimes maple syrup
- **tarte à la ferlouche:** a pie made with molasses or maple syrup and raisins

Language Note

After the passage of **la Loi 101** in 1976, which required all advertising and documentation to be in French, the **Office de la langue française** was created to help develop appropriate French terminology. **La Loi 101** was declared unconstitutional in 1988.

Connections and Comparisons

Language-to-Language

Because the owners of the logging companies in Quebec were generally English speakers, much of the lumberjack's language contained anglicisms. For example, the men who floated the lumber downriver were called **draveurs** *(drivers),* they used **bécosses** *(backhouse* or *outhouse),* and they ate in the **cookerie.**

Geography Link

Due to its northern location, the region around Quebec City receives approximately 130 inches of snow each winter and has average temperatures of −16 to −7 degrees Celsius (3 to 19 degrees Fahrenheit) in January, and 13 to 25 degrees Celsius (55 to 77 degrees Fahrenheit) in July. As they say in Quebec, there are two seasons: winter and July.

STANDARDS: 2.2, 3.1, 4.1

Using the Photo Essay

1 Typical houses in Vieux-Québec The narrow streets and stone structures of the older parts of Quebec City are reminiscent of European cities, but many buildings also represent the long, low, one-story construction typical of French-Canadian houses.

Geography Link

2 The Canadian Shield **(le bouclier canadien),** a range of mountains and peaks, reaches down toward the Great Lakes. Many of the rivers that empty into the St. Lawrence River "fall off" the edge of this shield in impressive waterfalls.

2 Les chutes Montmorency Overlooking these impressive falls is the Manoir Montmorency, built in 1780 for Edward, Duke of Kent, then governor-general of the colony and future father of Queen Victoria. Today, it is a restaurant and conference center.

3 La Grande Allée This boulevard holds the same place in **Québécois** hearts as the Champs-Elysées does in the hearts of Parisians. It was originally an Indian trail used to transport furs to sell to the French. In the seventeenth century, it was only a country lane separating two properties, and in later centuries, the address of several luxurious residences. Today, it is a busy street lined with many restaurants, cafés, shops, and offices.

4 La terrasse Dufferin This 671-meter walkway overlooks the lower town and the river. The part facing the château Frontenac was built over the remains of the château Saint-Louis (the governor-general's residence), which burned down in 1834.

Québec

Quebec City, one of the oldest cities in North America, is the capital of La Nouvelle-France, as the French-speaking province of Quebec used to be called. The Québécois people are fiercely proud of their heritage and traditions, and they work hard to maintain their language and culture. The narrow streets and quaint cafés of Vieux-Québec have an old-world feeling, but Quebec is also a dynamic, modern city — as exciting as any you'll find in North America!

Visit Holt Online
go.hrw.com
KEYWORD: WA3 QUEBEC CITY
Activités Internet

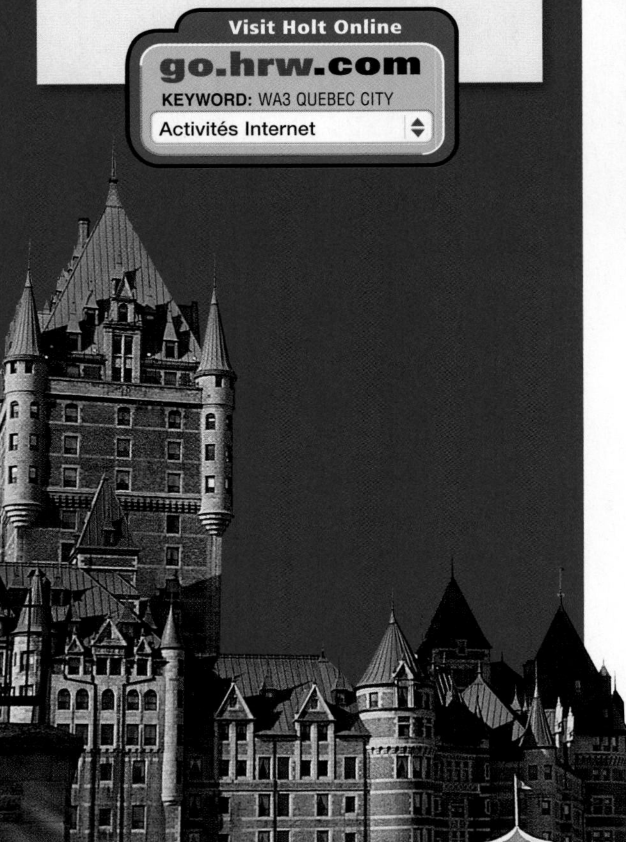

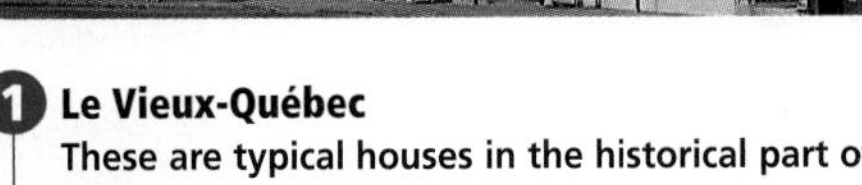

1 Le Vieux-Québec
These are typical houses in the historical part of the city.

2 Les chutes Montmorency
Spectacular waterfalls are found just outside of the city.

3 La Grande Allée
A boulevard lined with businesses and cafés, it is the longest road in Quebec.

4 La terrasse Dufferin
This bustling boardwalk overlooks the St. Lawrence River.

Cultures and Communities

Culture Notes

- The early European inhabitants of Quebec included settlers **(colons),** fur trappers, and **voyageurs,** who traveled by canoe to the interior to trade with the Indians.

1 Following several disastrous fires in Quebec City, new regulations require structures to be made of stone with slate roofs and to have high fire walls between buildings.

5 **La rue du Trésor**
This street in the heart of the old section of town is very popular among tourists. Local artists sell their work here.

6 **Les plaines d'Abraham**
This 250-acre park was the site of the battle in which the English defeated the French on September 13, 1759.

In chapter 4, you will meet Leticia and her Canadian pen pal, Emilie. Emilie and her friends will take you on a video tour of Quebec City. You will also find out what activities they do at different times of the year.

7 **Le quartier Petit-Champlain**
This picturesque shopping district is filled with boutiques and cafés.

8 **Le Vieux-Québec**
Musicians, jugglers, and other entertainers frequently perform in the streets.

Connections and Comparisons

Thinking Critically

6 **Drawing Inferences** Ask students to suggest other activities that people might do in the park. (Cycling, jogging, and walking are common pastimes. In the winter, one might find sledders or cross-country skiers.)

Thinking Critically

7 **Observing** Ask students to identify the most striking feature of the buildings here. The proliferation of plants and flowers is typically **québécois,** but at the same time, very reminiscent of the French love of flowers and gardens.

5 **La rue du Trésor** is a tiny pedestrian street **(rue piétonne)** where local artists sell their paintings, watercolors, drawings, and engravings.

6 **Les plaines d'Abraham,** located in **le parc des Champs de Bataille,** are named after Abraham Martin, a seventeenth-century settler.

History Link

6 During the famous battle in 1759, the British forces under General Wolfe scaled the cliff to attack and defeat the outnumbered French forces under General Montcalm.

7 **Le quartier Petit-Champlain** The cobblestone pedestrian street in this photo dates from 1680. It is linked with the upper part of the city by a cable car **(le funiculaire).** Recent restoration efforts have transformed the district into an animated gathering place with cafés, restaurants, and shops.

8 **Street performers** For years, **Québécois** families and friends have gathered for **veillées** where people sing, dance, and tell stories. This tradition lives on in the street performers often seen in Quebec City or Montreal. Each July, the **Festival d'été international** brings francophone musicians and performers from all over the world to play their music in Quebec City.

Thinking Critically

Comparing and Contrasting
Have students look at the photos on pages 104–105. Ask them to find features that seem European and others that seem North American.

Chapitre 4 : Sports et passe-temps

Chapter Overview

Mise en train pp. 108–110	***Nouvelles de Québec***			
	FUNCTIONS	**GRAMMAR**	**VOCABULARY**	**RE-ENTRY**
Première étape pp. 112–115	• Telling how much you like or dislike something, p. 114	• Expressions with **faire** and **jouer,** p. 113 • Question formation with **est-ce que,** p. 115	• Sports and hobbies, p. 112	• Expressing likes and dislikes **(Chapitre 1)** • The verb **aimer (Chapitre 2)** • Agreeing and disagreeing **(Chapitre 2)**
Deuxième étape pp. 116–120	• Exchanging information, p. 116	• **De** after a negative verb, p. 116 • The verb **faire,** p. 116 • The pronoun **on,** p. 117	• Weather expressions, p. 118 • Months of the year, p. 119 • Seasons, p. 120	• The verb **jouer,** regular **-er** verbs **(Chapitre 1)** • Agreeing and disagreeing **(Chapitre 2)** • Using **ne... pas (Chapitre 1)** • Expressing likes and dislikes **(Chapitre 1)** • Activities **(Chapitre 1)**
Troisième étape pp. 122–125	• Making, accepting, and turning down suggestions, p. 122	• Adverbs of frequency, p. 122		• Expressing opinions **(Chapitre 2)** • Expressing likes and dislikes **(Chapitre 1)**

Prononciation p. 125	**The sounds [u] and [y]** Audio CD 4, Tracks 12–14	**A écrire** (dictation) Audio CD 4, Tracks 15–17	
Lisons! pp. 126–127	**Allez, c'est à vous de choisir!**	**Reading Strategy:** Predicting what you're going to read	
Grammaire supplémentaire	**pp. 128-131** **Première étape,** pp. 128–129	**Deuxième étape,** pp. 129–130	**Troisième étape,** p. 131
Review pp. 132–135	**Mise en pratique,** pp. 132–133 **Ecrivons!** Arranging ideas logically Writing a letter	**Que sais-je?** p. 134	**Vocabulaire,** p. 135

CULTURE

- **Rencontre culturelle,** Old and new in Quebec City, p. 111
- **Note culturelle,** Celsius and Fahrenheit, p. 119
- **Panorama Culturel,** Sports in francophone countries, p. 121

Chapitre 4 : Sports et passe-temps

Chapter Resources

Visit Holt Online
go.hrw.com
KEYWORD: WA3 QUEBEC CITY-4
Online Edition

Lesson Planning

One-Stop Planner

Lesson Planner with Differentiated Instruction, pp. 18–22, 68

Student Make-Up Assignments
- Make-Up Assignment Copying Masters, Chapter 4

Listening and Speaking

TPR Storytelling Book, pp. 13–16

Listening Activities
- Student Response Forms for Listening Activities, pp. 27–29
- Additional Listening Activities 4-1 to 4-6, pp. 31–33
- Additional Listening Activities (song), p. 34
- Scripts and Answers, pp. 117–121

Video Guide
- Teaching Suggestions, pp. 26–27
- Activity Masters, pp. 28–30
- Scripts and Answers, pp. 95–97, 119

Activities for Communication
- Communicative Activities, pp. 19–24
- Realia and Teaching Suggestions, pp. 90–94
- Situation Cards, pp. 143–144

Reading and Writing

Reading Strategies and Skills Handbook, Chapter 4

Joie de lire 1, Chapter 4

Cahier d'activités, pp. 37–48

Grammar

Travaux pratiques de grammaire, pp. 25–34

Grammar Tutor for Students of French, Chapter 4

Assessment

Testing Program
- Grammar and Vocabulary Quizzes, **Etape** Quizzes, and Chapter Test, pp. 79–96
- Score Sheet, Scripts and Answers, pp. 97–104

Alternative Assessment Guide
- Portfolio Assessment, p. 21
- Performance Assessment, p. 35
- CD-ROM Assessment, p. 49

Student Make-Up Assignments
- Alternative Quizzes, Chapter 4

Standardized Assessment Tutor
- Reading, pp. 13–15
- Writing, p. 16
- Math, pp. 25–26

Middle School

Middle School Teaching Resources, Chapter 4

MEDIA

Online Activities
- **Jeux interactifs**
- **Activités Internet**

Video Program
- Videocassette 2
- Videocassette 5 (captioned version)

Interactive CD-ROM Tutor, Disc 1

DVD Tutor, Disc 1

Audio Compact Discs
- Textbook Listening Activities, CD 4, Tracks 1–18
- Additional Listening Activities, CD 4, Tracks 25–31
- Assessment Items, CD 4, Tracks 19–24

Teaching Transparencies
- Situation 4-1 to 4-3
- Vocabulary 4-A to 4-D
- **Mise en train**
- **Grammaire supplémentaire** Answers
- **Travaux pratiques de grammaire** Answers

One-Stop Planner CD-ROM

Use the **One-Stop Planner CD-ROM with Test Generator** to aid in lesson planning and pacing.

For each chapter, the **One-Stop Planner** includes:
- Editable lesson plans with direct links to teaching resources
- Printable worksheets from resource books
- Direct launches to the HRW Internet activities
- Video and audio segments
- Test Generator
- Clip Art for vocabulary items

Chapitre 4 : Sports et passe-temps

Projects

Le sport

Students will make a poster or collage presenting their favorite sport or team.

MATERIALS

Students may need
- Large sheets of paper or posterboard
- Magazines
- Scissors
- Colored pens and pencils
- Glue or tape

SUGGESTED SEQUENCE

1. **Prewriting** Have students do research on their favorite sport or team. They might want to look through the **Vocabulaire** sections of Chapters 1–4 to find useful vocabulary. You might also refer them to the Additional Vocabulary on page R13.
2. **First Draft** Have students write at least four sentences describing their poster topic and choose photos or drawings to illustrate their posters. They should also begin to organize the information for their poster and plan where they will write the information and position their photos and drawings.
3. **Peer-editing** Have students exchange their sentences with at least one other student. Have them check each other's work for comprehensibility and accuracy (spelling, verb forms, and word order). They should also comment on the poster layout and choice of illustrations.
4. **Final Draft** Have students rewrite their sentences, making any necessary corrections. Then, have them copy their information onto the poster and glue or tape their photos or illustrations in place. Have students display their posters in the classroom and describe them to the class.

GRADING THE PROJECT

Suggested Point Distribution: (total = 100 points)

Completeness of assignment	20 points
Presentation	30 points
Language use	20 points
Content	30 points

Games

Charades

In this game, students will review the verbs they've learned so far.

Have teams of three or four students recall the verbs they've learned in Chapters 1–4. Distribute index cards and have each group write a different verb on each one. Collect the cards, decide which team will start, and give the first player from that team one of the cards. The player has thirty seconds to mime the action and have his or her team call out the correct French verb. If the player succeeds, the team wins a point. In order to give all team members a chance to guess, no team member may make consecutive guesses. If the first team is unable to guess correctly, allow the other teams to try. Repeat the process with the other teams. After you have gone through all the verbs, use any that weren't guessed as tie-breakers.

Mémoire

This game provides an entertaining way for students to practice and review vocabulary.

Have students make two cards for each vocabulary word from this chapter. On one card, they should write the French word; on the other, they should illustrate the word or write the English equivalent. Mix the cards and number them on the blank side. You will need to write the number so that the vocabulary or illustration is right-side up when the card is flipped up. Tape the cards to the board so that the numbers show. Each player calls out two of the numbers in French. Turn up the two cards bearing those numbers to reveal the vocabulary word or illustration on the reverse side. The object is to find the two cards that match. Each player or team wins a point for each correct match. If the two cards do not match, be sure to turn the cards back to the number side so that they will remain in play.

STANDARDS: 1.3

Storytelling

Mini-histoire

This story accompanies Teaching Transparency 4-3. The ***mini-histoire*** *can be told and retold in different formats, acted out, written down, and read aloud, to give students additional opportunities to practice all four skills. The following story relates what different students are doing at the* **Ecole Secondaire Jacques-Cartier** *after school closes on Wednesday.*

C'est mercredi après-midi, et les élèves sont libres. Cédric aime jouer au football. Il invite Michelle et Thuy à jouer avec lui, mais elles préfèrent jouer au tennis. Marcia et Paul parlent de roller en ligne, mais Marcia ne fait pas de roller en ligne. Marc et Alexandre font souvent de la vidéo, et ils invitent Jean-Louis à faire de la vidéo. Pauvre Jean-Louis! Il ne peut pas faire de la vidéo. Il a un examen d'anglais vendredi, et il décide d'étudier pour l'examen. Le reste des élèves jouent au volley-ball. Rose ne fait pas souvent de sport. Elle trouve que le volley-ball, c'est barbant!

Traditions

Carnaval

The **Carnaval de Québec,** the largest winter carnival in Canada, has been held every winter since 1954. The carnival is celebrated over a period of 17 days, beginning in late January and lasting through mid-February. People from around the world and across Canada come to participate in the festival's events and see **Bonhomme Carnaval,** a snowman wearing a red hat and scarf who participates in most of the festivities, and the magnificent Ice Castle built from more than 2,500 blocks of ice. Some of the carnival's highlights are the **Soirée de la Bougie,** a night when thousands of candles light up the city, a winter softball tournament, ice-wall climbing, canoe races across the frozen St. Lawrence River, snow-sculpting demonstrations by teams from several different countries, and the snow bath. This latter event features people parading in bathing suits despite freezing temperatures, then rolling around in the snow until they can no longer stand the cold. Have students plan and put on their own winter carnival, adapting events to their region and giving them French names.

Recette

When you think of Canada, you usually think of maple syrup. The leaf of the maple tree even appears on the Canadian flag. Native Americans knew how to harvest the ***eau sucrée*** *(sugar water) from the maple tree and make syrup with it before the French or English ever settled in Canada. The harvesting season in Canada is commonly called the* ***Temps des sucres.***

SUCRE A LA CREME

pour 4 personnes

- 2 tasses de sirop d'érable
- 3/4 tasse de crème légère
- 3/4 tasse de noix hachées
- 1 cuillère à café d'extrait de vanille
- 1 cuillère à soupe de sirop de maïs

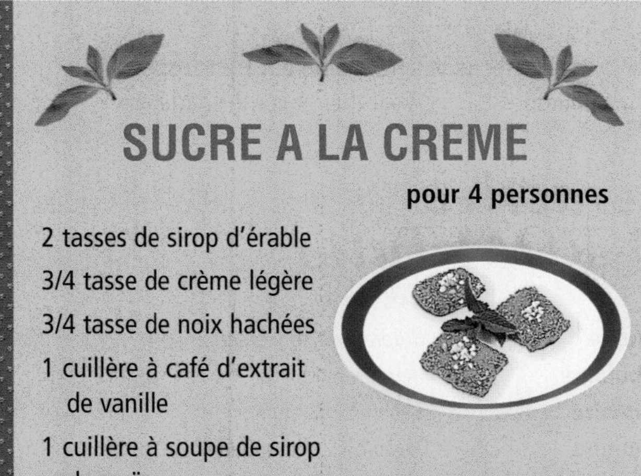

Mettre le sirop d'érable, le sirop de maïs et la crème légère dans une casserole et faire bouillir jusqu'à ce le mélange forme une boule molle (température de 234°F). Laisser tiédir (100° F) et remuer jusqu'à ce que le mélange s'épaississe. Ajouter la vanille et les noix.

Verser sur un plat beurré. Laisser refroidir. Découper en carrés.

STANDARDS: 1.1, 1.2, 1.3

Technology

Videocassette 2, Videocassette 5 (captioned version)
DVD Tutor, Disc 1
See Video Guide, pp. 23–28.

DVD/Video

Mise en train • Nouvelles de Québec

In this segment of the video, Emilie is making a video for Leticia, her pen pal in San Diego, to tell her about Quebec City and the sports and hobbies she likes. Emilie introduces her friends Michel, François, and Marie. Emilie and her friends talk about the sports and hobbies they like, the weather, and the different things you can do in each season in Quebec. We see scenes of Emilie, her friends, and other people participating in these activities.

Nouvelles de Québec (suite)

The story continues with Michel filming Emilie as she talks about Quebec City. We see scenes of different parts of the city as Emilie goes window-shopping and Michel goes to a hockey match. Next, Emilie and some friends go to **mont Sainte-Anne,** where they hike and ride mountain bikes. Finally, Emilie and Michel go to a skating rink. Emilie and Michel say goodbye to Leticia and suggest that she make a video for them about San Diego.

Qu'est-ce que tu fais comme sport?

Several teenagers from different French-speaking countries tell us what their favorite sports are.

Vidéoclips

- **Noky®**: advertisement for paper products
- **Casino®**: advertisement for a store

Interactive CD-ROM Tutor

Activity	Activity Type	Pupil's Edition Page
En contexte	*Interactive conversation*	
1. Vocabulaire	Jeu des paires	p. 112
2. Grammaire	Les mots qui manquent	p. 113
3. Grammaire	Les mots qui manquent	p. 116
4. Vocabulaire	Chasse au trésor Explorons!/Vérifions!	pp. 118, 120
5. Comment dit-on... ?	Chacun à sa place	p. 122
6. Grammaire	Le bon choix	pp. 112, 116, 122
Panorama Culturel	Qu'est-ce que tu fais comme sport? Le bon choix	p. 121
A toi de parler	*Guided recording*	pp. 132–133
A toi d'écrire	*Guided writing*	pp. 132–133

Teacher Management System

Launch the program, simply type "admin" in the password area and press RETURN. Log on to www.hrw.com/CDROMTUTOR for a detailed explanation of the Teacher Management System.

DVD Tutor

The *DVD Tutor* contains all material from the *Video Program* as described above. French captions are available for use at your discretion for all sections of the video. The *DVD Tutor* also provides a variety of video-based activities that assess students' understanding of the **Mise en train, Suite,** and **Panorama Culturel.**

This part of the *DVD Tutor* may be used on any DVD video player connected to a television or video monitor.

In addition to the video material and the video-based comprehension activities, the *DVD Tutor* also contains the entire *Interactive CD-ROM Tutor* in DVD-ROM format. Each DVD disc contains the activities from all 12 chapters of the *Interactive CD-ROM Tutor.*

This part of the *DVD Tutor* may be used on a Macintosh® or Windows® computer with a DVD-ROM drive.

To preview all resources available for this chapter, use the **One-Stop Planner CD-ROM,** Disc 1.

Go.Online!

Online Edition

The Online Edition for Allez, viens! *allows students access to their textbooks anytime anywhere.*

- *Audio at point of use*
- *Additional practice activities*
- *Self-test activities*
- *Online reference tools*
- *Entire Video Program (Enhanced version)*
- *Interactive Notebook (Enhanced version)*

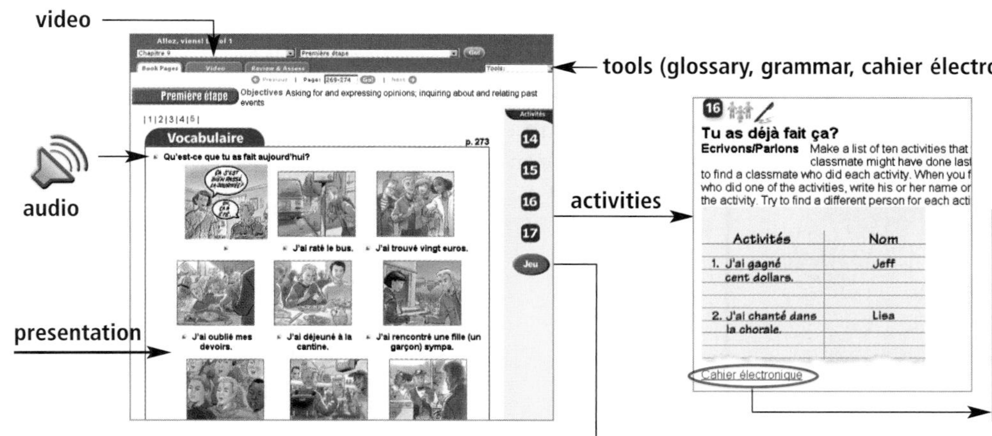

HRW Atlas

Internet Activités

Activités Internet

These guided internet activities include a worksheet and pre-selected and pre-screened authentic web sites from the francophone world. You can use these activities

- to help students develop research skills in the target language
- to introduce students to authentic cultural information
- as a project

Jeux interactifs

You can use the interactive activities in this chapter

- to practice grammar, vocabulary, and chapter functions
- as homework
- as an assessment option
- as a self-test
- to prepare for the Chapter Test

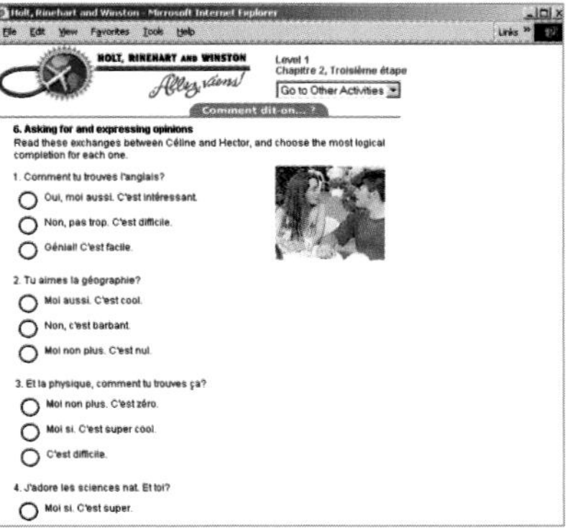

Projet Have students do a Web search for places in the French-speaking world other than Quebec City where people might practice their favorite sport, and the best time to go to those places. With that information, have them create a travel brochure in which fans of a certain sport can find places to go to practice the sport year-round. Have students document their sources by noting the names and URLs of all the sites they consulted.

Chapitre 4 : Sports et passe-temps
Textbook Listening Activities Scripts 

Première étape

6 p. 112

PHILIPPE Eh, salut, Pascal! Tu vas en vacances à la montagne! Quelle chance! Tu vas faire des photos?

PASCAL Des photos? Non, je ne fais jamais de photos.

PHILIPPE Tu vas faire du ski?

PASCAL Non, pas moi. Je n'aime pas le ski.

PHILIPPE Qu'est-ce que tu aimes faire, alors?

PASCAL Mais des tas de choses. J'aime faire de la natation. Et puis, le champion du patin à glace, c'est moi. J'adore ça. J'aime aussi beaucoup faire de la vidéo. A la rentrée, on va regarder une vidéo formidable de mes vacances.

Answers to Activity 6
Likes: swimming, ice-skating, making videos
Dislikes: taking pictures, skiing

9 p. 114

— Tu aimes faire du sport?
— Le sport, j'adore ça, surtout le roller en ligne et le hockey. Par contre, je n'aime pas beaucoup le volley. Et toi, tu aimes faire du sport?
— Le volley, pas du tout. Le roller en ligne, pas tellement. Je n'aime pas les sports d'équipe. J'aime bien faire du ski, et je fais du jogging tous les matins à sept heures.

Answers to Activity 9
Canadian student likes: in-line skating, hockey
Canadian student dislikes: volleyball
Your classmate likes: skiing, jogging
Your classmate dislikes: volleyball, in-line skating, team sports

Deuxième étape

21 p. 119

JOURNALISTE Bonjour, Paul. Qu'est-ce que tu aimes faire en hiver?

PAUL J'écoute de la musique et je regarde la télévision.

JOURNALISTE Tu ne fais pas de sport?

PAUL Si. Je fais du ski et je joue au hockey.

JOURNALISTE Est-ce que tu fais du sport, Anne?

ANNE De temps en temps, mais j'aime mieux aller au cinéma. Je regarde souvent la télé aussi.

JOURNALISTE Et toi, Julie, tu regardes la télévision?

JULIE Jamais. Je fais du sport. J'adore faire du ski et du patin.

JOURNALISTE Tu es sportive! Est-ce que tu écoutes de la musique aussi?

JULIE Oui, très souvent.

JOURNALISTE Et toi, Anne, tu aimes la musique?

ANNE Oui, beaucoup. Et j'aime aussi danser.

Answers to Activity 21
1. Julie
2. Paul, Julie, Anne
3. Paul
4. Anne
5. Anne

The following scripts are for the listening activities found in the *Pupil's Edition*. For Student Response Forms, see *Listening Activities,* pages 27–29. To provide additional listening practice, see *Listening Activities* book, pages 31–34.

One-Stop Planner CD-ROM

To preview all resources available for this chapter, use the **One-Stop Planner CD-ROM**, Disc 1.

Troisième étape

26 p. 122

1. — Allô?
— Allô, Lise? C'est Germain. Tiens, vendredi après-midi, on joue au volley-ball?
— Vendredi après-midi? D'accord. Bonne idée.

2. — Allô, oui?
— Salut, Renaud! Dis, tu fais quoi vendredi après-midi?
— Eh ben, rien. Pourquoi?
— On joue au volley-ball?
— Le volley... euh, ça ne me dit rien, le volley. C'est barbant.

3. — Allô?
— Salut, Philippe. C'est Germain. Qu'est-ce que tu fais ce week-end?
— Je ne sais pas. Et toi?
— J'ai une idée. On joue au volley-ball?
— Bonne idée! Le volley, c'est le fun!

4. — Allô?
— Allô, Monique? C'est Germain. On joue au volley?
— Je n'aime pas tellement le volley.

Answers to Activity 26
1. Lise: accepts
2. Renaud: turns down
3. Philippe: accepts
4. Monique: turns down

28 p. 123

1. EMILE Thierry, tu fais souvent du sport?
THIERRY Oui, je fais du jogging une fois par semaine.

2. EMILE Salut, Odile. Dis-moi, tu fais du sport?
ODILE Non, jamais. Je déteste le sport.

3. EMILE Et toi, Martine?
MARTINE Oh, de temps en temps. J'aime bien jouer au basket-ball.

4. EMILE Dis, François, tu fais souvent du sport?
FRANÇOIS Euh, pas vraiment. Quelquefois, je joue au tennis ou au base-ball.

5. EMILE Et toi, Vincent?
VINCENT Ouais, je fais de l'aérobic deux fois par semaine.

Answers to Activity 28
1. Thierry: once a week
2. Odile: never
3. Martine: from time to time
4. François: sometimes
5. Vincent: twice a week

PRONONCIATION, P. 125

For the scripts for Parts A and B, see page 125. The script for Part C is below.

C. A écrire *(dictation)*

— Salut! On joue au foot?
— Non. J'ai musique.
— Tu aimes la musique?
— Oui, bien sûr. C'est super.

Mise en pratique

1 p. 132

Vous aimez le ski, le patin, le hockey? Venez au Village des Sports. C'est le fun en hiver! Au printemps aussi, c'est le fun. Faites de l'athlétisme et du roller en ligne. Vous venez en été? Eh bien, c'est aussi le fun quand il fait chaud. Jouez au base-ball et faites du ski nautique. Et l'automne au Village des Sports, c'est super! Avec du volley et du football, Le Village des Sports, c'est le fun des quatre saisons!

Answers to Mise en pratique, Activity 1
Winter: skiing, skating, hockey
Spring: track and field, in-line skating
Summer: baseball, water-skiing
Fall: volleyball, soccer

Chapitre 4 : Sports et passe-temps
50-Minute Lesson Plans

Day 1

CHAPTER OPENER **5 min.**
- Present Chapter Objectives, p. 107.
- Focusing on Outcomes, ATE, p. 107
- Photo Flash!, ATE, p. 107
- Culture Note, ATE, p. 106

MISE EN TRAIN **40 min.**
- Presenting **Mise en train** and Preteaching Vocabulary, ATE, p. 108
- Language Note, ATE, p. 108
- Do Activities 1–5, p. 110.
- Presenting **Rencontre culturelle,** ATE, p. 111
- Read and discuss **Qu'en penses-tu?** and **Savais-tu que... ?,** p. 111.
- Thinking Critically, ATE, p. 111

Wrap-Up **5 min.**
- Challenge, ATE, p. 111.

Homework Options
Cahier d'activités, p. 37, Act. 1
Postcards, Teaching Suggestion, ATE, p. 111

Day 2

PREMIERE ETAPE
Quick Review **10 min.**
- Check homework.
- Bell Work, ATE, p. 112

Vocabulaire, p. 112 **15 min.**
- Presenting **Vocabulaire,** ATE, p. 112, using Teaching Transparencies 4-A and 4-B.
- Play Audio CD for Activity 6, p. 112.

Grammaire, p. 113 **15 min.**
- Presenting **Grammaire,** ATE, p. 113
- Language Notes, ATE, p. 113
- Do Activities 7–8, p. 113.

Wrap-Up **10 min.**
- Play Charades, ATE, p. 105C.

Homework Options
Cahier d'activités, pp. 38–39, Acts. 3–5
Travaux pratiques de grammaire, pp. 25–26, Acts. 1–4

Day 3

PREMIERE ETAPE
Quick Review **10 min.**
- Check homework.
- Mime sports and activities for students to guess in French.

Comment dit-on... ?, p. 114 **10 min.**
- Presenting **Comment dit-on... ?,** ATE, p. 114
- Play Audio CD for Activity 9, p. 114.
- Do Activity 11, p. 115, as a class, and Activity 10, p. 114, in pairs.

Grammaire, p. 115 **15 min.**
- Presenting **Grammaire,** ATE, p. 115
- **Grammaire supplémentaire,** p. 129, Activity 3
- Do Activity 12 or Activity 13, p. 115.

Wrap-Up **15 min.**
- Travaux pratiques de grammaire, p. 27, Acts. 5–6

Homework Options
Study for **Première étape** quiz.

Day 4

PREMIERE ETAPE
Quiz 4–1 **20 min.**
- Administer Quiz 4-1A or Quiz 4-1B.

DEUXIEME ETAPE
Comment dit-on... ?, p. 116 **10 min.**
- Presenting **Comment dit-on... ?,** ATE, p. 116
- Discuss **Note de grammaire**, p. 116.
- Do Activity 14, p. 116.

Grammaire, p. 116 **10 min.**
- Presenting **Grammaire**, ATE, p. 116
- Do Activity 15, p. 116.

Grammaire, p. 117 **5 min.**
- Presenting **Grammaire,** ATE, p. 117
- Do Activity 17, p. 117.

Wrap-Up **5 min.**
- Have partners find two activities they do that they have in common and tell the class about them, using the pronoun **on.**

Homework Options
Grammaire supplémentaire, pp. 129–130, Acts. 4–7
Travaux pratiques de grammaire, pp. 28–30, Acts. 7–11

Day 5

DEUXIEME ETAPE
Quick Review **10 min.**
- Do a "chain" activity, in which the first student asks another student, **Qu'est-ce que tu fais comme sport?** The second student replies, then poses the question to another student.

Vocabulaire, p. 118 **10 min.**
- Presenting **Vocabulaire,** ATE, p. 118, using Teaching Transparency 4–C
- Do Activity 18, p. 118.
- Do Activity 19, p. 118.

Vocabulaire, p. 119 **20 min.**
- Presenting **Vocabulaire,** ATE, p. 119
- Discuss **Note culturelle,** p. 119.
- Do Activity 20, p. 119.
- Play Audio CD for Activity 21, p. 119.
- Discuss **Tu te rappelles?,** p. 119.

Wrap-Up **10 min.**
- Game: Verb Bee, ATE, p. 130

Homework Options
Travaux pratiques de grammaire, pp. 30–32, Acts. 12–15

Day 6

DEUXIEME ETAPE
Quick Review **10 min.**
- Check homework.
- Name different holidays and have students tell you the month in which each holiday occurs.

Vocabulaire, p. 120 **30 min.**
- Present **Vocabulaire,** ATE, p. 120, using Teaching Transparency 4-D.
- Do Activities 23–24, p. 120.
- Cahier d'activités, pp. 42–43, Acts. 12–16

Wrap-Up **10 min.**
- Have students write their birthday in French on a slip of paper. Instruct them to ask each other their birthday and to arrange themselves in four groups by season.

Homework Options
Study for **Deuxième étape** quiz.

One-Stop Planner CD-ROM

For alternative lesson plans by chapter section, to create your own customized plans, or to preview all resources available for this chapter, use the **One-Stop Planner CD-ROM**, Disc 1.

For additional homework suggestions, see activities accompanied by this symbol throughout the chapter.

Day 7

DEUXIEME ETAPE

Quiz 4–2 20 min.
- Administer Quiz 4-2A or Quiz 4-2B.

PANORAMA CULTUREL 25 min.
- Presenting **Panorama Culturel**, ATE, p. 121, using Videocassette 2.
- Do **Qu'en penses-tu?** and **Savais-tu que… ?**, p. 121
- **Panorama Culturel**, Interactive CD-ROM Tutor (Disc 1)

Wrap-Up 5 min.
- Thinking Critically, ATE, p. 121

Homework Options
Cahier d'activités, p. 48, Acts. 26–27

Day 8

TROISIEME ETAPE

Quick Review 10 min.
- Check homework.

Comment dit-on... ?, p. 122 30 min.
- Presenting **Comment dit-on... ?**, ATE, p. 122
- Play Audio CD for Activity 26, p. 122.
- Do Activity 27, p. 122.
- Communicative Activity 4-3A and 4-3B, Activities for Communication, pp. 23–24

Wrap-Up 10 min.
- Situation Card 4-3: Role-play, Activities for Communication, p.144

Homework Options
Have students draw a comic strip summarizing the conversation they had with their partner while acting out Situation Card 4-3: Role-play, Activities for Communication, p. 144.

Day 9

TROISIEME ETAPE

Quick Review 10 min.
- Check homework. Have students present their comic strips to the class.

Grammaire, p. 122 15 min.
- Presenting **Grammaire,** ATE, p. 122
- Play Audio CD for Activity 28, p. 123.
- Do Activity 29, p. 123.
- Cahier d'activités, pp. 45–46, Acts. 20–23

Prononciation, p. 125 15 min.
- Play Audio CD for Activities A–C, p. 125.

Wrap-Up 10 min.
- Do Activity 30, p. 123.

Homework Options
Study for **Troisième étape** quiz.

Day 10

TROISIEME ETAPE

Quiz 4–3 20 min.
- Administer Quiz 4-3A or Quiz 4-3B.

LISONS! 25 min.
- Prereading Activities A–C, ATE, p. 126
- Reading Activities D–M, ATE, pp. 126–127
- Postreading Activity N, ATE, p. 127
- Thinking Critically, ATE, p. 127

Wrap-Up 5 min.
- Do the Using Text Organizers suggestion, ATE, p. 127, in which students create a conversation based on the reading.

Homework Options
Cahier d'activités, p. 47, Acts. 24–25

Day 11

LISONS!

Quick Review 5 min.
- Check homework.

MISE EN PRATIQUE 35 min.
- Play Audio CD for Activity 1, p. 132.
- Do Activity 2, p. 132.
- Challenge, ATE, p. 132
- Do Activity 3, p. 133.
- Do **Ecrivons!**, p. 133, with Process Writing, ATE, p. 132.

Wrap-Up 10 min.
- Have partners complete **Jeu de rôle,** p. 133.

Homework Options
Que sais-je?, p. 134

Day 12

MISE EN PRATIQUE

Quick Review 15 min.
- Check homework and collect final draft of **Ecrivons!**
- Game: **Mémoire,** ATE, p. 105C

Chapter Review 35 min.
- Review Chapter 4. Choose from **Grammaire supplémentaire,** Grammar Tutor for Students of French, Activities for Communication, Listening Activities, Interactive CD-ROM Tutor, or **Jeux interactifs.**

Homework Options
Study for Chapter 4 Test.

Assessment

Test, Chapter 4 50 min.
- Administer Chapter 4 Test. Select from Testing Program, Alternative Assessment Guide, Test Generator, or Standardized Assessment Tutor.

Chapitre 4 : Sports et passe-temps
90-Minute Lesson Plans

Block 1

CHAPTER OPENER 5 min.
- Present Chapter Objectives, p. 107
- Photo Flash!, ATE, p. 107
- Culture Note, ATE, p. 106

MISE EN TRAIN 45 min.
- Presenting **Mise en train,** ATE, p. 108.
- Language Note, ATE, p. 108
- View video of **Mise en train,** Videocassette 2, Video Guide, p. 25. Video Guide, p. 28, Activities 1–3

RENCONTRE CULTURELLE, p. 111 15 min.
- Presenting **Rencontre culturelle,** ATE, p. 111
- Read **Savais-tu que...?,** ATE, p. 111

PREMIERE ETAPE
Vocabulaire, p. 112 20 min.
- Presenting **Vocabulaire,** ATE, p. 112
- Additional Practice, ATE, p. 112
- Language-to-Language, ATE, p. 113
- Play Audio CD for Activity 6, p. 112.

Wrap-Up 5 min.
- Use the Chapter 4 **Mise en train** Transparencies to summarize what happened in the **Mise en train.**

Homework Options
Cahier d'activités, p. 38, Acts. 3–4
Travaux pratiques de grammaire, p. 25, Acts. 1–2

Block 2

PREMIERE ETAPE
Quick Review 5 min.
- Show pictures of activities presented on p. 112. Ask: **Qu'est-ce qu'ils aiment faire?**

Grammaire, p. 113 30 min.
- Presenting **Grammaire,** p. 113, Language Notes, ATE, p. 113
- Do Activity 7, p. 113, orally, with Challenge, ATE, p. 113
- **Grammaire supplémentaire** p. 128, Activities 1–2

Comment dit-on... ?, p. 114 20 min.
- Motivating Activity: Ask students if they always answer in complete sentences. Have them suggest short answers they might give in English if someone asked whether they liked or disliked something.
- Presenting **Comment dit-on...?,** ATE, p. 114
- Additional Practice, ATE, p. 114
- Play Audio CD for Activity 9, p. 114.
- Do Activity 10, p. 114.

Grammaire, p. 115 30 min.
- **Vocabulaire à la carte,** p. 115
- Presenting **Grammaire,** ATE, p. 115
- Do Activity 13, p. 115.
- **Grammaire supplémentaire,** p. 129, Activity 3
- Situation 4-1: Role-Play, Activities for Communication, p. 144

Wrap-Up 5 min.
- Additional Practice, ATE, p. 115

Homework Options
Study for **Première étape** quiz.
Travaux pratiques de grammaire, pp. 26–27, Acts. 3–6
Cahier d'activités, p. 40, Acts. 7–8

Block 3

PREMIERE ETAPE
Quick Review 10 min.
- Communicative Activity 4-1A and 4-1B, Activities for Communication, pp. 19–20

Quiz 4-1 20 min.
- Administer Quiz 4-1A or 4-1B.

DEUXIEME ETAPE
Quick Review 5 min.
- Bell Work, ATE, p. 116

Comment dit-on...?, p. 116 15 min.
- Presenting **Comment dit-on...?,** ATE, p. 116
- **Note de grammaire,** p. 116
- Do Activity 14, p. 116.

Grammaire: verb *faire*, p. 116 20 min.
- Presenting **Grammaire: verb *faire*,** ATE, p. 116
- Do Activities 15 and 16, pp. 116–117.
- **Grammaire supplémentaire,** p. 129, Activities 4–5

Grammaire: the pronoun *on*, p. 117 15 min.
- Presenting **Grammaire: the pronoun *on*,** ATE, p. 117
- Do Activity 17, p. 117.
- **Grammaire supplémentaire,** p. 130, Activities 6–7

Wrap-Up 5 min.
- Review **–er** verb conjugations.

Homework Options
Cahier d'activités, p. 41, Acts. 10–11
Travaux pratiques de grammaire, pp. 28–30, Acts. 7–11

For alternative lesson plans by chapter section, to create your own customized plans, or to preview all resources available for this chapter, use the **One-Stop Planner CD-ROM**, Disc 1.

For additional homework suggestions, see activities accompanied by this symbol throughout the chapter.

Block 4

DEUXIEME ETAPE

Quick Review 10 min.
- Game: **Mémoire,** ATE, p. 105C, with variation: match the subject pronoun to the correct form.

Vocabulaire, p. 118 20 min.
- Presenting **Vocabulaire,** ATE, p. 118
- Do Activity 18, p. 118. See Visual/Auditory Learners, ATE, p. 118.
- Do Activity 19, p. 118. Students should answer in complete sentences.

Vocabulaire, p. 119 25 min.
- Presenting **Vocabulaire**, ATE, p. 119
- **Note culturelle,** p. 119, Math Link, ATE, p. 119
- Do Activity 20, p. 119, with Challenge, ATE, p. 119.
- **Tu te rappelles?,** p. 119
- Play Audio CD for Activity 21, p. 119.

Vocabulaire, p. 120 10 min.
- Presenting **Vocabulaire,** ATE, p. 120
- Do Activity 24, p. 120.

PANORAMA CULTUREL 20 min.
- Presenting **Panorama Culturel**, ATE, p. 121 with Videocassette 2
- Have students answer **Qu'en penses-tu?** questions.
- Read **Savais-tu que... ?** with Culture Note, ATE, p. 121.
- Thinking Critically, ATE, p. 121

Wrap-Up 5 min.
- Visual Learners, ATE, p. 120.

Homework Options

Study for **Deuxième étape** quiz.
Pupil's Edition, Activity 22, p. 119
Cahier d'activités, p. 42, Acts. 12–14 and p. 48, Act. 26
Travaux pratiques de grammaire, pp. 30–32, Acts. 12–16

Block 5

DEUXIEME ETAPE

Quick Review 10 min.

Quiz 4-2 20 min.
- Administer Quiz 4-2A or 4-2B.

TROISIEME ETAPE

Comment dit–on...?, p. 122 15 min.
- Presenting **Comment dit-on... ?,** ATE, p. 122
- Play Audio for Activity 26, p. 122.
- Do Activity 27, p. 122.
- **Grammaire supplémentaire**, p. 131, Activities 9–10

Grammaire, p. 122 20 min.
- Presenting **Grammaire,** ATE, p. 122 and Language Note, ATE, p. 123
- Play Audio CD for Activity 28, p. 123.
- Do Activity 29, p. 123 and Culture Note, ATE, p. 123.

Prononciation, p. 125 15 min.
- Play Audio CD for **Prononciation,** Activities A, B, and C, p. 125.
- Auditory Learners, ATE, p. 125

Wrap-Up 10 min.
- Communicative Activity 4-3A and 4-3B, Activities for Communication, pp. 23–24

Homework Options

Study for **Troisième étape** quiz.
Travaux pratiques de grammaire, pp. 33–34, Acts. 17–20
Cahier d'activités, pp. 45–46, Acts. 19–22

Block 6

TROISIEME ETAPE

Quick Review 10 min.

Quiz 4-3 20 min.
- Administer Quiz 4-3A or 4-3B.

LISONS! 20 min
- Prereading Activities A–C, ATE, p. 126
- Reading Activities D–M, ATE, pp. 126–127
- Postreading Activity N, ATE, p. 127

MISE EN PRATIQUE 35 min.
- Play Audio CD for Activity 1, p. 132.
- Do Activities 2 and 4, pp. 132–133.
- Culture Note, ATE, p. 132
- Do **Ecrivons!**, p. 132, with Process Writing, ATE, p. 132.

Wrap-Up 5 min.
- Tell students, in French, to do a certain activity and have them respond by miming the activity.

Homework Options

Que sais-je?, p. 134
Finish final draft of **Ecrivons!,** p. 132.
Study for Chapter 4 Test.

Block 7

MISE EN PRATIQUE

Chapter Review 40 min.
- Check homework and collect final draft of **Ecrivons!**
- Review Chapter 4. Choose from **Grammaire supplémentaire,** Grammar Tutor for Students of French, Activities for Communication, Listening Activities, Interactive CD-ROM Tutor, or **Jeux interactifs.**

Test, Chapter 4 50 min.
- Administer Chapter 4 Test. Select from Testing Program, Alternative Assessment Guide, Test Generator, or Standardized Assessment Tutor.

Chapter Opener

CHAPITRE 4

One-Stop Planner CD-ROM

For resource information, see the **One-Stop Planner,** Disc 1.

Pacing Tips

Keep in mind while planning your lessons that the **Deuxième étape** in this chapter presents the verb **faire** and expressions with **faire** and **jouer.** The vocabulary for the seasons, months of the year, and weather are also covered in this **étape.** The **Troisième étape** is the lightest. For Lesson Plans and timing suggestions, see pages 105I–105L.

Meeting the Standards

Communication

- Telling how much you like or dislike something, p. 114
- Exchanging information, p. 116
- Making, accepting, and turning down suggestions, p. 122

Cultures

- Rencontre culturelle, p. 111
- Multicultural Link, p. 111
- Note culturelle, p. 119
- Panorama Culturel, p. 121
- Culture Note, pp. 106, 121, 123, 132

Connections

- Geography Link, p. 111
- History Link, p. 111
- Math Link, p. 119

Comparisons

- Thinking Critically: Drawing Inferences, p. 109
- Thinking Critically: Comparing and Contrasting, p. 111
- Thinking Critically: Analyzing, p. 121
- Thinking Critically: Comparing and Contrasting, p. 127

Communities

De l'école au travail, p. 125

Career Path, p. 133

Cultures and Communities

Culture Note

Centres d'animation and **Maisons des jeunes** are French organizations that offer teenagers a place to meet with other young people who share the same interests. These are also places where teenagers can find information on summer jobs, student travel opportunities, and many other topics. Classes are taught here on a variety of subjects, such as dancing, music, art, acting, and various sports. **Centres Communautaires** offer the same type of activities, but they are open to people of all ages. Some of them may focus on issues of interest to specific demographic groups. For more information on the **Maisons des jeunes,** see page 178.

CHAPITRE

4

Sports et passe-temps

Objectives

In this chapter you will learn to

Première étape

- tell how much you like or dislike something

Deuxième étape

- exchange information

Troisième étape

- make, accept, and turn down suggestions

Visit Holt Online
go.hrw.com
KEYWORD: WA3 QUEBEC CITY-4
Online Edition

On aime faire du théâtre!

Chapter Opener

CHAPITRE 4

Focusing on Outcomes

Have students read the three functional objectives listed on this page. Ask them which objectives correspond to the photo on pages 106 and 107. You might also ask students if they like the activity that is pictured.
NOTE: The self-check activities in **Que sais-je?** on page 134 help students assess their achievement of the objectives.

Photo Flash!

The young people in this photo are rehearsing a play during a drama class at a recreation center.

Connections and Comparisons

Sports Link

- There are many options that teenagers have in Quebec when they want to have fun. Activities include hiking or cycling in the many parks in Quebec, ice-skating in the indoor arena at **Le Colisée** or in the Saint Charles river in the winter, skiing, horseback riding, and many more. Have students make a list of the things that they like to do when they have free time. Are there attractions in their area where they go for fun?
- Have students research one of the sports in this chapter and any famous events or athletes associated with that sport in francophone countries. Have them share what they have learned with their classmates.

STANDARDS: 4.2, 5.2

Mise en train

CHAPITRE 4

Teaching Resources
pp. 108–110

PRINT 
- Lesson Planner, p. 18
- Video Guide, pp. 26, 28
- Cahier d'activités, p. 37

MEDIA 
- One-Stop Planner
- Video Program
  Mise en train
  Videocassette 2, 03:26–08:31
  Videocassette 5 (captioned version), 26:12–31:14
  Suite
  Videocassette 2, 08:34–18:14
  Videocassette 5 (captioned version), 31:20–41:00
- DVD Tutor, Disc 1
- Audio Compact Discs, CD 4, Trs. 1–2
- **Mise en train** Transparencies

Presenting
Mise en train

Since the letter is not read on the video, you might first read the letter aloud to students and have them listen with their books closed. Ask them what they understood, or have them answer the questions in Activity 1 on page 110. Then, tell students they're going to see the video Emilie made for Leticia. Play the video and then, have students open their books and read the letter and photo captions.

Mise en train Transparencies

Language Note

You might explain that the expression **C'est le fun** is Canadian slang; it is often contracted as **l'fun.**

This is an abridged version of the video episode.

MISE EN TRAIN ▪ *Nouvelles de Québec*

CD 4 Trs. 1–2

Stratégie pour comprendre

Emilie is eager to get to know her American pen pal Leticia. What kind of information do you think Emilie might include in a letter to her new pen pal? Look at the photos she included, and see if you can guess what Emilie is telling Leticia. What sort of questions might Emilie ask Leticia?

Salut, Leticia!

Comment ça va? Juste une petite lettre pour accompagner ces photos, une brochure sur le mont Sainte-Anne, une montagne près de Québec et aussi une cassette vidéo sur Québec... et sur moi! Comme ça, tu as une idée des activités ici... C'est l'automne à Québec et il fait déjà froid! Heureusement, il y a du soleil, mais il y a du vent. Quel temps est-ce qu'il fait à San Diego? Est-ce qu'il fait froid aussi? J'aime beaucoup Québec. C'est très sympa. Il y a beaucoup de choses à faire. En automne, je fais du patin et de la natation. J'adore le sport. En été, je fais du deltaplane et de la voile. Au printemps, je fais de l'équitation et je joue au tennis. Et en hiver, bien sûr, je fais du ski. C'est super ici pour le ski. Il neige de novembre à avril! Tu imagines? Est-ce qu'il neige à San Diego? Qu'est-ce qu'on fait comme sport? Du ski? Du base-ball? Quand il fait trop froid, je regarde la télévision et j'écoute de la musique. J'adore le rock et la musique québécoise. Et toi? Qu'est-ce que tu écoutes comme musique? Qu'est-ce qu'on fait à San Diego les fins de semaine? J'ai aussi une autre passion : de temps en temps, je fais des films avec un caméscope. C'est l'fun! Tu sais, c'est super, Québec. Et la Californie, c'est comment? C'est l'fun ou pas?

A très bientôt

Emilie

Preteaching Vocabulary

Guessing words from context

Ask students what they would include in a videotape to a French pen pal. Would they show their city, their friends, or what they like to do? Have them guess what Emilie might have included in her videotape to Leticia. Ask students to keep the context in mind, and have them identify expressions in ***Nouvelles de Québec*** that describe activities that Emilie and her friends like to do. **(Je joue au tennis. Je fais du ski. Je regarde la télévision. On fait du vélo.)** For each activity mentioned, have students tell in which season the characters participate in that activity.

STANDARDS: 1.2

Ça, c'est notre café préféré.

La musique, c'est super! Tu fais de la musique, toi?

Au printemps, on joue au tennis. J'adore!

C'est mon copain Michel. En été, on fait du vélo.

En automne, on fait de l'équitation.

C'est moi! En hiver, on fait du patin.

Cahier d'activités, p. 37, Act. 1

Using the Captioned Video/DVD

If students have difficulty understanding French spoken at a normal speed, use Videocassette 5 to allow students to see the French captions for ***Nouvelles de Québec*** and ***Nouvelles de Québec (suite).*** Hearing the language and watching the story will reduce anxiety about the new language and facilitate comprehension. The reinforcement of seeing the written vocabulary words as they watch the gestures and actions will help prepare students to do the comprehension activities on page 110. NOTE: The *DVD Tutor* contains captions for all sections of the *Video Program.*

Mise en train

CHAPITRE 4

Thinking Critically

Drawing Inferences Have students try to guess the seasons, climate, and activities shown on page 109. Ask if they can think of an English word that looks like **hiver** and has to do with winter? (Some animals *hibernate* in winter, living off their stored energy sources.)

Kinesthetic Learners

Have students or pairs of students come to the front of the class and mime the action in one of the photos. The first person to call out the number of the corresponding photo takes the next turn. As a challenge, you might also have students find the sentence in Emilie's letter where she talks about the activity being mimed.

Nouvelles de Québec (suite)

The story continues with Michel filming Emilie as she talks about Quebec City. We see scenes of different parts of the city as Emilie goes window-shopping and Michel goes to a hockey match. Next, Emilie and some friends go to **mont Sainte-Anne,** where they hike and ride mountain bikes. Finally, Emilie and Michel go to a skating rink. They interview a man who talks about the sports that he likes to practice throughout the year. Emilie and Michel say good-bye to Leticia and suggest that she make a video for them about San Diego.

Mise en train

CHAPITRE 4

Visual/Auditory Learners

3 You may want to play ***Nouvelles de Québec*** on Videocassette 5 to help students find the targeted expressions.

Language Note

4 Tell students that a good way to remember whether to use **en** or **au** with the seasons is that **en** is used with the seasons that begin with a vowel sound **(été, automne,** and **hiver)**, and **au** is used with **printemps,** which doesn't begin with a vowel sound.

These activities check for comprehension only. Students should not yet be expected to produce language modeled in **Mise en train.**

1 Tu as compris?

Answer the following questions about Emilie's letter to Leticia. Don't be afraid to guess. See answers below.

1. What is Emilie sending to Leticia along with her letter?
2. What are some of Emilie's hobbies and pastimes?
3. What would she like to know about Leticia and San Diego?
4. What does Emilie tell Leticia about the city of Quebec?
5. What else have you learned about Emilie from her letter?

2 C'est Emilie?

Tell whether Emilie would be likely or unlikely to say each of the statements below.

1. «J'adore faire du sport.» likely
2. «Le ski? Ici on n'aime pas beaucoup ça.» unlikely
3. «Pour moi, Québec, c'est barbant en hiver.» unlikely
4. «Faire des films avec un caméscope, pour moi, c'est passionnant.» likely
5. «Je regarde la télé en hiver quand il fait trop froid.» likely
6. «La musique? Bof! Je n'aime pas beaucoup ça.» unlikely

3 Cherche les expressions

In ***Nouvelles de Québec,*** what does Emilie say to . . . See answers below.

1. greet Leticia?
2. ask how Leticia is?
3. ask about the weather?
4. tell what she likes?
5. express her opinion about something?
6. inquire about California?
7. say goodbye?

C'est super. **Comment ça va?** **J'adore...** **A très bientôt.** **J'aime...** **C'est très sympa.** **Quel temps est-ce qu'il fait?** **Salut!** **C'est l'fun.** **Et la Californie, c'est comment?**

4 Les saisons et les sports

D'après la lettre d'Emilie, quels sports est-ce qu'elle fait? En quelle saison? Choisis des sports pour compléter ces phrases.

1. Au printemps, Emilie fait... de l'équitation.
2. En hiver, elle fait... du ski.
3. En automne, elle fait... du patin et de la natation.
4. En été, elle fait... du deltaplane et de la voile.

de l'équitation **du ski** **de la voile** **du deltaplane** **du patin** **de la natation**

5 Et maintenant, à toi

Emilie fait beaucoup de choses! Tu fais les mêmes choses? Pour chaque activité, réponds **Moi aussi** ou **Moi, non.**

1. Emilie fait du ski.
2. Elle écoute de la musique.
3. Emilie fait des films avec un caméscope.
4. Elle fait de l'équitation.
5. Quand il fait trop froid pour sortir, Emilie regarde la télé.
6. Emilie joue au tennis.

Comprehension Check

Auditory Learners

2 This activity can be used as a listening comprehension exercise. Read the sentences aloud and have students write **Oui** or **Non** on their papers.

Slower Pace

4 Go over the list of sports with students to make sure they understand them before completing the activity. You might mime the sports to avoid using English.

Answers

1
1. photographs, a brochure, and a videocassette
2. ice-skating, swimming, hang gliding, sailing, horseback riding, tennis, skiing, watching TV, listening to music, and making video films
3. her favorite hobbies and pastimes, what the weather is like, what music she listens to, what California is like
4. It's already cold in autumn. It's sunny, but windy. There are a lot of things to do there. It snows from November to April.
5. *Possible answer:* She's athletic, active, friendly, and extroverted.

3
1. Salut!
2. Comment ça va?
3. Quel temps est-ce qu'il fait?
4. J'aime...; J'adore...
5. C'est super. C'est l'fun. C'est très sympa.
6. Et la Californie, c'est comment?
7. A très bientôt.

STANDARDS: 1.2

What do you know about Quebec?

What impressions do you get of Quebec when you look at these photos?

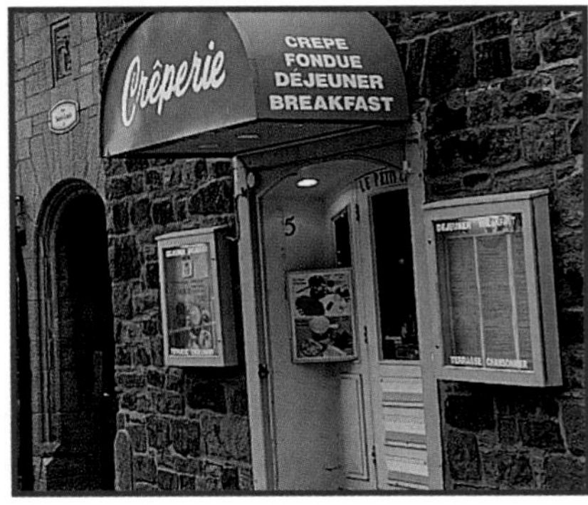

Qu'en penses-tu? See answers below.

1. What things do you see that are typically American?
2. What do you see in these photos that you might not see in the United States?

Savais-tu que... ?

One of the first things you'll notice about Quebec City is its fascinating blend of styles—old and new, European and North American. Old Quebec (**le Vieux-Québec**) is filled with quaint neighborhood cafés and shops that maintain the old-world flavor of Europe. And yet, it is surrounded by a vibrant, modern city with high-rise hotels, office buildings, and a complex network of freeways. All of these elements together give the city its unique character.

Presenting Rencontre culturelle

Have students describe the photos orally, and then answer the questions in **Qu'en penses-tu?** Ask them if they would like to visit or study in Quebec and have them explain why or why not.

History Link
Have students look up information about the founding of Quebec, the exploration of the region, and the important people involved. You might also have them refer to the Location Opener on pages 102–105.

Challenge
Have students choose one of the pictures of Quebec and write a short note as if they were sending it as a postcard.

Multicultural Link
Have students research cities in the United States where there is evidence of more than one major culture. They might choose New Orleans (French), Miami (Hispanic), or any city with a large Asian population (San Francisco). Have students research how these cultures have enriched the city and what contributions citizens of these cultures have made to their city and state.

Connections and Comparisons

Geography Link
Have students find Quebec on a map of Canada. You might have them calculate the distance between their city and Quebec. Have them look at a globe or world map to find out what other cities are on the same latitude as Quebec.

Thinking Critically
Comparing and Contrasting In English, have students compare their city with Quebec, writing or naming several similarities and differences. You might have them consult an encyclopedia to obtain more information about Quebec.

Possible answers
1. freeways, freeway signs, skyscrapers, and other modern buildings
2. cobblestone streets, European-style cafés and shops, French signs

STANDARDS: 2.2, 3.1, 3.2, 4.2

Première étape

CHAPITRE 4

Teaching Resources
pp. 112–115

PRINT

- Lesson Planner, p. 19
- TPR Storytelling Book, pp. 13, 16
- Listening Activities, pp. 27, 31
- Activities for Communication, pp. 19–20, 90, 93, 143–144
- Travaux pratiques de grammaire, pp. 25–27
- Grammar Tutor for Students of French, Chapter 4
- Cahier d'activités, pp. 38–40
- Testing Program, pp. 79–82
- Alternative Assessment Guide, p. 35
- Student Make-Up Assignments, Chapter 4

MEDIA 

- One-Stop Planner
- Audio Compact Discs, CD 4, Trs. 3–4, 19, 25–26
- Teaching Transparencies: 4-1, 4-A, 4-B; **Grammaire supplémentaire** Answers; Travaux pratiques de grammaire Answers
- Interactive CD-ROM Tutor, Disc 1

Bell Work
Have students write sentences telling two things they like to do after school and two things they don't like to do.

Presenting Vocabulaire

Write the activities on a transparency and cover it. Then, mime the activities one at a time. After you mime each one, say the French equivalent and have students repeat it as you uncover that expression. Then, hold up magazine pictures of people playing various sports and make true-false statements. **(Il joue au tennis.)**

Première étape

Objective Telling how much you like or dislike something

WA3 QUEBEC CITY-4

Vocabulaire

Sports et activités

CD-ROM 1 DVD 1

jouer au foot(ball)

jouer au football américain

faire de la vidéo

faire du roller en ligne

faire du patin à glace

faire du théâtre

faire de l'athlétisme

faire du vélo

faire de la natation*

You can probably guess what these activities are:

faire de l'aérobic	**faire du ski (nautique)**	**jouer au basket(-ball)**
faire du jogging	**jouer aux cartes**	**jouer au golf**
faire de la/des photo(s)	**jouer au base-ball**	**jouer au hockey**
jouer à des jeux vidéo	**jouer au tennis**	**jouer au volley(-ball)**

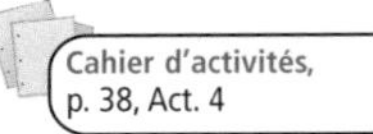
Cahier d'activités, p. 38, Act. 4

Travaux pratiques de grammaire, p. 25, Act. 1–2

*Remember that **nager** also means *to swim.*

6 Pascal à la montagne See scripts and answers on p. 105G.

Ecoutons Listen to this conversation between Philippe and Pascal. List at least two activities Pascal likes and two he doesn't like.

CD 4 Tr. 3

Communication for All Students

Additional Practice

- Have students categorize the activities by season and keep their notes to use in later activities.
- Show *Teaching Transparencies 4-A* and *4-B* and ask students which sport each person likes.

Kinesthetic Learners

Tell students to do some of these activities **(Joue au tennis!)** and have them mime the activity in response to your instruction.

STANDARDS: 1.2, 3.1

Grammaire

Expressions with *faire* and *jouer*

CD-ROM 1 DVD 1

You use **faire** *(to make, to do)* followed by the preposition **de** with activities, including sports.

- When the sport is a masculine noun, **de** becomes **du.**

  faire **du** ski   faire **du** patin

- If the activity is plural, **de** becomes **des.**

  faire **des** photos

- The preposition **de** doesn't change before **la** or **l'.**

  faire **de la** natation   faire **de l'**aérobic

You use **jouer** *(to play)* with games or sports that you play. It is followed by the preposition **à.**

- When the game or sport is a masculine noun **à** becomes **au.**

  jouer **au** football

- When the game or sport is plural, **à** becomes **aux.**

  jouer **aux** cartes

- The preposition **à** doesn't change before **la, l'** or **des.**

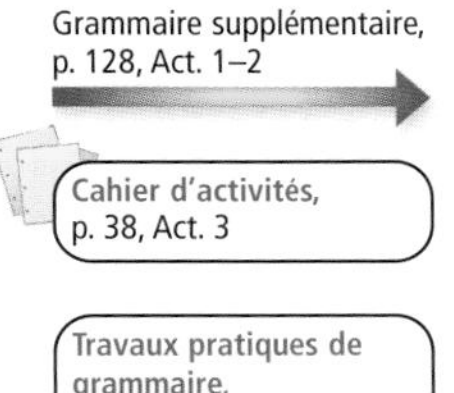

Grammaire supplémentaire, p. 128, Act. 1–2

Cahier d'activités, p. 38, Act. 3

Travaux pratiques de grammaire, p. 26, Act. 3–4

7 Grammaire en contexte

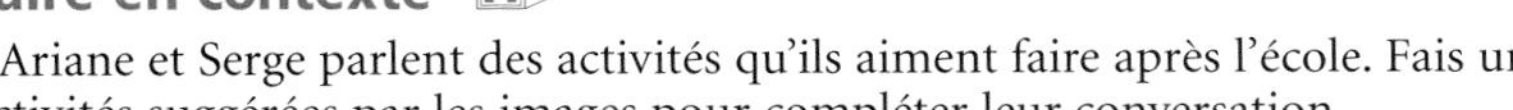

Ecrivons Ariane et Serge parlent des activités qu'ils aiment faire après l'école. Fais une liste des activités suggérées par les images pour compléter leur conversation.

ARIANE Qu'est-ce que tu aimes faire après l'école?

SERGE Moi, j'aime  avec mes copains. Et toi?
jouer au football

ARIANE Moi, j'aime  et j'adore  .
faire du roller en ligne
faire des photos

SERGE Tu aimes ? On va jouer à la plage demain. Tu viens?
jouer au volley-ball

ARIANE Non, merci. J'aime mieux  avec des copains.
faire du ski nautique

8 Grammaire en contexte

Parlons You and a Canadian student are discussing what you like to do after school on different days of the week. Create the conversation with one of your classmates.

EXEMPLE
—Qu'est-ce que tu aimes faire le lundi après l'école?
— J'aime jouer au basket le lundi. Et toi?
— Moi, j'aime faire du vélo.

Communication for All Students

Language Notes

- You may want to explain to students that **faire de la photo** means *to do photography,* while **faire des photos** means *to take pictures.*
- Some other activities using **faire** that students might like to know are **faire du vélo tout terrain** *(to mountain bike),* **faire de la gymnastique** *(to do gymnastics, to exercise in general),* **faire de la boxe** *(to box),* and **faire de l'alpinisme** *(to climb mountains).*

Challenge

7 After students have completed the activity, have them pair off and rewrite the dialogue to express their own preferences.

Presenting Grammaire

Expressions with *faire* and *jouer* Play **Jeter et attraper** (see page 139C) with activities. First, have students look back at the **Vocabulaire** on page 112, noticing which activities use **faire** and which ones use **jouer** and explain why. Then, have them close their books. Call out an activity **(ski)** and toss a ball to a student, who catches it and calls out the full expression **(faire du ski).** For an extra challenge, students who drop the ball should be given two activities.

Teacher Note

Students will learn more about contractions with **à** in Chapter 6 and contractions with **de** in Chapter 12. You may want to refer to these presentations on pages 177 and 369.

Language-to-Language

In Canada, *soccer* is called **le soccer** instead of **le foot(ball)** because Canadian football, which is similar to American football, also exists.

Première étape

CHAPITRE 4

Teaching Resources
pp. 112–115

PRINT 

- Lesson Planner, p. 19
- TPR Storytelling Book, pp. 13, 16
- Listening Activities, pp. 27, 31
- Activities for Communication, pp. 19–20, 90, 93, 143–144
- Travaux pratiques de grammaire, pp. 25–27
- Grammar Tutor for Students of French, Chapter 4
- Cahier d'activités, pp. 38–40
- Testing Program, pp. 79–82
- Alternative Assessment Guide, p. 35
- Student Make-Up Assignments, Chapter 4

MEDIA 

- One-Stop Planner
- Audio Compact Discs, CD 4, Trs. 3–4, 19, 25–26
- Teaching Transparencies: 4-1, 4-A, 4-B; **Grammaire supplémentaire** Answers; Travaux pratiques de grammaire Answers
- Interactive CD-ROM Tutor, Disc 1

Presenting
Comment dit-on... ?

Have a volunteer ask you if you like soccer. Then, give all of the short answers listed here, delivering each with exaggerated facial expressions and gestures to get the meaning across. Tell students how much you like certain activities. (**J'aime beaucoup nager.**) Have them indicate what they understood by using the thumbs-up gesture, the **comme ci comme ça** gesture, or the thumbs-down gesture.

Comment dit-on...?

Telling how much you like or dislike something

To tell how much you like something:
J'aime **beaucoup** le sport. *I like . . . a lot!*
J'aime **surtout** faire du ski. *I especially like . . .*

To tell how much you dislike something:
Je n'aime **pas tellement** le football. *I don't like . . . too much.*
Je n'aime **pas beaucoup** le volley-ball. *I don't like . . . very much.*
Je n'aime **pas du tout** la natation. *I don't like . . . at all.*

You can use the expressions in bold type alone as short answers:
—Tu aimes faire du sport?
—Oui, **beaucoup!** or
Non, **pas tellement.**

Cahier d'activités, p. 39, Act. 5

9 Qu'est-ce qu'ils aiment? See scripts and answers on p. 105G.

CD 4 Tr. 4

Ecoutons On a school trip to Quebec, you listen to your classmate talk to a Canadian student. Write down at least one sport or game each speaker likes and one each speaker dislikes.

10 Pas d'accord!

Parlons You and a Canadian exchange student want to watch sports on TV, but you can't agree on what to watch. Each time one of you finds something you like, the other doesn't like it and changes the channel. Act this out with a partner.

EXEMPLE **—Oh! J'aime bien le football. Et toi, tu aimes?**
—Pas beaucoup. Regarde, un match de tennis. Tu aimes le tennis?

le patin à glace
le hockey
le football américain
oui, beaucoup
le basket-ball
pas tellement
pas du tout
pas beaucoup
le ski
moi, si
la natation

Communication for All Students

Additional Practice
Give each student a card with a smiling face, a face with a straight line for a mouth, or a frowning face drawn on it. Then, have partners ask each other about certain activities and respond according to the card they have.

Slower Pace
9 Play the recording twice. The first time, tell students to listen only for those activities the speakers say they like. The second time, have students listen for those activities the speakers dislike.

STANDARDS: 1.1, 1.2, 5.1

11 Qu'est-ce qu'ils aiment faire?

Parlons The Canadian exchange student is visiting your school. He'd like to get to know your friends better, so he asks you about their interests. Tell him how much each of your friends likes or dislikes the activity pictured, using the cue provided.

Exemple **—Est-ce que Marc aime... ?** **—Non, il n'aime pas trop...**

(–) (+) (+) (–) (+)

Marc Isabelle Antoine Jean-Paul Anne-Marie

Answers may vary.

1. Est-ce que Marc aime... ? Non, il n'aime pas trop jouer au tennis.
2. Est-ce qu'Isabelle aime... ? Oui, elle aime beaucoup jouer aux cartes.
3. Et Antoine, est-ce qu'il aime... ? Oui, il aime surtout faire du ski nautique.
4. Et Jean-Paul, est-ce qu'il aime... ? Non, il n'aime pas tellement faire des photos.
5. Est-ce qu'Anne-Marie aime... ? Oui, elle aime beaucoup faire du patin à glace.

Grammaire

Question formation

You've already learned to make a yes-or-no question by raising the pitch of your voice at the end of a sentence. Another way to ask a yes-or-no question is to say **est-ce que** before a statement and raise your voice at the very end.

Est-ce que tu aimes faire du vélo?

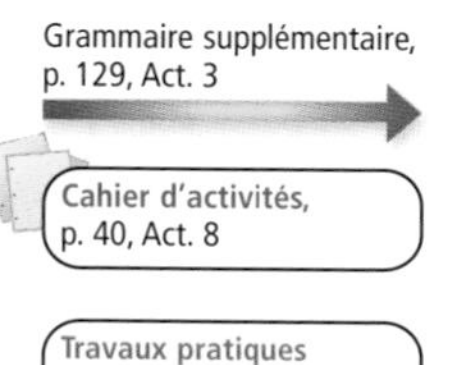

Grammaire supplémentaire, p. 129, Act. 3

Cahier d'activités, p. 40, Act. 8

Travaux pratiques de grammaire, p. 27, Act. 5–6

12 Grammaire en contexte

Parlons Avec un camarade, discutez des sports et des passe-temps que vous aimez tous les deux. Posez des questions et répondez à tour de rôle. Variez vos questions.

Exemple — **Est-ce que tu aimes jouer au football américain?**
— **Non! J'aime mieux faire de l'aérobic, du théâtre et du roller en ligne.**

Vocabulaire à la carte

faire un pique-nique	*to have a picnic*
faire de la randonnée	*to go hiking*
faire des haltères	*to lift weights*
faire de la gymnastique	*to do gymnastics*
faire du surf	*to surf*
faire de la voile	*to go sailing*

13 Grammaire en contexte

Parlons Poll five of your classmates about the sports and hobbies they like to do. Which activity is the most popular? Which is the least popular?

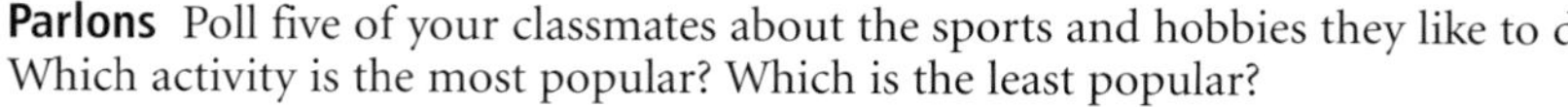

Communication for All Students

Additional Practice

Have students give all appropriate responses to the following questions and statements:

1. **Tu aimes le sport? (Oui, beaucoup! Non, pas trop. Oui, un peu. Pas tellement. Pas du tout.)**
2. **Moi, j'aime le volley-ball. (Moi aussi! Moi, non.)**
3. **Je n'aime pas le ski. (Moi, si! Moi non plus.)**

Visual Learners

13 Have students poll the whole class about each person's favorite and least favorite sport or activity. When they have finished collecting the data, have them present the results of their poll visually, in the form of a chart or graph.

Presenting Grammaire

Question formation Before students look at the explanation, write the sentence *You like to go bike riding* on the board. Ask students to turn it into a question in as many different ways as they can. (They might just use a rising intonation, place *Do* at the beginning of the sentence, or put *don't you?* at the end.) Next, have them look at the expression in the box and repeat it after you. Write the following sentences on the board and have students use **est-ce que** to turn them into questions:

1. **Tu aimes faire du roller en ligne.**
2. **Tu aimes faire de la natation.**
3. **Tu aimes étudier.**
4. **Tu aimes faire le ménage.**

Then, using the questions they form, have pairs of students ask and answer them.

Teacher Note

Grammaire You might tell students that a third, more formal way to form questions in French is by using *inversion,* reversing the order of the subject pronoun and the verb.

Assess

- Testing Program, pp. 79–82
  Quiz 4-1A, Quiz 4-1B
  Audio CD 4, Tr. 19
- Student Make-Up Assignments, Chapter 4, Alternative Quiz
- Alternative Assessment Guide, p. 35

Teaching Resources
pp. 116–120

PRINT

- Lesson Planner, p. 20
- TPR Storytelling Book, pp. 14, 16
- Listening Activities, pp. 28, 32
- Activities for Communication, pp. 21–22, 91, 93, 143–144
- Travaux pratiques de grammaire, pp. 28–32
- Grammar Tutor for Students of French, Chapter 4
- Cahier d'activités, pp. 41–44
- Testing Program, pp. 83–86
- Alternative Assessment Guide, p. 35
- Student Make-Up Assignments, Chapter 4

MEDIA

- One-Stop Planner
- Audio Compact Discs, CD 4, Trs. 5, 20, 27–28
- Teaching Transparencies: 4-2, 4-C, 4-D; **Grammaire supplémentaire** Answers; Travaux pratiques de grammaire Answers
- Interactive CD-ROM Tutor, Disc 1

Bell Work
Have students draw pictures of three activities from the previous **étape**.

Presenting
Comment dit-on... ?

Explain that **qu'est-ce que** means *what* and is used to begin an information question. Have students find examples of **qu'est-ce que** in Emilie's letter on page 108.

Grammaire

Have students repeat the forms of **faire** after you. Then, call out a subject pronoun and have students tell the appropriate verb form.

Deuxième étape

Objective Exchanging information

WA3 QUEBEC CITY-4

Comment dit-on...?

Exchanging information

To find out a friend's interests:

Qu'est-ce que tu fais comme sport? *What sports do you play?*
Qu'est-ce que tu fais pour t'amuser? *What do you do to have fun?*

To tell about your interests:

Je fais de l'athlétisme. *I do . . .*
Je joue au volley-ball. *I play . . .*
Je ne fais pas de ski. *I don't . . .*
Je ne joue pas au foot. *I don't play . . .*

Note de grammaire

Du, de la, and **de l'** usually become **de** (or **d'**) in a negative sentence.

Je ne fais pas **de** jogging.

Je ne fais pas **d'**athlétisme.

Cahier d'activités, p. 41, Act. 10
Grammaire supplémentaire, p. 129, Act. 4
Travaux pratiques de grammaire, p. 28, Act. 7–8

14 Grammaire en contexte

Parlons With a partner, take turns asking each other about your sports and hobbies.

EXEMPLE — **Qu'est-ce que tu fais pour t'amuser?**
— **Je fais du jogging et du ski. Et toi?**
— **Moi, je...**

Grammaire

The verb *faire*

CD-ROM 1 DVD 1

The irregular verb **faire** is used in many different expressions.

faire
(*to do, to play,* or *to make*)

Je	**fais**	Nous	**faisons**
Tu	**fais**	Vous	**faites**
Il/Elle/On	**fait**	Ils/Elles	**font**

Cahier d'activités, p. 41, Act. 11
Grammaire supplémentaire, pp. 129–130, Act. 5–6
Travaux pratiques de grammaire, p. 29, Act. 9–10

15 Grammaire en contexte

Ecrivons Complete the following conversation with the correct forms of the verb **faire.**

— Tu __1__ quels sports? fais
— Moi, je __2__ surtout du ski et du patin. fais
— Et tes copains, qu'est-ce qu'ils __3__ comme sport? font
— Michel __4__ de la natation et Hélène __5__ du roller en ligne. fait, fait
— Hélène et toi, est-ce que vous __6__ du sport ensemble? faites
— Oui, nous __7__ souvent du vélo. faisons

Teacher to Teacher

Todd Bowen
Adlai E. Stevenson High School
Lincolnshire, IL

Todd's students make "living sentences".

"On index cards I write several different subject pronouns, all forms of **faire** and **jouer,** the prepositions **à, au, aux, de, du, des,** and leisure activities. I distribute the cards evenly among my students. I will then say a sentence in English (I play soccer.), and the students holding the cards with **je, joue, au,** and **football** come to the front of the room and position themselves to create a **phrase vivante.**"

16 Grammaire en contexte

Parlons Jean and Luc are identical twins. They even enjoy the same activities. Tell what activities they do, based on what you see in their room. See answers below.

Grammaire

The pronoun *on*

- The subject pronoun **on** is used with the **il/elle** form of the verb. In conversational French, **on** usually means *we.*

  Le samedi, **on fait** du sport. *On Saturdays, we play sports.*
- **On** can mean *they* or *you* when it refers to people in general.

  En France, **on** parle français.
- You will have to use context, the surrounding words and phrases, to tell how a speaker is using **on.**

Grammaire supplémentaire, p. 130, Act. 7

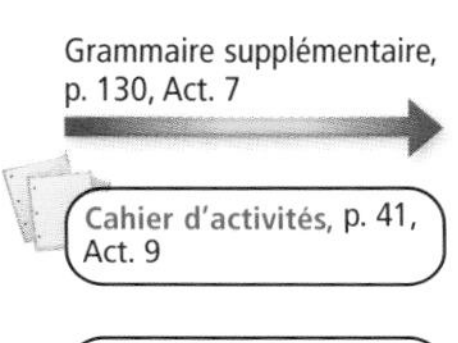

Cahier d'activités, p. 41, Act. 9

Travaux pratiques de grammaire, p. 30, Act. 11

17 Grammaire en contexte

Parlons Tell whether you and your friends do or don't do the activities shown in the photos.

Mes copains et moi, on fait...

1.

2.

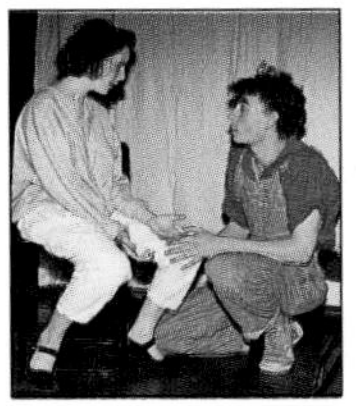
3.

4.

5.

Communication for All Students

Additional Practice

16 Have partners ask and answer questions about what Jean and Luc like to do, based on the illustration. Remind them to use **est-ce que.** **(Est-ce qu'ils aiment faire du ski? Est-ce qu'ils aiment jouer au hockey?)**

Challenge

17 Students might work in pairs to do this activity, asking their partner **Et toi?** after each activity they identify. You might also ask students to include the time and day of the week when they do these activities. **(Mes copains et moi, on fait du théâtre le lundi à 6h00 après l'école.).**

STANDARDS: 4.1

Presenting Grammaire

The pronoun *on* Hold up several pictures of various sports and activities and make some generalizations about the sport or activity pictured. **(On joue au foot au Texas. On fait du ski en France.)** Have students guess the meaning of **on** based on what you say and the pictures they see. Tell students that **on** can mean *we, they,* or *you* when referring to people in general. You might want to mention that **on** corresponds to *one* in English. (In order to be healthy, *one* needs to get enough sleep.) Then, have students complete the statement **Après l'école, on...**

Possible answers

16 Ils font du ski, du patin à glace, des photos et du théâtre. Ils jouent au football et au hockey.

Deuxième étape

CHAPITRE 4

Teaching Resources
pp. 116–120

PRINT 

- Lesson Planner, p. 20
- TPR Storytelling Book, pp. 14, 16
- Listening Activities, pp. 28, 32
- Activities for Communication, pp. 21–22, 91, 93, 143–144
- Travaux pratiques de grammaire, pp. 28–32
- Grammar Tutor for Students of French, Chapter 4
- Cahier d'activités, pp. 41–44
- Testing Program, pp. 83–86
- Alternative Assessment Guide, p. 35
- Student Make-Up Assignments, Chapter 4

MEDIA

- One-Stop Planner
- Audio Compact Discs, CD 4, Trs. 5, 20, 27–28
- Teaching Transparencies: 4-2, 4-C, 4-D; **Grammaire supplémentaire** Answers; Travaux pratiques de grammaire Answers
- Interactive CD-ROM Tutor, Disc 1

Presenting Vocabulaire

Present the weather expressions by talking about the weather conditions that prevail on the day of your presentation. Present other weather conditions by miming, drawing on the board, or showing pictures or props, such as an umbrella, mittens, and suntan lotion. Then, have students repeat the expressions after you as they read along in their book. Make several statements about weather conditions and have students point to the appropriate prop.

Vocabulaire

Quel temps fait-il?

Il fait beau.

Il fait chaud.

Il fait froid.

Il fait frais.

Il pleut.

Il neige.

Travaux pratiques de grammaire, p. 30, Act. 12

18 C'est agréable ou désagréable?

Parlons Is each of these activities pleasant (**agréable**) or unpleasant (**désagréable**)?

1. faire du vélo quand il fait froid désagréable
2. faire de la natation quand il fait chaud agréable
3. regarder la télé quand il neige agréable
4. faire du jogging quand il fait frais agréable
5. jouer au football américain quand il pleut désagréable

19 Et toi?

Ecrivons Qu'est-ce que tu aimes faire quand...

1. il fait froid?
2. il pleut?
3. il fait beau?
4. il neige?

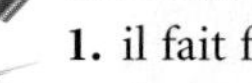

Communication for All Students

Additional Practice

Have the class keep a local weather chart for a week, with a different student responsible for recording the weather conditions each day. After the data has been recorded each day, ask students about the weather.

Visual/Auditory Learners

18 You might hold up a magazine picture or drawing of each type of weather (a rainy day) and name an activity **(jouer au football américain).** Have students respond with a thumbs-up gesture if they find it pleasant **(agréable)** and a thumbs-down gesture if they think it's unpleasant **(désagréable).**

STANDARDS: 3.1, 5.2

Vocabulaire

Les mois de l'année

janvier *juillet*
février *août*
mars *septembre*
avril *octobre*
mai *novembre*
juin *décembre*

Cahier d'activités, p. 44, Act. 17

Travaux pratiques de grammaire, p. 31, Act. 13–14

Note culturelle

Francophone countries, like most other countries of the world, use the metric system, so temperature is measured in degrees centigrade or Celsius rather than Fahrenheit. This means that the freezing point of water is 0°C, and its boiling point is 100°C. A comfortable temperature would be 25°C (77°F). If the temperature were more than 35°C, it would be very hot. If the temperature were 18°C (64.4°F), you would probably need a jacket. If the temperature were 15°C, what month might it be?

20 Il fait quel temps?

Lisons/Parlons In these months, what is the weather usually like where you live?

1. en mai
2. en février
3. en juillet
4. en octobre
5. en avril
6. en décembre

Il fait froid. Il fait frais. Il pleut. Il neige. Il fait beau. Il fait chaud.

Tu te rappelles?

Do you remember the endings that you learned to use with the verb **aimer** in Chapter 1? Those endings are exactly the same for all regular **-er** verbs, which include many French verbs. Here's how the verb **jouer** fits the pattern.

Grammaire supplémentaire, p. 130, Act. 8

jouer *(to play)*

Je **joue** / Tu **joues** / Il/Elle/On **joue** au tennis.

Nous **jouons** / Vous **jouez** / Ils/Elles **jouent** au tennis.

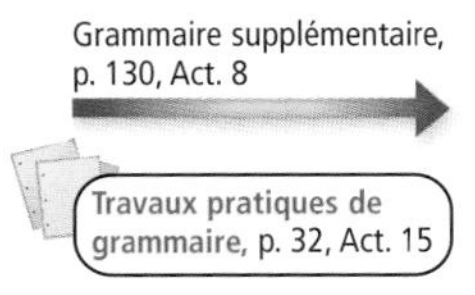

Travaux pratiques de grammaire, p. 32, Act. 15

21 Qu'est-ce que vous faites en hiver? See scripts and answers on p. 105G.

CD 4 Tr. 5

Ecoutons Listen as a newspaper reporter asks three Canadian teenagers, Paul, Anne, and Julie, about their hobbies and pastimes. Then, answer the questions below.

1. Which teenagers don't watch TV?
2. Which ones like to listen to music?
3. Which ones play hockey?
4. Which ones like to dance?
5. Which teenagers like to go to the movies?

22 Prisonnier des neiges

Ecrivons Imagine that you're snowed in during a winter storm. Write a note to a friend telling him or her about the weather, what you're doing to pass the time, and how you feel about the situation.

Connections and Comparisons

Math Link

Note culturelle To convert Fahrenheit to Celsius, subtract 32 and then multiply by 5/9. To convert Celsius to Fahrenheit, multiply by 9/5 and then add 32. Ask students if they know the freezing and boiling temperatures for water in degrees Celsius and Fahrenheit (Answers: 32° and 212° in Fahrenheit and 0° and 100° in Celsius).

Language-to-Language

If you have native speakers of Spanish in your classroom, you may want to point out the similarity between the verbs **hacer** (*to make* or *to do*) and **faire** when talking about the weather. **(Hace calor. = Il fait chaud.)** Have students tell how using **faire** and **hacer** is different from the way weather is described in English.

Presenting Vocabulaire

Divide a transparency into four sections. Label each section with a simple drawing to represent a season (a flower for spring, a sun for summer, and so on). Write the names of the months in French under the appropriate season. Present the months a season at a time, having students repeat each one after you. Then, call out months at random and have students raise their hand if their birthday is in that month. You might also hold up an illustration or an object associated with a holiday and have students name the month in which that holiday falls.

Challenge

20 Have students answer in complete sentences, either orally or in writing. Then, have them give at least one activity they do in each weather condition and/or in each month. **(En juillet, j'aime nager. En mai, je fais du vélo. Quand il neige, je fais du ski.)**

Building on Previous Skills

22 You might orally review some activities students learned in Chapter 1 **(regarder la télévision, écouter de la musique, étudier, parler au téléphone, danser).**

Teaching Suggestion

22 Students might prefer to write about a heat wave **(une vague de chaleur)** instead.

Portfolio

22 **Written** This activity could be a portfolio entry or a writing assessment activity. For portfolio suggestions, see *Alternative Assessment Guide,* pages iv–17.

STANDARDS: 1.2, 2.1, 3.1, 3.2, 4.1, 4.2

Presenting Vocabulaire

Show or draw pictures of the four seasons. Write the French words for the seasons on the board next to the pictures. Name an activity that one does. **(On fait du patin à glace.)** Have students identify the appropriate season. Re-enter some activities from previous chapters, such as **faire de l'équitation, nager,** and **voyager**. Present **en vacances** and **le week-end** using these activities. Present **le matin, l'après-midi,** and **le soir** by drawing the route of the sun from sunrise to sunset on the board. Give various times in the 24-hour system **(13h30, 8h50, 23h15)** and have students tell whether it's **le matin, l'après-midi,** or **le soir.** Teach the phrase **en vacances** by referring to the calendar as you talk about school vacations.

Assess

- Testing Program, pp. 83–86 Quiz 4-2A, Quiz 4-2B Audio CD 4, Tr. 20
- Student Make-Up Assignments, Chapter 4, Alternative Quiz
- Alternative Assessment Guide, p. 35

Vocabulaire

CD-ROM 1
DVD 1

Qu'est-ce que tu fais...

en vacances?

le soir?

le week-end?

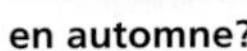
en automne?

en hiver?

au printemps?

en été?

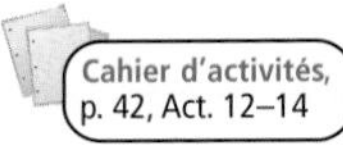
Cahier d'activités, p. 42, Act. 12–14

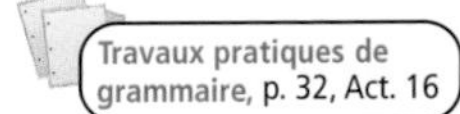
Travaux pratiques de grammaire, p. 32, Act. 16

23 Un questionnaire

Lisons/Parlons To help pair up campers for activities, a camp counselor has sent out the survey you see on the right. Give one answer in each category.

1. En automne, je...
   a. fais du patin à glace.
   b. joue au hockey.
   c. écoute de la musique.
   d. fais du ski.
   e. fais autre chose.
2. En hiver, je...
   a. joue au football américain.
   b. joue au foot.
   c. fais du théâtre.
   d. joue au volley.
   e. fais autre chose.
3. Au printemps, je...
   a. joue au base-ball.
   b. fais de l'athlétisme.
   c. fais du vélo.
   d. fais de la vidéo.
   e. fais autre chose.
4. En été, je...
   a. fais de la natation.
   b. fais du roller en ligne.
   c. regarde la télé.
   d. fais du ski nautique.
   e. fais autre chose.

24 J'aime faire...

Parlons Dis à tes camarades de classe ce que tu fais à chaque saison et demande-leur ce qu'ils font. Essaie de trouver quelqu'un qui fait au minimum deux des choses que tu fais.

EXEMPLE — **En hiver, je fais du patin à glace. Et toi?**
— **Moi, non! Quand il fait froid, j'écoute de la musique.**

25 Une lettre

Ecrivons Tu prépares un voyage au Canada et tu as décidé d'écrire à ton correspondant canadien. Ecris un paragraphe pour lui demander quels sont ses sports et ses passe-temps préférés. Ecris aussi ce que tu fais et ce que tu ne fais pas.

Communication for All Students

Additional Practice

23 Have students give their own preferred activity if they choose **fais autre chose.**

Slower Pace

25 Before students write their letters, have them think of activities a Canadian pen pal might enjoy.

Visual Learners

Show *Teaching Transparencies 4-A* and *4-2.* Have students describe the activities and weather conditions shown. You might prompt students with **Quand il..., ils...**

Qu'est-ce que tu fais comme sport?

What sports do you play? Where do you go to practice them? We asked some young people about their favorite sports. Here's what they had to say.

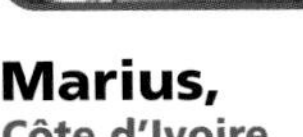

Marius,
Côte d'Ivoire

«Je fais beaucoup de sport, mais surtout le football. Je fais le football et le skate, le patin à roulettes et puis j'aime aussi le tennis.» Tr. 7

Aljosa,
France

«Comme sport, j'aime bien faire le tennis. J'aime bien aller à la piscine, voilà. J'aime bien [le] bowling.» Tr. 8

Mélanie,
Québec

«Avec mes amies, moi je fais beaucoup de sport. Je fais partie de l'équipe interscolaire de volley-ball et de badminton de l'école. Je fais de la natation. Je fais du patinage. Je fais de la course. Je fais du tennis aussi souvent l'été. L'hiver, je patine.» Tr. 9

Qu'en penses-tu?

1. Which of these students enjoy the same sports that you do?
2. Which sports that they mention are not played in your area?
3. Can you guess which sports are associated with the following events and places?*
   - a. La Coupe du monde
   - b. Le Grand Prix de Monaco
   - c. Le Tour de France
   - d. Le stade Roland-Garros

Savais-tu que... ?

While schools in francophone countries do offer extracurricular sports, serious athletes often participate through clubs outside of school. Activities such as swimming, tennis, or volleyball are often organized by parent volunteers or communities. In France, recreation centers (**Maisons des jeunes et de la culture** or **MJC**) sponsor all kinds of social, cultural, and educational activities for young people.

* a. soccer b. auto racing c. cycling d. tennis (the French Open)

Cultures and Communities

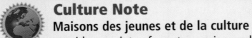

Culture Note

Maisons des jeunes et de la culture provide a variety of sports, movies, and other activities, such as music, dance, computer science, photography, and arts and crafts. Annual dues are charged based on the number of activities in which a person participates.

Community Link

Have students prepare short reports in English on sporting events in francophone countries. They might look up in *The World Almanac* the most recent winners of the events listed in question 3 of **Qu'en penses-tu?**

Teaching Resources
p. 121

PRINT
- Video Guide, pp. 27, 28–29
- Cahier d'activités, p. 48

MEDIA
- One-Stop Planner
- Video Program Videocassette 2, 18:31–20:45
- DVD Tutor, Disc 1
- Audio Compact Discs, CD 4, Trs. 6–9
- Interactive CD-ROM Tutor, Disc 1

Presenting
Panorama Culturel

Tell students to listen for the sports that each interviewee mentions. Play the video, and then hold up pictures of various activities, asking **Qui fait ça?** Students call out the name of the interviewee who mentioned that activity.

Questions

1. **Qu'est-ce que Marius fait comme sport?** (du football, du skate, du patin à roulettes, du tennis)
2. **Est-ce qu'Aljosa aime le bowling?** (Oui)
3. **Est-ce que Mélanie fait du sport à l'école?** (Oui)
4. **Qu'est-ce qu'elle fait en été?** (du tennis) **En hiver?** (Elle patine.)

Thinking Critically

Analyzing Have students give advantages and disadvantages of having school-sponsored sports teams (football, cheerleaders, drill team).

Teaching Resources
pp. 122–125

PRINT 

- Lesson Planner, p. 21
- TPR Storytelling Book, pp. 15, 16
- Listening Activities, pp. 28–29, 33
- Activities for Communication, pp. 23–24, 92, 93–94, 143–144
- Travaux pratiques de grammaire, pp. 33–34
- Grammar Tutor for Students of French, Chapter 4
- Cahier d'activités, pp. 45–46
- Testing Program, pp. 87–90
- Alternative Assessment Guide, p. 35
- Student Make-Up Assignments, Chapter 4

MEDIA 

- One-Stop Planner
- Audio Compact Discs, CD 4, Trs. 10–11, 21, 29–30
- Teaching Transparencies: 4-3; **Grammaire supplémentaire** Answers; Travaux pratiques de grammaire Answers
- Interactive CD-ROM Tutor, Disc 1

Bell Work
Have students write six sentences using a different form of **faire** and a different activity in each.

Presenting
Comment dit-on... ?
Write the new expressions on the board. Name a sport and ask a student to suggest doing that sport. Respond by accepting or turning down the suggestion.

Grammaire
Draw a timeline with the adverbs of frequency. Name pastimes **(le vélo)** and have individual students indicate on the timeline how often they do each activity. Then, say the complete sentence and have students repeat.

Troisième étape

Objective Making, accepting, and turning down suggestions

WA3 QUEBEC CITY-4

Comment dit-on...?

Making, accepting, and turning down suggestions

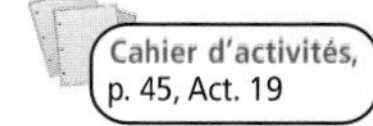

To make a suggestion:

On fait du patin?
How about . . . ?
On joue au foot?
How about . . . ?

To turn down a suggestion:

Désolé(e), mais je ne peux pas.
Sorry, but I can't.
Ça ne me dit rien.
That doesn't interest me.
Non, c'est barbant!

To accept a suggestion:

D'accord. *OK.*
Bonne idée. *Good idea.*
Oui, c'est génial!
Allons-y! *Let's go!*

Cahier d'activités, p. 45, Act. 19

26 **On joue au volley?** See scripts and answers on p. 105H.

Ecoutons Listen as Germain calls his friends Lise, Renaud, Philippe, and Monique to suggest activities for the weekend. Do his friends accept or turn down his suggestions?
CD 4 Tr. 10

27 **Qu'est-ce qu'on fait?**

Parlons Write down one or two things that you'd like to do this weekend. Then, find three classmates who'd like to join you.

EXEMPLE — **On fait du jogging ce week-end?**
— **Le jogging, c'est barbant!** *or* **D'accord. C'est génial, le jogging.**

Grammaire

Adverbs of frequency

- To tell how often you do something, use **quelquefois** (*sometimes*), **de temps en temps** (*from time to time*), une **fois par semaine** (*. . . time(s) a week*), **souvent** (*often*), **d'habitude** (*usually*), **rarement** (*rarely*), and **ne... jamais** (*never*).
- Short adverbs usually come after the verb. Longer adverbs can be placed at the beginning or the end of a sentence. Put **d'habitude** at the beginning of a sentence and **une fois par semaine** at the end. Put **ne... jamais** around the verb, as you do with **ne... pas.**

Je fais **souvent** du ski.
D'habitude, je fais du ski au printemps.
Je fais du ski **une fois par semaine.**
Je **ne** fais **jamais** de ski.

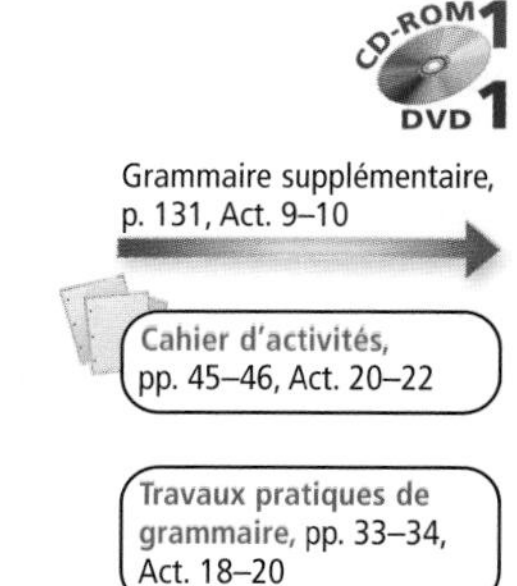

CD-ROM 1
DVD 1
Grammaire supplémentaire, p. 131, Act. 9–10
Cahier d'activités, pp. 45–46, Act. 20–22
Travaux pratiques de grammaire, pp. 33–34, Act. 18–20

Communication for All Students

Additional Practice
26 Ask your students if they would like to do certain activities. Students should respond by accepting your suggestion or turning it down.

Game
Your class has to send teams to the "school olympics". The goal is to form teams of 5 students per sport. Choose 5 or 6 sports. Choose a captain for each team sport. Each captain will ask a student if he/she accepts to be on the team. The student should either accept or refuse. Once every captain has asked a student, the new member of the team (or again the captain if he was turned down) will then ask other students to become part of the team. The first team to successfully recruit five students wins the game.

STANDARDS: 1.1, 1.2, 4.1

Grammaire en contexte See scripts and answers on p. 105H.

Ecoutons Listen as Emile, a reporter for a school newspaper in Quebec City, interviews his classmates about sports. How often does each person practice sports?
CD 4 Tr. 11

Grammaire en contexte

Parlons Pauline is an active, French-Canadian teenager. Based on her calendar, take turns with a partner asking about her activities and how often she does them.

EXEMPLE — **Est-ce qu'elle fait de l'aérobic?**
— **Oui, de temps en temps.**

NOVEMBRE

DIMANCHE	LUNDI	MARDI	MERCREDI	JEUDI	VENDREDI	SAMEDI
		1 jogging	2 photo	3 jogging	4 théâtre	5 patin à glace
6 aérobic	7 jogging	8 photo	9	10 jogging	11	12 jogging
13 photo	14 jogging	15	16 aérobic	17 jogging	18 théâtre	19
20 patin à glace	21 jogging	22 jogging	23 photo	24 ski	25	26 aérobic
27 jogging	28	29 jogging	30 photo			

30 Grammaire en contexte

Parlons With a partner, discuss your favorite pastimes and how often you do them. Ask questions to keep the conversation going.

EXEMPLE — **Qu'est-ce que tu fais pour t'amuser?**
— **En été, je fais souvent du ski nautique. Et toi?**
— **Je fais du vélo. Et toi? Tu fais du vélo... ?**

le week-end?
en vacances?
en été?
quand il fait froid?
quand il fait beau?

Troisième étape

CHAPITRE 4

Challenge

28 Have students give the sport that each person practices and tell how often he or she does the activity as well.

Challenge

29 Have students make two calendars of their own, one blank and one with their activities filled in, like Pauline's. Have them give the blank calendar to a partner, who asks questions about the other's activities and fills in the blank calendar appropriately. They should compare the newly completed calendar to the original, and then reverse roles.

Kinesthetic Learners

30 You might have students create interview skits based on this activity.

Culture Note

Tell students that weekly calendars in France begin with Monday, but those in Canada begin with Sunday, as in the United States.

Language Note

You might point out that students can replace the number in **une fois par semaine** to fit their situation **(deux fois... , trois fois...).**

Communication for All Students

Slower Pace

28 Stop the recording after each interview and have students write the adverb of frequency. You may prefer to have individuals volunteer an oral answer.

Slower Pace

29 You might want to go over Pauline's schedule orally before students pair off to discuss it. You might also call out the activity and have students give the days and times when Pauline does that activity, and vice versa.

STANDARDS: 1.1, 1.2, 5.1

Troisième étape

CHAPITRE 4

Teaching Resources
pp. 122–125

PRINT
- Lesson Planner, p. 21
- TPR Storytelling Book, pp. 15, 16
- Listening Activities, pp. 28–29, 33
- Activities for Communication, pp. 23–24, 92, 93–94, 143–144
- Travaux pratiques de grammaire, pp. 33–34
- Grammar Tutor for Students of French, Chapter 4
- Cahier d'activités, pp. 45–46
- Testing Program, pp. 87–90
- Alternative Assessment Guide, p. 35
- Student Make-Up Assignments, Chapter 4

MEDIA 
- One-Stop Planner
- Audio Compact Discs, CD 4, Trs. 10–11, 21, 29–30
- Teaching Transparencies: 4-3; **Grammaire supplémentaire** Answers; Travaux pratiques de grammaire Answers
- Interactive CD-ROM Tutor, Disc 1

Portfolio

31 **Written** This activity is suitable for students' written portfolios. Students may also want to record the conversation they have with their classmates. For portfolio suggestions, see *Alternative Assessment Guide*, page 21.

33 **Written** This activity might be added to students' portfolios or used at the end of this **étape** as an assessment activity. For portfolio suggestions, see *Alternative Assessment Guide*, pages iv–17.

31 Sondage

a. **Ecrivons** Make a chart like the one shown here. In the left-hand column, list the activities you enjoy. In the middle column, tell when you do them, and in the right-hand column, tell how often.

ACTIVITE	SAISON	FREQUENCE
Je fais du ski. Je fais...	en hiver	de temps en temps

b. **Parlons** Now, share this information with three other classmates. Ask questions to find out what you have in common and what you don't.

EXEMPLE — **Je fais du ski de temps en temps.**
— **Pas moi! Je ne fais jamais de ski.**

32 Le sportif

Lisons/Parlons Your French pen pal Lucien is coming to visit soon. Read his letter and tell whether he would answer **D'accord** or **Ça ne me dit rien** if you were to suggest the following activities.

1. On fait de la vidéo ce week-end? D'accord.
2. On fait du ski nautique? Ça ne me dit rien.
3. On joue au foot? D'accord.
4. On fait de la natation ce soir? D'accord.
5. On joue au football américain ce week-end? Ça ne me dit rien.

Salut!
J'espère que ça va. Moi, ça va bien. Je fais beaucoup de sport maintenant. Et toi, tu aimes faire du sport? Moi, j'aime jouer au foot, mais je n'aime pas trop le football américain; c'est barbant. D'habitude, le week-end, je joue au tennis ou je fais de la natation. La natation, c'est génial. Mais je n'aime pas faire du ski nautique; c'est nul. Quand il fait froid, je fais de l'aérobic. A part le sport, quelquefois, je fais de la vidéo. Et toi? Qu'est-ce que tu fais le week-end? Ecris-moi vite!
A bientôt,
Lucien

33 Cher Lucien, ... 

Ecrivons Now, answer Lucien's letter. Be sure to . . .
- tell him what activities you like and why you like them.
- tell him when and how often you do each activity.
- tell him what you don't like to do and why not.
- suggest one or two things you might do together and when.

Communication for All Students

Slower Pace
31 You might give students examples of questions for this activity **(Tu aimes... ? Comment tu trouves... ? Est-ce que tu fais/joues... ?)**. You might also have students recall ways to express their opinion of activities. **(C'est super, génial, nul, barbant.)**

Auditory Learners
32 Students might read the letter aloud in small groups, or you might read it aloud to the class.

Challenge
32 Type copies of Lucien's letter, deleting all the activities and the opinion words. Have students fill in the blanks with their own activities and opinions.

STANDARDS: 1.2, 1.3, 3.1

  **De l'école au travail** 

Ecrivons/Parlons Some well-known athletes from Canada are training in your town for the summer. You've been working as an intern for the local newspaper, and a reporter needs your help to interview one of the French-speaking athletes. Work with a partner to create a list of interview questions in French. You may want to ask what sports he or she likes to do, what the weather is like in Canada during the winter and the summer, and what he or she likes to do for fun. Then, choose the role of interviewer or athlete and practice the interview.

35 Mon journal

Ecrivons Using the information in the chart you made for Activity 31, write about your favorite weekend and after-school activities and how often you do them. Give your opinions of the activities, too.

PRONONCIATION

CD 4
Trs. 12–17

The sounds [u] and [y]

See scripts and answers on p. 105H.

The sound [u] occurs in such English words as *Sue, shoe,* and *too.* The French [u] is shorter, tenser, and more rounded than the vowel sound in English. Listen to these French words: **tout, nous, vous.** The sound [u] is usually represented by the letter combination **ou.**

The sound [y] is represented in the words s**alut, super,** and **musique.** This sound does not exist in English. To pronounce [y], start by saying [i], as in the English word *me.* Then, round your lips as if you were going to say the English word *moon,* keeping your tongue pressed behind your lower front teeth.

A. A prononcer

Now, practice first the sound [u] and then [y]. Repeat these words.

1. vous
2. nous
3. douze
4. rouge
5. cours
6. joue
7. tu
8. musique
9. nul
10. étude
11. une
12. du

B. A lire

Take turns with a partner reading the following sentences aloud.

1. Salut! Tu t'appelles Louis?
2. J'ai cours aujourd'hui.
3. Tu aimes la trousse rouge?
4. Elle n'aime pas du tout faire du ski.
5. Nous aimons écouter de la musique.
6. Vous jouez souvent au foot?

C. A écrire

You're going to hear a short dialogue. Write down what you hear.

Communication for All Students

Slower Pace

Have students copy the sentences from **Prononciation,** Part B, into their notebook as you write them on the board or on a transparency. Have students circle all the [u] sounds. As they read the words aloud that contain this sound, circle the correct words in your sentences so students can correct their papers. Then, have students pair off to practice reading the sentences aloud. Do the same for the sound [y].

Kinesthetic Learners

Tell students in French to do a certain activity and have them respond by miming the activity.

STANDARDS: 1.1, 1.3, 4.1, 5.1, 5.2

Auditory Learners

Prononciation Tell students that when they see the letter *u* by itself, it always represents the sound [y]. Have them make their own lists of words containing the sounds [u] and [y]. Read aloud words from the students' lists and ask them to raise their left hand to signal [u] and their right hand to signal [y]. You might also read the list of words from Part A.

Writing Assessment

35 You might refer students to p. R13 for additional vocabulary related to sports and activities. You may wish to use the following rubric in assessing this or other writing activities.

Writing Rubric	Points			
	4	3	2	1
Content (Complete–Incomplete)				
Comprehensibility (Comprehensible–Incomprehensible)				
Accuracy (Accurate–Seldom accurate)				
Organization (Well organized–Poorly organized)				
Effort (Excellent–Minimal)				

18–20: A 16–17: B 14–15: C 12–13: D Under 12: F

Mon journal

35 For an additional journal entry suggestion for Chapter 4, see *Cahier d'activités,* page 148.

Assess

- Testing Program, pp. 87–90
  Quiz 4-3A, Quiz 4-3B
  Audio CD 4, Tr. 21
- Student Make-Up Assignments, Chapter 4, Alternative Quiz
- Alternative Assessment Guide, p. 35

Teaching Resources
pp. 126–127

PRINT 

- Lesson Planner, p. 22
- Cahier d'activités, p. 47
- Reading Strategies and Skills Handbook, Chapter 4
- Joie de lire 1, Chapter 4
- Standardized Assessment Tutor, Chapter 4

MEDIA

- One-Stop Planner

Prereading

Activities A–C

Making Predictions

A.–C. Ask students to read the introduction silently. Ask them what they think it means. Then, have students try to guess what type of information will be provided in the selection. List their responses on the board. Then, have students scan the article. Have them see how many of the items they listed on the board are in the article.

Answers

A. *Come on, it's your choice!;* choosing different activities to do in your spare time

B. *Pour les artistes:* information about artistic activities
Pour les sportifs: Information about sports/athletic activities
Answers will vary.

C. required equipment; best ages to begin the activity; how often the activity should be done; addresses and telephone numbers for more information; No, some sections tell how much equipment might cost. Also, there is no address or telephone number under the section entitled **La musique.**

D. *Possible answers:* musique, âge, commencer, important, motivé, instrument, début, possible, rythme, général, progresser, théâtre, adolescence, improvisation, textes, danse, muscles, tee-shirt, mouvements, rythmiques, fédération

Lisons!

ALLEZ, C'EST A VOUS DE CHOISIR!

Stratégie pour lire

When you first glance at a reading selection, you might try to predict what information the article will give you. This will give you a better idea of what you're going to read. Remember to use headings, subheadings, and the organization of the text to help you understand what you're reading.

A. The title of this selection is **Allez, c'est à vous de choisir!** What do you think this title means? What do you think the article will be about? See answers below.

B. Look at the organization of the article and the two major headings. What type of information do you think will be included under **Pour les artistes?** What about **Pour les sportifs?** What do you know about the activities in each category? See answers below.

C. What type of information do you find in each section? Do all the sections have the same type of information? If not, how do they differ? See answers below.

Pour les artistes

D. Scan the sections titled **La musique, Le théâtre,** and **La danse.** Make a list of the cognates you find. You should find at least ten. See answers below.

ALLEZ, C'EST A VOUS DE CHOISIR!

Cette année, c'est décidé, vous vous lancez dans une activité! Nous vous en proposons ici quelques exemples, à vous de choisir...

POUR LES ARTISTES

LA MUSIQUE

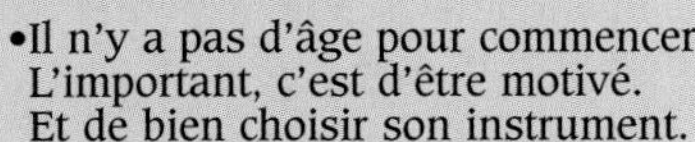

- Il n'y a pas d'âge pour commencer. L'important, c'est d'être motivé. Et de bien choisir son instrument.
- Vous devez avoir votre instrument. Au début, il est possible de le louer.
- Rythme : en général 1 heure de solfège par semaine et 1/2 h de cours d'instrument. Pour progresser, il faut prévoir 1/4 h de travail chaque jour.

LE THEATRE

- C'est souvent à l'adolescence qu'on commence. On découvre à la fois les joies (et les doutes) de l'improvisation et les grands auteurs.
- Rythme : entre 2 et 3 heures par semaine, plus des textes à apprendre.
- Renseignez-vous auprès de votre mairie ou à l'École de Musique, 4, rue Beaubourg, 75004 Paris. Tél : 01 42 71 25 07.

LA DANSE

- Peu de garçons s'inscrivent au cours de danse et c'est bien dommage car la danse apprend à aimer et maîtriser son corps... et à s'éclater aussi!
- Débutant à tout âge!
- Pour commencer, un caleçon chaud (pour les muscles) et un tee-shirt près du corps (pour que le prof voie vos mouvements) peuvent suffire. Et des chaussures ballerines ou rythmiques.
- Rythme : 1 heure et demie par semaine.
- Fédération française de danse : 12, rue Saint-Germain-d'Auxerrois, 75013 Paris. Tél : 01 42 36 12 61.

Communication for All Students

Additional Practice

Ask students what sports and activities they would like to participate in. Have them tell what they would need to do to get started and identify the equipment they would need.

Group Work

Have students work in groups to find out the requirements to join a club or organization that offers the same activities in their area. Are the requirements similar to or different than the ones in the reading selection? Is the minimum age for the activity the same?

STANDARDS: 1.2, 3.1, 4.1

POUR LES SPORTIFS

LE TENNIS

- Des matchs sont organisés par les clubs. Ils permettent de se préparer à la compétition.
- Le coût varie selon les clubs et votre niveau. Choisissez un forfait qui comprend les cours et l'accès aux courts.
- Comptez au moins 38 euros pour une raquette de bonne qualité et choisissez des chaussures adaptées, pas les tennis mode que vous portez tous les jours!
- Rythme : 1 heure par semaine, plus les tournois. Si vous jouez beaucoup, faites un autre sport en complément, pour éviter les problèmes de dos.
- Fédération française de tennis : Stade Roland-Garros, 2, avenue Gordon Bennett, 75016 Paris. Tél : 01 47 43 48 00.

LE FOOTBALL

- Avec quelques copains et un ballon, on peut s'amuser presque partout. Mais pour jouer dans les règles de l'art, mieux vaut s'inscrire dans un club.

- Souvent, le short et le maillot sont fournis par le club, mais les chaussures à crampons vissés coûtent entre 23 et 137 euros.
- Rythme : en général 2 heures par semaine. Rencontres entre clubs le samedi ou le dimanche.
- Fédération française de football : 60 bis, avenue d'Iéna, 75763 Paris cédex 16. Tél : 01 44 31 73 00.

LE KARTING

- Il existe une formule de location de kart avec cours adaptés dès 12 ans.
- Coût : environ 457 euros par an, comprenant les cours et le matériel.
- Rythme : 1 heure par semaine, plus quelques courses (souvent le samedi ou le dimanche).
- Groupement national de karting : 203, rue Lafayette, 75010 Paris. Tél : 01 42 05 09 44.

E. What do you think the word **débutant** means? Can you think of any words in English that are related to this word? *beginning; debutante, debut*

F. At what age do people usually. . .
1. learn how to play an instrument *any age*
2. begin drama? *as a teenager/adolescent*
3. learn how to dance? *any age*

G. According to the article, how often do you need to practice playing an instrument to improve quickly? *1/4 hour per day*

Pour les sportifs

H. What do you think **Rythme** means? How do you know? *pace; Answers will vary.*

I. What do you think **Le Karting** means? Is this an activity that is popular in your area? *go–carting; Answers will vary.*

J. According to the article, how much does a tennis racket cost? *about 38 €*

K. Which of these activities . . .
1. require(s) special shoes? *tennis and soccer*
2. require(s) two or more hours a week? *soccer*

L. For which activities is it recommended that you join a club? *tennis and soccer*

M. Which activity costs the most to participate in? Why?

N. Conduct a survey among your classmates to see which of these activities are the most and least popular and why. You might also find out in how many of these activities your classmates have participated, which ones are the most interesting, and why. Make a list of questions you need to include in your survey.

M. *go-carting; Participants must pay for classes and materials.*

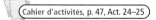

Cahier d'activités, p. 47, Act. 24–25

Connections and Comparisons

Language-to-Language

Ask students to think about the origin of the word **karting.** How did they recognize what the word means? Can they think of any other words used in the French language that end in —*ing*? Students might want to know **le bowling, le parking, le jogging,** and **le camping.**

Thinking Critically

N. Comparing and Contrasting After students have conducted their survey, ask them whether young people in France seem to have interests similar to those of young people in the United States. What activities listed here are not common in the United States? What popular activities aren't suggested here?

Reading

Activities D–M

Language Note

Students might want to know the following words: **rythme** *(rate, pace);* **solfège** *(music theory);* **s'inscrire** *(to join, to enroll);* and **corps** *(body).*

Monitoring Comprehension

Form six groups and assign each group one section of the reading. Have them find at what age they should start the activity, how often they should participate, the cost and/or items needed to begin, and where to find more information. Have each group report its findings to the class.

Postreading

Activity N

Analyzing

What activities seem to take the greatest amount of dedication and practice? Which activities are most mentally or physically beneficial?

Drawing on your Experience

Have pairs of students create a conversation in which they discuss which activity from this article they would prefer to do and why. Have them support their opinions with details from the reading.

Using Text Organizers

Have students find out more information about an activity they would like to pursue that is not included in this article. You might have them research what equipment or supplies they might need, a good age to start, and how often they would probably do the activity. Have them share their findings by creating a poster with the information in French.

Grammaire supplémentaire

CHAPITRE 4

For **Grammaire supplémentaire** Answer Transparencies, see the *Teaching Transparencies* binder.

Answers

1
1. jouer
   faire
2. faire
   faire
3. jouer
   faire
4. faire
   jouer

2
1. Il aime faire du ski nautique.
2. Elle aime faire du vélo.
3. Ils aiment jouer à des jeux vidéo.
4. Moi, j'aime faire du ski.
5. Tu aimes jouer au tennis.
6. Nous aimons jouer au foot.
7. Ils aiment faire du patin à glace.
8. Elle aime faire du théâtre.

Grammaire supplémentaire

Première étape

Objective Telling how much you like or dislike something

1 Complète les conversations suivantes avec **faire** ou **jouer**. (**p. 113**)

1. —Corinne, est-ce-que tu aimes _____ au golf?
   —Non. Je préfère _____ du ski.
2. —Frédéric et Arthur, est-ce que vous aimez _____ de la vidéo?
   —Pas tellement. Nous aimons mieux _____ du théâtre.
3. —Et Malika, est-ce qu'elle aime _____ aux cartes?
   —Pas du tout. Mais elle aime _____ de la natation.
4. —Georges, est-ce que tu aimes _____ du jogging?
   —Oui. Mais je préfère _____ au hockey.

2 According to their interests, what do Sandrine and her friends do in their spare time? Write six sentences telling what they do, using the verbs **faire** or **jouer** and an expression from the box in each sentence. Use each expression only once. (**p. 113**)

jeux vidéo	vélo	ski nautique
tennis	natation	ski
théâtre	football	patin à glace

EXEMPLE Ariane aime la piscine.
Elle aime faire de la natation.

1. Claude aime tellement la plage.
2. Suzanne aime les bicyclettes.
3. Olivier et Victor aiment les ordinateurs.
4. Moi, j'aime la neige.
5. Tu aimes le sport.
6. Marc et moi, nous aimons le foot.
7. Emilie et Michel aiment le hockey.
8. Louise aime Shakespeare et Molière.

Grammar Resources for Chapter 4

The **Grammaire supplémentaire** activities were designed as supplemental activities for the grammatical concepts presented in the chapter. You might use them as additional practice, for review, or for assessment.

For more grammar presentations, review, and practice, refer to the following:
- Travaux pratiques de grammaire
- Grammar Tutor for Students of French
- Grammar Summary on pp. R15-R28
- Cahier d'activités
- Grammar and Vocabulary quizzes (Testing Program)
- Test Generator
- Interactive CD-ROM Tutor
- **Jeux interactifs** at go.hrw.com

3 You have made a list of the activities your classmates like to do. Double-check your list by asking your classmates if your information is correct, using **est-ce que,** and **tu** or **vous** as appropriate. (**p. 115**)

EXEMPLE Paul et Aurélie aiment faire du ski.
Est-ce que vous aimez faire du ski?

1. Anne-Marie et Louise aiment jouer au foot.
2. Marc aime jouer à des jeux vidéo.
3. Elodie aime faire de la photo.
4. Jacques et Jules aiment jouer au tennis.
5. Alexandrine aime faire du ski nautique.
6. Véronique et Céline aiment faire de l'athlétisme.
7. Miriam aime faire du vélo.
8. Jean et Françoise aiment jouer aux cartes.

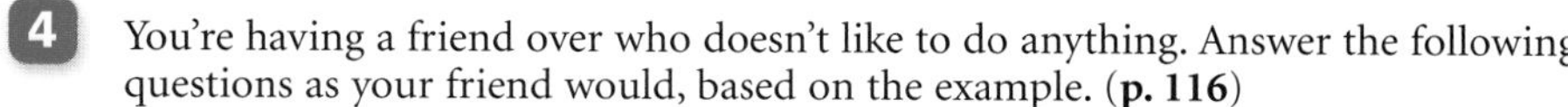

Deuxième étape

Objective Exchanging information

4 You're having a friend over who doesn't like to do anything. Answer the following questions as your friend would, based on the example. (**p. 116**)

EXEMPLE	Tu joues au volley?	**Non, je ne joue pas au volley.**
	Tu fais du ski?	**Non, je ne fais pas de ski.**

1. Tu fais de la natation?
2. Tu joues à des jeux vidéo?
3. Tu fais de l'athlétisme?
4. Tu fais du jogging?
5. Tu joues aux cartes?
6. Tu fais des photos?
7. Tu fais du patin à glace?
8. Tu fais du roller en ligne?

5 Pauline et Louise ont des projets pour la soirée. Complète leur conversation avec les formes correctes de **faire.** (**p. 116**)

LOUISE Dis, Pauline, on __1__ de la natation ce soir?

PAULINE Non. Quand il fait froid, moi, je ne __2__ pas de natation! J'aime mieux __3__ du patin à glace! Tu __4__ du patin à glace, toi?

LOUISE Non, ça ne me dit rien. En hiver, quand il neige, mes copines et moi, nous __5__ du ski. C'est génial, le ski!

PAULINE En été, Gilles et Félix __6__ du ski nautique. J'adore le ski nautique! Mais ce soir, moi, je __7__ du patin à glace. C'est décidé!

LOUISE D'accord. Allons-y!

Grammaire supplémentaire

CHAPITRE 4

Answers

3
1. Est-ce que vous aimez jouer au foot?
2. Est-ce que tu aimes jouer à des jeux vidéo?
3. Est-ce que tu aimes faire de la photo?
4. Est-ce que vous aimez jouer au tennis?
5. Est-ce que tu aimes faire du ski nautique?
6. Est-ce que vous aimez faire de l'athlétisme?
7. Est-ce que tu aimes faire du vélo?
8. Est-ce que vous aimez jouer aux cartes?

4
1. Non, je ne fais pas de natation.
2. Non, je ne joue pas à des jeux vidéo.
3. Non, je ne fais pas d'athlétisme.
4. Non, je ne fais pas de jogging.
5. Non, je ne joue pas aux cartes.
6. Non, je ne fais pas de photos.
7. Non, je ne fais pas de patin à glace.
8. Non, je ne fais pas de roller en ligne.

5
1. fait
2. fais
3. faire
4. fais
5. faisons
6. font
7. fais

Teacher to Teacher

June Ricks
Fort Zumwalt West HS
O'Fallon, MO

A "family feud" works well in June's class.

"To practice expressions with **faire** and **jouer,** I play a game similar to Family Feud. Divide the class into two families. Each family sends one representative outside the room while I ask team members to answer multiple-choice questions: **"Tu aimes mieux jouer au foot ou jouer au football americain?"** When the family representative returns, I ask him or her the same questions about the family: **"Ils aiment mieux jouer au foot ou jouer au football américain?"** The representative has to answer in complete sentences. The family with the most correct matches wins."

STANDARDS: 1.2

Grammaire supplémentaire

CHAPITRE 4

For **Grammaire supplémentaire** Answer Transparencies, see the *Teaching Transparencies* binder.

Grammaire supplémentaire

Visit Holt Online
go.hrw.com
KEYWORD: WA3 QUEBEC CITY-4
Jeux interactifs

6 Odile is asking her friends if they play certain sports. Based on their answers, what are her questions? Remember to use the correct forms of **faire.** (**p. 116**)

EXEMPLE ODILE **Vous faites du vélo?**
JEREMY ET VALENTINE Oui, on adore faire du vélo.

1. ODILE ______________________
   SYLVIE Oui, j'aime beaucoup faire du jogging.
2. ODILE ______________________
   PIERRE Oui, Sophie et Marie adorent faire de l'aérobic.
3. ODILE ______________________
   DAVID Oui, Arthur aime faire de la natation.
4. ODILE ______________________
   MARION ET FRANCINE Oui, nous aimons bien faire du ski.
5. ODILE ______________________
   VANESSA Oui, Elodie et Jérôme aiment beaucoup faire du roller en ligne.
6. ODILE ______________________
   CHRISTINE Oui, Thérèse aime faire de la randonnée.

7 Rewrite the following sentences, replacing the subject with the pronoun **on.** Be sure to make any necessary changes. (**p. 117**)

1. Nous adorons le théâtre.
2. Marcel et moi aimons faire de la natation après l'école.
3. Est-ce que vous faites du ski nautique au Texas?
4. Vous jouez aux cartes?
5. Nous faisons de l'aérobic.
6. Est-ce que nous faisons du roller en ligne ce week-end?
7. Est-ce que vous faites du théâtre dans votre école?

8 Complete the following sentences with the activity most appropriate for the weather condition or time of year stated. (**p. 119**)

jouer au football américain
regarder la télé
jouer au tennis
jouer au hockey
nager
jouer à des jeux vidéo

1. En automne, mon frère _____.
2. Quand il fait chaud, les enfants _____.
3. Quand il neige, Jacqueline _____.
4. Quand il pleut, je _____.
5. Quand il fait frais, mon frère et moi _____.

Answers

6
1. Tu fais du jogging?
2. Sophie et Marie font de l'aérobic?
3. Arthur fait de la natation?
4. Vous faites du ski?
5. Elodie et Jérôme font du roller en ligne?
6. Thérèse fait de la randonnée?

7
1. On adore le théâtre.
2. On aime faire de la natation après l'école.
3. Est-ce qu'on fait du ski nautique au Texas?
4. On joue aux cartes?
5. On fait de l'aérobic.
6. Est-ce qu'on fait du roller en ligne ce week-end?
7. Est-ce qu'on fait du théâtre dans votre école?

8
1. joue au football américain
2. nagent
3. joue à des jeux vidéo.
4. regarde la télé
5. jouons au tennis

Communication for All Students

Game

Verb Bee Play this game to review **-er** verbs. Divide the class into two teams and have one player from each team go to the board. Call out an infinitive **(jouer)** and a subject **(vous).** Award a point to the team of the first player to write the correct verb form.

Visual Learners

Cut pictures from a magazine of activities and different weather conditions and seasons. Hold up a picture of an activity and a weather condition. Students should make a sentence based on whether the two pictures go together logically or not. **(Je fais du tennis quand il fait beau/au printemps. Je ne fais pas de tennis/quand il fait froid/en hiver.)**

STANDARDS: 1.2

Troisième étape

Objective Making, accepting, and turning down suggestions

Grammaire supplémentaire

CHAPITRE 4

9 François is asking Janine how often she plays certain sports. Rewrite their conversation, using the fragments below. Remember to use the correct form of the verb and to put the adverb in the correct position. (**p. 122**)

FRANÇOIS tu/est-ce que/souvent/faire/de la natation
JANINE faire/de la natation/je/souvent/au printemps/oui
FRANÇOIS faire/du ski/de temps en temps/tu/est-ce que
JANINE faire/du ski/oui/je/quand il neige
FRANÇOIS quelquefois/tu/est-ce que/jouer/au foot
JANINE ne...jamais/jouer/non/au foot/je

10 Vanessa has taken a survey to find out how often teenagers play certain sports. Rewrite her notes, using the adverbs from the box. The meaning of the sentences should remain the same. Use each adverb only once. (**p. 122**)

EXEMPLE Camille fait du vélo trois fois par semaine.
Camille fait souvent du vélo.

ne ... jamais d'habitude quelquefois
souvent une fois par semaine

1. Koffi joue au tennis de temps en temps.
2. Estelle et Olivia font du patin à glace le samedi matin.
3. Quand il pleut, Fatima ne fait pas de jogging.
4. Sébastien joue au golf tous les jours au printemps.

Answers

9
1. Est-ce que tu fais souvent de la natation?
2. Oui, je fais souvent de la natation au printemps.
3. Est-ce que tu fais du ski de temps en temps?
4. Oui, je fais du ski quand il neige.
5. Est-ce que tu joues quelquefois au foot?
6. Non, je ne joue jamais au foot.

10
1. Quelquefois, Koffi joue au tennis.
2. Estelle et Olivia font du patin à glace une fois par semaine.
3. Quand il pleut, Fatima ne fait jamais de jogging.
4. D'habitude, Sébastien joue au golf au printemps.

Review and Assess

You may wish to assign the **Grammaire supplémentaire** activities as additional practice or homework after presenting material throughout the chapter. Assign Activities 1–2 after **Grammaire** (p. 113), Activity 3 after **Grammaire** (p. 115), Activity 4 after **Note de grammaire** (p. 116), Activities 5–6 after **Grammaire** (p. 116), Activity 7 after **Grammaire** (p. 117), Activity 8 after **Tu te rappelles?** (p. 119), Activities 9–10 after **Grammaire** (p. 122). To prepare students for the **Etape** Quizzes and Chapter Test, we suggest doing the **Grammaire supplémentaire** activities in the following order. Have students complete Activities 1–3 before taking Quizzes 4-1A or 4-1B; Activities 4–8 before Quizzes 4-2A or 4-2B; and Activities 9–10 before Quizzes 4-3A or 4-3B.

STANDARDS: 1.2

Mise en pratique

CHAPITRE 4

The **Mise en pratique** reviews and integrates all four skills and culture in preparation for the Chapter Test.

Teaching Resources
pp. 132–133

PRINT 

- Lesson Planner, p. 22
- Listening Activities, p. 29
- Video Guide, pp. 27, 30
- Grammar Tutor for Students of French, Chapter 4
- Standardized Assessment Tutor, Chapter 4

MEDIA 

- One-Stop Planner
- Video Program Videocassette 2, 20:46-22:06
- DVD Tutor, Disc 1
- Audio Compact Discs, CD 4, Tr. 18
- Interactive CD-ROM Tutor, Disc 1

Additional Practice

2 Have students describe each of the photos in the ad. They should identify the season, give the weather conditions, and tell where the people are and what they are doing.

Culture Note

You might point out to students that Canadian phone numbers follow the American rather than the French pattern, with a three-digit area code and numbers of three and four digits separated by a dash. To call long-distance, Canadians dial 1 before the area code and number, just as in the United States.

Mise en pratique

CD-ROM 1 DVD 1

1 Listen to this radio commercial for the **Village des Sports,** a resort in Quebec. List at least one activity offered in each season. See scripts and answers on p. 105H.

CD 4 Tr. 18

2 You've decided to spend part of your vacation at the **Village des Sports.** Read the information you've received about the resort. Then, answer the questions that follow.

Village des Sports

c'est l'fun fun fun!

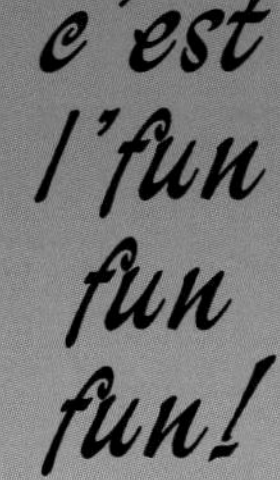

en hiver comme en été

Le plus grand centre du sport au Canada offre du plaisir pour toute la famille.
Services d'accueil, de restauration et de location sur place.

EN ETE
- le tennis
- le volley
- l'athlétisme
- le base-ball
- le roller en ligne
- le ski nautique
- la natation
- l'équitation
- la voile

EN AUTOMNE
- le football
- l'équitation
- la randonnée
- le volley

EN HIVER
- le hockey
- le ski
- le patin à glace
- la luge

AU PRINTEMPS
- le base-ball
- la randonnée
- le roller en ligne
- le tennis

Village des Sports
1860, boul. Valcartier
(418) 844-3725
à 24 km du centre-ville de Québec via la route 371 Nord

Apply and Assess

Challenge

1 Have students list more than one activity mentioned for each season. You might give a small prize to the student who lists the most activities mentioned on the recording.

Additional Practice

2 Have students choose one activity that they like from the choices listed under each season in the ad and tell why they like that particular activity. Ask them if there are any other activities that they participate in during each of the four seasons.

STANDARDS: 1.2

See answers below.

1. Would the **Village des Sports** be good for a family vacation? Why or why not?
2. According to the brochure, in what season(s) can you go . . .
   a. in-line skating? **c.** hiking?
   b. water skiing? **d.** horseback riding?
3. You have a friend who doesn't like cold weather. What three activities could your friend do at the **Village des Sports?**

3 **a.** You've arrived at the **Village des Sports.** You meet your three roommates, get to know them, and ask them about the activities they enjoy.

b. You and your roommates decide to participate in an activity together. Each of you suggests an activity until you all agree on one.

4 What differences are there between the way students in your area and students in Quebec spend their free time?

5 Ecrivons!

You're going to write a letter to your French class back home describing your activities at the **Village des Sports.** Organizing your ideas using the strategy below will help you create your letter.

Stratégie pour écrire

Arranging ideas logically is a helpful way to organize your ideas before you begin writing.

1. Divide a sheet of paper into three separate columns.
2. Label the first column on your paper **J'aime...** , the next column **Je n'aime pas...** , and the third column **Le temps.**
3. In the first column, list the activities that you like to participate in at the **Village des Sports.** In the next column, list the activities you dislike, and in the third column, tell what the weather is like there.
4. Now you are ready to write your letter.

J'aime	Je n'aime pas	Le temps
faire du ski		Il fait froid.

6 Jeu de rôle

You're a famous Canadian athlete. Your partner, a reporter for the local television station, will interview you about your busy training routine. Tell the interviewer what you do at different times of the year, in various weather conditions, and how often. Then, take the role of the reporter and interview your partner, who will assume the identity of a different Canadian athlete.

Mise en pratique

CHAPITRE 4

Teaching Suggestion

3 Either of these activities could be used in addition to, or in place of, one of the chapter projects. Have students write and practice these skits and then perform them in front of the class. Students might record them as an oral portfolio entry.

Career Path

6 Have students think about why knowing French would be valuable for a career in journalism. Have them tell how their skills in French would help them with research, interviewing, writing, and reporting. You might also have students use the Internet to find sites of French news magazines.

Portfolio

6 **Oral** This activity is appropriate as an oral portfolio entry. For portfolio suggestions, see *Alternative Assessment Guide,* pages iv–17.

Apply and Assess

Challenge

5 Have students add another column to their charts to record how often they do each activity **(Quand?).** Have them include this information in their letters as well.

Process Writing

5 Students may want to describe their stay at a summer camp **(une colonie de vacances)** instead. Have students exchange their first draft for peer-editing and feedback. Help them create a checklist of things to look for as they edit their partner's paper. After the editing is done, have volunteers read their letter to the class.

Answers

2 1. Yes; the resort offers activities for all the family.
2. a. in-line skating: summer and spring; b. waterskiing: summer; c. hiking: fall and spring; d. horseback riding: summer and fall
3. *Answers may vary. Possible answers:* swimming, waterskiing, volleyball

STANDARDS: 1.1, 1.2, 1.3, 3.1, 5.1

Que sais-je?

CHAPITRE 4

Teaching Resources
p. 134

PRINT 
- Grammar Tutor for Students of French, Chapter 4

MEDIA 
- Interactive CD-ROM Tutor, Disc 1
- Online self-test

go.hrw.com
WA3 QUEBEC-4

Answers

1 *Like:* J'aime beaucoup... ; J'aime surtout...
Dislike: Je n'aime pas tellement... ; Je n'aime pas beaucoup... ; Je n'aime pas du tout...
1. jouer au golf.
2. faire de la natation.
3. jouer au tennis.
4. faire de la photo.
5. faire du roller en ligne.

2 *Enjoy:* J'aime beaucoup... ; J'aime surtout...
Don't enjoy: Je n'aime pas tellement... ; Je n'aime pas beaucoup... ; Je n'aime pas du tout...

3 Je joue... ; Je fais...

4 **1.** Tu joues au football?/Est-ce que tu joues au football?
2. Tu joues au hockey?/Est-ce que tu joues au hockey?
3. Tu joues au volley-ball?/Est-ce que tu joues au volley-ball?

5 **1.** Au printemps/En été/En automne/En hiver, je...
2. En janvier/février/mars/avril/mai/juin/juillet/août/septembre/octobre/novembre/décembre, j'aime...
3. Quand il fait froid/il fait frais/il fait beau/il fait chaud/il pleut/il neige, je...
4. Le matin/L'après-midi/Le soir, j'aime...

7 *Accept:* D'accord. Bonne idée. Oui, c'est génial.
Oui, c'est super! Allons-y!
Turn down: Désolé(e), mais je ne peux pas. Ça ne me dit rien. Non, c'est barbant. Non, c'est nul!

Que sais-je?

WA3 QUEBEC CITY-4

Can you use what you've learned in this chapter?

Can you tell how much you like or dislike something?
p. 114

1 Can you tell someone how much you like or dislike these activities? See answers below.

1.

2.

3.

4.

5.

2 Can you tell someone which sports and activities you enjoy a lot? Which ones you don't enjoy at all? See answers below.

Can you exchange information?
p. 116

3 How would you tell someone about a few of your sports and hobbies, using the verbs **jouer** and **faire?** See answers below.

4 How would you find out if someone plays these games? See answers below.

1.

2.

3.

5 How would you tell someone in French . . . See answers below.
1. what you do in a certain season?
2. what you like to do in a certain month?
3. what you do in certain weather?
4. what you like to do at a certain time of day?

Can you make, accept, and turn down suggestions?
p. 122

6 How would you suggest that . . .
1. you and a friend go waterskiing? On fait du ski nautique?
2. you and your friends play baseball? On joue au base-ball?

7 If a friend asked you to go jogging, how would you accept the suggestion? How would you turn it down? See answers below.

Review and Assess

Teaching Suggestions

1 4 To review the months and seasons of the year, have students tell in which month(s) and/or season(s) the people in the illustrations are doing the activities.

5 You might have students tell how frequently they do each activity, using appropriate adverbs.

6 7 For further practice, students might use the illustrations on this page to make, accept, and turn down suggestions.

Première étape

Telling how much you like or dislike something

Beaucoup.	*A lot.*
surtout	*especially*
Pas tellement.	*Not too much.*
Pas beaucoup.	*Not very much.*
Pas du tout.	*Not at all.*

Sports and hobbies

faire de l'aérobic	*to do aerobics*
de l'athlétisme	*to do track and field*
du jogging	*to jog*
de la natation	*to swim*
du patin à glace	*to ice-skate*
de la photo	*to do photography*
des photos	*to take pictures*
du roller en ligne	*to in-line skate*
du ski	*to ski*
du ski nautique	*to water-ski*
du théâtre	*to do drama*
du vélo	*to bike*
de la vidéo	*to make videos*
jouer au base-ball	*to play baseball*
au basket(-ball)	*to play basketball*
au foot(ball)	*to play soccer*
au football américain	*to play football*
au golf	*to play golf*
au hockey	*to play hockey*
à des jeux vidéo	*to play video games*
au tennis	*to play tennis*
au volley(-ball)	*to play volleyball*
aux cartes	*to play cards*

Other useful expressions

Est-ce que	*(introduces a yes-or-no question)*

Vocabulaire

Deuxième étape

Exchanging information

Qu'est-ce que tu fais comme sport?	*What sports do you play?*
Qu'est-ce que tu fais pour t'amuser?	*What do you do to have fun?*
Je fais...	*I play/do . . .*
Je joue...	*I play . . .*
Je ne fais pas de...	*I don't play/do . . .*
Je ne joue pas...	*I don't play . . .*
faire	*to do, to play, to make*
jouer	*to play*

Weather

Quel temps fait-il?	*What's the weather like?*
Il fait beau.	*It's nice weather.*
Il fait chaud.	*It's hot.*
Il fait frais.	*It's cool.*
Il fait froid.	*It's cold.*
Il pleut.	*It's raining.*
Il neige.	*It's snowing.*

Seasons, months, and times

Qu'est-ce que tu fais...	*What do you do . . .*
le week-end?	*on weekends?*
le soir?	*in the evening?*
en vacances?	*on vacation?*
au printemps?	*in the spring?*
en été?	*in the summer?*
en automne?	*in the fall?*
en hiver?	*in the winter?*
en janvier?	*in January?*
en février?	*in February?*
en mars?	*in March?*
en avril?	*in April?*
en mai?	*in May?*
en juin?	*in June?*
en juillet?	*in July?*
en août?	*in August?*
en septembre?	*in September?*
en octobre?	*in October?*
en novembre?	*in November?*
en décembre?	*in December?*

Other useful expressions

on	*we, they, you*

Troisième étape

Making, accepting, and turning down suggestions

On... ?	*How about . . . ?*
D'accord.	*OK.*
Bonne idée.	*Good idea.*
Allons-y!	*Let's go!*
Oui, c'est...	*Yes, it's . . .*
Désolé(e), mais je ne peux pas.	*Sorry, but I can't.*
Ça ne me dit rien.	*That doesn't interest me.*
Non, c'est...	*No, it's (that's) . . .*

Expressions of frequency

quelquefois	*sometimes*
...fois par semaine	*. . . time(s) a week*
de temps en temps	*from time to time*
souvent	*often*
rarement	*rarely*
ne... jamais	*never*
d'habitude	*usually*

Review and Assess

Projet

Mon calendrier Have students make a calendar for one month showing the sport and/or activities they practice each day. Students may want to include illustrations or photos on their calendars. Have them fill in the days on the calendar with the names of the activities, and, on a separate sheet of paper, write at least four sentences describing their activities. They can say how much they like them and how often they practice them. Have them write the information around the calendar and glue or tape the illustrations on the appropriate days. Have students display and describe their calendars to the class.

Vocabulaire

CHAPITRE 4

Additional Practice

- To review vocabulary, you might have students list all of the cognates they can find on this page.
- You might play the game **Mémoire** described on page 105C.

Chapter 4 Assessment

- **Testing Program**
  Chapter Test, pp. 91–96

  Audio Compact Discs, CD 4, Trs. 22–24
  Speaking Test, p. 344
- **Alternative Assessment Guide**
  Performance Assessment, p. 35
  Portfolio Assessment, p. 21
  CD-ROM Assessment, p. 49
- **Interactive CD-ROM Tutor, Disc 1**
  CD-ROM 1 A toi de parler
  DVD 1 A toi d'écrire
- **Standardized Assessment Tutor**
  Chapter 4
- **One-Stop Planner, Disc 1**

  Test Generator
  Chapter 4

Location Opener

CHAPTERS 5, 6, 7

Teaching Resources
pp. 136–139

PRINT 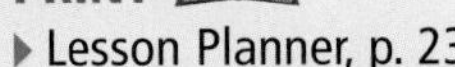
- Lesson Planner, p. 23
- Video Guide, pp. 31, 32

MEDIA 
- One-Stop Planner
- Video Program
  Videocassette 2, 22:40–25:07
- DVD Tutor, Disc 1
- Interactive CD-ROM Tutor, Disc 2
- Map Transparency 1

go.hrw.com
WA3 PARIS

Using the Almanac and Map

Terms in the Almanac
- **La basilique du Sacré-Cœur,** built between 1876 and 1914, is located on Montmartre, the highest point in Paris.
- **Le musée du Louvre,** the largest museum in the world, houses such works as the *Mona Lisa* **(La Joconde)** and the *Venus de Milo.*
- **Le musée d'Orsay,** formerly a train station, was turned into a museum in 1986. It is devoted to sculpture, painting, and architecture of the nineteenth century.
- **Le musée Rodin** houses many of Rodin's most famous sculptures, including *Le Penseur* and *Les Bourgeois de Calais.*
- **Le jardin du Luxembourg** is a famous Parisian park.
- **Les Tuileries** is a park **à l'italienne** with fountains and sculptures.

CHAPITRES 5,6,7

Allez, viens à Paris!

Capitale de la France

Population : plus de 2.150.000; région parisienne : plus de 10.000.000

Points d'intérêt : la tour Eiffel, l'Arc de triomphe, la cathédrale Notre-Dame, le centre Georges Pompidou, la basilique du Sacré-Cœur

Musées : l'Orangerie, le musée du Louvre, le musée d'Orsay, le musée de l'Homme, le musée Rodin

Parcs et jardins : le jardin du Luxembourg, le Champ-de-Mars, les Tuileries

Parisiens célèbres : Charles Baudelaire, Colette, Victor Hugo, Edith Piaf, Auguste Rodin, Jean-Paul Sartre

Industries : haute couture, finance, technologie, transport, tourisme

ANGLETERRE
BELGIQUE
ALLEMAGNE
LUXEMBOURG
Paris
Strasbourg
Chartres
Tours
Poitiers
SUISSE
Océan Atlantique
FRANCE
Lyon
ITALIE
Bordeaux
Arles
Nice
Aix-en-Provence
CORSE
ESPAGNE
Mer Méditerranée

go.hrw.com WA3 PARIS
VIDEO
CD-ROM 2
DVD 1

L'avenue des Champs-Elysées et l'Arc de triomphe

Cultures and Communities

Background Information
The earliest known inhabitants of Paris were the **Parisii,** who settled on the **Ile de la Cité** in the third century B.C. Paris has often played a central role in the political and cultural evolution of France. The major political events of the French Revolution occurred in Paris in 1789. Today, Paris is an important university center. The **Quartier latin** has been home to many students since the Middle Ages. In the mid-nineteenth century, Baron Haussmann, working under Emperor Napoléon III, razed many areas of the city and created **les grands boulevards.**

STANDARDS: 2.2, 3.1, 5.1

Connections and Comparisons

Architecture Link

L'avenue des Champs-Elysées extends from the place de la Concorde to the place Charles de Gaulle. In the courtyard of the Louvre museum is the Arc de triomphe du Carrousel; in the center of the place de la Concorde is the obélisque de Louxor, at the end of the avenue is the famous Arc de Triomphe. These monuments are all perfectly aligned.

History Link

L'Arc de Triomphe, situated in the middle of the place Charles de Gaulle (the former place de l'Etoile) where twelve avenues intersect, was constructed on the orders of Napoléon I. Underneath the Arc is the tomb of the French Unknown Soldier, placed there after World War I.

Map Activity

Have students look at the map and try to determine why Paris was an important crossroads throughout history.

Art Link

Have students research various French artists (David, Monet, Manet, Degas, Rodin, Matisse, Renoir, Chagall) or artists who worked in France (Van Gogh and Picasso).

History Link

Even though **Notre-Dame** is one of the most famous cathedrals, it was not the scene of royal coronations or funerals. Kings of France were crowned in the cathedral in Reims where Clovis, the first Christian king of France, was baptized. Many of the French kings are buried in the basilica of Saint-Denis, just north of Paris.

Location Opener

CHAPTERS 5, 6, 7

Using the Photo Essay

1 **Le centre Georges Pompidou,** a museum named after the second president of the Fifth Republic, offers a splendid view of Paris. The upper floors are reached via escalators encased in glass tubes that allow visitors to look out over Paris as they ascend. The public square in front of the museum is always bustling with all kinds of entertainment, from magicians, to fire-eaters, to mimes.

2 **Montmartre** is the highest point in Paris. Many of its steep, narrow streets end in staircases. Both Sacré-Cœur and Saint-Pierre-de-Montmartre, one of the earliest Roman-Gothic churches, are located in Montmartre. There is some disagreement about how the name **Montmartre** originated. Some speculate that it came from the *mount of Mars,* because of the Roman temple that stood on top of the hill. Others say it means *mount of martyrs,* referring to the site of the execution of Saint Denis, the first bishop of Paris.

3 Each **bouquiniste** has a green, metal box affixed to the stone wall along the Seine. When the **bouquinistes** are not there, their wares are locked inside the box.

Paris

Paris is a city that has no equal. It is the intellectual and cultural capital of the French-speaking world and also the largest city in Europe, if you include the greater Parisian area. Whether you like to visit museums, go to the theater, sit in cafés, or stroll along tree-lined boulevards, there's something for everyone here. Paris is one of the world's most beautiful and exciting cities!

Visit Holt Online
go.hrw.com
KEYWORD: WA3 PARIS
Activités Internet

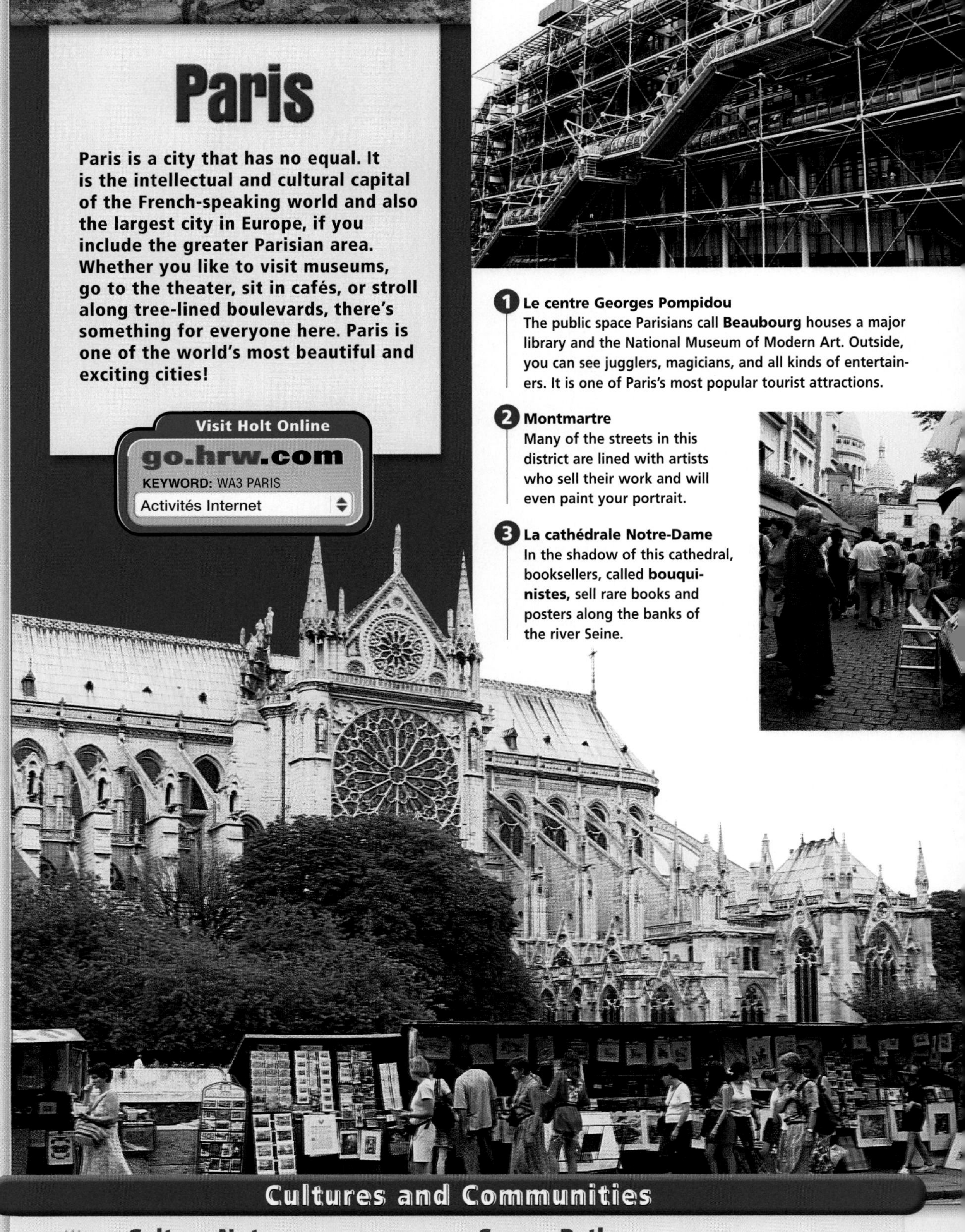

1 **Le centre Georges Pompidou**
The public space Parisians call **Beaubourg** houses a major library and the National Museum of Modern Art. Outside, you can see jugglers, magicians, and all kinds of entertainers. It is one of Paris's most popular tourist attractions.

2 **Montmartre**
Many of the streets in this district are lined with artists who sell their work and will even paint your portrait.

3 **La cathédrale Notre-Dame**
In the shadow of this cathedral, booksellers, called **bouquinistes,** sell rare books and posters along the banks of the river Seine.

Cultures and Communities

Culture Note

3 Efforts were made in the past to limit or reduce the number of **bouquinistes** along the Seine. However, the public outcry was so great that the project was abandoned, and these traditional fixtures remain along the banks of the Seine.

Career Path

Have students discuss why knowing several languages would be useful in a city like Paris. Ask students to think of cities in the United States that, like Paris, receive tourists from around the world. How would knowing a foreign language be beneficial in these places? Which languages would be most helpful?

STANDARDS: 2.1, 5.1

4 Les cafés
In Paris, the terrace of a café is a wonderful place to sit and watch the world go by.

5 La tour Eiffel
This iron skyscraper was erected as a temporary exhibit for the Centennial Exposition in 1889 and has been the object of controversy ever since. It is 320.75 meters tall, including the television antenna added in 1957. To reach the top platform, ride one of the hydraulic elevators or climb the 1,792 stairs!

In chapters 5, 6, and 7, you'll meet some Parisians. Paris is a very old city; it is thought to be named after a tribe called the Parisii that settled there 2,300 years ago. Many of the buildings around Paris are several hundred years old, giving it a special character completely different from that of most American cities. At the same time, Paris has all the amenities of a large modern city—a transportation system that is the envy of the world, well-maintained public phones, and streets that are cleaned every morning, for example.

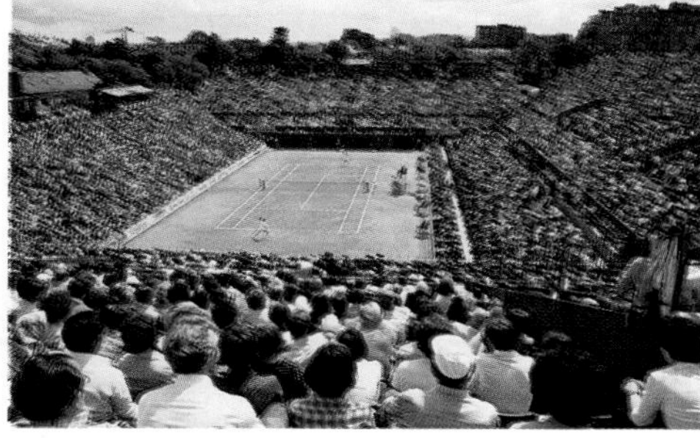

6 Le stade Roland-Garros
The famous French Open tennis tournament takes place in this stadium every summer.

7 Le métro
The Paris subway is one of the world's most efficient mass-transit systems.

4 Paris is full of sidewalk cafés, some of which date from the eighteenth century. The most famous include **Les Deux Magots** (see photo, pages 140–141), the nearby **Café de Flore,** and the **Café Procope,** frequented by Voltaire in the eighteenth century.

5 Among the many illuminated monuments in Paris is **la tour Eiffel.** Until 1986, it was illuminated by giant projectors located on the ground. In 1986, lights were installed on the tower itself. These lights give the tower greater depth, making it look like a jewel.

6 **Roland Garros** was a famous French aviator who, in 1913, was the first to fly successfully across the Mediterranean.

7 The Paris **métro** began service with the Vincennes-Maillot line in 1900, several years after both the London and Boston subways. Today, there are 16 lines with over 350 stations. The system extends to the suburbs with four **RER (Réseau express régional)** lines. **RER** trains are slightly larger than **métro** trains, and outside the city limits, they travel above ground.

Culture Note

7 French transportation systems are among the best in the world. A network of **autoroutes** crisscrosses the country. The **TGV (Train à grande vitesse)** and other trains run by the **SNCF (Société nationale des chemins de fer français)** reach every corner of France. French firms have also designed and built subways in Cairo and Mexico City.

Connections and Comparisons

Architecture Link

1 The structure of the **centre Georges Pompidou,** because of its skeletal design of pipes and tubes, is referred to as **la raffinerie,** *the refinery.* In reality, the pipes and tubes are quite functional, as they serve as casing for the heating, air-conditioning, electrical, and telephone conduits.

History Link

7 Ask students if they can figure out why the names of so many metro lines include the word **porte,** such as **Porte de Clignancourt** and **Porte d'Orléans.** (In the Middle Ages, Paris was a walled city whose gates were closed at dusk. Gates were located around the city and named. As the city grew, the wall was extended several times.)

Chapitre 5 : On va au café?

Chapter Overview

Mise en train pp. 142–144	***Qu'est-ce qu'on prend?***			
	FUNCTIONS	**GRAMMAR**	**VOCABULARY**	**RE-ENTRY**
Première étape pp. 145–150	• Making suggestions, p. 145 • Making excuses, p. 145 • Making a recommendation, p. 148	• The verb **prendre,** p. 149	• Food and beverages, p. 147	• Accepting and turning down a suggestion **(Chapitre 4)** • Likes and dislikes **(Chapitre 1)** • Activities **(Chapitre 1)**
Deuxième étape pp. 151–153	• Getting someone's attention, p. 151 • Ordering food and beverages, p. 151	• The imperative, p. 152		• Expressing likes, dislikes, and preferences **(Chapitre 1)**
Troisième étape pp. 154–157	• Inquiring about and expressing likes and dislikes, p. 154 • Paying the check, p. 155			• Expressing likes and dislikes **(Chapitre 1)** • Numbers 20–100 **(Chapitres 2, 3)**

Prononciation p. 157	**The nasal sound [ã]** Audio CD 5, Tracks 12–14	**A écrire** (dictation) Audio CD 5, Tracks 15–17	
Lisons! pp. 158–159	**Des menus de cafés**	**Reading Strategy:** Using what you already know	
Grammaire supplémentaire	**pp. 160–163** **Première étape,** p. 160	**Deuxième étape,** pp. 161–162	**Troisième étape,** p. 163
Review pp. 164–167	**Mise en pratique,** pp. 164–165 **Ecrivons!** Arranging ideas spatially Creating a poster	**Que sais-je?** p. 166	**Vocabulaire,** p. 167

CULTURE

- **Panorama Culturel,** Meeting friends, p. 150
- Realia: Café menu, p. 152
- **Note culturelle,** Waitpersons as professionals, p. 153
- Realia: Menu from **La Crêperie Normande,** p. 153
- **Note culturelle, La litote,** p. 154
- **Note culturelle,** Tipping, p. 156
- Realia: Café bill, p. 156
- Realia: Menu from **Café Sport,** p. 156

Chapitre 5 : On va au café?
Chapter Resources

Visit Holt Online
go.hrw.com
KEYWORD: WA3 PARIS-5
Online Edition

Lesson Planning

One-Stop Planner

Lesson Planner with Differentiated Instruction, pp. 23–27, 69

Student Make-Up Assignments
- Make-Up Assignment Copying Masters, Chapter 5

Listening and Speaking

TPR Storytelling Book, pp. 17–20

Listening Activities
- Student Response Forms for Listening Activities, pp. 35–37
- Additional Listening Activities 5-1 to 5-6, pp. 39–41
- Additional Listening Activities (song), p. 42
- Scripts and Answers, pp. 122–126

Video Guide
- Teaching Suggestions, pp. 34–35
- Activity Masters, pp. 36–38
- Scripts and Answers, pp. 98–100, 120

Activities for Communication
- Communicative Activities, pp. 25–30
- Realia and Teaching Suggestions, pp. 95–99
- Situation Cards, pp. 145–146

Reading and Writing

Reading Strategies and Skills Handbook, Chapter 5

Joie de lire 1, Chapter 5

Cahier d'activités, pp. 49–60

Grammar

Travaux pratiques de grammaire, pp. 35–40

Grammar Tutor for Students of French, Chapter 5

Assessment

Testing Program
- Grammar and Vocabulary Quizzes, **Etape** Quizzes, and Chapter Test, pp. 105–122
- Score Sheet, Scripts and Answers, pp. 123–130

Alternative Assessment Guide
- Portfolio Assessment, p. 22
- Performance Assessment, p. 36
- CD-ROM Assessment, p. 50

Student Make-Up Assignments
- Alternative Quizzes, Chapter 5

Standardized Assessment Tutor
- Reading, pp. 17–19
- Writing, p. 20
- Math, pp. 25–26

Middle School

Middle School Teaching Resources, Chapter 5

Online Activities
- **Jeux interactifs**
- **Activités Internet**

Video Program
- Videocassette 2
- Videocassette 5 (captioned version)

2 **Interactive CD-ROM Tutor,** Disc 2

1 **DVD Tutor,** Disc 1

Audio Compact Discs
- Textbook Listening Activities, CD 5, Tracks 1–18
- Additional Listening Activities, CD 5, Tracks 25–31
- Assessment Items, CD 5, Tracks 19–24

Teaching Transparencies
- Situation 5-1 to 5-3
- Vocabulary 5-A and 5-B
- **Mise en train**
- **Grammaire supplémentaire** Answers
- **Travaux pratiques de grammaire** Answers

Use the **One-Stop Planner CD-ROM with Test Generator** to aid in lesson planning and pacing.

For each chapter, the **One-Stop Planner** includes:
- Editable lesson plans with direct links to teaching resources
- Printable worksheets from resource books
- Direct launches to the HRW Internet activities
- Video and audio segments
- Test Generator
- Clip Art for vocabulary items

Chapitre 5 : On va au café?

Projects

Notre café

Have groups of three or four students design a menu for a café they will open.

MATERIALS

Students may need

- Construction paper
- Markers or colored pencils
- Magazines
- Tape or glue
- Scissors

SUGGESTED SEQUENCE

1. **Prewriting** Students should come up with ideas for their café, including the theme or style of the café and the price range. One student should write down the different ideas; the group should then decide which ideas to follow.
2. **First Draft** Different tasks should be assigned to individual group members: writing down menu items, designing the menu, editing, and choosing appropriate prices in euros for each item.
3. **Peer-editing** Have students check one another's work. Are there enough items for the menu? Do the items have reasonable and consistent prices? Is the spelling correct, and are the items in the correct section of the menu? Is the menu design attractive, and does it reflect the restaurant's style?
4. **Final Draft** Students should add their assigned parts to the menu and complete it with illustrations or graphics according to the design. They should also check for any mistakes before handing it in.

GRADING THE PROJECT

Suggested Point Distribution: (total = 100 points)
Content ....25 points
Menu design ....25 points
Spelling/placement of items ....25 points
Participation ....25 points

TEACHING SUGGESTION

These menus might be displayed in the classroom and/or used in skits or for reading comprehension.

Games

Jeter et attraper

This game will help students review vocabulary. It is recommended at the end of the first ***étape.***

Procedure List various categories (food, drink, activities, the infinitive of a particular verb, and so on) on the board or on a transparency. Call out a category and toss a ball or other soft object to a student. The student must catch the ball and name an appropriate item in that category within three seconds. Then, that student will call out a category and toss the ball to another student. The game continues in this manner.

Jeu de concours

This game will help students review words and expressions in a variety of categories.

Procedure Draw a game grid on a large sheet of paper hanging on the wall. The grid should have six columns, each headed by a category. Below each category are five boxes that contain numbers ranging from 100–500 and English words or expressions. The game grid below can be used as a model. The object of the game is to give the French equivalents for the expressions in the boxes. Players who do so are awarded the points in the box they selected. Divide the class into two teams and decide the order of play. The first player selects a category and a box, and then attempts to say in French the word or expression given in the box. For example, if a student selects the category "Ordering" and the box "200, ask for menu," then that student should say **"La carte, s'il vous plaît."** If the player answers correctly, the box is crossed out, and the team receives the given number of points. If the player answers incorrectly, the other team will have the opportunity to give the correct response.

Example:

Suggestions/ Excuses	Menu	Prendre	Ordering	Commands	Potpourri
100 play basketball	100 coffee	100 je	100 get attention	100 watch a film	100 homework
200 go jogging	200 steak & fries	200 elle	200 ask for menu	200 play soccer	200 yummy
300 I have homework	300 hot chocolate	300 nous	300 ask for check	300 do sports	300 how much
400 I have errands to do	400 apple juice	400 vous	400 ask for hot dog	400 have a sandwich	400 gross
500 I have things to do	500 grilled ham & cheese	500 ils	500 ask for types of drinks	500 bring me…	500 to be hungry and thirsty

STANDARDS: 1.3, 5.1, 5.2

Storytelling

Mini-histoire

*This story accompanies Teaching Transparency 5-1. The **mini-histoire** can be told and retold in different formats, acted out, written down, and read aloud, to give students additional opportunities to practice all four skills. The following story relates what students like to do at lunch time.*

Tous les midis, les amis vont au café. Nicolas, Caroline et Stéphanie aiment discuter. Ils prennent leur repas rapidement. Nicolas regarde Stéphanie et dit : «Pourquoi est-ce que tu bois de l'eau avec ton croque-monsieur? Regarde, je prends un coca avec mon hot-dog. C'est tellement bon!» «C'est vrai, mais quand j'ai soif, je préfère boire de l'eau. Et toi Caroline?» «Moi aussi. Aujourd'hui, je vais boire de l'eau et un café avec mon sandwich au jambon» «Qu'est-ce qu'il y a Philippe? Tu ne dis rien!» Philippe ne parle pas. Il a faim et il mange un steak-frites avec plaisir.

Traditions

Café, bistro, brasserie

For the past three hundred years, Parisians have been meeting their friends for a meal or drink at a **café, bistro,** or **brasserie.** The first **café** in Paris opened in 1702 and quickly became a place where Parisians discussed current events, read, or played chess over a cup of coffee or some other beverage. This tradition continues today, the **café** or **bistro** being a place where friends meet to have a drink or light snack and to watch the world go by. Although **bistros** have been around for about 300 years, the word **bistro** only dates back to the Russian occupation of Paris in 1814. The Russians used to yell **Bistro!** (Quickly!) in an effort to hurry French waiters, thus giving this type of restaurant its name. The other popular hang-out for Parisians, a **brasserie,** is a restaurant that specializes in Alsatian **choucroute** (sausage and sauerkraut) and seafood. Have students read *A Moveable Feast,* by Ernest Hemingway or one of George Simenon's books, featuring Detective Maigret, to find out more about the **café, bistro,** and **brasserie** tradition.

Recette

*The **croque-monsieur** is a dish typically found in any **café** or **brasserie** throughout France. It is a grilled, ham-and-cheese sandwich that is often served open-faced. The first one was probably made at the turn of the twentieth century in Paris. French people eat them most often at lunch time because they are quick and easy to make. They can be served with a salad or French fries. There is also a **croque-madame,** which is a **croque-monsieur** topped with a fried egg.*

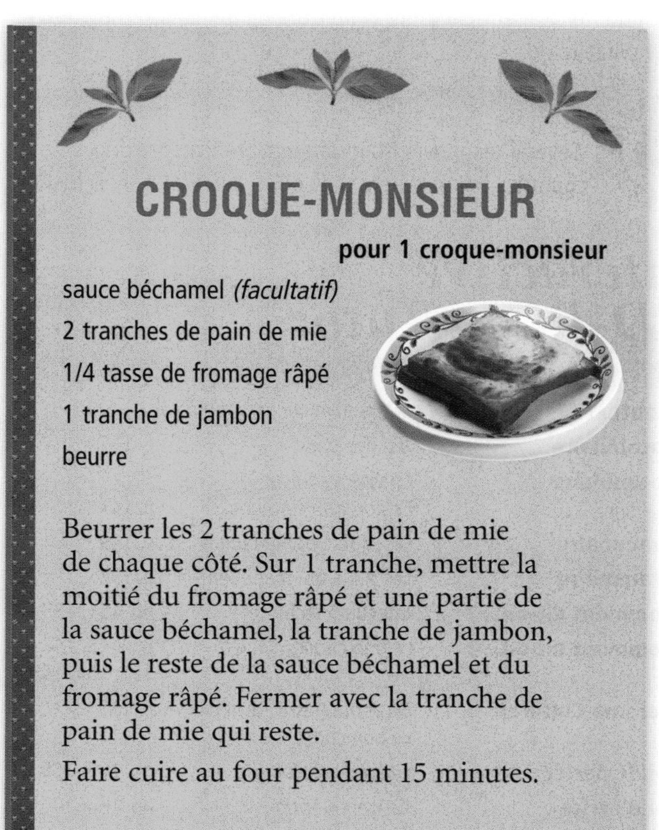

CROQUE-MONSIEUR

pour 1 croque-monsieur

sauce béchamel *(facultatif)*
2 tranches de pain de mie
1/4 tasse de fromage râpé
1 tranche de jambon
beurre

Beurrer les 2 tranches de pain de mie de chaque côté. Sur 1 tranche, mettre la moitié du fromage râpé et une partie de la sauce béchamel, la tranche de jambon, puis le reste de la sauce béchamel et du fromage râpé. Fermer avec la tranche de pain de mie qui reste.

Faire cuire au four pendant 15 minutes.

STANDARDS: 1.3, 3.2, 5.1

Technology

Videocassette 2, Videocassette 5 (captioned version)
DVD Tutor, Disc 1
See Video Guide, pp. 33–38.

DVD/Video

Mise en train • Qu'est-ce qu'on prend?

In this segment of the video, Cécile, Thomas, and Chloé decide to go to a café. Their friend Sébastien is busy and makes an excuse. At the café, they ask for a menu and discuss what they will have. When the waiter arrives, Thomas and Cécile order right away. Chloé has trouble deciding, but finally orders a **croque-monsieur**. When they've finished eating, Thomas asks for the check. Chloé discovers that she can't find her wallet. When the waiter brings the check, they don't know what to do.

Qu'est-ce qu'on prend? (suite)

When the story continues, Thomas, Cécile, and Chloé find that they don't have enough money to pay the bill. Then, they learn that they have been given the bill for another table. They need even more money for their own! As they try to figure out what to do, some tourists start a conversation with them. When the tourists learn of the situation, they insist on paying the difference. As Thomas, Cécile, and Chloé are leaving, Chloé finds her wallet on the ground.

Où retrouves-tu tes amis?

Several teenagers from different French speaking countries tell us where they go to meet with their friends.

Vidéoclips

- **Badoit®**: advertisement for mineral water
- **Orangina®**: advertisement for orange drink

Interactive CD-ROM Tutor

Activity	Activity Type	Pupil's Edition Page
En contexte	*Interactive conversation*	
1. Vocabulaire	Jeu des paires	p. 147
2. Vocabulaire	Chasse au trésor Explorons!/Vérifions!	p. 147
3. Grammaire	Les mots qui manquent	p. 149
4. Grammaire	Les mots qui manquent	p. 152
5. Comment dit-on... ?	Chacun à sa place	pp. 151, 155
6. Comment dit-on... ?	Le bon choix	pp. 145, 148, 151, 154, 155
Panorama Culturel	Où retrouves-tu tes amis? Le bon choix	p. 150
A toi de parler	*Guided recording*	pp. 164–165
A toi d'écrire	*Guided writing*	pp. 164–165

Teacher Management System

Launch the program, type "admin" in the password area and press RETURN. Log on to **www.hrw.com/CDROMTUTOR** for a detailed explanation of the Teacher Management System.

DVD Tutor

The *DVD Tutor* contains all material from the *Video Program* as described above. French captions are available for use at your discretion for all sections of the video. The *DVD Tutor* also provides a variety of video-based activities that assess students' understanding of the **Mise en train, Suite,** and **Panorama Culturel.**

This part of the *DVD Tutor* may be used on any DVD video player connected to a television or video monitor.

In addition to the video material and the video-based comprehension activities, the *DVD Tutor* also contains the entire *Interactive CD-ROM Tutor* in DVD-ROM format. Each DVD disc contains the activities from all 12 chapters of the *Interactive CD-ROM Tutor.*

This part of the *DVD Tutor* may be used on a Macintosh® or Windows® computer with a DVD-ROM drive.

To preview all resources available for this chapter, use the **One-Stop Planner CD-ROM,** Disc 2.

Visit Holt Online
go.hrw.com
KEYWORD: WA3 PARIS-5
Online Edition

Go.Online!

Online Edition

The Online Edition for Allez, viens! *allows students access to their textbooks anytime anywhere.*

- *Audio at point of use*
- *Additional practice activities*
- *Self-test activities*
- *Online reference tools*
- *Entire Video Program (Enhanced version)*
- *Interactive Notebook (Enhanced version)*

HRW Atlas

Internet Activités

video

audio

presentation

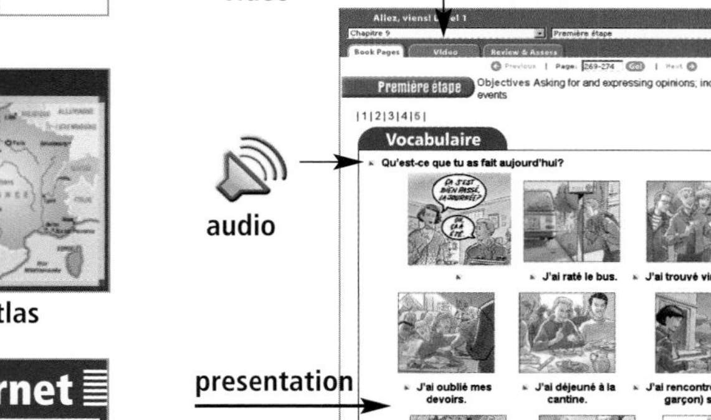

tools (glossary, grammar, cahier électronique)

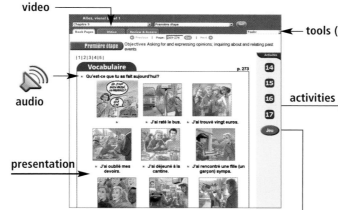

activities

16 Tu as déjà fait ça?
Ecrivons/Parlons Make a list of ten activities that classmate might have done last to find a classmate who did each activity. When you f who did one of the activities, write his or her name or the activity. Try to find a different person for each acti

Activités	Nom
1. J'ai gagné cent dollars.	Jeff
2. J'ai chanté dans la chorale.	Lisa

Cahier électronique

Notebook

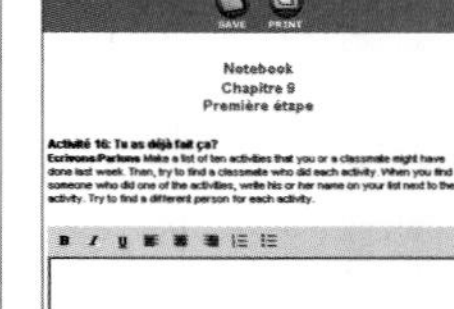

Activités Internet

These guided internet activities include a worksheet and pre-selected and pre-screened authentic web sites from the francophone world. You can use these activities

- to help students develop research skills in the target language
- to introduce students to authentic cultural information
- as a project

Jeux interactifs

You can use the interactive activities in this chapter

- to practice grammar, vocabulary, and chapter functions
- as homework
- as an assessment option
- as a self-test
- to prepare for the Chapter Test

Projet You are publishing a new travel guide named "Gastronomic weekend in France." First, have your students pick one or two different regions in France. Then, have them do a Web search to find hotels or bed and breakfasts in that area. They should write an article describing an ideal getaway weekend in that region. Have them describe the lodging conditions, the meals offered, and the price for two nights.

Chapitre 5 : On va au café?

Textbook Listening Activities Scripts 

Première étape

6 p. 145

1. — On va au café?
— Oui, allons-y!
2. — On fait du jogging?
— Ça ne me dit rien.
3. — On écoute de la musique?
— Oui, d'accord. C'est une bonne idée.
4. — On joue au basket?
— Je ne peux pas. J'ai des devoirs à faire.
5. — On fait des photos?
— Désolé, mais j'ai des courses à faire.

Answers to Activity 6
1. accepts
2. turns down
3. accepts
4. turns down
5. turns down

9 p. 148

1. Moi, je voudrais une pizza et un coca, s'il vous plaît.
2. Un croque-monsieur, s'il vous plaît.
3. Je voudrais un jus de fruit.
4. Et moi, je vais prendre un steak-frites, s'il vous plaît.
5. Un sandwich au fromage pour moi.

Answers to Activity 9
1. Paul
2. Minh
3. Didier
4. Mamadou
5. Nabil

Deuxième étape

14 p. 151

1. Je vais prendre un steak-frites, s'il vous plaît.
2. Vous avez choisi?
3. Donnez-moi un croque-monsieur, s'il vous plaît.
4. Qu'est-ce que vous avez comme sandwiches?
5. Vous prenez?
6. Apportez-moi un jus de pomme, s'il vous plaît.

Answers to Activity 14
1. le client
2. le serveur
3. le client
4. le client
5. le serveur
6. le client

The following scripts are for the listening activities found in the *Pupil's Edition*. For Student Response Forms, see *Listening Activities,* pages 35–37. To provide students with additional listening practice, see *Listening Activities,* pages 39–42.

One-Stop Planner CD-ROM

To preview all resources available for this chapter, use the **One-Stop Planner CD-ROM**, Disc 2.

Troisième étape

21 p. 154

1. Cette pizza, elle n'est pas très bonne.
2. La glace au chocolat, c'est délicieux!
3. Il n'est pas terrible, ce hot-dog.
4. Ne mange pas ça! C'est dégoûtant!
5. Il est bon, ce croque-monsieur.

Answers to Activity 21

1. dislikes
2. likes
3. dislikes
4. dislikes
5. likes

25 p. 155

1. Apportez-moi un coca, s'il vous plaît.
2. L'addition, s'il vous plaît.
3. Je vais prendre un jus de pomme, s'il vous plaît.
4. Ça fait combien, s'il vous plaît?
5. Donnez-moi une limonade, s'il vous plaît.

Answers to Activity 25

1. ordering
2. getting ready to pay the check
3. ordering
4. getting ready to pay the check
5. ordering

PRONONCIATION, P. 157

For the scripts for Parts A and B, see p. 157.
The script for Part C is below.

C. A écrire *(dictation)*

— Ça fait combien, un jus d'orange et un sandwich?
— Huit euros trente-cinq.

Mise en pratique

1 p. 164

1. — Michel, on prend un sandwich?
— D'accord. Je voudrais un sandwich au jambon et de l'eau minérale.

2. — Je vais prendre une pizza.
— Moi aussi.

3. — Vous avez choisi?
— Apportez-moi un steak-frites et un coca, s'il vous plaît.

4. — Je voudrais une coupe Melba.
— Bonne idée.

Answers to Mise en pratique, Activity 1

1. Café de la gare
2. Café Américain
3. Café Américain
4. Café de Paris

Chapitre 5 : On va au café?

50-Minute Lesson Plans

Day 1

CHAPTER OPENER 5 min.
- Thinking Critically suggestions, ATE, p. 140
- Present Chapter Objectives, p. 141. See Focusing on Outcomes, ATE, p. 141.
- Photo Flash!, ATE, p. 141

MISE EN TRAIN 40 min.
- Presenting **Mise en train** and Preteaching Vocabulary, ATE, p. 142, using Videocassette 2
- Do Activities 1–5, p. 144.

Wrap-Up 5 min.
- Have pairs of students present their solution to Isabelle's problem by role-playing the situation between Isabelle and the waiter.

Homework Options
Cahier d'activités, p. 49, Act. 1

Day 2

PREMIERE ETAPE
Quick Review 10 min.
- Check homework.
- Bell Work, ATE, p. 145

Comment dit-on... ?, p. 145 15 min.
- Presenting **Comment dit-on... ?,** ATE, p. 145
- Play Audio CD for Activity 6, p. 145.
- Do Activity 7 and 8, p. 146.

Vocabulaire, p. 147 15 min.
- Presenting **Vocabulaire,** ATE, p. 147, using Teaching Transparencies 5-A and 5-B.
- Language Notes, and Language-to-Language, ATE, p. 147
- Play Audio CD for Activity 9, p. 148.
- Do Activity 10, p. 148.

Wrap-Up 10 min.
- Select food or beverage items and have students in teams illustrate them to their teammates. The first team to guess and name the item wins a point.

Homework Options
Cahier d'activités, p. 50, Acts. 3–4
Travaux pratiques de grammaire, pp. 35–36, Acts. 1–4

Day 3

PREMIERE ETAPE
Quick Review 10 min.
- Check homework.
- Name local restaurants and have students tell you the food items they serve there.

Comment dit-on... ?, p. 148 10 min.
- Presenting **Comment dit-on... ?,** ATE, p. 148

Grammaire, p. 149 20 min.
- Presenting **Grammaire,** ATE, p. 149
- **De bons conseils,** p. 149 and Thinking Critically, ATE, p. 149
- Do Activities 12–13, p. 149.
- Do Travaux pratiques de grammaire, p. 37, Acts. 6–7.

Wrap-Up 10 min.
Have students pair off and take turns recommending five things to eat and telling why.

Homework Options
Study for **Première étape** quiz.

Day 4

PREMIERE ETAPE
Quiz 5-1 20 min.
- Administer Quiz 5-1A or 5-1B.

PANORAMA CULTUREL 25 min.
- Present **Panorama Culturel,** p. 150, using Videocassette 2.
- Do **Qu'en penses-tu?** and read **Savais-tu que... ?,** p. 150.
- See Language Note, ATE, p. 150.
- **Panorama Culturel,** Interactive CD-ROM Tutor, Disc 2

Wrap-Up 5 min.
- Thinking Critically, ATE, p. 150

Homework Options
Cahier d'activités, p. 60, Act. 27

Day 5

DEUXIEME ETAPE
Quick Review 10 min.
- Bell Work, ATE, p. 151

Comment dit-on... ?, p. 151 30 min.
- Presenting **Comment dit-on... ?,** ATE, p. 151
- **A la française,** p. 151
- Play Audio CD for Activity 14, p. 151.
- Do Activity 15, p. 151.
- Have students prepare and present Activity 16 on p. 152, to the class. You might videotape each pair of students and have a viewing and "awards ceremony" for best actor and actress on another class day.

Wrap-Up 10 min.
- Have students imagine that they are about to go on a long journey. Have them say which food and beverage items they would pack in their lunch box for the journey.

Homework Options
Cahier d'activités, p. 53, Acts. 10–11

Day 6

DEUXIEME ETAPE
Quick Review 10 min.
- Check homework.
- Say statements that either a server or a customer might say. Have students raise their left hand for server statements and their right hand for customer statements.

Grammaire, p. 152 30 min.
- Presenting **Grammaire,** ATE, p. 152
- Review the classroom commands learned in the Preliminary Chapter, p. 11.
- Kinesthetic Learners, ATE, p. 152
- Do Activity 17, p. 152.
- **Note culturelle,** p. 153.
- Do Activity 18 or 19, p. 153.
- Travaux pratiques de grammaire, p. 38, Acts. 8–10

Wrap-Up 10 min.
- Play Game: **Jacques a dit** with new commands, ATE, p. 15C.

Homework Options
Study for **Deuxième étape** quiz.

For alternative lesson plans by chapter section, to create your own customized plans, or to preview all resources available for this chapter, use the **One-Stop Planner CD-ROM**, Disc 2.

For additional homework suggestions, see activities accompanied by this symbol throughout the chapter.

Day 7

DEUXIEME ETAPE

Quiz 5-2 20 min.
- Administer Quiz 5-2A or 5-2B.

Project 25 min.
- Have students begin the project **Notre café,** ATE, p. 139C.

Wrap-Up 5 min.
- Discuss **Note culturelle,** ATE, p. 153. Have students ask each other if they play the games mentioned in the **Note culturelle,** ATE and which video games they like to play.

Homework Options

Have students search for photos of food with which they can decorate their project menus.

Day 8

TROISIEME ETAPE

Quick Review 20 min.
- Have students complete their project menus.

Comment dit-on... ?, p. 154 20 min.
- Presenting **Comment dit-on... ?,** ATE, p. 154
- Play Audio CD for Activity 21, p. 154.
- Discuss **Note culturelle,** p. 154.
- Do Activity 22 or 23, pp. 154–155.

Wrap-Up 10 min.
- Write a variety of foods and drinks on the board and ask students' opinions of them.

Homework Options

Cahier d'activités, pp. 56–57, Acts. 18–21
Travaux pratiques de grammaire, p. 39, Acts. 11–12

Day 9

TROISIEME ETAPE

Quick Review 10 min.
- Check homework.

Comment dit-on... ?, p. 155 15 min.
- Presenting **Comment dit-on... ?,** ATE, p. 155
- Play Audio CD for Activity 25, p. 155.
- **Tu te rappelles?,** p. 155, and **Note culturelle,** p. 156
- Cahier d'activités, pp. 57–58, Acts. 22–24

Prononciation, p. 157 15 min.
- Complete presentation and do Activities A–C, p. 157, using Audio CD 5.

Wrap-Up 10 min.
- Do Activity 28, p. 156. Have students use the menus they created as they act out their scene.

Homework Options

Study for **Troisième étape** quiz.

Day 10

TROISIEME ETAPE

Quiz 5-3 20 min.
- Administer Quiz 5-3A or Quiz 5-3B.

LISONS! **25 min.**
- Discuss the **Stratégie pour lire,** p. 158, then do Prereading Activity A, ATE, p. 158.
- Do Reading Activities B–H, pp. 158–159. Monitoring Comprehension, ATE, p. 158.
- Postreading Activity I, Using Text Organizers, ATE, p. 159.

Wrap-Up 5 min.
- Math Link, ATE, p. 158

Homework Options

Cahier d'activités, p. 59, Act. 26

Day 11

LISONS!

Quick Review 5 min.
- Check homework.

MISE EN PRATIQUE 35 min.
- Play Audio CD for Activity 1, p. 164.
- Do Activity 2, p. 164.
- Math Link, ATE, p. 164
- Do Activity 3, p. 165.
- Begin **Ecrivons!,** p. 165.

Wrap-Up 10 min.
- Have partners complete **Jeu de rôle,** p. 165.

Homework Options

Que sais-je?, p. 166
Finish **Ecrivons!,** Pupil's Edition, p. 165.

Day 12

MISE EN PRATIQUE

Quick Review 15 min.
- Check homework and collect **Ecrivons!** posters.
- Play Game: **Jeu de concours,** ATE, p. 139C.

Chapter Review 35 min.
- Review Chapter 5. Choose from **Grammaire supplémentaire,** Grammar Tutor for Students of French, Activities for Communication, Listening Activities, Interactive CD-ROM Tutor, or **Jeux interactifs.**

Homework Options

Study for Chapter 5 Test.

Assessment

Test, Chapter 5 50 min.
- Administer Chapter 5 Test. Select from Testing Program, Alternative Assessment Guide, Test Generator, or Standardized Assessment Tutor.

Chapitre 5 : On va au café?

90-Minute Lesson Plans

Block 1

CHAPTER OPENER 5 min.
- Present Chapter Objectives, p. 141. See Focusing on Outcomes, ATE, p. 141.
- Thinking Critically suggestions, ATE, p. 140
- Photo Flash!, ATE, p. 141

MISE EN TRAIN 45 min.
- Presenting **Mise en train,** ATE, p. 142
- Preteaching Vocabulary, ATE, p. 142
- View video of **Mise en train,** Videocassette 2, Video Guide, p. 33. Do Activity Master 1, Viewing and Postviewing activities, Video Guide, p. 36

PREMIERE ETAPE

Comment dit-on… ?, p. 145 20 min.
- Ask students which French foods they have heard of or eaten. Ask them to suggest French words we use to talk about food (**purée, à la mode, sauté, entrée**).
- Presenting **Comment dit-on… ?,** ATE, p. 145
- Language Note, ATE, p. 145
- Slower Pace, ATE, p. 145
- Play Audio CD for Activity 6, p. 145.
- Do Activity 7, p. 146. See **Tu te rappelles?,** p. 146.

Vocabulaire, p. 147 15 min.
- Presenting **Vocabulaire,** ATE, p. 147
- Language Notes, Language-to-Language, and Culture Notes, ATE, p. 147
- Language Note, ATE, p. 148

Wrap-Up 5 min.
- Summarize what happened in the **Mise en train** using Chapter 5 **Mise en train** Transparencies.

Homework Options
Travaux pratiques de grammaire, pp. 35–36, Acts. 1–4
Cahier d'activités, p. 50, Act. 2

Block 2

PREMIERE ETAPE

Quick Review 15 min.
- Play Audio CD for Activity 9, p. 148. See Slower Pace, ATE, p. 148. Combine with Activity 10, p. 148, and then call on some students to present to the rest of the class.

Grammaire: the verb *prendre,* p. 149 45 min.
- Presenting **Grammaire,** ATE, p. 149. See Language Note, ATE, p. 149.
- Do Activities 12 and 13, p. 149.
- **De bons conseils,** p. 149
- Thinking Critically, ATE, p. 149
- **Grammaire supplémentaire,** pp. 160–161, Acts. 1–2

Comment dit-on... ?, p. 148 5 min.
- Presenting **Comment dit-on… ?,** ATE, p. 148

PANORAMA CULTUREL 20 min.
- Presenting **Panorama Culturel,** ATE, p. 150, using Videocassette 2
- Thinking Critically and Language Note, ATE, p. 150
- Read **Savais-tu que… ?,** p. 150.
- Do **Qu'en penses-tu?,** p. 150.

Wrap-Up 5 min.
- Have students pair off taking turns recommending five things to eat and drink and telling why.

Homework Options
Study for **Première étape** quiz.
Travaux pratiques de grammaire, pp. 36–37, Acts. 5–7
Cahier d'activités, pp. 51–52, Acts. 5–9

Block 3

PREMIERE ETAPE

Quick Review 10 min.
- Activities for Communication, p. 145, Situation Card 5-1: Interview

Quiz 5-1 20 min.
- Administer Quiz 5-1A or 5-1B.

DEUXIEME ETAPE

Quick Review 5 min.
- Activities for Communication, pp. 25–26, Communicative Activities 5-1A and 5-1B

Comment dit-on... ?, p. 151 40 min.
- Bell Work, ATE, p. 151
- Presenting **Comment dit-on... ?,** ATE, p. 151
- Play Audio CD for Activity 14, p. 151.
- Do Activity 15, p. 151.
- **A la française,** p. 151
- TPR Storytelling, p. 18: Give students a copy of the **mini-histoire** (cartoon) without the script and have them recreate the dialogue. Allow 10 minutes to prepare and 10 minutes to present to the class.

Grammaire, p. 152 5 min.
- Presenting **Grammaire,** ATE, p. 152

Wrap-Up 10 min.
- Game: **Jacques a dit,** ATE, p. 15C

Homework Options
Cahier d'activités, pp. 53–54, Acts. 10–13
Travaux pratiques de grammaire, p. 38, Acts. 8–10

One-Stop Planner CD-ROM

For alternative lesson plans by chapter section, to create your own customized plans, or to preview all resources available for this chapter, use the **One-Stop Planner CD-ROM**, Disc 2.

For additional homework suggestions, see activities accompanied by this symbol throughout the chapter.

Block 4

DEUXIEME ETAPE

Quick Review 10 min.
- Activities for Communication, pp. 27–28, Communicative Activities 5-2A and 5-2B

Grammaire, p. 152 40 min.
- Do Activity 17, p. 152.
- **Grammaire supplémentaire,** pp. 161–162, Acts. 3–5
- **Note culturelle,** p. 153
- Do Activity 19, p. 153 with Cooperative Learning, Culture Notes, and **Note culturelle,** ATE, p. 153.

TROISIEME ETAPE

Comment dit-on... ?, p. 154 35 min.
- Presenting **Comment dit-on... ?,** ATE, p. 154
- Play Audio CD for Activity 21, p. 154.
- **Note culturelle,** p. 154
- Do Activity 22, p. 154.
- Do Activity 24, p. 155. See Slower Pace and Language Note, ATE, p. 155.

Wrap-Up 5 min.
- Bell Work, ATE, p. 154

Homework Options

Study for **Deuxième étape** quiz.
Cahier d'activités, p. 54, Acts. 14–15 and p. 56, Acts. 19–20
Travaux pratiques de grammaire , p. 39, Acts. 11–12

Block 5

DEUXIEME ETAPE

Quick Review 10 min.

Quiz 5-2 20 min.
- Administer Quiz 5-2A or 5-2B.

TROISIEME ETAPE

Comment dit-on... ?, p. 155 30 min.
- Presenting **Comment dit-on... ?,** ATE, p. 155.
- Culture Notes, ATE, p. 155
- **Tu te rappelles?,** p. 155
- Play Audio CD for Activity 25, p. 155.
- **Note culturelle,** p. 156
- Do Activity 27, p. 156 and Group Work, ATE, p. 156.

Prononciation, p. 157 20 min.
- Present **Prononciation,** ATE, p. 157.
- Play Audio CD for Activities A, B, and C, p. 157. See Language Note, ATE, p. 157.

Wrap-Up 10 min.
- Activities for Communication, pp. 29-30, Communicative Activity 5-3A and 5-3B

Homework Options

Study for **Troisième étape** quiz.
Grammaire supplémentaire, p. 163, Acts. 8–9
Cahier d'activités, p. 57, Acts. 21–23
Travaux pratiques de grammaire, pp. 39–40, Acts. 13–14

Block 6

TROISIEME ETAPE

Quick Review 10 min.

Quiz 5-3 20 min.
- Administer Quiz 5-3A or 5-3B.

LISONS! 20 min
- Discuss the **Stratégie pour lire,** p. 158, then do Prereading Activity A, ATE, p. 158
- Do Reading Activities B–H, pp. 158–159, ATE, p. 158.
- Do Postreading Activity I, Using Text Organizers, ATE, p. 159.

MISE EN PRATIQUE 20 min.
- Play Audio CD for Activity 1 p. 164.
- Do Activity 3, p. 164.
- Begin **Ecrivons!,** p. 165.

Wrap-Up 20 min.
- Activity 28, p. 156 and Culture Note, ATE, p. 156. Allow 10 min. to prepare and 10 min. to present to class.

Homework Options

Que sais-je?, p. 166
Finish **Ecrivons!,** Pupil's Edition, p. 165.
Study for Chapter 5 Test.

Block 7

MISE EN PRATIQUE

Quick Review 10 min.
- Check homework and collect **Ecrivons!** posters.

Chapter Review 30 min.
- Review Chapter 5. Choose from **Grammaire supplémentaire,** Grammar Tutor for Students of French, Activities for Communication, Listening Activities, Interactive CD-ROM Tutor, or **Jeux interactifs.**

Test, Chapter 5 50 min.
- Administer Chapter 5 Test. Select from Testing Program, Alternative Assessment Guide, Test Generator, or Standardized Assessment Tutor.

CHAPITRE 5

One-Stop Planner CD-ROM

For resource information, see the **One-Stop Planner**, Disc 2.

Pacing Tips

Keep in mind while planning your lessons that the **Première étape** in this chapter covers a lot of new vocabulary, grammar and functions. The **Troisième étape** is the lightest. For Lesson Plans and timing suggestions, see pages 139I–139L.

Meeting the Standards

Communication

- Making suggestions; making excuses, p. 145
- Making a recommendation, p. 148
- Getting someone's attention; ordering food and beverages, p. 151
- Inquiring about and expressing likes and dislikes, p. 154
- Paying the check, p. 155

Cultures

- Culture Notes, pp. 147, 153, 155
- Panorama Culturel, p. 150
- Note culturelle, p. 153
- Note culturelle, p. 154
- Note culturelle, p. 156

Connections

- Math Link, pp. 158, 164

Comparisons

- Language-to-Language, p. 147
- Thinking Critically: Synthesizing, p. 149
- Language-to-Language, p. 149
- Thinking Critically: Comparing and Contrasting, p. 150
- Language-to-Language, p. 153

Communities

- De l'école au travail, p. 156

Connections and Comparisons

Thinking Critically

Comparing and Contrasting Ask students if they have any preconceptions about French cafés and if they can imagine going there and enjoying themselves. Have them discuss how their experience at a French café might be different from that at a café in the U.S.

Thinking Critically

Evaluating Ask students if there are any restaurants where they live that have both indoor and outdoor seating. Do many people choose to eat outside? Ask students what factors they consider when deciding whether to eat inside or outside. Ask if they have a preference and why.

STANDARDS: 4.2

CHAPITRE 5

On va au café?

Objectives

In this chapter you will learn to

Première étape

- make suggestions
- make excuses
- make a recommendation

Deuxième étape

- get someone's attention
- order food and beverages

Troisième étape

- inquire about and express likes and dislikes
- pay the check

Visit Holt Online
go.hrw.com
KEYWORD: WA3 PARIS-5
Online Edition

◀ On va au café?

Chapter Opener

CHAPITRE 5

Focusing on Outcomes

After reading the list of outcomes with students, have them imagine how the functions could be used in a café setting.
NOTE: The self-check activities in **Que sais-je?** on page 166 help students assess their achievement of the objectives.

Cultures and Communities

Photo Flash!

As was the practice in the 1920s in Paris, young writers, such as Ernest Hemingway and F. Scott Fitzgerald, frequented **Les Deux Magots** to discuss their ideas with other writers and even to do some of their writing. Other cafés, such as the **Café de Flore,** were also frequented by such intellectuals as Simone de Beauvoir and Jean-Paul Sartre, who discussed philosophy and current events.

STANDARDS: 2.1

CHAPITRE 5

Teaching Resources
pp. 142–144

PRINT

- Lesson Planner, p. 23
- Video Guide, pp. 34, 36
- Cahier d'activités, p. 49

MEDIA 

- One-Stop Planner
- Video Program
  Mise en train
  Videocassette 2, 25:09–28:22
  Videocassette 5 (captioned version), 41:06–44:21
  Suite
  Videocassette 2, 28:25–32:15
  Videocassette 5 (captioned version), 44:27–48:14
- DVD Tutor, Disc 1
- Audio Compact Discs, CD 5, Trs. 1–2
- **Mise en train** Transparencies

Presenting
Mise en train

Have students quickly scan the text to pick out any menu items they might recognize. Have them guess which items are food and which are beverages. You might have them figure out the price of the Coupe Melba in dollars, using the current exchange rates. Then, have students view the video and read the episode in groups.

Mise en train Transparencies

The **roman-photo** is an abridged version of the video episode.

MISE EN TRAIN ▪ *Qu'est-ce qu'on prend?*

CD 5 Trs. 1–2

DVD VIDEO

Stratégie pour comprendre
Where does this story take place? What do you expect Chloé, Cécile, Thomas, and Sébastien to talk about in that setting? What could happen at the end to make them upset?

Chloé

Thomas

Cécile

Le serveur

1 **Chloé :** Allô? Sébastien? Salut. C'est Chloé. Dis, on va au café. Tu viens avec nous?

2 **Chloé :** Sébastien ne peut pas venir avec nous. Il a des devoirs à faire. Bon. On y va?

3 **Thomas :** Qu'est-ce que vous prenez?
Cécile : Je vais prendre une menthe à l'eau.
Chloé : Euh... je ne sais pas.
Thomas : Moi, je vais prendre une glace.

4 **Thomas :** C'est combien, les coupes Melba?
Chloé : Trois trente-cinq.

Preteaching Vocabulary

Guessing words from context

Tell students to begin by thinking about what usually happens when they go to a restaurant. You may wish to write the following sentence on the board and ask students to finish the sequence: 1. The waitperson arrives and asks what you'll be drinking. 2. ... Then, tell students to follow the story, using the sequence they have created while guessing at the meaning of these expressions:

3 **Qu'est-ce que vous prenez?**
4 **C'est combien?**
5 **Vous avez choisi?**
9 **L'addition, s'il vous plaît.**

STANDARDS: 1.2

5
Le serveur : Vous avez choisi?
Cécile : Apportez-moi une menthe à l'eau, s'il vous plaît.

6
Thomas : Tu aimes le fromage?
Chloé : Oui.
Thomas : Prends un croque-monsieur.
Chloé : D'accord. Un croque-monsieur pour moi, s'il vous plaît!

7
Chloé : Qu'est-ce que vous avez comme jus de fruit?
Le serveur : Nous avons du jus d'orange, du jus de pomme...
Chloé : Un jus d'orange, s'il vous plaît.

8
Le serveur : Une coupe Melba, une coupe Melba, une menthe à l'eau, une eau minérale, un croque-monsieur et un jus d'orange. Bon appétit!

9
Thomas : Monsieur! L'addition, s'il vous plaît.
Le serveur : Tout de suite.

10
Chloé : Eh, je ne trouve pas mon porte-monnaie! Je n'ai pas d'argent!
Cécile : C'est pas vrai!

Cahier d'activités, p. 49, Act. 1

Using the Captioned Video/DVD

If students have difficulty understanding French spoken at a normal speed, use Videocassette 5 to allow students to see the French captions for ***Qu'est-ce qu'on prend?*** and ***Qu'est-ce qu'on prend? (suite).*** Hearing the language and watching the story will reduce anxiety about the new language and facilitate comprehension. The reinforcement of seeing the written vocabulary words as they watch the gestures and actions will help prepare students to do the comprehension activities on page 144.
NOTE: The *DVD Tutor* contains captions for all sections of the *Video Program.*

Challenge

You might type and distribute copies of the dialogue with some of the words deleted. Have students work in pairs to complete the dialogue. You might give a small prize to the pair that finishes first.

Qu'est-ce qu'on prend? (suite)

When the story continues, Chloé, Cécile, and Thomas find out they don't have enough money to pay the bill. Then, they learn that they got the wrong bill and they need even more money for their own! Some tourists at the next table learn of the situation and insist on paying the difference. As the three friends are leaving, Chloé finds her wallet on the ground.

STANDARDS: 1.2

Mise en train

CHAPITRE 5

Additional Practice

2 As a variation, make the actual remarks that are paraphrased here **(Apportez-moi une menthe à l'eau, s'il vous plaît.)** and have students choose the correct paraphrase. **(Cécile commande une menthe à l'eau.)**

These activities check for comprehension only. Students should not yet be expected to produce language modeled in **Mise en train.**

1 Tu as compris? See answers below.

Answer the following questions about ***Qu'est-ce qu'on prend?***

1. What is the relationship between the teenagers in ***Qu'est-ce qu'on prend?***
2. Where are they at the beginning of the story?
3. Where do they decide to go?
4. Who has trouble deciding what to order?
5. What is the problem at the end of the story?

2 Mets en ordre

Mets les phrases suivantes en ordre d'après ***Qu'est-ce qu'on prend?***

1. Cécile commande une menthe à l'eau. 2
2. Thomas demande l'addition. 5
3. Chloé invite Sébastien à aller au café. 1
4. Chloé ne retrouve pas son argent. 6
5. Le serveur dit «Bon appétit!». 4
6. Chloé commande un jus d'orange. 3

3 Les deux font la paire

Choisis la bonne réponse d'après ***Qu'est-ce qu'on prend?***

1. On va au café? c
2. Qu'est-ce que vous prenez? b
3. C'est combien, les coupes Melba? d
4. Qu'est-ce que vous avez comme jus de fruit? a

a. Nous avons du jus d'orange, du jus de pomme...
b. Je vais prendre une menthe à l'eau.
c. Désolé. J'ai des devoirs à faire.
d. Trois trente-cinq.

4 Cherche les expressions

Look back at ***Qu'est-ce qu'on prend?*** What do the students say to . . . See answers below.

1. give an excuse for someone?
2. ask if someone's ready to order?
3. order food?
4. ask what kind of fruit juice the restaurant serves?
5. ask how much something costs?
6. ask for the check?

Apportez-moi...
Vous avez choisi?
Il a des devoirs à faire.
L'addition, s'il vous plaît.
Je vais prendre...
C'est combien,... ?
Qu'est-ce que vous avez comme jus de fruit?

5 Et maintenant, à toi

Chloé is in an embarrassing situation. What do you think she is going to do? Take turns with a partner suggesting ways Chloé and her friends might resolve their problem.

Answers

1
1. friends, classmates
2. at someone's house
3. to a café
4. Chloé
5. Chloé can't find her wallet. She has no money.

4
1. Il a des devoirs à faire.
2. Vous avez choisi?
3. Apportez-moi...
4. Qu'est-ce que vous avez comme jus de fruit?
5. C'est combien, ... ?
6. L'addition, s'il vous plaît.

Comprehension Check

Slower Pace

2 Before they begin, have students look for cognates in the title and the sentences in this activity **(en ordre, serveur, invite).**

3 You might choose to have students work in pairs, taking turns asking a question and finding an appropriate response.

Challenge

5 Have each pair of students brainstorm several solutions to this situation. Then, have them explain the solution they prefer to the class. Once all the solutions have been presented, ask the class to vote on the best one.

STANDARDS: 1.1, 1.2, 5.1

Objectives Making suggestions; making excuses; making a recommendation

WA3 PARIS-5

Comment dit-on...?

Making suggestions; making excuses

To make suggestions:

On va au café? *How about going to the café?*
On fait du ski?
On joue au base-ball?

To make excuses:

Désolé(e). J'ai des devoirs à faire. *Sorry. I have homework to do.*
J'ai des courses à faire. *I have errands to do.*
J'ai des trucs à faire. *I have some things to do.*
J'ai des tas de choses à faire. *I have lots of things to do.*
Je ne peux pas parce que... *I can't because . . .*

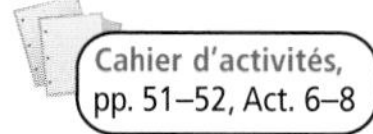
Cahier d'activités, pp. 51–52, Act. 6–8

6 Qu'est-ce que tu as envie de faire? See scripts and answers on p. 139G.

Ecoutons Listen to the following dialogues. Do the speakers accept or turn down the suggestions?

CD 5 Tr. 3

Communication for All Students

Language Note

The term **trucs** is informal and very commonly used. Students can use **truc(s)** when they don't know the word for something: **J'aime bien ces trucs.** *(I like these things.)*; **Tu as vu ce truc-là?** *(Did you see that thingamajig over there?)*. Ask students if they know other words in English that can be used in this situation.

Slower Pace

6 Before students listen to the recording, have them practice distinguishing acceptance from refusal. Say aloud several expressions **(D'accord./Bonne idée./Ça ne me dit rien.)** and tell students to gesture thumbs-up if they hear an acceptance and thumbs-down if they hear a refusal.

Première étape

CHAPITRE 5

Teaching Resources
pp. 145–149

PRINT

- Lesson Planner, p. 24
- TPR Storytelling Book, pp. 17, 20
- Listening Activities, pp. 35, 39
- Activities for Communication, pp. 25–26, 95, 98, 145–146
- Travaux pratiques de grammaire, pp. 35–37
- Grammar Tutor for Students of French, Chapter 5
- Cahier d'activités, pp. 50–52
- Testing Program, pp. 105–108
- Alternative Assessment Guide, p. 36
- Student Make-Up Assignments, Chapter 5

MEDIA 

- One-Stop Planner
- Audio Compact Discs, CD 5, Trs. 3–4, 19, 25–26
- Teaching Transparencies: 5-1, 5-A, 5-B; **Grammaire supplémentaire** Answers; Travaux pratiques de grammaire Answers
- Interactive CD-ROM Tutor, Disc 2

Bell Work

Have students write whether they like or dislike the following foods: **le chocolat, la glace, les escargots, les hamburgers, les frites, la pizza.**

Presenting
Comment dit-on... ?

Read aloud the conversation in the cartoon. Ask students which student is going to the café and which one isn't and why. Then, suggest activities to students **(On joue au basket?),** prompting various excuses. Write activities on the board and have partners use them to make suggestions and respond with excuses.

Première étape

CHAPITRE 5

Teaching Resources
pp. 145–149

PRINT 

- Lesson Planner, p. 24
- TPR Storytelling Book, pp. 17, 20
- Listening Activities, pp. 35, 39
- Activities for Communication, pp. 25–26, 95, 98, 145–146
- Travaux pratiques de grammaire, pp. 35–37
- Grammar Tutor for Students of French, Chapter 5
- Cahier d'activités, pp. 50–52
- Testing Program, pp. 105–108
- Alternative Assessment Guide, p. 36
- Student Make-Up Assignments, Chapter 5

MEDIA

- One-Stop Planner
- Audio Compact Discs, CD 5, Trs. 3–4, 19, 25–26
- Teaching Transparencies: 5-1, 5-A, 5-B; **Grammaire supplémentaire** Answers; Travaux pratiques de grammaire Answers
- Interactive CD-ROM Tutor, Disc 2

Teaching Suggestion

8 Have students exchange papers and edit each other's work. They should not make any corrections, but simply underline whatever is incorrect and return the papers. Students should then make their own corrections and rewrite their notes.

Portfolio

8 **Written** This item is appropriate for students' written portfolios. For portfolio suggestions, see *Alternative Assessment Guide,* pages iv–17.

Tu te rappelles?

Do you remember the following ways to accept a suggestion?

D'accord.
Bonne idée.

Do you remember the following ways to turn down a suggestion?

Ça ne me dit rien. J'aime mieux...
Désolé(e), mais je ne peux pas.

7 Qu'est-ce qu'on fait?

Parlons Suggest to your friends that you all do these activities after class. They will either accept your suggestions or turn them down and make excuses. Take turns making suggestions.

EXEMPLE —On... ?
—D'accord,... *or* Désolé(e),...

1. On va au café?

2. On joue au foot(ball)?

3. On regarde la télévision?

4. On écoute de la musique?

5. On va au concert?

8 Un petit mot

Ecrivons You and your friend have agreed to go to the café on Saturday. You can't make it. Write your friend a note. Say that you can't go, make an excuse, and suggest another activity at another time.

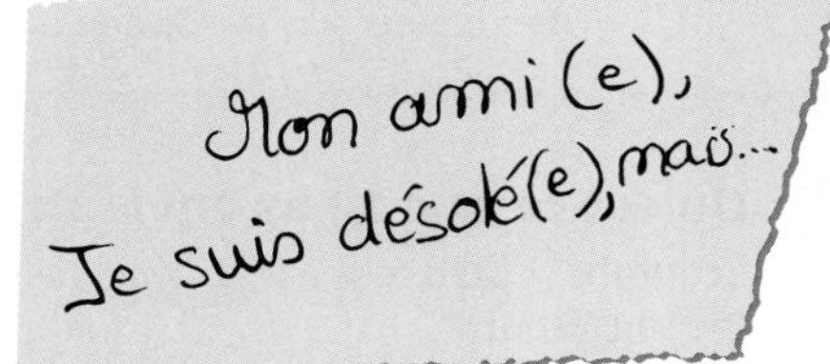
Mon ami (e),
Je suis désolé(e), mais...

Communication for All Students

Building on Previous Skills

7 Have students recall or look up expressions for accepting and refusing from previous chapters. (Examples include **C'est l'fun! Allons-y! Oui, c'est génial/super. Non, c'est barbant/zéro/nul.**)

Language Note

8 Ask students why they think **désolé** is sometimes spelled with an extra **-e.** Tell them that because it is an adjective, the spelling depends on the gender of the speaker. Point out that the pronunciation doesn't change, however.

STANDARDS: 1.1, 1.3, 5.1

Vocabulaire

Cahier d'activités, p. 50, Act. 3

Travaux pratiques de grammaire, pp. 35–36, Act. 1–4

CD-ROM 2 DVD 1

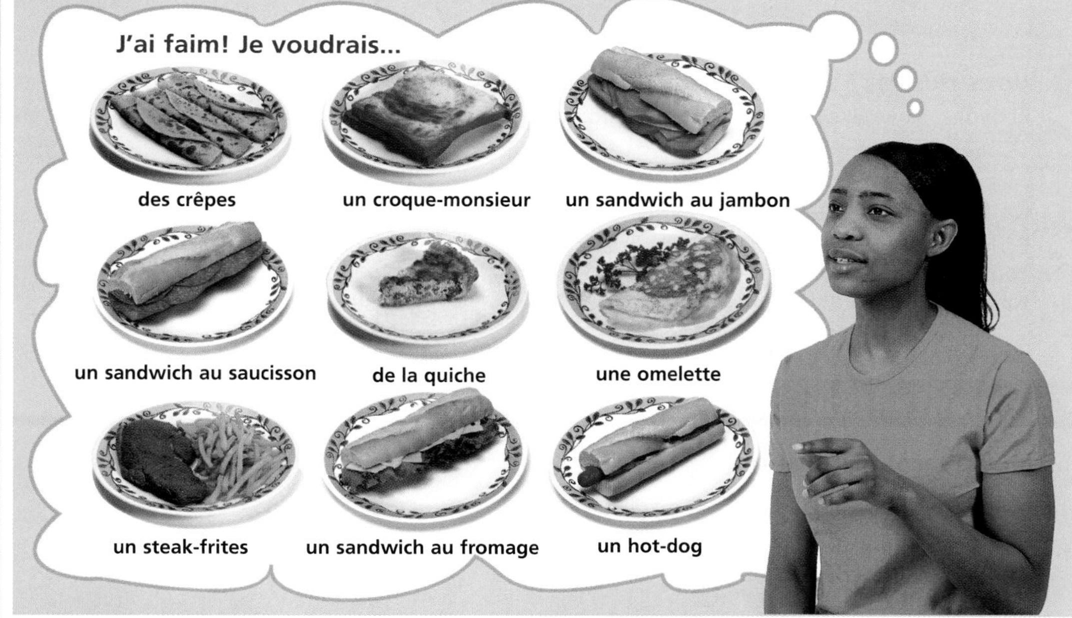

Presenting Vocabulaire

Collect containers of the beverages shown in the illustration. Or, draw or paste pictures of the containers on large file cards. Present the terms for the drinks first. Say **J'ai soif** aloud with appropriate gestures to get the meaning across. Then, say **Je voudrais...**, showing a container and naming the beverage. Repeat this with the food items, using pictures, drawings, or toys.

Language Notes

- Another way to say *lemonade* is **une citronnade.**
- Slang terms for *to eat* and *food* are **bouffer** and **la bouffe.** The slang term for water is **la flotte.**
- Make sure students don't pronounce the final **-m** of **faim.** Ask if they can think of an English word related to **faim** *(famished).*

Language-to-Language

Remind students that one way languages influence one another is through "loan words," words one language adopts from another. Food is a category with many borrowed words. Ask students to give examples in French of food related items (from this lesson or from previous chapters) that have been borrowed from English. Then, have students brainstorm words related to food that English has borrowed from other languages (**hors-d'œuvres, sauerkraut, tortilla**). Discuss why words for food might be so readily shared among languages.

Cultures and Communities

Culture Notes

- In France, flavored syrups are used in several popular drinks. Syrups are served with either non-carbonated water or lemon soda. Flavors of syrups include **fraise** *(strawberry),* **framboise** *(raspberry),* **groseille** *(red currant),* and **orgeat** *(barley water).* When ordering a syrup drink in a café, it is a good idea to specify that you want non-alcoholic syrup (**sirop sans alcool**).
- In France, milk is generally not drunk at meals. Coffee is generally taken black after meals. At breakfast, people might have **café au lait** in a bowl (**un bol de café**).
- You might want to let students know that most café sandwiches are made with pieces of **baguettes.**

STANDARDS: 3.1, 3.2, 4.1

Première étape

CHAPITRE 5

Teaching Resources
pp. 145–149

PRINT

- Lesson Planner, p. 24
- TPR Storytelling Book, pp. 17, 20
- Listening Activities, pp. 35, 39
- Activities for Communication, pp. 25–26, 95, 98, 145–146
- Travaux pratiques de grammaire, pp. 35–37
- Grammar Tutor for Students of French, Chapter 5
- Cahier d'activités, pp. 50–52
- Testing Program, pp. 105–108
- Alternative Assessment Guide, p. 36
- Student Make-Up Assignments, Chapter 5

MEDIA 

- One-Stop Planner
- Audio Compact Discs, CD 5, Trs. 3–4, 19, 25–26
- Teaching Transparencies: 5-1, 5-A, 5-B; **Grammaire supplémentaire** Answers; Travaux pratiques de grammaire Answers
- Interactive CD-ROM Tutor, Disc 2

Presenting
Comment dit-on... ?

Place various food and drink items or pictures of them on a table and recommend them to students. Students should pick up the item or picture you recommend. Then, hold up pictures of various food and drink items and prompt students to recommend them to you.

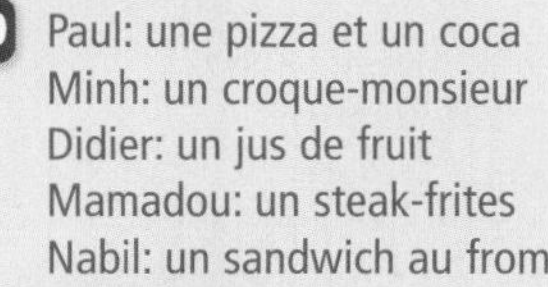

Answers

10 Paul: une pizza et un coca
Minh: un croque-monsieur
Didier: un jus de fruit
Mamadou: un steak-frites
Nabil: un sandwich au fromage

9 Qu'est-ce qu'il commande? See scripts and answers on p. 139G.

Ecoutons Look at the picture. As the boys tell the waiter what they would like, decide which boy is ordering.

CD 5 Tr. 4

10 Vous désirez? See answers below.

Ecrivons Now, take the role of the server in Activity 9. Write down each boy's order.

11 La fête internationale 

Ecrivons Your French class is going to participate in an international food fair at school. You've been assigned to poll your classmates about the types of food and drink they would like to have at the fair. Make a list of five questions you might ask.

Comment dit-on...?

Making a recommendation

To recommend something to eat or drink:

Prends une limonade. (informal) *Have . . .*
Prenez un sandwich. (formal) *Have . . .*

Travaux pratiques de grammaire, p. 36, Act. 5

Communication for All Students

Language Note
Point out to students that the spelling of **croque-monsieur** doesn't change in the plural: **les croque-monsieur.**

Slower Pace
9 Have students identify in French the food shown in the thought bubbles. Stop the recording after each person orders and have students write or say the name of the boy who is ordering.

Additional Practice
9 Have students write or say **Il a faim** or **Il a soif,** as appropriate for each of the boys.

STANDARDS: 1.2, 5.2

Grammaire

The verb *prendre*

Prendre is an irregular verb.

prendre *(to take; to have food or drink)*

Je	**prends**	Nous	**prenons**
Tu	**prends**	Vous	**prenez**
Il/Elle/On	**prend**	Ils/Elles	**prennent**

Tu **prends** des frites?
Nous **prenons** un croque-monsieur.

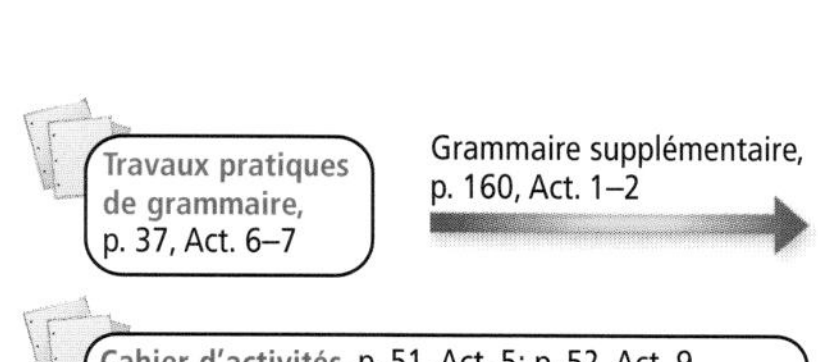

Cahier d'activités, p. 51, Act. 5; p. 52, Act. 9

12 **Grammaire en contexte**

Ecrivons You and your friends are deciding what to have in a café. Complete the conversation with the appropriate forms of the verb **prendre.**

1. prenez 2. prends 3. prends 4. prenons 5. prend 6. prennent

—Alors, qu'est-ce que vous ___1___ ?
—Moi, j'ai très faim, je ___2___ un steak-frites.
—Et toi, Anne, qu'est-ce que tu ___3___ ?
—Michel et moi, nous ___4___ une pizza.
—Et Isabelle, qu'est-ce qu'elle ___5___ ?
—Isabelle et Sylvie n'ont pas faim, mais elles ont très soif. Alors elles ___6___ un coca.

De bons conseils

Resist the temptation to match English with French word-for-word. In many cases, it doesn't work. For example, in English you say *I am hungry,* while in French you say **J'ai faim** (literally, *I have hunger*).

Michel prend un steak-frites. Paul et Julie prennent un sandwich. Sandrine et Eric prennent un hot-dog. Fabienne prend une eau minérale.

13 **Au café**

Parlons What are these people having?

Connections and Comparisons

Thinking Critically

Synthesizing — De bons conseils Ask students to think of expressions they've learned that can't be matched word for word with an English equivalent. **(Tu t'appelles comment? Tu as quel âge?)**

Language-to-Language

You might want to tell students who are native speakers of Spanish that the verb **prendre** is similar in meaning and usage to the verb **tomar** in Spanish.

Presenting Grammaire

The verb *prendre* Introduce the singular forms of **prendre** first, asking students what they notice about the pronunciation (they all sound the same). Then, present the plural forms, making sure students pronounce the **[n]** sound. Next, say the forms in random order, having students tell whether the form is singular or plural. Finally, give pictures of food **(des frites)** to various students and have the class tell what the students are having **(Ils prennent des frites.)**

Language Note

Have students compare the plural forms of **prendre** to the infinitive. Point out that the **d** of the infinitive does not appear in the plural forms. Point out also that the singular forms are pronounced with the nasal vowel **[ã],** while the plurals have an **[n]** sound.

Assess

- Testing Program, pp. 105–108
  Quiz 5-1A, Quiz 5-1B
  Audio CD 5, Tr. 19
- Student Make-Up Assignments, Chapter 5, Alternative Quiz
- Alternative Assessment Guide, p. 36

CHAPITRE 5

Teaching Resources
p. 150

PRINT 
- Video Guide, pp. 34–35, 36–37
- Cahier d'activités, p. 60

MEDIA
- One-Stop Planner
- Video Program
  Videocassette 2, 32:18–34:39
- DVD Tutor, Disc 1
- Audio Compact Discs, CD 5, Trs. 5–8
- Interactive CD-ROM Tutor, Disc 2

Presenting Panorama Culturel

Have students view the video. To check comprehension, ask the **Questions** below. Then, replay the video, pausing after each interview to ask questions 1 and 2 of **Qu'en penses-tu?**

Language Note

Students may want to know the following words: **baby (-foot)** *(Foosball®, table soccer);* **flipper** *(pinball);* **piscine** *(swimming pool).*

Questions

1. **Où est-ce que Déjan va après l'école?** (au café) **Qu'est-ce qu'il fait là-bas?** (Il joue au baby et au flipper.)
2. **Quand est-ce que Clémentine va à la piscine?** (quand il fait beau)
3. **Qu'est-ce qu'Armande fait à l'Alocodrome?** (Elle prend de l'aloco.)

Answers
1. café, park, friends' houses, Alocodrome

Où retrouves-tu tes amis?

Where do you go to meet with your friends? Here's what some francophone students had to say about where they go and what they do.

Déjan,
France

«J'aime bien aller au café après l'école. On va jouer un peu au baby, au flipper et après, je rentre chez moi faire les devoirs. On a un parc à côté de chez nous et on rencontre tous nos amis.» Tr. 6

Clémentine,
France

«Nous allons dans des cafés ou chez d'autres amis. Quand il fait beau, [on va] à la piscine. Ça dépend du temps qu'il fait.» Tr. 7

Armande,
Côte d'Ivoire

«Je vais à la maison, soit chez moi, ou bien chez eux [mes amis]. Puis on va à l'Alocodrome, enfin pour prendre un peu d'aloco, puis on revient à la maison.» Tr. 8

Qu'en penses-tu?

1. Where do these students go to meet their friends? See answers below.
2. Do you and your friends like to go to the same places and do the same things as these teenagers? Where do you go? What do you do?

Savais-tu que... ?

Many cultures have a particular kind of place where people gather. In many francophone countries, a café is more than just a place to eat; it's a social institution! Cafés primarily serve beverages. They may also serve bread (**pain**) or flaky crescent rolls (**croissants**) in the morning, and some cafés serve lunch. If you order something, you may stay in most cafés as long as you like. In some African countries, people like to go to open-air restaurants called **maquis.** They usually open only in the evening and serve traditional snack foods such as fried plantains (**aloco**), as well as full meals.

Connections and Comparisons

Thinking Critically

Comparing and Contrasting Have students discuss or list similarities and differences between a fast-food restaurant in the United States and a French café. You might pick a specific local establishment to use in the comparison.

Math Link

Have students poll one another to find out where they go to meet friends, either on weekends or after school. Then, have the class prepare a graph on large posterboard to represent visually the results of their poll.

STANDARDS: 2.2, 4.2

Deuxième étape

Objectives Getting someone's attention; ordering food and beverages

WA3 PARIS-5

Comment dit-on...?

Getting someone's attention; ordering food and beverages

To get the server's attention:

Excusez-moi.
Monsieur! Madame! Mademoiselle!
La carte, s'il vous plaît. *The menu, please.*

The server may ask:

Vous avez choisi? *Have you decided/chosen?*
Vous prenez? *What are you having?*

You might want to ask:

Vous avez des jus de fruit?
Qu'est-ce que vous avez comme boissons? *What kind of drinks do you have?*
Qu'est-ce qu'il y a à boire? *What is there to drink?*

To order:

Je voudrais un hamburger.
Je vais prendre un coca, **s'il vous plaît.** *I'll have . . . , please.*
Un sandwich, **s'il vous plaît.** *. . . , please.*
Donnez-moi un hot-dog, **s'il vous plaît.** *Please give me . . .*
Apportez-moi une limonade, **s'il vous plaît.** *Please bring me . . .*

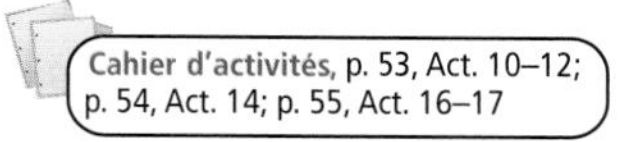
Cahier d'activités, p. 53, Act. 10–12; p. 54, Act. 14; p. 55, Act. 16–17

14 C'est le serveur ou le client? See scripts and answers on p. 139G.

Ecoutons Listen to these remarks and decide whether the server (**le serveur/la serveuse**) or the customer (**le client/la cliente**) is speaking.

CD 5 Tr. 9

15 Méli-mélo!

Lisons/Parlons Unscramble the following conversation between a server and a customer. Then, act it out with a partner.

—Qu'est-ce qu'il y a comme sandwiches? 2
—Bien sûr. 5
—Eh bien, donnez-moi un sandwich au fromage, s'il vous plaît. 4
—Vous avez choisi? 1
—Il y a des sandwiches au jambon, au saucisson, au fromage... 3

A la française

If you need time to think during a conversation, you can say **Eh bien...** and pause for a moment before you continue speaking.

—Vous prenez, mademoiselle?
—Eh bien... un steak-frites, s'il vous plaît.

At first you'll have to make a conscious effort to do this. The more you practice, the more natural it will become.

Communication for All Students

Building on Previous Skills

Ask students what expressions they would need if they wanted to order something in a café or restaurant.

Kinesthetic Learners

14 Play the recording again and have the students mime the appropriate gestures (the waiter writing down an order, the client pointing to an item on a menu as he or she orders, etc.).

Challenge

15 Have students expand the conversation after they have unscrambled it, by adding their own food and drink choices.

Deuxième étape

CHAPITRE 5

Teaching Resources pp. 151–153

PRINT 

- Lesson Planner, p. 25
- TPR Storytelling Book, pp. 18, 20
- Listening Activities, pp. 36, 40
- Activities for Communication, pp. 27–28, 96, 98, 145–146
- Travaux pratiques de grammaire, p. 38
- Grammar Tutor for Students of French Chapter 5
- Cahier d'activités, pp. 53–55
- Testing Program, pp. 109–112
- Alternative Assessment Guide, p. 36
- Student Make-Up Assignments, Chapter 5

MEDIA 

- One-Stop Planner
- Audio Compact Discs, CD 5, Trs. 9, 20, 27–28
- Teaching Transparencies: 5-2; **Grammaire supplémentaire** Answers; Travaux pratiques de grammaire Answers
- Interactive CD-ROM Tutor, Disc 2

Bell Work

On a transparency, write a list of foods and beverages and several adverbs of frequency. Have students write sentences using the verb **prendre,** telling how often they have each item.

Presenting Comment dit-on... ?

Have students repeat the expressions after you. Then, play the video of the **Mise en train,** and have students tell you to stop it when they hear the waiter ask for the order and again when they hear the young people order. Then, take various students' orders by asking **Vous prenez?**

Deuxième étape

CHAPITRE 5

Teaching Resources
pp. 151–153

PRINT

- Lesson Planner, p. 25
- TPR Storytelling Book, pp. 18, 20
- Listening Activities, pp. 36, 40
- Activities for Communication, pp. 27–28, 96, 98, 145–146
- Travaux pratiques de grammaire, p. 38
- Grammar Tutor for Students of French Chapter 5
- Cahier d'activités, pp. 53–55
- Testing Program, pp. 109–112
- Alternative Assessment Guide, p. 36
- Student Make-Up Assignments, Chapter 5

MEDIA 

- One-Stop Planner
- Audio Compact Discs, CD 5, Trs. 9, 20, 27–28
- Teaching Transparencies: 5-2; **Grammaire supplémentaire** Answers; Travaux pratiques de grammaire Answers
- Interactive CD-ROM Tutor, Disc 2

Presenting
Grammaire

The imperative Contrast a command and a declarative statement that have the same verb. **(Va au tableau! Elle va au tableau.)** Ask students what the structural difference is between the command and the statement (no subject in the command). Finally, say some declarative sentences and have students restate them as commands.

Possible Answers

17
1. Prenez un coca.
2. Ecoute la radio/un CD.
3. Joue(z) au foot.
4. Etudiez!
5. Prenez un pull.
6. Joue au base-ball.

16 On prend un sandwich?

Lisons/Parlons You've stopped at a café for lunch. Get the server's attention, look at the menu, and order. Take turns playing the role of the server.

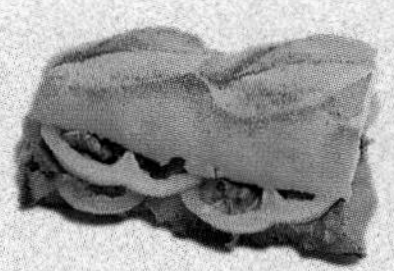

LA MAISON DU SANDWICH

NOS SANDWICHES

au jambon de Paris	3,00€	au gruyère	3,00€
au jambon de pays	3,50€	au camembert	3,00€
au saucisson	3,00€	au saumon	4,50€
au pâté	3,50€	au crabe	4,00€
mixte (jambon et gruyère)	3,50€	végétarien	3,50€

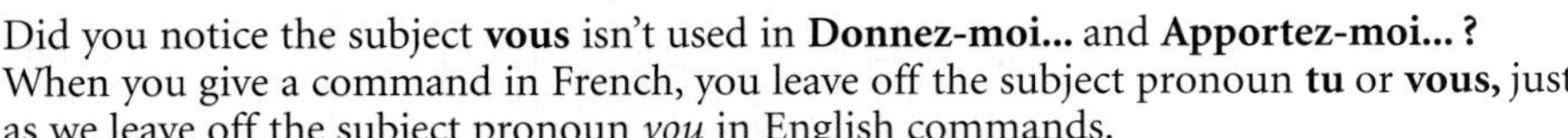

Grammaire

The imperative

CD-ROM 2 DVD 1

Did you notice the subject **vous** isn't used in **Donnez-moi...** and **Apportez-moi... ?** When you give a command in French, you leave off the subject pronoun **tu** or **vous,** just as we leave off the subject pronoun *you* in English commands.

- When you write the **tu** form of a regular **-er** verb as a command, drop the final **s** of the usual verb ending.

  Tu écoutes... → **Ecoute!**
  Tu regardes... → **Regarde!**

- If the verb isn't a regular **-er** verb, the spelling of the command form doesn't change.

  Tu fais... → **Fais** les devoirs!
  Tu prends... → **Prends** un hot-dog, Paul!

- Remember to use the **tu** form when you talk with family members and people your own age or younger. Use the **vous** form when you talk with people older than you or with more than one person.

  Prenez un coca, Marc et Eve.

Grammaire supplémentaire, pp. 161–162, Act. 3–6

Cahier d'activités, p. 54, Act. 13, 15

Travaux pratiques de grammaire, p. 38, Act. 8–10

17 Grammaire en contexte

Parlons Your friends can't decide how they want to spend their Saturday afternoon. You're the one they always turn to for advice. Respond to each of their statements below by telling them what they should do. See answers below.

Exemple —Nous avons faim.
—Prenez un sandwich.

1. Nous avons soif.
2. J'aime beaucoup la musique.
3. Il fait beau aujourd'hui.
4. Nous avons un examen demain.
5. Il fait frais.
6. Je voudrais faire du sport.

Communication for All Students

Language Note

16 The counter in a café is often referred to as **le zinc,** because in the past, it was covered with zinc.

Slower Pace

16 You might model the pronunciation of the menu items before beginning this activity.

Kinesthetic Learners

Give students or pairs of students the following commands and have them perform the actions. **Apporte(z)-moi un stylo! Parle(z) français! Donne(z)-moi une feuille de papier! Danse(z)! Nage(z)! Apporte(z)-moi un crayon jaune! Prends/Prenez ce livre!** After some practice, have students give the commands to one another.

STANDARDS: 1.1, 1.2, 4.1

18 Grammaire en contexte

Parlons You don't know what to order at the café. The server makes some suggestions for you, but you don't like the suggestions. Take turns playing the server.

Exemple
—**Prenez un sandwich au fromage.**
—**Non, je n'aime pas le fromage.**
—**Alors, prenez un sandwich au jambon.**
—**Non, apportez-moi un hot-dog, s'il vous plaît.**

Note culturelle

In France, waiters and waitresses are considered professionals. In better restaurants, waiters and waitresses must not only be good servers but they must also be knowledgeable about food and wine. Even in simple restaurants or cafés, servers take great pride in their work. Contrary to what you may have seen in American movies, it is impolite to address a waiter as **Garçon.** It is more polite to say **Monsieur** to a waiter, and **Madame** or **Mademoiselle** to a waitress. It is expected that diners will take time to enjoy their food, so service in French restaurants may seem slow to Americans. It is not uncommon for a meal to last several hours.

19 A la crêperie

Lisons/Parlons You and some friends get together at a **crêperie.** Look at the menu and order. Take turns playing the server.

La Crêperie Normande

Crêpes salées :

Jambon - fromage	4,50€
Epinards - crème fraîche	4,50€
Champignons	5,00€

Crêpes sucrées :

Sucre	3,50€
Banane - Chantilly	4,50€
Chocolat	4,00€
Glace vanille - sauce noisette	5,00€

20 Mon journal 

Ecrivons Make a list of the foods and drinks you like to have when you go out with your friends. Then, mention several items you'd try if you were at a café in France.

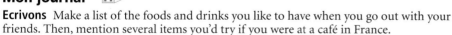

Cultures and Communities

Culture Notes

19 • Crêpes are a specialty of Brittany **(Bretagne)**. Traditionally, they are served during **la fête de la chandeleur,** a Christian, religious holiday in February celebrating the presentation of Jesus in the temple. **Crêperies** usually serve both dessert and dinner **crêpes,** as well as sparkling apple cider.

• **Note culturelle** In some cafés, you will find pinball machines **(les flippers)**, table soccer **(le baby-foot)**, and video games **(les jeux vidéo).** Video games may be located in a separate room at the back of the café. Decks of cards and checker games are also available in many cafés.

Language-to-Language

If you have students who speak Spanish, you might have them tell how informal commands in Spanish are similar to informal commands for **-er** verbs in French. (They both drop the final **-s.**) You might also stress that verbs in French that do not end in **-er** keep the final **-s** in informal commands, but in Spanish, the **-s** is dropped from all regular verbs.

Challenge

19 Have students give their reactions to some of the items **(J'aime beaucoup... , Nous n'aimons pas... , Je voudrais...).**

Mon journal

20 For an additional journal entry suggestion for Chapter 5, see *Cahier d'activités*, page 149.

Cooperative Learning

After students practice the vocabulary orally, have groups of four or five role-play a restaurant scene. One student is the server, one is the chef, and the others are the customers. The customers give their orders to the server, who writes them down. The server then goes to the chef and reads aloud the orders. The chef writes down the items, while repeating the orders aloud. Finally, the server "serves" the customers, restating each person's order.

Assess

- Testing Program, pp. 109–112
  Quiz 5-2A, Quiz 5-2B
  Audio CD 5, Tr. 20
- Student Make-Up Assignments, Chapter 5, Alternative Quiz
- Alternative Assessment Guide, p. 36

Teaching Resources
pp. 154–157

PRINT

- Lesson Planner, p. 26
- TPR Storytelling Book, pp. 19, 20
- Listening Activities, pp. 36–37, 41
- Activities for Communication, pp. 29–30, 97, 99, 145–146
- Travaux pratiques de grammaire, pp. 39–40
- Grammar Tutor for Students of French, Chapter 5
- Cahier d'activités, pp. 56–58
- Testing Program, pp. 113–116
- Alternative Assessment Guide, p. 36
- Student Make-Up Assignments, Chapter 5

MEDIA 

- One-Stop Planner
- Audio Compact Discs, CD 5, Trs. 10–11, 21, 29–30
- Teaching Transparencies: 5-3; **Grammaire supplémentaire** Answers; Travaux pratiques de grammaire Answers
- Interactive CD-ROM Tutor, Disc 2

Bell Work
Have students write commands with the **tu** forms of **écouter, faire, regarder, prendre,** and **jouer.**

Presenting
Comment dit-on... ?

Model the expressions and have students repeat them. Using magazine pictures of food, point to an item and ask a student **Comment tu trouves ça?** Students should use the new expressions to express their opinion of the given food item.

Troisième étape

Objectives Inquiring about and expressing likes and dislikes; paying the check

WA3 PARIS-5

Comment dit-on...?

Inquiring about and expressing likes and dislikes

To ask how someone likes the food or drink:

Comment tu trouves ça? *How do you like it?*

To say you like your food/drink:

C'est... *It's . . .*
bon! *good!*
excellent! *excellent!*
délicieux! *delicious!*
pas mauvais. *pretty good.*

To say you don't like your food/drink:

C'est... *It's . . .*
pas bon. *not good.*
pas terrible. *not so great.*
dégoûtant. *gross.*
mauvais. *bad.*

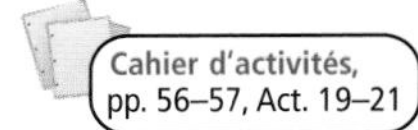

Cahier d'activités, pp. 56–57, Act. 19–21

Travaux pratiques de grammaire, p. 39, Act. 11–12

21 C'est bon, ça? See scripts and answers on p. 139H.

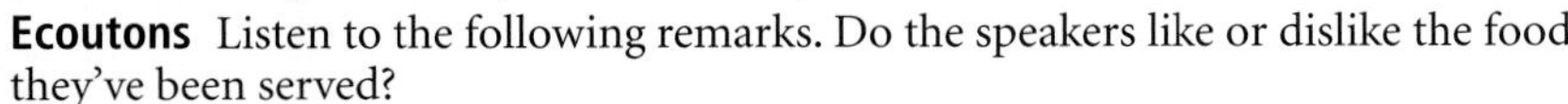

Ecoutons Listen to the following remarks. Do the speakers like or dislike the food they've been served?

CD 5
Tr. 10

Note culturelle

French speakers have a tendency to use understatement **(la litote).** For instance, if the food were bad, they might say **C'est pas terrible.** Similarly, rather than saying something is good, they would say **C'est pas mauvais.**

22 A mon avis...

Parlons The school cafeteria is thinking of adding some items to the menu. A poll is being taken among the students. Discuss each of the items below with a partner.

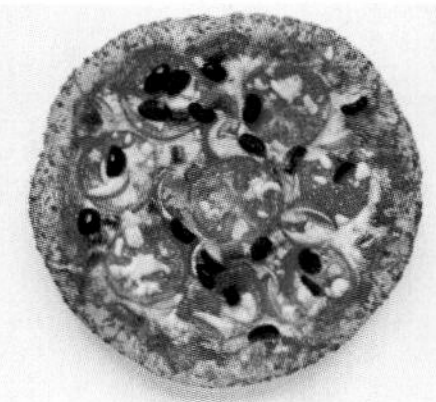

1.

2.

3.

4.

Communication for All Students

Building on Previous Skills
Ask students what else they need to know about eating in a café, now that they know how to get a waiter's attention and order.

Slower Pace
21 Before playing the recording, write on the board the expressions of opinion students will hear. Then, ask them if each one expresses a like or a dislike.

STANDARDS: 1.2, 2.1, 3.2, 5.2

Ça, c'est bon.

Parlons You and your partner are in a café. Ask if your partner has decided what to order and tell what you think of his or her choice.

EXEMPLE

— **Tu as choisi? Qu'est-ce que tu vas prendre?**
— **Euh... je vais prendre un hot-dog.**
— **Un hot-dog? C'est dégoûtant!** *or* **Bonne idée. C'est délicieux.**

Chère correspondante 

Ecrivons Your French pen pal Cécile asked you what teenagers in America eat or drink when they get together. Write a brief note in French telling her what you and your friends have when you go out and what you think of each item.

Comment dit-on...?

Paying the check

CD-ROM 2
DVD 1

To ask for the check:	The server might answer:
L'addition, s'il vous plaît. *The check, please.*	**Oui, tout de suite.** *Yes, right away.* **Un moment, s'il vous plaît.**

To ask how much something is:	
C'est combien, un sandwich?	**C'est** huit **euros.**
Ça fait combien, s'il vous plaît?	**Ça fait** cinquante **euros.**
How much is it, . . . ? (total)	*It's . . . euros.* (total)

Cahier d'activités, pp. 57–58, Act. 23–24

Grammaire supplémentaire, p. 163, Act. 9

25 Au restaurant

See scripts and answers on p. 139H.

Ecoutons Listen to the following remarks. Are the speakers ordering or getting ready to pay the check?

CD 5 Tr. 11

Tu te rappelles?

Do you remember the numbers from 20–100?

20 **vingt**	50 **cinquante**	80 **quatre-vingts**
30 **trente**	60 **soixante**	90 **quatre-vingt-dix**
40 **quarante**	70 **soixante-dix**	100 **cent**

Travaux pratiques de grammaire, pp. 39–40, Act. 13–14

Grammaire supplémentaire, p. 163, Act. 7–8

Troisième étape

CHAPITRE 5

Building on Previous Skills

23 Students will need to practice **Tu as choisi?** before doing this activity. You might have students look at the food items on page 147 or the menus in the **Lisons!** section as they do this activity.

Language Note

24 Remind students that in negative sentences, **de** replaces the indefinite article. **(Nous prenons un sandwich au jambon, mais nous ne prenons jamais de hot-dog.)**

Slower Pace

24 Before starting this activity, review the food items orally. You might also want to make a list of adverbs of frequency on the board: **souvent, une fois par semaine, quelquefois, ne... jamais.**

Presenting
Comment dit-on... ?

Ask students to look back at the **Mise en train** or view the video to identify these functions. Then, act out both asking for and paying the check in front of the class. Act out the dialogue a second time, having students repeat after you. You might have students refer to the menu on page 156 as you ask the prices of various items. **(C'est combien, un croque-monsieur?)** Finally, have students practice both roles with a partner.

Portfolio

24 **Written** This activity is appropriate for students' written portfolios. You might have students edit one another's note before they write a final draft. For portfolio suggestions, see *Alternative Assessment Guide,* page 22.

Cultures and Communities

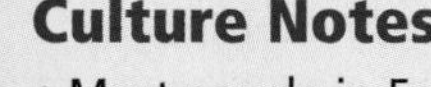

Culture Notes

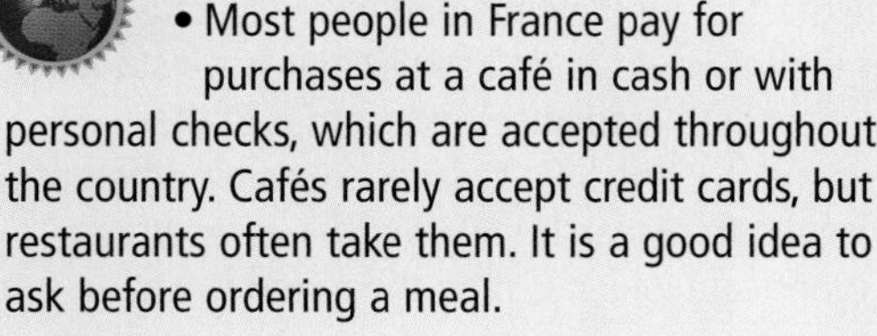

• Most people in France pay for purchases at a café in cash or with personal checks, which are accepted throughout the country. Cafés rarely accept credit cards, but restaurants often take them. It is a good idea to ask before ordering a meal.

• You might want to discuss French table manners with students: keep both hands above the table (people sometimes rest their wrists on the table edge); keep your fork in your left hand to eat; avoid eating with your hands (even fries and pizza).

Troisième étape

CHAPITRE 5

Teaching Resources
pp. 154–157

PRINT

- Lesson Planner, p. 26
- TPR Storytelling Book, pp. 19, 20
- Listening Activities, pp. 36–37, 41
- Activities for Communication, pp. 29–30, 97, 99, 145–146
- Travaux pratiques de grammaire, pp. 39–40
- Grammar Tutor for Students of French, Chapter 5
- Cahier d'activités, pp. 56–58
- Testing Program, pp. 113–116
- Alternative Assessment Guide, p. 36
- Student Make-Up Assignments, Chapter 5

MEDIA 

- One-Stop Planner
- Audio Compact Discs, CD 5, Trs. 10–11, 21, 29–30
- Teaching Transparencies: 5-3; **Grammaire supplémentaire** Answers; Travaux pratiques de grammaire Answers
- Interactive CD-ROM Tutor, Disc 2

Language Note

26 Have students look at the receipt next to Activity 26. Point out that capital letters in French are sometimes printed without accents.

Group Work

27 While students are writing their captions, draw four large columns on the board and number them 1–4. Ask for volunteers to come to the board and write one of their captions in the appropriate column. Then, have students tell as many logical stories as they can by combining the captions.

26 Ça fait combien?

Parlons You and your friend have just finished eating at a café. Look at this check, tell what you had (**Moi, j'ai pris...**), and figure out how much each of you owes.

EXEMPLE —**Moi, j'ai pris...**
—**Ça fait... euros.**

LA GIRAFE
Port de Cavalaire
Tél : 04 94 64 40 31

28-09-02

CROQUE-MONSIEUR	3,50€
STEAK-FRITES	4,50€
EAU MINERALE	1,50€
COCA	2,00€
TOTAL	11,50€

La Direction souhaite
que cet instant de
détente vous ait été
AGREABLE

Note culturelle

In cafés and restaurants, a 15% tip is included in the check if the words **service compris** are posted or written on the menu. If you're not sure, it's acceptable to ask **Le service est compris?** It's customary, however, to leave a little extra if the service is particularly good.

27 Qu'est-ce qu'on dit?

Ecrivons Write what you think the people in this scene are saying. Then, with a partner, compare what you both have written.

28 De l'école au travail

Parlons During the summer you found a job as a waitperson at the Café Sport. Ask your customers if they have decided what to order and what they would like to eat and drink. They'll tell you what they like to eat and you'll suggest dishes according to their tastes. At the end, tell them how much they have to pay and hand them the check.

CAFE SPORT

Sandwiches		**BOISSONS**	
Fromage	2,50 €	Jus de fruit orange, pomme, pamplemousse	2,00 €
Jambon	3,00 €		
Saucisson	3,00 €		
Hamburger	3,50 €	Limonade	1,50 €
Hot-dog	2,50 €	Café	1,50 €
Steak-frites	5,00 €	Cola	2,00 €
Croque-monsieur	3,50 €	Eau minérale	1,50 €
Pizza	3,50 €	Chocolat	2,50 €
Frites	1,50 €		
Glace	1,50 €		

Teacher to Teacher

Jacqueline Donnelly
Holland High School
Holland, MI

Jacqueline suggests the following idea to close this étape.

"Students enjoy expressing artistically how they imagine a French café to be, through a collage or by doing their own artwork. I sometimes have students create their own café (menu, décor, and ambiance) in a corner of the classroom and invite other students to visit. What makes this a bit different is that the students are encouraged to research and consider cafés from different eras, maybe even a cyber-café which is now the rage."

STANDARDS: 1.2, 1.3, 2.1, 3.1, 3.2, 4.2

PRONONCIATION

CD 5
Trs. 12–17

The nasal sound [ã] See scripts and answers on p. 139H.

Listen carefully to the vowel sounds in the following words: **ans, en.** These words contain the nasal sound [ã]. It's called a nasal sound because part of the air goes through the back of your mouth and nose when you make the sound. Listen to the English word *sandwich,* and the French **sandwich.** Is the first syllable pronounced the same in the two words? The sound in French is a pure nasal sound, with no trace of the *n* sound in it. In English you say *envy,* but in French you say **envie.** The nasal sound [ã] has four possible spellings: **an, am, en,** and **em.**

These letter combinations don't always represent a nasal sound. If another vowel follows the **n** or the **m,** or if the **n** or **m** is doubled, there may not be a nasal sound. You'll have to learn the pronunciation when you learn the word.

Listen to the following pairs of words and compare the sounds.

Fr*ance*/*ani*mal   pr*end*/pr*en*ez   *jam*bon/*ami*   *en*vie/*enn*emi

A. A prononcer

Repeat the following words.

en France	attendez	comment	soixante
anglais	dimanche	jambon	temps
orange	tellement	vent	souvent

B. A lire

Take turns with a partner reading the following sentences aloud.

1. Il a cent francs.
2. J'ai un excellent roman allemand.
3. Elle a danse et sciences nat vendredi.
4. Moi, je vais prendre un sandwich au jambon.

C. A écrire

You're going to hear a short dialogue. Write down what you hear.

Assess

- Testing Program, pp. 113–116 Quiz 5-3A, Quiz 5-3B Audio CD 5, Tr. 21
- Student Make-Up Assignments, Chapter 5, Alternative Quiz
- Alternative Assessment Guide, p. 36

Communication for All Students

Language Note

Prononciation Have students read the second paragraph above. In French, syllables usually begin with a consonant. When a consonant has a vowel on each side, the consonant will attach itself to the following vowel, preventing the nasal sound. This can be illustrated by dividing words into syllables: **a-ni-mal, pre-nez.**

Additional Practice

Prononciation Write the sentences in Part B on the board or on a transparency. Have students tell you which words contain the nasal sound and circle or underline them. Practice these words first, making sure students pronounce them correctly. Then, have students practice reading the sentences.

Lisons!

CHAPITRE 5

Teaching Resources
pp. 158–159

PRINT
- Lesson Planner, p. 27
- Cahier d'activités, p. 59
- Reading Strategies and Skills Handbook, Chapter 5
- Joie de lire 1, Chapter 5
- Standardized Assessment Tutor, Chapter 5

MEDIA
- One-Stop Planner

Prereading
Activity A

Using Prior Knowledge
You might use the first question of Activity A as an opener to get students thinking about menus and what they reveal about a restaurant. Have students look at the illustrations on the menus. What do they notice?

Reading
Activities B–H

Monitoring Comprehension
Have students work in pairs or small groups to skim the menus quickly and answer the questions in Activities B, C, and D.

Lisons!

Des menus de cafés

Stratégie pour lire
When you're faced with something new to read, look for anything that is familiar, anything that will help you identify the type of reading selection that you're dealing with. For example, a quick glance at these reading selections tells you that they're menus. Since you're familiar with menus, you should have a general idea of the kind of information these will contain, even if you don't know what all the words mean.

A. When you look at menus, what information are you usually looking for? Can you find this type of information on these menus? See answers below.

B. French cuisine is enjoyed the world over. However, you can often find dishes from other cultures at French cafés and restaurants. See answers below.
1. Which items on the menus are typical American dishes?
2. What French words might you find on American menus?
3. What other French words do you know that are related to food and restaurants?

C. In the Café des Lauriers, what ingredients do the **salade niçoise,** the **salade mexicaine,** and the **salade sicilienne** have in common? green lettuce and tomatoes

Salade verte . . . . 3,00€
Salade niçoise . . . . 5,75€
(salade verte, tomates, œufs, haricots verts, thon, olives)
Salade mexicaine . . . . 6,00€
(salade verte, tomates, maïs, poivrons, thon, olives)
Salade sicilienne . . . . .6,00€
(salade verte, tomates, basilic, mozzarella, huile d'olive)
Assiette anglaise . . . . .6,75€
(jambon blanc, saucisson, rôti de porc, beurre)
Sandwiches
jambon blanc . . . . .4,25€
saucisson . . . . .4,25€
pâté . . . . .4,50€
fromage . . . . .4,00€
Croque-monsieur . . . . 4,00€
Portion fromage . . . . .2,75€
Pizza . . . . .4,50€
Quiche . . . . 4,50€
Hamburger . . . . .4,50€

Connections and Comparisons

Math Link
Have students calculate in dollars the price of the most expensive item at each café. You may need to review with students how to convert euros to dollars.

Geography Link
Ask students what different countries or regions are referred to in the menu. Ask them if specific foods might sometimes be associated with a certain country (for example, corn with Mexico). Have them think of or create a menu item associated with the region or city where they live. What ingredients would be typical?

Answers
A. food choices, prices; yes
B. 1. hamburger, hot-dog, pizza, banana split, cola
2. *Answers will vary.*
3. *Possible answers:* Bon appétit!, bistro, à la mode, soupe du jour, entrée, à la carte, hors-d'œuvre, chef, sauté, parfait

STANDARDS: 1.2, 2.2, 3.1, 4.1

FONTAINE ELYSÉE

SANDWICHES

Jambon cru	4,50€
Jambon de Paris	4,00€
Pâté	4,00€
Mixte	5,50€
Roquefort aux noix	4,50€

OMELETTES

Jambon	5,50€
Fromage	5,50€
Mixte	6,00€

PLATS DIVERS

Croque-monsieur	4,50€
Escargots (les 6)	7,75€
Hot-Dog 1 Saucisse	4,50€
Hot-Dog 2 Saucisses	8,50€

BOISSONS CHAUDES

Café express	2,25€
Décaféiné	2,25€
Café ou chocolat viennois	4,50€
Café crème	4,00€
Cappuccino	4,75€

BOISSONS FRAICHES

Eau minérale, limonade	4,25€
Cola	4,50€
Jus de fruit raisin, poire, abricot, pamplemousse, ananas	4,50€

SPECIALITES

COUPE CHAMPS-ELYSEES : Chocolat - Pistache - Caramel - Sauce Chocolat - Mandarine Impériale - Chantilly	8,00€
BANANA SPLIT : Glace -Vanille - Chocolat - Banane Fruit - Sauce Chocolat - Chantilly	6,25€
COUPE MELBA : Vanille - Pêche Fruit - Chantilly - Sauce Fraise	6,25€

For Activities D–G, see answers below.

D. Which café lists the beverages served? Do you recognize any of them? What is the difference between **BOISSONS FRAICHES** and **BOISSONS CHAUDES?**

E. How many different cognates can you find on the menus? (You should be able to find at least ten!)

F. Read the following statements about your friends' likes and dislikes. Which café would you recommend to each one?

1. **Chantal a soif, mais elle n'a pas faim. Elle aime les jus de fruit.**
2. **Michel adore la glace.**
3. **Jean-Paul est végétarien.**
4. **Mai voudrait une omelette.**
5. **Alain aime les quiches.**

G. Judging from the menus, what are the differences between the two cafés? What are the specialties of each one?

H. If you were invited to go out and were given a choice, which café would you choose? Why? Which one would you choose if you had to pay?

I. If you had 15 € to spend, what would you order?

J. Now, make your own menu. Plan what you want to serve and how you want the menu to look. Will you have any illustrations? Don't forget to include prices.

Cahier d'activités, p. 59, Act. 26

Postreading
Activities I–J

Using Text Organizers
J. This activity could be expanded as the Chapter Project. See page 139C for the project description.

Answers

D. Fontaine Elysée; boissons fraîches *(cold drinks),* boissons chaudes *(hot drinks)*

E. *Possible answers:* salade, tomates, olives, porc, omelette, vanille, sauce, banane, abricot, caramel, spécialités, sandwiches, mexicaine

F. 1. Fontaine Elysée
2. Fontaine Elysée
3. Café des Lauriers
4. Fontaine Elysée
5. Café des Lauriers

G. Fontaine Elysée has more choices; Café des Lauriers has no specialty. Fontaine Elysée's specialty is ice cream.

Communication for All Students

Additional Practice
F. Have students pair off to create a conversation in French in which one person asks the other how he or she likes each café.

— **Comment tu trouves le café Fontaine Elysée?**

— **C'est très cher, mais les sandwiches sont très bons.**

Challenge
H. You might have students work in groups of three to create a conversation in French that might take place in this situation.

STANDARDS: 1.2, 2.2, 3.1, 4.1, 5.2

Grammaire supplémentaire

CHAPITRE 5

For **Grammaire supplémentaire** Answer Transparencies, see the *Teaching Transparencies* binder.

Grammaire supplémentaire

Première étape

Objectives Making suggestions; making excuses; making a recommendation

1 Choose the appropriate completion for each sentence. (**p. 149**)

1. Guillaume et Ludovic...	**a.** prend un jus de pomme; elle a soif.
2. Paul...	**b.** prenons des hot-dogs.
3. Anne et Lucie...	**c.** prenez un chocolat.
4. Marie-Lise et toi...	**d.** prennent du jus d'orange; elles ont très soif.
5. André et moi...	**e.** prends un croque-monsieur.
6. Alice...	**f.** prennent un sandwich.
7. Moi, je...	**g.** prend un steak-frites; il a faim.

2 You and your friends are deciding what to order in a café. Complete the sentences that follow with the correct forms of **prendre.** (**p. 149**)

1. Tu ______ un jus de pomme?
2. Eric ______ un hot-dog.
3. Vous ______ un café?
4. Moi, je ______ une limonade.
5. Elles ______ des sandwiches.
6. Nous ______ des cocas.
7. Jean et Alphonse ______ un steak-frites.
8. Le professeur ______ un croque-monsieur.

Answers

1
1. f
2. g
3. d
4. c
5. b
6. a
7. e

2
1. prends
2. prend
3. prenez
4. prends
5. prennent
6. prenons
7. prennent
8. prend

Grammar Resources for Chapter 5

The **Grammaire supplémentaire** activities were designed as supplemental activities for the grammatical concepts presented in the chapter. You might use them as additional practice, for review, or for assessment.

For more grammar presentations, review, and practice, refer to the following:
- Travaux pratiques de grammaire
- Grammar Tutor for Students of French
- Grammar Summary on pp. R15–R28
- Cahier d'activités
- Grammar and Vocabulary quizzes (Testing Program)
- Test Generator
- Interactive CD-ROM Tutor
- **Jeux interactifs** at go.hrw.com

STANDARDS: 1.2

Deuxième étape

Objectives Getting someone's attention; ordering food and beverages

3 You and your friends are browsing through a basket full of items on sale. Tell your friends what to get (**prendre**) based on what they tell you about their favorite colors. (**p. 152**)

un jean noir
des baskets bleues
des sweat-shirts orange
un tee-shirt rouge
des pull-overs verts
un short blanc
un bracelet rose

Exemple Céline : J'aime le rouge. **Prends le tee-shirt rouge!**

1. Valentine et Sophie : On adore l'orange.
2. Jérôme : Moi, j'aime bien le noir.
3. Clément : Moi, j'aime le blanc.
4. Anne et Lydie : On aime bien le bleu.
5. Aurélie : Moi, j'aime le rose.
6. Marcel et Pascal : On adore le vert.

4 A physical education teacher is encouraging her students to exercise. Based on their objections, write what she had told them to do. (**p. 152**)

Exemple —**Faites du sport!**
—Mais on n'aime pas faire du sport!

1. —Mais je n'aime pas faire de la natation!
2. —Mais on n'aime pas faire du jogging!
3. —Mais on n'aime pas jouer au basket!
4. —Mais je n'aime pas jouer au tennis!
5. —Mais nous n'aimons pas jouer au football!
6. —Mais je n'aime pas faire du roller en ligne!

Communication for All Students

Challenge

3 Have students work in pairs to do the activity once. Then, have them "refill" the basket with different colors and items of clothing, and do the activity again, with names of classmates or friends and the colors that they like.

Kinesthetic Learners

4 Have students work in pairs to practice giving each other the commands. They should take turns acting them out. Volunteers might wish to act out the activities in front of the class.

Grammaire supplémentaire

CHAPITRE 5

Answers

3
1. Prenez les sweat-shirts orange!
2. Prends le jean noir!
3. Prends le short blanc!
4. Prenez les baskets bleues!
5. Prends le bracelet rose!
6. Prenez les pull-overs verts!

4
1. Fais de la natation!
2. Faites du jogging!
3. Jouez au basket!
4. Joue au tennis!
5. Jouez au football!
6. Fais du roller en ligne!

STANDARDS: 1.2

For **Grammaire supplémentaire** Answer Transparencies, see the *Teaching Transparencies* binder.

Grammaire supplémentaire

5 Rewrite the following requests, using the imperative of the verbs in parentheses followed by **-moi.** (**p. 152**)

EXEMPLE —Monsieur, je voudrais un café, s'il vous plaît. (apporter)
—**Apportez-moi un café,** s'il vous plaît.

1. —Maman, je voudrais une limonade, s'il te plaît. (apporter)
   —_______, s'il te plaît.
2. —Jérémy, je voudrais un sandwich au fromage, s'il te plaît. (donner)
   —_______, s'il te plaît.
3. —Monsieur, je voudrais une eau minérale, s'il vous plaît. (donner)
   —_______, s'il vous plaît.
4. —Mademoiselle, je voudrais un coca, s'il vous plaît. (apporter)
   —_______, s'il vous plaît.
5. —Bérénice, je voudrais un chocolat, s'il te plaît. (apporter)
   —_______, s'il te plaît.

6 Mr. and Mrs. Laforge are in a restaurant with their two children. Complete their conversation below with the correct forms of the verbs in parentheses. (**pp. 149, 151, 152**)

ERIC — Maman, j'__1__ (avoir) faim. Est-ce que je peux __2__ (prendre) une pizza?

MME LAFORGE — Oui, c'est une bonne idée. Et toi, Emilie, tu __3__ (avoir) faim?

EMILIE — Non, mais j'__4__ (avoir) soif. Est-ce que je peux __5__ (prendre) un coca?

MME LAFORGE — Non. __6__ (Prendre) un jus de fruit, ils sont délicieux ici. Et toi, Marc, tu __7__ (prendre) un croque-monsieur ou tu __8__ (préférer) un sandwich au fromage?

M. LAFORGE — Un sandwich au fromage. Et toi, Marie?

MME LAFORGE — Moi, j'__9__ (adore) les œufs. Je __10__ (prendre) une omelette.

LE SERVEUR — Vous __11__ (avoir) choisi?

M. LAFORGE — Oui, __12__ (apporter)-nous une pizza, une omelette, un sandwich au fromage, deux jus d'orange et deux eaux minérales, s'il vous plaît.

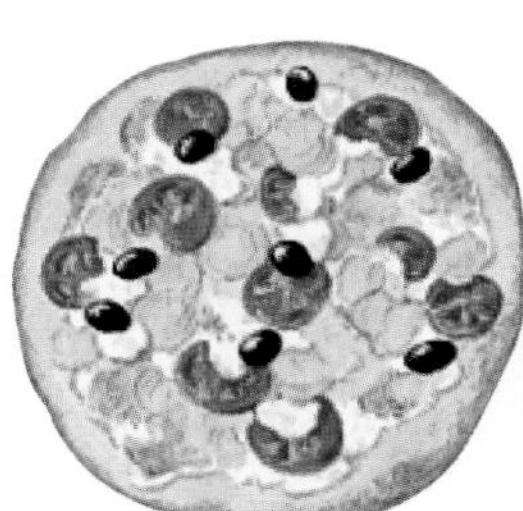

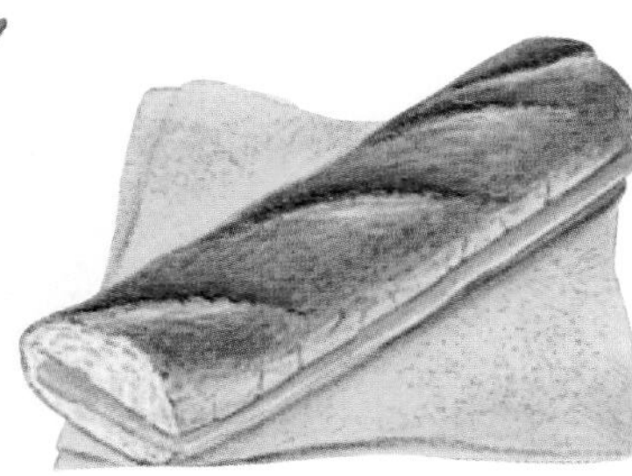

Answers

5
1. Apporte-moi une limonade ...
2. Donne-moi un sandwich au fromage ...
3. Donnez-moi une eau minérale ...
4. Apportez-moi un coca ...
5. Apporte-moi un chocolat ...

6
1. ai
2. prendre
3. as
4. ai
5. prendre
6. Prends
7. prends
8. préfères
9. adore
10. prends
11. avez
12. apportez

Teacher to Teacher

Colleen Webster
Olathe North High School
Olathe, KS

Here's an idea from Colleen to practice numbers.

"To practice numbers made up of more than one word **(cent quatre-vingt-douze)**, write the numbers on index cards, each word on a separate card. Make separate cards for hyphens and the word **et**. Distribute the cards to the students. Then, call out a number in English and have students go to the front of the room and arrange themselves in the correct order."

Troisième étape

Objectives **Inquiring about and expressing likes and dislikes; paying the check**

7 Maud would like to know how much the following items cost. Write the waiter's answers to her questions. The prices are given in parentheses. Write out the amounts in French. (**p. 155**)

EXEMPLE C'est combien, la pizza suprême? (10, 50 €) **C'est dix euros cinquante.**

1. C'est combien, le steak-frites? (6,50 €)
2. C'est combien, l'omelette au jambon? (5,75 €)
3. C'est combien, la salade niçoise? (7,75 €)
4. C'est combien, trois sandwiches au rosbif? (13,25 €)
5. C'est combien, le couscous? (11,50 €)
6. C'est combien, le croque-monsieur et le café? (9,75 €)

8 Write out in French the number that would come next in each of the series below. (**p. 155**)

1. vingt-deux, quarante-quatre, soixante-six...
2. seize, trente-deux, quarante-huit...
3. onze, trente et un, cinquante et un...
4. quatre-vingt-quinze, quatre-vingt-dix, quatre-vingt-cinq...
5. soixante-dix, quatre-vingts, quatre-vingt-dix...
6. vingt-cinq, trente-cinq, quarante-cinq...

9 Choose the correct form of the verb. (**pp. 151, 152, 155**)

1. C' _______ combien un hamburger?
   a. est
   b. a
   c. es

2. Mathieu, _______ ton hot-dog.
   a. manges
   b. mange
   c. mangez

3. Sabine et Laure, _______ une pizza.
   a. prends
   b. prenez
   c. prendre

4. _______-moi un coca, s'il vous plaît.
   a. Apportez
   b. Apportes
   c. Apporter

5. Comment tu _______ ça?
   a. trouves
   b. trouve
   c. trouvez

6. Ça _______ combien?
   a. fait
   b. fais
   c. faire

Review and Assess

You may wish to assign the **Grammaire supplémentaire** activities as additional practice or homework after presenting material throughout the chapter. Assign Activities 1–2 after **Grammaire** (p. 149), Activities 3–6 after **Grammaire** (p. 152), and Activities 7–8 after **Tu te rappelles?** (p. 155). To prepare students for the **Etape** Quizzes and Chapter Test, we suggest doing the **Grammaire supplémentaire** activities in the following order. Have students complete Activities 1–2 before taking Quizzes 5-1A or 5-1B; Activities 3–6 before Quizzes 5-2A or 5-2B; and Activities 7–9 before Quizzes 5-3A or 5-3B.

Answers

7
1. C'est six euros cinquante.
2. C'est cinq euros soixante-quinze.
3. C'est sept euros soixante-quinze.
4. C'est treize euros vingt-cinq.
5. C'est onze euros cinquante.
6. C'est neuf euros soixante-quinze.

8
1. quatre-vingt-huit
2. soixante-quatre
3. soixante et onze
4. quatre-vingts
5. cent
6. cinquante-cinq

9
1. a
2. b
3. b
4. a
5. a
6. a

STANDARDS: 1.2

Mise en pratique

CHAPITRE 5

The **Mise en pratique** reviews and integrates all four skills and culture in preparation for the Chapter Test.

Teaching Resources

pp. 164–165

PRINT 

- Lesson Planner, p. 27
- Listening Activities, p. 37
- Video Guide, pp. 35, 38
- Grammar Tutor for Students of French, Chapter 5
- Standardized Assessment Tutor, Chapter 5

MEDIA

- One-Stop Planner
- Video Program Videocassette 2, 34:41–35:56
- DVD Tutor, Disc 1
- Audio Compact Discs, CD 5, Tr. 18
- Interactive CD-ROM Tutor, Disc 2

Challenge

1 Have students write down the items that are ordered in each dialogue.

Portfolio

2 **Oral** You might want to have students add this to their oral portfolios or use it as an oral assessment tool. For portfolio suggestions, see *Alternative Assessment Guide,* page 22.

Mise en pratique

Visit Holt Online
go.hrw.com
KEYWORD: WA3 PARIS-5
Self-Test

1 In which café would you most likely hear these conversations? See scripts and answers on p. 139H.

CD 5 Tr. 18

Café de Paris

15, Place du Palais - 75004 Paris
Téléphone 01-43-54-20-21

Nos ***glaces***

Coupe Melba	7,50
Coupe Nougat	7,00
Banana Split	6,50

Nos ***boissons***

Eau minérale	2,00
Jus de fruit	2,25
Café	1,75
Thé	1,25

SERVICE COMPRIS 15%

Café de la gare

87, Avenue Victor Hugo -
75017 Paris
Tél. 01-45-62-52-53

Sandwiches

Croque-monsieur	4,50
Sandwich au jambon	3,75
Sandwich au fromage	3,00
Sandwich au rosbif	3,75

Boissons

Orangina, Coca	1,50
Eau minérale	1,75
Café	1,25
Jus de fruit	2,00

Café Américain

135, Boulevard d'Argençon • 75008 Paris
• Téléphone 01-44-15-30-33

★ **Pizzas** ★

Trois fromages	7,50
Suprême	9,75

★ **Plats** ★

Couscous	7,50
Steak-frites	6,75

★ **Boissons** ★

Coca	2,00
Limonade	2,25
Eau minérale	2,50

SERVICE COMPRIS 15%

2 You and your partner are hungry. Suggest that you go to a café, decide what you both want to eat, and choose one of the cafés above.

Apply and Assess

Slower Pace

1 Before doing this activity, go over the menus with students. Ask them to identify as many differences as they can among the cafés, particularly concerning the type of food offered.

Math Link

1 Replay the recording. Pause the recording after each dialogue and ask students to calculate the amount of the check.

STANDARDS: 1.1, 1.2, 3.1

3 From what you know about French cafés, are these statements true or false?

1. If you don't see **service compris** on the menu, you should leave a tip. true
2. To call the waiter, you should say **Garçon!** false
3. It is usually acceptable to stay in a French café for a long time, as long as you've ordered something to eat or drink. true
4. If a French person says **C'est pas mauvais,** he or she doesn't like the food. false

4 Ecrivons!

The French Club at your school is going to have a picnic to raise money. Plan the picnic with two classmates and then create your own poster announcing it.

First, create a name and catchy slogan to attract attention to your event. Determine the time and place of the picnic, the food, and the activities planned. Include a brief description of the purpose of the event. You should also decide how much each item will cost. Jot down all of your decisions.

Stratégie pour écrire
Arranging ideas spatially is a useful way to organize information before you write. It's a way of creating a type of blueprint to show how your finished product will look.

Now, you're ready to create your blueprint. On a sheet of paper, draw a box for each item that you will include on your poster (title, slogan, date, time, place, food, and so on) in the place where you want the information to appear. Label each box with the type of information that will go in that space.

Next, using the blueprint you've developed, create your poster promoting the French Club picnic. Use what you've learned in this chapter, such as commands. You might add drawings or magazine cutouts to illustrate your poster.

Title

Slogan

5 Jeu de rôle

The day of the French Club picnic has arrived. One person in your group will act as host, the others will be the guests. The host will ask people what they want. Guests will tell what they want and talk about how they like the food and drink. After eating, suggest activities and decide which one you'll participate in.

Mise en pratique

CHAPITRE 5

Writing Assessment

4 You might use the following rubric when grading your students on this activity.

Writing Rubric	Points			
	4	3	2	1
Content (Complete–Incomplete)				
Comprehensibility (Comprehensible–Incomprehensible)				
Accuracy (Accurate–Seldom accurate)				
Organization (Well organized–Poorly organized)				
Effort (Excellent–Minimal)				

18–20: A
16–17: B
14–15: C
12–13: D
Under 12: F

Apply and Assess

Process Writing

4 Have students work in groups to create a radio announcement for the picnic they're planning. They might record their announcements for their class and play them for other French classes.

Teaching Suggestion

4 5 Both of these activities could be used as class projects.

STANDARDS: 1.1, 1.3, 3.1, 5.1, 5.2

Que sais-je?

CHAPITRE 5

Teaching Resources
p. 166

PRINT 
- Grammar Tutor for Students of French, Chapter 5

MEDIA 
- Interactive CD-ROM Tutor, Disc 2
- Online self-test

go.hrw.com WA3 PARIS-5

Teacher Note
This page is intended to help students prepare for the Chapter Test. It is a brief checklist of the major points covered in the chapter. The students should be reminded that this is only a checklist and does not necessarily include everything that will appear on the test.

Answers

2 *Possible answers:* Désolé(e), j'ai des devoirs à faire. J'ai des courses à faire. J'ai des trucs à faire.

4
1. Excusez-moi. Monsieur! Madame! Mademoiselle!
2. Qu'est-ce que vous avez comme sandwiches?
3. Qu'est-ce qu'il y a à boire?

6 *Possible answers:* Je voudrais... ; Je vais prendre... ; Donnez-moi... ; Apportez-moi... , s'il vous plaît.

7
1. Il prend un sandwich au jambon.
2. Tu prends un steak-frites.
3. Nous prenons un jus d'orange.
4. Ils prennent une limonade.

9 *Possible answers:* C'est bon! C'est délicieux! C'est pas bon. C'est pas terrible. C'est dégoûtant.

10
1. C'est combien, un hot-dog?
2. C'est combien, une pizza?
3. C'est combien, une glace?
4. C'est combien, une salade?

Que sais-je?

WA3 PARIS-5

Can you use what you've learned in this chapter?

Can you make suggestions, excuses, and recommendations? pp. 145, 148

1 How would you suggest to a friend that you . . .
1. go to the café? On va au café?
2. play tennis? On joue au tennis?

2 How would you turn down a suggestion and make an excuse? See answers below.

3 How would you recommend to a friend something . . . Possible answers:
1. to eat? Prends un sandwich au jambon.
2. to drink? Prends un coca.

Can you get someone's attention and order food and beverages? p. 151

4 In a café, how would you . . . See answers below.
1. get the server's attention?
2. ask what kinds of sandwiches they serve?
3. ask what there is to drink?

5 How would you say that you're . . .
1. hungry? J'ai faim.
2. thirsty? J'ai soif.

6 How would you order . . . See answers below.
1. something to eat?
2. something to drink?

7 How would you tell what people are having, using the verb **prendre?** See answers below.

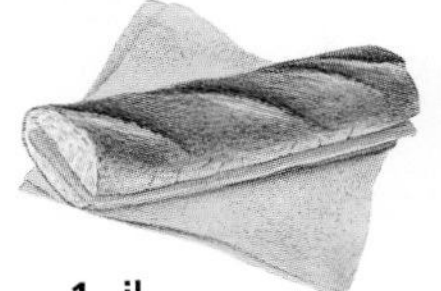
1. il

2. tu

3. nous

4. ils

Can you inquire about and express likes and dislikes? p. 154

8 How would you ask a friend how he or she likes a certain food? Comment tu trouves ça?

9 How would you tell someone what you think of these items? See answers below.

1.

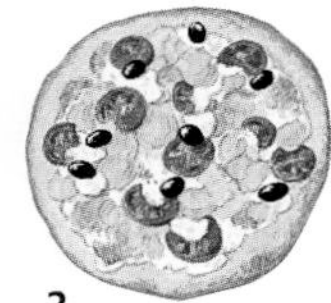
2.

3.

4.

Can you pay the check? p. 155

10 How would you ask how much each item in number 9 costs? See answers below.

11 How would you ask for the check? L'addition, s'il vous plaît.

12 How would you ask what the total is? Ça fait combien, s'il vous plaît?

Review and Assess

Additional Practice
9 Have students include the name of the item as they give their opinion of it. Then, have them find a partner in the class whose likes and dislikes match their own. Which of these four foods is the most popular? Which food is the least popular? Which foods would students include in their menu if they were planning a party?

Game
Le Base-ball Draw a baseball diamond on the board. Divide the class into two teams. The player up first may try to answer a single question for one base, two questions for a double, and so on. You might want to use the more difficult questions for players trying for extra-base hits.

STANDARDS: 1.1

Vocabulaire

Première étape

Making suggestions; making excuses

On va au café?	*How about going to the café?*
On... ?	*How about . . . ?*
Désolé(e). J'ai des devoirs à faire.	*Sorry. I have homework to do.*
J'ai des courses à faire.	*I have errands to do.*
J'ai des trucs à faire.	*I have some things to do.*
J'ai des tas de choses à faire.	*I have lots of things to do.*
Je ne peux pas parce que...	*I can't because . . .*

Foods and beverages

un croque-monsieur	*toasted ham and cheese sandwich*
un sandwich	*ham sandwich*
au jambon	
au saucisson	*salami sandwich*
au fromage	*cheese sandwich*
un hot-dog	*hot dog*
un steak-frites	*steak and French fries*
une quiche	*quiche*
une omelette	*omelet*
une crêpe	*very thin pancake*
une eau minérale	*mineral water*
une limonade	*lemon soda*
un citron pressé	*lemonade*
un sirop de fraise (à l'eau)	*water with strawberry syrup*
un coca	*cola*
un jus d'orange	*orange juice*
un jus de pomme	*apple juice*
un café	*coffee*
un chocolat	*hot chocolate*

Making a recommendation

Prends/Prenez...	*Have . . .*
prendre	*to take; to have food or drink*

Other useful expressions

avoir soif	*to be thirsty*
avoir faim	*to be hungry*

Deuxième étape

Getting someone's attention

Excusez-moi.	*Excuse me.*
Monsieur!	*Waiter!*
Madame!	*Waitress!*
Mademoiselle!	*Waitress!*
La carte, s'il vous plaît.	*The menu, please.*

Ordering food and beverages

Vous avez choisi?	*Have you decided/chosen?*
Vous prenez?	*What are you having?*
Vous avez... ?	*Do you have . . . ?*
Qu'est-ce que vous avez comme boissons?	*What do you have to drink?*
Qu'est-ce qu'il y a à boire?	*What is there to drink?*
Je voudrais...	*I'd like . . .*
Je vais prendre..., s'il vous plaît.	*I'll have . . ., please.*
..., s'il vous plaît.	*. . ., please.*
Donnez-moi..., s'il vous plaît.	*Please give me . . .*
Apportez-moi..., s'il vous plaît.	*Please bring me . . .*

Troisième étape

Inquiring about and expressing likes and dislikes

Comment tu trouves ça?	*How do you like it?*
C'est...	*It's . . .*
bon!	*good!*
excellent!	*excellent!*
délicieux!	*delicious!*
pas mauvais!	*pretty good!*
pas bon.	*not good.*
pas terrible.	*not so great.*
dégoûtant.	*gross.*
mauvais.	*bad.*

Paying the check

L'addition, s'il vous plaît.	*The check, please.*
Oui, tout de suite.	*Yes, right away.*
Un moment, s'il vous plaît.	*One moment, please.*
C'est combien,... ?	*How much is . . . ?*
Ça fait combien, s'il vous plaît?	*How much is it, please?*
C'est... euros.	*It's . . . euros.*
Ça fait... euros.	*It's . . . euros.*

Vocabulaire

CHAPITRE 5

Building on Previous Skills

Have students write down all the cognates they can find on this page.

Chapter 5 Assessment

- **Testing Program**
  Chapter Test, pp. 117–122
  Audio Compact Discs, CD 5, Trs. 22–24
  Speaking Test, p. 345
- **Alternative Assessment Guide**
  Performance Assessment, p. 36
  Portfolio Assessment, p. 22
  CD-ROM Assessment, p. 50
- **Interactive CD-ROM Tutor, Disc 2**

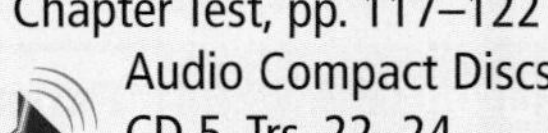

  A toi de parler
  A toi d'écrire
- **Standardized Assessment Tutor**
  Chapter 5
- **One-Stop Planner, Disc 2**
  Test Generator
  Chapter 5

Review and Assess

Challenge

As a comprehensive review of vocabulary, have students write a conversation among two customers and a server in a café using vocabulary from all three **étapes.** Students might do this with a partner or in groups of three.

Visual Learners

Have students work in pairs or small groups to draw a comic strip depicting a scene in a café. Have them write a conversation between a waiter and a customer. Groups can then exchange their comic strips and perform each other's dialogues for additional practice.

STANDARDS: 1.1, 1.2

Chapitre 6 : Amusons-nous!
Chapter Overview

Mise en train pp. 170–172	***Projets de week-end***			
	FUNCTIONS	**GRAMMAR**	**VOCABULARY**	**RE-ENTRY**
Première étape pp. 173–178	• Making plans, p. 173	• Using **le** with days of the week, p. 173 • The verb **aller** and **aller** + infinitive, p. 174 • Contractions with **à**, p. 177	• Leisure time activities, p. 173 • Places to go in one's spare time, p. 176	• Expressing likes and dislikes **(Chapitre 1)** • Days of the week **(Chapitre 2)**
Deuxième étape pp. 179–182	• Extending and responding to invitations, p. 179	• The verb **vouloir**, p. 180		• Making, accepting, and turning down suggestions **(Chapitre 4)** • Sports and hobbies **(Chapitre 4)**
Troisième étape pp. 183–187	• Arranging to meet someone, p. 183	• Information questions, p. 185		• Official time **(Chapitre 2)** • **Est-ce que (Chapitre 4)** • Days of the week **(Chapitre 2)** • Time expressions **(Chapitre 2)**

Prononciation p. 187	**The vowel sounds [ø] and [œ]** Audio CD 6, Tracks 12–14	**A écrire** (dictation) Audio CD 6, Tracks 15–17	
Lisons! pp. 188–189	**Parcs d'attractions**	**Reading Strategy:** Using context to determine meaning	
Grammaire supplémentaire	**pp. 190–193** **Première étape,** pp. 190–192	**Deuxième étape,** p. 192	**Troisième étape,** p. 193
Review pp. 194–197	**Mise en pratique,** pp. 194–195 **Ecrivons!** Arranging ideas chronologically Planning a day in Paris	**Que sais-je?** p. 196	**Vocabulaire,** p. 197

CULTURE

- **Panorama Culturel,** Going out with friends, p. 178
- Realia: Leisure activities, p. 179
- **Rencontre culturelle,** Dating in France, p. 182
- **Note culturelle,** Conversational time, p. 184
- Realia: Movie schedule, p. 186

Chapitre 6 : Amusons-nous!

Chapter Resources

Lesson Planning

One-Stop Planner

Lesson Planner with Differentiated Instruction, pp. 28–32, 70

Student Make-Up Assignments
- Make-Up Assignment Copying Masters, Chapter 6

Listening and Speaking

TPR Storytelling Book, pp. 21–24

Listening Activities
- Student Response Forms for Listening Activities, pp. 43–45
- Additional Listening Activities 6-1 to 6-6, pp. 47–49
- Additional Listening Activities (song), p. 50
- Scripts and Answers, pp. 127–131

Video Guide
- Teaching Suggestions, pp. 40–41
- Activity Masters, pp. 42–44
- Scripts and Answers, pp. 100–102, 120

Activities for Communication
- Communicative Activities, pp. 31–36
- Realia and Teaching Suggestions, pp. 100–104
- Situation Cards, pp. 147–148

Reading and Writing

Reading Strategies and Skills Handbook, Chapter 6

Joie de lire 1, Chapter 6

Cahier d'activités, pp. 61–72

Grammar

Travaux pratiques de grammaire, pp. 41–50

Grammar Tutor for Students of French, Chapter 6

Assessment

Testing Program
- Grammar and Vocabulary Quizzes, **Etape** Quizzes, and Chapter Test, pp. 131–148
- Score Sheet, Scripts and Answers, pp. 149–156
- Midterm Exam, pp. 157–164
- Score Sheet, Scripts, and Answers, pp. 165–170

Alternative Assessment Guide
- Portfolio Assessment, p. 23
- Performance Assessment, p. 37
- CD-ROM Assessment, p. 51

Student Make-Up Assignments
- Alternative Quizzes, Chapter 6

Standardized Assessment Tutor
- Reading, pp. 21–23 • Writing, p. 24 • Math, pp. 25–26

Middle School

Middle School Teaching Resources, Chapter 6

Online Activities
- **Jeux interactifs**
- **Activités Internet**

Video Program
- Videocassette 2
- Videocassette 5 (captioned version)

Interactive CD-ROM Tutor, Disc 2

DVD Tutor, Disc 1

Audio Compact Discs
- Textbook Listening Activities, CD 6, Tracks 1–18
- Additional Listening Activities, CD 6, Tracks 31–37
- Assessment Items, CD 6, Tracks 19–24
- Midterm Exam, CD 6, Tracks 25–30

Teaching Transparencies
- Situation 6-1 to 6-3
- Vocabulary 6-A and 6-B
- **Mise en train**
- **Grammaire supplémentaire** Answers
- **Travaux pratiques de grammaire** Answers

One-Stop Planner CD-ROM

Use the **One-Stop Planner CD-ROM with Test Generator** to aid in lesson planning and pacing.

For each chapter, the **One-Stop Planner** includes:
- Editable lesson plans with direct links to teaching resources
- Printable worksheets from resource books
- Direct launches to the HRW Internet activities
- Video and audio segments
- Test Generator
- Clip Art for vocabulary items

Chapitre 6 : Amusons-nous!

Projects

Les vacances parfaites

Students will create a poster or brochure of a vacation spot in the francophone world. This can be done in English or French.

MATERIALS

✂ **Students may need**
- Travel information
- Reference books
- Scissors
- Glue or tape
- Colored pens and pencils
- Construction paper

PREPARATION

Have students choose a vacation spot in the francophone world that interests them. Then, have them gather information about the place, using atlases, magazines, catalogs, newspaper articles, and travel brochures.

SUGGESTED SEQUENCE

1. Have students make a list of information tourists might need for their particular destination, including attractions, average weather conditions, local customs, currency, and so on.
2. Have students organize their materials and notes and begin planning their posters. If the posters are to be in French, students might also look up unfamiliar words they will need.
3. Next, students either show you their organized materials, or have classmates look over their work to check spelling and provide feedback on the appropriateness of the content and arrangement of the layout.
4. Students then finish putting their posters together, adding illustrations, captions, and other written information.

GRADING THE PROJECT

Suggested Point Distribution: (total = 100 points)

Content	30 points
Presentation/appearance	30 points
Language use (if in French)	20 points
Creativity	20 points

Games

Le mot juste

This game will help your students develop the skill of circumlocution, the linguistic art of communicating when a person doesn't know the precise word he or she needs. Explain to students that they will learn to paraphrase, use synonyms, describe essential elements, and apply key phrases to communicate when they find themselves at a loss for the exact word.

Materials To play this game, you will need index cards.

Preparation Create a list of words related to the vocabulary presented in the chapter or **étape.** On each card, write one word from the list. Arrange four desks at the front of the room so that the two partners from each team can face each other. Place the cards face down where they can easily be reached by the players from any of the desks. On the board or a transparency, write the following key phrases:

C'est un(e)...
C'est un(e) truc, personne, animal que/qui...
Il/Elle est grand(e)/âgé(e). C'est... rouge/grand.
Ça ressemble à...
C'est le contraire de...
C'est un endroit où...
Il/Elle a...
... est fait(e) en plastique/bois/verre/coton.
On l'utilise pour...

Procedure Divide the class into two teams and select a scorekeeper and a timekeeper. Have two players from each team sit at the desks. A player from Team A selects a card and shows it to only one of the players from Team B. Using circumlocution, the Team A player makes a statement about the vocabulary word without saying the word itself. (For an elephant, one could say **C'est un animal gris.**) If the player's partner guesses the word, Team A receives five points. (Allow 30 seconds per guess.) If not, the Team B player in turn gives a clue to his or her partner. If the partner guesses correctly, Team B receives four points. Play alternates between the two teams, with point value dropping by one after each incorrect guess. If no team scores a point after five clues, any student on Team A may guess to earn one point. If Team A can't guess correctly, a student from Team B is given the same opportunity. Announce the answer if no one guesses correctly. After four words, select four new players for the next round.

STANDARDS: 1.3, 3.2, 5.1, 5.2

Storytelling

Mini-histoire

*This story accompanies Teaching Transparency 6-1. The **mini-histoire** can be told and retold in different formats, acted out, written down, and read aloud, to give students additional opportunities to practice all four skills. The following story relates the weekly schedule of two friends.*

Marc et Sophie vont au Lycée Voltaire du lundi matin à 9 heures au vendredi soir à 17 heures. Tous les midis, ils mangent au café «Chez Pierre». Après l'école, ils aiment jouer dans le parc. Le mercredi après-midi, il n'y a pas classe. Marc joue au football de 15 heures à 17 heures au stade du Rey. Sophie préfère lire et va choisir de nouveaux livres à la bibliothèque municipale. Le week-end, ils sont aussi très occupés. Le samedi, quand il fait beau, Marc veut aller pique-niquer et Sophie veut faire les vitrines. Quand il pleut, ils adorent aller au cinéma ou au musée. Le dimanche, ils sont fatigués et ils ne veulent rien faire. Ils dorment.

Traditions

Loisirs

Every day, Parisians escape the hustle and bustle of Paris by taking a stroll or sitting in one of the city's many parks and gardens. One of the most popular parks is the **Jardin du Luxembourg.** As the day passes, the park fills with children playing, workers enjoying a picnic lunch or snack, and retirees playing chess or **pétanque,** a type of lawn bowling. However, it is on the weekends that the grounds really come alive. Children ride ponies or the 100 year-old carousel and watch the marionette show at the **Grand Guignol.** Teens and adults play tennis, jog, or sit on the many park benches, chatting with friends or reading. As is the case in many of the parks in France, walking or sitting on the grass is forbidden. Have students conduct an Internet search to get more information about this and other famous parks in Paris.

Recette

*The **steak-frites** is a very simple dish that is served everywhere in France. Most of the time, children order a **steak-frites** when they go to restaurants with their parents, not so much for the steak as for the French fries. However, it is said that the best fries are to be found in Belgium.*

STEAK-FRITES

Steak

2 steaks

4 cuillères à café de poivre noir

3 cuillères à café de beurre

1 cuillère à café d'huile végétale

2 cuillères à soupe de farine

3/4 tasse de bouillon

sel

Frites

6 pommes de terre

huile végétale

sel

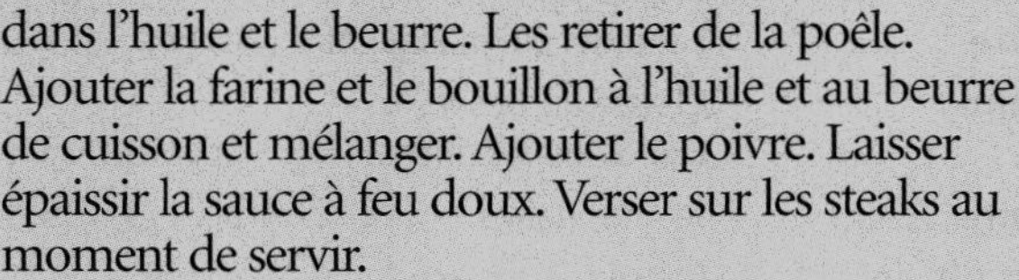

Faire cuire les steaks dans l'huile et le beurre. Les retirer de la poêle. Ajouter la farine et le bouillon à l'huile et au beurre de cuisson et mélanger. Ajouter le poivre. Laisser épaissir la sauce à feu doux. Verser sur les steaks au moment de servir.

Eplucher les pommes de terre et les couper dans le sens de la longueur. Faire chauffer l'huile. Plonger les pommes de terre dans l'huile jusqu'à ce qu'elles soient entièrement cuites mais pas dorées. Sortir les pommes de terre de l'huile et les égoutter à l'aide de serviettes en papier.

Ne faire cuire que quelques frites à la fois.

Replonger les frites dans l'huile. Les retirer de nouveau de l'huile. Les égoutter et les garder au chaud dans le four.

Technology

DVD/Video

Videocassette 2, Videocassette 5 (captioned version)
DVD Tutor, Disc 1
See Video Guide, pp. 39–44.

Mise en train • Projets de week-end

In this segment of the video, Mathieu asks Isabelle what she plans to do the next day. She tells him about her plans for the day and says she is free for the evening. Mathieu asks her if she would like to go to a concert, but she is not interested. Mathieu suggests they go to the zoo, but Isabelle doesn't like zoos. They each make several more suggestions but cannot agree on any of them. During their conversation, we see scenes of their suggested activities. They finally agree to go to the movies, but then can't agree on what film to see!

Projets de week-end (suite)

When the story continues, Mathieu and Isabelle agree on a film. Mathieu and Isabelle invite Simon to join them, but he is too busy with schoolwork. Mathieu and Isabelle then meet Thuy, who is interested in going to the movies but wants to see a different film. Mathieu checks the times in his *Pariscope.* They all meet in front of the theater, but the movie is not playing. Mathieu discovers that he has last week's *Pariscope!*

Qu'est-ce que tu fais quand tu sors?

Several teenagers from different French-speaking countries tell us where they go and what they like to do on weekends with their friends.

Vidéoclips

- **Panach'®**: advertisement for beverage
- **Folie's®**: chocolat liégeois: advertisement for dessert

Interactive CD-ROM Tutor

Activity	Activity Type	Pupil's Edition Page
En contexte	*Interactive conversation*	
1. Grammaire	Les mots qui manquent	p. 174
2. Vocabulaire	Chasse au trésor Explorons!/Vérifions!	pp. 173, 176
3. Vocabulaire	Jeu des paires	pp. 173, 176
4. Comment dit-on... ?	Chacun à sa place	p. 179
5. Grammaire	Les mots qui manquent	p. 180
6. Comment dit-on... ?	Le bon choix	p. 183
Panorama Culturel	Qu'est-ce que tu fais quand tu sors? Le bon choix	p. 178
A toi de parler	*Guided recording*	pp. 194–195
A toi de d'écrire	*Guided writing*	pp. 194–195

Teacher Management System

Launch the program, type "admin" in the password area and press RETURN. Log on to **www.hrw.com/CDROMTUTOR** for a detailed explanation of the Teacher Management System.

DVD Tutor

The *DVD Tutor* contains all material from the *Video Program* as described above. French captions are available for use at your discretion for all sections of the video. The *DVD Tutor* also provides a variety of video-based activities that assess students' understanding of the **Mise en train, Suite,** and **Panorama Culturel.**

This part of the *DVD Tutor* may be used on any DVD video player connected to a television or video monitor.

In addition to the video material and the video-based comprehension activities, the *DVD Tutor* also contains the entire *Interactive CD-ROM Tutor* in DVD-ROM format. Each DVD disc contains the activities from all 12 chapters of the *Interactive CD-ROM Tutor.*

This part of the *DVD Tutor* may be used on a Macintosh® or Windows® computer with a DVD-ROM drive.

To preview all resources available for this chapter, use the **One-Stop Planner CD-ROM,** Disc 2.

Visit Holt Online
go.hrw.com
KEYWORD: WA3 PARIS-6
Online Edition

Go.Online!

Online Edition

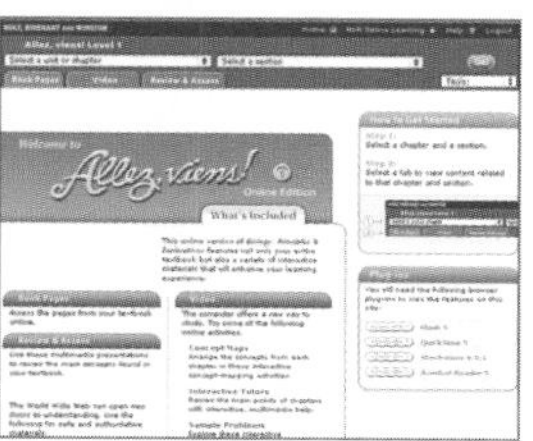

The Online Edition for Allez, viens! *allows students access to their textbooks anytime anywhere.*

- *Audio at point of use*
- *Additional practice activities*
- *Self-test activities*
- *Online reference tools*
- *Entire Video Program (Enhanced version)*
- *Interactive Notebook (Enhanced version)*

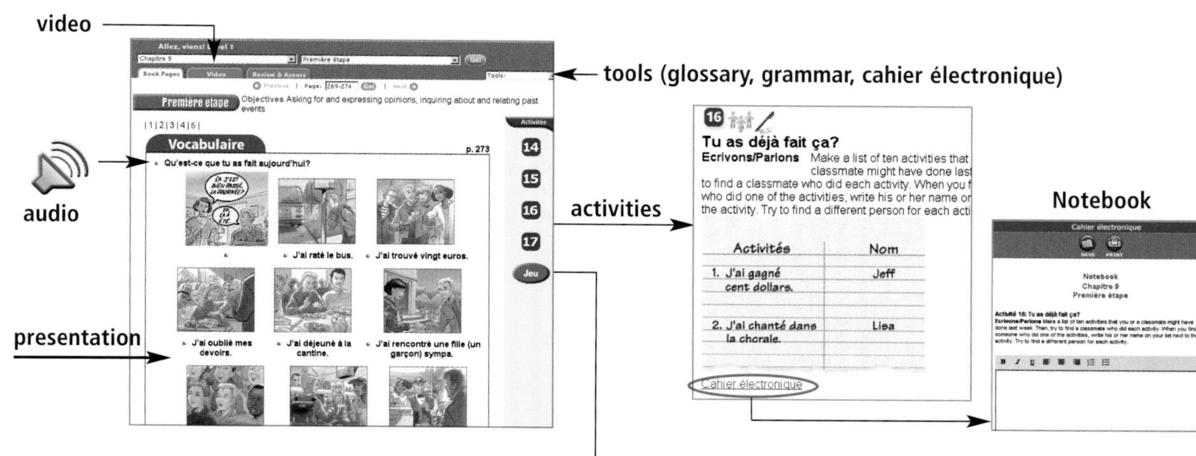

HRW Atlas

Internet Activités

Activités Internet

These guided internet activities include a worksheet and pre-selected and pre-screened authentic web sites from the francophone world. You can use these activities

- to help students develop research skills in the target language
- to introduce students to authentic cultural information
- as a project

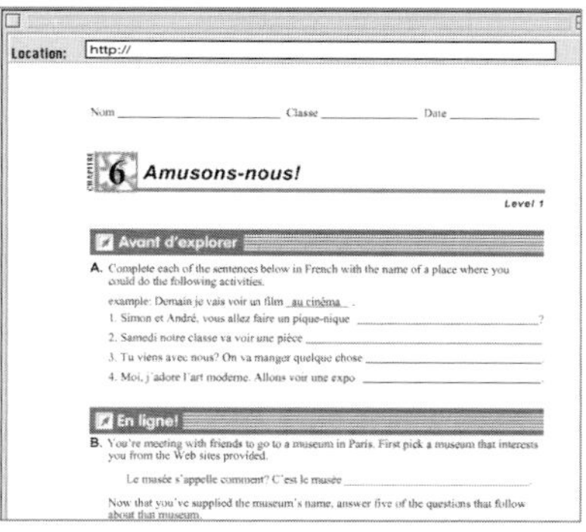

Jeux interactifs

You can use the interactive activities in this chapter

- to practice grammar, vocabulary, and chapter functions
- as homework
- as an assessment option
- as a self-test
- to prepare for the Chapter Test

Projet Have students imagine that they are tour guides and they love to entertain the tourists! Have them do a Web search and select a destination for a tour: a museum, a church, a monument, or a bus or **bateau-mouche** tour of Paris. Have them introduce their tour, describe the place they are about to show, give some historical background, tell a funny story related to the place, and give general instructions to the tourists. Students might want to record their guided tours on a cassette and play it for the class.

Chapitre 6 : Amusons-nous!

Textbook Listening Activities Scripts

Première étape

7 p. 173

SOPHIE Alors, qu'est-ce que tu vas faire ce week-end?

THERESE Ce week-end? Oh là là! Plein de choses! Samedi matin, je vais faire une vidéo à la Maison des jeunes. Samedi après-midi, je vais faire les magasins et le soir, je vais au cinéma avec des copains.

SOPHIE C'est tout?

THERESE Non, attends, ce n'est pas fini! Dimanche matin, je vais au café et l'après-midi, je vais aller au Parc Astérix.

SOPHIE Eh bien, bon week-end!

Possible answers to Activity 7
make a video, go shopping, go to the movies, go to a café, go to Parc Astérix

9 p. 174

1. Samedi après-midi, je vais jouer au football.
2. Michel et moi, nous regardons la télévision.
3. Je prends un sandwich et un coca.
4. Tu vas faire un pique-nique?
5. Nous allons faire une promenade.

Answers to Activity 9
1. going to do
2. doing
3. doing
4. going to do
5. going to do

Deuxième étape

17 p. 179

1. — Dis, Marc, tu veux aller nager?
— Désolé, je ne peux pas.

2. — Tu veux bien faire les magasins avec nous, Nathalie?
— A quelle heure?
— Vers cinq heures.
— Pourquoi pas?

3. — On va jouer au foot ce week-end. Tu viens, Malika?
— Oui, je veux bien.

4. — Stéphane, on va faire un pique-nique. Tu viens?
— Un pique-nique? Désolé, je suis occupé. J'ai un match de tennis.

5. — Salut, Ferdinand. On va écouter de la musique?
— Je ne peux pas. J'ai des trucs à faire.
— Dommage.

6. — Tu veux venir manger un sandwich avec nous, Serge?
— Oui, je veux bien. A quelle heure?
— Maintenant.
— D'accord. J'arrive.

Answers to Activity 17
1. refuse
2. accepte
3. accepte
4. refuse
5. refuse
6. accepte

The following scripts are for the listening activities found in the *Pupil's Edition*. For Student Response Forms, see *Listening Activities,* pages 43–45. To provide students with additional listening practice, see *Listening Activities,* pages 47–50.

One-Stop Planner CD-ROM

To preview all resources available for this chapter, use the **One-Stop Planner CD-ROM**, Disc 2.

Troisième étape

24 p. 184

Salut, Paul. C'est moi, Sylvie! Ça va?... Demain, je vais au musée d'Orsay. Tu veux venir avec moi?... Oui, demain... A quelle heure? Bon, vers midi. Tu viens?... Super! Alors, on se retrouve devant le musée... C'est ça. Midi, devant le musée, demain. A demain, Paul...

Answers to Activity 24

1. c
2. a
3. c
4. c

26 p. 184

1. Salut. C'est Laurent. On va au zoo ce week-end avec Nathalie. Est-ce que tu veux venir avec nous? Voilà. On y va samedi après-midi, vers trois heures. On se retrouve devant le zoo à trois heures moins le quart. D'accord? Alors, à demain peut-être.
2. Allô! C'est moi, Patricia. Comment ça va? Je vais au stade dimanche avec Pascal. Tu veux venir avec nous? On va voir un match de foot. On se retrouve à huit heures au métro Saint-Michel. A dimanche. Tchao!
3. Bonjour. Ici Eric. Je vais à la piscine demain matin à dix heures. Est-ce que tu peux venir? Rendez-vous devant la piscine. Au revoir.

Answers to Activity 26

1. Laurent; to the zoo; Saturday afternoon at 2:45; in front of the zoo
2. Patricia; to the stadium; Sunday at 8:00; at the Saint-Michel metro stop
3. Eric; to the swimming pool; tomorrow morning at 10:00; in front of the swimming pool

PRONONCIATION, P. 187

For the scripts for Parts A and B , see p. 187. The script for Part C is below.

C. A écrire *(dictation)*

— Tu veux aller à la Maison des jeunes jeudi?

— A quelle heure?

— Vers neuf heures.

— Désolé, je ne peux pas.

Mise en pratique

2 p. 194

— Tu viens avec moi visiter la tour Montparnasse? J'ai un bon de réduction. On a une vue magnifique de la terrasse.

— Bof. Je vais avoir le vertige là-haut.

— Tu veux aller au cinéma ou au musée?

— Non, je voudrais aller écouter les grandes orgues de Notre-Dame. C'est tellement beau.

— D'accord. Tu veux y aller quand?

— Dimanche, si tu veux.

— Pourquoi pas? On se retrouve à quelle heure?

— Le concert est à six heures moins le quart. On peut se donner rendez-vous vers cinq heures et demie.

— Où ça?

— Devant la cathédrale.

— O.K. Notre-Dame, dimanche, à cinq heures et demie. Bonne idée. Ça coûte cher?

— Mais non, c'est gratuit.

— Génial! C'est vraiment une excellente idée.

Answers to Mise en pratique, Activity 2

Notre-Dame; Sunday at 5:30, in front of the cathedral

Chapitre 6 : Amusons-nous!
50-Minute Lesson Plans

Day 1

CHAPTER OPENER **5 min.**
- Present Chapter Objectives, ATE, p. 169.
- Background Information, ATE, p. 168
- Thinking Critically, ATE, p. 169

MISE EN TRAIN **40 min.**
- Presenting **Mise en train** and Preteaching Vocabulary, ATE, p. 170
- Culture Note, ATE, p. 170, and Culture Notes, ATE, p. 171
- Do Activities 1–6, p. 172.

Wrap-Up **5 min.**
- Show Map Transparency 5 (Paris). Call on students to point out the places mentioned in the **Mise en train.** Point out other major places of interest. Ask students which of the places they would like to visit and why.

Homework Options
Cahier d'activités, p. 61, Acts. 1–2

Day 2

PREMIERE ETAPE
Quick Review **10 min.**
- Check homework.
- Bell Work, ATE, p. 173

Comment dit-on... ?, p. 173 **10 min.**
- Presenting **Comment dit-on... ?,** ATE, p. 173
- Play Audio CD for Activity 7, p. 173.

Vocabulaire, p. 173 **20 min.**
- Presenting **Vocabulaire,** ATE, p. 173, using Teaching Transparency 6-A
- Presenting **Note de grammaire,** ATE, p. 173
- **Grammaire supplémentaire,** p. 190, Act. 1
- Travaux pratiques de grammaire, p. 41, Acts. 1–2

Wrap-Up **10 min.**
- Do Activity 8, p. 173, as a "chain" activity. The first student will ask the next student about his or her plans for the weekend. That student will respond and ask the next student and so forth.

Homework Options
Travaux pratiques de grammaire, p. 42, Acts. 3–4

Day 3

PREMIERE ETAPE
Quick Review **10 min.**
- Check homework.
- Motivating Activity: Write clues for the activities on page 173 on slips of paper, such as "Romeo and Juliette" for **voir une pièce.** Distribute the slips and then ask each student **Qu'est-ce que tu vas faire ce week-end?** Students will respond with the activity prompted by the clue they received.

Grammaire, p. 174 **30 min.**
- Presenting **Grammaire,** ATE, p. 174
- Challenge, ATE, p. 174
- Play Audio CD for Activity 9, p. 174.
- Do Activities 10–11, pp. 174–175.
- **Grammaire supplémentaire,** pp. 190–191, Acts. 2–3

Wrap-Up **10 min.**
- Kinesthetic Learners, ATE, p. 175

Homework Options
Cahier d'activités, p. 63, Act. 7
Travaux pratiques de grammaire, p. 43, Acts. 5–6

Day 4

PREMIERE ETAPE
Quick Review **10 min.**
- Check homework.
- Play Game: **Trop à faire,** ATE, p. 191.

Vocabulaire, p. 176 **10 min.**
- Presenting **Vocabulaire,** ATE, p. 176, using Teaching Transparency 6-B
- Do Activity 13, p. 176.

Grammaire, p. 177 **15 min.**
- Presenting **Grammaire,** ATE, p. 177
- Do Activity 14, p. 177.
- Travaux pratiques de grammaire, pp. 44–45, Acts. 7–11

Wrap-Up **15 min.**
- Challenge, ATE, p. 177

Homework Options
Study for the **Première étape** quiz.

Day 5

PREMIERE ETAPE
Quiz 6-2 **20 min.**
- Administer Quiz 6-1A or Quiz 6-1B.

PANORAMA CULTUREL **25 min.**
- Present **Panorama Culturel** using Videocassette 2, p. 178.
- Do **Qu'en penses-tu?** questions, p. 178
- Read **Savais-tu que... ?,** p. 178.
- Panorama Culturel, Interactive CD-ROM Tutor, Disc 2

Wrap-Up **5 min.**
- Visual Learners, ATE, p. 178

Homework Options
Cahier d'activités, p. 72, Acts. 25–26

Day 6

DEUXIEME ETAPE
Quick Review **10 min.**
- Bell Work, ATE, p. 179

Comment dit-on... ?, p. 179 **15 min.**
- Presenting **Comment-dit-on... ?,** ATE, p. 179
- Play Audio CD for Activity 17, p. 179.
- Do Activity 18, p. 180.
- Cahier d'activités, p. 65, Acts. 11–12

Grammaire, p. 180 **15 min.**
- Presenting **Grammaire,** ATE, p. 180
- Do Activity 20, p. 181.
- Cahier d'activités, pp. 66–67, Acts. 15–16

Wrap-Up **10 min.**
- Have students pair off. Provide one student in each pair with a vocabulary card depicting a place in town or a sports activity. Give the other student a card with *accept* or *refuse* written on it. Have students act out a dialogue according to their cards.

Homework Options
Study for **Deuxième étape** quiz.

One-Stop Planner CD-ROM

For alternative lesson plans by chapter section, to create your own customized plans, or to preview all resources available for this chapter, use the **One-Stop Planner CD-ROM**, Disc 2.

For additional homework suggestions, see activities accompanied by this symbol throughout the chapter.

Day 7

DEUXIEME ETAPE

Quiz 6-2 20 min.
- Administer Quiz 6-2A or 6-2B

RENCONTRE CULTURELLE 20 min.
- Presenting **Rencontre culturelle,** ATE, p. 182
- Thinking Critically/Comparing and Contrasting, ATE, p. 182
- Do **Qu'en penses-tu?** questions, p. 182.
- Read **Savais-tu que.... ?,** p. 182.

Wrap-Up 10 min.
- Expand the Motivating Activity, ATE, p. 182, by having students sketch pictures of the places they would take photos of to send their French penpal.

Homework Options

Multicultural Link, ATE, p. 182

Day 8

TROISIEME ETAPE

Quick Review 10 min.
- Have students present the information they gathered for the Multicultural Link activity, ATE, p. 182.

Comment dit-on... ?, p. 183 30 min.
- Presenting **Comment dit-on... ?,** ATE, p. 183
- Discuss **Note culturelle,** p. 184.
- Play Audio CD for Activity 24, p. 184.
- Do Activity 25, p. 184.
- Play Audio CD for Activity 26, p. 184.

Wrap-Up 10 min.
- Do Activity 27, p. 185, as a whole-class activity.

Homework Options

Cahier d'activités, pp. 68–69, Acts. 18–20
Travaux pratiques de grammaire, pp. 47–48, Acts. 14–17

Day 9

TROISIEME ETAPE

Quick Review 5 min.
- Check homework.

Grammaire, p. 185 20 min.
- Presenting **Grammaire,** ATE, p. 185
- Do Activities 28 and 30, pp. 185–186.
- Travaux pratiques de grammaire, pp. 49–50, Acts. 18–20

Prononciation, p. 187 15 min.
- Complete presentation and do Activities A–C, p. 187, using Audio CD 6.

Wrap-Up 10 min.
- Have students write a sentence about their plans for the weekend, omitting the activity: **Samedi, après-midi, à trois heures, je vais __ à la piscine avec des copains.** Have students read their sentences to a partner, who will try to fill in the blanks.

Homework Options

Study for the **Troisième étape** quiz.

Day 10

TROISIEME ETAPE

Quiz 6-3 20 min.
- Administer Quiz 6-3A or Quiz 6-3B.

LISONS! 25 min.
- Motivating Activity: Bring in brochures or advertisements from amusement parks or tourist attractions. Have students look at them and ask if they have gone to any of these places or if they would like to go to these places.
- Discuss the **Stratégie pour lire,** p. 188, then do Prereading Activity A, ATE, p. 188.
- Culture Note, ATE, p. 188
- Do Reading Activities B–D, ATE, p. 188.
- Do Activity E, p. 189.

Wrap-Up 5 min.
- Do Postreading Activity E, Thinking Critically, ATE, p. 189.

Homework Options

Cahier d'activités, p. 71, Act. 24

Day 11

LISONS!

Quick Review 5 min.
- Check homework.

MISE EN PRATIQUE 35 min.
- Do Activity 1, p. 194.
- Play Audio CD for Activity 2, p. 194.
- Career Path, ATE, p. 194
- Do Activity 3, p. 195.
- Begin **Ecrivons!,** p. 195. See Portfolio, Written, ATE, p. 195.

Wrap-Up 10 min.
- Have partners complete **Jeu de rôle,** p. 195.

Homework Options

Que sais-je?, p. 196
Finish **Ecrivons!,** Pupil's Edition, p. 195.

Day 12

MISE EN PRATIQUE

Quick Review 15 min.
- Check homework and have students read their **Ecrivons!** aloud for extra-credit.
- Play Game: Around the World, p. 185.

Chapter Review 35 min.
- Review Chapter 6. Choose from **Grammaire supplémentaire,** Grammar Tutor for Students of French, Activities for Communication, Listening Activities, Interactive CD-ROM Tutor, or **Jeux interactifs.**

Homework Options

Study for Chapter 6 Test.

Assessment

Test, Chapter 6 50 min.
- Administer Chapter 6 Test. Select from Testing Program, Alternative Assessment Guide, Test Generator, or Standardized Assessment Tutor.

Chapitre 6 : Amusons-nous!

90-Minute Lesson Plans

Block 1

CHAPTER OPENER 5 min.
- Present Chapter Objectives, ATE, p. 169.
- Motivating Activity: Ask students to recall what they have learned about Paris from the Location Opener on pages 136–139
- Background Information, ATE, p. 168, and Thinking Critically, ATE, p. 169

MISE EN TRAIN 45 min.
- Presenting **Mise en train,** ATE, p. 170, Culture Note, ATE, p. 170, and Culture Notes, ATE, p. 171
- Motivating Activity: Show Map Transparency 5 of Paris. Call on students to point out the places mentioned in the **Mise en train.** Point out other places of interest.
- View video of **Mise en train,** Videocassette 2, Video Guide, p. 39. Do Activity Master 1, Activities 1 and 2, Video Guide, p. 42.

PREMIERE ETAPE

Comment dit-on... ?, p. 173 10 min.
- Bell Work, ATE, p. 173
- Presenting **Comment dit-on... ?,** ATE, p. 173
- Play Audio CD for Activity 7, p. 173.

Vocabulaire, p. 173 15 min.
- Presenting **Note de Grammaire,** ATE, p. 173
- **Grammaire supplémentaire,** p. 190, Act. 1
- Presenting **Vocabulaire,** ATE, p. 173

Grammaire: the verb *aller,* p. 174 10 min.
- Presenting **Grammaire,** ATE, p. 174
- Challenge, ATE, p. 174
- Play Audio CD for Activity 9, p. 174.

Wrap-Up 5 min.
- Summarize what happened in the video episode using Chapter 6 **Mise en train** Transparencies.

Homework Options

Travaux pratiques de grammaire, pp. 41–43, Acts. 1–5

Cahier d'activités, p. 63, Acts. 5–7

Block 2

PREMIERE ETAPE

Quick Review 10 min.
- Kinesthetic Learners, ATE, p. 175

Grammaire: the verb *aller,* p. 174 cont. 20 min.
- Game: **Trop à faire,** ATE, p. 191
- Play Audio CD for Activity 9, p. 174.
- Do Activities 10–11, pp. 174–175.
- **A la française,** p. 175
- **Grammaire supplémentaire,** pp. 190–191, Acts. 2–3

Vocabulaire, p. 176 20 min.
- Presenting **Vocabulaire,** ATE, p. 176
- Teacher-to-Teacher activity, ATE, p. 176
- Teacher Note, ATE, p. 175
- Do Activity 13, p. 176, orally.

Grammaire, p. 177 25 min.
- Presenting **Grammaire,** ATE, p. 177
- Do Activity 14, p. 177. Have students read the sentences out loud.
- **Grammaire supplémentaire,** p. 191, Act. 4
- Do Activity 15, p. 177.

Wrap-Up 15 min.
- Challenge, ATE, p. 177

Homework Options

Study for **Première étape** quiz.

Travaux pratiques de grammaire, pp. 43–45, Acts. 6–11

Cahier d'activités, p. 64, Acts. 8–10

Block 3

PREMIERE ETAPE

Quick Review 20 min.
- TPR Storytelling Book, p. 21: Give students copies of the TPR story without the **Mini-histoire,** then have the students re-write the story told by the pictures.

Quiz 6-1 20 min.
- Administer Quiz 6-1A or 6-1B.

PANORAMA CULTUREL 15 min.
- Presenting **Panorama Culturel,** ATE, p. 178
- Culture Notes, ATE, p. 178
- Answer the **Qu'en penses-tu?** questions, p. 178.
- Read **Savais-tu que... ?,** p. 178.

DEUXIEME ETAPE

Comment dit-on... ?, p. 179 25 min.
- Presenting **Comment dit-on... ?,** ATE, p. 179
- Additional Practice, ATE, p. 179
- Play Audio CD for Activity 17, p. 179. See Challenge, ATE, p. 179.
- Do Activity 18, p. 180, orally.
- Do Activity 19, p. 180.

Wrap-Up 10 min.
- Activities for Communication, p. 148, Situation Card 6-1: Role-Play

Homework Options

Travaux pratiques de grammaire, p. 46, Acts. 12–13

Cahier d'activités, p. 65, Acts. 11–12

For alternative lesson plans by chapter section, to create your own customized plans, or to preview all resources available for this chapter, use the **One-Stop Planner CD-ROM**, Disc 2.

For additional homework suggestions, see activities accompanied by this symbol throughout the chapter.

Block 4

DEUXIEME ETAPE

Quick Review 10 min.
- Activities for Communication, pp. 31–32, Communicative Activity 6-1A and 6-1B

Grammaire: the verb *vouloir,* p. 180 30 min.
- Presenting **Grammaire: the verb *vouloir,*** ATE, p. 180
- Kinesthetic Learners, ATE, p. 180
- Do Activity 20, p. 181. Have students write their answers on the board.
- **Grammaire supplémentaire,** pp. 191–192, Acts. 5–6

RENCONTRE CULTURELLE 15 min.
- Thinking Critically/Comparing and Contrasting, ATE, p. 182
- Answer **Qu'en penses-tu?** questions, p. 182.
- Read **Savais-tu que... ?,** p. 182.

TROISIEME ETAPE

Comment dit-on… ?, p. 183 30 min.
- Presenting **Comment dit-on… ?,** ATE, p. 183 and Additional Practice, ATE, p. 183
- Play Audio CD for Activity 24, p. 184.
- Do **Note culturelle,** p. 184. See Language-to-Language, ATE, p. 184.
- Do Activity 25, p. 184.
- Play Audio CD for Activity 26, p. 184.

Wrap-Up 5 min.
- Have students pair off. Provide one student in each pair with a vocabulary card picturing a place in town or a sports activity. Give the other student a card with *accept* or *refuse* written on it. Have students act out a dialogue according to their cards.

Homework Options

Study for **Deuxième étape** quiz.

Travaux pratiques de grammaire, pp. 47–48, Acts. 14–17

Cahier d'activités, pp. 66–67, Acts. 13–17

Block 5

DEUXIEME ETAPE

Quick Review 10 min.

Quiz 6-2 20 min.
- Administer Quiz 6-2A or 6-2B.

TROISIEME ETAPE

Grammaire, p. 185 35 min.
- Presenting **Grammaire,** ATE, p. 185
- Additional Practice, ATE, p. 185
- Do Activity 28, p. 185. See Challenge, ATE, p. 185.
- Game: Around the World, ATE, p. 185
- Culture Notes, ATE, p. 186
- Do Activity 31, p. 186.

Prononciation, p. 157 20 min.
- Presenting **Prononciation,** ATE, p. 187
- Play Audio CD for Activities A, B, and C. See Additional Practice, ATE, p. 187.

Wrap-Up 5 min.
- Have students write a sentence about their plans for the weekend, omitting the activity: **Samedi, après-midi, à trois heures, je vais __ à la piscine avec des copains.** Have students read their sentences to a partner, who will try to fill in the blanks.

Homework Options

Study for **Troisième étape** quiz.

Travaux pratiques de grammaire, pp. 49–50, Acts. 18–21

Cahier d'activités, pp. 68–69, Acts. 18–22

Block 6

TROISIEME ETAPE

Quick Review 10 min.

Quiz 6-3 20 min.
- Administer Quiz 6-3A or 6-3B.

LISONS! 20 min
- Discuss the **Stratégie pour lire,** p. 188, then do Prereading Activity A, ATE, p. 188. See Culture Note, ATE, p. 188.
- Do Reading Activities B–D, Monitoring Comprehension, ATE, p. 188
- Do Postreading Activity E, Thinking Critically, ATE, p. 189. See Portfolio, Written, ATE, p. 195.

MISE EN PRATIQUE 20 min.
- Do Activity 1, p. 194.
- Play Audio CD for Activity 2, p. 194.
- Begin **Ecrivons!,** p. 195.

Wrap-Up 20 min.
- Do **Mise en Pratique** Activity 3, p. 195, as a class discussion.

Homework Options

Que sais-je?, p. 196

Study for Chapter 6 Test.

Block 7

MISE EN PRATIQUE

Quick Review 10 min.
- Check homework and have students read their **Ecrivons!** aloud for extra-credit.

Chapter Review 30 min.
- Review Chapter 6. Choose from **Grammaire supplémentaire,** Grammar Tutor for Students of French, Activities for Communication, Listening Activities, Interactive CD-ROM Tutor, or **Jeux interactifs.**

Test, Chapter 6 50 min.
- Administer Chapter 6 Test. Select from Testing Program, Alternative Assessment Guide, Test Generator, or Standardized Assessment Tutor.

Chapter Opener

CHAPITRE 6

For resource information, see the **One-Stop Planner,** Disc 2.

Pacing Tips

Keep in mind while planning your lessons that the **Première étape** in this chapter covers a lot of new vocabulary, grammar and functions. The **Deuxième** and **Troisième étapes** are fairly evenly balanced in terms of new content. For Lesson Plans and timing suggestions, see pages 167I–167L.

Meeting the Standards

Communication

- Making plans, p. 173
- Extending and responding to invitations, p. 179
- Arranging to meet someone, p. 183

Cultures

- Culture Note, pp. 170, 171, 178, 186, 188
- Panorama Culturel, p. 178
- Rencontre culturelle, p. 182
- Multicultural Link, p. 182
- Note culturelle, p. 184

Connections

- Social Studies/Government Link, p. 169
- Language Arts Link, p. 188
- Math Link, p. 188

Comparisons

- Thinking Critically: Comparing and Contrasting, pp. 169, 182
- Language-to-Language, p. 184

Communities

- Career Path, p. 194
- De l'école au travail, p. 187

Cultures and Communities

Background Information

The **Jardin du Luxembourg** is the site of the **Palais du Luxembourg,** built in the 1600s for Marie de Médicis, the Italian widow of Henri IV. Rubens painted the original interiors, which are now in the Louvre. Today, the palace is the home of the French senate, while the grounds (**le jardin**) are a popular relaxation spot for locals and tourists alike. There is a large pond in the park, where children often sail their toy boats. The beautiful Médicis fountain, built in 1627, is said to be one of the most romantic spots in Paris. Many visitors enjoy the park by simply strolling along the numerous pathways and enjoying the 19th-century sculptures found throughout the park.

STANDARDS: 2.2

CHAPITRE 6
Amusons-nous!

Objectives

In this chapter you will learn to

Première étape

- make plans

Deuxième étape

- extend and respond to invitations

Troisième étape

- arrange to meet someone

Visit Holt Online
go.hrw.com
KEYWORD: WA3 PARIS-6
Online Edition

◀ Ici, les Parisiens se relaxent dans le jardin devant le palais du Luxembourg.

Chapter Opener

CHAPITRE 6

Focusing on Outcomes

Have students look at the chapter outcomes and match them with the photo.
NOTE: The self-check activities in **Que sais-je?** on page 196 help students assess their achievement of the objectives.

Connections and Comparisons

Thinking Critically

Comparing and Contrasting Are there similar parks where you live? Who goes to them? What do people do there? Which activities in the photo do people also do in the parks where you live? Can you think of some U.S. cities with famous parks? Where do you prefer to meet your friends for outdoor activities?

Social Studies/Government Link

The French senate, which has been meeting in the **Palais du Luxembourg** since 1852, is not the only governing body in France. The **Assemblée nationale** has more members and more power, since its **députés** are directly elected, unlike the senators. Together, both bodies make up the French **Parlement.**

STANDARDS: 3.1, 4.2

Mise en train

CHAPITRE 6

Teaching Resources

pp. 170–172

PRINT 

- Lesson Planner, p. 28
- Video Guide, pp. 40, 42
- Cahier d'activités, p. 61

MEDIA 

- One-Stop Planner
- Video Program
  Mise en train
  Videocassette 2, 36:14–39:22
  Videocassette 5 (captioned version), 48:20–51:30
  Suite
  Videocassette 2, 39:24–44:52
  Videocassette 5 (captioned version), 51:32–56:00
- DVD Tutor, Disc 1
- Audio Compact Discs, CD 6, Trs. 1–2
- **Mise en train** Transparencies

Culture Note

The Louvre was first used as a defensive structure in 1204 by Philippe II Auguste. Over the years, it has served as a royal residence to several kings, notably Francis I. Now one of the largest museums in the world, the Louvre welcomes visitors through its newly renovated main entrance under the huge glass pyramid designed by I. M. Pei.

Presenting Mise en train

Have students guess what Mathieu and Isabelle are talking about. Play the video and ask students to listen for what the two friends will do on Saturday, what Mathieu suggests for Sunday, and what, if anything, the two friends finally decide to do.

Mise en train Transparencies

The **roman-photo** is an abridged version of the video episode.

MISE EN TRAIN • *Projets de week-end*

CD 6
Trs. 1–2

DVD VIDEO

Stratégie pour comprendre
What do you think the title of this episode means? What do you think Mathieu and Isabelle are talking about? Can you guess from what you see in the photos?

Isabelle

Mathieu

Vendredi après-midi...

1

Mathieu : Salut, Isabelle. Dis, qu'est-ce que tu vas faire demain?
Isabelle : Oh, pas grand-chose. Le matin, je vais aller à mon cours de danse. L'après-midi, je vais faire les magasins. Mais le soir, je suis libre.

2

Mathieu : Il y a un concert super à Bercy : Patrick Bruel. J'aimerais bien y aller. Tu veux venir avec moi?
Isabelle : Oh non, je n'ai pas envie d'aller à un concert.
Mathieu : Ah, dommage...

3

Mathieu : Et dimanche après-midi, tu es libre?
Isabelle : Dimanche? Oui, je n'ai rien de prévu.
Mathieu : Tu veux aller au zoo?
Isabelle : Ah, non, je déteste les zoos.

4

Mathieu : Alors, allons au Louvre.
Isabelle : Non, je n'aime pas trop les musées.

Preteaching Vocabulary

Recognizing Cognates

Tell students that the **Mise en train** has plenty of cognates that will allow them to guess what Isabelle and Mathieu are talking about doing this weekend. Then, read aloud the following expressions, which contain cognates, and have students look for them in the text:

2 **...je n'ai pas envie d'aller à un concert.**
3 **...je déteste les zoos.**
4 **Non, je n'aime pas trop les musées.**
9 **...aller au cinéma; Moi, je propose *Dracula.***
10 **les films d'horreur, un film comique, c'est bizarre.**

STANDARDS: 1.2, 2.2, 4.2

5 **Mathieu :** Qu'est-ce que tu veux faire, alors?

6 **Isabelle :** S'il fait beau, on peut faire une promenade au palais de Chaillot. On peut même monter au sommet de la tour Eiffel.
Mathieu : Bof.

7 **Isabelle :** J'ai une idée! Tu ne veux pas aller faire un tour dans un bateau-mouche?
Mathieu : Ça, non. C'est pas terrible.

8 **Isabelle :** On va au Sacré-Cœur?
Mathieu : Non, je n'ai pas envie.

9 **Mathieu :** On peut tout simplement aller au cinéma. Tu veux?
Isabelle : D'accord. Je veux bien. Qu'est-ce que tu veux voir comme film?
Mathieu : Moi, je propose *Dracula.* Ça passe à 16h40 et à 18h55.

10 **Isabelle :** Oh non, je n'aime pas les films d'horreur. Je préfère aller voir un film comique.
Mathieu : Oh non! Encore un film comique?! Tu sais, c'est bizarre. On n'est jamais d'accord!

Cahier d'activités, p. 61, Act. 1–2

Using the Captioned Video/DVD

If students have difficulty understanding French spoken at a normal speed, use Videocassette 5 to allow students to see the French captions for ***Projets de week-end*** and ***Projets de week-end (suite).*** Hearing the language and watching the story will reduce anxiety about the new language and facilitate comprehension. The reinforcement of seeing the written vocabulary words as they watch the gestures and actions will help prepare students to do the comprehension activities on page 172. NOTE: The *DVD Tutor* contains captions for all sections of the *Video Program.*

Mise en train

Culture Notes

- To verify movie listings, Mathieu and Isabelle consult *Pariscope,* a weekly entertainment guide that lists movies, shows, and exhibits in Paris. Other major cities have similar publications available.
- The **palais de Chaillot** was built in 1937 on the site of the old **palais du Trocadéro.** Its two curving wings house five different museums: the **musée de la Marine,** the **musée de l'Homme,** the **musée des Monuments français,** the **Cinémathèque française,** and the **musée du Cinéma.** Its beautifully terraced gardens and fountains lead down to the Seine River.
- The huge Romanesque-Byzantine church, **Sacré-Cœur,** offers a breathtaking view of Paris. It was built after France was defeated in the Franco-Prussian War of 1870–1871. Its belltower houses the **Savoyarde,** a bell weighing over 18,000 kilos.

Projets de week-end (suite)

When the story continues, Mathieu and Isabelle agree on a film. Mathieu and Isabelle meet Thuy, who is interested in going to the movies but wants to see a different film. Mathieu checks the times in his *Pariscope.* They all meet in front of the theater, but the movie is not playing. Mathieu discovers that he has last week's *Pariscope!*

Mise en train

CHAPITRE 6

Building on Previous Skills

5 You might want to review expressions for making excuses in Chapter 5. (See page 145.)

6 Students might refer to the activities in Activity 4, or they might reread the story.

These activities check for comprehension only. Students should not yet be expected to produce language modeled in **Mise en train**.

1 Tu as compris?

Answer the following questions according to ***Projets de week-end.*** Don't be afraid to guess. See answers below.

1. What are Isabelle's plans for tomorrow?
2. What day and time of day is it?
3. Can you name three places where Mathieu suggests they go?
4. Can you name three things that Isabelle prefers to do?
5. What do they finally agree to do? What problem remains?

2 Vrai ou faux?

1. Isabelle aime aller au zoo. faux
2. Isabelle a un cours de danse. vrai
3. Mathieu aime la musique de Patrick Bruel. vrai
4. Isabelle aime bien les musées. faux
5. Isabelle veut voir un film d'horreur dimanche après-midi. faux

3 Mets en ordre

Mets les phrases en ordre d'après ***Projets de week-end.***

1. Isabelle propose d'aller au palais de Chaillot. 3
2. Mathieu propose d'aller au zoo. 2
3. Isabelle propose d'aller au Sacré-Cœur. 5
4. Mathieu ne veut pas faire de promenade. 4
5. Isabelle refuse d'aller au concert. 1
6. Isabelle accepte d'aller au cinéma. 6

4 Où est-ce qu'on veut aller?

Choisis les activités qu'Isabelle veut faire et les activités que Mathieu préfère. See answers below.

aller voir un film comique
aller voir un film d'horreur
faire une promenade au palais de Chaillot
aller à un concert
aller au musée
aller au zoo
faire un tour en bateau
aller au Sacré-Cœur

5 Invitations et refus

Match Mathieu's suggestions for weekend activities with Isabelle's refusals.

Tu veux...

1. aller au concert de Patrick Bruel? d
2. aller au Louvre? c
3. aller au zoo? a
4. aller voir *Dracula?* b

Désolée, mais...

a. je déteste les zoos.
b. je préfère aller voir un film comique.
c. je n'aime pas trop les musées.
d. je n'ai pas envie.

6 Et maintenant, à toi

How would you react to Mathieu and Isabelle's suggestions for the weekend? Which would you choose to do? Why? Compare your answers with a partner's.

Comprehension Check

Slower Pace

1 Have students indicate the photos where the answers can be found. (1. Photo ①; 2. Photo ①; 3. Photos ②, ③, ④, and ⑨; 4. Photos ⑥, ⑦, ⑧, and ⑩; 5. Photos ⑨ and ⑩).

Additional Practice

2 If the sentence is true, have students find the text that verifies it.

Slower Pace

3 Play the video of the **Mise en train.** Ask students to watch and listen carefully for any mention of places to go or things to do. Compile a list on the board and then have pairs or small groups do the activity.

Answers

1
1. A.M. dance class, P.M. shopping, free evening
2. Friday afternoon
3. concert, zoo, museum, movies
4. take a walk at the palais de Chaillot, go to the top of the Eiffel Tower, take a boat ride, go to Sacré-Cœur
5. Isabelle and Mathieu decide to go to a movie, but they cannot agree on which one to see.

4 *Isabelle:* aller voir un film comique, faire une promenade au palais de Chaillot, faire un tour en bateau, aller au Sacré-Cœur
Mathieu: aller à un concert, aller au zoo, aller voir un film d'horreur, aller au musée

STANDARDS: 1.2, 4.2

Première étape

Objective Making plans

WA3 PARIS-6

Comment dit-on...?

Making plans

To ask what a friend's planning to do:

Qu'est-ce que tu vas faire demain? *What are you going to do . . . ?*
Tu vas faire quoi ce week-end? *What are you going to do . . . ?*

To tell what you're going to do:

Vendredi, **je vais** faire du vélo.
Samedi après-midi, **je vais** aller au café. } *I'm going to . . .*
Dimanche, **je vais** regarder la télé.
Pas grand-chose. *Not much.*
Rien de spécial. *Nothing special.*

7 Les projets de Thérèse See scripts and answers on p. 167G.

Ecoutons Listen as Sophie asks Thérèse about her plans for the weekend. Write down at least three things Thérèse plans to do.

CD 6 Tr. 3

Vocabulaire

regarder un match	*to watch a game (on TV)*
manger quelque chose	*to eat something*
voir un film	*to see a movie*
aller voir un match	*to go see a game*
voir une pièce	*to see a play*
faire une promenade	*to go for a walk*
faire les vitrines	*to window-shop*
faire un pique-nique	*to have a picnic*
aller à une boum	*to go to a party*

Note de grammaire

If you want to say that you do an activity regularly on a certain day of the week, use the article **le** before the day of the week.

Je fais du patin à glace **le mercredi** *(on Wednesdays).*

To say that you are doing something only on one particular day, use the day of the week without an article before it.

Je vais faire du patin à glace **mercredi** *(on Wednesday).*

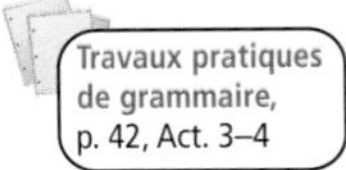

Grammaire supplémentaire, p. 190, Act. 1–2

8 Grammaire en contexte

a. **Ecrivons** Ecris trois activités que tu vas faire cette semaine.

b. **Parlons** Maintenant, dis à ton/ta camarade ce que tu vas faire et demande-lui ce qu'il/elle va faire.

EXEMPLE **Cette semaine, je vais faire de l'athlétisme et jouer au football. Vendredi soir, je vais voir un film. Et toi, qu'est-ce que tu vas faire?**

Communication for All Students

Challenge

7 Have students write down all five of the activities Thérèse has planned. Tell them that Sophie has completely different plans. Have them suggest five possible things that Sophie has planned for the weekend. Ask students whose weekend appeals to them more. Why or why not?

Visual Learners

8 You might have students draw the activities that they have planned and then show them to their partners. Students can then change partners and do the activity using each other's pictures in order to practice the new vocabulary.

Teaching Resources
pp. 173–177

PRINT
- Lesson Planner, p. 29
- TPR Storytelling Book, pp. 21, 24
- Listening Activities, pp. 43, 47
- Activities for Communication, pp. 31–32, 100, 103, 147–148
- Travaux pratiques de grammaire, pp. 41–45
- Grammar Tutor for Students of French, Chapter 6
- Cahier d'activités, pp. 62–64
- Testing Program, pp. 131–134
- Alternative Assessment Guide, p. 37
- Student Make-Up Assignments, Chapter 6

MEDIA
- One-Stop Planner
- Audio Compact Discs, CD 6, Trs. 3–4, 19, 31–32
- Teaching Transparencies: 6-1, 6-A, 6-B; **Grammaire supplémentaire** Answers; Travaux pratiques de grammaire Answers
- Interactive CD-ROM Tutor, Disc 2

Bell Work
Have students suggest doing four activities.

Presenting
Comment dit-on... ?
Tell students what you're going to do next weekend. Then, ask students about their weekends.

Note de grammaire
Ask individual students questions such as, **Qu'est-ce que tu fais le mardi à 10h?**

Vocabulaire
Bring in pictures of activities and say what you're going to do. Ask volunteers to tape the appropriate picture to the board.

STANDARDS: 1.1, 1.2, 4.1

Première étape

CHAPITRE 6

Teaching Resources
pp. 173–177

PRINT 
- Lesson Planner, p. 29
- TPR Storytelling Book, pp. 21, 24
- Listening Activities, pp. 43, 47
- Activities for Communication, pp. 31–32, 100, 103, 147–148
- Travaux pratiques de grammaire, pp. 41–45
- Grammar Tutor for Students of French, Chapter 6
- Cahier d'activités, pp. 62–64
- Testing Program, pp. 131–134
- Alternative Assessment Guide, p. 37
- Student Make-Up Assignments, Chapter 6

MEDIA
- One-Stop Planner
- Audio Compact Discs, CD 6, Trs. 3–4, 19, 31–32
- Teaching Transparencies: 6-1, 6-A, 6-B; **Grammaire supplémentaire** Answers; Travaux pratiques de grammaire Answers
- Interactive CD-ROM Tutor, Disc 2

Presenting Grammaire

The verb *aller* After introducing **aller,** explain that it is also used with an infinitive to express the immediate future. Mention a certain day and time of day **(mercredi à 6h),** and tell students what you're going to do then. **(Je vais voir un film.)** Then, give a certain day and time and have students tell what they are going to do. To practice the third-person forms, ask students to tell about their classmates' plans. **(Qu'est-ce que José va faire mercredi à 6h?)**

Grammaire

The verb *aller*

Aller is an irregular verb.

aller *(to go)*

Je	**vais**	Nous	**allons**
Tu	**vas**	Vous	**allez**
Il/Elle/On	**va**	Ils/Elles	**vont**

- You can use a form of the verb **aller** with the infinitive of another verb to say that you're *going to do something* in the future.

  Je vais jouer au base-ball demain.
- To say that you're not going to do something in the near future, put **ne... pas** around the conjugated form of the verb **aller.**

  Je ne vais pas jouer au base-ball demain.

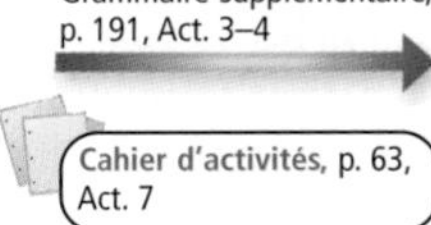

Grammaire supplémentaire, p. 191, Act. 3–4

Cahier d'activités, p. 63, Act. 7

Travaux pratiques de grammaire, p. 43, Act. 5–6

9 Grammaire en contexte See scripts and answers on p. 167G.

Ecoutons Listen to the following sentences and decide whether the people are talking about what they're doing or what they're going to do.

CD 6 Tr. 4

10 Grammaire en contexte

Parlons You have a busy weekend planned! Tell what you're going to do and on what day you plan to do it. Answers may vary. Possible answers:

1. Je vais voir un match dimanche.

2. Je vais voir un film vendredi.

3. Je vais faire un pique-nique dimanche.

4. Je vais aller à une boum vendredi.

5. Je vais faire les vitrines vendredi.

6. Je vais manger quelque chose samedi.

Communication for All Students

Challenge
Grammaire On the board or on a transparency, draw three columns. Write the six subject pronouns in the first column, the infinitive **aller** in the second, and activities students suggest in the third. Ask students to write as many sentences as possible in five minutes, using the items in the three columns.

Slower Pace
9 Before they do this activity, ask students for examples of sentences in the present **(Ils jouent au foot.)** and in the immediate future. **(Ils vont jouer au foot.)**

STANDARDS: 1.2, 1.3, 4.1

11 Qu'est-ce qu'ils vont faire?

Parlons/Ecrivons What are these people going to do?

1. **Elles** Elles vont faire les vitrines.

2. **Ils** Ils vont manger/aller au café.

3. **Je** Je vais jouer au football.

4. **Nous** Nous allons faire un pique-nique.

5. **Vous** Vous allez voir un film.

6. **Elle** Elle va faire une promenade.

A la française

The French often use the present tense of a verb to say that something will happen in the near future, just as we do in English.

Samedi matin, je vais jouer au tennis. *Saturday morning, I'm going to play tennis.*
Samedi matin, je joue au tennis. *Saturday morning, I'm playing tennis.*

12 Enquête

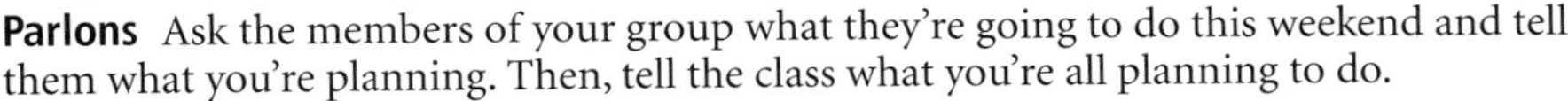

Parlons Ask the members of your group what they're going to do this weekend and tell them what you're planning. Then, tell the class what you're all planning to do.

EXEMPLE

—Qu'est-ce que tu fais ce week-end, Nicole?
—Samedi, je vais faire du ski nautique. Et toi?
—Moi, je vais à une boum.
—Je vais à une boum et Nicole va faire du ski nautique samedi.
(to the class)

Teacher Notes

You might make the following suggestions to students.

- Encourage students to visualize new vocabulary as they study it. To learn the word **la bibliothèque,** for example, they might visualize their local library as they say the French word aloud.
- You might suggest that students create memory devices to learn new material. For example, students might use the first letters (BCCMMPP) of a list of new words **(bibliothèque, centre commercial, cinéma, Maison des jeunes, musée, parc, piscine)** to make a sentence. (Bruno Couldn't Cook Mom's Meat Pizza Precisely.)

Challenge

12 Have two groups compare their activities and summarize the results. **(Maria, Pam et Damon font du ski nautique samedi, mais Tori joue au tennis.)**

Communication for All Students

Slower Pace

11 As you tell in French what the people in the photos are going to do, have students write down the numbers of the photos you describe. Then, have students pair off and take turns telling each other what the people in the photos are going to do.

Kinesthetic Learners

Have small groups of students play "Charades." One member of the group acts out an activity he or she plans to do, and the other students try to guess the activity the person is miming. The first student to say what the person is going to do **(Tu vas faire du jogging.)** chooses who will take the next turn.

STANDARDS: 1.1, 1.3, 4.1, 5.1, 5.2

Première étape

CHAPITRE 6

Teaching Resources
pp. 173–177

PRINT 

- Lesson Planner, p. 29
- TPR Storytelling Book, pp. 21, 24
- Listening Activities, pp. 43, 47
- Activities for Communication, pp. 31–32, 100, 103, 147–148
- Travaux pratiques de grammaire, pp. 41–45
- Grammar Tutor for Students of French, Chapter 6
- Cahier d'activités, pp. 62–64
- Testing Program, pp. 131–134
- Alternative Assessment Guide, p. 37
- Student Make-Up Assignments, Chapter 6

MEDIA

- One-Stop Planner
- Audio Compact Discs, CD 6, Trs. 3–4, 19, 31–32
- Teaching Transparencies: 6-1, 6-A, 6-B; **Grammaire supplémentaire** Answers; Travaux pratiques de grammaire Answers
- Interactive CD-ROM Tutor, Disc 2

Presenting Vocabulaire

After introducing the **Vocabulaire,** hold up illustrations (a zebra, a movie star) or props (sunglasses, a shopping bag) to suggest the places, asking **On va où?** Name some local places and have students call out the French term for the place (for example, *the Galleria*—**un centre commercial).** Tell students to go to a certain place **(Va à la plage!).** To show they understand, have them mime what they would do there.

Vocabulaire

Where do you and your friends like to go in your spare time?

au restaurant

au cinéma

au parc

au stade

au zoo

au centre commercial

à la plage

à la piscine

au musée

à la Maison des jeunes

au théâtre

à la bibliothèque

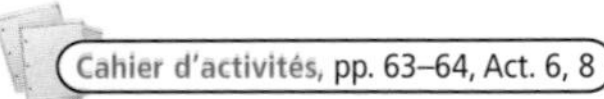
Cahier d'activités, pp. 63–64, Act. 6, 8

Travaux pratiques de grammaire, pp. 44–45, Act. 7–9

13 Où vas-tu?

Lisons Où est-ce que tu vas pour faire ces activités?

1. Je vais faire de la natation... d
2. Je vais faire les vitrines... c
3. Je vais voir un film... a
4. Je vais manger quelque chose... e
5. Je vais voir un match... f
6. Je vais voir une pièce... b

a. au cinéma.
b. au théâtre.
c. au centre commercial.
d. à la piscine.
e. au café.
f. au stade.

Teacher to Teacher

James C. May
Rufus King High School
Milwaukee, WI

Here's a unique way that James uses the Clip Art in the *One-Stop Planner.*

"To practice the vocabulary on page 176, I make photocopies of the Clip Art from the *One-Stop Planner CD* that corresponds to the places on this page. Each student receives a copy and they separate the different pictures. They then line these pictures up at the top of their desk. I say a vocabulary word and they move the picture down. I do the same thing on the overhead projector so students can verify their responses. When the class is responding well to individual words, I say the words in groups of three. Students must move the corresponding pictures down in the order in which I said them."

Grammaire

Contractions with *à*

The preposition **à** usually means *to* or *at*.
When you use **à** before **le** or **les**, make the following contractions:

à + le = au Je vais **au** stade.

à + les = aux Martine va aller **aux** Tuileries.

The preposition **à doesn't contract with l' or la:**

Cet après-midi, on ne va pas **à la** Maison des jeunes. On va **à l'**école.

Grammaire supplémentaire, pp. 191–192, Act. 5–6

Travaux pratiques de grammaire, p. 45, Act. 10–11

14 Grammaire en contexte

Lisons/Ecrivons Christine et Alain parlent des endroits où ils aiment aller le week-end. Regarde les images et complète leur conversation.

CHRISTINE Moi, j'adore aller 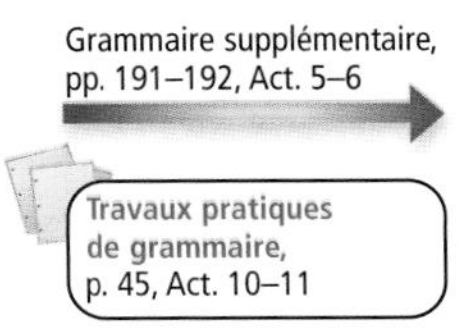 avec mes copains. Après, on va

au cinéma

souvent ______. Et toi?
au café

ALAIN Moi, j'aime mieux aller ______. J'adore le sport. J'aime bien
au stade

aller ______ aussi. On y joue souvent au foot.
au parc

CHRISTINE Qu'est-ce que tu vas faire ce week-end? On va  ?
à la piscine/à la plage

ALAIN Ah, non, je n'aime pas trop nager. Tu veux aller  ?
au zoo

15 Qu'est-ce qu'on fait?

Parlons You're trying to decide what to do after school. With a partner, take turns suggesting places to go. Then, accept or reject each other's suggestions.

le café, le musée, la piscine, le parc, la piscine, la Maison des jeunes, le zoo, la bibliothèque, le centre commercial

16 Mon journal

Ecrivons Tu as des projets pour le week-end? Qu'est-ce que tu vas faire? Où vas-tu? Quand?

EXEMPLE **Vendredi après-midi, je vais faire mes devoirs. Samedi, je...**

Communication for All Students

Game

Concentration® For each vocabulary word or expression, make two cards. On one card, write the phrase in French **(au théâtre)**. On the other, draw a picture or tape a magazine picture of the item. Number the back of each card and tape them to the board with the numbers visible. Divide the class into two teams. Have the first player from the first team call out two numbers. Turn over the corresponding cards. If the cards match, the player keeps them and takes another turn. If not, the turn passes to the other team.

Presenting Grammaire

Contractions with *à* Draw two columns on the board. One should be labeled *masculine* and the other *feminine*. Have students look at the **Vocabulaire** on page 176. Ask volunteers to come to the board and write each word, including its definite article, in the appropriate column, according to the gender of the word. Then, have other volunteers come to the board and write either **au** or **à la** with each of the words listed. Ask students to try to deduce when to use **au** and **à la.** Then, read the **Grammaire** and point out that while **à** never combines with **l'**, it always contracts with **les** to form **aux,** regardless of the gender of the word.

Challenge

14 Have partners rewrite the conversation to reflect their own interests. They could then include this in their written portfolios. Students could also rewrite their conversations on posterboard, inserting pictures of the places they like to go.

Assess

- Testing Program, pp. 131–134
  Quiz 6-1A, Quiz 6-1B
  Audio CD 6, Tr. 19
- Student Make-Up Assignments, Chapter 6, Alternative Quiz
- Alternative Assessment Guide, p. 37

STANDARDS: 1.1, 3.1, 5.1

CHAPITRE 6

Teaching Resources
p. 178

PRINT 

- Video Guide, pp. 41, 42–43
- Cahier d'activités, p. 72

MEDIA

- One-Stop Planner
- Video Program Videocassette 2, 43:55–46:56
- DVD Tutor, Disc 1
- Audio Compact Discs, CD 6, Trs. 5–8
- Interactive CD-ROM Tutor, Disc 2

Presenting Panorama Culturel

Have students view the video and write down the activities that the interviewees mention. To check comprehension, you might ask yes-no questions, such as **Arnaud achète des disques?**, as well as the **Questions** below.

Visual Learners

Hold up magazine illustrations of the activities and ask **Qui fait ça?**

Questions

1. **Julie fait quels sports?** (Elle joue au tennis, au basket.)
2. **Arnaud va où quand il sort?** (au cinéma, dans une discothèque)
3. **Où est-ce que Céline va quand elle sort?** (à la patinoire, dans les restaurants, dans les fast-foods)
4. **Qu'est-ce qu'elle fait comme sport?** (Elle fait du tennis; elle nage.)

Qu'est-ce que tu fais quand tu sors?

When you go out with your friends, where do you go? What do you do? We asked some French-speaking students what they like to do on weekends with their friends. Here's what they said.

Julie,
Côte d'Ivoire

«Quand je sors, je me balade. Je vais manger un peu. Souvent, on va jouer de la musique. On joue au tennis... souvent, au basket aussi.» Tr. 6

Arnaud,
France

«Je vais au cinéma. Je vais dans une discothèque. J'achète des disques.» Tr. 7

Céline,
Viêt-nam

«Je vais à la patinoire, ou [je vais] faire les boutiques, ou [je vais] au restaurant, enfin dans les fast-foods, ou alors je vais faire du sport, du tennis. Je vais nager.» Tr. 8

Qu'en penses-tu?

1. Do you and your friends like to do any of the things these teenagers mentioned?
2. Do they mention anything that you wouldn't do? Why wouldn't you do these things?
3. What do you and your friends like to do that these teenagers haven't mentioned?

Savais-tu que...?

Teenagers around the world generally like to do the same things. They usually have favorite places where they go to meet with their friends, just as you do. In most towns, students can find films, plays, concerts, and **discothèques** to go to in their free time. Dance parties (**boums**) are very popular. Most cities in France also have a **Maison des jeunes et de la culture (la MJC)** where a variety of activities, such as photography, music, dance, drama, arts and crafts, and computer science, is available to young people.

Cultures and Communities

Culture Notes

- Many French movie theaters and museums have student rates **(tarif réduit)** that are usually available to young tourists with student ID cards or proof of age.
- In Paris, most **métro** trains begin their final run between midnight and 1:00 A.M. Thus, parties or evenings out usually end in time for everyone to get to the closest subway station in time for the last train.

STANDARDS: 2.1, 3.2, 4.2

Deuxième étape

Objective Extending and responding to invitations

WA3 PARIS-6

Comment dit-on...?

Extending and responding to invitations

CD-ROM 2 DVD 1

To extend an invitation:

Allons au parc! *Let's go . . . !*
Tu veux aller au café **avec moi?** *Do you want to . . . with me?*
Je voudrais aller faire du vélo. **Tu viens?** *Will you come?*
On peut faire du ski. *We can . . .*

To accept an invitation:

D'accord.
Bonne idée.
Je veux bien. *I'd really like to.*
Pourquoi pas? *Why not?*

To refuse an invitation:

Ça ne me dit rien.
J'ai des trucs à faire.
Désolé(e), je ne peux pas.
Désolé(e), je suis occupé(e). *Sorry, I'm busy.*

Cahier d'activités, pp. 65–66, Act. 11–14

Les loisirs préférés	15-25 ans
Cinéma	90
Discothèque	69
Fête foraine	58
Concert de rock	42
Parc d'attractions	37
Match (payant)	36
Monument historique	31
Bal public	30
Musée	27
Théâtre	17
Concert de jazz	11
Cirque	10
Concert classique	6
Spectacle de danse	5
Opéra	3

See scripts and answers on p. 167G.

17 On accepte ou on refuse?

Ecoutons Ecoute ces dialogues. Est-ce qu'on accepte ou refuse l'invitation?

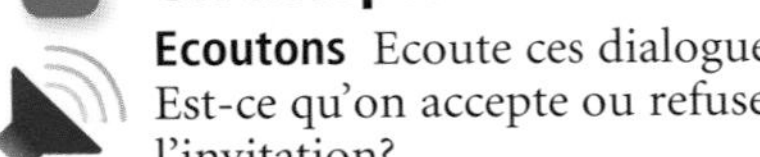

CD 6 Tr. 9

Communication for All Students

Additional Practice

Have two students stand up. Call out an expression from **Comment dit-on... ?** The first student to identify it correctly as an invitation, an acceptance, or a refusal remains standing, while the other sits down, and the next student stands up. Continue until all students have had a chance to respond.

Challenge

17 Have students listen to the recording again, and ask them what clues (other than the words) might indicate whether the response is positive or negative. For example, intonation and the response of the person extending the invitation can also indicate how the offer was received **(Dommage)**.

Deuxième étape

CHAPITRE 6

Teaching Resources
pp. 179–182

PRINT

- Lesson Planner, p. 30
- TPR Storytelling Book, pp. 22, 24
- Listening Activities, pp. 44, 48
- Activities for Communication, pp. 33–34, 101, 103, 147–148
- Travaux pratiques de grammaire, p. 46
- Grammar Tutor for Students of French, Chapter 6
- Cahier d'activités, pp. 65–67
- Testing Program, pp. 135–138
- Alternative Assessment Guide, p. 37
- Student Make-Up Assignments, Chapter 6

MEDIA

- One-Stop Planner
- Audio Compact Discs, CD 6, Trs. 9, 20, 33–34
- Teaching Transparencies: 6-2; **Grammaire supplémentaire** Answers; Travaux pratiques de grammaire Answers
- Interactive CD-ROM Tutor, Disc 2

Bell Work

Have students write their plans for next weekend.

Presenting
Comment dit-on... ?

Have students tell which animal in the cartoon is extending an invitation, which one is refusing, and which one is accepting. Ask students for expressions they've already learned for inviting someone and for accepting and refusing an invitation (see Chapter 5). Then, present the new expressions with gestures and have students tell whether you are extending, accepting, or refusing an invitation.

Deuxième étape

CHAPITRE 6

Teaching Resources
pp. 179–182

PRINT 

- Lesson Planner, p. 30
- TPR Storytelling Book, pp. 22, 24
- Listening Activities, pp. 44, 48
- Activities for Communication, pp. 33–34, 101, 103, 147–148
- Travaux pratiques de grammaire, p. 46
- Grammar Tutor for Students of French, Chapter 6
- Cahier d'activités, pp. 65–67
- Testing Program, pp. 135–138
- Alternative Assessment Guide, p. 37
- Student Make-Up Assignments, Chapter 6

MEDIA

- One-Stop Planner
- Audio Compact Discs, CD 6, Trs. 9, 20, 33–34
- Teaching Transparencies: 6-2; **Grammaire supplémentaire** Answers; Travaux pratiques de grammaire Answers
- Interactive CD-ROM Tutor, Disc 2

Presenting
Grammaire

The verb *vouloir* Ask students **Qu'est-ce que tu veux faire après l'école?** Then, as students give different answers **(écouter de la musique, faire les magasins, jouer au tennis),** write them on the board or on a transparency. Next, have partners ask each other whether they want to do those activities. **(Tu veux... ?)** Finally, ask students when they might use **Je voudrais** (when asking for something in a store or restaurant; when asking permission to do something).

18 Et toi? Tu veux?

Lisons Choisis la bonne réponse.

1. J'ai faim. d
2. Je voudrais faire un pique-nique. a
3. Tu ne viens pas? b
4. Je voudrais voir un match de foot. e
5. Tu veux voir une pièce? c

a. Allons au parc!
b. J'ai des trucs à faire.
c. Pourquoi pas? Allons au théâtre!
d. Tu veux aller au café?
e. Allons au stade!

19 Tu acceptes?

Parlons Your partner will invite you to participate in some of the following activities. Accept or refuse, telling where you're going or what you're going to do instead. Then, reverse roles.

Possible answers:

1. On peut regarder la télévision.

2. Tu veux faire les vitrines?

3. Allons danser!

4. Tu veux jouer au tennis?

5. Je vais voir un film. Tu viens?

6. Tu veux aller à la piscine?

Grammaire

The verb *vouloir*

Vouloir is an irregular verb.

vouloir *(to want)*

Je	**veux**	Nous	**voulons**
Tu	**veux**	Vous	**voulez**
Il/Elle/On	**veut**	Ils/Elles	**veulent**

Je voudrais *(I would like)* is a more polite form of **je veux.**

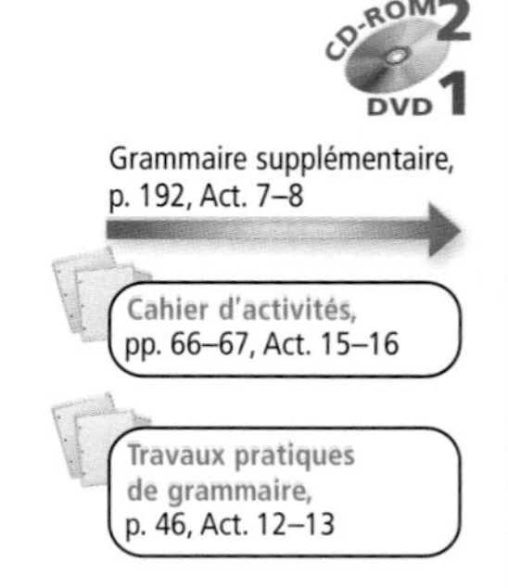

Grammaire supplémentaire, p. 192, Act. 7–8

Cahier d'activités, pp. 66–67, Act. 15–16

Travaux pratiques de grammaire, p. 46, Act. 12–13

Communication for All Students

Additional Practice

18 Ask students to suggest different ways to make the same invitations. This could be done orally or as a written assignment.

Slower Pace

19 First, have students identify the activities shown. Then, ask them to suggest other places or activities that could be used in refusing the invitations.

Kinesthetic Learners

Toss a ball to a student as you call out a subject pronoun **(il, singulier).** The student catches the ball, calls out the corresponding verb form of **vouloir (veut),** and tosses the ball to a classmate while calling out a different subject pronoun.

20 Grammaire en contexte  See answers below.

Parlons Qu'est-ce qu'on veut faire ce soir?

1. Pierre et Marc

2. Alain

3. Moi, je...

4. Elodie et Guy

5. Mes copains et moi, nous...

6. David et Monique

21 Invitations pour le week-end

Parlons You're making plans for the upcoming weekend. Take turns with a partner suggesting activities and accepting or politely refusing the suggestions.

22 Vous voulez faire quoi?

Parlons You and your friends can't decide what to do this weekend. Each of you makes a suggestion, and the others react to it. See if you can find three things you'd all like to do.

Exemple —**Vous voulez faire du vélo?**
—**Oui, je veux bien.**
—**Moi, je ne veux pas. Je n'aime pas faire du vélo.**

23 A la boum!

Lisons/Parlons Le Cercle Français organise une fête. Tu vas inviter trois camarades. Avant d'accepter ou de refuser ton invitation, ils veulent savoir quelles activités tu veux faire. Dis-leur ce que tu veux faire et tes camarades vont accepter ou refuser.

danser
écouter de la musique québécoise
parler français avec des copains
voir un film français
manger des escargots

L'ambiance sera extra!

Le Cercle Français
t'invite
à une fête
le 10 mai
de 7h à 10h

Si tu viens, ce sera plus sympa!

Deuxième étape

CHAPITRE 6

Speaking Assessment

23 You might use the following rubric when grading your students on this activity.

Speaking Rubric	Points			
	4	3	2	1
Content (Complete–Incomplete)				
Comprehension (Total–Little)				
Comprehensibility (Comprehensible–Incomprehensible)				
Accuracy (Accurate–Seldom accurate)				
Fluency (Fluent–Not fluent)				

18–20: A 14–15: C Under
16–17: B 12–13: D 12: F

Assess

- Testing Program, pp. 135–138
  Quiz 6-2A, Quiz 6-2B
  Audio CD 6, Tr. 20
- Student Make-Up Assignments, Chapter 6, Alternative Quiz
- Alternative Assessment Guide, p. 37

Communication for All Students

Building on Previous Skills

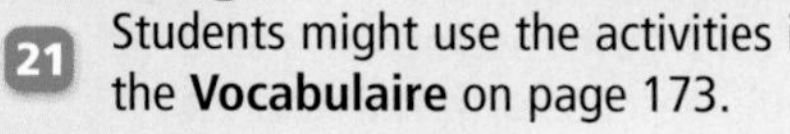

21 Students might use the activities in the **Vocabulaire** on page 173.

Challenge

23 Have students also decide upon a time and place for the party and then create colorful invitations to send out to guests. They might include illustrations or a list of the activities offered to encourage people to come.

Visual Learners

Show *Teaching Transparency 6-2* and assign each person in the illustration to a student or group of students. Provide them with a strip of transparency and a pen and have them create a speech bubble for that person.

Answers

20
1. Ils veulent aller au zoo.
2. Il veut aller à la Maison des jeunes.
3. Moi, je veux aller au restaurant.
4. Ils veulent faire du vélo.
5. Nous voulons aller au théâtre.
6. Ils veulent aller au musée.

STANDARDS: 1.1, 1.2, 1.3, 5.1, 5.2

CHAPITRE 6

Presenting Rencontre culturelle

Give each photo a number. Then, have students, individually or in pairs, write at least three phrases or sentences in English to describe each photo. They might want to tell what the people are doing or wearing, where they are, and any other details they notice. Collect students' papers and read aloud one or two sentences from each. Ask students to identify the photo you are describing by saying **un, deux,** or **trois.**

Motivating Activity
Tell students that their French pen pal has asked some questions about going out in the United States. Ask them what they would take pictures of (a movie theater, the mall, their favorite restaurant) to make an informative photo-collage about going out in their town, similar to the one on this page.

Teacher Note
You may want to refer to the list of professional resources on page T46 for a list of publications that students may want to read to learn more about the habits of francophone teenagers.

Qu'en penses-tu? See answer below.

1. Judging from these photos, how would you describe a typical date in France?
2. Do American teenagers usually go out on dates in groups or in couples? Which do you think is preferable? Why?
3. What do you think is the best age to begin dating? Why?

Savais-tu que... ?

French teenagers tend to go out in groups. They usually do not "date" in the same way American teenagers do. They do not generally pair off into couples until they are older. Those who do have a boyfriend or girlfriend still go out with a group — but they almost always pay their own way.

Connections and Comparisons

Multicultural Link
Have students research dating habits and customs in other countries. They might interview exchange students or community members with different cultural backgrounds to find out the normal age to begin dating, popular places to go on dates, and who pays.

Thinking Critically
Comparing and Contrasting Ask students how they would describe a typical American date to someone from France or another francophone country. They might include who goes out, where they might go, and who pays.

Answer
1. French teenagers go out in groups rather than in couples.

STANDARDS: 2.1, 3.2, 4.2

Troisième étape

Objective Arranging to meet someone

WA3 PARIS-6

Comment dit-on...?

Arranging to meet someone

CD-ROM 2 DVD 1

To ask when: **Quand?** **Quand ça?**	To tell when: **Lundi./Demain matin./Ce week-end.** **Tout de suite.** *Right away.*
To ask where: **Où?** **Où ça?**	To tell where: **Au** café. *At the . . .* **Devant** le cinéma. *In front of . . .* **Dans** le café. *In . . .* **Au métro** Saint-Michel. *At the . . . subway stop.* **Chez** moi. *At . . . house.*
To ask with whom: **Avec qui?**	To tell with whom: **Avec** Ahmed et Nathalie.
To ask at what time: **A quelle heure?**	To tell at what time: **A dix heures du matin.** *At ten in the morning.* **A cinq heures de l'après-midi.** *At five in the afternoon.* **A cinq heures et quart.** *At quarter past five.* **A cinq heures et demie.** *At half past five.* **Vers six heures.** *About six o'clock.*
To ask the time: **Quelle heure est-il?** *What time is it?* To confirm: **Bon, on se retrouve** à trois heures. *OK, we'll meet . . .* **Rendez-vous** mardi au café. *We'll meet . . .* **Entendu.** *OK.*	To give the time: **Il est six heures.** *It's six o'clock.* **Il est six heures moins le quart.** *It's a quarter to six.* **Il est six heures dix.** *It's ten after six.* **Il est midi.** *It's noon.* **Il est minuit.** *It's midnight.*

Cahier d'activités, pp. 68–69, Act. 19–20

Travaux pratiques de grammaire, pp. 47–48, Act. 14–17

Communication for All Students

Additional Practice

To practice question words, give possible answers **(Au stade.)** and have students say the appropriate question word. **(Où?)**

Challenge

Have students imagine a fictitious meeting between two famous personalities from the past. Have them write down the time and the place. For example, **Napoléon et Marilyn Monroe se retrouvent devant le cinéma lundi vers sept heures.** Students can then work in pairs to produce a parody of a gossip magazine, with drawings and captions describing the **rendez-vous** of the famous couples.

Troisième étape

CHAPITRE 6

Teaching Resources
pp. 183–187

PRINT
- Lesson Planner, p. 31
- TPR Storytelling Book, pp. 23, 24
- Listening Activities, pp. 44–45, 49
- Activities for Communication, pp. 35–36, 102, 104, 147–148
- Travaux pratiques de grammaire, pp. 47–50
- Grammar Tutor for Students of French, Chapter 6
- Cahier d'activités, pp. 68–70
- Testing Program, pp. 139–142
- Alternative Assessment Guide, p. 37
- Student Make-Up Assignments, Chapter 6

MEDIA
- One-Stop Planner
- Audio Compact Discs, CD 6, Trs. 10–11, 21, 35–36
- Teaching Transparencies: 5-3; **Grammaire supplémentaire** Answers; Travaux pratiques de grammaire Answers
- Interactive CD-ROM Tutor, Disc 2

Bell Work

Write three invitations on a transparency and have students write a different response to each one.

Presenting
Comment dit-on... ?

Act out both sides of a phone conversation in which you arrange to meet someone. Check comprehension by asking **Où ça? Quand ça?** and so on. Then, pretend to arrange a meeting with the class by asking individual students when, where, and at what time to meet. Show students various times on a clock and have them repeat the time expressions.

STANDARDS: 4.1

Troisième étape

Teaching Resources
pp. 183–187

PRINT

- Lesson Planner, p. 31
- TPR Storytelling Book, pp. 23, 24
- Listening Activities, pp. 44–45, 49
- Activities for Communication, pp. 35–36, 102, 104, 147–148
- Travaux pratiques de grammaire, pp. 47–50
- Grammar Tutor for Students of French, Chapter 6
- Cahier d'activités, pp. 68–70
- Testing Program, pp. 139–142
- Alternative Assessment Guide, p. 37
- Student Make-Up Assignments, Chapter 6

MEDIA 

- One-Stop Planner
- Audio Compact Discs, CD 6, Trs. 10–11, 21, 35–36
- Teaching Transparencies: 6-3; **Grammaire supplémentaire** Answers; Travaux pratiques de grammaire Answers
- Interactive CD-ROM Tutor, Disc 2

Building on Previous Skills

Note culturelle Call out official times in French and have students tell you the time in the 12-hour system, adding **du matin, de l'après-midi,** or **du soir.**

Cooperative Learning

25 Have students form groups of three. For each illustration, one person gives the time, a second gives the activity or place, and the third puts these elements into a sentence.

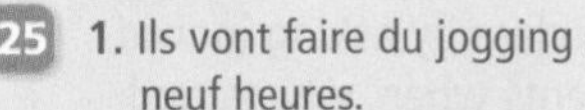

Answers

25
1. Ils vont faire du jogging à neuf heures.
2. Ils vont à la bibliothèque à midi.
3. Ils vont au zoo à six heures moins le quart.
4. Ils vont au musée à huit heures et demie.

24 L'invitation de Sylvie See scripts on p. 167H.

CD 6 Tr. 10

Ecoutons While you're waiting to use a public phone in Paris, you overhear a young woman inviting a friend to go out. Listen to the conversation and then choose the correct answers to these questions.

1. Sylvie parle avec qui?
   a. Marc **b.** Anna **c.** Paul
2. Elle va où?
   a. au musée **b.** au parc **c.** au stade
3. A quelle heure?
   a. 1h30 **b.** 10h15 **c.** 12h00
4. Où est-ce qu'ils se retrouvent?
   a. au métro Solférino **b.** dans un café **c.** devant le musée

Note culturelle

You've already learned that train, airline, school, and other official schedules use a 24-hour system called **l'heure officielle.** When you look in an entertainment guide such as *Pariscope,* you may see that a movie starts at 20h00, which is 8:00 P.M. In everyday conversation, however, people use a 12-hour system. For example, for 1:30 P.M., you may hear, **une heure et demie de l'après-midi,** rather than **treize heures trente.** Expressions such as **et demie, et quart,** and **moins le quart** are used only in conversational time, never in official time.

25 A quelle heure?

Parlons Où est-ce que Christian et Noëlle vont aujourd'hui? Qu'est-ce qu'ils vont faire? A quelle heure? See answers below.

1. 9h00

2. 12h00

3. 5h45

4. 8h30

26 Qui et où? See scripts and answers on p. 167H.

CD 6 Tr. 11

Ecoutons Listen to these three messages on your answering machine and write down who they're from and where you're being invited to go. Listen a second time and write down the meeting time and place.

Connections and Comparisons

Language-to-Language

If you have students who speak Spanish, you may want to point out the similarities in telling time in Spanish and French. **Moins** in French and *menos* in Spanish function the same way. (**Il est dix heures moins dix.** *Son las diez menos diez.*) The expressions **et quart** and **et demie** are equivalent to *y cuarto* and *y media.* Have your Spanish-speaking students identify some differences in telling time in the two languages. (For minutes past the hour, Spanish uses *y* while French does not. French uses the word **heure** while Spanish does not. **Il est deux heures cinq.** *Son las dos y cinco.*)

STANDARDS: 1.1, 1.2, 2.1, 3.2, 4.1, 4.2

27 Qu'est-ce que tu vas faire ce soir?

a. **Ecrivons** Fais une liste de trois choses que tu vas faire ce soir. Dis à quelle heure et où tu vas les faire.

b. **Parlons** Maintenant, demande à ton/ta camarade ce qu'il/elle va faire ce soir. Ensuite, continue à lui poser des questions sur ses projets.

Grammaire

Information questions

There are several ways to ask information questions in French.

- People often ask information questions using only a question word or phrase. They will sometimes add **ça** after the question word to make it sound less abrupt.
  Où ça?
  Quand ça?
- Another way to ask an information question is to attach the question word or phrase at the end of a statement.
  Tu vas **où?**
  Tu veux faire **quoi?**
  Tu vas au cinéma **à quelle heure?**
  Tu vas au parc **avec qui?**
- Still another way is to begin an information question with the question word or phrase, followed by **est-ce que (qu')**.
  Où est-ce que tu vas?
  Qu'est-ce que tu veux faire ce soir?
  Avec qui est-ce que tu vas au cinéma?
  A quelle heure est-ce qu'on se retrouve?

Grammaire supplémentaire, p. 193, Act. 9–10

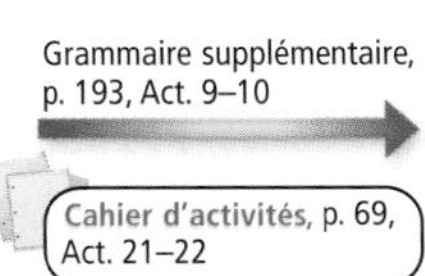

Cahier d'activités, p. 69, Act. 21–22

Travaux pratiques de grammaire, pp. 49–50, Act. 18–21

28 Grammaire en contexte

Parlons Some friends are inviting you to join them. Ask questions to get more information about their plans. Complete the conversation with the appropriate question words or phrases.

— Tu veux aller au cinéma?
— Quand ça?
— Demain soir.
— A quelle heure?
— Vers six heures.
— Où ça?
— Au cinéma Gaumont.
— Avec qui?
— Avec Catherine et Michel.
— D'accord!
— Bon, on se retrouve...

Communication for All Students

Additional Practice

Ask a question using the informal pattern with the question word(s) at the end. **(Tu études à quelle heure?)** Ask students to restate the question using the formal pattern with **est-ce que. (A quelle heure est-ce que tu études?)** Then, reverse the procedure.

Challenge

28 Have partners supply their own information for the invitation (what, when, where, with whom, what time). You might have several students present their conversations to the class. As the other students listen, have them write down the information they hear.

Portfolio

27 **Oral** Part **b** of this activity might be recorded and included in students' oral portfolios. For portfolio suggestions, see *Alternative Assessment Guide,* page 23.

Presenting Grammaire

Information questions Ask students to recall all the question words they can **(comment, à quelle heure, combien, qu'est-ce que, quoi, quand, où,** and **avec qui).** Using these words, ask students simple questions and have them give short answers. **(Tu vas où après l'école?)** Next, write on the board these three questions: **Où? Tu vas où? Où est-ce que tu vas?** Then, have students follow this model to write more questions, substituting **quand, avec qui,** and **à quelle heure** for **où.**

Game

Around the World In this game, students will practice asking information questions. Have students stand in rows. The first two students in the first row are the two players. Call out an answer to a question, such as **A l'école.** The first student to call out an appropriate question **(Où est-ce que tu vas?)** wins and moves to stand beside the next person in the row. The player who loses sits down. The round continues in this manner until each player has had a chance to play. Play as many rounds as needed until there is only one student left.

STANDARDS: 1.1, 4.1

Troisième étape

CHAPITRE 6

Teaching Resources
pp. 183–187

PRINT 

- Lesson Planner, p. 31
- TPR Storytelling Book, pp. 23, 24
- Listening Activities, pp. 44–45, 49
- Activities for Communication, pp. 35–36, 102, 104, 147–148
- Travaux pratiques de grammaire, pp. 47–50
- Grammar Tutor for Students of French, Chapter 6
- Cahier d'activités, pp. 68–70
- Testing Program, pp. 139–142
- Alternative Assessment Guide, p. 37
- Student Make-Up Assignments, Chapter 6

MEDIA

- One-Stop Planner
- Audio Compact Discs, CD 6, Trs. 10–11, 21, 35–36
- Teaching Transparencies: 5-3; **Grammaire supplémentaire** Answers; Travaux pratiques de grammaire Answers
- Interactive CD-ROM Tutor, Disc 2

Auditory Learners

30 Before students do this activity, read aloud several true-false statements about the movies and have students respond **vrai** or **faux.** For example, you might say *La Guerre des étoiles* **est à quinze heures (faux),** or *Les Visiteurs* **est à seize heures trente (vrai).**

Slower Pace

31 Before students begin writing, you might write the following questions on the board or on a transparency. **Fabienne veut faire quoi vendredi soir? Et samedi après-midi? On va au ciné à quelle heure samedi soir? Qu'est-ce qu'elle veut faire dimanche matin?** Have students write down these questions and their answers and include them as part of the writing assignment.

29 Grammaire en contexte

Ecrivons You'd like to find out more about what teenagers in France normally do. Write down at least six questions to ask your pen pal about his or her classes, activities, and hobbies.

30 Allons au cinéma!

Parlons Look at the movie schedule below. Choose a movie you want to see and invite your partner to go with you. When you've agreed on a movie to see, decide at which time you want to go and arrange a time and place to meet.

Le Beaumont — **15, Bd des Italiens • 75002 PARIS**

- **Astérix chez les Bretons,** *v.f. Séances : 12h, 14h15, 16h30, 18h45, 21h00*
- **Les Randonneurs,** *v.f. Séances : 11h55, 13h55, 15h55*
- **Roméo et Juliette,** *v.f. Séances : 13h40, 16h15, 18h55, 21h30*
- **La Guerre des étoiles,** *v.o. Séances : 11h30, 14h, 16h30, 19h, 21h30*
- **Mon chien Skip,** *v.f. Séances : 13h30, 15h, 16h30*
- **Les 101 Dalmatiens,** *v.o. Séances : 11h05, 13h45, 16h20, 19h, 21h35*
- **Hercule,** *v.f. Séance : 21h*
- **Les Visiteurs,** *v.f. Séances : 13h30, 16h30*
- **Le Journal d'Anne Frank,** *v.f. Séances : 12h30, 14h, 16h*
- **Casablanca,** *v.o. Séances : 16h30, 19h*

31 Ça te dit?

Ecrivons A friend has written you this note suggesting some things to do this weekend. Write an answer, accepting the invitations or making suggestions of your own.

Salut! Ça va? Tu veux faire quoi ce week-end? Moi, je voudrais faire les magasins vendredi soir et jouer au tennis samedi après-midi. On va au ciné samedi soir vers huit heures et demie. Tu viens? Et dimanche matin, tu veux aller au café? Qu'est-ce que tu en penses? Fabienne

Cultures and Communities

Culture Notes

30 • Have students try to guess the English titles of some of the films in this activity and those of other films as well. *(Cendrillon, Cinderella).* Tell students that the terms **v.o.** and **v.f.** mean **version originale** (in the original language with subtitles) and **version française.**

30 • In 2000, the two main cinema chains in France, UGC and Gaumont-MK2, launched a system of cards. Movie goers can buy a card for 14.94 euros. The card is valid for a whole month and entitles the holder to see as many movies as they want in a month.

STANDARDS: 1.1, 3.1, 5.1, 5.2

Parlons This summer you're working as a camp counselor. You're trying to set up a group meeting some time during the evening this week, and you need to find out when is a good time and place for everyone to meet. Work with a partner and find out what he or she is planning on doing each evening and at what time. Agree on a possible day and time to schedule the meeting.

PRONONCIATION

CD 6
Trs. 12–17

The vowel sounds [ø] and [œ]

See scripts and answers on p. 167H.

The vowel sound [ø] in **veux** is represented by the letter combination **eu.** It is pronounced with the lips rounded and the tongue pressed against the back of the lower front teeth. To produce this sound, first make the sound **è,** as in **algèbre,** and hold it. Then, round the lips slightly to the position for closed **o,** as in **photo.** Repeat these words.

jeudi veux peu deux

The vowel sound [œ] in the word **heure** is similar to the sound in **veux** and is also represented by the letters **eu.** This sound is more open, however, and occurs when these letters are followed by a consonant sound in the same syllable. To produce this sound, first make the sound **è,** as in **algèbre,** and hold it. Then, round the lips slightly to the position for open **o,** as in **short.** Repeat these words.

classeur feuille heure

A. A prononcer

Repeat the following words.

1. jeudi	déjeuner	peux
2. deux	veut	mieux
3. ordinateur	jeunes	heure
4. feuille	classeur	veulent

B. A lire

Take turns with a partner reading each of the following sentences aloud.

1. Tu as deux ordinateurs? On peut étudier chez toi jeudi?
2. Tu veux manger des escargots? C'est délicieux!
3. On va à la Maison des jeunes? A quelle heure?
4. Tu as une feuille de papier? Je n'ai pas mon classeur.

C. A écrire

You're going to hear a short dialogue. Write down what you hear.

Troisième étape

CHAPITRE 6

Assess

- Testing Program, pp. 139–142 Quiz 6-3A, Quiz 6-3B Audio CD 6, Tr. 21
- Student Make-Up Assignments, Chapter 6, Alternative Quiz
- Alternative Assessment Guide, p. 37

Communication for All Students

Visual Learners

31 Bring in magazine photos of several different activities and places. Have students work in pairs, one to rewrite the letter and the other to respond, using activities based on the photos.

Additional Practice

Prononciation Have students scan the end-of-chapter **Vocabulaire** to find all the words that contain the **eu** combination. Then, have them write sentences like the ones in Part B, using as many of these words as possible. Remind them that the sentences must be logical!

STANDARDS: 1.3

Teaching Resources
pp. 188–189

PRINT 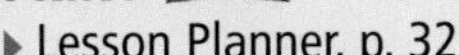

- Lesson Planner, p. 32
- Cahier d'activités, p. 71
- Reading Strategies and Skills Handbook, Chapter 6
- Joie de lire 1, Chapter 6
- Standardized Assessment Tutor, Chapter 6

MEDIA 

- One-Stop Planner

Culture Note
The photo of model castles on the **France Miniature** brochure shows several châteaux of the Loire Valley, including Chenonceau (foreground) and Chambord (background).

Prereading
Activity A

Using Context Clues
Begin by having students scan the brochures to answer the question in this activity. You might also ask what types of brochures these are and what information students would expect to find in them.

Reading
Activities B–D

Monitoring Comprehension
B. Have students correct the inaccurate statements.

Lisons!

Parcs d'attractions

Le Pays FRANCE MINIATURE, c'est la France comme vous ne l'avez jamais vue! Sur une immense carte en relief, sont regroupées les plus belles richesses de notre patrimoine : 166 monuments historiques, 15 villages typiques de nos régions, les paysages et les scènes de la vie quotidienne à l'échelle 1/30ème... au cœur d'un environnement naturel extraordinaire.

CALENDRIER :
Ouverture : 15 mars au 15 novembre.
Tous les jours de 10h à 19h.

TARIFS :
Individuels : Adultes : 12 €.
Enfants : 8 € (de 11 à 16 ans).

RESTAURATION
Deux restaurants de 300 places chacun et 2 kiosques proposent des menus de différentes régions de France (un restaurant ouvert le samedi soir).
Aire de pique-nique aménagée.

Parcs d'attractions

Stratégie pour lire
When you run across a word you don't know, use context to guess the meaning of the word. You automatically use this strategy in your own language. For example, you may not know the English word *dingo*, but when you see it in a sentence, you can make an intelligent guess about what it means. Read this sentence: *He thought that the kangaroos and the koala bears were cute, but that the dingos were mean-looking.* You can guess that a dingo is a possibly vicious animal found in Australia. It is, in fact, a wild dog.

Where do you like to go on the weekend? Look at these brochures to see where Parisians go for fun.

A. What kinds of places do these brochures describe? theme parks and zoo

B. One of your friends visited **France Miniature** and told you about it. Check the brochure to see if what he said was accurate or not.

1. "I saw more than 150 monuments!" accurate
2. "There were twenty villages represented." inaccurate
3. "The size of everything was on a scale of 1/25." inaccurate
4. "It was more expensive than **Parc Astérix.**" inaccurate
5. "We stayed until midnight." inaccurate
6. "We went on my birthday, June 15th." accurate

Connections and Comparisons

Language Arts Link
Read aloud (or have students read) **Stratégie pour lire.** Choose a passage from a Language Arts reading selection and delete every seventh word. Have students use the context to suggest words that could complete the passage.

Math Link
France Miniature Make sure students understand the concept of building on a scale of 1/30. How tall would a 60-meter building be on this reduced scale? (2 meters)

STANDARDS: 1.2, 2.2, 3.1

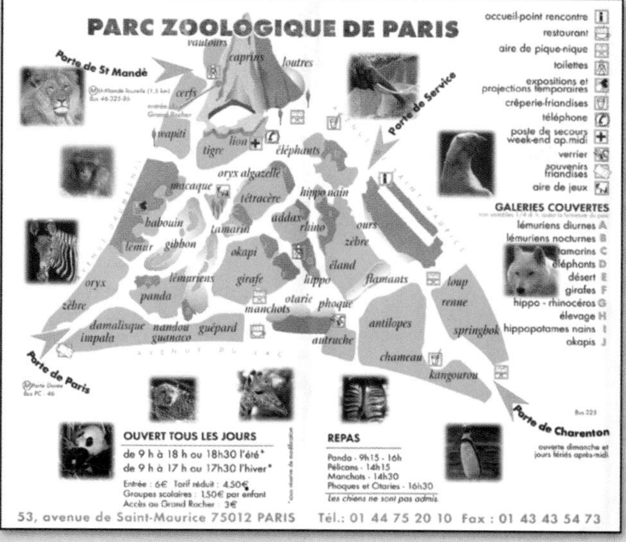

PARC ASTERIX

Bienvenue en Gaule pour une journée mémorable!

Pour passer une journée partagée entre l'émotion et l'aventure.
Pour retrouver cette bonne humeur légendaire et communicative.
Pour faire un voyage mémorable en Gaule, au pays du bien-vivre et de l'histoire...

Venez au Parc Astérix! Astérix et tous ses amis vous y attendent...

Départ de Paris les mercredis et samedis à 9h, du 10 avril au 2 octobre. Retour du site à 18h et arrivée à Paris vers 19h30.

Prix par personne : 52 €
Enfants de 3 à 11 ans inclus : 40 €
Le prix inclut l'hébergement.

C. Look at the brochure for **Parc Astérix** and answer the following questions. See answers below.

1. During which months would you not be able to go on this trip?
2. On which days of the week can you take this trip to **Parc Astérix?**
3. If you took the trip in the advertisement, at what time would you leave Paris?
4. At what time would you leave the park for the trip back?
5. If you go with three friends and one of you brings your ten-year-old sister, how much will it cost?

D. Imagine you and a friend want to go to the **Parc zoologique de Paris.** See answers below.

1. Is the park open on Sundays? Is there a restaurant?
2. How much is it going to cost? Will it make a difference if you're students?
3. How late can you stay in the summer? In the winter?
4. What are some of the animals you'll get to see?
5. At what time do the pelicans eat? The pandas?
6. How many picnic areas are there? What is near the first-aid station? Where can you buy a gift?

E. Which of these places would you like to go to most? Why?

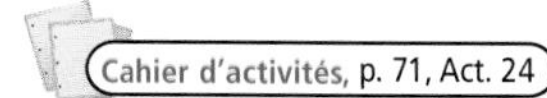
Cahier d'activités, p. 71, Act. 24

Communication for All Students

Additional Practice

D. Have students make a list, in French, of animals that they might see during a visit to the zoo. You might refer them to the names of animals in the Preliminary Chapter.

Challenge

Have students create their own brochure in French for a local amusement park. Students could also invent their own ideal amusement park, after polling one another to find out about some of the most popular features.

Lisons!

CHAPITRE 6

Terms in Lisons!

- An important expression from **France Miniature** is **aire de pique-nique aménagée**—*equipped picnic area.*
- Terms that might interest students from the **Parc Astérix** brochure include:
  retrouver—*to find again*
  bien-vivre—*good living, the good life*
- Students might want to know some of the other expressions from the zoo brochure:
  friandises—*sweets, desserts*
  manchots—*penguins*
  fauves—*wildcats*
  otaries—*sea lions*

Postreading

Activity E

Thinking Critically

Evaluating Use Activity E as a closing discussion question. You might also ask students to name the brochures that give them the most and the least information. Students might enjoy creating a brochure in French to advertise a nearby attraction in their own community to French tourists.

Answers

C. 1. November through March
2. Wednesdays and Saturdays
3. 9:00 A.M.
4. 6:00 P.M.
5. 248 euros.

D. 1. Yes; Yes
2. 6€ or 4,50€; student groups: 1,50€ per child
3. summer: 6:00 or 6:30 P.M.; winter: 5:00 or 5:30 P.M.
4. *Possible answers:* elephants, tigers, kangaroos
5. pelicans: 2:15 P.M.; pandas: 9:15 A.M. and 4:00 P.M.
6. four picnic areas; lions and tigers; souvenirs, friandises *(souvenir shop)*

Grammaire supplémentaire

CHAPITRE 6

For **Grammaire supplémentaire** Answer Transparencies, see the *Teaching Transparencies* binder.

Grammaire supplémentaire

Première étape

Objective Making plans

1 Malika is leaving a message on Axel's answering machine. Complete her message with **le** when appropriate. Be careful! In some cases, you won't need to add anything. (**p. 173**)

Salut, Axel! C'est moi, Malika! Ça va? Ecoute! On va au Café Américain ___1___ lundi soir. Tu viens? On va souvent à la crêperie ___2___ lundi, mais cette semaine, on va aller au café. Bonne idée, non? ___3___ mercredi après-midi, on va aller voir une pièce. On va quelquefois au théâtre ___4___ mercredi. C'est super, le théâtre! Est-ce que tu peux venir? Ah, oui, ___5___ samedi, on va à la boum de Nadine. Qu'est-ce que tu fais d'habitude ___6___ samedi soir? Tu veux venir avec nous? Eh bien, à bientôt peut-être. Tchao!

2 Véronique and Elodie are trying to choose a convenient time to go to the movies. Complete Elodie's responses according to her schedule below. (**p. 173**)

LUNDI	MARDI	MERCREDI	JEUDI	VENDREDI	SAMEDI	DIMANCHE
sortie de l'école 17h15	sortie de l'école 16h00	sortie de l'école 12h15	sortie de l'école 17h15	sortie de l'école 16h00	sortie de l'école 11h15	
devoirs! étudier pour l'examen	18h00–19h30 danse	14h00–16h00 natation	18h00–19h30 danse	20h00 dîner au restaurant	14h00–16h00 natation	
					20h00 boum de Michèle	20h30 concert de I AM

1. J'ai danse ______ et ______ de 18h00 à 19h30.
2. ______ soir, j'ai des devoirs à faire.
3. ______ la sortie de l'école est à 12h15, mais j'ai natation à 14h00.
4. ______ et ______, j'ai natation de 14h00 à 16h00.
5. Je vais au restaurant ______ soir.
6. ______ soir, il y a le concert de I AM.
7. Tu es libre ______ après-midi?

Grammar Resources for Chapter 6

The **Grammaire supplémentaire** activities were designed as supplemental activities for the grammatical concepts presented in the chapter. You might use them as additional practice, for review, or for assessment.

For more grammar presentations, review, and practice, refer to the following:

- Travaux pratiques de grammaire
- Grammar Tutor for Students of French
- Grammar Summary on pp. R15–R28
- Cahier d'activités
- Grammar and Vocabulary quizzes (Testing Program)
- Test Generator
- Interactive CD-ROM Tutor
- **Jeux interactifs** at go.hrw.com

Answers

1
1. X
2. le
3. X
4. le
5. X
6. le

2
1. le mardi / le jeudi
2. Lundi
3. Le mercredi
4. Le mercredi / le samedi
5. vendredi
6. Dimanche
7. dimanche

STANDARDS: 1.2

3

Fernand and Michèle are discussing what to do this coming Saturday. Complete their conversation with the correct forms of **aller.** (**p. 174**)

FERNAND Dis, Michèle, tu ___1___ faire quoi demain?
MICHELE Bof. Rien de spécial. D'habitude, le samedi, je fais les vitrines.
FERNAND Eric et moi, on ___2___ faire un pique-nique. Tu viens avec nous?
MICHELE Désolée, mais ça ne me dit rien, les pique-niques.
FERNAND Mais écoute, Michèle! Les pique-niques, c'est génial! Tous les copains ___3___ venir! On ___4___ jouer au foot! Julien et Juliette ___5___ apporter des hot-dogs! Nous ___6___ nous amuser!
MICHELE D'accord. Pourquoi pas? On se retrouve où?
FERNAND Devant la MJC. Vers trois heures.
MICHELE Entendu. Je ___7___ passer chez toi vers deux heures et demie.

4

Fais une phrase avec les mots proposés. Utilise la forme correcte du verbe **aller.** (**p. 174**)

EXEMPLE Marc et Li/faire les vitrines **Marc et Li vont faire les vitrines.**

1. Toi, tu/aller au café
2. Moi, je/aller au théâtre
3. Marc/voir un film
4. Simone et moi, nous/voir un match
5. Pascal et Maurice, vous/faire une promenade
6. Michèle et François/aller à une boum
7. Nous/faire un pique-nique
8. Vous/manger quelque chose

5

Christelle and Alain are talking about what they like to do during their free time. Complete the following sentences according to the photos. (**p. 177**)

1. Je vais  pour faire du jogging.
2. J'aime aller  pour nager.
3. En été, j'aime aller  .
4. Mes amis et moi, nous aimons aller  .

Grammaire supplémentaire

CHAPITRE 6

Answers

3
1. vas
2. va
3. vont
4. va
5. vont
6. allons
7. vais

4
1. Toi, tu vas aller au café.
2. Moi, je vais aller au théâtre.
3. Marc va voir un film.
4. Simone et moi, nous allons voir un match.
5. Pascal et Maurice, vous allez faire une promenade.
6. Michèle et François vont aller à une boum.
7. Nous allons faire un pique-nique.
8. Vous allez manger quelque chose.

5
1. au parc
2. à la piscine
3. à la plage
4. au zoo

Communication for All Students

Game

Trop à faire Begin the game by telling what you're going to do tomorrow. **(Je vais jouer au volley-ball.)** Then, have a student repeat what you're going to do and add what he or she is planning to do. **(...va jouer au volley-ball, mais moi, je vais étudier.)** Each student continues by repeating all the previous activities and adding another. If someone makes a mistake, the next student starts a new sequence with an activity he or she is going to do. Encourage students to use **et** or **mais,** where appropriate.

Grammaire supplémentaire

CHAPITRE 6

For **Grammaire supplémentaire** Answer Transparencies, see the *Teaching Transparencies* binder.

Answers

6
1. à la
2. au, au
3. aux
4. à la
5. au
6. au
7. au

7
1. veulent
2. veux
3. voulez
4. voulons
5. veux
6. veut

8
1. Elles veulent aller à la piscine.
2. Je veux aller à la bibliothèque.
3. Vous voulez voir une pièce.
4. Il veut voir un film.
5. Nous voulons aller à une boum.
6. Tu veux regarder un match de foot à la télé.

Grammaire supplémentaire

WA3 PARIS-6

6 Imagine que tu vas faire un voyage à Paris avec tes amis cet été. Utilise **à, à la, au,** et **aux** pour compléter les phrases suivantes. (**p. 177**)

1. Christine va aller ___ cathédrale (f.).
2. Nous allons aller ___ théâtre et ___ restaurant.
3. Marc va aller ___ concerts de rock du festival de la musique.
4. Moi, je vais ___ Maison des jeunes.
5. Les garçons ne vont pas aller ___ centre commercial.
6. Je vais voir un film français ___ cinéma.
7. Et Mark et Jeanne vont voir un match de foot ___ stade.

Deuxième étape

Objective Extending and responding to invitations

7 Complète les phrases suivantes avec la forme correcte du verbe **vouloir.** (**p. 180**)

1. Mes copines _____ aller au restaurant.
2. Mais moi, je _____ aller au café.
3. Et vous, vous _____ manger quelque chose?
4. Non. Nous _____ voir un film.
5. Et toi, Eric, tu _____ faire quoi?
6. Patricia et moi, on _____ faire les vitrines.

8 Based on their preferences, write what the following students want to do. Be sure to use the appropriate subject pronoun, the correct form of **vouloir,** and an expression from the box. Use each expression only once. (**p. 180**)

> voir un film — regarder un match de foot à la télé — voir une pièce — manger quelque chose — aller à une boum — aller à la bibliothèque — aller à la piscine

EXEMPLE Marianne a faim. **Elle veut manger quelque chose.**

1. Suzanne et Monique adorent nager.
2. J'aime lire.
3. Vous adorez le théâtre.
4. Gilles aime bien le cinéma.
5. Anne et moi, nous aimons danser.
6. Tu aimes le football.

Teacher to Teacher

Susan Hayden
Aloha High School
Beaverton, OR

Try Susan's use of kinesthetic skills to practice *au, à la,* and *à l'*.

"I ask each student to draw one of the places they've learned, for example, a movie theater. I then tape the pictures on the walls. In a circle, the students walk around the room, naming the places they are going to **(au zoo, à la piscine).** After this productive cacophony, they work with a partner and invite him/her to three places, moving to those places in the room. I then have them switch roles from inviter to invitee."

STANDARDS: 1.2

Troisième étape

Objective Arranging to meet someone

9 Complète la conversation suivante avec la réponse correcte. (**p. 185**)

Avec Lise.	A sept heures et demie.
Chez moi.	Ce soir.

DIANE Tu viens manger avec nous, Isabelle?
ISABELLE Oui. Je veux bien. Quand ça?
DIANE ___1___
ISABELLE Où est-ce qu'on se retrouve?
DIANE ___2___
ISABELLE Avec qui on va manger?
DIANE ___3___
ISABELLE On se retrouve à quelle heure?
DIANE ___4___

10 Fais correspondre la réponse de la colonne A à la question posée dans la colonne B. (**p. 185**)

A	B
1. Mireille et Matthieu.	**a.** Où est-ce qu'on se retrouve?
2. On va voir *Les Randonneurs.*	**b.** Qu'est-ce tu vas voir?
3. Demain, à deux heures et demie.	**c.** Tu vas avec qui?
4. Je vais voir un film.	**d.** Quand ça?
5. Au cinéma Beaubourg.	**e.** Qu'est-ce que tu vas faire ce week-end?

Review and Assess

You may wish to assign the **Grammaire supplémentaire** activities as additional practice or homework after presenting material throughout the chapter. Assign Activities 1–2 after **Note de grammaire** (p. 173), Activities 3–4 after **Grammaire** (p. 174), Activities 5–6 after **Grammaire** (p. 177), Activities 7–8 after **Grammaire** (p. 180), and Activities 9–10 after **Grammaire** (p. 185). To prepare students for the **Etape** Quizzes and Chapter Test, we suggest doing the **Grammaire supplémentaire** activities in the following order. Have students complete Activities 1–6 before taking Quizzes 6-1A or 6-1B; Activities 7–8 before Quizzes 6-2A or 6-2B; and Activities 9–10 before Quizzes 6-3A or 6-3B.

Answers

9
1. Ce soir.
2. Chez moi.
3. Avec Lise.
4. A sept heures et demie.

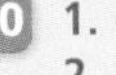

10
1. c
2. b
3. d
4. e
5. a

STANDARDS: 1.2

Mise en pratique

CHAPITRE 6

The **Mise en pratique** reviews and integrates all four skills and culture in preparation for the Chapter Test.

Teaching Resources

pp. 194–195

PRINT 

- Lesson Planner, p. 32
- Listening Activities, p. 45
- Video Guide, pp. 41, 44
- Grammar Tutor for Students of French, Chapter 6
- Standardized Assessment Tutor, Chapter 6

MEDIA

- One-Stop Planner
- Video Program
  Videocassette 2, 46:57–48:00
- DVD Tutor, Disc 1
- Audio Compact Discs, CD 6, Tr. 18
- Interactive CD-ROM Tutor, Disc 2

Additional Practice

1 Ask students which place they would prefer to visit and why.

Answers

1
1. la tour Eiffel
2. Notre-Dame de Paris; Sundays
3. yes; la tour Eiffel, le musée d'Orsay
4. au musée d'Orsay
5. Notre-Dame de Paris
6. all of them
7. le musée d'Orsay
8. la tour Eiffel
9. à la tour Eiffel

Mise en pratique

Visit Holt Online
go.hrw.com
KEYWORD: WA3 PARIS-6
Self-Test

La tour Eiffel est le monument parisien le plus connu au monde. Elle a été construite pour l'Exposition universelle de 1889. Jusqu'à la construction de l'Empire State Building de New York en 1931, la tour Eiffel était la plus haute tour du monde avec ses 320 mètres, antenne comprise. La tour a trois étages. Il y a un restaurant au premier et au deuxième étages. Le troisième étage offre un superbe point de vue sur la ville. Horaires : 9h30 à 23h. Tarifs : 3 € à 8,50 €.

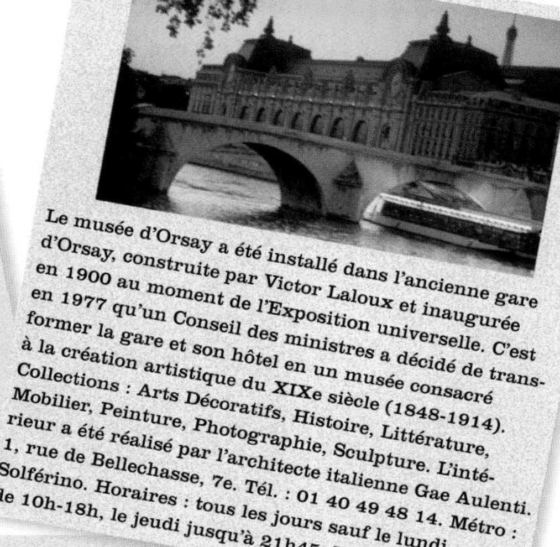

Le musée d'Orsay a été installé dans l'ancienne gare d'Orsay, construite par Victor Laloux et inaugurée en 1900 au moment de l'Exposition universelle. C'est en 1977 qu'un Conseil des ministres a décidé de transformer la gare et son hôtel en un musée consacré à la création artistique du XIXe siècle (1848-1914). Collections : Arts Décoratifs, Histoire, Littérature, Mobilier, Peinture, Photographie, Sculpture. L'intérieur a été réalisé par l'architecte italienne Gae Aulenti. 1, rue de Bellechasse, 7e. Tél. : 01 40 49 48 14. Métro : Solférino. Horaires : tous les jours sauf le lundi de 10h-18h, le jeudi jusqu'à 21h45. Tarifs : 5,50 €.

Notre-Dame de Paris est un chef-d'œuvre de l'art gothique français, construite entre 1163 et 1330. La façade principale est composée de trois gigantesques portails. Visite guidée et gratuite de la cathédrale tous les jours : à 12h du lundi au vendredi, à 14h30 le samedi, à 14h le dimanche. Visite payante des tours tous les jours de 10h à 17h30. Concerts gratuits tous les dimanches à 17h45. Pas de visite les jours fériés.
Tél : 01 42 34 56 10.
Tarifs : Visite des tours : 5 €.

1 Look over the advertisements and answer the questions below. See answers below.

1. Which place(s) offer(s) a view of Paris?
2. Where can you go to a free concert? On what day?
3. Are any of these places open in the evening? If so, which ones?
4. Where can you see nineteenth-century French art?
5. Which attraction is closed on holidays?
6. Which places list their prices?
7. Which attraction is closed on Mondays?
8. Which attraction costs the most to visit?
9. At which place can you buy something to eat?

2 Your French friends are discussing which Paris attraction to visit. Listen to their conversation and write down the attraction they decide on. Listen again and tell when and where they agree to meet. See scripts and answers on p. 167H.

CD 6 Tr. 18

Apply and Assess

Challenge

1 You might use this activity as a game. Have students form small groups and give them a time limit to answer as many questions as possible. You might give a prize to the group that correctly answers the most questions.

Career Path

Have students list the types of services provided by a travel agency for someone planning to visit Paris. Have students identify the services on the list that would require knowing French. You might have students visit travel agency sites on the Internet for more ideas.

STANDARDS: 1.2, 2.2, 3.1, 5.1

3 Using what you've learned about French culture, answer the following questions. See answers below.

1. Where do French teenagers like to go to have fun?
2. Would a French teenager be surprised at American dating customs? Why?

4 

Ecrivons!

You have one day in Paris to do whatever you like. Write a note to your French class back home telling everyone what you plan to do during your day in Paris.

Stratégie pour écrire

Arranging your ideas chronologically is helpful when planning activities for the day. To do this, take a sheet of paper, turn it sideways, and divide it into five columns. Label the first column de 8h à 10h, the second column de 10h à midi, and so on, in two-hour increments up to 6:00 in the evening. Next, decide what you would like to do at these times and write the information in the appropriate columns.

de 8h à 10h	de 10h à midi	de midi à 2h
aller au café	aller au zoo	
faire une promenade dans le jardin des Tuileries.		

Now, using the information from the chart you've prepared, write the note to your French class. Tell everyone what you plan to see and do throughout the day. Here are some connecting words that may help your writing flow more smoothly: **d'abord** *(first)*, **ensuite** *(next)*, and **après ça** *(after that)*.

5

Jeu de rôle

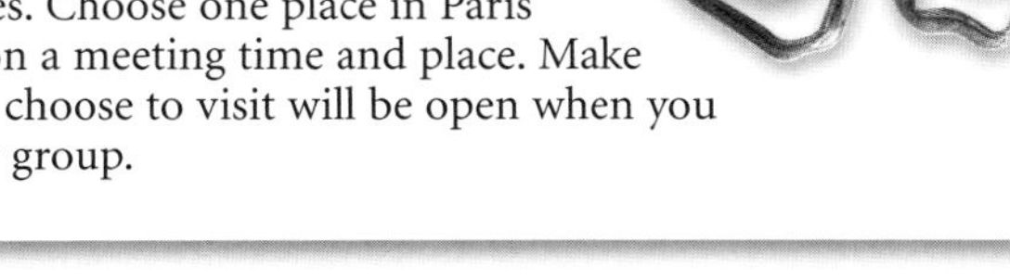

Get together with some classmates. Choose one place in Paris you'd all like to visit and decide on a meeting time and place. Make sure that the Paris attraction you choose to visit will be open when you plan to go. Act this out with your group.

Mise en pratique

CHAPITRE 6

Portfolio

4 **Written** You might have students include this assignment in their written portfolios. For portfolio suggestions, see *Alternative Assessment Guide,* pages iv–17.

5 **Oral** Students might include this conversation in their oral portfolios.

Apply and Assess

Process Writing

4 If students have problems getting started or would like more options, refer them to the Location Opener on pages 136–139 for places and activities in Paris.

Challenge

5 Extend this activity by having students find several classmates who have planned an activity similar to theirs. Then, ask the groups to research three of the sights or attractions they want to see. Have each group do a short, oral presentation about the attractions they research.

Possible answers

3
1. films, plays, concerts, discothèques, dance parties, **Maisons des jeunes**
2. Yes, because French teenagers tend to go out in groups rather than couples.

STANDARDS: 1.1, 1.3, 5.1, 5.2

Que sais-je?

CHAPITRE 6

Teaching Resources
p. 196

PRINT 
- Grammar Tutor for Students of French, Chapter 6

MEDIA 
- Interactive CD-ROM Tutor, Disc 2
- Online self-test

go.hrw.com
WA3 PARIS-6

Teacher Note
This page is intended to help students prepare for the Chapter Test. It is a brief checklist of the major points covered in the chapter. Students should be reminded that this is only a checklist and does not necessarily include everything that will appear on the test.

Teaching Suggestion
3 **4** Encourage students to vary the ways they express each function.

Answers

3 *Possible answers:*
1. Tu veux faire les vitrines avec moi?
2. Je voudrais faire une promenade. Tu viens?
3. On peut aller voir un match de basket.
4. Allons au café!

4 *Accepting:* D'accord. Bonne idée. Je veux bien. Pourquoi pas?
Refusing: Ça ne me dit rien. J'ai des trucs à faire. Désolé(e), je ne peux pas. Je suis occupé(e).

5
1. Ahmed veut aller à la bibliothèque.
2. Isabelle et Ferdinand veulent aller au théâtre.
3. Mon amie et moi, nous voulons aller au musée.

7
1. au cinéma, devant le stade, au café
2. avec Anne, avec mes amis
3. vers trois heures, à huit heures et demie, à midi
4. demain, ce soir, lundi après-midi

Que sais-je?

WA3 PARIS-6

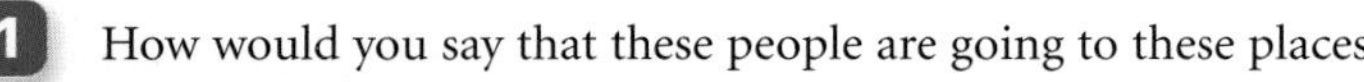

Can you use what you've learned in this chapter?

Can you make plans?
p. 173

1 How would you say that these people are going to these places?

1. Je vais au match de base-ball.

2. Nous allons au centre commercial.

3. Anne et Etienne vont au cinéma.

2 How would you tell what you're planning to do this weekend? Je vais... ce week-end.

Can you extend and respond to invitations?
p. 179

3 How would you invite a friend to . . . See answers below.
1. go window shopping?
2. go for a walk?
3. go see a basketball game?
4. go to the café?

4 How would you accept the following invitations? How would you refuse them? See answers below.
1. Je voudrais aller faire du ski. Tu viens?
2. Allons à la Maison des jeunes!
3. On va au restaurant. Tu viens?
4. Tu veux aller au cinéma?

5 How would you say that the following people want to go to these places? See answers below.

1. Ahmed

2. Isabelle et Ferdinand

3. Mon amie et moi

Can you arrange to meet someone?
p. 183

6 If someone invited you to go to the movies, what are three questions you might ask to find out more information?
Possible answers: Où ça? Quand ça? A quelle heure? Avec qui?

7 What are some possible answers to the following questions? See answers below.
1. Où ça?
2. Avec qui?
3. A quelle heure?
4. Quand ça?

Review and Assess

Building on Previous Skills
1 Have students add a day and time to their answers. You might have them practice with the **tu, vous, il,** and **elle** forms as well.

Additional Practice
5 Suggest other places these or other people might want to visit.

Auditory Learners
7 Read the following message left on an answering machine and have students answer the questions in this activity based on the message. **(Salut, c'est Monique! Ecoute, tu veux aller au musée? On y va samedi avec Daniel vers deux heures—il veut y voir une exposition de photos. Alors, tu peux? Rendez-vous devant le musée—à bientôt!)**

STANDARDS: 1.1, 1.2

Vocabulaire

Première étape

Making plans

Qu'est-ce que tu vas faire... ?	*What are you going to do . . . ?*
Tu vas faire quoi...?	*What are you going to do . . . ?*
Je vais...	*I'm going . . .*
Pas grand-chose.	*Not much.*
Rien de spécial.	*Nothing special.*

Things to do

aller à une boum	*to go to a party*
faire une promenade	*to go for a walk*
faire un pique-nique	*to have a picnic*
faire les vitrines	*to window-shop*
manger quelque chose	*to eat something*
regarder un match	*to watch a game (on TV)*
voir un film	*to see a movie*
aller voir un match	*to go see a game*
voir une pièce	*to see a play*

Places to go

la bibliothèque	*library*
le centre commercial	*mall*
le cinéma	*movie theater*
la Maison des jeunes et de la culture (MJC)	*recreation center*
le musée	*museum*
le parc	*park*
la piscine	*swimming pool*
la plage	*beach*
le restaurant	*restaurant*
le stade	*stadium*
le théâtre	*theater*
le zoo	*zoo*

Other useful expressions

aller	*to go*
au/à la/à l'/aux	*to, at*

Deuxième étape

Extending invitations

Allons... !	*Let's go . . . !*
Tu veux... avec moi?	*Do you want . . . with me?*
Tu viens?	*Will you come?*
On peut...	*We can . . .*

Accepting invitations

D'accord.	*OK.*
Bonne idée.	*Good idea.*
Je veux bien.	*I'd really like to.*
Pourquoi pas?	*Why not?*

Refusing invitations

Ça ne me dit rien.	*I don't feel like it.*
J'ai des trucs à faire.	*I've got things to do.*
Désolé(e), je ne peux pas.	*Sorry, I can't.*
Désolé(e), je suis occupé(e).	*Sorry, I'm busy.*

Other useful expressions

je voudrais...	*I'd like . . .*
vouloir	*to want*

Troisième étape

Arranging to meet someone

Quand (ça)?	*When?*
tout de suite	*right away*
Où (ça)?	*Where?*
dans	*in*
devant	*in front of*
au (métro)...	*at the . . . (metro stop)*
chez...	*at . . . ('s) house*
Avec qui?	*With whom?*
avec...	*with . . .*
A quelle heure?	*At what time?*
A cinq heures.	*At five o'clock.*
et demie	*half past*
et quart	*quarter past*
moins le quart	*quarter to*
moins cinq	*five to*
Quelle heure est-il?	*What time is it?*
Il est midi.	*It's noon.*
Il est minuit.	*It's midnight.*
Il est midi (minuit) et demi.	*It's half past noon (midnight).*
vers	*about*
Bon, on se retrouve...	*OK, we'll meet . . .*
Rendez-vous...	*We'll meet . . .*
Entendu.	*OK.*

Other useful expressions

ce week-end	*this weekend*
demain	*tomorrow*
est-ce que	*(introduces a yes-no question)*

Review and Assess

Circumlocution

Have students act out a conversation in which a tourist in a French city wants to visit certain places, but hasn't yet learned the French words for them. One partner will play the role of the tourist, and the other partner will guess the name of the place based on what the tourist says. **(—Où est-ce qu'on peut faire les vitrines? –Au centre commercial.)** Students can use vocabulary for activities and places from previous chapters as well. You may want to give students the list of circumlocution expressions on page 167C .

Vocabulaire

CHAPITRE 6

Game

Mots croisés Have groups of students choose five or six vocabulary words and design a crossword puzzle with pictures or fill-in-the-blank sentences as clues. Have groups exchange and complete the puzzles.

Chapter 6 Assessment

- **Testing Program**
  Chapter Test, pp. 143–148

  Audio Compact Discs, CD 6, Trs. 22–24
  Speaking Test, p. 345
  Midterm Exam, pp. 157–164
  Score Sheet, pp. 165–167
  Listening Scripts, pp. 168–169
  Answers, p. 170

  Audio Compact Discs, CD 6, Trs. 25–30
- **Alternative Assessment Guide**
  Performance Assessment, p. 37
  Portfolio Assessment, p. 23
  CD-ROM Assessment, p. 51
- **Interactive CD-ROM Tutor, Disc 2**

  A toi de parler
  A toi d'écrire
- **Standardized Assessment Tutor**
  Chapter 6
- **One-Stop Planner, Disc 2**
  Test Generator
  Chapter 6

STANDARDS: 1.1, 1.2, 1.3

Chapitre 7 : La famille
Chapter Overview

Mise en train pp. 200–202	***Sympa, la famille!***			
	FUNCTIONS	**GRAMMAR**	**VOCABULARY**	**RE-ENTRY**
Première étape pp. 203–207	• Identifying people, p. 203 • Introducing people, p. 207	• Possession with **de,** p. 204 • Possessive adjectives, p. 205	• Family relationships, p. 204	• Asking for and giving people's names and ages **(Chapitre 1)** • Sports and hobbies **(Chapitre 4)** • Adverbs of frequency **(Chapitre 4)**
Deuxième étape pp. 208–212	• Describing and characterizing people, p. 209	• Adjective agreement, p. 210 • The verb **être,** p. 211	• Describing and characterizing people, p. 208	• Adjective agreement and placement **(Chapitre 3)** • **Et** and **mais (Chapitre 1)**
Troisième étape pp. 213–215	• Asking for, giving, and refusing permission, p. 213		• Household chores, p. 213	• Sports and activities **(Chapitres 1, 4)** • The verb **vouloir (Chapitre 6)**

Prononciation p. 215	**The nasal sounds [ɔ̃], [ɛ̃], and [œ̃]** Audio CD 7, Tracks 14–16	**A écrire** (dictation) Audio CD 7, Tracks 17–19	
Lisons! pp. 216–217	**En direct des refuges**	**Reading Strategy:** Finding the main idea	
Grammaire supplémentaire	**pp. 218–221** **Première étape,** pp. 218–219	**Deuxième étape,** pp. 219–221	**Troisième étape,** p. 221
Review pp. 222–225	**Mise en pratique,** pp. 222–223 **Ecrivons!** Using details to describe people Describing a family photo	**Que sais-je?** p. 224	**Vocabulaire,** p. 225

CULTURE

- **Note culturelle,** Family life, p. 206
- **Panorama Culturel,** Pets in France, p. 212

Chapitre 7 : La famille

Chapter Resources

Lesson Planning

One-Stop Planner

Lesson Planner with Differentiated Instruction, pp. 33–37, 71

Student Make-Up Assignments
- Make-Up Assignment Copying Masters, Chapter 7

Listening and Speaking

TPR Storytelling Book, pp. 25–28

Listening Activities
- Student Response Forms for Listening Activities, pp. 51–53
- Additional Listening Activities 7-1 to 7-6, pp. 55–57
- Additional Listening Activities (song), p. 58
- Scripts and Answers, pp. 132–136

Video Guide
- Teaching Suggestions, pp. 46–47
- Activity Masters, pp. 48–50
- Scripts and Answers, pp. 102–104, 120–121

Activities for Communication
- Communicative Activities, pp. 37–42
- Realia and Teaching Suggestions, pp. 105–109
- Situation Cards, pp. 149–150

Reading and Writing

Reading Strategies and Skills Handbook, Chapter 7

Joie de lire 1, Chapter 7

Cahier d'activités, pp. 73–84

Grammar

Travaux pratiques de grammaire, pp. 51–60

Grammar Tutor for Students of French, Chapter 7

Assessment

Testing Program
- Grammar and Vocabulary Quizzes, **Etape** Quizzes, and Chapter Test, pp. 171–188
- Score Sheet, Scripts and Answers, pp. 189–196

Alternative Assessment Guide
- Portfolio Assessment, p. 24
- Performance Assessment, p. 38
- CD-ROM Assessment, p. 52

Student Make-Up Assignments
- Alternative Quizzes, Chapter 7

Standardized Assessment Tutor
- Reading, pp. 27–29
- Writing, p. 30
- Math, pp. 51–52

Middle School

Middle School Teaching Resources, Chapter 7

Online Activities
- **Jeux interactifs**
- **Activités Internet**

Video Program
- Videocassette 3
- Videocassette 5 (captioned version)

Interactive CD-ROM Tutor, Disc 2

DVD Tutor, Disc 1

Audio Compact Discs
- Textbook Listening Activities, CD 7, Tracks 1–20
- Additional Listening Activities, CD7, Tracks 27–33
- Assessment Items, CD 7, Tracks 21–26

Teaching Transparencies
- Situation 7-1 to 7-3
- Vocabulary 7-A to 7-D
- **Mise en train**
- **Grammaire supplémentaire** Answers
- **Travaux pratiques de grammaire** Answers

Use the **One-Stop Planner CD-ROM with Test Generator** to aid in lesson planning and pacing.

For each chapter, the **One-Stop Planner** includes:
- Editable lesson plans with direct links to teaching resources
- Printable worksheets from resource books
- Direct launches to the HRW Internet activities
- Video and audio segments
- Test Generator
- Clip Art for vocabulary items

Projects

Mon album de famille

Students will make a family photo album, with descriptions of each family member, similar to the one on pages 200–201. Students might describe a cartoon, television, or royal family instead of their own.

MATERIALS

✂ **Students may need**

- Construction paper
- Stapler and staples
- Colored markers or pens
- Family photos or magazine pictures
- Tape or glue

SUGGESTED SEQUENCE

1. Have students choose at least five family members to present in their photo albums. They should make a list of words and phrases to describe each member. For each person, have students list his or her age, at least three adjectives, and two things that he or she likes or dislikes.
2. Have students choose photos or draw sketches of the family members they are featuring in their album.
3. Have students write rough drafts of their descriptions. They might give their descriptions to a classmate to edit.
4. Give students some construction paper and have them tape or glue one photo or drawing on each page and copy their final description of that family member below it.
5. Have students design and draw a cover for their album and staple it to the other pages.

GRADING THE PROJECT

Suggested Point Distribution: (total = 100 points)

Completion of assignment	25 points
Vocabulary use	25 points
Presentation/creativity	25 points
Language use	25 points

TEACHER NOTE

Encourage students to take their projects home to share with their families.

Games

Qui suis-je?

In this game, students will interact and practice question formation.

Procedure The day before the game, have each student write the name of a well-known person on an index card. Collect the cards and make sure there are no duplicates. You might want to include the principal or other staff members. On the day of the game, tape a card to each student's back, without letting him or her see the card. Have students try to determine their new identity by asking members of their group yes-no questions. (**Je suis grand(e)?**) Circulate to monitor and help out as needed. You might set a time limit for this game and give prizes to the first few students who guess the name affixed to their back.

Variation An alternate way to play this game is to have students write their own names and a brief but detailed description of themselves on an index card. Have them include their likes and dislikes, their hobbies, and so on. Collect and redistribute the cards, taping one to each student's back. Continue with the game as described above.

Possessifs

In this game, students will practice using possessive adjectives.

Procedure Prepare in advance two sets of flash cards, one set with subject pronouns and the other set with nouns from the first seven chapters. Divide the class into two or three teams and appoint a timekeeper. One player from each team will play at a time. Hold up two flash cards, one showing a subject pronoun and the other a noun. The player must say the possessive adjective appropriate to the subject together with the noun within a set amount of time (five seconds should be long enough). For example, if **ils** and **amis** are shown on the two cards, the player should say **leurs amis.** Give points for all correct answers. Make sure all players have a turn and play as many rounds as you choose. By mixing the pronouns and nouns, you can use the same cards over and over.

Variation This game can also be played by forming smaller teams so all of the students can play at once. In this case, each team would write their answer on a piece of paper within a specific time limit (perhaps 5–10 seconds). This way, all students and all teams will play each round.

STANDARDS: 1.3, 5.1

Storytelling

Mini-histoire

This story accompanies Teaching Transparency 7-3. The ***mini-histoire*** *can be told and retold in different formats, acted out, written down, and read aloud, to give students additional opportunities to practice all four skills. The following story relates what Albert's family does on Saturday morning.*

Aujourd'hui, c'est samedi. Albert veut jouer au football avec son oncle Patrick; Pauline doit jouer au tennis avec sa cousine Julie. Leurs parents sont d'accord, mais d'abord, il faut faire le ménage! «Pauline, range ta chambre et fais la vaisselle pendant que je passe l'aspirateur. Dépêche-toi parce que je dois aller faire des courses et échanger cette plante verte car elle est trop grande» dit la mère. Papa dit «Et toi, Albert, sors les poubelles, et s'il te plaît, lave ma voiture. Je suis en retard». Le père sort. Pour lui, pas question de faire le ménage. Il n'aime pas ça. Alors, il va promener le chien!

Traditions

Quatorze juillet

Bastille Day, **la fête nationale,** is celebrated on July 14. It commemorates the storming of the Bastille prison in 1789, the event that symbolizes the end of the French monarchy and the beginning of the Republic. It is a French national holiday and each community celebrates this day with its local parades, dances, and fireworks.

In Paris, locals and tourists line up along the Champs-Elysées to watch the spectacular military parade in the presence of the head of state. At night, families from entire neighborhoods gather to eat, drink, talk, and dance at the **petits bals de quartier.** The most popular **bal** takes place at the **place de la Bastille,** where the prison used to stand. Late in the evening, revelers watch fireworks displays throughout the city. Have students compare the Bastille Day celebrations in Paris to those of July 4th in their hometown.

Recette

The neighborhood in Paris called **les Halles** *was once full of markets that sold produce to restaurants and stores in the early hours of the morning. Farmers and store managers would gather in cafés before or after work to enjoy a hot bowl of onion soup.* **Les Halles** *is now a shopping mall, but many cafés in the area have kept the tradition alive and stay open 24 hours a day. Artists often meet there after their evening performances in local theatres or concert halls.*

GRATINEE DES HALLES

pour 6 personnes

4 gros oignons
4 cuillères à soupe de beurre
1 cuillère à soupe d'huile
1 cuillère à soupe de farine
4 tasses de bouillon
1 cuillère à café de sucre
3 tasses de gruyère
1 baguette
sel et poivre

Peler et couper les oignons. Faire cuire les oignons dans le mélange beurre-huile jusqu'à ce qu'ils deviennent bruns. Ajouter la farine. Ajouter le bouillon. Saler et poivrer. Laisser cuire pendant 20 minutes.

Faire griller la baguette. Mettre le pain grillé dans des bols individuels. Recouvrir de gruyère râpé. Verser la soupe par-dessous, rajouter du fromage râpé et gratiner.

STANDARDS: 1.3, 3.2, 4.2

Chapitre 7 : La famille

Technology

DVD/Video

Videocassette 3, Videocassette 5 (captioned version)
DVD Tutor, Disc 1
See Video Guide, pp. 45–50.

Mise en train • Sympa, la famille!

In this segment of the video, Thuy arrives at Isabelle's house for a visit. Isabelle introduces Thuy to her father. Thuy notices Isabelle's family photo album and asks if she can look at it. As they look at the photos, Isabelle explains who all the family members are and describes them. Thuy says that she is an only child and asks about Isabelle's brother Alexandre. Isabelle tells her that he can be difficult.

Tu as un animal domestique? Il est comment?

Several teenagers from different French-speaking countries tell us about their pets.

Sympa, la famille! (suite)

When the story continues, Alexandre enters Isabelle's room, without knocking or saying hello, and asks where his CD is. Isabelle is annoyed with Alexandre but introduces him to Thuy. Next, the doorbell rings. It is Aunt Véronique, who has brought a kitten as a surprise for Isabelle and Alexandre. Isabelle introduces Thuy. Isabelle's father is not enthusiastic about the kitten, but the others convince him to let them keep it.

Vidéoclips

- **César®:** advertisement for dog food
- **Jockey®:** advertisement for yogurt

Interactive CD-ROM Tutor

Activity	Activity Type	Pupil's Edition Page
En contexte	*Interactive conversation*	
1. Vocabulaire	Chasse au trésor Explorons! Vérifions!	p. 204
2. Grammaire	Les mots qui manquent	p. 210
3. Vocabulaire	Chasse au trésor Explorons! Vérifions!	pp. 208, 210
4. Grammaire	Les mots qui manquent	p. 211
5. Comment dit-on... ?	Chacun à sa place	p. 213
6. Vocabulaire	Jeu des paires	p. 213
Panorama Culturel	Tu as un animal domestique? Il est comment? Le bon choix	p. 212
A toi de parler	*Guided recording*	pp. 222–223
A toi d'écrire	*Guided writing*	pp. 222–223

Teacher Management System

Launch the program, type "admin" in the password area and press RETURN. Log on to www.hrw.com/CDROMTUTOR for a detailed explanation of the Teacher Management System.

DVD Tutor

The *DVD Tutor* contains all material from the *Video Program* as described above. French captions are available for use at your discretion for all sections of the video. The *DVD Tutor* also provides a variety of video-based activities that assess students' understanding of the **Mise en train, Suite,** and **Panorama Culturel.**

This part of the *DVD Tutor* may be used on any DVD video player connected to a television or video monitor.

In addition to the video material and the video-based comprehension activities, the *DVD Tutor* also contains the entire *Interactive CD-ROM Tutor* in DVD-ROM format. Each DVD disc contains the activities from all 12 chapters of the *Interactive CD-ROM Tutor.*

This part of the *DVD Tutor* may be used on a Macintosh® or Windows® computer with a DVD-ROM drive.

To preview all resources available for this chapter, use the **One-Stop Planner CD-ROM,** Disc 2.

Go.Online!

Online Edition

The Online Edition for Allez, viens! *allows students access to their textbooks anytime anywhere.*

- *Audio at point of use*
- *Additional practice activities*
- *Self-test activities*
- *Online reference tools*
- *Entire Video Program (Enhanced version)*
- *Interactive Notebook (Enhanced version)*

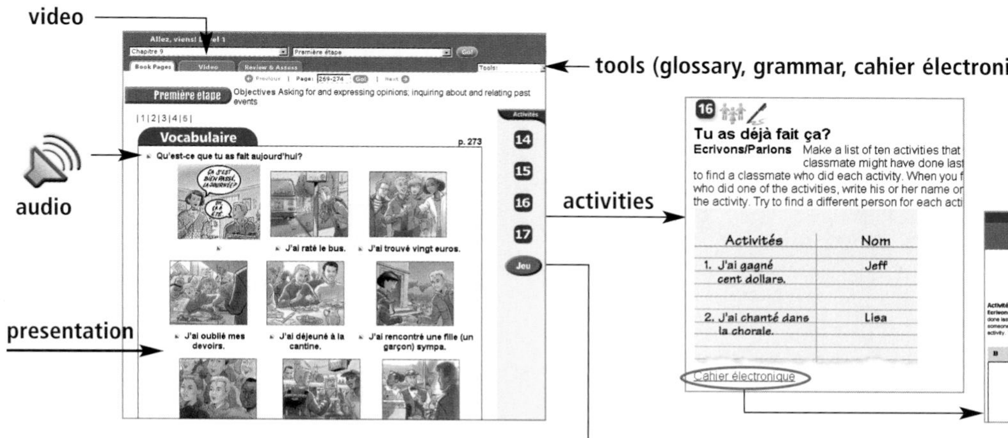

Activités Internet

These guided internet activities include a worksheet and pre-selected and pre-screened authentic web sites from the francophone world. You can use these activities

- to help students develop research skills in the target language
- to introduce students to authentic cultural information
- as a project

Jeux interactifs

You can use the interactive activities in this chapter

- to practice grammar, vocabulary, and chapter functions
- as homework
- as an assessment option
- as a self-test
- to prepare for the Chapter Test

Projet Have students do a Web search on a famous family and gather information about the different members of the family. Then, have them draw the family tree. Have students document their sources by noting the names and URLs of all sites they consulted.

Chapitre 7 : La famille

Textbook Listening Activities Scripts 

Première étape

8 **p. 205**

1. Voilà mon grand-père. Il n'est pas jeune, mais il est toujours actif. Regarde. Là, il fait du vélo.

2. Et voici ma mère et mon père. Là, ils sont en vacances à la Martinique. Qu'est-ce qu'il fait beau, hein?

3. Et ça, c'est ma sœur. Elle adore jouer au volley!

4. Ce sont mes deux frères. Ils jouent souvent au football.

5. Et ça, c'est moi avec mon chien. Il est mignon, n'est-ce pas?

Answers to Activity 8

1. d
2. b
3. a
4. e
5. c

9 **p. 205**

1. Notre chien s'appelle Chouchou.

2. Nos poissons aiment beaucoup manger.

3. Leurs chats aiment sortir le matin.

4. Son canari est jaune.

5. Votre chien, il a quel âge?

6. Et vos chats, est-ce qu'ils aiment beaucoup dormir?

7. Ses poissons sont noirs ou rouges?

Answers to Activity 9

1. their own; dog
2. their own; fish
3. someone else's; cats
4. someone else's; canary
5. someone else's; dog
6. someone else's; cats
7. someone else's; fish

12 **p. 207**

1. Salut, Michèle! Je te présente mon amie Anne-Marie.

2. Regarde. Voilà Mademoiselle Simonet.

3. Maman, je te présente Annick.

4. Voilà Isabelle. C'est une amie.

5. Madame Martin, je vous présente Monsieur Poulain.

Answers to Activity 12

1. introducing
2. identifying
3. introducing
4. identifying
5. introducing

Deuxième étape

15 **p. 209**

1. Elle est grande et blonde.

2. Il est petit, roux et très fort.

3. Il est grand et brun.

4. Elle est petite, mince et brune.

5. Elle est petite et rousse.

Answers to Activity 15

1. Julie
2. Martin
3. Roger
4. Carmen
5. Denise

16 **p. 209**

1. Dominique est grande, brune et très intelligente.

2. Ça, c'est Andrée. Andrée est mince et blonde. Euh, un peu pénible.

3. Tu vois, là, c'est Joëlle. Joëlle aime bien faire du sport. Petite mais assez forte. Elle est amusante.

4. Ici, c'est Gabriel. Gabriel est mignon et tellement gentil!

5. Et Danielle. Danielle est brune. Toujours embêtante. Pas facile du tout!

Answers to Activity 16

1. Dominique — favorable
2. Andrée — unfavorable
3. Joëlle — favorable
4. Gabriel — favorable
5. Danielle — unfavorable

The following scripts are for the listening activities found in the *Pupil's Edition*. For Student Response Forms, see *Listening Activities*, pages 51–53. To provide students with additional listening practice, see *Listening Activities*, pages 55–58.

One-Stop Planner CD-ROM

To preview all resources available for this chapter, use the **One-Stop Planner CD-ROM**, Disc 2.

Troisième étape

23 p. 213

1. — Je voudrais sortir. Tu es d'accord?
— Non. C'est impossible.

2. — Je peux aller à la plage?
— Pas question.

3. — Je voudrais aller au restaurant avec mes amis. Tu es d'accord?
— Oui, si tu fais d'abord tes devoirs.

4. — On va jouer au football. Je peux y aller?
— Oui, bien sûr.

5. — Est-ce que je peux aller au cinéma?
— Oui, si tu veux.

Answers to Activity 23
1. refused
2. refused
3. given
4. given
5. given

24 p. 214

1. — Maman, Stéphanie et Emilie vont au cinéma ce soir. Je peux y aller?
— Non, tu dois garder ta sœur.

2. — Je voudrais sortir avec Jean-Luc. Je peux?
— Si tu promènes le chien, c'est d'accord.

3. — Maman, je peux sortir avec Marc ce soir?
— Si tu passes d'abord l'aspirateur.

4. — On va au parc cet après-midi pour faire un pique-nique. Je voudrais y aller.
— Mais non. Tu sais bien, tu dois ranger ta chambre!

5. — Je voudrais aller à la piscine avec Elise et Cécile. D'accord?
— D'accord, si tu fais d'abord tes devoirs.

6. — Je peux aller au centre commercial ce soir avec Arnaud?
— Oui, si tu fais d'abord la vaisselle.

Answers to Activity 24
1. c
2. e
3. d
4. a
5. f
6. b

PRONONCIATION, P. 215

For the scripts for Parts A and B, see p. 215. The script for Part C is below.

C. A écrire *(dictation)*

— Voilà mon cousin américain.
— Son chien est très mignon.

Mise en pratique

1 p. 222

1. Je m'appelle Nathalie. Ma famille habite à Paris. J'ai un frère qui s'appelle Jean-Paul. Il a douze ans. Il est très gentil avec moi. J'ai aussi un chat. Il s'appelle Câlin. Il n'est pas vieux, il a deux ans seulement. Et moi, quel âge j'ai? Eh bien, j'ai quinze ans.

Answers to Mise en pratique, Activity 1
1. Jean-Paul
2. douze ans
3. un chat
4. Il n'est pas vieux, il a deux ans.

Chapitre 7 : La famille
50-Minute Lesson Plans

Day 1

CHAPTER OPENER 10 min.
- Discuss the Culture Note, ATE, p. 198, and Thinking Critically, ATE, p. 199.
- Present Chapter Objectives, ATE, p. 199.

MISE EN TRAIN 30 min.
- Motivating Activity: Ask students if they keep a photo album and of whom they have photos. What else might they keep in the album?
- Presenting **Mise en train** and Preteaching Vocabulary, ATE, p. 200
- Do Activities 1–5, p. 202.

Wrap-Up 10 min.
- Challenge, ATE, p. 201

Homework Options
Cahier d'activités, p. 73, Act. 1

Day 2

PREMIERE ETAPE
Quick Review 10 min.
- Check homework and do Bell Work, ATE, p. 203.

Comment dit-on... ?, p. 203 15 min.
- Presenting **Comment dit-on... ?,** ATE, p. 203
- Play Audio CD for Activity 6, p. 203.

Vocabulaire, p. 204 15 min.
- Presenting **Vocabulaire,** ATE, p. 204, using Teaching Transparency 7-A
- Present the **Note de grammaire,** ATE, p. 204, using the Slower Pace suggestion, ATE, p. 204.
- Do Activity 7, p. 204. See Additional Practice, ATE, p. 204.
- Play Audio CD for Activity 8, p. 205.
- Cahier d'activités, p. 74, Acts. 2–3

Wrap-Up 10 min.
Have students write sentences identifying the relationship between two celebrities or cartoon characters.

Homework Options
Cahier d'activités, p. 75, Act. 4
Travaux pratiques de grammaire, pp. 51–52, Acts. 1–4

Day 3

PREMIERE ETAPE
Quick Review 10 min.
- Check homework.

Grammaire, p. 205 20 min.
- Presenting **Grammaire,** ATE, p. 205
- **Grammaire supplémentaire,** p. 218, Acts. 2–3
- Play Audio CD for Activity 9, p. 205.
- Discuss **Note culturelle,** p. 206.
- Do Activity 10 or Activity 11, p. 206.
- Travaux pratiques de grammaire, p. 53, Acts. 5–7

Comment dit-on... ?, p. 207 10 min.
- Presenting **Comment dit-on... ?,** ATE, p. 207
- Do Activities 12–13, p. 207.

Wrap-Up 10 min.
- Show Teaching Transparency 7-A and have students identify the familly members and explain their relationship to Isabelle.

Homework Options
Study for **Première étape** quiz.

Day 4

PREMIERE ETAPE
Quiz 7-1, 20 min.
- Administer Quiz 7-1A or 7-1B.

DEUXIEME ETAPE
Vocabulaire, p. 208 10 min.
- Presenting **Vocabulaire,** ATE, p. 208, using Teaching Transparencies 7-B and 7-C.
- Play Audio CD for Activity 15, p. 209.

Comment dit-on... ?, p. 209 15 min.
- Presenting **Comment dit-on... ?,** ATE, p. 209
- Play Audio CD for Activity 16, p. 209.
- Do Activity 17, p. 209.

Wrap-Up 5 min.
- Additional Practice, ATE, p. 208

Homework Options
Cahier d'activités, pp. 77–78, Acts. 9–10, 13
Travaux pratiques de grammaire, p. 54, Acts. 8–9

Day 5

DEUXIEME ETAPE
Quick Review 10 min.
- Check homework.
- Write the names of celebrities or TV characters on the chalk board. Describe each person in French and have students guess which person you are describing.

Grammaire, p. 210 25 min.
- Presenting **Grammaire,** ATE, p. 210
- Do Activities 18–19, p. 210.
- **Grammaire supplémentaire,** p. 219, Act. 5

Wrap-Up 15 min.
- Activities for Communication, pp. 39–40, Communicative Activity 7-2A and 7-2B

Homework Options
Cahier d'activités, pp. 77–78, Acts. 11–12
Travaux pratiques de grammaire, pp. 55–57, Acts. 10–14

Day 6

DEUXIEME ETAPE
Quick Review 10 min.
- Check homework.
- Motivating Activity: Name celebrities or mythical characters and ask students to describe them.

Grammaire, p. 211 30 min.
- Present **Grammaire,** ATE, p. 211.
- Do Activities 20–21, p. 211.
- **Grammaire supplémentaire,** p. 219, Act. 6
- Travaux pratiques de grammaire, pp. 57–58, Acts. 15–17

Wrap-Up 10 min.
- Pass out mazagine photos to students and have each student describe the physical characteristics of the person in his or her photo to the class.

Homework Options
Study for **Deuxième étape** quiz.

One-Stop Planner CD-ROM

For alternative lesson plans by chapter section, to create your own customized plans, or to preview all resources available for this chapter, use the **One-Stop Planner CD-ROM**, Disc 2.

For additional homework suggestions, see activities accompanied by this symbol throughout the chapter.

Day 7

DEUXIEME ETAPE

Quiz 7-2 20 min.
- Administer Quiz 7-2A or 7-2B.

PANORAMA CULTUREL 25 min.
- Present **Panorama Culturel** using Videocassette 3, p. 212.
- Have students answer **Qu'en penses-tu?** questions, p. 212.
- Read **Savais-tu que… ?,** p. 212.
- **Panorama Culturel,** Interactive CD-ROM Tutor, Disc 2

Wrap-Up 5 min.
- Thinking Critically, ATE, p. 212

Homework Options

Cahier d'activités, p. 84, Acts. 26–27

Day 8

TROISIEME ETAPE

Quick Review 10 min.
- Activities for Communication, pp. 37–38, Communicative Activity 7-1A and 7-1B

Comment dit-on... ?, p. 213 30 min.
- Presenting **Comment dit-on... ?,** ATE, p. 213
- Play Audio CD for Activity 23, p. 213.
- **Grammaire supplémentaire,** p. 220, Act. 7
- Have students draw a comic strip in which a child asks a parent permission to do two activities. The parent will give permission for one of the activities and refuse permission for the other.

Wrap-Up 10 min.
- Have students imagine that they are your parents. Ask them permission to do different activities. The students will give and refuse permission.

Homework Options

Cahier d'activités, p. 81, Act. 21

Day 9

TROISIEME ETAPE

Quick Review 10 min.
- Check homework.

Vocabulaire, p. 213 15 min.
- Presenting **Vocabulaire,** ATE, p. 213, using Teaching Transparency 7-D.
- Tell students to do various chores and have them respond by miming the appropriate activity.
- Do Activity 25, p. 214.
- Travaux pratiques de grammaire, pp. 59–60, Acts. 18–21

Prononciation, p. 187 15 min.
- Complete presentation and Activities A–C, p. 215, using Audio CD 5.

Wrap-Up 10 min.
- Play Game: **Chasse au trésor**, ATE, p. 215.

Homework Options

Study for the **Troisième étape** quiz.

Day 10

TROISIEME ETAPE

Quiz 7-3 20 min.
- Administer Quiz 7-3A or 7-3B.

LISONS! 25 min.
- Read and discuss the **Stratégie pour lire,** p. 216, then do Prereading Activities A–B, with using Prior Knowledge, ATE, p. 216.
- Reading Activities C–G, Monitoring Comprehension, ATE, p. 216

Wrap-Up 5 min.
- Do Additional Practice, ATE, p. 217.

Homework Options

Cahier d'activités, p. 83, Act. 25

Have students select or draw a real or fictional family photo to bring to class (for **Ecrivons!** assignment).

Day 11

LISONS!

Quick Review 10 min.
- Check homework.
- Postreading Activity H, Using Text Organizers, ATE, p. 217

MISE EN PRATIQUE 30 min.
- Play Audio CD for Activity 1, p. 222.
- Do Activities 2–3, pp. 222–223.
- Do the Tactile Learners activity, ATE, p. 222.
- Do **Ecrivons!**, p. 223, using the Process Writing suggestion, ATE, p. 223.

Wrap-Up 10 min.
- Have partners complete **Jeu de rôle,** p. 223.

Homework Options

Que sais-je?, p. 224

Day 12

MISE EN PRATIQUE

Quick Review 15 min.
- See second half of Process Writing, ATE, p. 223.
- Play Game: **Qui suis-je?,** ATE, p. 197C.

Chapter Review 35 min.
- Review Chapter 7. Choose from **Grammaire supplémentaire,** Grammar Tutor for Students of French, Activities for Communication, Listening Activities, Interactive CD-ROM Tutor, or **Jeux interactifs.**

Homework Options

Study for Chapter 7 Test.

Assessment

Test, Chapter 7 50 min.
- Administer Chapter 7 Test. Select from Testing Program, Alternative Assessment Guide, Test Generator or Standardized Assessment Tutor.

Chapitre 7 : La Famille
90-Minute Lesson Plans

Block 1

CHAPTER OPENER 5 min.
- Culture Note, ATE, p. 198 and Thinking Critically ATE, p. 199
- Present Chapter Objectives, ATE, p. 199.

MISE EN TRAIN 45 min.
- Presenting **Mise en train,** ATE, p. 200 and Challenge, ATE, p. 201
- View video of **Mise en train,** Videocassette 3, Video Guide, p. 45.
- Do Activity Master 1, Video Guide, p. 48, Acts. 1–3.

PREMIERE ETAPE

Comment dit-on... ?, p. 203 10 min.
- Bell Work, ATE, p. 203
- Presenting **Comment dit-on... ?,** ATE, p. 203
- Do Activity 6, p. 203. See Slower Pace, ATE, p. 203.

Vocabulaire, p. 204 25 min.
- Presenting **Vocabulaire,** ATE, p. 204.
- Present **Note de grammaire,** p. 204. See Slower Pace, ATE, p. 204.
- Do Activity 7, p. 204, orally.
- Play Audio CD for Activity 8, p. 205.
- Listening Activities, p. 55, Additional Listening Activities 7-1 and 7-2
- Do Activities for Communication, pp. 105, 108, Realia 7-1, p. 105. See Suggestion 1, p. 108.

Wrap-Up 5 min.
- Summarize what happened in the **Mise en train** using Chapter 7 **Mise en train** Transparencies.

Homework Options

Travaux pratiques de grammaire, pp. 51–52, Acts. 1–4

Cahier d'activités, p. 74, Acts. 2–3

Block 2

PREMIERE ETAPE

Quick Review 10 min.
- Activities for Communication, pp. 37–38, Communicative Activity 7-1A and 7-1B

Grammaire, p. 205 45 min.
- Do Presenting **Grammaire,** ATE, p. 205. See Teacher to Teacher, ATE, p. 205.
- Play Audio CD for Activity 9, p. 205. See Slower Pace, ATE, p. 205.
- **Grammaire supplémentaire,** pp. 218–219, Acts. 1–4
- **Note culturelle,** p. 206
- Do Activity 10, p. 206. See Reteaching and Slower Pace, ATE, p. 206.
- Do Activity 11, p. 206.

Comment dit-on... ?, p. 207 15 min.
- Presenting **Comment dit-on... ?,** ATE, p. 207
- Play Audio CD for Activity 12, p. 207.
- **Tu te rappelles?,** p. 207
- **Vocabulaire à la carte,** p. 207

Wrap-Up 20 min.
- Have students form groups of three. In each group, one person will introduce another to the third member. This person asks questions to get to know the newcomer. Then have students present these introductions to the class.

Homework Options

Study for **Première étape** quiz.

Travaux pratiques de grammaire, p. 53, Acts. 5–7

Cahier d'activités, pp. 75–76, Acts. 4–8

Block 3

PREMIERE ETAPE

Quick Review 10 min.
- Bell Work, ATE, p. 208

Quiz 7-1 20 min.
- Administer Quiz 7-1A or Quiz 7-1B.

DEUXIEME ETAPE

Vocabulaire, p. 208 15 min.
- Presenting **Vocabulaire,** ATE, p. 208
- Do **De bons conseils,** p. 208. See Visual Learners, ATE, p. 208.
- Additional Practice, ATE, p. 208
- Play Audio CD for Activity 15, p. 209.

Comment dit-on... ?, p. 209 10 min.
- Presenting **Comment dit-on... ?,** ATE, p. 209
- Play Audio CD for Activity 16, p. 209.
- Do Activity 17, p. 209.

Grammaire, p. 210 30 min.
- Do Presenting **Grammaire,** ATE, p. 210. See Language Note, ATE, p. 210.
- Do Activities 18, p. 210, orally.
- Name celebrities or mythical characters and ask students to describe them.
- Do Activity 19, p. 210, in writing.

Wrap-Up 5 min.
- Have students mime adjectives before the whole class or a small group, who will try to guess the adjectives. The mimers might select adjectives from a stack of flash cards or mime an adjective of his/her choice.

Homework Options

Travaux pratiques de grammaire, pp. 54–56, Acts. 8–13

Cahier d'activités, p. 77, Acts. 9–11

One-Stop Planner CD-ROM

For alternative lesson plans by chapter section, to create your own customized plans, or to preview all resources available for this chapter, use the **One-Stop Planner CD-ROM**, Disc 2.

For additional homework suggestions, see activities accompanied by this symbol throughout the chapter.

Block 4

DEUXIEME ETAPE

Quick Review 10 min.
- Activities for Communication, pp. 39–40, Communicative Activity 7-2A and 7-2B

Grammaire: the verb *être,* p. 211 35 min.
- Presenting **Grammaire: the verb *être,*** ATE, p. 211
- Do Activities 20–21, p. 211. See Additional Practice, ATE, p. 211
- **Grammaire supplémentaire,** p. 219, Acts. 5–6
- Do Activity 22, p. 211. See **Mon journal,** ATE, p. 211.

PANORAMA CULTUREL 15 min.
- Presenting **Panorama Culturel,** ATE, p. 212
- Language Note, ATE, p. 212
- Answer the **Qu'en penses-tu?** questions, p. 212.
- Read **Savais-tu que... ?,** p. 212.

TROISIEME ETAPE

Comment dit-on... ?, p. 213 10 min.
- Presenting **Comment dit-on... ?,** ATE, p. 213
- Play Audio CD for Activity 23, p. 213.

Vocabulaire, p. 213 10 min.
- Presenting **Vocabulaire,** ATE, p. 213
- Tell students to do various chores and have them respond by miming the appropriate activitiy.

Wrap-Up 10 min.
- Activities for Communication, p. 150, Situation Card: Role-play 7-2

Homework Options

Study for **Troisième étape** quiz.
Travaux pratiques de grammaire, pp. 57–58, Acts. 14–17
Cahier d'activités, pp. 78–79, Acts. 12–16

Block 5

DEUXIEME ETAPE

Quick Review 10 min.

Quiz 7-2 20 min.
- Administer Quiz 7-2A or 7-2B

TROISIEME ETAPE

Vocabulaire, p. 213, con't 35 min.
- Play Audio CD for Activity 24, p. 214.
- Do Activities 25 and 26, p. 214.
- Do Activity 28, p. 215. Allow 10 min. to prepare and 10 min. to present to class.

Prononciation, p. 215 15 min.
- Present **Prononciation,** p. 215. See Language Note, ATE, p. 215.
- Play Audio CD for Activities A, B, and C, p. 215.

Wrap-Up 10 min.
- Game: **Chasse au Trésor**, ATE, p. 215

Homework Options

Study for **Troisième étape** quiz.
Travaux pratiques de grammaire, pp. 59–60, Acts. 18–21
Cahier d'activités, pp. 80–82, Acts. 19–24

Block 6

TROISIEME ETAPE

Quick Review 10 min.

Quiz 7-3 20 min.
- Administer Quiz 7-3A or Quiz 7-3B.

LISONS! 20 min
- Read and discuss the **Stratégie pour lire,** p. 216, then do Prereading Activities A–B, Using Prior Knowledge, ATE, p. 216.
- Do Reading Activities C–G, Monitoring Comprehension, ATE, p. 216.
- Postreading Activity H, Using Text Organizers, ATE, p. 217

MISE EN PRATIQUE 30 min.
- Play Audio CD for Activity 1, p. 222.
- Do Activities 2 and 3, pp. 222–223.
- Do **Ecrivons!,** p. 223, using the Process Writing suggestion, ATE, p. 223.

Wrap-Up 10 min.
- Activities for Communication, pp. 41–42, Communicative Activity 7-3A and 7-3B

Homework Options

Que sais-je?, p. 224
Study for Chapter 7 Test.

Block 7

MISE EN PRATIQUE

Quick Review 10 min.
- See second half of Process Writing, ATE, p. 223.

Chapter Review 30 min.
- Review Chapter 7. Choose from **Grammaire supplémentaire,** Grammar Tutor for Students of French, Activities for Communication, Listening Activities, Interactive CD-ROM Tutor, or **Jeux interactifs.**

Test, Chapter 6 50 min.
- Administer Chapter 7 Test. Select from Testing Program, Alternative Assessment Guide, Test Generator, or Standardized Assessment Tutor.

Chapter Opener

CHAPITRE 7

For resource information, see the **One-Stop Planner,** Disc 2.

Pacing Tips

Keep in mind while planning your lesson that the **Première** and **Deuxième étapes** in this chapter cover a lot of new vocabulary, grammar and functions. The verb **être** and adjective agreement are both presented in the **Deuxième étape.** The **Troisième étape** is the lightest in terms of new material. For Lesson Plans and timing suggestions, see pages 197I–197L.

Meeting the Standards

Communication

- Identifying people, p. 203
- Introducing people, p. 207
- Describing and characterizing people, p. 209
- Asking for, giving, and refusing permission, p. 213

Cultures

- Culture Note, p. 198
- Note culturelle, p. 206
- Panorama Culturel, p. 212

Connections

- Thinking Critically: Comparing and Contrasting, p. 216

Comparisons

- Thinking Critically: Comparing and Contrasting, p. 199
- Language-to-Language, p. 210
- Thinking Critically: Analyzing, pp. 212, 216

Communities

- Family Link, p. 202
- Career Path, p. 214
- De l'école au travail, p. 215

Cultures and Communities

Culture Note

French weddings are similar to traditional American weddings. However, some customs that American students might be familiar with aren't practiced in France. For example, no showers are held before the wedding, and there are no bridesmaids or groomsmen in the wedding party. Instead, **demoiselles d'honneur** and **garçons d'honneur,** who are usually young children from the bride's and groom's families, accompany the bride down the aisle. In addition to a civil ceremony, which is required to make the marriage legally binding, some French couples also choose to have a religious service.

CHAPITRE

7 La famille

Objectives

In this chapter you will learn to

Première étape

- identify and introduce people

Deuxième étape

- describe and characterize people

Troisième étape

- ask for, give, and refuse permission

Visit Holt Online
go.hrw.com
KEYWORD: WA3 PARIS-7
Online Edition

◀ **Elle est comment, ta famille?**

Chapter Opener

CHAPITRE 7

Focusing on Outcomes

Have students read the chapter outcomes and match them to the photo. Ask them to think of some situations in which these functions would be used, such as introducing people at parties or telling stories.
NOTE: The self-check activities in **Que sais-je?** on page 224 help students assess their achievement of the objectives.

Teacher Notes

- Also included in this chapter are possessive adjectives and vocabulary describing family relationships, as well as household chores.
- Some suggestions in this chapter ask students to cut pictures from magazines. Consider keeping old issues in the classroom for this purpose. You might also want to begin a subscription to a French magazine. See page T46 for a list of periodicals and subscription services.

Connections and Comparisons

Thinking Critically

Comparing and Contrasting In Africa, members of the extended family often live under the same roof as the nuclear family. It is normal for all family members to be intimately involved in every aspect of one another's lives, including business matters, health care, education, child care, and employment. Ask students how this compares to family structures in the U.S. Have them discuss the advantages and disadvantages of the nuclear family versus the extended family.

Mise en train

CHAPITRE 7

Teaching Resources
pp. 200–202

PRINT 
- Lesson Planner, p. 33
- Video Guide, pp. 46, 48
- Cahier d'activités, p. 73

MEDIA
- One-Stop Planner
- Video Program
  Mise en train
  Videocassette 3, 01:14–05:08
  Videocassette 5 (captioned version), 56:02–59:57
  Suite
  Videocassette 3, 05:11–09:19
  Videocassette 5 (captioned version), 1:00:00–1:04:08
- DVD Tutor, Disc 1
- Audio Compact Discs, CD 7, Trs. 1–2
- **Mise en train** Transparencies

Teaching Suggestion
Have students look at the pictures on pages 200–201 and guess how the people are related to Isabelle.

Presenting Mise en train
Show the video, stopping after each photo Isabelle describes to ask students to name and describe the relatives in English. You might draw Isabelle's family tree, without the names, and have students fill them in as they view the video.

Mise en train Transparencies

The **roman-photo** is an abridged version of the video episode.

MISE EN TRAIN ▪ *Sympa, la famille!*

CD 7 Trs. 1–2

Stratégie pour comprendre
Look at the people pictured in the photo album. Can you guess how they're related to Isabelle?

Thuy

Isabelle

1 **Thuy :** Tiens, j'adore regarder les photos. Je peux les voir?
Isabelle : Bien sûr!

2 Ce sont mes grands-parents. Ils sont heureux sur cette photo. Ils fêtent leur quarantième anniversaire de mariage.

3 C'est une photo de Papa et Maman.

4 Là, c'est mon oncle et ma tante, le frère de ma mère et sa femme. Et au milieu, ce sont leurs enfants, mes cousins. Ils habitent tous en Bretagne. Ça, c'est Loïc. Il a 18 ans. C'est Julie. Elle a 8 ans. Elle est adorable. Et elle, c'est ma cousine Patricia. Elle est très intelligente. En maths, elle a toujours 18 sur 20!

Preteaching Vocabulary

Recognizing Cognates
First, have students match the following French words with their English equivalent.

2 **1. grands-parents**	**a.** mom
3 **2. Papa**	**b.** uncle
3 **3. Maman**	**c.** baby
4 **4. oncle**	**d.** dad
5 **5. bébé**	**e.** grandparents

Using the context, have them guess what the words 6 **frère,** 7 **tante,** and 8 **sœurs** might mean. Then, tell them to match who they think the people in the photos are to the French words in the list.

STANDARDS: 1.2, 4.2

5 Là, c'est moi. Quel amour de bébé, n'est-ce pas? Je suis toute petite... peut-être un an et demi.

6 C'est mon frère Alexandre. Il a 11 ans. Il est parfois pénible.

7 C'est ma tante du côté de mon père. Elle s'appelle Véronique. Ça, c'est son chat Musica. Elle adore les animaux. Elle a aussi deux chiens!

8
Isabelle : Et toi, tu n'as pas de frères ou de sœurs?
Thuy : Non. Je suis fille unique.
Isabelle : Tu as de la chance.

Cahier d'activités, p. 73, Act. 1

Using the Captioned Video/DVD

If students have difficulty understanding French spoken at a normal speed, use Videocassette 5 to allow students to see the French captions for ***Sympa, la famille!*** and ***Sympa, la famille! (suite).*** Hearing the language and watching the story will reduce anxiety about the new language and facilitate comprehension.

The reinforcement of seeing the written vocabulary words as they watch the gestures and actions will help prepare students to do the comprehension activities on page 202.
NOTE: The *DVD Tutor* contains captions for all sections of the *Video Program.*

Mise en train

CHAPITRE 7

Challenge

You might have partners read the text together. As they read, have them draw a family tree to illustrate the relationships that are mentioned. They can check their drawing by looking at Isabelle's family tree in the **Vocabulaire** on page 204.

Visual Learners

Have students watch the video without the sound to encourage them to use visual clues to figure out who the people are and what they're like.

Sympa, la famille! (suite)

When the story continues, Alexandre enters Isabelle's room, without knocking, and asks where his CD is. Isabelle is annoyed with Alexandre but introduces him to Thuy. Next, the doorbell rings. It's Aunt Véronique, who has brought a kitten as a surprise for Isabelle and Alexandre. Isabelle's father is not very enthusiastic about the kitten, but agrees to let them keep it.

Mise en train

CHAPITRE 7

Family Link

5 Students might want to talk about their own family, invent an imaginary family, select a TV or comic book family, or refer to the photo of the family on page 203 to compare to Isabelle's.

These activities check for comprehension only. Students should not yet be expected to produce language modeled in **Mise en train.**

1 Tu as compris?

Réponds aux questions suivantes sur ***Sympa, la famille!***

1. What are Isabelle and Thuy talking about? Isabelle's family photos
2. Does Isabelle have brothers or sisters? If so, what are their names? yes, a brother; Alexandre
3. How many cousins does she have? three
4. Who are some of the other family members she mentions? grandparents, parents, an uncle, two aunts
5. How does Isabelle feel about her family? How can you tell? She likes her family. She speaks favorably of them.

2 Vrai ou faux?

1. Julie a huit ans. vrai
2. Julie est blonde. faux
3. Les cousins d'Isabelle habitent à Paris. faux
4. Tante Véronique n'a pas d'animaux. faux
5. Thuy a un frère. faux

3 Quelle photo?

De quelle photo est-ce qu'Isabelle parle?

1. Il a onze ans. b
2. En maths, elle a toujours 18 sur 20. a
3. J'ai un an et demi, je crois... c
4. Elle a huit ans. d

a.

b.

c.

d.

4 Cherche les expressions See answers below.

In ***Sympa, la famille!,*** what does Isabelle or Thuy say to . . .

1. ask permission?
2. identify family members?
3. describe someone?
4. pay a compliment?
5. tell someone's age?
6. complain about someone?

Je peux... ? **C'est...** **Elle est très intelligente.** **Elle est adorable.** **Il/Elle a... ans.** **Ce sont...** **Il est parfois pénible.** **Ils sont heureux.**

5 Et maintenant, à toi

Est-ce que la famille d'Isabelle est comme les familles que tu connais? Est-ce qu'elle est différente? Pourquoi?

Comprehension Check

Challenge

2 Have students find a quote from the story to confirm the true statements.

Auditory Learners

4 You might have students view the video or listen to the recording of ***Sympa, la famille!*** to find these expressions.

Visual Learners

4 To help students identify the expressions in Activity 4, play the captioned version of ***Sympa, la famille!*** on Videocassette 5.

5 Students might also sketch a family tree in their journal and write a comparison in English.

Answers

4
1. Je peux... ?
2. C'est... ; Ce sont...
3. *Possible answers:* Ils sont heureux. Elle est adorable. Elle est très intelligente.
4. *Possible answers:* Elle est adorable. Elle est très intelligente.
5. Il/Elle a... ans.
6. Il est parfois pénible.

STANDARDS: 1.2, 4.2

Première étape

Objectives Identifying and introducing people

WA3 PARIS-7

Comment dit-on...?

Identifying people

C'est qui, ce gros bébé?
C'est moi. Et voilà ma grand-mère.

To identify people:

C'est ma tante Véronique.
Ce sont mes cousins Loïc et Julie. *These/Those are . . .*
Voici mon frère Alexandre. *Here's . . .*
Voilà Patricia. *There's . . .*

6 C'est qui?

Parlons Avec un(e) partenaire, inventez des identités pour les personnes qui sont sur cette photo.

Communication for All Students

Slower Pace

6 If students need help with French names, refer them to page 5 of the Preliminary Chapter.

Additional Practice

Show the transparency for the **Mise en train** and call on volunteers to identify the various family members.

Première étape

CHAPITRE 7

Teaching Resources
pp. 203–207

PRINT

- Lesson Planner, p. 34
- TPR Storytelling Book, pp. 25, 28
- Listening Activities, pp. 51, 55
- Activities for Communication, pp. 37–38, 105, 108, 149–150
- Travaux pratiques de grammaire, pp. 51–53
- Grammar Tutor for Students of French, Chapter 7
- Cahier d'activités, pp. 74–76
- Testing Program, pp. 171–174
- Alternative Assessment Guide, p. 38
- Student Make-Up Assignments, Chapter 7

MEDIA

- One-Stop Planner
- Audio Compact Discs, CD 7, Trs. 3–5, 21, 27–28
- Teaching Transparencies: 7-1, 7-A; **Grammaire supplémentaire** Answers; Travaux pratiques de grammaire Answers
- Interactive CD-ROM Tutor, Disc 2

Bell Work

Have students write answers to the following questions: **Tu t'appelles comment? Tu as quel âge? Ça va?**

Presenting
Comment dit-on... ?

Before students open their book, use the expressions in the box to identify several students in the classroom and some pictures you've brought in of faculty members or of family members. After several examples, point to one or more people and ask **C'est qui?** Then, identify students who are close by or far away, using **voici** and **voilà.**

Teaching Resources
pp. 203–207

PRINT

- Lesson Planner, p. 34
- TPR Storytelling Book, pp. 25, 28
- Listening Activities, pp. 51, 55
- Activities for Communication, pp. 37–38, 105, 108, 149–150
- Travaux pratiques de grammaire, pp. 51–53
- Grammar Tutor for Students of French, Chapter 7
- Cahier d'activités, pp. 74–76
- Testing Program, pp. 171–174
- Alternative Assessment Guide, p. 38
- Student Make-Up Assignments, Chapter 7

MEDIA 

- One-Stop Planner
- Audio Compact Discs, CD 7, Trs. 3–5, 21, 27–28
- Teaching Transparencies: 7-1, 7-A; **Grammaire supplémentaire** Answers; Travaux pratiques de grammaire Answers
- Interactive CD-ROM Tutor, Disc 2

Presenting Vocabulaire

Draw a transparency of the family tree with no labels. Uncover one generation at a time and identify each family member, writing in the person's relationship to Isabelle **(ma tante Véronique).** Then, create fill-in-the-blank sentences, such as **Véronique est la ____ d'Alexandre. (tante),** and have students complete them.

Vocabulaire

CD-ROM 2 DVD 1

Les membres de la famille d'Isabelle

Other family relationships:
la femme *wife*
le mari *husband*
la fille *daughter*
le fils *son*
l'enfant *child*
le parent *parent, relative*

Ma grand-mère et mon grand-père, Eugénie et Jean-Marie Ménard

Ma tante Véronique, la sœur de mon père

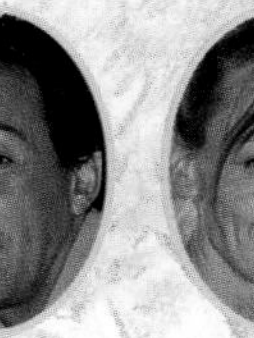

Mon père et ma mère, Raymond et Josette Guérin

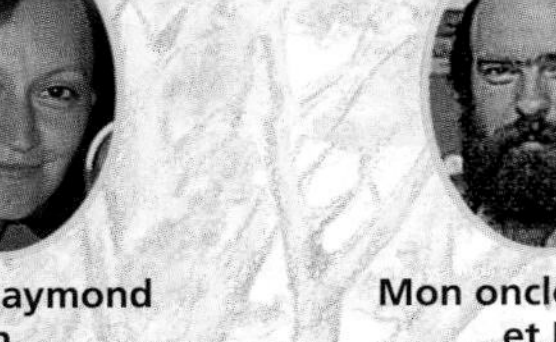

Mon oncle et ma tante, Guillaume et Micheline Ménard

Mon frère Alexandre

C'est moi!

Mes cousines Patricia et Julie, et mon cousin Loïc

Mon chien

Mon chat

Mon canari

Mon poisson

Cahier d'activités, pp. 74–75, Act. 2a, 4a

Travaux pratiques de grammaire, p. 51, Act. 1–2

Note de grammaire

Use **de (d')** to indicate relationship or ownership.

C'est la mère **de** Paul.
That's Paul's mother.
Voici le chien **d'**Ophélie.
Here's Ophélie's dog.
C'est un ami **du** prof.
That's the teacher's friend.

Grammaire supplémentaire, p. 218, Act. 1

Cahier d'activités, pp. 74, 76, Act. 2b, 7b

Travaux pratiques de grammaire, p. 52, Act. 3–4

7 Grammaire en contexte

Parlons Quels membres de la famille d'Isabelle sont décrits dans les phrases suivantes?

EXEMPLE Le frère de Véronique, c'est Raymond.

1. C'est le père d'Alexandre.
2. C'est la femme de Guillaume.
3. C'est le grand-père de Julie.
4. C'est la mère de Patricia.
5. Ce sont les sœurs de Loïc.
6. C'est le cousin de Patricia.

Communication for All Students

Slower Pace

Note de grammaire Demonstrate this structure by pointing out students' school supplies and telling to whom they belong. For example, pick up a notebook and say **C'est le cahier de Steven.** Then, pick up an object and have a student tell whose it is.

Additional Practice

7 Say the names of two of the people on the family tree **(Julie et Loïc).** Have students write the relationship between them. You might also have students write sentences identifying the relationship between two celebrities or cartoon characters. **(Bart Simpson est le frère de Lisa Simpson.)**

8 La famille d'Alain

See scripts on p. 197G. 1. d 2. b 3. a 4. e 5. c

Ecoutons Alain montre des photos de sa famille à Jay. De quelle photo est-ce qu'il parle?

CD 7 Tr. 3

a. b. c. d. e.

Grammaire

Possessive adjectives

	Before a masculine singular noun	Before a feminine singular noun	Before a plural noun
my	**mon**	**ma**	**mes**
your	**ton**	**ta**	**tes**
his/her/its	**son** frère	**sa** sœur	**ses** frères
our	**notre**	**notre**	**nos**
your	**votre**	**votre**	**vos**
their	**leur**	**leur**	**leurs**

- **Son, sa,** and **ses** may mean either *her* or *his*.

  C'est **son** père. That's *her* father. *or* That's *his* father.

  C'est **sa** mère. That's *her* mother. *or* That's *his* mother.

  Ce sont **ses** parents. Those are *her* parents. *or* Those are *his* parents.

- **Mon, ton,** and **son** are used before all singular nouns that begin with a vowel sound, whether the noun is masculine or feminine.

  C'est **ton amie** Marianne?

  C'est **mon oncle** Xavier.

- Liaison is always made with **mon, ton,** and **son,** and with all the plural forms.

  mon école **nos amis**

- Use **ton, ta,** and **tes** with people you would normally address with **tu.** Use **votre** and **vos** with people you would normally address with **vous.**

Grammaire supplémentaire, pp. 218–219, Act. 2–4

Cahier d'activités, pp. 75–76, Act. 6–7a

Travaux pratiques de grammaire, p. 53, Act. 5–7

9 Grammaire en contexte

See scripts and answers on p. 197G.

Ecoutons Listen to Roland and Odile. Are they talking about their own pets or someone else's? Then, listen again to find out what kind of pets they're talking about.

CD 7 Tr. 4

Teacher to Teacher

Bernadette Takano
Norman North High School
Norman, OK

Here's a useful tip from Bernadette on teaching the possessive adjectives.

"Possessive adjectives always seemed confusing to my students until I came up with a means to help them remember the rule. I give them a little magic sentence:

WHAT MATTERS IS WHAT IS POSSESSED.

Then, I immediately give a few examples, such as:
I am a girl, BUT my book is **MON livre,** because **livre** is masculine. It has helped many students grasp the concept of possessive adjectives."

Slower Pace

8 You might have students describe the pictures before you play the recording. Tell them to listen for key words to get the general meaning and to try not to translate every word.

Presenting Grammaire

Possessive adjectives Before students see these structures, ask them for the different ways to say *the* **(le, la, l', les).** Ask them how they choose the correct article (gender, number). Then, pick up classroom objects and say they belong to you. **(C'est mon livre.)** You might also ask about ownership by asking **C'est ton livre?** Next, pick up a boy's pencil and say **C'est son crayon.** Do the same with a girl's pencil. Ask students what they notice about **son** (it means both *his* and *her*). Finally, pick up items belonging to various students and ask the class **C'est mon stylo?,** prompting the response **Non, c'est son stylo!** You might also pick up an item from your desk to prompt the response **Oui, c'est votre...** or choose a book that two students are sharing to prompt **Non, c'est leur livre!**

Slower Pace

9 Before starting this activity, you might ask students to determine which of the possessive adjectives they would use to speak about their own pets **(mon, ma, mes, notre, nos)** and which they would use to speak about someone else's **(son, sa, ses, leur, leurs, ton, ta, tes, votre, vos).**

STANDARDS: 1.2, 4.1

Première étape

CHAPITRE 7

Teaching Resources
pp. 203–207

PRINT

- Lesson Planner, p. 34
- TPR Storytelling Book, pp. 25, 28
- Listening Activities, pp. 51, 55
- Activities for Communication, pp. 37–38, 105, 108, 149–150
- Travaux pratiques de grammaire, pp. 51–53
- Grammar Tutor for Students of French, Chapter 7
- Cahier d'activités, pp. 74–76
- Testing Program, pp. 171–174
- Alternative Assessment Guide, p. 38
- Student Make-Up Assignments, Chapter 7

MEDIA 

- One-Stop Planner
- Audio Compact Discs, CD 7, Trs. 3–5, 21, 27–28
- Teaching Transparencies: 7-1, 7-A; **Grammaire supplémentaire** Answers; Travaux pratiques de grammaire Answers
- Interactive CD-ROM Tutor, Disc 2

Slower Pace

10 Have students tell how they think the people in the illustration are related. Then, have them identify the activities the people like to do. You might write their suggestions on the board or on a transparency. Finally, have partners use this information in their questions and answers.

Additional Practice

11 Ask students to find a picture in a magazine that illustrates a familial relationship. Have students write what they think the relationship between the people in the picture might be.

Note culturelle

Family life plays an important role in French society. Although modern times have brought changes to the family's daily life (more working mothers, less time for family activities, more divorces, and so on), France is working hard to maintain the family unit. To do this, the French government provides subsidies **(allocations familiales)** to all families with two or more children. Other social benefits also encourage larger families in a country with an ever-decreasing birth rate. These benefits include a paid maternity leave of at least 14 weeks, a renewable maternity or paternity leave of one year, free day-care, and a birth allowance **(allocation de naissance)** for every child after the second. Families also receive subsidies for each child attending school or college.

10 Grammaire en contexte

Parlons Tu habites avec une famille française. Tu montres une photo de ta famille à ton/ta camarade. Explique-lui qui sont les personnes sur la photo. Il/Elle va te poser des questions. Ensuite, changez de rôle.

EXEMPLE

—C'est qui, ça?
—C'est ma sœur.
—Elle joue souvent au tennis?
—Oui. Une fois par semaine.

11 Devine!

Parlons Identifie les personnes sur les images suivantes et explique leurs relations. Travaille avec un(e) camarade, puis changez de rôle.

EXEMPLE **C'est Nadine et son grand-père.**

Nadine

Hassan

Thierry

Liliane

Monique et Annie

Communication for All Students

Tactile Learners

Have students cut out three magazine pictures of men, four of women, two of boys, and three of girls. Give each student an unlabeled drawing of a family tree, then have students pair off. One student will call out a family member **(C'est le père de famille.)**, and the other will tape a picture in the appropriate place on the family tree.

Reteaching

10 **Adverbs of frequency** To review adverbs of frequency give students a subject and a verb phrase **(ils/jouer au golf)**. Ask them to form a sentence, by adding an adverb. **(Ils jouent souvent au golf.)**

STANDARDS: 2.1, 3.2, 4.2

Comment dit-on...?

Introducing people

To introduce someone to a friend:

C'est Jean-Michel.
Je te présente mon ami Jean-Michel.
I'd like you to meet . . .

To introduce someone to an adult:

Je vous présente Jean-Michel.

To respond to an introduction:

Salut, Jean-Michel. **Ça va?**
Bonjour.
Très heureux (heureuse).
Pleased to meet you. (formal)

Cahier d'activités, p. 76, Act. 8

12 **Les présentations** See scripts and answers on p. 197G.

Ecoutons Are the people in these conversations identifying someone or introducing someone?

CD 7 Tr. 5

13 **Je te présente...**

Parlons Il y a un(e) nouvel(le) élève français(e) dans ton école. Il/Elle te demande comment tes camarades s'appellent et quel âge ils ont. Travaillez en groupe et faites les présentations. Ensuite, changez de rôle.

14 **Mon journal**

Ecrivons Ecris un paragraphe sur ta famille. Donne le nom et l'âge de chaque personne et explique ce que cette personne aime bien faire. Si tu préfères, tu peux aussi inventer une famille ou décrire une famille célèbre ou une famille de la télé.

Tu te rappelles?

Do you remember how to ask for and give people's name and age?

—Elle s'appelle comment?
—Magali.
—Elle a quel âge?
—Seize ans.

Vocabulaire à la carte

Here are some other words you might need to talk about your family.

des petits-enfants	*grandchildren*
un demi-frère	*stepbrother; half brother*
une demi-sœur	*stepsister; half sister*
un(e) enfant unique	*an only child*
une belle-mère	*stepmother/mother-in-law*
un beau-père	*stepfather/father-in-law*
un petit-fils	*grandson*
une petite-fille	*granddaughter*
une nièce	*niece*
un neveu	*nephew*

Cultures and Communities

Community Link

If possible, have French-speaking exchange students from your local community come in and speak to the class. You might also try contacting your local **Alliance française** or a nearby university. Have students introduce themselves and their classmates to the guests in French.

Career Path

Have students list reasons why it would be important to know how to introduce people in different languages. Have students do research on French business etiquette. How is it the same as American business etiquette? How is it different? For example, the appropriate amount of time spent exchanging pleasantries might vary considerably.

Presenting
Comment dit-on... ?

Demonstrate the expressions by introducing students to stuffed animals you have brought in, and then by introducing one student to another. Next, use **Je vous présente...** to introduce one student to the entire class.

Portfolio

13 **Oral** This activity can be used for oral assessment or can be added to students' oral portfolios. For portfolio information, see *Alternative Assessment Guide,* pages iv–17.

Mon journal

For additional family vocabulary, refer students to the Additional Vocabulary on page R10. Students might want to include a family tree or photos in their journal entry. For an additional journal entry suggestion for Chapter 7, see *Cahier d'activités,* page 151.

Assess

- Testing Program, pp. 171–174
  Quiz 7-1A, Quiz 7-1B
  Audio CD 7, Tr. 21
- Student Make-Up Assignments, Chapter 7, Alternative Quiz
- Alternative Assessment Guide, p. 38

STANDARDS: 1.1, 1.3, 3.1, 5.1, 5.2

Teaching Resources
pp. 208–211

PRINT 

- Lesson Planner, p. 35
- TPR Storytelling Book, pp. 26, 28
- Listening Activities, pp. 52, 56
- Activities for Communication, pp. 39–40, 106, 108–109, 149–150
- Travaux pratiques de grammaire, pp. 54–58
- Grammar Tutor for Students of French, Chapter 7
- Cahier d'activités, pp. 77–79
- Testing Program, pp. 175–178
- Alternative Assessment Guide, p. 38
- Student Make-Up Assignments, Chapter 7

MEDIA

- One-Stop Planner
- Audio Compact Discs, CD 7, Trs. 6–7, 22, 29–30
- Teaching Transparencies: 7-2, 7-B, 7-C; **Grammaire supplémentaire** Answers; Travaux pratiques de grammaire Answers
- Interactive CD-ROM Tutor, Disc 2

Bell Work

Write **stylos, mère, livre, amie, feuilles de papier,** and **sport préféré** on the board. Have students write sentences claiming ownership. **(Ce sont mes stylos.)**

Presenting Vocabulaire

Present the vocabulary using magazine pictures. Then, ask students to name celebrities whom these adjectives describe. **(Qui est amusant?)** You might also ask about the hair color of class members. **(Qui est blond(e)? brun(e)? roux(rousse)?)**

Deuxième étape

Objective Describing and characterizing people

go.hrw.com
WA3 PARIS-7

Vocabulaire

Ils sont comment?

You can also use these descriptive words:

mignon(mignonne)(s) *cute* **ne... ni grand(e)(s) ni petit(e)(s)** . . . *neither tall nor short*

You can use these words to characterize people:

amusant(e)(s)	*funny*	**intelligent(e)(s)**	*smart*	**embêtant(e)(s)**	*annoying*
timide(s)	*shy*	**content(e)(s)**	*happy*	**pénible(s)**	*a pain in the neck*
gentil(le)(s)	*nice*	**fort(e)(s)**	*strong*	**méchant(e)(s)**	*mean*
sympathique(s)/sympa(s)	*nice*				

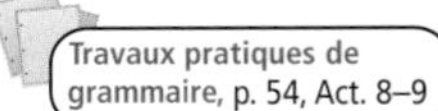

Cahier d'activités, p. 77, Act. 9–10

Travaux pratiques de grammaire, p. 54, Act. 8–9

DE BONS CONSEILS

Organizing vocabulary in various ways can help you remember words. Group words by categories, like foods, sports, numbers, colors, and so forth. Try to associate words with a certain context, such as school (school subjects, classroom objects) or a store (items for sale, salesperson). Try to use associations like opposites, such as **petit—grand** or **gros—mince.**

Communication for All Students

Visual Learners

De bons conseils Suggest that students make flash cards, pairing adjectives that are opposites **(gentil/méchant),** associating a person with an adjective (**fort** — Superman®), or drawing a facial expression to represent each adjective.

Additional Practice

Create true-false statements about celebrities or fictitious characters and have the class respond to them. **(Michael Jordan est grand. Tiger Woods est blond. Superman est fort.)**

15 De qui est-ce qu'on parle? See scripts and answers on p. 197G.

Ecoutons Match the descriptions you hear with the students' names.

CD 7 Tr. 6

Roger Denise Julie Martin Carmen

Comment dit-on...?

Describing and characterizing people

To ask what someone is like:

Il est comment? *What is he like?*
Elle est comment? *What is she like?*
Ils/Elles sont comment? *What are they like?*

To describe someone:

Il n'est ni grand **ni** petit.
Elle est brune.
Ils/Elles sont âgé(e)s.

To characterize someone:

Il est pénible.
Elle est timide.
Ils/Elles sont amusant(e)s.

Cahier d'activités, p. 78, Act. 13

16 Les cousins d'Ariane See scripts and answers on p. 197G.

Ecoutons Ariane is telling a friend about her cousins. Does she have a favorable or unfavorable opinion of them?

CD 7 Tr. 7

17 Des familles bizarres

Parlons Comment sont les membres de ces familles?
See answers below.

Communication for All Students

Slower Pace

15 Before playing the recording, ask students to suggest adjectives they might use to describe each person in the picture. Write their suggestions on a transparency for them to refer to as they listen to the recording.

Slower Pace

16 Before students hear the recording, have them suggest what Ariane might say that would be favorable or unfavorable. Remind students that these categories are matters of opinion.

STANDARDS: 1.2, 5.2

Deuxième étape

CHAPITRE 7

Presenting Comment dit-on... ?

Begin by asking **Je suis comment? Grand(e)? Petit(e)? Jeune? Agé(e)? Amusant(e)?** Then, hold up pictures of people and ask what they are like. **(Il/Elle est comment? Ils/Elles sont comment?)** Next, name or show a photo of a celebrity and ask the class various questions about the person, such as **Il est petit? Il est fort? Il est brun? Il est comment?** You might also play the **Mise en train** video episode, pausing after each person is described to ask **Il/Elle est comment?**

Language Note

17 Tell students that they should not add an **-s** to family names in French: **Ce sont les Simpson. Voilà les Ménard.**

Portfolio

17 **Written** This activity could be included in students' written portfolios. For portfolio information, see *Alternative Assessment Guide,* pages iv–17.

Answers

17 *Possible answers for first photo:* L'oncle est gros, et la mère est mince. Les enfants sont pénibles.
Possible answers for second photo: Bart est petit, pénible et jaune. Maggie est mignonne. Lisa est intelligente et gentille. Homer est gros et amusant.

Teaching Resources
pp. 208–211

PRINT

- Lesson Planner, p. 35
- TPR Storytelling Book, pp. 26, 28
- Listening Activities, pp. 52, 56
- Activities for Communication, pp. 39–40, 106, 108–109, 149–150
- Travaux pratiques de grammaire, pp. 54–58
- Grammar Tutor for Students of French, Chapter 7
- Cahier d'activités, pp. 77–79
- Testing Program, pp. 175–178
- Alternative Assessment Guide, p. 38
- Student Make-Up Assignments, Chapter 7

MEDIA 

- One-Stop Planner
- Audio Compact Discs, CD 7, Trs. 6–7, 22, 29–30
- Teaching Transparencies: 7-2, 7-B, 7-C; **Grammaire supplémentaire** Answers; Travaux pratiques de grammaire Answers
- Interactive CD-ROM Tutor, Disc 2

Presenting Grammaire

Adjective agreement Draw stick figures of a boy, a girl, two boys, and two girls on the board. Have students suggest descriptions for each one, using adjectives they can recall. Write the adjectives in the correct form under each figure. Then, point to the appropriate stick figure as you say the sentences in the grammar box. Have students suggest reasons for the differences. Repeat this with adjectives that don't change and ask students what they notice about these adjectives.

Grammaire

Adjective agreement

CD-ROM 2 DVD 1

As you may remember from Chapter 3, you often change the pronunciation and spelling of adjectives according to the nouns they describe.

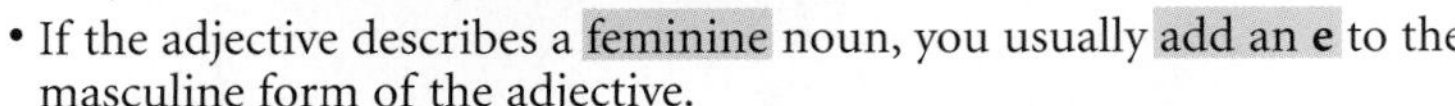

- If the adjective describes a feminine noun, you usually add an **e** to the masculine form of the adjective.
- If the adjective describes a plural noun, you usually add an **s** to the singular form, masculine or feminine.
- If an adjective describes both males and females, you always use the masculine plural form.
- Some adjectives have special (irregular) feminine or plural forms. Here are some irregular adjectives that you've seen in this chapter.

Il est **roux.**	Elle est **rousse.**
Ils sont **roux.**	Elles sont **rousses.**
Il est **mignon.**	Elle est **mignonne.**
Ils sont **mignons.**	Elles sont **mignonnes.**
Il est **gentil.**	Elle est **gentille.**
Ils sont **gentils.**	Elles sont **gentilles.**
Il est **gros.**	Elle est **grosse.**
Ils sont **gros.**	Elles sont **grosses.**
Il est **sympa.**	Elle est **sympa.**
Ils sont **sympas.**	Elles sont **sympas.**

- In the masculine forms, the final consonant sound is silent. In the feminine forms, the final consonant sound is pronounced.
- A few adjectives don't ever change. Here are some that you've already seen.

marron **orange** **cool** **super**

Grammaire supplémentaire, p. 219, Act. 5–6

Cahier d'activités, pp. 77–78, Act. 11–12

Travaux pratiques de grammaire, pp. 55–57, Act. 10–14

18 **Grammaire en contexte**

Parlons Frédéric et Denise sont frère et sœur. Regarde l'image et dis s'ils sont semblables ou différents.

EXEMPLE **Frédéric est grand, mais Denise est petite.**

19 **Grammaire en contexte**

Parlons Décris ton/ta meilleur(e) ami(e) à un(e) camarade. Dis comment il/elle est physiquement. Décris sa personnalité et ce qu'il/elle aime. Ensuite, changez de rôle.

Connections and Comparisons

Language Note

Tell students that some adjectives, such as **cool** and **super,** are invariable because they come from another language. Others, such as **marron** and **orange,** are invariable because their adjective forms were derived from nouns *(chestnut* and *orange).*

Language-to-Language

Ask Spanish-speaking students in your class how the rules of adjective agreement in Spanish and French might be similar. Have volunteers come to the board to show the similarities, using examples like the ones in the **Grammaire.**

Grammaire

The verb *être*

Grammaire supplémentaire, pp. 220–221, Act. 7–9

Cahier d'activités, pp. 78–79, Act. 14–15

Travaux pratiques de grammaire, pp. 57–58, Act. 15–17

Etre is an irregular verb.

être *(to be)*

Je	**suis**	intelligent(e).	Nous	**sommes**	intelligent(e)s.
Tu	**es**	intelligent(e).	Vous	**êtes**	intelligent(e)(s).
Il/Elle/On	**est**	intelligent(e).	Ils/Elles	**sont**	intelligent(e)s.

20 Grammaire en contexte

Ecrivons Albain décrit tout le monde. Complète ses descriptions avec la forme appropriée du verbe **être.** **1.** suis **2.** sont **3.** êtes **4.** es **5.** est **6.** est **7.** sont **8.** sommes

Je __1__ blond, mais Rénato et Jacob, ils __2__ bruns. Francette et Babette, vous __3__ rousses. Et toi, Francette, tu __4__ grande aussi. Rénato aussi __5__ grand, et pénible. Babette __6__ très gentille et mignonne. Mais les différences ne __7__ pas importantes. Nous __8__ tous intelligents.

21 Grammaire en contexte

Parlons Décris un membre de la famille Louvain à un(e) camarade. Attention! Ne dis pas comment il/elle s'appelle. Ton/Ta camarade doit deviner de qui tu parles. Ensuite, changez de rôle.

22 Mon journal

Ecrivons Ecris un paragraphe pour décrire une personne de ta famille que tu admires. Dis ce qu'il/elle aime faire et où il/elle aime aller. Si tu préfères, tu peux décrire un personnage de la télé.

Communication for All Students

Slower Pace

20 Before doing this activity, review the forms of **être** using yourself and the students as subjects of descriptive sentences.

Additional Practice

21 Extend this activity by having partners also tell how the person described might be related to Gabrielle.

Visual Learners

21 Have one partner draw the family member, without looking at the illustration, as the other partner describes the person. Then, have the partner who described the family member check the drawing for accuracy and label it with the correct name. Students can then extend this activity by taking turns describing and drawing famous people.

Presenting Grammaire

The verb *être* Make two sets of flash cards, one with the forms of **être** and the other with the subject pronouns. Tape the flash cards in random order on the board and have students match the subjects and verbs. Then, remove the verb cards from the board and ask for volunteers to write the verb forms next to the subject cards. Finally, divide the class into two teams. Have the first player from each team come to the board. Name a subject pronoun and an adjective **(elle/ brun).** The first player to combine them in a correct sentence on the board wins a point. **(Elle est brune.)** Continue until all players have had a turn.

Mon journal

22 As a prewriting activity, name a member of a popular TV family and ask students to describe him or her. For an additional journal entry suggestion for Chapter 7, see *Cahier d'activités,* page 151.

Assess

- Testing Program, pp. 175–178 Quiz 7-2A, Quiz 7-2B, Audio CD 7, Tr. 22
- Student Make-Up Assignments, Chapter 7, Alternative Quiz
- Alternative Assessment Guide, p. 38

STANDARDS: 1.3, 3.1

CHAPITRE 7

Teaching Resources
p. 212

PRINT 
- Video Guide, pp. 47, 48–49
- Cahier d'activités, p. 84

MEDIA 
- One-Stop Planner
- Video Program
  Videocassette 3, 09:21–11:58
- DVD Tutor, Disc 1
- Audio Compact Discs, CD 7, Trs. 8–11
- Interactive CD-ROM Tutor, Disc 2

Presenting Panorama Culturel

Ask students for common pet names for dogs, cats, and other pets in the United States. Then, play the video and have them listen for the kind of pet each person has and its name.

Language Note

Students might want to know these words: **se promener** *(to go for a walk);* **au garrot** *(at the withers);* **faire des balades** *(to go for walks).*

Questions

1. **Qui est Chopine? Et Fabécar? Et Viêt?** (le chien d'Olivier; le chat d'Onélia; le cheval de Marie-Emmanuelle)
2. **Comment sont-ils?** (Chopine—pas trop gros, vivant; Fabécar—très affectueux; Viêt—brun et grand)
3. **Qu'est-ce que Chopine aime faire?** (s'amuser, manger)

Panorama Culturel

Tu as un animal domestique? Il est comment?

We talked to some French-speaking people about their pets. Here's what they had to say.

Olivier,
Martinique

«Oui, j'ai un animal à la maison, un chien. Son nom, c'est Chopine. Il n'est pas trop gros, [il est] vivant. Il aime beaucoup s'amuser et beaucoup manger aussi.» Tr. 9

Onélia,
France

«J'ai un chat. Il s'appelle Fabécar. Il a trois ans. C'est un mâle. On le voit assez rarement. On le voit seulement quand il veut manger, sinon il se promène dans les jardins. Il est très affectueux.» Tr. 10

Marie-Emmanuelle,
France

«J'ai un cheval. Il est grand. Il fait 1 mètre 78 au garrot. Il est brun. Il s'appelle Viêt. Et on fait des balades à cheval.» Tr. 11

Qu'en penses-tu?

1. What names do these people give their pets? Chopine, Fabécar, Viêt
2. Do you take your pets out in public? Why or why not? If so, where?
3. What kind of system is used in the United States to identify lost pets? identification tags

Savais-tu que...?

More than half of French households have pets. City dwellers often take them along when they shop. In many francophone countries, people sometimes carry small animals in baskets (**paniers**) made just for them! It isn't unusual to see dogs and cats on trains or in subways, restaurants, department stores, and other public places. Most pet owners have their four-legged friends tattooed with a number that allows them to be identified in case they are lost. Various groups in France have launched poster campaigns to encourage dog owners to teach their pets to use the gutter instead of the sidewalk: **Apprenez-leur le caniveau!**

Connections and Comparisons

Thinking Critically

Analyzing Have students consider the advantages of tatooing pets versus using identification tags. Which system is more effective?

Language Note

Students might want to know these animal-related expressions: **minou** *(kitty,* used to call a cat, or as a generic name for a cat); **ouah! ouah!** *(bow-wow);* **aboyer** *(to bark);* **miaou** *(meow);* **miauler/faire miaou** *(to mew, whine).*

STANDARDS: 2.1, 3.2, 4.2

Troisième étape

Objective Asking for, giving, and refusing permission

WA3 PARIS-7

Comment dit-on...?

Asking for, giving, and refusing permission

CD-ROM 2 DVD 1

To ask for permission:

Je voudrais aller au cinéma. **Tu es d'accord?** *Is that OK with you?*
(**Est-ce que**) **je peux** sortir? *May I . . .*

To give permission:

Oui, si tu veux. *Yes, if you want to.*
Pourquoi pas?
Oui, bien sûr.
D'accord, si tu fais **d'abord** la vaisselle. *OK, if you . . . first.*

To refuse permission:

Pas question! *Out of the question!*
Non, c'est impossible. *No, that's impossible.*
Non, tu dois faire tes devoirs. *No, you've got to . . .*
Pas ce soir. *Not . . .*

PAPA, JE PEUX ALLER AU CAFE CE SOIR?
DEMANDE A TA MERE.

Grammaire supplémentaire, p. 221, Act. 10

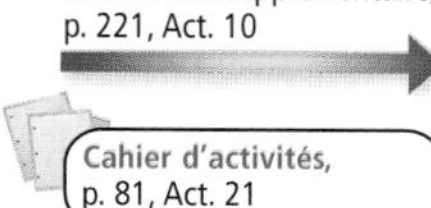
Cahier d'activités, p. 81, Act. 21

23 Je peux... ? See scripts and answers on p. 197H.

Ecoutons Listen to these people ask for permission. Are they given or refused permission?

CD 7 Tr. 12

Vocabulaire

CD-ROM 2 DVD 1

débarrasser la table	*to clear the table*
faire les courses	*to do the shopping*
faire le ménage	*to clean house*
faire la vaisselle	*to do the dishes*
garder ta petite sœur	*to look after . . .*
laver la voiture	*to wash the car*
passer l'aspirateur	*to vacuum*
promener le chien	*to walk the dog*
ranger ta chambre	*to pick up your room*
sortir la poubelle	*to take out the trash*
tondre le gazon	*to mow the lawn*

Tu peux sortir si tu ranges d'abord ta chambre.

Cahier d'activités, pp. 80–82, Act. 17–18, 20, 22–23

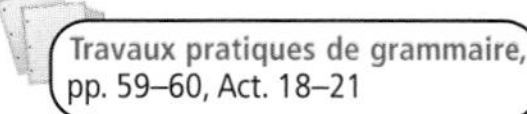
Travaux pratiques de grammaire, pp. 59–60, Act. 18–21

Communication for All Students

Slower Pace

23 To give an example, have a student ask you for permission. Give a positive or negative response and then ask the class if you granted or refused permission.

Kinesthetic Learners

Tell students to do various chores and have them respond by miming the appropriate activity.

Teaching Resources pp. 213–215

PRINT

- Lesson Planner, p. 36
- TPR Storytelling Book, pp. 27, 28
- Listening Activities, pp. 52–53, 57
- Activities for Communication, pp. 41–42, 107, 109, 149–150
- Travaux pratiques de grammaire, pp. 59–60
- Grammar Tutor for Students of French, Chapter 7
- Cahier d'activités, pp. 80–82
- Testing Program, pp. 179–182
- Alternative Assessment Guide, p. 38
- Student Make-Up Assignments, Chapter 7

MEDIA

- One-Stop Planner
- Audio Compact Discs, CD 7, Trs. 12–13, 23, 31–32
- Teaching Transparencies: 7-3, 7-D; **Grammaire supplémentaire** Answers; Travaux pratiques de grammaire Answers
- Interactive CD-ROM Tutor, Disc 2

Bell Work

Ask students to write the opposites of **gros, grand, méchant,** and **âgé.**

Presenting Comment dit-on... ?

Model the new expressions, using gestures. Repeat a new expression and have students identify the function.

Vocabulaire

Using props (a leash, trash bag, dishes), demonstrate the activities and tell students in French what you're doing.

STANDARDS: 1.2

Teaching Resources
pp. 213–215

PRINT
- Lesson Planner, p. 36
- TPR Storytelling Book, pp. 27, 28
- Listening Activities, pp. 52–53, 57
- Activities for Communication, pp. 41–42, 107, 109, 149–150
- Travaux pratiques de grammaire, pp. 59–60
- Grammar Tutor for Students of French, Chapter 7
- Cahier d'activités, pp. 80–82
- Testing Program, pp. 179–182
- Alternative Assessment Guide, p. 38
- Student Make-Up Assignments, Chapter 7

MEDIA
- One-Stop Planner
- Audio Compact Discs, CD 7, Trs. 12–13, 23, 31–32
- Teaching Transparencies: 7-3, 7-D; **Grammaire supplémentaire** Answers; Travaux pratiques de grammaire Answers
- Interactive CD-ROM Tutor, Disc 2

Additional Practice
24 You might have students tell or write what is happening in the pictures.

Group Work
26 After students have written their captions, make four columns on the board, each representing one of the illustrations. Have students write one of their captions in the appropriate column. Then, have small groups make up a story, using one caption from each column.

Auditory Learners
26 For additional listening practice, suggest two expressions for each illustration and have students choose the correct one. For example, for the second illustration, you might say **Oui, si tu veux** or **Pas question.**

24 Permission donnée ou refusée See scripts and answers on p. 197H.

Ecoutons Listen to some French teenagers ask permission to go out with their friends. Which picture represents the outcome of each dialogue?

CD 7 Tr. 13

a.

b.

c.

d.

e.

f.

25 Qui doit le faire?

Parlons Demande à un(e) camarade qui fait les corvées ménagères dans sa famille. Ensuite, changez de rôle.

EXEMPLE —**Qui promène le chien?**
—**Mon frère. Et moi aussi quelquefois.**

26 Tu es d'accord?

Ecrivons Qu'est-ce que ces personnes disent?

1.

2.

3.

4.

Cultures and Communities

Career Path
Have students imagine that they work for a French family as an **au pair** or a nanny. How would the vocabulary they have learned in this chapter help them with their daily tasks? (family vocabulary, vocabulary for chores around the house). Have them discuss their ideas, and then have them suggest other categories of vocabulary that would help them in that situation.

STANDARDS: 1.2, 1.3

Et toi?

Parlons Donne la permission ou refuse la permission dans les situations suivantes.

1. Ta petite sœur ou ton petit frère veut écouter ta cassette.
2. Ton ami(e) veut lire ton livre.
3. Ta petite sœur ou ton petit frère veut aller avec tes amis et toi au cinéma.

28 De l'école au travail

Parlons This summer, you're going to work for a French family as a babysitter. Your partner is going to play the role of one of the children, and he is going to ask you permission to do different things this weekend. Give permission for some activities and say no for others. Explain why you gave or refused permission. Then, change roles.

PRONONCIATION

CD 7
Trs. 14–19

The nasal sounds [ɔ̃], [ɛ̃], and [œ̃]

See scripts and answers on p. 197H.

In Chapter 5 you learned about the nasal sound [ɑ̃]. Now listen to the other French nasal sounds [ɔ̃], [ɛ̃], and [œ̃]. As you repeat the following words, try not to put a trace of the consonant **n** in your nasal sounds.

on hein un

How are these nasal sounds represented in writing? The nasal sound [ɔ̃] is represented by a combination of **on** or **om.** Several letter combinations can represent the sound [ɛ̃], for example, **in, im, ain, aim, (i)en.** The nasal sound [œ̃] is spelled **un** or **um.** A vowel after these groups of letters or, in some cases, a doubling of the consonant **n** or **m** will result in a non-nasal sound, as in **limonade** and **ennemi.**

A. A prononcer

Repeat the following words.

1. ton	blond	pardon	nombre
2. cousin	impossible	copain	faim
3. un	lundi	brun	humble

B. A lire

Take turns with a partner reading the following sentences aloud.

1. Ils ont très faim. Ils vont prendre des sandwiches au jambon. C'est bon!
2. Allons faire du patin ou bien, allons au concert!
3. Ce garçon est blond et ce garçon-là est brun. Ils sont minces et mignons!
4. Pardon. C'est combien, cette montre?

C. A écrire

You're going to hear a short dialogue. Write down what you hear.

Communication for All Students

Language Note

Point out that even though the nasal sound **[ɛ̃]** can be spelled in a variety of ways, the letter **i** is always part of the syllable. Make sure that students pronounce the nasal **[ɔ̃]** with their mouths small and rounded, with most of the sound passing through the nose **(pardon).** For the nasal **[ɛ̃],** the mouth is wider, but still not very open **(jardin).** For the nasal **[œ̃] (lundi),** the jaw should be dropped more than for the **[ɛ̃]** sound.

Auditory Learners

Prononciation To have students listen to the nasal sound in words like **ton** and **blond,** play the song *Il était une bergère,* on Audio CD 10.

Troisième étape

CHAPITRE 7

Speaking Assessment

27 You might use the following rubric when grading your students on this activity.

Speaking Rubric	Points			
	4	3	2	1
Content (Complete–Incomplete)				
Comprehension (Total–Little)				
Comprehensibility (Comprehensible–Incomprehensible)				
Accuracy (Accurate–Seldom accurate)				
Fluency (Fluent–Not fluent)				

18–20: A　14–15: C　Under 12: F
16–17: B　12–13: D

Game

Chasse au trésor Provide each student with a list of ten instructions, such as **Trouve quelqu'un qui... (1) a deux tantes. (2) a un poisson. (3) ne fait jamais les courses.** Students circulate, asking questions in French to find someone who meets the qualifications. They should then have that student sign his or her name next to the item. The first student to complete the list wins.

Assess

- Testing Program, pp. 179–182 Quiz 7-3A, Quiz 7-3B Audio CD 7, Tr. 23
- Student Make-Up Assignments, Chapter 7, Alternative Quiz
- Alternative Assessment Guide, p. 38

Lisons!

CHAPITRE 7

Teaching Resources
pp. 216–217

PRINT 

- Lesson Planner, p. 37
- Cahier d'activités, p. 83
- Reading Strategies and Skills Handbook, Chapter 7
- Joie de lire 1, Chapter 7
- Standardized Assessment Tutor, Chapter 7

MEDIA 

- One-Stop Planner

Prereading
Activities A–B

Using Prior Knowledge
Ask students if they've ever adopted a pet and how they went about finding and choosing one (newspaper, animal shelter, pet shop).

Reading
Activities C–G

Monitoring Comprehension
You might form small groups and assign each group one of the animals. Students should look for a physical description, personality characteristics, where the pet is located, and how it got to be in the shelter. Have groups share their information with the class. You might also have groups read their information aloud and have the class guess which pet they are describing.

Answers

B. *Possible answers:* what kinds of animals are available, how to adopt the animals, each animal's age, appearance, and personality

C. Mayo is no longer up for adoption.; Mayo has found a family.; where Mayo was adopted, the name of Mayo's new owner, Mayo's color, the fact that the owner already has a thirteen-year-old Siamese cat

Lisons!

En direct des refuges

Stratégie pour lire
When you read something, it's important to separate the main idea from the supporting details. Sometimes the main idea is clearly stated at the beginning, other times it's just implied.

A. Which completion best expresses the main idea of these articles?
These articles are about . . .
1. animals that are missing.
2. animals that have performed heroic rescues.
3. animals that are up for adoption.
4. animals that have won prizes at cat and dog shows.

B. Now that you've decided what the main idea of the reading is, make a list of the kinds of details you expect to find in each of the articles. See answers below.

C. How is Mayo different from the other animals? What is the main idea of the article about him? What other details are given? See answers below.

D. Each of the articles includes a description of the animal. Look at the articles again and answer these questions.
1. Which animal is the oldest? The youngest? Camel; Jupiter
2. Which animals get along well with children? Camel, Jupiter, Flora

EN DIRECT DES REFUGES

Cet animal vous attend au refuge de la Société normande de protection aux animaux, 7 bis, avenue Jacques-Chastellain, Ile Lacroix 76000 Rouen. Tél.: (02) 35.70.20.36. Si Camel a été adopté, pensez à ses voisins de cage.

IL VOUS ATTEND, ADOPTEZ-LE

CAMEL, 5 ANS

Ce sympathique bobtail blanc et gris est arrivé au refuge à la suite du décès accidentel de son maître. Il est vif, joyeux, a bon caractère et s'entend très bien avec les enfants. En échange de son dévouement et de sa fidélité, ce sportif robuste demande un grand espace afin de pouvoir courir et s'ébattre à son aise.

Continuez à nous écrire, et envoyez-nous votre photo avec votre protégé, une surprise vous attend!

Cet animal vous attend au refuge de l'Eden, Rod A'char, 29430 Lanhouarneau. Tél.: (02) 98.61.64.55. Colette Di Faostino tient seule, sans aucune subvention, ce havre exemplaire mais pauvre. Si Dady a été adoptée, pensez à ses compagnons de malchance !

ELLE VOUS ATTEND, ADOPTEZ-LA

DADY, 2 ANS

Toute blanche, à l'exception de quelques petites taches et des oreilles noires bien dressées, Dady a un petit air de spitz, opulente fourrure en moins. Gentille, enjouée, très attachante, elle a été abandonnée après la séparation de ses maîtres et attend une famille qui accepterait de s'occuper d'elle un peu, beaucoup, passionnément.

Mayo a trouvé une famille

Mayo a été adopté à la SPA de Valenciennes par Françoise Robeaux qui rêvait d'un chat gris ! Il a ainsi rejoint l'autre «fils» de la famille, un superbe siamois âgé de 13 ans.

Connections and Comparisons

Thinking Critically
Comparing and Contrasting Have students research and compare attitudes in the U.S. about pets with attitudes about them in France. You might also have them find out if there are large stores for pets like the ones here. Have students search the Internet for pet-supply sites in both countries and compare the types of products available.

Thinking Critically
Analyzing Ask students to pay careful attention to the way the pets are described in the article. What can they say about the style of the article? What is the writer's purpose? How might the article be different if it were written for veterinarians?

STANDARDS: 1.2, 3.1, 4.2

Cet animal vous attend avec espoir au refuge Grammont de la SPA 30, av. du Général-de-Gaulle 92230 Gennevilliers. Tél.: (01) 47.98.57.40. Rens. sur Minitel: 36.15 SPA. Si Poupette est déjà partie, pensez aux autres!

ELLE VOUS ATTEND, ADOPTEZ-LA

POUPETTE, 3 ANS

Cette jolie chatte stérilisée au regard tendre et étonné a été recueillie à l'âge de quelques semaines par une vieille dame, dont elle a été la dernière compagne. Sa maîtresse est malheureusement décédée après un long séjour à l'hôpital. Poupette, l'orpheline, ne comprend pas ce qui lui arrive et commence à trouver le temps long ! Elle a hâte de retrouver un foyer «sympa», des bras caressants et une paire de genoux pour ronronner.

Cet animal vous attend au refuge de la fondation Assistance aux animaux, 8, rue des Plantes 77410 Villevaudé. Tél.: (01) 60.26.20.48 (l'après-midi seulement).

IL VOUS ATTEND, ADOPTEZ-LE

JUPITER, 7 MOIS

Cet adorable chaton tigré et blanc vient tout juste d'être castré et est dûment tatoué. Très joueur et affectueux, il a été recueilli au refuge parce que, malheureusement, sa maîtresse a dû être hospitalisée pour un séjour de longue durée. Sociable, il s'entend très bien avec les jeunes enfants et accepterait volontiers un chien pour compagnon.

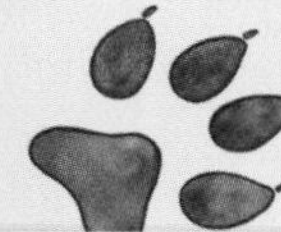

Elle vous attend au refuge de l'Eden, Rod A'char, 29430 Lanhouarneau. Tél.: (02) 98.61.64.55. Colette Di Faostino tient seule, sans aucune subvention, ce havre exemplaire mais pauvre. Si Flora a déjà été adoptée, pensez à ses compagnons !

ELLE VOUS ATTEND, ADOPTEZ-LA

FLORA, 3 ANS

C'est une pure braque Saint Germain roux et blanc. Elle ne pense qu'à jouer, s'entend bien avec les enfants et témoigne d'une gentillesse infatigable. Flora a été abandonnée car elle ne s'intéressait pas à la chasse. Son sport passion : la course derrière la «baballe».

Vous avez recueilli un animal par notre intermédiaire ? Envoyez-nous votre photo avec votre protégé, une surprise vous attend!

3. Which animal needs a lot of space? Camel
4. Which animals love to play? Jupiter, Flora

E. Make a list of all the adjectives of physical description that you can find in the articles. Now, list the adjectives that describe the animals' characteristics. See answers below.

F. Each article also explains why these animals were sent to the animal shelter. See answers below.
1. Which animal wasn't interested in hunting?
2. Whose owner was involved in an accident?
3. Whose owner had to go to the hospital for a long time?
4. Whose family got separated?

G. A third kind of detail tells where you can go to adopt these animals. Can you find the French word for *animal shelter*? le refuge

H. Now, write your own classified ad to try to find a home for a lost pet. Remember to give the animal's name and age, tell what the animal looks like, and describe his or her character.

or

Write a letter to the animal shelter telling them what kind of pet you would like to adopt.
1. First, make a list of all of the characteristics you're looking for in a pet. Will you choose to adopt a cat or a dog? What will he or she look like? Act like? Like to do?
2. Write a short letter, including all the important information about your desired pet.
3. Don't forget to give your address and telephone number!

Cahier d'activités, p. 83, Act. 25

Lisons!

CHAPITRE 7

Terms in Lisons!

Write the following terms on the board or on a transparency to help students in their reading:
recueilli *(picked up)*
maître(-sse) *(pet owner)*
course *(race)*
courir *(to run)*
s'entendre bien avec *(to get along well with)*

Visual/Auditory Learners

Have students cover the text and only look at the pictures. Read out some of the descriptions of the animals without giving their names and have students identify the animals by calling out its name.

Postreading

Activity H

Using Text Organizers

Have students convert their ads into posters or into a class newspaper, with the information neatly displayed and a drawing or photo of the pet, if possible. Display the posters around the room and have each student choose a pet to "adopt." They might write a short paragraph, explaining why they chose that particular pet.

Portfolio

H. Written Activity H is appropriate as an entry in students' written portfolios. For portfolio information, see the *Alternative Assessment Guide,* pages iv–17.

Communication for All Students

Challenge

Have students write three or four true-false statements about the selections. They should then exchange papers, mark the items either **vrai** or **faux,** and return them to be corrected.

Additional Practice

Ask students to explain which of the animals pictured they might like to adopt and why.

Visual Learners

Bring some stuffed animals to class and have students describe their physical characteristics. Then have students invent personality traits for the animals, based on what they read in the descriptions of the pets up for adoption. Students could then bid to "adopt" the stuffed animals, giving their reasons for choosing one "pet" over another.

Answers

E. *Physical:* blanc et gris, robuste, toute blanche, noires, opulente, gris, jolie, adorable, tigré et blanc, tatoué, pure, roux et blanc *Character:* sympathique, vif, joyeux, gentille, enjouée, attachante, tendre, étonné, joueur, affectueux, sociable, infatigable

F. 1. Flora
2. Camel's
3. Jupiter's, Poupette's
4. Dady's

STANDARDS: 1.2, 1.3, 3.1, 5.2

Grammaire supplémentaire

CHAPITRE 7

For **Grammaire supplémentaire** Answer Transparencies, see the *Teaching Transparencies* binder.

Answers

1
1. C'est la grand-mère de Guy.
2. Ce sont les frères de Marie.
3. C'est le fils de Fatima.
4. Ce sont les tantes de Paul.
5. C'est le grand-père de Saïdou.
6. C'est la fille de Jean.
7. C'est le petit-fils de Mme Lominé.

2
1. nos
2. ma
3. mes
4. notre
5. notre
6. nos

3
1. vos
2. ta
3. tes
4. votre
5. ta
6. vos

Grammaire supplémentaire

Première étape

Objectives Identifying and introducing people

1 Ahmed est nouveau dans ton quartier. Aide-le à identifier certaines personnes. Pour répondre à ses questions, utilise **c'est** et **ce sont** et les mots entre parenthèses dans l'ordre où ils se trouvent. (**pp. 203, 204**)

EXEMPLE —C'est qui, Karim et Mohammed? (les oncles/Samira)
—Ce sont les oncles de Samira.

1. C'est qui, Claudette? (la grand-mère/Guy)
2. C'est qui, Arnaud et Martin? (les frères/Marie)
3. C'est qui, Mourad? (le fils/Fatima)
4. C'est qui, Jacqueline et Jeanne? (les tantes/Paul)
5. C'est qui, Ismaïl? (le grand-père/Saïdou)
6. C'est qui, Hélène? (la fille/Jean)
7. C'est qui, Stéphane? (le petit-fils/Mme Lominé)

2 Sabine and Claire are asking their younger brother Luc to bring them some items they forgot in their room. Complete their statements with the appropriate possessive adjectives. (**p. 205**)

EXEMPLE Luc, apporte-nous <u>**nos**</u> calculatrices, s'il te plaît!

1. Apporte-nous _____ stylos, s'il te plaît!
2. Apporte-moi _____ trousse, s'il te plaît!
3. Apporte-moi _____ cahiers, s'il te plaît!
4. Apporte-nous _____ dictionnaire, s'il te plaît!
5. Apporte-moi _____ calculatrice, s'il te plaît!
6. Apporte-nous _____ sacs, s'il te plaît!

3 Luc ne trouve pas ce que ses sœurs veulent. Il leur demande où ces choses se trouvent. Complète ses questions avec les adjectifs possessifs appropriés. (**p. 205**)

1. (à Claire et à Sabine) Ils sont où, _____ stylos?
2. (à Claire) Elle est où, _____ trousse?
3. (à Sabine) Ils sont où, _____ cahiers?
4. (à Sabine et à Claire) Il est où, _____ dictionnaire?
5. (à Claire) Elle est où, _____ calculatrice?
6. (à Sabine et à Claire) Ils sont où, _____ sacs?

Grammar Resources for Chapter 7

The **Grammaire supplémentaire** activities were designed as supplemental activities for the grammatical concepts presented in the chapter. You might use them as additional practice, for review, or for assessment.

For more grammar presentations, review, and practice, refer to the following:

- Travaux pratiques de grammaire
- Grammar Tutor for Students of French
- Grammar Summary on pp. R15–R28
- Cahier d'activités
- Grammar and Vocabulary quizzes (Testing Program)
- Test Generator
- Interactive CD-ROM Tutor
- DVD Tutor
- **Jeux interactifs** at <u>**go.hrw.com**</u>

STANDARDS: 1.2

4 Mazarine et Jean-Luc parlent de leurs animaux domestiques. Complète leurs phrases avec les adjectifs possessifs appropriés. (**p. 205**)

MAZARINE	Il a quel âge, ___1___ chien, Jean-Luc?
JEAN-LUC	___2___ chien? Je n'ai pas de chien. Par contre, j'ai des poissons rouges!
MAZARINE	Ah, c'est cool, ça! Ils s'appellent comment, ___3___ poissons?
JEAN-LUC	Elvis et Presley. Tu aimes les poissons rouges, toi?
MAZARINE	Oui, beaucoup, mais j'aime mieux les chats et les canaris. ___4___ sœur a deux chats et trois canaris.
JEAN-LUC	Ils sont comment, les chats de ___5___ sœur?
MAZARINE	Très mignons!
JEAN-LUC	Et ___6___ canaris?
MAZARINE	Eh bien, ils sont jaunes.
JEAN-LUC	Ah! Très drôle! Est-ce que ___7___ parents aiment bien les animaux?
MAZARINE	Oui. Chez moi, tout le monde adore les animaux.

Grammaire supplémentaire

CHAPITRE 7

Deuxième étape

Objective Describing and characterizing people

5 Déchiffre chaque adjectif, et ensuite, fais l'accord avec le sujet, si c'est nécessaire. (**p. 210**)

1. Daniel est UNBR.
2. Ses amis sont LNBOD.
3. Ses tantes sont NILTEG.
4. Ses frères sont OFRT.
5. Ses sœurs sont TNSUAMA.
6. Son chien est BNTAMEET.
7. Sa grand-mère est ETPIT.
8. Ses chats sont ROGS.
9. Sa mère est XRUO.
10. Son cousin est ENBLEPI.

6 Complète chaque phrase avec l'adjectif approprié et fais l'accord nécessaire. (**p. 210**)

1. J'aime beaucoup ta cousine Mathilde. Elle est ________. (pénible/sympa)
2. Cette quiche est ________! (super/timide)
3. Tes yeux sont ________. (orange/marron)
4. J'aime bien ta grand-mère. Elle est ________. (embêtant/amusant)
5. Ta mère est ________, non? (roux/orange)

Answers

4
1. ton
2. Mon
3. tes
4. Ma
5. ta
6. ses
7. tes

5
1. brun
2. blonds
3. gentilles
4. forts
5. amusantes
6. embêtant
7. petite
8. gros
9. rousse
10. pénible

6
1. sympa
2. super
3. marron
4. amusante
5. rousse

Teacher to Teacher

Judy Eames
Pulaski County High
Somerset, KY

Try Dr. Eames' game to practice possessive adjectives and family vocabulary.

"On 3x5 index cards, write a family vocabulary word **(la mère)** on one side and label it as the question side. Label the other side as the answer side and write another vocabulary word **(le père).** On another card, write the word **la mère** on the answer side and another vocabulary word on the question side. Repeat each word on the question side of one card on the answer side of another card. The first student uses the question side to ask, **Qui est ma mère?** The student with **la mère** as the answer should reply **Moi, je suis ta mère.** The student who replies asks the next question. Continue until all the questions are answered."

STANDARDS: 1.2

Grammaire supplémentaire

CHAPITRE 7

For **Grammaire supplémentaire** Answer Transparencies, see the *Teaching Transparencies* binder.

Grammaire supplémentaire

7 Complète chaque phrase logiquement. (**p. 211**)

1. Je...	**a.** est très gentille.
2. Elles...	**b.** suis grand et fort.
3. Tu...	**c.** sont embêtants.
4. Julien et moi, on...	**d.** sommes très minces.
5. Jeanne...	**e.** es méchant!
6. Alice et moi, nous...	**f.** êtes un peu pénibles!
7. Mes frères...	**g.** est roux.
8. Marie et toi, vous...	**h.** sont intelligentes.

8 Choose the expression from the box below that completes each sentence logically. Be sure to consider adjective agreement while making your choices. (**p. 211**)

1. ____________ rousses mais toi, tu es blonde.
2. ____________ très gentille. Tu l'invites à ma boum, d'accord?
3. ____________ très cool. Je peux les écouter?
4. ____________ brun mais toi, tu es blonde.
5. ____________ mignon comme tout! Viens ici, Médor.
6. ____________ timides et ne parlent jamais.
7. ____________ orange. C'est bizarre.

Ton chien est
Tes CD sont
Ton père est
Ta sœur est
Tes baskets sont
Tes cousines sont
Tes amis sont

Answers

7
1. b
2. h
3. e
4. g
5. a
6. d
7. c
8. f

8
1. Tes cousines sont
2. Ta sœur est
3. Tes CD sont
4. Ton père est
5. Ton chien est
6. Tes amis sont
7. Tes baskets sont

Communication for All Students

Challenge

7 Have students work in pairs and create an activity for their classmates using this activity as a model. Students could complete each other's activities and then compile them to use as a review for the chapter test (after you have checked them for accuracy).

Slower Pace

8 Review adjective agreement with students before doing this exercise. Then have them underline the endings for each of the adjectives and make predictions about what the possible answers could be. Check answers together as a class, allowing volunteers to write them on the board or on an overhead transparency.

STANDARDS: 1.2

9 Emma veut savoir comment sont les personnes qui sont dans l'album de photos de Gustave. Ecris ses questions en utilisant la forme correcte du verbe **être** et l'adjectif possessif approprié. (**pp. 205, 211**)

EXEMPLE GUSTAVE Ça, ce sont mes cousines Arianne et Aurélie.
EMMA **Elles sont comment, tes cousines?**

1. Ça, c'est mon cousin Jean-Pierre.
2. Voilà mes tantes Yvette et Claudette.
3. Ça, ce sont mes oncles André et Auguste.
4. Voilà mes grands-parents.
5. Voilà ma sœur Rosalie.

Troisième étape

Objective **Asking for, giving, and refusing permission**

10 Onélia veut faire beaucoup de choses, mais, d'abord, elle doit demander la permission à ses parents. Complète ses questions avec la forme appropriée du verbe **être.** (**pp. 211, 213**)

1. Je voudrais sortir avec mes copains. Tu _____ d'accord, Maman?
2. Je voudrais aller au cinéma. Vous _____ d'accord?
3. Je voudrais aller à la MJC. Tu _____ d'accord, Papa?
4. Je _____ invitée à la boum de Pierre. Vous _____ d'accord?

11 Mme Ménard demande à ses enfants de l'aider. Complète leurs réponses avec la forme correcte du verbe **être.** (**pp. 211, 213**)

1. MME MENARD Fabienne, tu fais les courses, s'il te plaît?
FABIENNE Désolée, je _____ occupée. J'ai des devoirs à faire.
2. MME MENARD Anne et Eva, vous faites la vaisselle, s'il vous plaît?
ANNE ET EVA Désolées, nous _____ occupées.
3. MME MENARD Paul et Eric, vous pouvez débarrasser la table?
PAUL ET ERIC Désolés, on _____ occupés. On a des trucs à faire.
4. MME MENARD Lise, tu peux promener le chien?
LISE Oui, bien sûr!
MME MENARD Merci. Tu _____ très gentille!

Grammaire supplémentaire

CHAPITRE 7

Answers

9
1. Il est comment, ton cousin?
2. Elles sont comment, tes tantes?
3. Ils sont comment, tes oncles?
4. Ils sont comment, tes grands-parents?
5. Elle est comment, ta sœur?

10
1. es
2. êtes
3. es
4. suis; êtes

11
1. suis
2. sommes
3. est
4. es

Review and Assess

You may wish to assign the **Grammaire supplémentaire** activities as additional practice or homework after presenting material throughout the chapter. Assign Activity 1 after **Note de grammaire** (p. 204), Activities 2–4 after **Grammaire** (p. 205), Activities 5–6 after **Grammaire** (p. 210), Activities 7–9 after **Grammaire** (p. 211) and Activities 10–11 after **Vocabulaire** (p. 213). To prepare students for the **Etape** Quizzes and Chapter Test, we suggest doing the **Grammaire supplémentaire** activities in the following order. Have students complete Activities 1–4 before taking Quizzes 7-1A or 7-1B; Activities 5–9 before Quizzes 7-2A or 7-2B; and Activities 10–11 before Quizzes 7-3A or 7-3B.

STANDARDS: 1.2

Mise en pratique

CHAPITRE 7

The **Mise en pratique** reviews and integrates all four skills and culture in preparation for the Chapter Test.

Teaching Resources
pp. 222–223

PRINT 

- Lesson Planner, p. 37
- Listening Activities, p. 53
- Video Guide, pp. 47, 50
- Grammar Tutor for Students of French, Chapter 7
- Standardized Assessment Tutor, Chapter 7

MEDIA  

- One-Stop Planner
- Video Program Videocassette 3, 12:00–13:07
- DVD Tutor, Disc 1
- Audio Compact Discs, CD 7, Tr. 20
- Interactive CD-ROM Tutor, Disc 2

Language Note

You might tell students that the announcements shown here, as well as other official announcements, are called **les faire-part.** The birth announcement would be **un faire-part de naissance,** and the wedding announcement would be **un faire-part de mariage.**

Answers

1. birth announcement; *Possible answers:* It is similar to an American birth announcement. The names at the bottom have the same last name.
2. the son of Denise Morel-Tissot and Raymond Tissot
3. the parents
4. Michel Louis Raymond was born.
5. wedding announcement; *Possible answers:* The word **mariage** looks like *marriage.* Christelle and Nicolas are a couple.
6. a couple announcing their wedding plans
7. Christelle and Nicolas got married.
8. Christelle's or Nicolas's parents

Mise en pratique

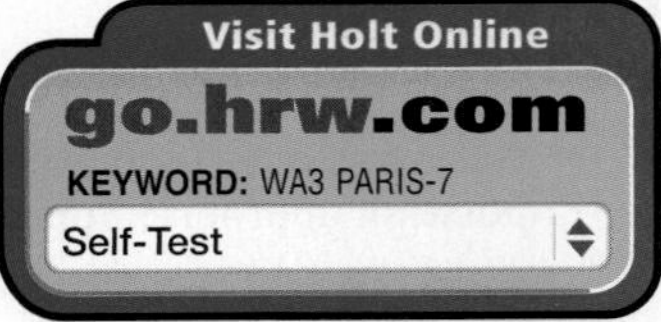

1 Ecoute Nathalie qui va te parler de sa famille. Puis, réponds aux questions. See scripts and answers on p. 197H.

CD 7 Tr. 20

1. Comment s'appelle le frère de Nathalie?
2. Il a quel âge?
3. Est-ce qu'elle a un chien ou un chat?
4. Comment est son animal?

2 D'abord, lis ces documents rapidement. Ensuite, relis chaque document et réponds aux questions suivantes. See answers below.

1. What kind of document is this? How do you know?
2. Who is Michel Louis Raymond?
3. Who are Denise Morel-Tissot and Raymond Tissot?
4. What happened on May 20, 2003?

Nous avons la joie de vous annoncer la naissance de notre fils

Michel Louis Raymond
20 mai 2003

Denise Morel-Tissot
Raymond Tissot

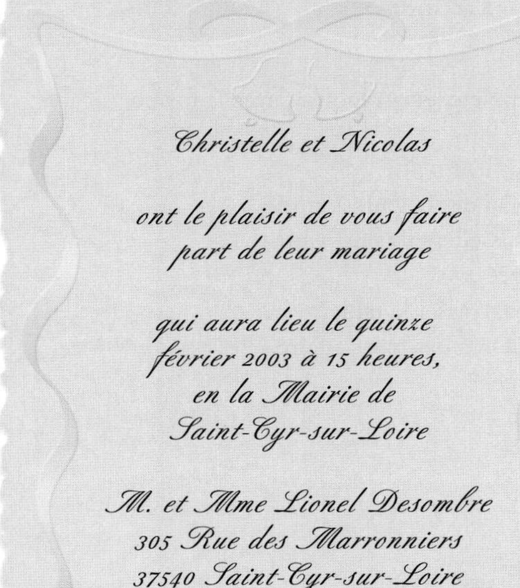

Christelle et Nicolas

ont le plaisir de vous faire part de leur mariage

qui aura lieu le quinze février 2003 à 15 heures, en la Mairie de Saint-Cyr-sur-Loire

M. et Mme Lionel Desombre
305 Rue des Marronniers
37540 Saint-Cyr-sur-Loire

5. What kind of document is this? How do you know?
6. Who are Christelle and Nicolas?
7. What happened on February 15, 2003, at three o'clock?
8. Who do you think M. and Mme Lionel Desombre are?

Apply and Assess

Group Work

2 Have students form small groups. Assign one of the announcements to each group. Have the groups read the announcement and answer the related questions. Reporters from each group can give the group's answers to the class. Ask groups to share any other details they gleaned from the announcement.

Tactile Learners

2 Have students make their own birth announcements. Supply stationery or construction paper and markers. You might also have students bring in a baby picture of themselves to attach to the announcement. If students don't want to make their own birth announcements, have them create one for a TV or cartoon character.

STANDARDS: 1.2

3 Est-ce que ces phrases décrivent la culture française, la culture américaine ou les deux?

1. Dogs are not allowed in restaurants or department stores. American culture
2. The government gives money to all families with two or more children. French culture
3. Pets are tattooed with an identification number. French culture
4. Women have a paid maternity leave of 14 weeks. French culture

Ecrivons!

Write a paragraph describing the family in the picture. Give French names to all the family members, tell their ages, give brief physical descriptions, say something about their personalities, and mention one or two things they each like to do.

Stratégie pour écrire
Using details to describe people will enable you to help your reader develop a clearer mental picture of what you're writing about. The more detailed the writing, the sharper the mental image the reader gets of the subject.

A cluster diagram, like the one you created in Chapter 3, will help you organize your thoughts. Make a large circle for each family member, then attach smaller circles for age, physical description, and so on.

Using the information you organized in your cluster diagram, write a paragraph describing the family in the picture. Imagine that your readers have never seen this picture before. After reading your paragraph, they should feel as if they know the members of the family personally. Be sure to use descriptive words you learned in this chapter, but remember those you've learned in previous chapters as well!

Jeu de rôle

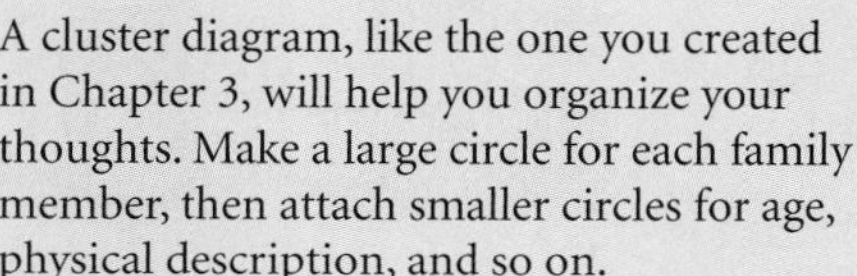

Your friends arrive at your door and suggest that you go out with them. Your parent tells them that you can go out if you finish your chores, so your friends offer to help. As you work around the house, you discuss where to go and what to do. Create a conversation with your classmates. Be prepared to act out the scene, using props.

Apply and Assess

Teaching Suggestion

4 Give each person in the illustration a name **(Adèle, Jean-Paul, Sophie, Laurent, Céline, Danielle, Emile)** and write the names across the board. Have students read their description of one of the people and have the class tell which person is being described.

Process Writing

4 Have students bring pictures of other families (real or fictional). Have them write a short description of the family they chose. Collect the papers and tape the pictures students brought to the board. Divide the class into several teams. Then, read aloud one of the descriptions to the class. The first team to correctly identify the family being described wins a point.

Que sais-je?

CHAPITRE 7

Teaching Resources
p. 224

PRINT 

- Grammar Tutor for Students of French, Chapter 7

MEDIA 

- Interactive CD-ROM Tutor, Disc 2
- Online self-test

 go.hrw.com
WA3 PARIS-7

Teacher Note

This page is intended to help students prepare for the Chapter Test. It is a brief checklist of the major points covered in the chapter. The students should be reminded that this is only a checklist and does not necessarily include everything that will appear on the test.

Answers

3 *Possible answers:*
1. La femme est brune, l'homme est blond et le garçon est roux.
2. Ils sont forts.

5
1. Je peux aller au cinéma? Est-ce que je peux aller au cinéma?
2. Je peux sortir avec des copains? Est-ce que je peux sortir avec des copains?
3. Je peux faire les magasins? Est-ce que je peux faire les magasins?
4. Je peux faire du patin à glace? Est-ce que je peux faire du patin à glace?

6 *Possible answers:*
Giving permission: Oui, si tu veux. Pourquoi pas? Oui, bien sûr. D'accord, si tu... d'abord...
Refusing: Pas question! Non, c'est impossible. Non, tu dois... Pas ce soir.

7 *Possible answers:*
faire la vaisselle, faire le ménage, ranger ma chambre, promener le chien, garder ma petite sœur, sortir la poubelle, débarrasser la table, laver la voiture, tondre le gazon, passer l'aspirateur

Que sais-je?

WA3 PARIS-7

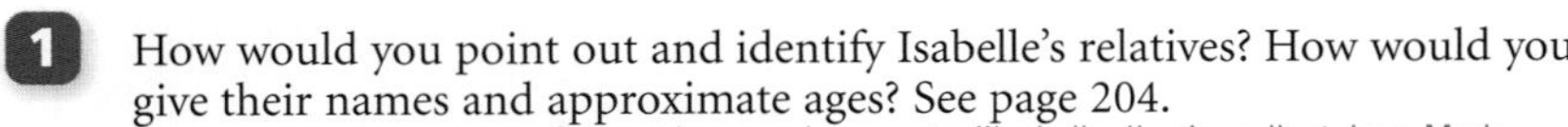

Can you use what you've learned in this chapter?

Can you identify people?
p. 203

1 How would you point out and identify Isabelle's relatives? How would you give their names and approximate ages? See page 204.
1. her grandparents Ce sont les grands-parents d'Isabelle. Ils s'appellent Jean-Marie et Eugénie Ménard. Ils ont soixante ans.
2. her uncle C'est l'oncle d'Isabelle. Il s'appelle Guillaume Ménard. Il a quarante ans.
3. her cousin Loïc C'est le cousin d'Isabelle. Il s'appelle Loïc. Il a dix-huit ans.
4. her brother C'est le frère d'Isabelle. Il s'appelle Alexandre. Il a onze ans.

Can you introduce people?
p. 207

2 How would you introduce your friend to . . .
1. an adult relative? Je vous présente...
2. a classmate? C'est... ; Je te présente...

Can you describe and characterize people?
p. 209

3 How would you describe these people? See answers below.

1.

2.

4 How would you . . .
1. tell a friend that he or she is nice? Tu es gentil(gentille).
2. tell several friends that they're annoying? Vous êtes embêtant(e)s/pénibles.
3. say that you and your friend are intelligent? Nous sommes intelligent(e)s.

Can you ask for, give, and refuse permission?
p. 213

5 How would you ask permission to . . . See answers below.
1. go to the movies?
2. go out with your friends?
3. go shopping?
4. go ice-skating?

6 How would you give someone permission to do something? How would you refuse? See answers below.

7 What are three things your parents might ask you to do before allowing you to go out with your friends? See answers below.

Review and Assess

Auditory Learners

3 Have students write descriptions of the people in the illustrations. Collect the papers, read some of the descriptions at random, and have students write the number of the illustration that fits each description you read.

Challenge

7 Have pairs of students use the answers they gave in Activity 7 to create and act out a conversation between a child and a parent. The child should ask for permission to go somewhere. The parent should grant permission on the condition that the child do the three things the students mentioned in Activity 7. Then, have students reverse roles.

STANDARDS: 1.1

Vocabulaire

Première étape

Identifying people

C'est...	*This/That is . . .*
Ce sont...	*These/those are . . .*
Voici...	*Here's . . .*
Voilà...	*There's . . .*

Family members

la famille	*family*
le grand-père	*grandfather*
la grand-mère	*grandmother*
la mère	*mother*
le père	*father*
le parent	*parent, relative*
la femme	*wife*
le mari	*husband*
la sœur	*sister*
le frère	*brother*
la fille	*daughter*
le fils	*son*
l'enfant (m./f.)	*child*
l'oncle (m.)	*uncle*
la tante	*aunt*
la cousine	*girl cousin*
le cousin	*boy cousin*
le chat	*cat*
le chien	*dog*
le canari	*canary*
le poisson	*fish*

Possessive adjectives

mon/ma/mes	*my*
ton/ta/tes	*your*
son/sa/ses	*his, her*
notre/nos	*our*
votre/vos	*your*
leur/leurs	*their*

Introducing people

C'est...	*This is . . .*
Je te/vous présente...	*I'd like you to meet . . .*
Très heureux (heureuse).	*Pleased to meet you.* (formal)

Other useful expressions

de	*of* (indicates relationship or ownership)

Deuxième étape

Describing and characterizing people

Il est comment?	*What is he like?*
Elle est comment?	*What is she like?*
Ils/Elles sont comment?	*What are they like?*
Il est...	*He is . . .*
Elle est...	*She is . . .*
Ils/Elles sont...	*They're . . .*
amusant(e)	*funny*
content(e)	*happy*
embêtant(e)	*annoying*
fort(e)	*strong*
gentil (gentille)	*nice*
intelligent(e)	*smart*
méchant(e)	*mean*
pénible	*annoying; a pain in the neck*
sympa(thique)	*nice*
timide	*shy*
âgé(e)	*older*
blond(e)	*blond*
brun(e)	*brunette*
grand(e)	*tall*
gros (grosse)	*fat*
jeune	*young*
mince	*slender*
mignon (mignonne)	*cute*
ne... ni grand(e) ni petit(e)	*neither tall nor short*
petit(e)	*short*
roux (rousse)	*redheaded*
être	*to be*

Troisième étape

Asking for, giving, and refusing permission

Tu es d'accord?	*Is that OK with you?*
(Est-ce que) je peux... ?	*May I . . . ?*
Oui, si tu veux.	*Yes, if you want to.*
Pourquoi pas?	*Why not?*
Oui, bien sûr.	*Yes, of course.*
D'accord, si tu... d'abord...	*OK, if you . . . first.*
Pas question!	*Out of the question!*
Non, c'est impossible.	*No, that's impossible.*
Non, tu dois...	*No, you've got to . . .*
Pas...	*Not . . .*

Chores

débarrasser la table	*to clear the table*
faire la vaisselle	*to do the dishes*
faire le ménage	*to clean house*
faire les courses	*to do the shopping*
garder...	*to look after . . .*
laver la voiture	*to wash the car*
passer l'aspirateur	*to vacuum*
promener le chien	*to walk the dog*
ranger ta chambre	*to pick up your room*
sortir la poubelle	*to take out the trash*
tondre le gazon	*to mow the lawn*

Review and Assess

Game

Jeu d'association Have students form small groups and arrange their desks in circles. You will need a small ball for each group. Start the game by calling out a word or expression from the **Vocabulaire (le chien)** and tossing the ball to a member of the group, who calls out a related word or expression **(le chat)**. Then, that student calls out another word and tosses the ball to another student who must catch the ball and say a related word, and so on. If a student drops the ball or can't think of a word, he or she is out. You might assign an arbiter to monitor each group. The last remaining player wins. As an alternative, you might play for points instead of eliminating players.

Vocabulaire

CHAPITRE 7

Circumlocution

Have students use the vocabulary from this chapter to come up with riddles for their partner to figure out. **(—C'est la femme du père. —La mère.)** You may want to award a prize to the student who can think of the most riddles, or to the pair who can answer the riddles with the fewest guesses.

Chapter 7 Assessment

- **Testing Program**
  Chapter Test, pp. 183–188

  Audio Compact Discs, CD 7, Trs. 24–26
  Speaking Test, p. 346
- **Alternative Assessment Guide**
  Performance Assessment, p. 38
  Portfolio Assessment, p. 24
  CD-ROM Assessment, p. 52
- **Interactive CD-ROM Tutor, Disc 2**

  A toi de parler
  A toi d'écrire
- **Standardized Assessment Tutor**
  Chapter 7
- **One-Stop Planner, Disc 2**
  Test Generator
  Chapter 7

STANDARDS: 1.1

Location Opener

CHAPTER 8

Teaching Resources
pp. 226–229

PRINT
- Lesson Planner, p. 38
- Video Guide, pp. 51–52

MEDIA
- One-Stop Planner
- Video Program
  Videocassette 3, 13:37–15:52
- DVD Tutor, Disc 2
- Interactive CD-ROM Tutor, Disc 2
- Map Transparency 2

go.hrw.com
WA3 ABIDJAN

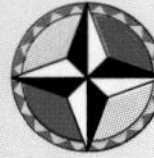

Using the Almanac and Map

Terms in the Almanac

- **L'Assemblée nationale**, the legislative body whose chamber is located in the Plateau, has 124 representatives, most of whom belong to the ruling political party, the **Parti Démocratique de Côte d'Ivoire (PDCI).**
- **Le palais du Président** is the residence of the Ivorian president. Overlooking the Ebrié Lagoon, the palace has several magnificent gardens.
- **Le parc national du Banco,** a 7,500-acre park outside of Abidjan, is the site of a thriving laundry business. Every morning in the park, hundreds of laundrymen come to the Banco River, pound the clothes on stones to get them clean, and spread them out to dry.
- **Le Musée national** gives ample evidence of Côte d'Ivoire's rich cultural heritage. The collection of over 20,000 art objects includes wooden statues and masks, jewelry, pottery, musical instruments, and furniture.

CHAPITRE 8

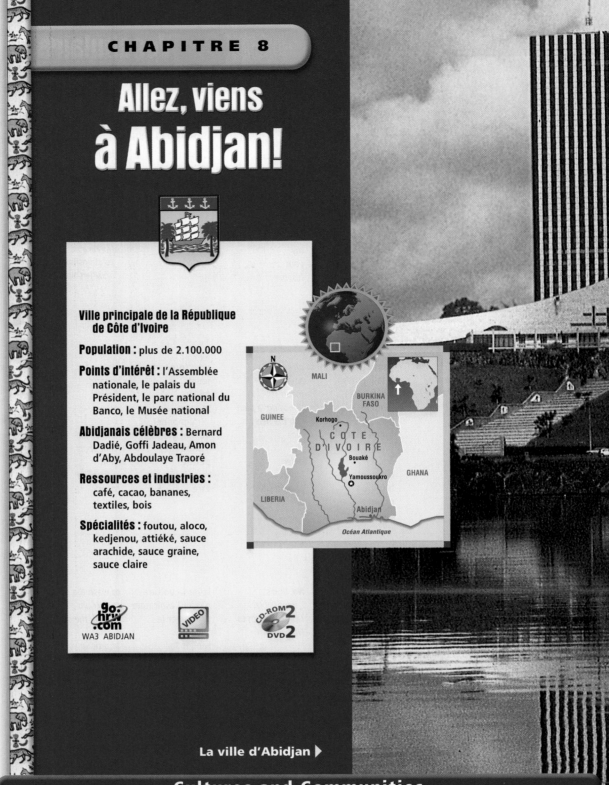

Allez, viens à Abidjan!

Ville principale de la République de Côte d'Ivoire

Population : plus de 2.100.000

Points d'intérêt : l'Assemblée nationale, le palais du Président, le parc national du Banco, le Musée national

Abidjanais célèbres : Bernard Dadié, Goffi Jadeau, Amon d'Aby, Abdoulaye Traoré

Ressources et industries : café, cacao, bananes, textiles, bois

Spécialités : foutou, aloco, kedjenou, attiéké, sauce arachide, sauce graine, sauce claire

N
MALI
BURKINA FASO
GUINEE
Korhogo
CÔTE D'IVOIRE
Bouaké
Yamoussoukro
GHANA
LIBERIA
Abidjan
Océan Atlantique

go.hrw.com WA3 ABIDJAN

VIDEO

CD-ROM 2 DVD 2

La ville d'Abidjan ▶

Cultures and Communities

Photo Flash!
Call students' attention to the skyline of Abidjan on these pages and point out the **Cathédrale Saint-Paul.** This eye-catching modern cathedral was consecrated by the Pope in 1985.

Background Information
Abidjan, the largest city of Côte d'Ivoire, is considered to be the economic capital of the country. Abidjan is located on a series of islands and drained lowlands and lies along the Ebrié Lagoon. In 1950, the construction of the Vridi Canal provided an effective passageway between the lagoon and the Gulf of Guinea, part of the Atlantic Ocean. This construction, along with Côte d'Ivoire's independence from France in 1960, has allowed the city to expand into one of the busiest seaports and financial centers of francophone West Africa.

STANDARDS: 2.2, 3.1, 5.1

Map Activity

As students look at the map, ask them to name the five countries that share a border with Côte d'Ivoire (Liberia, Guinée *(Guinea),* Mali, Burkina Faso, and Ghana). Ask students if they know that the former name of Burkina Faso was Upper Volta. Have students identify the capital city of Côte d'Ivoire (Yamoussoukro).

Connections and Comparisons

Geography/Architecture Link

Ask students to research other cities on the same latitude as Abidjan, which might have the same climate and vegetation. Ask students to find out how the buildings in Abidjan and other tropical cities are built to withstand the heavy rains of the wet season. What modifications do architects make for this kind of weather?

Thinking Critically

Comparing and Contrasting Ask students if Abidjan looks more like a European city or a North American city. Ask them to explain the reasons for their answers (for example, Abidjan looks more like Europe because Côte d'Ivoire is a former French colony and the French influence can still be seen; or it looks more like a North American city because of the preponderance of modern buildings).

STANDARDS: 2.2, 3.1, 4.2

Location Opener

CHAPTER 8

Using the Photo Essay

(1) A variety of fabrics, such as wax prints, kente cloth, indigo fabric, and woven cloth can be found in the markets in Abidjan. Kente cloth is a brightly colored fabric with intricate patterns made by the Ashanti in Ghana.

(3) **Le Plateau** is sometimes known as "little Manhattan" because of its imposing, tall buildings and its dominant position overlooking the water of the lagoon.

Architecture Link

(3) **La Pyramide,** the building shown in this photo, is located in the heart of the **Plateau** on avenue Franchet-d'Esperey. Because of its triangular, asymmetrical structure, **la Pyramide** is one of the city's most impressive examples of modern architecture.

History Link

In the eighteenth century, Queen Abla Pokou, the niece of King Osei Toutou, was leading several families out of Ghana after the king's death when they came upon the Comoë River and could not continue. The high priest asked that a child be given up in exchange for safe passage across the river. Legend has it that Pokou threw her only child into the waters, crying **"Baoulé"** *("The child is dead"),* and a group of hippos formed a "bridge" on which the families crossed the river. Through this experience, Queen Pokou gave the name **Baoulé** to the people who had followed her into what is now central Côte d'Ivoire.

Abidjan

Cette ville moderne est située sur la baie de Cocody en Côte d'Ivoire. C'est une ville pleine d'animation qu'on appelle souvent «le creuset de l'Afrique». Les bureaux et les hôtels du quartier du Plateau contrastent avec Treichville, un quartier pittoresque et très animé qui est le centre culturel d'Abidjan.

Visit Holt Online
go.hrw.com
KEYWORD: WA3 ABIDJAN
Activités Internet

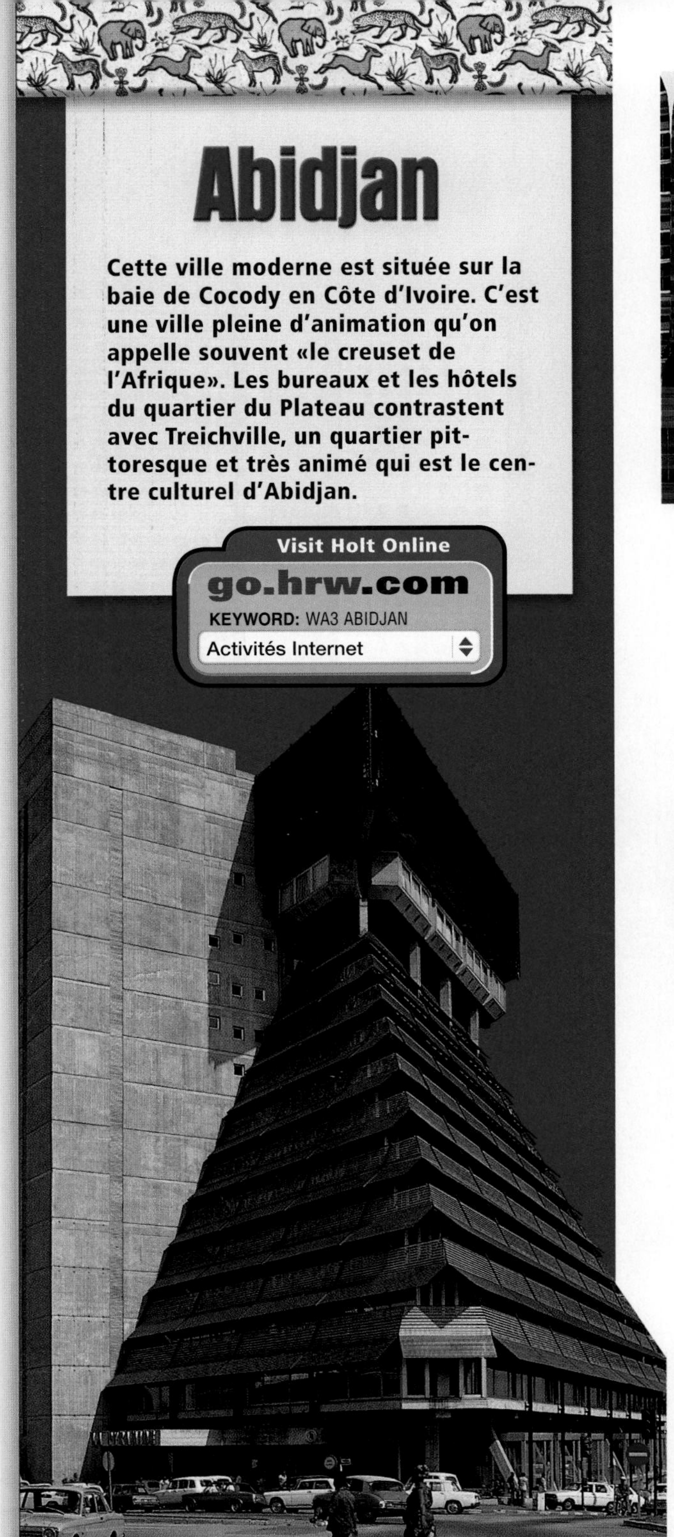

(1) Les tissus colorés
La Côte d'Ivoire est connue pour ses tissus très colorés.

(2) Les masques traditionnels
On peut voir beaucoup de masques traditionnels au Musée national d'Abidjan.

(3) Le Plateau
C'est le centre des affaires et du gouvernement à Abidjan.

Cultures and Communities

Culture Note

(2) Several ethnic groups in Côte d'Ivoire are known for their traditional masks. For example, the **Poro** system of life, on which the **Sénoufo** culture is based, follows a complex social code and philosophy. These people use wooden masks to communicate the teachings of their society. Many of these masks are made in artisan villages surrounding Korhogo in northern Côte d'Ivoire. The ceremonial masks of the **Dan** people, who belong to the larger **Malinké** region surrounding the city of Man in western Côte d'Ivoire, represent the powerful traditions of their group and can be found in museums all over the world.

STANDARDS: 2.2, 3.1, 5.1

5 **Treichville**
C'est le principal quartier commerçant d'Abidjan. On y découvre toutes sortes de couleurs, de sons et d'arômes. Ce quartier animé est un vrai plaisir pour les sens.

4 **Le parc Banco**
C'est un parc national depuis 1953, et une très belle réserve naturelle située dans la forêt tropicale.

Au chapitre 8, on va faire la connaissance de Djeneba, de sa famille, de sa prof d'anglais et d'Aminata. Djeneba nous fait visiter le marché d'Abidjan et on apprend comment faire du foutou qui est une spécialité de Côte d'Ivoire. Abidjan est une ville de contrastes. C'est une grande ville moderne, mais riche en traditions africaines.

6 **Le port d'Adjamé**
C'est un des ports les plus importants de l'Afrique occidentale.

Location Opener

CHAPTER 8

4 Parts of **le parc Banco** serve as coffee and cocoa plantations, managed by villagers who live in the area. There is also a small zoo in the center of the park near the lake.

Building on Previous Skills

4 Ask students if they have ever visited a national park. Have them brainstorm activities in French that they might do there **(faire du vélo, faire des photos).** Have them come up with a list of any animals that they might see in a national park.

5 **Treichville** is the African hub of Abidjan and is a very lively section of town, day and night. The Treichville market is the largest market in the city and is located across the street from the headquarters of the PDCI, the major political party of the country. This neighborhood is also known for its African restaurants and nightclubs, many of which are situated around the **avenue de la Reine-Pokou,** named for the ancient queen who gave the **Baoulé** people their name.

6 Many of the workers who built the city of Abidjan originally settled in the **Adjamé** area (a neighborhood north of the **Plateau**) before moving on to Treichville. In the Ebrié language, **Adjamé** means *place of meeting.* The busy port allows Côte d'Ivoire to maintain its trade in cocoa, coffee, and other products, although economic problems have slowed this trade in recent years.

Connections and Comparisons

Geography Link

4 **Le parc Banco** was established in 1926 outside of Abidjan as a forest reserve and was declared a national park in 1953. The southern part of Côte d'Ivoire, including **le parc Banco,** is dominated by tropical rain forests, which include many varieties of trees, such as palms, fruit trees, ebony, and mahogany. As you move north in the direction of the desert, the land becomes savannah, which is grassland covered with plants that withstand drought and fire. Côte d'Ivoire is fairly flat, except for the hills of Man and Odienné in the western and northwestern parts of the country.

STANDARDS: 2.2, 3.1

Chapitre 8 : Au marché

Chapter Overview

Mise en train pp. 232–234	***Une invitée pour le déjeuner***

	FUNCTIONS	GRAMMAR	VOCABULARY	RE-ENTRY
Première étape pp. 235–239	• Expressing need, p. 238	• The partitive and indefinite articles **du, de la, de l',** and **des,** p. 236 • **Avoir besoin de,** p. 238	• Grocery items, p. 235	• Food vocabulary **(Chapitre 5)** • The verb **avoir (Chapitre 2)** • Asking others what they need and telling what you need **(Chapitre 3)**
Deuxième étape pp. 240–244	• Making, accepting, and declining requests, p. 240 • Telling someone what to do, p. 240	• The verb **pouvoir**, p. 241 • **De** with expressions of quantity, p. 242	• Quantities of food and beverages, 242	• Activities **(Chapitre 1)** • The imperative **(Chapitre 5)**
Troisième étape pp. 245–249	• Offering, accepting, or refusing food, p. 247	• The pronoun **en,** p. 248	• Meals of the day, p. 245	• The verb **vouloir (Chapitre 6)**

Prononciation p. 249	**The sounds [o] and [ɔ]** Audio CD 8, Tracks 13–15	**A écrire** (dictation) Audio CD 8, Tracks 16–18	
Lisons! pp. 250–251	**La cuisine africaine**	**Reading Strategy:** Recognizing false cognates	
Grammaire supplémentaire	**pp. 252–255** **Première étape,** pp. 252–253	**Deuxième étape,** p. 253	**Troisième étape,** pp. 254–255
Review pp. 256–259	**Mise en pratique,** pp. 256–257 **Ecrivons!** Arranging ideas spatially Writing a food ad	**Que sais-je?** p. 258	**Vocabulaire,** p. 259

CULTURE

- **Panorama Culturel,** Shopping for groceries in francophone countries, p. 239
- **Note culturelle,** The metric system, p. 242
- **Rencontre culturelle,** Foods of Côte d'Ivoire, p. 244
- **Note culturelle,** Mealtimes in francophone countries, p. 246

Chapitre 8 : Au marché
Chapter Resources

Lesson Planning

One-Stop Planner

Lesson Planner with Differentiated Instruction, pp. 38–42, 72

Student Make-Up Assignments
- Make-Up Assignment Copying Masters, Chapter 8

Listening and Speaking

TPR Storytelling Book, pp. 29–32

Listening Activities
- Student Response Forms for Listening Activities, pp. 59–61
- Additional Listening Activities 8-1 to 8-6, pp. 63–65
- Additional Listening Activities (song), p. 66
- Scripts and Answers, pp. 137–141

Video Guide
- Teaching Suggestions, pp. 54–55
- Activity Masters, pp. 56–58
- Scripts and Answers, pp. 105–106, 121

Activities for Communication
- Communicative Activities, pp. 43–48
- Realia and Teaching Suggestions, pp. 110–114
- Situation Cards, pp. 151–152

Reading and Writing

Reading Strategies and Skills Handbook, Chapter 8

Joie de lire 1, Chapter 8

Cahier d'activités, pp. 85–96

Grammar

Travaux pratiques de grammaire, pp. 61–70

Grammar Tutor for Students of French, Chapter 8

Assessment

Testing Program
- Grammar and Vocabulary Quizzes, **Etape** Quizzes, and Chapter Test, pp. 197–214
- Score Sheet, Scripts and Answers, pp. 215–222

Alternative Assessment Guide
- Portfolio Assessment, p. 25
- Performance Assessment, p. 39
- CD-ROM Assessment, p. 53

Student Make-Up Assignments
- Alternative Quizzes, Chapter 8

Standardized Assessment Tutor
- Reading, pp. 31–33
- Writing, p. 34
- Math, pp. 51–52

Middle School

Middle School Teaching Resources, Chapter 8

Online Activities
- **Jeux interactifs**
- **Activités Internet**

Video Program
- Videocassette 3
- Videocassette 5 (captioned version)

Interactive CD-ROM Tutor, Disc 2

DVD Tutor, Disc 2

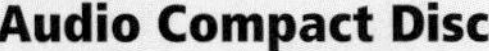

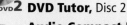

Audio Compact Discs
- Textbook Listening Activities, CD 8, Tracks 1–19
- Additional Listening Activities, CD 8, Tracks 26–32
- Assessment Items, CD 8, Tracks 20–25

Teaching Transparencies
- Situation 8-1 to 8-3
- Vocabulary 8-A to 8-D
- **Mise en train**
- **Grammaire supplémentaire** Answers
- **Travaux pratiques de grammaire** Answers

One-Stop Planner CD-ROM

Use the **One-Stop Planner CD-ROM with Test Generator** to aid in lesson planning and pacing.

For each chapter, the **One-Stop Planner** includes:
- Editable lesson plans with direct links to teaching resources
- Printable worksheets from resource books
- Direct launches to the HRW Internet activities
- Video and audio segments
- Test Generator
- Clip Art for vocabulary items

Chapitre 8 : Au marché

Projects

Jour de marché

Students will role-play a marketplace scene, acting as vendors and customers.

TEACHER NOTE

You might have students do this project after they complete the **Première étape,** where they will learn about a variety of food items from Côte d'Ivoire.

MATERIALS

✂ **Students may need**

- A variety of foods
- Plates, platters, or bowls
- A small knife for cutting food
- Cardboard
- Tape or glue
- Colored markers
- Paper, pen, pencil

SUGGESTED SEQUENCE

1. Before "market day," ask students to find out if there are any tropical fruits available locally. Have them refer to the **Vocabulaire** on page 235. Then, bring in or have students bring in some of these foods.
2. Ask for five or six volunteers to be the vendors; the others will be the customers. Have the vendors make signs for their stands and set up the marketplace. Several students might work together on one stand. Have the customers make paper money.
3. On "market day," have the vendors set up their stands and clean and cut the foods into portions so that everyone can "buy" some. All the shopping, bargaining, and purchasing should then be conducted in French.
4. After everyone has shopped and tried some of the foods, have students clean up. Then, have them write about the experience, giving their opinions of the foods they tried.

GRADING THE PROJECT

This is an ungraded project, but you might choose to give participation grades or a grade for the writing assignment.

TEACHER NOTE

In the Postreading section of **Lisons!** on page 251, you will find another suggested project that can be graded.

Games

Quels ingrédients?

In this game, students will practice expressing need as well as food vocabulary.

Procedure The game begins with one student naming a particular dish or meal: **un sandwich, une salade, une salade de fruits, une omelette, le déjeuner.** The next student names one ingredient needed for that particular dish or meal. Subsequent students repeat all the previously mentioned ingredients and add another. For example, the first student might say **un sandwich.** The next student would say **Il faut du pain.** The third student would say **Il faut du pain et du jambon.** When a student is unable to repeat the order correctly, start a new round with a different food item. This game can be played either by going in order around the class, or by randomly calling on students, which is more difficult. You might want to have one or two students act as judges, who write down the ingredients as they are mentioned to verify the correct order.

Qu'est-ce qu'on fait?

This game will test students' recognition of the ingredients for various recipes.

Procedure This game can be played by individuals, partners, or small groups. Read aloud a list of ingredients for a particular dish that students are familiar with. Students will try to guess what dish it is within a given time. You might want to consult a cookbook for recipes, or use the recipes that students create for the **Lisons!** activity on page 251. Students may guess in English if they have not learned the French name of a particular dish.

Example:

du pain, du fromage, du jambon, du beurre
(un croque-monsieur)

STANDARDS: 1.3, 5.2

Storytelling

Mini-histoire

*This story accompanies Teaching Transparency 8-2. The **mini-histoire** can be told and retold in different formats, acted out, written down, and read aloud, to give students additional opportunities to practice all four skills. The following story is about shopping.*

La mère dit à Martine : «Tu peux aller faire des courses?» «Bon, d'accord» dit Martine. «J'y vais tout de suite. Qu'est-ce que tu veux?» La mère prépare une liste et dit : «J'ai besoin d'un litre de lait, de deux kilos de pommes de terre, de deux kilos de riz, de trois kilos de tomates, d'une douzaine d'œufs, de fromage et de mangues».
Martine court au supermarché. Elle a faim. Elle adore les gâteaux et elle achète une tarte aux fraises qu'elle mange tout de suite. Elle aime faire les courses; il y a des tas de choses à voir, à goûter. Elle va acheter les fruits, les légumes et le lait. Elle n'a rien oublié et sa mère est contente.

Traditions

Masques

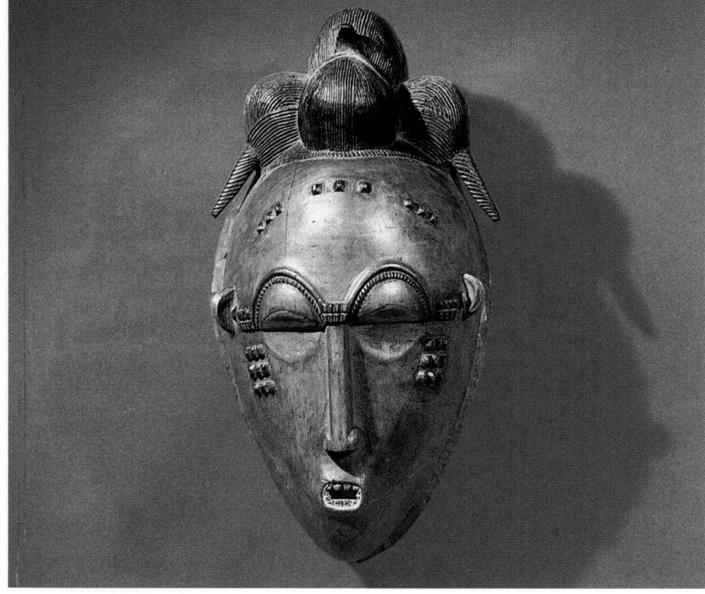

The people of Côte d'Ivoire use masks in many of their public celebrations and private rituals, ranging from funerals and harvest celebrations to coming-of-age ceremonies and initiations. Masks do not hide the identity of the wearer, but rather create a new identity for him. Carved from wood and decorated with beads, metals, and ivory by experienced craftsmen, masks represent entities from the spirit world, legendary animals, or mythological beings. Some masks are made for a single special occasion while others are passed down from one generation to the next. Have students use the Internet or books from their local library to research masks from Côte d'Ivoire. Then, have them choose one and recreate it using materials available to them.

Recette

***Ignames** (yams) are celebrated in Côte d'Ivoire the whole year round. The celebrations mark the end of each good harvest season. They occur in February in the West and during the summer months in the North and the South. The festivals go on all year long in the eastern part of the country.*

IGNAMES A LA TOMATE

pour 4 personnes

2 ignames *(patates douces)*
2 oignons coupés
1/2 tasse de pâte de tomates
2 tasses d'eau
2 cuillères à soupe d'huile végétale
poivre
piments (à volonté)

Eplucher et couper les oignons et les faire cuire dans l'huile. Ajouter la pâte de tomates et l'eau. Mélanger. Ajouter les ignames, le poivre et les piments. Laisser mijoter jusqu'à ce que les ignames soient bien cuites. Servir avec du riz, du poisson ou de la viande.

STANDARDS: 1.3, 2.2, 3.2

Chapitre 8 : Au marché
Technology

DVD/Video

Videocassette 3, Videocassette 5 (captioned version)
DVD Tutor, Disc 2
See Video Guide, pp. 53–58.

Mise en train • Une invitée pour le déjeuner

In this segment of the video, Djeneba's mother (Mme Diomandé) and aunt (Aminata) are discussing what to prepare for lunch. Djeneba's mother asks Djeneba to go shopping at the market. She tells her what she needs for lunch. At the market, Djeneba buys fish, tomatoes, rice, and other things her mother asked for. When she returns home, she and her mother prepare lunch. When they are almost done, someone knocks at the door, and Djeneba realizes that she forgot to tell her mother that she had invited a guest for lunch!

Où est-ce que tu aimes faire des provisions?

Several teenagers from different French-speaking countries tell us where they go shopping for groceries.

Une invitée pour le déjeuner (suite)

When the story continues, we discover that Miss Riggs, Djeneba's English teacher, is at the door. The next scene is a flashback to the market where Miss Riggs is asking Djeneba how to make **sauce arachide.** Djeneba tells her that her mother is making it for lunch and invites Miss Riggs. Back home, Djeneba's mother tells Miss Riggs about **sauce arachide.** At the table, Djeneba's mother offers everyone **foutou** and **sauce arachide.**

Vidéoclips

- **Andros®**: advertisement for fruit compote
- **Garbit®**: advertisement for paëlla (a popular Spanish dish made with rice and seafood)

Interactive CD-ROM Tutor

Activity	Activity Type	Pupil's Edition Page
En contexte	*Interactive conversation*	
1. Vocabulaire	Chasse au trésor Explorons!/Vérifions!	p. 235
2. Vocabulaire	Chacun à sa place	p. 235
3. Grammaire	Le bon choix	p. 236
4. Grammaire	Les mots qui manquent	p. 241
5. Vocabulaire	Jeu des paires	p. 242
6. Comment dit-on... ?	Chacun à sa place	pp. 240, 247
Panorama Culturel	Où est-ce que tu aimes faire des provisions? Le bon choix	p. 239
A toi de parler	*Guided recording*	pp. 256–257
A toi d'écrire	*Guided writing*	pp. 256–257

Teacher Management System

Launch the program, type "admin" in the password area, and press RETURN. Log on to **www.hrw.com/CDROMTUTOR** for a detailed explanation of the Teacher Management System.

DVD Tutor

The *DVD Tutor* contains all material from the *Video Program* as described above. French captions are available for use at your discretion for all sections of the video. The *DVD Tutor* also provides a variety of video-based activities that assess students' understanding of the **Mise en train, Suite,** and **Panorama Culturel.**

This part of the *DVD Tutor* may be used on any DVD video player connected to a television or video monitor.

In addition to the video material and the video-based comprehension activities, the *DVD Tutor* also contains the entire *Interactive CD-ROM Tutor* in DVD-ROM format. Each DVD disc contains the activities from all 12 chapters of the *Interactive CD-ROM Tutor.*

This part of the *DVD Tutor* may be used on a Macintosh® or Windows® computer with a DVD-ROM drive.

To preview all resources available for this chapter, use the **One-Stop Planner CD-ROM,** Disc 2.

Go.Online!

Online Edition

The Online Edition for Allez, viens! *allows students access to their textbooks anytime anywhere.*

- *Audio at point of use*
- *Additional practice activities*
- *Self-test activities*
- *Online reference tools*
- *Entire Video Program (Enhanced version)*
- *Interactive Notebook (Enhanced version)*

video

audio

presentation

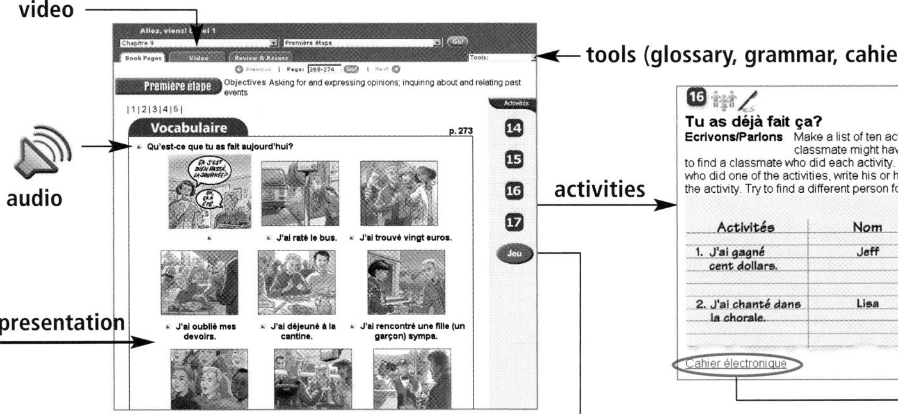

tools (glossary, grammar, cahier électronique)

activities

Notebook

HRW Atlas

Internet Activités

Activités Internet

These guided internet activities include a worksheet and pre-selected and pre-screened authentic web sites from the francophone world. You can use these activities

- to help students develop research skills in the target language
- to introduce students to authentic cultural information
- as a project

Jeux interactifs

You can use the interactive activities in this chapter

- to practice grammar, vocabulary, and chapter functions
- as homework
- as an assessment option
- as a self-test
- to prepare for the Chapter Test

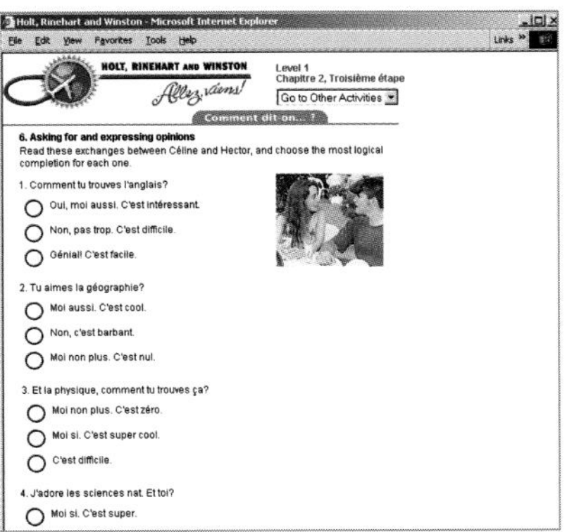

Projet Tell students that they are at a friend's place in Abidjan. They love Ivorian cuisine and want to help their hostess prepare a special dish. Have them search the Web for a typical Ivorian recipe. Then, have them do a search to find out where they can purchase all the ingredients necessary to prepare that dish. They should describe the shopping place (name, location, size, atmosphere).

Chapitre 8 : Au marché

Textbook Listening Activities Scripts 

Première étape

7 p. 236

1. — Comment sont ces fraises?
— Bof, elles ne sont pas très mûres.

2. — Tu aimes ce poisson?
— Ça va. Rien de spécial.

3. — Elle est comment, cette mangue?
— Elle est délicieuse. Mais moi, j'adore les mangues!

4. — Comment est ce poulet?
— Pas mauvais.

5. — Alors? Ces haricots? Ils sont bons?
— Pas terribles.

Answers to Activity 7
1. fruit
2. fish
3. fruit
4. poultry
5. vegetables

Deuxième étape

14 p. 241

1. — Eh bien, Jean-Luc, tu peux aller faire les courses aujourd'hui?
— Euh, je regrette, mais je n'ai pas le temps.

2. — Sylvie, tu me rapportes du lait cet après-midi?
— Bon, d'accord.

3. — Robert! Rapporte-moi du beurre! N'oublie pas!
— Mais, Maman, je ne peux pas maintenant!

4. — Annie, tu peux acheter des fraises pour le dîner?
— Tout de suite.

5. — Euh, Chantal, achète-moi un paquet de riz cet après-midi!
— Je veux bien.

Answers to Activity 14

a. 1. making a request
2. making a request
3. telling someone what to do
4. making a request
5. telling someone what to do

b. 1. declines
2. accepts
3. declines
4. accepts
5. accepts

17 p. 243

1. — Bonjour, monsieur. Je voudrais douze tranches de jambon, s'il vous plaît.
— Voilà.
— C'est combien?
— Six euros vingt.

2. — Bonjour, madame. Est-ce que vous avez des fraises, s'il vous plaît?
— Oui, regardez, elles sont mûres!
— Alors, je vais prendre un kilo de fraises.
— Voilà. Ça fait trois euros vingt-neuf.
— Tenez.
— Merci bien. Au revoir.

3. — Bonjour, madame. C'est combien, l'eau minérale, s'il vous plaît?
— Un euro soixante la bouteille.
— Bien, je vais prendre trois bouteilles.
— Tenez.
— Merci. Ça fait combien?
— Quatre euros quatre-vingts.
— Tenez.
— Merci.

4. — Je voudrais un morceau de fromage, s'il vous plaît, monsieur.
— Voilà.
— Je vais aussi prendre une douzaine d'œufs.
— C'est tout?
— Oui.
— Alors, ça vous fait... cinq euros.
— Voilà.
— Merci.

Answers to Activity 17
1. twelve slices of ham
2. a kilo of strawberries
3. three bottles of mineral water
4. a piece of cheese, a dozen eggs

The following scripts are for the listening activities found in the *Pupil's Edition.* For Student Response Forms, see *Listening Activities,* pages 59–61. To provide students with additional listening practice, see *Listening Activities,* pages 63–66.

One-Stop Planner CD-ROM

To preview all resources available for this chapter, use the **One-Stop Planner CD-ROM,** Disc 2.

Troisième étape

21 p. 246

1. — Dis, Anne, qu'est-ce que tu prends d'habitude au petit déjeuner?
— Oh, d'habitude, je prends un chocolat, du pain, du beurre et de la confiture.

2. — Pardon, monsieur. Qu'est-ce que vous prenez en général au petit déjeuner?
— Je prends un café, un jus d'orange et des fruits.

3. — Bonjour, madame. Qu'est-ce que vous prenez d'habitude au petit déjeuner?
— J'aime bien prendre du lait avec des céréales, du pain avec du beurre et un jus d'orange.

Answers to Activity 21
1. c
2. a
3. b

25 p. 247

1. Vous prenez de la salade?
2. Merci. Je n'ai plus faim.
3. Oui, avec plaisir.
4. Encore du poisson?
5. Non, merci.

Answers to Activity 25
1. offering
2. refusing
3. accepting
4. offering
5. refusing

PRONONCIATION, P. 249

For the scripts for Parts A and B, see p. 249. The script for Part C is below.

C. A écrire *(dictation)*

— Tu peux aller faire les courses aujourd'hui?
— D'accord. Qu'est-ce qu'il te faut?
— Il me faut deux kilos de pommes de terre, du fromage et un gâteau.

Mise en pratique

1 p. 256

Mesdames, messieurs, aujourd'hui, profitez de nos prix exceptionnels sur l'alimentation! Le kilo de carottes à un euro vingt-cinq, le kilo de pommes de terre à un euro treize et les deux kilos d'oranges, trois euros cinq. Et ce n'est pas fini! Cinq euros trente-quatre, le poulet. Sept euros soixante-quinze, le kilo de jambon. Des prix aussi sur les produits laitiers! Les six litres de lait à trois euros quatre-vingt-seize; un euro cinquante-quatre, la douzaine d'œufs! Alors, vous hésitez encore? Dépêchez-vous. Remplissez vos placards! Faites de bonnes affaires!

Possible answers to Mise en pratique, Activity 1
1 kilo of carrots, 1.25€;
1 kilo of potatoes, 1.13€;
2 kilos of oranges, 3.05€;
1 chicken, 5.34€;
1 kilo of ham, 7.75€;
6 liters of milk, 3.96€;
1 dozen eggs, 1.54€

Chapitre 8 : Au marché

50-Minute Lesson Plans

Day 1

CHAPTER OPENER 5 min.
- Culture Note, ATE, p. 230
- Thinking Critically, ATE, p. 231.
- Present Chapter Objectives, ATE, p. 231.

MISE EN TRAIN 40 min.
- Presenting **Mise en train** and Preteaching Vocabulary, ATE, p. 232
- Teaching Suggestion and Photo Flash, ATE, p. 233
- Do Activities 1–6, p. 234.

Wrap-Up 5 min.
- Multicultural Link, ATE, p. 233

Homework Options
Cahier d'activités, p. 85, Acts. 1–2

Day 2

PREMIERE ETAPE
Quick Review 10 min.
- Check homework.
- Bell Work, ATE, p. 235

Vocabulaire, p. 235 15 min.
- Presenting **Vocabulaire,** ATE, p. 235, using Teaching Transparencies 8-A and 8-B
- Language Notes, ATE, p. 235
- Play Audio CD for Activity 7, p. 236.

Grammaire, p. 236 15 min.
- Presenting **Grammaire,** ATE, p. 236
- Do Activities 8–9, pp. 236–237.
- Additional Practice, ATE, p. 236
- Discuss **Note culturelle,** p. 237, and Culture Note, ATE, p. 237.

Wrap-Up 10 min.
- Play Game: **Attrape-le!,** ATE, p. 235.

Homework Options
Cahier d'activités, pp. 86–87, Acts. 3–6
Travaux pratiques de grammaire, pp. 61–65, Acts. 1–9

Day 3

PREMIERE ETAPE
Quick Review 10 min.
- Check homework.
- Write **Légumes, Fruits, Produits laitiers,** and **Viandes** on the chalk board. Place flash cards of the food items written in French under the categories in random order. Have students tell in which category to correctly place the food items.

Comment dit-on... ?, p. 238 10 min.
- Presenting **Comment dit-on... ?,** ATE, p. 238
- Discuss **A la française,** p. 238 and Language-to-Language, ATE, p. 238.
- Cahier d'activités, p. 88, Act. 8

Note de grammaire, p. 238 20 min.
- Discuss **Note de grammaire,** p. 238.
- Do Activities 11–12, p. 238.
- Travaux pratiques de grammaire, p. 65, Act. 10.

Wrap-Up 10 min.
- Activities for Communication, pp. 43–44, Communicative Activity 8-1A and 8-1B

Homework Options
Study for the **Première étape** quiz.

Day 4

PREMIERE ETAPE
Quiz 8-1 20 min.
- Administer Quiz 8-1A or 8-1B.

PANORAMA CULTUREL 25 min.
- Presenting **Panorama Culturel,** p. 239, using Videocassette 3
- Have students answer **Qu'en penses-tu?** questions, p. 239.
- Read **Savais-tu que... ?,** p. 239.
- **Panorama Culturel,** Interactive CD-ROM Tutor, Disc 2

Wrap-Up 5 min.
- Prepare short lists of the food items in French with their spellings scrambled. Write one of the scrambled lists on the chalkboard and have teams of students race to unscramble the words to earn points.

Homework Options
Cahier d'activités, p. 96, Acts. 26–28

Day 5

DEUXIEME ETAPE
Quick Review 10 min.
- Bell Work, ATE, p. 240

Comment dit-on... ?, p. 240 15 min.
- Presenting **Comment dit-on... ?,** ATE, p. 240
- Play Audio CD for Activity 14, p. 241.

Grammaire, p. 241 15 min.
- Presenting **Grammaire,** ATE, p. 241
- Do Activity 15, p. 241.
- **Grammaire supplémentaire,** p. 253, Acts. 4–5

Wrap-Up 10 min.
- Write activities that students have learned to say in French on the board (such as **nager, danser, faire du ski,...**). Have students interview each other to see if they can do the activities listed.

Homework Options
Cahiers d'activités, pp. 89–90, Acts. 10–14
Travaux pratiques de grammaire, p. 66, Acts. 11–12

Day 6

DEUXIEME ETAPE
Quick Review 10 min.
- Check homework.
- Visual Learners, ATE, p. 240

Vocabulaire, p. 242 30 min.
- Presenting **Vocabulaire,** ATE, p. 242, using Teaching Transparency 8-C
- Discuss **Note de grammaire,** p. 242.
- **Grammaire supplémentaire,** p. 253, Activity 6
- Discuss **Note culturelle,** p. 242. See Thinking Critically, ATE, p. 242.
- Travaux pratiques de grammaire, pp. 67–68, Acts. 13–16

Wrap-Up 10 min.
- Activities for Communication, p. 152, Situation Card 8-2: Role-play

Homework Options
Study for the **Deuxième étape** quiz.

For alternative lesson plans by chapter section, to create your own customized plans, or to preview all resources available for this chapter, use the **One-Stop Planner CD-ROM**, Disc 2.

For additional homework suggestions, see activities accompanied by this symbol throughout the chapter.

Day 7

DEUXIEME ETAPE

Quiz 8-2 20 min.
- Administer Quiz 8-2A or 8-2B.

RENCONTRE CULTURELLE 25 min.
- Presenting **Rencontre culturelle,** ATE, p. 244
- Do **Qu'en penses-tu?** questions, p. 244.
- Read **Savais-tu que... ?,** p. 244.
- Discuss Culture Notes, ATE, p. 244.

Wrap-Up 5 min.
- Discuss with students the most unusual dishes they have ever tried and how they liked them.

Homework Options
Have students search for recipes for other Ivorian dishes at the library or on the Internet.

Day 8

TROISIEME ETAPE

Quick Review 10 min.
- Have students share any recipes they found for Ivorian dishes.
- Bell Work, ATE, p. 245

Vocabulaire, p. 245 30 min.
- Presenting **Vocabulaire,** ATE, p. 245, using Teaching Transparency 8-D
- Culture Notes, ATE, p. 246
- Play Audio CD for Activity 21, p. 246.
- Discuss **Note culturelle,** p. 246.
- Do Activities 22–24, pp. 246–247.

Wrap-Up 10 min.
- Play Game: **Qu'est-ce qu'on fait?,** ATE, p. 229C. Have students guess the dish as well as the meal at which it would most likely be served.

Homework Options
Cahier d'activités, p. 92, Acts. 19–20
Travaux pratiques de grammaire, p. 69, Acts. 17–18

Day 9

TROISIEME ETAPE

Quick Review 5 min.
- Check homework.

Comment dit-on... ?, p. 247 15 min.
- Presenting **Comment dit-on... ?,** ATE, p. 247
- Play Audio CD for Activity 25, p. 247.
- Cahier d'activités, p. 92, Act. 21

Grammaire, p. 248 15 min.
- Presenting **Grammaire,** ATE, p. 248
- Do Activity 27, p. 248.
- Travaux pratiques de grammaire, p. 70, Acts. 19–20

Prononciation, p. 249 10 min.
- Complete presentation and do Activities A–C, p. 249, using Audio CD 8.

Wrap-Up 5 min.
- Review for Quiz 8-3, pp. 245–249.

Homework Options
Study for **Troisième étape** quiz.

Day 10

TROISIEME ETAPE

Quiz 8-3 20 min.
- Administer Quiz 8-3A or 8-3B.

LISONS! 25 min.
- Motivating Activity: Have students look at the photos and describe the foods.
- Read and discuss the **Stratégie pour lire,** p. 250. Then do Prereading Activities A–D, Using Prior Knowledge, ATE, p. 250.
- Do Reading Activities E–H, p. 250.

Wrap-Up 5 min.
- Math Link, ATE, p. 251

Homework Options
Cahier d'activités, p. 95, Act. 25

Day 11

LISONS!

Quick Review 10 min.
- Check homework.
- Postreading Activity I, Thinking Critically, ATE, p. 251

MISE EN PRATIQUE 30 min.
- Play Audio CD for Activity 1, p. 256.
- Do Activities 2–3, pp. 256–257.
- Begin **Ecrivons!,** p. 257.

Wrap-Up 10 min.
- Have partners complete **Jeu de rôle,** p. 257.

Homework Options
Que sais-je?, p. 258
Finish **Ecrivons!,** p. 257.

Day 12

MISE EN PRATIQUE

Quick Review 15 min.
- Check homework and collect **Ecrivons!**
- Play Game: **Quels ingrédients?** ATE, p. 229C.

Chapter Review 35 min.
- Review Chapter 8. Choose from **Grammaire supplémentaire,** Grammar Tutor for Students of French, Activities for Communication, Listening Activities, Interactive CD-ROM Tutor, or **Jeux interactifs.**

Homework Options
Study for Chapter 8 Test.

Assessment

Test, Chapter 8 50 min.
- Administer Chapter 8 Test. Select from Testing Program, Alternative Assessment Guide, Test Generator, or Standardized Assessment Tutor.

Chapitre 8 : Au marché
90-Minute Lesson Plans

Block 1

CHAPTER OPENER **5 min.**
- Culture Note, Career Path, ATE, p. 230
- Thinking Critically, ATE, p. 231
- Present Chapter Objectives, ATE, p. 231.

MISE EN TRAIN **45 min.**
- Motivating Activity: Ask students what they normally eat for lunch. What would they make if a guest were coming for lunch?
- Presenting **Mise en train,** ATE, p. 232
- Photo Flash, ATE p. 233; Teaching Suggestion and Multicultural Link, ATE, p. 233
- View video of **Mise en train,** Videocassette 3, Video Guide, p. 53. Do Activities 1–2, Video Guide, p. 56, Activity Master 1.

PREMIERE ETAPE
Vocabulaire, p. 235 **35 min.**
- Bell Work, ATE, p. 235
- Presenting **Vocabulaire,** ATE, p. 235, with Language Notes, ATE, p. 235.
- Play Audio CD for Activity 7, p. 236. See Challenge, ATE, p. 236.
- Culture Note, ATE, p. 237

Wrap-Up **5 min.**
- Summarize what happened in the **Mise en train** using Chapter 8 **Mise en train** Transparencies.

Homework Options
Travaux pratiques de grammaire, pp. 61–62, Acts. 1–4
Cahier d'activités, p. 86, Acts. 3–4

Block 2

PREMIERE ETAPE
Quick Review **10 min.**
- Check homework.
- Show pictures of food items presented on p. 235 and ask students: **Qu'est-ce que c'est?**

Grammaire, p. 236 **30 min.**
- Presenting **Grammaire,** ATE, p. 236
- Do Activity 8, p. 236. See Additional Practice, ATE, p. 236.
- **Grammaire supplémentaire,** p. 252, Acts. 1–2
- **Note culturelle,** p. 237
- Do Activity 10, p. 237.

Comment dit-on... ?, p. 238 **30 min.**
- Presenting **Comment dit-on... ?,** ATE, p. 238
- **Note de grammaire,** p. 238
- Do Activity 11, p. 238, orally.
- **Grammaire supplémentaire,** p. 252, Act. 3
- **A la française,** p. 238 and Language-to-Language, ATE, p. 238
- **Vocabulaire à la carte,** p. 238
- Do Activity 13, p. 238.

PANORAMA CULTUREL **15 min.**
- Presenting **Panorama Culturel,** ATE, p. 239
- Answer the **Qu'en penses-tu?** questions, p. 239.
- Read **Savais-tu que... ?,** p. 239.

Wrap-Up **5 min.**
- Game: **Attrape-le!,** ATE, p. 235

Homework Options
Study for **Première étape** quiz.
Travaux pratiques de grammaire, pp. 63–65, Acts. 5–10
Cahier d'activités, pp. 87–88, Acts. 5–9

Block 3

PREMIERE ETAPE
Quick Review **10 min.**
- Activities for Communication, p. 151, Situation Card 8-1: Interview

Quiz 8-1 **20 min.**
- Administer Quiz 8-1A or 8-1B.

DEUXIEME ETAPE
Comment dit-on... ?, p. 240 **20 min.**
- Bell Work, ATE, p. 240
- Presenting **Comment dit-on... ?,** ATE, p. 240, Language Note, ATE, p. 240
- Play Audio CD for Activity 14, p. 241.
- **A la française,** p. 241. See Language Note, ATE, p. 241

Grammaire: the verb *pouvoir,* p. 241 **25 min.**
- Presenting **Grammaire: the verb *pouvoir,*** ATE, p. 241, Language-to-Language, ATE, p. 241
- Do Activity 15, p. 241.
- **Grammaire supplémentaire,** p. 253, Acts. 4 and 5
- Do Activity 16, p. 241. See Challenge, ATE, p. 241.

Wrap-Up **15 min.**
- Activities for Communication, pp. 43–44, Communicative Activity 8-1A and 8-2B. Present to class.

Homework Options
Travaux pratiques de grammaire, p. 66, Acts. 11–12
Cahier d'activités, pp. 89–90, Acts. 10–14

One-Stop Planner CD-ROM

For alternative lesson plans by chapter section, to create your own customized plans, or to preview all resources available for this chapter, use the **One-Stop Planner CD-ROM**, Disc 2.

For additional homework suggestions, see activities accompanied by this symbol throughout the chapter.

Block 4

DEUXIEME ETAPE

Quick Review 10 min.
- Activities for Communication, pp. 45–46, Communicative Activity 8-2A and 8-2B

Vocabulaire, p. 242 35 min.
- Presenting **Vocabulaire,** ATE, p. 242. See Language Notes and Culture Note, ATE, p. 243
- **Note de grammaire,** p. 242. See Teacher Note, ATE, p. 243
- Play Audio CD for Activity 17, p. 243.
- Do Activity 18, p. 243.
- **Grammaire supplémentaire,** p. 253, Act. 6
- **Note culturelle,** p. 242 and Math Link, ATE, p. 242

RENCONTRE CULTURELLE 15 min.
- Presenting **Rencontre culturelle,** ATE, p. 244
- Culture Notes, ATE, p. 244
- Answer the **Qu'en penses-tu?** questions, p. 244.
- Read **Savais-tu que... ?,** p. 244.

TROISIEME ETAPE

Vocabulaire, p. 245 25 min.
- Presenting **Vocabulaire,** ATE, p. 245 with Culture Notes, ATE p. 246 and Language Note, ATE, p. 247
- Play Audio CD for Activity 21, p. 246. See Slower Pace, ATE, p. 246.
- **Note culturelle,** p. 246
- Do Activity 22, p. 246.
- Thinking Critically, ATE, p. 248 and Thinking Critically, ATE, p. 249

Wrap-Up 5 min.
- Hold up various food items and have students ask you for a specific quantity of each one.

Homework Options
Study for **Deuxième étape** quiz.
Travaux pratiques de grammaire, pp. 67–68, Acts. 13–16
Cahier d'activités, pp. 90–91, Acts. 13–18, p. 96, Act. 26

Block 5

DEUXIEME ETAPE

Quick Review 10 min.

Quiz 8-2 20 min.
- Administer Quiz 8-2A or 8-2B.

TROISIEME ETAPE

Vocabulaire, p. 245, con't 10 min.
- Bell Work, ATE, p. 245
- Do Activity 23, p. 247 and Slower Pace, ATE, p. 247.

Grammaire, p. 248 35 min.
- Presenting **Comment dit-on... ?,** ATE, p. 247 and Language Note, ATE, p. 247
- Play Audio CD for Activity 25, p. 247.
- Presenting **Grammaire,** ATE, p. 248. See Music Link, ATE, p. 248
- Do Activity 27, p. 248.
- **Grammaire supplémentaire,** pp. 253–254, Acts. 7–8

Wrap-Up 15 min.
- Do Activity 26, p. 248. Present to class.

Homework Options
Study for **Troisième étape** quiz.
Travaux pratiques de grammaire, pp. 69–70, Acts. 17–20
Cahier d'activités, pp. 92–94, Acts. 19–24

Block 6

TROISIEME ETAPE

Quick Review 10 min.

Quiz 8-3 20 min.
- Administer Quiz 8-3A or 8-3B.

Prononciation, p. 249 15 min.
- Present **Prononciation,** p. 249. See Teacher Note, ATE, p. 249.
- Play Audio CD for Activities A, B, and C p. 249 and see Teaching Suggestion, ATE, p. 249.

LISONS! 20 min
- Read and discuss the **Stratégie pour lire,** p. 250, then do Prereading Activities A–D, Using Prior Knowledge, ATE, p. 250.
- Do Reading Activities E–H, Language Note p. 250.
- Postreading Activity I, Teaching Suggestion and Thinking Critically, ATE, p. 251
- Math Link, ATE, p. 251

MISE EN PRATIQUE 15 min.
- Play Audio CD for Activity 1, p. 256.
- Do Activity 3, p. 256.
- Begin **Ecrivons!,** p. 257.

Wrap-Up 10 min.
- Activities for Communication, pp. 47–48, Communicative Activity 8-3A and 8-3B

Homework Options
Que sais-je?, p. 258
Finish **Ecrivons!,** p. 257.
Study for Chapter 8 Test.

Block 7

MISE EN PRATIQUE

Quick Review 10 min.
- Check homework and collect **Ecrivons!**

Chapter Review 35 min.
- Review chapter 8. Choose from **Grammaire supplémentaire,** Grammar Tutor for Students of French, Activities for Communication, Listening Activities, Interactive CD-ROM Tutor, or **Jeux interactifs.**

Test, Chapter 8 45 min.
- Administer Chapter 8 Test. Select from Testing Program, Alternative Assessment Guide, Test Generator, or Standardized Assessment Tutor.

Chapter Opener

CHAPITRE 8

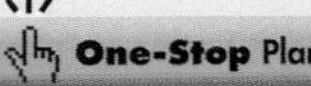

One-Stop Planner CD-ROM

For resource information, see the **One-Stop Planner,** Disc 2.

Pacing Tips

Keep in mind while planning your lessons that the **Première** and **Deuxième étape** have about the same amount of content. The **Troisième étape** is the lightest in terms of new material. For Lesson Plans and timing suggestions, see pages 229I–229L.

Meeting the Standards

Communication

- Expressing need, p. 238
- Making, accepting, and declining requests; telling someone what to do, p. 240
- Offering, accepting, or refusing food, p. 247

Cultures

- Culture Note, pp. 230, 243, 244, 246
- Multicultural Link, p. 233
- Note culturelle, p. 237
- Panorama Culturel, p. 239
- Note culturelle, p. 242
- Rencontre culturelle, p. 244
- Note culturelle, p. 246

Connections

- Math Link, p. 242
- Music Link, p. 248
- Math Link, p. 251

Comparisons

- Thinking Critically: Comparing and Contrasting, p. 231
- Language-to-Language, pp. 238, 241
- Thinking Critically: Analyzing, p. 242
- Thinking Critically: Comparing and Contrasting, p. 251

Communities

- Career Path, p. 230
- Community Link, p. 244
- De l'école au travail, p. 249

Cultures and Communities

Culture Note

The photo on pages 230–231 shows a typical outdoor market in Côte d'Ivoire. Although there are no set rules as to who sells what, generally women sell fruits, vegetables, and fish, while men sell bread and meat. Both men and women sell fabric.

Career Path

Have students imagine themselves as owners of a market stall or buyers for a market. What would be their job responsibilities? What if they worked for a market that imported goods from other countries? How would knowing French or other languages help them in this career?

STANDARDS: 2.2, 5.1

CHAPITRE 8

Au marché

Objectives

In this chapter you will learn to

Première étape

- express need

Deuxième étape

- make, accept, and decline requests
- tell someone what to do

Troisième étape

- offer, accept, or refuse food

Visit Holt Online
go.hrw.com
KEYWORD: WA3 ABIDJAN-8
Online Edition

◀ Un marché d'Abidjan

Chapter Opener

CHAPITRE 8

Focusing on Outcomes

Have students think of different situations in which the functions listed in the outcomes might be used. You might write their ideas on the board or on a transparency. Ask students to match the outcomes to the photo. NOTE: The self-check activities in **Que sais-je?** on page 258 help students assess their achievement of the objectives.

Connections and Comparisons

Thinking Critically

Observing Ask students to share their knowledge, experiences, and/or impressions of Africa. Then, direct students' attention to the photo. Ask them to identify features that are uniquely African.

Thinking Critically

Comparing and Contrasting Have students compare the Ivorian market they see to outdoor markets they've seen in the U.S. or photos they've seen of French markets. How are they similar? Different?

STANDARDS: 4.2

Mise en train

CHAPITRE 8

Teaching Resources
pp. 232–234

PRINT 
- Lesson Planner, p. 38
- Video Guide, pp. 54, 56
- Cahier d'activités, p. 85

MEDIA 
- One-Stop Planner
- Video Program
  Mise en train
  Videocassette 3, 15:56–20:18
  Videocassette 5 (captioned version), 1:04:12–1:08:37
  Suite
  Videocassette 3, 20:20–24:11
  Videocassette 5 (captioned version), 1:08:39–1:12:31
- DVD Tutor, Disc 2
- Audio Compact Discs, CD 8, Trs. 1–2
- **Mise en train** Transparencies

Presenting Mise en train

Before students watch the video, introduce the characters in the story. Write their names on the board and ask students to guess what their relationships are. Then, have students watch the episode to get the gist of the story. When they have finished watching the episode for the first time, ask them to tell what they think is happening in the story. You might have students look over the questions in Activity 1 on page 234 and keep them in mind as they watch the episode again. Ask students to name the items that Djeneba buys at the market.

Mise en train Transparencies

The **roman-photo** is an abridged version of the video episode.

MISE EN TRAIN ▪ *Une invitée pour le déjeuner*

CD 8
Trs. 1–2

Stratégie pour comprendre
Where does Djeneba go to do the grocery shopping? Do you recognize any of the food items she buys?

Djeneba

Mme Diomandé

Aminata

Le matin chez les Diomandé, à Abidjan. C'est l'heure du petit déjeuner.

1 kilo de riz
250 grammes de pâte d'arachide
1 poisson
7 oignons
1 douzaine de tomates
3 citrons
un paquet de beurre
du pain

1
Mme Diomandé : Encore du pain, Aminata?
Aminata : Non, merci. Je n'ai plus faim.
Mme Diomandé : Je pense faire du foutou avec de la sauce arachide pour le déjeuner.

2
Plus tard...
Mme Diomandé : Tiens, te voilà, Djeneba. Tu me fais le marché?
Djeneba : Volontiers! Qu'est-ce qu'il te faut?

3
Mme Diomandé : Il me faut des légumes, du riz, du poisson... Tu me rapportes aussi du pain... Et prends de la pâte de tomates.
Djeneba : Bon, d'accord.

Preteaching Vocabulary

Identifying keywords

Help students understand the story by identifying the following key vocabulary: ❶ **le déjeuner,** ❷ **le marché; Qu'est-ce qu'il te faut?** You might show pictures from pages 232–233 and 245 to demonstrate **le marché** and **le déjeuner,** and you could remind students of the expression **Qu'est-ce qu'il te faut... ?** from Chapter 3 by asking them **Qu'est-ce qu'il te faut pour le sport?** Call attention to what Madame Diomandé says she needs in order to make lunch: ❸ **Il me faut des légumes...** Tell students to try to identify names of particular food items by matching images to words.

STANDARDS: 1.2, 2.2, 3.2, 4.2

4 Djeneba va au marché...

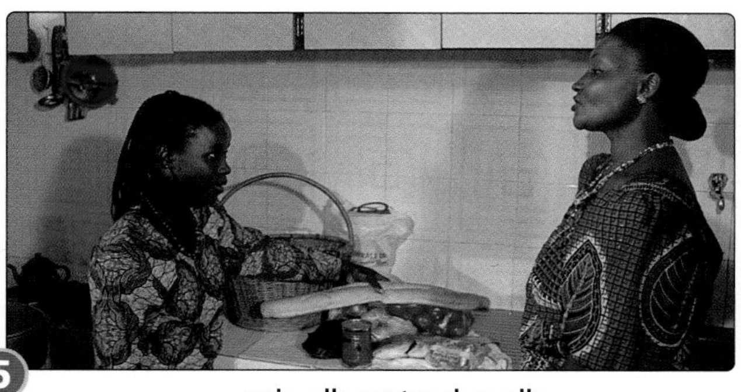

5 ... puis, elle rentre chez elle.

Djeneba : Voilà le poisson, les 250 grammes de pâte d'arachide, les oignons, les tomates et les citrons. J'ai aussi acheté un paquet de beurre, de la pâte de tomates, du pain et du riz.

Mme Diomandé : Merci, chérie.

6 Mme Diomandé fait la cuisine.

7 **Mme Diomandé :** Viens. Goûte voir. C'est bon?

Djeneba : Oui, très bon.

8

9 **Djeneba :** Ah, j'ai oublié... Devine qui j'ai vu au marché.

Mme Diomandé : Aucune idée... Va voir qui est à la porte.

Cahier d'activités, p. 85, Act. 1–2

Using the Captioned Video/DVD

If students have difficulty understanding French spoken at a normal speed, use Videocassette 5 to allow students to see the French captions for ***Une invitée pour le déjeuner*** and ***Une invitée pour le déjeuner (suite).*** Hearing the language and watching the story will reduce anxiety about the new language and facilitate comprehension. The reinforcement of seeing the written vocabulary words as they watch the gestures and actions will help prepare students to do the comprehension activities on page 234. NOTE: The *DVD Tutor* contains captions for all sections of the *Video Program.*

Mise en train

CHAPITRE 8

Teaching Suggestion

Ask students if they are familiar with the units of measurement used in the shopping list. The metric system is presented on page 242.

Photo Flash!

7 9 In these photos, Djeneba is holding a pestle that she is using to make **foutou.** This dish is usually made by pounding boiled yams, **manioc** *(cassava),* or plantains in a mortar until they are the consistency of paste. They are then shaped into round balls for serving (see page 244).

Multicultural Link

Ask students if they have tried food specialties from other countries and how they liked them. You might also have them choose a country and research its food specialties. Have students list specialties of their own town or area.

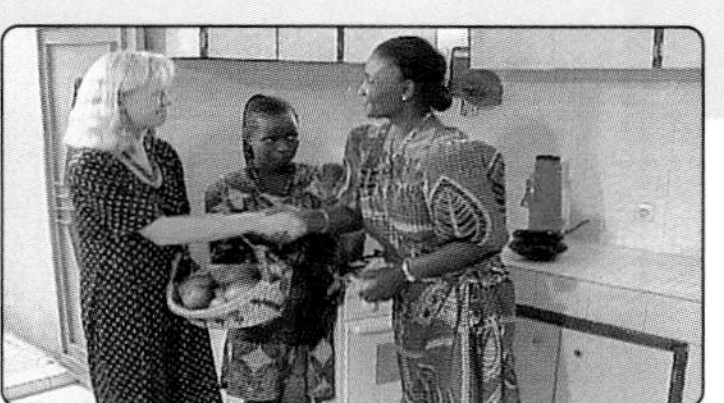

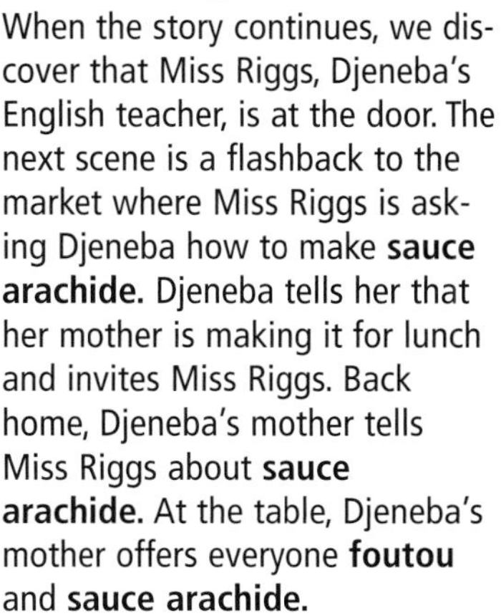

Une invitée pour le déjeuner (suite)

When the story continues, we discover that Miss Riggs, Djeneba's English teacher, is at the door. The next scene is a flashback to the market where Miss Riggs is asking Djeneba how to make **sauce arachide.** Djeneba tells her that her mother is making it for lunch and invites Miss Riggs. Back home, Djeneba's mother tells Miss Riggs about **sauce arachide.** At the table, Djeneba's mother offers everyone **foutou** and **sauce arachide.**

STANDARDS: 1.2, 2.2, 3.2, 4.2

Mise en train

CHAPITRE 8

Teaching Suggestions

1 You might have students work in pairs to answer these questions.

2 3 4 Have students do these activities individually or in pairs. You might check answers orally.

These activities check for comprehension only. Students should not yet be expected to produce language modeled in **Mise en train**.

1 Tu as compris? See answers below.

1. What time of day is it?
2. What does Mme Diomandé want Djeneba to do? Why?
3. What are some of the things Djeneba buys?
4. What happens at the end of the story?
5. Judging from the story title, what do you think Djeneba forgot to tell Mme Diomandé?

2 Vrai ou faux?

1. Aminata va au marché. faux
2. Mme Diomandé va faire du foutou avec de la sauce arachide. vrai
3. Djeneba ne veut pas aller au marché. faux
4. Djeneba achète des bananes au marché. faux
5. Djeneba oublie le pain. faux

3 Choisis la photo

Choisis les photos qui représentent ce que Djeneba a acheté.

1. du poisson b 2. des tomates d 3. des oignons e 4. des citrons a 5. du pain c

a.

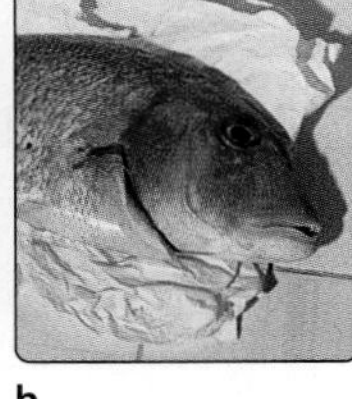
b.

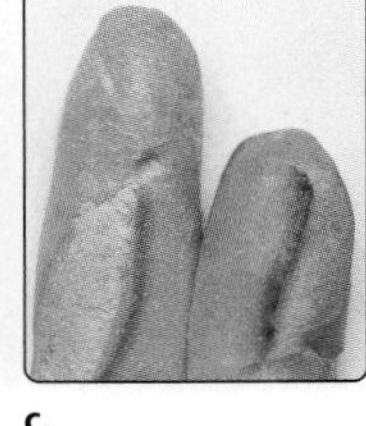
c.

d.

e.

4 C'est qui?

1. «Non, merci. Je n'ai plus faim.» Aminata
2. «Tu me fais le marché?» Mme Diomandé
3. «J'ai aussi acheté un paquet de beurre, de la pâte de tomates, du pain et du riz.» Djeneba
4. «Ah, j'ai oublié... » Djeneba
5. «Va voir qui est à la porte.» Mme Diomandé

5 Cherche les expressions See answers below.

In ***Une invitée pour le déjeuner,*** how does . . .

1. Mme Diomandé offer more food to Aminata?
2. Aminata refuse the offer?
3. Mme Diomandé ask Djeneba to do the shopping?
4. Mme Diomandé tell Djeneba what she needs?
5. Djeneba agree to do what Mme Diomandé asks?

Volontiers! Tu me fais le marché?
Non, merci. Je n'ai plus faim.
Bon, d'accord. Il me faut...
Encore du pain?

6 Et maintenant, à toi

Qui fait les courses dans ta famille? Où est-ce que vous faites les courses?

Answers

1
1. morning
2. She wants her to go to the market. Mme Diomandé needs some ingredients for a dish she is planning to make.
3. fish, peanut butter, onions, tomatoes, lemons, rice, butter, bread, and tomato paste
4. Someone knocks at the door.
5. Djeneba forgot to tell her that she had invited a guest for lunch.

5
1. Encore du pain?
2. Non, merci. Je n'ai plus faim.
3. Tu me fais le marché?
4. Il me faut...
5. Volontiers!/Bon, d'accord.

Comprehension Check

Challenge

2 Have students identify the photo that proves or disproves each statement.

3 Bring in these food items or pictures of them and hold them up. Have students call out the numbers of the corresponding names.

Additional Practice

4 Have students tell who said each of the following:

1. **Qu'est-ce qu'il te faut?** (Djeneba)
2. **Encore du pain... ?** (Mme Diomandé)
3. **Et prends de la pâte de tomates.** (Mme Diomandé)
4. **Oui, très bon.** (Djeneba)

STANDARDS: 1.2, 4.2

Première étape

Objective Expressing need

WA3 ABIDJAN-8

Vocabulaire

Qu'est-ce qu'on trouve au marché? Au supermarché?

CD-ROM 2 DVD 2

Légumes

du maïs — des petits pois (m.) — des pommes de terre (f.)

des carottes (f.) — des gombos (m.)

Produits laitiers

du beurre — du fromage — du lait

Viandes

du porc — du poulet

du bœuf

Fruits

des fraises (f.)

des poires (f.)

des noix de coco (f.)

des citrons (m.)

des goyaves (f.)

des papayes (f.)

des pommes (f.)

des mangues (f.)

du raisin

des ananas (m.)

des yaourts (m.) *yogurt*
des œufs (m.) *eggs*
du poisson *fish*
du riz *rice*
du pain *bread*
de la farine *flour*

du sucre *sugar*
de la confiture *jam*
des gâteaux (m.) *cakes*
de la tarte *pie*
des oranges (f.) *oranges*
des bananes (f.) *bananas*
des pêches (f.) *peaches*

des tomates (f.) *tomatoes*
des avocats (m.) *avocados*
une/de la salade *a/some salad*
des salades (f.) *heads of lettuce*
des oignons (m.) *onions*
des haricots verts (m.) *green beans*
des champignons (m.) *mushrooms*

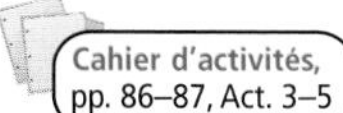

Travaux pratiques de grammaire, pp. 61–62, Act. 1–4

Cahier d'activités, pp. 86–87, Act. 3–5

Communication for All Students

Language Notes

- Make sure students pronounce **poisson** with an **s** sound, not with a **z** sound as in **poison.**
- The final **-f** is pronounced in **œuf,** but not in the plural **œufs.** Teach students the sentence *One egg is* **un œuf** *("enough")* to help them remember to pronounce the **-f** only in the singular form.

Game

Attrape-le! Place three food items on a table **(une mangue, une tomate, un citron).** Call two students to the table. Say what you'd like to have. The first student to grab the item and hand it to you wins. The winner stays at the table and another player comes forward. You might add more items to make the game more challenging.

Première étape

CHAPITRE 8

Teaching Resources
pp. 235–238

PRINT

- Lesson Planner, p. 39
- TPR Storytelling Book, pp. 29, 32
- Listening Activities, pp. 59, 63
- Activities for Communication, pp. 43–44, 110, 113, 151–152
- Travaux pratiques de grammaire, pp. 61–65
- Grammar Tutor for Students of French, Chapter 8
- Cahier d'activités, pp. 86–88
- Testing Program, pp. 197–200
- Alternative Assessment Guide, p. 39
- Student Make-Up Assignments, Chapter 8

MEDIA

- One-Stop Planner
- Audio Compact Discs, CD 8, Trs. 3, 20, 26–27
- Teaching Transparencies: 8-1, 8-A, 8-B; **Grammaire supplémentaire** Answers; Travaux pratiques de grammaire Answers
- Interactive CD-ROM Tutor, Disc 2

Bell Work

Have students list three things they might order in a café.

Presenting Vocabulaire

Bring in real or toy food items or magazine pictures to present this vocabulary. Present the new words by food groups, holding up the object or illustration as you say the word for each one. Then, hold up the items or pictures again, asking **Qu'est-ce que c'est?** Encourage students to make charts for each food group. Have them create a set of picture flash cards.

Teaching Resources
pp. 235–238

PRINT

- Lesson Planner, p. 39
- TPR Storytelling Book, pp. 29, 32
- Listening Activities, pp. 59, 63
- Activities for Communication, pp. 43–44, 110, 113, 151–152
- Travaux pratiques de grammaire, pp. 61–65
- Grammar Tutor for Students of French, Chapter 8
- Cahier d'activités, pp. 86–88
- Testing Program, pp. 197–200
- Alternative Assessment Guide, p. 39
- Student Make-Up Assignments, Chapter 8

MEDIA 

- One-Stop Planner
- Audio Compact Discs, CD 8, Trs. 3, 20, 26–27
- Teaching Transparencies: 8-1, 8-A, 8-B; **Grammaire supplémentaire** Answers; Travaux pratiques de grammaire Answers
- Interactive CD-ROM Tutor, Disc 2

Presenting
Grammaire

The partitive and indefinite articles To present the partitive article, first draw a whole pizza and a whole cake on the board. Identify them orally, using the indefinite article: **une pizza, un gâteau.** Then, divide each into pieces and shade one of the pieces. Identify the portions, using the partitive article: **de la pizza, du gâteau.** Next, bring in a whole food item **(une tarte, un pain, une orange)** and have students ask for some or all of it. Remind students that they learned how to use **de** after **ne... pas** in Chapter 3.

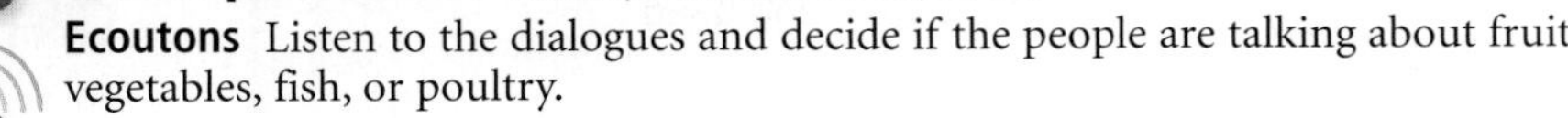

7 **Qu'en penses-tu?** See scripts and answers on p. 229G.

Ecoutons Listen to the dialogues and decide if the people are talking about fruit, vegetables, fish, or poultry.

CD 8 Tr. 3 

Grammaire

CD-ROM 2 DVD 2

The partitive and indefinite articles

You already know how to use **un** and **une** with singular nouns and **des** with plural nouns. Use **du, de la, de l',** or **des** to indicate *some of* or *part of* something.

Je voudrais **du** gâteau.
Tu veux **de la** salade?
Elle va prendre **de l'**eau minérale.
Il me faut **des** oranges.

- If you want to talk about a whole item, use the indefinite articles **un** and **une.**

Il achète **une** tarte.

Il prend **de la** tarte.

- In a negative sentence, **du, de la, de l',** and **des** change to **de/d'** *(none* or *any).*

—Tu as **du** pain?
—Désolée, je n'ai pas **de** pain.

—Tu prends **de la** viande?
—Merci, je ne prends jamais **de** viande.

- You can't leave out the article in French as you do in English.
Elle mange **du** fromage. *She's eating cheese.*

Grammaire supplémentaire, p. 252, Act. 1–3

Cahier d'activités, p. 87, Act. 6

Travaux pratiques de grammaire, pp. 63–65, Act. 5–9

8 **Grammaire en contexte**

Lisons/Ecrivons Complète ce dialogue avec **du, de la, de l', de, d',** ou **des.**

ASSIKA Dis, Maman, qu'est-ce qu'on mange à midi? J'ai très faim!
MAMAN ___1___ poisson, ___2___ riz et ___3___ haricots verts. Du, du, des
ASSIKA Est-ce qu'on a encore ___4___ pain? du
MAMAN Non. Et on n'a pas ___5___ bananes non plus. Est-ce que tu peux aller en acheter? de
ASSIKA Bon, d'accord. C'est tout?
MAMAN Non. Prends aussi ___6___ yaourts, ___7___ farine et ___8___ sucre. Je vais faire un gâteau pour ce soir. des, de la, du
ASSIKA Super!
MAMAN Merci, ma chérie.

Communication for All Students

Challenge

7 Before playing the recording, distribute the flash cards (see the **Vocabulaire** presentation on page 235) randomly to students. Write **Fruits, Légumes, Viandes, Volailles** *(poultry),* **Poissons,** and **Produits laitiers** on the board at the top of six columns, and ask students to tape their flash cards under the correct categories.

Additional Practice

8 Have students rewrite the dialogue, substituting their favorite foods for the items mentioned and leaving the numbered blanks empty. Have them exchange papers with a partner, who fills in the blanks and then returns the paper for correction.

9 Grammaire en contexte

Parlons Qu'est-ce que Prisca, Clémentine et Adjoua achètent au marché? See answers below.

1.

2.

3.

Note culturelle

Shopping at a market in Côte d'Ivoire can be an exciting and colorful experience. Every city, town, and village has an open- air market where people come to buy and sell food, cloth, housewares, medicine, and herbal remedies.

Although French is the official language in Côte d'Ivoire, more than 60 different African languages are spoken there. To make shopping easier for everyone, there is a common market language called **Djoula.** Here are a few phrases in **Djoula.**

í ní sɔ̀gɔ̀ma	(ee nee *sogoma*)	*Good morning.*
í ní wúla	(ee *nee* woulah)	*Good afternoon./Hello.*
í ká kɛ́nɛ wá?	(ee kah keh*neh* wah)	*How are you?/How's it going?*
n ká kɛ́nɛ kósobɛ	(nnkah keh*neh* kuh*soh*beh)	*I'm fine.*

10 Qu'est-ce qu'il y a dans le chariot?

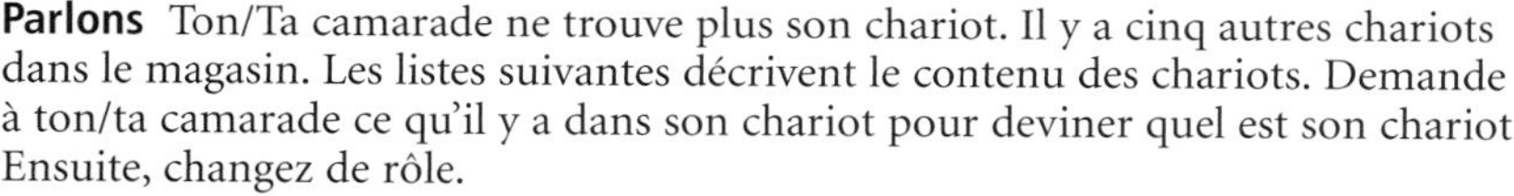

Parlons Ton/Ta camarade ne trouve plus son chariot. Il y a cinq autres chariots dans le magasin. Les listes suivantes décrivent le contenu des chariots. Demande à ton/ta camarade ce qu'il y a dans son chariot pour deviner quel est son chariot. Ensuite, changez de rôle.

EXEMPLE
— Tu as acheté des tomates? — Non.
— Tu as acheté du poisson? — Oui.
— Ton chariot, c'est le numéro... ? — Oui.

1. du poisson, des tomates, des bananes, du fromage, du lait
2. du pain, des œufs, des oignons, du poisson, des haricots verts
3. du sucre, des ananas, du lait, du maïs, des tomates
4. des tomates, des haricots verts, des œufs, du sucre, du maïs
5. des ananas, des bananes, du fromage, des oignons, des haricots verts
6. des bananes, des œufs, du poisson, du pain, des tomates

Cultures and Communities

Culture Note

In Côte d'Ivoire, it is common to see women carrying food, firewood, a bucket of water, or various other loads on their head. If the object is heavy, two women might lift it onto a third woman's head. High school girls will sometimes carry their books on their head as they walk to and from school. In the market, it is not uncommon to see a woman carrying a bowl of food items on her head, a bag in one hand, and a baby riding on her back. With this arrangement, the woman still has the other hand free to carry on her business, and the baby has a cozy place to sleep!

Première étape

CHAPITRE 8

Additional Practice

Note culturelle Have partners practice greeting each other in Djoula. They might also choose to use these greetings in activities and skits later in the chapter.

Language Note

For *seller* or *merchant,* the words **vendeur(-euse)** and **commerçant(e)** are generally interchangeable.

Slower Pace/ Visual Learners

10 Hold up pictures of the foods mentioned in this activity and have students give the number of the cart that contains each one. For example, if you hold up a picture of pineapples, the class would respond **trois et cinq.**

Community Link

You might invite someone from West Africa or someone who has traveled there to speak to your class. Try contacting the international student office at a local college or university. Returned Peace Corps volunteers might also be classroom visitors. Write to Peace Corps, Office of World Wise Schools, 1990 K Street, Washington, D.C. 20526, or call the Peace Corps Africa desk at 1-800-424-8580.

Answers

9
1. du riz, un ananas, des citrons, des œufs, du beurre, une banane
2. des tomates, des œufs, du maïs, un oignon
3. du riz, un oignon, des pommes de terre, une tomate, une orange

Première étape

CHAPITRE 8

Presenting Comment dit-on... ?

Distribute vocabulary cards to students. Then, ask various students **De quoi est-ce que tu as besoin?** or **Qu'est-ce qu'il te faut?** and have them respond by naming the item on their card **(ananas).** Then, have groups of five or six play the game **Quels ingrédients?** To play, each student repeats all the previously mentioned ingredients and adds another. This game is explained in more detail on page 229C.

Assess

- Testing Program, pp. 197–200 Quiz 8-1A, Quiz 8-1B Audio CD 8, Tr. 20
- Student Make-Up Assignments, Chapter 8, Alternative Quiz
- Alternative Assessment Guide, p. 39

Comment dit-on...?

Expressing need

— **Qu'est-ce qu'il te faut?**
— **Il me faut** des bananes, du riz et de l'eau minérale.
— **De quoi est-ce que tu as besoin?** *What do you need?*
— **J'ai besoin de** riz pour faire du foutou. *I need . . .*

Note de grammaire

The expression **avoir besoin de** can be followed by a noun or a verb. The partitive article is not used with this expression.

Tu **as besoin de** tomates?
Nous **avons besoin d'**œufs pour l'omelette.
J'**ai besoin d'**aller au marché.

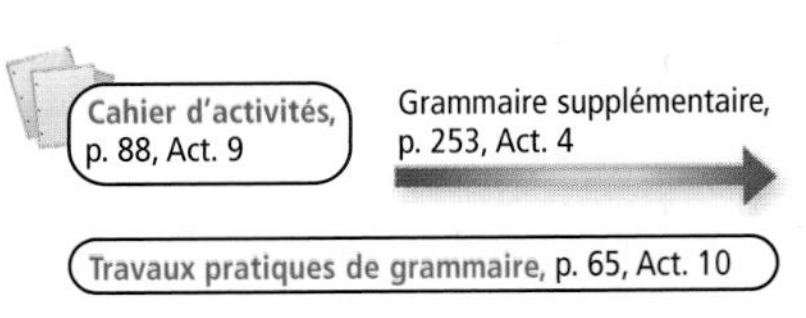

Cahier d'activités, p. 88, Act. 9
Grammaire supplémentaire, p. 253, Act. 4
Travaux pratiques de grammaire, p. 65, Act. 10

11 Grammaire en contexte

Lisons/Parlons Sandrine fait une fête, mais le menu est secret. Regarde les listes suivantes et devine ce qu'elle prépare.

1. J'ai besoin de salade, de tomates, de carottes, d'oignons... une salade
2. J'ai besoin de fromage, de pain, de jambon... un sandwich
3. J'ai besoin d'œufs, de champignons, de fromage, de lait... une omelette
4. J'ai besoin de bananes, de pommes, d'oranges... une salade de fruits

une tarte aux pommes
un banana split
une salade de fruits
un sandwich
une salade
une omelette

12 Grammaire en contexte

 See answers below.

Ecrivons Tu as besoin de quoi pour faire...

1. un bon sandwich?
2. une quiche?
3. une salade?
4. une salade de fruits?
5. un banana split?

13 Que faut-il?

Parlons Tu veux préparer un repas pour ta famille française. D'abord, fais un menu. Ensuite, va au supermarché et achète ce qu'il te faut. Ton/ta camarade va jouer le rôle du/de la marchand(e). Ensuite, changez de rôle.

A la française

Many French expressions involve foods: **On est dans la purée** *(We're in trouble)*; **C'est pas de la tarte** *(It's not easy)*. Can you guess what **C'est du gâteau** means?*

Vocabulaire à la carte

Here are some additional words you may want to know:

du concombre	*cucumber*
des cornichons (m.)	*pickles*
de la mayonnaise	*mayonnaise*
de la moutarde	*mustard*
des noix (f.)	*nuts*
du poivre	*pepper*
du sel	*salt*

* It means *It's easy; it's a piece of cake.*

Answers

12 *Possible answers:*

1. de pain, de fromage, de viande, de cornichons, de moutarde
2. d'œufs, de fromage, de lait, de champignons, d'oignons
3. de salade, de tomates, de carottes, de champignons, de concombre
4. d'oranges, de fraises, de bananes, d'un ananas
5. de bananes, de glace, de noix

Connections and Comparisons

Language-to-Language

A la française Have students think of additional expressions in English that involve food. *(It's food for thought. Don't cry over spilled milk.)* You might want to have your students guess what these French expressions mean: **Ça baigne dans le beurre!** *It's going very well.* **Il mange son pain blanc le premier.** *He eats his cake first.* **Ce n'est pas mes oignons.** *It's none of my business.* Ask students who speak Spanish to share similiar expressions involving food. **Es una papa sin sal.** *He or she is a dull person (literally, a potato without salt).* **Ese huevo quiere sal.** *He or she wants to take advantage of you (literally, that egg wants salt).*

STANDARDS: 1.1, 1.3, 4.1, 5.1

Où est-ce que tu aimes faire des provisions?

Where does your family go to shop for groceries? People in francophone countries have several options. We asked these people where they shop. Here's what they had to say.

Louise, France

«Je vais le plus souvent au supermarché, mais je préfère le marché, parce que le marché, c'est dehors et puis, l'ambiance est meilleure.» Tr. 5

Angèle, Côte d'Ivoire

«Je préfère aller au supermarché pour aller faire des achats parce que là-bas, c'est plus sûr et bien conservé.» Tr. 6

Micheline, Belgique

«Je préfère aller au marché, chez les petits commerçants, parce qu'il y a le contact personnel, il y a le choix, il y a les odeurs, les couleurs, le plaisir de la promenade aussi dans le marché.» Tr. 7

Qu'en penses-tu? See answers below.

1. Where do these people shop for groceries?
2. What are the advantages and disadvantages of shopping in these different places?
3. Are there outdoor farmers' markets in your community? What can you buy there?
4. Does your family sometimes shop in small specialty stores? If so, what do they buy there?

Savais-tu que... ?

Many people in francophone countries grocery shop in supermarkets (**supermarchés**) or hypermarkets (**hypermarchés**) because it's convenient. Others prefer to shop in small grocery stores (**épiceries**) or outdoor markets (**marchés en plein air**). **Supermarchés** are similar to their American counterparts. **Hypermarchés** are very large stores that carry just about anything you can imagine—all under one roof! Americans may be surprised to learn, however, that stores are not open 24 hours a day or even late in the evening. **Epiceries** are usually closed between 12:30 P.M. and 4 P.M. and all day on either Sunday or Monday.

Cultures and Communities

Culture Notes

- Prices in West African markets are not fixed and customers are expected to bargain. With the buyer's first inquiry, the vendor often extols the virtues of the item and quotes a high price, sometimes triple the price usually paid. The customer should never pay this price, but make a counteroffer of approximately half the usual price. The vendor and customer will usually bargain to a happy compromise.
- In many African countries, it is believed that a vendor who allows the first customer of the day to leave without purchasing something will have bad luck for the rest of the day.

CHAPITRE 8

Teaching Resources
p. 239

PRINT
- Video Guide, pp. 55, 56–57
- Cahier d'activités, p. 96

MEDIA
- One-Stop Planner
- Video Program Videocassette 3, 24:13–26:49
- DVD Tutor, Disc 2
- Audio Compact Discs, CD 8, Trs. 4–7
- Interactive CD-ROM Tutor, Disc 2

Presenting Panorama Culturel

After students view the video and read the interviews, ask them the **Questions** below. Have them tell where they would prefer to shop and why. They might respond orally or in writing. Ask students if they choose different places to shop for different things.

Questions

1. **Pourquoi est-ce que Louise préfère aller au marché?** (C'est dehors; l'ambiance est meilleure.)
2. **Pourquoi est-ce qu'Angèle préfère aller au supermarché pour faire ses achats?** (C'est plus sûr et bien conservé.)
3. **Pourquoi est-ce que Micheline préfère aller au marché?** (Il y a le contact personnel, le choix, les odeurs, les couleurs, le plaisir de la promenade.)

Answers

1. in the supermarket and market
2. *Answers will vary.*

STANDARDS: 2.1, 3.2, 4.2

CHAPITRE 8

Teaching Resources
pp. 240–243

PRINT

- Lesson Planner, p. 40
- TPR Storytelling Book, pp. 30, 32
- Listening Activities, pp. 59–60, 64
- Activities for Communication, pp. 45–46, 111, 113, 151–152
- Travaux pratiques de grammaire, pp. 66–68
- Grammar Tutor for Students of French, Chapter 8
- Cahier d'activités, pp. 89–91
- Testing Program, pp. 201–204
- Alternative Assessment Guide, p. 39
- Student Make-Up Assignments, Chapter 8

MEDIA

- One-Stop Planner
- Audio Compact Discs, CD 8, Trs. 8–10, 21, 28–29
- Teaching Transparencies: 8-2, 8-C; **Grammaire supplémentaire** Answers; Travaux pratiques de grammaire Answers
- Interactive CD-ROM Tutor, Disc 2

Bell Work
Display pictures of several food items and have students name them in French, using the indefinite or partitive article.

Presenting
Comment dit-on... ?

Have students tell what is happening in the illustration on this page and repeat the requests after you. Ask them to suggest other ways to complete **Tu peux... ?** and **Tu me rapportes... ?** Ask students to get various items for you. **(Tu me rapportes du jambon?)**

Deuxième étape

Objectives Making, accepting, and declining requests; telling someone what to do

go.hrw.com
WA3 ABIDJAN-8

Comment dit-on...?

Making, accepting, and declining requests; telling someone what to do

To make requests:

Tu peux aller faire les courses?
Can you . . . ?
Tu me rapportes des œufs?
Will you bring me . . . ?

To accept:

Pourquoi pas?
Bon, d'accord.
Je veux bien. *Gladly.*
J'y vais tout de suite.
I'll go right away.

To tell someone what to do:

Rapporte(-moi) du beurre.
Bring (me) back . . .
Prends du lait. *Get . . .*
Achète(-moi) du riz. *Buy (me) . . .*
N'oublie pas d'acheter le lait.
Don't forget to . . .

To decline:

Je ne peux pas maintenant.
Je regrette, mais je n'ai pas le temps.
I'm sorry, but I don't have time.
J'ai des trucs à faire.
J'ai des tas de choses à faire.

Cahier d'activités, p. 89, Act. 10–12

Communication for All Students

Building on Previous Skills
Ask students when or of whom they might ask a favor. When would they tell someone to do something? What might they tell someone to do?

Language Note
Remind students that they must drop the final **-s** in the **tu** command for **-er** verbs, but not for other types of verbs.

Visual Learners
Place pictures of food items or real food items on a table. Give various students commands **(Rapporte-moi du lait.)** and have them respond by handing you the appropriate picture or item.

Un petit service See scripts and answers on p. 229G.

CD 8
Trs. 8–9

a. Ecoutons Listen to these dialogues. Is the first speaker making a request or telling someone what to do?

b. Ecoutons Now, listen again. Does the second speaker accept or decline the request or command?

A la française

You already know that the verb **faire** means *to do.* What do you think the verb **refaire** might mean? The prefix **re-** in front of a verb means *to redo* something; to do something again. Use **r-** in front of a verb that begins with a vowel.

Tu dois **re**lire ce livre. *You need to reread this book.*

On va **r**acheter du lait. *We'll buy milk again.*

Rouvre la porte, s'il te plaît. *Reopen the door, please.*

Does this same rule apply in English?

Grammaire

The verb *pouvoir*

CD-ROM 2
DVD 2

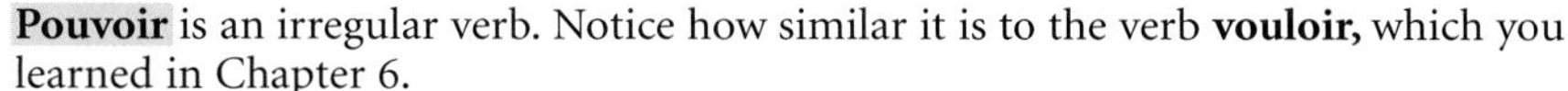

Pouvoir is an irregular verb. Notice how similar it is to the verb **vouloir,** which you learned in Chapter 6.

pouvoir *(to be able to, can, may)*

Je	**peux**	Nous	**pouvons**
Tu	**peux**	Vous	**pouvez**
Il/Elle/On	**peut**	Ils/Elles	**peuvent**

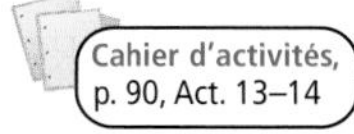

Cahier d'activités, p. 90, Act. 13–14

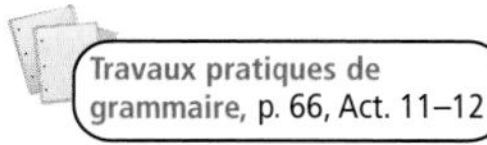

Travaux pratiques de grammaire, p. 66, Act. 11–12

Grammaire supplémentaire, p. 253, Act. 5–6

15 Grammaire en contexte

Lisons/Ecrivons Complète la conversation avec les formes appropriées du verbe **pouvoir.**

M. BONFILS Sim, tu __1__ aller au marché pour moi? peux

SIM Non, je ne __2__ pas. J'ai des trucs à faire! peux

ARMANDE Papa, Julie et moi, nous __3__ y aller si tu veux. pouvons

M. BONFILS Merci, les filles. Vous __4__ me prendre un ananas et des mangues? pouvez
Ah, et du pain aussi.

JULIE On __5__ acheter les fruits, mais Sim et Marius ne font jamais rien.
Ils __6__ bien acheter le pain pour une fois! peut, peuvent

16 Grammaire en contexte

Parlons Demande à tes camarades s'ils peuvent faire les choses suivantes pour toi ou avec toi.

EXEMPLE —**Vous pouvez écouter de la musique après l'école?**
—**Non, nous ne pouvons pas.**

- regarder la télé après l'école
- aller nager
- faire des courses avec moi
- me rapporter un sandwich
- sortir ce soir
- jouer au foot demain

Connections and Comparisons

Language-to-Language

Review with students the difference between the use of *can* and *may* in English. Point out that the verb **pouvoir** means both *can* and *may.*

Language Notes

- **A la française** Ask students to try to guess the meanings of the following verbs that are formed with the prefix **re-: reprendre, redonner, recommencer** *(to take back, to give back, to begin again).*
- A famous French proverb is **Vouloir, c'est pouvoir.** Have students try to guess the English equivalent. *(Where there's a will, there's a way.)*

Deuxième étape

CHAPITRE 8

Teaching Suggestion

14 Ask students to listen to the speakers' intonation for clues, as well as to what they say.

Presenting Grammaire

The verb *pouvoir* First, ask students to recall the forms of the verb **vouloir.** Have individuals write one form they remember on the board until the paradigm is complete. Write the forms of **pouvoir** next to those of **vouloir.** Next, name a subject pronoun and toss a ball to a student, who must say the correct verb form as he or she catches the ball. Then, that student continues by tossing the ball to another student while calling out a subject pronoun.

Challenge

16 Encourage students to offer excuses for declining their classmates' requests. Have students find at least two classmates who accept to do each activity with them.

Deuxième étape

CHAPITRE 8

Teaching Resources
pp. 240–243

PRINT

- Lesson Planner, p. 40
- TPR Storytelling Book, pp. 30, 32
- Listening Activities, pp. 59–60, 64
- Activities for Communication, pp. 45–46, 111, 113, 151–152
- Travaux pratiques de grammaire, pp. 66–68
- Grammar Tutor for Students of French, Chapter 8
- Cahier d'activités, pp. 89–91
- Testing Program, pp. 201–204
- Alternative Assessment Guide, p. 39
- Student Make-Up Assignments, Chapter 8

MEDIA

- One-Stop Planner
- Audio Compact Discs, CD 8, Trs. 8–10, 21, 28–29
- Teaching Transparencies: 8-2, 8-C; **Grammaire supplémentaire** Answers; Travaux pratiques de grammaire Answers
- Interactive CD-ROM Tutor, Disc 2

Presenting Vocabulaire, Note de grammaire

Say the expressions of quantity as you hold up the corresponding amount or container of each item. Have partners or small groups list other items that are packaged or sold in these quantities **(un litre de coca)**. Collect their lists, call out the foods or beverages, and have students give a possible quantity for each one.

Vocabulaire

Vous en voulez combien?

CD-ROM 2 DVD 2

un kilo(gramme) de pommes de terre et **une livre d'**oignons

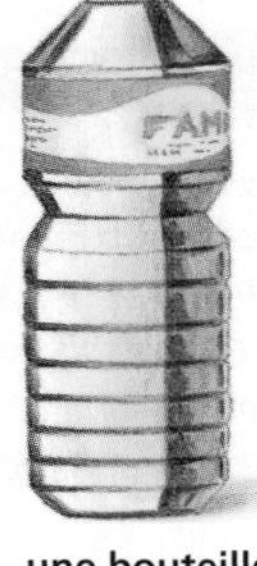

une bouteille d'eau minérale

une douzaine d'œufs

une boîte de tomates

un paquet de sucre

une tranche de jambon

un morceau de fromage

un litre de lait

Cahier d'activités, pp. 90–91, Act. 15–17

Travaux pratiques de grammaire, p. 67, Act. 13

Note de grammaire

Notice that you use **de** or **d'** after these expressions of quantity.

Une tranche **de** jambon, s'il vous plaît.

Je voudrais un kilo **d'**oranges.

Travaux pratiques de grammaire, pp. 67–68, Act. 14–16

Grammaire supplémentaire, pp. 253–254, Act. 7–8

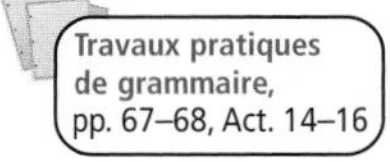

Note culturelle

The metric system was created shortly after the French Revolution and has since been adopted by nearly all countries in the world. Although the United States is officially trying to convert to the metric system, many people aren't yet used to it. In the metric system, lengths are measured in centimeters and meters, rather than inches and yards. Distances are measured in kilometers. Grams and kilograms are the standard measures of weight. **Une livre** is half a kilogram. Liquids, including gasoline, are measured in liters. To convert metric measurements, use the following table:

1 centimeter = .39 inches	1 gram = .035 ounces
1 meter = 39.37 inches	1 kilogram = 2.2 pounds
1 kilometer = .62 miles	1 liter = 1.06 quarts

Connections and Comparisons

Math Link

Note culturelle Have students figure out their height in meters and centimeters or their weight in kilos. They could also calculate speed limits in kilometers per hour (55 mph = 89 kph; 65 mph = 105 kph). Students may be sensitive about discussing their own measurements, so you might discuss the height and weight of various celebrities instead.

Thinking Critically

Analyzing Ask students to give advantages of the American system of weights and measures. Have them discuss the advantages and disadvantages of changing to the metric system.

STANDARDS: 2.1, 2.2, 3.1, 4.2

Vous en voulez combien? See scripts and answers on p. 229G.

Ecoutons Listen to Sophie as she does her shopping. Write down the items and the quantities she asks for.

CD 8 Tr. 10

18 Grammaire en contexte

Lisons/Ecrivons Ta mère et ta grand-mère préparent un dîner. Elles te demandent d'aller au marché. Complète la conversation suivante avec une quantité logique de chaque article. Utilise les expressions proposées. See answers below.

une boîte de/d' | une douzaine de/d' | un morceau de/d' | un litre de/d' | une bouteille de/d' | un paquet de/d' | une livre de/d' | un kilo de/d'

—Alors, Maman, qu'est-ce qu'il te faut?
—Il me faut __1__ bœuf, __2__ fromage et __3__ eau minérale.
—Et pour le dessert?
—Achète-moi __4__ farine, __5__ pêches et __6__ œufs.
—Et toi, Mémé, de quoi est-ce que tu as besoin?
—Rapporte-moi __7__ oignons et __8__ lait, s'il te plaît.
—D'accord. A tout à l'heure.

Allons au marché!

Parlons Tu fais les courses. Achète les articles sur ta liste. Demande une quantité logique pour chaque article. Ton/Ta camarade joue le rôle du/de la marchand(e). Ensuite, changez de rôle.

Vous avez choisi? | Voilà. | Et avec ça? | C'est tout? | Vous désirez? | Je voudrais... | Il me faut... | Je prends...

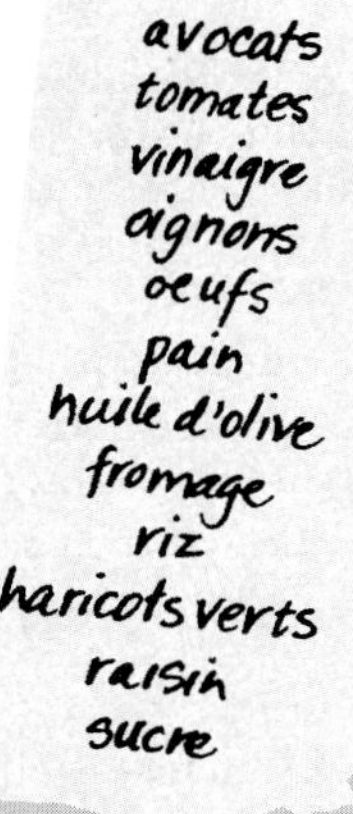

Jeu de rôle

Parlons Tu fais des courses pour des personnes âgées. Fais une liste des articles que tu dois acheter. Donne aussi les quantités. Ton/Ta camarade va jouer le rôle de la personne âgée que tu aides. Ensuite, changez de rôle.

Deuxième étape

CHAPITRE 8

Teacher Note

Note de grammaire Make sure students understand that only **de** or **d'** is used after expressions of quantity, regardless of the gender and number of the noun that follows.

Language Notes

- Other common expressions of quantity are **une brique de lait, un pot de yaourt,** and **une plaquette de beurre** (two quarter-pound sticks).
- Explain that **une livre** is an old unit of measure equivalent to half a kilo (1 kilo equals 2.2 pounds), so it equals approximately one pound.

Culture Note

In Côte d'Ivoire, meat, potatoes, flour, sugar, popcorn, rice, and milk are sold by weight (kilos or grams). Vegetables and fruits are priced according to size, freshness, and availability. Items such as hot peppers **(piments)** and okra are sold in bunches. Small items are often placed in large banana leaves that are folded to make containers.

Assess

- Testing Program, pp. 201–204
  Quiz 8-2A, Quiz 8-2B
  Audio CD 8, Tr. 21
- Student Make-Up Assignments, Chapter 8, Alternative Quiz
- Alternative Assessment Guide, p. 39

Communication for All Students

Teaching Suggestions

17 You might have partners listen to the recording together, with one writing the item as the other writes the quantity.

19 Have partners list the quantities they intend to buy before they work together.

20 Before they begin the activity, have students make a list of what they need to get. Then, after the partners have read their lists to each other, they might exchange them to check for accuracy.

Additional Practice

Show *Teaching Transparency 8-2* and have partners act out the situation.

Possible answers

1. une livre de
2. un morceau de
3. une bouteille d'
4. un paquet de
5. une boîte de
6. une douzaine d'
7. un kilo d'
8. un litre de

STANDARDS: 1.1, 1.2, 5.1, 5.2

Building on Previous Skills

Ask students if they've ever tried food from another country. Have them describe what the food looked like and how it tasted. Ask them if they used any special utensils or if certain customs were connected with eating the food.

Presenting Rencontre culturelle

Have students look at the pictures and guess what each dish is made of. Then, have three volunteers read the descriptions. Have small groups of students answer the questions in **Qu'en penses-tu?** and report back to the class.

Culture Notes

- Since most meals are not made with prepared foods, a typical meal might take from six to seven hours, including a visit to the market and cleaning up afterwards. For this reason, the sauce that is eaten for lunch is often eaten for dinner on the same day.
- Tell students that when they are guests for dinner in Africa, they should at least taste everything that they are served. When they are offered a second helping, it is polite to accept at least some, even though they may not want more.

◄ **Le foutou,** the national dish of Côte d'Ivoire, is a paste made from boiled plantains, manioc, or yams. It is eaten with various sauces, such as peanut sauce or palm oil nut sauce.

▼ **La sauce arachide** is one of the many sauces eaten in Côte d'Ivoire. It is made from peanut butter with beef, chicken, or fish, hot peppers, peanut oil, garlic, onions, tomato paste, tomatoes, and a variety of other vegetables. It is usually served over rice.

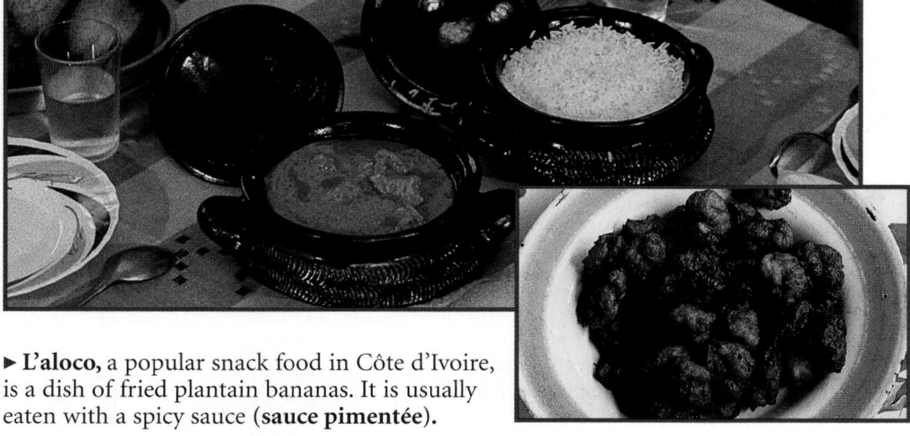

► **L'aloco,** a popular snack food in Côte d'Ivoire, is a dish of fried plantain bananas. It is usually eaten with a spicy sauce (**sauce pimentée**).

Qu'en penses-tu?

1. Do these dishes resemble any that are eaten in the United States? See answers below.
2. Which ingredients in these dishes can you find in your neighborhood grocery store? Which ingredients are unfamiliar?
3. What dishes are typical of your part of the country? Why are they more common than others?

Savais-tu que... ?

Yams (**ignames**) and plantains are abundant in the Republic of Côte d'Ivoire, which explains why **foutou** is a popular dish. A typical lunch consists of one main course — often **foutou,** rice, or **attiéké** (ground manioc root) with a sauce, and a dessert, usually tropical fruits such as guavas, pineapples, or papayas. Lunch is traditionally followed by an hour-long siesta. To accommodate this custom, stores are closed from noon until 3:00 P.M., even in large cities such as Abidjan. Unlike lunch, dinner tends to be a much lighter meal. Heavy foods are rarely eaten in the evening.

Cultures and Communities

Community Link

Call a local community education program or community college and try to find someone who teaches African cooking. Invite this person to come and speak to your students about popular recipes and their ingredients, or even prepare a dish.

Culture Note

In Ivorian villages, **foutou** is eaten without silverware and only with the right hand. It is considered rude to eat with the left hand, which is reserved for personal hygiene. To eat **foutou,** individuals break off a piece, form a small ball, and then dip it in the sauce accompanying the meal.

Possible answers

1. **Le foutou** is a unique dish that has no American equivalent. **La sauce arachide** resembles a dark sauce, stew, or soup. **L'aloco** resembles banana fritters.

STANDARDS: 2.1, 2.2, 3.2, 4.2

Objective Offering, accepting, or refusing food

go.hrw.com WA3 ABIDJAN-8

Vocabulaire

Qu'est-ce qu'on mange au...

petit déjeuner?

déjeuner?

goûter?

dîner?

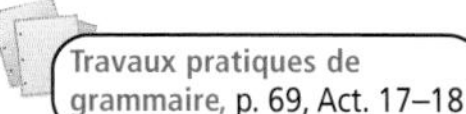
Travaux pratiques de grammaire, p. 69, Act. 17–18

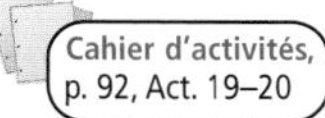
Cahier d'activités, p. 92, Act. 19–20

Communication for All Students

Building on Previous Skills

Ask students if they have ever been served food they didn't like and what they did in that situation. Discuss how to avoid being rude in such a situation. Have students consider the consequences of being an inconsiderate guest. Ask students how they would feel if a guest refused to taste something they had prepared.

Troisième étape

Teaching Resources
pp. 245–249

PRINT 

- Lesson Planner, p. 41
- TPR Storytelling Book, pp. 31, 32
- Listening Activities, pp. 60–61, 65
- Activities for Communication, pp. 47–48, 112, 114, 151–152
- Travaux pratiques de grammaire, pp. 69–70
- Grammar Tutor for Students of French, Chapter 8
- Cahier d'activités, pp. 92–94
- Testing Program, pp. 205–208
- Alternative Assessment Guide, p. 39
- Student Make-Up Assignments, Chapter 8

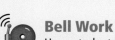

MEDIA 

- One-Stop Planner
- Audio Compact Discs, CD 8, Trs. 11–12, 22, 30–31
- Teaching Transparencies: 8-3, 8-D; **Grammaire supplémentaire** Answers; Travaux pratiques de grammaire Answers
- Interactive CD-ROM Tutor, Disc 2

Bell Work

Have students first write a sentence to say that they need two items, and then a question to ask someone to get a specified quantity of each item.

Presenting Vocabulaire

Ask students to name the different foods shown on each table. Hold up pictures of various foods and beverages and have students name the meal at which they would have them.

Troisième étape

CHAPITRE 8

Teaching Resources
pp. 245–249

PRINT 

- Lesson Planner, p. 41
- TPR Storytelling Book, pp. 31, 32
- Listening Activities, pp. 60–61, 65
- Activities for Communication, pp. 47–48, 112, 114, 151–152
- Travaux pratiques de grammaire, pp. 69–70
- Grammar Tutor for Students of French, Chapter 8
- Cahier d'activités, pp. 92–94
- Testing Program, pp. 205–208
- Alternative Assessment Guide, p. 39
- Student Make-Up Assignments, Chapter 8

MEDIA

- One-Stop Planner
- Audio Compact Discs, CD 8, Trs. 11–12, 22, 30–31
- Teaching Transparencies: 8-3, 8-D; **Grammaire supplémentaire** Answers; Travaux pratiques de grammaire Answers
- Interactive CD-ROM Tutor, Disc 2

Slower Pace

21 Before playing the recording, have pairs of students name the foods shown in each illustration, or you might name the items in each breakfast and have students identify the letter of the illustration you're describing.

21 Le petit déjeuner See scripts and answers on p. 229H.

CD 8 Tr. 11

Ecoutons Listen to these people tell what they have for breakfast. Match each speaker with his or her breakfast.

a.

b.

c.

Note culturelle

In the morning, most people in francophone countries have a very light breakfast. Coffee with hot milk **(café au lait)** and hot chocolate are the drinks of choice. They are usually served with bread or croissants, butter, and jam. Children may eat cereal for breakfast as well, sometimes with warm milk. The largest meal of the day, **le déjeuner,** has traditionally been between noon and 1:00 P.M. Dinner **(le dîner)** is eaten after 7:00 P.M.

22 Un repas typique

Parlons Regarde les images suivantes et dis à quel(s) repas tu manges chaque plat. Ensuite, décide si ces plats sont typiquement américains, français ou les deux.
See answers below.

1.

2.

3.

4.

5.

6.

Possible answers

22
1. au dîner; both
2. au goûter; both
3. au déjeuner; francophone country
4. au petit déjeuner; United States
5. au dîner; francophone country
6. au petit déjeuner; francophone country

Cultures and Communities

Culture Notes

- Explain that in France, **le déjeuner** is usually the main meal of the day, whereas **le dîner** is typically a light, simple meal.
- In Côte d'Ivoire, people might have popcorn **(du pop-corn)**, peanuts **(des arachides)**, roasted yams, or **aloco** with hot sauce **(sauce pimentée)** for an afternoon snack.
- **Nutella®** is a spread made from hazelnuts and chocolate. It is very popular in Europe and is sometimes eaten at breakfast or for a snack **(le goûter)**. It is now available in many supermarkets in the U.S.

STANDARDS: 1.2, 2.1, 3.2, 4.2

Quel repas?

Parlons Décris un des repas suivants à ton/ta camarade. Il/Elle doit deviner quelle image tu décris. Ensuite, changez de rôle.

EXEMPLE **Il y a du poulet,...**

1.

2.

3.

Devine!

Ecrivons/Parlons Fais des menus pour tes trois repas de demain. Utilise le **Vocabulaire** de la page 235. Ton/Ta camarade fait aussi trois menus. Ensuite, devinez le contenu de vos menus.

EXEMPLE **—Au petit déjeuner, tu vas manger... ?**
—Oui, c'est ça. *or* **Non, pas de...**

Comment dit-on...?

Offering, accepting, or refusing food

CD-ROM 2 DVD 2

To offer food to someone:

Tu veux du riz?
Vous voulez de l'eau minérale?
Vous prenez du fromage?
Tu prends du fromage?
Encore du pain? *More . . . ?*

To accept:

Oui, s'il vous/te plaît.
Oui, j'en veux bien. *Yes, I'd like some.*
Oui, avec plaisir. *Yes, with pleasure.*

To refuse:

Non, merci.
Je n'en veux plus. *I don't want any more.*
Non, merci. Je n'ai plus faim. *No thanks. I'm not hungry anymore.*

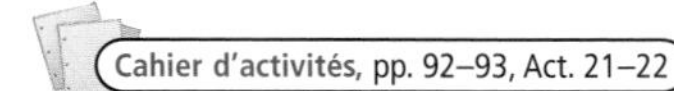
Cahier d'activités, pp. 92–93, Act. 21–22

A table See scripts and answers on p. 229H.

Ecoutons Is the speaker offering, accepting, or refusing food?

CD 8 Tr. 12

Communication for All Students

Slower Pace

23 Before doing the activity, have students point out the differences among the three meals.

Challenge

23 This activity could also be done by having students write a description of one of the meals. Then, have them exchange papers with a partner, who will guess which meal is described.

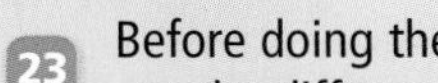

Tactile Learners

Bring in mineral water, sliced bread, or food that can be broken into pieces. Offer some to the first person in each row. After that student responds, give him or her the food. He or she then offers some to the next student, and so on.

Language Note

Tell students that responding to an offer of food by saying **Merci** alone might be taken as a refusal. Another expression of acceptance is **Oui, je veux bien.**

Presenting Comment dit-on... ?

Bring in real food items or pictures of them. Offer different items to individuals, varying your expressions. **(Tu veux du poulet? Tu prends de l'eau?)** Next, have students offer you the food items, using the **vous** form. Alternately accept and refuse the various food items, having students repeat after you.

Writing Assessment

24 You might use the following rubric when grading your students on this activity.

Writing Rubric	Points			
	4	3	2	1
Content (Complete–Incomplete)				
Comprehensibility (Comprehensible–Incomprehensible)				
Accuracy (Accurate–Seldom accurate)				
Organization (Well organized–Poorly organized)				
Effort (Excellent–Minimal)				

18–20: A 14–15: C Under 12: F
16–17: B 12–13: D

STANDARDS: 1.2, 1.3, 3.1, 5.2

Teaching Resources
pp. 245–249

PRINT 

- Lesson Planner, p. 41
- TPR Storytelling Book, pp. 31, 32
- Listening Activities, pp. 60–61, 65
- Activities for Communication, pp. 47–48, 112, 114, 151–152
- Travaux pratiques de grammaire, pp. 69–70
- Grammar Tutor for Students of French, Chapter 8
- Cahier d'activités, pp. 92–94
- Testing Program, pp. 205–208
- Alternative Assessment Guide, p. 39
- Student Make-Up Assignments, Chapter 8

MEDIA

- One-Stop Planner
- Audio Compact Discs, CD 8, Trs. 11–12, 22, 30–31
- Teaching Transparencies: 8-3, 8-D; **Grammaire supplémentaire** Answers; Travaux pratiques de grammaire Answers
- Interactive CD-ROM Tutor, Disc 2

Presenting
Grammaire

The pronoun *en* On five cards, write each word and the question mark of **Tu veux des mangues?** Write **en** on a sixth card. Give one card, with the exception of **en**, to each of five students. Have them stand side-by-side so their cards read **Tu veux des mangues?** Then, remove the students holding the cards for **des** and **mangues.** Substitute another student holding the card for **en** in the proper position to form **Tu en veux?** Repeat this procedure for the other examples.

26 Encore du pain?

Parlons Un élève ivoirien dîne chez toi. Tu veux qu'il goûte plusieurs plats. Encourage-le. Ton ami accepte ou refuse poliment.

Look for opportunities to practice your French wherever you go. Try to meet French-speaking people and talk with them. Ask your teacher to help you find a pen pal in a French-speaking country. Rent videocassettes of French films. See how many French products you can find at the grocery store and the cosmetic counter, and how many French dishes you can find on restaurant menus.

Grammaire

The pronoun *en*

En takes the place of a phrase beginning with **du, de la, de l', des,** or **de** to avoid repetition. **En** usually means *some (of it/of them)* or simply *it/them.*

— Tu veux **des mangues?**
— Oui, j'**en** veux bien.
— Tu manges **des légumes?**
— Oui, j'**en** mange souvent.

In a negative sentence, **en** means *any* or *none.*

— Tu veux **du beurre?**
— Merci, je n'**en** veux pas.

Grammaire supplémentaire, pp. 254–255, Act. 9–12

Cahier d'activités, p. 93, Act. 23

Travaux pratiques de grammaire, p. 70, Act. 19–20

27 Grammaire en contexte

Lisons/Ecrivons Regarde les articles dans le panier d'Aïssata. Combien est-ce qu'elle en a? Donne la quantité de chaque article.

EXEMPLE Des haricots? **Elle en a un kilo.**

1. Du lait? Elle en a un litre.
2. Du beurre? Elle en a un paquet.
3. Des tomates? Elle en a trois.
4. Du riz? Elle en a un kilo.
5. Des œufs? Elle en a six.
6. De l'eau minérale? Elle en a une bouteille.
7. Des ananas? Elle n'en a pas.

Connections and Comparisons

Thinking Critically

Evaluating In Africa, as in France, people almost never drink milk with meals. Ask students which French or African eating habits might be difficult to adopt.

Music Link

Grammaire To have students listen to the pronoun **en** modeled in a song, play *Il n'y en a pas comme nous* available on Audio CD 8.

28 Grammaire en contexte

Parlons Demande à un(e) camarade s'il ou si elle aime les plats de l'activité 26. Utilise le pronom **en** dans tes questions. Ensuite, changez de rôle.

Exemple — **Tu manges du poulet?**
— **Oui, j'en mange souvent.**

29 De l'école au travail

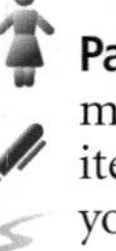

Parlons/Ecrivons You work part-time in a French restaurant where the chef speaks mostly French. The chef, Pierre Leroux, asks you to go to the supermarket to buy some items he needs to prepare certain dishes. Make a list of what he needs and verify that you have all of the items. Your partner will play the role of the chef. Then switch roles.

PRONONCIATION

CD 8
Trs. 13–18

The sounds [o] and [ɔ] See scripts and answers on p. 229H.

The sound [o] is similar to the vowel sound in the English word *boat.* To make the sound [o], hold your mouth in a whistling position. Keep the lips and tongue steady to avoid the glide heard in *boat.* Repeat each of these words: **trop, kilo, mot.** The spellings **au, eau, ô,** and sometimes **o** represent the sound [o]. Now, repeat these words: **jaune, chaud, beau, rôle.**

The sound [ɔ] is between the vowel sounds in the English words *boat* and *bought.* Usually, this sound is followed by a consonant sound in the same syllable. The sound [ɔ] is more open, so hold your mouth in a semi-whistling position to produce it. This sound is usually spelled with the letter **o.** Now, repeat these words: **bof, donne, fort, carotte.**

A. A prononcer

Repeat the following words and phrases.

1. au revoir	un stylo jaune	au restaurant
2. un gâteau	moi aussi	des haricots verts
3. des pommes	d'abord	une promenade
4. encore	dormir	l'école

B. A lire

Take turns with a partner reading each of the following sentences aloud.

1. Elle a une gomme violette et un stylo jaune.
2. Tu aimes les carottes? Moi, j'adore. J'aime bien aussi les escargots et le porc.
3. Elle est occupée aujourd'hui. Elle a informatique et biologie.
4. Il me faut un short parce qu'il fait trop chaud.
5. Tu peux sortir si tu promènes d'abord le chien.

C. A écrire

You're going to hear a short dialogue. Write down what you hear.

Teacher to Teacher

Lynn Payne
Hidden Valley High School
Roanoke, VA

Here's Lynn's idea for a culture project.

"My culture project for Chapitre 8 is a travel brochure of Abidjan with pictures and captions in simple French. The cover of the brochure has the title **Allez, viens à Abidjan** and a small map. The first panel of the brochure contains three "sights to see". The middle panel is for "things to do". On the third panel, students are to list hotels and restaurants with Ivorian foods, which can be obtained from the Internet. Finally, on the back of the brochure, students put pictures of festivals and special holidays in Côte d'Ivoire."

Troisième étape

Thinking Critically

Comparing and Contrasting
Ask students to compare a French breakfast with what Americans normally eat for breakfast. Ask students if they generally have a light breakfast or a heavy one.

Teacher Note

Prononciation Notice that in Part A, rows 1 and 2 contain examples of the **[o]** sound, and rows 3 and 4 present examples of the **[ɔ]** sound.

Teaching Suggestion

Prononciation After correcting the dictation in Part C, have students underline the letters that represent the **[o]** sound and circle the letters that represent **[ɔ]**.

Assess

- Testing Program, pp. 205–208
  Quiz 8-3A, Quiz 8-3B
  Audio CD 8, Tr. 22
- Student Make-Up Assignments, Chapter 8, Alternative Quiz
- Alternative Assessment Guide, p. 39

STANDARDS: 1.1, 1.3, 4.1, 4.2

Lisons!

CHAPITRE 8

Teaching Resources
pp. 250–251

PRINT 
- Lesson Planner, p. 42
- Cahier d'activités, p. 95
- Reading Strategies and Skills Handbook, Chapter 8
- Joie de lire 1, Chapter 8
- Standardized Assessment Tutor, Chapter 8

MEDIA
- One-Stop Planner

Prereading
Activities A–D

Using Prior Knowledge
Have students compile a list of French cooking terms used in English, such as **sauté, julienne,** and **purée.**

Reading
Activities E–H

Terms in Lisons!
Students may want to know the following expressions: **pâte** *(dough);* **étaler** *(to roll out);* **cuire** *(to cook);* **four** *(oven);* **ail** *(garlic);* **éplucher** *(to peel);* **évider** *(to empty out).*

Language Note
Students might notice that the recipe directions are given in the infinitive form. This is common in written instructions to a general audience. Ask students why they think this is done.

TPR Give various cooking instructions and have students mime the actions. You might provide props, such as a bowl, a spoon, and a baking pan.

Lisons!

LA CUISINE AFRICAINE

Stratégie pour lire
Remember to look for cognates to help you figure out what you're reading. Occasionally, you will encounter false cognates, words that look alike in two languages but have different meanings.

Context clues can sometimes help you recognize false cognates. An example of a false cognate is the French phrase fruits de mer. Fruits de mer may make you think of the English word *fruit,* but it means *seafood.*

A. You already know a few false cognates. Try to figure out the meaning of the false cognates in the sentences below.

1. Je vais à San Francisco à 11h00. Maintenant, il est 10h40, et **j'attends** le train.
   - **a.** I'm attending
   - **b.** I'm late for
   - **c.** I'm waiting for
2. J'adore les sciences. Ce soir, je vais **assister** à une conférence sur l'ozone.
   - **a.** to attend
   - **b.** to assist
   - **c.** to teach

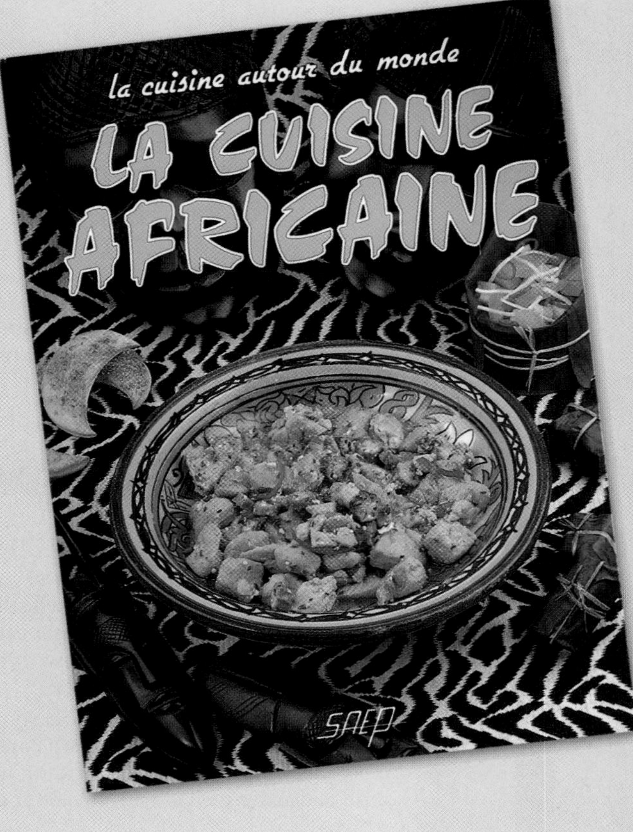

Les desserts

Croissants au coco et au sésame
(Afrique occidentale)
Prép. : 30 mn. - Cuiss. : 10 mn.
Repos : 1 h. - 8 pers.

2 œufs	*170 g de farine*
140 g de sucre	*Vanille en poudre*
190 g de noix de coco râpée	*Graines de sésame.*

Mélanger la noix de coco râpée, le sucre, la vanille et les œufs entiers. Incorporer la farine. Travailler la pâte. Former une boule. Laisser reposer 1 heure au frais.

Etaler la pâte sur 1/2 cm. Découper en croissants. Les rouler dans le sésame. Cuire au four à 200 °C, (th. 6-7), 10 minutes.

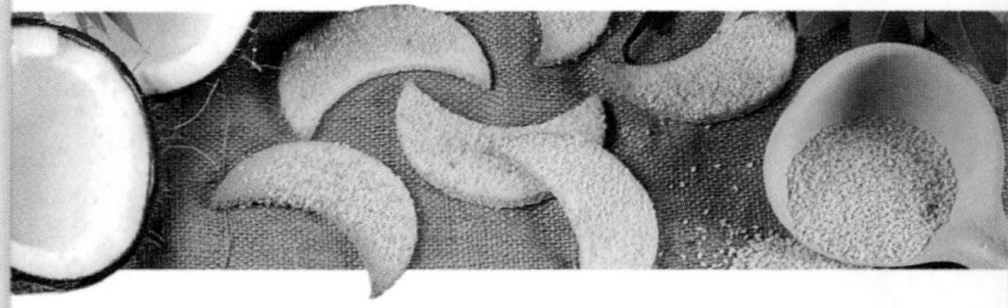

Connections and Comparisons

Thinking Critically
Organizing Have students create a list of common cooking instructions in English, such as *bake, slice, stir, mix,* and so on. Tell students to place them in the order in which they are usually performed. For example, *stir* would come before *bake.* Tell students that they will be able to guess the meanings of some unfamiliar French instructions by their order in the recipe.

STANDARDS: 1.2, 2.2, 3.1, 3.2, 4.1

Signification des symboles accompagnant les recettes

Recettes		Recettes	
✕	élémentaire	○	peu coûteuse
✕✕	facile	○○	raisonnable
✕✕✕	difficile	○○○	chère

Les entrées

Mousseline africaine de petits légumes ✕ ○○
(Afrique occidentale - Bénin - Togo)

Prép. : 40 mn. - Cuiss. : 15 mn.
4 pers.

2 petits concombres	*1 avocat*
Ail	*1 épi de maïs*
1 lime	*Graines de carvi*
1 radis noir	*4 petites brioches*
1/2 papaye	*Sel.*

Eplucher les concombres. Les détailler en dés. Faire la même chose avec l'avocat.

Débarrasser l'épis de maïs des feuilles et des barbes. Le faire cuire durant 15 minutes à l'eau bouillante. Saler en fin de cuisson.

Egréner le maïs. Débarrasser la papaye de ses graines. La découper en petits dés. **Emincer le radis noir. Parfumer de graines de carvi et d'ail haché. Arroser la salade de jus de lime.**

Retirer le chapeau des brioches. Les évider. Les garnir de la salade parfumée.

Les brioches ne doivent pas être sucrées. Si on les fabrique, il convient d'ôter le sucre.

Ne pas saler l'épi de maïs au début de la cuisson mais à la fin afin d'éviter qu'il durcisse.

B. With a partner, scan the reading and write down all of the cognates you can find in these selections. See answers below.

C. Did you find any false cognates? Were you able to figure out what they mean? If so, how? See answers below.

D. Where would you expect to find these reading selections? Where are these dishes from? cookbook; Africa

E. Which of the dishes would make a good dessert? croissants

F. Are these dishes easy or difficult to make? How do you know? Are they expensive or inexpensive to make? How do you know? See answers below.

G. To make **croissants,** how long do you need to chill the dough? At what temperature do you bake them? What temperature is that on the Fahrenheit scale? (To convert from Celsius to Fahrenheit, multiply by $\frac{9}{5}$ and add 32.) See answers below.

H. To make **mousseline,** how long do you have to cook the corn? Do you think this dish would taste sweet or salty? How many people does this dish serve? See answers below.

I. Now, with a partner, write the instructions for an easy recipe that you know how to make. Include the ingredients, the steps required to prepare the dish, and the cooking and preparation time required.

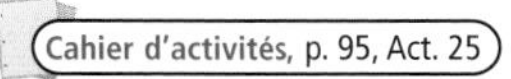
Cahier d'activités, p. 95, Act. 25

Postreading
Activity I

Kinesthetic Learners

I. Ask students to use metric measurements in their recipes. You might have students demonstrate how to prepare their dishes in front of the class, using props if they choose. Have one partner read aloud the recipe while the other acts out the instructions. You might prefer to have students make their dishes at home and bring them in for the class to sample.

Challenge

As an additional chapter project, students might compile all the recipes into a class cookbook. They might design and draw a cover and illustrate each recipe. You might have them make copies to distribute to the entire class.

Connections and Comparisons

Math Link

- Have students figure out the American measurements of the ingredients in the cookie recipe. They might refer to the conversion chart in the **Note culturelle** on page 242.
- **I.** If students use the oven for their recipes, have them give the oven temperature in Celsius. The formula for converting Fahrenheit to Celsius is $F - 32 \times 5/9$.

Thinking Critically

Comparing and Contrasting After students have read the recipes carefully, ask them if the ingredients listed would be difficult to find in local stores. Ask students if the recipes sound appetizing and if they are similar to dishes that they have eaten.

Answers

B. *Possible answers:* africaine, coco, sésame, vanille, symboles, raisonnable, desserts, avocat

C. *Possible answers:* parfumer *(to flavor),* détailler *(to cut separately),* fabriquer *(to make)*

F. Symbols show that both recipes are very easy **(élémentaire)** and moderately priced **(raisonnable).**

G. one hour; 200°C; 392°F

H. 15 minutes; salty; four people

STANDARDS: 1.2, 1.3, 2.2, 3.1, 3.2, 4.1, 5.2

Grammaire supplémentaire

CHAPITRE 8

For **Grammaire supplémentaire** Answer Transparencies, see the *Teaching Transparencies* binder.

Answers

1 du; du; du; de la; des; du; des; des; des; des

2 1. de la farine; des œufs; du beurre; du sel; de la levure; du jus de pomme; du lait
2. des oignons; des tomates; de l'huile d'arachide; de la pâte d'arachide; de la pâte de tomates; du sel; des piments rouges.

3
1. du
2. des
3. des
4. d'
5. de la
6. du
7. du
8. de
9. de l'
10. une

Grammaire supplémentaire

Visit Holt Online
go.hrw.com
KEYWORD: WA3 ABIDJAN-8
Jeux interactifs

Première étape

Objective Expressing need

1 Eric is planning a party and has made a list of what he needs to do to get ready. Complete his list with **du, de la, de l',** and **des** as needed. (**p. 236**)

Pour ma boum, je vais faire des sandwiches, alors je vais acheter __1__ pain, __2__ fromage et __3__ jambon. Mes amis aiment manger __4__ salade. Dans la salade, je vais mettre __5__ tomates, __6__ maïs et __7__ champignons. Pour le dessert, je vais préparer une salade de fruits avec __8__ oranges, __9__ bananes et __10__ pommes.

2 Lis les recettes ci-dessous. Ensuite, écris une note pour te rappeler les choses que tu dois acheter au marché. Utilise les articles **du, de la, de l'** et **des.** (**p. 236**)

EXEMPLE **Il me faut de la farine...**

1. **Les crêpes bretonnes**
500 g de farine
3 œufs
20 g de beurre
3 g de sel
5 g de levure
1 cl de jus de pomme
1/4 litre de lait

2. **La sauce arachide**
4 oignons
2 tomates
5 cl d'huile d'arachide
100 g de pâte d'arachide
100 g de pâte de tomates
10 g de sel
3 piments rouges

3 Anne and Odile are talking about items they have to bring to a picnic. Complete their conversation with the partitive or indefinite articles. (**p. 236**)

— Alors, moi, j'ai __1__ raisin, __2__ pommes et __3__ tomates. Je n'ai pas __4__ avocats. Et toi, qu'est-ce que tu as?

— J'ai __5__ confiture, __6__ pain et __7__ fromage. Je n'ai pas __8__ jus de pomme, mais j'ai __9__ eau minérale. Est-ce que tu veux acheter __10__ tarte?

—Oui, c'est une bonne idée.

Grammar Resources for Chapter 8

The **Grammaire supplémentaire** activities were designed as supplemental activities for the grammatical concepts presented in the chapter. You might use them as additional practice, for review, or for assessment.

For more grammar presentations, review, and practice, refer to the following:

- Travaux pratiques de grammaire
- Grammar Tutor for Students of French
- Grammar Summary on pp. R15–R28
- Cahier d'activités
- Grammar and Vocabulary quizzes (Testing Program)
- Test Generator
- Interactive CD-ROM Tutor
- DVD Tutor
- **Jeux interactifs** at go.hrw.com

STANDARDS: 1.2

Grammaire supplémentaire

CHAPITRE 8

4 Rewrite the following sentences, using the expressions **avoir besoin de** or **il me/te faut** and the partitive article. (**pp. 236, 238**)

EXEMPLE Il me faut des bananes. **J'ai besoin de bananes.**
Tu as besoin de lait? **Il te faut du lait?**

1. Il me faut des noix de coco.
2. Il te faut des papayes?
3. Tu as besoin de confiture?
4. Il me faut du raisin.
5. J'ai besoin d'eau minérale.
6. Il te faut des ananas?
7. Tu as besoin de sucre?
8. Il te faut de la farine?
9. Il me faut des œufs, aussi.
10. Tu as besoin de pêches?

Deuxième étape

Objectives Making, accepting, and declining requests; telling someone what to do

5 Combine les expressions des deux colonnes pour faire des phrases complètes. (**p. 241**)

A	B
1. Est-ce que tu...	a. ne peuvent pas aller au cinéma ce soir. Ils sont occupés.
2. Elle...	b. ne peux pas sortir la poubelle. Je n'ai pas le temps.
3. Nous...	c. peux débarrasser la table, s'il te plaît?
4. Angèle et toi, vous...	d. ne pouvons pas faire la vaisselle. Nous avons des trucs à faire.
5. Moi, je...	e. ne peut pas sortir avec ses copines. Elle a des devoirs à faire.
6. Mes copains...	f. pouvez promener le chien?

6 Ton ami(e) et toi, vous allez faire une fête. Ecrivez les choses que les invités peuvent apporter. Utilise les formes correctes du verbe **pouvoir.** (**p. 241**)

1. Isabelle _____ acheter des avocats et des tomates.
2. Moi, je _____ acheter des tartes.
3. Henri, tu _____ acheter des fraises et des citrons?
4. Carol et Sylvain, vous _____ acheter de la salade et du pain.
5. Barbara, Serge et Françoise _____ acheter des boissons.

7 Unscramble the names of the food items. Then, combine the fragments to create sentences that tell Djeneba what to get you from the market. (**p. 242**)

EXEMPLE RUERBE / un paquet de/s'il te plaît/prends
Prends un paquet de beurre, s'il te plaît!

1. ITESPT OSPI / une boîte de/rapporte-moi/s'il te plaît
2. NDVAIE / s'il te plaît/un morceau de/achète-moi
3. EFOSU D' / prends/une douzaine
4. SJU ASANAN D' / une bouteille de/acheter/n'oublie pas de
5. AMCHNONPIGS / tu peux/s'il te plaît/une livre de/acheter
6. IRNAFE / un kilo de/s'il te plaît/rapporte-moi

Teacher to Teacher

Beth Pierce
Columbia High School
Columbia, MS

Beth suggests this game to review the partitive and indefinite articles.
"Each person draws a picture of a different food item. All desks are in a circle, one less desk than there are people playing. One student stands in the center with a rolled-up piece of poster paper held by a rubber band. One student stands up and names, in French, any food item pictured using a partitive or definite article. The person who has that picture in front of him or her has to quickly say another food item *before* the person in the center hits him or her with the paper "bat." If the person in the middle manages to hit someone, they exchange places. The new person in the circle now has to say a food item before he or she sits down."

Answers

4
1. J'ai besoin de noix de coco.
2. Tu as besoin de papayes?
3. Il te faut de la confiture?
4. J'ai besoin de raisin.
5. Il me faut de l'eau minérale.
6. Tu as besoin d'ananas?
7. Il te faut du sucre?
8. Tu as besoin de farine?
9. J'ai besoin d'œufs, aussi.
10. Il te faut des pêches?

5
1. c
2. e
3. d
4. f
5. b
6. a

6
1. peut
2. peux
3. peux
4. pouvez
5. peuvent

7
1. Rapporte-moi une boîte de petits pois, s'il te plaît!
2. Achète-moi un morceau de viande, s'il te plaît!
3. Prends une douzaine d'œufs!
4. N'oublie pas d'acheter une bouteille de jus d'ananas!
5. Tu peux acheter une livre de champignons, s'il te plaît?
6. Rapporte-moi un kilo de farine, s'il te plaît!

STANDARDS: 1.2

Grammaire supplémentaire

CHAPITRE 8

For **Grammaire supplémentaire** Answer Transparencies, see the *Teaching Transparencies* binder.

Grammaire supplémentaire

WA3 ABIDJAN-8

8 Your mom has asked you to pick up some items at the neighborhood grocery store. Write a sentence for each of the items on the list that you will need to purchase. Choose the appropriate quantity from the box for each item you request. (**p. 242**)

EXEMPLE **Il me faut un paquet de sucre./J'ai besoin d'un paquet de sucre.**

une tranche, un litre, un morceau, un kilo, un paquet, une boîte, une douzaine, une bouteille

sucre
farine
fromage
lait
eau minérale
œufs
pommes de terre
jambon

Troisième étape

Objective Offering, accepting, or refusing food

9 Tu demandes à Didier ce que sa famille aime manger. Ecris les réponses de Didier. Utilise **en** et le verbe **prendre.** (**pp. 149, 248**)

EXEMPLE Tu prends du café au lait au petit déjeuner?
Oui, j'en prends.

1. Tu prends du lait au dîner? Non, ...
2. Tes parents prennent du pain avec leur fromage? Oui, ...
3. Ta sœur prend des légumes au déjeuner? Oui, ...
4. Ton petit frère prend des gâteaux au goûter? Non, ...
5. Ta cousine et toi, vous prenez de la viande au déjeuner? Non, ...
6. Tu prends de la sauce arachide avec ton riz? Oui, ...

10 Joël dîne avec sa famille française pour la première fois. Mets les morceaux de phrases dans le bon ordre pour recréer la conversation du dîner. Mets les formes correctes des verbes et ajoute les articles nécessaires. N'oublie pas la ponctuation! (**pp. 236, 247, 248**)

1. — petits pois/vouloir/tu
2. — en/bien/je/oui/vouloir
3. — vouloir/pain/tu
4. — plaisir/oui/avec
5. — tu/poulet/vouloir
6. — vouloir/ne...plus/merci/en/je/non
7. — vouloir/fromage/tu
8. — merci/je/non/laitiers/manger/ne...pas/produits

Answers

8
1. Il me faut un paquet de sucre.
2. J'ai besoin d'un paquet de farine, aussi.
3. J'ai besoin d'un morceau de fromage.
4. Il me faut un litre de lait.
5. J'ai besoin d'une bouteille d'eau minérale.
6. Il me faut une douzaine d'œufs.
7. J'ai besoin d'un kilo de pommes de terre.
8. Il me faut une tranche de jambon.

9
1. je n'en prends pas.
2. ils en prennent.
3. elle en prend.
4. il n'en prend pas.
5. on n'en prend pas.
6. j'en prends.

10
1. Tu veux des petits pois?
2. Oui, j'en veux bien.
3. Tu veux du pain?
4. Oui, avec plaisir.
5. Tu veux du poulet?
6. Non, merci. Je n'en veux plus.
7. Tu veux du fromage?
8. Non merci, je ne mange pas de produits laitiers.

Communication for All Students

Slower Pace

9 You might have students do this activity orally first, answering each question without using the pronoun *en*. Then, have students work in pairs to practice using *en* in their answers.

Challenge

10 Have students work in groups of five and use this activity as a model to create their own dinner conversation. Have each group perform their conversation in the form of a skit in front of the class.

STANDARDS: 1.2

11 Lis les quatre phrases ci-dessous pour avoir des informations sur les amis d'Armelle. Utilise ces informations pour écrire leurs réponses aux questions d'Armelle. Utilise **en** et le verbe **vouloir** dans chaque réponse. (**p. 248**)

> **Marius n'a plus faim, mais il a très soif.**
>
> **Irène aime les fruits, mais elle n'aime pas tellement le fromage.**
>
> **Isabelle n'aime pas la viande, mais elle adore le poisson.**
>
> **Léopold a très faim, mais il n'a plus soif.**

EXEMPLE Irène, encore du fromage? **Non, merci. Je n'en veux plus.**

1. Marius, tu veux de l'eau?
2. Irène, tu veux des pêches?
3. Isabelle, encore du rosbif?
4. Léopold, tu veux du gâteau?
5. Isabelle, tu veux du poisson?
6. Marius, encore du riz?

12 A nutritionist is visiting your school to interview students about their eating habits and to advise them on how to have a well-balanced diet. Complete the following sentences with the necessary articles. (**pp. 236, 238, 248**)

—Est-ce que tu manges __1__ fruits?
—Oui, j'__2__ mange souvent.
—Est-ce que tu manges __3__ bœuf?
—Non, je ne mange pas __4__ viande, mais je mange __5__ œufs de temps en temps.
—Est-ce que tu aimes __6__ lait?
—Non, je n'__7__ bois jamais, mais je mange __8__ yaourt et __9__ fromage.
—Est-ce que tu bois __10__ eau?
—Oui. J'__11__ bois beaucoup. Je bois au moins un litre __12__ eau par jour.
—Bon, tu manges très bien, mais tu as besoin de manger __13__ légumes.

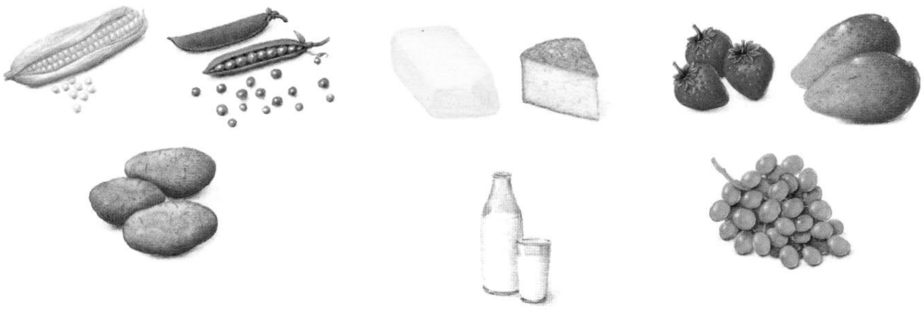

Answers

11
1. Oui, j'en veux bien.
2. Oui, j'en veux bien.
3. Non, merci. Je n'en veux plus.
4. Oui, j'en veux bien.
5. Oui, j'en veux bien.
6. Non, merci. Je n'en veux plus.

12
1. des
2. en
3. du
4. de
5. des
6. le
7. en
8. du
9. du
10. de l'
11. en
12. d'
13. des

Review and Assess

You may wish to assign the **Grammaire supplémentaire** activities as additional practice or homework after presenting material throughout the chapter. Assign Activities 1–3 after **Grammaire** (p. 236), Activity 4 after **Note de grammaire** (p. 238), Activities 5–6 after **Grammaire** (p. 241), Activities 7–8 after **Note de grammaire** (p. 242), and Activities 9–12 after **Grammaire** (p. 248). To prepare students for the **Etape** Quizzes and Chapter Test, we suggest doing the **Grammaire supplémentaire** activities in the following order. Have students complete Activities 1–4 before taking Quizzes 8-1A or 8-1B; Activities 5–8 before Quizzes 8-2A or 8-2B; and Activities 9–12 before Quizzes 8-3A or 8-3B.

Mise en pratique

CHAPITRE 8

The **Mise en pratique** reviews and integrates all four skills and culture in preparation for the Chapter Test.

Teaching Resources
pp. 256–257

PRINT 

- Lesson Planner, p. 42
- Listening Activities, p. 61
- Video Guide, pp. 55, 58
- Grammar Tutor for Students of French, Chapter 8
- Standardized Assessment Tutor, Chapter 8

MEDIA 

- One-Stop Planner
- Video Program Videocassette 3, 26:51–27:58
- Audio Compact Discs, CD 8, Tr. 19
- Interactive CD-ROM Tutor, Disc 2

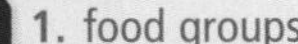

Answers

2
1. food groups
2. milk and milk products; meats, fish, and eggs; breads (starches); fruits and vegetables; fats; sugar
3. a. calcium, protein, vitamins A, B, and D
   b. protein, iron, vitamin B
   c. carbohydrates, fiber
   d. fiber, vitamins A and B, carbohydrates
   e. lipids, vitamins A and E
   f. carbohydrates
4. *Possible answers:*
   Lait: lait, fromage, yaourt
   Viandes: poulet, bœuf, porc
   Pain/féculents: pain, pommes de terre, riz
   Fruits/légumes: oranges, petits pois, carottes
   Matières grasses: beurre
   Sucre: gâteau, glace, confiture
5. *Answers will vary.*

Mise en pratique

1 Listen to this supermarket advertisement. List four of the foods that are on sale. Then, listen again for the prices of the four items you listed.

See scripts and answers on p. 229H.

CD 8 Tr. 19

2

LES GROUPES D'ALIMENTS

Les aliments sont regroupés en 6 catégories selon leurs caractéristiques nutritionnelles :

- **Le lait et les produits laitiers** sont nos principaux fournisseurs de calcium.
- **Viandes, poissons et œufs** sont nos sources essentielles de protéines de bonne qualité.
- **Le groupe du pain, des féculents et des légumes secs** apporte les «glucides lents» libérant progressivement l'énergie nécessaire à notre organisme.
- **Légumes et fruits** sont nos sources de fibres, vitamines et minéraux.
- **Les matières grasses** sont les sources énergétiques les plus importantes pour notre corps.
- **Le sucre et ses dérivés** apportent les «glucides rapides» nécessaires au bon fonctionnement cérébral et musculaire.

Groupe	Lait Produits Laitiers	Viandes Poissons Œufs	Pains Féculents	Fruits Légumes	Matières Grasses	Sucre Dérivés
Intérêt Principal	Calcium	Protéines	Glucides	Fibres Vitamines A et B	Lipides	Glucides
Intérêt Secondaire	Protéines Vitamines A, B, D	Fer Vitamine B	Fibres	Glucides	Vitamines (A, E, selon mat. grasses)	

L'ensemble de ces catégories permet, au sein d'une alimentation diversifiée, de couvrir tous nos besoins.

See answers below.

1. What kind of chart is this?
2. What do the six categories listed mean?
3. According to the chart, what are some of the nutrients found in . . .
   a. produits laitiers?
   b. viandes?
   c. pain?
   d. fruits et légumes?
   e. matières grasses?
   f. sucre et ses dérivés?
4. Give some examples of foods you know in French that fall into each category.
5. Name three foods that are high in protein and three that are high in calcium.

Apply and Assess

Slower Pace

1 Before you play the recording, tell students that they should not expect to hear the prices given immediately after the food item. You might pause the recording after one or two items are mentioned to give students time to write.

Challenge

1 As a follow-up activity, students might prepare and record similar advertisements.

Health Link

Have students bring in the latest charts of recommended foods and of foods to avoid. If possible, have them describe the foods in French.

STANDARDS: 1.2, 3.1

3 Quelles différences est-ce qu'il y a entre les repas africains, français et américains?
See answers below.

Ecrivons!

Imagine that you're the producer of a certain food item that you're trying to market. Write an ad that encourages people to buy the item, telling when they might eat it and why it's good. Consider who would be likely to buy your product. Include logos and pictures in your ad as well.

Persuasive writing encourages people to do a certain thing or to think a certain way. Advertisements are a type of persuasive writing because advertisers try to convince people that their products are better than any others.

Stratégie pour écrire

Arranging your ideas spatially is a good way to organize ideas for your advertisement. First, brainstorm some catchy phrases and convincing arguments you might write in your ad to persuade people to buy your product. Also, decide what types of illustrations you might use (photos, logos, and so on) and where to place them in your ad. Then, create a sketch of how you want your ad to look.

Using the sketch you prepared, create the ad for your product. Structure is very important in persuasive writing. You should choose what you feel is the greatest benefit or most appealing characteristic of the product and draw attention to it. You can do this by writing it in larger print or in an eye-catching color. Less attention should be drawn to what you feel are your product's weaker points. However, try to avoid relying too heavily on illustrations and layout; your ad should be informative as well as eye-catching. Be sure to use descriptive terms that illustrate the qualities of your product.

5

Jeu de rôle

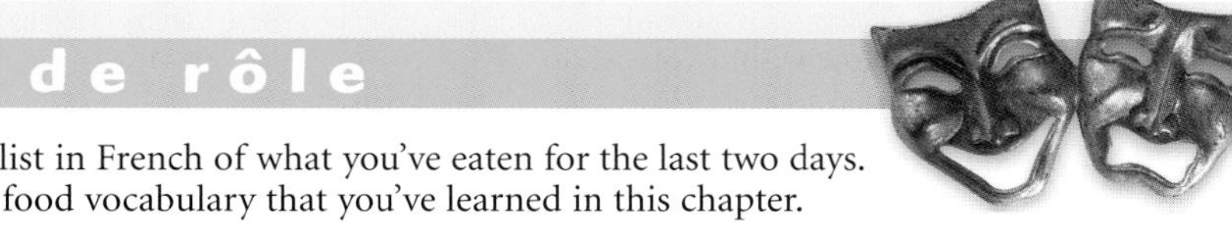

a. Make a list in French of what you've eaten for the last two days. Use the food vocabulary that you've learned in this chapter.

b. Now, you go to a nutrition counselor. The counselor will evaluate your diet, telling you what you need to eat more of and what you shouldn't eat anymore. Act out this scene with a partner. Then, change roles.

Mise en pratique

CHAPITRE 8

Portfolio

5 **Oral** This activity might be included in students' oral portfolios and/or performed as a skit for the class. For portfolio information, see the *Alternative Assessment Guide,* pages iv–17.

Apply and Assess

Process Writing

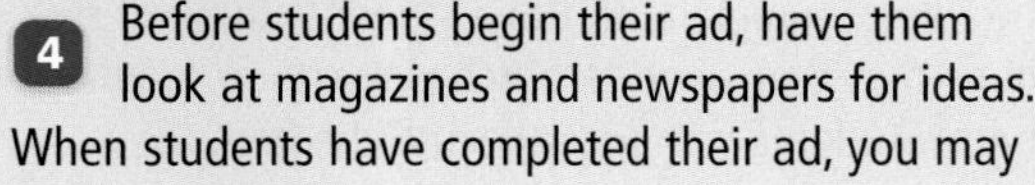

4 Before students begin their ad, have them look at magazines and newspapers for ideas. When students have completed their ad, you may want to compile them all into a food catalog that can be displayed in the classroom, or award a prize for the most creative advertisement.

Answers

3 *Possible answers:*
In Africa and France, lunch is often the largest meal of the day, while in the United States, dinner is the largest meal. Dinner is eaten later in Africa and France than in the United States. In Africa, lunch is followed by an hour-long siesta and stores are generally closed from noon to 3:00 P.M.

Que sais-je?

CHAPITRE 8

Teaching Resources
p. 258

PRINT 
- Grammar Tutor for Students of French, Chapter 8

MEDIA 
- Interactive CD-ROM Tutor, Disc 2
- Online self-test

go.hrw.com
WA3 ABIDJAN-8

Teacher Note
This page is intended to help students prepare for the Chapter Test. It is a brief checklist of the major points covered in the chapter. The students should be reminded that this is only a checklist and does not necessarily include everything that will appear on the test.

Answers

1
1. Il me faut du poisson. J'ai besoin de poisson.
2. Il me faut des pommes de terre. J'ai besoin de pommes de terre.
3. Il me faut du riz. J'ai besoin de riz.
4. Il me faut du gâteau. J'ai besoin de gâteau.
5. Il me faut un ananas. J'ai besoin d'ananas.

4 *Possible answers:*
Je voudrais... ; Je prends... ; Il me faut...
1. une douzaine d'œufs.
2. un litre de lait.
3. un kilo d'oranges.
4. un paquet de beurre.
5. une tranche de jambon.
6. une bouteille d'eau minérale.

5 *Possible answers:*
Tu veux... ; Vous voulez... ; Tu prends... ; Vous prenez... ; Encore...
1. du riz?
2. des oranges?
3. du lait?

7 *Possible answers:*
1. Pour le petit déjeuner, je prends...
2. Pour le déjeuner, je prends...
3. Pour le goûter, je prends...
4. Pour le dîner, je prends...

Que sais-je?

WA3 ABIDJAN-8

Can you use what you've learned in this chapter?

Can you express need?
p. 238

1 How would you tell someone that you need these things? See answers below.

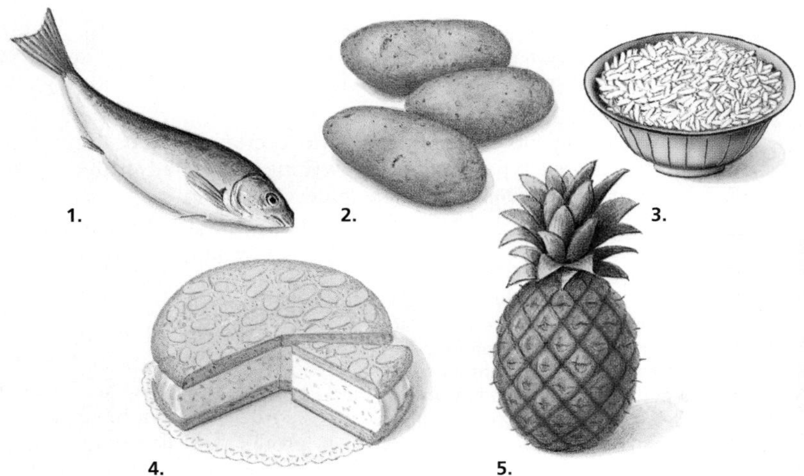

Can you make, accept, and decline requests and tell someone what to do?
p. 240

2 How would you . . .
1. ask someone to go grocery shopping for you? Tu peux aller faire les courses?
2. tell someone to bring back some groceries for you? Tu me rapportes... ?

3 How would you accept the requests in Activity 2? How would you refuse?
Accept: Bon, d'accord. Je veux bien. J'y vais tout de suite.
Refuse: Je ne peux pas maintenant. Je regrette, mais je n'ai pas le temps.

4 How would you ask for a specific quantity of these foods? See answers below.
1. œufs
2. lait
3. oranges
4. beurre
5. jambon
6. eau minérale

Can you offer, accept, or refuse food?
p. 247

5 How would you offer someone these foods? See answers below.
1. some rice
2. some oranges
3. some milk

6 How would you accept the foods listed in number 5 if they were offered? How would you refuse them?
Accept: Oui, s'il vous/te plaît. Oui, avec plaisir.
Refuse: Non, merci. Je n'en veux plus. Je n'ai plus faim.

7 How would you tell someone what you have for . . . See answers below.
1. breakfast?
2. lunch?
3. an afternoon snack?
4. dinner?

Review and Assess

Additional Practice
1 Have students write a grocery list, specifying quantities of these items.

Circumlocution
Have students imagine that they're shopping in a food market in Côte d'Ivoire, but they don't know the vocabulary for food items very well. Have them work with a partner, who will play the role of a merchant. Have students think of five items that they need to purchase, without naming them. Students will circumlocute the item they need to the merchant, who will try to help them with their purchase. **(—C'est un fruit jaune. —C'est une banane?—Oui, c'est ça.)**

STANDARDS: 1.1

Vocabulaire

Première étape

Expressing need

Qu'est-ce qu'il te faut?	*What do you need?*
Il me faut...	*I need . . .*
De quoi est-ce que tu as besoin?	*What do you need?*
J'ai besoin de...	*I need . . .*
du, de la, de l', des	*some*

Foods; Shopping

des ananas (m.)	*pineapples*
des avocats (m.)	*avocados*
des bananes (f.)	*bananas*
du beurre	*butter*
du bœuf	*beef*
des carottes (f.)	*carrots*
des champignons (m.)	*mushrooms*
des citrons (m.)	*lemons*
de la confiture	*jam*
de la farine	*flour*
des fraises (f.)	*strawberries*
du fromage	*cheese*
des fruits (m.)	*fruit*
des gâteaux (m.)	*cakes*
des gombos (m.)	*okra*
des goyaves (f.)	*guavas*
des haricots verts (m.)	*green beans*
du lait	*milk*
des légumes (m.)	*vegetables*
du maïs	*corn*
des mangues (f.)	*mangoes*
des noix de coco (f.)	*coconuts*
des œufs (m.)	*eggs*
des oignons (m.)	*onions*
des oranges (f.)	*oranges*
du pain	*bread*
des papayes (f.)	*papayas*
des pêches (f.)	*peaches*
des petits pois (m.)	*peas*
des poires (f.)	*pears*
du poisson	*fish*
des pommes (f.)	*apples*
des pommes de terre (f.)	*potatoes*
du porc	*pork*
du poulet	*chicken*
des produits (m.) **laitiers**	*dairy products*
du raisin	*grapes*
du riz	*rice*
une/de la salade	*a/some salad*
des salades	*heads of lettuce*
du sucre	*sugar*
de la tarte (f.)	*pie*
des tomates (f.)	*tomatoes*
de la viande	*meat*
des yaourts (m.)	*yogurt*
le marché	*market*
le supermarché	*supermarket*

Deuxième étape

Making, accepting, and declining requests

Tu peux... ?	*Can you . . . ?*
Tu me rapportes... ?	*Will you bring me . . . ?*
Bon, d'accord.	*Well, OK.*
Je veux bien.	*Gladly.*
J'y vais tout de suite.	*I'll go right away.*
Je regrette, mais je n'ai pas le temps.	*I'm sorry, but I don't have time.*
Je ne peux pas maintenant.	*I can't right now.*

Telling someone what to do

Rapporte(-moi)...	*Bring (me) back . . .*
Prends...	*Get . . .*
Achète(-moi)...	*Buy (me) . . .*
N'oublie pas de...	*Don't forget to . . .*
pouvoir	*to be able to, can, may*

Quantities

une boîte de	*a can of*
une bouteille de	*a bottle of*
une douzaine de	*a dozen*
un kilo(gramme) de	*a kilogram of*
un litre de	*a liter of*
une livre de	*a pound of*
un morceau de	*a piece of*
un paquet de	*a package/box of*
une tranche de	*a slice of*

Troisième étape

Offering, accepting, or refusing food

Tu veux... ?	*Do you want . . . ?*
Vous voulez... ?	*Do you want . . . ?*
Vous prenez... ?	*Will you have . . . ?*
Tu prends... ?	*Will you have . . . ?*
Encore de... ?	*More . . . ?*
Oui, s'il vous/te plaît.	*Yes, please.*
Oui, j'en veux bien.	*Yes, I'd like some.*
Oui, avec plaisir.	*Yes, with pleasure.*
Non, merci.	*No, thank you.*
Je n'en veux plus.	*I don't want any more.*
Non, merci. Je n'ai plus faim.	*No thanks. I'm not hungry anymore.*
en	*some, of it, of them, any*

Meals

le petit déjeuner	*breakfast*
le déjeuner	*lunch*
le goûter	*afternoon snack*
le dîner	*dinner*

Review and Assess

Game

Concours de vocabulaire Have students bring in pictures of the food listed on this page. Form two teams and have one player from each team go to the board. Show them one of the pictures. Writing on the board, the players must identify the item **(du lait),** give an appropriate quantity of it **(un litre de lait),** say that they need the item **(J'ai besoin de lait),** ask someone to buy it **(Tu peux acheter du lait?),** and offer it to someone **(Encore du lait?).** Give a point to the player who first writes all the information correctly.

Vocabulaire

CHAPITRE 8

Teaching Suggestion

To review vocabulary, you might play the game **Quels ingrédients?** described on page 229C.

Language Note

Point out to students that in French, unlike in English, **carotte** is spelled with one **r** and two **t**'s.

Chapter 8 Assessment

- **Testing Program**
  Chapter Test, pp. 209–214

  Audio Compact Discs, CD 8, Trs. 23–25
  Speaking Test, p. 346
- **Alternative Assessment Guide**
  Performance Assessment, p. 39
  Portfolio Assessment, p. 25
  CD-ROM Assessment, p. 53
- **Interactive CD-ROM Tutor, Disc 2**

  A toi de parler
  A toi d'écrire
- **Standardized Assessment Tutor**
  Chapter 8
- **One-Stop Planner, Disc 2**

  Test Generator
  Chapter 8

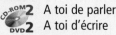

STANDARDS: 1.1, 1.2

Location Opener

CHAPTERS 9, 10, 11

Teaching Resources
pp. 260–263

PRINT 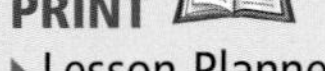

- Lesson Planner, p. 43
- Video Guide, pp. 59–60

MEDIA 

- One-Stop Planner
- Video Program
  Videocassette 3, 28:27–31:14
- DVD Tutor, Disc 2
- Interactive CD-ROM Tutor, Disc 3
- Map Transparency 1

go.hrw.com
WA3 ARLES

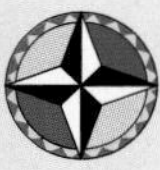

Using the Almanac and Map

Terms in the Almanac

- **Les Baux-de-Provence**, the ruins of a medieval city, sits on a rock promontory in the **Alpilles** (*little Alps*). The mineral bauxite, discovered in the area in 1821, was named after **Les Baux**.
- **Les Antiques à St-Rémy-de-Provence** is home to the best preserved mausoleum in the world and a small **arc de triomphe**.
- **Alphonse Daudet** (1840–1897), the author of several short stories and novels that celebrate Provence, including *Les Aventures prodigieuses de Tartarin de Tarascon* (1872) and *Les Lettres de mon moulin* (1866)
- **Frédéric Mistral** (1830–1914) wrote a narrative poem, *Mirèio* (1859) in Provençal, a language spoken in Provence.
- **Le Museon Arlaten** is a folklore museum of Provençal life founded in 1896 by Frédéric Mistral.

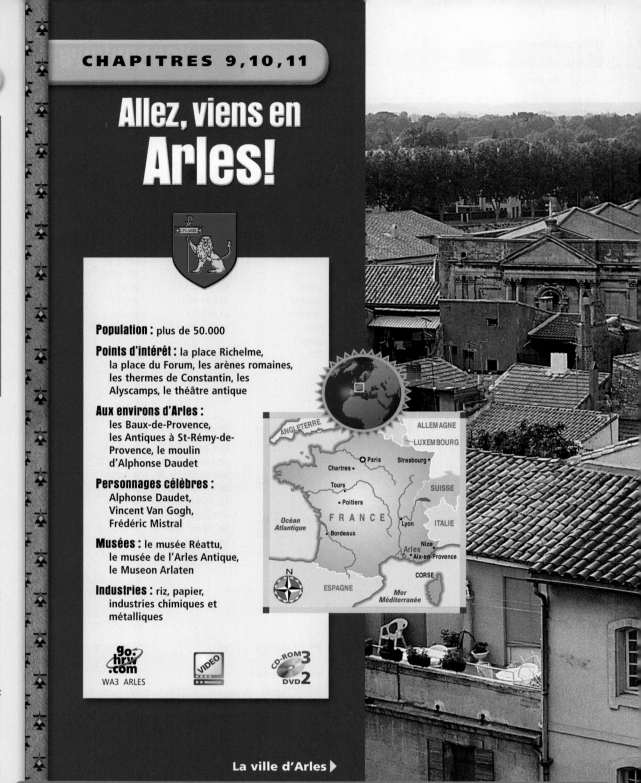

CHAPITRES 9,10,11

Allez, viens en Arles!

Population : plus de 50.000

Points d'intérêt : la place Richelme, la place du Forum, les arènes romaines, les thermes de Constantin, les Alyscamps, le théâtre antique

Aux environs d'Arles : les Baux-de-Provence, les Antiques à St-Rémy-de-Provence, le moulin d'Alphonse Daudet

Personnages célèbres : Alphonse Daudet, Vincent Van Gogh, Frédéric Mistral

Musées : le musée Réattu, le musée de l'Arles Antique, le Museon Arlaten

Industries : riz, papier, industries chimiques et métalliques

go.hrw.com WA3 ARLES

VIDEO

CD-ROM 3 DVD 2

La ville d'Arles ▶

Cultures and Communities

Background Information
In 46 B.C., Julius Caesar established a Roman colony in Arles, and in 306 A.D., Constantine the Great made the city a capital in his empire. In 1239, Arles became part of Provence, which, in 1481, became part of France.

Culture Note
The red-tiled roofs on the houses in the photo on pages 260–261 are typical of the south of France. The distinctive roofs are made from red-canal, curved, clay tiles. The roofs are gently sloped to keep the tiles from sliding off.

STANDARDS: 2.2, 3.1, 5.1

Location Opener

CHAPTERS 9, 10, 11

Map Activities

- Ask students if they can name any cities in southern France **(Nice, Cannes, Marseille, Avignon).** You might have students turn to the detailed map of France on page xxiii, or show them *Map Transparency 1*.
- Ask students if they can name the mountain ranges in France (**les Pyrénées, les Alpes, le Jura, le Massif Central,** and **les Vosges**).
- Have students look at the map on page 260, or at the map of the francophone world on page xxvi, and suggest reasons why the Greeks and Romans were the first to colonize what is now southern France.

Geography Link

The smallest administrative division of France is a **commune**, which consists of a town and some of the surrounding area. Arles is the largest **commune** in France because of its location near the **Camargue**. The entire area covers approximately 190,000 acres.

Connections and Comparisons

Thinking Critically

Observing Have students compare the photo of the city of Arles on pages 260–261 with the photos of Poitiers on pages 12–15. Ask students if they notice any differences (the tiled roofs) or similarities (the window shutters). What mixture of ancient and modern times can they find? (The ancient church on this page is surrounded by television antennas and even a satellite dish.)

History Link

Ask students if they can name any other areas of the world where the Romans established settlements (southern Europe, the Middle East, North Africa, Germany, Belgium, and Great Britain).

Location Opener

CHAPTERS 9, 10, 11

Using the Photo Essay

1 Les Alyscamps is a famous cemetery that was used from Roman times through the Middle Ages. Tombs of more than 80 generations of people who were buried there were discovered in three layers. Unfortunately, in later centuries, stones and sarcophagi were taken for building projects and souvenirs. Today, a shaded pathway lined with ancient tombs offers the visitor an eerie glimpse of history.

1 Vincent Van Gogh (1853–1890) was a post-impressionistic Dutch painter who spent most of his life in France. From 1888–1890, he lived in Arles, where he produced 300 paintings, including *Starry Night, The Bridge at Arles*, and *L'Arlésienne*. His use of bright colors and harsh brush strokes was revolutionary. In fact, one of his paintings, *Sunflowers*, sold at that time for the highest price ever paid for a painting. Van Gogh suffered from mental problems and spent time in an asylum. He cut off one of his ears after an argument with painter Paul Gauguin and eventually committed suicide. Many of his works are now on display in Paris at the **musée d'Orsay**.

2 Les arènes romaines, when originally built in the first century, could seat approximately 25,000 spectators. After the fall of the Roman Empire, 200 houses, and even a church, were constructed inside the arena. Restoration began in 1825. The structure had been severely damaged throughout the centuries as stones were removed for other construction. In fact, the third level of galleries is completely gone. The view from the upper level, overlooking the Rhône River and the surrounding countryside, is magnificent.

Arles

Les Grecs ont fondé la ville d'Arles au cinquième siècle avant Jésus-Christ. Arles était la plus grande ville de Provence et la capitale de la Gaule ancienne. Arles est devenu une ville française en 1481. En 1888, Vincent Van Gogh est venu habiter en Arles. Il y a peint beaucoup de tableaux très célèbres. Aujourd'hui, Arles attire toujours les artistes, les historiens et les archéologues. De nombreux visiteurs viennent aussi en Arles chaque année pour ses festivals, ses musées et pour visiter ses environs. Arles est une ville très spéciale qu'on appelle souvent «le cœur de la Provence».

Visit Holt Online
go.hrw.com
KEYWORD: WA3 ARLES
Activités Internet

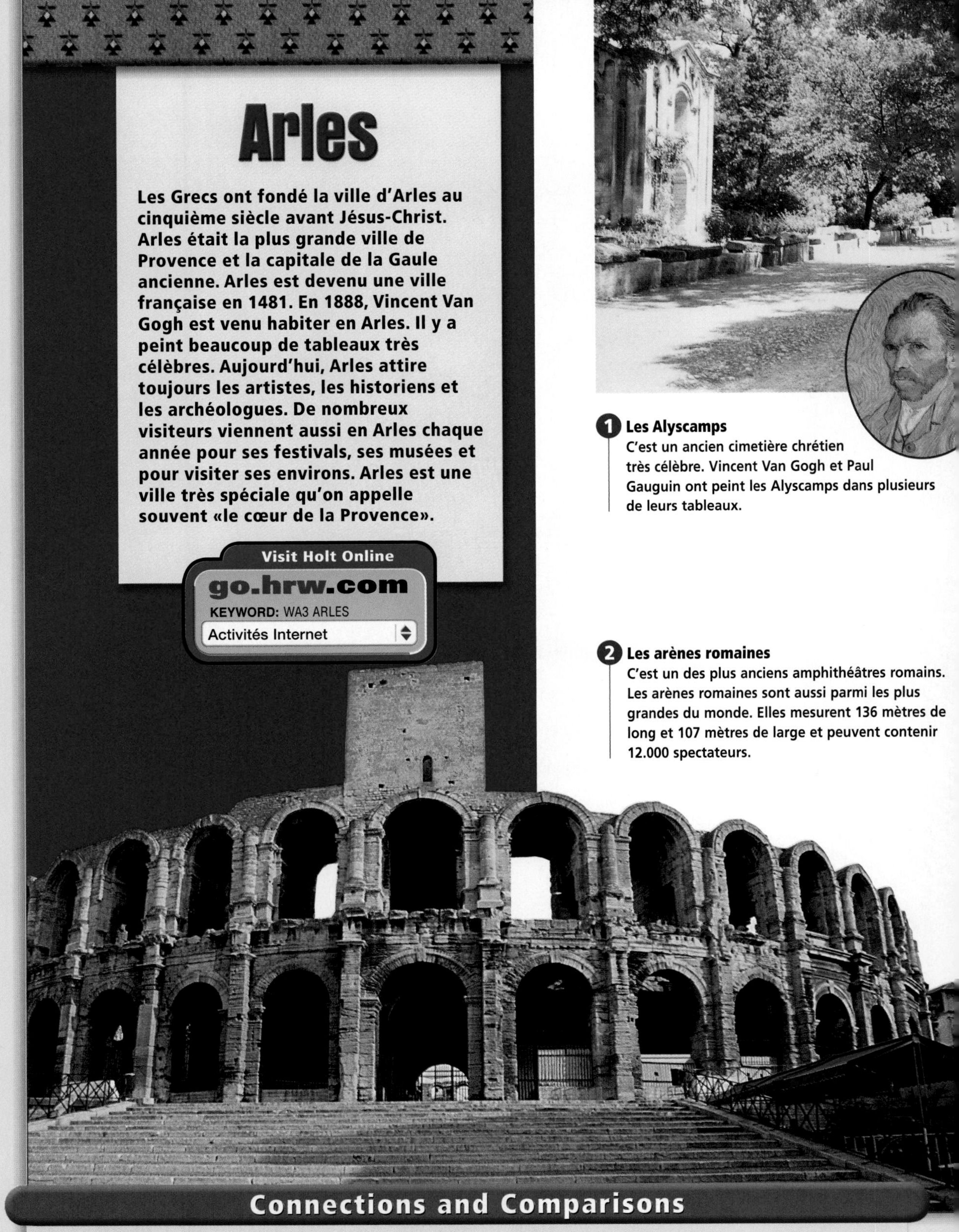

1 Les Alyscamps
C'est un ancien cimetière chrétien très célèbre. Vincent Van Gogh et Paul Gauguin ont peint les Alyscamps dans plusieurs de leurs tableaux.

2 Les arènes romaines
C'est un des plus anciens amphithéâtres romains. Les arènes romaines sont aussi parmi les plus grandes du monde. Elles mesurent 136 mètres de long et 107 mètres de large et peuvent contenir 12.000 spectateurs.

Connections and Comparisons

Art Link

Van Gogh generally painted three types of subjects: still life, landscape, and figure, most of which portrayed the daily lives of the peasants, the hardships they endured, and the countryside they cultivated. During the time Van Gogh spent in Arles, he painted blossoming fruit trees, views of the town, self-portraits, portraits of Roulin the postman, his own family and friends, interiors and exteriors of houses, a series of sunflowers, and a sky full of stars.

Geography Link

Located on the Rhône River, the city of Arles is officially known as Arles-sur-Rhône to distinguish it from Arles-sur-Tech, which is located in the eastern Pyrenees Mountains.

STANDARDS: 2.2

3 La Camargue
La Camargue est une région de marais magnifique. C'est un endroit protégé qui est célèbre pour ses flamants roses et ses chevaux sauvages.

Aux chapitres 9, 10 et 11,

tu vas faire la connaissance d'Hélène, de Magali et de leurs amis Florent et Ahmed. Ils vont te faire visiter la très belle ville d'Arles qui est située en Provence, dans le sud de la France. C'est une ville très ancienne, célèbre pour ses ruines romaines, mais aussi pour ses nombreux festivals et ses traditions provençales...

4 les festivals
Arles est une ville célèbre pour ses nombreux festivals. On peut y admirer des danseurs en costumes traditionnels qui viennent de toute la Provence.

5 Le théâtre antique
On utilise encore aujourd'hui ce théâtre construit au premier siècle avant Jésus-Christ. Le Festival d'Arles, les Rencontres internationales de la photographie et d'autres spectacles ont lieu au théâtre antique.

Location Opener

CHAPTERS 9, 10, 11

3 **La Camargue**, established as a nature preserve in 1927, is the delta of the Rhône River. The river splits into two arms: **le Grand Rhône**, which makes up nine-tenths of the volume, and **le Petit Rhône**, just upstream from Arles. In certain areas, the delta area advances from 10 to 50 meters a year because of silt deposits, but it has receded in other areas. **La Camargue** is famous for its pink flamingos, bulls, and the white horses shown in the photo. Scattered throughout the delta are **mas**, or *farms*, where the **gardians** work herding the bulls.

4 Many festivals are held in Arles every year. **Le festival d'Arles** lasts the entire month of July and consists of concerts, theatrical and dance performances, and exhibitions. **La fête des gardians**, a version of a rodeo, takes place on May 1. **Le Salon international des santonniers**, held every December, is famous for its Nativity scenes (**crèches**) and ornamental figures (**santons**).

5 **Le théâtre antique**, a Roman theater located a short distance from the **arènes**, is the site for many drama and dance performances, as well as the **festival d'Arles**, held every July. When the **théâtre antique** was built, it was able to hold approximately 7,000 spectators. After the fifth century A.D., it was used as a quarry, and all that remains today are some of the seats and two marble Corinthian columns from the original wall behind the acting area.

Cultures and Communities

Culture Notes

3 The village of Saintes-Maries-de-la-Mer, the unofficial capital of the **Camargue**, is the destination of an annual pilgrimage on May 24 and 25 by European gypsies.

3 The bulls raised in the **Camargue** are often reluctant participants in bullfights. Bullfights in France are different from those in Spain; the bull lives after the fight. Have students search on the Internet or at a library in what cities Provengal bullfights take place.

Chapitre 9 : Au téléphone
Chapter Overview

Mise en train pp. 266–268	***Un week-end spécial***			
	FUNCTIONS	**GRAMMAR**	**VOCABULARY**	**RE-ENTRY**
Première étape pp. 269–274	• Asking for and expressing opinions, p. 269 • Inquiring about and relating past events, p. 270	• The **passé composé** with **avoir,** p. 271 • Placement of adverbs with the **passé composé,** p. 272	• Activities you have done during the day, p. 273	• Chores **(Chapitre 7)** • Asking for, giving, and refusing permission **(Chapitre 7)** • The verb **avoir (Chapitre 2)** • Activities **(Chapitre 1)**
Deuxième étape pp. 275–278	• Making and answering a telephone call, p. 276	• The **-re** verbs: **répondre,** p. 277		• **Aller** + infinitive **(Chapitre 6)** • The verb **pouvoir (Chapitre 6)**
Troisième étape pp. 279–281	• Sharing confidences and consoling others, p. 279 • Asking for and giving advice, p. 279	• The object pronouns **le, la, les, lui,** and **leur,** p. 279		• The imperative **(Chapitre 6)** • The verb **pouvoir (Chapitre 8)**

Prononciation p. 281	**The vowel sounds [e] and [ɛ]** Audio CD 9, Tracks 13–15	**A écrire** (dictation) Audio CD 9, Tracks 16–18	
Lisons! pp. 282–283	**Je passe ma vie au téléphone**	**Reading Strategy:** Combining different reading strategies	
Grammaire supplémentaire	**pp. 284–287** **Première étape,** pp. 284–285	**Deuxième étape,** p. 286	**Troisième étape,** p. 287
Review pp. 288–291	**Mise en pratique,** pp. 288–289 **Ecrivons!** Answering the five "w" questions Writing a letter asking advice	**Que sais-je?** p. 290	**Vocabulaire,** p. 291

CULTURE

- **Note culturelle,** History of Arles, p. 272
- Realia: Ad for phone services, p. 275
- **Note culturelle,** The French telephone system, p. 276
- Realia: **Télécartes** from **France Télécom,** p. 276
- **Panorama Culturel,** Telephone habits of French-speaking teenagers, p. 278

Chapitre 9 : Au téléphone

Chapter Resources

Visit Holt Online
go.hrw.com
KEYWORD: WA3 ARLES-9
Online Edition

Lesson Planning

One-Stop Planner

Lesson Planner with Differentiated Instruction, pp. 43–47, 73

Student Make-Up Assignments
- Make-Up Assignment Copying Masters, Chapter 9

Listening and Speaking

TPR Storytelling Book, pp. 33–36

Listening Activities
- Student Response Forms for Listening Activities, pp. 67–69
- Additional Listening Activities 9-1 to 9-6, pp. 71–73
- Additional Listening Activities (song), p. 74
- Scripts and Answers, pp. 142–146

Video Guide
- Teaching Suggestions, pp. 62–63
- Activity Masters, pp. 64–66
- Scripts and Answers, pp. 105–107, 122

Activities for Communication
- Communicative Activities, pp. 49–54
- Realia and Teaching Suggestions, pp. 115–119
- Situation Cards, pp. 153–154

Reading and Writing

Reading Strategies and Skills Handbook, Chapter 9

Joie de lire 1, Chapter 9

Cahier d'activités, pp. 97–108

Grammar

Travaux pratiques de grammaire, pp. 71–78

Grammar Tutor for Students of French, Chapter 9

Assessment

Testing Program
- Grammar and Vocabulary Quizzes, **Etape** Quizzes, and Chapter Test, pp. 223–240
- Score Sheet, Scripts and Answers, pp. 241–248

Alternative Assessment Guide
- Portfolio Assessment, p. 26
- Performance Assessment, p. 40
- CD-ROM Assessment, p. 54

Student Make-Up Assignments
- Alternative Quizzes, Chapter 9

Standardized Assessment Tutor,
- Reading, pp. 35–37
- Writing, p. 38
- Math, pp. 51–52

Middle School

Middle School Teaching Resources, Chapter 9

MEDIA

Online Activities
- **Jeux interactifs**
- **Activités Internet**

Video Program
- Videocassette 3
- Videocassette 5 (captioned version)

Interactive CD-ROM Tutor, Disc 3

DVD Tutor, Disc 2

Audio Compact Discs
- Textbook Listening Activities, CD 9, Tracks 1–19
- Additional Listening Activities, CD 9, Tracks 26–32
- Assessment Items, CD 9, Tracks 20–25

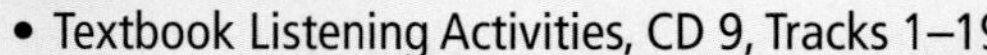

Teaching Transparencies
- Situation 9-1 to 9-3
- Vocabulary 9-A to 9-B
- **Mise en train**
- **Grammaire supplémentaire** Answers
- **Travaux pratiques de grammaire** Answers

One-Stop Planner CD-ROM

Use the **One-Stop Planner CD-ROM with Test Generator** to aid in lesson planning and pacing.

For each chapter, the **One-Stop Planner** includes:
- Editable lesson plans with direct links to teaching resources
- Printable worksheets from resource books
- Direct launches to the HRW Internet activities
- Video and audio segments
- Test Generator
- Clip Art for vocabulary items

Chapitre 9 : Au téléphone

Projects

La Provence

Have students work individually to research topics associated with the region of Provence. Projects should include a written report and an oral and visual presentation, all in English.

MATERIALS

✂ **Students may need**
- Reference Books
- Posterboard
- Colored markers

PREPARATION

Ask each student to select a topic. Possible topics include:
- tourist attractions or history of the region
- natural resources or geography of the region
- regional dishes or products
- the Roman occupation or architecture

SUGGESTED SEQUENCE

1. Students choose a topic and begin looking for reference materials.
2. Students gather information and begin organizing their reports and creating their visuals.
3. Once students have a rough draft of their report, have them peer-edit their work. Students should submit an outline of their oral presentation to be checked for clarity and organization.
4. After making any necessary changes in their rough drafts, students should edit them again for accuracy. They should also prepare and organize their visual aids.
5. Have students give their oral presentations. You might display their posters around the classroom.

GRADING THE PROJECT

Suggested Point Distribution: (total = 100 points)

Completion of assignment....................20 points
Creativity...30 points
Language use...20 points
Presentation ....30 points

Games

Message téléphonique

In this game, students will practice using telephone vocabulary.

Procedure Whisper one of the short messages below only once to one student. Then, have that student whisper what you said to the next student, and so on. Once the message reaches the last student, ask that person to say the message aloud to compare it with the original. Follow the same procedure with the other messages. If the class is very large, this game might be played by two or three groups simultaneously. You might whisper the message to the first person in each group, wait for all groups to finish, and have the final student in each group say the message aloud. Try to begin each time with different students so that the same students aren't always first and last. The suggested messages here can be shortened or extended, depending on the class' success with the first few messages.

Ne quittez pas.
C'était épouvantable.
Qui est à l'appareil?
J'ai un petit problème.
Vous pouvez rappeler plus tard?
Qu'est-ce que tu me conseilles?
Qu'est-ce que tu as fait vendredi soir?

Verb Tense Race

In this game, students will practice various verb conjugations.

Procedure This game can be played by two to five teams. Begin by naming a regular **-er** verb, a subject pronoun, and a tense (past, present, or future). Students should write the subject and the correct verb form. For example, if you say **apporter, nous, passé composé,** the students should write **nous avons apporté.** Vary the subjects and tenses. You might point out the accent changes in **acheter** and **répéter.** To play with two teams, have one student from each team race to the board to write the correct verb form when you give a verb, a subject, and a tense. To play with three or more teams, provide each team with an overhead transparency and marker or pieces of scrap paper. Have students work together to figure out and write down the answer. The first team to hold up a correctly written answer wins. If you need a tiebreaker, give two points for correct irregular past participles. For a list of -**er** verbs and irregular past participles that students know, see the vocabulary list for the **Première étape** on page 291.

STANDARDS: 1.1, 1.3, 3.1, 3.2

Storytelling

Mini-histoire

This story accompanies Teaching Transparency 9-A. The ***mini-histoire*** *can be told and retold in different formats, acted out, written down, and read aloud, to give students additional opportunities to practice all four skills. The following story tells about Robert's challenging day.*

Robert a passé une très mauvaise matinée! Il a raté le bus et il a oublié ses devoirs. Mais, il a passé un très bon après-midi. D'abord, il a trouvé cinq euros devant le lycée. Ensuite, il a déjeuné à la cantine et il a rencontré une fille sympa qui s'appelle Brigitte. Après ses cours, il a chanté dans la chorale et il a acheté un CD super. Le soir, il a travaillé au fast-food. Devine qui est venu au fast-food—Brigitte!

Traditions

Santons

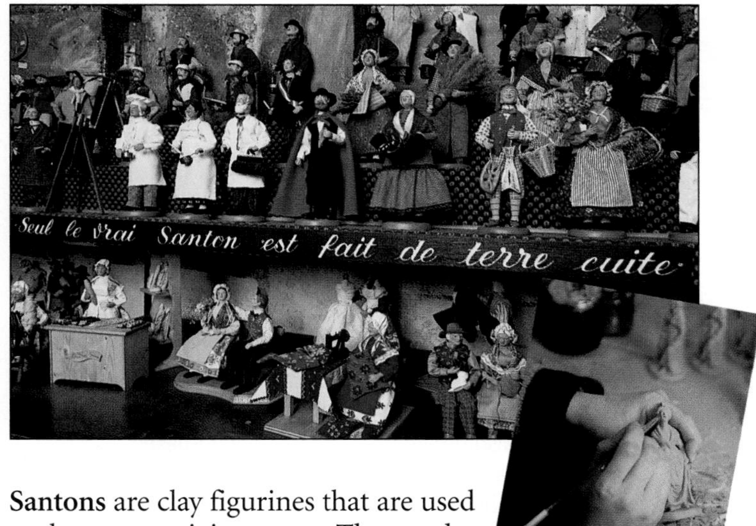
Seul le vrai Santon est fait de terre cuite

Santons are clay figurines that are used to decorate nativity scenes. The word **santon** means *little saint.* The first ones appeared at the end of the eighteenth century. Their creator was Jean-Louis Lagnel, a monk who was born in Marseilles in 1764. The **santons** also represent the many professions associated with the food service industry. Some of the more popular ones are the baker, the cook, the goose breeder, the cheese maker, the olive picker, and the grape picker, but there are many others. The **santons** have become a traditional decoration at Christmas time. Have students do research on **santons** and present the results to the rest of the class.

Recette

Tomatoes come from Peru. For many years, people's feelings toward tomatoes were divided. Southern Europeans and North Africans liked them from the moment they were imported there, and tomatoes changed their way of cooking forever. However, in England, and then in the U.S., tomatoes were believed to be poisonous. Nowadays, tomatoes are part of everyday dishes.

TOMATES PROVENÇALES

pour 4 personnes

4 tomates fermes
4 gousses d'ail
1 cuillère à soupe de persil
1/2 tasse de chapelure (ou biscottes écrasées)
2 cuillères à soupe de beurre
sel
poivre

Hacher le persil et l'ail. Faire chauffer le beurre ou l'huile dans le plat à cuisiner. Couper les tomates en deux, les disposer sur la face fraîchement coupée. Laisser frire une minute, puis les retourner. Saupoudrer d'ail et de persil hachés, et d'une cuillère à café de chapelure sur chaque moitié de tomate. Saler et poivrer et laisser cuire doucement 15 minutes.

STANDARDS: 1.3, 2.2, 3.2, 5.1, 5.2

Technology

Videocassette 3, Videocassette 5 (captioned version)
DVD Tutor, Disc 2
See Video Guide, pages 61–66.

DVD/Video

Mise en train • Un week-end spécial

Magali calls her friend Hélène, and they tell each other what they did over the weekend. We see a flashback of Magali with her friends at **les arènes,** where Florent introduced her to Ahmed. Magali tells Hélène about Ahmed and how she and her friends went to les Baux-de-Provence on Sunday. Hélène is anxious to hear the rest, but Magali's father needs to use the telephone, so she tells Hélène that she will call back.

Tu aimes téléphoner?

Three teenagers from France and Martinique tell us about their telephone habits. In additional interviews, people from various French-speaking countries tell us whether or not they like to talk on the phone.

Mise en train (suite)

When the story continues, Magali calls Hélène back and tells her about her trip to les Baux-de-Provence; we see flashbacks of Magali and her friends there. Magali tells Hélène about the sights they visited. At the end of the episode, we see a flashback of Magali opening a package. It is a gift from Ahmed, a **santon** that Magali admired at the souvenir boutique at les Baux-de-Provence. Magali asks Hélène for advice about getting to know Ahmed.

Vidéoclips

- **Groupe Azur®**: advertisement for insurance
- **Petits Cœurs®**: advertisement for cookies

Interactive CD-ROM Tutor

Activity	Activity Type	Pupil's Edition Page
En contexte	*Interactive conversation*	
1. Grammaire	Les mots qui manquent	p. 271
2. Vocabulaire	Jeux des paires	p. 273
3. Vocabulaire	Chasse au trésor Explorons!/Vérifions!	pp. 271, 273
4. Comment dit-on... ?	Méli-Mélo	p. 276
5. Comment dit-on... ?	Chacun à sa place	pp. 269, 276
6. Comment dit-on... ?	Le bon choix	p. 279
Panorama Culturel	Tu aimes téléphoner? Le bon choix	p. 278
A toi de parler	*Guided recording*	pp. 288–289
A toi d'écrire	*Guided writing*	pp. 288–289

Teacher Management System

Launch the program, type "admin" in the password area, and press RETURN. Log on to www.hrw.com/CDROMTUTOR for a detailed explanation of the Teacher Management System.

DVD Tutor

The *DVD Tutor* contains all material from the *Video Program* as described above. French captions are available for use at your discretion for all sections of the video. The *DVD Tutor* also provides a variety of video-based activities that assess students' understanding of the **Mise en train, Suite,** and **Panorama Culturel.**

This part of the *DVD Tutor* may be used on any DVD video player connected to a television or video monitor.

In addition to the video material and the video-based comprehension activities, the *DVD Tutor* also contains the entire *Interactive CD-ROM Tutor* in DVD-ROM format. Each DVD disc contains the activities from all 12 chapters of the *Interactive CD-ROM Tutor.*

This part of the *DVD Tutor* may be used on a Macintosh® or Windows® computer with a DVD-ROM drive.

To preview all resources available for this chapter, use the **One-Stop Planner CD-ROM,** Disc 3.

Go.Online!

Online Edition

The Online Edition for Allez, viens! *allows students access to their textbooks anytime anywhere.*

- *Audio at point of use*
- *Additional practice activities*
- *Self-test activities*
- *Online reference tools*
- *Entire Video Program (Enhanced version)*
- *Interactive Notebook (Enhanced version)*

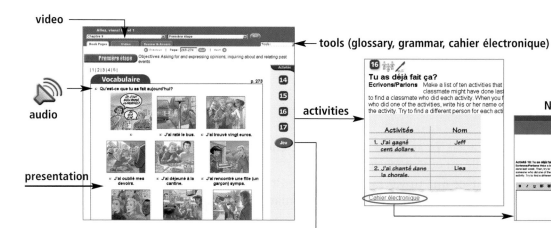

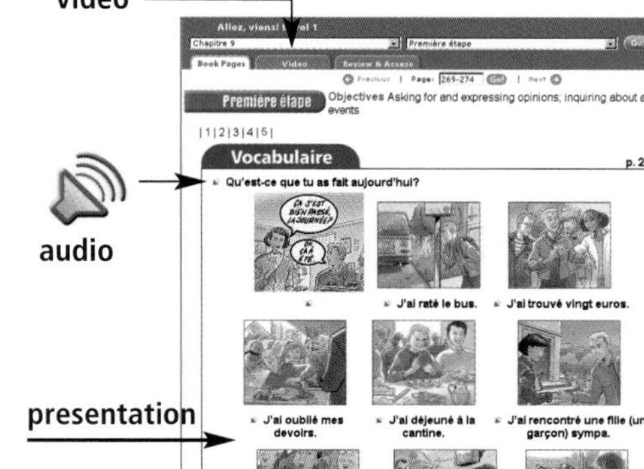

HRW Atlas

Activités Internet

These guided internet activities include a worksheet and pre-selected and pre-screened authentic web sites from the francophone world. You can use these activities

- to help students develop research skills in the target language
- to introduce students to authentic cultural information
- as a project

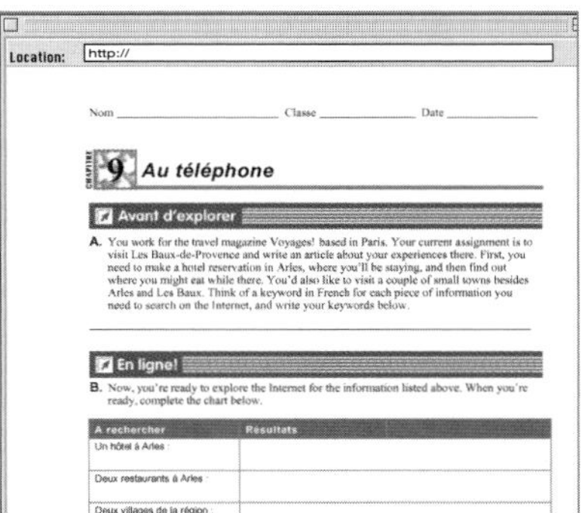

Jeux interactifs

You can use the interactive activities in this chapter

- to practice grammar, vocabulary, and chapter functions
- as homework
- as an assessment option
- as a self-test
- to prepare for the Chapter Test

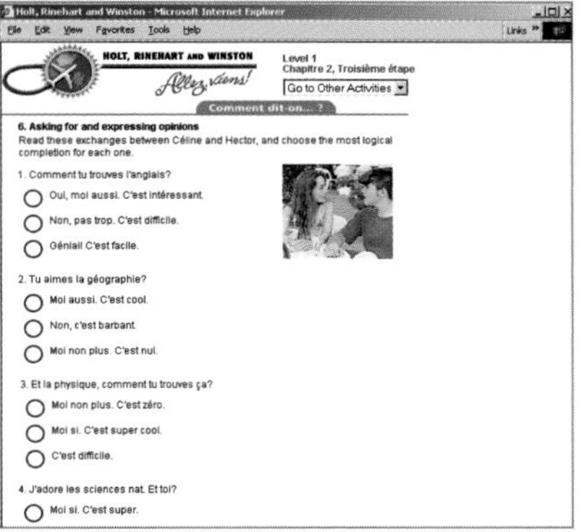

Projet Have students choose another town in the Provence region and search the Web for information on that town. They should find out about tourist attractions in the area, restaurants, local specialties, lodging, and activities to do. Have students prepare a travelogue based on their online research.

Chapitre 9 : Au téléphone
Textbook Listening Activities Scripts 

Première étape

7 p. 269

1. —Salut. Alors, tu as passé un bon week-end?
   —Oh, c'était épouvantable!
2. —Dis, tu as passé un bon week-end?
   —Ça a été.
3. —Tu as passé un bon week-end?
   —Oui, très bon.
4. —Tiens, tu as passé un bon week-end?
   —Oui, très chouette.
5. —Tu as passé un bon week-end?
   —Oh, pas mauvais.

Answers to Activity 7
1. no fun at all
2. mildly good
3. really good
4. really good
5. mildly good

10 p. 271

1. —Bonjour, Serge. Ça va? Tu as passé un bon week-end?
   —Ça a été. Je suis allé au cinéma avec Sandrine.
2. —Tiens, Eric! Qu'est-ce que tu vas faire ce week-end?
   —Oh, je ne sais pas. Je vais peut-être regarder un match à la télé.
3. —Dominique, ça va?
   —Oui, ça va bien. Et toi?
   —Ça va. Ecoute. On va danser samedi soir. Tu viens?
   —Bonne idée!
4. —Salut, Christine!
   —Salut!
   —Tu as passé un bon week-end?
   —Oui, très bon.
   —Qu'est-ce que tu as fait?
   —Je suis allée à la plage, et j'ai rencontré des copains.
5. —Tiens, Sylvie, tu es allée où ce week-end?
   —Je suis allée au café avec Patrick.
   —Tu as passé un bon week-end?
   —Oui, très chouette.

Answers to Activity 10
1. last weekend
2. next weekend
3. next weekend
4. last weekend
5. last weekend

Deuxième étape

19 p. 276

1. —Allô?
   —Bonjour. Je suis bien chez Michel Perrault?
   —Oui. Qui est à l'appareil?
   —C'est Françoise.
   —Salut, Françoise! C'est moi, Paul.
   —Ah salut, Paul. Michel est là?
   —Une seconde, s'il te plaît.
   —D'accord.
2. —Allô?
   —Salut, Suzanne! C'est Jeanne à l'appareil. Ça va?
   —Oui, ça va bien.
   —Je peux parler à Thierry?
   —Thierry n'est pas là. Tu peux rappeler plus tard?
   —D'accord.
3. —Allô?
   —Bonjour, Anne?
   —Non, c'est Brigitte.
   —Ah, Anne est là?
   —Euh, je ne sais pas. Une seconde, s'il vous plaît. Vous pouvez rappeler? Elle est occupée.
   —Je peux lui laisser un message?
   —Bien sûr.
   —Vous pouvez lui dire que Daniel a téléphoné?
   —D'accord. C'est noté.

Answers to Activity 19
1. Françoise; Michel
2. Jeanne; Thierry
3. Daniel; Anne

21 p. 277

1. —Allô?
   —Bonjour. Est-ce que Madame Tissot est là?
   —Non, elle n'est pas là.
   —Je peux laisser un message?
   —Bien sûr.
   —Vous pouvez lui dire que Madame Morel a téléphoné?
   —Madame Moran?
   —Non, Morel. M-O-R-E-L.
   —Ah, Morel. D'accord.
   —Merci. Au revoir.
   —Au revoir.
2. —Allô?
   —Bonjour. Je peux parler à Monsieur Tissot? C'est son frère, Roger.
   —Désolé, mais il n'est pas là.
   —Vous pouvez lui dire que je ne peux pas aller au restaurant samedi soir?
   —D'accord.
   —Merci. Allez, au revoir.
   —Au revoir.
3. —Allô?
   —Bonjour! C'est Claire Laroche à l'appareil. Anne est là, s'il vous plaît?
   —Non, elle n'est pas là. Vous pouvez rappeler plus tard?
   —Oui. Mais, est-ce que je peux laisser un message?
   —Bien sûr.

The following scripts are for the Listening Activities found in the *Pupil's Edition*. For Student Response Forms, see *Listening Activities,* pages 67–69. To provide students with additional listening practice, see *Listening Activities,* pages 71–74.

To preview all resources available for this chapter, use the **One-Stop Planner CD-ROM**, Disc 3.

—Vous pouvez lui dire qu'on va au cinéma à neuf heures moins le quart?
—Euh, à quelle heure? Vous pouvez répéter?
—A neuf heures moins le quart.
—D'accord.
—Bon, merci. Au revoir.
—Au revoir.

4. —Allô?
—Bonjour. Je suis bien chez Philippe?
—Oui. Qui est à l'appareil?
—C'est Marc. Je peux lui parler?
—Désolé, mais il n'est pas là.
—Alors, je peux laisser un message?
—Bien sûr.
—Vous pouvez lui dire qu'on va jouer au foot samedi après-midi?
—D'accord.
—Merci bien. Au revoir.
—Au revoir.

Possible answers to Activity 21
1. Mme Tissot — Mme Morel a téléphoné.
2. M. Tissot — Votre frère Roger ne peut pas aller au restaurant samedi soir.
3. Anne — Claire Laroche a téléphoné. Vous allez au cinéma à neuf heures moins le quart.
4. Philippe — Marc a téléphoné. Vous allez jouer au foot samedi après-midi.

Troisième étape

24 p. 279

1. —Je veux sortir avec Jean-Luc. Tu crois que je peux l'inviter?

2. —Eh bien, si tu ne veux pas rater ton examen, tu devrais étudier.

3. —Bruno? Moi, je trouve qu'il n'est pas très gentil. Oublie-le!

4. —Moi, je voudrais bien aller au concert de Vanessa Paradis, mais ça coûte très cher! Qu'est-ce que je fais?

5. —Alors, si tu veux acheter une voiture, pourquoi tu ne travailles pas cet été?

6. —Je ne mange pas beaucoup, mais je trouve que je suis un peu gros quand même. Qu'est-ce que tu me conseilles?

7. —Si elle n'a pas encore téléphoné, téléphone-lui!

Answers to Activity 24
1. asking 2. giving 3. giving 4. asking 5. giving 6. asking 7. giving

25 p. 279

—Allô?
—Salut, Mireille. C'est Simone. Ça va?
—Oui, ça va. Et toi?
—Pas terrible. Je peux te parler? Tu as une minute?
—Oui.
—J'ai un petit problème.
—Je t'écoute.
—Ben, j'ai raté mon examen de maths. Je ne sais pas quoi faire.
—Ne t'en fais pas, Simone!
—Mais, j'ai beaucoup étudié. J'ai bien préparé mes réponses et j'ai quand même raté.
—Qu'est-ce que je peux faire?
—Je peux étudier avec toi, Mireille?
—Bien sûr! Ne t'en fais pas. Ça va aller mieux!

Answers to Activity 25
Elle a raté son examen de maths.

PRONONCIATION, P. 281

For the scripts for Parts A and B, see p. 281. The script for Part C is below.

C. A écrire *(dictation)*

—Allô?
—Salut, Hélène. Tu peux parler? J'ai un problème.
—Je t'écoute.

Mise en pratique

1 p. 288

Salut, c'est Martin. Comment vas-tu? Tu as passé un bon week-end? Moi, j'ai passé un week-end génial. Je suis allé à la plage. Il a fait un temps superbe. Samedi, j'ai fait du ski nautique et après, j'ai joué au volley-ball. Ensuite, dimanche, j'ai fait du jogging. Et toi, qu'est-ce que tu as fait? Appelle-moi quand tu rentres. Salut!

Answers to Mise en pratique, Activity 1
1. false 2. true 3. true 4. false 5. true 6. false

Chapitre 9 : Au téléphone

50-Minute Lesson Plans

Day 1

CHAPTER OPENER 5 min.
- Present Chapter Objectives, p. 265
- Culture Note, ATE, p. 264
- Thinking Critically/Comparing and Contrasting and Thinking Critically/Evaluating, ATE, p. 265

MISE EN TRAIN, 40 min.
- Presenting **Mise en train** and Preteaching Vocabulary, ATE, p. 266
- Culture Notes, ATE, p. 267
- Do Activities 1–6, p. 268.
- Visual Learners and Tactile Learners, ATE, p. 268

Wrap-Up 5 min.
- Have students summarize the events from **Un week-end spécial** using the **Mise en train** Transparencies.

Homework Options
Cahier d'activités, p. 97, Act. 1

Day 2

PREMIERE ETAPE
Quick Review 5 min.
- Check homework.
- Bell Work, ATE, p. 269

Comment dit-on... ?, p. 269 20 min.
- Presenting **Comment dit-on... ?,** ATE, p. 269
- Play Audio CD for Activity 7, p. 269.
- Do Activity 8, p. 269

Comment dit-on... ?, p. 270 20 min.
- Presenting **Comment dit-on... ?,** ATE, p. 270
- Do Activity 9, p. 270, using Teaching Transparency 9-1.

Wrap-Up 5 min.
- Students tell each other how their weekends were.

Homework Options
Cahier d'activités, p. 98, Acts. 2–3

Day 3

PREMIERE ETAPE
Quick Review 5 min.
- Check homework.

Grammaire, p. 271 25 min.
- Presenting **Grammaire,** ATE, p. 271
- Language-to-Language, ATE, p. 271
- Play Audio CD for Activity 10, p. 271.
- Do Activities 11–12, pp. 271–272.
- **Grammaire supplémentaire,** pp. 284–285, Activities 1–3

Note de grammaire, p. 272 10 min.
- Discuss **Note de grammaire** and do Activity 13, p. 272.
- **Grammaire supplémentaire,** p. 285, Activity 5

Wrap-Up 10 min.
- Game: **Loto!,** ATE, p. 272

Homework Options
Travaux pratiques de grammaire, pp. 71–74, Acts. 1–8
Cahier d'activités, pp. 98–99, Acts. 4, 6–7

Day 4

PREMIERE ETAPE
Quick Review 10 min.
- Check homework.

Note culturelle, p. 240 5 min.
- Discuss **Note culturelle,** p. 272
- History Link/Language Link, ATE, p. 273

Vocabulaire, p. 273 30 min.
- Present **Vocabulaire** using Teaching Transparencies 9-A and 9-B.
- Language Note, ATE, p. 273
- Do Activity 14, p. 274.
- Activities for Communication, pp. 49–50, Communicative Activity 9-1A and 9-B
- **De bons conseils,** p. 274
- Do Activities 16–17, p. 274.

Wrap-Up 5 min.
- Travaux pratiques de grammaire, p. 75, Acts. 9–10

Homework Options
Study for Quiz 9-1.

Day 5

PREMIERE ETAPE
Quiz 9-1 20 min.
- Administer Quiz 9-1A or 9-1B.

DEUXIEME ETAPE
Comment dit-on... ?, p. 276 25 min.
- Career Path, ATE, p. 275
- Do Activity 18, p. 275.
- Presenting **Comment dit-on... ?,** ATE, p. 276
- Play Audio CD for Activity 19, p. 276.
- Discuss **Note culturelle,** p. 276 and Culture Note, ATE, p. 276.
- Complete Activity 22, p. 277, in pairs.

Wrap-Up 5 min.
- Say some of the telephone expressions and have students tell whether you are the caller or the person receiving the call.

Homework Options
Cahier d'activités, p. 102, Acts. 13–14
Travaux pratiques de grammaire, p. 76, Acts. 11–12

Day 6

DEUXIEME ETAPE
Quick Review 10 min.
- Check homework.

Grammaire, p. 277 30 min.
- Presenting **Grammaire,** ATE, p. 277
- Play Audio CD for Activity 21, p. 277.
- **Grammaire supplémentaire,** pp. 286–287, Activities 7–8
- Activities for Communication, p. 154, Situation Card 9-2: Role-play
- Game: **Message téléphonique,** ATE, p. 263C

Wrap-Up 10 min.
- Travaux pratiques de grammaire, p. 77, Activities 13–14

Homework Options
Study for Quiz 9-2.

For alternative lesson plans by chapter section, to create your own customized plans, or to preview all resources available for this chapter, use the **One-Stop Planner CD-ROM**, Disc 3.

For additional homework suggestions, see activities accompanied by this symbol throughout the chapter.

Day 7

DEUXIEME ETAPE

Quiz 9-2 20 min.
- Administer Quiz 9-2A or 9-2B.

PANORAMA CULTUREL 25 min.
- Presenting **Panorama Culturel,** using Videocassette 3, ATE, p. 278
- Answer **Qu'en penses-tu?** questions, p. 278
- Read **Savais-tu que... ?,** p. 278
- **Panorama Culturel,** Interactive CD-ROM Tutor, Disc 3

Wrap-Up 5 min.
- Thinking Critically, Synthesizing, ATE, p. 278

Homework Options
Cahier d'activités, p. 108, Acts. 26–27

Day 8

TROISIEME ETAPE

Quick Review 10 min.
- Check homework.
- Bell Work, ATE, p. 279

Comment dit-on... ?, p. 269 20 min.
- Presenting **Comment dit-on... ?,** ATE, p. 279
- Play Audio CD for Activity 24, p. 279.
- Discuss **De bons conseils**, p. 279.

Note de grammaire, p. 279 15 min.
- Discuss **Note de grammaire,** p. 279.
- Play Audio CD for Activity 25, p. 279.
- Complete Activities 26–29, p. 280. See Slower Pace, ATE, p. 280.
- Cahier d'activités, pp. 104–105, Acts. 18–22

Wrap-Up, 5 min.
- Copy onto a transparency some problems and solutions from the **Comment dit-on... ?** box. Have students match the problems with the solutions.

Homework Options
Pupil's Edition, Acts. 10–11, p. 287
Travaux pratiques de grammaire, p. 78, Acts. 15–16

Day 9

TROISIEME ETAPE

Quick Review 10 min.
- Check homework.

Prononciation, p. 281 30 min.
- Complete presentation and Activities A–C, p. 281, using Audio CD 9.
- Activities for Communication, pp. 53–54, Communicative Activity 9-3A and 9-3B

Wrap-Up 10 min.
- Additional Practice, ATE, p. 281

Homework Options
Study for Quiz 9-3.

Day 10

TROISIEME ETAPE

Quiz 9-3 20 min.
- Administer Quiz 9-3A or 9-3B.

LISONS! 25 min.
- Prereading Activities A–B, ATE, p. 282
- Culture Note, ATE, p. 283
- Reading Activities C–J, pp. 282–283
- Using Prior Knowledge, ATE, Thinking Critically, Analyzing, ATE, p. 282

Wrap-Up, 5 min.
- Have students recall the different reading strategies they have learned.

Homework Options
Cahier d'activités, p. 107, Act. 26

Day 11

LISONS!

Quick Review 15 min.
- Check homework.
- Postreading Activity K, ATE, p. 283

MISE EN PRATIQUE 30 min.
- Play Audio CD for Activity 1 and do Activities 2–3 in pairs, p. 288.
- Discuss the strategy for **Ecrivons!** as a class and then have students work on their letters to Agnès.
- Have partners complete **Jeu de rôle,** p. 289.

Wrap-Up 5 min.
- Game: **Ce week-end,** ATE, p. 290

Homework Options
Que sais-je?, p. 290

Day 12

MISE EN PRATIQUE

Quick Review 25 min.
- Challenge, ATE, p. 289
- See Teacher Note for Activity 4, ATE, p. 290.

Student Review 25 min.
- Review Chapter 9. Choose from **Grammaire supplémentaire**, Grammar Tutor for Students of French, Activities for Communication, Listening Activities, Interactive CD-ROM Tutor, or **Jeux interactifs.**

Homework Options
Study for Chapter 9 Test.

Assessment

Test, Chapitre 9 50 min.
- Administer Chapitre 9 Test. Select from Assessment Program, Alternative Assessment Guide, Test Generator, or Standardized Assessment Tutor.

Chapitre 9 : Au téléphone
90-Minute Lesson Plans

Block 1

CHAPTER OPENER 5 min.
- Present Chapter Objectives, p. 265.
- Thinking Critically/Comparing and Contrasting and Thinking Critically/Evaluating, ATE, p. 265
- Culture Note, ATE, p. 264

MISE EN TRAIN 40 min.
- Presenting **Mise en train,** ATE, p. 266. See Preteaching Vocabulary, ATE, p. 266.
- Do Activities 1–2, p. 268
- View video of Mise en train, using Videocassette 3. See Video Guide, p. 60.

PREMIERE ETAPE

Comment dit-on... ?, p. 269 20 min.
- Presenting **Comment dit-on... ?,** ATE, p. 269
- Do Visual Learners, ATE, p. 269
- Play Audio CD for Activity 7, p. 269.
- Do Activity 8, p. 269. See Kinesthetic Learners, ATE, p. 269.

Comment dit-on... ?, p. 270 20 min.
- Presenting **Comment dit-on... ?,** ATE, p. 270, using Teaching Transparency 9-1
- Preview **Grammaire:** The **passé composé** with **avoir,** p. 271. Have students observe construction of **passé composé** in sentences of **Comment dit-on... ?,** p. 270.
- Do Activity 9, p. 270.

Wrap-Up 5 min.
- Summarize what happened in the **Mise en train** using the **Mise en train** Transparencies.

Homework Options
Cahier d'activités, pp. 97–98, Acts. 1–3

Block 2

PREMIERE ETAPE

Quick Review 5 min.
- Talk about the previous evening or weekend. Have students guess what you're saying in the past tense, what you did first, etc.

Grammaire, p. 270 25 min.
- Presenting **Grammaire,** ATE, p. 271. Recycle verbs from "Things to do," Chapter 6.
- Play Audio CD for Activity 10, p. 271
- Do Activities 11–12, pp. 271–272.

Note de grammaire, p. 272 15 min.
- Present **Note de grammaire,** p. 272.
- Challenge, ATE, p. 272
- Do Activity 13, p. 272.

Note Culturelle, p. 272 10 min.
- Read **Note culturelle,** p. 272.
- History Link/Language Link, ATE, p. 273

Vocabulaire, p. 273 30 min.
- Presenting **Vocabulaire,** ATE, p. 273 with Teaching Transparencies 9-A or 9-B. See Language Note, ATE, p. 273.
- Do Activities 14 and 16, p. 274.
- Game: **Loto!,** ATE, p. 272. Students prepare **Loto!** cards.

Wrap-Up 5 min.
- Review **passé composé** with negation and adverbs and new vocabulary. As a class, reassemble scrambled sentence strips on transparency.

Homework Options
Finish **Loto!** cards
Pupil's Edition, Activity 17, p. 242
Travaux pratiques de grammaire, pp. 71–75, Acts. 1–10

Block 3

PREMIERE ETAPE

Quick Review 30 min.
- Review **passé composé** with negation and adverb placement.
- Activities for Communication, p. 153, Situation Cards: Interview 9-1
- Activities for Communication, pp. 49–50, Communicative Activity 9-1A and 9-1B
- Listening Activities, p. 71, Additional Listening Activity 9-2

DEUXIEME ETAPE

Comment dit-on... ?, p. 276 45 min.
- Motivate Suggestion: Have students brainstorm expressions needed for answering the phone and taking messages that a non-English speaker might need when visiting the U.S.
- Read conversation for Activity 18, p. 275.
- Slower Pace Suggestion, ATE, p. 275. Complete Activity 18, p. 275.
- Presenting **Comment dit-on... ?,** ATE, p. 276
- Do Activity 20, p. 277.
- Discuss **Note culturelle,** p. 276.

Wrap-Up 15 min.
- Game: **Loto!,** ATE, p. 272. Play **Loto!** using students **Loto!** cards to review **passé composé** and expressions.

Homework Options
Study for Quiz 9-1
Cahier d'activités, pp. 98–101, Acts. 4–12
Grammaire supplémentaire, pp. 284–285, Acts. 1–5

For alternative lesson plans by chapter section, to create your own customized plans, or to preview all resources available for this chapter, use the **One-Stop Planner CD-ROM**, Disc 3.

For additional homework suggestions, see activities accompanied by this symbol throughout the chapter.

Block 4

PREMIERE ETAPE

Quick Review 5 min.
- Check homework.

Quiz 9-1 20 min.
- Administer Quiz 9-1A or 9-1B.

DEUXIEME ETAPE

Comment dit-on... ?, p. 276 30 min.
- Review **Comment dit-on... ?,** p. 276, with Additional Practice, ATE, p. 277.
- Play Audio CD for Activities 19 and 21, pp. 276–277.
- Activities for Communication, p. 116, Realia 9-2
- Activities for Communication, pp. 153 Situation Cards: Interview 9-2

Grammaire: -re verbs 10 min.
- Presenting **Grammaire: -re** verbs, ATE, p. 277
- Do Activity 23, p. 277.

LISONS! 20 min.
- Prereading Activities A–B, ATE, p. 282
- Reading Activities C–J, Teaching Suggestion, ATE, pp. 282–283
- Do Postreading Activity K, p. 283. See Thinking Critically: Analyzing suggestion, ATE, p. 282.
- Have students work in groups to read and summarize parts of the article, then have each group present their summary to the class.

Wrap-Up 5 min.
- Say some of the telephone expressions and have students tell whether you are the caller or the person receiving the call.

Homework Options

Cahier d'activités, pp. 102–103, Acts. 13–17
Travaux pratiques de grammaire, pp. 76–77, Acts. 11–14
Study for Quiz 9-2.

Block 5

DEUXIEME ETAPE

Quick Review 5 min.
- Check homework.

Quiz 9-2 20 min.
- Administer Quiz 9-2A or 9-2B.

PANORAMA CULTUREL 10 min.
- Present **Panorama Culturel** with Audio CD, ATE, p. 278.
- Have students answer **Qu'en penses-tu?** questions, p. 278.
- **Read Savais-tu que... ?,** p. 278.

TROISIEME ETAPE

Comment dit-on... ?, 50 min.
- Motivate Suggestion: Ask students when they might ask for a friend's help or in what circumstances they might need to help a friend.
- Presenting **Comment dit-on... ?,** ATE, p. 279
- Present **Note de grammaire,** p. 279.
- Play Audio CD for Activities 24–25, p. 279.
- Do Activities 27 and 28, p. 280, as a whole class.
- Activities for Communication, p. 153, Situation Interview 9-3
- Activities for Communication, p. 117, Realia 9-3

Wrap-Up 5 min.
- Suggest a problem to the class and ask for advice from students.

Homework Options

Travaux pratiques de grammaire, p. 78, Acts. 15–16
Cahier d'activités, pp. 104–106, Acts. 18–24
Pupil's Edition, p. 289, **Ecrivons!**

Block 6

TROISIEME ETAPE

Quick Review 20 min.
- Check homework.
- Do Activity 29, p. 280.

Quiz 9-3 20 min.
- Administer Quiz 9-3A or 9-3B.

Prononciation 15 min.
- Present Prononciation, p. 281: See Language Note, ATE, p. 281.
- Play Audio CD for Activities A, B, and C.

MISE EN PRATIQUE 30 min.
- Students create a final version of their rough draft, p. 289
- Students trade papers and give written advice to their partners.
- Play Audio CD for Activity 1, p. 288.
- Do Activity 3, p. 288.

Wrap-Up 5 min.
- Challenge, ATE, p. 289

Homework Options

Que sais-je?, p. 290
Study for Chapter 9 Test.

Block 7

MISE EN PRATIQUE

Quick Review 10 min.
- Check homework and have students perform radio talk show skits.

Warm-up/Review for Chapter Test 30 min.
- Review Chapter 9. Choose from **Grammaire supplémentaire,** Grammar Tutor for Students of French, Activities for Communication, Listening Activities, Interactive CD-ROM Tutor, or **Jeux interactifs.**

Test, Chapter 9 50 min.
- Administer Chapter 9 Test. Select from Assessment Program, Alternative Assessment Guide, Test Generator, or Standardized Assessment Tutor.

Chapter Opener

CHAPITRE 9

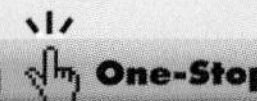
One-Stop Planner CD-ROM

For resource information, see the **One-Stop Planner**, Disc 3.

Pacing Tips

In this chapter, the most important grammar concept (the **passé composé** with **avoir**), along with new vocabulary to practice it, is presented in the first **étape**. Plan your lessons so that you can spend the bulk of classroom time with the first **étape.** For Lesson Plans and timing suggestions, see pages 263I–263L.

Meeting the Standards

Communication

- Asking for and expressing opinions, p. 269
- Inquiring about and relating past events, p. 270
- Making and answering a telephone call, p. 276
- Sharing confidences and consoling others, p. 279
- Asking for and giving advice, p. 279

Cultures

- Culture Notes, pp. 264, 267, 276
- Note culturelle, pp. 272, 276

Connections

- History Link/Language Link, p. 273

Comparisons

- Thinking Critically: Comparing and Contrasting, pp. 265, 266, 273, 281
- Language-to-Language, pp. 271, 274
- Multicultural Link, p. 265

Communities

- Career Path, p. 275
- De l'école au travail, p. 280

Cultures and Communities

Culture Note

In West Africa, telephone service is limited. Smaller towns and villages may not have service at all. Even in large cities, every household may not have a telephone. Public phones are scarce as well, but calls can be made from the post office. International calls can be made through hotel operators or long-distance operators in local post offices and are usually expensive. Since telephones are not always available, visits to friends and relatives often replace phone calls. In fact, it is not uncommon for visitors to drop by unannounced to catch up on the latest news of friends and family.

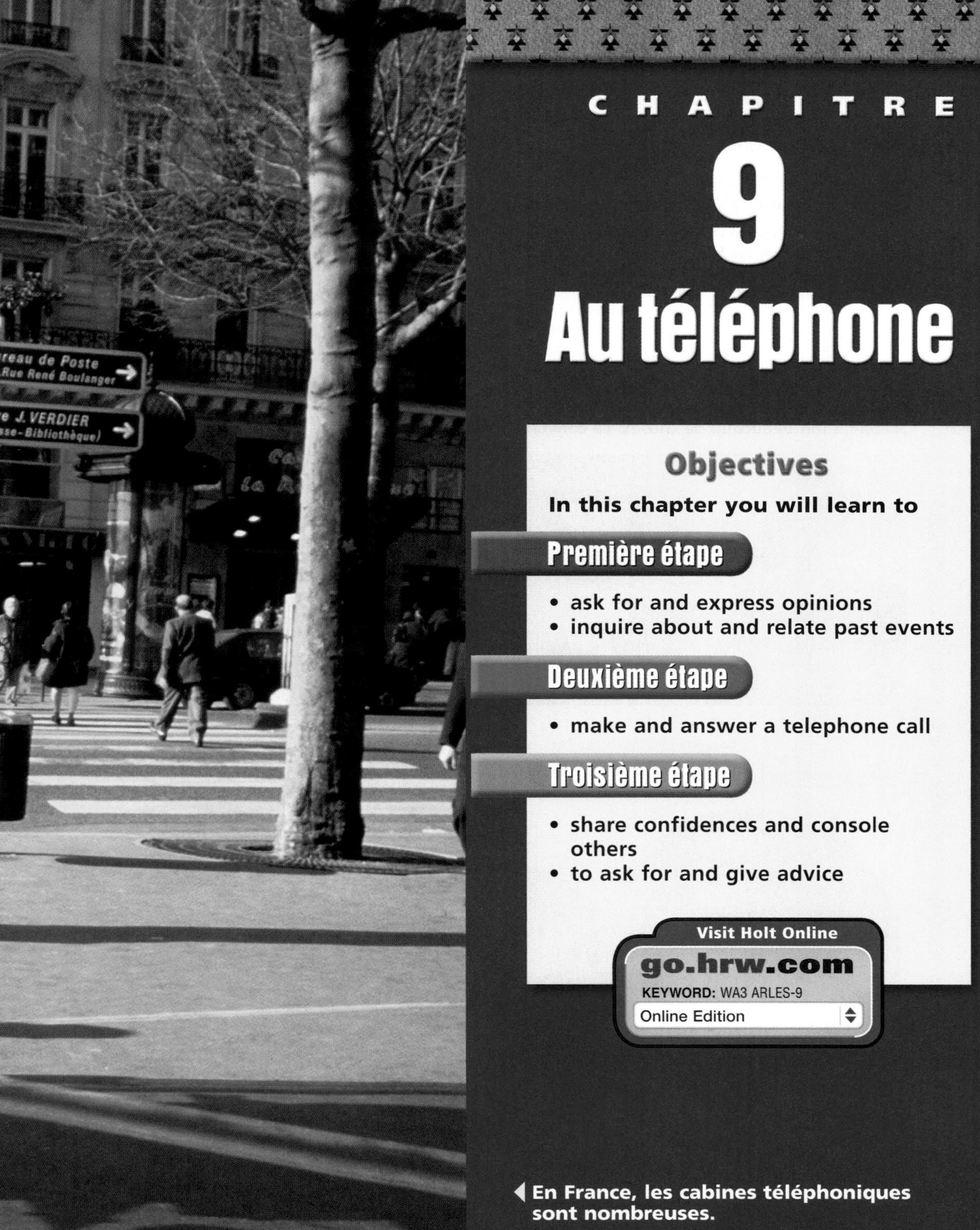

CHAPITRE

9

Au téléphone

Objectives

In this chapter you will learn to

Première étape

- ask for and express opinions
- inquire about and relate past events

Deuxième étape

- make and answer a telephone call

Troisième étape

- share confidences and console others
- to ask for and give advice

Visit Holt Online
go.hrw.com
KEYWORD: WA3 ARLES-9
Online Edition

◀ En France, les cabines téléphoniques sont nombreuses.

Chapter Opener

CHAPITRE 9

Focusing on Outcomes

Have students describe situations when they last performed the functions in the list of outcomes. Ask them how often they do these things. Then, ask what expressions they might expect to learn in this chapter. NOTE: The self-check activities in **Que sais-je?** on page 290 help students assess their achievement of the objectives.

Thinking Critically

Analyzing Ask students why understanding a phone conversation might be difficult in a foreign language. (There are no hints from body language or facial expressions.)

Multicultural Link

Have students compare the French public phone system to the one they're used to. You might want to assign countries to students and have them find out how public phones work there. They might ask someone who has traveled to their assigned country, or call or write to the nearest tourist office. Then, have them report their findings to the class.

Connections and Comparisons

Thinking Critically

Comparing and Contrasting Ask students when they last used a public telephone and why? Have students research phone use habits in France and the U.S. Which country has the most users of cellular phones? Are teens in France likely to have their own phone line or cell phones? Ask students why they think this is the case.

Thinking Critically

Evaluating Have students find out the differences between **télécartes** and phone cards in the U.S. (**Télécartes** are read directly by the public phone itself, whereas phone cards are used by dialing a toll-free number and then accessing service through a code). Have them discuss the advantages and disadvantages of phone cards.

STANDARDS: 2.1, 4.2

Mise en train

CHAPITRE 9

Teaching Resources
pp. 266–268

PRINT 
- Lesson Planner, p. 43
- Video Guide, pp. 62, 64
- Cahier d'activités, p. 97

MEDIA
- One-Stop Planner
- Video Program
  Mise en train
  Videocassette 3, 31:16–34:56
  Videocassette 5 (captioned version), 1:12:35–1:16:18
  Suite
  Videocassette 3, 34:58–38:56
  Videocassette 5 (captioned version),1:16:20–1:20:18
- DVD Tutor, Disc 2
- Audio Compact Discs, CD 9, Trs. 1–2
- **Mise en train** Transparencies

Presenting Mise en train

Have students look at the photos in ***Un week-end spécial*** and answer the general questions at the top of the page. You might also use the Preteaching Vocabulary suggestion below. Show the video. Then, have students read the dialogue and use the photos to understand the general meaning. Ask them to answer the questions in Activity 1 on page 268 as they read.

Mise en train Transparencies

Thinking Critically

Comparing and Contrasting Ask students to discuss the girls' weekend in small groups or as a class. Have them compare their recent weekend with Magali's and Hélène's. Ask if they discuss their weekend on the phone with friends and if they ever have to get off the phone.

The **roman-photo** is an abridged version of the video episode.

MISE EN TRAIN ▪ *Un week-end spécial*

CD 9 Trs. 1–2

Stratégie pour comprendre

Before you watch the video, think about the title of the story and look at the photos on these two pages. What is the subject of Hélène and Magali's telephone conversation? How did you figure that out?

Hélène

Magali

Florent

Ahmed

Hélène et Magali sont au téléphone et racontent ce qu'elles ont fait pendant le week-end. Magali a fait beaucoup de choses. La conversation dure...

1
Hélène : Allô?
Magali : Hélène? C'est Magali à l'appareil. Tu as passé un bon week-end?
Hélène : Bof, ça a été. Je n'ai rien fait de spécial.

2 **Hélène :** Samedi, j'ai fait mes devoirs.

3 **Hélène :** Dimanche, j'ai regardé la télévision...

4 **Hélène :** ...et j'ai lu un peu.

Preteaching Vocabulary

Identifying keywords

First ask students to guess the context of the **Mise en train** (a telephone conversation). Then, have them use their prior knowledge of French and the images in frames 1–8 to identify keywords or phrases that tell them what is happening. Here are some words they might identify as helpful: ❶ **rien de spécial;** ❷ **j'ai fait mes devoirs;** ❸ **télévision;** ❹ **j'ai lu;** ❺ **super;** ❻ **garçon, sympa;** ❼ **parlé;** ❽ **Les Baux-de-Provence.** Can students identify the two sentences that tell what kind of weekend each girl had? (**Je n'ai rien fait de spécial. J'ai passé un week-end super**.) What words or phrases in frames 2–4 and 6–8 support that conclusion?

STANDARDS: 1.2

5

Hélène : Et toi? Tu as passé un bon week-end?
Magali : Excellent! J'ai passé un week-end super!
Hélène : Ah oui? Qu'est-ce que tu as fait?
Magali : Je suis allée au théâtre antique avec Florent.

6 **Magali :** Il m'a présenté un garçon très sympa. Il s'appelle Ahmed. Il est super gentil.

7 **Magali :** Nous avons beaucoup parlé. Tu sais, il adore le sport. Il aime le tennis, comme moi.

8 **Magali :** Dimanche, nous sommes tous allés aux Baux-de-Provence.

9

Hélène : Qu'est-ce que vous avez fait là-bas?
Magali : Je vais te raconter une histoire incroyable!
Hélène : Je t'écoute.
Magali : Attends une seconde... Ecoute, Hélène, mon père veut téléphoner. Je te rappelle plus tard.

10

Hélène : Mais, qu'est-ce qui s'est passé aux Baux-de-Provence?

Cahier d'activités, p. 97, Act. 1

Using the Captioned Video/DVD

If students have difficulty understanding French spoken at a normal speed, use Videocassette 5 to allow students to see the French captions for ***Un week-end spécial*** and ***Un week-end spécial (suite).*** Hearing the language and watching the story will reduce anxiety about the new language and facilitate comprehension. The reinforcement of seeing the written vocabulary words as they watch the gestures and actions will help prepare students to do the comprehension activities on page 268.

NOTE: The *DVD Tutor* contains captions for all sections of the *Video Program.*

Culture Notes

- The **théâtre antique** in downtown Arles dates back to the time of the Emperor Augustus.
- **Les Baux-de-Provence** is a lively village of winding streets and small shops perched on a rocky promontory. A medieval castle dating from the thirteenth century offers a beautiful view of the surrounding countryside.
- **Santons** are ceramic figures that depict characters from Nativity scenes, as well as people of different occupations, such as shepherds or weavers, dressed in traditional provençal attire. See page 263D for more information.

Un week-end spécial (suite)

In the second part of the story, Magali calls Hélène back and tells her about her trip to **les Baux-de-Provence,** as we see flashbacks of Magali and her friends there. Magali tells Hélène about the sights they visited. At the end of the episode, we see a flashback of Magali opening a package. It is a gift from Ahmed, a **santon** that Magali admired at the souvenir boutique in **les Baux-de-Provence**. Magali asks Hélène for advice about getting to know Ahmed.

Mise en train

CHAPITRE 9

Challenge

1 **2** Have students do these activities first without looking back at the text. Then, have them look back to check their answers.

Group Work

6 Form small groups. Have each group imagine a sequel to the story and share it with the class. Have the class choose the most imaginative, the most realistic, the most probable, and so on.

These activities check for comprehension only. Students should not yet be expected to produce language modeled in **Mise en train.**

1 Tu as compris?

1. How was Hélène's weekend? OK.
2. Did Magali have a good weekend? Yes. Why? Why not? She met a nice boy.
3. Do you think Magali likes Ahmed? Yes. How can you tell? She says he is very nice.
4. Why does Magali have to hang up? Her father needs to make a phone call.

2 Magali ou Hélène?

Qui a fait ça, Magali ou Hélène?

1. aller aux Baux Magali
2. faire ses devoirs Hélène
3. lire Hélène
4. aller au théâtre antique Magali
5. regarder la télévision Hélène
6. ne rien faire de spécial Hélène

3 Mets en ordre

Put Magali's activities in order according to ***Un week-end spécial.*** 1, 4, 2, 3

1. Elle est allée au théâtre antique.
2. Elle est allée aux Baux-de-Provence.
3. Elle a parlé avec Hélène au téléphone.
4. Elle a rencontré un garçon sympa.

4 C'est qui?

A quelle personne correspond chaque phrase?

Magali

Hélène

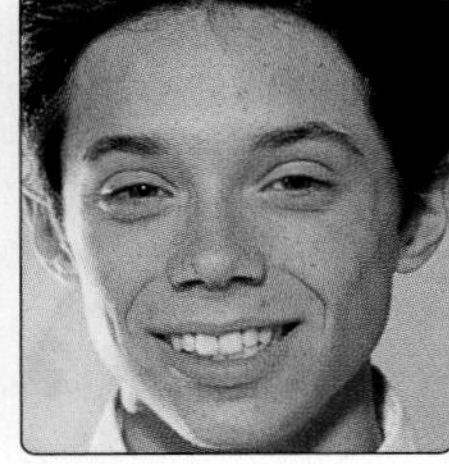
Ahmed

le père de Magali

1. Cette personne veut téléphoner. le père de Magali
2. Cette personne a passé un bon week-end. Magali
3. Cette personne est super gentille. Ahmed
4. Pendant le week-end, cette personne n'a rien fait de spécial. Hélène
5. Cette personne va téléphoner plus tard. Magali

5 Cherche les expressions

According to ***Un week-end spécial,*** what do you say in French . . . See answers below.

1. to answer the phone?
2. to identify yourself on the phone?
3. to ask if someone had a good weekend?
4. to ask what someone did?
5. to tell someone to hold?
6. to ask what happened?

C'est... à l'appareil.
Qu'est-ce qui s'est passé?
Attends une seconde.
Allô?
Qu'est-ce que tu as fait?
Tu as passé un bon week-end?

6 Et maintenant, à toi

What do you think happened to Magali at les Baux?

Comprehension Check

Visual Learners

2 On a transparency, draw pictures to illustrate the activities the girls did over the weekend. For example, you might draw a book to illustrate Hélène's statement, **J'ai lu un peu.** Then, write the girls' dialogue in speech bubbles on strips of transparency. Call on students to match the speech bubbles to the illustrations.

Tactile Learners

3 You might write the statements on strips of paper and tape them in random order on the board. Then, write the numbers 1–4 to the side. Have a student move one sentence to its correct position. Repeat the process until all sentences are in order. If there is a mistake, a student can use his or her turn to correct it.

Answers

5
1. Allô?
2. C'est... à l'appareil.
3. Tu as passé un bon week-end?
4. Qu'est-ce que tu as fait?
5. Attends une seconde.
6. Qu'est-ce qui s'est passé?

STANDARDS: 1.2

Première étape

Objectives Asking for and expressing opinions; inquiring about and relating past events

WA3 ARLES-9

Comment dit-on...?

Asking for and expressing opinions

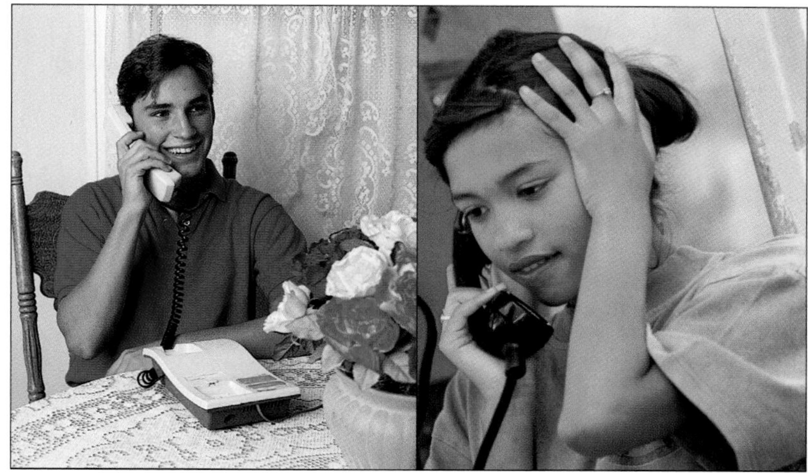

To ask for someone's opinion:

Tu as passé un bon week-end? *Did you have a good weekend?*

To express satisfaction:

Oui, très chouette. *Yes, super.*
Oui, excellent.
Oui, très bon.

To express indifference:

Oui, ça a été. *Yes, it was OK.*
Oh, pas mauvais.

To express dissatisfaction:

Très mauvais.
C'était épouvantable. *It was horrible.*

Cahier d'activités, p. 98, Act. 2

7 Le week-end! See scripts and answers on p. 263G.

Ecoutons Listen to these people talk about their weekend. Tell if they had a really good time, a mildly good time, or no fun at all.

CD 9 Tr. 3

8 Tu as passé un bon week-end?

Parlons Demande à tes camarades s'ils ont passé un bon week-end ou pas. Ensuite, dis-leur si toi, tu as passé un bon week-end ou pas.

Communication for All Students

Visual Learners

7 Show magazine pictures of people who are happy, indifferent, or unhappy and ask **Il/Elle a passé un bon week-end?**

Kinesthetic Learners

7 Have students respond by making the thumbs-up gesture, the **comme ci comme ça** gesture, or the thumbs-down gesture.

Teaching Resources
pp. 269–274

PRINT
- Lesson Planner, p. 44
- TPR Storytelling Book, pp. 33, 36
- Listening Activities, pp. 67, 71
- Activities for Communication, pp. 49–50, 115, 118, 153–154
- Travaux pratiques de grammaire, pp. 71–75
- Grammar Tutor for Students of French, Chapter 9
- Cahier d'activités, pp. 98–101
- Testing Program, pp. 223–226
- Alternative Assessment Guide, p. 40
- Student Make-Up Assignments, Chapter 9

MEDIA

- One-Stop Planner
- Audio Compact Discs, CD 9, Trs. 3–4, 20, 26–27
- Teaching Transparencies: 9-1, 9-A, 9-B; **Grammaire supplémentaire** Answers; Travaux pratiques de grammaire Answers
- Interactive CD-ROM Tutor, Disc 3

Bell Work

Have students write their opinions of three of their favorite classes or activities and three of their least favorite. **(Le français, c'est génial. La biologie, c'est nul.)**

Presenting
Comment dit-on... ?

Draw three faces showing satisfaction, indifference, and dissatisfaction on the board. Read each response, making appropriate facial expressions, and have students tell which face expresses it.

STANDARDS: 1.1, 1.2, 5.1

Première étape

CHAPITRE 9

Teaching Resources
pp. 269–274

PRINT
- Lesson Planner, p. 44
- TPR Storytelling Book, pp. 33, 36
- Listening Activities, pp. 67, 71
- Activities for Communication, pp. 49–50, 115, 118, 153–154
- Travaux pratiques de grammaire, pp. 71–75
- Grammar Tutor for Students of French, Chapter 9
- Cahier d'activités, pp. 98–101
- Testing Program, pp. 223–226
- Alternative Assessment Guide, p. 40
- Student Make-Up Assignments, Chapter 9

MEDIA 

- One-Stop Planner
- Audio Compact Discs, CD 9, Trs. 3–4, 20, 26–27
- Teaching Transparencies: 9-1, 9-A, 9-B; **Grammaire supplémentaire** Answers; Travaux pratiques de grammaire Answers
- Interactive CD-ROM Tutor, Disc 3

Presenting
Comment dit-on... ?

Tell students that you're going to talk about your weekend. Have them listen for what you did and in what order. Then, tell about your weekend activities again, writing **d'abord, ensuite, après, après ça,** and **finalement** on the board as you proceed. Next, write five of the activities you mentioned on five flash cards, and give the flash cards to five students. Have them recall in what order you recounted your activities and hold the flash cards under the appropriate sequencing expressions on the board.

Comment dit-on...?

Inquiring about and relating past events

To inquire about past events:

Qu'est-ce qui s'est passé (hier)?
What happened (yesterday)?
Qu'est-ce que tu as fait vendredi?
What did you do . . . ?
Et après? *And then?*
Tu es allé(e) où? *Where did you go?*

To relate past events:

Nous avons parlé. *We talked.*
D'abord, j'ai fait mes devoirs.
First, . . .
Ensuite, j'ai téléphoné à un copain.
Then, . . .
Après, je suis sorti(e).
Afterwards, I went out.
Et après ça, j'ai téléphoné à Luc.
And after that, . . .
Finalement/Enfin, je suis allé(e) chez Paul.
Finally, I went . . .

Cahier d'activités, p. 98, Act. 3

9 Méli-mélo!

Lisons Remets la conversation entre Albert et Marcel dans le bon ordre.

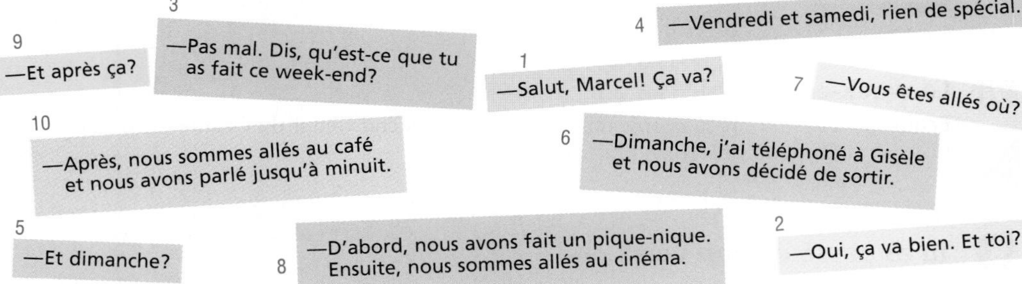

9 —Et après ça?
3 —Pas mal. Dis, qu'est-ce que tu as fait ce week-end?
1 —Salut, Marcel! Ça va?
4 —Vendredi et samedi, rien de spécial.
7 —Vous êtes allés où?
10 —Après, nous sommes allés au café et nous avons parlé jusqu'à minuit.
6 —Dimanche, j'ai téléphoné à Gisèle et nous avons décidé de sortir.
5 —Et dimanche?
8 —D'abord, nous avons fait un pique-nique. Ensuite, nous sommes allés au cinéma.
2 —Oui, ça va bien. Et toi?

Communication for All Students

Slower Pace

9 Copy these sentences randomly on a sheet of paper and give copies to pairs of students. Have partners begin by finding the sentence that might start the conversation. Then, have them underline or circle the sequencing expressions and number the sentences to show the correct order.

Challenge

9 After they complete the activity, have students work in groups to write their own telephone conversation with a friend, using Albert's and Marcel's as a model. Have them write each line of the conversation on a strip of paper and scramble the strips. Then, have the groups exchange their scrambled conversations and unscramble them.

STANDARDS: 1.2

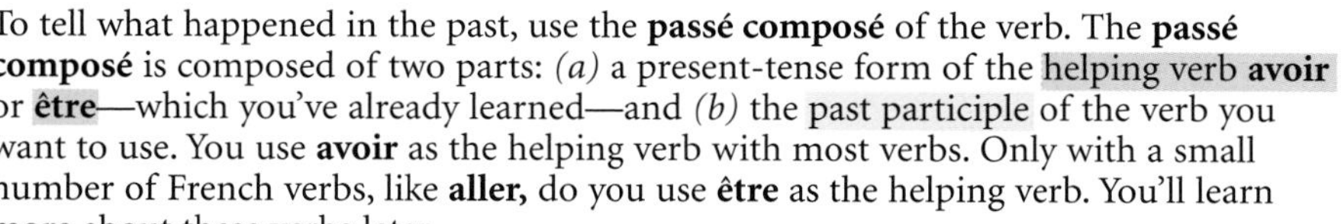

Grammaire

The *passé composé* with *avoir*

To tell what happened in the past, use the **passé composé** of the verb. The **passé composé** is composed of two parts: *(a)* a present-tense form of the helping verb **avoir** or **être**—which you've already learned—and *(b)* the past participle of the verb you want to use. You use **avoir** as the helping verb with most verbs. Only with a small number of French verbs, like **aller,** do you use **être** as the helping verb. You'll learn more about these verbs later.

Helping Verb		+ *Past Participle*
J'	**ai**	**parlé** au téléphone.
Tu	**as**	
Il/Elle/On	**a**	
Nous	**avons**	
Vous	**avez**	
Ils/Elles	**ont**	

- To form the past participle of a verb that ends in **-er,** drop the **-er** and add **-é.**
- To make a verb in the **passé composé** negative, put **ne (n')... pas** around the helping verb.

Je **n'**ai **pas** étudié.

- Some French verbs have irregular past participles—that is, they don't follow a regular pattern. You'll have to memorize them when you learn the verb. Here are the past participles of some irregular verbs that you've already seen.

faire → fait	J'ai **fait** mes devoirs.
prendre → pris	Ils ont **pris** un taxi.
voir → vu	Il a **vu** sa grand-mère.
lire → lu	Elle a **lu** un roman français.

Grammaire supplémentaire, pp. 284–285, Act. 1–3

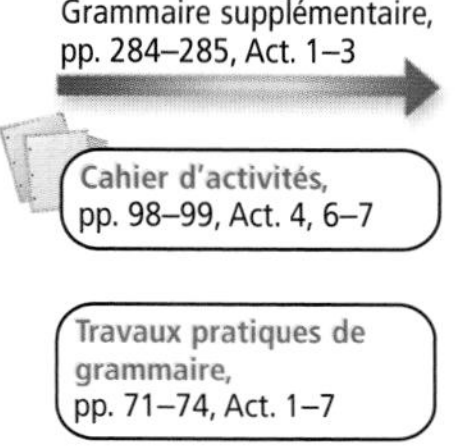

Cahier d'activités, pp. 98–99, Act. 4, 6–7

Travaux pratiques de grammaire, pp. 71–74, Act. 1–7

10 Grammaire en contexte See scripts and answers on p. 263G.

Ecoutons Listen to these conversations and decide whether the speakers are talking about what they did last weekend or what they're going to do next weekend.

CD 9 Tr. 4

11 Grammaire en contexte

Parlons Qu'est-ce que Claire et ses amis ont fait à la plage?

1. Ils ont joué au volley.

2. Ils ont fait un pique-nique.

3. Claire a écouté de la musique.

Connections and Comparisons

Language-to-Language

Some students may be confused by the **passé composé** in French **(j'ai parlé),** since they are used to using one verb for the past in English *(I spoke).* Have them think about compound tenses that exist in English (*I had spoken, I will have spoken,* and so on) and point out the similarities. If you have native speakers of Spanish in your classroom, explain to them that the **passé composé** is very similar in usage (although not in form) to the preterite in Spanish. Have these students give examples.

Presenting Grammaire

The *passé composé* with *avoir* Write the sentence **Nous avons parlé** on the board and ask students to tell what they can deduce about the past tense. Then, review the forms of **avoir** by handing students items such as a book or some pencils and asking **Qui a mon livre/mes crayons? (Tim a votre livre. Alicia et John ont vos crayons.)** Explain that the **passé composé** is formed with the present tense of **avoir** plus a past participle. Then, hold up pictures that illustrate activities such as **voir un film, manger du gâteau,** and **faire du jogging.** Call on students to give the correct past participle of each verb.

Slower Pace

10 Before starting this activity, review the use of **aller** + infinitive to express future time. Write an activity on the board **(faire les devoirs)** and have one volunteer create a sentence, using that verb in the **passé composé.** Then, have a second volunteer create a second sentence with the same verb, using **aller.** You might also ask students **Qu'est-ce que tu vas faire demain?**

Visual Learners

11 As a variation, make up several sentences about the pictures. **(Ils ont joué au volley-ball. Ils ont fait un pique-nique. Elle a écouté la radio.)** Say them at random and have students write the number of the picture each one refers to.

Teaching Resources
pp. 269–274

PRINT 

- Lesson Planner, p. 44
- TPR Storytelling Book, pp. 33, 36
- Listening Activities, pp. 67, 71
- Activities for Communication, pp. 49–50, 115, 118, 153–154
- Travaux pratiques de grammaire, pp. 71–75
- Grammar Tutor for Students of French, Chapter 9
- Cahier d'activités, pp. 98–101
- Testing Program, pp. 223–226
- Alternative Assessment Guide, p. 40
- Student Make-Up Assignments, Chapter 9

MEDIA 

- One-Stop Planner
- Audio Compact Discs, CD 9, Trs. 3–4, 20, 26–27
- Teaching Transparencies: 9-1, 9-A, 9-B; **Grammaire supplémentaire** Answers; Travaux pratiques de grammaire Answers
- Interactive CD-ROM Tutor, Disc 3

Game

Loto! Have each student draw a 4 x 4 grid and fill the squares with different past tense forms **(j'ai pris, il a lu)**. Write the infinitives of these verbs on slips of paper **(prendre, lire)** and put them in a box. Then, begin the "bingo" game. Select a slip of paper, call out the infinitive in French, and have students mark the square on the grid if it contains the past tense of the verb you called. When a student has marked four squares in a row, horizontally, vertically, or diagonally, he or she calls out **Loto!** and reads the items in French.

Possible answers

13
1. Elle a bien étudié.
2. Il a beaucoup travaillé.
3. Elle n'a pas encore vu *Les Misérables*.
4. Il a trop mangé.
5. Il a déjà lu *Le Petit Prince*.

12 Qu'est-ce qu'on a fait?

Parlons Avec un camarade, parlez de ce que vous avez fait et de ce que vous n'avez pas fait le week-end dernier. Ensuite, raconte le week-end de ton camarade à un troisième élève.

EXEMPLE **J'ai promené le chien samedi matin.**

faire mes devoirs — laver la voiture — sortir la poubelle — promener le chien — acheter une montre — ranger ma chambre — prendre un café avec mes amis — faire le ménage — voir un film français — faire un pique-nique — lire un roman

Note de grammaire

When you use the **passé composé** with adverbs such as **trop, beaucoup, pas encore** *(not yet)*, **bien** *(well)*, **mal** *(badly)*, and **déjà** *(already)*, place the adverb before the past participle of the verb.

J'ai **déjà** mangé.

Nadine n'a **pas encore** vu ce film.

Travaux pratiques de grammaire, p. 74, Act. 8

Grammaire supplémentaire, p. 285, Act. 4–5

Note culturelle

Arles est situé sur le Rhône, un fleuve du sud de la France. Pendant les premiers siècles après Jésus-Christ, Arles est devenu le port le plus important de la province romaine du sud de la Gaule appelée Provincia. Arles est aussi devenu le plus grand centre de commerce. Aujourd'hui, on peut toujours voir l'influence romaine en Arles. On peut y visiter l'amphithéâtre romain, un ancien théâtre, qui est toujours utilisé et les plus grands thermes de Provence.

13 Grammaire en contexte

See answers below.

Parlons Donne une raison logique pour expliquer pourquoi chaque chose est arrivée. Utilise les mots dans la boîte et le **passé composé**.

EXEMPLE Céline a gagné le match de tennis.
Elle a bien joué.

1. Marie-Louise a eu 18 à son interro de maths!
2. Jérôme n'a pas d'énergie.
3. Sabine veut aller voir *Les Misérables*.
4. Luc n'a plus faim.
5. Etienne ne veut pas lire *Le Petit Prince*.

bien — étudier — travailler — pas encore — déjà — voir — lire — trop — manger — beaucoup

Communication for All Students

Slower Pace

12 Have students look at the expressions in the word box and form the **passé composé** of the infinitives given in each expression.

Challenge

Note de grammaire Have one student suggest an activity **(voyager)**. Then, have a second student give the **passé composé. (J'ai voyagé.)** Have a third student repeat the sentence, adding an adverb that relates to his or her own experience. **(J'ai beaucoup voyagé.)**

STANDARDS: 1.1, 1.3, 2.2, 3.1, 5.1, 5.2

Vocabulaire

Qu'est-ce que tu as fait aujourd'hui?

ÇA S'EST BIEN PASSÉ, LA JOURNÉE?
OH, ÇA A ÉTÉ.

J'ai raté le bus.

J'ai trouvé vingt euros.

J'ai oublié mes devoirs.

J'ai déjeuné à la cantine.

J'ai rencontré une fille (un garçon) sympa.

J'ai chanté dans la chorale.

J'ai acheté un CD.

J'ai travaillé au fast-food.

Here are some other verbs and expressions you may want to use to talk about what you've done during your day.

apporter	*to bring*	**passer un examen**	*to take an exam*
chercher	*to look for*	**rater une interro**	*to fail a quiz*
commencer	*to begin, to start*	**répéter**	*to rehearse, to practice music*
dîner	*to have dinner*	**retrouver**	*to meet with*
gagner	*to win, to earn*	**visiter**	*to visit (a place)*
montrer	*to show*		

Travaux pratiques de grammaire, p. 75, Act. 9–10

Connections and Comparisons

History Link/Language Link

The French word **Provence** comes from the Latin word **Provincia,** the name the Romans gave to their province in Gaul. Have students find out more about the Roman occupation and different Roman ruins in the area. Students might research how the aqueducts and baths functioned and were used. (See page 263C for project ideas.)

Thinking Critically

Comparing and Contrasting Have students compare their typical school day to the one pictured here. What are some of the differences they notice? (The bus is a city bus and not a school bus, as public schools in France do not provide transportation.)

Presenting Vocabulaire

Gather props to help present the sentences (a 50 euro bill, a fork, a CD). Act out each sentence and have students repeat it, imitating your gestures. Next, call on eight students to mime one sentence each and have the class tell what happened to them. Then, make statements using the verbs at the bottom of the page and have students respond by miming the actions.

Kinesthetic Learners

Write several sentences with words from the **Vocabulaire** on strips of transparency. **(Après l'école, j'ai cherché mon chat. Ensuite, Emile et Laurent ont retrouvé des amis.)** Cut the sentences into sequencing words, subjects, auxiliary verbs, past participles, and objects or complements and shuffle them. Have two students come up to the overhead and arrange the pieces to make sentences.

Challenge

Have students write down three activities from the **Vocabulaire** that they did last week. Then, have them try to find one other student who also did these activities by saying **J'ai déjeuné à la cantine. Et toi?** Have them report back to the class.

Additional Practice

Write each sequencing expression on a strip of transparency and distribute them to five students. Have students write an activity they did over the weekend on their strips. Then, display the strips on the overhead and have the class use them to create a story. You might use this activity as a writing assignment.

Language Note

Point out that **commencer** is followed by **à** when used with an infinitive.

CHAPITRE 9

Language Note
Remind students that **du, de la, de l', des, un,** and **une** all become **de** after a negative expression, but the definite articles **le, la,** and **les** do not change.

Visual Learners
14 Have students bring in magazine pictures of people engaged in different activities. As they hold up each picture, have the class tell what the people did last weekend.

Challenge
16 Set either a time limit or a goal of five names.

Mon journal
17 For an additional journal entry suggestion for Chapter 9, see *Cahier d'activités,* page 153.

Assess
- Testing Program, pp. 223–226
  Quiz 9-1A, Quiz 9-1B
  Audio CD 9, Tr. 20
- Student Make-Up Assignments
  Chapter 9, Alternative Quiz
- Alternative Assessment Guide, p. 40

14 Le week-end dernier Answers may vary.

Parlons Dis ce que les personnes suivantes ont fait le week-end dernier.

1. Elle a étudié.

2. Elle a rencontré un garçon sympa.

3. Il a raté une interro.

4. Il a dîné avec sa grand-mère.

5. Il a écouté de la musique.

6. Elles ont acheté des livres.

15 Pierre a fait quoi? See answers below.

Parlons Pierre a passé une semaine dans une colonie de vacances. Regarde les activités dans la boîte. Qu'est-ce qu'il a fait à ton avis? Qu'est-ce qu'il n'a pas fait?

chanter avec des copains
rater le bus
gagner un match
nager
faire du ski nautique
acheter un CD
rater un examen
manger des escargots

French words that look similar are often related in meaning, so you can use words you already know to guess the meanings of new words. If you already know what **chanter** means, you can probably guess the meaning of **une chanteuse.** You know what **commencer** means, so what do you think le **commencement** means? Likewise, you should be able to figure out **le visiteur** from the verb **visiter**.

16 Tu as déjà fait ça?

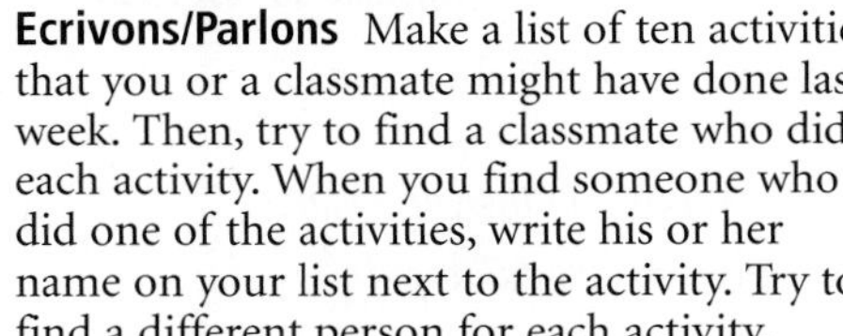

Ecrivons/Parlons Make a list of ten activities that you or a classmate might have done last week. Then, try to find a classmate who did each activity. When you find someone who did one of the activities, write his or her name on your list next to the activity. Try to find a different person for each activity.

Activités	Nom
1. J'ai gagné cent dollars.	Jeff
2. J'ai chanté dans la chorale.	Lisa

17 Mon journal

Write down five things you did last weekend. Be sure to tell when you did each activity, with whom, and add as many other details as you can think of.

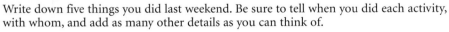

Connections and Comparisons

Language-to-Language
De bons conseils To show students how words that look alike are often related in meaning, in other languages as well as French and English, give them the following examples in Spanish. Ask students to guess what a **pintor**, a **patinador**, and a **cantante** are if **pintar** means *to paint*, **patinar** means *to skate*, and **cantar** means *to sing* (*painter, skater,* and *singer*). If you have native speakers of Spanish in your classroom, have them give other examples.

Answers

15 Pierre a : gagné un match, fait du ski nautique, nagé, chanté avec des copains.
Pierre n'a pas : raté d'examen, mangé d'escargots, raté le bus, acheté de CD.

STANDARDS: 1.3, 3.1, 4.1, 5.2

Objective Making and answering a telephone call

WA3 ARLES-9

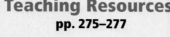

—Allô, Anita?
—Oui. C'est moi.
—Salut. C'est François.

—Allô? C'est Michel. Véronique est là, s'il vous plaît?
—Une seconde.
—Merci.

—Allô? Est-ce que Xuan est là, s'il vous plaît?
—Non, il est chez Robert.
—Est-ce que je peux laisser un message?
—Bien sûr.
—Vous pouvez lui dire qu'Emmanuelle a téléphoné?
—D'accord.
—Merci.

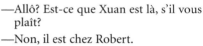

18 **Au téléphone**

Parlons Answer these questions about the conversations.

1. What do the people say to begin the conversation? Allô?
2. Who has to wait a few seconds to speak to his or her friend? Michel
3. Who gets to talk right away to the person he or she is calling? François
4. Who isn't home? Xuan

Allô, allô?
Les spécialistes du téléphone
Microcommutateurs • Téléphones sans fil • Téléphones de voiture • Répondeurs • Télécopieurs personnels • Interphones • Alarmes
18, rue Lafayette — **13200 ARLES** **04-90-96-45-75**
26, rue de la Liberté — **13200 ARLES** **04-90-49-54-16**

Communication for All Students

Slower Pace

18 Have students tell who the caller is and who is answering the phone in each conversation. Have them list the words that helped them decide.

Additional Practice

18 Act out the conversations for students. Then, distribute typed copies of the dialogues. Have students underline the expressions they used to answer the questions. Finally, have them practice reading the conversations aloud.

Teaching Resources
pp. 275–277

PRINT 

- Lesson Planner, p. 45
- TPR Storytelling Book, pp. 34, 36
- Listening Activities, pp. 67–68, 72
- Activities for Communication, pp. 51–52, 116, 118–119, 153–154
- Travaux pratiques de grammaire, pp. 76–77
- Grammar Tutor for Students of French, Chapter 9
- Cahier d'activités, pp. 102–103
- Testing Program, pp. 227–230
- Alternative Assessment Guide, p. 40
- Student Make-Up Assignments, Chapter 9

MEDIA 

- One-Stop Planner
- Audio Compact Discs, CD 9, Trs. 5–6, 21, 28–29
- Teaching Transparencies: 9-2; **Grammaire supplémentaire** Answers; Travaux pratiques de grammaire Answers
- Interactive CD-ROM Tutor, Disc 3

Bell Work

Have students write three sentences telling what they did or didn't do after school yesterday. Students might exchange and edit each other's papers.

Career Path

Ask students why learning telephone expressions would be valuable in a career in telecommunications. Ask them how they would use their French for a career in this field.

Deuxième étape

Teaching Resources
pp. 275–277

PRINT

- Lesson Planner, p. 45
- TPR Storytelling Book, pp. 34, 36
- Listening Activities, pp. 67–68, 72
- Activities for Communication, pp. 51–52, 116, 118–119, 153–154
- Travaux pratiques de grammaire, pp. 76–77
- Grammar Tutor for Students of French, Chapter 9
- Cahier d'activités, pp. 102–103
- Testing Program, pp. 227–230
- Alternative Assessment Guide, p. 40
- Student Make-Up Assignments, Chapter 9

MEDIA

- One-Stop Planner
- Audio Compact Discs, CD 9, Trs. 5–6, 21, 28–29
- Teaching Transparencies: 9-2; **Grammaire supplémentaire** Answers; Travaux pratiques de grammaire Answers
- Interactive CD-ROM Tutor, Disc 3

Presenting
Comment dit-on... ?

Act as both the caller and the person called in a simple conversation, using the expressions from **Comment dit-on... ?** Then, dial a number, make telephone ringing sounds, turn to the class, and say **Ça ne répond pas.** Dial again, making busy signal sounds, and tell the class **C'est occupé.** Then, pretend to answer the phone, pause, and say **Ne quittez pas.** Turn to the class and hand the phone to a student, saying **C'est pour toi.** Have students repeat the new expressions.

Comment dit-on...?

CD-ROM 3 DVD 2

Making and answering a telephone call

To make a phone call:	To answer a phone call:
Bonjour. **Je suis bien chez** Véronique? *Is this . . . 's house?*	**Allô?** **Qui est à l'appareil?** *Who's calling?*
C'est Michel. (**Est-ce que**) Véronique **est là, s'il vous plaît?**	**Vous pouvez rappeler plus tard?** *Can you call back later?*
Je peux parler à Véronique? **Je peux laisser un message?** *May I leave a message?*	**Une seconde, s'il vous plaît.** **D'accord.**
Vous pouvez lui dire que j'ai téléphoné? *Can you tell her/him that I called?*	**Bien sûr.**

Here are some additional phrases you may need:

Ne quittez pas. *Hold on.*

Ça ne répond pas. *There's no answer.*

C'est occupé. *It's busy.*

Cahier d'activités, p. 102, Act. 13–14

Travaux pratiques de grammaire, p. 76, Act. 11–12

19 Un coup de fil See scripts and answers on p. 263G.

Ecoutons Ecoute ces conversations téléphoniques. Qui téléphone? A qui voudrait-il/-elle parler?

CD 9 Tr. 5

Note culturelle

En France, quand on veut téléphoner, on peut aller à la poste. Il y a toujours des cabines téléphoniques à la poste. On peut aussi téléphoner d'une cabine publique. Pour réduire le vandalisme, France Télécom remplace de plus en plus les téléphones à pièces par des publiphones à cartes. Ces téléphones modernes utilisent des télécartes. On peut acheter sa télécarte à la poste ou dans un bureau de tabac. Chaque carte contient un certain nombre d'unités. Pour téléphoner, on met sa télécarte dans le publiphone. On utilise plusieurs unités à chaque fois. Le publiphone a un écran qui dit combien d'unités il reste sur la télécarte. On utilise plus d'unités si on téléphone loin ou longtemps. Quand on a utilisé toutes les unités d'une télécarte, il faut en acheter une autre.

Cultures and Communities

Culture Notes

- In France, local calls are charged by the minute, just like long-distance calls in the United States. **France Télécom** is the national public phone company responsible for all local and long-distance service.
- French phone numbers consist of five sets of two digits, separated by periods (03.24.13.93.12). With the exception of Paris that has its own rules, the first set represents the region, the second set the department, the next three sets your personal number. If you call France from the United States, you drop the first digit (zero) when you dial the number.

20 Méli-mélo!

Lisons Mets cette conversation dans le bon ordre.

9 D'accord.
1 Allô?
4 C'est Aurélie.
8 Tu peux lui dire que j'ai téléphoné?
5 Salut, Aurélie. Désolée, elle n'est pas là.
2 Allô, bonjour. Je peux parler à Nicole?
3 Qui est à l'appareil?
7 Bien sûr.
6 Est-ce que je peux laisser un message?

21 Messages téléphoniques See scripts and answers on pp. 263G–263H.

CD 9 Tr. 6

Ecoutons During your exchange visit to France, you stay with a French family, **les Tissot.** You're the only one at home today. Several of their friends call and leave messages. Write down the messages and compare your notes with a classmate's.

22 Jeu de rôle

Parlons Tu téléphones à un(e) ami(e) mais il/elle n'est pas à la maison. Laisse un message pour ton ami(e). Ton (ta) camarade va jouer la rôle du père ou de la mère de ton ami(e). Ensuite, changez de rôle.

Grammaire

-re verbs

Like **-er** verbs, most verbs that end in **-re** follow a regular pattern. Drop the **-re** from the infinitive and add the endings indicated in the box to the right. Notice that you don't add an ending to the **il/elle/on** form of the verb.

répondre *(to answer)*

je répond**s**	nous répond**ons**
tu répond**s**	vous répond**ez**
il/elle/on répond	ils/elles répond**ent**

- **Répondre** is followed by a form of the preposition **à**. Nathalie répond **à** Lucas. Je réponds **au** professeur.
- Some other **-re** verbs you might want to use are **vendre** *(to sell)*, **attendre** *(to wait for)*, and **perdre** *(to lose)*.
- To form the past participle of an **-re** verb, drop the **-re** and add **-u**. Il a **répondu** à sa lettre. Nous avons **perdu** nos cahiers.

Grammaire supplémentaire, p. 286, Act. 6–8

Cahier d'activités, p. 103, Act. 15–16

Travaux pratiques de grammaire, p. 77, Act. 13–14

23 Grammaire en contexte

Ecrivons Sébastien overhears the following comments before class. Complete the comments with the appropriate forms of the verbs **répondre, vendre, attendre,** and **perdre.**

1. «Nous _____ le professeur. Il est en retard.» attendons
2. «Attention, Luc! Tu _____ ton argent. Tu dois fermer ton sac à dos.» perds
3. «Ils _____ toujours bien aux questions du professeur!» répondent
4. «Est-ce qu'on _____ des calculatrices à la Papeterie Simonet? Il me faut une calculatrice.» vend
5. «Je _____ à la lettre de Marianne. Elle est à Nice avec sa famille.» réponds
6. «On va _____ des tee-shirts pour gagner de l'argent pour le Cercle français.» vendre

Communication for All Students

Teacher Note

Students might want to know these terms: *cellular phone* **(un téléphone mobile)**; *cordless phone* **(un téléphone sans fil)**.

Additional Practice

20 Have students give an appropriate response to each of the following questions: **Allô? Qui est à l'appareil? Je peux parler à Nicole? Tu peux rappeler plus tard?**

Slower Pace

21 Stop the recording after each phone call to allow students time to jot down a few words to help them recall the message.

Language Notes

- Other useful telephone expressions are: **composer le numéro** *(to dial the number);* **l'annuaire** *(phone book);* **décrocher** *(to pick up the receiver);* **raccrocher** *(to hang up).*
- You might point out that **un coup de téléphone** or **un coup de fil** is an informal way of saying *a phone call.* One might give someone a call **(donner un coup de téléphone/un coup de fil à quelqu'un)** or get a call from someone **(recevoir un coup de téléphone/un coup de fil de quelqu'un).**

Presenting Grammaire

***-re* verbs** Bring in props to help you illustrate the four **-re** verbs presented. For example, you might hold up a sign that says "For Sale" and tell the students **Je vends ma maison.** You might look in your desk drawer and say **Où est mon stylo... ? J'ai perdu mon stylo.** To present the other forms, you might hold up pictures of people doing various activities. For example, you might hold up a picture of some people at a bus stop and tell the students **Ils attendent le bus.** Write the forms on the board as you present them and then have students identify the endings. As the class becomes familiar with the forms, ask them questions such as **Qu'est-ce que je fais?,** as you act out the different verbs.

Assess

- Testing Program, pp. 227–230
  Quiz 9-2A, Quiz 9-2B
  Audio CD 9, Tr. 21
- Student Make-Up Assignments, Chapter 9, Alternative Quiz
- Alternative Assessment Guide, p. 40

STANDARDS: 1.1, 1.2, 5.1, 5.2

CHAPITRE 9

Teaching Resources
p. 278

PRINT 
- Video Guide, pp. 63, 64–65
- Cahier d'activités, p. 108

MEDIA
- One-Stop Planner
- Video Program
  Videocassette 3, 38:59–41:47
- DVD Tutor, Disc 2
- Audio Compact Discs, CD 9, Trs. 7–10
- Interactive CD-ROM Tutor, Disc 3

Presenting
Panorama Culturel

Play the video. Pause after each interview to ask **Il/Elle aime téléphoner?** Ask what else students understand from the first viewing. Then, write the **Questions** below on the board or on a transparency and have students answer them as they read the interviews with a partner.

Questions

1. **Pourquoi est-ce que les parents de Nicole rouspètent?** (parce qu'elle reste longtemps au téléphone)
2. **Pourquoi est-ce que Virgile aime téléphoner?** (Ça permet de discuter, de prendre des nouvelles. C'est pratique.)
3. **A qui est-ce que Marie aime téléphoner?** (à ses copines et à ses copains, à Caroline)
4. **Est-ce que Marie aime téléphoner aux gens qu'elle ne connaît pas?** (Non)

Tu aimes téléphoner?

How often do you call your friends? We asked some francophone teenagers about their telephone habits. Here's what they told us.

Nicole,
Martinique

«Oui, j'aime beaucoup téléphoner. Mes parents rouspètent souvent parce que je reste longtemps au téléphone, parce que ça coûte cher, le téléphone, et donc ils me demandent d'éviter de parler trop souvent au téléphone, de rester moins longtemps. Le plus souvent, je téléphone à peu près une heure de temps.» Tr. 8

Virgile,
France

«Ah oui, j'aime beaucoup téléphoner. Ça permet de discuter, de prendre des nouvelles un peu partout. C'est pratique.» Tr. 9

Marie,
France

«Ben, j'aime bien téléphoner... Ça dépend à qui, mes copines, mes copains. J'aime bien parce que j'aime bien leur parler, surtout à ma meilleure amie Caroline. J'aime beaucoup lui parler. On reste très longtemps. Mais sinon, téléphoner aux gens que je connais pas, j'aime pas trop.» Tr. 10

Qu'en penses-tu?

1. How do your phone habits compare with those of these people?
2. How might your life be different if you did or didn't have a phone in your room?
3. What restrictions on the use of the phone do you have at your house?

Savais-tu que... ?

The French telecommunications network is one of the best in the world. However, talking on the telephone in France and other francophone countries is still expensive, even when calling locally. For this reason, teenagers are not usually allowed to spend long periods of time on the phone, and most do not have a phone in their room.

Connections and Comparisons

Thinking Critically

Drawing Inferences Have students guess what **rouspètent** means from the context of Nicole's interview *(moan, grumble, complain)*. Have students ever seen adults do this? Under what circumstances?

Thinking Critically

Synthesizing Ask students how they would keep in touch with friends and family in a French home where phone calls are very expensive.

STANDARDS: 2.1, 3.2, 4.2

Troisième étape

Objectives Sharing confidences and consoling others; asking for and giving advice

go.hrw.com WA3 ARLES-9

Comment dit-on...?

Sharing confidences and consoling others; asking for and giving advice

To share a confidence:

J'ai un petit problème. *I've got a little problem.*
Je peux te parler? *Can I talk to you?*
Tu as une minute? *Do you have a minute?*

To console someone:

Je t'écoute. *I'm listening.*
Qu'est-ce que je peux faire? *What can I do?*
Ne t'en fais pas! *Don't worry!*
Ça va aller mieux! *It's going to get better!*

To ask for advice:

A ton avis, qu'est-ce que je fais? *In your opinion, what do I do?*
Qu'est-ce que tu me conseilles? *What do you advise me to do?*

To give advice:

Oublie-le/-la/-les! *Forget him/her/it/them!*
Téléphone-lui/-leur! *Call him/her/them!*
Tu devrais lui/leur parler. *You should talk to him/her/them.*
Pourquoi tu ne téléphones **pas?** *Why don't you . . . ?*

Cahier d'activités, pp. 104–105, Act. 18–22

24 Des conseils

See scripts and answers on p. 263H.

Ecoutons Are these people giving advice or asking for advice?

CD 9 Tr. 11

Many language students feel nervous about speaking. You might be worried about making mistakes, or you might think you won't sound right. To sharpen your speaking skills, practice aloud at home in French, using situations and material covered in class. You could role-play two friends talking on the phone about a problem that one person has. What would each person say? This is a good time to incorporate grammar points (like the object pronouns) that you covered in class in your conversation. These practice conversations will help prepare you to speak confidently in class.

Note de grammaire

In the expressions above, **le, la,** and **les** *(him, her, it, them)* are object pronouns that refer to people or things. The pronouns **lui** *(to him, to her)* and **leur** *(to them)* refer only to people. You will learn more about these pronouns later.

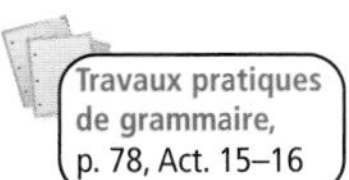

Travaux pratiques de grammaire, p. 78, Act. 15–16

Grammaire supplémentaire, p. 287, Act. 9–10

25 Grammaire en contexte

See scripts and answers on p. 263H.

Ecoutons Ecoute cette conversation entre Mireille et Simone. Simone a un problème. Quel est son problème?

CD 9 Tr. 12

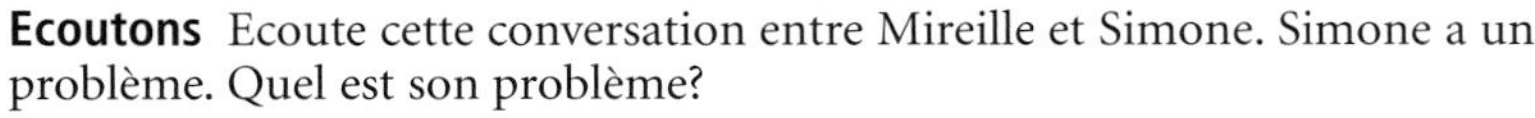

Teacher to Teacher

Nicole Mitescu
Claremont High School
Claremont, CA

Nicole's students make connections with other French students.

"This requires audio tapes and tape recorders or a language lab. I have students in one French class record messages for students in the second French class. The students in the second class respond to the messages. Students use the tapes to "leave messages" for a friend, either describing a problem and asking for advice, or describing something exciting they did over the weekend. If you don't have a language lab, the students enjoy working on this at home, too. I don't grade this assignment, but I do listen to the tapes before giving them to the second class. The kids have a lot of fun with this activity!"

Troisième étape

CHAPITRE 9

Teaching Resources

pp. 279–281

PRINT

- Lesson Planner, p. 46
- TPR Storytelling Book, pp. 35, 36
- Listening Activities, pp. 69, 73
- Activities for Communication, pp. 53–54, 117, 119, 153–154
- Travaux pratiques de grammaire, p. 78
- Grammar Tutor for Students of French, Chapter 9
- Cahier d'activités, pp. 104–106
- Testing Program, pp. 231–234
- Alternative Assessment Guide, p. 40
- Student Make-Up Assignments, Chapter 9

MEDIA

- One-Stop Planner
- Audio Compact Discs, CD 9, Trs. 11–12, 22, 30–31
- Teaching Transparencies: 9-3; **Grammaire supplémentaire** Answers; Travaux pratiques de grammaire Answers
- Interactive CD-ROM Tutor, Disc 3

Bell Work

Have students write responses to the following: **Bonjour! Je peux laisser un message? Qui est à l'appareil? Vous pouvez lui dire que j'ai téléphoné?**

Presenting

Comment dit-on... ?

Act out the following scenes with a toy telephone, having students guess which functions you're demonstrating:

1. Call a friend to get help with a problem.
2. Answer a call from a friend who has a problem.

Continue your conversation until all the new expressions have been identified.

STANDARDS: 1.1, 1.2

Troisième étape

CHAPITRE 9

Teaching Resources
pp. 279–281

PRINT 

- Lesson Planner, p. 46
- TPR Storytelling Book, pp. 35, 36
- Listening Activities, pp. 69, 73
- Activities for Communication, pp. 53–54, 117, 119, 153–154
- Travaux pratiques de grammaire, p. 78
- Grammar Tutor for Students of French, Chapter 9
- Cahier d'activités, pp. 104–106
- Testing Program, pp. 231–234
- Alternative Assessment Guide, p. 40
- Student Make-Up Assignments, Chapter 9

MEDIA 

- One-Stop Planner
- Audio Compact Discs, CD 9, Trs. 11–12, 22, 30–31
- Teaching Transparencies: 9-3; **Grammaire supplémentaire** Answers; Travaux pratiques de grammaire Answers
- Interactive CD-ROM Tutor, Disc 3

Cooperative Learning

28 Have students do this activity in small groups. One student poses a problem and each of the others offers advice. Then, they all collaborate to decide on the best advice. You might want to re-enter expressions for agreeing and disagreeing, such as **Tu es d'accord?** and **Je ne suis pas d'accord.**

Portfolio

28 **Oral** This activity is suitable for students' oral portfolios. For portfolio suggestions, see *Alternative Assessment Guide,* page 26.

26 J'ai un petit problème 

Lisons Trouve la solution logique à chaque problème.

1. Mon frère ne me parle plus depuis cinq jours. d
2. Je veux acheter un vélo, mais je n'ai pas d'argent. b
3. J'ai oublié mes devoirs. c
4. Je vais rater l'interro d'anglais. a

a. Tu devrais étudier plus souvent.
b. Pourquoi tu ne travailles pas?
c. Refais-les!
d. Parle-lui!

27 Pauvre Hervé!

Ecrivons Console Hervé.

Possible answers: 1. Ça va aller mieux! 2. Oublie-la! 3. Ne t'en fais pas!

28 Et à ton avis?

Parlons Your friend phones and asks to speak to you. He or she has some problems and wants to ask your advice about them. Console your friend and offer some advice. Then, change roles.

Il/Elle...

- n'a pas d'argent pour acheter des baskets.
- n'a pas acheté de cadeau pour l'anniversaire de sa sœur.
- n'aime pas le prof de biologie.
- n'a pas parlé avec son petit ami (sa petite amie) depuis 3 jours.
- ne peut pas trouver de travail pour l'été.
- a raté un examen.
- veut rencontrer de nouveaux copains.
- n'a pas gagné son match de tennis.
- veut faire une boum, mais ses parents ne sont pas d'accord.

29 De l'école au travail

Parlons You're the host of a radio talk show called ***A l'écoute des jeunes.*** You receive many calls from teenagers asking for your advice. Your job is to answer the phone, listen to their problems, ask them questions, and console them or give them some advice.

Communication for All Students

Group Work

26 Have groups of students make up additional problems with a solution for each, using this activity as a model. Have them number the problems and letter the solutions. They should provide an answer key on a separate sheet of paper. Then, have groups exchange papers with another group and match their problems to the suggested solutions.

Slower Pace

28 Review the suggested problems by having students match them to props you hold up, such as want ads **(ne peut pas trouver de travail pour l'été),** a party hat **(veut faire une boum...),** a toy phone, and tennis shoes. Have students change the verbs and possessive adjectives to the **je** and **tu** forms in preparation for the activity.

STANDARDS: 1.1, 1.3, 5.1, 5.2

PRONONCIATION

CD 9
Trs. 13–18

The vowel sounds [e] and [ɛ]

See scripts and answers on p. 263H.

Listen to the vowels in the word **préfère.** How are they different? The first one is pronounced [e], and the second one [ɛ]. To make the vowel sound [e], hold your mouth in a closed, smiling position. Keep your lips and tongue steady to avoid the glide, as in the English word *day.* Repeat these words.

été désolé occupé répondre

Now, take a smiling position once again, but this time open your mouth wider. This will produce the vowel sound [ɛ]. Repeat these words.

règle algèbre achète frère

In the examples, you can see that **é** represents the sound [e], while **è** represents the sound [ɛ] in writing. You've probably noticed that **e** with no accent and some other letter combinations can represent these sounds as well. Repeat these words.

apportez trouver

You see that the spellings **ez** and **er** normally represent the sound [e]. This is true of all infinitives ending in **-er.**

Some spellings of the vowel sound [ɛ] are **ait, ais, ei,** and **ê.** An unaccented **e** is pronounced as open [ɛ] when it is followed by a double consonant, such as **ll** or **tt,** when followed by **x,** and, in most cases, when followed by **r,** or by any pronounced consonant. Now repeat these words.

fait français neige bête

elle cassette examen cherche

A. A prononcer

Repeat the following words.

1. délicieux	méchant	théâtre	vélo
2. après-midi	père	mère	très
3. février	chanter	chez	prenez
4. cette	française	treize	pêches

B. A lire

Take turns with a partner reading each of the following sentences aloud.

1. Ne quittez pas! Je vais chercher mon frère.
2. Marcel a visité Arles en mai. Il est allé au musée, à la cathédrale et aux arènes.
3. Elle n'aime pas trop l'algèbre et la géométrie, mais elle aime bien l'espagnol.
4. Tu ne peux pas aller au cinéma. Tu n'as pas fait la vaisselle.

C. A écrire

You're going to hear a short dialogue. Write down what you hear.

Teaching Suggestion

Prononciation Make sure students look over their work for accents before the dictation in Part C is corrected. Look over their sentences for common errors and review accent-sound correlations, if necessary.

Language Note

Prononciation Make sure students don't make a diphthong out of the **[e]** sound, commonly pronounced by Americans as *ay-ee.*

Additional Practice

Show *Teaching Transparency 9-3* and ask students to state the problem each situation illustrates. Then, have volunteers role-play, asking a friend or family member for advice about one of the problems.

Assess

- Testing Program, pp. 231–234 Quiz 9-3A, Quiz 9-3B, Audio CD 9, Tr. 22
- Student Make-Up Assignments, Chapter 9, Alternative Quiz
- Alternative Assessment Guide, p. 40

Connections and Comparisons

Thinking Critically

Analyzing After students have practiced the pronunciations, have them think about how they would teach the vowel sounds in the English words **day** and **pet** to French speakers. What do they think French speakers would tend to do, given the way similar vowel sounds are pronounced in French?

Thinking Critically

Comparing and Contrasting Point out that regional variations exist in French, just as in English. Ask students how vowels are pronounced differently in different regions in the U.S. Ask them how they pronounce **pen** and **pin,** for example. You might show a film made from one of Marcel Pagnol's books, such as *Manon des Sources,* so that students can hear a regional variant.

Lisons!

CHAPITRE 9

Teaching Resources
pp. 282–283

PRINT 
- Lesson Planner, p. 47
- Cahier d'activités, p. 107
- Reading Strategies and Skills Handbook, Chapter 9
- Joie de lire 1, Chapter 9
- Standardized Assessment Tutor, Chapter 9

MEDIA 
- One-Stop Planner

Prereading
Activities A–B

Terms in Lisons!
Students might want to know the following words:
chaleureux *(warm)*
gâterie *(little treat)*
maîtrise *(mastery)*
combiné magique *(magic receiver),*
quotidiennement *(daily)*
fil *(cord).*

Reading
Activities C–J

Using Prior Knowledge
Complete Activities C, D, and E as a class and then have partners complete Activities F–J. Encourage them to use the strategies they have previously learned to guess the meaning of unfamiliar words.

Answers
Possible answers:
A. telephone habits of teenagers
B. The first and second sections are personal statements from teenagers. The third section is more general information.
C. around the age of 10 or 11; Her parents punished her for using the phone too much.

Lisons!

Je passe ma vie au téléphone

Stratégie pour lire
As you read, you use many different reading strategies at the same time. You may start by looking at illustrations, then move on to the titles and subtitles. You may need to skim the passage to get the general idea, then scan for specific details, and finally read the passage for more complete comprehension.

A. Skim the article. What kind of information do you expect to find? See answers below.
B. What is the purpose of each section? How does the second section differ from the others? See answers below.

Emmanuelle
C. How old was Emmanuelle when she started using the telephone? How did her parents feel about her using the telephone? See answers below.
D. Read Emmanuelle's statement and list all the cognates you find. Then, match these terms with their English equivalents.

1. carte téléphonique b	a. stationery
2. réprimander c	b. phone card
3. remboursement d	c. reprimand
4. cabine téléphonique e	d. reimbursement
5. papier à lettres a	e. telephone booth

Et moi, et moi...et eux!

Je passe ma vie au téléphone

Il y en a qui chantent : «Qui a eu cette idée folle, un jour, d'inventer l'école?» Moi, si j'en avais le talent, je chanterais : «Qui a eu cette idée folle, un jour, d'inventer le phone?»

Je ne pouvais plus me passer du téléphone. Et pourtant, j'ai tout essayé : punitions des parents, remboursement des communications, cures de quinze jours et plus en colonie... J'en ai découvert l'usage à dix ou onze ans, l'utilisation quasi quotidienne à treize ans. Et cela pour n'importe quel motif : discuter du travail scolaire, appeler les copains de colo qui habitent parfois à plus de 100 km de chez moi...

C'est à ce moment-là que mes parents sont intervenus. Au début, mes coups de fil ne se voyaient pas sur la note car mes parents restent assez longtemps, eux aussi, au téléphone. Mais du coup, j'ai pris l'habitude des longues conversations et des cris se sont fait entendre. Jusqu'au jour où, las de me réprimander, ils ont décidé de m'acheter une carte téléphonique et des timbres. J'ai vite eu la flemme d'aller à la cabine téléphonique et j'ai donc jeté mon dévolu sur le papier à lettres. En écrivant, j'utilise ma petite cervelle et quel plaisir de recevoir en retour une lettre que je peux lire et relire où et quand je veux!

Emmanuelle: «Qui a eu l'idée, un jour, d'inventer le phone?»

Il ne se passe pas une journée sans que je reçoive ma lecture préférée, celle qui vient du fond du cœur, celle des copains. D'accord, le téléphone est rapide et chaleureux, mais la lettre l'est peut-être encore plus. Bref, le téléphone est une gâterie à consommer avec modération.

Emmanuelle, 15 ans

Connections and Comparisons

Thinking Critically
- **Analyzing** Ask students how their lives would be different if local calls in the United States were charged by the minute.
- **Analyzing** In Emmanuelle's letter, she writes **"Qui a eu cette idée folle, un jour, d'inventer le phone?"**. Ask students to think of other forms of communication that have been invented in the last decade. Have them discuss the positive and negative ways in which these new inventions and the speed and accessibility of communication have changed people's lives. Have any of the new inventions changed the way students communicate?

STANDARDS: 1.2, 3.1, 4.1

Le bon usage du téléphone passe par une certaine maîtrise de l'appareil. Il faut savoir se présenter, être clair, précis, articuler... Après quelques années de pratique s'installe une véritable relation avec le combiné magique, merveilleux messager des peines et des espoirs. On attend une soirée entière une hypothétique sonnerie, on sursaute à chaque «Dring!», redoutant que Sylvain annule le rendez-vous pour lequel il a fallu passer trois heures dans la salle de bains. Combien de fois ai-je tourné, hésitante, autour de cet objet mystérieux au clavier soudain terrifiant? Combien de fois a-t-il, avec patience et sans jamais rien dire, recueilli mes rires et mes larmes? C'est pourquoi, aujourd'hui, je tiens à confesser publiquement et solennellement que j'aime mon téléphone!

Géraldine, 17 ans

Géraldine: «Je le confesse: mon téléphone, je l'aime!»

Pour dire bonjour, pour un rien...

Un quart d'heure, une demi-heure, une heure pendus au bout du fil... L'opération se répète quotidiennement. «Mes enfants téléphonent à leurs amis pour un rien, pour se dire bonjour et parfois pour faire leurs devoirs. Ça commence dès qu'ils rentrent du lycée et ça peut durer très longtemps... C'est à croire qu'ils sont nés avec un téléphone à l'oreille!», confie Véronique. Comme le dit Aurélie : «De retour chez soi, la seule façon de conserver un lien avec ceux qu'on vient de quitter, c'est le téléphone.»

Le téléphone, c'est un fil qui vous relie au monde, qui rassure sur l'amitié des copains. Et c'est ce qui est le plus important.

Au sens propre comme au sens figuré, l'appareil est un fil qui vous relie au monde, qui vous rassure sur l'amitié des copains. C'est-à-dire sur ce qui est le plus important. Parce que dans l'amitié, on trouve la confiance, le respect, la tolérance et la sécurité dont on a tant besoin, à tout moment. Faute de lien, le risque est de se retrouver seul face à ses angoisses.

D'ailleurs, peu importe parfois qui vous appelez; quand l'interlocuteur décroche, vous finissez toujours par trouver quelque chose à raconter ou une confidence à partager.

E. How did Emmanuelle break her telephone addiction? How does she communicate with her friends now? Why does she prefer this means of communication? See answers below.

Géraldine

F. What advice does Géraldine give at the beginning of her statement? How does she describe her relationship with the telephone? See answers below.

G. Who might have made each of the following statements?

"My telephone is my best friend." Géraldine

"Finally, Arlette answered the letter I wrote her last week!" Emmanuelle

"You may not make any more long-distance calls!" Emmanuelle's parents

H. Which people give the following reasons for talking on the phone? See answers below.

1. to say hello to friends
2. to do homework

Pour dire bonjour, pour un rien...

I. In this section, Véronique and Aurélie each make a statement. Which person is a parent? How do you know? See answers below.

J. Read the selection again and find three reasons why people enjoy talking on the phone. Which reason do you think is most important? See answers below.

K. In English, write a statement similar to Emmanuelle's and Geraldine's in which you tell how you feel about the telephone. Give examples to show why you feel the way you do.

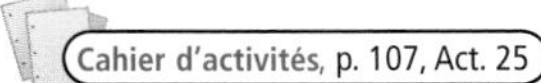
Cahier d'activités, p. 107, Act. 25

Lisons!

CHAPITRE 9

Postreading
Activity K

Thinking Critically

Analyzing You might ask students to discuss the following questions about **Je passe ma vie au téléphone:** Which of the reasons given for talking on the phone are valid? Which are not? What are some other justifiable reasons for staying on the phone?

Culture Note

You might tell students that in Germany, people often answer the phone by giving their last name. In Italy, they're likely to hear **Pronto.** In Spanish-speaking countries, they might hear various expressions, such as **Bueno, Diga,** and **Aló.**

Teacher Note

For an additional reading, see *Cahier d'activités,* page 107.

Answers

Possible answers:

E. She started writing letters. Now, she writes letters all the time. She can read and reread the letters whenever she likes.

F. She says you need to know how to present yourself and how to be precise and clear on the telephone. She loves her telephone.

H. 1. les enfants de Véronique
2. les enfants de Véronique, Emmanuelle

I. Véronique: she says "mes enfants..."

J. Students sometimes talk on the phone about assignments; the phone keeps you connected to the world and to your friends; there is always something to share.

Communication for All Students

Visual Learners

H. Have students imagine that they are marketing executives for **France Télécom.** Using the reasons that they find in Activity H, have them create print advertisements to encourage more telephone use by the French. They might wish to use drawings or cut-out photos from magazines. Have them present their ads to the class and then display them around the room.

Kinesthetic/ Auditory Learners

K. Have students work in pairs to produce skits about their telephone use as they described it in Activity K. Have them read their statements out loud and then perform their skits. Bring in props, such as toy telephones, if available. Some students might wish to play the roles of exasperated parents receiving their phone bills, or needing to use the phone for another call or Internet access.

STANDARDS: 1.2, 1.3, 3.1, 4.1

Grammaire supplémentaire

CHAPITRE 9

For **Grammaire supplémentaire** Answer Transparencies, see the *Teaching Transparencies* binder.

Grammaire supplémentaire

Visit Holt Online
go.hrw.com
KEYWORD: WA3 ARLES-9
Jeux interactifs

Première étape

Objectives Asking for and expressing opinions; inquiring about and relating past events

1 Emmanuelle téléphone à Julie pour lui raconter son week-end. Pour compléter leur conversation, utilise le passé composé des verbes entre parenthèses. (**p. 271**)

EMMANUELLE Salut Julie. Tu __1__ (passer) un bon week-end?

JULIE Oh, oui. J'__2__ (regarder) un match de tennis, j' __3__ (parler) avec ma grand-mère et j' __4__ (lire) un roman. Et toi? Qu'est-ce que tu __5__ (faire)?

EMMANUELLE J' __6__ (prendre) la voiture de ma mère, et ma sœur et moi, nous __7__ (voir) un film.

2 Complète ce que Pierre a écrit dans son journal à propos de son week-end. Utilise le passé composé des verbes entre parenthèses. (**p. 271**)

Hier, j' __1__ (retrouver) mes amis Jean et Françoise au café. Nous __2__ (déjeuner) ensemble, puis, nous __3__ (parler) de notre week-end. Samedi, Françoise __4__ (lire) un livre et Jean __5__ (étudier). Le soir, ils __6__ (acheter) un billet de loto mais ils __7__ (ne pas gagner). Dimanche, j'__8__ (voir) un bon film et ensuite, j' __9__ (faire) mes devoirs.

Answers

1
1. as passé
2. ai regardé
3. ai parlé
4. ai lu
5. as fait
6. ai pris
7. avons vu

2
1. ai retrouvé
2. avons déjeuné
3. avons parlé
4. a lu
5. a étudié
6. ont acheté
7. n'ont pas gagné
8. ai vu
9. ai fait

Grammar Resources for Chapter 9

The **Grammaire supplémentaire** activities were designed as supplemental activities for the grammatical concepts presented in the chapter. You might use them as additional practice, for review, or for assessment.

For more grammar presentations, review, and practice, refer to the following:

- Travaux pratiques de grammaire
- Grammar Tutor for Students of French
- Grammar Summary on pp. R15–R28
- Cahier d'activités
- Grammar and Vocabulary quizzes (Testing Program)
- Test Generator
- Interactive CD-ROM Tutor
- DVD Tutor
- **Jeux interactifs** at **go.hrw.com**

STANDARDS: 1.2

3 Edouard veut toujours faire ce que Milo a fait. Lis ce qu'Edouard va faire et ensuite, dis ce que Milo a fait hier. Mets les verbes au passé composé et fais les changements nécessaires. (**p. 271**)

EXEMPLE Demain, je vais acheter des baskets.
Hier, Milo a acheté des baskets.

1. Je vais laver la voiture de mon père demain. Hier,...
2. Je vais déjeuner à la cantine demain. Hier,...
3. Demain, je vais retrouver mes copains. Hier,...
4. Demain, je vais répéter avec la chorale. Hier,...
5. Je vais dîner avec ma grand-mère demain. Hier,...
6. Demain, je vais ranger ma chambre. Hier,...

4 Complète chaque phrase avec l'adverbe approprié. (**pp. 271, 272**)

1. Hélène a (demain / pas encore / trop) mangé hier soir.
2. Tu vas parler avec Sullivan (demain / ce matin / hier)?
3. J'ai (bientôt / déjà / hier) fait mes devoirs.
4. Marianne et Roger, vous avez (maintenant / bien / hier) lu ce roman?
5. Les Saint-Martin ont pris un taxi pour aller à la gare (demain / maintenant / ce matin).

5 La maman d'Elissa lui demande si elle et ses frères et sœurs ont fait leur tâches domestiques. Réponds pour Elissa. Dans tes réponses, utilise **déjà** ou **ne (n')... pas encore.** N'oublie pas de faire tous les changements nécessaires. (**p. 272**)

EXEMPLE MAMAN Tu as passé l'aspirateur?
ELISSA **Non, je n'ai pas encore passé l'aspirateur.**

1. MAMAN Claire et toi, vous avez rangé vos chambres?
   ELISSA Non, ______________________________
2. MAMAN Tu as débarrassé la table?
   ELISSA Oui, ______________________________
3. MAMAN Et Guillaume, est-ce qu'il a fait les courses?
   ELISSA Oui, ______________________________
4. MAMAN Est-ce que tu as promené le chien?
   ELISSA Non, ______________________________
5. MAMAN Est-ce que Claire et Sophie ont fait le ménage?
   ELISSA Non, ______________________________

Teacher to Teacher

Elaine Bind
McDonogh School
Ownings Mills, MD

Elaine's activity practices the *passé composé* in the negative forms.

"To practice the placement of "**ne...pas**" in the **passé composé,** I paste pictures from magazines onto cards, or draw simple pictures, representing different activities. I then put on the board a list of time frames: **été 2000, le week-end dernier, hiver 1999, les vacances, hier soir,** etc. I hold up a card and specify a time for the students. Students say whether they did or didn't do the activity at that time."

Variation: Students select the picture and the time for each activity.

Answers

3
1. Milo a lavé la voiture de son père.
2. Milo a déjeuné à la cantine.
3. Milo a retrouvé ses copains.
4. Milo a répété avec la chorale.
5. Milo a dîné avec sa grand-mère.
6. Milo a rangé sa chambre.

4
1. trop
2. demain
3. déjà
4. bien
5. ce matin

5
1. nous n'avons pas encore rangé nos chambres.
2. j'ai déjà débarrassé la table.
3. il a déjà fait les courses.
4. je n'ai pas encore promené le chien.
5. elles n'ont pas encore fait le ménage.

Grammaire supplémentaire

CHAPITRE 9

For **Grammaire supplémentaire** Answer Transparencies, see the *Teaching Transparencies* binder.

Grammaire supplémentaire

WA3 ARLES-9

Deuxième étape

Objective Making and answering a telephone call

6 Ecris six phrases logiques en utilisant des mots de chaque colonne. Utilise le passé composé et n'oublie pas de faire tous les changements nécessaires. (**p. 277**)

Toi, tu		**devant le cinéma**
Moi, je	**prendre**	**le bus de 10 h**
Tes cousins	**répondre**	**le téléphone**
La mère de Serge	**vendre**	**la question du professeur**
Vous	**perdre**	**la voiture**
Nous	**attendre**	**mon portefeuille**
		pendant 15 minutes

7 Pierre, David et Yves parlent de ce que leurs amis vont faire aujourd'hui. Complète leur conversation avec les formes correctes des verbes **répondre** et **attendre.** (**p. 277**)

PIERRE Tiens, salut! Vous ___1___ le bus?
YVES Non, nous ___2___ Paul. Il va au stade avec nous.
PIERRE Où est Lise?
DAVID Elle est chez elle. Elle ___3___ sa mère pour aller au musée.
PIERRE Ah oui! C'est vrai. Et Bruno, qu'est-ce qu'il fait ce matin?
YVES Il ___4___ à la lettre de son correspondant américain. Et toi, qu'est-ce que tu fais, alors?
PIERRE Rien de spécial.
DAVID Tu ___5___ Paul avec nous?
PIERRE Oui, pourquoi pas?

8 Mets chaque phrase dans un ordre logique. Utilise le passé composé quand c'est nécessaire. (**p. 277**)

1. hier/Paul/perdre/son portefeuille/au centre commercial
2. nous/répondre/au téléphone/quand/notre père/travailler
3. ne/pas/perdre/votre argent
4. mes parents/vendre/leur voiture/bleu/la semaine dernière
5. Michel/vendre/des bonbons/pour/gagner de l'argent

Answers

6 *Answers will vary.*

7
1. attendez
2. attendons
3. attend
4. répond
5. attends

8
1. Hier, Paul a perdu son portefeuille au centre commercial.
2. Nous répondons au téléphone quand notre père travaille.
3. Ne perdez pas votre argent!
4. Mes parents ont vendu leur voiture bleue la semaine dernière.
5. Michel vend des bonbons pour gagner de l'argent.

Communication for All Students

Additional Practice

7 To extend this activity, have the students create a phone conversation between Pierre and Lise. Pierre should tell what he did with his friends, Yves, David, and Paul. Lise should say if she liked her visit to the museum or not. Have students act out the phone conversation in front of the class.

Kinesthetic learners

8 You may want to write each word of the 5 sentences on a separate index card. Scramble the words for the first sentence and have a student put them back in the right order. Once all the words are in the correct order, have the student conjugate the verb in the appropriate tense and then write the complete sentence on the board.

STANDARDS: 1.2

Troisième étape

Objectives **Sharing confidences and consoling others; asking for and giving advice**

9 Léon appelle Magali pour lui demander son avis. Complète leur conversation avec **le, la, l', les, lui** ou **leur.** (**p. 279**)

MAGALI Allô?
LEON Salut, Magali, ça va? J'ai un petit problème. Tu as une minute?
MAGALI Oui. Bien sûr. Je t'écoute.
LEON Ben, hier, au café, j'ai rencontré une fille. On a parlé pendant deux heures. Ce matin, elle m'a téléphoné pour me dire qu'elle veut sortir avec moi. A ton avis, qu'est-ce que je fais?
MAGALI Elle est comment, cette fille? Tu ___1___ (l', les) aimes bien?
LEON Oui. Je ___2___ (l', la) aime beaucoup. Elle est super sympa.
MAGALI Qu'est-ce que tu ___3___ (lui, leur) as répondu, alors?
LEON Je ne ___4___ (la, lui) ai pas répondu. A ton avis, qu'est-ce que je fais?
MAGALI Téléphone- ___5___ (lui, leur) tout de suite!
LEON Mais je ne trouve plus son numéro de téléphone!
MAGALI Cherche- ___6___ (le, leur)!
LEON Non, c'est pas possible. Je ne peux pas ___7___ (le, lui) téléphoner. Je suis trop timide!
MAGALI Ah, bon! Alors, oublie- ___8___ (la, les)!

10 Ton ami Max et toi, vous donnez des conseils à Odile. Répète les conseils de Max et utilise les pronoms **le, la, les, lui** ou **leur.** (**p. 279**)

EXEMPLE MAX Achète les pommes rouges!
TOI **Oui. Achète-les!**

1. Téléphone à tes copains! ____________
2. Prends la trousse violette! ____________
3. Apporte tes disques compacts! ____________
4. Oublie ce garçon! ____________
5. Attends les vacances! ____________
6. Ecris à Caroline! ____________
7. Parle à tes parents! ____________
8. Achète ces stylos! ____________

Review and Assess

You may wish to assign the **Grammaire supplémentaire** activities as additional practice or homework after presenting material throughout the chapter. Assign Activities 1–3 after **Grammaire** (p. 271), Activities 4–5 after **Note de grammaire** (p. 272), Activities 6–8 after **Grammaire** (p. 277), and Activities 9–10 after **Note de grammaire** (p. 279). To prepare students for the **Etape** Quizzes and Chapter Test, we suggest doing the **Grammaire supplémentaire** activities in the following order. Have students complete Activities 1–5 before taking Quizzes 9-1A or 9-1B; Activities 6–8 before Quizzes 9-2A or 9-2B; and Activities 9–10 before Quizzes 9-3A or 9-3B.

Answers

9
1. l'
2. l'
3. lui
4. lui
5. lui
6. le
7. lui
8. la

10
1. Oui. Téléphone-leur!
2. Oui. Prends-la!
3. Oui. Apporte-les!
4. Oui. Oublie-le!
5. Oui. Attends-les!
6. Oui. Ecris-lui!
7. Oui. Parle-leur!
8. Oui. Achète-les!

Mise en pratique

CHAPITRE 9

The **Mise en pratique** reviews and integrates all four skills and culture in preparation for the Chapter Test.

Teaching Resources
pp. 288–289

PRINT 

- Lesson Planner, p. 47
- Listening Activities, p. 69
- Video Guide, pp. 63, 66
- Grammar Tutor for Students of French, Chapter 9
- Standardized Assessment Tutor, Chapter 9

MEDIA

- One-Stop Planner
- Video Program, Videocassette 3, 41:49–42:56
- DVD Tutor, Disc 2
- Audio Compact Discs, CD 9, Tr. 19
- Interactive CD-ROM Tutor, Disc 3

Teacher Note

3 If students have problems with any of these questions, tell them to reread the **Note culturelle** on page 276.

Answers

2
1. A boy asked her out, and she doesn't know if he's serious.
2. She tells Monique not to be discouraged and to approach the boy.
3. her family
4. She tells S not to pay attention to the negative comments and to tell her family she's unhappy.

Mise en pratique

1 A friend has left a message on your answering machine telling you what he did over the weekend. Listen, then decide if these sentences are true or false. See scripts and answers on p. 263H.

CD 9 Tr. 19

1. Martin a passé un mauvais week-end.
2. Il est allé à la plage.
3. Il a fait beau pendant le week-end.
4. Il a joué au football samedi.
5. Il n'a pas joué au tennis.
6. Dimanche, il a fait de l'aérobic.

2 D'abord, lis ces lettres rapidement. Ensuite, relis chaque lettre plus attentivement. De quoi est-ce que ces lettres parlent? Qui est Agnès? Ensuite, réponds aux questions suivantes. See answers below.

Chère Agnès

Agnès vous comprend. Vous pouvez lui confier tous vos problèmes. Elle trouve toujours une solution!

Il me dit qu'il veut sortir avec moi. Est-ce vrai?

Chère Agnès,
J'aime beaucoup un garçon, Pierre, qui me dit, dans une lettre très tendre, qu'il veut sortir avec moi. Mais il ne m'appelle jamais. Se moque-t-il de moi? Aide-moi car je suis dingue de lui!
--Monique...

Ne te décourage pas! Tu aimes ce garçon et il t'aime également. Tu t'imagines qu'il se moque de toi, mais lui aussi doit se demander s'il a ses chances. A toi d'aller vers lui. Bonne chance!

Toute ma famille me déteste.

Chère Agnès,
J'ai 14 ans et j'ai un problème : tout le monde dans ma famille me déteste, sauf ma mémé. Mes parents et ma sœur se moquent toujours de moi et me disent que je suis laide. Je suis très déprimée. Au secours!
--S

Ah S...! N'écoute pas ce que ta famille te dit. Et puis, il y a toujours ta mémé qui t'aime. Tu as 14 ans et tes parents ont sûrement peur de perdre leur petite fille. Parle-leur de tes sentiments et tu verras, tout ira mieux.

1. What is Monique's problem?
2. How does Agnès respond?
3. Who is S having difficulties with?
4. What does Agnès advise her to do?

3 D'après ce que tu sais sur le système de téléphone français, est-ce que les phrases suivantes sont vraies ou fausses?

1. The only way to make a call from a public phone in France is to use coins. false
2. You can generally find a public phone at the post office. true
3. You can't buy phone cards at the post office. false
4. Card-operated phones are being replaced by coin-operated ones. false
5. If you make a call using a phone card, you will be charged based on the distance and duration of the call. true

Apply and Assess

Slower Pace

1 Have students read the statements before they listen to the recording.

Challenge

1 Have students correct the false statements to make them true. You might also have them tell whether or not they did the activities the speaker mentioned last weekend.

STANDARDS: 1.2

4 

Ecrivons!

Think of a problem that many teenagers face. Describe the problem in a letter to Agnès and ask her to give you some advice. Then, exchange letters with a classmate and write a response offering advice about his or her problem as if you were Agnès.

Prewriting

On a sheet of paper, brainstorm ways to explain the problem by asking yourself the "W" questions. Who is involved in the problem? What exactly is the problem? Where do you see the problem? At home? At school? When is the problem most evident? Why do you think this problem occurs?

Stratégie pour écrire

Answering the five "W" questions (Who? What? Where? When? Why?) can help you clarify your ideas. It can also help you make sure you don't leave out important information for your readers.

Writing

Using the answers to your "W" questions, write a letter to Agnès describing the problem. Be as specific as you can in your description. However, don't try to use vocabulary and expressions you don't know or aren't familiar with. Use what you know as effectively as you can; other words and expressions will come later.

Now, exchange letters with a classmate. Each of you should write a response to the other's letter, offering advice on the problem. In writing your response, try to use some of the expressions you've learned for giving advice. After your classmate has read your response, have him or her return it to you, along with the letter you wrote. You're now ready for the final step of the writing process.

Revising

Evaluating your work is another important part of writing. This process involves several steps:

1. Self-evaluation: Reread both your letter and the response you wrote. Are they both arranged well? Are they easy to understand? Are they too wordy, or are they lacking information?
2. Proofreading: Now, go over your writing again. This time, look just for misspelled words, punctuation errors, and grammatical mistakes.
3. Revising: Make any changes you feel are necessary.

After these steps are completed, you can submit or publish the final copy of your work.

5

Jeu de rôle

You haven't seen your friend in a while. You want to find out what he or she has been doing. Phone and ask to speak to your friend. Talk about what you both did last weekend. Find out also what your friend is planning to do next summer. Act this out with a partner.

Apply and Assess

Challenge

4 Students could also use their letters as material for a radio talk show skit in which callers discuss their problems on the air with someone like Agnès. Have students work in groups of four in which one person takes the role of Agnès and the other three play the roles of the callers. Have them perform the skit in front of the class.

Process Writing

4 You may want to have the class make up some imaginary problems. Write a list on the board and allow students to either choose a problem from this list or think up one on their own.

Portfolio

4 **Written** This activity is appropriate for students' written portfolios. For portfolio suggestions, see *Alternative Assessment Guide,* pages iv–17.

Writing Assessment

4 You might also use the following rubric when grading your students on this activity.

Writing Rubric	Points			
	4	3	2	1
Content (Complete–Incomplete)				
Comprehensibility (Comprehensible–Incomprehensible)				
Accuracy (Accurate–Seldom accurate)				
Organization (Well organized–Poorly organized)				
Effort (Excellent–Minimal)				

18–20: A 14–15: C Under
16–17: B 12–13: D 12: F

Teacher Note

To help students edit one another's work for the **Ecrivons!** writing assignments, you might give them the Peer-Editing Rubric on page 9 of the *Alternative Assessment Guide.* Students complete the rubric by checking content and proofreading their classmate's work.

Que sais-je?

CHAPITRE 9

Teaching Resources
p. 290

PRINT
- Grammar Tutor for Students of French, Chapter 9

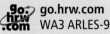

MEDIA 
- Interactive CD-ROM Tutor, Disc 3
- Online self-test

go.hrw.com
WA3 ARLES-9

Teacher Note
This page is intended to help students prepare for the Chapter Test. It is a brief checklist of the major points covered in the chapter. The students should be reminded that this is only a checklist and does not necessarily include everything that will appear on the test.

Additional Practice
2 To extend this activity and review the **passé composé,** have students tell what they did during their weekend, after they have told how it was.

Additional Practice
4 You might have students review other forms of the **passé composé** in addition to the **je** form suggested in the activity.

Answers

5
1. C'est...
2. Je suis bien chez... ?
3. (Est-ce que) ...est là, s'il vous plaît? (Est-ce que) je peux parler à... ?
4. Je peux laisser un message?
5. Vous pouvez lui dire que j'ai téléphoné?
6. C'est occupé.

Que sais-je?

WA3 ARLES-9

Can you use what you've learned in this chapter?

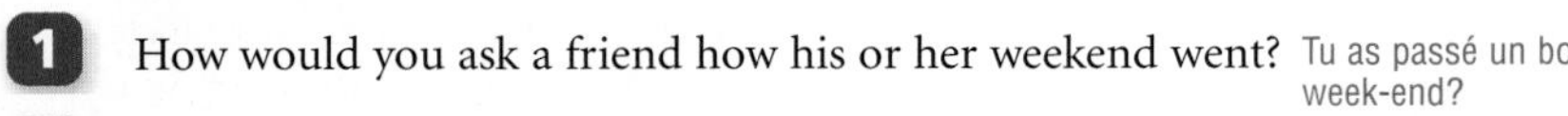

Can you ask for and express opinions? p. 269

1 How would you ask a friend how his or her weekend went? Tu as passé un bon week-end?

2 How would you tell someone that your weekend was . . .
1. great? C'était très chouette.
2. OK? Ça a été. Pas mauvais.
3. horrible? C'était épouvantable. Très mauvais.

Can you inquire about and relate past events, using the passé composé? p. 270

3 If you were inquiring about your friend's weekend, how would you ask . . .
1. what your friend did? Qu'est-ce que tu as fait?
2. where your friend went? Tu es allé(e) où?
3. what happened? Qu'est-ce qui s'est passé?

4 How would you tell someone that you did these things?

1. J'ai chanté.

2. J'ai gagné le match de tennis.

3. J'ai raté le bus.

Can you make and answer a telephone call? p. 276

5 If you were making a telephone call, how would you . . . See answers below.
1. tell who you are?
2. ask if it's the right house?
3. ask to speak to someone?
4. ask to leave a message?
5. ask someone to say you called?
6. tell someone the line's busy?

6 If you were answering a telephone call, how would you . . .
1. ask who's calling? Qui est à l'appareil?
2. ask someone to hold? Une seconde, s'il vous plaît.
3. ask someone to call back later? Vous pouvez rappeler plus tard?

Can you share confidences, console others, and ask for and give advice? p. 279

7 How would you approach a friend about a problem you have?
J'ai un petit problème. Je peux te parler? Tu as une minute?

8 What would you say to console a friend?
Ne t'en fais pas! Ça va aller mieux!

9 How would you ask a friend for advice?
A ton avis, qu'est-ce que je fais? Qu'est-ce que tu me conseilles?

10 How would you tell a friend what you think he or she should do?
Tu devrais.... Pourquoi tu ne... pas?

Review and Assess

Game
Ce week-end Have students form groups of five or six. The first person in each group begins by telling one thing he or she did last weekend. **(Ce week-end, j'ai dîné au restaurant avec mes parents.)** The next person repeats the first activity and adds another. **(Ce week-end, j'ai dîné au restaurant avec mes parents et j'ai étudié.)** Groups compete to see which one can go on the longest without making a mistake.

STANDARDS: 1.1, 1.2

Première étape

Asking for and expressing opinions

Tu as passé un bon week-end?	*Did you have a good weekend?*
Oui, très chouette.	*Yes, super.*
Oui, excellent.	*Yes, excellent.*
Oui, très bon.	*Yes, very good.*
Oui, ça a été.	*Yes, it was OK.*
Oh, pas mauvais.	*Oh, not bad.*
Très mauvais.	*Very bad.*
C'était épouvantable.	*It was horrible.*

Inquiring about and relating past events

Qu'est-ce qui s'est passé (hier)?	*What happened (yesterday)?*
Nous avons parlé.	*We talked.*
Qu'est-ce que tu as fait... ?	*What did you do . . . ?*
D'abord,...	*First, . . .*
Ensuite,...	*Then, . . .*
Après, je suis sorti(e).	*Afterwards, I went out.*
Et après (ça)...	*And after (that) . . .*
Finalement/Enfin,...	*Finally, . . .*
Tu es allé(e) où?	*Where did you go?*
Je suis allé(e)...	*I went . . .*
j'ai fait	*I did, I made*
j'ai pris	*I took*
j'ai vu	*I saw*
j'ai lu	*I read*
déjà	*already*
bien	*well*
mal	*badly*
ne... pas encore	*not yet*
acheter	*to buy*
apporter	*to bring*
chanter	*to sing*
chercher	*to look for*
commencer	*to begin, to start*
déjeuner à la cantine	*to have lunch at the cafeteria*
dîner	*to have dinner*
gagner	*to win, to earn*
montrer	*to show*
oublier	*to forget*
passer un examen	*to take an exam*
rater le bus	*to miss the bus*
rater une interro	*to fail a quiz*
rencontrer	*to meet for the first time*
répéter	*to rehearse, to practice music*
retrouver	*to meet with*
travailler au fast-food	*to work at a fast-food restaurant*
trouver	*to find*
visiter	*to visit (a place)*
une fille	*girl*
un garçon	*boy*

Deuxième étape

Making and answering a telephone call

Allô?	*Hello?*
Je suis bien chez...?	*Is this . . . 's house?*
Qui est à l'appareil?	*Who's calling?*
(Est-ce que)... est là, s'il vous plaît?	*Is . . . there, please?*
Une seconde, s'il vous plaît.	*One second, please.*
(Est-ce que) je peux parler à...?	*May I speak to . . . ?*
Bien sûr.	*Certainly.*
Vous pouvez rappeler plus tard?	*Can you call back later?*
Je peux laisser un message?	*May I leave a message?*
Vous pouvez lui dire que j'ai téléphoné?	*Can you tell her/him that I called?*
Ne quittez pas.	*Hold on.*
Ça ne répond pas.	*There's no answer.*
C'est occupé.	*It's busy.*
attendre	*to wait for*
perdre	*to lose*
répondre (à)	*to answer*
vendre	*to sell*

Troisième étape

Sharing confidences and consoling others

J'ai un petit problème.	*I've got a little problem.*
Je peux te parler?	*Can we talk?*
Tu as une minute?	*Do you have a minute?*
Je t'écoute.	*I'm listening.*
Qu'est-ce que je peux faire?	*What can I do?*
Ne t'en fais pas!	*Don't worry!*
Ça va aller mieux!	*It's going to get better!*

Asking for and giving advice

A ton avis, qu'est-ce que je fais?	*In your opinion, what do I do?*
Qu'est-ce que tu me conseilles?	*What do you advise me to do?*
Oublie-le/-la/-les!	*Forget him/her/it/them!*
Téléphone-lui/-leur!	*Call him/her/them!*
Tu devrais lui/leur parler.	*You should talk to him/her/them.*
Pourquoi tu ne... pas?	*Why don't you . . . ?*
le	*him, it*
la	*her, it*
les	*them*
lui	*to him, to her*
leur	*to them*

Review and Assess

Game

Réponds! For each student, write a question from one of the **Comment dit-on... ?** boxes on an index card. **(Tu as passé un bon week-end? Je peux parler à... ? Qu'est-ce que tu me conseilles?)** Have students stand in two lines facing one another. Each student reads the question on his or her card, and the student facing him or her has ten seconds to respond. At your signal, the students in one line move down one, and the person at the end moves to the front. The other row of students remains stationary. Repeat the process until students are back in their original positions.

Vocabulaire

Chapter 9 Assessment

- **Testing Program**
  Chapter Test, pp. 235–240
   Audio Compact Discs, CD 9, Trs. 23–25
  Speaking Test, p. 347
- **Alternative Assessment Guide**
  Performance Assessment, p. 40
  Portfolio Assessment, p. 26
  CD-ROM Assessment, p. 54
- **Interactive CD-ROM Tutor, Disc 3**
   CD-ROM 3 A toi de parler!
  DVD 2 A toi d'écrire!
- **Standardized Assessment Tutor**
  Chapter 9
- **One-Stop Planner, Disc 3**
  Test Generator
  Chapter 9

STANDARDS: 1.1, 5.2

Chapitre 10 : Dans un magasin de vêtements
Chapter Overview

Mise en train pp. 294–296	***Chacun ses goûts***

	FUNCTIONS	GRAMMAR	VOCABULARY	RE-ENTRY
Première étape pp. 297–300	• Asking for and giving advice, p. 300	• The verbs **mettre** and **porter,** p. 299	• Clothes and accessories, p. 297	• The future with **aller** **(Chapitre 6)** • Sequencing adverbs **(Chapitre 9)** • Colors **(Chapitre 3)** • Family members **(Chapitre 7)**
Deuxième étape pp. 301–305	• Expressing need; inquiring, p. 301	• Adjectives used as nouns, p. 301 • The **-ir** verbs: **choisir,** p. 303		• Likes and dislikes **(Chapitre 1)** • The **passé composé** with **avoir** **(Chapitre 9)** • Expressing need **(Chapitre 8)**
Troisième étape pp. 306–311	• Asking for an opinion; paying a compliment; criticizing, p. 306 • Hesitating; making a decision, p. 310	• The direct object pronouns **le, la,** and **les,** p. 309 • **C'est** versus **il/elle est,** p. 310		• Demonstrative adjectives **(Chapitre 3)** • The imperative **(Chapitre 5)**

Prononciation p. 311	**The glides [j], [w], and [ɥ]** Audio CD 10, Tracks 13–15	**A écrire** (dictation) Audio CD 10, Tracks 16–18	
Lisons! pp. 312–313	**La mode au lycée**	**Reading Strategy:** Distinguishing fact from opinion	
Grammaire supplémentaire	**pp. 314–317** **Première étape,** p. 314	**Deuxième étape,** pp. 315–316	**Troisième étape,** pp. 316–317
Review pp. 318–321	**Mise en pratique,** pp. 318–319 **Ecrivons!** Paraphrasing Writing an article on fashion trends	**Que sais-je?** p. 320	**Vocabulaire,** p. 321

CULTURE

- Realia: Clothing ad, p. 302
- Realia: French size chart, p. 303
- **Note culturelle,** Clothing sizes, p. 303
- **Panorama Culturel,** Fashion in francophone countries, p. 305
- **Rencontre culturelle,** Responding to compliments, p. 308

Chapitre 10 : Dans un magasin de vêtements
Chapter Resources

Lesson Planning

One-Stop Planner

Lesson Planner with Differentiated Instruction, pp. 48–52, 74

Student Make-Up Assignments
- Make-Up Assignment Copying Masters, Chapter 10

Listening and Speaking

TPR Storytelling Book, pp. 37–40

Listening Activities
- Student Response Forms for Listening Activities, pp. 75–77
- Additional Listening Activities 10-1 to 10-6, pp. 79–81
- Additional Listening Activities (song), p. 82
- Scripts and Answers, pp. 147–151

Video Guide
- Teaching Suggestions, pp. 68–69
- Activity Masters, pp. 70–72
- Scripts and Answers, pp. 109–111, 122

Activities for Communication
- Communicative Activities, pp. 55–60
- Realia and Teaching Suggestions, pp. 120–124
- Situation Cards, pp. 155–156

Reading and Writing

Reading Strategies and Skills Handbook, Chapter 10

Joie de lire 1, Chapter 10

Cahier d'activités, pp. 109–120

Grammar

Travaux pratiques de grammaire, pp. 79–87

Grammar Tutor for Students of French, Chapter 10

Assessment

Testing Program
- Grammar and Vocabulary Quizzes, **Etape** Quizzes, and Chapter Test, pp. 249–266
- Score Sheet, Scripts and Answers, pp. 267–274

Alternative Assessment Guide
- Portfolio Assessment, p. 27
- Performance Assessment, p. 41
- CD-ROM Assessment, p. 55

Student Make-Up Assignments
- Alternative Quizzes, Chapter 10

Standardized Assessment Tutor
- Reading, pp. 39–41
- Writing, p. 42
- Math, pp. 51–52

Middle School

Middle School Teaching Resources, Chapter 10

MEDIA

Online Activities
- **Jeux interactifs**
- **Activités Internet**

Video Program
- Videocassette 4
- Videocassette 5 (captioned version)

Interactive CD-ROM Tutor, Disc 3

DVD Tutor, Disc 2

Audio Compact Discs
- Textbook Listening Activities, CD 10, Tracks 1–19
- Additional Listening Activities, CD 10, Tracks 26–32
- Assessment Items, CD 10, Tracks 20–25

Teaching Transparencies
- Situation 10-1 to 10-3
- Vocabulary 10-A
- **Mise en train**
- **Grammaire supplémentaire** Answers
- **Travaux pratiques de grammaire** Answers

Use the **One-Stop Planner CD-ROM with Test Generator** to aid in lesson planning and pacing.

For each chapter, the **One-Stop Planner** includes:
- Editable lesson plans with direct links to teaching resources
- Printable worksheets from resource books
- Direct launches to the HRW Internet activities
- Video and audio segments
- Test Generator
- Clip Art for vocabulary items

Projects

Un défilé de mode

This project may be oral or written. Students will organize a fashion show. They may actually model clothes on a runway, accompanied by an oral commentary, or draw their designs and provide a written description on a poster.

MATERIALS

✂ **Students may need**
- Clothing or fabric
- Posterboard
- Colored pencils
- Fashion magazines
- French-English dictionaries

SUGGESTED SEQUENCE

1. Have students form groups of three or four. Have each group decide on the general style of their fashion line: grunge, evening wear, retro, modern, and so on.
2. Have students look through fashion magazines for ideas.
3. Have students sketch or collect the items for their show. Remind students that their goal is to sell the clothes, so their commentaries should include when and where they can be worn as well as a description of the overall look.
4. Have students organize their projects and decide in what order to present the items or plan the layout of their poster.
5. Have students type their descriptions and finalize their visuals if they are doing a written project.

If they are making a poster, they might attach samples of fabric or jewelry to add texture to their illustrations. If they are doing a runway presentation, have them present the fashions to the class as a narrator from the group reads the description of each item.

GRADING THE PROJECT

Suggested Point Distribution: (total = 100 points)

Completion of assignment	20 points
Creativity	30 points
Language use	20 points
Presentation	30 points

Games

Dessinez-moi!

In this game, students will review clothing vocabulary.

Procedure Describe an outfit to students (see examples below) and have them draw the outfit on a piece of paper as they listen to you. Say each item of clothing only once. After the outfit is complete, have students hold up their drawings and award a point for each correct one, or you might have volunteers draw their version of the outfit on the board. The outfits might be serious, humorous, or even bizarre.

Examples of outfits:

1. **un maillot de bain, un chapeau, un manteau large, une ceinture trop serrée, des bottes moches, des lunettes de soleil**
2. **un sweat-shirt court, des baskets trop grandes, une écharpe, un jean, des boucles d'oreilles longues, un cardigan large**
3. **un pantalon court, une chemise, une petite cravate, une casquette, de grandes chaussettes**

Variation Give students pieces of paper and crayons or transparencies and colored markers and have them draw color illustrations as you describe them.

Mémoire

This game will test students' recognition of clothing vocabulary.

Procedure This game is played like Concentration®. First, assign sections of the **Vocabulaire** on page 321 to groups of students. Have them create two cards for each item: one with the French word or expression on it, and the other with an illustration of the item. Collect the cards, mix them thoroughly, and number them consecutively on the back. Tape them to the board or wall in numerical order so that only the numbers show. Then, have players ask to see two cards by saying the numbers in French (**trois, douze**). Turn over the two cards. If they match, the player wins a point, keeps the cards, and the next player takes a turn. Continue until all students have had a chance to guess or until all cards have been matched. You might want to give out small prizes to the students who get the most points.

STANDARDS: 1.3

Storytelling

Mini-histoire

*This story accompanies Teaching Transparency 10-1. The **mini-histoire** can be told and retold in different formats, acted out, written down, and read aloud, to give students additional opportunities to practice all four skills. The following story tells about three friends looking for the appropiate clothes to wear to go out.*

Coralie ne sait pas quoi mettre pour aller au cinéma ce soir avec Christian. Elle demande à ses amies Patricia et Florence : «Qu'est-ce que je vais mettre pour sortir ce soir?» Patricia lui répond : «Tu peux mettre cette jupe rouge avec ton chemisier blanc et tes chaussures noires.» «Cette jupe ne me va plus.» dit Coralie. «J'ai grandi et elle est trop petite. Je la trouve aussi un peu démodée. Et toi, Florence, qu'en penses-tu?» «Je suis d'accord avec toi. Mets plutôt ce pull bleu avec ton jean rose.» «Ce pull est trop large; ce n'est pas mon style. Je vais mettre ma nouvelle robe jaune, verte et bleue avec mes sandales jaunes.»

Traditions

Parfum

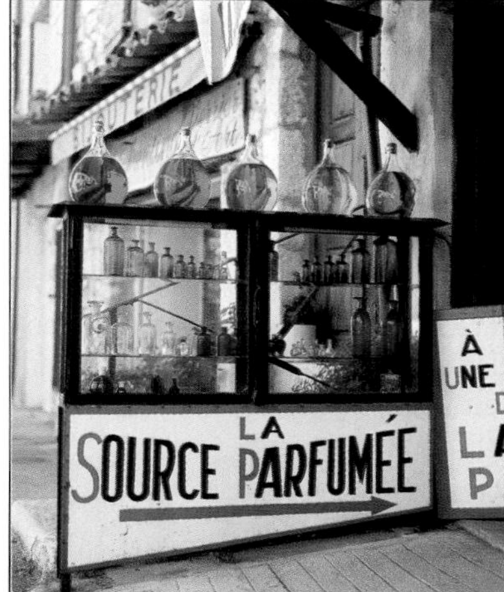

Wearing perfume first became fashionable when Catherine de Médicis began wearing scented gloves in the 16th century. This trend made the city of Grasse, which was already the heart of the leather tanning industry, the center of the perfume industry as well. Business flourished under the reign of Louis XIV when people used perfume to mask body odors. Forty perfume houses were eventually established in Grasse in the 18th and 19th centuries as perfume became more a fashion accessory rather than a means to disguise unpleasant odors. These same houses continue their perfume-making traditions today. Using thousands of flowers, such as lavender, rose, and jasmine, and other natural products, they make the essences that are blended by a master perfumer, or **nez,** who with one whiff can pick from among 6,000 scents to create a perfume. Have students smell and compare different perfumes. What essences do they smell? Which ones do they like and why?

Recette

***Herbes de Provence** is a mixture of different herbs that grow naturally on the dry land of Provence. The blend may vary from producer to producer. Thyme and rosemary are always included in the mixture. Then, some combination of the following herbs are added: summer savory, marjoram, oregano, sage, basil, fennel, tarragon and bay leaf. Sometimes, a little lavender is also added to the mixture. **Herbes de Provence** are usually sold pre-packaged and are available in gourmet food stores.*

OMELETTE PROVENÇALE

pour 4 personnes

8 œufs
1/2 tasse de lait
1 oignon
3 tomates
2 cuillères à soupe d'huile d'olive
persil
thym
herbes de Provence
sel
poivre

Eplucher et couper l'oignon en petits morceaux. Faire cuire les oignons dans une poêle avec l'huile d'olive. Laver et couper les tomates en tranches. Dans un bol, mélanger les œufs, le lait et les différentes herbes (herbes de Provence, persil, thym), le sel et le poivre. Ajouter les tomates. Une fois que les oignons sont cuits, les ajouter aux œufs, puis verser le tout dans la poêle qui a servi à cuire les oignons. Laisser cuire pendant 5 à 10 minutes. Servir.

Chapitre 10 : Dans un magasin de vêtements

Technology

Videocassette 4, Videocassette 5 (captioned version)
DVD Tutor, Disc 2
See Video Guide, pp. 67–72.

DVD/Video

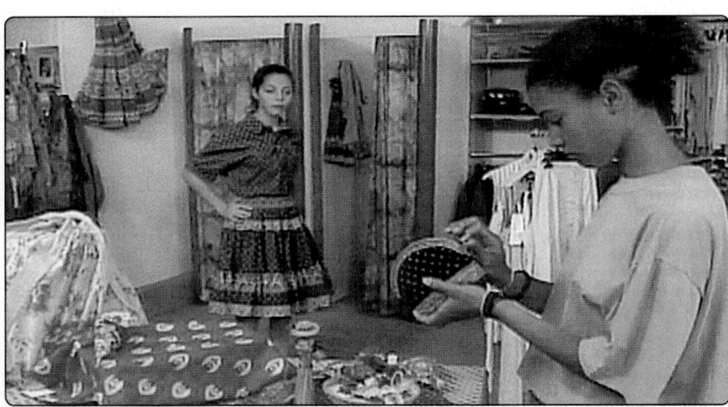

Mise en train • Chacun ses goûts

In this segment of the video, Magali and Hélène discuss what they are going to wear to Sophie's birthday party. Later, we see Sophie leaving a clothing boutique. Magali enters the same boutique. Inside, she is helped by a saleswoman and tries on several items. Finally, Magali finds a skirt and a shirt that she likes.

Qu'est-ce que tu aimes comme vêtements?

Several teenagers from different French-speaking countries tell us what they like to wear.

Chacun ses goûts (suite)

When the story continues, Hélène enters the clothing boutique and sees Magali. Magali asks her about the outfit she has on, and Hélène compliments her on it. Magali is unsure and still can't figure out what to do. Later, at Sophie's, everything is ready for the party. Malika arrives, and then Ahmed, Charles, and Florent. When Magali arrives, she and Sophie discover they've bought the same shirt! Magali is upset at first, but then smiles. Florent takes a photo of Magali and Sophie.

Vidéoclips

- **Groupe Kelton®:** advertisement for watches
- **Alain Afflelou®:** advertisement for eyeglasses

Interactive CD-ROM Tutor

Activity	Activity Type	Pupil's Edition Page
En contexte	*Interactive conversation*	
1. Vocabulaire	Jeu des paires	p. 297
2. Vocabulaire	Chasse au trésor Explorons!/Vérifions!	p. 297
3. Grammaire	Les mots qui manquent	pp. 299, 303
4. Grammaire	Méli-mélo	p. 309
5. Comment dit-on... ?	Chacun à sa place	pp. 301, 306
6. Grammaire	Le bon choix	pp. 309–310
Panorama Culturel	Qu'est-ce que tu aimes comme vêtements? Le bon choix	p. 305
A toi de parler	*Guided recording*	pp. 318–319
A toi d'écrire	*Guided writing*	pp. 318–319

Teacher Management System

Launch the program, type "admin" in the password area and press RETURN. Log on to www.hrw.com/CDROMTUTOR for a detailed explanation of the Teacher Management System.

DVD Tutor

The *DVD Tutor* contains all material from the *Video Program* as described above. French captions are available for use at your discretion for all sections of the video. The *DVD Tutor* also provides a variety of video-based activities that assess students' understanding of the **Mise en train, Suite,** and **Panorama Culturel.**

This part of the *DVD Tutor* may be used on any DVD video player connected to a television or video monitor.

In addition to the video material and the video-based comprehension activities, the *DVD Tutor* also contains the entire *Interactive CD-ROM Tutor* in DVD-ROM format. Each DVD disc contains the activities from all 12 chapters of the *Interactive CD-ROM Tutor.*

This part of the *DVD Tutor* may be used on a Macintosh® or Windows® computer with a DVD-ROM drive.

To preview all resources available for this chapter, use the **One-Stop Planner CD-ROM,** Disc 3.

Go.Online!

Online Edition

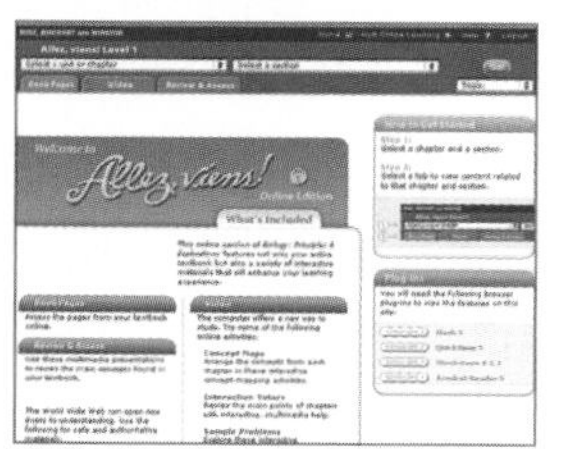

The Online Edition for Allez, viens! *allows students access to their textbooks anytime anywhere.*

- *Audio at point of use*
- *Additional practice activities*
- *Self-test activities*
- *Online reference tools*
- *Entire Video Program (Enhanced version)*
- *Interactive Notebook (Enhanced version)*

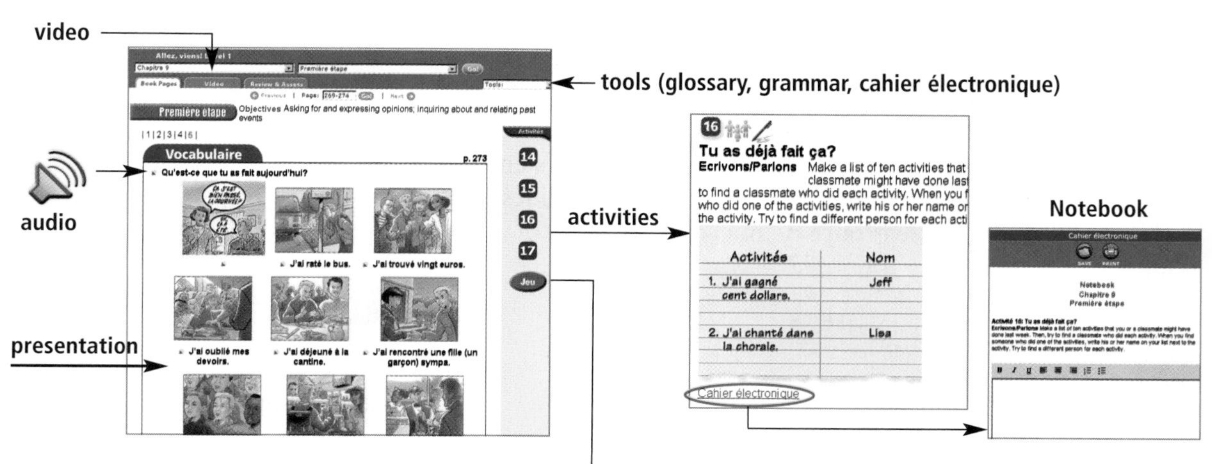

Activités Internet

These guided internet activities include a worksheet and pre-selected and pre-screened authentic web sites from the francophone world. You can use these activities

- to help students develop research skills in the target language
- to introduce students to authentic cultural information
- as a project

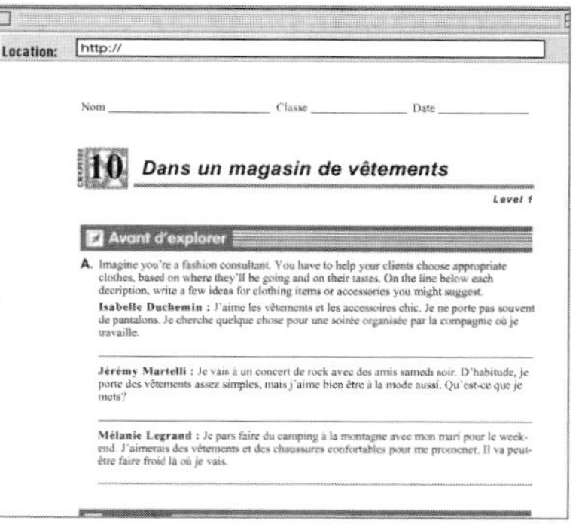

Jeux interactifs

You can use the interactive activities in this chapter

- to practice grammar, vocabulary, and chapter functions
- as homework
- as an assessment option
- as a self-test
- to prepare for the Chapter Test

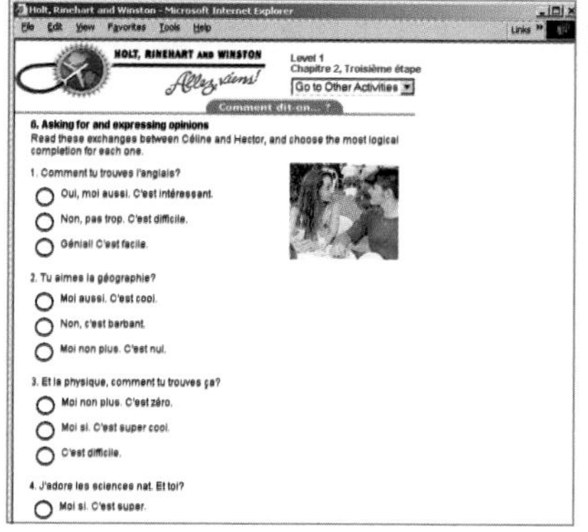

Projet Tell students that they need to buy a "cool" outfit to wear to a friend's birthday party and also find a special gift for their friend. Have students search the Web for the best places in Arles to go shopping according to the clothes they plan to purchase and the gift they want to offer. Then, have them write an e-mail to a friend where they describe their online shopping experience and tell about their purchases.

Chapitre 10 : Dans un magasin de vêtements

Textbook Listening Activities Scripts 

Première étape

7 p. 298

ARMELLE J'ai acheté des tas de vêtements pour la rentrée. J'ai trouvé une jupe orange en coton avec la ceinture qui va avec. Elle est super, tu vas voir. Je vais la mettre demain. J'ai aussi acheté un chemisier noir avec le cardigan assorti. Très chic.

AMIE Tu n'as pas acheté de chaussures cette fois-ci? C'est ton habitude.

ARMELLE Non, il me faut des chaussures, mais c'était trop cher. Mais j'ai acheté des chaussettes en solde et aussi une paire de boucles d'oreilles pour l'anniversaire de ma sœur.

Answer to Activity 7

c

13 p. 300

1. — Je vais au cinéma avec Chantal ce soir. Dis, Pierre, qu'est-ce que je mets?

2. — Si tu veux être chic, Dianne, pourquoi tu ne mets pas ta nouvelle robe?

3. — Mais non! Il ne faut pas mettre ton jean! Pourquoi est-ce que tu ne mets pas un pantalon?

4. — Je ne sais pas quoi mettre pour aller à la boum. J'aimerais quelque chose de joli.

5. — Tu vas avoir trop chaud, Luc. Mets un short et des sandales!

Answers to Activity 13

1. asking
2. giving
3. giving
4. asking
5. giving

Deuxième étape

17 p. 301

1. — Je cherche un maillot de bain.

2. — Vous avez ça en quarante?

3. — Je peux vous aider?

4. — J'aimerais des chaussures pour aller avec ma robe.

5. — Non, mais nous l'avons en bleu.

6. — Je peux l'essayer?

7. — Vous avez choisi?

Answers to Activity 17

1. customer
2. customer
3. salesperson
4. customer
5. salesperson
6. customer
7. salesperson

18 p. 302

1. — Vous avez ça en quarante-quatre?

2. — Il me faut des chaussettes noires.

3. — Ça coûte vingt-cinq euros soixante.

4. — Je peux essayer la jupe blanche?

5. — Le blouson en cuir, c'est cent quarante et un euros.

6. — Vous l'avez en trente-huit?

Answers to Activity 18

1. size
2. color
3. price
4. color
5. price
6. size

Troisième étape

26 p. 307

1. — Dis, comment tu trouves ma jupe?
— Euh, je la trouve un peu démodée.

2. — Elle est super chic, ta robe!
— Tu trouves?

3. — Dis, Nicole, tu sais, ces chaussures, elles ne vont pas du tout avec ta jupe!
— Ah oui? C'est vrai?

The following scripts are for the listening activities found in the *Pupil's Edition*. For Student Response Forms, see *Listening Activities,* pages 75–77. To provide students with additional listening practice, see *Listening Activities,* pages 79–82.

To preview all resources available for this chapter, use the **One-Stop Planner CD-ROM**, Disc 3.

4. — Il n'est pas trop serré, ce chemisier?
— Euh, si, je le trouve un peu serré.

5. — Il est sensass, ton pantalon!
— Tu crois?
— Oui, il te va très bien!

6. — Elle me va, cette robe?
— C'est tout à fait ton style!

Answers to Activity 26

1. criticizing
2. complimenting
3. criticizing
4. criticizing
5. complimenting
6. complimenting

31 p. 310

1. VENDEUSE Ce manteau vous va très bien, monsieur. Vous le prenez?
CLIENT Il me plaît, mais il est beaucoup trop cher.

2. VENDEUSE Alors, vous avez décidé de prendre cette casquette, monsieur?
CLIENT Elle est super. Je la prends.

3. VENDEUSE Et ces baskets? Vous les prenez?
CLIENT Euh, j'hésite. Elles sont sensass, mais pas vraiment mon genre.

4. VENDEUSE Très bien, monsieur. Et vous avez décidé pour ces bottes?
CLIENT Pourquoi pas? Je les prends aussi.

5. VENDEUSE Et cette chemise, vous la prenez, monsieur?
CLIENT Je ne sais pas. J'aime la couleur, mais elle est chère.

6. VENDEUSE C'est tout à fait votre style, ce blouson. Vous le prenez?
CLIENT Euh, je ne sais pas. Il est un peu trop court.

Answers to Activity 31

1. doesn't take
2. takes
3. can't decide
4. takes
5. can't decide
6. can't decide

PRONONCIATION, P. 311

For the scripts for Parts A and B, see p. 311. The script for Part C is below.

C. A écrire *(dictation)*

— Je cherche un maillot de bain.
— Voilà.
— Je peux l'essayer?
— Oui, bien sûr.

Mise en pratique

1 p. 318

VENDEUSE Bonjour. Je peux vous aider?
PHILIPPE Oui, euh... je voudrais une chemise.

VENDEUSE Quel genre de chemise cherchez-vous?
PHILIPPE Bof, je ne sais pas. Quelque chose de cool, de branché. Une chemise bleue ou kaki, à carreaux peut-être.

VENDEUSE Eh bien, nous avons des chemises américaines, style western. Ça vous intéresse?
PHILIPPE Ouais, ...

VENDEUSE Les voilà. Comment les trouvez-vous?
PHILIPPE Pas mal. Ouais, j'aime bien celle-ci.

VENDEUSE Vous faites quelle taille?
PHILIPPE Euh... je ne sais pas... Vous l'avez en trente-sept/trente-huit?

VENDEUSE Voici.
PHILIPPE Je peux l'essayer?

VENDEUSE Bien sûr.

(plus tard)

VENDEUSE Elle vous va très bien. C'est tout à fait votre style! Et c'est tellement à la mode!
PHILIPPE Mais moi, je la trouve un peu serrée. Vous avez ça en trente-neuf/quarante?

VENDEUSE Oui, en trente-neuf/quarante, mais en rouge.
PHILIPPE Euh... j'hésite. J'aime pas trop la rouge. J'aime mieux la bleue. Bon, alors. Ça va. C'est combien?

VENDEUSE Quarante-huit euros.
PHILIPPE Ah? Quarante-huit euros?! Je regrette, c'est trop cher. Je ne la prends pas.

Answers to Mise en pratique, Activity 1

1. a shirt
2. blue and khaki
3. The shirt suits him. It's his style, and it's in fashion.
4. It's a little tight.
5. No.

Chapitre 10 : Dans un magasin de vêtements

50-Minute Lesson Plans

Day 1

CHAPTER OPENER **5 min.**
- Thinking Critically, ATE, p. 293.
- Present Chapter Objectives, p. 293.
- Culture Note, ATE, p. 292
- Language Note, ATE, p. 293
- Career Path, ATE, p. 292.

MISE EN TRAIN **40 min.**
- Presenting **Mise en train** and Preteaching Vocabulary, ATE, p. 294
- Language Note, ATE, p. 294
- Thinking Critically, ATE, p. 295.
- Do Activities 1–6, p. 296

Wrap-Up 5 min.
- Auditory Learners, p. 295

Homework Options
Cahier d'activités, p. 109, Act. 1

Day 2

PREMIERE ETAPE
Quick Review 10 min.
- Check homework.
- Bell Work, ATE, p. 297

Vocabulaire, p. 297 15 min.
- Presenting **Vocabulaire,** ATE, p. 297, using Teaching Transparency 10-A
- Reteaching Adjective agreement, ATE, p. 298
- Play Audio CD for Activity 7, p. 298.
- Do Activity 8, p. 298.

Grammaire, p. 299 15 min.
- Presenting **Grammaire,** ATE, p. 299
- Do Activities 11–12, p. 299.
- Additional Practice, ATE, p. 299
- Discuss **De bons conseils,** p. 299.

Wrap-Up 10 min.
- Teacher to Teacher, ATE, p. 297

Homework Options
Cahier d'activités, pp. 110–111, Acts. 2–7
Travaux pratiques de grammaire, pp. 79–81, Acts. 1–6

Day 3

PREMIERE ETAPE
Quick Review 10 min.
- Check homework.
- Have pairs of students describe what their partner is wearing.

Comment dit-on... ?, p. 300 30 min.
- Presenting **Comment dit-on... ?,** ATE, p. 300
- Play Audio CD for Activity 13, p. 300.
- Do Activity 13, p. 300.
- Cahier d'activités, p. 112, Acts. 8–9

Wrap-Up 10 min.
- List various situations on the board **(à l'école, à un mariage).** Have one student ask a second student **Qu'est-ce que je mets pour aller... ?** The second student gives advice, and then asks a third student what to wear for another occasion. Continue until all students have asked a question.

Homework Options
Study for Quiz 10-1.

Day 4

PREMIERE ETAPE
Quiz 10-1 20 min.
- Administer Quiz 10-1A or 10-1B.

DEUXIEME ETAPE
Comment dit-on... ?, p. 301 10 min.
- Presenting **Comment dit-on... ?,** ATE, p. 301

Note de grammaire, p. 301 15 min.
- Present **Note de grammaire,** p. 301.
- Visual Learners, ATE, p. 301
- Play Audio CD for Activities 17–18, pp. 301–302.
- Do Activities 19–20, p. 302.
- Discuss **Note culturelle,** p. 303.

Wrap-Up 5 min.
- Activities for Communication, p.156, Situation Card 10-1: Role-play

Homework Options
Cahier d'activités, pp. 113–114, Acts. 10–13
Travaux pratiques de grammaire, p. 82, Acts. 7–8

Day 5

DEUXIEME ETAPE
Quick Review 5 min.
- Review the expressions from **Comment dit-on... ?,** p. 301, using Teaching Transparency 10-2.

Grammaire, p. 303 35 min.
- Presenting **Grammaire,** ATE, p. 303
- Do Activities 23–24, p. 304.
- Cahier d'activités, p. 115, Acts. 14–16
- Travaux pratiques de grammaire, pp. 83–84, Acts. 9–12
- Challenge, ATE, p. 302

Wrap-Up 10 min.
- Visual Learners, ATE, p. 304

Homework Options
Study for Quiz 10-2.

Day 6

DEUXIEME ETAPE
Quiz 10-2 20 min.
- Administer Quiz 10-2A or 10-2B.

PANORAMA CULTUREL, p. 305 25 min.
- Present Panorama Culturel, using Videocassette 4, p. 305 or DVD Tutor.
- Answer **Qu'en penses-tu?** questions, p. 305
- Read **Savais-tu que... ?,** p. 305
- **Panorama Culturel,** Interactive CD-ROM Tutor, Disc 3

Wrap-Up 5 min.
- Culture Note, ATE, p. 305

Homework Options
Cahier d'activités, p. 120, Acts. 26–27

For alternative lesson plans by chapter section, to create your own customized plans, or to preview all resources available for this chapter, use the **One-Stop Planner CD-ROM**, Disc 3.

For additional homework suggestions, See activities accompanied by this symbol throughout the chapter.

Day 7

TROISIEME ETAPE

Quick Review 10 min.
- Check homework.
- Bell Work, ATE, p. 306

Comment dit-on... ?, p. 306 20 min.
- Presenting **Comment dit-on... ?,** ATE, p. 306
- TPR Storytelling Book, pp. 39–40
- Play Audio CD for Activity 26, p. 307.
- Do Activities 27–28, p. 307.

RENCONTRE CULTURELLE 15 min.
- Presenting **Rencontre culturelle,** ATE, p. 308
- Discuss Thinking Critically and Culture Note, ATE, p. 308.

Wrap-Up 5 min.
- Additional Practice, ATE, p. 308

Homework Options
Cahier d'activités, pp. 116–117, Acts. 17–20
Travaux pratiques de grammaire, pp. 85–86, Acts. 13–15

Day 8

TROISIEME ETAPE

Quick Review 10 min.
- Check homework.

Grammaire, p. 309 30 min.
- Presenting **Grammaire,** ATE, p. 309
- Do Activity 30, p. 309.
- **Grammaire supplémentaire,** p. 316, Activities 7–8
- Activities for Communication, pp. 59–60, Communicative Activity 10-3A and 10-3B

Wrap-Up 10 min.
- Game: **Dessinez-moi!,** ATE, p. 291C

Homework Options
Cahier d'activités, p. 117, Act. 21
Travaux pratiques de grammaire, pp. 86–87, Acts. 16–17

Day 9

TROISIEME ETAPE

Quick Review 10 min.
- Check homework.

Comment dit-on... ?, p. 310 15 min.
- Presenting **Comment dit-on... ?,** ATE, p. 310
- Discuss **Note de grammaire,** p. 310, and do Additional Practice, ATE, p. 310.
- Play Audio CD for Activity 31, p. 310.
- Do Activity 33, p. 310.

Prononciation, p. 311 15 min.
- Complete presentation and do Activities A–C, p. 311, using Audio CD 10.

Wrap-Up 10 min.
- Activities for Communication, p. 156, Situation Card 10-3: Role-play

Homework Options
Study for Quiz 10-3.

Day 10

TROISIEME ETAPE

Quiz 10-3 20 min.
- Administer Quiz 10-3A or Quiz 10-3B.

LISONS! 25 min.
- Thinking Critically, Evaluating, ATE, p. 312
- Prereading Activities A–C, p. 312
- Thinking Critically, Comparing and Contrasting, ATE, p. 312
- Reading Activities D–H, pp. 312–313
- Do Activity I, p. 313.

Wrap-Up 5 min.
- Game: **C'est qui?,** ATE, p. 313

Homework Options
Cahier d'activités, p. 119, Act. 25

Day 11

LISONS!

Quick Review 10 min.
- Check homework.
- Review **Comment dit-on... ?,** p. 306, using Realia 10-3, Activities for Communication, p. 122.

MISE EN PRATIQUE 30 min.
- Play Audio CD for Activity 1, p. 318.
- Do Activities 2–3, p. 318.
- Do **Ecrivons!,** p. 319.

Wrap-Up 10 min.
- Game: **Mémoire,** ATE, p. 291C

Homework Options
Que sais-je?, p. 320

Day 12

MISE EN PRATIQUE

Quick Review 10 min.
- Have partners complete **Jeu de rôle,** p. 319.

Chapter Review 40 min.
- Review Chapter 10. Choose from **Grammaire supplémentaire,** Grammar Tutor for Students of French, Activities for Communication, Listening Activities, Interactive CD-ROM Tutor, or **Jeux interactifs.**

Homework Options
Study for Chapter 10 Test.

Assessment

Test, Chapter 10 50 min.
- Administer Chapter 10 Test. Select from Testing Program, Alternative Assessment Guide, Test Generator, or Standardized Assessment Tutor.

Chapitre 10 : Dans un magasin de vêtements

90-Minute Lesson Plans

Block 1

CHAPTER OPENER 5 min.
- Thinking Critically, ATE, p. 293
- Present Chapter Objectives, p. 293
- Culture Note, ATE, p. 292
- Career Path, ATE, p. 292

MISE EN TRAIN 40 min.
- Language Note, ATE, p. 294
- Presenting **Mise en train,** ATE, p. 294
- Preteaching Vocabulary, ATE, p. 294
- View video of **Mise en train,** Videocassette 4. See Video Guide, pp. 67–68, 69, Activity Master 1, **Mise en train.**

PREMIERE ETAPE

Vocabulaire, p. 297 40 min.
- Bell Work, ATE, p. 297
- Presenting **Vocabulaire,** ATE, p. 297
- Play Audio CD for Activity 7, p. 298. See Slower Pace, ATE, p. 298.
- Do Activity 8, p. 298. See Building on Previous Skills, ATE, p. 298. Have students tell the colors of the items.
- Language Note, ATE, p. 298
- Do Activity 9, p. 298.
- Game: **Dessinez-moi!,** ATE, p. 291C

Wrap-Up 5 min.
- Summarize what happened in the **Mise en train,** using **Mise en train** Transparencies.

Homework Options

Travaux pratiques de grammaire, p. 79, Acts. 1–2

Cahier d'activités, p. 110, Acts. 2–4

Block 2

PREMIERE ETAPE

Quick Review 5 min.
- Play Audio CD for Additional Listening Activities 10-1 and 10-2, Listening Activities, p. 79

Grammaire, verbs *mettre* and *porter,* p. 299 25 min.
- Presenting **Grammaire: verbs *mettre* and *porter,*** ATE, p. 299 with Language Note, ATE, p. 299
- Additional Practice, ATE, p. 299
- Do Activities 11 and 12, p. 299.
- **Grammaire supplémentaire,** p. 314, Acts. 1–2
- **De bons conseils,** p. 299

Comment dit-on... ?, p. 300 35 min.
- Presenting **Comment dit-on... ?,** ATE, p. 300, Language Note, ATE, p. 300
- Play Audio CD for Activity 13, p. 300.
- Do Activities 14–15, p. 300.
- Have partners write and act out a short conversation between friends who are deciding what to wear to a school party that will include a picnic and dancing. Allow 10 min. to prepare and 10 min. to perform.

DEUXIEME ETAPE

Comment dit-on... ?, p. 301 20 min.
- Presenting **Comment dit-on... ?,** ATE, p. 301
- Play Audio CD for Activity 17, p. 301.
- **Note de grammaire,** p. 301 with Visual Learners, ATE, p. 301
- Play Audio CD for Activity 18, p. 302. See Challenge, ATE, p. 302.
- **Grammaire supplémentaire,** p. 314, Act. 3

Wrap-Up 5 min.
- Have students imagine an outfit and then describe it to a partner who will draw it.

Homework Options

Study for Quiz 10-1

Travaux pratiques de grammaire, pp. 80–81, Acts. 3–6

Cahier d'activités, pp. 111–113, Acts. 5–11

Block 3

PREMIERE ETAPE

Quick Review 10 min.
- Bell Work, ATE, p. 301
- Activities for Communication, p. 155, Situation Card 10-1: Interview

Quiz 10-1 20 min.
- Administer Quiz 10-1A or 10-1B.

DEUXIEME ETAPE

Comment dit–on... ?, p. 301, cont. 20 min.
- Do Activity 20, p. 302.
- Do Activity 19, p. 302. Have students prepare then act out the conversation.
- Do Activity 21, p. 302.
- **Note culturelle,** p. 303 with Building on Previous Skills, ATE, p. 303
- **Vocabulaire à la carte,** p. 303 with Language Notes, ATE, p. 303
- Do Activity 22, p. 303.

Grammaire: -ir verbs, p. 303 35 min.
- Presenting **Grammaire: -ir verbs,** ATE, p. 303, Language Notes, ATE, p. 303
- Do Activities 23 and 24, p. 304, in partners.
- **Grammaire supplémentaire,** p. 315, Acts. 4–6

Wrap-Up 5 min.
- Visual Learners, ATE, p. 304

Homework Options

Study for Quiz 10-2

Travaux pratiques de grammaire, pp. 82–84, Acts. 7–12

Cahier d'activités, pp. 114–115, Acts. 12–16

One-Stop Planner CD-ROM

For alternative lesson plans by chapter section, to create your own customized plans, or to preview all resources available for this chapter, use the **One-Stop Planner CD-ROM**, Disc 3.

For additional homework suggestions, see activites accompanied by this symbol throughout the chapter.

Block 4

DEUXIEME ETAPE

Quick Review 5 min.
- Ask students to describe their favorite outfit. Ask what is important when choosing clothes (color, comfort, style, fabric, cost).

PANORAMA CULTUREL 15 min
- Presenting **Panorama Culturel**, p. 305
- Culture Note, ATE, p. 305
- Answer the **Qu'en penses-tu?** questions, p. 305
- Read **Savais-tu que... ?**, p. 305

Quick Review 10 min.
- Activities for Communication, pp. 57–58, Communicative Activities 10-2A and 10-2B

Quiz 10-2 20 min.
- Administer Quiz 10-2A or 10-2B.

TROISIEME ETAPE

Comment dit-on... ?, p. 306 30 min.
- Bell Work, ATE, p. 306
- Presenting **Comment dit-on... ?**, ATE, p. 306 with Language-to-Language, ATE, p. 306
- Play Audio CD for Activity 26, p. 307. See Challenge, ATE, p. 307.
- Do Activity 27, p. 307 with Group Work and Teacher Note, ATE, p. 307.
- Do Activity 28, p. 307 with Teaching Suggestions, ATE, p. 307

Wrap-Up 10 min.
- Activities for Communication, p. 155, Situation Card 10-2: Interview

Homework Options

Travaux pratiques de grammaire, pp. 85–86, Acts. 13–15

Cahier d'activités, p. 116, Acts. 17–18

Block 5

TROISIEME ETAPE

Quick Review 5 min.
- Do Activity 29, p. 309.

RENCONTRE CULTURELLE 15 min.
- Presenting **Rencontre culturelle,** ATE, p. 308
- Thinking Critically, Culture Note, ATE, p. 308
- Discuss **Qu'en penses-tu?**, p. 308
- Read **Savais-tu que... ?**, p. 308

Grammaire, p. 309 15 min.
- Presenting **Grammaire,** ATE, p. 309
- Do Activity 30, p. 309.
- **Grammaire supplémentaire,** p. 316, Act. 7

Comment dit-on... ?, p. 310 30 min.
- Presenting **Comment dit-on... ?**, p. 310, ATE with Visual Learners, ATE, p. 310
- **Note de grammaire,** p. 310 with Additional Practice, ATE, p. 310
- Play Audio CD for Activity 31, p. 310.
- **Grammaire supplémentaire,** pp. 316–317, Acts. 8 and 9

Prononciation, p. 311 15 min.
- Present **Prononciation,** p. 311.
- Play Audio CD for Activities A, B, and C. See Language Note, ATE, p. 311.

Wrap-Up 10 min.
- Supply students with a picture of an outfit from a magazine. Have students work in groups of three, with one person acting as the salesperson and the other two as friends. The friends ask for and give their opinions of each other's outfits and compliment and criticize the outfits. The salesperson offers help and compliments.

Homework Options

Study for Quiz 10-3

Travaux pratiques de grammaire, pp. 86–87, Acts. 16–18

Cahier d'activités, pp. 117–118, Acts. 19–24

Block 6

TROISIEME ETAPE

Quick Review 10 min.
- Activities for Communication, pp. 59–60, Communicative Activities 10-3A and 10-3B

Quiz 10-3 20 min.
- Administer Quiz 10-3A or 10-3B.

LISONS! 20 min
- Prereading Activities A–B, Thinking Critically, ATE, p. 312
- Reading Activities D–H, ATE, pp. 312–313
- Postreading Activity I, Portfolio, ATE, p. 313
- Terms in **Lisons!**, ATE, p. 312

MISE EN PRATIQUE 30 min.
- Play Audio CD for Activity 1, p. 318.
- Do Activities 2–3.
- Do **Ecrivons!**, p. 319.

Wrap-Up 10 min.
- Activities for Communication, p. 155, Situation Card 10-3: Interview

Homework Options

Que sais-je?, p. 320

Finish **Ecrivons!**, Pupil's Edition, p. 319.

Study for Chapter 10 Test

Block 7

MISE EN PRATIQUE

Quick Review 10 min.
- Check homework and collect **Ecrivons!**

Warm-Up / Review for Chapter Test 30 min.
- Review Chapter 10. Choose from **Grammaire supplémentaire,** Grammar Tutor for Students of French, Activities for Communication, Listening Activities, Interactive CD-ROM Tutor, or **Jeux interactifs.**

Test, Chapter 10 50 min.
- Administer Chapter 10 Test. Select from Testing Program, Alternative Assessment Guide, Test Generator, or Standardized Assessment Tutor.

Chapter Opener

CHAPITRE 10

One-Stop Planner CD-ROM

For resource information, see the **One-Stop Planner,** Disc 3.

Pacing Tips

Keep in mind while planning your lessons that all three **étapes** in this chapter are more or less balanced. The **Première étape** presents the new vocabulary for this chapter. The **–ir** verbs are introduced in the **Deuxième étape.** All three **étapes** present new functional expressions. For Lesson Plans and timing suggestions, see pages 291I–291L.

Meeting the Standards

Communication
- Asking for and giving advice, p. 300
- Expressing need; inquiring, p. 301
- Asking for an opinion, paying a compliment, and criticizing, p. 306
- Hesitating; making a decision, p. 310

Cultures
- Culture Note, pp. 292, 305, 308
- Note culturelle, p. 303
- Panorama Culturel, p. 305
- Rencontre culturelle, p. 308

Connections
- Family Link, p. 305
- Math Link, p. 303
- Multicultural Link, p. 308

Comparisons
- Thinking Critically: Analyzing, p. 295
- Thinking Critically: Analyzing, p. 308
- Thinking Critically: Comparing and Contrasting, p. 312

Communities
- Career Path, p. 292
- De l'école au travail, p. 311

Cultures and Communities

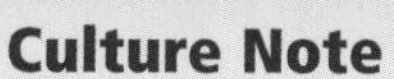

Culture Note

The skirts that Magali is looking at are made of **provençal** fabric. These prints are characterized by one or more distinctive **provençal** motifs, which are recognizable by their floral designs, medallions, or paisleys.

Career Path

Ask students to name some international designers and some cities that they associate with the fashion industry. You might clip out pages from men's and women's fashion magazines showing names and clothing of international designers. Ask students which languages would be useful if they were to work in the fashion industry.

STANDARDS: 2.2, 5.1, 5.2

CHAPITRE

10

Dans un magasin de vêtements

Objectives

In this chapter you will learn to

Première étape

- ask for and give advice

Deuxième étape

- express need
- inquire

Troisième étape

- ask for an opinion
- pay a compliment
- criticize
- hesitate
- make a decision

Visit Holt Online
go.hrw.com
KEYWORD: WA3 ARLES-10
Online Edition

◀ **Je ne sais pas quoi mettre pour aller à la boum.**

Chapter Opener

CHAPITRE 10

Focusing on Outcomes

Ask students to tell how the outcomes could be used to discuss clothing. Then, have them suggest other situations in which these outcomes could be used and how (when buying school supplies or gifts, when discussing new hairstyles).
NOTE: The self-check activities in **Que sais-je?** on page 320 help students assess their achievement of the objectives.

Language Note

You might want to tell your students that **faire les boutiques** or **faire les magasins** refers to *shopping,* while **faire les vitrines** or **faire du lèche-vitrines** refers to *window shopping,* or shopping without the intent to buy.

Connections and Comparisons

Thinking Critically

Analyzing Ask students which times of the year they notice more advertising in newspapers and on television for buying new clothing. Have students look in French magazines for clothing ads. What occasions seem to be common to both cultures for buying new clothes (back-to-school)? Have them discuss how fashion designers and the media help create a constant demand for new styles.

History Link

Have students do research on some of the traditional costumes of the different regions of France. Students could also research why and how France became a fashion capital and report on some famous designers such as Coco Chanel and Yves Saint-Laurent.

STANDARDS: 1.2, 2.2, 3.1

Mise en train

CHAPITRE 10

Teaching Resources
pp. 294–296

PRINT 
- Lesson Planner, p. 48
- Video Guide, pp. 68, 70
- Cahier d'activités, p. 109

MEDIA 
- One-Stop Planner
- Video Program
  Mise en train
  Videocassette 4, 01:13–05:42
  Videocassette 5 (captioned version), 1:20:22–1:24:53
  Suite
  Videocassette 4, 05:47–09:57
  Videocassette 5 (captioned version), 1:25:00–1:29:10
- DVD Tutor, Disc 2
- Audio Compact Discs, CD 10, Trs. 1–2
- **Mise en train** Transparencies

Presenting Mise en train

After viewing the video, play the recording and have students follow along in their books. Stop the recording to ask the questions in Activity 1 on page 296 to check students' comprehension: after the first scene, question 1; after the second, question 2; after the third, question 3; after the ninth, question 4.

Mise en train Transparencies

Language Note

The expression **Chacun ses goûts** is the French equivalent of *To each his own.*

The **roman-photo** is an abridged version of the video episode.

MISE EN TRAIN ▪ *Chacun ses goûts*

CD 10
Trs.1–2

Stratégie pour comprendre
What event are Hélène and Magali discussing at the beginning of the story? Where does Magali go? Why do you think Hélène doesn't go with her?

Magali

Hélène

La vendeuse

1
Magali : Oh là là! Je ne sais pas quoi mettre demain. C'est l'anniversaire de Sophie. J'ai envie d'acheter quelque chose de joli. Et toi, qu'est-ce que tu vas mettre?
Hélène : Oh, je ne sais pas. Sans doute un jean et un tee-shirt.

2
Magali : Pourquoi est-ce que tu ne trouves pas quelque chose d'original? De mignon?
Hélène : Ecoute, Magali. Moi, j'aime bien être en jean et en tee-shirt. C'est simple et agréable à porter. Chacun ses goûts.

3
Au magasin...
La vendeuse : Bonjour. Je peux vous aider?
Magali : Je cherche quelque chose pour aller à une fête. J'aimerais quelque chose d'original et pas trop cher.

4
La vendeuse : Qu'est-ce que vous faites comme taille?
Magali : Je fais du 38.

Preteaching Vocabulary

Guessing words from context

Tell students to think about what usually happens when they go to a clothing store. You may wish to write the following phrases on the board and allow students to finish the sequence: 1. You look around, 2. The salesperson approaches you and asks, "Can I help you?" 3. ... Then, have students use this context to guess the meaning of the following expressions:

- ❸ **Je peux vous aider?**
- ❹ **Qu'est-ce que vous faites comme taille?**
- ❺ **C'est pas tellement mon style.**
- ❽ **Ah, très chic!**

You can also ask students to identify the following items of clothing by pointing to articles that their classmates are wearing while you say the words:

- ❶ **un tee-shirt, un jean**
- ❾ **une jupe, un chemisier**

STANDARDS: 1.2

5

La vendeuse : Nous avons des jupes, si vous voulez. Tenez, celle-ci fait jeune. Comment la trouvez-vous?

Magali : Bof. C'est pas tellement mon style.

6

Magali : J'aime bien cette jupe-ci. Est-ce que vous l'avez en vert?

La vendeuse : Elle est jolie, n'est-ce pas? Nous l'avons en bleu, en rouge et en vert. La voilà en 38.

7

Magali essaie la jupe...

La vendeuse : Très joli. Ça vous va très bien.

Magali : Oui, c'est pas mal, mais elle est un peu large, non? Est-ce que vous l'avez en 36?

8

Quelques minutes plus tard...

La vendeuse : Ah, très chic! C'est tout à fait votre style.

Magali : Vous trouvez? Mais, je ne sais pas quoi mettre avec.

9

La vendeuse : Nous avons ces chemisiers, si vous aimez. Taille unique. Ça va très bien avec la jupe.

Cahier d'activités, p. 109, Act. 1

Using the Captioned Video/DVD

If students have difficulty understanding French spoken at a normal speed, use Videocassette 5 to allow students to see the French captions for ***Chacun ses goûts*** and ***Chacun ses goûts (suite).*** Hearing the language and watching the story will reduce anxiety about the new language and facilitate comprehension.

The reinforcement of seeing the written vocabulary words as they watch the gestures and actions will help prepare students to do the comprehension activities on page 296.

NOTE: The *DVD Tutor* contains captions for all sections of the *Video Program.*

Mise en train

CHAPITRE 10

Thinking Critically

Analyzing Have students discuss the questions that Magali asks at the clothing store. Ask students if they ask the same questions and if there are other things to consider when buying clothes. Ask them whether they agree with the saleswoman that it's worth any price to look original.

Auditory Learners

Describe each photo aloud in random order. For example, for Photo 5, you might say **Magali trouve une jupe, mais ce n'est pas son style.** Have students call out the number of the photo you're describing.

Chacun ses goûts (suite)

When the story continues, Hélène enters the clothing boutique and sees Magali. Magali asks her about the outfit she has on, and Hélène compliments her on it. Magali is unsure and still can't figure out what to do. Later, when Magali arrives at Sophie's, she and Sophie discover they've bought the same shirt! Magali is upset at first, but then smiles.

STANDARDS: 1.2, 5.2

Mise en train

CHAPITRE 10

Auditory Learners

4 Read the sentences aloud in random order and have students tell whether the salesperson or customer is speaking.

Teaching Suggestion

6 This activity might be done orally as a class or in pairs. You might also have students write down their answers.

Answers

5
1. Je ne sais pas quoi mettre.
2. C'est simple et agréable à porter.
3. J'aimerais quelque chose de...
4. Je fais du...
5. C'est pas tellement mon style.
6. Est-ce que vous l'avez en... ?

These activities check for comprehension only. Students should not yet be expected to produce language modeled in **Mise en train.**

1 Tu as compris?

1. Why does Magali want to buy something new? She is going to a birthday party.
2. What is Hélène going to wear? Why? jeans and a T-shirt; They are simple and comfortable.
3. What type of clothing is Magali looking for? something original and not too expensive
4. What outfit does Magali like? a green skirt and a shirt

2 C'est qui?

Qui parle? C'est Magali, Hélène ou la vendeuse?

1. «J'aimerais quelque chose d'original et pas trop cher.» Magali
2. «Je peux vous aider?» la vendeuse
3. «Moi, j'aime bien être en jean et en tee-shirt. C'est simple et agréable à porter.» Hélène
4. «Qu'est-ce que vous faites comme taille?» la vendeuse
5. «Chacun ses goûts.» Hélène
6. «Est-ce que vous l'avez en vert?» Magali
7. «C'est tout à fait votre style.» la vendeuse
8. «Ce n'est pas tellement mon style.» Magali

3 Chacun ses goûts

Qu'est-ce que Magali dit de ces vêtements?

1. le jean et le tee-shirt d'Hélène Pourquoi est-ce que tu ne trouves pas quelque chose d'original? De mignon?
2. la première jupe que la vendeuse propose. Bof. Ce n'est pas tellement mon style.
3. la jupe verte en 38 C'est pas mal, mais elle est un peu large.

4 Qu'est-ce qu'elle répond?

Qu'est-ce que Magali répond à la vendeuse?

1. Qu'est-ce que vous faites comme taille? b
2. Comment la trouvez-vous? d
3. Je peux vous aider? c
4. Ah, très chic! C'est tout à fait votre style. a

a. Vous trouvez? Mais, je ne sais pas quoi mettre avec.
b. Je fais du 38.
c. Je cherche quelque chose pour aller à une fête.
d. Bof. Ce n'est pas tellement mon style.

5 Cherche les expressions See answers below.

According to ***Chacun ses goûts,*** how would you . . .

1. express indecision?
2. express satisfaction with your clothes?
3. tell a salesperson what you want?
4. tell what size you wear?
5. express dissatisfaction with clothes?
6. ask for a certain color or size?

Je fais du...
J'aimerais quelque chose de...
C'est simple et agréable à porter.
C'est pas tellement mon style.
Je ne sais pas quoi mettre.
Est-ce que vous l'avez en... ?

6 Et maintenant, à toi

Est-ce que tu préfères le style de Magali ou d'Hélène? Qu'est-ce que tu aimes comme vêtements?

Comprehension Check

Slower Pace/Visual Learners

2 If students have difficulty with this activity, show the video, stop it when you come to each of these quotes, and have students identify the speaker.

Additional Practice

Write down some sentences from the conversation between Magali and the salesperson on strips of transparency and place the strips on the overhead in random order. Have students identify the person who said each sentence. Then, have students put the sentences in order to recreate the conversation.

Objective Asking for and giving advice

WA3 ARLES-10

Vocabulaire

Les vêtements

CD-ROM 3 DVD 2

Here are some other words you may want to use to talk about what you're wearing.

un bracelet	**un manteau** *coat*	**des sandales** (f.)
un cardigan	**un pantalon**	**un short**
un jean	**un pull**(-over)	**un sweat-shirt**

Travaux pratiques de grammaire, pp. 79–80, Act. 1–3

Cahier d'activités, pp. 110–111, Act. 2–5

Teacher to Teacher

Carol Chadwick
Taipei American School
Taipei, Taiwan

Try Carol's game to practice clothing vocabulary and colors.

"This game is called **Qui est le criminel?** Cut 26 full-page pictures from magazines, labeled A-Z. Attach the pictures to the board using magnets. I begin by telling students there is a criminal among the group of people in the pictures (which I secretly choose). Students have to ask yes/no questions about what the "criminal" is wearing until they can identify him or her **("Est-ce qu'il /elle porte un blouson noir?")**. The person who correctly identifies the "criminal" chooses another one and the game continues."

Première étape

CHAPITRE 10

Teaching Resources
pp. 297–300

PRINT

- Lesson Planner, p. 49
- TPR Storytelling Book, pp. 37, 40
- Listening Activities, pp. 75, 79
- Activities for Communication, pp. 55–56, 120, 123, 155–156
- Travaux pratiques de grammaire, pp. 79–81
- Grammar Tutor for Students of French, Chapter 10
- Cahier d'activités, pp. 110–112
- Testing Program, pp. 249–252
- Alternative Assessment Guide, p. 41
- Student Make-Up Assignments, Chapter 10

MEDIA

- One-Stop Planner
- Audio Compact Discs, CD 10, Trs. 3–4, 20, 26–27
- Teaching Transparencies: 10-1, 10-A; **Grammaire supplémentaire** Answers; Travaux pratique de grammaire Answers
- Interactive CD-ROM Tutor, Disc 3

Bell Work
Have students list three colors they're wearing today.

Presenting
Vocabulaire

Present the vocabulary with real clothing items or magazine pictures. Then, ask individuals how much various items in the ads cost. **(Combien coûte la montre noire?)** Next, point to various items of clothing that students are wearing, asking **Qu'est-ce que c'est?** You might also hold up an item and ask students what other item(s) of clothing they would suggest to go with it.

STANDARDS: 1.1

Première étape

CHAPITRE 10

Teaching Resources
pp. 297–300

PRINT 

- Lesson Planner, p. 49
- TPR Storytelling Book, pp. 37, 40
- Listening Activities, pp. 75, 79
- Activities for Communication, pp. 55–56, 120, 123, 155–156
- Travaux pratiques de grammaire, pp. 79–81
- Grammar Tutor for Students of French, Chapter 10
- Cahier d'activités, pp. 110–112
- Testing Program, pp. 249–252
- Alternative Assessment Guide, p. 41
- Student Make-Up Assignments, Chapter 10

MEDIA 

- One-Stop Planner
- Audio Compact Discs, CD 10, Trs. 3–4, 20, 26–27
- Teaching Transparencies: 10-1, 10-A; **Grammaire supplémentaire** Answers; Travaux pratique de grammaire Answers
- Interactive CD-ROM Tutor, Disc 3

Slower Pace

7 Before playing the recording, have students identify the items in the illustrations. Have them point out the similarities and differences among the three groups. You might want to play the recording twice.

Language Note

Another term for **un cardigan** is **un gilet.** A sweatsuit is called **un jogging.**

Answers

8 Lise a acheté une cravate pour son père, des boucles d'oreilles pour sa mère, une casquette pour son frère, des chaussettes pour sa sœur, un bracelet pour sa grand-mère et une écharpe pour son grand-père.

7 Qu'est-ce qu'Armelle a acheté? See scripts on p. 291G.

CD 10
Tr. 3

Ecoutons Listen as Armelle tells her friend about her big shopping trip. Then, choose the illustration that represents her purchases. c

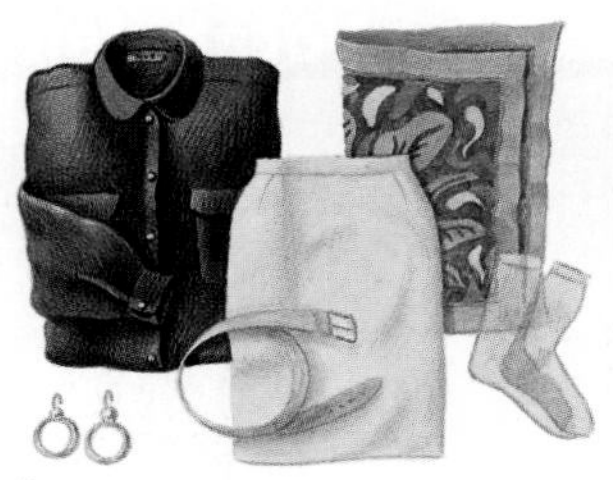

a.

b.

c.

8 Des cadeaux See answers below.

Parlons Regarde l'image et dis ce que Lise a acheté pour sa famille.

EXEMPLE **Elle a acheté... pour...**

9 Pas de chance!

Ecrivons Imagine que tu voyages en France. A l'arrivée, tu ne trouves pas tes bagages. Alors, la compagnie aérienne te donne 500 dollars pour acheter de nouveaux vêtements. Fais une liste de ce que tu vas acheter.

EXEMPLE **D'abord, je vais acheter...**

10 La fête

Parlons Tu es invité(e) à une fête. Dis quels vêtements tu vas porter. Choisis des articles de la liste de l'activité 9. Est-ce que tu vas avoir besoin d'autres vêtements?

EXEMPLE **Je vais mettre...**

Communication for All Students

Building on Previous Skills

8 Before students begin, you might review family vocabulary from Chapter 7 by showing *Teaching Transparency 7-A.* Ask questions about the family members. **(Raymond est le père ou la mère d'Isabelle?)** Have students recall the use of **son, sa,** and **ses** as well. This activity might also be written.

Reteaching

Adjective agreement Ask students to recall how they form the feminine and the plural of most adjectives. Then, remind them that the last consonant may be doubled before the **-e** is added: **violet(te),** or that the feminine form may be irregular: **blanc (blanche).** Show various clothing articles and have students describe them, including colors.

STANDARDS: 1.2, 5.2

Grammaire

The verbs *mettre* and *porter*

Mettre is an irregular verb.

mettre *(to put, to put on, to wear)*

Je	**mets**	Nous	**mettons**
Tu	**mets**	Vous	**mettez**
Il/Elle/On	**met**	Ils/Elles	**mettent**

- **Mets** and **met** are pronounced alike. You don't pronounce the final consonant(s) **ts** and **t.**
- The past participle of **mettre** is **mis:** Elle **a mis** une jupe.
- You can also use the regular **-er** verb **porter** to tell what someone is wearing: Elle **porte** une robe.

Grammaire supplémentaire, p. 314, Act. 1–3

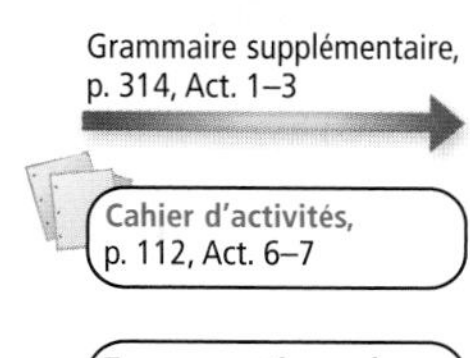

Cahier d'activités, p. 112, Act. 6–7

Travaux pratiques de grammaire, pp. 80–81, Act. 4–6

11 **Grammaire en contexte**

Parlons Dis ce que les personnes suivantes mettent pour sortir.

1. Pour aller à l'école, Sophie...

2. Pour aller à une boum, elles...

3. Pour aller au café, toi, tu...

4. Pour aller au stade, nous...

1. met une jupe, une ceinture et un pull.
2. mettent des robes et des chaussures.
3. mets un blouson.
4. mettons des baskets.

12 **Grammaire en contexte**

Parlons Demande à ton/ta camarade quels vêtements il/elle a mis hier et dis-lui ce que toi, tu as mis.

De bons conseils

Although it's common to feel a little uncomfortable when speaking a new language, the best way to overcome it is to talk and talk and talk. Whenever you answer a question or have a conversation with a partner, try to keep the conversation going as long as possible. Don't worry about making a mistake. The more you think about making mistakes, the less likely you will be to talk.

Connections and Comparisons

Thinking Critically

11 **Comparing and Contrasting** Have students look throughout the book for other illustrations and photos of French-speaking students at school, a party, a café, or sports event. Have students compare what these illustrations show as well as what they would wear in similar situations.

Language-to-Language

If you have any Spanish-speaking students, tell them that when speaking about wearing and putting on clothes, **porter** (to wear) and **mettre** (to put on) correspond to **llevar** and **poner** in Spanish.

Presenting Grammaire

The verbs *mettre* and *porter* Write the forms of **mettre** on large flashcards and shuffle them. Write the subject pronouns on the board. As you show each card, have students tell you what they think the subject pronouns might be. Have them repeat the subject and verb as you tape the card next to the subject pronoun on the board. Then, bring in magazine photos of boys and girls and ask students **Qu'est-ce qu'il/elle met pour la boum ce soir?** You might also tell students there's a party tonight and ask them what they're going to wear. **(Qu'est-ce que tu mets pour la boum ce soir?)**

Language Note

Porter also means *to wear,* but most people prefer to use **mettre** *(to put on, to wear)* in everyday conversation. Caution your students, however, that **mettre** cannot be used to tell what someone is wearing now. **Elle met une robe** means either *She is putting on a dress,* or *She is going to wear a dress (tonight).* To say that someone is wearing a dress now, **porter** must be used. **(Elle porte une robe aujourd'hui.)**

Additional Practice

Grammaire Describe what a student is wearing, asking the class **Qui a mis des baskets, un jean et un tee-shirt rouge?** The first person to call out the correct student's name asks the next question. You might also show *Teaching Transparency 10-1* and ask students **Qu'est-ce qu'elles mettent?**

Auditory Learners

11 Tell students what the people in the pictures are putting on. Have students write the number of the appropriate illustration.

STANDARDS: 1.1, 4.1, 4.2

Première étape

CHAPITRE 10

Presenting Comment dit-on... ?

Ask individuals for advice on what to wear to a party **(à une boum),** to school **(à l'école),** and to a restaurant **(au restaurant).** Write prompts for their responses on the board. Then, have them ask you for advice.

Language Note

Remind students that the **tu** form of **mettre** retains the final **-s** in the command form since it is not an **-er** verb.

Visual Learners

14 Assign a clothing item to each student. Have them draw and color a picture of their assigned item on one side of an index card and write the French word for it on the other side. Distribute the cards to partners and have them ask for and give advice about what to wear with the item.

Mon journal

16 For an additional journal entry suggestion for Chapter 10, see *Cahier d'activités,* page 154.

Assess

- Testing Program, pp. 249–252 Quiz 10-1A, Quiz 10-1B, Audio CD 10, Tr. 20
- Student Make-Up Assignments Chapter 10, Alternative Quiz
- Alternative Assessment Guide, p. 41

Comment dit-on...?

Asking for and giving advice

To ask for advice:

Je ne sais pas quoi mettre pour aller à la boum. *I don't know what to wear for (to) . . .*
Qu'est-ce que je mets? *What shall I wear?*

To give advice:

Pourquoi est-ce que tu ne mets pas ta robe? *Why don't you wear . . . ?*
Mets ton jean. *Wear . . .*

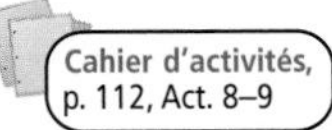
Cahier d'activités, p. 112, Act. 8–9

JE NE SAIS PAS QUOI METTRE POUR ALLER VOIR NICOLE!
POURQUOI EST-CE QUE TU NE METS PAS MA CRAVATE AVEC CETTE CHEMISE?

13 Des conseils
See scripts and answers on p. 291G.

CD 10 Tr. 4

Ecoutons Are these people asking for or giving advice?

14 Harmonie de couleurs

Parlons Demande à ton/ta camarade ce que tu devrais mettre avec les vêtements suivants. Il/Elle va te donner des conseils. Ensuite, changez de rôle.

Exemple —**Qu'est-ce que je mets avec ma jupe noire?**
—**Pourquoi est-ce que tu ne mets pas ton pull gris?**

1. Avec mon pantalon bleu?
2. Avec ma chemise rouge?
3. Avec mes baskets violettes?
4. Avec mon pull gris?
5. Avec mon short orange?
6. Avec ma veste verte?

15 Qu'est-ce que je mets?

Parlons Cette année, tu vas habiter avec une famille française. Dis à ton/ta camarade où tu vas aller en France et explique ce que tu vas faire. Demande-lui quels vêtements tu devrais porter pour les occasions suivantes. Il/Elle va te donner des conseils. Ensuite, changez de rôle.

Exemple —**Pour aller au café, qu'est-ce que je mets?**
—**Mets un jean et un sweat-shirt.**

pour aller à une boum
pour aller à la plage
pour aller au café
pour dîner dans un restaurant élégant
pour jouer au football
pour aller au parc
pour aller au théâtre
pour faire du patin à glace
pour aller au musée
pour faire du ski

16 Mon journal

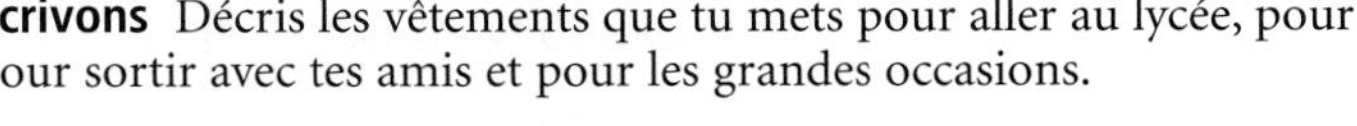

Ecrivons Décris les vêtements que tu mets pour aller au lycée, pour aller à des fêtes, pour sortir avec tes amis et pour les grandes occasions.

Cultures and Communities

Community Link

Have volunteer students bring in photos from a recent special occasion in their community (wedding, graduation, bar mitzvah, **quinceñera,** etc.). Have them present the photos and then have the class comment on the clothing worn. Ask students how they can tell who the focal participants in the event are (special clothing worn by the bride and the groom, etc.).

Career Path

Ask students what would be appropriate to wear to a job interview for different types of jobs (professional, retail, food service, etc.). Students who have after-school jobs might wish to describe what they wore for their initial interviews and then say what they normally wear to work.

STANDARDS: 1.1, 1.2, 1.3, 3.1, 5.1

Objectives Expressing need; inquiring

WA3 ARLES-10

Comment dit-on...?

Expressing need; inquiring

The salesperson might ask you:

Vous désirez?
(Est-ce que) je peux vous aider?
May I help you?

BONJOUR, J'AIMERAIS UN PANTALON POUR ALLER AVEC MON TEE-SHIRT!
VOUS AVEZ CES CHAUSSURES EN 43?

To express need, you might answer:

Oui, il me faut un chemisier vert.
Oui, vous avez des chapeaux?
Je cherche quelque chose pour aller à une boum.
I'm looking for something to . . .
J'aimerais un chemisier **pour aller avec** ma jupe.
I'd like . . . to go with . . .
Non, merci, je regarde.
No, thanks, I'm just looking.
Je peux l'/les essayer?
Can I try it/them on?
Je peux essayer le/la/l'/les bleu(e)(s)?
Can I try on the . . . ?

To inquire about prices:

C'est combien,... ?
Ça fait combien?

To ask about sizes, colors, and fabrics:

Vous avez ça en (taille) 36?
Do you have that in (size) . . . ?
en bleu?
en coton? *cotton?*
en jean? *denim?*
en cuir? *leather?*

Travaux pratiques de grammaire, p. 82, Act. 7

Cahier d'activités, p. 113, Act. 10–11

Note de grammaire

You can use colors and other adjectives as nouns by putting **le, la,** or **les** before them. Change their spelling according to the things they refer to: **le bleu, la bleue** = *the blue one;* **les verts, les vertes** = *the green ones.*

Travaux pratiques de grammaire, p. 82, Act. 8

Grammaire supplémentaire, p. 315, Act. 4

Cahier d'activités, p. 114, Act. 12

17 Qui parle? See scripts and answers on p. 291G.

Ecoutons Listen and decide whether a customer or salesperson is speaking.

CD 10 Tr. 5

Communication for All Students

Building on Previous Skills

Ask students what they would need to say when shopping for clothes in France. Then, ask them to list appropriate expressions they already know in French. You might also ask students if they have ever worked in a clothing store and, if so, how they addressed their customers.

Visual Learners

Note de grammaire Practice this structure by holding up two items, such as notebooks, which are the same except for the color. Ask individual students to choose the one they prefer. **(Tu aimes mieux le blanc ou le jaune?)**

Teaching Resources
pp. 301–304

PRINT

- Lesson Planner, p. 50
- TPR Storytelling Book, pp. 38, 40
- Listening Activities, pp. 75–76, 80
- Activities for Communication, pp. 57–58, 121, 123, 155–156
- Travaux pratiques de grammaire, pp. 82–84
- Grammar Tutor for Students of French, Chapter 10
- Cahier d'activités, pp. 113–115
- Testing Program, pp. 253–256
- Alternative Assessment Guide, p. 41
- Student Make-Up Assignments, Chapter 10

MEDIA 

- One-Stop Planner
- Audio Compact Discs, CD 10, Trs. 5–6, 21, 28–29
- Teaching Transparencies: 10-2; **Grammaire supplémentaire** Answers; Travaux pratiques de grammaire Answers
- Interactive CD-ROM Tutor, Disc 3

Bell Work

Display a picture of an outfit and have students write a description of it.

Presenting
Comment dit-on... ?

Begin by playing the video for ***Chacun ses goûts,*** pausing it for students to repeat each of the expressions in **Comment dit-on... ?** as they are used in the video. Then, act as a salesperson and ask students **Je peux vous aider?** Criticize the fit and color to encourage students to ask for different sizes and colors.

STANDARDS: 1.2, 4.1

Deuxième étape

CHAPITRE 10

Teaching Resources
pp. 301–304

PRINT 
- Lesson Planner, p. 50
- TPR Storytelling Book, pp. 38, 40
- Listening Activities, pp. 75–76, 80
- Activities for Communication, pp. 57–58, 121, 123, 155–156
- Travaux pratiques de grammaire, pp. 82–84
- Grammar Tutor for Students of French, Chapter 10
- Cahier d'activités, pp. 113–115
- Testing Program, pp. 253–256
- Alternative Assessment Guide, p. 41
- Student Make-Up Assignments, Chapter 10

MEDIA 
- One-Stop Planner
- Audio Compact Discs, CD 10, Trs. 5–6, 21, 28–29
- Teaching Transparencies: 10-2; **Grammaire supplémentaire** Answers; Travaux pratiques de grammaire Answers
- Interactive CD-ROM Tutor, Disc 3

Teaching Suggestion

18 You might have students write their answers, using C for color, S for size, and P for price.

Challenge

18 Have students tell the color, price, or size of each item.

18 Couleur, prix ou taille? See scripts and answers on p. 291G.

Ecoutons Listen and decide whether these people are talking about the color, price, or size of the items they're looking at.

CD 10 Tr. 6

19 Méli-mélo!

Lisons Mets cette conversation dans le bon ordre.

6 —C'est combien?
5 —Oui. Nous les avons en bleu, en rouge et en orange.
3 —Voilà, ces maillots de bain sont très chic.
8 —Oh là là! C'est trop cher, ça!
1 —Je peux vous aider?
7 —C'est 68 €.
4 —Euh, je n'aime pas trop la couleur. Vous les avez en bleu?
2 —Oui, je cherche un maillot de bain.

20 Grammaire en contexte

Lisons/Ecrivons Blondine et Claire se préparent pour aller à une fête. Complète leur conversation avec **le, la, l'** ou **les** et une couleur. Answers may vary.

—Et avec ma jupe bleue, est-ce que je mets mon chemisier orange ou mon chemisier blanc?
—Pas l'orange! Mets plutôt __1__. le blanc
—Et pour les chaussures? __2__ vont mieux avec ma jupe, non? Les blanches
—Mais non. Mets __3__. les bleues
—Et mon sac rose ou le noir? Le rose, non?
—Mmm... je n'aime pas __4__. Tu as une ceinture noire? le rose
—Oui, mais j'ai aussi une ceinture jaune.
—Ah non! Pas la jaune! Mets __5__. la noire

21 Préférences

Parlons Tu regardes des vêtements dans un catalogue avec ton/ta camarade. Dites quels articles vous aimez et en quelle couleur.

EXEMPLE —**J'aime bien ce polo bleu. Et toi?**
—**Moi, j'aime mieux le noir.**

Communication for All Students

Visual Learners

19 Show *Teaching Transparency 10-2.* Have partners write another conversation based on what they see, cut it into strips line by line, and exchange it with another pair. Students should then reassemble the conversation and hand it back to the pair who wrote it to be checked. You might also have students act out their conversation.

Visual Learners

21 Have students make their own clothing catalogue. Have them draw items or cut out pictures from magazines. They should label the items and give a price for each in euros. Be sure they give their store a name. You might choose to use this as a chapter project.

STANDARDS: 1.1, 1.2

Note culturelle

The French don't use the same clothing sizes as Americans. Look at this size conversion chart to find the size you'd ask for if you were shopping in France.

TABLE DE COMPARAISON DE TAILLES

Robes, chemisiers et pantalons femmes.						
France	34	36	38	40	42	44
USA	3	5	7	9	11	13

Chaussures femmes.						
France	36	37	38	38½	39	40
USA	5-5½	6-6½	7-7½	8	8½	9

Tricots, pull-overs, pantalons hommes.						
France	36	38	40	42	44	46
USA	26	28	30	32	34	36

Chemises hommes.						
France	36	37	38	39	40	41
USA	14	14½	15	15½	16	16½

Chaussures hommes.						
France	39	40	41	42	43	44
USA	6½-7	7½	8	8½	9-9½	10-10½

22 Jeu de rôle

Parlons Tu as besoin de quelque chose pour aller avec les vêtements proposés. Dis au vendeur/à la vendeuse ce que tu veux. Pose des questions sur les prix et sur les tailles. Joue cette scène avec ton/ta camarade. Ensuite, changez de rôle.

un jean
un blouson en jean
une veste en cuir noir
un pull jaune
un short noir
une chemise en coton

Vocabulaire à la carte

à rayures	*striped*	**en laine**	*wool*
à carreaux	*checked*	**en rayonne**	*rayon*
à pois	*polka dot*	**en lin**	*linen*
à fleurs	*flowered*	**en soie**	*silk*
bleu clair	*light blue*	**bleu foncé**	*dark blue*

Grammaire

-ir verbs

CD-ROM 3
DVD 2

You've already learned the forms of regular **-er** and **-re** verbs. There is one more regular verb pattern for you to learn. Here are the forms of regular **-ir** verbs.

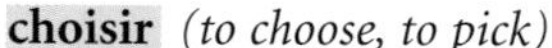

choisir *(to choose, to pick)*

Je	**choisis**	Nous	**choisissons**
Tu	**choisis**	Vous	**choisissez**
Il/Elle/On	**choisit**	Ils/Elles	**choisissent**

Je **choisis** un manteau noir.

- The past participle of regular **-ir** verbs ends in **-i:** Elle a chois**i** une belle robe.
- Other regular **-ir** verbs you might want to use when talking about clothes are: **grandir** *(to grow)*, **maigrir** *(to lose weight)*, and **grossir** *(to gain weight)*.

Grammaire supplémentaire, pp. 315–316, Act. 5–7

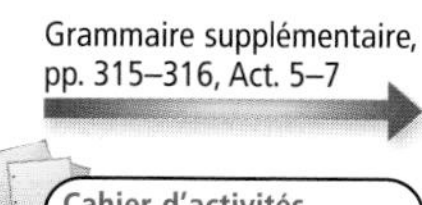

Cahier d'activités, p. 115, Act. 14–16

Travaux pratiques de grammaire, pp. 83–84, Act. 9–12

Connections and Comparisons

Building on Previous Skills

Note culturelle Re-enter numbers by naming a type of clothing, the gender of the wearer, and an American size. **(chemise, homme, quinze et demi.)** Have students give the corresponding French size. Then, reverse the procedure. You might also have students determine the French equivalents of their own sizes for shirts, shoes, dresses, and pants.

Math Link

Have students figure out the pattern of conversion from American to French sizes.

Portfolio

22 Oral This activity is appropriate for students' oral portfolios. For portfolio suggestions, see the *Alternative Assessment Guide,* pages iv–17.

Presenting Grammaire

***-ir* verbs** Write the stem **chois-** on a piece of paper. Then, write each subject pronoun and each of the verb endings on separate pieces of paper. Pass out all of the papers to students in the class. The student who receives the paper with **chois-** on it should come to the front of the class and remain there throughout the activity. As you call out a subject pronoun and the corresponding verb ending, the student holding the subject pronoun and the student holding the appropriate verb ending should come to the front of the class, displaying their papers on either side of the student with the stem **chois-** to form the correct subject and verb. Then, hold up pictures of two different hats. Ask a student **Quel chapeau est-ce que tu choisis?** When the student responds, ask the class **Quel chapeau est-ce que Pierre a choisi?** Continue with pictures of different clothing items.

Language Notes

Vocabulaire à la carte Point out that **bleu clair** and **bleu foncé** are invariable.

Grammaire Point out that a single **s** between vowels sounds like a *z,* while double **s** sounds like an *s.* Have students practice saying **choisissons,** pronouncing the first **s** like a *z* and the double **s** like an *s.*

Deuxième étape

CHAPITRE 10

Language Note
Point out to students that **un grand magasin** is a large department store, and a smaller shop is called **une boutique** or **un magasin.**

Assess
- Testing Program, pp. 253–256 Quiz 10-2A, Quiz 10-2B Audio CD 10, Tr. 21
- Student Make-Up Assignments, Chapter 10, Alternative Quiz
- Alternative Assessment Guide, p. 41

Possible answers

23
1. Elle choisit les chaussures rouges.
2. Nous choisissons le blouson noir.
3. Il choisit la cravate rouge.
4. Vous choisissez le chemisier bleu.

23 Grammaire en contexte See answers below.

Parlons Qu'est-ce qu'ils choisissent pour aller avec leurs vêtements?

1. **Elle...**

2. **Nous...**

3. **Il...**

4. **Vous...**

24 Ça ne me va plus! 1. Il a maigri. 2. Ils ont grandi. 3. Il a grossi. 4. Elle a grandi.

Parlons Pourquoi ces vêtements ne vont plus? Utilise le passé composé dans tes réponses.

1.

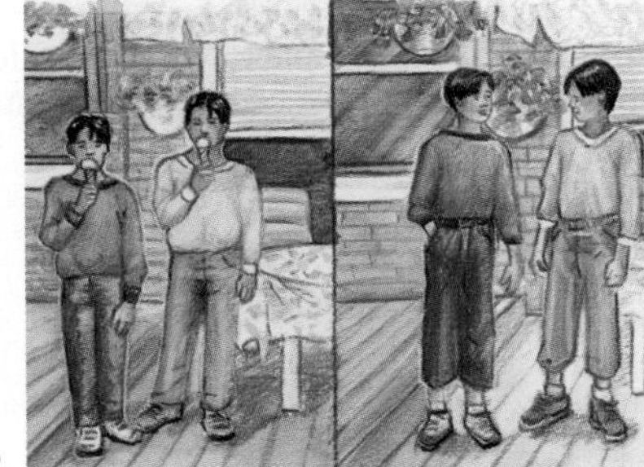
2.

3.

4.

25 Dans un grand magasin

Parlons Avec un(e) camarade, joue une scène entre un(e) client(e) et un vendeur/une vendeuse dans un grand magasin. Le/La client(e) va en vacances d'hiver. Il/Elle dit au vendeur/à la vendeuse ce qu'il/elle cherche. Il/Elle pose aussi des questions sur les tailles, les couleurs, les styles, les tissus et les prix. Il/Elle veut essayer plusieurs articles. Le vendeur/la vendeuse répond au/à la client(e). Ensuite, changez de rôle.

Communication for All Students

Additional Practice

23 Have partners ask and tell each other what they would choose. For example, one student says **Elle choisit les chaussures rouges** and asks **Et toi?** The other answers **Moi, je choisis...** and tells which shoes he or she would wear with the outfit. Students might suggest an item not shown in the illustration. They might also use the past tense or the future with **aller.**

Visual Learners

Show pictures of a baby, Santa Claus, and a stick figure. Ask students **Qu'est-ce qu'ils doivent** *(should)* **faire? (grandir, maigrir, grossir).** You might write **grandir, grossir,** and **maigrir** on the board and ask students to come up and write the different verb forms.

STANDARDS: 1.1, 1.3, 5.1, 5.2

Qu'est-ce que tu aimes comme vêtements?

We asked some francophone people what they like to wear. Here's what they said.

Marie-Emmanuelle,
France

«J'aime bien mettre des jeans, des tee-shirts, des affaires simples, mais de temps en temps, j'aime bien être originale et porter des jupes longues, ou euh... quelque chose de plus classique ou plus moderne.» Tr. 8

Thomas,
France

«J'aime les jeans, les chemises, les grosses chaussures et les casquettes aussi.» Tr. 9

Aminata,
Côte d'Ivoire

«J'adore beaucoup les jupes droites, les robes, les pagnes. J'aime beaucoup me mettre aussi en tissu.» Tr. 10

Qu'en penses-tu?

1. How do you and your friends like to dress? How is this different from the way these people like to dress?
2. Which of these people share your tastes in clothing?

Savais-tu que...?

In France and other francophone countries, it is common to see people dressed quite well on the streets, on trains, at work, and in restaurants, even fast-food restaurants. In Africa, women commonly drape themselves in brightly-colored fabrics called **pagnes.** Martinique is famous for its **madras** patterns, and southern France is known for its pretty **provençal** prints. Although Paris has the reputation of being a fashion capital, ordinary Parisians don't wear fashions created by well-known designers. Most young people like to wear jeans, just like American teenagers.

Cultures and Communities

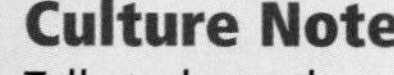

Culture Note

Tell students that **madras** is a brightly colored plaid fabric commonly worn in Martinique. See Photo 4 on page 353. A **pagne** is a length of cloth that African women wrap around their waist to make a skirt.

Family Link

Ask students to interview their family members about what they like to wear and why. Have students report their results to the class and give possible explanations for the different preferences.

CHAPITRE 10

Teaching Resources
p. 305

PRINT

- Video Guide, pp. 68–69, 70–71
- Cahier d'activités, p. 120

MEDIA 

- One-Stop Planner
- Video Program
  Videocassette 4, 09:59–12:55
- DVD Tutor, Disc 2
- Audio Compact Discs, CD 10, Trs. 7–10
- Interactive CD-ROM Tutor, Disc 3

Presenting Panorama Culturel

Have students write the interviewees' names at the top of three columns on a sheet of paper. Tell them to listen for and write down two things that each person likes to wear. Then, play the video. You might compile a complete list on a transparency and have students check their answers.

Questions

1. **Qu'est-ce que Marie-Emmanuelle aime mettre comme vêtements?** (des jeans, des tee-shirts, des jupes longues)
2. **Comment sont les vêtements qu'elle préfère?** (simples, classiques, modernes)
3. **Thomas aime quelles sortes de vêtements?** (les jeans, les chemises, les grosses chaussures et les casquettes)
4. **Aminata adore quelles sortes de vêtements?** (les jupes droites, les robes, les pagnes) **En quoi est-ce qu'elle aime se mettre?** (en tissu)

STANDARDS: 2.1, 2.2, 3.2, 4.2, 5.1

Teaching Resources
pp. 306–307, 309–311

PRINT

- Lesson Planner, p. 51
- TPR Storytelling Book, pp. 39, 40
- Listening Activities, pp. 76–77, 81
- Activities for Communication, pp. 59–60, 122, 124, 155–156
- Travaux pratiques de grammaire, pp. 85–87
- Grammar Tutor for Students of French, Chapter 10
- Cahier d'activités, pp. 116–118
- Testing Program, pp. 257–260
- Alternative Assessment Guide, p. 41
- Student Make-Up Assignments, Chapter 10

MEDIA

- One-Stop Planner
- Audio Compact Discs, CD 10, Trs. 11–12, 22, 30–31
- Teaching Transparencies: 10-3; **Grammaire supplémentaire** Answers; Travaux pratiques de grammaire Answers
- Interactive CD-ROM Tutor, Disc 3

Bell Work
Write the following questions on the board and have students write an appropriate response: **Je peux vous aider? Qu'est-ce que vous faites comme taille? Qu'est-ce que vous allez mettre avec ce pantalon vert?**

Presenting
Comment dit-on... ?

Bring in pictures from magazines that show a variety of clothing and fits (short, tight, baggy, and so on). Comment on each one and have students repeat the expressions after you. You might bring in some old clothes you no longer wear and ask for opinions of them **(Vous le trouvez chic ou démodé?).**

Troisième étape

Objectives Asking for an opinion; paying a compliment; criticizing; hesitating; making a decision

WA3 ARLES-10

Comment dit-on...?

Asking for an opinion, paying a compliment, and criticizing

CD-ROM 3 DVD 2

To ask for an opinion:

Comment tu trouves... ?
Elle me va, cette robe?
Does . . . suit me?
Il te/vous plaît, ce jean?
Do you like . . . ?
Tu aimes mieux le bleu **ou** le noir?

ÇA ME VA, CE JEAN?
IL VOUS VA TRÈS BIEN. C'EST TOUT À FAIT VOTRE STYLE!

To pay a compliment:

C'est parfait. *It's perfect.*
C'est tout à fait ton/votre style.
It looks great on you!
Elle te/vous va très bien, cette jupe.
. . . suits you really well.
Il/Elle va très bien avec ta chemise.
It goes very well with . . .
Je le/la/les trouve... *I think it's/they're . . .*
très à la mode. *in style.*
chic.
mignon(mignonne)(s). *cute.*
sensationnel(le)/sensass. *fantastic.*
rétro.

To criticize:

Il/Elle ne te/vous va pas du tout. *That doesn't look good on you at all.*
Il/Elle est (Ils/Elles sont) trop serré(e)(s). *It's/They're too tight.*
large(s). *baggy.*
petit(e)(s). *small.*
grand(e)(s). *big.*
court(e)(s). *short.*
long(longue)(s). *long.*
Il/Elle ne va pas du tout avec tes chaussures. *That doesn't go at all with . . .*
Je le/la/les trouve moche(s). *I think it's/they're tacky.*
démodé(e)(s). *out of style.*
horrible(s). *terrible.*

Cahier d'activités, pp. 116–117, Act. 17–20

Travaux pratiques de grammaire, pp. 85–86, Act. 13–15

Connections and Comparisons

Language-to-Language
Clothing and adjectives to describe clothing represent another category of "loan" words that languages borrow from one other. Have students suggest clothing items *(jean, short,* and so on) and adjectives to describe them *(chic, sensass)* that are similar in both French and English. Ask them in which language they think the word originated and explain why.

26 **Compliment ou critique?** See scripts and answers on pp. 291G–291H.

Ecoutons Listen to the following conversations and decide if the speakers are complimenting or criticizing each other's clothing.

CD 10
Tr. 11

27 **Un après-midi au grand magasin** See answers below.

Parlons Tu es vendeur/vendeuse au magasin Le Printemps. Ces personnes ont besoin de conseils. Qu'est-ce que tu leur dis?

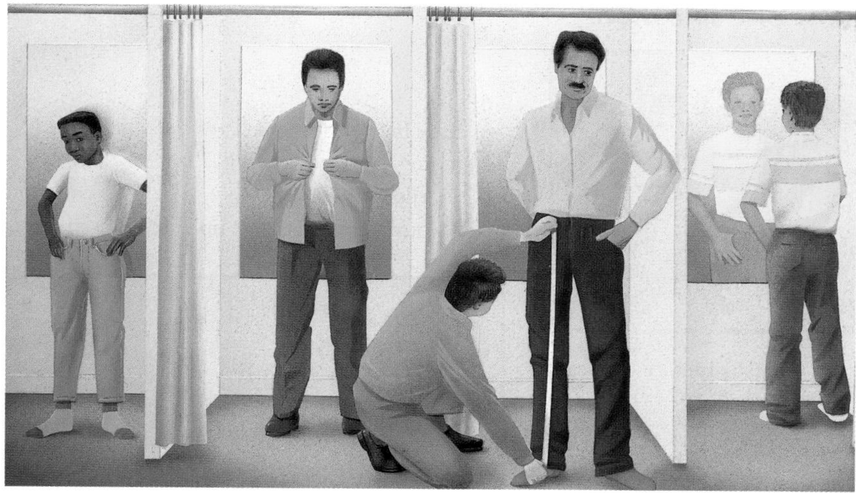

28 **Sondage**

Lisons/Parlons Fais ce petit test d'un magazine de mode français. Combien de points est-ce que tu as au total? Comment es-tu d'après le test? Compare ton résultat avec le résultat d'un(e) camarade.

ENQUETE : LA MODE

Es-tu à la mode?

Fais notre petit test pour savoir si tu es vraiment à la dernière mode.

En général, quelle sorte de vêtements est-ce que tu portes?
a. Des vêtements super chic. (3 points)
b. Ça dépend de l'occasion. (2 points)
c. Des jeans, des tee-shirts et des baskets. (1 point)

Tu achètes de nouveaux vêtements...
a. très souvent. (3 points)
b. quelquefois. (2 points)
c. presque jamais. (1 point)

Quand tu achètes des vêtements, en général, tu...
a. achètes ce qui est à la dernière mode. (3 points)
b. achètes quelque chose que tu aimes. (2 points)
c. achètes ce qui est en solde. (1 point)

Dans un magazine de mode, tu vois que les chemises en plastique fluorescentes sont très populaires. Tu...
a. achètes 4 chemises de 4 couleurs différentes. (3 points)
b. attends patiemment pour voir si les autres en portent. (2 points)
c. refuses d'en acheter! Tu ne veux pas être ridicule! (1 point)

Réponses :
10 -12 points : Tu es vraiment à la mode! Attention! Tu risques de perdre ton originalité.
5 - 9 points : Parfaitement raisonnable! Tu es à la mode tout en gardant ton propre style.
0 - 4 points : Tu ne t'intéresses pas à la mode! Tu sais, il y a quelquefois des styles uniques. Essaie de les trouver.

NE PRENDS PAS CE TEST TROP AU SERIEUX!

Communication for All Students

Challenge

26 Have students write a plus sign to indicate a compliment and a minus sign to indicate criticism. You might also ask them to write the key words that support their answers: **démodé(e), super chic, trop serré(e),** and so on.

Group Work

27 Have groups of three students act out the scene. One is trying on the clothes, the friend offers criticism, and the salesperson offers compliments and help finding different colors and sizes.

Troisième étape

CHAPITRE 10

Teacher Note

27 **Le Printemps** is a major French department store.

Teaching Suggestions

28 Before students complete the survey, have them guess what the following words mean from context: **la dernière mode** *(the latest fashion),* and **en solde** *(on sale).* You might also have them read the descriptions under **Réponses** in the right-hand column and try to guess which description fits them.

28 Have students hand in their results anonymously and have a few volunteers compile them to find out which styles are most common in the class.

Additional Practice

28 Have groups create their own three- or four-question fashion survey and administer it to the class.

Answers

27 Ce pantalon bleu est trop court. Cette chemise bleue est trop serrée. Ce pantalon noir est trop long. Ce pantalon rouge est trop large et trop long.

STANDARDS: 1.2, 3.1, 5.2

CHAPITRE 10

Motivating Activity
Ask students when they might compliment someone and what they would say. Ask how they respond to compliments. You might have two students role-play a scene in English in which one compliments an item of clothing and the other responds.

Presenting Rencontre culturelle
Have two students read each dialogue for the class. Then, ask students the first question in **Qu'en penses-tu?** Next, have partners act out one of the dialogues. You might have volunteers perform their dialogue for the class.

Additional Practice
Have partners pay each other compliments and respond in French.

Visual Learners
Have students draw their own scenes, illustrating a situation in which one person is paying a compliment and the other person is responding. Have them write the French dialogue in speech bubbles. This item would be appropriate for students' written portfolios.

Culture Note
In some countries in West Africa, it is wise to use caution when paying compliments. Normally, when someone compliments you on what you are wearing or on something you own, you are expected to offer it to that person. Likewise, when you compliment someone on something, he or she will often offer it to you, even if it is the last shirt a man owns or a woman's favorite earrings.

Read the following dialogues to find out how French people compliment one another.

—J'aime bien ta chemise.
—Ah oui?
—Oui, elle est pas mal.
—Tu trouves? Tu sais, c'est une vieille chemise.

—Il est super, ce chapeau!
—Tu crois?
—Oui, il te va très bien.
—C'est gentil.

—Tu es ravissante aujourd'hui!
—Vraiment? Je n'ai rien fait de spécial.

Qu'en penses-tu?
1. How do these people react to a compliment? They downplay the compliment.
2. How do you usually react to a compliment? How is that different from the French reactions you've just read?
Answers will vary; Americans often say thank you, while the French tend to downplay compliments.

Savais-tu que...?
The French do not compliment freely and generally do so only in exceptional cases. It is common to respond to compliments with **Merci.** However, French people will often respond with a modest expression of disbelief, such as **Vraiment? Tu crois? Tu trouves? Ah oui?** or a comment downplaying the importance of the item complimented, such as **Oh, c'est vieux.**

Connections and Comparisons

Thinking Critically
Analyzing Have students read **Savais-tu que... ?** and give possible reasons why the French don't pay compliments freely. Ask them how they think the French might view people from other cultures who pay compliments frequently and why.

Multicultural Link
You might have students interview people from different cultures or people who have studied other cultures to find out acceptable ways to pay and accept compliments in those cultures. Discuss their findings in class.

STANDARDS: 2.1, 3.2, 4.2

Fais des compliments!

Parlons Fais des compliments à un(e) camarade sur deux vêtements qu'il/elle porte. Il/Elle va te répondre à la française.

EXEMPLE —**Elles sont sensass, tes baskets!**
—**Vraiment?**
—**Oui, elles sont très à la mode!**

Grammaire

The direct object pronouns *le, la,* and *les*

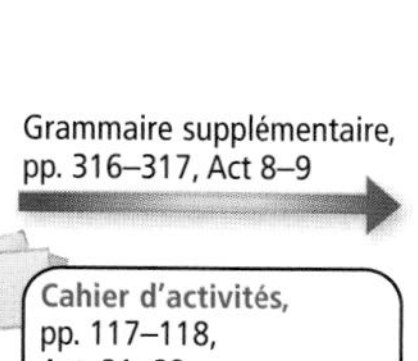

The pronouns **le,** *him* or *it,* **la,** *her* or *it,* and **les,** *them,* refer to people or things. In the sentences below, what do the pronouns **le, la,** and **les** refer to?*

— Ce pull, il te plaît? — Oui, je **le** trouve assez chic.
— Comment tu trouves cette robe? — Je **la** trouve démodée.
— Vous aimez ces chaussures? — Oui, je vais **les** prendre.

- You normally place the direct object pronouns before the conjugated verb.
  Je **le** prends. Je **l'**ai pris.
  Je ne **la** prends pas. Ne **les** prends pas!
- There are two exceptions to this rule. You place the direct object pronoun after the conjugated verb in a positive command and before an infinitive.
  Prends-**le!**
  Je vais **la** prendre.
- When **le** or **la** comes before a verb that starts with a vowel sound, it changes to **l'**.
  Je vais essayer **le pull.** Je vais **l'**essayer.

* the pullover, the dress, the shoes

Grammaire supplémentaire, pp. 316–317, Act 8–9

Cahier d'activités, pp. 117–118, Act. 21–22

Travaux pratiques de grammaire, pp. 86–87, Act. 16–17

Qu'en penses-tu?

Lisons/Ecrivons Elise et Karim font des courses. Complète leur conversation avec **le, la, l',** et **les.**

ELISE Dis, Karim, tu aimes ce pantalon, toi?
KARIM Bof... Je __1__ trouve un peu démodé, mais enfin... le
ELISE Et cette chemise-là?
KARIM Oui, je __2__ aime bien. Eh! Tu as vu ces chaussures? Elles sont super, non? l'
ELISE Oui! Tu vas __3__ prendre? les
KARIM Oh, je sais pas...
ELISE Si, allez! Prends- __4__! les
KARIM Bon. Je vais __5__ essayer. Et toi, essaie la chemise. Je __6__ trouve vraiment chouette. les, la
ELISE D'accord. Mmm... et ce pull violet, il est beau, non?
KARIM Oui, mais je __7__ préfère en bleu. le

Communication for All Students

Kinesthetic Learners

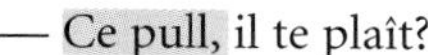

29 Have students bring in clothing items and arrange them around the classroom, simulating departments of a clothing store. Have students pair off and walk around the room to shop and compliment each other on the items they select.

Visual Learners

Have students work in pairs to write sentences complimenting their partner's clothing on strips of a transparency. Create a small strip of a transparency for each direct object pronoun. Have each student display the complete sentence on the overhead in the correct order. Have the class replace the object with the appropriate direct object pronoun and rearrange the sentence in the correct order.

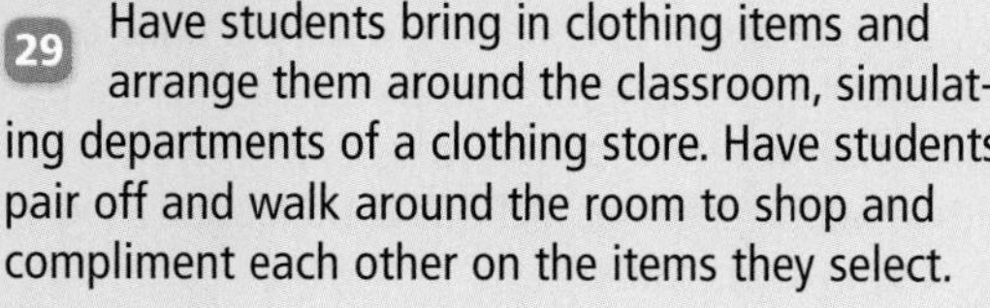

Portfolio

29 **Oral** This item is appropriate for students' oral portfolios. For portfolio suggestions, see *Alternative Assessment Guide,* pages iv–17.

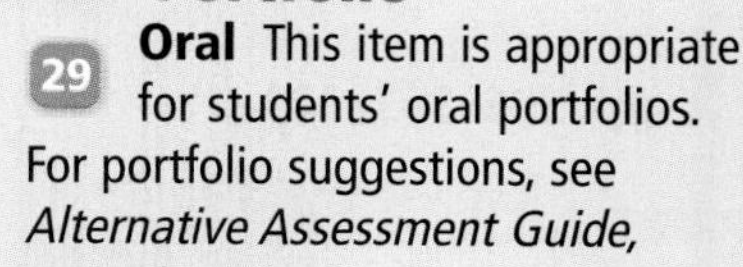

Presenting Grammaire

The direct object pronouns Bring to class the following items or pictures of them: a sweater, a dress, and a pair of shoes. Show each item, ask **Qu'est-ce que c'est?** and write the responses on the board. Then, ask the question **Ce pull (cette robe, ces chaussures), comment tu le (la, les) trouves?** as you hold up each item. Model the answers **Je le/la/les trouve...** Then, ask individual students how they like each item. Continue with additional items or illustrations. Read the grammar explanation. Then, pretend to be a salesperson and ask individuals **Tu prends ce pull (cette robe, ces chaussures)?** Have students answer **Oui, je le/la/les prends** or **Non,...**

Teacher Note

Students are not required to use the direct object pronouns with the past tense in this chapter. The agreement of the past participle with the direct object pronoun is presented in Level 2.

Teaching Resources
pp. 306–307, 309–311

PRINT 

- Lesson Planner, p. 51
- TPR Storytelling Book, pp. 39, 40
- Listening Activities, pp. 76–77, 81
- Activities for Communication, pp. 59–60, 122, 124, 155–156
- Travaux pratiques de grammaire, pp. 85–87
- Grammar Tutor for Students of French, Chapter 10
- Cahier d'activités, pp. 116–118
- Testing Program, pp. 257–260
- Alternative Assessment Guide, p. 41
- Student Make-Up Assignments, Chapter 10

MEDIA 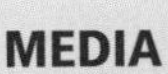 

- One-Stop Planner
- Audio Compact Discs, CD 10, Trs. 11–12, 22, 30–31
- Teaching Transparencies: 10-3; **Grammaire supplémentaire** Answers; Travaux pratiques de grammaire Answers
- Interactive CD-ROM Tutor, Disc 3

Presenting
Comment dit-on... ?

Write the expressions for *hesitating* and *making a decision* on a transparency. Then, hold up various clothing items or pictures of them. Give a price for each and ask students **Vous le/la/les prenez?** Make some prices outrageously high (300 € for a pair of socks) and some unbelievably low (2 € for a dress).

Additional Practice

31 Type the listening script with some of the words deleted. Make copies and have partners fill in the blanks.

Comment dit-on...?

Hesitating; making a decision

When the salesperson asks you:

Vous avez choisi?
Vous avez décidé de prendre ce pantalon?
Have you decided to take . . . ?
Vous le/la/les prenez?
Are you going to take it/them?

To hesitate, say:

Je ne sais pas.
Euh... J'hésite.
Oh, I'm not sure.
Il/Elle me plaît, mais il/elle est cher/chère.
I like it, but it's expensive.

To make a decision, say:

Je le/la/les prends.
I'll take it/them.
C'est trop cher.
It's too expensive.

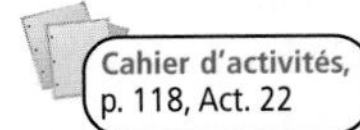
Cahier d'activités, p. 118, Act. 22

Note de grammaire

- Use **il/elle/ils/elles** when you are referring to a specific item.
  Comment tu trouves cette robe?
  Elle est chouette, non?
- Use **c'est** when you are speaking in general about an action or something that happened.
  J'aime porter des pantalons parce que **c'est** pratique.
  J'ai réussi à mon examen de maths! **C'est** super!

In the sentences above, **c'est** refers to the general ideas of wearing pants and passing a test.

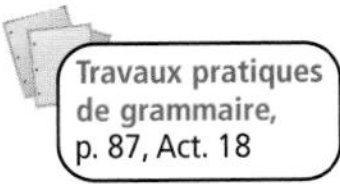
Travaux pratiques de grammaire, p. 87, Act. 18

Grammaire supplémentaire, p. 317, Act. 10

Cahier d'activités, p. 118, Act. 23

31 Oui ou non? See scripts and answers on p. 291H.

CD 10 Tr. 12

Ecoutons Listen to these exchanges between a customer and a salesperson. Tell whether the customer takes the item, doesn't take it, or can't decide.

32 Qu'est-ce qu'ils disent?

Ecrivons/Parlons Ecris ce que tu crois que ces personnes disent. Ensuite, compare tes réponses avec les réponses d'un(e) camarade.

1.

2.

3.

4.

Communication for All Students

Kinesthetic Learners

32 Have partners act out their conversation and ask students to guess which illustration they're dramatizing.

Auditory Learners

32 Collect the conversations students wrote and read one scene aloud. Have students write the number of the corresponding illustration.

Visual Learners

Write **Je le/la/les prends** or **C'est trop cher** on cards for each student. Then, give a card and a picture of an item of clothing to pairs of students. Have them create and act out the dialogues suggested by their cards.

STANDARDS: 1.1, 1.3, 5.1

Parlons Tu travailles au rayon vêtements du grand magasin Le Printemps, à Paris. Un client/Une cliente veut acheter des vêtements pour aller à un mariage. Il/elle hésite, alors tu vas l'aider à trouver quelque chose et lui donner des conseils.

PRONONCIATION

CD 10 Trs. 13–18

The glides [j], [w], and [ɥ]

See scripts and answers on p. 291H.

As you listen to people speak French, you may notice a sound that reminds you of the first sound in the English word *yes.* This sound is called a *glide,* because one sound glides into another. Now, try making the sound [j] in these common French words: **mieux, chemisier, bien.** Did you notice that this gliding sound often occurs when the letter **i** is followed by **e?** The sound is also represented by the letters **ill** in words such as **maillot** and **gentille.**

There are two more glides in French. [w] sounds similar to the *w* sound you hear in *west wind.* Listen to these French words: **moi, Louis, jouer.**

The last glide sound is the one you hear in the French word **lui.** It sounds like the French vowel sounds [y] and [i] together. This sound is often written as **ui.** Listen to the glide [ɥ] in these words: **cuir, huit, juillet.**

A. A prononcer

Repeat the following words.

1. travailler	monsieur	combien	conseiller
2. pouvoir	soif	poires	moins
3. suis	minuit	suite	juillet

B. A lire

Take turns with a partner reading each of the following sentences aloud.

1. J'aime bien tes boucles d'oreilles. Elles sont géniales!
2. Il me faut des feuilles de papier, un taille-crayon et un cahier.
3. Elle a choisi un blouson en cuir et une écharpe en soie. C'est chouette!
4. Tu as quoi aujourd'hui? Moi, j'ai histoire et ensuite, je vais faire mes devoirs.
5. —Tu veux promener le chien avec moi?
—Pourquoi pas?

C. A écrire

You're going to hear a short dialogue. Write down what you hear.

Communication for All Students

Slower Pace

Have students begin by breaking the sentences in Part B into three- or four-word phrases, and work up to saying entire sentences.

Visual Learners

Show *Teaching Transparency 10-3* and have students suggest what the customers and salespeople might be saying. You might have partners write a brief dialogue between a customer and a salesperson.

Language Note

Prononciation Make sure students don't split the glides into two separate syllables.

Additional Practice

Note de grammaire Write the following sentences on the board or on a transparency and have students complete them:

___ est trop serrée, cette robe. On n'a pas école demain. ___ est génial! Tu aimes ce pantalon? ___ est chic, n'est-ce pas? J'aime parler au téléphone parce que ___ est agréable.

Portfolio

33 **Oral** This activity is appropriate for students' oral portfolios. For portfolio suggestions, see the *Alternative Assessment Guide,* pages iv–17.

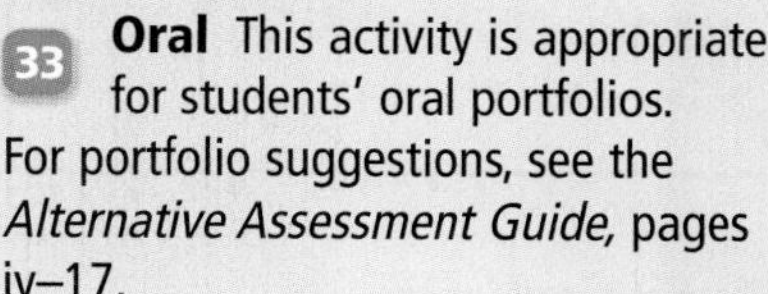

Assess

- Testing Program, pp. 257–260 Quiz 10-3A, Quiz 10-3B, Audio CD 10, Tr. 22
- Student Make-Up Assignments, Chapter 10, Alternative Quiz
- Alternative Assessment Guide, p. 41

STANDARDS: 4.1

Lisons!

CHAPITRE 10

Teaching Resources
pp. 312–313

PRINT 
- Lesson Planner, p. 52
- Cahier d'activités, p. 119
- Reading Strategies and Skills Handbook, Chapter 10
- Joie de lire 1, Chapter 10
- Standardized Assessment Tutor, Chapter 10

MEDIA
- One-Stop Planner

Prereading
Activities A–C

Thinking Critically
Evaluating Ask students why they think fashion is important to some people and not to others. Have them look at the photos and tell what they can guess about the personalities of these people based on their clothing.

Teaching Suggestion
A., B. Have students answer the questions in these activities in small groups.

Using Graphic Organizers
B. Provide large sheets of paper and have students draw the styles pictured and write their opinions of them.

Reading
Activities D–H

Monitoring Comprehension
D. Have students suggest words or phrases in French that teenagers might say if they consider fashion important and if they consider it unimportant. **(C'est cool; C'est nul.)**

Lisons!

LA MODE AU LYCÉE

Stratégie pour lire
When you read, be careful to separate facts from opinions. A fact is something that can be proven by observation or specific information. Le jean est rouge is a fact that you could prove by looking at the jeans to see if they're red or not. An opinion is someone's personal view of something. La mode, c'est important is an opinion. While some people may believe that to be true, it cannot be proven.

A. Think for a moment about the role fashion plays in your life.
1. Do you follow trends you see in magazines or at school?
2. How much influence do your parents have on your wardrobe?
3. Do you think clothing is a reflection of a person's personality or lifestyle?

B. How would you categorize styles that are popular at your school or in your town? What words would you use to describe them?

C. What can you tell about the people who wrote these essays? Answers will vary.

D. Which of the students consider fashion important? Which consider it unimportant? Answers will vary.

LA MODE AU LYCÉE

Mélanie
• 15 ans. En seconde au lycée Théodore Aubanel, Avignon.

Ce que je trouve dommage aujourd'hui, c'est que les filles ressemblent de plus en plus à des garçons. Au lycée, presque toutes mes copines portent des jeans ou des pantalons avec des sweat-shirts. Moi aussi, j'aime bien les jeans, mais de temps en temps, je préfère m'habiller «en fille» avec des robes ou des jupes. Je porte aussi beaucoup de bijoux, surtout des boucles d'oreilles; j'adore ça. Et puis en même temps, ça fait plaisir à mes parents quand je suis habillée comme ça; ils préfèrent ça au look garçon manqué.

Christophe
• 17 ans. En terminale au lycée Henri IV, Paris.

Moi, ce qui m'énerve avec la mode, c'est que si tu ne la suis pas, tout le monde te regarde d'un air bizarre au lycée. Moi, par exemple, le retour de la mode des années 70, les pattes d'eph et le look grunge, c'est vraiment pas mon truc. Je trouve ça horrible. Alors, je ne vois pas pourquoi je devrais m'habiller comme ça, simplement parce que c'est la mode. Je préfère porter des pantalons à pinces, des blazers et des chemises avec des cravates. Mes copains trouvent que ça fait trop sérieux, trop fils-à-papa, mais ça m'est égal. Je suis sûr que dans quelques années, quand ils travailleront, ils seront tous habillés comme moi et quand ils regarderont des photos de terminale, ils rigoleront bien en voyant les habits qu'ils portaient à 18 ans!

Connections and Comparisons

Thinking Critically
Comparing and Contrasting Have students compare present styles with those of the past and discuss the differences.

Thinking Critically
Analyzing Have students discuss their reactions to the reading. Would these teenagers fit in at their school? Why or why not? Do students agree or disagree with the attitudes expressed in the interviews?

STANDARDS: 1.2, 2.1, 3.1, 4.1, 4.2

Serge

• 16 ans. En première au lycée Ampère de Lyon.

Pour moi, ce qui est vraiment important, c'est d'avoir des vêtements confortables. Je suis très sportif et j'aime pouvoir bouger dans mes habits. Mais, je veux aussi des trucs cool. Pas question de porter des vêtements très serrés ou très chers, par exemple. Je ne vois pas l'intérêt d'avoir un blouson qui coûte 610 €. Je préfère un blouson bon marché dans lequel je peux jouer au foot avec les copains. Comme ça, si je tombe ou si je l'abîme, c'est pas tragique. En général, je mets des jeans parce que c'est pratique et sympa. En été, je porte des tee-shirts très simples et en hiver, des sweat-shirts. Et comme chaussures, je préfère les baskets.

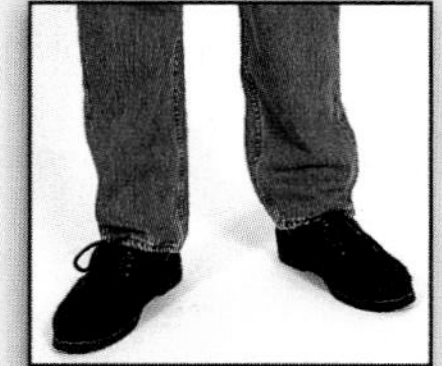

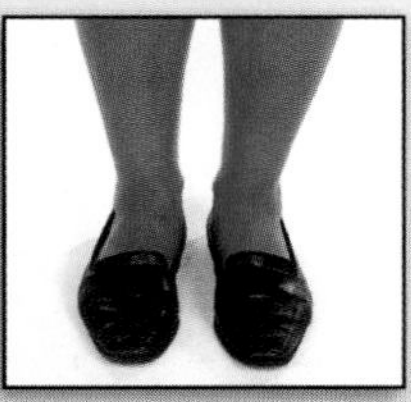

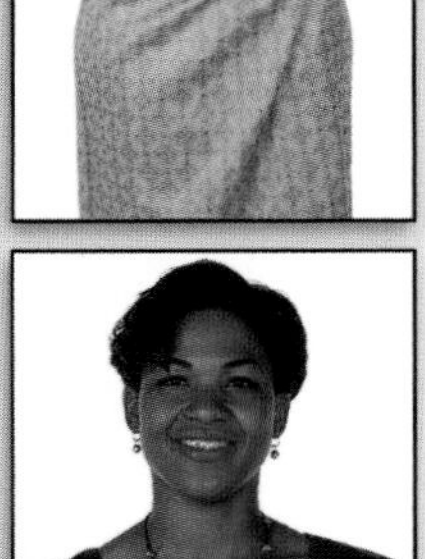

Emmanuelle

• 17 ans et demi. Lycée Mas de Tesse, Montpellier.

Pour moi, la façon dont quelqu'un s'habille est un reflet de sa personnalité. Au lycée, j'étudie les arts plastiques, et comme on le dit souvent, les artistes sont des gens originaux et créatifs. Je n'aime pas dépenser beaucoup pour mes vêtements. Je n'achète jamais de choses très chères, mais j'utilise mon imagination pour les rendre plus originales. Par exemple, j'ajoute toujours des accessoires sympas : bijoux fantaisie que je fabrique souvent moi-même, foulards, ceintures, sacs... Parfois, je fais même certains de mes vêtements, surtout les jupes car c'est facile. Et comme ça, je suis sûre que personne ne portera la même chose que moi!

E. Although many people consider France a fashion capital, the U.S. also influences fashion. What English words can you find in the essays? See answers below.

F. Look for the words in the box below in the essays. Then, try to match them with their English equivalents.

1. bijoux d	**a.** fashion
2. la mode a	**b.** things
3. pattes d'eph f	**c.** ruin
4. bouger e	**d.** jewelry
5. abîme c	**e.** to move
6. les trucs b	**f.** bell-bottoms

G. Which student . . .

1. likes clothes that are practical and comfortable? Serge
2. makes some of his or her clothing and jewelry? Emmanuelle
3. doesn't buy expensive clothes? Serge, Emmanuelle
4. thinks girls should wear feminine clothes sometimes? Mélanie

H. Which of the following sentences are facts and which are opinions?

1. En été, je porte des tee-shirts. fact
2. Les artistes sont des gens originaux et créatifs. opinion
3. Les filles ressemblent de plus en plus à des garçons. opinion
4. Je n'achète jamais de choses très chères. fact
5. La façon dont on s'habille est un reflet de sa personnalité. opinion

I. Write a short paragraph in French telling what you like to wear. Mention colors and any other details you feel are important.

Cahier d'activités, p. 119, Act. 25

Lisons!

CHAPITRE 10

Terms in Lisons!

Some useful expressions that you might write on the board or on a transparency are **ce qui m'énerve** *(what annoys me);* **fabriquer** *(to make);* **un foulard** (*a decorative scarf*).

Thinking Critically

Evaluating Have students give their reactions to each of the statements in Activity H. If they disagree, have them tell why.

Postreading

Activity I

Portfolio

I. Written Students may want to add a drawing of themselves to illustrate their paragraphs. Have them use pictures from magazines to make a collage that illustrates their sense of fashion. This activity is appropriate for students' written portfolios. For portfolio information, see *Alternative Assessment Guide,* pages iv–17.

Communication for All Students

Additional Practice

H. Have students write two sentences, one fact and one opinion. You might have them form groups to compile their statements and determine whether they are labeled accurately. Then, have the groups turn in their statements.

Game

C'est qui? In small groups, one student names an item worn by one of the teenagers or quotes from one of the essays. The other students try to identify the teenager. The student who guesses correctly takes the next turn.

Answers

E. jeans, sweat-shirts, look grunge, blazers, cool, tee-shirts, baskets

STANDARDS: 1.2, 1.3, 2.1, 3.1, 3.2, 4.1

Grammaire supplémentaire

CHAPITRE 10

For **Grammaire supplémentaire** Answer Transparencies, see the *Teaching Transparencies* binder.

Grammaire supplémentaire

Première étape

Objective Asking for and giving advice

1 Complète les phrases suivantes avec le présent du verbe **mettre.** (**p. 299**)

1. Qu'est-ce que je __ E __ __ pour la boum de Charles?
2. Pourquoi tu ne M __ T __ pas ta robe blanche?
3. Odile et Béatrice __ __ T __ E __ __ souvent des robes à fleurs.
4. Boris et moi, nous __ E __ __ __ N __ des lunettes de soleil pour aller à des boums.
5. Vous __ __ T __ E __ des lunettes de soleil quand il pleut comme ça?
6. Oui, on __ E __ toujours des lunettes de soleil et des baskets.

2 Complète les phrases suivantes avec le sujet approprié. (**p. 299**)

je/j'	vous	nous
Sylvie	mes parents	Jeannette

1. ______ a mis une robe rouge pour aller à l'opéra.
2. ______ portent toujours des jeans le week-end.
3. Pour aller nager, ______ met son maillot de bain rose et blanc.
4. A la plage, ______ portons toujours des lunettes de soleil.
5. ______ mettez des bottes quand il pleut?
6. Il faisait froid hier, alors ______ ai mis mon cardigan noir pour aller à l'école.

3 Marie-France demande à Patricia ce qu'elle devrait porter pour aller au théâtre. Complète leur conversation avec la forme correcte des verbes entre parenthèses. N'oublie pas d'utiliser le **passé composé** quand c'est nécessaire. (**p. 299**)

MARIE-FRANCE Je ne sais pas quoi __1__ (mettre) pour aller au théâtre.
PATRICIA __2__ (mettre) ta jupe noire avec ton chemisier blanc.
MARIE-FRANCE Non, ce n'est pas très chic. Et j' __3__ (déjà mettre) mon chemisier blanc avec ma veste cette semaine.
PATRICIA Pourquoi tu ne __4__ (mettre) pas ton chemisier bleu avec une écharpe alors?
MARIE-FRANCE Non, j' __5__ (déjà porter) mon écharpe à la boum de Jean-Marc.
PATRICIA __6__ (mettre) ta robe noire.
MARIE-FRANCE Bonne idée. Et je vais __7__ (mettre) aussi mes chaussures noires. Enfin, c'est décidé.

Answers

1
1. M T S
2. E S
3. M E T N T
4. M T T O S
5. M E T Z
6. M T

2
1. Jeannette
2. Mes parents
3. Sylvie
4. nous
5. Vous
6. j'

3
1. mettre
2. Mets
3. ai déjà mis
4. mets
5. ai déjà porté
6. Mets
7. mettre

Grammar Resources for Chapter 10

The **Grammaire supplémentaire** activities were designed as supplemental activities for the grammatical concepts presented in the chapter. You might use them as additional practice, for review, or for assessment.

For more grammar presentations, review, and practice, refer to the following:
- Travaux pratiques de grammaire
- Grammar Tutor for Students of French
- Grammar Summary on pp. R15–R28
- Cahier d'activités
- Grammar and Vocabulary quizzes (Testing Program)
- Test Generator
- Interactive CD-ROM Tutor
- **Jeux interactifs** at go.hrw.com

STANDARDS: 1.2

 Objectives Expressing need; inquiring

4 Nadia demande à Clara ce qu'elle devrait mettre pour aller à la boum de Raphaël. Utilise le verbe **mettre** à l'impératif et la forme correcte de l'adjectif entre parenthèses. (**pp. 299, 301**)

Exemple NADIA Je mets ma robe violette? (gris)
CLARA Je la trouve trop serrée. **Mets la grise!**

1. NADIA Je mets mes sandales jaunes? (blanc)
   CLARA Je les trouve un peu démodées. _____
2. NADIA Je mets mon cardigan orange? (noir)
   CLARA C'est pas ton style. _____
3. NADIA Je mets mon écharpe rouge? (rose)
   CLARA Elle ne te va pas. _____
4. NADIA Je mets ma ceinture verte? (bleu)
   CLARA Elle ne va pas avec ta robe. _____
5. NADIA Je mets mes boucles d'oreilles marron? (vert)
   CLARA Je les trouve trop grosses. _____

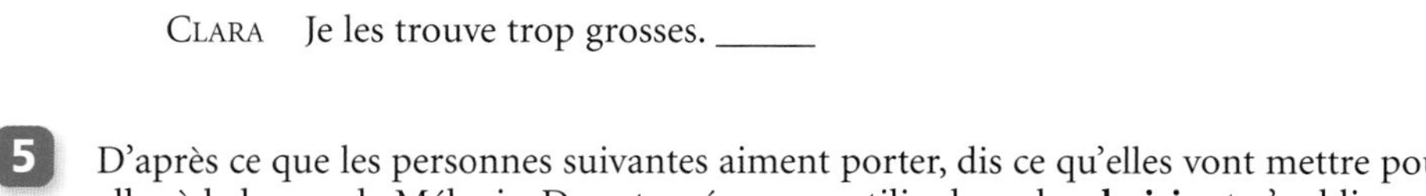

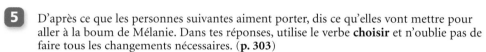

5 D'après ce que les personnes suivantes aiment porter, dis ce qu'elles vont mettre pour aller à la boum de Mélanie. Dans tes réponses, utilise le verbe **choisir** et n'oublie pas de faire tous les changements nécessaires. (**p. 303**)

Exemple Suzanne aime les jupes courtes. **Elle choisit une jupe courte.**

1. Pierre et Philippe aiment bien les cravates à pois.
2. Armelle adore les robes rétro.
3. Moi, j'aime les boucles d'oreilles noires.
4. Tu préfères les chemisiers à fleurs.
5. Elsa et toi, vous aimez bien les chaussures en cuir.
6. Toi et moi, nous adorons les blousons en jean.

6 Ecris des phrases complètes avec les mots suivants. N'oublie pas de mettre les verbes au présent et de faire tous les changements nécessaires. (**p. 303**)

1. vous/ne/pas/grossir/parce que/vous/faire du sport
2. on/grandir/si/on/manger/assez
3. tu/maigrir/parce que/tu/jouer au foot/tous les jours
4. nous/grossir/facilement/si/nous/ne/pas/faire du jogging
5. je/grossir/parce que/je/manger/beaucoup de gâteaux
6. mes petites sœurs/grandir/tous les jours
7. il/maigrir/si/il/ne/pas/manger/trois fois par jour
8. vous/grandir/quand/vous/manger vos légumes
9. ma sœur/maigrir/facilement/quand/elle/faire de l'aérobic
10. tu/manger/beaucoup/mais/tu/ne/jamais/grossir

Communication for All Students

Slower Pace

4 Before students complete Activity 4, have them circle the object of the first sentence and label it singular or plural and masculine or feminine.

Challenge

4 Have students work in pairs to use this activity as a model to create their own activity. Have them change the clothes and colors. Partners might exchange their activity with another pair of students. You might also have volunteers perform their conversations in front of the class.

Answers

4
1. Mets les blanches!
2. Mets le noir!
3. Mets la rose!
4. Mets la bleue!
5. Mets les vertes!

5
1. Ils choisissent des cravates à pois.
2. Elle choisit une robe rétro.
3. Je choisis des boucles d'oreilles noires.
4. Tu choisis un chemisier à fleurs.
5. Vous choisissez des chaussures en cuir.
6. Nous choisissons des blousons en jean.

6
1. Vous ne grossissez pas parce que vous faites du sport.
2. On grandit si on mange assez.
3. Tu maigris parce que tu joues au foot tous les jours.
4. Nous grossissons facilement si nous ne faisons pas de jogging.
5. Je grossis parce que je mange beaucoup de gâteaux.
6. Mes petites sœurs grandissent tous les jours.
7. Il maigrit s'il ne mange pas trois fois par jour.
8. Vous grandissez quand vous mangez vos légumes.
9. Ma sœur maigrit facilement quand elle fait de l'aérobic.
10. Tu manges beaucoup mais tu ne grossis jamais.

STANDARDS: 1.2

Grammaire supplémentaire

CHAPITRE 10

For **Grammaire supplémentaire** Answer Transparencies, see the *Teaching Transparencies* binder.

Grammaire supplémentaire

WA3 ARLES-10

7 Dis pourquoi les personnes suivantes ne peuvent plus mettre leurs vêtements. Utilise le **passé composé** des verbes entre parenthèses. (**p. 303**)

EXEMPLE Armelle, ce cardigan ne te va plus. (grandir) **J'ai grandi.**

1. Sophie, ce pantalon ne te va plus. (maigrir)
2. Pierre et Jean, ces chemises ne vous vont plus. (grandir)
3. Valentine, cette robe ne te va plus. (grossir)
4. Ce pantalon ne me va plus. (grandir)
5. Ahmed et Karim, ces vestes ne vous vont plus. (maigrir)
6. Dis donc, ce blouson ne me va plus. (grossir)

Troisième étape

Objectives Asking for an opinion; paying a compliment; criticizing; hesitating; making a decision

8 Tu fais les magasins avec une amie et elle te demande ton avis sur les vêtements qu'elle voudrait acheter. Dans tes réponses, utilise **le, la, les** et **l'**. (**p. 309**)

1. Est-ce que tu aimes cette robe?
2. Comment tu trouves ce pantalon?
3. Je veux acheter cette veste, mais j'hésite.
4. J'aime bien cette veste, mais elle est chère et un peu grande.
5. Qu'est-ce que tu penses de ces chaussures?

Answers

7
1. J'ai maigri.
2. Nous avons grandi.
3. J'ai grossi.
4. Tu as grandi.
5. Nous avons maigri.
6. Tu as grossi.

8 *Answers may vary.*
1. Oui, je l'aime bien.
2. Je le trouve démodé.
3. Prends-la.
4. Ne la prends pas.
5. Je les trouve chic!

Teacher to Teacher

Paula Bernard
Sandy Creek High School
Fayette County, GA

Review both vocabulary and verb forms with Paula's activity.

"This is a pair activity. On a sheet of paper, write as many of the chapter vocabulary words and conjugated forms of the new verbs **porter, mettre, choisir, grandir** and **maigrir** in French as will fit. Include at least a few different conjugated forms of each verb. Make copies of the sheet—one for each pair of students. Each student has a different color pen, with which he or she writes his or her name. I call out words in English (for the verbs, I call out the subject pronoun also). The student in each pair who circles the most correct words first, wins a prize or extra points."

STANDARDS: 1.2

9 Anne est dans un magasin de vêtements. Complète la conversation qu'elle a avec le vendeur. Utilise le pronom approprié **le, la, les** ou **l'** dans tes réponses. (**p. 309**)

EXEMPLE
ANNE Ces bottes vont très bien avec mon manteau. **Je peux les essayer?**
VENDEUR Elles vous vont très bien, mademoiselle! **Vous les prenez?**
ANNE Oui. **Je les prends.**

1. ANNE Ce blouson va très bien avec mon pantalon noir. _____?
VENDEUR Il vous va très bien, mademoiselle. _____?
ANNE Oui. _____.
2. ANNE Ces sandales vont très bien avec ma jupe en jean. _____?
VENDEUR Elles vous vont très bien, mademoiselle. _____?
ANNE Euh... J'hésite... Non. _____. Elles sont trop chères.
3. ANNE Cette robe va très bien avec mes chaussures. _____?
VENDEUR Elle vous va très bien, mademoiselle. _____?
ANNE Elle me plaît beaucoup. Oui. _____.
4. ANNE Ces lunettes de soleil vont très bien avec mon maillot de bain. _____?
VENDEUR Elles vous vont très bien, mademoiselle. _____?
ANNE Elles sont super cool. Oui. _____.

10 Complète les phrases suivantes avec **il est, elle est** ou **c'est.** (**p. 310**)

1. Comment tu trouves ce chapeau? _____ sensass, non?
2. Moi, j'aime beaucoup porter un chapeau parce que _____ sympa.
3. Cédric porte souvent une casquette. _____ en cuir, sa casquette. Très chic!
4. Tu aimes les choses en cuir, toi? Moi, non. Je préfère le jean. _____ plus pratique!
5. Tu dis? Ah, oui. J'adore le look rétro. _____ chouette, le rétro!
6. Moi, j'ai une chemise rétro! _____ super cool!
7. Je vais essayer le pull vert, mais je pense que/qu' _____ trop grand.
8. J'aime porter des jeans et des tee-shirts parce que _____ toujours à la mode.

Qu'est-ce que tu penses de mon nouveau look?

Grammaire supplémentaire

CHAPITRE 10

Answers

9
1. Je peux l'essayer? Vous le prenez? Je le prends.
2. Je peux les essayer? Vous les prenez? Je ne les prends pas.
3. Je peux l'essayer? Vous la prenez? Je la prends.
4. Je peux les essayer. Vous les prenez? Je les prends.

10
1. Il est
2. c'est
3. Elle est
4. C'est
5. C'est
6. Elle est
7. il est
8. c'est

Review and Assess

You may wish to assign the **Grammaire supplémentaire** activities as additional practice or homework after presenting material throughout the chapter. Assign Activities 1–3 after **Grammaire** (p. 299), Activity 4 after **Note de grammaire** (p. 301), Activities 5–7 after **Grammaire** (p. 303), Activities 8–9 after **Grammaire** (p. 309), and Activity 10 after **Note de grammaire** (p. 310).

To prepare students for the **Etape** Quizzes and Chapter Test, we suggest doing the **Grammaire supplémentaire** activities in the following order. Have students complete Activities 1–3 before taking Quizzes 10-1A or 10-1B; Activities 4–7 before Quizzes 10-2A or 10-2B; and Activities 8–10 before Quizzes 10-3A or 10-3B.

STANDARDS: 1.2

Mise en pratique

CHAPITRE 10

The **Mise en pratique** reviews and integrates all four skills and culture in preparation for the Chapter Test.

Teaching Resources
pp. 318–319

PRINT

- Lesson Planner, p. 52
- Listening Activities, p. 77
- Video Guide, pp. 69, 72
- Grammar Tutor for Students of French, Chapter 10
- Standardized Assessment Tutor, Chapter 10

MEDIA 

- One-Stop Planner
- Video Program, Videocassette 4, 12:57–14:16
- DVD Tutor, Disc 2
- Audio Compact Discs, CD 10, Tr. 19
- Interactive CD-ROM Tutor, Disc 3

Challenge

2 Have students create an ad for an article of clothing they're wearing or for a favorite article of clothing, using this ad as a model.

Mise en pratique

CD-ROM 3
DVD 2

Visit Holt Online
go.hrw.com
KEYWORD: WA3 ARLES-10
Self-Test

1 Listen to this conversation between Philippe and a saleswoman at a French department store. Then, answer these questions. See scripts and answers on p. 291H.

CD 10 Tr. 19

1. What does Philippe want to buy?
2. What colors does he prefer?
3. What does the salesperson say about the first item Philippe tries on?
4. How does Philippe feel about the way the item fits?
5. Does he end up buying it?

2 Look over the advertisement below. Then, answer the questions that follow.

NOUVELLE COLLECTION ARIELLE DE LA BRETTINIERE

FEMME : Pantalon à pinces uni, 100 % soie. Du 36 au 44, **60€**. Existe en vert, bleu, rouge, blanc et noir. **Cardigan** en coton, taille unique, **45,50€**. Existe en noir et blanc cassé. **Tee-shirt** cache-cœur noir, manches courtes, **19,50€**. **Boucles d'oreilles** et **bracelet** fantaisie, **6,80€** et **9,90€**. **ENFANT : Robe** bleu clair à fleurs multicolores, 100 % coton. De 2 à 8 ans, **12€**. **Tee-shirt** uni rose, 100 % coton, **4,40€**. De 2 à 8 ans. Existe en 17 coloris. **Sandales** en cuir blanc, **18,10€**. Du 24 au 34. **HOMME : Pantalon** à pinces, 100 % lin. Du 38 au 52, **66,90€**. Existe en noir, bleu marine, beige et marron. **Chemise** en jean, manches longues. Du 2 au 6, **39,40€**. **Pull** rouge, 100 % coton. Du 2 au 6, **45,50€**.

VENDUE DANS LES GRANDS MAGASINS

1. Who does **Arielle de la Brettinière** make clothes for? men, women, and children
2. How many colors does the child's T-shirt come in? 17
3. The women's pants are available in what sizes? 36 to 44
4. What material is the men's shirt made of? denim
5. What's the most expensive men's item on the page? The most expensive women's item? *Most expensive:* men's pants, 66,90€; women's pants, 60€

3 From what you know about French culture, are these statements true or false?

1. The French are famous for giving lots of compliments. false
2. The French tend to downplay the compliments they receive. true
3. **Merci** is the only appropriate response to a compliment. false
4. A common French way to respond to a compliment on something you're wearing is to say **Tu trouves?** true

Apply and Assess

Slower Pace

1 Tell students to read the questions before they listen to the recording. Encourage them to listen to the entire conversation before they write their answers. Then, play the recording again so students can check their work or complete the activity.

Additional Practice

2 Have students give the price and color of each clothing item in the ad. You might assign each item to a group of students. Have them note the sizes and colors it is available in, the price, and the fabric. Since most of the colors in the ad are cognates, encourage students to guess what the colors might be.

STANDARDS: 1.2, 3.1

4 

Ecrivons!

You've been hired by a French magazine to write about fashion trends among American teenagers today. Interview two or three classmates about their tastes in clothing. Then, write a short article in French based on your interviews.

Prewriting

First, brainstorm a list of interview questions that you might ask your classmates about their fashion preferences. You might ask what they like to wear, what they wear to parties **(les boums)**, what colors they like, and what their favorite article of clothing is. Arrange your questions in a logical order. You may want to arrange them so that you begin with more general questions and progress to more specific ones.

Next, conduct your interview with two or three classmates. Be sure to take notes on their responses to each of your questions.

Before you begin your article, rearrange the information you've collected into a logical order. For example, you might group different answers to each question together.

Stratégie pour écrire

Paraphrasing is a useful tool for organizing and simplifying information for your readers. To paraphrase a quote or other piece of information you collect, you state the main points in your own words. At the same time, be sure you don't change the meaning of what was said.

Writing

Expository writing is a process of converting information you've collected into a readable or easily understandable form. Newspaper and magazine articles are good examples of expository writing. Reporters collect information on newsworthy events, fashion trends, etc., and then take that information and turn it into articles that readers can easily understand.

Now, referring to the information you've collected and organized, write a short article that reveals what you found out. It's not necessary to include every detail of the information you collect. For example, if a quote from your interview is too long, you may paraphrase the main points of the quote in your own words.

Revising

Peer evaluation is another helpful step in the evaluation process. Give your article to a classmate and have him or her give you suggestions on how to improve it. After your classmate evaluates your article, make any revisions you feel are necessary, including those you find in proofreading. Now you're ready to submit your finished article.

5 

Jeu de rôle

Choose one of the items from the advertisement on page 318 and ask the salesperson about it. Do they have it in your size? Can you try it on? The salesperson should compliment the way it looks, and you should decide whether to buy it or not. Take turns playing the role of the salesperson.

Mise en pratique

CHAPITRE 10

Additional Practice

You may also want to have students paraphrase the three interviews from the **Panorama Culturel** on page 305.

Writing Assessment

4 You might use the following rubric when grading your students on this activity.

Writing Rubric	Points			
	4	3	2	1
Content (Complete–Incomplete)				
Comprehensibility (Comprehensible–Incomprehensible)				
Accuracy (Accurate–Seldom accurate)				
Organization (Well organized–Poorly organized)				
Effort (Excellent–Minimal)				

18–20: A 14–15: C Under
16–17: B 12–13: D 12: F

Apply and Assess

Process Writing

4 Give students the following quotes and have them paraphrase them.

a. "I like to wear skirts and shorts to parties, well, sometimes dresses too. It just depends on the party. Also, I like to wear shorts in the winter sometimes and always in the summer, and on the weekends, I really love to wear them. I love to wear shorts at school too. I like black and red ones the best."

b. "I really don't care what I wear most of the time. I just wear warm clothes in winter and cool clothes in summer, and in the other seasons, it just depends on weather. I just go day by day, you know. And I don't like to shop at the mall, either. I let my mom do it for me."

Que sais-je?

CHAPITRE 10

Teaching Resources
p. 320

PRINT 
- Grammar Tutor for Students of French, Chapter 10

MEDIA  
- Interactive CD-ROM Tutor, Disc 3
- Online self-test

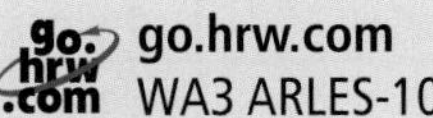
go.hrw.com
WA3 ARLES-10

Teacher Note
This page is intended to help students prepare for the test. It is a brief checklist of the major points covered in the chapter. The students should be reminded that this is only a checklist and does not necessarily include everything that will appear on the test.

Answers

2
1. Pourquoi est-ce que tu ne mets pas ton pantalon noir? Mets ton pantalon noir.
2. Pourquoi est-ce que tu ne mets pas ton pull? Mets ton pull.

5
1. Charles choisit une veste bleue et verte.
2. Jean-Marc et Farid choisissent un manteau en cuir bleu.
3. Astrid choisit des chaussures en cuir.
4. Delphine et Camille choisissent des chaussettes blanches.

7 *Possible answers:*
Complimenting: C'est tout à fait ton style. Il/Elle te va très bien. Il/Elle va très bien avec ... ; Je le/la/les trouve chic/à la mode/ mignon(ne)(s)/ sensass. C'est parfait.
Criticizing: Il/Elle ne te va pas du tout. Il/Elle ne va pas du tout avec ... ; Il/Elle est (Ils/Elles sont) trop serré(e)(s)/large(s)/petit(e)(s)/grand (e)(s)/court(e)(s). Je le/la/les trouve moche(s)/démodé(e)(s)/horrible(s).

Que sais-je?

WA3 ARLES-10

Can you use what you've learned in this chapter?

Can you ask for and give advice? p. 300

1 How would you ask a friend what you should wear to a party?
Qu'est-ce que je mets pour aller à la boum?

2 How would you advise a friend to wear these clothes, using the verb **mettre?**
See answers below.

1.

2.

Can you express need and inquire? p. 301

3 How would you tell a salesperson . . .
1. that you're just looking? Je regarde.
2. what you would like? J'aimerais... ; Je cherche...

4 How would you ask a salesperson . . . 1. Je peux l'/les essayer? Je peux essayer le/la/les... ?
1. if you can try something on?
2. if they have what you want in a different size? Vous avez ça en... (36)?
3. if they have what you want in a particular color? Vous avez ça en... (rouge)?
4. how much something costs? C'est combien? Ça fait combien?

5 How would you tell what these people are choosing?

Charles

Jean-Marc et Farid

Astrid

Delphine et Camille

Can you ask for an opinion, pay a compliment, and criticize? p. 306

6 If you were shopping with a friend, how would you ask . . .
1. if your friend likes what you have on? Comment tu trouves... ? Ça te plaît?
2. if something looks good on you? Ça me va?
3. if it's too short? Il/Elle est trop court(e)?

7 How would you compliment a friend's clothing? How would you criticize it?
See answers below.

Can you hesitate and make a decision? p. 310

8 How can you express your hesitation?
J'hésite. Je ne sais pas. Ça me plaît, mais c'est cher.

9 How would you tell a salesperson what you've decided to do?
Je le/la/les prends. C'est trop cher.

Review and Assess

Additional Practice

2 To practice the **passé composé,** have students say that their friend wore these clothes to a party yesterday.

6 Ask students what else they might ask a friend when they try on clothing.

9 Remind students to give examples of both positive and negative responses.

STANDARDS: 1.2

Vocabulaire

Première étape

Clothes

un blouson	jacket
des bottes (f.)	boots
des boucles d'oreilles (f.)	earrings
un bracelet	bracelet
un cardigan	cardigan
une casquette	cap
une ceinture	belt
un chapeau	hat
des chaussettes (f.)	socks
des chaussures (f.)	shoes
une chemise	shirt (men's)
un chemisier	shirt (women's)
une cravate	tie
une écharpe	scarf
une jupe	skirt
des lunettes (f.) de soleil	sunglasses
un maillot de bain	bathing suit
un manteau	coat
un pantalon	(a pair of) pants
une robe	dress
des sandales (f.)	sandals
une veste	suit jacket, blazer
des vêtements (m.)	clothes

Asking for and giving advice

Je ne sais pas quoi mettre pour...	I don't know what to wear for (to) . . .
Qu'est-ce que je mets?	What shall I wear?
Pourquoi est-ce que tu ne mets pas... ?	Why don't you wear . . . ?
Mets...	Wear . . .
mettre	to put, to put on, to wear
porter	to wear

Deuxième étape

Expressing need; inquiring

Vous désirez?	What would you like?
(Est-ce que) je peux vous aider?	May I help you?
Je cherche quelque chose pour...	I'm looking for something to . . .
J'aimerais... pour aller avec...	I'd like . . . to go with . . .
Non, merci, je regarde.	No, thanks, I'm just looking.
Je peux l'/les essayer?	Can I try it/them on?
Je peux essayer le/la/les... ?	Can I try on the . . . ?
Vous avez ça... ?	Do you have that. . . ? (size, fabric, color)
en (taille)... ?	in size . . . ?
en bleu	in blue
en coton	cotton
en jean	denim
en cuir	leather

Other useful expressions

choisir	to choose, to pick
grandir	to grow
maigrir	to lose weight
grossir	to gain weight

Troisième étape

Asking for an opinion; paying a compliment; criticizing

Comment tu trouves... ?	How do you like . . . ?
Il/Elle me va?	Does . . . suit me?
Il/Elle te/vous plaît?	Do you like it?
C'est parfait.	It's perfect.
C'est tout à fait ton/votre style.	It looks great on you!
Il/Elle te/vous va très bien.	It suits you really well.
Il/Elle va très bien avec...	It goes very well with . . .
Il/Elle est (Ils/Elles sont) trop...	It's/They're too . . .
Je le/la/les trouve...	I think it's/they're . . .
très à la mode	in style
chic	chic
mignon(mignonne)(s)	cute
sensationnel(le)(s)/sensass	fantastic
rétro	retro
serré(e)(s)	tight
large(s)	baggy
petit(e)(s)	small
grand(e)(s)	big
court(e)(s)	short
long(longue)(s)	long
moche(s)	tacky
démodé(e)(s)	out of style
horrible(s)	terrible
Il/Elle ne te/vous va pas du tout.	It doesn't look good on you at all.
Il/Elle ne va pas du tout avec...	It doesn't go at all with . . .

Hesitating; making a decision

Vous avez choisi?	Have you decided?
Vous avez décidé de prendre... ?	Have you decided to take . . . ?
Vous le/la/les prenez?	Are you taking it/them?
Je ne sais pas.	I don't know.
Euh... J'hésite.	Well, I'm not sure.
Il/Elle me plaît, mais il/elle est cher/chère.	I like it, but it's expensive.
Je le/la/les prends.	I'll take it/them.
C'est trop cher.	It's too expensive.

Review and Assess

Game

Concours de famille This game is played like Family Feud®. First, group the chapter vocabulary into categories: what you wear every day, what you wear for special occasions, what a salesperson might say, what you might say if something doesn't fit, and so on. Then, divide the class into two or more teams and have a player from each team go to the board. Call out a category. The team whose player first gives an appropriate expression has one minute to list on the board all the words or expressions that fit into that category. Award points for correctly spelled answers. You may play up to a certain number of points or until you have exhausted all the categories.

Vocabulaire

CHAPITRE 10

Circumlocution

Have students imagine that they are staying with a French family and that they're looking for a certain item of their clothing they have misplaced. They are having difficulty remembering the French word for the item and are trying to communicate to the host family member what they need. **(On le porte pour nager.)** Have students work with a partner, one playing the role of the exchange student and the other playing the role of the host family member. Then have students change roles.

Chapter 10 Assessment

- **Testing Program**
  Chapter Test, pp. 261–266

  Audio Compact Discs, CD 10, Trs. 23–25
  Speaking Test, p. 347
- **Alternative Assessment Guide**
  Performance Assessment, p. 41
  Portfolio Assessment, p. 27
  CD-ROM Assessment, p. 55
- **Interactive CD-ROM Tutor, Disc 3**
  CD-ROM 3 A toi de parler
  DVD 2 A toi d'écrire
- **Standardized Assessment Tutor**
  Chapter 10
- **One-Stop Planner, Disc 3**
  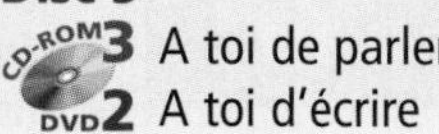
  Test Generator
  Chapter 10

STANDARDS: 1.3

Chapitre 11 : Vive les vacances!
Chapter Overview

Mise en train pp. 324–326	***Bientôt les vacances!***			

	FUNCTIONS	GRAMMAR	VOCABULARY	RE-ENTRY
Première étape pp. 327–332	• Inquiring about and sharing future plans, p. 329 • Expressing indecision; expressing wishes, p. 329	• The prepositions **à** and **en,** p. 330	• Vacation spots and activities, p. 327	• The verb **aller** + infinitive **(Chapitre 6)** • Asking for advice **(Chapitre 9)** • Making, accepting, and refusing suggestions **(Chapitres 4, 5)** • Telling what you like and what you'd like to do **(Chapitre 3)**
Deuxième étape pp. 333–336	• Reminding; reassuring, p. 333 • Seeing someone off, p. 336	• The **-ir** verbs: **partir, sortir,** and **dormir,** p. 334	• Things to pack for a vacation, p. 333	• Clothing **(Chapitre 10)** • The imperative **(Chapitre 5)** • Weather expressions **(Chapitre 4)** • **L'heure officielle (Chapitre 2)**
Troisième étape pp. 337–339	• Asking for and expressing opinions, p. 337 *Review* • Inquiring about and relating past events, p. 337			• The **passé composé (Chapitre 9)** • The verb **vouloir (Chapitre 6)** • Asking for and expressing opinions **(Chapitre 9)**

Prononciation p. 339	**Aspirated h; th, ch, and gn** Audio CD 11, Tracks 13–15	**A écrire** (dictation) Audio CD 11, Tracks 16–18	
Lisons! pp. 340–341	**Un guide touristique**	**Reading Strategy:** Reading for a purpose	
Grammaire supplémentaire	**pp. 342–345** **Première étape,** pp. 342–343	**Deuxième étape,** pp. 343–344	**Troisième étape,** p. 345
Review pp. 346–349	**Mise en pratique,** pp. 346–347 **Ecrivons!** Using connecting words Writing a letter to an exchange student	**Que sais-je?** p. 348	**Vocabulaire,** p. 349

CULTURE

- **Note culturelle,** Colonies de vacances, p. 328
- **Panorama Culturel,** Annual vacations in France, p. 332

Realia: Itinerary for Provence, p. 335

Chapitre 11 : Vive les vacances!

Chapter Resources

Lesson Planning

One-Stop Planner

Lesson Planner with Differentiated Instruction, pp. 53–57, 75

Student Make-Up Assignments

- Make-Up Assignment Copying Masters, Chapter 11

Listening and Speaking

TPR Storytelling Book, pp. 41–44

Listening Activities

- Student Response Forms for Listening Activities, pp. 83–85
- Additional Listening Activities 11-1 to 11-6, pp. 87–89
- Additional Listening Activities (song), p. 90
- Scripts and Answers, pp. 152–156

Video Guide

- Teaching Suggestions, pp. 74–75
- Activity Masters, pp. 76–78
- Scripts and Answers, pp. 111–114, 122–123

Activities for Communication

- Communicative Activities, pp. 61–66
- Realia and Teaching Suggestions, pp. 125–129
- Situation Cards, pp. 157–158

Reading and Writing

Reading Strategies and Skills Handbook, Chapter 11

Joie de lire 1, Chapter 11

Cahier d'activités, pp. 121–132

Grammar

Travaux pratiques de grammaire, pp. 88–97

Grammar Tutor for Students of French, Chapter 11

Assessment

Testing Program

- Grammar and Vocabulary Quizzes, **Etape** Quizzes, and Chapter Test, pp. 275–292
- Score Sheet, Scripts and Answers, pp. 293–300

Alternative Assessment Guide

- Portfolio Assessment, p. 28
- Performance Assessment, p. 42
- CD-ROM Assessment, p. 56

Student Make-Up Assignments

- Alternative Quizzes, Chapter 11

Standardized Assessment Tutor

- Reading, pp. 43–45
- Writing, p. 46
- Math, pp. 51–52

Middle School

Middle School Teaching Resources, Chapter 11

MEDIA

Online Activities

- **Jeux interactifs**
- **Activités Internet**

Video Program

- Videocassette 4
- Videocassette 5 (captioned version)

Interactive CD-ROM Tutor, Disc 3

DVD Tutor, Disc 2

Audio Compact Discs

- Textbook Listening Activities, CD 11, Tracks 1–19
- Additional Listening Activities, CD 11, Tracks 26–32
- Assessment Items, CD 11, Tracks 20–25

Teaching Transparencies

- Situation 11-1 to 11-3
- Vocabulary 11-A to 11-C
- **Mise en train**
- **Grammaire supplémentaire** Answers
- **Travaux pratiques de grammaire** Answers

One-Stop Planner CD-ROM

Use the **One-Stop Planner CD-ROM with Test Generator** to aid in lesson planning and pacing.

For each chapter, the **One-Stop Planner** includes:

- Editable lesson plans with direct links to teaching resources
- Printable worksheets from resource books
- Direct launches to the HRW Internet activities
- Video and audio segments
- Test Generator
- Clip Art for vocabulary items

Chapitre 11 : Vive les vacances!

Projects

Le Monde du voyageur

Students will create posters of travel scenes.

MATERIALS

✂ **Students may need**
- French-English dictionary
- Markers or colored pencils
- Magazines and catalogues
- Posterboard or construction paper

SUGGESTED SEQUENCE

1. Students might work alone or in small groups. Tell them that they will depict an airport, train station, or vacation scene, with labels on important items and speech bubbles for the people in the scene. You might show *Teaching Transparency 11-2* as an example of a travel scene.
2. Students choose the location for their scenes and begin gathering or drawing pictures to illustrate it. They may wish to present a story or simply show people doing different things.
3. Before they create the final draft, have students plan the layout of their pictures and look up words they don't know in the dictionary. They might cut out pictures from magazines as well. Have them label as many items as possible, such as clothes, travel items, objects in the scene, activities, and so on. Remind them to check their spelling.
4. Next, have students write speech bubbles for the people shown. They might choose to demonstrate greeting or seeing people off, giving advice, or other appropriate functions.
5. Have students edit one another's work; they should make any corrections in labels or language use. They should then add any final touches to their posters to make them complete and attractive.

GRADING THE PROJECT

Suggested Point Distribution: (total = 100 points)

Completion of assignment	30 points
Creativity	30 points
Language use	20 points
Appearance	20 points

Games

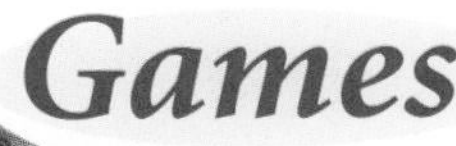

Dessin animé

In this game, students will review vocabulary related to vacation activities.

Procedure First, divide the class into two or more teams and have a player from the first team go to the board. Give the player the name of a vacation place or activity in French and have him or her draw a representation of that activity or place. If the player's team correctly guesses the activity or place within 15 seconds, that team wins a point. The turn then goes to the second team.

Variation This game can also be played in small groups. In this case, students choose an activity from the vocabulary list at the end of the chapter and draw their illustrations on paper or on a transparency.

Je l'ai trouvé!

The object of this game is to have students recognize the names of francophone countries and identify their location on a map.

Procedure Before playing this game, give students a few minutes to look over the map of the francophone world on pages xxvi–1 in their book. You might also show *Map Transparency 4.* Then, display two world maps and divide the class into two teams. Have a player from each team stand by a map. Call out the name of a country in French. The first player to point out the country on the map and say **Je l'ai trouvé!** wins a point. Give each team a point in case of a tie.

Réponds vite!

In this game, students will practice verb forms.

Procedure Divide the class into two teams and place a bell or squeaky toy on top of a desk. Then, have one player from each team come forward. Name a subject, a verb, and a tense (**je, partir, présent**). Give the first student to ring the bell a chance to respond with the correct verb form. If that student is wrong, the other player has a chance to respond. A correct answer wins a point for the team. Then, both players return to their seats, and two other players come forward. In case of confusion due to mispronunciation, have the player write the verb form on the board. In addition to verb forms, you can also ask students to give functional expressions, such as *see someone off* or *suggest that someone go to the beach.*

STANDARDS: 1.3

Storytelling

Mini-histoire

This story accompanies Teaching Transparency 11-3. The ***mini-histoire*** *can be told and retold in different formats, acted out, written down, and read aloud, to give students additional opportunities to practice all four skills. The following story involves several friends who meet at a café and tell about their favorite activities during their vacation.*

«Alors Florent, qu'est-ce que tu as fait pendant les vacances?» «J'ai travaillé dans un fast-food. Je voulais m'acheter un ordinateur. Et toi, Brigitte, où est-ce que tu es allée?» «Je suis allée avec mes deux cousines chez mes grands-parents au bord de la mer. Nous avons joué au volley-ball et nous avons fait de la plongée sous-marine».

Simone et Raphaël parlent ensemble des vacances prochaines. Simone dit : «Je n'ai encore rien de prévu. Je vais rester chez moi pour lire. Et toi, Raphaël?» «J'ai l'intention d'aller faire du camping. J'aime faire des randonnées et découvrir la nature», répond Raphaël.

Traditions

Course camarguaise

The largest Roman amphitheater in Provence, **les arènes,** once held chariot races, sporting events, and popular spectacles in which gladiators were pitted against one another or against wild animals. Nearly two thousand years later, people continue to attend sporting events here. Every year, crowds of up to 12,000 people fill the arena to watch bullfights from around Easter to September.

There are two types of bullfighting featured in the arena: the traditional bullfight (**mise à mort**) and the **course camarguaise.** The **course camarguaise** is a unique style of bullfighting specific to this region. It is a spectacle in which **raseteurs** dressed in white, use hooks held between their fingers to remove ribbons tied to the bull's horns. The bulls are a pure breed found only in the Camargue region. They have distinctive horns that point upwards. Have students do research on the Roman presence in Arles or find out more about the Camarguaise style of bullfighting.

Recette

Ratatouille *is probably the most famous of all the traditional dishes of the South of France. Each French person prepares it differently, even though the ingredients are always more or less the same. The name* ***"ratatouille"*** *is made of two French words:* ***rata,*** *which refers to a type of stew that used to be served to soldiers, and* ***touiller,*** *a colloquial expression meaning "to mix".*

RATATOUILLE

pour 4 personnes

1 aubergine
3 courgettes moyennes coupées en morceaux
1 oignon coupé en tranches
2 gousses d'ail hachées
2 tomates coupées en tranches
2 cuillères à soupe de beurre
2 cuillères à soupe d'huile d'olive
sel et poivre
laurier
persil
thym

Eplucher et couper en morceaux l'aubergine et les courgettes. Couper les tomates en cubes. Faire chauffer l'huile et le beurre dans une grande poêle et faire cuire l'oignon et l'ail avec le sel et le poivre pendant environ 10 minutes. Ajouter l'aubergine, les courgettes et les tomates, ainsi que le thym, le laurier et le persil.

Couvrir et laisser mijoter pendant 30 à 40 minutes. Servir chaud avec du riz, du poisson ou de la viande, ou froid avec du pain.

Chapitre 11 : Vive les vacances!

Technology

DVD/Video

Videocassette 4, Videocassette 5 (captioned version)
DVD Tutor, Disc 2
See Video Guide, pp. 73–78.

Mise en train • Bientôt les vacances!

In this segment of the video, Ahmed and Florent are playing soccer when Magali comes up to greet them. They talk about their plans for the summer. Magali is going to a summer camp, and Ahmed plans to go camping and then work at a gas station in Arles. Florent doesn't have any vacation plans yet. Magali and Ahmed each make suggestions. Florent wants to do something interesting, but he doesn't know what!

Qu'est-ce que tu fais pendant les vacances?

Several teenagers from different French-speaking countries tell us where they go and what they do on vacation.

Bientôt les vacances! (suite)

When the story continues, Florent's father sees an ad for a **séjour linguistique** in England and thinks Florent should participate. Florent tells Ahmed of his plans. Ahmed says that it won't be fun and it rains all the time in England. Florent is reluctant to go to England, but his parents finally persuade him to go. At the end of the story, Florent's parents receive a package from him. He has sent back his rain gear and is having a great time after all!

Vidéoclips

- **TGV Atlantique®**: advertisement for train service
- **SNCF Carte Kiwi®**: advertisement for discount train travel

Interactive CD-ROM Tutor

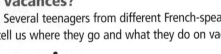

Activity	Activity Type	Pupil's Edition Page
En contexte	*Interactive conversation*	
1. Vocabulaire	Le bon choix	p. 327
2. Vocabulaire	Jeu des paires	p. 333
3. Grammaire	Les mots qui manquent	p. 334
4. Comment dit-on... ?	Le bon choix	pp. 329, 333 336–337
5. Grammaire	Méli-mélo	p. 338
6. Grammaire	Les mots qui manquent	p. 338
Panorama Culturel	Qu'est-ce que tu fais pendant les vacances? Le bon choix	p. 332
A toi de parler	*Guided recording*	pp. 346–347
A toi d'écrire	*Guided writing*	pp. 346–347

Teacher Management System

Launch the program, type "admin" in the password area and press RETURN. Log on to **www.hrw.com/CDROMTUTOR** for a detailed explanation of the Teacher Management System.

DVD Tutor

The *DVD Tutor* contains all material from the *Video Program* as described above. French captions are available for use at your discretion for all sections of the video. The *DVD Tutor* also provides a variety of video-based activities that assess students' understanding of the **Mise en train, Suite,** and **Panorama Culturel.**

This part of the *DVD Tutor* may be used on any DVD video player connected to a television or video monitor.

In addition to the video material and the video-based comprehension activities, the *DVD Tutor* also contains the entire *Interactive CD-ROM Tutor* in DVD-ROM format. Each DVD disc contains the activities from all 12 chapters of the *Interactive CD-ROM Tutor.*

This part of the *DVD Tutor* may be used on a Macintosh® or Windows® computer with a DVD-ROM drive.

To preview all resources available for this chapter, use the **One-Stop Planner CD-ROM,** Disc 3.

Go.Online!

Online Edition

The Online Edition for Allez, viens! *allows students access to their textbooks anytime anywhere.*

- *Audio at point of use*
- *Additional practice activities*
- *Self-test activities*
- *Online reference tools*
- *Entire Video Program (Enhanced version)*
- *Interactive Notebook (Enhanced version)*

HRW Atlas

video

audio

presentation

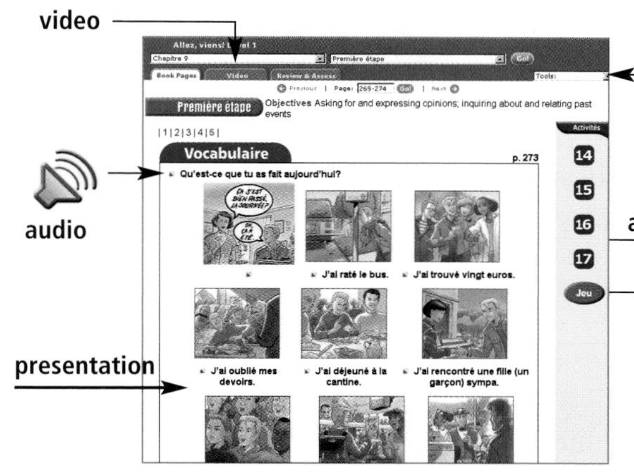

tools (glossary, grammar, cahier électronique)

activities

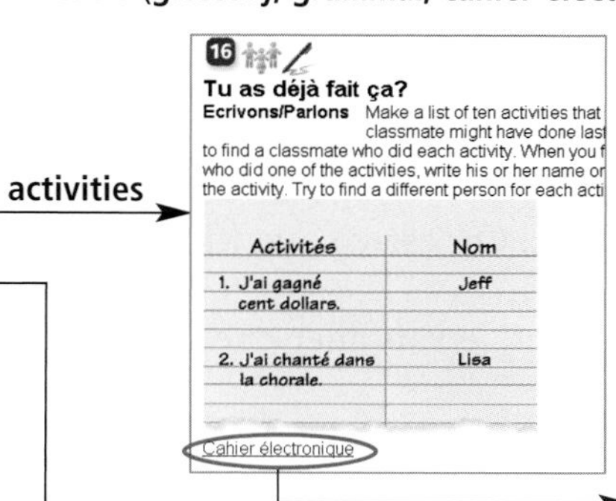

Notebook

Activités Internet

These guided internet activities include a worksheet and pre-selected and pre-screened authentic web sites from the francophone world. You can use these activities

- to help students develop research skills in the target language
- to introduce students to authentic cultural information
- as a project

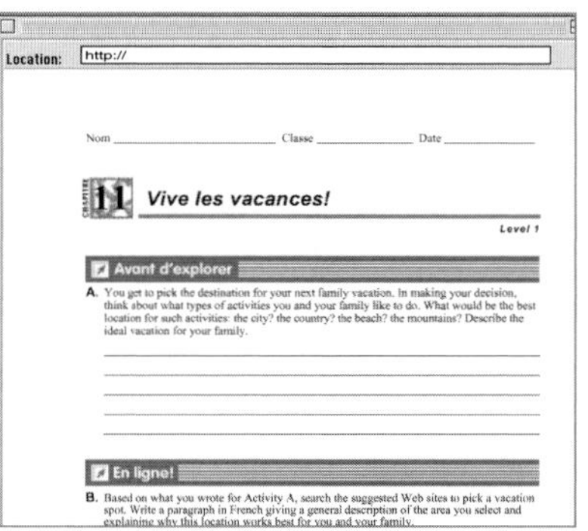
Location: http://

Nom ______ Classe ______ Date ______

11 Vive les vacances!

Level 1

Avant d'explorer

A. You get to pick the destination for your next family vacation. In making your decision, think about what types of activities you and your family like to do. What would be the best location for such activities: the city? the country? the beach? the mountains? Describe the ideal vacation for your family.

En ligne!

B. Based on what you wrote for Activity A, search the suggested Web sites to pick a vacation spot. Write a paragraph in French giving a general description of the area you select and explaining why this location works best for you and your family.

Jeux interactifs

You can use the interactive activities in this chapter

- to practice grammar, vocabulary, and chapter functions
- as homework
- as an assessment option
- as a self-test
- to prepare for the Chapter Test

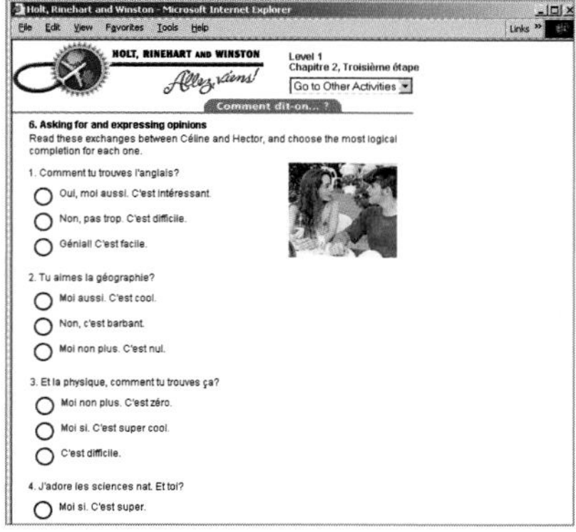

Projet Have students do a Web search to plan the vacation of their dreams in a francophone country. They should provide all kinds of information about the place they choose, including tourist attractions, activities, and accomodations. Then, have them prepare a poster to display the information they find.

STANDARDS: 1.2, 1.3, 3.2

Chapitre 11 : Vive les vacances!
Textbook Listening Activities Scripts 

Première étape

6 p. 327

Answers to Activity 6
1. Nathalie is going boating on the coast.
2. Bruno is going to Paris with his parents.
3. Pauline is going to visit her cousins in La Rochelle.
4. Emile is going hiking in the mountains.

1. — Bonjour, Nathalie. Qu'est-ce que tu vas faire pendant tes vacances?
— Je ne sais pas encore, mais je voudrais aller au bord de la mer et faire du bateau.
— Eh bien, bonnes vacances.
— Merci beaucoup.

2. — Alors, Bruno. Qu'est-ce que tu vas faire cet été?
— Je vais aller à Paris avec mes parents.
— Ah, c'est génial. Tu aimes Paris, toi?
— Je n'y suis jamais allé.
— Tu vas voir, c'est très joli. J'espère qu'il va faire beau.
— Moi aussi!

3. — Bonjour, Pauline. Où est-ce que tu vas aller en vacances?
— Au mois de juillet, je vais aller chez mes cousins à La Rochelle.
— C'est chouette, La Rochelle.
— Je sais, mais, moi, j'aimerais mieux aller en colonie de vacances avec des copains.
— Amuse-toi bien quand même.
— Merci.

4. — Alors, Emile, tu as décidé? Où est-ce que tu vas aller en vacances?
— Euh, je pense aller à la montagne.
— Pour faire de la randonnée?
— Oui, mais c'est cher.
— Dommage. Tu n'y vas pas alors?
— Si. J'y vais quand même.
— Eh bien, bonnes vacances.
— Merci beaucoup.

8 p. 329

Answers to Activity 8
1. undecided
2. definite plans
3. undecided
4. undecided
5. definite plans

1. — Qu'est-ce que tu vas faire pendant les vacances, Sabine?
— Euh, je n'ai rien de prévu. Je voudrais bien aller chez mes grands-parents, mais j'ai envie de travailler aussi.

2. — Dis, Gilbert, où est-ce que tu vas aller pendant les vacances?
— Oh, ça va être super! En juillet, je vais voir mon oncle au Canada, et en août, je vais voyager en Afrique.

3. — Qu'est-ce que tu vas faire cet été, Ariane?
— Euh, j'hésite. Je voudrais bien aller à la plage, mais je ne sais pas.

4. — Tu vas travailler cet été?
— Euh, je me demande. Je voudrais bien si je peux trouver du travail. Est-ce qu'il y a du travail à la station-service?

5. — Qu'est-ce que tu vas faire pendant les vacances?
— Je vais dans un camp de tennis. C'est chouette, hein? On va jouer au tennis trois heures par jour.

13 p. 331

Answers to Activity 13
1. vrai 2. faux 3. vrai 4. faux

ALAIN Je ne sais pas où aller pendant les vacances. Tu as une idée?
VALERIE Tu devrais aller à la Martinique.
ALAIN Ah oui?
VALERIE Oui, j'y suis allée plusieurs fois.
ALAIN C'est comment?
VALERIE C'est chouette. Il fait toujours beau. Les gens sont très sympas.
ALAIN Qu'est-ce qu'on peut y faire?
VALERIE Oh, plein de choses. Il y a des plages superbes. Tu peux y faire de la planche à voile, du bateau, de la plongée. Tu peux aussi visiter Fort-de-France. C'est une ville très intéressante.
ALAIN Qu'est-ce qu'on peut voir à Fort-de-France?
VALERIE Le marché aux poissons, le marché aux fruits et aux légumes ou la place de la Savane, qui est très belle.
ALAIN Eh bien, c'est une bonne idée. J'ai envie d'y aller!

Deuxième étape

18 p. 334

Answers to Activity 18
1. reminding
2. reassuring
3. reminding
4. reassuring
5. reminding
6. reassuring
7. reminding

1. — Tu as les cadeaux, Frédéric? N'oublie surtout pas les cadeaux!

2. — J'ai mon manteau, mon écharpe, ma cravate. J'ai pensé à tout!

3. — Tu as pensé à ton dictionnaire? Il ne faut pas que tu l'oublies. Il te faut absolument un dictionnaire.

4. — Eh bien, j'ai regardé ma liste deux fois. Je suis sûr, je n'ai rien oublié.

5. — Tu n'as pas oublié tes sandales? Tu sais, il va faire très chaud.

The following scripts are for the listening activities found in the *Pupil's Edition*. For Student Response Forms, see *Listening Activities,* pages 83–85. To provide students with additional listening practice, see *Listening Activities,* pages 87–90.

To preview all resources available for this chapter, use the **One-Stop Planner CD-ROM**, Disc 3.

6. — Oui, j'ai mon appareil-photo. Ne t'en fais pas.

7. — Tu ne prends pas ton maillot de bain? Pourquoi? Tu vas en avoir besoin.

25 p. 336

1. — Salut, Michel! Ça va? Ça fait longtemps! Qu'est-ce que tu fais?

2. — A bientôt, Nathalie! Amuse-toi bien!

3. — Eh bien, bon voyage, Luc! N'oublie pas de m'écrire! Je vais penser à toi!

4. — Salut, Amira! Tu vas mieux? On va au cinéma ce soir. Tu viens?

5. — Salut, Paul! Tu as de la chance, toi, d'aller en Italie! Passe de bonnes vacances!

6. — Salut, Albert! Ça s'est bien passé, le week-end? Qu'est-ce que tu as fait?

Answers to Activity 25
1. arrive 2. part 3. part 4. arrive 5. part 6. arrive

Troisième étape

29 p. 337

1. — Tu as passé un bon été?
— Oh, pas mauvais. J'ai beaucoup travaillé, mais j'ai gagné de l'argent.

2. — Ça s'est bien passé, tes vacances en Italie?
— C'était un véritable cauchemar! Il a fait tellement chaud et c'était trop cher!

3. — Tu t'es bien amusée en vacances, Fabienne?
— Ah oui, c'était formidable! Il a fait très beau! On est allés à la plage tous les jours!

4. — Dis, Etienne, tu as passé un bon week-end?
— Euh, pas vraiment. Je suis allé chez mes cousins à la montagne. C'est barbant chez eux!

5. — Tu t'es bien amusé en colonie de vacances?
— Oh, ça a été. On a beaucoup joué au football, mais moi, j'aime mieux le tennis.

6. — Ça s'est bien passé, tes vacances à la montagne?
— C'était épouvantable! J'y suis allée pour faire du ski et il n'y avait pas de neige!

7. — Tu t'es bien amusée à Paris?
— C'était formidable! On est allés au Louvre, à Notre-Dame, à la tour Eiffel et au Sacré-Cœur.

Answers to Activity 29
1. fair 3. good 5. fair 7. good
2. bad 4. bad 6. bad

PRONONCIATION, P. 339

For the scripts for Parts A and B , see p. 339. The script for Part C is below.

C. A écrire *(dictation)*

— Salut, Michel! Qu'est-ce que tu fais cet été?

— Je vais chez mon oncle à la campagne. Il a trois chats mignons et quatre chiens méchants.

Mise en pratique

1 p. 346

Vous voulez découvrir de nouveaux horizons? Vous avez l'esprit d'aventure? Pierre et Vacances peut vous aider à partir au bout du monde! Grands voyages pour petits budgets!

Envie de soleil, de plages tranquilles, de musique exotique? Sortez votre maillot de bain et votre crème solaire. Venez passer une semaine au Maroc faire de la planche à voile et de la plongée sous-marine.

Envie de neige et de descentes olympiques? Les montagnes de Grenoble vous attendent. Hôtel, location de skis et chaussures, forfait téléski, voyage en train compris, au départ de Paris, quatre cent cinquante euros.

Envie de sensation forte et de paysages spectaculaires? La randonnée de votre vie vous attend! Descente du Grand Canyon avec un guide. Campez au bord des eaux vertes du Colorado. Pour les amoureux du risque, rafting possible.

Pour profiter des prix hors saison, voyagez avant le quinze juin. Nous avons des prix étudiant et des prix de groupes. Si les voyages vous intéressent, venez nous voir ou téléphonez à Pierre et Vacances, zéro deux, quarante-sept, vingt-trois, trente-deux, vingt-deux.

Answers to Mise en pratique, Activity 1
1. travel agency/tour company
2. *Possible answers:* Morocco, Grenoble, the Grand Canyon, Colorado River
3. windsurfing, scuba diving, skiing, hiking, camping, rafting
4. students and groups

Chapitre 11 : Vive les vacances!
50-Minute Lesson Plans

Day 1

CHAPTER OPENER **5 min.**
- Ask students where they would go on vacation if they had unlimited time and money. You might also have them recall popular vacation spots mentioned in previous chapters.
- Photo Flash!, ATE, p. 322
- Present Chapter Objectives, p. 323.
- Building on Previous Skills, p. 323
- Language Note, ATE, p. 323
- Culture Note, ATE, p. 323

MISE EN TRAIN **40 min.**
- Presenting **Mise en train** and Preteaching Vocabulary, ATE, p. 324
- Geography Link, ATE, p. 323
- Do Activities 1–5, p. 326.

Wrap-Up **5 min.**
- Have student volunteers discuss summer jobs they have had. Students should tell where they worked and whether, like Ahmed, they were working so they could buy something special.

Homework Options
Cahier d'activités, p. 121, Act. 1

Day 2

PREMIERE ETAPE
Quick Review **10 min.**
- Check homework.
- Bell Work, ATE, p. 327

Vocabulaire, p. 327 **15 min.**
- Presenting **Vocabulaire,** ATE, p. 327, using Teaching Transparencies 11-A and 11-B
- Play Audio CD for Activity 6, p. 327.
- Discuss **Tu te rappelles?,** p. 328, then do Activity 7, p. 328.

Note culturelle, p. 328 **15 min.**
- Discuss **Note culturelle,** p. 328, and do Thinking Critically, **Note culturelle,** ATE, p. 328.
- Discuss **De bon conseils,** p. 328, and do Language-to-Language, **De bons conseils,** ATE, p. 328.

Wrap-Up **10 min.**
- Game: **Dessin animé,** ATE, p. 321C

Homework Options
Cahier d'activités, p. 122, Acts. 2–4
Travaux pratiques de grammaire, pp. 88–90, Acts. 1–6

Day 3

PREMIERE ETAPE
Quick Review **10 min.**
- Check homework.
- Describe three different vacation "packages" and have students tell the one they would most like to go on.

Comment dit-on... ?, p. 329 **10 min.**
- Presenting **Comment dit-on... ?,** ATE, p. 329
- Play Audio CD for Activity 8, p. 328.
- Do Activity 9, p. 329.

Note de grammaire, p. 330 **20 min.**
- Presenting **Note de grammaire,** ATE, p. 330.
- **Grammaire supplémentaire,** p. 342, Activity 2
- Do Activities 10–11, p. 330.
- Play Audio CD for Activity 13, p. 331
- Cahiers d'activités, p. 123, Acts. 5–6
- Do Travaux pratiques de grammaire, p. 91, Act. 7.

Wrap-Up **10 min.**
- Game: **Les vacances,** ATE, p. 329

Homework Options
Study for Quiz 11-1.

Day 4

PREMIERE ETAPE
Quiz 11-1 20 min.
- Administer Quiz 11-1A or 11-1B.

PANORAMA CULTUREL **15 min.**
- Present **Panorama Culturel**, p. 332, using Videocassette 4 or DVD Tutor, Disc 2.
- Answer **Qu'en penses-tu?** questions, p. 332.
- Read **Savais-tu que... ?,** p. 332.
- **Panorama Culturel,** Interactive CD-ROM Tutor, Disc 3

Wrap-Up **5 min.**
- Thinking Critically, ATE, p. 332

Homework Options
Cahier d'activités, p. 132, Acts. 24–25

Day 5

DEUXIEME ETAPE
Quick Review **10 min.**
- Bell Work, ATE, p. 333

Vocabulaire, p. 333 **15 min.**
- Presenting **Vocabulaire,** ATE, p. 333, using Teaching Transparency 11-C
- Do Activity 17, p. 333
- Additional Practice, ATE, p. 333

Comment dit-on... ?, p. 333 **15 min.**
- Presenting **Comment dit-on... ?,** ATE, p. 333
- Play Audio CD for Activity 18, p. 334.
- Do Activities 19–20, p. 334.

Wrap-Up **10 min.**
- Activities for Communication, p. 158, Situation Card 11-2: Role-Play

Homework Options
Cahiers d'activités, p. 125, Acts. 10–11
Travaux pratiques de grammaire, pp. 92–93, Acts. 8–10

Day 6

DEUXIEME ETAPE
Quick Review **10 min.**
- Check homework.
- Bring to class articles of clothing and the vocabulary items from **Vocabulaire,** p. 333. Hold up each item and have pairs of students take turns reminding and reassuring each other.

Grammaire, p. 334 **30 min.**
- Presenting **Grammaire,** ATE, p. 334
- Discuss **A la française,** p. 334.
- Do Activities 21–22, p. 335.
- **Grammaire supplémentaire,** p. 343, Activities 4–5

Wrap-Up **10 min.**
- Do Activity 23, p. 335.

Homework Options
Cahiers d'activités, p. 125, Act. 12
Travaux pratiques de grammaire, pp. 93–94, Acts. 11–12

One-Stop Planner CD-ROM

For alternative lesson plans by chapter section, to create your own customized plans, or to preview all resources available for this chapter, use the **One-Stop Planner CD-ROM**, Disc 3.

For additional homework suggestions, see activities accompanied by this symbol throughout the chapter.

Day 7

DEUXIEME ETAPE

Quick Review 20 min.
- Check homework.

Comment dit-on... ?, p. 336 15 min.
- Presenting **Comment dit-on... ?**, ATE, p. 336
- Discuss **Tu te rappelles?**, p. 336.
- Play Audio CD for Activity 25.
- Do Activity 26, p. 334.
- Cahier d'activités, p. 127, Act. 14
- Review weather expressions, p. 118, then do Activity 27, p. 336.
- Travaux pratiques de grammaire, pp. 94–95, Acts. 13 and 15

Wrap-Up 5 min.
- Game: **N'oublie pas!**, ATE, p. 336

Homework Options
Study for Quiz 11-2.

Day 8

DEUXIEME ETAPE

Quiz 11-2 20 min.
- Administer Quiz 11-2A or 11-2B.

TROISIEME ETAPE

Comment dit-on... ?, p. 337 20 min.
- Presenting **Comment dit-on... ?**, ATE, p. 337
- Discuss **Tu te rappelles?**, p. 337.
- Play Audio CD for Activity 29, p. 337.
- Do Activity 30, p. 337.
- Discuss **Tu te rappelles?**, p. 338.
- Do Activities 31–32, p. 338.

Wrap-Up 10 min.
- Additional Practice, ATE, p. 338

Homework Options
Cahier d'activités, p. 128–129, Acts. 17–22
Travaux pratiques de grammaire, pp. 96–97, Acts. 16–18

Day 9

TROISIEME ETAPE

Quick Review 5 min.
- Check homework.

Project: Le monde du voyageur, ATE, **p. 321C 25 min.**
- Have students begin project **Le monde du voyageur,** ATE, p. 321C.

Prononciation, p. 249 15 min.
- Complete presentation and play Audio CD for Activities A–C, p. 339.

Wrap-Up 5 min.
- Have students report on the progress they made on their projects.

Homework Options
Study for Quiz 11-3.
Complete Project: **Le monde du voyageur.**

Day 10

TROISIEME ETAPE

Quiz 11-3 20 min.
- Administer Quiz 11-3A or 11-3B.

LISONS! 25 min.
- Motivating Activity, ATE, p. 340
- Do Prereading Activities, A–B, p. 340.
- Do Reading Activities C–H, Thinking Critically, ATE, p. 341.
- Do Postreading Activity I, using Teaching Suggestion, ATE, p. 341.

Wrap-Up 5 min.
- Have students present their projects to the class.

Homework Options
Cahier d'activités, p. 131, Act. 23

Day 11

LISONS!

Quick Review 10 min.
- Check homework.

MISE EN PRATIQUE 30 min.
- Play Audio CD for Activity 1, p. 346.
- Do Activities 2–3, p. 346.
- Do **Ecrivons!**, p. 347.

Wrap-Up 10 min.
- Do Revising of **Ecrivons!**, p. 347.

Homework Options
Que sais-je?, p. 348
Finish **Ecrivons!**, Pupil's Edition, p. 347

Day 12

MISE EN PRATIQUE

Quick Review 15 min.
- Check homework and collect **Ecrivons!**
- Have partners complete **Jeu de rôle**, p. 347.

Student Review 35 min.
- Review Chapter 11. Choose from **Grammaire supplémentaire,** Grammar Tutor for Students of French, Activities for Communication, Listening Activities, Interactive CD-ROM Tutor, or **Jeux interactifs.**

Homework Options
Study for Chapter 11 Test.

Assessment

Test, Chapter 11 50 min.
- Administer Chapter 11 Test. Select from Testing Program, Alternative Assessment Guide, Test Generator, or Standardized Assessment Tutor.

Chapitre 11 : Vive les vacances!
90-Minute Lesson Plans

Block 1

CHAPTER OPENER 5 min.
- Motivating Activity: Ask students where they would go on vacation if they had unlimited time and money. You might also have them recall popular vacation spots mentioned in previous chapters.
- Present Chapter Objectives, p. 323
- Language Note, ATE, p. 323
- Photo Flash! and Culture Note, ATE, p. 323

MISE EN TRAIN 40 min.
- Thinking Critically, ATE, p. 325
- Presenting **Mise en train,** ATE, p. 324
- Geography Link, ATE, p. 322
- Slower Pace, ATE, p. 325
- View video of **Mise en train,** using Videocassette 4. See Video Guide, p. 73–74, 75, Activity Master 1, **Mise en train.**

PREMIERE ETAPE
Vocabulaire, p. 327 40 min.
- Presenting **Vocabulaire,** ATE, p. 327
- Play Audio CD for Activity 6, p. 327.
- Visual/Kinesthetic Learners, ATE, p. 327
- **De bons conseils,** p. 328, and Language-to-Language, ATE, p. 328
- **Tu te rappelles?,** p. 328
- **Grammaire supplémentaire,** p. 342, Act. 1
- Do Activity 7, p. 328.
- **Note culturelle,** p. 328 and Language Notes, ATE, p. 328

Wrap-Up 5 min.
- Summarize what happened in the **Mise en train,** using **Mise en train** Transparencies.

Homework Options
Travaux pratiques de grammaire, pp. 88–89, Acts. 1–4
Cahier d'activités, p. 122, Acts. 2–4

Block 2

PREMIERE ETAPE
Quick Review 5 min.
- Bell Work, ATE, p. 327

Comment dit-on... ?, p. 329 75 min.
- Presenting **Comment dit-on... ?,** ATE, p. 329
- Play Audio CD for Activity 8, p. 329. See Additional Practice, ATE, p. 329.
- Game: **Les vacances,** ATE, p. 329
- Presenting **Note de grammaire,** p. 330 and Language Note, ATE, p. 330
- **Vocabulaire à la carte,** p. 330
- Do Activity 10, p. 330, orally.
- Game: **Où se trouve... ?,** ATE, p. 330
- **Tu te rappelles?,** p. 330
- Play Audio CD for Activity 13, p. 331.
- **A la française,** p. 331, Additional Practice, ATE, p. 331
- Do Activity 14, p. 331 and Career Path, ATE, p. 331.

Wrap-Up 10 min.
- Activities for Communication, p. 125, Realia 11-1. See Speaking suggestion #7.

Homework Options
Study for Quiz 11-1
Travaux pratiques de grammaire, pp. 90–91, Acts. 5–7
Cahier d'activités, pp. 123–124, Acts. 5–9

Block 3

PREMIERE ETAPE
Quick Review 5 min.
- Motivating Activity: Give students cards with vacation destinations written on them. Have students list at least two things they're going to do there.

Quiz 11-1 20 min.
- Administer Quiz 11-1A or 11-1B.

PANORAMA CULTUREL 15 min.
- Presenting **Panorama Culturel,** ATE, p. 332
- Answer the **Qu'en penses-tu?** questions, p. 332
- Read **Savais-tu que... ?,** p. 332 and do Thinking Critically, ATE, p. 332

DEUXIEME ETAPE
Vocabulaire, p. 333 10 min.
- Bell Work, ATE, p. 333
- Presenting **Vocabulaire,** ATE, p. 333
- Do Activity 17, p. 333.

Comment dit-on... ?, p. 333 10 min.
- Presenting **Comment dit-on... ?,** ATE, p. 333
- Play Audio CD for Activity 18, p. 334.
- Do Activity 19, p. 334 with Challenge, ATE, p. 334
- Do Activity 20, p. 334.

Grammaire: the verb partir, p. 334 20 min.
- Presenting **Grammaire:** the verb **partir,** ATE, p. 334, Language Note, ATE, p. 334
- **A la française,** p. 334
- Game: Tic Tac Toe, p. 344

Wrap-Up 10 min.
- Activities for Communication, pp. 61–62, Communicative Activity 11-1A and 11-1B

Homework Options
Travaux pratiques de grammaire, pp. 92–93, Acts. 8–11
Cahier d'activités, pp. 125–126, Acts. 10–13

For alternative lesson plans by chapter section, to create your own customized plans, or to preview all resources available for this chapter, use the **One-Stop Planner CD-ROM**, Disc 3.

For additional homework suggestions, see activities accompanied by this symbol throughout the chapter.

Block 4

DEUXIEME ETAPE

Quick Review 10 min.
- Activities for Communication, pp. 63–64, Communicative Activity 11-2A and 11-2B.

Grammaire: the verb *partir,* con't, p. 334 25 min.
- Do Activity 21, p. 335 with Additional Practice, ATE, p. 335.
- **Grammaire supplémentaire,** p. 343, Acts. 4–5
- Do Activity 22, p. 335, orally.
- Do Activity 24, p. 335 with Teaching Suggestion and Teacher Note, ATE, p. 335.

Comment dit-on... ?, p. 336 35 min.
- Presenting **Comment dit-on... ?,** ATE, p. 336
- Play Audio CD for Activity 25, p. 336. See Additional Practice, ATE, p. 336.
- **Tu te rappelles?,** p. 336
- Do Activity 26, p. 336.
- Game: **N'oublie pas!,** ATE, p. 336
- Do Activity 28, p. 336.

Wrap-Up 20 min.
- Activities for Communication, p. 158 Situation Card 11-2: Role-Play

Homework Options

Study for Quiz 11-2

Travaux pratiques de grammaire, pp. 94–95, Acts. 12–15

Cahier d'activités, p. 127, Acts. 14–16

Block 5

DEUXIEME ETAPE

Quick Review 10 min.
- Bell Work, ATE, p. 337

Quiz 11-2 20 min.
- Administer Quiz 11-2A or 11-2B.

TROISIEME ETAPE

Comment dit-on... ?, p. 337 40 min.
- Presenting **Comment dit-on... ?,** ATE, p. 337
- Play Audio CD for Activity 29, p. 337. See Challenge, ATE, p. 337.
- **Tu te rappelles?,** p. 337
- Do Activity 30, p. 337.
- **Tu te rappelles?,** p. 338 with Reteaching and Additional Practice, ATE, p. 338
- Do Activity 31, p. 338.
- **Grammaire supplémentaire,** p. 344, Act. 7
- Have students act out a phone conversation between two friends who are comparing their weekends. Students should tell how their weekends were and what they did.

Prononciation, p. 339 15 min.
- Present **Prononciation,** p. 339 with Language-to-Language, ATE, p. 339.
- Play Audio CD for Activities A, B, and C, p. 339.

Wrap-Up 5 min.
- Using Teaching Transparency 11-3, ask students what the teenagers did on vacation and how they felt about it.

Homework Options

Study for Quiz 11-3

Travaux pratiques de grammaire, pp. 96–97, Acts. 16–18

Cahier d'activités, pp. 128–130, Acts. 17–22

Block 6

TROISIEME ETAPE

Quick Review 10 min.
- Activities for Communication, pp. 65–66, Communicative Activities 11-3A and 11-3B

Quiz 11-3 20 min.
- Administer Quiz 11-3A or 11-3B.

LISONS! 20 min
- Prereading Activities A–B, Motivating Activity, ATE, p. 340
- Reading Activities D–H, Thinking Critically, ATE, p. 341
- Postreading Activity I, ATE, p. 341

MISE EN PRATIQUE 30 min.
- Play Audio CD for Activity 1, p. 346.
- Do Activities 2–3, p. 346.
- Do **Ecrivons!,** p. 347.

Wrap-Up 10 min.
- Activities for Communication, p. 157, Situation Card 11-3: Interview

Homework Options

Que sais-je?, p. 348

Finish **Ecrivons!,** Pupil's Edition, p. 347.

Study for Chapter 11 Test

Block 7

MISE EN PRATIQUE

Quick Review 10 min.
- Check homework and collect **Ecrivons!**

Chapter Review 30 min.
- Review Chapter 11. Choose from **Grammaire supplémentaire,** Grammar Tutor for Students of French, Activities for Communication, Listening Activities, Interactive CD-ROM Tutor, or **Jeux interactifs.**

Test, Chapter 11 50 min.
- Administer Chapter 11 Test. Select from Testing Program, Alternative Assessment Guide, Test Generator, or Standardized Assessment Tutor.

CHAPITRE 11

One-Stop Planner CD-ROM

For resource information, see the **One-Stop Planner**, Disc 3.

Pacing Tips

Both the **Première** and **Deuxième étapes** in this chapter present new vocabulary, functions, and grammar. Keep in mind while planning your lessons that the **Troisième étape** is the lightest. For Lesson Plans and timing suggestions, see pages 321I–321L.

Meeting the Standards

Communication

- Inquiring about and sharing future plans; expressing indecision; expressing wishes, p. 329
- Reminding; reassuring, p. 333
- Seeing someone off, p. 336
- Asking for and expressing opinions, p. 337

Cultures

- Culture Note, p. 322
- Multicultural Link, p. 323
- Note culturelle, p. 328
- Panorama Culturel, p. 332

Connections

- Geography Link, pp. 323, 339
- History Link, p. 335
- Science Link, p. 341
- Math Link, p. 341

Comparisons

- Thinking Critically: Comparing and Contrasting, p. 325
- Thinking Critically: Synthesizing, p. 326
- Thinking Critically: Drawing Inferences, pp. 332, 341

Communities

- Career Path, p. 331
- De l'école au travail, p. 339

Cultures and Communities

Photo Flash!

The Verdon is a river located in the South of France in the **Alpes du Sud.** It runs through a deeply cut valley with abrupt, twisted rocks and cone-shaped peaks. The **gorges du Verdon** are 21 kilometers long, and in places, 700 meters deep (2,297 feet), passing through mainly uninhabited country, between the natural amphitheater of Moutiers-Ste-Marie and the narrow streets of Castellane. Tourists come here for camping, rafting and kayaking, but mostly to enjoy the wild, scenic excursions.

Culture Note

Workers in France have 5 weeks paid vacation per year. The normal work week consists of 35 hours. More and more French people are taking long weekends to discover other parts of France.

CHAPITRE 11

Vive les vacances!

Objectives

In this chapter you will learn to

Première étape

- inquire about and share future plans
- express indecision
- express wishes
- ask for advice
- make, accept, and refuse suggestions

Deuxième étape

- remind
- reassure
- see someone off

Troisième étape

- ask for and express opinions
- inquire about and relate past events

Visit Holt Online
go.hrw.com
KEYWORD: WA3 ARLES-11
Online Edition

C'était formidable, les vacances en Provence!

Connections and Comparisons

Geography Link

Ask students to look in an atlas or on the Internet and locate **Sisteron** and **les gorges du Verdon.** Have them find information on the attractions at these places and what the weather is like.

Multicultural Link

Ask students which holidays they have off from school. Have them suggest both national holidays, such as Martin Luther King Day or Columbus Day, and religious holidays, such as Yom Kippur, Christmas, or Ramadan. Then, have them research national and religious holidays in other countries and how they're celebrated.

Chapter Opener

CHAPITRE 11

Focusing on Outcomes

Ask students to describe a vacation they have taken, or an imaginary vacation, and tell why they enjoyed it. Then, have partners suggest how they would express the chapter outcomes, using vocabulary and expressions they already know. Ask them to list English expressions that accomplish the same functions. NOTE: The self-check activities in **Que sais-je?** on page 348 help students assess their achievement of the objectives.

Language Note

Have students guess what **Vive** in the expression **Vive les vacances!** means. You might write **Vive le roi!** or **Vive la France!** on the board as additional examples.

Building on Previous Skills

Ask students to recall and name in French particular sports and activities they might do on vacation.

STANDARDS: 3.1, 4.2

Mise en train

CHAPITRE 11

Teaching Resources
pp. 324–326

PRINT

- Lesson Planner, p. 53
- Video Guide, pp. 74, 76
- Cahier d'activités, p. 121

MEDIA

- One-Stop Planner
- Video Program
  Mise en train
  Videocassette 4, 14:32–16:56
  Videocassette 5 (captioned version), 1:29:16–1:31:41
  Suite
  Videocassette 4, 17:00–24:17
  Videocassette 5 (captioned version), 1:32:44–1:39:03
- DVD Tutor, Disc 2
- Audio Compact Discs, CD 11, Trs. 1–2
- **Mise en train** Transparencies

Presenting Mise en train

As a prereading activity, have students answer the questions at the top of page 324. Play the video and then have students answer the questions in Activity 1 on page 326. Ask them to suggest advantages and disadvantages of each teenager's vacation plans.

Mise en train Transparencies

The **roman-photo** is an abridged version of the video episode.

MISE EN TRAIN ▪ *Bientôt les vacances!*

CD 11 Trs. 1–2

Stratégie pour comprendre
Judging from clues in this episode, what time of year is it? What do you think Magali, Florent, and Ahmed might be talking about? What is Florent's dilemma at the end?

Ahmed

Florent

Magali

1
Florent : Alors, les copains, qu'est-ce que vous allez faire pendant les vacances?
Magali : Moi, je pars en colonie de vacances.
Florent : C'est sympa!

2
Magali : Et en août, je vais voir mes cousins à la montagne. Ils habitent à Sisteron, dans les Alpes de Haute-Provence. C'est super joli là-bas.

3
Magali : Et toi, Ahmed, tu vas à l'étranger?
Ahmed : Non. En juillet, je vais faire du camping dans les gorges du Verdon.

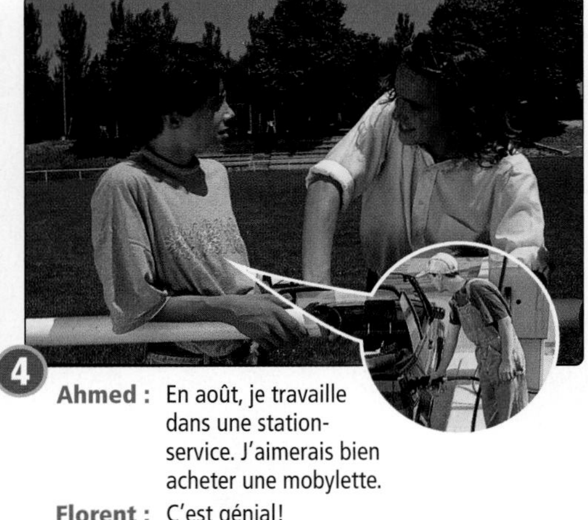

4
Ahmed : En août, je travaille dans une station-service. J'aimerais bien acheter une mobylette.
Florent : C'est génial!

Preteaching Vocabulary

Guessing words from context

Tell students that Magali, Ahmed, and Laurent are talking about their plans for the summer holidays which are illustrated in the bubbles attached to each image on page 324. Then, have students infer the meaning of these expressions by using the corresponding photos and keeping the context of vacation plans in mind:

1. **une colonie de vacances**
2. **la montagne**
3. **les gorges du Verdon**
4. **une station-service**

STANDARDS: 1.2

5

Magali : Et toi, Florent?
Florent : Je vais peut-être rester en Arles. J'ai envie d'être ici pour le Festival de la photographie. A part ça, je n'ai rien de prévu. Je n'ai pas encore décidé.
Ahmed : Pourquoi est-ce que tu ne travailles pas comme pompiste avec moi?
Florent : J'aimerais bien, mais je préfère partir en vacances.

6

Magali : Tu peux aller en colonie de vacances aussi.
Florent : C'est possible.

7

Magali : Bon, je dois m'en aller.
Ahmed : Moi aussi. Au revoir à tous!
Magali : Salut!
Florent : Tchao!

8

Florent : Qu'est-ce que je vais faire, moi?

Cahier d'activités, p. 121, Act.1

Using the Captioned Video/DVD

If students have difficulty understanding French spoken at a normal speed, use Videocassette 5 to allow students to see the French captions for ***Bientôt les vacances!*** and ***Bientôt les vacances! (suite).*** Hearing the language and watching the story will reduce anxiety about the new language and facilitate comprehension. The reinforcement of seeing the written vocabulary words as they watch the gestures and actions will help prepare students to do the comprehension activities on page 326. NOTE: The *DVD Tutor* contains captions for all sections of the *Video Program.*

Mise en train

CHAPITRE 11

Slower Pace

Stop the recording or video periodically to ask students where the teenagers are going on vacation. **(Il/Elle va où en vacances?)**

Thinking Critically

Comparing and Contrasting
Ask students to compare what these French teenagers are planning to do for the summer with what they themselves usually do. Do they find any of the activities mentioned by the French students unusual? Why? What might an American teenager do that these French teenagers didn't mention?

Bientôt les vacances! (suite)

When the story continues, Florent's father sees an ad for a **séjour linguistique** in England and thinks Florent should participate. Florent is reluctant to go to England because of the rainy weather there, but his parents finally persuade him to go. At the end of the story, Florent's parents receive a package from him. He has sent back his rain gear and is having a great time after all!

STANDARDS: 1.2, 4.2

Mise en train

CHAPITRE 11

Teaching Suggestion

5 This activity could be a class discussion or a writing assignment for individuals or groups.

These activities check for comprehension only. Students should not yet be expected to produce language modeled in **Mise en train.**

1 Tu as compris? See answers below.

1. What time of year is it? How do you know?
2. Who is planning to travel during the vacation? Where?
3. Who is going to work during the vacation? Why?
4. What is Florent going to do?

2 C'est qui?

D'après ***Bientôt les vacances!,*** qui a l'intention de (d')...

Florent

Ahmed

Magali

- aller dans les Alpes? — Magali
- travailler en Arles? — Ahmed
- rester en Arles? — Florent
- partir en colonie de vacances? — Magali
- aller voir ses cousins? — Magali
- aller à la montagne? — Magali
- faire du camping? — Ahmed

3 Vrai ou faux?

1. Les trois jeunes restent en France pendant les vacances. vrai
2. Les cousins de Magali habitent à la montagne. vrai
3. Ahmed va faire du camping dans les Alpes. faux
4. Ahmed va travailler dans un café. faux
5. Ahmed veut aller au Festival de la photographie. faux
6. Florent part en colonie de vacances. faux

4 Cherche les expressions

According to ***Bientôt les vacances!,*** what can you say in French. . . See answers below.

1. to ask what someone is going to do?
2. to tell what a place looks like?
3. to express an opinion?
4. to express indecision?
5. to make a suggestion?
6. to express a preference?

C'est génial! **C'est super joli...** **Je préfère...**
Pourquoi est-ce que tu ne... pas?
Qu'est-ce que vous allez faire... ?
Je n'ai pas encore décidé.

5 Et maintenant, à toi

Quels projets de vacances est-ce que tu préfères? Pourquoi?

Comprehension Check

Challenge

3 Have students create one or two additional true-false statements based on ***Bientôt les vacances!*** They might read their statements aloud to the class, or they might exchange papers with a partner.

Thinking Critically

4 **Synthesizing** Ask students to name other situations in which these expressions might be used.

Answers

1
1. almost summer; July and August are mentioned.
2. Magali: colonie de vacances and Sisteron, dans les Alpes de Haute-Provence; Ahmed: les gorges du Verdon
3. Ahmed; He needs money to buy a moped.
4. He doesn't know.

4
1. Qu'est-ce que vous allez faire... ?
2. C'est super joli...
3. C'est génial!
4. Je n'ai pas encore décidé.
5. Pourquoi est-ce que tu ne... pas... ?
6. Je préfère...

STANDARDS: 1.2

Objectives Inquiring about and sharing future plans; expressing indecision; expressing wishes; asking for advice; making, accepting, and refusing suggestions

WA3 ARLES-11

Vocabulaire

Où est-ce que tu vas aller pendant tes vacances?

CD-ROM 3 DVD 2

à la montagne

à la campagne

au bord de la mer

en forêt

en colonie de vacances

chez mes grands-parents

Qu'est-ce qu'on peut y faire? On peut y...

faire du camping.

faire de la randonnée.

faire du bateau.

faire de la plongée.

faire de la planche à voile.

faire de la voile.

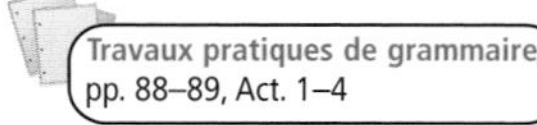
Travaux pratiques de grammaire, pp. 88–89, Act. 1–4

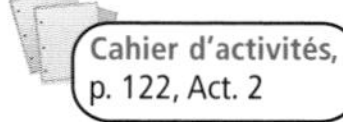
Cahier d'activités, p. 122, Act. 2

6 Les vacances See scripts and answers on p. 321G.

Ecoutons Listen as Nathalie, Bruno, Pauline, and Emile tell about their vacation plans. What is each teenager going to do?
CD 11 Tr. 3

Communication for All Students

Slower Pace

6 Stop the recording after each person speaks to elicit answers.

Visual/Kinesthetic Learners

To practice the vacation vocabulary, have students play the game **Dessin animé,** described on page 321C.

Challenge

Tell students to imagine they are starting a summer camp for their friends and classmates. Ask them where they would have the camp and what activities they would offer.

Première étape

CHAPITRE 11

Teaching Resources
pp. 327–331

PRINT

- Lesson Planner, p. 54
- TPR Storytelling Book, pp. 41, 44
- Listening Activities, pp. 83–84, 87
- Activities for Communication, pp. 61–62, 125, 128, 157–158
- Travaux pratiques de grammaire, pp. 88–91
- Grammar Tutor for Students of French, Chapter 11
- Cahier d'activités, pp. 122–124
- Testing Program, pp. 275–278
- Alternative Assessment Guide, p. 42
- Student Make-Up Assignments, Chapter 11

MEDIA 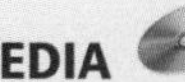

- One-Stop Planner
- Audio Compact Discs, CD 11, Trs. 3–5, 20, 26–27
- Teaching Transparencies: 11-1, 11-A, 11-B; **Grammaire supplémentaire** Answers; Travaux pratiques de grammaire Answers
- Interactive CD-ROM Tutor, Disc 3

Bell Work

Have students write sentences telling whether or not they do the following: **faire de l'aérobic, faire de la natation, faire du vélo, jouer au football, jouer au tennis.**

Presenting Vocabulaire

Use magazine illustrations to present the new vocabulary. Then, ask **On est où?** as you show pictures of the places, and **Qu'est-ce qu'on fait?** as you show pictures of activities. Next, ask if students have been to these places.

STANDARDS: 1.2, 3.1

Première étape

CHAPITRE 11

Teaching Resources
pp. 327–331

PRINT

- Lesson Planner, p. 54
- TPR Storytelling Book, pp. 41, 44
- Listening Activities, pp. 83–84, 87
- Activities for Communication, pp. 61–62, 125, 128, 157–158
- Travaux pratiques de grammaire, pp. 88–91
- Grammar Tutor for Students of French, Chapter 11
- Cahier d'activités, pp. 122–124
- Testing Program, pp. 275–278
- Alternative Assessment Guide, p. 42
- Student Make-Up Assignments, Chapter 11

MEDIA

VIDEO

- One-Stop Planner
- Audio Compact Discs, CD 11, Trs. 3–5, 20, 26–27
- Teaching Transparencies: 11-1, 11-A,11-B; **Grammaire supplémentaire** Answers; Travaux pratiques de grammaire Answers
- Interactive CD-ROM Tutor, Disc 3

Building on Previous Skills

De bons conseils Have students look back at the vocabulary pages in previous chapters to find examples of words with these endings. Examples include **éducation, sortie, vaisselle, piscine, heure, plage, ménage, devoir, classeur,** and **manteau.** You might have groups compete to find the most words.

Language Notes

- The word **animateur (animatrice)** is also used to describe hosts of TV shows or anyone who plans and leads group activities.
- You might point out that **au bord de la mer** *(to/on the coast)* is not exactly synonymous with **à la plage,** which refers specifically to the beach.

DE BONS CONSEILS

Although there are few hard-and-fast rules to help you remember if a noun is masculine or feminine, you can often predict the gender of a word by its ending. Some of the endings that usually indicate a feminine word are **-tion, -sion, -ie, -ette, -elle, -ine, -ude,** and **-ure.** Endings that often signal a masculine word are **-ment, -age, -oir, -ier, -et,** and **-eau.** But be careful! There are exceptions.

Tu te rappelles?

Do you remember how to tell what is going to happen? Use a form of the verb **aller** *(to go)* plus the infinitive of another verb.

Demain, **je vais** faire du bateau.

Grammaire supplémentaire, p. 342, Act. 1–2

Si tu as oublié
the verb *aller*
va à la page 174.

Cahier d'activités, p. 122, Act. 4

Travaux pratiques de grammaire, p. 90, Act. 5–6

7 En colonie de vacances

Parlons Qu'est-ce que Vincent et Roland vont faire en colonie de vacances?

Ils vont... **1.** faire de la planche à voile.

2. faire de la plongée.

3. faire du ski nautique.

4. jouer au football.

5. faire de l'équitation.

6. faire de la voile.

Note culturelle

In francophone countries, many children and teenagers attend summer camps **(colonies de vacances),** where they learn folklore, folk dances, arts and crafts, foreign languages, and learn about many other subjects. Of course, they also participate in sports. The camps are usually run by young adults called **animateurs.** In France alone there are hundreds of **colonies de vacances.**

Connections and Comparisons

Thinking Critically

Comparing and Contrasting Take a poll of how many students have ever attended a summer camp. Ask them if they enjoyed it, how long they stayed there, and what activities were offered. Have students compare the activities they've enjoyed at summer camps or seen in movies about summer camps with the types of activities offered in the **colonies de vacances.**

Language-to-Language

De bons conseils You might tell students that many languages, in addition to French, assign genders to nouns. Nouns in Spanish are masculine or feminine, and nouns in German are masculine, feminine, or neuter. Ask students to think of English words that are thought of as feminine. (A *ship* is often referred to as *she.*)

STANDARDS: 2.1, 3.2, 4.1, 4.2

Comment dit-on...?

Inquiring about and sharing future plans; expressing indecision; expressing wishes

Qu'est-ce que tu vas faire pendant tes vacances?
Je ne sais pas. J'hésite. Je voudrais bien aller à la montagne...mais j'ai aussi envie de rester ici pour voir mes grands-parents!

To inquire about someone's plans:

Qu'est-ce que tu vas faire cet été?
Où est-ce que tu vas aller pendant les vacances?

To share your plans:

En juillet, **je vais** travailler.
En août, **j'ai l'intention d'**aller en Italie.
. . . I intend to . . .

To express indecision:

J'hésite.
Je ne sais pas.
Je n'en sais rien. *I have no idea.*
Je n'ai rien de prévu. *I don't have any plans.*

To express wishes:

Je voudrais bien aller chez mes cousins.
J'ai envie de travailler.
I feel like . . .

Cahier d'activités, p. 123, Act. 6

8 Les projets de vacances See scripts and answers on p. 321G.

Ecoutons Listen to these speakers talk about their vacations. Do they have definite plans or are they undecided?
CD 11 Tr. 4

9 Les vacances en France

Parlons Imagine que tu vas aller en vacances en France cet été. Ton/Ta camarade va te poser des questions sur tes projets. Dis-lui ce que tu as envie de faire et ce que tu vas faire là-bas. Ensuite, changez de rôle.

Exemple — **Qu'est-ce que tu vas faire cet été?**
— **Je vais faire du camping à la campagne.**

visiter le Louvre
faire des photos
faire du ski
rencontrer de jeunes Français
voir la tour Eiffel
parler français
aller à un concert de rock français
aller au café

Teacher to Teacher

Laura Grable
Riverhead Middle School
Riverhead, NY

Laura's students make math connections.

"As a group, we decide on possible answers to the question **Qu'est-ce que tu vas faire cet été?** I have students come up with ten places and activities they might do there. Each student then surveys his/her classmates by asking the question and keeping tally. The students then put the results in a bar graph format. I ask them to be prepared to do a mini-presentation of the results of their survey. Students get to display their graphs in a prominent place in the classroom."

Presenting
Comment dit-on... ?

To introduce the new expressions, prompt three students to ask you the questions. In response to the first student, express indecision. In response to the second student, share your plans. In response to the third, express your wishes. Then, ask students what they're going to do tonight.

Additional Practice

8 You might have students write down the destination(s) or activities mentioned by the speakers.

9 Have students suggest other things they'd like to do. Write their suggestions on a transparency for reference during the activity. Remind students to reverse roles.

Visual Learners

9 Show *Teaching Transparency 11-1.* Have students look at the posters displayed in the travel agency for additional vacation destinations and activities.

Game

Les vacances Write different answers to the question **Qu'est-ce que tu vas faire cet été?** on index cards. Write each answer on two separate cards. Include plans that your students would be likely to have, such as **Je vais travailler comme maître nageur** *(lifeguard)* **à la piscine.** Distribute one card to each student. Students circulate and ask about one another's plans until they find the person whose card matches theirs.

Teaching Resources
pp. 327–331

PRINT

- Lesson Planner, p. 54
- TPR Storytelling Book, pp. 41, 44
- Listening Activities, pp. 83–84, 87
- Activities for Communication, pp. 61–62, 125, 128, 157–158
- Travaux pratiques de grammaire, pp. 88–91
- Grammar Tutor for Students of French, Chapter 11
- Cahier d'activités, pp. 122–124
- Testing Program, pp. 275–278
- Alternative Assessment Guide, p. 42
- Student Make-Up Assignments, Chapter 11

MEDIA

- One-Stop Planner
- Audio Compact Discs, CD 11, Trs. 3–5, 20, 26–27
- Teaching Transparencies: 11-1, 11-A,11-B; **Grammaire supplémentaire** Answers; Travaux pratiques de grammaire Answers
- Interactive CD-ROM Tutor, Disc 3

Presenting
Note de grammaire

After explaining the use of **à** with cities and **en** and **au** with countries, have students practice by asking one another where they would like to go for their next vacation. You might also have small groups make suggestions and decide together on a vacation destination. Write **Pourquoi pas aller... ?** and **On peut aller... ?** on the board as prompts.

Language Note
The preposition **en** is used instead of **à** with the town of Arles.

Note de grammaire

- To say *to* or *in* before the names of most cities, use **à.**
  Tu vas **à** Paris pendant les vacances?
- Names of countries are either masculine or feminine. Feminine countries end in **-e**, but there are exceptions, such as **le Mexique.** Use **au** (*to, in*) before masculine names, **en** (*to, in*) before feminine names and before names of countries that begin with a vowel. Before plural names, use **aux.**
  Vous allez **au** Canada?
  Hélène va **en** Allemagne.
  Nous allons **aux** Etats-Unis.
- States and provinces follow slightly different rules.

Grammaire supplémentaire, pp. 342–343, Act. 3–4

Travaux pratiques de grammaire, p. 91, Act. 7

Vocabulaire à la carte

en Angleterre	au Brésil	en Espagne	en Italie	au Sénégal
en Allemagne	en Californie	aux Etats-Unis	au Maroc	en Suisse
en Australie	en Chine	en France	au Mexique	au Texas
en Belgique	en Egypte	en Floride	en Russie	au Viêt-nam

10 Grammaire en contexte

Parlons Dans quel pays vont-ils passer leurs vacances?

au Canada — aux Etats-Unis — au Maroc — en Russie — en Angleterre — en Egypte — en France

1. Murielle va prendre des photos de la tour Eiffel. en France
2. Monique va visiter le château Frontenac. au Canada
3. Joseph va visiter la tour de Londres. en Angleterre
4. Mathieu va voir les pyramides. en Egypte
5. Than et Laure vont visiter le Texas. aux Etats-Unis
6. Dominique va voir le Kremlin. en Russie
7. Paul et Gilles vont aller à Casablanca. au Maroc

Tu te rappelles?

Do you remember how to ask for advice? Make, accept, and refuse suggestions?

To ask for advice:
Je ne sais pas quoi faire (où aller).
Tu as une idée?
Qu'est-ce que tu me conseilles?

To make suggestions:
Je te conseille de...
Tu devrais...

To accept suggestions:
C'est une bonne idée!
Pourquoi pas?
D'accord!
Allons-y!

To refuse suggestions:
Non, ce n'est pas possible.
Non, je ne peux pas.
Ça ne me dit rien.
C'est trop cher.

11 Grammaire en contexte

Parlons Choisis deux pays de l'activité 10. Avec un groupe de camarades, trouve au moins trois activités que tout le monde veut faire dans chaque pays.

12 Un voyage gratuit

Parlons Tu as gagné un voyage pour aller où tu veux dans le monde. Où est-ce que tu vas aller? Pourquoi? Qu'est-ce que tu vas y faire? Parle de ton voyage avec un(e) camarade. Ensuite, changez de rôle.

Communication for All Students

Game

Où se trouve... ? Hold a geography contest. Students on one team name a well-known city; their opponents tell in which country or state it is located. Refer students to the Additional Vocabulary on pages R13–R14 for additional country names.

Challenge

10 Have students write one or two sentences describing what they would like to see or do on vacation, read them aloud, and have the class guess where each student would like to go. Encourage them to use the locations previously presented in the book (Poitiers, Quebec, Paris, Abidjan, Arles).

En vacances à la Martinique

See scripts and answers on p. 321G.

Ecoutons Ecoute Alain et Valérie qui parlent de leurs vacances. Est-ce que ces phrases sont vraies ou fausses?

CD 11 Tr. 5

1. Alain ne sait pas quoi faire.
2. Valérie n'a pas d'idées.
3. Valérie est déjà allée à la Martinique.
4. Alain ne veut pas aller à la Martinique.

A la française

Use the words **alors** *(so, then, well, in that case)* and **donc** *(so, then, therefore)* to connect your sentences.

J'adore faire de la plongée, **donc** je vais en Australie.

Tu aimes faire du bateau? **Alors,** tu devrais aller à Marseille.

14 **Des conseils**

Parlons Ces élèves rêvent de ce qu'ils aiment. Ils ne savent pas où aller pendant les vacances. Tu as une idée?

Exemple **Tu devrais aller...**
Je te conseille d'aller...

Malika au musée.

Marion en forêt.

Hai en Egypte.

Christian au bord de la mer.

Adrienne en Afrique.

Ali à la montagne

Où aller?

Parlons Dis à ton/ta camarade ce que tu aimes faire en vacances. Il/Elle va te dire où tu devrais aller pour faire ces choses. Accepte ou refuse ses suggestions et quand tu refuses, dis pourquoi. Ensuite, changez de rôle.

16 **Mon journal** 

Ecrivons Décris un voyage que tu vas faire ou que tu voudrais faire. Où veux-tu aller? Quand? Avec qui? Qu'est-ce que tu vas y faire?

Cultures and Communities

Career Path

Tourism is an industry in which speaking a foreign language is almost a necessity. Tour guides generally speak three or more languages fluently. Some of the job responsibilities include meeting the tour group upon their arrival, assisting with hotel accommodations, and accompanying the tourists on tours during their vacation. Tour guides with a historical or specialized knowledge of a region might conduct specific tours and work with many tour groups during any given day. Have students discuss which languages would be most useful for someone who works as a tour guide and why.

Slower Pace

13 Before playing the recording, read the statements aloud. Ask students what they think the conversations will be about, based on these statements.

Additional Practice

A la française Write the following sentences on a transparency. Have students match and then combine them, using **donc** or **alors.**

1. **J'aime faire du camping.**
2. **Je vais chez ma tante.**
3. **J'aime faire de la voile.**
4. **Je vais au bord de la mer.**

a. **Je vais au Québec.**
b. **Je vais au bord de la mer.**
c. **J'apporte un cadeau.**
d. **J'ai besoin de mon maillot de bain.**

Mon journal

16 For an additional journal entry suggestion for Chapter 11, see *Cahier d'activités,* page 155.

Assess

- Testing Program, pp. 275–278
  Quiz 11-1A, Quiz 11-1B
  Audio CD 11, Tr. 20
- Student Make-Up Assignments, Chapter 11, Alternative Quiz
- Alternative Assessment Guide, p. 42

STANDARDS: 1.1, 1.2, 1.3, 5.1

CHAPITRE 11

Teaching Resources
p. 332

PRINT
- Video Guide, pp. 75, 76–77
- Cahier d'activités, p. 132

MEDIA
- One-Stop Planner
- Video Program Videocassette 4, 24:19–27:36
- DVD Tutor, Disc 2
- Audio Compact Discs, CD 11, Trs. 6–9
- Interactive CD-ROM Tutor, Disc 3

Presenting Panorama Culturel

Before playing the video, ask students to listen for what the people do on vacation. Remind them that they don't need to understand every word, just the general idea. After playing the video, have students work in groups to read the interviews and write answers to the questions in **Qu'en penses-tu?** Then, have the groups share their answers.

Questions

1. **Pourquoi est-ce que Sim va au village?** (pour voir les parents, parce que ça fait changer de climat)
2. **Qu'est-ce que Nicole fait aux fêtes de ses amis?** (Elle danse, s'amuse, rigole, joue aux cartes.)
3. **Nicole a combien de mois de vacances?** (deux)
4. **Avec qui est-ce que Céline part en vacances?** (avec des amis)

Answers

1. parents' village, the beach, the movies, parties, friends' homes, Spain, Corsica; dance, have fun, laugh, play cards

Qu'est-ce que tu fais pendant les vacances?

We asked some francophone people where they go and what they do on vacation. Here are their responses.

Sim,
Côte d'Ivoire

«Pendant les vacances, d'habitude je vais au village chez les parents qui sont restés au village. Et après une année scolaire, il faut aller les voir parce que ça... il y a longtemps qu'on se voit pas. Donc, ça fait plaisir aux parents de revoir les enfants quand ils vont au village. Voilà. Ça fait changer de climat. On va se reposer un peu.» Tr. 7

Nicole,
Martinique

«Pendant les vacances, alors, je vais généralement à la plage, au cinéma. Le soir, je sors, enfin je vais dans des fêtes, chez des amis. On danse. On s'amuse. On rigole. On joue aux cartes. Les vacances se passent comme ça.»

Quand est-ce que tu as des vacances?

«J'ai des vacances en juillet, à partir de juillet. Les vacances durent deux mois et nous reprenons l'école en septembre.» Tr. 8

Céline,
France

«Ben, pendant les vacances, bon, des fois je pars. L'année dernière, je suis partie en Espagne, cette année je pars en Corse. Je pars souvent avec des copains ou... sinon, je reste à Aix.» Tr. 9

Qu'en penses-tu? See answers below.

1. Where do these people like to go and what do they like to do during their vacations?
2. Where do you go and what do you do on vacation? How does this differ from what these people do?

Savais-tu que...?

Salaried employees in France are guaranteed five weeks of vacation time per year. Most people take a month off in July or August and take the fifth week at some other time of the year, often in winter.

Connections and Comparisons

Thinking Critically

Drawing Inferences After reading **Savais-tu que... ?**, have groups discuss the following questions: Why do you think people in the United States aren't guaranteed five weeks of vacation a year? Why do you think it is different in France?

Multicultural Link

Have students choose a country and find out how much vacation time people there have and when they usually take their vacations.

STANDARDS: 2.1, 3.2, 4.2

Deuxième étape

Objectives Reminding; reassuring; seeing someone off

WA3 ARLES-11

Vocabulaire

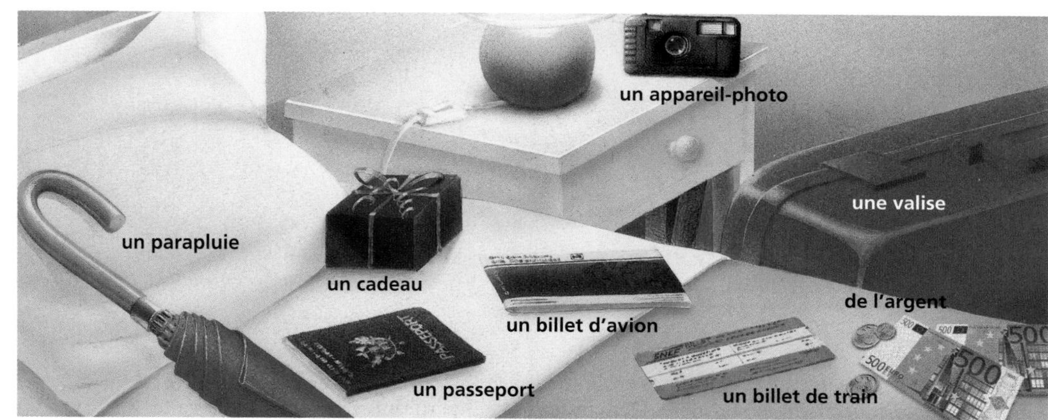

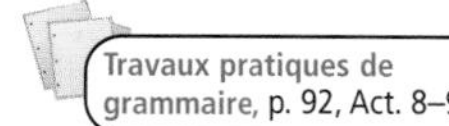
Travaux pratiques de grammaire, p. 92, Act. 8–9

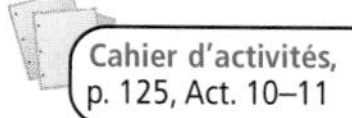
Cahier d'activités, p. 125, Act. 10–11

17 Qu'est-ce qu'il te faut?

Parlons Réponds aux questions suivantes.

1. Qu'est-ce qu'il faut quand il pleut? un parapluie
2. Qu'est-ce qu'il faut pour prendre le train? L'avion? un billet de train, un billet d'avion
3. Qu'est-ce qu'il faut pour acheter des souvenirs? de l'argent
4. Qu'est-ce qu'il faut pour prendre des photos? un appareil-photo

Comment dit-on...?

Reminding; reassuring

To remind someone of something:

N'oublie pas ton passeport!
Tu n'as pas oublié ton billet d'avion?
You didn't forget . . . ?
Tu ne peux pas partir sans ton écharpe!
You can't leave without . . . !
Tu prends ton manteau? *Are you taking . . . ?*

To reassure someone:

Ne t'en fais pas.
J'ai pensé à tout. *I've thought of everything.*
Je n'ai rien oublié. *I didn't forget anything.*

Cahier d'activités, p. 126, Act. 13

Communication for All Students

Visual/Kinesthetic Learners

17 As you read the questions out loud, have students respond by drawing the items. Have them check one another's work. You might also extend the activity by having students think of other situations in which the items might be necessary.

Additional Practice

Name a variety of destinations and have students suggest items you should take with you. Ask students to keep in mind the weather conditions and types of activities associated with the place as they make their suggestions.

Teaching Resources
pp. 333–336

PRINT

- Lesson Planner, p. 55
- TPR Storytelling Book, pp. 42, 44
- Listening Activities, pp. 84, 88
- Activities for Communication, pp. 63–64, 126, 128–129, 157–158
- Travaux pratiques de grammaire, pp. 92–95
- Grammar Tutor for Students of French, Chapter 11
- Cahier d'activités, pp. 125–127
- Testing Program, pp. 279–282
- Alternative Assessment Guide, p. 42
- Student Make-Up Assignments, Chapter 11

MEDIA 

- One-Stop Planner
- Audio Compact Discs, CD 11, Trs. 10–11, 21, 28–29
- Teaching Transparencies: 11-2, 11-C; **Grammaire supplémentaire** Answers; Travaux pratiques de grammaire Answers
- Interactive CD-ROM Tutor, Disc 3

Bell Work

Have students write where the following people could be going on vacation: **Nous voulons voir les pyramides. Anne-Marie et Yvette aiment faire du ski. Marco veut pratiquer son espagnol.**

Presenting Vocabulaire, Comment dit-on... ?

To present the vocabulary, bring in a suitcase with items from the **Vocabulaire.** Then, introduce the expressions from **Comment dit-on... ?** Say an expression for reminding with the new vocabulary **(N'oublie pas ton passeport!)** and have students pack the suitcase as they reassure you.

STANDARDS: 1.2

Deuxième étape

CHAPITRE 11

Teaching Resources
pp. 333–336

PRINT

- Lesson Planner, p. 55
- TPR Storytelling Book, pp. 42, 44
- Listening Activities, pp. 84, 88
- Activities for Communication, pp. 63–64, 126, 128–129, 157–158
- Travaux pratiques de grammaire, pp. 92–95
- Grammar Tutor for Students of French, Chapter 11
- Cahier d'activités, pp. 125–127
- Testing Program, pp. 279–282
- Alternative Assessment Guide, p. 42
- Student Make-Up Assignments, Chapter 11

MEDIA 

- One-Stop Planner
- Audio Compact Discs, CD 11, Trs. 10–11, 21, 28–29
- Teaching Transparencies: 11-2, 11-C; **Grammaire supplémentaire** Answers; Travaux pratiques de grammaire Answers
- Interactive CD-ROM Tutor, Disc 3

Presenting Grammaire

The verb *partir* Walk out the door, saying **Salut! Je pars!** Then, have various students walk toward the door as you describe their actions, using the forms of **partir.** Have students repeat the forms after you, and then have them deduce the forms of **sortir** and **dormir.** Write their guesses on a transparency, correcting any mistakes. Next, have students mime sleeping or leaving and ask the class **Qu'est-ce qu'il/elle fait?**

18 Tu n'as rien oublié? See scripts and answers on pp. 321G–321H.

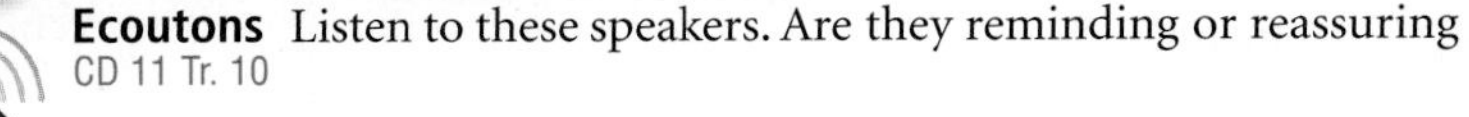

Ecoutons Listen to these speakers. Are they reminding or reassuring someone?
CD 11 Tr. 10

Si tu as oublié
clothing
va à la page 297.

19 Qu'est-ce qu'il a oublié?

Lisons/Parlons Regarde la liste de choses que Jean-Paul doit prendre avec lui pour son voyage. Fais une liste des choses qu'il a oubliées. Avec un(e) camarade, joue le rôle d'un parent de Jean-Paul et dis-lui ce qu'il doit prendre. Ensuite, changez de rôle.

Travaux pratiques de grammaire, p. 93, Act. 10

appareil-photo	casquette
billet d'avion	baskets
billet de train	shorts
passeport	chaussures
dictionnaire	chaussettes
magazines	cadeaux

20 Jeu de rôle

Parlons Cet été, tu vas en vacances en France avec ton club de français. Ton ami(e) est allé(e) en France l'année dernière. Demande-lui ce que tu dois prendre. Il/Elle va te répondre. Joue cette scène avec un(e) camarade, puis, changez de rôle.

EXEMPLE **—Qu'est-ce que je devrais prendre?**
—N'oublie pas ton appareil-photo.

Grammaire

The verb *partir*

A small group of verbs whose infinitives end in **-ir** follow a pattern different than the one you learned in Chapter 10.

partir *(to leave)*

Je	**pars**	Nous	**partons**
Tu	**pars**	Vous	**partez**
Il/Elle/On	**part**	Ils/Elles	**partent**

Elles **partent** à dix heures.

- Don't pronounce the **s** or **t** in **pars** or **part.**
- **Sortir** *(to go out)* and **dormir** *(to sleep)* also follow this pattern.

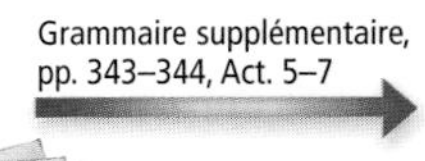

Cahier d'activités, p. 125, Act. 12

Travaux pratiques de grammaire, pp. 93–94, Act. 11–12

A la française

French speakers often use the present tense to talk about the future.
Je **pars** à neuf heures. *I'm leaving/I'm going to leave/I will leave . . .*
Je **sors** avec Aline ce soir. *I'm going out/I'm going to go out/I will go out . . .*

Communication for All Students

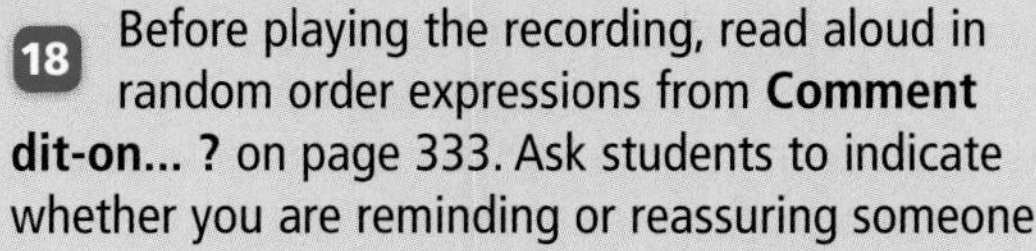

Slower Pace

18 Before playing the recording, read aloud in random order expressions from **Comment dit-on... ?** on page 333. Ask students to indicate whether you are reminding or reassuring someone.

19 Before students list what Jean-Paul has forgotten, have them copy his list and check off what he remembered to pack.

Challenge

19 You might also have students make a list of things Jean-Paul may have packed that are not on his list.

Slower Pace

20 Before they do this activity, have students make a short list of items they might need.

STANDARDS: 1.1, 1.2, 4.1

21 Grammaire en contexte

Ecrivons Tu parles de ta routine quotidienne avec la famille française chez qui tu habites. Complète chaque phrase avec la forme correcte de **partir, sortir** ou **dormir.**

1. Je __________ pour l'école à huit heures du matin. pars
2. Ma sœur et moi, nous __________ jusqu'à dix heures le samedi matin. dormons
3. Mon père et ma mère __________ toujours avant moi le matin. partent
4. Mon frère Emile __________ le vendredi soir avec son amie Agnès. sort

22 Vacances en Provence

See answers below.

Parlons Regarde l'itinéraire de Marianne. Ensuite, réponds aux questions.

1. D'où part Marianne samedi?
2. Où est-ce qu'elle va?
3. Son voyage va durer combien de temps?
4. Qu'est-ce qu'elle a l'intention de faire?

SAMEDI :
départ d'Arles, bus de 9h35;
arrivée aux Baux-de-Provence à 10h10;
* visite de la Cathédrale d'Images;
dîner : Auberge de la Benvengudo

DIMANCHE :

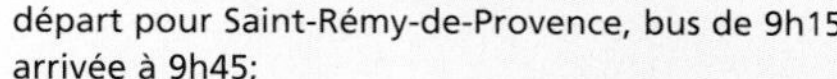

départ pour Saint-Rémy-de-Provence, bus de 9h15;
arrivée à 9h45;
* visite du musée Van Gogh; déjeuner : pique-nique à Fontvieille;
* visite du moulin de Daudet; retour aux Baux-de-Provence; départ pour Avignon, bus de 18h16; arrivée à 19h10 Hôtel le Midi; dîner

LUNDI :

* visite de la Cité des Papes, le Pont St-Bénezet, promenade du Rocher des Doms, le musée du Petit-Palais;
* spectacle folklorique; départ pour Grasse 20h15; arrivée à 22h10 Hôtel les Arômes

MARDI :
* visite de la Parfumerie Fragonard;
* Musée d'Art et d'Histoire de Provence; départ de Grasse à 17h42; arrivée en Arles à 19h20

23 Jeu de rôle

Parlons Tu vas faire le même voyage que Marianne. Ton/Ta camarade va te poser des questions sur ton voyage et va te dire ce que tu dois prendre avec toi.

EXEMPLE —**Tu vas aller aux Baux-de-Provence? N'oublie pas ton appareil-photo.**
—**Ah! C'est une bonne idée.**

24 Bonjour de Provence!

Ecrivons Pendant ton voyage en Provence, écris une carte postale à ton ami(e), à tes camarades de classe ou à ton professeur.

Language Notes

- You might explain to your students that **partir** means *to leave* and is used to stress the action of going away. **Sortir,** however, implies that one is *going out* for a short period of time and will be returning soon.
- Remind students that **partir, sortir,** and **dormir** follow a different pattern than **-ir** verbs like **choisir** and **finir.**

Additional Practice

21 To practice the other forms of these verbs, you might use large flash cards with different subject pronouns written on them and a clock with moveable hands. Set the clock to a certain time and hold up a subject flash card, asking **On part à quelle heure?**

Challenge

22 Have students write a short paragraph describing what Marianne is going to do during one day of her vacation. This might also be done orally. This activity is appropriate for students' written or oral portfolios.

Teaching Suggestion

24 Students might write their message on one side of an index card and illustrate it on the reverse side. Refer them to the Location Opener on pages 260–263 for illustration ideas.

Teacher Note

The postcard in Activity 24 features fields of lavender **(la lavande),** a flower native to the Provence region.

Connections and Comparisons

History Link

23 Before they do this activity, you might have groups of students research the historical significance of each of the places Marianne is visiting: **la Cathédrale d'Images, le musée Van Gogh, le moulin de Daudet, la Cité des Papes, le Pont Saint-Bénezet, le Rocher des Doms, le musée du Petit-Palais, la Parfumerie Fragonard,** and **le Musée d'Art et d'Histoire de Provence.**

Answers

22
1. d'Arles
2. aux Baux-de-Provence, à Saint-Rémy-de-Provence, à Avignon et à Grasse
3. quatre jours
4. *Possible answers:* visiter une cathédrale, des musées et une parfumerie, assister à un spectacle folklorique

Presenting
Comment dit-on... ?

Ask students what they say in English to see someone off at the airport or at the train or bus station. Have several students read the text in the speech bubbles. Then, introduce the expressions while waving goodbye and have students practice them with a partner.

Game

N'oublie pas! Name a vacation destination and have a student remind you of one thing to take. The next student should repeat the first item and remind you of another. Continue until everyone has had a chance to add an item or until a mistake is made, in which case, you might give another destination and restart the game.

Assess

- Testing Program, pp. 279–282 Quiz 11-2A, Quiz 11-2B Audio CD 11, Tr. 21
- Student Make-Up Assignments, Chapter 11, Alternative Quiz
- Alternative Assessment Guide, p. 42

Comment dit-on...?

Seeing someone off

To wish someone a good trip:

Bon voyage! *Have a good trip!*
Bonnes vacances! *Have a good vacation!*
Amuse-toi bien! *Have fun!*
Bonne chance! *Good luck!*

Cahier d'activités, p. 127, Act. 14–16

25 On arrive ou on part?

See scripts and answers on p. 321H.

Ecoutons Ecoute ces conversations. On arrive ou on part?
CD 11 Tr. 11

26 Au revoir!

Parlons Ton ami(e) français(e) part en France. Tu vas à l'aéroport avec lui/elle. Dis-lui au revoir. Joue cette scène avec un(e) camarade.

27 Un grand voyage

Parlons Ton ami(e) et toi, vous allez faire un voyage dans un autre pays. Choisissez le pays où vous voulez aller et les activités que vous allez faire. Parlez du temps qu'il fait dans ce pays et dites quand vous voulez partir. Parlez aussi des vêtements et des autres choses que vous allez prendre.

28 Un petit mot

Ecrivons Ton ami(e) va partir en voyage demain. Ecris-lui une lettre pour lui dire bon voyage. Suggère des activités qu'il/elle peut faire pendant ses vacances.

Tu te rappelles?

Do you remember how to give commands? Use the **tu** or **vous** form of the verb without a subject pronoun.

Attends! Allez!

When you use an **-er** verb, remember to drop the final **s** of the **tu** form.

Ecoute!

When you use an object pronoun with a positive command, place it after the verb, separated by a hyphen in writing.

Donnez-moi votre billet, s'il vous plaît.

Travaux pratiques de grammaire, p. 94, Act. 13

Grammaire supplémentaire, p. 344, Act. 8

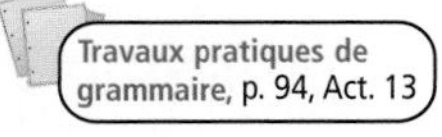

Si tu as oublié weather va à la page 118.

Travaux pratiques de grammaire, p. 95, Act. 14–15

Communication for All Students

Additional Practice

Ask students what they would say to a friend who was leaving on a long car trip; who was leaving on vacation; who was going to Disneyland™; who was leaving for a band competition.

Challenge

26 Encourage students to expand their goodbyes by telling the person what to do during the flight or after he or she gets home. They might use **N'oublie pas de...** or **Pense à...**

STANDARDS: 1.1, 1.2, 1.3, 5.1

Troisième étape

Objectives Asking for and expressing opinions; inquiring about and relating past events

WA3 ARLES-11

Comment dit-on...?

Asking for and expressing opinions

To ask someone's opinion:

Tu as passé un bon été?

Ça s'est bien passé? *Did it go well?*

Tu t'es bien amusé(e)? *Did you have fun?*

To express an opinion:

Oui, très chouette.
Oui, c'était formidable! *Yes, it was great!*
Oui, ça a été.
Oh, pas mauvais.
C'était épouvantable.
Non, pas vraiment. *No, not really.*
C'était un véritable cauchemar! *It was a real nightmare!*
C'était ennuyeux. *It was boring.*
C'était barbant.

Cahier d'activités, pp. 128–129, Act. 17–19

See scripts and answers on p. 321H.

29 C'était comment, les vacances?

CD 11 Tr. 12

Ecoutons Listen to these conversations and then tell whether these people had a good, fair, or bad vacation.

30 Méli-mélo!

Lisons Remets la conversation entre Thierry et Hervé dans le bon ordre.

Tu te rappelles?

Do you remember how to inquire about and relate events that happened in the past?

Tu es allé(e) où?
Qu'est-ce que tu as fait?
D'abord,... Ensuite,... Après,... Finalement,...

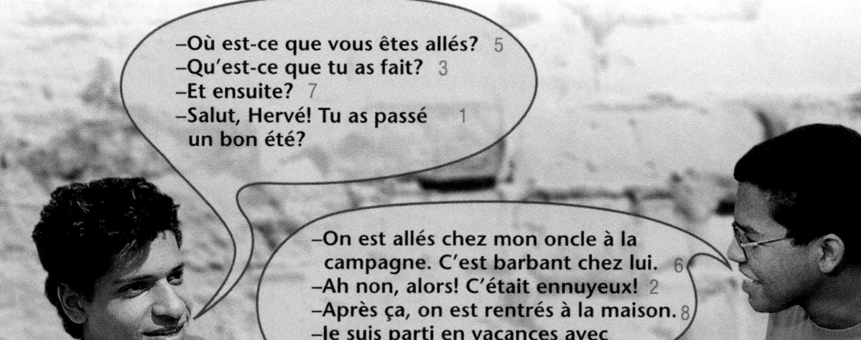

–Où est-ce que vous êtes allés? 5
–Qu'est-ce que tu as fait? 3
–Et ensuite? 7
–Salut, Hervé! Tu as passé un bon été? 1
–On est allés chez mon oncle à la campagne. C'est barbant chez lui. 6
–Ah non, alors! C'était ennuyeux! 2
–Après ça, on est rentrés à la maison. 8
–Je suis parti en vacances avec mes parents. 4

Communication for All Students

Challenge

29 Have students imagine they spent their vacation in a certain place and have them write a sentence telling how it was. Then, have them read their sentence to a partner, who will indicate whether the student had a good, fair, or bad time.

Building on Previous Skills

Have students list French expressions they've already learned for giving opinions. Have them recall the French gestures that indicate if something was great, so-so, and not so good. Then, have them work with a partner to talk about a vacation they took, using these gestures and previously learned vocabulary.

Troisième étape

CHAPITRE 11

Teaching Resources pp. 337–339

PRINT

- Lesson Planner, p. 56
- TPR Storytelling Book, pp. 43, 44
- Listening Activities, pp. 85, 89
- Activities for Communication, pp. 65–66, 127, 129, 157–158
- Travaux pratiques de grammaire, pp. 96–97
- Grammar Tutor for Students of French, Chapter 11
- Cahier d'activités, pp. 128–130
- Testing Program, pp. 283–286
- Alternative Assessment Guide, p. 42
- Student Make-Up Assignments, Chapter 11

MEDIA

- One-Stop Planner
- Audio Compact Discs, CD 11, Trs. 12, 22, 30–31
- Teaching Transparencies: 11-3; **Grammaire supplémentaire** Answers; Travaux pratiques de grammaire Answers
- Interactive CD-ROM Tutor, Disc 3

Bell Work

Have students write a note to a French friend who is coming to visit, reminding him or her of three things to pack for the trip.

Presenting Comment dit-on... ?

Draw three columns on the board and label them with a question mark, a happy face and an unhappy face. Teach these expressions, using appropriate gestures or facial expressions. Then, name vacation activities **(garder ma petite sœur, aller à la plage)** and have students react with an expression from the board as if they had done the activity while on vacation.

Troisième étape

CHAPITRE 11

Teaching Resources
pp. 337–339

PRINT 

- Lesson Planner, p. 56
- TPR Storytelling Book, pp. 43, 44
- Listening Activities, pp. 85, 89
- Activities for Communication, pp. 65–66, 127, 129, 157–158
- Travaux pratiques de grammaire, pp. 96–97
- Grammar Tutor for Students of French, Chapter 11
- Cahier d'activités, pp. 128–130
- Testing Program, pp. 283–286
- Alternative Assessment Guide, p. 42
- Student Make-Up Assignments, Chapter 11

MEDIA 

- One-Stop Planner
- Audio Compact Discs, CD 11, Trs. 12, 22, 30–31
- Teaching Transparencies: 11-3; **Grammaire supplémentaire** Answers; Travaux pratiques de grammaire Answers
- Interactive CD-ROM Tutor, Disc 3

Portfolio

32 **Written** This activity could also be written and would be appropriate for students' written portfolios. For portfolio suggestions, see *Alternative Assessment Guide,* pages iv–17.

Tu te rappelles?

CD-ROM 3 DVD 2

Si tu as oublié **le passé composé** va à la page 271.

Grammaire supplémentaire, p. 345, Act. 9–10

Cahier d'activités, p. 130, Act. 21

Travaux pratiques de grammaire, pp. 96–97, Act. 16–18

Do you remember how to form the **passé composé?** Use a form of **avoir** as a helping verb with the past participle of the main verb. The past participles of regular **-er, -re,** and **-ir** verbs end in **é, u,** and **i.**

Nous **avons** beaucoup **mangé.** J'**ai répondu** à leur lettre. Ils **ont fini.**

You have to memorize the past participles of irregular verbs.

J'**ai fait** du camping. Ils **ont vu** un film.

To make a verb in the **passé composé** negative, you place **ne... pas** around the helping verb.

Il **n'**a **pas** fait ses devoirs.

With **aller, partir,** and **sortir,** you use **être** as the helping verb instead of **avoir.**

31 Qu'est-ce qu'elle a fait?  See answers below.

Lisons/Ecrivons Mets ces activités dans le bon ordre d'après l'itinéraire de Marianne à la page 335 en utilisant le passé composé.

EXEMPLE **D'abord, elle...**

visiter la Parfumerie Fragonard
visiter le musée Van Gogh
voir un spectacle folklorique
visiter la Cité des Papes
voir le moulin de Daudet
faire la promenade du Rocher des Doms
faire un pique-nique

32 On fait la même chose?

Parlons Ton/Ta camarade et toi, vous avez pris ces photos pendant vos vacances en France l'année dernière. Expliquez où vous êtes allé(e)s et ce que vous avez fait. Donnez votre opinion sur chaque activité ou sur chaque endroit.

Un café sur le Cours Mirabeau

Le palais des Papes, c'est formidable.

La mer Méditerranée

Les arènes en Arles

La Côte d'Azur

Communication for All Students

Reteaching

Passé composé Review the forms of **avoir** on a transparency. Ask students if they remember how to form the past participles of regular **-er, -re,** and **-ir** verbs and if they can recall the irregular past participles of verbs like **faire, lire,** and **voir.** To practice verb forms, you might also want to play the verb game **Réponds vite!,** described on page 321C.

Additional Practice

Tu te rappelles? You might conduct a short, oral practice of the **passé composé** by asking simple questions such as **Qu'est-ce que tu as mis hier? Qu'est-ce que tu as fait pendant le week-end? Qu'est-ce que tu as mangé ce matin?** Then, have partners ask each other what they did yesterday and tell three things they did.

Answers

31 D'abord, elle a visité le musée Van Gogh. Ensuite, elle a fait un pique-nique, et elle a vu le moulin de Daudet. Après ça, elle a visité la Cité des Papes, et elle a fait la promenade du Rocher des Doms. Ensuite, elle a vu un spectacle folklorique. Enfin, elle a visité la Parfumerie Fragonard.

  De l'école au travail 

Ecrivons You work for a company that organizes tours for young people. One of your clients has requested that you write him a note telling what he needs to bring on the trip. Study the itinerary on page 335 that you've put together for his tour group and write him a short fax detailing what he should pack.

EXEMPLE **Le samedi 7 juin tu vas prendre le bus pour les Baux-de-Provence. N'oublie pas ton argent pour acheter le billet.**

PRONONCIATION

CD 11
Trs. 13–18

Aspirated h, th, ch, and gn See scripts and answers on p. 321H.

You've learned that you don't pronounce the letter **h** in French. Some words begin with an aspirated **h** (**h aspiré**). This means that you don't make elision and liaison with the word that comes before. Repeat these phrases: **le haut-parleur; le houx; les halles; les haricots.**

Haut and **houx** begin with an aspirated **h,** so you can't drop the **e** from the article **le. Halles** and **haricots** also begin with an aspirated **h,** so you don't pronounce the **s** in the article **les.** How will you know which words begin with an aspirated **h?** If you look the words up in the dictionary, you may find an asterisk (*) before an aspirated **h.**

How do you pronounce the combination **th?** Just ignore the letter **h** and pronounce the **t.** Repeat these words: **mathématiques, théâtre, athlète.**

What about the combination **ch?** In French, **ch** is pronounced like the English *sh,* as in the word *show.* Compare these English and French words: *change*/**change,** *chocolate*/**chocolat,** *chance*/**chance.** In some words, **ch** is pronounced like *k.* Listen to these words and repeat them: **chorale, Christine, archéologie.**

Finally, how do you pronounce the combination **gn?** The English sound /ny/, as in the word *onion* is similar. Pronounce these words: **oignon, montagne, magnifique.**

A. A prononcer

Repeat the following words.

1. le héros	la harpe	le hippie	le hockey
2. thème	maths	mythe	bibliothèque
3. Chine	choisir	tranche	pêches
4. espagnol	champignon	montagne	magnifique

B. A lire

Take turns with a partner reading each of the following sentences aloud.

1. J'aime la Hollande, mais je veux aller à la montagne en Allemagne.
2. Je cherche une chemise, des chaussures et un chapeau.
3. Il n'a pas fait ses devoirs de maths et de chimie à la bibliothèque dimanche.
4. Charles a gagné trois hamsters. Ils sont dans ma chambre! Quel cauchemar!

C. A écrire

You're going to hear a short dialogue. Write down what you hear.

Connections and Comparisons

Geography Link

33 Encourage students to use atlases or other reference materials to find out more about the climate and topography of the Provence region.

Language-to-Language

- The word **le houx** means *holly.*
- Many words with the **h aspiré** are of Germanic, rather than Latin, origin or were borrowed from modern German or English. You might point out that words of these origins generally do not have **l'** preceding them.

Portfolio

32 **Oral** This might be included in students' oral portfolios. For portfolio suggestions, see *Alternative Assessment Guide,* page 28.

Speaking Assessment

32 You might use the following rubric when grading your students on this activity.

Speaking Rubric	Points			
	4	3	2	1
Content (Complete–Incomplete)				
Comprehension (Total–Little)				
Comprehension (Comprehensible–Incomprehensible)				
Accuracy (Accurate–Seldom accurate)				
Fluency (Fluent–Not fluent)				

18–20: A
16–17: B
14–15: C
12–13: D
Under 12: F

Teaching Suggestion

Prononciation You might have students prepare to read aloud any two of the sentences in Part B for oral assessment.

Assess

- Testing Program, pp. 283–286 Quiz 11-3A, Quiz 11-3B Audio CD 11, Tr. 22
- Student Make-Up Assignments, Chapter 11, Alternative Quiz
- Alternative Assessment Guide, p. 42

STANDARDS: 1.1, 1.3, 4.1, 5.1, 5.2

Lisons!

CHAPITRE 11

Teaching Resources
pp. 340–341

PRINT 

- Lesson Planner, p. 57
- Cahier d'activités, p. 131
- Reading Strategies and Skills Handbook, Chapter 11
- Joie de lire 1, Chapter 11
- Standardized Assessment Tutor, Chapter 11

MEDIA 

- One-Stop Planner

Prereading
Activities A–B

Motivating Activity
Before they begin the activities, have students look at travel guides for New York City, Chicago, Dallas, and so on. You might also ask them to bring in travel guides. Have groups of students go through the guides that are available and identify the general categories of information found in them. Then, do Activities A–B as a class.

Lisons!

Un guide touristique

Stratégie pour lire
When you read for a purpose, it's a good idea to decide beforehand what kind of information you want. If you're looking for an overview, a quick, general reading may be all that is required. If you're looking for specific details, you'll have to read more carefully.

A. The information at the top of both pages is from a book entitled *Le Guide du Routard.* Do you think this is
1. a history book?
2. a travel guide?
3. a geography book?

B. You usually read a book like this to gather general information about what is going on, or to find details about a certain place or event. What general categories of information can you find? Under what titles? See answers below.

C. Where should you stay if . . .
1. you plan to visit Provence in November?
2. you want a balcony?
3. you want the least expensive room you can get?
4. you have a tent and a sleeping bag? See answers below.

D. Do you think the descriptions of the hotels were written by the hotel management? How do you know? No; Some remarks are unfavorable.

Où dormir?

Très bon marché
Auberge de jeunesse : 20, av. Foch. ☎ 04-90-96-18-25. Fax : 04-90-96-31-26. Fermée du 20 décembre au 10 février. 100 lits. 12,2€ la première nuit, 10,4€ les suivantes, draps et petit déjeuner compris. Fait aussi restaurant. Repas à 7,2€.

Prix modérés
Hôtel Gaugin : 5, place Voltaire. ☎ 04-90-96-14-35. Fax : 04-90-18-98-87. Fermé en novembre. De 27,5 à 32€ la chambre double. Chambres simples, bien aménagées. Les six qui donnent sur la place ont un balcon et la vue sur la place Voltaire. Peu de charme cependant dans ce quartier de l'après-guerre. Le petit plus : tous les matins la météo locale est affichée à la réception!

Plus chic
Hôtel du Musée : 11, rue du Grand-Prieuré. ☎ 04-90-93-88-88. Fax : 04-90-49-98-15. Fermé en janvier. De 45,7 à 61€ la chambre double. Joli patio pour le petit déjeuner. Dans une belle demeure du XVIIe siècle, face au musée Réattu et à deux pas du Rhône, une excellente adresse. Très bien situé et très bon accueil.

Camping
Camping City : 67, route de Crau. ☎ 04-90-93-08-86. Fax : 04-90-93-91-07. Fermé du 30 octobre au 1er mars. Assez ombragé, mais plutôt bruyant. Attention aux moustiques, car situé près d'un marécage. Piscine, épicerie, plats à emporter. Animations en été.

BATEAU «MIREIO»
Bateau restaurant de 250 places, chauffé, climatisé. Croisières déjeuner sans escale vers Châteauneuf-du-Pape ou avec escale en Arles – visite de la capitale de la Camargue –, à Roquemaure avec dégustation des vins de Côtes du Rhône, à Villeneuve avec visite du village et de ses monuments. Croisières dîner et soirées spectacle devant Avignon et Villeneuve. Animation dansante et commentaires sur toutes les croisières.

84000 AVIGNON -
Tél. : 04 90 85 62 25
Fax : 04 90 85 61 14

CATHEDRALE D'IMAGES
Aux Baux-de-Provence, dans les anciennes carrières du Val-d'Enfer, CATHEDRALE D'IMAGES propose un spectacle permanent en IMAGE TOTALE.4.000m2 d'écrans naturels, 40 sources de projection, 2 500 diapos créent une féerie visuelle et sonore où déambule le spectateur.–Couvrez-vous car les carrières sont fraîches!–

13520 LES BAUX-DE-PROVENCE -
Tél. : 04 90 54 38 65
Fax : 04 90 54 42 65

Communication for All Students

Building on Previous Skills
Point out Provence on a map. Have students share information they have already learned about Provence through the Location Opener for Chapters 9–11, the **Notes culturelles,** and their projects for Chapter 9. Ask students what they would do if they were to go on a vacation to Provence.

Slower Pace
You might assign small groups a category each, such as meals, food, months of the year, days of the week, and so on. Ask them to scan the travel information and list words they recognize that fit their category.

Answers
B. what to see (various titles), where to eat *(Où manger?)*, where to sleep *(Où dormir?)*
C. 1. Auberge de jeunesse en Arles, Hôtel du Musée
2. Hôtel Gauguin
3. Auberge de jeunesse en Arles
4. Camping City

STANDARDS: 1.2, 2.2, 3.1

Où manger?

Bon marché

Vitamine : 16, rue du Docteur-Fanton, ☎ 04-90-93-77-36. derrière la place du Forum. Fermé le samedi soir et le dimanche sauf pendant la féria et le mois de la Photo. Une carte de 50 salades différentes, de 2,8 à 7,6€, 15 spécialités de pâtes de 5,3 à 7,3€, le tout dans une salle agréablement décorée (expos photos) et avec un accueil décontracté.

Le Grillon : 36, rond-point des Arènes. ☎ 04-90-96-70-97. Fermé le dimanche soir et le mercredi. Menu à 12,8€, très honnête, le midi, le soir et le week-end, avec soupe de poisson, fricassée de canard à la graine de moutarde, fromage ou dessert. À la carte, comptez 18,3 € pour un repas complet. Ce restaurant-brasserie-crêperie-glacier ne paie pas de mine, mais il y a une agréable terrasse avec une très belle vue sur les arènes. On y découvre de bons petits plats sympathiques.

Le Poisson Banane : 6, rue du Forum. ☎ 04-90-96-02-58. Ouvert uniquement le soir. Fermé le dimanche seulement hors saison. Menus à 12€ jusqu'à 21 h, 18,3 et 20,6€. Avec sa grande terrasse et sa tonnelle, ce petit resto caché derrière la place du Forum passe facilement inaperçu et c'est dommage. Il est agréable d'aller y goûter une cuisine sucrée-salée inventive avec une spécialité antillaise : le «poisson banane», bien sûr.

CHATEAU MUSEE DE L'EMPERI

Le CHATEAU DE L'EMPERI,

la plus importante forteresse médiévale en Provence, abrite une des plus somptueuses collections d'art et d'histoire militaire qui soit en Europe. Cette collection unique illustre l'évolution des uniformes et de l'art militaire de Louis XIV à 1918. La période napoléonienne est la plus présente. Le Château de l'Empéri est situé en plein cœur de la ville ancienne.

13300 SALON DE PROVENCE - Tél : 04 90 56 22 36

GROTTES DE THOUZON

Les décors de stalactites qui parent « le ciel » de ce réseau naturel forment des paysages souterrains merveilleux. (Photo : M. CROTET) Grotte réputée pour la finesse de ses stalactites (fistuleuses). Parcours aisé pour les personnes âgées et les enfants. Seule grotte naturelle aménagée pour le tourisme en Provence. Ouvert du 1/04 au 31/10. Groupe toute l'année sur rendez-vous.

84250 LE THOR
Tél. : 04 90 33 93 65
Fax : 04 90 33 74 90

E. Which restaurant should you try if . . . See answers below.

1. you want the most expensive meal available?
2. you love salad?
3. you want to go out on Saturday night?

F. At the bottom of both pages, you will find descriptions of several tourist attractions in Provence. After you've read them, match the attractions listed below with the sites where you would find them.

1. a dinner cruise b
2. stalactites c
3. thousands of projection screens a
4. a collection of military art and uniforms d

a. Cathédrale d'Images
b. Bateau «Miréio»
c. Grottes de Thouzon
d. Château Musée de l'Empéri

G. If you were working at a tourist information office, what would you recommend to someone who . . . See answers below.

1. wants a comfortable cruise package?
2. would like to visit a medieval castle?
3. likes to explore caves?
4. is interested in military art?

H. Are there similar tourist attractions in your area? What are they?

I. You and your friend have three days to spend in Arles. You're on a very tight budget, but you still want to enjoy your trip. Where will you stay? Where will you eat your lunches and dinners? How much will you spend for these three days?

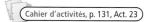

Cahier d'activités, p. 131, Act. 23

Lisons!

CHAPITRE 11

Reading

Activities C–H

Thinking Critically

Drawing Inferences Ask students to suggest reasons why the places listed under **Où dormir?** are closed during various times of the year.

Postreading

Activity I

Teaching Suggestion

I. Using Marianne's itinerary on page 335 as an example, students might write out their final itinerary and hand it in.

Challenge

Have students research lodgings and restaurants in a city they'd like to visit or in their own city. Have them create a brochure for French tourists that rates the hotels and restaurants. Price categories might include **très bon marché, bon marché, prix modérés,** and **plus chic.** They might also find out hotel rates and average menu prices and list them in euros. Current exchange rates can be obtained from the newspaper or from larger banks and the Internet.

Connections and Comparisons

Science Link

You might have your students do research to find out how caves such as the **Grottes de Thouzon** are formed.

Math Link

I. Give students a specific amount for their budget and have them itemize everything that they spend. You might have a contest to see which student can spend the least amount of money and still have some of the budgeted amount left over. You might also stipulate that they must follow common-sense guidelines for health and safety, so they must eat and stay in a hotel or hostel.

Answers

E. 1. Le Poisson Banane
2. Vitamine
3. Le Grillon, Le Poisson Banane

G. 1. Bateau «Miréio»
2. Château Musée de l'Empéri
3. Grottes de Thouzon
4. Château Musée de l'Empéri

STANDARDS: 1.2, 2.2, 3.1, 5.2

Grammaire supplémentaire

CHAPITRE 11

For **Grammaire supplémentaire** Answer Transparencies, see the *Teaching Transparencies* binder.

Answers

1 **Il fait beau, alors...**
1. je vais faire de la randonnée avec des copains.
2. on va prendre des photos dans le parc.
3. nous allons passer la journée à la plage.

Il pleut, alors...
4. mes tantes vont regarder un film à la télévision.
5. vous n'allez pas sortir de chez vous.
6. tu vas lire un roman.

2
1. Antoine va faire du bateau.
2. Sophie et sa sœur vont faire de la voile.
3. Nous allons aller au bord de la mer.
4. Vous allez faire de la randonnée.

3
1. l'Australie; Elle va aller en Australie.
2. les Etats-Unis; Elle va aller aux Etats-Unis.
3. le Mexique; Elle va aller au Mexique.
4. l'Italie; Elle va aller en Italie.
5. le Canada; Elle va aller au Canada.

Grammaire supplémentaire

Première étape

Objectives Inquiring about and sharing future plans; expressing indecision; expressing wishes; asking for advice; making, accepting, and refusing suggestions

1 Lis chaque phrase et décide si on parle d'une activité à faire quand il fait beau ou quand il pleut. Ensuite, écris les phrases dans la catégorie appropriée. (**p. 328**)

- je vais faire de la randonnée avec des copains.
- on va prendre des photos dans le parc.
- mes tantes vont regarder un film à la télévision.
- vous n'allez pas sortir de chez vous.
- nous allons passer la journée à la plage.
- tu vas lire un roman.

Il fait beau, alors...	Il pleut, alors...
1. . . .	**4.** . . .
2. . . .	**5.** . . .
3. . . .	**6.** . . .

2 Voici ce que ces gens font d'habitude en été. Mets ces phrases au futur en utilisant le verbe **aller.** (**pp. 174, 328**)

1. Antoine fait du bateau.
2. Sophie et sa sœur font de la voile.
3. Ma famille et moi, nous allons au bord de la mer.
4. Anne et toi, vous faites de la randonnée.

3 Le nom de ces étudiants étrangers commence par la première lettre de leur pays d'origine. Trouve le pays d'origine de chaque étudiant et dis où ils vont aller en vacances cet été. (**p. 330**)

EXEMPLE Bélinda/**le Brésil** -> **Elle va aller au Brésil.**

1. ANNE/ ______ - ______
2. ERIN/______ - ______
3. MARIA/______ - ______
4. ISABELLA/______ - ______
5. CÉLINE/ ______ - ______

le Canada — le Mexique — les Etats-Unis — le Brésil — l'Australie — l'Italie

Grammar Resources for Chapter 11

The **Grammaire supplémentaire** activities were designed as supplemental activities for the grammatical concepts presented in the chapter. You might use them as additional practice, for review, or for assessment.

For more grammar presentations, review, and practice, refer to the following:
- Travaux pratiques de grammaire
- Grammar Tutor for Students of French
- Grammar Summary on pp. R15–R28
- Cahier d'activités
- Grammar and Vocabulary quizzes (Testing Program)
- Test Generator
- Interactive CD-ROM Tutor
- **Jeux interactifs** at **go.hrw.com**

STANDARDS: 1.2

Grammaire supplémentaire

CHAPITRE 11

4 Jeanne et ses amis ne savent pas où aller en vacances et te demandent conseil. Lis ce qu'ils aiment faire et suggère-leur un des pays proposés. (**p. 330.**)

EXEMPLE J'aime faire de la randonnée! **Pourquoi tu ne vas pas en Suisse?**

1. J'adore les quiches et les croque-monsieur!
   ____
2. Nous aimons la plage.
   ____
3. Je voudrais visiter les pyramides.
   ____
4. Nous adorons parler espagnol.
   ____

la Californie
l'Egypte
la Suisse
le Mexique
la France

Deuxième étape

Objectives Reminding; reassuring; seeing someone off

5 Pour chaque phrase, choisis le sujet qui va avec le verbe, et ensuite, décide si ce qu'on dit est **une bonne idée** ou **une mauvaise idée.** (**p. 334**)

1. (Elle/Vous) partez à midi pour aller au lycée?
   C'est une ______ idée.
2. (Tu/Nous) dors pendant que le prof parle?
   C'est une ______ idée.
3. (Vous/Elle) part souvent en vacances.
   C'est une ______ idée.
4. (Je/Nous) ne pars jamais sans mon parapluie quand il pleut.
   C'est une ______ idée.
5. (Je/Ils) sortent souvent sans prendre leurs portefeuilles.
   C'est une ______ idée.
6. (Nous/Ils) ne sortons jamais sans nos lunettes de soleil quand il fait beau.
   C'est une ______ idée.

Teacher to Teacher

Ricky Adamson
Forrest City High School
Forrest City, AK

Ricky's students put the pieces together.

"To practice the forms of **partir, sortir,** and **dormir,** have students make verb puzzles with separate pieces for each subject pronoun, the stem of the verb and the verb endings. For example, for the **je** form of **partir,** students would have 3 puzzle pieces—the subject pronoun **je,** the verb stem **par,** and the ending **s.** When the puzzle is put together, students will see **je pars.**"

Answers

4
1. Pourquoi tu ne vas pas en France?
2. Pourquoi vous n'allez pas en Californie?
3. Pourquoi tu ne vas pas en Egypte?
4. Pourquoi vous n'allez pas au Mexique?

5
1. Vous / mauvaise
2. Tu / mauvaise
3. Elle / bonne
4. Je / bonne
5. Ils / mauvaise
6. Nous / bonne

CHAPITRE 11

For **Grammaire supplémentaire** Answer Transparencies, see the *Teaching Transparencies* binder.

Grammaire supplémentaire

WA3 ARLES-11

6 Ecris cinq phrases pour dire quand tes amis et toi, vous allez à l'école. Utilise le verbe **partir.** (**p. 334**)

EXEMPLE Marianne (8h30) **Elle part à huit heures et demie.**

1. Antoine et moi (6h15)
2. Et toi, Maryse (7h00)
3. Lise et Marie (7h30)
4. Philippe et toi (8h00)
5. Stéphane (8h45)

7 Omar et Larissa se préparent pour aller chez leur grand-mère. Complète leur conversation avec les formes appropriées des verbes entre parenthèses. (**p. 334**)

OMAR Dis, Larissa, tu __1__ (dormir) toujours?

LARISSA Oui. Je __2__ (dormir)!

OMAR Mais c'est pas possible! On __3__ (partir) dans une heure!

LARISSA On __4__ (aller) où?

OMAR Tu ne te rappelles pas? Nous __5__ (partir) en vacances aujourd'hui! Au bord de la mer! Chez Mémé!

LARISSA Ah, mais c'est vrai! J'avais oublié! C'est super! Qu'est-ce que je __6__ (prendre)? Mon maillot de bain?

OMAR Oui. __7__ (prendre)-le! Il __8__ (aller) faire chaud! Et n' __9__ (oublier) pas une robe! On va __10__ (sortir) avec les copains tous les soirs.

LARISSA Je __11__ (pouvoir) prendre la valise de Maman?

OMAR Oui. Si tu __12__ (vouloir).

LARISSA Dis, Omar, tu n' __13__ (avoir) pas oublié le cadeau pour Mémé?

OMAR Mais non. Je n' __14__ (avoir) rien oublié. J' __15__ (avoir) pensé à tout.

8 Il y a des choses que tes amis et toi, vous devez prendre quand vous partez en vacances. Vos parents vous disent de les prendre. Ecris ce qu'ils vous disent et utilise le pronom approprié **le, la** ou **les**. (**pp. 279, 336**)

EXEMPLE Je ne peux pas partir sans mon blouson en jean.
Eh bien, prends-le!

1. Je ne peux pas partir sans ma valise!
2. Je ne peux pas partir sans mon passeport!
3. Nous ne pouvons pas partir sans nos chaussures en cuir!
4. Je ne peux pas partir sans mon appareil-photo!
5. Nous ne pouvons pas partir sans nos lunettes de soleil!
6. Je ne peux pas partir sans ma cravate à fleurs.

Answers

6
1. Nous partons à six heures et quart.
2. Tu pars à sept heures.
3. Elles partent à sept heures et demie.
4. Vous partez à huit heures.
5. Il part à neuf heures moins le quart.

7
1. dors
2. dors
3. part
4. va
5. partons
6. prends
7. Prends
8. va
9. oublie
10. sortir
11. peux
12. veux
13. as
14. ai
15. ai

8
1. Eh bien, prends-la!
2. Eh bien, prends-le!
3. Eh bien, prenez-les!
4. Eh bien, prends-le!
5. Eh bien, prenez-les!
6. Eh bien, prends-la!

Communication for All Students

Game

Tic Tac Toe Draw a Tic Tac Toe grid on the board. Write a subject pronoun and the infinitive **sortir, dormir,** or **partir** in each square, and have students copy the grid. In order to mark an *X* or an *O* in a square, players must write the correct verb form in that square. Have students play the game with a partner.

Challenge

7 Have students work in pairs to create a similar conversation. They should pick a different destination and remind each other to take the necessary items. You might have volunteers perform their skit in front of the classroom.

STANDARDS: 1.2

Troisième étape

Objectives Asking for and expressing opinions; inquiring about and relating past events

Grammaire supplémentaire

CHAPITRE 11

9 Hélène raconte ce qu'elle a fait pendant ses vacances l'année dernière et parle de ce qu'elle va faire cette année. En lisant chaque phrase, décide de quelles vacances elle parle et ensuite, choisis la photo qui dépeint le mieux ses vacances. (**pp. 328, 338**)

1. Ça va être une aventure!
2. Je suis restée chez moi tout le temps.
3. Il va faire beau.
4. Je vais mettre un short et des lunettes de soleil dans ma valise avant de partir.
5. J'ai eu le temps de lire un roman.
6. Il n'a pas fait beau.
7. Je vais aller à la plage.
8. J'ai regardé la télé.

a.

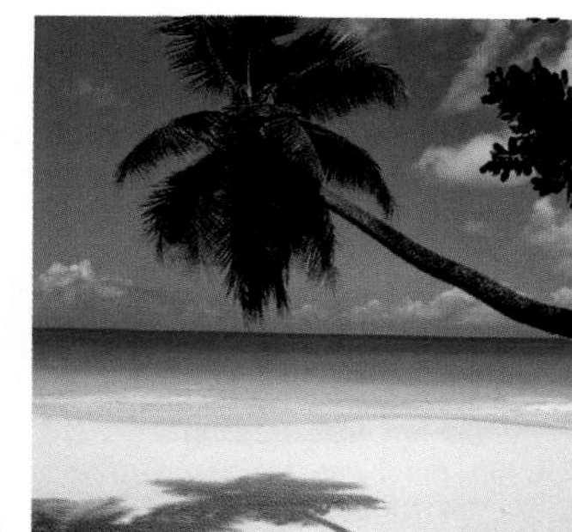
b.

10 Mets les mots dans un ordre logique pour dire ce que tes amis et toi, vous avez fait pendant les vacances. N'oublie pas de mettre les verbes au passé composé. (**pp. 271, 338**)

EXEMPLE On/faire/ne/rien/de/spécial **On n'a rien fait de spécial.**

1. Karim et moi/pièce/voir/une/super/nous
2. Tu/de/au bord de/la/faire/mer/voile/la/non?
3. Christelle/jusqu'à midi/dormir
4. Jacques et Simon/la télé/regarder/pendant des heures
5. Jonathan et toi/de/randonnée?/vous/la/faire
6. Larissa et moi/des/sensass/lire/romans/nous
7. Véra et Julie/visiter/le Louvre
8. Moi/à/des/répondre/lettres/je

Review and Assess

You may wish to assign the **Grammaire supplémentaire** activities as additional practice or homework after presenting material throughout the chapter. Assign Activities 1–2 after **Tu te rappelles?** (p. 328), Activities 3–4 after **Note de grammaire** (p. 330), Activities 5–7 after **Grammaire** (p. 334), Activity 8 after **Tu te rappelles?** (p. 336), and Activities 9–10 after **Tu te rappelles?** (p. 338).

To prepare students for the **Etape** Quizzes and Chapter Test, we suggest doing the **Grammaire supplémentaire** activities in the following order. Have students complete Activities 1–4 before taking Quizzes 11-1A or 11-1B; Activities 5–8 before Quizzes 11-2A or 11-2B; and Activities 9–10 before Quizzes 11-3A or 11-3B.

Answers

9
1. cette année (b)
2. l'année dernière (a)
3. cette année (b)
4. cette année (b)
5. l'année dernière (a)
6. l'année dernière (a)
7. cette année (b)
8. l'année dernière (a)

10
1. Karim et moi, nous avons vu une pièce super.
2. Tu as fait de la voile au bord de la mer, non?
3. Christelle a dormi jusqu'à midi.
4. Jacques et Simon ont regardé la télé pendant des heures.
5. Jonathan et toi, vous avez fait de la randonnée?
6. Larissa et moi, nous avons lu des romans sensass.
7. Véra et Julie ont visité le Louvre.
8. Moi, j'ai répondu à des lettres.

Mise en pratique

CHAPITRE 11
The **Mise en pratique** reviews and integrates all four skills and culture in preparation for the Chapter Test.

Teaching Resources
pp. 346–347

PRINT 

- Lesson Planner, p. 57
- Listening Activities, p. 85
- Video Guide, pp. 75, 78
- Grammar Tutor for Students of French, Chapter 11
- Standardized Assessment Tutor, Chapter 11

MEDIA

- One-Stop Planner
- Video Program Videocassette 4, 27:38–29:11
- DVD Tutor, Disc 2
- Audio Compact Discs, CD 11, Tr. 19
- Interactive CD-ROM Tutor, Disc 3

Teaching Suggestion
1 You might first have students listen to the recording, read the questions, and then listen again for the answers.

Mise en pratique

1 Listen to the radio advertisement and then answer the questions below. See scripts and answers on p. 321H.

CD 11 Tr. 19

1. What is being advertised?
2. Can you name two places that are mentioned in the advertisement?
3. What activities are mentioned in the advertisement?
4. For whom do they offer discounts?

2 Regarde cette brochure et réponds aux questions suivantes.

Le rêve américain devient réalité, en séjour Immersion avec EF

Vivre à l'américaine
Qui n'a rêvé un jour de vivre une autre vie ? Ce rêve devient réalité, grâce à la formule EF Immersion : pendant quelques semaines, vous devenez totalement américain. Parce que les familles d'accueil sont soigneusement séléctionnées par EF, votre intégration est immédiate, et vos progrès linguistiques sont aussi spectaculaires que durables. C'est, sans nul doute, la formule qui vous assure la connaissance la plus directe et la plus profonde du mode de vie américain.

Vacances de Printemps

N° de séjour	Date de départ	Date de retour	Durée du séjour	Région	Frais de séjour*
550	11 avril	25 avril	2 sem.	Côte Est	1.179
551	18 avril	2 mai	2 sem.	Côte Est	1.179
552	18 avril	2 mai	2 sem.	Sud-Est	1.246

1. Where do students go if they sign up for this trip? the United States
2. Where do they stay? with a family
3. What do they learn? English language, American lifestyle
4. In what months can students make this trip? April, May
5. How long does it last? 2 weeks
6. To what regions of the country can students go? the East Coast, the Southeast
7. How much does this trip cost? 1.179€ for the East Coast, 1.246€ for the Southeast

3 Dis si les phrases suivantes sont vraies ou fausses.

1. Only a few French children attend summer camp. false
2. French children can study foreign languages at summer camp. true
3. Most French people take a one-week summer vacation. false

Apply and Assess

Slower Pace
1 Have students write a list of the vacation words and expressions they expect to hear in this advertisement; they can look at this list while they listen to the recording. You might pause the recording after each type of vacation to assess comprehension.

Challenge
2 After students have answered the questions, have them discuss or write about their reaction to the ad. You might have them design a similar ad aimed at Americans who might like to experience the culture of France or of other francophone countries.

 STANDARDS: 1.2

4 Ecrivons!

Write a letter to a French-speaking exchange student who is coming to your school. Tell him or her what there is to see and do where you live, what the weather is like there, and what to bring.

Prewriting

Before you begin your letter, arrange your ideas logically to make your letter flow more smoothly. You might want to divide a sheet of paper into columns and label each column with a subject you'll address in your letter (**le temps, il te faut...**, and so on). Write each of your ideas in the appropriate column.

> **Stratégie pour écrire**
> Using connecting words such as **donc** and **alors** to link your ideas can help your writing flow more naturally.

Writing

Using the ideas you organized, write a letter to describe the place where you live. Include a lot of detail in your description to help form an image of the places to visit. Try to use connecting words to tie sentences together in the letter. Remember to use expressions you've learned for making suggestions and reminding someone to do something.

Revising

Proofreading is one of the most important steps in the evaluation process. It gives you a chance to correct any mistakes you might have made while you were writing. While writing your first draft, concentrate on being creative. You can make corrections to the grammar, punctuation, and spelling when you proofread.

It's a good idea to proofread in several passes. First, read through your letter to check only for grammar and punctuation mistakes. On your second pass, check for spelling errors. This way, there will be fewer errors in your final draft.

5 Jeu de rôle

a. You want to take a trip for your vacation, but you're not sure where. Tell your travel agent what you like to do and what you'd like to see. The travel agent will make some suggestions about where you might go and what there is to do there. He or she will also describe the weather conditions and tell you what clothes to take, where you can stay, and when and from where you can leave. The travel agent will also remind you of things you shouldn't forget to take. Act this out with your partner. Then, change roles.

b. You've returned from your trip and your friend wants to know how it went. Tell your friend about your trip and answer any questions he or she has about what you did. Act this out with your partner and then change roles.

Mise en pratique

CHAPITRE 11

Building on Previous Skills

5 For this activity, students might use information they learned about Canada and Côte d'Ivoire from previous chapters, the research they did for projects, or the activities they did in this chapter.

Apply and Assess

Process Writing

4 To expand the Prewriting phase, have students list the sights that they think the French exchange student visiting their town would most like to see and the activities he or she would most like to do **(la plage)**. Beside each activity, have students write the best time of year or season to visit the sight or to do the activity **(en été)**. Then, next to the time of year, have students list any specific items the French exchange student might need to bring for visiting the sight or doing the activity **(un maillot de bain)**.

STANDARDS: 1.1, 1.3, 3.1, 5.1, 5.2

Que sais-je?

CHAPITRE 11

Teaching Resources
p. 348

PRINT
- Grammar Tutor for Students of French, Chapter 11

MEDIA
- Interactive CD-ROM Tutor, Disc 3
- Online self-test

go.hrw.com
WA3 ARLES-11

Teacher Note
This page is intended to help students prepare for the Chapter Test. It is a brief checklist of the major points covered in the chapter. The students should be reminded that this is only a checklist and does not necessarily include everything that will appear on the test.

Answers

1 *Possible answers:*
Où est-ce que tu vas aller pendant les vacances? Qu'est-ce que tu vas faire?; Je vais... J'ai l'intention de...

2 1. J'hésite. Je ne sais pas.
2. Je voudrais bien aller...

4 Je te conseille de (d')... /Tu devrais...
1. aller à la campagne.
2. faire du camping.
3. travailler.
4. aller au Canada.

5 *Accept:* Pourquoi pas? D'accord! Allons-y!
Refuse: Non, ce n'est pas possible. Non, je ne peux pas.

6 N'oublie pas...
1. ton appareil-photo.
2. les cadeaux.
3. ton manteau.

8 1. Didier part à quatorze heures vingt-huit.
2. Désirée et Annie partent à vingt heures quarante-six.
3. Nous partons à onze heures quinze.
4. Tu pars à vingt-trois heures cinquante-neuf.

Que sais-je?

WA3 ARLES-11

Can you use what you've learned in this chapter?

Can you inquire about and share future plans? Express indecision and wishes? p. 329

1 How would you ask where a friend is going on vacation and what he or she is going to do? How would you answer these questions? See answers below.

2 How would you tell someone . . . See answers below.
1. you're not sure what to do?
2. where you'd really like to go?

Can you ask for advice? Make, accept, and refuse suggestions? p. 330

3 How would you ask a friend for advice about your vacation?
Je ne sais pas quoi faire (où aller). Tu as une idée? Qu'est-ce que tu me conseilles?

4 How would you suggest to a friend that he or she . . . See answers below.
1. go to the country?
2. go camping?
3. work?
4. go to Canada?

5 How would you accept and refuse the suggestions in number 4? See answers below.

Can you remind and reassure someone? p. 333

6 How would you remind a friend to take these things on a trip? See answers below.

1.

2.

3.

7 How would you reassure someone you haven't forgotten these things?

Je n'ai pas oublié...

1. mon passeport.

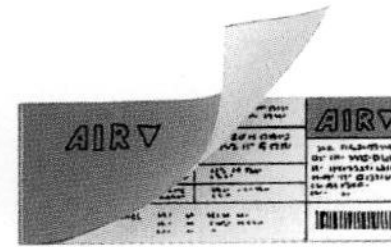

2. mon billet d'avion.

3. mon billet de train.

Can you see someone off? p. 336

8 How would you tell when these people are leaving, using the verb **partir?**
1. Didier / 14h28
2. Désirée et Annie / 20h46
3. Nous / 11h15
4. Tu / 23h59

See answers below.

9 How would you wish someone a good trip?
Bon voyage! Bonnes vacances! Amuse-toi bien!

Can you ask for and express opinions? p. 337

10 How would you ask a friend how his or her vacation went?
Tu as passé un bon été? Ça s'est bien passé? Tu t'es bien amusé(e)?

11 How would you tell how your vacation went? C'était formidable/très chouette. Ça a été. Pas mauvais. C'était épouvantable. C'était un véritable cauchemar! C'était ennuyeux.

Can you inquire about and relate past events? p. 337

12 How would you find out what a friend did on vacation?
Qu'est-ce que tu as fait? Tu es allé(e) où?

13 How would you tell what you did on vacation?

Review and Assess

Challenge
4 Have students add other activities, such as hiking or sailing, and other destinations, such as Mexico, England, or Vietnam.

5 Have students offer several different ways to accept and reject the suggestions.

Additional Practice
8 You might suggest other subjects and times for more practice with **partir.** Have students give the times in both conversational and official style.

STANDARDS: 1.2

Première étape

Inquiring about and sharing future plans

Qu'est-ce que tu vas faire...?	*What are you going to do . . . ?*
Où est-ce que tu vas aller... ?	*Where are you going to go . . . ?*
Je vais...	*I'm going to . . .*
J'ai l'intention de/d'...	*I intend to . . .*

Expressing indecision

J'hésite.	*I'm not sure.*
Je ne sais pas.	*I don't know.*
Je n'en sais rien.	*I have no idea.*
Je n'ai rien de prévu.	*I don't have any plans.*

Expressing wishes

Je voudrais bien...	*I'd really like to . . .*
J'ai envie de/d'...	*I feel like . . .*

Vacation places and activities

à la montagne	*to/in the mountains*
en forêt	*to/in the forest*
à la campagne	*to/in the countryside*
en colonie de vacances	*to/at a summer camp*
au bord de la mer	*to/on the coast*
chez...	*to/at . . . 's house*
faire du camping	*to go camping*
faire de la randonnée	*to go hiking*
faire du bateau	*to go boating*
faire de la plongée	*to go scuba diving*
faire de la planche à voile	*to go windsurfing*
faire de la voile	*to go sailing*
à	*to, in (a city or place)*
en	*to, in (before a feminine noun)*
au	*to, in (before a masculine noun)*
aux	*to, in (before a plural noun)*

Asking for advice; making, accepting, and refusing suggestions

See Tu te rappelles? on page 330.

Deuxième étape

Travel items

un passeport	*passport*
un billet de train	*train ticket*
un billet d'avion	*plane ticket*
une valise	*suitcase*
de l'argent	*money*
un appareil-photo	*camera*
un cadeau	*gift*
un parapluie	*umbrella*

Reminding, reassuring

N'oublie pas...	*Don't forget . . .*
Tu n'as pas oublié... ?	*You didn't forget . . . ?*
Tu ne peux pas partir sans...	*You can't leave without . . .*
Tu prends... ?	*Are you taking . . . ?*
Ne t'en fais pas.	*Don't worry.*
Je n'ai rien oublié.	*I didn't forget anything.*
J'ai pensé à tout.	*I've thought of everything.*
partir	*to leave*

Seeing someone off

Bon voyage!	*Have a good trip!*
Bonnes vacances!	*Have a good vacation!*
Amuse-toi bien!	*Have fun!*
Bonne chance!	*Good luck!*

Troisième étape

Asking for and expressing opinions

Tu as passé un bon... ?	*Did you have a good . . . ?*
Ça s'est bien passé?	*Did it go well?*
Tu t'es bien amusé(e)?	*Did you have fun?*
Oui, très chouette.	*Yes, very cool.*
C'était formidable!	*It was great!*
Oui, ça a été.	*Yes, it was OK.*
Oh, pas mauvais.	*Oh, not bad.*
C'était épouvantable.	*It was horrible.*
Non, pas vraiment.	*No, not really.*
C'était un véritable cauchemar!	*It was a real nightmare!*
C'était ennuyeux.	*It was boring.*
C'était barbant.	*It was boring.*

Inquiring about and relating past events

See Tu te rappelles? on page 337.

Vocabulaire

CHAPITRE 11

Chapter 11 Assessment

- **Testing Program**
  Chapter Test, pp. 287–292
   Audio Compact Discs, CD 11, Trs. 23–25
  Speaking Test, p. 348
- **Alternative Assessment Guide**
  Performance Assessment, p. 42
  Portfolio Assessment, p. 28
  CD-ROM Assessment, p. 56
- **Interactive CD-ROM Tutor, Disc 3**
  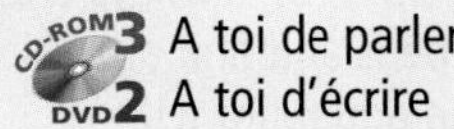
  CD-ROM 3 A toi de parler
  DVD 2 A toi d'écrire
- **Standardized Assessment Tutor**
  Chapter 11
- **One-Stop Planner, Disc 3**
  Test Generator
  Chapter 11

Review and Assess

Circumlocution

Tell students to imagine that they are traveling in a francophone country and they have lost several necessary travel items. Then, tell them that they don't know the words for these travel items, but they need to make a list of the missing items. Have them describe the items they lost to a partner, without naming them. The partner will guess the items that are missing. You might give them the expression **On l'utilise pour...** Then, have partners switch roles and describe different items.

STANDARDS: 1.1

Location Opener

CHAPTER 12

Teaching Resources
pp. 350–353

PRINT 
- Lesson Planner, p. 58
- Video Guide, pp. 79–80

MEDIA 
- One-Stop Planner
- Video Program
  Videocassette 4, 29:42–32:00
- DVD Tutor, Disc 2
- Interactive CD-ROM Tutor, Disc 3
- Map Transparency 3

 go.hrw.com
WA3 FORT-DE-FRANCE

Using the Almanac and Map

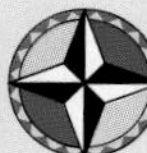

Terms in the Almanac
- **Créole,** one of two languages spoken in Martinique, is a blend of French, Spanish, English, and African languages. Words in Creole are usually written the way they sound.
- **Le musée départemental,** a museum devoted to the history of the island, includes artifacts of the Pre-Columbian Arawak and Carib civilizations, exhibits on Napoleon I and Josephine, and information on **la montagne Pelée** and the history of slavery on the island.
- **La cathédrale Saint-Louis,** a Romanesque cathedral built in 1671, has beautiful, stained-glass windows. Many of the island's governors are interred beneath it.
- **Le Parc floral et culturel** introduces visitors to the flowers and plants of the island and also contains an aquarium with native fish.
- **crabes farcis:** deviled land crabs
- **blanc-manger:** coconut pudding
- **boudin créole:** spicy creole sausage
- **acras de morue:** cod fritters

CHAPITRE 12

Allez, viens à Fort-de-France!

Ville principale de la Martinique

Population : plus de 100.000

Langues : français, créole

Points d'intérêt : la bibliothèque Schœlcher, le musée départemental, le fort Saint-Louis, la cathédrale Saint-Louis

Parcs et jardins : la Savane, le Parc floral

Spécialités : crabes farcis, blanc-manger, boudin créole, acras de morue

Evénements : Carnaval, le Festival de Fort-de-France, les Tours des yoles rondes de la Martinique

WA3 FORT-DE-FRANCE

La ville de Fort-de-France

Cultures and Communities

Background Information
Located on the beautiful Baie des Flamands, Fort-de-France is the largest city and busiest commercial center in the French West Indies. As the region's chief port, its exports include sugar cane, cocoa, and various fruits. Formerly known as Fort-Royal, Fort-de-France is now the **chef-lieu** *(administrative seat or capital)* of Martinique, which is a **département d'outre-mer** *(overseas department)* of France. Fort-de-France became the administrative capital of Martinique in 1902, when Saint-Pierre, formerly the largest city of the island, was destroyed by an eruption of Mount Pelée that killed approximately 30,000 people.

STANDARDS: 2.2, 3.1, 5.1

Map Activity

Ask students if they know on which body of water Fort-de-France is located (the Caribbean Sea). Ask if they can identify other countries that are located near Martinique (Cuba, Haiti, Dominican Republic, Colombia, Panama, Venezuela).

Culture Note

Several holidays and festivals take place every year in Fort-de-France and throughout Martinique. **Carnaval,** a festival of music, parades, and costumes, is celebrated for four days preceding Ash Wednesday **(le mercredi des Cendres). Le Festival de Fort-de-France** in July offers exhibits, concerts, and theatrical productions.

Connections and Comparisons

History Link

France began to colonize Martinique with d'Esnambuc's arrival in 1635, and the island became a domain of the French crown in 1674. The British had possession of the island three times in the eighteenth and early nineteenth centuries (1762, 1794–1802, 1809– 1814). In 1815, the island was ceded by treaty to France, and in 1946, it became an overseas department. Martinique sends four deputies to the French National Assembly and is governed by a prefect, appointed by the French Minister of the Interior, and a general council, elected by the people of the island.

Using the Photo Essay

1 La Savane Located here are statues of Pierre Belain d'Esnambuc, who led 80 settlers to Fort Saint-Pierre in 1635, and of Josephine, the first wife of French Emperor Napoleon I. Josephine, the daughter of a Martinique planter, was born on the island in 1763.

2 La bibliothèque Schœlcher is a public library named after Victor Schœlcher, who fought to abolish slavery in the nineteenth century. Slavery was officially abolished in Martinique in 1848.

Fort-de-France

La ville de Fort-de-France est sur la baie des Flamands, entre les montagnes et la mer des Caraïbes. Presque un tiers de la population martiniquaise habite à Fort-de-France ou dans ses environs. C'est une ville où il y a un mélange de cultures. La Martinique est à 6.817 km (*4,261 miles*) de Paris, mais c'est un département français. L'influence française est évidente. Les bâtiments aux couleurs pastel et les balcons en fer forgé rappellent la Nouvelle-Orléans, mais les sons de la langue créole et de la musique zouk sont purement antillais.

Visit Holt Online
go.hrw.com
KEYWORD: WA3 FORT-DE-FRANCE
Activités Internet

1 La Savane
C'est un magnifique parc plein d'arbres tropicaux, de fontaines, de bancs et de jardins. On y va pour rencontrer ses amis, se promener ou jouer au football.

2 La bibliothèque Schœlcher
C'est un bâtiment de styles divers (byzantin, égyptien et roman). Comme la tour Eiffel, elle a été construite pour l'Exposition universelle de 1889. Plus tard, on l'a démontée et reconstruite à Fort-de-France.

3 Le clocher de la cathédrale Saint-Louis
Il domine le centre-ville de Fort-de-France.

Cultures and Communities

Background Information

The original inhabitants of Martinique were Indians from South America who gradually migrated through the islands of the Caribbean, most likely reaching Martinique and Guadeloupe in the second century A.D. Gradually, the Arawaks, another Indian people, settled there. Subsequently, a cannibalistic warrior race called the Caribs (who gave their name to the Caribbean Sea) conquered the Arawaks. In the early sixteenth century, when Columbus arrived in Martinique for the first time, he encountered the descendants of the Caribs, whose excellent fighting skills prevented the Europeans from immediately gaining possession of the island.

STANDARDS: 2.1

4 Le madras
La Martinique est connue pour ses tissus colorés qu'on appelle madras.

5 Le fort Saint-Louis
Il est construit sur une presqu'île rocheuse. Il domine la ville de Fort-de-France.

Au chapitre 12,
tu vas faire la connaissance de Lucien, de sa famille et de son amie Mireille. Ils vont te faire visiter Fort-de-France, la ville principale de la Martinique. C'est une ville moderne qui conserve ses traditions et l'art de vivre créole. Elle a toutes les caractéristiques d'une ville française, mais située sous le soleil des tropiques.

6 Au marché
On peut acheter des fruits et des légumes frais tous les jours. C'est un endroit pittoresque.

Connections and Comparisons

Thinking Critically

4 Drawing Inferences Have students suggest reasons why head coverings are important. (In Martinique, the intense heat and sun of the tropical climate create the need for some sort of head covering. Scarf-like head coverings serve to hold one's hair in place, are decorative and stylish, and often match the outfit being worn.)

6 Observing Have students try to identify the different fruits and vegetables in the photos. Moving from left to right, you can see *yams* **(des ignames)**, *star fruit* **(des caramboles)**, *breadfruit* **(fruit de l'arbre à pain)** sitting in front of the pineapples, and *hot peppers* **(piments)** in the bowl behind the star fruit and tomatoes. The flowers behind the pineapples are called *anthuriums,* the official flower of Martinique.

5 Le fort Saint-Louis was built in the seventeenth century to defend the island of Martinique. Today, special permission is needed to visit the fort.

5 Call students' attention to the French flag flying atop **fort Saint-Louis.** Explain that since Martinique is a French **département,** its people are French citizens.

Thinking Critically

6 Comparing and Contrasting Have students recall from Chapter 8 the differences between shopping in an open-air market and in a store. How might the produce be different? What quantities might one buy? Are prices fixed? How does the shopper carry his or her purchases? In Martinique, most produce sold in open-air markets is fresh, and women will often carry their purchases on their heads, as students will notice in Photo 6. Shoppers generally bring their own shopping bags and pay in cash. They might bargain with the seller on the price of a particular item. Tasting is also common before one buys something.

STANDARDS: 2.2, 3.2

Chapitre 12 : En ville

Chapter Overview

Mise en train pp. 356–358	***Un petit service***			
	FUNCTIONS	**GRAMMAR**	**VOCABULARY**	**RE-ENTRY**
Première étape pp. 359–363	• Pointing out places and things, p. 361	• Contractions with **à,** p. 360	• Names of stores and businesses, p. 359	• School supplies **(Chapitre 3)** • Food items **(Chapitre 8)** • The **passé composé** **(Chapitre 9)**
Deuxième étape pp. 364–368	• Making and responding to requests, p. 364 • Asking for advice and making suggestions, p. 366	• The partitive, p. 364 • The pronoun **y,** p. 367	Means of transportation, p. 366	• Expressing need **(Chapitre 8)** • Making an excuse **(Chapitre 5)** • Inviting **(Chapitre 6)**
Troisième étape pp. 369–373	• Asking for and giving directions, p. 371	• Contractions with **de,** p. 369	Prepositions of location, p. 369	• Family vocabulary **(Chapitre 7)** • Possessive adjectives **(Chapitre 7)**

Prononciation p. 373	**Review** Audio CD 12, Tracks 12–14	**A écrire** (dictation) Audio CD 12, Tracks 15–17	
Lisons! pp. 374–375	**Cheval de bois**	**Reading Strategy:** Combining different reading strategies	
Grammaire supplémentaire	**pp. 376–379** **Première étape,** pp. 376–377	**Deuxième étape,** pp. 377–378	**Troisième étape,** p. 379
Review pp. 380–383	**Mise en pratique,** pp. 380–381 **Ecrivons!** Making a writing plan Writing a conversation	**Que sais-je?** p. 382	**Vocabulaire,** p. 383

CULTURE

- **Note culturelle,** Store hours in France and Martinique, p. 360
- **Rencontre culturelle,** Making "small talk" in francophone countries, p. 363
- Realia: A French stamp, p. 365
- **Panorama Culturel,** Getting a driver's license in francophone countries, p. 368
- **Note culturelle, DOMs** and **TOMs,** p. 370
- **Note culturelle,** Public areas downtown, p. 371

Chapter Resources

Visit Holt Online
go.hrw.com
KEYWORD: WA3 FORT-DE-FRANCE-12
Online Edition

PRINT

Lesson Planning

One-Stop Planner

Lesson Planner with Differentiated Instruction, pp. 58–62, 76

Student Make-Up Assignments
- Make-Up Assignment Copying Masters, Chapter 12

Listening and Speaking

TPR Storytelling Book, pp. 45–48

Listening Activities
- Student Response Forms for Listening Activities, pp. 91–93
- Additional Listening Activities 11-1 to 11-6, pp. 95–97
- Additional Listening Activities (song), p. 98
- Scripts and Answers, pp. 157–161

Video Guide
- Teaching Suggestions, pp. 82–83
- Activity Masters, pp. 84–86
- Scripts and Answers, pp. 114–117, 123

Activities for Communication
- Communicative Activities, pp. 67–72
- Realia and Teaching Suggestions, pp. 130–134
- Situation Cards, pp. 159–160

Reading and Writing

Reading Strategies and Skills Handbook, Chapter 12

Joie de lire 1, Chapter 12

Cahier d'activités, pp. 133–144

Grammar

Travaux pratiques de grammaire, pp. 98–107

Grammar Tutor for Students of French, Chapter 12

Assessment

Testing Program
- Grammar and Vocabulary Quizzes, **Etape** Quizzes, and Chapter Test, pp. 301–318
- Score Sheet, Scripts and Answers, pp. 319–326
- Final Exam, pp. 327–334
- Score Sheet, Scripts and Answers, pp. 335–340

Alternative Assessment Guide
- Portfolio Assessment, p. 29
- Performance Assessment, p. 43
- CD-ROM Assessment, p. 57

Student Make-Up Assignments
- Alternative Quizzes, Chapter 12

Standardized Assessment Tutor
- Reading, pp. 47–49 • Writing, p. 50 • Math, pp. 51–52

Middle School

Middle School Teaching Resources, Chapter 12

MEDIA

Online Activities
- **Jeux interactifs**
- **Activités Internet**

Video Program
- Videocassette 4
- Videocassette 5 (captioned version)

Interactive CD-ROM Tutor, Disc 3

DVD Tutor, Disc 2

Audio Compact Discs
- Textbook Listening Activities, CD 12, Tracks 1–18
- Additional Listening Activities, CD 12, Tracks 31–37
- Assessment Items, CD 12, Tracks 19–24, 25–30

Teaching Transparencies
- Situation 12-1 to 12-3
- Vocabulary 12-A to 12-C
- **Mise en train**
- **Grammaire supplémentaire** Answers
- **Travaux pratiques de grammaire** Answers

One-Stop Planner CD-ROM

Use the **One-Stop Planner CD-ROM with Test Generator** to aid in lesson planning and pacing.

For each chapter, the **One-Stop Planner** includes:
- Editable lesson plans with direct links to teaching resources
- Printable worksheets from resource books
- Direct launches to the HRW Internet activities
- Video and audio segments
- Test Generator
- Clip Art for vocabulary items

Projects

Ma ville

Students will create a brochure for visitors with maps of their town or neighborhood and written directions to important places.

MATERIALS

Students may need

- Construction paper
- Scissors, glue
- Local maps
- Markers or colored pens
- Telephone directories
- Tourist brochures

SUGGESTED SEQUENCE

1. Have students make a list of interesting and important places in their area that visitors might want to visit.
2. Have students find out exactly where each place is located. Then, have them sketch a rough map of the city with each place correctly indicated. They should also begin to gather or draw pictures to illustrate their maps.
3. Have students write directions to the points of interest from main streets or designated locations. They might use the following vocabulary: **l'autoroute** *(highway);* **Prenez la 35 jusqu'à ...** *(Take highway 35 to . . .);* **la sortie** Main Street *(the . . . exit);* **un pont** *(bridge);* **faire demi-tour** *(to make a U-turn);* **un carrefour** *(intersection);* **une rue à sens unique** *(one-way street).*
4. Have students exchange their written directions for peer-editing. Partners should check the clarity and accuracy of the directions by trying to follow them on a city map.
5. Have students select their final illustrations and plan the final layout of their maps.
6. Have students finalize their maps. They should copy the final version of the written directions at the bottom or on the reverse side of the map.

These brochures might be displayed at school, added to portfolios, or sent to local tourist offices or Chambers of Commerce.

GRADING THE PROJECT

Suggested Point Distribution (total = 100 points)

Completion of assignment.....................20 points
Content/creativity.................................30 points
Language use...25 points
Presentation..25 points

Games

Chasse l'intrus

In this game, students will practice new and previously learned vocabulary.

Procedure Give each student an index card. Ask students to write four words on their card: three should have something in common, and the fourth should be unrelated. For example, students might write **banque, pharmacie, avion,** and **boulangerie.** Words can be related according to their meanings or their parts of speech. Collect and shuffle the cards. Divide the class into two teams. Give a card to the first player on the first team. The player says **Chasse l'intrus!** to his or her opponent and reads aloud the four words on the card. If the opposing player correctly identifies the word that doesn't belong within a specified amount of time, his or her team wins a point. Teams take turns, asking questions until all the cards have been read. The team with the most points wins. NOTE: If pronunciation is a problem, have students show their card to the opposing player.

Les Mots en famille

In this game, students will review vocabulary from all twelve chapters.

Procedure Skim the French-English vocabulary list at the back of the book and make a list under several general categories, such as **les vêtements, l'école, à manger,** and **les sports.** Have students pair off or form small groups. Give each pair or group a transparency and a marker. Then, announce a category and give partners or groups 2 or 3 minutes to write down as many related words as they can think of, without consulting their book or dictionaries. Then, project the transparencies and have the class verify the spelling and appropriateness of each item. Give one point for each appropriate word that is spelled correctly. The team with the most points wins. This game might be played with functional expressions as well as with vocabulary words.

Storytelling

Mini-histoire

This story accompanies Teaching Transparency 12-2. The ***mini-histoire*** *can be told and retold in different formats, acted out, written down, and read aloud, to give students additional opportunities to practice all four skills. The following story is about the Martin family asking Céline to run some errands for them in town.*

Céline doit aller en ville faire des courses. Rémi lui demande : «Est-ce que tu peux passer à la poste pour moi et porter ces lettres?» «Bien sûr», dit Céline. Son père lui demande : «Est-ce que tu peux passer à la pharmacie? J'ai commandé un médicament et il est arrivé». «D'accord». La mère de Céline lui dit : «Est-ce que tu peux aller au marché et acheter un kilo d'abricots et six bananes? Et si tu as le temps, est-ce que tu peux passer à l'épicerie prendre un litre de lait et à la boulangerie prendre une baguette?» «Si tu veux», répond Céline. Martine lui demande aussi : «Est-ce que tu peux rendre ces livres à la bibliothèque?» «Je suis désolée, mais je n'ai pas le temps», répond Céline.

Traditions

Costume

The traditional costume of Martinique is a skirt, made of brightly colored cotton or silk worn over a lace petticoat, and an embroidered bodice. A scarf over the shoulder and a turban made from **madras** fabric complete the outfit.

The turban is the most important part of the costume, because the manner in which it is tied communicates information about the wearer. If tied with one point (**tête à un bout**), the wearer indicates "my heart is for the taking." Two points (**tête à deux bouts**) indicate "my heart is taken," and three points (**tête à trois bouts**) state "my heart is spoken for, but you can still try your luck." Ask students what the woman's turban on page 353 in their book indicates. Then, have them make their own turbans with one, two, or three points.

Recette

The Aztecs and the Mayas began trading chocolate long ago. Christopher Columbus knew of it, but it was the explorer Hernando Cortés who first brought chocolate to Europe. Originally, chocolate was used as a drink ingredient. The nineteenth century saw the invention of the first chocolate bar. Today, Switzerland and Belgium are reputed to produce the best chocolate. Europeans consume a lot of dark chocolate, while Americans tend to consume more milk chocolate.

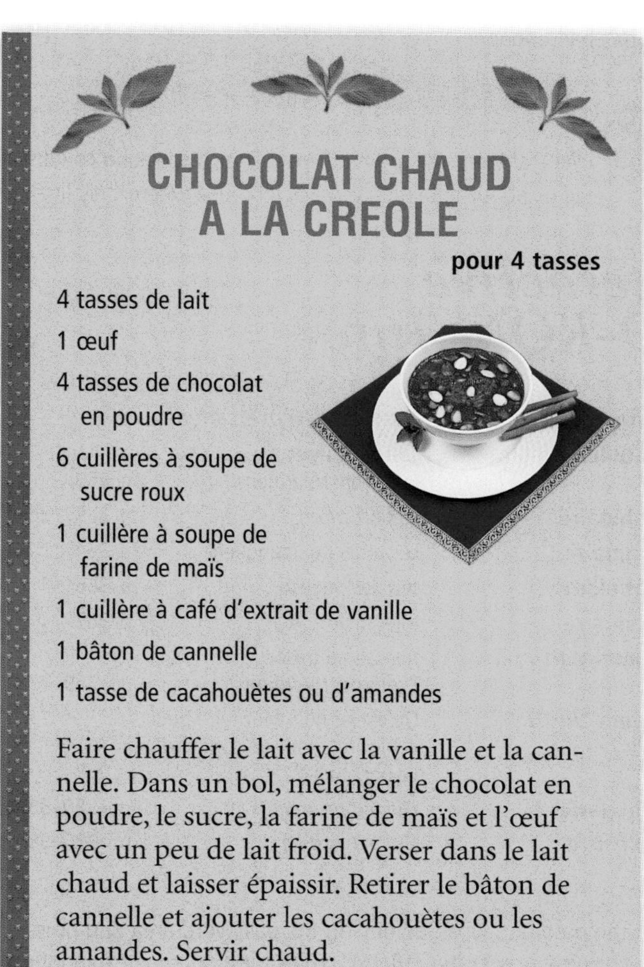

CHOCOLAT CHAUD A LA CREOLE

pour 4 tasses

4 tasses de lait
1 œuf
4 tasses de chocolat en poudre
6 cuillères à soupe de sucre roux
1 cuillère à soupe de farine de maïs
1 cuillère à café d'extrait de vanille
1 bâton de cannelle
1 tasse de cacahouètes ou d'amandes

Faire chauffer le lait avec la vanille et la cannelle. Dans un bol, mélanger le chocolat en poudre, le sucre, la farine de maïs et l'œuf avec un peu de lait froid. Verser dans le lait chaud et laisser épaissir. Retirer le bâton de cannelle et ajouter les cacahouètes ou les amandes. Servir chaud.

Chapitre 12 : En ville

Technology

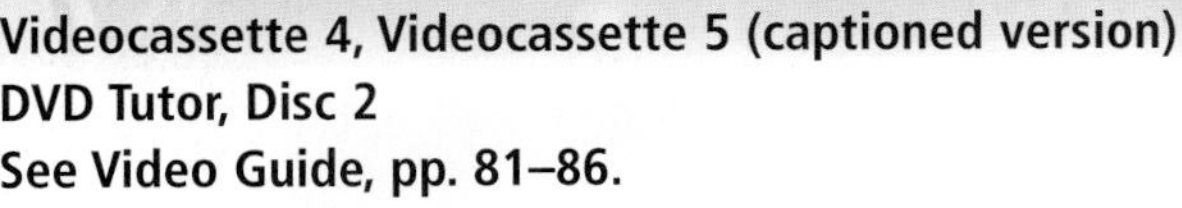

Videocassette 4, Videocassette 5 (captioned version)
DVD Tutor, Disc 2
See Video Guide, pp. 81–86.

DVD/Video

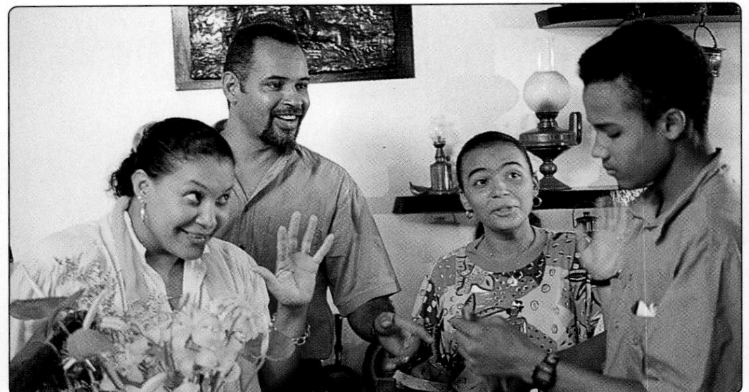

Mise en train • Un petit service

In this episode, Lucien plans to meet his friend Mireille in town and visit the Fort Saint-Louis. As he is getting ready to leave, his mother, father, and sister all ask favors of him. Although they ask him to do a lot of errands, Lucien reluctantly agrees to everyone's request. When a neighbor enters and asks if anyone is going to town, however, Lucien has had enough.

Qu'est-ce qu'il faut faire pour avoir un permis de conduire?

Several teenagers from different French-speaking countries tell us about obtaining a driver's license where they live.

Un petit service (suite)

When the story continues, Mireille accompanies Lucien on his errands. They get lost trying to find a record store and ask a man for directions. Then, they take a ferry to deliver a package, and Lucien points out landmarks in Fort-de-France. When Lucien returns home, they all thank him for doing their errands. His mother asks him about the fort, and he realizes he completely forgot about visiting it!

Vidéoclips

- **RATP®:** advertisement for Parisian transport system
- **Banette®:** advertisement for bread (1)
- **Banette®:** advertisement for bread (2)

Interactive CD-ROM Tutor

Activity	Activity Type	Pupil's Edition Page
En contexte	*Interactive conversation*	
1. Vocabulaire	Chasse au trésor Explorons!/Vérifions!	p. 359
2. Vocabulaire	Le bon choix	p. 359
3. Grammaire	Les mots qui manquent	p. 364
4. Vocabulaire	Jeu des paires	p. 366
5. Grammaire	Méli-mélo	p. 367
6. Comment dit-on... ?	Chasse au trésor Explorons!/Vérifions!	pp. 369, 371
Panorama Culturel	Qu'est-ce qu'il faut faire pour avoir un permis de conduire? Le bon choix	p. 368
A toi de parler	*Guided recording*	pp. 380–381
A toi d'écrire	*Guided writing*	pp. 380–381

Teacher Management System

Launch the program, type "admin" in the password area and press RETURN. Log on to www.hrw.com/CDROMTUTOR for a detailed explanation of the Teacher Management System.

DVD Tutor

The *DVD Tutor* contains all material from the *Video Program* as described above. French captions are available for use at your discretion for all sections of the video. The *DVD Tutor* also provides a variety of video-based activities that assess students' understanding of the **Mise en train, Suite,** and **Panorama Culturel.**

This part of the *DVD Tutor* may be used on any DVD video player connected to a television or video monitor.

In addition to the video material and the video-based comprehension activities, the *DVD Tutor* also contains the entire *Interactive CD-ROM Tutor* in DVD-ROM format. Each DVD disc contains the activities from all 12 chapters of the *Interactive CD-ROM Tutor.*

This part of the *DVD Tutor* may be used on a Macintosh® or Windows® computer with a DVD-ROM drive.

To preview all resources available for this chapter, use the **One-Stop Planner CD-ROM,** Disc 3.

Visit Holt Online
go.hrw.com
KEYWORD: WA3 FORT-DE-FRANCE-12
Online Edition

Go.Online!

Online Edition

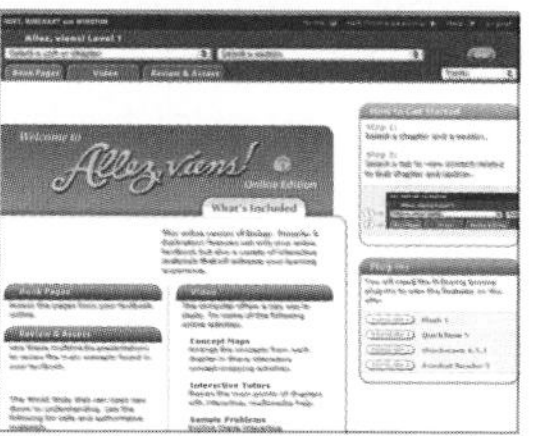

The Online Edition for Allez, viens! *allows students access to their textbooks anytime anywhere.*

- *Audio at point of use*
- *Additional practice activities*
- *Self-test activities*
- *Online reference tools*
- *Entire Video Program (Enhanced version)*
- *Interactive Notebook (Enhanced version)*

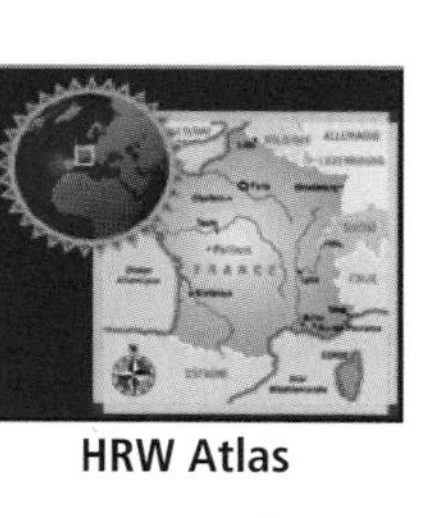

HRW Atlas

Internet Activités

video

audio

presentation

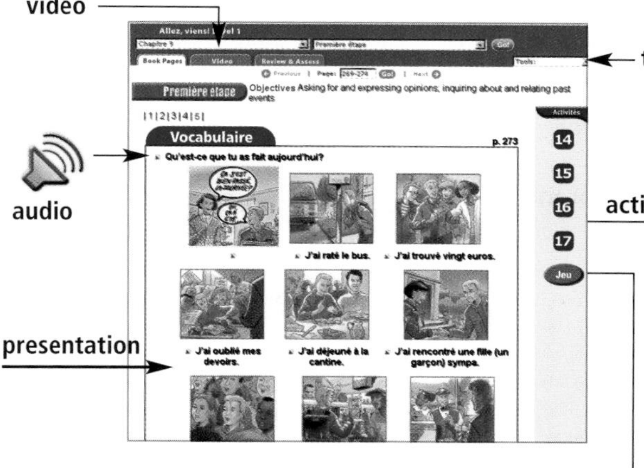

tools (glossary, grammar, cahier électronique)

activities

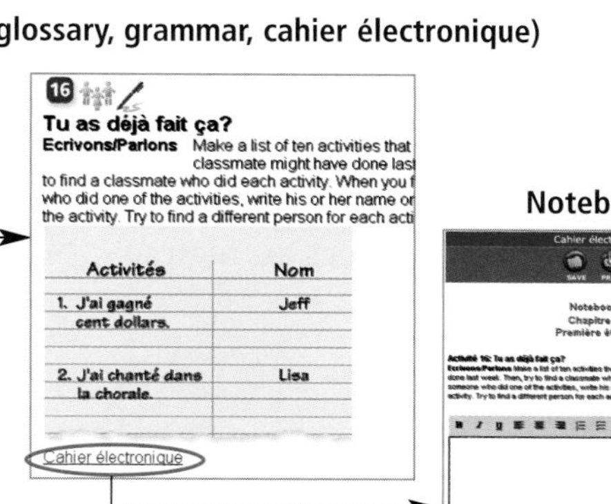

Notebook

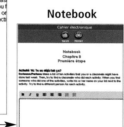

Activités Internet

These guided internet activities include a worksheet and pre-selected and pre-screened authentic web sites from the francophone world. You can use these activities

- to help students develop research skills in the target language
- to introduce students to authentic cultural information
- as a project

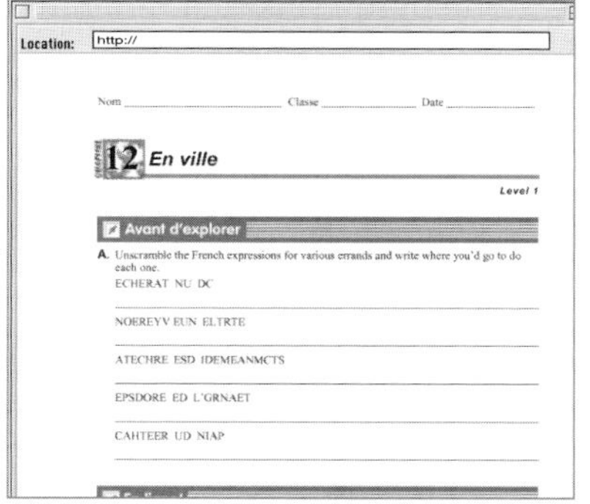

Jeux interactifs

You can use the interactive activities in this chapter

- to practice grammar, vocabulary, and chapter functions
- as homework
- as an assessment option
- as a self-test
- to prepare for the Chapter Test

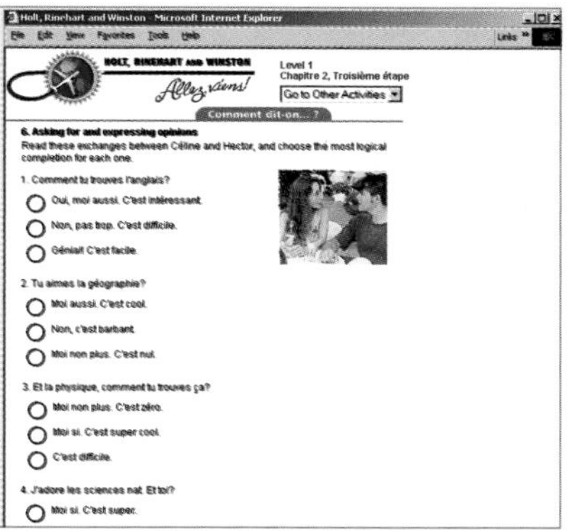

Projet Tell students that they're working for a company in Fort-de-France that organizes day tours for visitors. Have them work in groups of two or three to decide what the focus of their tour will be. They might either organize a day tour that includes a little of everything, or they might choose a specific theme for their tour. For example, they might have a tour that focuses on local arts and crafts, music, an architectural tour, or a historical tour. Have students search the Web for all the necessary information. Have them prepare a detailed tour itinerary, based on their online research.

Chapitre 12 : En ville

Textbook Listening Activities Scripts 

Première étape

7 p. 360

1. — De l'aspirine, s'il vous plaît.
   — Voilà. C'est tout?
2. — Vous avez des disques compacts en espagnol?
   — Oui, bien sûr.
3. — Je voudrais déposer cent euros.
   — Le numéro de votre compte, s'il vous plaît?
4. — Je voudrais des timbres.
   — Vous en voulez combien?
5. — Il me faut du papier, des stylos et des enveloppes.
   — Ça fait huit euros quarante-neuf.
6. — Mmm... Il a l'air très bon, ce gâteau-là. Je vais le prendre.
   — N'oublie pas, tu es au régime!

Answers to Activity 7

1. at the drugstore
2. at the record store
3. at the bank
4. at the post office
5. at the book/stationery store
6. at the pastry shop/bakery

Deuxième étape

15 p. 364

1. — Marie, tu peux aller à la poste acheter des timbres?
   — Désolée, mais je n'ai pas le temps!
2. — Est-ce que tu peux aller à la pharmacie? J'ai mal à la tête, mais je n'ai plus d'aspirine.
   — Oui, d'accord. J'y vais tout de suite.
3. — Tu peux me rendre un petit service? J'ai besoin d'argent. Est-ce que tu peux aller à la banque ce matin?
   — Oui, si tu veux.
4. — Au retour, tu peux passer à la boulangerie? Prends deux baguettes, s'il te plaît.
   — Oui, Maman. C'est tout?
5. — Tu pourrais passer par la bibliothèque aujourd'hui? Je veux rendre ces livres.
   — Désolé, je ne peux pas. J'ai des tas de choses à faire.
6. — Zut alors! J'ai oublié les tomates! Tu peux passer au marché pour moi?
   — Oui, je veux bien. Je pars tout de suite.

Answers to Activity 15

1. refuses
2. agrees
3. agrees
4. agrees
5. refuses
6. agrees

19 p. 367

1. — Comment est-ce qu'on va en ville?
   — On peut y aller à vélo, si tu veux.
2. — J'aimerais bien aller au cinéma.
   — Bonne idée. Comment veux-tu y aller?
   — On peut prendre le bus.
3. — Je vais à Paris cet été.
   — Ah oui? Comment est-ce que tu y vas?
   — J'y vais en avion.
4. — Tu veux aller à la plage ce week-end?
   — Oui, on peut y aller à pied.
5. — Comment est-ce que tu vas à Fort-de-France demain?
   — J'y vais en voiture avec mes parents.
6. — Tu ne veux pas aller au musée samedi?
   — Si. On peut prendre un taxi collectif.

Answers to Activity 19

1. to town, by bike
2. to the movies, by bus
3. to Paris, by plane
4. to the beach, on foot
5. to Fort-de-France, by car
6. to the museum, by taxi

The following scripts are for the listening activities found in the *Pupil's Edition*. For Student Response Forms, see *Listening Activities*, pages 91–93. To provide students with additional listening practice, see *Listening Activities*, pages 95–98.

To preview all resources available for this chapter, use the **One-Stop Planner CD-ROM**, Disc 3.

Troisième étape

23 p. 369

1. La boulangerie est à côté du cinéma.

2. La banque est au coin de la rue.

3. La pharmacie est loin de la papeterie.

4. Le café est entre la poste et le cinéma.

5. Le cinéma est en face du lycée.

6. La poste est près du café.

Answers to Activity 23
1. false
2. true
3. false
4. true
5. true
6. true

27 p. 371

En sortant de la gare routière, prenez à gauche. Vous serez sur le boulevard du Général de Gaulle. Ensuite, prenez la première rue à gauche. C'est la rue Schœlcher. Continuez jusqu'à la rue Victor Sévère et tournez à gauche. Vous allez passer devant la bibliothèque. Juste après la bibliothèque, prenez à droite, rue de la Liberté. Allez tout droit jusqu'à la rue Antoine Siger. Là, tournez à droite et ce sera le premier bâtiment sur votre gauche.

Answer to Activity 27
to the post office

PRONONCIATION, P. 373

For the scripts for Parts A and B, see page 373. The script for Part C is below.

C. A écrire *(dictation)*

— Tu pourrais faire des courses pour moi?

— Volontiers!

— Passe à la poste. Prends des timbres. Et n'oublie pas les enveloppes à la papeterie.

— Bon, d'accord.

Mise en pratique

2 p. 380

1. — La bibliothèque Schœlcher est très grande, et elle est aussi très belle, n'est-ce pas?

2. — Les plages de sable blanc de la Martinique sont magnifiques. On peut à la fois s'y baigner et y faire du bateau.

3. — Ça, c'est le marché. C'est un vrai paradis pour les yeux : on y trouve des légumes de toutes les couleurs.

4. — Là, c'est le disquaire où j'ai acheté le dernier CD de Kassav', un groupe de musique zouk qui est très populaire ici.

Answers to Mise en pratique, Activity 2
c, d, a, b

Chapitre 12 : En ville

Review Chapter

50-Minute Lesson Plans

Day 1

CHAPTER OPENER 5 min.

- Motivating Activity: Ask students if they have ever been lost and how they reacted. Ask them to imagine getting lost in another country. Ask students what communication skills they might use, other than speaking the foreign language.
- Present Chapter Objectives, p. 355.
- Photo Flash!, ATE, p. 354
- Multicultural Link, ATE, p. 355

MISE EN TRAIN 40 min.

- Presenting **Mise en train** and Preteaching Vocabulary, ATE, p. 356
- Auditory Learners, ATE, p. 357
- Do Activities 1–6, p. 358.

Wrap-Up 5 min.

- Visual Learners, ATE, p. 357

Homework Options

Cahier d'activités, p. 133, Act. 1

Day 2

PREMIERE ETAPE

Quick Review 10 min.

- Check homework.
- Bell Work, ATE, p. 359

Vocabulaire, p. 359 30 min.

- Present **Vocabulaire,** p. 359, using Teaching Transparency 12-A.
- Discuss **Tu te rappelles?,** p. 360.
- Play Audio CD for Activity 7, p. 360.
- Do Activities 8–9, p. 360.
- Discuss **Note culturelle**, p. 360.
- Thinking Critically, ATE, p. 360

Wrap-Up 10 min.

- Additional Practice, ATE, p. 359

Homework Options

Cahier d'activités, pp. 134–135, Acts. 2–5
Travaux pratiques de grammaire, pp. 98–101, Acts. 1–8

Day 3

PREMIERE ETAPE

Quick Review 10 min.

- Check homework.
- Distribute copies of the Teaching Transparency 12-A Transparency Master. Tell students the errands you need to do, using **d'abord, ensuite, finalement,** and so forth. Have students number the places on the Transparency Master in the order you mention them.

Comment dit-on... ?, p. 361 30 min.

- Presenting **Comment dit-on... ?,** ATE, p. 361
- Discuss **De bons conseils,** p. 361 and Language-to-Language, ATE, p. 361.
- Do Activity 12, p. 362.
- Discuss **A la française,** p. 362 and do Circumlocution, ATE, p. 362.
- Cahier d'activités, pp. 135–136, Acts. 6–8

Wrap-Up 10 min.

- Have students point out places on the map, using expressions from **Comment dit-on... ?,** using Transparency 12-3.

Homework Options

Study for Quiz 12-1.

Day 4

PREMIERE ETAPE

Quiz 12-1 20 min.

- Administer Quiz 12-1A or 12-1B.

RENCONTRE CULTURELLE 25 min.

- Presenting **Rencontre culturelle,** ATE, p. 363
- Answer **Qu'en penses-tu?** questions, p. 363
- Read **Savais-tu que... ?,** p. 363
- Discuss Culture Notes, ATE, p. 363.

Wrap-Up 5 min.

Thinking Critically, Comparing and Contrasting, ATE, p. 363

Homework Options

Have students write a conversation between an American visiting Martinique and a shopkeeper at a Martinique store.

Day 5

DEUXIEME ETAPE

Quick Review 10 min.

- Have student volunteers read or act out the conversations they wrote for homework.
- Bell Work, ATE, p. 364

Comment dit-on... ?, p. 364 30 min.

- Presenting **Comment dit-on... ?,** ATE, p. 364
- Language Note, ATE, p. 364
- Discuss **Tu te rappelles?,** p. 364.
- Play Audio CD for Activity 15, p. 364.
- Do Activities 16–17, p. 365.

Wrap-Up 10 min.

- Additional Practice, ATE, p. 365

Homework Options

Cahier d'activités, p. 137, Acts. 9–11
Travaux pratiques de grammaire, p. 102, Acts. 9–10

Day 6

DEUXIEME ETAPE

Quick Review 5 min.

- Check homework.

Comment dit-on... ?, p. 366 10 min.

- Presenting **Comment dit-on... ?,** ATE, p. 366

Vocabulaire, p. 366 15 min.

- Presenting **Vocabulaire,** ATE, p. 366, using Teaching Transparency 12-B
- Language Notes, ATE, p. 367
- Play Audio CD for Activity 19, p. 367.

Grammaire, p. 367 15 min.

- Presenting **Grammaire,** ATE, p. 367
- Do Activity 21, p. 367.
- Travaux pratiques de grammaire, pp. 103–105, Acts. 11–13, 16–17

Wrap-Up 5 min.

- Activities for Communication, p. 160, Situation Card 12-2: Role-play

Homework Options

Study for Quiz 12-2.

One-Stop Planner CD-ROM

For alternative lesson plans by chapter section, to create your own customized plans, or to preview all resources available for this chapter, use the **One-Stop Planner CD-ROM**, Disc 3.

For additional homework suggestions, see activities accompanied by this symbol throughtout the chapter.

Day 7

DEUXIEME ETAPE

Quiz 12-2 20 min.
- Administer Quiz 12-2A or 12-2B.

PANORAMA CULTUREL 25 min
- Presenting **Panorama Culturel,** p. 368, ATE, using Videocassette 4 or DVD Tutor, Disc 2.
- Answer **Qu'en penses-tu?** questions, p. 368.
- **Panorama Culturel,** Interactive CD-ROM Tutor, Disc 3

Wrap-Up 5 min.
- Thinking Critically, ATE, p. 368

Homework Options
Cahier d'activités, p. 144, Acts. 26–27

Day 8

TROISIEME ETAPE

Quick Review 10 min.
- Check homework.

Vocabulaire, p. 369 30 min.
- Presenting **Vocabulaire,** ATE, p. 369, using Teaching Transparency 12-C
- Discuss **Note de grammaire,** p. 369.
- Play Audio CD for Activity 23, p. 369.
- Do Activities 25–26, p. 370.
- Discuss **Note culturelle,** p. 370.

Wrap-Up 10 min.
- Do Activity 24, p. 369. See Game, ATE, p. 369.

Homework Options
Cahier d'activités, pp. 140–141, Acts. 18–21
Travaux pratiques de grammaire, pp. 106–107, Acts. 18–20

Day 9

TROISIEME ETAPE

Quick Review 10 min.
- Check homework.

Comment dit-on... ?, p. 371 15 min.
- Presenting **Comment dit-on... ?,** p. 371
- Play Audio CD for Activity 27, p. 371.
- Discuss **Note culturelle,** p. 371.
- Do Activity 28, p. 371.
- Cahier d'activités, pp. 141–142, Acts. 22–24

Prononciation, p. 373 15 min.
- Complete presentation and Activities A–C, p. 373, using Audio CD 12.

Wrap-Up 10 min.
- Activities for Communication, p. 158, Situation Card 12-3: Role-play

Homework Options
Study for Quiz 12-3.

Day 10

TROISIEME ETAPE

Quiz 12-3 20 min.
- Administer Quiz 12-3A or 12-3B.

LISONS! 25 min.
- Prereading Activity A, Using Prior Knowledge, ATE, p. 374
- Reading Activities B–F, Language Note, ATE, pp. 374–375
- Postreading Activities G–I, Thinking Critically, ATE, p. 375

Wrap-Up 5 min.
- Cooperative Learning, ATE, p. 375

Homework Options
Cahier d'activités, p. 143, Act. 25

Day 11

LISONS!

Quick Review 5 min.
- Check homework.

MISE EN PRATIQUE 35 min.
- Do Activity 1, p. 380.
- Additional Practice, ATE, p. 380
- Play Audio CD for Activity 2, p. 380.
- Do **Ecrivons!,** p. 381.

Wrap-Up 10 min.
- Do Revising step of **Ecrivons!**

Homework Options
Que sais-je?, p. 382
Finish **Ecrivons!,** Pupil's Edition, p. 381.

Day 12

MISE EN PRATIQUE

Quick Review 15 min.
- Check homework and collect **Ecrivons!**
- **Jeu de rôle,** p. 381.

Chapter Review 35 min.
- Review Chapter 12. Choose from **Grammaire supplémentaire,** Grammar Tutor for Students of French, Activities for Communication, Listening Activities, Interactive CD-ROM Tutor, or **Jeux interactifs.**

Homework Options
Study for Chapter 12 Test.

Assessment

Test, Chapter 12 50 min.
- Administer Chapter 12 Test. Select from Testing Program, Alternative Assessment Guide, Test Generator, or Standardized Assessment Tutor.

Chapitre 12 : En ville
90-Minute Lesson Plans

Block 1

CHAPTER OPENER 5 min.
- Motivating Activity: Ask students if they have ever been lost and how they reacted. Ask them to imagine getting lost in another country. Ask students what other communication skills they might use, besides speaking the foreign language.
- Photo Flash, ATE, p. 354
- Present Chapter Objectives, p. 355
- Multicultural Link, ATE, p. 354

MISE EN TRAIN 45 min.
- **Stratégie pour comprendre,** p. 356
- Preteaching Vocabulary, ATE, p. 356
- Presenting **Mise en train,** ATE, p. 356
- View video of **Mise en train,** Videocassette 4, Video Guide, p. 81.

PREMIERE ETAPE

Vocabulaire, p. 359 35 min.
- Bell Work, ATE, p. 359
- Presenting **Vocabulaire,** ATE, p. 359 and Additional Practice, ATE, p. 359
- Play Audio CD for Activity 7, p. 360.
- **Tu te rappelles?,** p. 360, with Additional Practice, ATE, p. 360
- Do Activity 8, p. 360. See Challenge, ATE, p. 360.
- Do Activity 9, p. 360, orally.
- **Note culturelle,** p. 360, Thinking Critically, p. 360
- Do Activity 10, p. 361 orally. Teaching Suggestion, ATE, p. 361
- **De bons conseils,** p. 361
- Both Language-to-Language suggestions and Challenge, ATE, p. 361

Wrap-Up 5 min.
- Summarize what happened in the **Mise en train,** using **Mise en train** Transparencies.

Homework Options

Travaux pratiques de grammaire, pp. 98–99, Acts. 1–4

Cahier d'activités, pp. 134–135, Acts. 2–6

Block 2

PREMIERE ETAPE

Quick Review 5 min.
- Hold up items (or pictures) such as stamps, a **baguette,** jam, bank deposit slip and ask: **Qu'est-ce que c'est?** and **Où est-ce qu'on achète ça?**

Comment dit-on...?, p. 361 40 min.
- Presenting **Comment dit-on...?,** ATE, p. 361
- **Grammaire supplémentaire,** p. 376, Acts. 1–2
- Do Activity 12, p. 362 with Visual Learners, ATE, p. 362
- **A la française,** p. 362 and Circumlocution, ATE, p. 362
- Have students write a note to a friend, telling what they plan to do over the weekend. They should include at least three separate chores, errands, or activities.

RENCONTRE CULTURELLE 35 min.
- Presenting **Rencontre culturelle,** ATE, p. 363
- Culture Notes, Teaching Suggestion, Thinking Critically, Comparing and Contrasting, ATE, p. 363
- Answer the **Qu'en penses-tu?** questions, p. 363
- Read **Savais-tu que... ?,** ATE, p. 363
- Synthesizing, ATE, p. 363
- Activities for Communication, p. 133, Realia 12-1

Wrap-Up 10 min.
- Activities for Communication, p. 159, Situation Card 12-3: Interview

Homework Options

Study for Quiz 12-1

Travaux pratiques de grammaire, pp. 100–101, Act. 5–8

Cahier d'activités, p. 136, Act. 7–8

Block 3

PREMIERE ETAPE

Quick Review 10 min.
- Activities for Communication, pp. 67–68 Communicative Activities 12-1A and 12-1B

Quiz 12-1 20 min.
- Administer Quiz 12-1A or 12-1B.

DEUXIEME ETAPE

Comment dit-on... ?, 30 min.
- Bell Work, ATE, p. 364
- Presenting **Comment dit-on...?,** ATE, p. 364, Language Note, ATE, p. 364
- Play Audio CD for Activity 15, p. 364. See Challenge, ATE, p. 364.
- Do Activity 16, p. 365.
- **Tu te rappelles?,** p. 364 with Reteaching, ATE, p. 365
- Do Activity 17, p. 365. See Additional Practice, ATE, p. 365
- Do activity 18, p. 365

Comment dit–on...?, p. 366 5 min.
- Presenting **Comment dit–on...?** ATE, p. 366, using Transparency 12-2

Vocabulaire, p. 366, 20 min.
- Presenting **Vocabulaire,** ATE, p. 367 with Language Notes, ATE, p. 367
- Play Audio CD for Activity 19, p. 367. See Slower Pace, ATE, p. 367

Wrap-Up 5 min.
- **Grammaire supplémentaire**, p. 377, Act. 3

Homework Options

Travaux pratiques de grammaire, pp. 102–103, Acts. 9–12

Cahier d'activités, pp. 137–138, Acts. 9–14

For alternative lesson plans by chapter section, to create your own customized plans, or to preview all resources available for this chapter, use the **One-Stop Planner CD-ROM**, Disc 3.

For additional homework suggestions, see activities accompanied by this symbol throughout the chapter.

Block 4

DEUXIEME ETAPE

Quick Review 10 min.
- Do Activity 20, p. 367. See Challenge, ATE, p. 367

Grammaire, p. 367 25 min.
- Presenting **Grammaire,** ATE, p. 367 with Music Link, ATE, p. 367
- Do Activity 21, p. 367, in writing.
- Additional Practice, ATE, p. 367
- **Grammaire supplémentaire,** p. 377, Acts. 4–5

PANORAMA CULTUREL 15 min
- Presenting **Panorama Culturel,** p. 368, with Videocassette 4 or DVD Tutor, Disc 2
- Language Note, ATE, p. 368
- Answer the **Qu'en penses-tu?** questions, p. 368
- Thinking Critically, ATE, p. 368

TROISIEME ETAPE

Vocabulaire, p. 369, 30 min.
- Presenting **Vocabulaire,** ATE, p. 369
- Play Audio CD for Activity 23, p. 369.
- **Note de grammaire,** p. 369
- Do Activity 24, p. 369.
- **Grammaire supplémentaire,** p. 378, Act. 6
- Do Activity 25, p. 370.
- Do Activity 26, p. 370 with Challenge, ATE, p. 370
- **Note culturelle,** p. 370

Wrap-Up 10 min.
- Have small groups review the forms of transportation by playing charades.

Homework Options
Study for Quiz 12-2
Travaux pratiques de grammaire, pp. 106–107, Acts. 18–21
Cahier d'activités, pp. 140–142, Acts. 18–24

Block 5

DEUXIEME ETAPE

Quick Review 10 min.
- Activities for Communication, pp. 69–70, Communicative Activities 12-2A and 12-2B

Quiz 12-2 20 min.
- Administer Quiz 12-2A or 12-2B.

TROISIEME ETAPE

Comment dit-on...?, p. 371 30 min.
- Motivating Activity: Modify Activity 24, p. 369: The teacher gives the clues and the students guess who it is.
- Presenting **Comment dit-on...?,** ATE, p. 371
- Play Audio CD for Activity 27, p. 371. See Challenge, ATE, p. 371.
- **Note culturelle,** p. 371
- Do Activity 28, p. 371.
- Do Activity 29, ATE, p. 372.
- Activities for Communication, p. 132, Realia 12-3

Prononciation, p. 373 15 min.
- Present **Prononciation,** p. 373 with Teaching Suggestion with ATE, p. 373
- Play Audio CD for Activities A, B, and C. See Language Note, ATE, p. 373.

Wrap-Up 15 min.
- Game: **Les mots en famille,** ATE, p. 353C

Homework Options
Study for Quiz 12-3
Travaux pratiques de grammaire, pp. 106–107, Acts. 18–21
Cahier d'activités, pp. 140–142, Acts. 18–24

Block 6

TROISIEME ETAPE

Quick Review 10 min.
- Activities for Communication, pp. 71–72, Communicative Activities 12-3A and 12-3B

Quiz 12-3 20 min.
- Administer Quiz 12-3A or 12-3B.

LISONS! 20 min
- Do Prereading Activity A, Using Prior Knowledge, ATE, p. 374.
- Do Reading Activities B–F, Language Note, ATE, pp. 374–375.
- Do Postreading Activities G–I, Thinking Critically, ATE, p. 375.

MISE EN PRATIQUE 30 min.
- Do Activity 1, p. 380.
- Play Audio CD for Activity 2.
- Do **Ecrivons!,** p. 381.

Wrap-Up 10 min.
- Activities for Communication, p. 160, Situation Card 12-3: Role-Play

Homework Options
Que sais-je?, p. 382
Study for Chapter 12 Test
Finish **Ecrivons!,** Pupil's Edition, p. 381.

Block 7

MISE EN PRATIQUE

Quick Review 10 min.
- Check homework and collect **Ecrivons!**

Chapter Review 30 min.
- Review Chapter 12. Choose from **Grammaire supplémentaire,** Grammar Tutor for Students of French, Activities for Communication, Listening Activities, Interactive CD-ROM Tutor, or **Jeux interactifs.**

Test, Chapter 12 50 min.
- Administer Chapter 12 Test. Select from Testing Program, Alternative Assessment Guide, Test Generator, or Standardized Assessment Tutor.

Chapter Opener

CHAPITRE 12

One-Stop Planner CD-ROM

For resource information, see the **One-Stop Planner**, Disc 3.

Pacing Tips

All three **étapes** in this chapter present new vocabulary and functions. Keep in mind while planning your lessons, that the **Première étape** is the lightest. For Lesson Plans and timing suggestions, see pages 353I–353L.

Meeting the Standards

Communication

- Pointing out places and things, p. 361
- Making and responding to requests, p. 364
- Asking for advice and making suggestions, p. 366
- Asking for and giving directions, p. 371

Cultures

- Note culturelle, pp. 360, 370, 371
- Rencontre culturelle, p. 363
- Culture Notes, pp. 363, 366, 370
- Panorama Culturel, p. 368

Connections

- Multicultural Link, pp. 354, 366
- Music Link, p. 367
- History Links, p. 372
- Literature Link, p. 375
- Language Arts Link, p. 375

Comparisons

- Thinking Critically: Analyzing - Note culturelle, p. 360
- Thinking Critically: Synthesizing, p. 363
- Thinking Critically: Comparing and Contrasting, pp. 358, 363, 368, 371, 375

Communities

- Community Link, p. 371
- Career Path, p. 383
- De l'école au travail, p. 373

Cultures and Communities

Photo Flash!

Fort-de-France is the departmental seat of Martinique as well as the island's business center. This view of a busy downtown street in Fort-de France shows the commercial center of town with shops, cars, and people strolling on the sidewalks.

Multicultural Link

Most people in Martinique and Guadeloupe speak French at work and in other formal situations, but they are more likely to use **Créole** with family members and close friends. Ask students if they themselves or other members of their community speak a different language at home than at school.

CHAPITRE

12

En ville

Objectives

In this chapter you will review and practice

Première étape

- pointing out places and things

Deuxième étape

- making and responding to requests
- asking for advice and making suggestions

Troisième étape

- asking for and giving directions

Visit Holt Online
go.hrw.com
KEYWORD: WA3 FORT-DE-FRANCE-12
Online Edition

◀ Les rues animées de Fort-de-France

Chapter Opener

CHAPITRE 12

Focusing on Outcomes

Begin by asking students how these functions relate to the photo on pages 354–355. Since some of these functions were presented in earlier chapters, you might review them by asking students to recall familiar expressions for each function.
NOTE: The self-check activities in **Que sais-je?** on page 382 help students assess their achievement of the objectives.

Connections and Comparisons

Social Studies Link

Ask students what kinds of government business might go on in Fort-de-France (promotion of tourism, implementation of policy from France, etc.). Have students do comparative research on U.S. territories, such as Puerto Rico and Guam. How is policy administered in those places? Are the people of those territories full citizens of the U.S.? How does their status compare with that of people in Martinique?

Thinking Critically

Comparing and Contrasting Ask students what connections there might be between some African cultures and the culture of Martinique. Have students do research on topics such as language, foods, beliefs, and customs that might have African origins.

STANDARDS: 3.1, 3.2

Mise en train

CHAPITRE 12

Teaching Resources
pp. 356–358

PRINT 
- Lesson Planner, p. 58
- Video Guide, pp. 82, 84
- Cahier d'activités, p. 133

MEDIA
- One-Stop Planner
- Video Program
  Mise en train
  Videocassette 4, 32:04–35:17
  Videocassette 5 (captioned version), 1:39:10–1:42:26
  Suite
  Videocassette 4, 35:20–44:30
  Videocassette 5 (captioned version), 1:42:30–1:51:39
- DVD Tutor, Disc 2
- Audio Compact Discs, CD 12, Trs. 1–2
- **Mise en train** Transparencies

Presenting Mise en train

Before students view the video episode, have them make a chart like this:

WHO? WHERE? WHY?
Mother
Lisette
Father
Lisette
Mother
Father

As students view the video, they should briefly note in English where Lucien's family members ask him to go and what they ask him to do there. Play the episode again to allow students to revise their notes. Then, as students tell you their answers, record them on a transparency so they can correct their own charts.

Mise en train Transparencies

The **roman-photo** is an abridged version of the video episode.

MISE EN TRAIN ▪ *Un petit service*

CD 12
Trs. 1–2

Stratégie pour comprendre
What do you think Un petit service means? Can you guess what Lucien's mother, father, and sister are asking him to do?

Lucien

Lisette

La mère

Le père

Une voisine

1 **Lucien :** Maman, je vais en ville. J'ai rendez-vous avec Mireille. On va passer la journée à Fort-de-France. Je vais lui faire visiter le fort Saint-Louis.

2 **La mère :** Avant de rentrer, passe au marché et prends de l'ananas, des oranges et des caramboles.

3 **Lisette :** Ah, tu peux rendre ces livres à la bibliothèque aussi, s'il te plaît? Et en échange, tu me prends trois autres livres. Voilà ma carte.

4 **Le père :** Est-ce que tu peux aller à la poste et envoyer ce paquet?
Lucien : Je ne sais pas si je vais avoir le temps.

Preteaching Vocabulary

Using Prior Knowledge
Have students use previous knowledge to identify the following place names:
- 2 **le marché**
- 3 **la bibliothèque**
- 4 **la poste**
- 6 **chez le disquaire**
- 7 **la boulangerie.**

If Lucien is going to run errands at all these places **en ville,** what could **ville** mean?

STANDARDS: 1.2, 4.2

5
Lucien : Je vais d'abord au fort Saint-Louis, puis je dois aller au marché et ensuite...
Le père : C'est important...
Lucien : Bon.

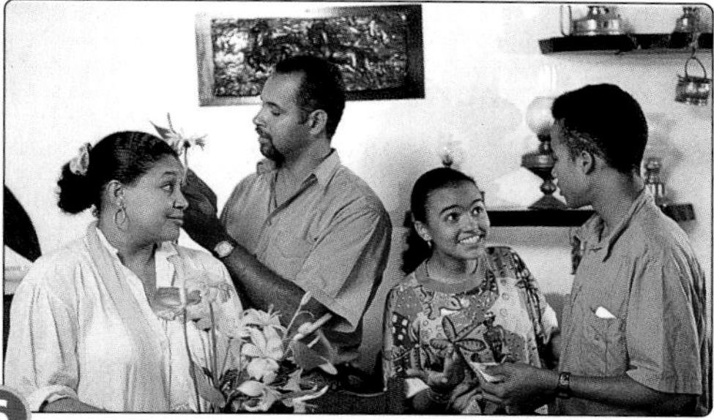

6
Lisette : Tu peux passer chez le disquaire? J'ai commandé un disque compact.
Lucien : Bien. C'est tout?

7
La mère : Au retour, tu peux aller à la boulangerie? Prends deux baguettes.

8
Lucien : Bon, ça suffit pour aujourd'hui!

9
Le père : Tu vas voir, c'est très intéressant, le fort Saint-Louis.
Lisette : Merci, Lucien. C'est sympa.

10
Une voisine : Bonjour. Est-ce que par hasard vous allez en ville aujourd'hui?
Lucien : Au secours!

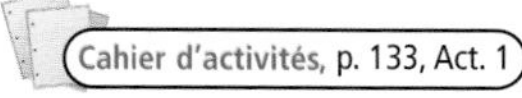
Cahier d'activités, p. 133, Act. 1

Using the Captioned Video/DVD

If students have difficulty understanding French spoken at a normal speed, use Videocassette 5 to allow students to see the French captions for ***Un petit service*** and ***Un petit service (suite).*** Hearing the language and watching the story will reduce anxiety about the new language and facilitate comprehension. The reinforcement of seeing the written vocabulary words as they watch the gestures and actions will help prepare students to do the comprehension activities on page 358.
NOTE: The *DVD Tutor* contains captions for all sections of the *Video Program.*

Mise en train

CHAPITRE 12

Auditory Learners

Play the recording of ***Un petit service.*** Have students read along in their book and repeat the text in the pauses provided on the recording. Then, have them form groups of five and read the story aloud.

Visual Learners

Copy the text from Photos 2, 3, 4, 6, 7, and 8 onto a transparency and label them with the letters **a** through **f**. Then, hold up objects to represent each of the errands (a **baguette**, an orange, a library book, a postage stamp, and so on). Have students match the family's requests to the items requested.

Un petit service (suite)

When the story continues, Mireille accompanies Lucien on his errands. They get lost trying to find a record store and ask a man for directions. Then, they take a ferry to deliver a package, and Lucien points out landmarks in Fort-de-France. When Lucien returns home, his mother asks him about the fort, and he realizes he completely forgot about visiting it!

STANDARDS: 1.2, 4.2

Mise en train

CHAPITRE 12

Thinking Critically

6 Comparing and Contrasting Have students list where they go to do each of their errands and compare their list with Lucien's errands.

These activities check for comprehension only. Students should not yet be expected to produce language modeled in **Mise en train.**

1 Tu as compris?

1. What are Lucien's plans for the day? to visit fort Saint-Louis in Fort-de-France with Mireille
2. What are Lucien and his family talking about? running errands in town
3. Is Lucien happy with the situation? Why or why not? No; He's afraid he won't have time for everything.
4. What happens at the end? Lucien calls for help when a neighbor starts to ask a favor.

2 Qui dit quoi?

Lucien

Lisette

M. Lapiquonne

Mme Lapiquonne

1. «Tu peux aller à la boulangerie?»
2. «Tu peux rendre ces livres à la bibliothèque aussi, s'il te plaît?»
3. «Est-ce que tu peux aller à la poste et envoyer ce paquet?»
4. «Tu peux passer chez le disquaire?»
5. «Passe au marché et prends de l'ananas, des oranges et des caramboles.»
6. «C'est très intéressant, le fort Saint-Louis.»

1. Mme Lapiquonne 2. Lisette 3. M. Lapiquonne 4. Lisette 5. Mme Lapiquonne 6. M. Lapiquonne

3 Où va-t-il?

Où est-ce que Lucien va aller pour...

1. acheter des caramboles?
2. envoyer le paquet?
3. rendre les livres?
4. acheter le disque compact?
5. acheter des baguettes?

1. au marché 2. à la poste 3. à la bibliothèque 4. chez le disquaire 5. à la boulangerie

à la boulangerie **à la poste** **chez le disquaire** **à la bibliothèque** **au marché**

4 Vrai ou faux?

1. Lucien va acheter des caramboles, des pêches et des pommes. faux
2. Il va rendre des livres à la bibliothèque. vrai
3. Lucien va à la boulangerie. vrai
4. Lisette lui donne de l'argent pour acheter un livre. faux
5. Lucien va chez le disquaire pour son père.
6. Il va acheter le journal pour la voisine.

5. faux 6. faux

5 Cherche les expressions

According to *Un petit service,* how do you . . . See answers below.

1. say you're meeting someone?
2. say you don't know if you'll have time?
3. ask someone to do something for you?
4. express your annoyance?
5. call for help?

Est-ce que tu peux... ? **Au secours!** **Ça suffit!** **J'ai rendez-vous avec...** **Je ne sais pas si je vais avoir le temps.**

6 Et maintenant, à toi

Quelles courses est-ce que tu fais pour ta famille et tes amis? Est-ce que tu vas aux mêmes endroits que Lucien?

Comprehension Check

Additional Practice

3 Have students match these errands with the people pictured in Activity 2 who requested them. Have students tell what else they could do in each place.

Challenge

4 Write the sentences on the board or a transparency, omitting several words. **(Lucien va acheter des ____ , des pêches et des _____.)** Have students complete these sentences to make them true.

Answers

5
1. J'ai rendez-vous avec...
2. Je ne sais pas si je vais avoir le temps.
3. Est-ce que tu peux... ?
4. Ça suffit!
5. Au secours!

STANDARDS: 1.2, 4.2

Première étape

Objective Pointing out places and things

WA3 FORT-DE-FRANCE-12

Vocabulaire

Où est-ce qu'on va pour faire les courses? On peut aller à ces endroits :

à la **boulangerie** pour acheter **des baguettes**

à la **pâtisserie** pour acheter **des pâtisseries**

à **l'épicerie** pour acheter de la confiture

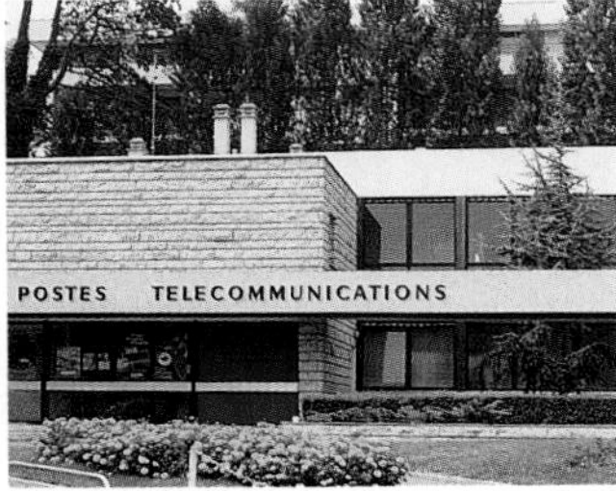

à la **poste** pour acheter **des timbres** et **envoyer des lettres**

à la **banque** pour **retirer** ou **déposer** de l'argent

à la **librairie-papeterie** pour acheter des livres ou **des enveloppes**

à la **pharmacie** pour acheter **des médicaments**

chez le disquaire pour acheter des disques compacts ou des cassettes

à la **bibliothèque** pour **emprunter** ou **rendre** des livres

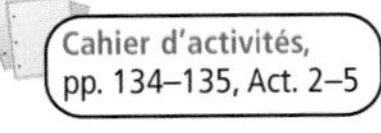
Cahier d'activités, pp. 134–135, Act. 2–5

Travaux pratiques de grammaire, pp. 98–99, Act. 1–4

Communication for All Students

Building on Previous Skills

Ask students to name three or four places where tourists might want to go in their town during a vacation and tell why.

Additional Practice

For listening practice, create and read aloud several true-false statements based on the **Vocabulaire,** such as **On va à la bibliothèque pour acheter du pain.** Call on individual students to correct the false statements.

Première étape

CHAPITRE 12

Teaching Resources

pp. 359–362

PRINT

- Lesson Planner, p. 59
- TPR Storytelling Book, pp. 45, 48
- Listening Activities, pp. 91, 95
- Activities for Communication, pp. 67–68, 130, 133, 159–160
- Travaux pratiques de grammaire, pp. 98–101
- Grammar Tutor for Students of French, Chapter 12
- Cahier d'activités, pp. 134–136
- Testing Program, pp. 301–304
- Alternative Assessment Guide, p. 43
- Student Make-Up Assignments, Chapter 12

MEDIA 

- One-Stop Planner
- Audio Compact Discs, CD 12, Trs. 3, 19, 31–32
- Teaching Transparencies: 12-1, 12-A; **Grammaire supplémentaire** Answers; Travaux pratiques de grammaire Answers
- Interactive CD-ROM Tutor, Disc 3

Bell Work

Have students make a shopping list in French of at least five things they need to buy. They might include groceries, school supplies, or clothing. Have them begin the list with **Il me faut...**

Presenting Vocabulaire

Hold up pictures of the items that can be purchased at each store, having students repeat after you. Write the store names and the items available at each one on strips of transparency. Have two students come to the projector and match the stores with the items available at each one.

Première étape

CHAPITRE 12

Teaching Resources
pp. 359–362

PRINT

- Lesson Planner, p. 59
- TPR Storytelling Book, pp. 45, 48
- Listening Activities, pp. 91, 95
- Activities for Communication, pp. 67–68, 130, 133, 159–160
- Travaux pratiques de grammaire, pp. 98–101
- Grammar Tutor for Students of French, Chapter 12
- Cahier d'activités, pp. 134–136
- Testing Program, pp. 301–304
- Alternative Assessment Guide, p. 43
- Student Make-Up Assignments, Chapter 12

MEDIA 

- One-Stop Planner
- Audio Compact Discs, CD 12, Trs. 3, 19, 31–32
- Teaching Transparencies: 12-1, 12-A; **Grammaire supplémentaire** Answers; Travaux pratiques de grammaire Answers
- Interactive CD-ROM Tutor, Disc 3

Thinking Critically
Analyzing — Note culturelle
Have students consider how late stores usually stay open in the United States. Have them compare these hours to the hours that French stores usually keep. What are the advantages and disadvantages of French hours? Of American hours?

7 Où sont-ils? See scripts and answers on p. 353G.

Ecoutons Listen to these conversations and tell where the people are.

CD 12
Tr. 3

Tu te rappelles?

Remember, **au, à la, à l',** and **aux** mean *to the* or *at the*. Use **au** before a masculine singular noun, **à la** before a feminine singular noun, **à l'** before any singular noun beginning with a vowel sound, and **aux** before any plural noun.

Je vais { **au** musée. / **à la** boulangerie. / **à l'**épicerie.

Je vais { **à l'**hôtel. / **aux** Etats-Unis.

Grammaire supplémentaire, p. 376, Act. 1

Travaux pratiques de grammaire, pp. 100–101, Act. 5–8

8 Un petit mot

Lisons/Ecrivons Lis ce petit mot que Frédéric a écrit à un ami. Ensuite, fais une liste de trois endroits où Frédéric est allé et explique ce qu'il y a fait. See answers below.

Cher Pierre,

Ici, rien de bien nouveau. Hier, mes parents sont allés passer la journée chez leurs amis, alors j'étais tout seul. J'en ai profité pour faire des courses. D'abord, je suis allé à la boulangerie acheter du pain. Ensuite, je suis allé à la poste parce que je n'avais plus de timbres, et j'en ai profité pour envoyer une lettre à Jules, mon correspondant québécois. Puis, je suis allé à la bibliothèque emprunter quelques livres parce que j'ai fini de lire toute ma collection. Je n'ai pas trouvé le dernier livre de Stephen King à la bibliothèque (il paraît qu'il est super!), alors je suis allé à la librairie pour l'acheter. Finalement, je suis passé à l'épicerie acheter des légumes et du fromage pour mon déjeuner. Voilà, c'est tout. Ecris-moi vite pour me dire comment tu trouves ton nouveau lycée. Salut.

Frédéric

9 Des courses en ville

Lisons Yvette fait des courses en ville. Où est-elle?

1. «Je voudrais ce gâteau au chocolat, s'il vous plaît.» à la pâtisserie
2. «Je voudrais emprunter ces trois livres, s'il vous plaît.» à la bibliothèque
3. «Eh bien, je voudrais des médicaments pour ma mère.» à la pharmacie
4. «C'est combien pour envoyer cette lettre aux Etats-Unis?» à la poste
5. «Zut, alors! Elle est fermée. Je ne peux pas déposer de l'argent!» à la banque

Note culturelle

Stores in France and Martinique don't stay open 24 hours a day. Between 12:30 P.M. and 3:30 P.M., very few small businesses are open; however, they usually remain open until 7:00 P.M. By law, businesses must close one day a week, usually Sunday. Only grocery stores, restaurants, and certain places related to culture and entertainment, such as museums and movie theaters, may stay open on Sunday.

Communication for All Students

Additional Practice
Tu te rappelles? You might have students recall the French names of other places where they might go after school **(au café, au ciné)**. Then, have partners ask and tell each other where they're going after school this weekend.

Challenge
8 Have students write a response to Frédéric's letter, describing a similar day they've had.

Visual Learners
9 One student draws a picture of a building that Yvette visited. The partner must identify the place, say what Yvette said there, and then draw a different building.

Possible answers

8 to the bakery to buy bread, to the post office to buy stamps and send a letter, to the library to borrow some books, to the bookstore to buy a book, to the grocery store to buy vegetables and cheese

STANDARDS: 1.2, 3.1, 3.2, 4.2

10 **Il va où?** See answers below.

a. **Lisons** Regarde la liste d'Armand. Où va-t-il?

b. **Lisons** Qu'est-ce qu'il peut acheter d'autre là où il va?

classeurs
gomme
enveloppes
CD
livre
aspirine
timbres
œufs
tarte
baguettes

DE BONS CONSEILS

You've already learned that an ending can often help you guess the gender of a word. An ending can also help you guess the meaning of a word. For example, the ending **-erie** often indicates a place where something is sold or made. Look at these words: **poissonnerie, fromagerie, chocolaterie, croissanterie.** What do you think they mean? Another common ending that carries a particular meaning is **-eur (-euse).** It indicates a person who performs a certain activity. In French, **chasser** means *to hunt.* A person who hunts is a **chasseur.** Since **chanter** means *to sing,* how do you think you would say *singer* in French? If **danser** means *to dance,* how would you say *dancer?**

11 **Devine!**

Parlons Pense à une chose que tu as achetée. Puis dis à ton/ta camarade où tu l'as achetée. Ton/Ta partenaire va essayer de deviner de quoi tu parles. Ensuite, changez de rôle.

EXEMPLE — **Je suis allé(e) à la boulangerie.**
— **Tu as acheté des croissants?**
— **Non.**

Si tu as oublié
le passé composé
va à la page 271.

Grammaire supplémentaire, pp. 376–377, Act. 2–3

Comment dit-on...?

Pointing out places and things

Voici tes timbres.
Regarde, voilà ma maison.
Look, here/there is/are . . .

Ça, c'est la banque.
This/That is . . .

Là, c'est mon disquaire préféré.
There, that is . . .

Là, tu vois, c'est la maison de mes grands-parents.
There, you see, this/that is . . .

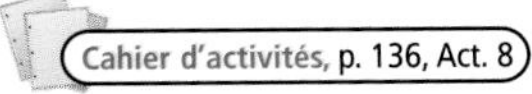
Cahier d'activités, p. 136, Act. 8

VOILÀ LA MAISON DE MES GRANDS-PARENTS.

*chanteur(euse), danseur(euse)

Première étape

CHAPITRE 12

Teaching Suggestions

10 You might have students work in pairs to answer these questions. Have them do **10a** first and then write their answers on the board. Students can then use these place names as the basis for answering **10b.**

Language-to-Language

De bons conseils The official French term for a *Walkman®* is **un baladeur,** which translates literally as *one who walks around.* A **conteur** is *someone who narrates stories.* **Rapporter** means *to tell on* or *to tattle,* so a **rapporteur** is not a very popular person!

Additional Practice

11 You might ask students to think of two or three additional things that they bought at different stores.

Presenting
Comment dit-on... ?

Begin by identifying students or pictures of celebrities that you have brought to class. Then, use the expressions to identify different items in the classroom and pictures of buildings. Finally, hold up pictures of different places or things or point to various objects in the classroom and have students identify them.

Connections and Comparisons

Language-to-Language

De bons conseils You might have students think of common suffixes in English, such as *-ly, -er,* and *-ment,* and suggest words that have these endings *(happily, buyer, punishment).*

Challenge

De bons conseils Have students guess what the ending **-ant** means from looking at the following words they're already familiar with: **barbant, intéressant, embêtant, dégoûtant.** You might have them go through the French vocabulary at the end of the book to find other endings that signal adjectives (**-é, -eux, -euse,** and so on).

Answers

10 a. à la librairie-papeterie (classeurs, gomme, enveloppes, livre), chez le disquaire (CD), à la pharmacie (aspirine), à la poste (timbres), à l'épicerie (œufs), à la pâtisserie (tarte), à la boulangerie (baguettes)

b. *Answers will vary.*

CHAPITRE 12

Portfolio

13 **Written** This activity might be expanded into the chapter project described on page 353C. This item is appropriate for students' written portfolios. For portfolio suggestions, see *Alternative Assessment Guide,* pages iv–17.

Assess

- Testing Program, pp. 301–304 Quiz 12-1A, Quiz 12-1B, Audio CD 12, Tr. 19
- Student Make-Up Assignments Chapter 12, Alternative Quiz
- Alternative Assessment Guide, p. 43

12 A la Martinique

Parlons Tu as pris les photos suivantes pendant ton voyage à la Martinique. Avec un(e) camarade, dites ce qu'il y a sur les photos. Possible answers:

le disquaire	la statue de Joséphine de Beauharnais
la pharmacie	la boulangerie
la bibliothèque Schœlcher	le marché

1. Voici la statue de Joséphine de Beauharnais.

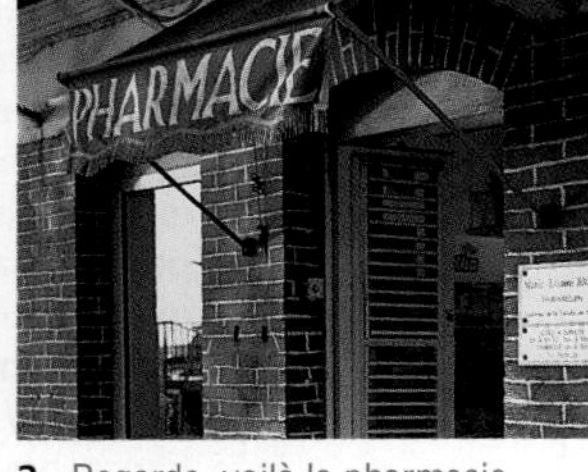

2. Regarde, voilà la pharmacie.

3. Ça, c'est le disquaire.

4. Là, c'est le marché.

5. Là, tu vois, c'est la bibliothèque Schœlcher.

6. Voici la boulangerie.

A la française

When you try to communicate in a foreign language, there will always be times when you can't remember or don't know the exact word you need. One way to get around this problem is to use *circumlocution*. Circumlocution means substituting words and expressions you do know to explain what you mean. For example, if you can't think of the French word for *pharmacy*, you might say **l'endroit où on peut acheter des médicaments** *(the place where you can buy medicine).* Other expressions you can use are **la personne qui/que** *(the person who/whom),* and **le truc qui/que** *(the thing that).*

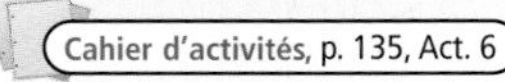

Cahier d'activités, p. 135, Act. 6

13 Mon quartier

Ecrivons Un(e) élève francophone va habiter avec ta famille pendant un semestre. Fais un plan de ton quartier et marque où se trouvent ton école, la poste, le supermarché, etc...

14 Jeu de rôle

Parlons L'élève francophone (ton/ta camarade) te demande où se trouvent plusieurs endroits. Montre-les sur le plan de l'activité 13. Explique ce qu'on y achète ou ce qu'on y fait. Ensuite, changez de rôle.

Communication for All Students

Visual Learners

12 You might also have students bring in photos they've taken on vacation, or pictures they've cut from magazines, and identify them to a partner or to the class.

Circumlocution

After reading **A la française** with students, have them practice using circumlocution to identify the photos in Activity 12. You might also give students some photos of additional places to describe to a partner in French. To help students, provide them with a list of circumlocution expressions from page 167C.

STANDARDS: 1.1, 1.3, 3.1, 5.1

Look at the illustrations below. Where are these people? What are they talking about?

— Bonjour, Madame Perrot. Vous avez passé de bonnes vacances?

— Très bonnes. On est allés à la Guadeloupe. Vous savez, ma sœur habite là-bas, et...

— Et votre père, il va bien?

— Oui, merci. Il va beaucoup mieux depuis...

— Qu'est-ce que vous allez faire avec ça?

— Ma voisine m'a donné une très bonne recette. C'est très simple. Tout ce qu'il faut faire, c'est...

Qu'en penses-tu?

1. What are the topics of these conversations? What does this tell you about the culture of Martinique? family, vacation, recipes; For the **Martiniquais**, it is more important to spend time finding out what's going on in one another's life than to get business done quickly.
2. What kind of relationships do you or your family have with the people who work in your town? Do you know them? Do you often make "small talk" with them?

Savais-tu que... ?

In Martinique, as in many parts of France, people like to take the time to say hello, ask how others are doing, and find out what's going on in one another's lives. Of course, the smaller the town, the more likely this is to occur. While it may be frustrating to Americans in a hurry, especially when they are conducting business, in West Indian culture it is considered rude not to take a few minutes to engage in some polite conversation before talking business.

Cultures and Communities

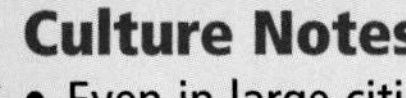

Culture Notes

- Even in large cities like Paris, owners of small shops often greet customers as they come into the store and say goodbye as they leave. Customers often respond with a polite **Bonjour, madame/monsieur** or **Merci, au revoir!**
- Small talk is also very common in Côte d'Ivoire and can be quite involved. When people run into a friend or acquaintance during the day, they often inquire at length about that person's health, job, and family situation. Friends will also inquire about the health, job, and general situation of that person's entire family and circle of friends.

CHAPITRE 12

Motivating Activity

Ask students for examples of "small talk" in English. Ask them in what situations and with whom they might make small talk.

Presenting
Rencontre culturelle

Have two students read each conversation aloud. After each one, ask the class where the people are, what they are talking about, and what the other people are doing. **(On est où? De quoi est-ce qu'on parle? Que font les autres?)** Then, have students answer the questions in **Qu'en penses-tu?** as a class or with a partner.

Teaching Suggestion

You might ask students if there are places or situations in the United States in which small talk is expected or discouraged.

Thinking Critically

Comparing and Contrasting Ask students how Americans behave when they have to stand in line and if their behavior is different from that shown here. Ask students if they consider themselves to be very patient.

Synthesizing Form small groups. Have each group adapt one of these conversations to a similar situation in their town. Have them expand the conversations by involving the other customers who are waiting in line. Groups should act out their conversation.

STANDARDS: 2.1, 3.2, 4.2

Teaching Resources
pp. 364–367

PRINT

- Lesson Planner, p. 60
- TPR Storytelling Book, pp. 46, 48
- Listening Activities, pp. 91–92, 96
- Activities for Communication, pp. 69–70, 131, 133–134, 159–160
- Travaux pratiques de grammaire, pp. 102–105
- Grammar Tutor for Students of French, Chapter 12
- Cahier d'activités, pp. 137–139
- Testing Program, pp. 305–308
- Alternative Assessment Guide, p. 43
- Student Make-Up Assignments, Chapter 12

MEDIA 

- One-Stop Planner
- Audio Compact Discs, CD 12, Trs. 4–5, 20, 33–34
- Teaching Transparencies: 12-2, 12-B; **Grammaire supplémentaire** Answers; Travaux pratiques de grammaire Answers
- Interactive CD-ROM Tutor, Disc 3

Bell Work
Have students list the places they'd go to get the following items: **du pain, des timbres, un livre, une gomme,** and **un CD.**

Presenting
Comment dit-on... ?

Begin by reviewing the previously learned expressions suggested under Building on Previous Skills. Then, use the expressions in **Comment dit-on... ?** to ask individual students for various favors.

Deuxième étape

Objectives Making and responding to requests; asking for advice and making suggestions

WA3 FORT-DE-FRANCE-12

Comment dit-on...?

Making and responding to requests

CD-ROM 3 DVD 2

To make a request:

(Est-ce que) tu peux aller au marché?
Tu me rapportes des timbres?
Tu pourrais passer à la poste acheter des timbres?
Could you go by . . . ?

To accept requests:

D'accord.
Je veux bien.
J'y vais tout de suite.
Si tu veux. *If you want.*

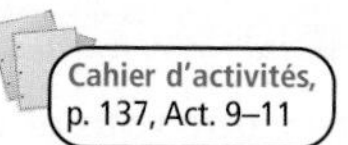
Cahier d'activités, p. 137, Act. 9–11

To decline requests:

Je ne peux pas maintenant.
Je suis désolé(e), mais je n'ai pas le temps.

Tu te rappelles?

Use the partitive articles **du, de la,** and **de l'** when you mean some of an item. If you mean a whole item instead of a part of it, use the indefinite articles **un, une,** and **des. Du, de la, de l', des, un,** and **une** usually become **de/d'** in negative sentences.

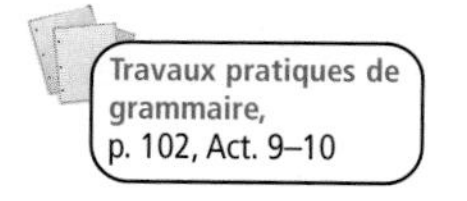
Travaux pratiques de grammaire, p. 102, Act. 9–10

Grammaire supplémentaire, p. 377, Act. 4

15 **Est-ce que tu peux...?** See scripts and answers on p. 353G.

Ecoutons Listen to the following conversations and decide if the person agrees to or refuses the request.

CD 12 Tr. 4

Communication for All Students

Building on Previous Skills
Have students recall French expressions they already know that they would use to tell someone to do something, such as cleaning one's room. **(Range ta chambre! Tu dois ranger ta chambre.)** Write their suggestions on the board. You might also ask students to recall possible responses to the commands.

Language Note
You might want to compare **pourrais** with **voudrais,** explaining that the **-ais** ending signals the polite form for **je** and **tu.**

Challenge
15 Have students also write down the errand that is requested. Have partners use these notes to make and respond to requests.

16 Un petit service

Parlons Qu'est-ce que ces jeunes te disent pour te demander un service? See answers below.

1.

2.

3.

4.

17 Il me faut...

Parlons Décide de quels articles tu as besoin et demande à ton/ta camarade d'aller les acheter au magasin approprié. Il/Elle va accepter ou refuser d'y aller. Ensuite, changez de rôle.

Si tu as oublié
expressing need
va à la page 238.

Grammaire supplémentaire, p. 377, Act. 5

1.

0,46 €
LA POSTE
RF
2.

LANCELOT DU LAC
3.

4.

5.

6.

18 Tu pourrais me rendre un service?

Parlons Demande à tes camarades de te rendre les services suivants. Ils vont accepter ou refuser et te donner une raison.

- aller chercher un livre à la bibliothèque
- acheter un dictionnaire de français à la librairie
- acheter un CD chez le disquaire
- acheter un sandwich au fast-food
- acheter une règle à la papeterie
- acheter des timbres à la poste

Si tu as oublié
making an excuse
va à la page 145.

Communication for All Students

Auditory Learners

16 Read aloud appropriate requests and have students match them with the illustrations.

Challenge

16 Encourage students to say or write other requests each person might make. Have them expand each person's request by telling why the errand needs to be done.

Slower Pace

17 Before students do the activity, have them tell which store they would go to for each item.

Challenge

18 Have students vary the way they request and respond to favors.

Deuxième étape

CHAPITRE 12

Additional Practice

17 You might also show the items you used for the **Vocabulaire** presentation on page 359 (a jar of jam, money, medicine, a croissant, and a library book) and have partners make appropriate requests.

Reteaching

17 **The partitive** Review the use of the partitive, using **Tu te rappelles?** on page 364. You might bring in a loaf of bread to demonstrate **un pain,** and then break off a piece and offer it to students to illustrate the partitive **du pain.** Have students name each item in the photos with the correct partitive article.

Additional Practice

Show *Teaching Transparency 12-2.* Assign each of the people shown to one of four groups. Have them write a speech bubble on a strip of transparency for the person they were assigned. Project their transparencies on top of the original transparency and have the class match the speech bubbles to the people.

Possible answers

16
1. (Est-ce que) tu peux aller à la poste envoyer des lettres?
2. (Est-ce que) tu pourrais passer à la bibliothèque rendre des livres?
3. Tu me rapportes un CD?
4. (Est-ce que) tu pourrais passer à la pharmacie acheter des médicaments?

Deuxième étape

CHAPITRE 12

Teaching Resources
pp. 364–367

PRINT 

- Lesson Planner, p. 60
- TPR Storytelling Book, pp. 46, 48
- Listening Activities, pp. 91–92, 96
- Activities for Communication, pp. 69–70, 131, 133–134, 159–160
- Travaux pratiques de grammaire, pp. 102–105
- Grammar Tutor for Students of French, Chapter 12
- Cahier d'activités, pp. 137–139
- Testing Program, pp. 305–308
- Alternative Assessment Guide, p. 43
- Student Make-Up Assignments, Chapter 12

MEDIA 

- One-Stop Planner
- Audio Compact Discs, CD 12, Trs. 4–5, 20, 33–34
- Teaching Transparencies: 12-2, 12-B; **Grammaire supplémentaire** Answers; Travaux pratiques de grammaire Answers
- Interactive CD-ROM Tutor, Disc 3

Presenting
Comment dit-on... ?, Vocabulaire

Name local places and ask **Comment est-ce qu'on peut y aller? En voiture? En bus?** Then, display a map of the United States or a world map and make true-false statements about how to get to and from certain locations. Have students say whether the statement is true or false. For example, **de San Francisco à New York, on peut y aller à vélo. (faux)** or **de Miami à la Martinique, on peut y aller en bateau. (vrai)**

Comment dit-on...?

Asking for advice and making suggestions

To ask for advice on how to get somewhere:
Comment est-ce qu'on y va?
How can we get there?

To suggest how to get somewhere:
On peut y aller en train.
We can go . . .
On peut prendre le bus.
We can take . . .

Vocabulaire

CD-ROM 3 DVD 2

Comment est-ce qu'on y va?

en bus (m.)

à pied (m.)

à vélo (m.)

en voiture (f.)

en taxi (m.)

en bateau (m.)

en avion (m.)

en train (m.)

en métro (m.)

Travaux pratiques de grammaire, pp. 103–104, Act. 11–15

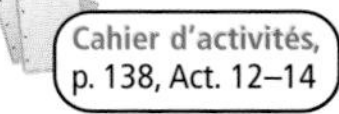

Cahier d'activités, p. 138, Act. 12–14

Cultures and Communities

Culture Note

In some former French colonies in West Africa, such as **Guinée** and **Sénégal**, people travel between cities in taxis that wait for passengers at **gare-voitures.** If you want to travel to a specific city, you go to the **gare-voiture** and ask for the taxi that is going to that city. There are no set schedules though, as the driver does not leave until the taxi is full of paying passengers.

Multicultural Link

Have students choose a foreign city or country and imagine the most popular and efficient form of transportation there. They may also want to find out about typical bus, train, metro, and plane fares there.

STANDARDS: 2.1, 4.2

19 On y va comment? See scripts and answers on p. 353G.

Ecoutons Listen to these conversations. Where are these people going and how are they going to get there?
CD 12 Tr. 5

20 Comment vont-ils voyager?

Parlons Dis comment ces gens voyagent.

1. en bateau

2. en métro

3. en train

4. en avion

Grammaire

The pronoun *y*

You've already seen the pronoun **y** *(there)* several times. Can you figure out how to use it?

—Je vais **à la bibliothèque.** Tu **y** vas aussi?
—Non, je n'**y** vais pas.
—Je vais **chez le disquaire.** Tu veux **y** aller?
—Non, j'**y** suis allé hier.

It can replace an entire phrase meaning *to, at,* or *in* any place that has already been mentioned. Place it before the conjugated verb, or, if there is an infinitive, place **y** before the infinitive: Je vais **y** aller demain.

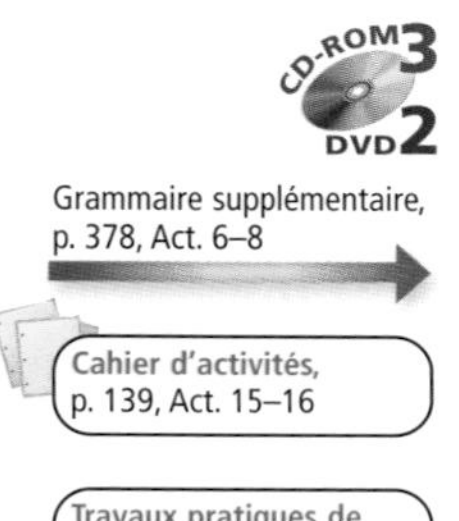
CD-ROM 3
DVD 2

Grammaire supplémentaire, p. 378, Act. 6–8

Cahier d'activités, p. 139, Act. 15–16

Travaux pratiques de grammaire, p. 105, Act. 16–17

21 Grammaire en contexte

Parlons Comment est-ce que tes amis et toi, vous allez aux endroits suivants?

EXEMPLE **Au cinéma? Nous y allons en bus.**

au cinéma, au supermarché, à la poste, à la bibliothèque, à la piscine, au centre commercial, au stade, au parc, à la librairie, au lycée, au concert

22 Qu'est-ce qu'on fait vendredi soir?

Parlons Tu téléphones à un(e) ami(e) pour l'inviter à sortir vendredi soir. Décidez où vous voulez aller et dites comment vous allez y aller.

Si tu as oublié
inviting
Va à la page 179.

Communication for All Students

Slower Pace

19 Before they do this activity, have students list expressions they might expect to hear.

Challenge

20 You might also have students write brief descriptions of what the people are going to do and why.

Additional Practice

Write destinations like **chez le disquaire** and **à la bibliothèque** on cards and distribute them. Then, have students pair off and ask questions until they find out where their partner is going.
—Tu vas à la bibliothèque?
—Non, je n'y vais pas.
—Tu vas chez le disquaire?
—Oui, je vais y aller aujourd'hui.

Deuxième étape

CHAPITRE 12

Language Notes

- Explain that **à** is used instead of **en** with **pied** and **vélo** because they aren't vehicles in which you ride.
- Point out that either the definite article or indefinite article can be used with transportation after **prendre (prendre le train, prendre un taxi).**

Presenting Grammaire

The pronoun *y* Write **Il, va, à la bibliothèque,** and **y** on separate strips of transparency. Arrange the first three strips to form the sentence **Il va à la bibliothèque** and have students repeat it. Then, replace **à la bibliothèque** with **y** to form the sentence **Il y va.** Write the subjects, verbs, and prepositional phrases of several similar sentences and the pronoun **y** on strips, scramble them, and call on students to arrange them into sentences, first without **y,** and then forming a new sentence using **y.**

Music Link

After teaching the pronoun **y,** you might play the song *Sur le pont d'Avignon* available on Audio CD 9. Have students raise their hand whenever they hear the pronoun **y.**

Assess

- Testing Program, pp. 305–308 Quiz 12-2A, Quiz 12-2B, Audio CD 12, Tr. 20
- Student Make-Up Assignments Chapter 12, Alternative Quiz
- Alternative Assessment Guide, p. 43

CHAPITRE 12

Teaching Resources
p. 368

PRINT 
- Video Guide, pp. 83, 84–85
- Cahier d'activités, p. 144

MEDIA
- One-Stop Planner
- Video Program Videocassette 4, 44:32–47:20
- DVD Tutor, Disc 2
- Audio Compact Discs, CD 12, Trs. 6–9
- Interactive CD-ROM Tutor, Disc 3

Presenting
Panorama Culturel

After students view the video, have them scan the interviews for cognates and skim for a general idea of what each person is saying. Then, ask the **Questions** below.

Language Note
You might define the following terms: **sur route** *(on the road)*; **conduite** *(driving)*; **trajet** *(route)*; **ailleurs** *(elsewhere)*.

Questions
1. **Est-ce que Lily-Christine a son permis de conduire?** (Non, elle a son permis probatoire.)
2. **D'après Lily-Christine, combien d'examens est-ce qu'on passe pour avoir le permis de conduire?** (deux)
3. **Est-ce qu'Emmanuel a son permis de conduire? Pourquoi ou pourquoi pas?** (Non; Il faut avoir 18 ans.)
4. **D'après Charlotte, qu'est-ce qu'il faut bien savoir?** (les signes, le code de la route)

Qu'est-ce qu'il faut faire pour avoir un permis de conduire?
Here's what some francophone people told us about obtaining a driver's license where they live.

Lily-Christine,
Québec

«J'ai mon permis probatoire, temporaire. Je n'ai pas encore mon permis de conduire. Premièrement, pour avoir ton permis, tu suis les cours théoriques. Après ça, tu passes ton examen. Si tu passes l'examen, tu as ton permis temporaire. Après, tu suis des cours pratiques. Tu passes un examen sur route. Et puis, si tu as l'examen sur route, eh bien, tu as ton permis.» Tr. 7

Emmanuel,
France

«Non, je n'ai pas encore de permis de conduire parce que je n'ai pas encore 16 ans. Je l'aurai peut-être, [mon] permis accompagné, à 16 ans. Autrement, [pour avoir] un permis de conduire normal, il faut attendre 18 ans en France. Pour avoir un permis de conduire, il faut passer le code. C'est un examen, quoi, c'est le code de la route. Et [il] faut passer la conduite. On est avec un moniteur. On doit faire un trajet qu'il nous indique et puis, suivant si on le fait bien ou pas, on a notre permis.» Tr. 8

Charlotte,
France

«Il faut sans doute bien savoir ses signes, son code de la route. [Il ne faut] pas avoir la tête ailleurs souvent, enfin... [Il] faut être bien dans sa tête. Voilà.» Tr. 9

Qu'en penses-tu?
1. Are the requirements for a driver's license that these people mention the same as those in your state?
2. What means of public transportation are available in your area? Do you use them? Why or why not?
3. How does transportation influence your lifestyle? How would your lifestyle change if you lived where these people do?

Connections and Comparisons

Motivating Activity
Ask whether they have, or would like to have, a driver's license and why or why not.

Thinking Critically
Comparing and Contrasting Have students compare the French, Canadian, and American requirements for a driver's license. Which requirements are most strict? What do students think the requirements for a license should be?

STANDARDS: 2.1, 3.2, 4.2

Objective Asking for and giving directions

go.hrw.com
WA3 FORT-DE-FRANCE-12

Vocabulaire

La bibliothèque est **entre** le lycée et la banque.
La poste est **à droite du** café.
Le cinéma est **à gauche du** café.

La boulangerie est **au coin de** la rue.
Le café est **en face de** la bibliothèque.

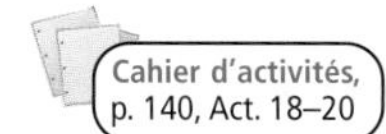

Cahier d'activités, p. 140, Act. 18–20

Travaux pratiques de grammaire, pp. 106–107, Act. 19–21

Here are some other prepositions you may want to use to give directions:

à côté de	*next to*	**loin de**	*far from*
devant	*in front of*	**près de**	*near*
derrière	*behind*		

Note de grammaire

The preposition **de** usually means *of* or *from.*

- When you use **de** before **le** or **les,** make the following contractions:

  de + le = du C'est près **du** musée.
  de + les = des La ville est près **des** Alpes.

- **De** doesn't change before **l'** or **la:**

  C'est au coin **de la** rue.
  La poste est à côté **de l'**école.

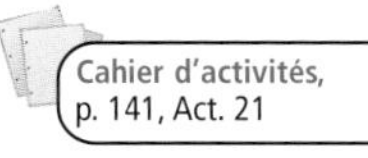

Cahier d'activités, p. 141, Act. 21

Grammaire supplémentaire, p. 379, Act. 9–10

Travaux pratiques de grammaire, p. 106, Act. 18

23 Vrai ou faux?
See scripts and answers on p. 353H.

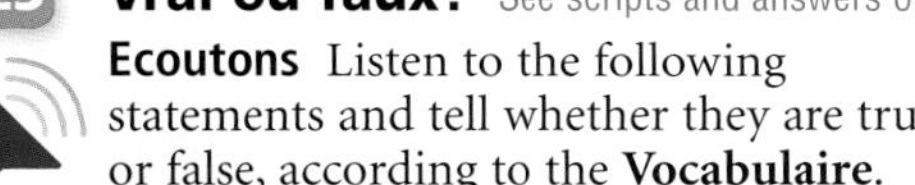

Ecoutons Listen to the following statements and tell whether they are true or false, according to the **Vocabulaire**.

CD 12 Tr. 10

24 Qui est-ce?

Parlons Explique où un(e) camarade est assis(e) en classe. Les autres élèves de ton groupe vont essayer de deviner de qui tu parles.

EXEMPLE **Cette personne est derrière David et à côté d'Isabelle.**

Communication for All Students

Building on Previous Skills

Have students suggest English expressions they might need in order to ask for directions if they were lost in a city. Have them list French expressions they already know.

Slower Pace

You might write incomplete sentences on a transparency **(La boulangerie est près de...)** and have students complete them.

Game

24 Have students form teams and award a point for a correct answer. They might give locations of objects as well as people.

Teaching Resources
pp. 369–373

PRINT 

- Lesson Planner, p. 61
- TPR Storytelling Book, pp. 47, 48
- Listening Activities, pp. 92–93, 97
- Activities for Communication, pp. 71–72, 132, 134, 159–160
- Travaux pratiques de grammaire, pp. 106–107
- Grammar Tutor for Students of French, Chapter 12
- Cahier d'activités, pp. 140–142
- Testing Program, pp. 309–312
- Alternative Assessment Guide, p. 43
- Student Make-Up Assignments, Chapter 12

MEDIA 

- One-Stop Planner
- Audio Compact Discs, CD 12, Trs. 10–11, 21, 35–36
- Teaching Transparencies: 12-3, 12-C; **Grammaire supplémentaire** Answers; Travaux pratiques de grammaire Answers
- Interactive CD-ROM Tutor, Disc 3

Bell Work

Have students write down the forms of transportation they take to go to the following places: **le cinéma, le fast-food, l'école.**

Presenting Vocabulaire

Have volunteers hold up signs with the names of different places written on them. Position the students at different locations in the classroom and tell the class where each "building" is located in relation to the others nearby. You might also position yourself near a particular "building" and ask questions about your location. **(Je suis près de la boulangerie?)**

STANDARDS: 1.2, 1.3, 4.1

Troisième étape

CHAPITRE 12

Teaching Resources
pp. 369–373

PRINT 

- Lesson Planner, p. 61
- TPR Storytelling Book, pp. 47, 48
- Listening Activities, pp. 92–93, 97
- Activities for Communication, pp. 71–72, 132, 134, 159–160
- Travaux pratiques de grammaire, pp. 106–107
- Grammar Tutor for Students of French, Chapter 12
- Cahier d'activités, pp. 140–142
- Testing Program, pp. 309–312
- Alternative Assessment Guide, p. 43
- Student Make-Up Assignments, Chapter 12

MEDIA

- One-Stop Planner
- Audio Compact Discs, CD 12, Trs. 10–11, 21, 35–36
- Teaching Transparencies: 12-3, 12-C; **Grammaire supplémentaire** Answers; Travaux pratiques de grammaire Answers
- Interactive CD-ROM Tutor, Disc 3

Reteaching

Family vocabulary Draw the family tree of a TV family or of a royal family and ask students to describe the relationships between the family members. You might expand this activity by having students tell where the families live and what they like to do. You might also ask questions about familial relationships, such as **Le frère de ton père, c'est ton oncle ou ta mère?**

Culture Note

Since Martinique is a **département** of France, people in Martinique refer to continental France as **la métropole.**

25 Il est perdu!

Parlons Ton ami Hervé n'a pas le sens de l'orientation. Tout ce qu'il décrit est dans la direction opposée de ce qu'il pense. Réponds aux questions d'Hervé pour l'aider.

EXEMPLE **—La poste est loin de la bibliothèque?**
—Mais non, elle est près de la bibliothèque.

1. Est-ce que la papeterie est près de la pharmacie?
2. Le cinéma est devant le centre commercial?
3. La bibliothèque est à droite?
4. Est-ce que le café est derrière le stade?

1. Mais non, elle est loin de la pharmacie.
2. Mais non, il est derrière le centre commercial.
3. Mais non, elle est à gauche.
4. Mais non, il est devant le stade.

Note culturelle

Martinique is an overseas possession of France known as a **département d'outre-mer,** or **DOM.** It has the same administrative status as a department in France, and the people of Martinique, who are citizens of France, have the same rights and responsibilities as other French citizens. Other DOMs include Guadeloupe, French Guiana, and Reunion Island. France also has overseas territories, like New Caledonia and French Polynesia. These territories are called **territoires d'outre-mer,** or **TOMs.**

26 La visite d'Arianne

Ecrivons Arianne a pris des photos pendant sa visite chez son oncle et sa tante. Complète les descriptions des photos avec des prépositions.

1. C'est mon oncle et ma tante dans le jardin ____ leur maison. devant

2. Là, ____ ma tante, c'est mon cousin Daniel. à côté de

3. Et voilà ma cousine Adeline, ____ mon oncle. derrière

4. Il y a une boulangerie ____ leur maison. Les croissants sont délicieux le matin! en face de/près de

5. Leur maison est ____ une autre maison et une épicerie. entre

6. Il y a un parc au coin de la rue, ____ leur maison. près de

Communication for All Students

Additional Practice

25 Have partners write one or two additional questions Hervé might ask about places in their own town. They might ask their partner these questions, or you might collect them to ask the class.

Challenge

26 You might also have students draw their own family pictures like Arianne's (or pictures of a famous or imaginary family) and exchange them with a partner. The partner will ask about the people and places in the drawings and help write appropriate captions. Students might include this "photo album" in their written portfolio.

STANDARDS: 1.1, 2.2, 3.2

Comment dit-on...?

Asking for and giving directions

CD-ROM 3
DVD 2

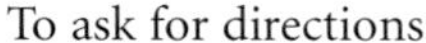

To ask for directions:

Pardon, madame. La poste, **s'il vous plaît?**
Pardon, mademoiselle. Où est la banque, **s'il vous plaît?**
Pardon, monsieur. Je cherche le musée, **s'il vous plaît.**
Excuse me, sir. I'm looking for . . . , please.

To give directions:

Vous continuez jusqu'au prochain feu rouge.
You keep going until the next light.
Vous allez tout droit jusqu'au lycée.
You go straight ahead until you get to . . .
Vous tournez à droite.
You turn . . .
Prenez la rue Lamartine, **puis traversez la rue** Isambert.
Take . . . Street, then cross . . . Street.
Vous passez devant la boulangerie.
You'll pass . . .
C'est tout de suite à gauche.
It's right there on the . . .

Cahier d'activités, pp. 141–142, Act. 22–24

27 Pardon, je cherche... See scripts on p. 353H.

Ecoutons Guy is at the bus station (**la gare routière**) in Fort-de-France. Follow M. Robinet's directions, using the map on page 372. Where does Guy want to go? to the post office

CD 12 Tr. 11

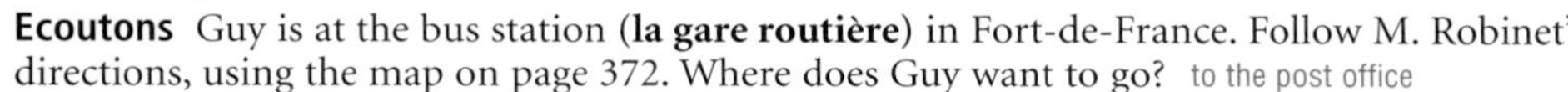

Note culturelle

In many French towns, intersections have a traffic circle **(un rond-point)** at the center, which is often decorated with flowers, fountains, or statues. Vehicles enter and continue around the center island, turning off at the various streets that open into the circle. Most towns have at least one public square, often located in front of a public building or a church. Numerous cities have closed off some of the tiny streets in the **centre-ville** and made pedestrian areas where people can stroll freely, without having to worry about traffic.

28 Où est-ce?

Parlons Explique à ton/ta camarade comment aller de l'école à ton restaurant favori ou à ton magasin de disques préféré. Ton/Ta camarade va essayer de deviner le nom de l'endroit. Ensuite, changez de rôle.

Teacher to Teacher

Melinda suggests setting up obstacles for the students.

Melinda Marks
Grant Union High School
Sacramento, CA

"I create an obstacle course in my classroom to practice the functions in this **étape.** I arrange the desks and chairs in the classroom to form "streets". I then blindfold a student. I point out a destination in the room to the rest of the class. The class gives the blindfolded student directions in French such as turn left, go straight, and so on, to arrive at the destination. Chaotic, but fun!"

Presenting Comment dit-on... ?

Use *Teaching Transparency 12-3* to give directions to several places and trace the route clearly with a pointer. Then, give directions to several places in town and have students tell whether or not your directions are accurate.

Challenge

27 Have students listen to the recording with their book closed and sketch the route.

Community Link

You might have students look up the history of a public square, town hall, local landmark, or building in their town.

Thinking Critically

Comparing and Contrasting
Ask students if there is a place comparable to a town square in their own town. Are there any statues, fountains, or public gardens? Where? Are there any areas that are off-limits to cars? What are the advantages and disadvantages of having an outdoor pedestrian mall?

Portfolio

28 **Oral** This activity is suitable for students' oral portfolios. For portfolio suggestions, see *Alternative Assessment Guide*, pages iv–17.

Troisième étape

CHAPITRE 12

Teaching Resources
pp. 369–373

PRINT 

- Lesson Planner, p. 61
- TPR Storytelling Book, pp. 47, 48
- Listening Activities, pp. 92–93, 97
- Activities for Communication, pp. 71–72, 132, 134, 159–160
- Travaux pratiques de grammaire, pp. 106–107
- Grammar Tutor for Students of French, Chapter 12
- Cahier d'activités, pp. 140–142
- Testing Program, pp. 309–312
- Alternative Assessment Guide, p. 43
- Student Make-Up Assignments, Chapter 12

MEDIA

- One-Stop Planner
- Audio Compact Discs, CD 12, Trs. 10–11, 21, 35–36
- Teaching Transparencies: 12-3, 12-C; **Grammaire supplémentaire** Answers; Travaux pratiques de grammaire Answers
- Interactive CD-ROM Tutor, Disc 3

Slower Pace

29 Before students do this activity, have them locate on the map the two sites in the photos. Then, have them locate the major landmarks and streets mentioned in the letter.

Challenge

29 Have students write directions to a different location on the map and read them to a partner, who follows the directions and tells where they lead.

Additional Practice

29 Give directions to various locations on the map. Have students tell where your directions lead.

29 Quel monument est-ce? la cathédrale Saint-Louis

Lisons Ton/ta correspondant(e) martiniquais(e) te conseille certains endroits à visiter. Il/Elle te dit comment y aller. Suis ses explications sur le plan de Fort-de-France et dis de quel endroit il/elle parle.

la bibliothèque Schœlcher

la cathédrale Saint-Louis

Quand tu sors de la gare routière, va à droite sur le boulevard du Général de Gaulle. Prends la première à droite — c'est la rue Félix Eboué — et continue tout droit. Tu vas passer devant la préfecture. Traverse l'avenue des Caraïbes et va tout droit dans la rue de la Liberté jusqu'à la poste. Ensuite, tourne à droite rue Blénac et continue tout droit. Ça sera à droite, tout de suite après la rue Schoelcher.

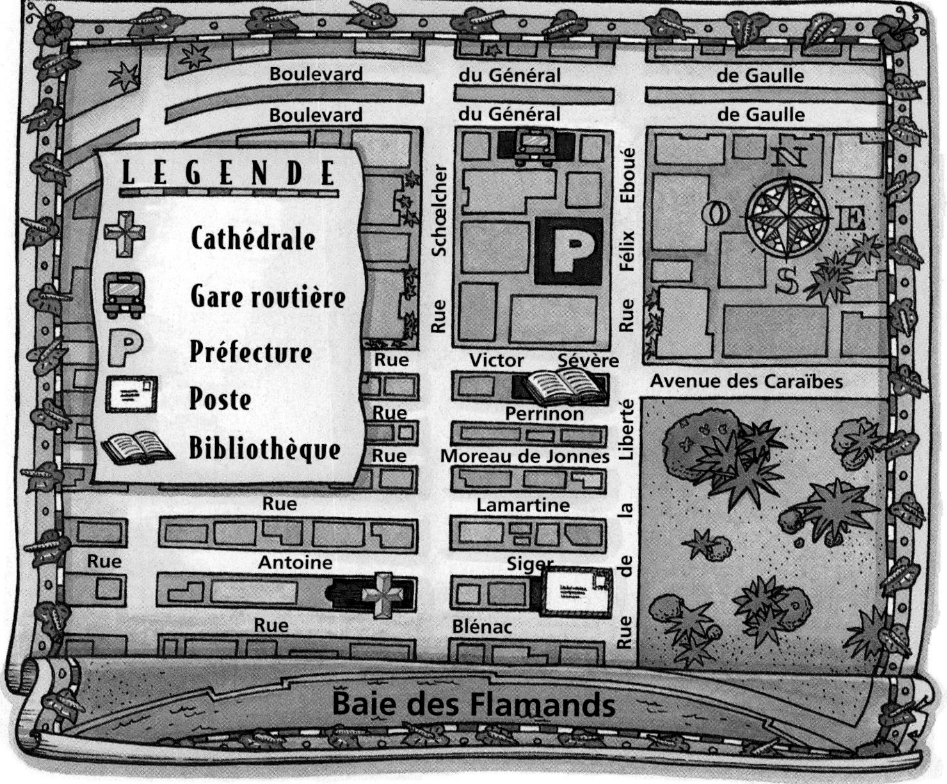

Connections and Comparisons

History Links

29 The Schœlcher Library is at the site of the old **Hôtel du Petit Gouvernement,** where Empress Josephine of France used to live. The library did not take the name Schœlcher to commemorate Victor Schœlcher's campaign to abolish slavery, but rather to acknowledge his gift of about 10,000 volumes to further the education of the people of Martinique.

29 You might have students find out about the people for whom the streets on the map were named and their major accomplishments (General Charles de Gaulle, Victor Schœlcher, Alphonse de Lamartine, or Antoine Siger). They might do the same for streets in their own town.

STANDARDS: 1.2, 3.1

30 De l'école au travail

Parlons Imagine que tu travailles comme hôte ou comme hôtesse dans le restaurant Chez Ana. Le restaurant est situé dans un quartier très touristique et beaucoup de touristes te demandent des renseignements. Crée une conversation avec ton/ta camarade qui va te demander comment trouver deux endroits en ville. Utilise le plan à la page 369 pour expliquer comment on va à ces deux endroits, puis changez de rôle.

PRONONCIATION

See scripts and answers on p. 353H.

CD 12 Trs. 12–17

Do you remember what you've learned about French pronunciation? Here is a quick pronunciation review. If you've forgotten how to produce any of these sounds, check the Pronunciation Index at the back of the book and go back to the chapters where they were introduced. Repeat these words.

[y]	**du**	é**tu**de	[u]	r**ou**ge	v**ou**drais
[o]	escar**got**s	gât**eau**	[ɔ]	p**o**mme	car**o**ttes
[ø]	v**eu**t	h**eu**r**eu**x	[œ]	s**œu**r	b**eu**rre
[e]	cin**é**ma	trouv**er**	[ɛ]	fr**è**re	angl**ai**se
[ã]	**an**glais	il pr**en**d	[ɔ̃]	all**on**s	poiss**on**
[ɛ̃]	qu**in**ze	p**ain**	[œ̃]	**lun**di	empr**un**ter
[j]	pap**ier**	v**i**ande	[w]	m**oi**	pouv**oi**r
[ɥ]	l**ui**	ens**ui**te	[t]	ma**th**s	**th**éâtre
[r]	t**r**ès	**r**oux	[ʃ]	**ch**at	**ch**er**ch**er
[']	le **h**éros	le **h**ockey	[ɲ]	monta**gne**	Allema**gne**

A. A prononcer

Repeat the following words.

1. nourriture	boutique	bateau	poste
2. feu	déposer	près	derrière
3. devant	avion	timbre	emprunter
4. pied	voiture	envoyer	tout de suite
5. rue	gauche	prochain	bibliothèque

B. A lire

Take turns with a partner reading each of the following sentences aloud.

1. Quand le chat n'est pas là, les souris dansent.
2. Il est mieux de travailler que de s'amuser.
3. Beaucoup de bruit pour rien.
4. Un poisson n'est jamais trop petit pour être frit.
5. On n'attrape pas les mouches avec du vinaigre.

C. A écrire

You're going to hear a short dialogue. Write down what you hear.

Communication for All Students

Teaching Suggestion

You might have students match the words in Part A with the corresponding sounds in the lists above.

Language Note

The sentences in Part B are well-known proverbs. You might have students quote similar English proverbs. Students might need to know **souris** *(mice)*, **bruit** *(noise, rumor)*, **frit** *(fried)*, and **mouches** *(flies)*.

Portfolio

30 **Written** This activity is also appropriate for students' written portfolios. For portfolio suggestions, see *Alternative Assessment Guide,* page 29.

Portfolio

Oral To assess students' pronunciation, have them record the list at the beginning of **Prononciation** for their oral portfolio. For portfolio suggestions, see *Alternative Assessment Guide,* pages iv–17.

Assess

- Testing Program, pp. 309–312 Quiz 12-3A, Quiz 12-3B, Audio CD 12, Tr. 21
- Student Make-Up Assignments Chapter 12, Alternative Quiz
- Alternative Assessment Guide, p. 43

STANDARDS: 1.3

CHAPITRE 12

Teaching Resources
pp. 374–375

PRINT 

- Lesson Planner, p. 62
- Cahier d'activités, p. 143
- Reading Strategies and Skills Handbook, Chapter 12
- Joie de lire 1, Chapter 12
- Standardized Assessment Tutor, Chapter 12

MEDIA

- One-Stop Planner

Prereading
Activity A

Using Prior Knowledge
Ask students what fairy tales or folk tales they remember from their childhood. Did they have a favorite? Have them describe characters or themes that are usually found in fairy tales. You might also have them discuss the purpose or moral of their favorite fairy tales.

Reading
Activity B–F

Language Note
Le flamboyant (used to describe the red horse) is a tree that is between 20 and 40 feet tall with feathery leaves and scarlet or orange flowers. You might ask students what the English word *flamboyant* means and point out the root word *flame*. **L'allamanda** (used to describe the yellow horse) is a shrub with large, funnel-shaped, golden flowers.

Answers

B. 1. The blue horse and Congo
2. There is a fair in town.
3. The mayor asked him to help.
4. He frees him and lets his dream come true.

Lisons!

Cheval de bois

Stratégie pour lire

When you read stories, newspaper and magazine articles, or novels that were written for native French speakers, you're bound to come across many unfamiliar words. Just remember to use all the reading tips that you know to try to understand what you're reading.

A. a wooden horse; in Saint-Pierre, Martinique

A. Regarde le titre et les illustrations qui accompagnent le texte. Quel est le sujet de l'histoire? Où se passe l'histoire?

B. Scan the story to see if you can find the answers to these questions. See answers below.

1. Who are the main characters in the story?
2. What is going on when the story starts?
3. Why does Congo come to help the horse?
4. How does Congo help the horse?

C. Lis l'histoire et ensuite mets ces événements dans le bon ordre.

1. Congo burns the blue horse. 5
2. A child is frightened by the blue horse. 2
3. Congo first comes to see the blue horse. 4
4. M. Quinquina and his sons play music. 1
5. The blue bird is freed. 6
6. The mayor goes to see Congo. 3

Cheval de bois

Cette année, la ville de Saint-Pierre accueille le manège de la famille Quinquina pour sa fête patronale. Le manège s'est installé sur la place du marché, face à la mer. Madame Quinquina tient une buvette où elle sert des limonades multicolores.

Monsieur Quinquina et ses deux fils jouent de la flûte de bambou et du "ti-bwa". Au rythme de cette musique, le manège de chevaux de bois, poussé par de robustes jeunes gens, tourne, tourne, tourne.

Cheval bleu, bleu comme l'océan.
Cheval noir, noir comme la nuit.
Cheval blanc, blanc comme les nuages.
Cheval vert, vert comme les bambous.
Cheval rouge, rouge comme le flamboyant.
Cheval jaune, jaune comme l'allamanda.

Les chevaux de bois tournent, tournent et, sur leur dos, tous les enfants sont heureux.

Mais quand la nuit parfumée caresse l'île, les chevaux de bois rêvent. Le cheval bleu, bleu comme l'océan, rêve de partir, partir loin, visiter les îles, visiter le monde. Il a entendu dire que la terre est ronde. Vrai ou faux? Il aimerait bien savoir ! Cela fait si longtemps qu'il porte ce rêve dans sa carcasse de bois que cette nuit-là, son rêve devient oiseau. L'oiseau bat des ailes dans le corps du cheval bleu, bleu comme l'océan.

Au matin, un enfant monte sur le cheval bleu. Tout à coup, il commence à hurler :
— Maman, maman, il y a une bête dans le cheval. J'ai peur! Je veux descendre.

Communication for All Students

Teaching Suggestions
A. You might want to do this activity with the entire class. Remind students just to look at the titles and pictures. Then, ask them how they arrived at their answers.

B. Remind students just to scan for the information and to skip over the other details.

Slower Pace
C. First, have students use the pictures and key words to find the page of the story on which each event takes place. Then, have them look more closely at each page to finalize the order.

STANDARDS: 1.2, 2.2, 3.1, 3.2, 4.1, 4.2

On arrête la musique, on arrête le manège. C'est un tollé général : les mères rassemblent leurs enfants. En quelques secondes, la place est vide. Le maire et ses conseillers décident d'aller chercher le sage Congo.

...Congo s'approche du manège et caresse les flancs du cheval bleu, bleu comme l'océan :
— Je vais te délivrer ! cheval bleu, bleu comme l'océan, car ton rêve est vivant, il s'est métamorphosé en oiseau.

Congo s'assied près du cheval bleu, bleu comme l'océan. Quand le maire voit Congo tranquillement assis, il sort de la mairie en courant et hurle :
— Que faites-vous?
— J'attends, dit doucement Congo.
— Vous attendez quoi? demande le maire.
— J'attends que la nuit mette son manteau étoilé et ouvre son œil d'or. Je ferai alors un grand feu.

Quand la nuit met son manteau étoilé et ouvre son œil d'or, Congo prend tendrement dans ses bras le cheval bleu, bleu comme l'océan, et le dépose dans les flammes. Le feu crépite, chante, et l'or des flammes devient bleu, bleu comme l'océan. Les habitants de Saint-Pierre voient un immense oiseau bleu, bleu comme l'océan, s'élever dans la nuit étoilée et s'envoler vers l'horizon.
Congo, heureux, murmure :
-Bon vent, oiseau-rêve !

RAPPEL As you read the story, you probably came across some unfamiliar words. Remember, you don't have to understand every word to get a sense of what you're reading. If you decide that the meaning of a particular word is necessary to help you understand the story, there are two techniques you've learned that can help: using the context to figure out the meaning of the word, and trying to see a cognate in the word.

D. Below are some cognates that appear in ***Cheval de bois.*** See if you can match them with their English equivalents.

1. habitants f	**a.** counselors
2. fête d	**b.** to descend; to get down
3. flammes e	**c.** island
4. conseillers a	**d.** festival
5. île c	**e.** flames
6. descendre b	**f.** inhabitants, people who live in a certain area

For Activities E and F, see answers below.

E. Make a list of all of the other cognates you can find in ***Cheval de bois.*** You should be able to find at least six more. Watch out for false cognates!

F. How can you tell this story was written for a young audience?

G. What stories, fairy tales, or myths have you read or heard that are similar to this story? In what ways are they similar? In what ways are they different?

H. Do you think there really was a bird inside the horse? What do you think the bird represents?

I. Compose a fairy tale of your own. Write it out or record it in French. Keep it simple so that your teacher can use it in the future with students who are beginning to learn French! Illustrate your story to make it easier to understand.

Cahier d'activités, p. 143, Act. 25

Terms in Lisons!

Students might want to know these words: **cheval** *(horse);* **bois** *(wood);* **manège** *(merry-go-round);* **rêve** *(dream);* **oiseau** *(bird);* **feu** *(fire);* **devient** *(becomes).*

Postreading

Activities G-I

Thinking Critically

Comparing and Contrasting
Have students compare the characters in this fairy tale to ones they're familiar with. How are they similar or different? Have them compare the ending of the story to the ending of *Cinderella* or *Beauty and the Beast.* Is there a moral to the story?

Using Text Organizers

I. You might have students write their stories in a book they make out of construction paper and illustrate them with drawings or magazine pictures. This would also be appropriate for students' written portfolios or as a chapter project.

Cooperative Learning

Have the class act out the story. In small groups, they should choose a director and a narrator, as well as actors to play the characters. You might videotape the performance to show to other classes.

Connections and Comparisons

Language Arts Link

Ask students how the use of repetition affects the story. Have them also find examples of symbolic or metaphoric language **(la nuit met son manteau étoilé, les chevaux de bois rêvent, le rêve devient oiseau).**

Literature Link

Famous Caribbean authors are Maryse Condé, Jacques Roumain, Léon-Gontran Damas, and Simone Schwartz-Bart. Damas joined Léopold Senghor of Senegal and Aimé Césaire of Martinique in founding the **Négritude** movement, which stressed African cultural, economic, social, and political values.

Answers

E. *Possible answers:*
flûte *(flute)*, bambou *(bamboo)*, rythme *(rhythm)*, musique *(music)*, robuste *(robust, strong)*, océan *(ocean)*, parfumée *(perfumed)*, caresse *(caress)*, ronde *(round)*, carcasse *(carcass)*, commence *(commence)*, secondes *(seconds)*, sage *(sage)*, flanc *(flank)*, tranquillement *(quietly, tranquilly)*, tendrement *(tenderly)*, immense *(immense)*, horizon *(horizon)*

F. It is short, relatively simple, and magical. The illustrations are colorful and simple.

Grammaire supplémentaire

CHAPITRE 12

For **Grammaire supplémentaire** Answer Transparencies, see the *Teaching Transparencies* binder.

Grammaire supplémentaire

Première étape

Objective Pointing out places and things

1 Ecris cinq phrases pour dire où ces gens vont aller pour trouver ce qu'ils veulent. Pour chaque phrase, utilise le présent d'**aller** et un des mot proposés. (**pp. 174, 177, 360**)

la boulangerie	la banque	la papeterie
la poste	l'épicerie	le marché	la pharmacie

EXEMPLE J'ai besoin de pain. **Je vais à la boulangerie.**

1. Il me faut des feuilles de papier et des gommes.
2. Tu as besoin de retirer de l'argent.
3. Il vous faut des timbres.
4. Mme Bonjean a besoin de farine et de beurre.
5. Pierre et moi, nous avons besoin de médicaments.

2 Tu demandes à tes amis ce qu'ils ont fait pendant le week-end. Regarde les photos et écris leurs réponses au passé composé. (**pp. 271, 361**)

1. Hélène, qu'est-ce que tu as fait pendant le week-end?
   J'...

2. Sandra et Pamela, vous avez passé un bon week-end?
   Oui, nous...

3. Tu as passé un bon week-end, Martin?
   Oui, j'...

4. Ahmed, tu as passé un bon week-end?
   Oui, j'...

Grammar Resources for Chapter 12

The **Grammaire supplémentaire** activities were designed as supplemental activities for the grammatical concepts presented in the chapter. You might use them as additional practice, for review, or for assessment.

For more grammar presentations, review, and practice, refer to the following:

- Travaux pratiques de grammaire
- Grammar Tutor for Students of French
- Grammar Summary on pp. R15–R28
- Cahier d'activités
- Grammar and Vocabulary quizzes (Testing Program)
- Test Generator on the One-Stop Planner CD-ROM
- Interactive CD-ROM Tutor
- **Jeux interactifs** at go.hrw.com

Answers

1
1. Je vais à la papeterie.
2. Tu vas à la banque.
3. Vous allez à la poste.
4. Elle va à l'épicerie.
5. Nous allons à la pharmacie.

2
1. ai lu un roman.
2. avons fait les magasins.
3. ai vu un film génial.
4. ai joué au football.

STANDARDS: 1.2

3 Delphine te raconte ses vacances à la Martinique. Complète les phrases avec les verbes indiqués au passé composé. (**pp. 271, 272, 277, 361**)

C'était chouette, mes vacances à la Martinique! Je n'ai pas reconnu mes cousins, ils __1__ (beaucoup grandir)! Le premier jour, nous __2__ (dîner) chez ma tante Liliane. On __3__ (parler) et on __4__ (regarder) des photos après le dîner. La première nuit, je/j' __5__ (dormir) longtemps. Le deuxième jour, nous __6__ (faire) de la plongée. C'était magnifique! Malheureusement, je/j' __7__ (perdre) mon appareil-photo et je/j' __8__ (ne pas prendre) de photos. Après, nous __9__ (visiter) la cathédrale Saint-Louis et la bibliothèque Schœlcher. Le dernier jour, nous __10__ (faire) un tour en bateau. Et après, nous __11__ (faire) des achats en ville où je/j' __12__ (acheter) un disque de musique zouk pour toi.

Deuxième étape

Objectives Making and responding to requests; asking for advice and making suggestions

4 Récris les phrases suivantes. Remplace les quantités précises par les articles appropriés **du, de la, de l'**, ou **des**. (**pp. 236, 364**)

EXEMPLE Tu pourrais me rapporter une bouteille de lait?
Tu pourrais me rapporter du lait?

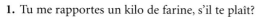

1. Tu me rapportes un kilo de farine, s'il te plaît?
2. Tu me prends un paquet de beurre, s'il te plaît?
3. Tu m'achètes une livre de carottes?
4. Rapporte-moi trois tranches de jambon, s'il te plaît!
5. Tu me rapportes deux bouteilles d'eau minérale?
6. Tu pourrais m'acheter dix enveloppes et vingt timbres, s'il te plaît?
7. Tu peux m'acheter deux baguettes et cinq pâtisseries?
8. Tu peux aller à la poste et envoyer deux paquets pour moi?

5 Chaque personne a besoin de quelque chose. Ecris des phrases en utilisant **J'ai besoin de...** ou **Il me faut...**, pour dire ce qu'il leur faut. (**pp. 238, 365**)

1. Tu pourrais passer à la pharmacie?
2. Est-ce que tu peux aller à la boulangerie, s'il te plaît?
3. Est-ce que tu peux aller chez le disquaire?
4. Tu peux passer à la bibliothèque, s'il te plaît?
5. Tu pourrais aller à la librairie-papeterie, s'il te plaît?

Teacher to Teacher

Tanya Stevenson
Terrill Middle School
Scotch Plains, NJ

Tanya uses this activity to practice and review the past tense.

"I model the past tense by showing students pictures of myself and telling them what I did and where I was. Students then show pictures of themselves, perhaps a yearbook or other photo, doing an activity. They tell the class what they did and where they were. I have also taken pictures of students in class and given them the pictures to report what they and other students did in French class. This activity gets students to apply the grammar in a real-life context."

Answers

3
1. ont beaucoup grandi
2. avons dîné
3. a parlé
4. a regardé
5. ai dormi
6. avons fait
7. ai perdu
8. n'ai pas pris
9. avons visité
10. avons fait
11. avons fait
12. ai acheté

4
1. Tu me rapportes de la farine, s'il te plaît?
2. Tu me prends du beurre, s'il te plaît?
3. Tu m'achètes des carottes?
4. Rapporte-moi du jambon, s'il te plaît!
5. Tu me rapportes de l'eau minérale?
6. Tu pourrais m'acheter des enveloppes et des timbres, s'il te plaît?
7. Tu peux m'acheter des baguettes et des pâtisseries?
8. Tu peux aller à la poste et envoyer des paquets pour moi?

5
1. Il me faut des médicaments.
2. J'ai besoin de pain.
3. Il me faut un disque compact.
4. J'ai besoin d'un livre.
5. Il me faut des enveloppes.

Grammaire supplémentaire

CHAPITRE 12

For **Grammaire supplémentaire** Answer Transparencies, see the *Teaching Transparencies* binder.

Answers

6
1. Nous y allons en train.
2. J'y vais à vélo.
3. Elle y va en bateau.
4. On y va en bus.
5. J'y vais en voiture.
6. On y va à pied.
7. J'y vais en taxi.
8. Nous y allons en métro.

7
1. Je vais y passer pour acheter des croissants.
2. Elle y a rendu mes livres.
3. Nous y avons acheté de l'aspirine.
4. Ma mère y a acheté des pâtisseries.
5. Nous y allons pour retirer de l'argent.
6. On y trouve de la musique zouk.

8
1. y vais
2. veux
3. y va
4. as trouvé
5. y ai trouvé
6. as
7. peux
8. ai
9. peux
10. y vais
11. y vas
12. pars

Grammaire supplémentaire

WA3 FORT-DE-FRANCE-12

6 Tu demandes à tes amis comment ils vont aller aux endroits suivants. Utilise le pronom **y** pour écrire leurs réponses. (**p. 367**)

Exemple Philippe, comment est-ce que tu vas aux Etats-Unis? (en avion)
J'y vais en avion.

1. Mohammed et Yasmina, comment est-ce que vous allez au bord de la mer? (en train)
2. Azzedine, comment tu vas à la campagne? (à vélo)
3. Comment est-ce que Fatima va en Angleterre? (en bateau)
4. Hannah et Raphaël, comment vous allez à la montagne? (en bus)
5. Aziz, comment est-ce que tu vas à Paris? (en voiture)
6. Comment est-ce qu'on va à la plage? (à pied)
7. Michel, quand tu vas à New York, comment est-ce que tu vas aux musées? (en taxi)
8. Agathe, quand tu vas à Paris avec ta mère, comment est-ce que vous allez de l'aéroport à l'hôtel? (en métro)

7 Récris les phrases suivantes en utilisant le pronom **y.** (**p. 367**)

1. Je vais passer à la boulangerie pour acheter des croissants.
2. Elle a rendu mes livres à la bibliothèque hier.
3. Nous avons acheté de l'aspirine à la pharmacie.
4. Ma mère a acheté des pâtisseries à la pâtisserie.
5. Nous allons à la banque pour retirer de l'argent.
6. On trouve de la musique zouk chez le disquaire Hit-Parade.

8 Complète les conversations suivantes avec **y** et la forme correcte du verbe entre parenthèses. Attention! Certains verbes vont être au présent et d'autres vont être au passé composé. (**p. 367**)

—Salut, Michèle, tu vas à la bibliothèque?
—Oui, je/j' __1__ (y/aller) cet aprèm. J'ai des livres à rendre. Tu __2__ (vouloir) venir?
—Oui, je veux bien. On __3__ (y/aller) à quelle heure?

—Dis, Florence, c'est vrai que tu __4__ (trouver) un billet de cent euros devant la banque?
—Pas tout à fait. Je/J' __5__ (y/trouver) une pièce de cinq euros.
—Tu __6__ (avoir) de la chance, quand même!

—Tu __7__ (pouvoir) me rendre un service, ma chérie!
—Oui, Maman.
—Je/J' __8__ (avoir) besoin de bananes et de citrons. Tu __9__ (pouvoir) aller au marché, s'il te plaît?
—Au marché? C'est loin! Comment est-ce que je/j' __10__ (y/aller)? A pied?
—Mais non. Pourquoi tu ne/n' __11__ (y/aller) pas à vélo?
—Bonne idée. Je __12__ (partir) tout de suite.

Communication for All Students

Challenge

6 You might have students rewrite the responses to each question in the past and future tenses. Ask them to pay attention to the placement of **y** in those tenses.

Additional Practice

10 Have students look at page 369 to write questions about different locations in the picture, for example, **Est-ce que le cinéma est loin du café?** Then, have students work in small groups to ask and respond to one another's questions.

STANDARDS: 1.2

Troisième étape

Objective Asking for and giving directions

9 Unscramble the following location words. Then, combine the fragments to create five sentences telling where the places are located. Use the places in the order in which they are given. (**p. 369**)

EXEMPLE EN CEFA ED/l'école/le café **L'école est en face du café.**

1. REDEIRER/la poste/le stade
2. ED TOIRDE A/la pharmacie/la boulangerie
3. SERP ED/l'épicerie/le cinéma
4. CHUGEA ED A/la pâtisserie/la bibliothèque
5. ED NOIL/la banque/la papeterie

10 Complète les phrases suivantes. (**p. 369**)

EXEMPLE La poste est à droite **du** café.

1. Le lycée est en face ______ cinéma.
2. Le marché est loin ______ lycée.
3. La pharmacie est à côté ______ arbres.
4. Le café est entre ______ poste et ______ cinéma.
5. La boulangerie est au coin ______ rue.
6. Le lycée est à gauche ______ bibliothèque.

Review and Assess

You may wish to assign the **Grammaire supplémentaire** activities as additional practice or homework after presenting material throughout the chapter. Assign Activity 1 after **Tu te rappelles?** (p. 360), Activities 2–3 after **Si tu as oublié** (p. 361), Activity 4 after **Tu te rappelles?** (p. 364), Activity 5 after **Si tu as oublié** (p. 365), Activities 6–8 after **Grammaire** (p. 367), and Activities 9–10 after **Note de grammaire** (p. 369).

To prepare students for the **Etape** Quizzes and Chapter Test, we suggest doing the **Grammaire supplémentaire** activities in the following order. Have students complete Activities 1–3 before taking Quizzes 12-1A or 12-1B; Activities 4–8 before Quizzes 12-2A or 12-2B; and Activities 9–10 before Quizzes 12-3A or 12-3B.

Answers

9
1. La poste est derrière le stade.
2. La pharmacie est à droite de la boulangerie.
3. L'épicerie est près du cinéma.
4. La pâtisserie est à gauche de la bibliothèque.
5. La banque est loin de la papeterie.

10
1. du
2. du
3. des
4. la, le
5. de la
6. de la

STANDARDS: 1.2

Mise en pratique

CHAPITRE 12

The **Mise en pratique** reviews and integrates all four skills and culture in preparation for the Chapter Test.

Teaching Resources

pp. 380–381

PRINT 

- Lesson Planner, p. 62
- Listening Activities, p. 93
- Video Guide, pp. 83, 86
- Grammar Tutor for Students of French, Chapter 12
- Standardized Assessment Tutor, Chapter 12

MEDIA 

- One-Stop Planner
- Video Program Videocassette 4, 47:22–49:12
- DVD Tutor, Disc 2
- Audio Compact Discs, CD 12, Tr. 18
- Interactive CD-ROM Tutor, Disc 3

Answers

1 motorcycle, taxi, rental car

1. Taxi Fort-de-France; 8:00 P.M.
2. Loca Center; Location Trois-Ilets
3. car: three days; motorcycle: one week
4. Location Trois-Ilets: 48 hours; Taxi Fort-de-France; advance reservation not necessary; Loca Center: high season, one month (if renting for at least 10 days) or 48 hours (if renting for 3–7 days); low season, the night before or the same day
5. Location Trois-Ilets and Loca Center: open on request; Taxi Fort-de-France: yes

Mise en pratique

1 You're planning a trip to Martinique and you'll need some transportation. Look at these ads. What kinds of transportation are available? See answers below.

LOCATION TROIS-ILETS
Anse à l'Ane - 97229 Trois-Ilets

68.40.37
Lundi à Vendredi
8 H - 13 H
et 15 H - 18 H
Week-end :
à la demande

Avec Location TROIS-ILETS, la moto que vous avez louée par téléphone, 48 heures plus tôt, vient à vous. Chez vous. Si vous vous trouvez dans la commune des Trois-Ilets. Location possible pour une semaine au moins.

TAXI FORT-DE-FRANCE
102 Rue de la République - 97200 Fort-de-France

70.44.08 Tous les jours : 5 H - 20 H

Nos taxis répondent sans délais quand vous téléphonez à Taxi Fort-de-France. Déplacement dans toute l'île.

LOCA CENTER
3 Km Route de Schœlcher n. 63 - 97233 Schœlcher

Livraison de voiture (Opel Corsa, Peugeot 106) à domicile (Nord Caraïbe, Schœlcher, Fort-de-France) pour une durée minimum de trois jours. Pas de frais de déplacement. Pendant la haute saison, pour une location de 10 jours au moins, réserver un mois à l'avance. Pour une location d'une durée de 3 à 7 jours, réserver 48 heures à l'avance. Pendant la basse saison, réserver la veille ou le jour même.

61.05.95
61.40.12
Lundi à Vendredi
7 H 30 - 16 H 30
Week-end : à la demande

1. Where can you call if you want a taxi? When is the latest you can call?
2. Where can you call if you want to rent a Peugeot? What about a motorcycle?
3. What's the minimum length of time you can rent these vehicles?
4. How far in advance do you need to make a reservation?
5. Are these places open on weekends?

2 Listen to Didier tell his family about his trip to Martinique. Put the pictures in order according to Didier's description. See scripts and answers on p. 353H.

CD 12
Tr. 18

a.

b.

c.

d.

Apply and Assess

Additional Practice

1 You might review the means of transportation by showing picture flash cards. After students identify the means of transportation, they might tell where they have gone using that form of transportation.

Slower Pace

2 Have students list words or phrases they associate with each picture before they listen to the recording.

Challenge

2 After doing this activity, have partners identify what is in the photos.

STANDARDS: 1.2

3
Ecrivons!

Write a logical conversation to accompany the picture below.

Prewriting

To help form your writing plan, look at the illustration and jot down ideas that immediately come to mind. You might imagine the situation, names for the people, and things they might be saying. Think about the types of vocabulary and structures you will need.

Stratégie pour écrire

Making a writing plan before you begin is important. Study the illustration carefully. Do you know all the vocabulary you'll need? Will you need to use certain verbs or structures frequently? You might want to use your textbook as a reference.

Writing

Now, using the notes you created in your writing plan, create the conversation that goes with the picture. Keep in mind expressions you've learned, such as asking for and giving directions, and vocabulary for telling where something is located.

Revising

When you've completed your writing, set it aside for a while before you do your self-evaluation. This will give you a fresh perspective on how to make it better. Also, when you evaluate what you've written, focus on only one area at a time. For example, don't look for spelling and punctuation mistakes while you're checking to see how well your writing flows. Focus on finding such mistakes when you proofread.

After you've revised your work, let a classmate give you feedback. Then, you can concentrate on making any other necessary revisions.

4
Jeu de rôle

While visiting Fort-de-France, you stop and mail some postcards at the post office. You ask the employee for directions to two places in town: the library and the cathedral. Using the map on page 372, the employee gives you directions from the post office to each of these places. Be sure to ask questions if something is not clear. Then, ask the employee what means of transportation you should use to get to these places.

Mise en pratique

Writing Assessment

3 You might use the following rubric when grading your students on this activity.

Writing Rubric	Points			
	4	3	2	1
Content (Complete–Incomplete)				
Comprehensibility (Comprehensible–Incomprehensible)				
Accuracy (Accurate–Seldom accurate)				
Organization (Well organized–Poorly organized)				
Effort (Excellent–Minimal)				

18–20: A 14–15: C Under
16–17: B 12–13: D 12: F

Apply and Assess

Process Writing

3 You might have students work in groups of three to write the conversation. Once each group has completed its conversation, have students act it out in front of the class.

Challenge

3 You might substitute different illustrations than the one shown here for students to write about. You might also have students find or draw their own illustration.

STANDARDS: 1.1, 1.3, 3.1, 5.1

Que sais-je?

CHAPITRE 12

Teaching Resources
p. 382

PRINT 
- Grammar Tutor for Students of French, Chapter 12

MEDIA
- Interactive CD-ROM Tutor, Disc 3
- Online self-test

go.hrw.com
WA3 FORT-DE-FRANCE-12

Teacher Note
This page is intended to help students prepare for the Chapter Test. It is a brief checklist of the major points covered in the chapter. The students should be reminded that this is only a checklist and does not necessarily include everything that will appear on the test.

Game
Où est... ? To practice giving directions, create a city in the classroom by labeling the aisles as streets and areas or objects in the room (your desk, the blackboard, the door) as buildings. Form two teams. A player from one team names a place, and a player from the opposing team must direct the first player there in French.

Que sais-je?

WA3 FORT-DE-FRANCE-12

Can you use what you've learned in this chapter?

Can you point out places and things? **p. 361**

1 How would you point out and identify . . . Possible answers:
1. a certain building? Voici...
2. a certain store? Regarde, voilà...
3. a certain person? Ça, c'est...

Can you make and respond to requests? **p. 364**

2 How would you ask someone to . . . Possible answers:
1. buy some stamps? Tu peux me rapporter des timbres?
2. go to the bookstore? Tu pourrais passer à la librairie?
3. deposit some money? (Est-ce que) tu peux déposer de l'argent?

3 How would you agree to do the favors you asked in number 2? How would you refuse? See answers below.

Can you ask for advice and make suggestions? **p. 366**

4 How would you ask a friend what means of transportation you should use to get to a certain store? Comment est-ce qu'on y va?

5 How would you suggest these means of transportation? On peut y aller... On peut prendre...

1.

en voiture.
la voiture.

3.
en taxi.
un taxi.

2.

en bateau.
un bateau.

4.

en bus.
le bus.

Can you ask for and give directions? **p. 371**

6 How would you tell someone that you're looking for a certain place?
Pardon, monsieur/madame/mademoiselle. Je cherche... , s'il vous plaît.

7 How would you ask someone where a certain place in town is?
Pardon, monsieur/madame/mademoiselle. Où est... , s'il vous plaît?

8 How would you give someone directions to your house from . . .
1. your school?
2. your favorite restaurant?

Review and Assess

Teaching Suggestions

1 You might review different types of buildings in town by naming a local place *(Prescriptions To Go)* and asking students to identify it. **(C'est une pharmacie.)**

2 **3** Encourage students to vary the ways they request and respond to favors.

Additional Practice

5 You might review other means of transportation in addition to the ones shown.

Visual/Kinesthetic Learners

8 Have students illustrate expressions for giving directions on the board or mime them for their classmates to guess.

Answers

3 *Agree:* D'accord. Je veux bien. J'y vais tout de suite. Si tu veux.
Refuse: Je ne peux pas maintenant. Je suis désolé(e), mais je n'ai pas le temps.

STANDARDS: 1.2

Vocabulaire

Première étape

Pointing out places and things

Voici...	*Here is/are . . .*
Regarde, voilà...	*Look, here/there is/are . . .*
Ça, c'est...	*This/That is . . .*
Là, c'est...	*There, that is . . .*
Là, tu vois, c'est...	*There, you see, this/that is . . .*
un endroit	*place*
chez	*at (at the place of) . . .*

Buildings

la banque	*bank*
la boulangerie	*bakery*
le disquaire	*record store*
l'épicerie (f.)	*small grocery store*
la librairie	*bookstore*
la papeterie	*stationery store*
la pâtisserie	*pastry shop*
la pharmacie	*drugstore*
la poste	*post office*

Things to do or buy in town

envoyer des lettres	*to send letters*
une baguette	*long, thin loaf of bread*
un timbre	*stamp*
retirer de l'argent (m.)	*to withdraw money*
déposer de l'argent	*to deposit money*
rendre	*to return something*
emprunter	*to borrow*
des médicaments (m.)	*medicine*
une enveloppe	*envelope*
une pâtisserie	*pastry*

Deuxième étape

Making and responding to requests

Tu peux... ?	*Can you . . . ?*
Tu me rapportes... ?	*Will you bring me . . . ?*
Tu pourrais passer à... ?	*Could you go by . . . ?*
D'accord.	*OK.*
Je veux bien.	*Gladly.*
J'y vais tout de suite.	*I'll go right away.*
Si tu veux.	*If you want.*
Je ne peux pas maintenant.	*I can't right now.*
Je suis désolé(e), mais je n'ai pas le temps.	*I'm sorry, but I don't have time.*

Asking for advice and making suggestions

Comment est-ce qu'on y va?	*How can we get there?*
On peut y aller...	*We can go . . .*
On peut prendre...	*We can take . . .*
y	*there*

Means of transportation

en bus (m.)	*by bus*
à pied (m.)	*on foot*
à vélo (m.)	*by bike*
en voiture (f.)	*by car*
en taxi (m.)	*by taxi*
en bateau (m.)	*by boat*
en avion (m.)	*by plane*
en train (m.)	*by train*
en métro (m.)	*by subway*

Troisième étape

Asking for and giving directions

Pardon, ..., s'il vous plaît?	*Excuse me, . . . please?*
Pardon, ... Où est..., s'il vous plaît?	*Excuse me, . . . Where is . . . , please?*
Pardon, ... Je cherche..., s'il vous plaît.	*Excuse me, . . . I'm looking for . . . , please.*
Vous continuez jusqu'au prochain feu rouge.	*You keep going until the next light.*
Vous allez tout droit jusqu'à...	*You go straight ahead until you get to . . .*
Vous tournez...	*You turn . . .*
Prenez la rue..., puis traversez la rue...	*Take . . . Street, then cross . . . Street.*
Vous passez...	*You'll pass . . .*
C'est tout de suite à...	*It's right there on the . . .*

Locations

à côté de	*next to*
loin de	*far from*
près de	*close to*
au coin de	*on the corner of*
en face de	*across from*
derrière	*behind*
devant	*in front of*
entre	*between*
à droite (de)	*to the right (of)*
à gauche (de)	*to the left (of)*

Review and Assess

Additional Practice

- To review pronunciation and vocabulary, have students find words in the **Vocabulaire** that contain the sounds listed in the **Prononciation** on page 373.
- To review vocabulary from all twelve chapters, play **Les Mots en famille** described on page 353C.

Game

You might have students play **Jacques a dit,** using the new expressions from this chapter as well as vocabulary they have already learned. **(Allez à gauche. Mettez le livre devant/derrière vous. Allez loin de la fenêtre.)**

Vocabulaire

CHAPITRE 12

Career Path

A career in banking provides many interesting opportunities for people who speak a foreign language, such as translating in the United States for customers who do not speak English, or working abroad with an international bank. Ask students to name cities or countries that have many international banks. What languages might be important in these locations?

Chapter 12 Assessment

- **Testing Program**
  Chapter Test, pp. 313–318

  Audio Compact Discs, CD 12, Trs. 22–24
  Speaking Test, p. 348
  Final Exam, pp. 327–334
  Score Sheet, pp. 335–337
  Listening Scripts, pp. 338–339
  Answers, p. 340

  Audio Compact Discs, CD 12, Trs. 25–30
- **Alternative Assessment Guide**
  Performance Assessment, p. 43
  Portfolio Assessment, p. 29
  CD-ROM Assessment, p. 57
- **Interactive CD-ROM Tutor, Disc 3**
  CD-ROM 3 A toi de parler
  DVD 2 A toi d'écrire
- **Standardized Assessment Tutor**
  Chapter 12
- **One-Stop Planner, Disc 3**

  Test Generator
  Chapter 12

STANDARDS: 1.2

Reference Section

Summary of Functions

Function is another word for the way in which you use language for a specific purpose. When you find yourself in specific situations, such as in a restaurant, in a grocery store, or at school, you'll want to communicate with those around you. In order to communicate in French, you have to "function" in the language.

Each chapter in this book focuses on language functions. You can easily find them in boxes labeled **Comment dit-on... ?** The other features in the chapter—grammar, vocabulary, culture notes—support the functions you're learning.

Here is a list of functions and the French expressions presented in this book. You'll need them in order to communicate in a wide range of situations. Following each function entry, you will find the chapter and page number where each function is presented.

Socializing

***Greeting people* Ch. 1, p. 22**
Bonjour.
Salut.

***Saying goodbye* Ch. 1, p. 22**
Salut. | A bientôt.
Au revoir. | A demain.
A tout à l'heure. | Tchao.

***Asking how people are and telling how you are* Ch. 1, p. 23**
(Comment) ça va? | Bof.
Ça va. | Pas mal.
Super! | Pas terrible.
Très bien. | Et toi?
Comme ci comme ça.

***Expressing and responding to thanks* Ch. 3, p. 90**
Merci.
A votre service.

***Extending invitations* Ch. 6, p. 179**
Allons... !
Tu veux... avec moi?
Tu viens?
On peut...

***Accepting invitations* Ch. 6, p. 179**
Je veux bien. | D'accord.
Pourquoi pas? | Bonne idée.

***Refusing invitations* Ch. 6, p. 179**
Désolé(e), je suis occupé(e).
Ça ne me dit rien.
J'ai des trucs à faire.
Désolé(e), je ne peux pas.

***Identifying people* Ch. 7, p. 203**
C'est...
Ce sont...
Voici...
Voilà...

***Introducing people* Ch. 7, p. 207**
C'est...
Je te/vous présente...
Très heureux (heureuse). (FORMAL)

***Inquiring about past events* Ch. 9, p. 270**
Qu'est-ce que tu as fait... ?
Tu es allé(e) où?
Et après?
Qu'est-ce qui s'est passé?

***Relating past events* Ch. 9, p. 270**
D'abord,...
Ensuite,...
Après,...
Je suis allé(e)...
Et après ça,...
Finalement,/Enfin,...

***Inquiring about future plans* Ch. 11, p. 329**
Qu'est-ce que tu vas faire... ?
Où est-ce que tu vas aller... ?

***Sharing future plans* Ch. 11, p. 329**
J'ai l'intention de...
Je vais...

***Seeing someone off* Ch. 11, p. 336**
Bon voyage!
Bonnes vacances!
Amuse-toi bien!
Bonne chance!

Exchanging Information

Asking someone's name and giving yours
Ch. 1, p. 24

Tu t'appelles comment?
Je m'appelle...

Asking and giving someone else's name **Ch. 1, p. 24**

Il/Elle s'appelle comment?
Il/Elle s'appelle...

Asking someone's age and giving yours **Ch. 1, p. 25**

Tu as quel âge?
J'ai... ans.

Asking for information **Ch. 2, p. 55**

Tu as quels cours... ?
Tu as quoi... ?
Vous avez... ?
Tu as... à quelle heure?

Giving information **Ch. 2, p. 55**

Nous avons...
J'ai...

Telling when you have class **Ch. 2, p. 58**

à... heure(s)
à... heure(s) quinze
à... heure(s) trente
à... heure(s) quarante-cinq

Making requests **Ch. 3, p. 80**

Tu as... ?
Vous avez... ?

Responding to requests **Ch. 3, p. 80**

Voilà.
Je regrette.
Je n'ai pas de...

Asking others what they need and telling what you need **Ch. 3, p. 82**

Qu'est-ce qu'il te faut pour... ?
Qu'est-ce qu'il vous faut pour... ?
Il me faut...

Expressing need **Ch. 8, p. 238; Ch. 10, p. 301**

Qu'est-ce qu'il te faut?
Il me faut...
De quoi est-ce que tu as besoin?
J'ai besoin de...
Oui, il me faut...
Oui, vous avez... ?
Je cherche quelque chose pour...
J'aimerais... pour aller avec...

Asking for information **Ch. 3, p. 90**

C'est combien?

Getting someone's attention
Ch. 3, p. 90; Ch. 5, p. 151

Pardon...
Excusez-moi.
... , s'il vous plaît.
Monsieur!
Madame!
Mademoiselle!

Exchanging information **Ch. 4, p. 116**

Qu'est-ce que tu fais comme sport?
Qu'est-ce que tu fais pour t'amuser?
Je fais...
Je ne fais pas de...
Je (ne) joue (pas)...

Ordering food and beverages **Ch. 5, p. 151**

Vous avez choisi?
Vous prenez?
Je voudrais...
Je vais prendre..., s'il vous plaît.
... , s'il vous plaît.
Donnez-moi... , s'il vous plaît.
Apportez-moi... , s'il vous plaît.
Vous avez... ?
Qu'est-ce que vous avez comme boissons?
Qu'est-ce qu'il y a à boire?

Paying the check **Ch. 5, p. 155**

L'addition, s'il vous plaît.
Oui, tout de suite.
Un moment, s'il vous plaît.
Ça fait combien, s'il vous plaît?
Ça fait... euros.
C'est combien, ... ?
C'est... euros.

Making plans **Ch. 6, p. 173**

Qu'est-ce que tu vas faire... ?
Tu vas faire quoi... ?
Je vais...
Pas grand-chose.
Rien de spécial.

Arranging to meet someone **Ch. 6, p. 183**

Quand (ça)?	et quart
Tout de suite.	moins le quart
Où (ça)?	moins cinq
Devant...	midi (et demi)
Au métro...	minuit (et demi)
Chez...	Vers...
Dans...	Quelle heure est-il?
Avec qui?	Il est...
A quelle heure?	On se retrouve...
A cinq heures...	Rendez-vous...
et demie	Entendu.

Describing and characterizing people **Ch. 7, p. 209**
Il est comment?
Elle est comment?
Ils/Elles sont comment?
Il/Elle est...
Ils/Elles sont...
Il/Elle n'est ni... ni...

Making a telephone call **Ch. 9, p. 276**
Bonjour.
Je suis bien chez... ?
C'est...
(Est-ce que)... est là, s'il vous plaît?
(Est-ce que) je peux parler à... ?
Je peux laisser un message?
Vous pouvez lui dire que j'ai téléphoné?
Ça ne répond pas.
C'est occupé.

Answering a telephone call **Ch. 9, p. 276**
Allô?
Qui est à l'appareil?
Une seconde, s'il vous plaît.
D'accord.
Bien sûr.
Vous pouvez rappeler plus tard?
Ne quittez pas.

Inquiring **Ch. 10, p. 301**
(Est-ce que) je peux vous aider?
Vous désirez?
Je peux l'(les) essayer?
Je peux essayer... ?
C'est combien, ... ?
Ça fait combien?
Vous avez ça en... ?

Pointing out places and things **Ch. 12, p. 361**
Là, tu vois, c'est...
Ça, c'est...
Regarde, voilà...
Là, c'est...
Voici...

Asking for advice **Ch. 12, p. 366**
Comment est-ce qu'on y va?

Making suggestions **Ch. 12, p. 366**
On peut y aller...
On peut prendre...

Asking for directions **Ch. 12, p. 371**
Pardon, ..., s'il vous plaît?
Pardon, ... Où est..., s'il vous plaît?
Pardon, ... Je cherche..., s'il vous plaît.

Giving directions **Ch. 12, p. 371**
Vous continuez jusqu'au prochain feu rouge.
Vous tournez...
Vous allez tout droit jusqu'à...
Prenez la rue..., puis traversez la rue...
Vous passez...
C'est tout de suite à...

Expressing Feelings and Emotions

Expressing likes, dislikes, and preferences **Ch. 1, pp. 26, 32**
J'aime (bien)...
Je n'aime pas...
Je préfère...
J'aime mieux...
J'adore...

Ch. 5, p. 154
C'est...
excellent!
pas mauvais!
pas terrible!
mauvais!
bon!
délicieux!
pas bon!
dégoûtant!

Telling what you'd like and what you'd like to do **Ch. 3, p. 85**
Je voudrais...
Je voudrais acheter...

Telling how much you like or dislike something **Ch. 4, p. 114**
Beaucoup.
Pas beaucoup.
Pas tellement.
Pas du tout.
surtout

Inquiring about likes and dislikes **Ch. 1, p. 26**
Tu aimes... ?

Ch. 5, p. 154
Comment tu trouves ça?

Sharing confidences **Ch. 9, p. 279**
J'ai un petit problème.
Je peux te parler?
Tu as une minute?

Consoling others **Ch. 9, p. 279**
Je t'écoute.
Ne t'en fais pas!
Ça va aller mieux!
Qu'est-ce que je peux faire?

Making a decision **Ch. 10, p. 310**
Vous avez décidé de prendre... ?
Vous avez choisi?
Vous le/la/les prenez?
Je le/la/les prends.
C'est trop cher.

Hesitating **Ch. 10, p. 310**
Euh... J'hésite.
Je ne sais pas.
Il/Elle me plaît, mais il/elle est...

Expressing indecision **Ch. 11, p. 329**
J'hésite.
Je ne sais pas.
Je n'en sais rien.
Je n'ai rien de prévu.

Expressing wishes **Ch. 11, p. 329**
J'ai envie de...
Je voudrais bien...

Expressing Attitudes and Opinions

Agreeing **Ch. 2, p. 54**
Oui, beaucoup.
Moi aussi.
Moi non plus.

Disagreeing **Ch. 2, p. 54**
Moi, non.
Non, pas trop.
Moi, si.
Pas moi.

Asking for opinions **Ch. 2, p. 61**
Comment tu trouves... ?
Comment tu trouves ça?

Ch. 9, p. 269
Tu as passé un bon week-end?

Ch. 10, p. 306
Il/Elle me va?
Il/Elle te/vous plaît?
Tu aimes mieux... ou... ?

Ch. 11, p. 337
Tu as passé un bon... ?
Tu t'es bien amusé(e)?
Ça s'est bien passé?

Expressing opinions **Ch. 2, p. 61**
C'est...

facile.	pas terrible.
génial.	pas super.
super.	zéro.
cool.	barbant.
intéressant.	nul.
passionnant.	pas mal.
difficile.	

Ça va.

Ch. 9, p. 269
Oui, très chouette.
Oui, excellent.
Oui, très bon.
Oui, ça a été.
Oh, pas mauvais.
C'était épouvantable.
Très mauvais.

Ch. 11, p. 337
C'était formidable!
Non, pas vraiment.
C'était ennuyeux.
C'était un véritable cauchemar!

Paying a compliment **Ch. 10, p. 306**
C'est tout à fait ton/ votre style.
Il/Elle te/vous va très bien.
Il/Elle va très bien avec...
Je le/la/les trouve...
C'est parfait.

Criticizing **Ch. 10, p. 306**
Il/Elle ne te/vous va pas du tout.
Il/Elle ne va pas du tout avec...
Il/Elle est (Ils/Elles sont) trop...
Je le/la/les trouve...

Persuading

Making suggestions **Ch. 4, p. 122**
On... ?
On fait... ?
On joue... ?

Ch. 5, p. 145
On va... ?

Accepting suggestions **Ch. 4, p. 122**
D'accord.
Bonne idée.
Oui, c'est...
Allons-y!

Turning down suggestions; making excuses
Ch. 4, p. 122
Non, c'est...
Ça ne me dit rien.
Désolé(e), mais je ne peux pas.

Ch. 5, p. 145
Désolé(e). J'ai des devoirs à faire.
J'ai des courses à faire.
J'ai des trucs à faire.
J'ai des tas de choses à faire.
Je ne peux pas parce que...

Making a recommendation **Ch. 5, p. 148**
Prends...
Prenez...

Asking for permission **Ch. 7, p. 213**
Tu es d'accord?
(Est-ce que) je peux... ?

Giving permission **Ch. 7, p. 213**
Oui, si tu veux.
Pourquoi pas?
D'accord, si tu... d'abord...
Oui, bien sûr.

Refusing permission **Ch. 7, p. 213**
Pas question!
Non, c'est impossible.
Non, tu dois...
Pas ce soir.

Making requests **Ch. 8, p. 240**
Tu peux (aller faire les courses)?
Tu me rapportes... ?

Ch. 12, p. 364
Est-ce que tu peux... ?
Tu pourrais passer à... ?

Accepting requests **Ch. 8, p. 240**
Pourquoi pas?
Bon, d'accord.
Je veux bien.
J'y vais tout de suite.

Ch. 12, p. 364
D'accord.
Si tu veux.

Declining requests **Ch. 8, p. 240**
Je ne peux pas maintenant.
Je regrette, mais je n'ai pas le temps.
J'ai des tas de choses (trucs) à faire.

Ch. 12, p. 364
Je suis désolé(e), mais je n'ai pas le temps.

Telling someone what to do **Ch. 8, p. 240**
Rapporte(-moi)...
Prends...
Achète(-moi)...
N'oublie pas de...

Offering food **Ch. 8, p. 247**
Tu veux... ?
Vous voulez... ?
Vous prenez... ?
Tu prends... ?
Encore... ?

Accepting food **Ch. 8, p. 247**
Oui, s'il vous/te plaît.
Oui, avec plaisir.
Oui, j'en veux bien.

Refusing food **Ch. 8, p. 247**
Non, merci.
Non, merci. Je n'ai plus faim.
Je n'en veux plus.

Asking for advice **Ch. 9, p. 279**
A ton avis, qu'est-ce que je fais?
Qu'est-ce que tu me conseilles?

Ch. 10, p. 300
Je ne sais pas quoi mettre pour...
Qu'est-ce que je mets?

Giving advice **Ch. 9, p. 279**
Oublie-le/-la/-les!
Téléphone-lui/-leur!
Tu devrais...
Pourquoi tu ne... pas?

Ch. 10, p. 300
Pourquoi est-ce que tu ne mets pas... ?
Mets...

Reminding **Ch. 11, p. 333**
N'oublie pas...
Tu n'as pas oublié... ?
Tu ne peux pas partir sans...
Tu prends... ?

Reassuring **Ch. 11, p. 333**
Ne t'en fais pas.
J'ai pensé à tout.
Je n'ai rien oublié.

Additional Vocabulary

This list presents additional vocabulary you may want to use when you're working on the activities in the textbook and in the workbooks. It also includes the optional vocabulary labeled **Vocabulaire à la carte** that appears in several chapters. If you can't find the words you need here, try the French-English and English-French vocabulary lists beginning on page R31.

Adjectives

absurd	*absurde*
awesome (impressive)	*impressionnant(e)*
boring	*ennuyeux/ennuyeuse*
chilly (weather)	*froid, frais*
colorful (thing)	*vif/vive*
despicable	*ignoble*
eccentric	*excentrique*
incredible	*incroyable*
tasteful (remark, object)	*de bon goût*
tasteless (flavor)	*insipide;* (remark, object) *de mauvais goût*
terrifying	*terrifiant(e)*
threatening	*menaçant(e)*
tremendous (excellent)	*formidable*
unforgettable	*inoubliable*
unique	*unique*

Clothing

blazer	*un blazer*
button	*un bouton*
coat	*un manteau*
collar	*un col*
eyeglasses	*des lunettes* (f.)
gloves	*des gants* (m.)
handkerchief	*un mouchoir*
high-heeled shoes	*des chaussures* (f.) *à talons*
lace	*de la dentelle*
linen	*du lin*
necklace	*un collier*
nylon	*du nylon*
pajamas	*un pyjama*
polyester	*du polyester*
raincoat	*un imperméable*
rayon	*de la rayonne*
ring	*une bague*
sale (discount)	*des soldes* (m.)
silk	*de la soie*
sleeve	*une manche*
slippers	*des pantoufles* (f.)
suit (man's)	*un costume;* (woman's) *un tailleur*
suspenders	*des bretelles* (f.)
velvet	*du velours*
vest	*un gilet*
wool	*de la laine*
zipper	*une fermeture éclair®*

Colors and Patterns

beige	*beige*
checked	*à carreaux*
colorful	*coloré(e), vif/vive*
dark blue	*bleu foncé*
dark-colored	*foncé(e)*
flowered	*à fleurs*
gold (adj.)	*d'or, doré(e)*
light blue	*bleu clair*
light-colored	*clair(e)*
patterned	*à motifs*
polka-dotted	*à pois*
striped	*à rayures*
turquoise	*turquoise*

Computers

CD-ROM	*le CD-ROM, le disque optique compact*
CD-ROM drive	*le lecteur de CD-ROM, l'unité* (f.) *de CD-ROM*
to click	*cliquer*
computer	*l'ordinateur* (m.)
delete key	*la touche d'effacement*
disk drive	*le lecteur de disquette, l'unité de disquettes* (f.)
diskette, floppy disk	*la disquette, la disquette souple*
to drag	*glisser, déplacer*
e-mail	*le courrier électronique, la messagerie électronique*
file	*le dossier*
file (folder)	*le fichier*
hard drive	*le disque dur*
homepage	*la page d'accueil*
Internet	*Internet* (m.)
keyboard	*le clavier*
keyword	*le mot-clé*
log on	*l'ouverture* (f.) *de session*
modem	*le modem*
monitor	*le moniteur, le logimètre*
mouse	*la souris*

password	*le mot de passe*
to print	*imprimer*
printer	*l'imprimante* (f.)
to quit	*quitter*
to record	*enregistrer*
return key	*la touche de retour*
to save	*sauvegarder, enregistrer*
screen	*l'écran* (m.)
to search	*chercher, rechercher*
search engine	*le moteur de recherche, l'outil* (m.) *de recherche*
to send	*envoyer*
software	*le logiciel*
Web site	*le site du Web, le site W3*
World Wide Web	*le World Wide Web, le Web, le W3*

Entertainment

blues	*le blues*
CD player	*le lecteur de CD*
camera flash	*le flash*
folk music	*la musique folklorique*
headphones	*les écouteurs*
hit (song)	*le tube*
lens	*l'objectif* (m.)
microphone	*le micro(phone)*
opera	*l'opéra* (m.)
pop music	*la musique pop*
reggae	*le reggae*
roll of film	*la pellicule (photo)*
screen	*l'écran* (m.)
speakers	*les enceintes* (f.), *les baffles* (m.)
to turn off	*éteindre*
to turn on	*allumer*
turntable	*la platine*
walkman	*le balladeur*

Family

adopted	*adopté(e), adoptif/adoptive*
brother-in-law	*le beau-frère*
child	*un(e) enfant*
couple	*un couple*
daughter-in-law	*la belle-fille*
divorced	*divorcé(e)*
engaged	*fiancé(e)*
goddaughter	*la filleule*
godfather	*le parrain*
godmother	*la marraine*
godson	*le filleul*
grandchildren	*les petits-enfants*
granddaughter	*la petite-fille*
grandson	*le petit-fils*
great-granddaughter	*l'arrière-petite-fille* (f.)
great-grandfather	*l'arrière-grand-père* (m.)
great-grandmother	*l'arrière-grand-mère* (f.)
great-grandson	*l'arrière-petit-fils* (m.)
half-brother	*le demi-frère*
half-sister	*la demi-sœur*
mother-in-law	*la belle-mère*
only child	*un/une enfant unique*
single	*célibataire*
sister-in-law	*la belle-sœur*

son-in-law	*le gendre; le beau-fils*
stepbrother	*le demi-frère*
stepdaughter	*la belle-fille*
stepfather	*le beau-père*
stepmother	*la belle-mère*
stepsister	*la demi-sœur*
stepson	*le beau-fils*
widow	*la veuve*
widower	*le veuf*

Foods and Beverages

appetizer	*une entrée*
apricot	*un abricot*
asparagus	*des asperges* (f.)
bacon	*du bacon*
bowl	*un bol*
Brussels sprouts	*des choux* (m.) *de Bruxelles*
cabbage	*du chou*
cauliflower	*du chou-fleur*
cereal	*des céréales* (f.)
chestnut	*un marron*
cookie	*un biscuit*
cucumber	*un concombre*
cutlet	*une escalope*
fried egg	*un œuf au plat;* **hard-boiled egg** *un œuf dur;* **scrambled eggs** *des œufs brouillés;* **soft-boiled egg** *un œuf à la coque*

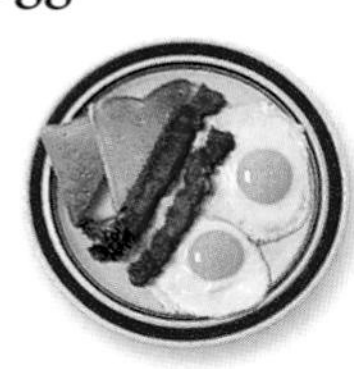

eggplant	*une aubergine*
French bread	*une baguette*
garlic	*de l'ail* (m.)
grapefruit	*un pamplemousse*
honey	*du miel*
liver	*du foie*
margarine	*de la margarine*
marshmallow	*une guimauve*
mayonnaise	*de la mayonnaise*
melon	*un melon*
mustard	*de la moutarde*
nuts	*des noix* (f.)
peanut butter	*du beurre de cacahouètes*
pepper (spice)	*du poivre;* (vegetable) *un poivron*
popcorn	*du pop-corn*
potato chips	*des chips* (f.)
raspberry	*une framboise*
salmon	*du saumon*
salt	*du sel*
shellfish	*des fruits* (m.) *de mer*
soup	*de la soupe*
spinach	*des épinards* (m.)
spoon	*une cuillère*
syrup	*du sirop*
veal	*du veau*
watermelon	*une pastèque*
zucchini	*une courgette*
bland	*doux (douce)*
hot (spicy)	*épicé(e)*
juicy (fruit)	*juteux/juteuse;* (meat) *tendre*
rare (cooked)	*saignant(e)*
medium (cooked)	*à point*
spicy	*épicé(e)*
well-done (cooked)	*bien cuit(e)*
tasty	*savoureux/savoureuse*

Housework

to clean	*nettoyer*
to dry	*faire sécher*
to dust	*faire la poussière*
to fold	*plier*
to hang	*pendre*
to iron	*repasser*
to put away	*ranger*
to rake	*ratisser*
to shovel	*enlever à la pelle*
to sweep	*balayer*

Pets

bird	*un oiseau*
cow	*une vache*
frog	*une grenouille*
goldfish	*un poisson rouge*
guinea pig	*un cochon d'Inde*
hamster	*un hamster*
horse	*un cheval*
kitten	*un chaton*
lizard	*un lézard*
mouse	*une souris*
parrot	*un perroquet*
pig	*un cochon*
puppy	*un chiot*
rabbit	*un lapin*
turtle	*une tortue*

Places Around Town

airport *l'aéroport* (m.)
beauty shop *le salon de coiffure*
bridge *le pont*
church *l'église* (f.)
consulate *le consulat*
hospital *l'hôpital* (m.)
mosque *la mosquée*
police station *le commissariat de police*
synagogue *la synagogue*
tourist office *l'office de tourisme* (m.)
town hall *l'hôtel* (m.) *de ville*

Professions

Note: If only one form is given, that form is used for both men and women. Note that you can also say **une femme banquier, une femme médecin,** and so forth.

archaeologist *un(e) archéologue*
architect *un(e) architecte*
athlete *un(e) athlète*
banker *un banquier*
businessman/ businesswoman *un homme d'affaires (une femme d'affaires)*
dancer *un danseur (une danseuse)*
dentist *un(e) dentiste*
doctor *un médecin*
editor *un rédacteur (une rédactrice)*
engineer *un ingénieur*
fashion designer *un(e) styliste de mode*
fashion model *un mannequin*
hairdresser *un coiffeur (une coiffeuse)*
homemaker *un homme au foyer (une femme au foyer)*
lawyer *un(e) avocat(e)*
manager (company) *un directeur (une directrice);* **(store, restaurant)** *un gérant (une gérante)*
mechanic *un mécanicien (une mécanicienne)*
painter (art) *un peintre; (buildings) un peintre en bâtiment*
pilot *un pilote*
plumber *un plombier*
scientist *un(e) scientifique*
secretary *un(e) secrétaire*
social worker *un assistant social (une assistante sociale)*
taxi driver *un chauffeur de taxi*
technician *un technicien (une technicienne)*
truck driver *un routier*
veterinarian *un(e) vétérinaire*
worker *un ouvrier (une ouvrière)*
writer *un écrivain*

School Subjects

accounting *la comptabilité*
business *le commerce*
foreign languages *les langues* (f.) *étrangères*
home economics *les arts* (m.) *ménagers*
marching band *la fanfare*
orchestra *l'orchestre* (m.)
social studies *les sciences* (f.) *sociales*
typing *la dactylographie*
woodworking *la menuiserie*
world history *l'histoire* (f.) *mondiale*

School Supplies

calendar *un calendrier*
colored pencils *des crayons* (m.) *de couleur*
compass *un compas*
correction fluid *du liquide correcteur*
glue *de la colle*
gym uniform *une tenue de gymnastique*
marker *un feutre*
rubber band *un élastique*
scissors *des ciseaux* (m.)
staple *une agrafe*
stapler *une agrafeuse*
transparent tape *du ruban adhésif*

Sports and Interests

badminton	*le badminton*
boxing	*la boxe*
fishing rod	*la canne à pêche*
foot race	*la course à pied*
to go for a ride (by bike, car, motorcycle, moped)	*faire une promenade, faire un tour (à bicyclette, en voiture, à moto, à vélomoteur)*
to do gymnastics	*faire de la gymnastique*
hunting	*la chasse*
to lift weights	*faire des haltères*
mountain climbing	*l'alpinisme* (m.)
to play checkers	*jouer aux dames*
to play chess	*jouer aux échecs*
to ride a skateboard	*faire de la planche à roulettes*
to sew	*coudre; faire de la couture*
speed skating	*le patinage de vitesse*
to surf	*faire du surf*

Weather

barometer	*le baromètre*
blizzard	*la tempête de neige*
cloudy	*nuageux*
drizzle	*la bruine*
fog	*le brouillard*
frost	*la gelée*
hail	*la grêle*
to hail	*grêler*
heat wave	*la canicule*
hurricane	*l'ouragan* (m.)
ice (on the road)	*le verglas*
It's pouring.	*Il pleut à verse.*
It's sleeting.	*Il tombe de la neige fondue.*
It's sunny.	*Il fait du soleil.*
lightning bolt	*l'éclair* (m.)
mist	*la brume*
shower (rain)	*l'averse* (f.)
storm	*la tempête*
thermometer	*le thermomètre*
thunder	*le tonnerre*
thunderstorm	*l'orage* (m.)
tornado	*la tornade*

Cities

Algiers	*Alger*
Brussels	*Bruxelles*
Cairo	*Le Caire*
Geneva	*Genève*
Lisbon	*Lisbonne*
London	*Londres*
Montreal	*Montréal*
Moscow	*Moscou*
New Orleans	*La Nouvelle-Orléans*
Quebec City	*Québec*
Tangier	*Tanger*
Venice	*Venise*
Vienna	*Vienne*

The Continents

Africa	*l'Afrique* (f.)
Antarctica	*l'Antarctique* (f.)
Asia	*l'Asie* (f.)
Australia	*l'Océanie* (f.)
Europe	*l'Europe* (f.)
North America	*l'Amérique* (f.) *du Nord*
South America	*l'Amérique* (f.) *du Sud*

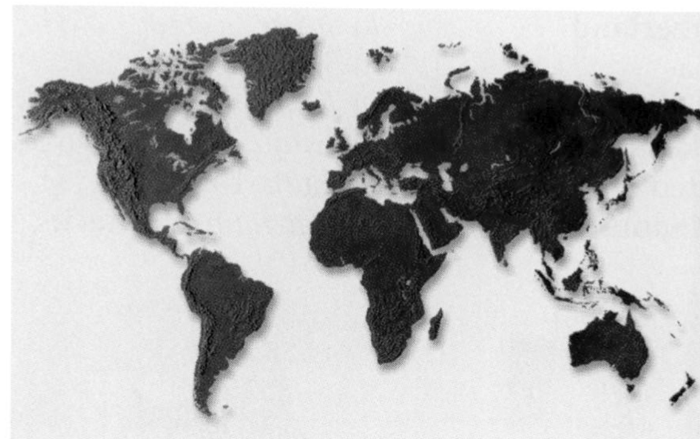

Countries

Algeria	*l'Algérie* (f.)
Argentina	*l'Argentine* (f.)
Australia	*l'Australie* (f.)
Austria	*l'Autriche* (f.)
Belgium	*la Belgique*
Brazil	*le Brésil*
Canada	*le Canada*
China	*la Chine*
Côte d'Ivoire	*la République de Côte d'Ivoire*
Egypt	*l'Egypte* (f.)
England	*l'Angleterre* (f.)
France	*la France*
Germany	*l'Allemagne* (f.)

Greece	*la Grèce*
Holland	*la Hollande*
India	*l'Inde* (f.)
Ireland	*l'Irlande* (f.)
Israel	*Israël* (m.)
Italy	*l'Italie* (f.)
Jamaica	*la Jamaïque*
Japan	*le Japon*
Jordan	*la Jordanie*
Lebanon	*le Liban*
Libya	*la Libye*
Luxembourg	*le Luxembourg*
Mexico	*le Mexique*
Monaco	*Monaco* (f.)
Morocco	*le Maroc*
Netherlands	*les Pays-Bas* (m.)
North Korea	*la Corée du Nord*
Peru	*le Pérou*
Philippines	*les Philippines* (f.)
Poland	*la Pologne*
Portugal	*le Portugal*
Russia	*la Russie*
Senegal	*le Sénégal*
South Korea	*la Corée du Sud*
Spain	*l'Espagne* (f.)
Switzerland	*la Suisse*
Syria	*la Syrie*
Tunisia	*la Tunisie*
Turkey	*la Turquie*
United States	*les Etats-Unis* (m.)
Vietnam	*le Viêt-nam*

States

California	*la Californie*
Florida	*la Floride*
Georgia	*la Géorgie*
Louisiana	*la Louisiane*
New Mexico	*le Nouveau Mexique*
North Carolina	*la Caroline du Nord*
Pennsylvania	*la Pennsylvanie*
South Carolina	*la Caroline du Sud*
Texas	*le Texas*
Virginia	*la Virginie*

Oceans and Seas

Atlantic Ocean	*l'Atlantique* (m.), *l'océan* (m.) *Atlantique*
Caribbean Sea	*la mer des Caraïbes*
English Channel	*la Manche*
Indian Ocean	*l'océan* (m.) *Indien*
Mediterranean Sea	*la mer Méditerranée*
Pacific Ocean	*le Pacifique, l'océan* (m.) *Pacifique*

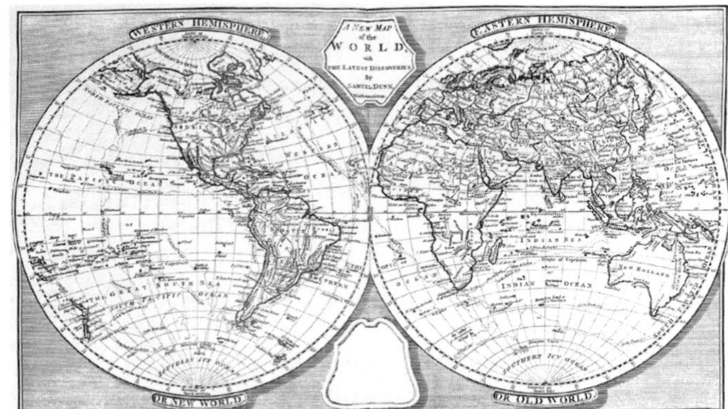

Other Geographical Terms

Alps	*les Alpes* (f.)
border	*la frontière*
capital	*la capitale*
continent	*le continent*
country	*le pays*
hill	*la colline*
lake	*le lac*
latitude	*la latitude*
longitude	*la longitude*
North Africa	*l'Afrique* (f.) *du Nord*
ocean	*l'océan* (m.)
plain	*la plaine*
Pyrenees	*les Pyrénées* (f.)
river	*la rivière, le fleuve*
sea	*la mer*
state	*l'état* (m.)
the North Pole	*le pôle Nord*
the South Pole	*le pôle Sud*
valley	*la vallée*

ADJECTIVES

REGULAR ADJECTIVES

In French, adjectives agree in gender and number with the nouns that they modify. A regular adjective has four forms: masculine singular, feminine singular, masculine plural, and feminine plural. To make a regular adjective agree with a feminine noun, add an **-e** to the masculine singular form of the adjective. To make one agree with a plural noun, add an **-s** to the masculine singular form. To make one adjective agree with a feminine plural noun, add **-es** to the masculine singular form. Adjectives ending in **-é,** like **désolé,** also follow these rules.

	SINGULAR	**PLURAL**
MASCULINE	un jean **vert**	des jeans **verts**
FEMININE	une ceinture **verte**	des ceintures **vertes**

ADJECTIVES THAT END IN AN UNACCENTED -E

When an adjective ends in an unaccented **-e,** the masculine singular and the feminine singular forms are the same. To form the plural of these adjectives, add an **-s** to the singular forms.

	SINGULAR	**PLURAL**
MASCULINE	un cahier **rouge**	des cahiers **rouges**
FEMININE	une trousse **rouge**	des trousses **rouges**

ADJECTIVES THAT END IN -S

When the masculine singular form of an adjective ends in an **-s,** the masculine plural form does not change. The feminine forms follow the regular adjective rules.

	SINGULAR	**PLURAL**
MASCULINE	un sac **gris**	des sacs **gris**
FEMININE	une robe **grise**	des robes **grises**

ADJECTIVES THAT END IN -EUX

Adjectives that end in **-eux** do not change in the masculine plural. The feminine singular form of these adjectives is made by replacing the **-x** with **-se.** To form the feminine plural, replace the **-x** with **-ses.**

	SINGULAR	PLURAL
MASCULINE	un garçon **heureux**	des garçons **heureux**
FEMININE	une fille **heureuse**	des filles **heureuses**

ADJECTIVES THAT END IN -IF

To make the feminine singular form of adjectives that end in **-if,** replace **-if** with **-ive.** To make the plural forms of these adjectives, add an **-s** to the singular forms.

	SINGULAR	PLURAL
MASCULINE	un garçon **sportif**	des garçons **sportifs**
FEMININE	une fille **sportive**	des filles **sportives**

ADJECTIVES THAT END IN -IEN

To make the feminine singular and feminine plural forms of adjectives that end in **-ien** in their masculine singular form, add **-ne** and **-nes.** Add an **-s** to form the masculine plural.

	SINGULAR	PLURAL
MASCULINE	un garçon **canadien**	des garçons **canadiens**
FEMININE	une fille **canadienne**	des filles **canadiennes**

ADJECTIVES THAT DOUBLE THE LAST CONSONANT

To make the adjectives **bon, gentil, gros, mignon, nul,** and **violet** agree with a feminine noun, double the last consonant and add an **-e.** To make the plural forms, add an **-s** to the singular forms. Note that with **gros,** the masculine singular and masculine plural forms are the same.

	SINGULAR					
MASCULINE	bon	gentil	gros	mignon	nul	violet
FEMININE	bonne	gentille	grosse	mignonne	nulle	violette

	PLURAL					
MASCULINE	bons	gentils	gros	mignons	nuls	violets
FEMININE	bonnes	gentilles	grosses	mignonnes	nulles	violettes

INVARIABLE ADJECTIVES

Some adjectives are invariable. They never change form. **Cool, marron, orange,** and **super** are examples of invariable adjectives.

Il me faut une montre **marron** et des baskets **orange.**

IRREGULAR ADJECTIVES

The forms of some adjectives must simply be memorized. This is the case for **blanc, sympa,** and **roux.**

Note that **sympathique,** the long form of the adjective, follows the rules for adjectives that end in an unaccented **-e,** like **rouge.**

	SINGULAR	PLURAL
MASCULINE	**blanc**	**blancs**
FEMININE	**blanche**	**blanches**

	SINGULAR	PLURAL
MASCULINE	**roux**	**roux**
FEMININE	**rousse**	**rousses**

	SINGULAR	PLURAL
MASCULINE	**sympa**	**sympas**
FEMININE	**sympa**	**sympas**

POSITION OF ADJECTIVES

In French, adjectives are usually placed after the noun that they modify.

C'est une femme **intelligente.**

Certain adjectives precede the noun. Some of these are **bon, jeune, joli, grand,** and **petit.**

C'est un **petit** village.

DEMONSTRATIVE ADJECTIVES

This, that, these, and *those* are demonstrative adjectives. There are two masculine singular forms of these adjectives in French: **ce** and **cet. Cet** is used with masculine singular nouns that begin with a vowel sound. Some examples are **cet ordinateur** and **cet homme.** Demonstrative adjectives always precede the noun that they modify.

	Singular Before a Consonant	Singular Before a Vowel Sound	Plural
MASCULINE	**ce** livre	**cet** ordinateur	**ces** posters
FEMININE	**cette** montre	**cette** école	**ces** gommes

POSSESSIVE ADJECTIVES

Possessive adjectives come before the noun that they modify and agree in gender and number with that noun. All nouns that begin with a vowel sound use the masculine singular form, for example **mon ami(e), ton ami(e), son ami(e).**

	Masculine Singular	Feminine Singular	Masc./Fem. Singular Before a Vowel Sound	Masc./Fem. Plural
my	**mon** père	**ma** mère	**mon** oncle	**mes** cousines
your	**ton** livre	**ta** montre	**ton** écharpe	**tes** cahiers
his, her, its	**son** chien	**sa** sœur	**son** école	**ses** cours

The possessive adjectives for *our, your,* and *their* have only two forms, singular and plural.

	Masc./Fem. Singular	Masc./Fem. Plural
our	**notre** frère	**nos** tantes
your	**votre** classeur	**vos** amis
their	**leur** copain	**leurs** trousses

ADJECTIVES AS NOUNS

To use an adjective as a noun, add a definite article before the adjective. The article that you use agrees in gender and number with the noun that the adjective is replacing.

—Tu aimes les chemises rouges ou **les blanches?**

Do you like the red shirts or the white ones?

—J'aime **les blanches.**

I like the white ones.

ADVERBS

POSITION OF ADVERBS

Most adverbs follow the conjugated verb. In the **passé composé,** they usually precede the past participle.

Nathalie fait **souvent** des photos. Je n'ai pas **bien** mangé ce matin.

Adverbs that are made up of more than one word can be placed at the beginning or at the end of a sentence. When you use **ne (n')... jamais,** place it around the conjugated verb.

D'habitude, je fais du tennis le soir.

J'aime faire de l'aérobic **deux fois par semaine.**

Je **n'**ai **jamais** fait de ski.

ARTICLES

DEFINITE ARTICLES

French has four definite articles: **le, la, l',** and **les.** The form that you use depends on the gender and number of the noun it modifies. Use **le** with masculine singular nouns, **le livre; la** with feminine singular nouns, **la chemise;** and **les** with both masculine and feminine nouns that are plural, **les crayons.** The form **l'** is used with both masculine and feminine nouns that begin with a vowel sound: **l'ami, l'amie, l'homme.** In French, you sometimes use a definite article when no article is required in English.

J'aime **le** chocolat et toi, tu préfères **le** café.

	Singular Before a Consonant	Singular Before a Vowel Sound	Plural
MASCULINE	**le** professeur	**l'**ami	**les** livres
FEMININE	**la** pharmacie	**l'**école	**les** pommes

INDEFINITE ARTICLES

In English, there are three indefinite articles: *a, an,* and *some.* In French there are also three: **un, une,** and **des.** The indefinite articles agree in number and gender with the nouns they modify.

	SINGULAR	PLURAL
MASCULINE	**un** poisson	**des** chats
FEMININE	**une** orange	**des** lunettes

PARTITIVE ARTICLES

To say that you want *part* or *some* of an item, use the partitive articles. Use **du** with a masculine noun and **de la** with a feminine noun. Use **de l'** with singular nouns that begin with a vowel sound whether they are masculine or feminine.

Je veux **de la** tarte aux pommes. *I want some apple pie.*

To indicate the whole as opposed to a part of the item, use the indefinite articles **un, une,** and **des.**

Pour la fête, il me faut **des** tartes. *I need (some) pies for the party.*

NEGATION AND THE ARTICLES

When the main verb of a sentence is negated, the indefinite and the partitive articles change to **de/d'.** Definite articles remain the same after a negative verb.

J'ai **le** livre de maths. —> Je n'ai pas **le** livre de maths.
J'ai **des** stylos. —> Je n'ai pas **de** stylos.
J'ai mangé **de la** pizza. —> Je n'ai pas mangé **de** pizza.

INTERROGATIVES

QUESTION FORMATION

There are several ways to ask yes-no questions. One of these is to raise the pitch of your voice at the end of a statement. The other is to place **est-ce que** in front of a statement.

Tu aimes le chocolat. —> **Tu aimes le chocolat?** (intonation) *or*
Est-ce que tu aimes le chocolat?

NEGATIVE QUESTIONS

The answer to a yes-no question depends on the way the question was stated. If the verb in a question is positive, then the answer is **oui** if you agree, and **non** if you don't. If the verb in a question is negative, then **non** is used to agree with the question and **si** to disagree.

Question	Agreeing with the Question	Disagreeing with the Question
Tu aimes lire?	**Oui,** j'aime lire.	**Non,** je n'aime pas lire.
Tu n'aimes pas lire?	**Non,** je n'aime pas lire.	**Si,** j'aime lire.

INFORMATION QUESTIONS

To ask for specific kinds of information, use the following question words:

A quelle heure? *At what time?* **Où?** *Where?*
Avec qui? *With whom?* **Quand?** *When?*

These words can be used by themselves, at the beginning of a question, at the beginning of a question, followed by **est-ce que,** or at the end of a question.

Avec qui? **Avec qui** est-ce qu'on va au cinéma?
Avec qui on va au cinéma? On va au cinéma **avec qui?**

NOUNS

PLURAL FORMS OF NOUNS

In French, you make most nouns plural by adding an **-s** to the end of the word, unless they already end in **-s** or **-x.** Nouns that end in **-eau** are made plural by adding an **-x,** and nouns that end in **-al** are generally made plural by replacing the **-al** with **-aux.**

	Regular Nouns	-s or -x	-eau	-al
SINGULAR	table	bus	manteau	hôpital
PLURAL	tables	bus	manteaux	hôpitaux

PREPOSITIONS

THE PREPOSITIONS A AND DE

The preposition **à** means *to, at,* or *in,* and **de** means *from* or *of.* When **à** and **de** are used in front of the definite articles **le** and **les**, they form contractions. If they precede any other definite article, there is no contraction.

Il va **à l'**école et **au** musée. *He's going to school and to the museum.*

Nous sommes loin **du** musée. *We are far from the museum.*

	Masculine Article	Feminine Article	Vowel Sound	Plural
à	à + le = **au**	à + la = **à la**	à + l' = **à l'**	à + les = **aux**
de	de + le = **du**	de + la = **de la**	de + l' = **de l'**	de + les = **des**

De can also indicate possession or ownership.

C'est le livre **de** Laurent. *It's Laurent's book.*

C'est le stylo **du** prof. *It's the professor's pen.*

PREPOSITIONS AND PLACES

To say that you are at or going to a place, you need to use a preposition. With cities, use the preposition **à : à Paris.** One notable exception is **en Arles.** When speaking about masculine countries, use **au : au Maroc.** With plural names of countries, use **aux : aux Etats-Unis.** Most countries ending in **-e** are feminine; in these cases, use **en : en France. Le Mexique** is an exception. If a country begins with a vowel, like **Israël,** use **en : en Israël.**

Cities	Masculine Countries	Feminine Countries or Masculine Countries that Begin with a Vowel	Plural Countries
à Nantes **à** Paris **en** Arles	**au** Canada **au** Maroc **au** Mexique	**en** Italie **en** Espagne **en** Israël	**aux** Etats-Unis **aux** Philippines **aux** Pays-Bas

PRONOUNS

In French, as in English, a pronoun can refer to a person, place, or thing. Pronouns are used to avoid repetition. In French, pronouns agree in gender and number with the noun that they replace.

SUBJECT PRONOUNS

Subject pronouns replace the subject in a sentence.

je (j')	*I*	**nous**	*we*
tu	*you* (familiar)	**vous**	*you* (plural or formal)
il	*he / it*	**ils**	*they*
elle	*she / it*	**elles**	*they*
on	*we / one / they*		

THE IMPERSONAL PRONOUN IL

Many statements in French begin with the personal pronoun **il.** In these statements, **il** does not refer to any particular person or thing. For this reason, these statements are called impersonal statements.

Il fait beau. *It's nice out.*

Il est huit heures. *It's eight o'clock.*

Il me/te faut... *I/You need . . .*

Il y a... *There is/are . . .*

DIRECT OBJECT PRONOUNS: LE, LA, LES

A direct object is a noun that receives the action of the verb. It answers the questions *What?* or *Whom?* To say *him, her, it,* or *them,* use the pronouns **le, la,** and **les.** In French, you place the direct object pronoun in front of the conjugated verb.

Il regarde **la télé.** —> Il **la** regarde.

If there is an infinitive in the sentence, the direct object pronoun comes before the infinitive.

Je vais attendre **Pierre.** —> Je vais **l'**attendre.

In an affirmative command, the direct object pronoun follows the verb and is connected to it with a hyphen.

Regarde **la télévision.** —> Regarde-**la!**

	SINGULAR	PLURAL
MASCULINE	**le / l'**	**les**
FEMININE	**la / l'**	**les**

INDIRECT OBJECT PRONOUNS: LUI, LEUR

The indirect object answers the question *To whom?* and refers only to people. In French an indirect object follows the preposition **à: Il parle à Marie.** The indirect object pronoun replaces the prepositional phrase **à + a person,** and precedes the conjugated verb.

Nous téléphonons **à Mireille.** —> Nous **lui** téléphonons.

If there is an infinitive in the sentence, the indirect object pronoun comes before the infinitive.

Il n'aime pas parler **à ses parents.** —> Il n'aime pas **leur** parler.

In an affirmative command, the indirect object pronoun follows the verb and is connected to it with a hyphen.

Téléphone **à ta sœur.** —> Téléphone-**lui!**

THE PRONOUN Y

To replace a phrase meaning *to, on, at,* or *in* any place that has already been mentioned, you can use the pronoun **y.** It can replace phrases beginning with prepositions of location such as **à, sur, chez, dans,** and **en + a place or thing.** Place **y** before the conjugated verb.

Elle va **à la pharmacie.** —> Elle **y** va.

If there is an infinitive, place **y** before the infinitive.

Elle va aller **à la poste** demain. —> Elle va **y** aller demain.

THE PRONOUN EN

The pronoun **en** replaces a phrase beginning with **de, du, de la, de l',** or **des.** It usually means *about it, some (of it/of them),* or simply *it/them,* and is placed before the conjugated verb.

Tu achètes **des haricots verts?** —> Oui, j'**en** achète pour le dîner.

En in a negative sentence means *not any* or *none.*

Tu ne bois pas **de café.** —> Tu n'**en** bois pas.

En is placed before the conjugated verb.

Je parle **de mes vacances.** —> J'**en** parle.

If there is an infinitive, place **en** before the infinitive.

Vous aimez manger **des fruits.** —> Vous aimez **en** manger.

Notice that with the **passé composé, en** precedes the helping verb.

Il a mangé **du pain.** —> Il **en** a mangé.

VERBS

THE PRESENT TENSE OF REGULAR VERBS

To conjugate a verb in French, use the following formulas. Which formula you choose depends on the ending of the infinitive. There are three major verb categories: **-er, -ir,** and **-re.** Each one has a different conjugation. Within these categories, there are regular and irregular verbs. To conjugate regular verbs, you drop the infinitive endings and add these endings.

	aimer *(to love, to like)*		**choisir** *(to choose)*		**vendre** *(to sell)*	
Subject	**Stem**	**Ending**	**Stem**	**Ending**	**Stem**	**Ending**
je/j'	aim	**-e**	chois	**-is**	vend	**-s**
tu		**-es**		**-is**		**-s**
il/elle/on		**-e**		**-it**		—
nous		**-ons**		**-issons**		**-ons**
vous		**-ez**		**-issez**		**-ez**
ils/elles		**-ent**		**-issent**		**-ent**

VERBS WITH STEM AND SPELLING CHANGES

Verbs listed in this section are not irregular, but they do have some stem and spelling changes.

With **acheter** and **promener**, add an **accent grave** over the second-to-last **e** for all forms except **nous** and **vous.** Notice that the accent on the second **e** in **préférer** changes from **é** to **è** in all forms except the **nous** and **vous** forms.

	acheter *(to buy)*	**préférer** *(to prefer)*	**promener** *(to walk (an animal))*
je/j'	**achète**	**préfère**	**promène**
tu	**achètes**	**préfères**	**promènes**
il/elle/on	**achète**	**préfère**	**promène**
nous	**achetons**	**préférons**	**promenons**
vous	**achetez**	**préférez**	**promenez**
ils/elles	**achètent**	**préfèrent**	**promènent**
Past Participle	**acheté**	**préféré**	**promené**

The following verbs have different stems for **nous** and **vous.**

	appeler *(to call)*	**essayer** *(to try)*
je/j'	**appelle**	**essaie**
tu	**appelles**	**essaies**
il/elle/on	**appelle**	**essaie**
nous	**appelons**	**essayons**
vous	**appelez**	**essayez**
ils/elles	**appellent**	**essaient**
Past Participle	**appelé**	**essayé**

The following verbs show a difference only in the **nous** form.

	commencer *(to start)*	**manger** *(to eat)*
je/j'	**commence**	**mange**
tu	**commences**	**manges**
il/elle/on	**commence**	**mange**
nous	**commençons**	**mangeons**
vous	**commencez**	**mangez**
ils/elles	**commencent**	**mangent**
Past Participle	**commencé**	**mangé**

	nager *(to swim)*	**voyager** *(to travel)*
je/j'	**nage**	**voyage**
tu	**nages**	**voyages**
il/elle/on	**nage**	**voyage**
nous	**nageons**	**voyageons**
vous	**nagez**	**voyagez**
ils/elles	**nagent**	**voyagent**
Past Participle	**nagé**	**voyagé**

VERBS LIKE DORMIR

These verbs follow a different pattern from the one you learned for regular **-ir** verbs. These verbs have two stems: one for the singular subjects, and one for the plural ones.

	dormir *(to sleep)*	**partir** *(to leave)*	**sortir** *(to go out, to take out)*
je/j'	dor**s**	par**s**	sor**s**
tu	dor**s**	par**s**	sor**s**
il/elle/on	dor**t**	par**t**	sor**t**
nous	dorm**ons**	part**ons**	sort**ons**
vous	dorm**ez**	part**ez**	sort**ez**
ils/elles	dorm**ent**	part**ent**	sort**ent**

VERBS WITH IRREGULAR FORMS

Verbs listed in this section do not follow the pattern of verbs like **aimer, choisir,** or **vendre.** Therefore, they are called *irregular verbs.* The following four irregular verbs are used frequently.

	aller *(to go)*	**avoir** *(to have)*
je/j'	**vais**	**ai**
tu	**vas**	**as**
il/elle/on	**va**	**a**
nous	**allons**	**avons**
vous	**allez**	**avez**
ils/elles	**vont**	**ont**

	être *(to be)*	**faire** *(to do, to make, to play)*
je/j'	**suis**	**fais**
tu	**es**	**fais**
il/elle/on	**est**	**fait**
nous	**sommes**	**faisons**
vous	**êtes**	**faites**
ils/elles	**sont**	**font**

Devoir, pouvoir, and **vouloir** are also irregular. They are usually followed by an infinitive.

Je peux chanter. *I can sing.*

	devoir *(must, to have to)*	**pouvoir** *(to be able to, can)*	**vouloir** *(to want)*
je/j' tu il/elle/on	**dois** **dois** **doit**	**peux** **peux** **peut**	**veux** **veux** **veut**
nous vous ils/elles	**devons** **devez** **doivent**	**pouvons** **pouvez** **peuvent**	**voulons** **voulez** **veulent**

These verbs also have irregular forms.

	dire *(to say)*	**écrire** *(to write)*	**lire** *(to read)*
je/j' tu il/elle/on	**dis** **dis** **dit**	**écris** **écris** **écrit**	**lis** **lis** **lit**
nous vous ils/elles	**disons** **dites** **disent**	**écrivons** **écrivez** **écrivent**	**lisons** **lisez** **lisent**
Past Participle	**dit**	**écrit**	**lu**

	mettre *(to put, to put on, to wear)*	**prendre** *(to take, to have food or drink)*	**voir** *(to see)*
je/j' tu il/elle/on	**mets** **mets** **met**	**prends** **prends** **prend**	**vois** **vois** **voit**
nous vous ils/elles	**mettons** **mettez** **mettent**	**prenons** **prenez** **prennent**	**voyons** **voyez** **voient**
Past Participle	**mis**	**pris**	**vu**

THE NEAR FUTURE (FUTUR PROCHE)

Like the past tense, the near future is made of two parts. The future tense of a verb consists of the present tense of **aller** plus the infinitive:

Vous **allez sortir** avec vos copains demain. *You're going to go out with your friends tomorrow.*

THE PAST TENSE (PASSE COMPOSE)

The past tense of most verbs is formed with two parts: the present tense form of the helping verb **avoir** and the past participle of the main verb. To form the past participle, use the formulas below. To make a sentence negative in the past, place the **ne... pas** around the helping verb **avoir.**

INFINITIVE	**aimer** *(to love, to like)*		**choisir** *(to choose)*		**vendre** *(to sell)*	
	Stem	**Ending**	**Stem**	**Ending**	**Stem**	**Ending**
PAST PARTICIPLE	aim	**-é**	chois	**-i**	vend	**-u**
	aimé		choisi		vendu	
PASSE COMPOSE	**j'ai aimé**		**j'ai choisi**		**j'ai vendu**	

J'**ai mangé** de la pizza.
Elle n'**a** pas **vendu** sa voiture.
Nous **avons choisi** le livre.
Nous n'**avons** pas **mangé** de pizza.

Some verbs have irregular past participles.

faire —> fait **prendre —> pris** **avoir —> eu**
lire —> lu **voir —> vu** **mettre —> mis**

With some verbs, such as **aller,** you use the helping verb **être** instead of **avoir.** The past participle of these verbs agrees in gender and number with the subject of the sentence.

Je **suis allé**(e) à l'école. Ils **sont allés** à la poste. Elle **est allée** au café.

THE IMPERATIVE (COMMANDS)

To make a request or a command of most verbs, use the **tu, nous,** or **vous** form of the present tense of the verb without the subject. Remember to drop the final **-s** in the **tu** form of an **-er** verb.

Mange!
Ecoute le professeur!
Faites vos devoirs!
Prenons un sandwich!

aimer *(to love, to like)*		**choisir** *(to choose)*		**vendre** *(to sell)*	
Stem	**Ending**	**Stem**	**Ending**	**Stem**	**Ending**
aim	**-e** **-ons** **-ez**	chois	**-is** **-issons** **-issez**	vend	**-s** **-ons** **-ez**

Pronunciation Index

Chapter	Letter Combination	IPA Symbol	Example
Ch. 1, p. 35 Intonation			
Ch. 2, p. 63 Liaison			vous‿avez des‿amis
Ch. 3, p. 91 The **r** sound	the letter **r**	/ʀ/	rouge vert
Ch. 4, p. 125 The sounds [y] and [u]	the letter **u** the letter combination **ou**	/y/ /u/	une nous
Ch. 5, p. 157 The nasal sound [ɑ̃]	the letter combination **an** the letter combination **am** the letter combination **en** the letter combination **em**	/ɑ̃/	anglais jambon comment temps
Ch. 6, p. 187 The vowel sounds [ø] and [œ]	the letter combination **eu** the letter combination **eu**	/ø/ /œ/	deux heure
Ch. 7, p. 215 The nasal sounds [ɔ̃], [ɛ̃], and [œ̃]	the letter combination **on** the letter combination **om** the letter combination **in** the letter combination **im** the letter combination **ain** the letter combination **aim** the letter combination **(i)en** the letter combination **un** the letter combination **um**	/ɔ̃/ /ɛ̃/ /œ̃/	pardon nombre cousin impossible copain faim bien lundi humble
Ch. 8, p. 249 The sounds [o] and [ɔ]	the letter combination **au** the letter combination **eau** the letter **ô** the letter **o**	/o/ /ɔ/	jaune beau rôle carotte
Ch. 9, p. 281 The vowel sounds [e] and [ɛ]	the letter combination **ez** the letter combination **er** the letter combination **ait** the letter combination **ais** the letter combination **ei** the letter **ê**	/e/ /ɛ/	apportez trouver fait français neige bête
Ch. 10, p. 311 The glides [j], [w], and [ɥ]	the letter **i** the letter combination **ill** the letter combination **oi** the letter combination **oui** the letter combination **ui**	/j/ /w/ /ɥ/	mieux maillot moi Louis huit
Ch. 11, p. 339 **h aspiré, th, ch,** and **gn**	the letter **h** the letter combination **th** the letter combination **ch** the letter combination **gn**	/'/ /t/ /ʃ/ /ɲ/	les halls théâtre chocolat oignon
Ch. 12, p. 373 Review			

Numbers

LES NOMBRES CARDINAUX

0	zéro	**20**	vingt	**80**	quatre-vingts
1	un(e)	**21**	vingt et un(e)	**81**	quatre-vingt-un(e)
2	deux	**22**	vingt-deux	**82**	quatre-vingt-deux
3	trois	**23**	vingt-trois	**90**	quatre-vingt-dix
4	quatre	**24**	vingt-quatre	**91**	quatre-vingt-onze
5	cinq	**25**	vingt-cinq	**92**	quatre-vingt-douze
6	six	**26**	vingt-six	**100**	cent
7	sept	**27**	vingt-sept	**101**	cent un
8	huit	**28**	vingt-huit	**200**	deux cents
9	neuf	**29**	vingt-neuf	**201**	deux cent un
10	dix	**30**	trente	**300**	trois cents
11	onze	**31**	trente et un(e)	**800**	huit cents
12	douze	**32**	trente-deux	**1.000**	mille
13	treize	**40**	quarante	**2.000**	deux mille
14	quatorze	**50**	cinquante	**3.000**	trois mille
15	quinze	**60**	soixante	**10.000**	dix mille
16	seize	**70**	soixante-dix	**19.000**	dix-neuf mille
17	dix-sept	**71**	soixante et onze	**40.000**	quarante mille
18	dix-huit	**72**	soixante-douze	**500.000**	cinq cent mille
19	dix-neuf	**73**	soixante-treize	**1.000.000**	un million

- The word **et** is used only in 21, 31, 41, 51, 61, and 71.
- **Vingt** (**trente, quarante,** and so on) **et une** is used when the number refers to a feminine noun: **trente et une cassettes.**
- The **s** is dropped from **quatre-vingts** and is not added to multiples of **cent** when these numbers are followed by another number: **quatre-vingt-cinq; deux cents,** *but* **deux cent six.** The number **mille** never takes an **s** to agree with a noun: **deux mille insectes.**
- **Un million** is followed by **de** + a noun: **un million de francs.**
- In writing numbers, a period is used in French where a comma is used in English.

LES NOMBRES ORDINAUX

1er, 1ère	premier, première	**9e**	neuvième	**17e**	dix-septième
2e	deuxième	**10e**	dixième	**18e**	dix-huitième
3e	troisième	**11e**	onzième	**19e**	dix-neuvième
4e	quatrième	**12e**	douzième	**20e**	vingtième
5e	cinquième	**13e**	treizième	**21e**	vingt et unième
6e	sixième	**14e**	quatorzième	**22e**	vingt-deuxième
7e	septième	**15e**	quinzième	**30e**	trentième
8e	huitième	**16e**	seizième	**40e**	quarantième

French-English Vocabulary

English-French Vocabulary

French-English Vocabulary

This list includes both active and passive vocabulary in this textbook. Active words and phrases are those listed in the **Vocabulaire** section at the end of each chapter. You are expected to know and be able to use active vocabulary. All entries in heavy black type in this list are active. All other words are passive. Passive vocabulary is for recognition only.

The number after each entry refers to the chapter where the word or phrase is introduced. Nouns are always given with an article. If it is not clear whether the noun is masculine or feminine, *m.* (masculine) or *f.* (feminine) follows the noun. Some nouns that are generally seen only in the plural, as well as ones that have an irregular plural form, are also given with gender indications and the abbreviation *pl.* (plural) following them. An asterisk (*) before a word beginning with *h* indicates an aspirate *h.* Phrases are alphabetized by the key word(s) in the phrase.

The following abbreviations are also used in this vocabulary: *pp.* (past participle), *inv.* (invariable), and *adj.* (adjective).

à *to, in (a city or place),* 11; **à côté de** *next to,* 12; **à la** *to, at,* 6; **A bientôt.** *See you soon.* 1; à carreaux *checked,* 10; **A demain.** *See you tomorrow.* 1; à fleurs *flowered,* 10; à la carte *pick and choose,* 3; à la française *French-style,* 1; **à la mode** *in style,* 10; à part ça *aside from that,* 11; à pois *polka dot,* 10; à propos de *in regard to, about,* 4; **A quelle heure?** *At what time?* 6; à rayures *striped,* 10; **A tout à l'heure!** *See you later!* 1; **A votre service.** *At your service; You're welcome.* 3; Et maintenant, à toi. *And now, it's your turn.* 1
l' abbaye (f.) *abbey,* 6
abîmer *to ruin,* 10
s' abonner *to subscribe;* abonnez-vous à... *subscribe to . . . ,* 3
l' abricot (m.) *apricot,* 5
abriter *to house,* 11
absent(e) *absent,* 2
accepter *to accept,* 6
accompagner *to accompany,* 4
l' accord (m.) *agreement;* Fais l'accord... *Make the agreement . . . ,* 7
l' accueil (m.) *reception, welcome,* 4
accueille (accueillir) *to welcome*
l' achat (m.) *purchase,* 3
acheter *to buy,* 9; **Achète (-moi)...** *Buy (me) . . . ,* 8; Je n'achète pas... *I don't buy / I'm not buying . . . ,* 3
l' acra de morue (m.) *cod fritter*
l' activité (f.) *activity,* 4
l' addition (f.) *check, bill,* 5; **L'addition, s'il vous plaît.** *The check, please.* 5
adhésif (-ive) *adhesive,* 3
admirer *to admire,* 7
adorable *adorable,* 7
adorer *to adore,* 1; **J'adore...** *I adore . . .* 1; J'adorerais... *I would adore . . . ,* 1
l' aérobic (f.) *aerobics,* 4; **faire de l'aérobic** *to do aerobics,* 4
l' aéroport (m.) *airport,* 11
les affaires (f.) *business, business affairs,* 8
affectueux (-euse) *affectionate,* 7
afin de *in order to,* 7
africain(e) (adj.) *African,* 8
l' Afrique (f.) *Africa,* 8
l' âge (m.) *age,* 1; **Tu as quel âge?** *How old are you?* 1
âgé(e) *older,* 7
l' agenda (m.) *planner,* 4
agit : il s'agit de *it's concerned with; it's about,* 6
agréable *pleasant,* 4
ai : J'ai... *I have . . . ,* 2; **J'ai... ans.** *I am . . . years old.* 1; **J'ai besoin de...** *I need . . . ,* 8; **J'ai faim.** *I'm hungry.* 5; **J'ai l'intention de...** *I intend to . . . ,* 11; **J'ai soif.** *I'm thirsty.* 5; **Je n'ai pas de...** *I don't have . . . ,* 3
l' aide-mémoire (m.) *memory aid,* 3
aider *to help,* 10; **(Est-ce que) je peux vous aider?** *May I help you?* 10
l' ail (m.) *garlic,* 8
les ailes (f.) *wings,* 12
aimé(e) (pp. of aimer) *loved,* 1
aimer *to like,* 1; **J'aime mieux...** *I prefer . . . ,*1; **J'aimerais... pour aller avec...** *I'd like . . . to go with . . . ,*10; **Je n'aime pas...** *I don't like . . . ,* 1; **Moi, j'aime (bien)...** *I (really) like . . . ,* 1; **Tu aimes... ?** *Do you like . . . ?* 1
l' aire de pique-nique aménagée (f.) *equipped picnic area,* 6
l' aise (f.) *ease,* 7
ajouter *to add,* 10
l' algèbre (f.) *algebra,* 2
l' Algérie (f.) *Algeria,* 0
l' alimentation (f.) *food,* 12
les aliments (m.) *nutrients,* 8
allé(e) (pp. of aller) *went,* 9; **Je suis allé(e)...** *I went . . . ,* 9; **Tu es allé(e) où?** *Where did you go?* 9
l' allée (f.) *path, driveway,* 4
l' allemand (m.) *German (language),* 2
aller *to go,* 6; **Ça va aller mieux!** *It's going to get better!* 9; **On peut y aller...** *We can go there . . . ,* 12
allez : Allez au tableau! *Go to the blackboard!* 0; **Allez, viens!** *Come along!* 0
Allô? *Hello?* 9
l' allocation de naissance (f.) *money provided as a birth allowance by the French government,* 7; l'allocation familiale (f.) *money provided by the French government to large families,* 7
allons : Allons-y! *Let's go!* 4; **Allons...** *Let's go . . . ,* 6
l' aloco (m.) *dish from West Africa made from fried plantain bananas and usually eaten as a snack,* 5
alors *well, then,* 3
l' alphabet (m.) *alphabet,* 0

l' ambiance (f.) *atmosphere,* 2
aménagé(e) *equipped,* 6
américain(e) *American* (adj.), 0
l' ami(e) *friend,* 1
amical(e) (pl. amicaux) *friendly,* 2
amicalement *sincerely (to close a letter),* 1
l' amitié (f.) *friendship,* 1
l' amour (m.) *love,* 1
l' amphithéâtre (m.) *amphitheater,* 9
amusant(e) *funny,* 7
s' amuser *to have fun,* 11; **Amuse-toi bien!** *Have fun!* 11; **Qu'est-ce que tu fais pour t'amuser?** *What do you do to have fun?* 4; **Tu t'es bien amusé(e)?** *Did you have fun?* 11
l' an (m.) *year,* 1; **J'ai... ans.** *I am . . . years old.* 1
l' ananas (m.) *pineapple,* 8
ancien(ne) *old; former,* 6; l'ancienne gare *the former train station,* 6
l' Andorre (article not commonly used) *Andorra,* 0
l' anglais (m.) *English (language),* 1
l' animal (m.) *animal,* 1; animal domestique *pet,* 7
l' animateur (m.) *camp counselor,* 11
les animations (f.) *activities,* 11
animé(e) *animated, lively,* 8
l' année (f.) *year,* 4
l' année scolaire (f.) *school year,* 2
l' anniversaire (m.) *anniversary; birthday,* 7
annoncer *to announce,* 7
les annonces (f.) *ads,* 1; les petites annonces *personal or business ads,* 1
anthracite *charcoal grey,* 10
antillais(e) (adj.) *Antillean, from the Antilles (islands in the Caribbean Sea),* 12
antique *ancient,* 9
les antiquités (f.) *antiquities, antiques,* 6
août *August,* 4; **en août** *in August,* 4
l' appareil (m.) *phone,* 9; **Qui est à l'appareil?** *Who's calling?* 9
l' appareil-photo (m.) *camera,* 11
appartient (appartenir) à *to belong to,* 9
s' appeler *to call oneself, to be called,* 1; **Il/Elle s'appelle comment?** *What's his/her name?* 1; **Il/Elle s'appelle...** *His/Her name is . . . ,* 1; **Je m'appelle...** *My name is . . . ,* 1; **Tu t'appelles comment?** *What's your name?* 1
apporter *to bring,* 9; **Apportez-moi..., s'il vous plaît.** *Please bring me . . . ,* 5
apprendre *to learn,* 0
approprié(e) *appropriate,* 7
l' aprèm (m.) *afternoon,* 2; cet aprèm *this afternoon,* 2
après *after, afterward,* 9; **Et après?** *And afterwards?* 9
l' après-guerre (m.) *post-war,* 11
l' après-midi (m.) *afternoon; in the afternoon,* 2; **l'après-midi libre** *afternoon off,* 2
l' arabe (m.) *Arabic (language),* 1
l' arbre (m.) *tree,* 12
l' archéologue (m.) *archaeologist,* 9
l' ardoise (f.) *writing slate,* 3
l' arène (f.) *amphitheater,* 9
l' argent (m.) *money,* 11
l' arôme (m.) *aroma, odor,* 8
l' arrivée (f.) *arrival,* 6
arroser *to sprinkle,* 8
l' art (m.) *art,* 1
l' article (m.) *article, item,* 8
l' artiste (m./f.) *artist,* 0
les arts plastiques (m. pl.) *art class,* 2
as : Tu as... ? *Do you have . . . ?* 3; **Tu as quel âge?** *How old are you?* 1; **De quoi est-ce que tu as besoin?** *What do you need?* 8
l' ascenseur (m.) *elevator,* 6
l' ascension (f.) *ascent, climb,* 6; ascension en haut de la tour *ascent/climb to the top of the tower,* 6
l' aspirateur (m.) *vacuum cleaner,* 7; **passer l'aspirateur** *to vacuum,* 7
l' aspirine (f.) *aspirin,* 12
Asseyez : Asseyez-vous! *Sit down!* 0
assez *enough, fairly,* 2
assis(e) *seated, sitting,* 12
assidu(e) *regular (punctual),* 2
l' assiette (f.) *plate,* 5
assuré(e) (pp. of assurer) *assured,* 1
l' athlétisme (m.) *track and field,* 4; **faire de l'athlétisme** *to do track and field,* 4
attachant(e) *loving,* 7
attendre *to wait for,* 9
Attention! *Watch out!* 7
attentivement *attentively,* 9
l' attiéké (m.) *ground manioc root,* 8
attirer *to attract,* 9
au *to, at,* 6; *to, in (before a masculine noun),* 11; **au métro...** *at the . . . metro stop,* 6; au milieu *in the middle,* 7; **au revoir** *goodbye,* 1; Au secours! *Help!* 9
l' auberge de jeunesse (f.) *youth hostel,* 11
aucun(e) *none,* 7
aujourd'hui *today,* 2
aussi *also,* 1; **Moi aussi.** *Me too.* 2
l' automne (m.) *autumn, fall,* 4; **en automne** *in the fall,* 4
autour de *around,* 8
autre *other,* 4
aux *to, in (before a plural noun),* 6
Av. (abbrev. of avenue) (f.) *avenue,* 6
avant *before,* 1
avec *with,* 1; **avec moi** *with me,* 6; **Avec qui?** *With whom?* 6
l' aventure (f.) *adventure,* 11
avez : Qu'est-ce que vous avez comme ... ? *What kind of . . . do you have?* 5; **Vous avez... ?** *Do you have . . . ?* 2
l' avion (m.) *plane,* 12; **en avion** *by plane,* 12, **un billet d'avion** *plane ticket,* 11
l' avis (m.) *opinion,* 9; **A ton avis, qu'est-ce que je fais?** *In your opinion, what do I do?* 9
l' avocat (m.) *avocado,* 8
avoir *to have,* 2; **avoir faim** *to be hungry,* 5; avoir hâte de *to be in a hurry (to do something),* 7; avoir la flemme *to be lazy,* 9; avoir lieu *to take place,* 7; avoir raison *to be right,* 2; **avoir soif** *to be thirsty,* 5
avons : Nous avons... *We have . . . ,* 2
avril April, 4; **en avril** *in April,* 4
ayant : ayant pu donner *having been able to give,* 2

B

le baby (foot) *table soccer game,* 5
le bac(calauréat) *secondary school exam for entering a university,* 2
le bachelier *someone who has passed the* **bac,** 2
le bagage *luggage,* 10
la baguette *long, thin loaf of bread,* 12
la baie *bay*
la balade à cheval *horseback ride,* 7
se balader *to stroll,* 6
le balcon *balcony,* 12
le ballon *ball,* 4
le bambou *bamboo,* 12
la banane *banana,* 8
le banc *(park) bench,* 12
les bandes dessinées (f.) *comic strips,* 2
la banque *bank,* 12
barbant(e) *boring,* 2
le base-ball *baseball,* 4; **jouer au base-ball** *to play baseball,* 4
le basilic *basil,* 5
le basket(-ball) *basketball,* 4; **jouer au basket(-ball)** *to play basketball,* 4
les baskets (f.) *sneakers,* 3
le bateau *boat,* 11; **en bateau** *by boat,* 12; **faire du bateau** *to go boating,* 11
le bateau-mouche *river boat,* 6
le bâtiment *building,* 12
bd (abbrev. of boulevard) (m.) *boulevard,* 6

beau (belle) *nice, pretty,* 4; **Il fait beau.** *It's nice weather.* 4
Beaucoup *A lot.* 4; **Oui, beaucoup.** *Yes, very much.* 2; **Pas beaucoup.** *Not very much.* 4
le beau-père *stepfather; father-in-law,* 7
le bébé *baby,* 7
belge *Belgian* (adj.), 1
la Belgique *Belgium,* 0
la belle-mère *stepmother; mother-in-law,* 7
le besoin *need,* 8; **De quoi est-ce que tu as besoin?** *What do you need?* 8; **J'ai besoin de...** *I need . . . ,* 8
la bête *animal,* 12
le beurre *butter,* 8
la bibliothèque *library,* 6
le bic *ballpoint pen,* 3
bien *well,* 1; **Je veux bien.** *Gladly.* 8; **Je veux bien.** *I'd really like to.* 6; **J'en veux bien.** *I'd like some.* 8; **Moi, j'aime (bien)...** *I (really) like . . . ,* 1; **Très bien.** *Very well.* 1
Bien sûr. *Of course.* 3; *certainly,* 9; **Oui, bien sûr.** *Yes, of course.* 7
bientôt *soon,* 1; **A bientôt.** *See you soon.* 1
Bienvenue! *Welcome!* 0
le bien-vivre *good living, the good life,* 6
le bifteck *steak,* 8
les bijoux (m.) *jewelry,* 10
le billet *ticket,* 11; **un billet d'avion** *plane ticket,* 11; **un billet de train** *train ticket,* 11
la biologie *biology,* 2
bizarre *strange,* 7
blanc(he) *white,* 3
le blanc-manger *coconut pudding*
bleu(e) *blue,* 3; bleu clair *light blue,* 10; bleu foncé *dark blue,* 10
blond(e) *blond,* 7
le blouson *jacket,* 10
le bœuf *beef,* 8
Bof! *(expression of indifference),* 1
boire *to drink,* 5; **Qu'est-ce qu'il y a à boire?** *What is there to drink?* 5
le bois *wood,* 12
la boisson *drink, beverage,* 5; **Qu'est-ce que vous avez comme boissons?** *What do you have to drink?* 5
la boîte *box, can,* 8; **une boîte de** *a can of,* 8
le bon *coupon,* 6
bon(ne) *good,* 5; **Bon courage!** *Good luck!* 2; **Bon voyage!** *Have a good trip!* 11; **Bon, d'accord.** *Well, OK.* 8; de bons conseils *good advice,* 1; **Oui, très bon.** *Yes, very good.* 9; **pas bon** *not good,* 5
Bonjour *Hello,* 1
bonne (f. of **bon**) *good,* 5; **Bonne chance!** *Good luck!* 11; **Bonne idée.** *Good idea.* 4; **Bonnes vacances!** *Have a good vacation!* 11
le bord *side, edge;* **au bord de la mer** *to/on the coast,* 11
les bottes (f.) *boots,* 10
les boucles d'oreilles (f.) *earrings,* 10
le boudin créole *spicy Creole sausage,* 12
bouger *to move,* 10
bouillant(e) *boiling,* 8
la boulangerie *bakery,* 12
la boule *ball,* 8
la boum *party,* 6; **aller à une boum** *to go to a party,* 6
le bouquiniste *bookseller who has a stand along the Seine River in Paris,* 5
la bouteille *bottle,* 8; **une bouteille de** *a bottle of,* 8
la boutique *store, shop,* 3; une boutique de souvenirs *souvenir shop,* 3
le bracelet *bracelet,* 3
la Bretagne *Brittany (region of northwest France),* 7
la brioche *brioche, light, slightly sweet bread made with a rich yeast dough,* 8
la brochure *brochure,* 4
la broderie *embroidery,* 10
brun(e) *brunette,* 7
le bulletin trimestriel *report card,* 2
le bureau *office, desk,* 8; bureau de tabac *newsstand,* 9
le bus *bus,* 12; **en bus** *by bus,* 12, **rater le bus** *to miss the bus,* 9
la buvette *refreshment stand,* 12
byzantin(e) *Byzantine; of the style of art and architecture developed in Eastern Europe between the 4th and 15th centuries (characterized by domes and elaborate mosaics),* 12

C'est... *It's . . . ,* 2; **C'est...** *This is . . . ,* 7; C'est qui? *Who is it?* 2; **C'est combien?** *How much is it?* 3; C'est du gâteau. *It's a piece of cake.* 8; C'est pas de la tarte. *It's not easy.* 8; C'est tout. *That's all.* 1; **Ça, c'est...** *This/That is . . . ,* 12; **Non, c'est impossible.** *No, that's impossible.* 7
C'était barbant! *It was boring!* 11
ça *that; it;* Ça boume? *How's it going?* 2; **Ça va.** *Fine.* 1; **Ça va?** *How are things going?* 1; **Ça, c'est...** *This/That is . . . ,* 12; Ça m'est égal *It doesn't matter; I don't care.* 10; **Ça ne me dit rien.** *That doesn't interest me.* 4; *I don't feel like it.* 6; ça suffit *that's enough,* 12; **Et après ça...** *And after that, . . . ,* 9; **Oui, ça a été.** *Yes, it was fine.* 9
ça fait : Ça fait combien, s'il vous plaît? *How much is it, please?* 5;
la cabine téléphonique *phone booth,* 9
le cabinet de toilette *small room with a sink and counter,* 11
caché(e) (pp. of cacher) *hidden,* 11
le cadeau *gift,* 11
le café *coffee, café,* 5; le café au lait *coffee with hot milk,* 8; le café crème *coffee with cream,* 5
le cahier *notebook,* 0
la calculatrice *calculator,* 3; une calculatrice-traductrice *translating calculator,* 3
le caleçon *leggings,* 4
le calendrier *calendar,* 6
la Californie *California,* 4
le camarade (la camarade) *friend;* camarade de classe *classmate,* 7
le camembert *Camembert cheese,* 5
le caméscope *camcorder,* 4
le camp de sport *sports camp,* 9
la campagne *countryside,* 11; **à la campagne** *to/in the country-side,* 11
le camping *camping,* 11; **faire du camping** *to go camping,* 11
le Canada *Canada,* 4
le canal *channel,* 3
le canari *canary,* 7
le caniveau *sidewalk gutter,* 7
la cantine *cafeteria,* 9; **à la cantine** *at the school cafeteria,* 9
la capitale *capital,* 5
car *because,* 4
la caractéristique *characteristic,* 8
la carambole *star fruit,* 12
la carcasse *body,* 12
le cardigan *sweater,* 10
le carnaval *carnival,* 11
la carotte *carrot,* 8
la carrière *quarry,* 11
la carte *map,* 0; *menu,* 12; à la carte *pick and choose,* 3; **La carte, s'il vous plaît.** *The menu, please.* 5
les cartes (f.) *cards,* 4; **jouer aux cartes** *to play cards,* 4
la cartouche *cartridge,* 3; cartouche d'encre *ink cartridge,* 3
le carvi *cumin* (Afrique), 8; graines de carvi *cumin seeds,* 8
la casquette *cap,* 10
la cassette *cassette tape,* 3
la cassette vidéo *videocassette,* 4
le catalogue *catalog,* 10
la catégorie *category,* 8
la cathédrale *cathedral,* 1
le cauchemar *nightmare,* 11; **C'était un véritable cauchemar!** *It was a real nightmare!* 11

ce *this; that,* 3; **Ce sont...** *These/Those are . . . ,* 7
la ceinture *belt,* 10
célèbre *famous, well-known,* 4
cent *one hundred,* 3; **deux cents** *two hundred,* 3
la centaine *a hundred or so;* des centaines d'années *hundreds of years,* 9
le centre *center,* 4
le centre commercial *mall,* 6
le centre-ville *city center,* 12
cependant *however,* 11
le cercle *circle, group,* 6; au cercle français *at French Club,* 4
certain(e) *certain, some,* 7
ces *these, those,* 3
cet *this, that,* 3
cette *this; that,* 3
chacun *each (person),* 5; Chacun ses goûts! *To each his own!* 1
la chaise *chair,* 0
chaleureux (-euse) *warm,* 9
la chambre *room,* 7; **ranger ta chambre** *to pick up your room,* 7
le champignon *mushroom,* 8
la chance *luck,* 11; **Bonne chance!** *Good luck!* 11
le changement *change,* 10
changer *to change,* 7
chanter *to sing,* 9
le chanteur *singer (male),* 9
la chanteuse *singer (female),* 9
Chantilly : la crème Chantilly *sweetened whipped cream,* 5
le chapeau *hat,* 10
le chapitre *chapter,* 9
chaque *each,* 4
chargé(e) *busy,* 2
le chariot *shopping cart,* 8
la chasse *hunting,* 7; une chasse au trésor *treasure hunt,* 3
le chat *cat,* 7
le chaton *kitten,* 7
chaud(e) *hot,* 4; **Il fait chaud.** *It's hot.* 4
chauffé(e) *heated,* 11
les chaussettes (f.) *socks,* 10
les chaussures (f.) *shoes,* 10; les chaussures à crampons *spikes,* 4
le chef-d'œuvre *masterpiece,* 6
la chemise *shirt (man's),* 10
la chemise *folder,* 3
le chemisier *shirt (woman's),* 10
le chèque *check,* 0
cher (chère) *dear,* 1; *expensive,* 3; **C'est trop cher.** *It's too expensive.* 10
chercher *to look for,* 9; **Je cherche quelque chose pour...** *I'm looking for something for . . . ,* 10
chéri(e) (noun) mon chéri/ma chérie *darling, sweetie,* 8
le cheval *horse,* 12; le cheval de bois *wooden horse, carousel horse,* 12
chez... *to/at . . . 's house,* 6; **chez le disquaire** *at the record store,* 12; **Je suis bien chez... ?** *Is this . . . 's house?* 9
chic *chic,* 10
le chien *dog,* 7; **promener le chien** *to walk the dog,* 7
le chiffre *number,* 0
la chimie *chemistry,* 2
chimique *chemical,* 9
le chocolat *chocolate,* 1; **un chocolat** *hot chocolate,* 5
la chocolaterie *chocolate shop,* 12
choisi (pp. of choisir) *decided, chosen;* **Vous avez choisi?** *Have you decided/chosen?* 5
choisir *to choose, to pick,* 10
le choix *choice,* 8
la chorale *choir,* 2
la chose *thing,* 5; **J'ai des tas de choses (trucs) à faire.** *I have lots of things to do.* 5
le chou *cabbage,* 1; mon chou *my darling, dear,* 1
chouette *cool,* 9; **Très chouette.** *Very cool.* 9
chrétien(ne) *Christian,* 9
la chute *waterfall,* 4
ci-dessous *below,* 8
le cimetière *cemetery,* 9
le cinéma *movie theater,* 6; *movies,* 1
cinq *five,* 9
cinquième *fifth,* 9
la Cité des Papes *monument in Avignon, France; a citadel of palaces where French popes lived and ruled in the 14th century,* 11
le citron *lemon,* 8
le citron pressé *lemonade,* 5
clair(e) *light (color),* 10
le classeur *loose-leaf binder,* 3
classique *classical,* 4
le client (la cliente) *customer,* 5
le climat *climate,* 11
climatisé(e) *air-conditioned,* 11
le clocher *steeple,* 12
le club *club,* 11
le coca *cola,* 5
le coco *coconut,* 8
le code de la route *rules of the road; test,* 12
le cœur *heart,* 9
le coin *corner,* 12; **au coin de** *on the corner of,* 12
le col *collar,* 10; au col montant *with turtleneck,* 10
le collant *hose,* 10
la colle *glue,* 3; un pot de colle *container of glue,* 3
la collection *collection,* 10
le collège *junior high school,* 2
la colonie de vacances *summer camp,* 11
coloré(e) *colorful,* 8
le coloris *color, shade,* 3
combien *how much, how many,* 3; **C'est combien,... ?** *How much is . . . ?* 5; **C'est combien?** *How much is it?* 3; **Ça fait combien, s'il vous plaît?** *How much is it, please?* 5
le combiné *(telephone) receiver,* 9
comique *comic, comical;* un film comique *comedy (movie),* 6
commander *to order,* 5
comme *like, as,* 4; **Comme ci comme ça.** *So-so.* 1; Qu'est-ce qu'ils aiment comme cours? *What subjects do they like?* 2; **Qu'est-ce que tu fais comme sport?** *What sports do you play?* 4; **Qu'est-ce que vous avez comme... ?** *What kind of . . . do you have?* 5
le commencement *beginning,* 9
commencer *to begin, to start,* 9
comment *what,* 0; *how,* 1; **(Comment) ça va?** *How's it going?* 1; Comment dit-on? *How do you say it?* 1; Comment le dire? How should you say it? 1; **Comment tu trouves... ?** *What do you think of . . . ?* 2; **Comment tu trouves ça?** *What do you think of that/it?* 2; **Il/Elle est comment?** *What is he/she like?* 7; **Ils/Elles sont comment?** *What are they like?* 7; **Tu t'appelles comment?** *What is your name?* 0
le commentaire *commentary,* 9
le commerçant *store owner,* 8
la Communauté financière africaine (CFA) *African Financial Community; the group of African countries that share a common currency (the CFA franc),* 3
la compagnie aérienne (f.) *airline company,* 10
le compagnon *companion,* 7
comparer *to compare,* 10
le compas *compass,* 3
compétent(e) *competent,* 2
compléter *to complete,* 4
le compliment *compliment,* 10
comprends : Tu comprends? *Do you understand?* 2
compris(e) *included,* 5
compris (pp. of comprendre): Tu as compris? *Did you understand?* 1
le concert *concert,* 1
le concombre *cucumber,* 8
conçu(e) (pp. of concevoir) *conceived,* 9
confier *to confide,* 9
la confiture *jam,* 8
connais : Tu les connais? *Do you know them?* 0; Tu connais ces nombres? *Do you recognize these numbers?* 2

la connaissance *acquaintance;* Faisons connaissance! *Let's get acquainted.* 1
connu(e) (pp. of connaître) *knew; known;* le plus connu *the best-known* (adj.), 6
le conseil *advice,* 1; de bons conseils *good advice,* 1; demander conseil *to ask for advice,* 11
conseiller *to advise, to counsel;* **Qu'est-ce que tu me conseilles?** *What do you advise me to do?* 9
le conseiller *adviser,* 12
la conseillère *adviser,* 12
conservé (pp. of conserver) *kept,* 2; ce bulletin doit être conservé(e) *this report card must be kept,* 2; *preserved (food);* c'est plus sûr et bien conservé *it's safer and better preserved,* 8
consoler *to console (someone), to make (someone) feel better, to comfort,* 9
construit(e) (pp. of construire) *constructed, built,* 9
contenir *to contain,* 9
content(e) *happy, pleased,* 7
le contenu *contents,* 8
continuer *to continue,* 12; **Vous continuez jusqu'au prochain feu rouge.** *You keep going until the next light.* 12
le contraste *contrast,* 8
contraster *to contrast,* 8
contre *against,* 2
la conversation *conversation,* 7
cool *cool,* 2
le copain (la copine) *friend,* 1
le cordon *cord, string;* le cordon de serrage *drawstring,* 10
le cornichon *pickle,* 8
le corps *body,* 8
correct(e) *correct, proper,* 9
le correspondant (la correspondante) *pen pal,* 1
correspondre *to write; to correspond,* 1; Fais correspondre... *Match . . . ,* 6
la corvée ménagère *household chore,* 7
le costume *costume, traditional dress,* 9
la côte *coast,* 11
le côté *side;* **à côté de** *next to,* 12; du côté de mon père *on my father's side (of the family),* 7
le coton *cotton,* 10; **en coton** *(made of) cotton,* 10
la couleur *color,* 3; **De quelle couleur est... ?** *What color is . . . ?* 3
le coup *hit, blow;* le coup de fil *phone call,* 9
la coupe *dish(ful),* 5
la coupe Melba *vanilla ice cream, peaches, whipped cream, and fruit sauce,* 5

courir *to run,* 7
le cours *course,* 2; **le cours de développement personnel et social (DPS)** *health,* 2; **Tu as quels cours... ?** *What classes do you have . . . ?* 2
les courses (f.) *shopping, errands,* 7; **faire les courses** *to do the shopping,* 7; **J'ai des courses à faire.** *I have errands to do.* 5
court(e) *short (length),* 10
le cousin *male cousin,* 7
la cousine *female cousin,* 7
coûteux (-euse) *expensive,* 8
le crabe *crab,* 5; les crabes farcis *deviled land crabs,* 9
la cravate *tie,* 10
le crayon *pencil,* 3; des crayons de couleur *colored pencils,* 3
créer *to create,* 11
la crème fraîche *thick cream like sour cream but without the sour flavor; used to make sauces and toppings,* 5
le créole *creole language,* 12
la crêpe *very thin pancake,* 5
la crêperie *café or restaurant which specializes in crêpes,* 5
crépiter *to crackle,* 12
le creuset *melting pot;* le creuset de l'Afrique *the melting pot of Africa,* 8
croire *to believe;* Tu crois? *Do you think so?* 10
la croisière *cruise,* 11
le croissant *croissant; flaky, buttery roll eaten at breakfast,* 5
la croissanterie *croissant shop,* 12
le croque-monsieur *toasted ham and cheese sandwich,* 5
cru(e) *uncooked,* 5
le cuir *leather,* 10; **en cuir** *(made of) leather,* 10
cuire *to cook, to bake,* 8
la culture *culture,* 7
culturel(le) *cultural,* 0

D'abord, ... *First, . . . ,* 9
D'accord. *O.K.* 4; **Bon, d'accord.** *Well, O.K.* 8; **D'accord, si tu... d'abord...** *O.K, if you . . . , first.* 7; **Tu es d'accord?** *Is that O.K. with you?* 7
d 'après *according to,* 4
d'habitude *usually,* 4
dans *in,* 6
danser *to dance,* 1
la danse *dance,* 2
le danseur (la danseuse) *dancer,* 9
de *from,* 0; *of,* 0; **de l'** *some,* 8; **de la** *some,* 8; **Je n'ai pas de...** *I don't have . . . ,* 3; **Je ne fais pas de...** *I don't play/do . . . ,* 4
déambuler *to stroll,* 11
débarrasser la table *to clear the table,* 7
le débutant (la débutante) *beginner,* 4
décaféiné(e) *decaffeinated,* 5
décédé(e) *deceased,* 7
décembre *December,* 4; **en décembre** *in December,* 4
le décès *death,* 7
déchiffrer *to decode,* 7
décider *to decide,* 5; **Vous avez décidé de prendre... ?** *Have you decided to take . . . ?* 10
décontracté(e) *relaxed,* 11
la découverte *discovery,* 3
découvrir *to discover,* 8
décrire *to describe,* 7
décrocher *to take down; to unhook;* quand l'interlocuteur décroche *when the speaker picks up (the phone),* 9
dedans *inside,* 3
défavorable *unfavorable, disapproving,* 7
dégoûtant(e) *gross,* 5
dehors *outside,* 8
déjà *already,* 9
déjeuner *to have lunch,* 9; **le déjeuner** *lunch,* 2
délicieux (-euse) *delicious,* 5
délirer *to be delirious;* La techno me fait délirer. *I'm wild about techno music.* 1
délivré(e) (pp. of delivrer) : il n'en sera pas délivré de duplicata *duplicates will not be issued,* 2
le deltaplane *hang-glider;* faire du deltaplane *to go hang-gliding,* 4
demain *tomorrow,* 2; **A demain.** *See you tomorrow.* 1
demander *to ask, to ask for,* 7; demander conseil *to ask for advice,* 11
demi(e) *half;* **et demi** *half past (after* **midi** *and* **minuit***),* 6; **et demie** *half past,* 6
le demi-frère *stepbrother,* 7; *half-brother,* 7
la demi-sœur *stepsister,* 7; *half-sister,* 7
démodé(e) *out of style,* 10
démonté(e) *dismantled,* 12
le dentiste (la dentiste) *dentist,* 1
le départ *departure,* 6
le département d'outre-mer *overseas department,* 12
dépêchez : Dépêchez-vous de... *hurry up and . . . ,* 1
déplorable *deplorable,* 2
déposer *to deposit,* 12
déprimé(e) *depressed,* 9

depuis *for (a certain amount of time),* 9; *since,* 12
le dérivé *derivative, by-product;* le sucre et ses dérivés *sugar and its by-products,* 8
dernier (-ière) *last;* la semaine dernière *last week,* 9
derrière *behind,* 12
des *some,* 3
les dés (m.) *dice;* découper en dés *to dice,* 8
dès que *as soon as,* 9
désagréable *unpleasant,* 4
la description *description,* 7
désirer *to desire, to want;* **Vous désirez?** *What would you like?* 10
désolé(e) : Désolé(e), je suis occupé(e). *Sorry, I'm busy.* 6; **Désolé(e), mais je ne peux pas.** *Sorry, but I can't.* 4
le dessert *dessert,* 0
le dessin *drawing,* 3
le détail *detail,* 9
détailler *to slice,* 8
détester *to hate, to detest,* 6
deux *two,* 0; les deux *both,* 7
la deuxième étape *second step,* 1
devant *in front of,* 6
devenir *to become,* 9
devez : vous devez *you must,* 11
deviennent : Que deviennent... ? *What happened to . . . ?* 7
deviner *to guess,* 7; Devine! *Guess!* 0
devoir *to have to, must,* 7
les devoirs (m.) *homework,* 2; **J'ai des devoirs à faire.** *I've got homework to do.* 5
le dévouement *devotion,* 7
devrais : Tu devrais... *You should . . . ,* 9
la diapo(sitive) *photographic slide,* 11
la dictée *dictation,* 0
le dictionnaire *dictionary,* 3
la différence *difference,* 2
différent(e) *different,* 7
difficile *difficult,* 2
dimanche *Sunday,* 2; **le dimanche** *on Sundays,* 2
dîner *to have dinner,* 9; **le dîner** *dinner,* 8
dingue *crazy,* 1; Je suis dingue de... *I'm crazy about . . . ,* 1
dire *to say;* 1; *to tell,* 9; Comment le dire? *How should you say it?* 1; Dis,... *Say, . . . ,* 2; **Ça ne me dit rien.** *That doesn't interest me.* 4; Comment dit-on... ? *How do you say . . . ?* 1; Jacques a dit... *Simon says . . . ,* 0; Qu'est-ce qu'on se dit? *What are they saying to themselves?* 2; **Vous pouvez lui dire que j'ai téléphoné?** *Can you tell her/him that I called?* 9
direct(e) *direct;* en direct *live,* 7
la direction *direction,* 12
la discothèque *dance club,* 6
discuter *to discuss,* 7; Ne discute pas! *Don't argue!* 3
disponible *available,* 8
le disquaire *record store,* 12; **chez le disquaire** *at the record store,* 12
le disque compact/CD *compact disc/CD,* 3
distant(e) *distant,* 2
la distribution *cast (of a movie, play, etc.),* 1; une distribution étincelante *a brilliant cast,* 1
divers(e) *various,* 3
le document *document,* 7
dois : Non, tu dois... *No, you've got to . . . ,* 7
le dolmen *dolmen,* 1
le dom-tom *abbreviation of* départements et territoires d'outre-mer; *overseas departments and territories of France such as Martinique and Réunion,* 3
domestique : animal domestique *pet,* 7
le domicile *place of residence,* 4
la domination *domination,* 9
dominer *to tower over,* 12
dommage *too bad,* 10
donc *so, therefore,* 11
donner *to give,* 5; **Donnez-moi..., s'il vous plaît.** *Please give me . . . ,* 5
donner sur *to overlook,* 11
dont *of which,* 7
dormir *to sleep,* 1
le dos *back,* 12; **un sac à dos** *backpack,* 3
doucement *gently,* 12
la douche *shower,* 11; avec douche ou bains *with shower or bath,* 11
doué(e) *gifted, talented,* 2
la douzaine *dozen,* 8; **une douzaine de** *a dozen,* 8
les draps (m.) *linens, sheets,* 11
dressé(e) *pointed,* 7
droit(e) *straight,* 10
la droite *right (direction);* **à droite (de)** *to the right,* 12
du *some,* 8
le duplicata (inv.) *duplicate;* il n'en sera pas délivré de duplicata *duplicates will not be issued,* 2
durable *long-lasting,* 11
durcir *to harden,* 8
la durée *duration,* 7
durer *to last,* 11

l' **eau** (f.) *water,* 5; **l'eau minérale** *mineral water,* 5; **le sirop de fraise (à l'eau)** *water with strawberry syrup,* 5
s' ébattre *to frolic,* 7
l' échange (m.) *exchange,* 7; en échange de *in exchange for,* 7
l' échantillon (m.) *sample,* 2
l' écharpe (f.) *scarf,* 10
l' échelle (f.) *scale,* 6
s' éclater *to have fun, to have a ball,* 4
l' école (f.) *school,* 1; A l'école *At school,* 0
l' écolier (m.), l'écolière (f.) *schoolboy/schoolgirl,* 3
l' économie (f.) *economics,* 2
écouter *to listen,* 1; Ecoute! *Listen!* 0; **écouter de la musique** *to listen to music,* 1; **Ecoutez!** *Listen!* 0; **Je t'écoute.** *I'm listening.* 9
l' écran (m.) *screen,* 11
l' écrin (m.) *case,* 6
écrire *to write,* 2; Ecris-moi. *Write me.* 1
écris : Ecris cinq phrases... *Write five sentences . . . ,* 12
l' édifice (m.) *edifice, building,* 6
l' éducation physique et sportive (EPS) (f.) *physical education,* 2; l'éducation civique et morale (f.) *civics class,* 2
efficace *efficient,* 9
égrener *to shell,* 8
égyptien(ne) *Egyptian* (adj.), 6
Eh bien... *Umm . . . (expression of hesitation),* 5
élastique *elastic* (adj.), 3
élémentaire *elementary; basic,* 8
l' éléphant (m.) *elephant,* 0
l' élève (m./f.) *student,* 2
l' emballage (m.) *packaging,* 9
embêtant(e) *annoying,* 7
émincer *to slice thinly,* 8
l' émission (f.) *TV program,* 4
empêche (empêcher) *to prevent, to keep from doing,* 2
l' emploi *use, job;* un emploi du temps *schedule,* 2
emprunter *to borrow,* 12
en *in,* 1; **en** *some, of it, of them, any, none,* 8; **en** *to, in (before a feminine country),* 11; **en coton** *(made of) cotton,* 10; **en cuir** *(made of) leather,* 10; en français *in French,* 1; **en jean** *(made of) denim,* 10; en retard *late,* 2; en solde *on sale,* 10; **en vacances** *on vacation,* 4; **Je n'en veux plus.** *I don't want anymore,* 8; **Oui, j'en veux bien.** *Yes, I'd like some.* 8; Qu'en penses-tu? *What do you think (about it)?* 1; **Vous avez ça en... ?** *Do you have that in . . . ? (size, fabric, color),* 10
encore *again, more;* **Encore de... ?** *More. . . ?* 8; *still,* 9

encourager *to encourage,* 8
l' **endroit** (m.) *place,* 12
énerver *to annoy,* 2
l' **enfant** (m./f.) *child,* 7; l'enfant unique *only child,* 7
enfin *finally,* 9
enjoué(e) *playful,* 7
ennuyer *to bore,* 2
ennuyeux (-euse) *boring,* 11; **C'était ennuyeux.** *It was boring,* 11
l' enquête (f.) *survey,* 1
l' enseignement (m.) *teaching,* 2
ensemble *together,* 4
l' ensemble (m.) *collection, ensemble,* 3
ensuite : Ensuite, ... *Next,/Then, . . . ,* 9
entendre *to hear;* s'entendre avec *to get along with,* 7
Entendu. *Agreed.* 6
entendu dire que : Il a entendu dire que... *He heard that . . . ,* 12
l' enthousiasme (m.) *enthusiasm,* 2
entier (-ière) *whole, entire;* le monde entier *all over the world,* 1
entrant *entering,* 2
entre *between,* 12
l' entrée (f.) *entry, entrance;* Entrée libre *"Browsers welcomed,"* 3
l' enveloppe (f.) *envelope,* 12
l' envie (f.) *desire; need;* **J'ai envie de...** *I feel like . . . ,* 11
les environs (m. pl.) *surroundings,* 9
s' envoler *to fly away,* 12
envoyer *to send,* 12; **envoyer des lettres** *to send letters,* 12
l' épi (m.) *ear (of a plant),* 8; l'épi de maïs *ear of corn,* 8
l' épicerie (f.) *grocery store,* 12
éplucher *to clean, to peel,* 8
l' éponge (f.) *sponge,* 3
épouvantable *terrible, horrible,* 9; **C'était épouvantable.** *It was horrible.* 9
l' EPS (l'éducation physique et sportive) *gym class,* 3
l' équipe interscolaire (f.) *school team,* 4
l' équitation (f.) *horseback riding,* 1; **faire de l'équitation** *to go horseback riding,* 1
es : Tu es d'accord? *Is that OK with you?* 7
l' escale (f.) *docking (of a boat),* 11
l' escalier (m.) *staircase,* 6
les escargots (m.) *snails,* 1
l' espace (m.) *space, area,* 7
l' espagnol (m.) *Spanish (language),* 2
espère : J'espère que oui. *I hope so.* 1
l' espoir (m.) *hope,* 7
essayer *to try; to try on,* 10; **Je peux essayer... ?** *Can I try on . . . ?* 10; **Je peux l'/les essayer?** *Can I try it/them on?* 10
est : Il/Elle est... *He/She is . . . ,* 7; **Quelle heure est-il?** *What time is it?* 6; **Qui est à l'appareil?** *Who's calling?* 9
Est-ce que *(Introduces a yes-or-no question),* 4; **(Est-ce que) je peux... ?** *May I . . . ?* 7
et *and,* 1; **Et après ça...** *And after that, . . . ,* 9; **Et toi?** *And you?* 1
l' étage (m.) *floor, story (of a building),* 6
était : C'était épouvantable. *It was horrible.* 9
étaler *to spread,* 8
l' étape (f.) *part,* 1; première étape *first part,* 1; deuxième étape *second part,* 1; troisième étape *third part,* 1
l' état (m.) *state,* 0
les Etats-Unis (m. pl.) United States, 0
l' été (m.) *summer,* 4; **en été** *in the summer,* 4
été (pp. of être) *was,* 9
étincelant(e) *brilliant,* 1
étoilé(e) *starry,* 12
étonné(e) (pp. of étonner) *surprised,* 7
étranger (-ère) *foreign,* 11
l' étranger (m.) *foreign countries;* à l'étranger *abroad,* 11
être *to be,* 7; **C'est...** *This is . . . ,* 7; **Ce sont...** *These (those) are . . . ,* 7; **Elle est...** *She is . . . ,* 7; **Il est...** *He is . . . ,* 7; **Il est...** *It is . . . (time),* 6; **Ils/Elles sont...** *They're . . . ,* 7; **Oui, ça a été.** *Yes, it was fine.* 9
l' étude (f.) *study hall,* 2
l' étudiant(e) (m./f.) *student,* 0
étudier *to study,* 1
eu (pp. of avoir) *had, got,* 9
l' euro *European Community monetary unit,* 3; Ça fait... euros./C'est... euros. *It's . . . euros.* 5
l' Europe (f.) *Europe,* 0
l' événement (m.) *event,* 9
évident(e) *evident, obvious,* 12
évider *to scoop out,* 8
éviter *to avoid,* 9
exactement *exactly,* 9
l' examen (m.) *exam,* 1; **passer un examen** *to take a test,* 9
excellent(e) *excellent,* 5; **Oui, excellent.** *Yes, excellent.* 9
excusez : Excusez-moi. *Excuse me.* 3
exemplaire *exemplary,* 7
l' explication (f.) *explanation,* 12
expliquer *to explain,* 7
l' exposition (f.) *exhibit,* 12
l' expression (f.) *expression,* 1

la face *face, side;* **en face de** *across from,* 12
facile *easy,* 2
la façon *way, manner,* 10
la faim *hunger;* **avoir faim** *to be hungry,* 5; **Non, merci. Je n'ai plus faim.** *No thanks. I'm not hungry anymore.* 8
faire *to do, to make, to play,* 4; **Désolé(e), j'ai des devoirs à faire.** *Sorry, I have homework to do.* 5; **J'ai des courses à faire.** *I have errands to do.* 5; **Qu'est-ce que tu vas faire... ?** *What are you going to do . . . ?* 6; **Tu vas faire quoi... ?** *What are you going to do . . . ?* 6; **faire de l'équitation** *to go horseback riding,* 1; faire de la course *to race (running),* 4; faire de la gymnastique *to do gymnastics,* 4; faire des haltères *to lift weights,* 4; **faire du bateau** *to go sailing,* **faire du sport** *to play sports,* 1; faire du surf *to surf,* 4; faire la cuisine *to cook, do the cooking,* 8; **faire la vaisselle** *to do the dishes,* 7; **faire le ménage** *to do housework,* 1; faire les boutiques *to go shopping,* 1; **faire les courses** *to do the shopping,* 7; **faire les magasins** *to go shopping,* 1; **faire les vitrines** *to window-shop,* 6; **faire un pique-nique** *to have a picnic,* 6; **faire une promenade** *to go for a walk,* 6
fais : A ton avis, qu'est-ce que je fais? *In your opinion, what do I do?* 9; Fais-moi... *Make me . . . ,* 3; **Je fais...** *I play/do . . . ,* 4; **Ne t'en fais pas!** *Don't worry!* 9; **Qu'est-ce que tu fais comme sport?** *What sports do you play?* 4; **Qu'est-ce que tu fais pour t'amuser?** *What do you do to have fun?* 4; **Qu'est-ce que tu fais... ?** *What do you do . . . ?* 4
faisons : Faisons connaissance! *Let's get acquainted.* 1
fait : Quel temps fait-il? *What's the weather like?* 4; **Il fait beau.** *It's nice weather.* 4; **Il fait chaud.** *It's hot.* 4; **Il fait frais.** *It's cool.* 4; **Il fait froid.** *It's cold.* 4
fait (pp. of faire) *done, made,* 9; **J'ai fait...** *I did/made . . . ,* 9; **Qu'est-ce que tu as fait?** *What did you do?* 9
la famille *family,* 7
la fantaisie *fancy,* 10
le fantôme *ghost,* 0

la farine *flour,* 8
le fast-food *fast-food restaurant,* 6
favorable *favorable, approving,* 7
favori(te) *favorite,* 12
faut : Il me faut... *I need . . . ,* 3; **Qu'est-ce qu'il te faut pour... ?** *What do you need for . . . ? (informal),* 3; **Qu'est-ce qu'il te faut?** *What do you need?* 8; **Qu'est-ce qu'il vous faut pour... ?** *What do you need for . . . ? (formal),* 3
le fauve *wildcat,* 6
faux (fausse) *false,* 2
les féculents (m.) *starches,* 8
la féerie *extravaganza,* 11
la femme *wife,* 7
la fenêtre *window,* 0
le fer forgé *wrought iron,* 12
ferai : je me ferai une joie de... *I'll gladly . . . ,* 1
fermez : Fermez la porte. *Close the door.* 0
le festival *festival,* 9
la fête *party,* 1; faire la fête *to live it up,* 1
fêter *to celebrate,* 7
le feu *fire,* 12
le feu rouge *traffic light,* 12; **Vous continuez jusqu'au prochain feu rouge.** *You keep going until the next light.* 12
la feuille *sheet; leaf;* **une feuille de papier** *sheet of paper,* 0
le feutre *marker,* 3
février *February,* 4; **en février** *in February,* 4
la fidélité *loyalty,* 7
le fil *cord, thread;* sans fil *cordless,* 9
le filet *a type of net or mesh bag,* 3
la fille *girl,* 0; **la fille** *daughter,* 7
le film *movie,* 6; **voir un film** *to see a movie,* 6; un film d'aventures *adventure film,* 1
le fils *son,* 7; fils-à-papa *daddy's boy,* 10
la fin *end,* 4
finalement *finally,* 9
fistuleux (-euse) *hollow,* 11
le flamant *flamingo;* flamant rose *pink flamingo,* 9
la flamme *flame,* 12
le flanc *side, flank,* 12
la fleur *flower,* 1
le fleuve *river,* 9
le flipper *pinball,* 5
la flûte *flute,* 0
la fois *time;* **une fois par semaine** *once a week,* 4
folklorique *folkloric, traditional,* 11
follement *madly,* 1
foncé(e) *dark (color),* 10
fonder *to found,* 9
la fontaine *fountain,* 12
le foot *soccer,* 4
le football *soccer,* 1; **le football américain** *football,* 4; **jouer au foot(ball)** *to play soccer,* 4; **jouer au football américain** *to play football,* 4
la forêt *forest,* 0; **en forêt** *to/in the forest,* 11
la forme *form, structure,* 7
formidable : C'était formidable! *It was great!* 11
le fort *fort,* 12
fort(e) *strong,* 7
fou (folle) *crazy,* 9
le foulard *scarf,* 10
le four *oven,* 8
le fournisseur *supplier,* 8
les fournitures (f. pl.) scolaires *school supplies,* 3
la fourrure *fur,* 7
le foutou *a paste made from boiled plantains, manioc, or yams; it is common in Côte d'Ivoire.* 8
le foyer home, 7
fraîche *cool, cold,* 5
le frais *cool place,* 8; au frais *in a cool place,* 8
les frais (m. pl.) *cost, expenses,* 11
frais *cool (temperature),* 4; **Il fait frais.** *It's cool.* 4 ; *fresh,* 12; des fruits et des légumes frais *fresh fruits and vegetables,* 12
la fraise *strawberry,* 8; **un sirop de fraises (à l'eau)** *water with strawberry syrup,* 5
le franc *(former monetary unit of France) franc,* 3
le franc de la Communauté financière africaine (CFA) *the currency of francophone Africa,* 8
le français *French (language),* 1; français(e) *French* (adj.), 0; *A la française* French-style, 2
francophone *French-speaking,* 0
la fréquence *frequency,* 4
le frère *brother,* 7
les friandises (f.) *sweets,* 6
les frites (f. pl.) *French fries,* 1
froid(e) *cold,* 4; **Il fait froid.** *It's cold.* 4
le fromage *cheese,* 5
la fromagerie *cheese shop,* 12
les fruits (m.) *fruit,* 8
fui (pp. of fuir) *fled,* 1
le fun *fun,* 4; C'est l' fun! (in Canada) *It's fun!* 4

gagner *to win, to earn,* 9
la garantie *guarantee,* 3
le garçon *boy,* 9
garder *to look after,* 7
la gare *train station,* 6 ; la gare routière *bus station,* 12
le garrot *withers, shoulder height of an animal such as a horse,* 7
le gâteau *cake,* 8
la gâterie *little treat,* 9
la gauche *left (direction);* **à gauche** *to the left,* 12
la Gaule *Gaul; the division of the ancient Roman Empire (in Western Europe) occupied by the Gauls,* 9
le gazon *lawn,* 7; **tondre le gazon** *to mow the lawn,* 7
généralement *in general, usually,* 11
génial(e) *great,* 2
le génie *genius,* 6
les genoux (m.) *knees,* 7; une paire de genoux *pair of knees, lap,* 7
les gens (m. pl.) *people,* 9
gentil(le) *nice,* 7
la géographie *geography,* 2
la géométrie *geometry,* 2
la glace *ice cream,* 1
la glace *ice;* **faire du patin à glace** *to ice-skate,* 4
le golf golf, 4; **jouer au golf** *to play golf,* 4
les gombos (m.) *okra,* 8
la gomme *eraser,* 3
les gorges (f.) *canyons,* 11
la/le gosse *kid,* 2; être traité comme un gosse *to be treated like a kid,* 2
la gouache *paint,* 3
le goût *taste,* 4
le goûter *afternoon snack,* 8
goûter *to taste,* 8
le gouvernement *government,* 8
la goyave *guava,* 8
grâce à *thanks to,* 11
gradué(e) *graduated,* 3; une règle graduée *graduated ruler,* 3
la graine *seed,* 8
la grammaire *grammar,* 1; grammaire en contexte *grammar in context,* 1
le gramme *gram (unit of measurement),* 8
grand(e) *tall,* 7; *big,* 10
grand-chose : Pas grand-chose. *Not much.* 6
grandir *to grow,* 10
la grand-mère *grandmother,* 7
le grand-père *grandfather,* 7
gratuit(e) *free,* 6
grec(que) *Greek* (adj.), 6
gris(e) *grey,* 3
gros(se) *fat,* 7
grossir *to gain weight,* 10
la grotte *cave,* 11
le groupe *musical group,* 2; le groupe *group,* 7
le gruyère *Gruyère cheese,* 5

la Guadeloupe *Guadeloupe,* 0
le guichet *ticket window,* 6
la Guyane française *French Guiana,* 0

H

habitant : habitant le monde entier *living all over the world,* 1
habite : J'habite à... *I live in . . . ,* 1
l' habitude (f.) *habit,* 4; **d'habitude** *usually,* 4
habituellement *usually,* 2
* haché(e) (pp. of hacher) *minced,* 8
Haïti (no article) *Haiti,* 0
***le hamburger** *hamburger,* 1
*les haricots (m.) *beans,* 8; **les haricots verts** (m. pl.) *green beans,* 8
l' harmonie (f.) *harmony,* 10
*la harpe *harp,* 11
*la hâte *hurry, haste;* Elle a hâte de... *She can't wait to . . . ,* 7
* haut(e) *tall, high,* 6
*le haut-parleur *loudspeaker,* 11
*le havre *haven,* 7
l' hébergement (m.) *lodging,* 6
l' hélicoptère (m.) *helicopter,* 0
*le héros *hero,* 11
hésite : Euh... J'hésite. *Well, I'm not sure.* 10
hésiter *to hesitate,* 10
l' heure (f.) *hour; time,* 1; **à l'heure de** *at the time of,* 1; **A quelle heure?** *At what time?* 6; **A tout à l'heure!** *See you later!* 1; l'heure officielle *official time (24-hour system),* 2; **Quelle heure est-il?** *What time is it?* 6; **Tu as... à quelle heure?** *At what time do you have . . . ?* 2
heures *o'clock,* 2; **à... heures** *at . . . o'clock,* 2; **à... heures quarante-cinq** *at . . . forty-five,* 2; **à... heures quinze** *at . . . fifteen,* 2; **à... heures trente** *at . . . thirty,* 2
heureusement *luckily, fortunately,* 4
heureux (-euse) *happy;* **Très heureux(-euse).** *Pleased to meet you.* 7
hier *yesterday,* 9
l' histoire (f.) *history,* 2
l' historien (m.) *historian,* 9
l' hiver (m.) *winter,* 4; **en hiver** *in the winter,* 4
***le hockey** *hockey,* 4; **jouer au hockey** *to play hockey,* 4
l' hôpital (pl. -aux) *hospital,* 0
l' horreur (f.) *horror;* un film d'horreur *horror movie,* 6
horrible *terrible,* 10
***le hot-dog** *hot dog,* 5
l' hôtel (m.) *hotel,* 0; l'hôtel de ville (m.) *town hall,* 1
*le houx *holly,* 11
l' huile d'olive (f.) *olive oil,* 5
* hurler *to shriek, to cry out,* 12
l' hypermarché (m.) *hypermarket,* 8

l' idée (f.) *idea,* 4; **Bonne idée.** *Good idea.* 4
identifier *to identify, to point out,* 7
l' identité (f.) *identity;* une photo d'identité *photo ID,* 1
l' igloo (m.) *igloo,* 0
l' igname (f.) *yam,* 8
il y a *there is, there are,* 5; il y a du soleil/du vent *it's sunny/windy,* 4; **Qu'est-ce qu'il y a à boire?** *What is there to drink?* 5
l' île (f.) *island,* 0
illogique *illogical,* 3
l' image (f.) *image,* 7
imagines : Tu imagines? *Can you imagine?* 4
l' impératif (m.) *command (verb form), imperative,* 10
important(e) *important,* 8
imprimé(e) *printed,* 10
inaperçu(e) *unnoticed,* 11
inclus(e) *included,* 6
incompétent(e) *incompetent,* 2
incroyable *unbelievable,* 9
l' industrie (f.) *industry,* 4
l' influence (f.) *influence,* 12
l' informatique (f.) *computer science,* 2
l' instrument de géométrie (m.) *instrument for geometry (compass, etc.),* 3
intelligent(e) *smart,* 7
l' intention (f.) *intention;* **J'ai l'intention de...** *I intend to . . . ,* 11
l' interclasse (m.) *break (between classes),* 2
intéressant(e) *interesting,* 2
international(e) *international,* 5
l' interphone (m.) *intercom,* 9
l' interro(gation) (f.) *quiz,* 9; **rater une interro** *to fail a quiz,* 9
intervenu(e) (pp. of intervenir) *intervened,* 9
l' interviewé(e) (m./f.) *interviewee,* 2
intime *personal,* 1
l' intonation (f.) *intonation,* 1
inventer *to invent,* 7
l' invitation (f.) *invitation,* 6
l' invité(e) (m./f.) *guest,* 8
inviter *to invite,* 7
ivoirien(ne) *from the Republic of Côte d'Ivoire,* 1

jamais : ne... jamais *never,* 4
le jambon *ham,* 5
janvier *January,* 4; **en janvier** *in January,* 4
le jardin *garden,* 0
jaune *yellow,* 3
le jazz *jazz,* 4
je *I,* 0
le jean *(pair of) jeans,* 3; **en jean** *made of denim,* 10
le jeu *game;* un jeu de rôle *role-playing exercise,* 1; **jouer à des jeux vidéo** *to play video games,* 4
jeudi *Thursday,* 2; **le jeudi** *on Thursdays,* 2
jeune *young,* 7; les jeunes *youths,* 4
le jogging *jogging,* 4; **faire du jogging** *to jog,* 4
la joie *joy,* 1
joignant (joindre) *attached,* 1
joli(e) *pretty,* 4
jouer *to play,* 4; **Je joue...** *I play . . . ,* 4; **Je ne joue pas...** *I don't play . . . ,* 4; **jouer à...** *to play (a game) . . . ,* 4
joueur (-euse) *playful,* 7
le jour *day,* 2; le jour férié (m.) *holiday,* 6
le journal *journal,* 1; *newspaper,* 12
la journée *day,* 2
juillet *July,* 4; **en juillet** *in July,* 4
juin *June,* 4; **en juin** *in June,* 4
la jupe *skirt,* 10
le jus d'orange *orange juice,* 5
le jus de fruit *fruit juice,* 5
le jus de pomme *apple juice,* 5
jusqu'à *up to, until,* 12; **Vous allez tout droit jusqu'à...** *You go straight ahead until you get to . . . ,* 12
juste *just,* 4

le kangourou *kangaroo,* 0
le kilo(gramme) *kilogram,* 8; **un kilo de** *a kilogram of,* 8
le kilomètre *kilometer,* 12

la *the,* 1; *her, it* (f.), 9
là *there,* 12; **-là** *there (noun suffix),* 3; **(Est-ce que)... est là, s'il**

vous plaît? *Is . . . , there, please?* 9; là-bas *there; over there,* 8
là-bas *there, over there,* 9
laid(e) *ugly,* 9
la laine *wool,* 10
laisser *to leave,* 9; **Je peux laisser un message?** *Can I leave a message?* 9
le lait *milk,* 8
laitier (-ière) *dairy,* 8; **les produits laitiers (m.)** *dairy products,* 8
la langue *language,* 1
large *baggy,* 10; *large wide;* 107 mètres de large *107 meters wide,* 9
le latin *Latin (language),* 2
laver *to wash,* 7; **laver la voiture** *to wash the car,* 7
le *the,* 1; *him, it,* 9
la légende *map key,* 12
la légèreté *lightness,* 6
les légumes (m.) *vegetables,* 8
les *the,* 1; *them,* 9
la lettre *letter,* 12; **envoyer des lettres** *to send letters,* 12
leur *to them,* 9
leur/leurs *their,* 7
levez : Levez la main! *Raise your hand!* 0; **Levez-vous!** *Stand up!* 0
la levure *yeast,* 8
la liaison *liaison; pronunciation of a normally silent consonant at the end of a word as if it were the first letter of the word that follows,* 2
la librairie *bookstore,* 12
la librairie-papeterie *bookstore and stationery store,* 3
libre *free,* 2
liégeois : café ou chocolat liégeois *coffee or chocolate ice cream with whipped cream,* 5
le lieu *place;* avoir lieu *to take place,* 7; ... aura lieu... *. . . will take place . . . ,* 7
la limonade *lemon soda,* 5
le lin *linen,* 10
le lion *lion,* 0
le liquide correcteur *correction fluid,* 3
lire *to read,* 1
lisant : en lisant *while reading,* 11
lisons : Lisons! *Let's read!* 1
la liste *list,* 8
la litote *understatement,* 5
le litre *liter,* 8; **un litre de** *a liter of,* 8
la livraison *delivery,* 12
la livre *pound,* 8; **une livre de** *a pound of,* 8
le livre *book,* 0
le livret scolaire *a student's personal gradebook,* 3
la location *rental,* 4
logique *logical,* 3
loin *far,* 12; **loin de** *far from,* 12
long(ue) *long,* 10
longtemps (adv.) *a long time,* 9
la longueur *length,* 10
louer *to rent,* 12
la Louisiane *Louisiana,* 0
lu (pp. of lire) *read,* 9
lui *to him, to her,* 9
lumineux (-euse) *luminous, lit up,* 3
lundi *Monday,* 2; **le lundi** *on Mondays,* 2
les lunettes de soleil (f. pl.) *sunglasses,* 10
le Luxembourg *Luxembourg,* 0
le lycée *high school,* 2
le lycéen *high school student,* 2

ma *my,* 7
madame (Mme) *ma'am, Mrs.,* 1; **Madame!** *Waitress!* 5
mademoiselle (Mlle) *miss, Miss,* 1; **Mademoiselle!** *Waitress!* 5
le madras *madras (fabric or pattern),* 10
le magasin *store,* 1; **faire les magasins** *to go shopping,* 1; grand magasin *department store,* 10
le magazine *magazine,* 3
le magnétoscope *videocassette recorder, VCR,* 0
magnifique *magnificent, splendid,* 9
mai *May,* 4; **en mai** *in May,* 4
maigrir *to lose weight,* 10
le maillot de bain *bathing suit,* 10
la main *hand,* 0
maintenant *now,* 2; **Je ne peux pas maintenant.** *I can't right now.* 8
le maire *mayor,* 12
la mairie *city hall,* 4
mais *but,* 1
le maïs *corn,* 8
la Maison des jeunes et de la culture (MJC) *recreation center,* 6
le maître *master, owner,* 7
maîtriser *to master,* 4
la majorité *majority,* 2
mal *bad,* 1; **Pas mal.** *Not bad.* 1
la malchance *misfortune,* 7
le mâle *male (refers to animals),* 7
malheureusement *unfortunately,* 7
le Mali *Mali,* 0
la manche *sleeve,* 10
le manchot *penguin,* 6
le manège *carousel,* 12
manger *to eat,* 6
la mangue *mango,* 8
manque : Qu'est-ce qui manque? *What's missing?* 2
manqué(e) (pp. of manquer) *missed;* garçon manqué *tomboy,* 10
le manteau *coat,* 10
le maquis *maquis; kind of outdoor restaurant in Côte d'Ivoire,* 5
le marchand (la marchande) *merchant, shopkeeper,* 8
le marché *market,* 8
mardi *Tuesday,* 2; **le mardi** *on Tuesdays,* 2
le mari *husband,* 7
le mariage *marriage,* 7
le Maroc *Morocco,* 0
marocain(e) *Moroccan* (adj.), 1
marron (inv.) *brown,* 3
mars *March,* 4; **en mars** *in March,* 4
martiniquais(e) *from Martinique,* 1
la Martinique *Martinique,* 0
le masque *mask,* 8
le match *game,* 6; **regarder un match** *to watch a game (on TV),* 6; **aller voir un match** *to go see a game (in person),* 6
les maths (les mathématiques) (f. pl.) *math,* 1
la matière *school subject,* 2; *fabric,* 10
les matières grasses (f.) *fat,* 8
le matin *morning, in the morning,* 2
mauvais(e) *bad,* 5; **C'est pas mauvais!** *It's pretty good!* 5; **Oh, pas mauvais.** *Oh, not bad.* 9; **Très mauvais.** *Very bad.* 9
méchant(e) *mean,* 7
mécontent(e) *unhappy,* 2
les médicaments (m.) *medicine,* 12
meilleur(e) *best,* 7; les meilleurs amis *best friends,* 7
le mélange *mixture,* 12
mélanger *to mix,* 8
méli-mélo *mishmash,* 1
le membre *member;* le membre de la famille *family member,* 7
même *same,* 4
la mémé *granny, grandma,* 9
le ménage *housework,* 1; **faire le ménage** *to do housework,* 1
le mensuel *monthly publication,* 9
la menthe à l'eau *beverage made with mint syrup and water,* 5
le menu *meal, menu,* 8
méprisant(e) *contemptuous,* 2
la mer *sea;* **au bord de la mer** *to/on the coast,* 11
Merci. *Thank you,* 3; **Non, merci.** *No, thank you.* 8
mercredi *Wednesday,* 2; **le mercredi** *on Wednesdays,* 2
la mère *mother,* 7
mes *my,* 7
le message *message,* 9; **Je peux laisser un message?** *May I leave a message?,* 9
mesurer *to measure,* 9
le mètre *meter,* 9
le métro *subway,* 12; **au métro...** *at the . . . metro stop,* 6; **en métro** *by subway,* 12

métropolitain(e) *metropolitan,* 2
mets : mets en ordre *put into order,* 6
mettre *to put, to put on, to wear,* 10; **Je ne sais pas quoi mettre pour...** *I don't know what to wear for (to) . . . ,* 10; **Mets...** *Wear . . . ,* 10; **Qu'est-ce que je mets?** *What shall I wear?* 10
meublé(e) *furnished,* 11
mexicain(e) (adj.) *Mexican,* 5
miam-miam *yum-yum,* 5
midi *noon,* 6; **Il est midi.** *It's noon.* 6; **Il est midi et demi.** *It's half past noon.* 6
mieux *better,* 9; **Ça va aller mieux!** *It's going to get better!* 9; **J'aime mieux...** *I prefer . . . ,* 1
mignon(ne) *cute,* 7
le milieu *middle;* au milieu *in the middle,* 7
millier (m.) *a thousand or so;* des milliers d'autres visiteurs *thousands of other tourists,* 9
mince *slender,* 7
minuit *midnight,* 6; **Il est minuit.** *It's midnight.* 6; **Il est minuit et demi.** *It's half past midnight.* 6
la minute *minute,* 9; **Tu as une minute?** *Do you have a minute?* 9
mis (pp. of mettre) *put, placed,* 10
la mise *putting, setting;* mise en pratique *putting into practice,* 1; mise en train *getting started,* 1
la mise en scène *production,* 1
mixte *mixed,* 5
le mobilier *furniture,* 6
la mobylette *motor scooter,* 11
moche *tacky,* 10
la mode *style,* 10; **à la mode** *in style,* 10; à la dernière mode *in the latest fashion,* 10
le mode d'emploi *instructions,* 9
modéré(e) *moderate,* 11
moderne *modern,* 8
moi *me,* 2; **Moi aussi.** *Me too.* 2; **Moi, non.** *I don't.* 2; **Moi non plus.** *Neither do I.* 2; **Moi, si.** *I do.* 2; **Pas moi.** *Not me.*
moins *(with numbers) minus, lower,* 0; **moins cinq** *five to,* 6; **moins le quart** *quarter to,* 6
le mois *month,* 4
le moment *moment,* 5; **Un moment, s'il vous plaît.** *One moment, please.* 5
mon *my,* 7
Monaco *Monaco,* 0
le monde *world,* 0
le moniteur *monitor,* 12
monsieur (M.) *sir, Mr.,* 1; **Monsieur!** *Waiter!* 5
le monstre *monster,* 0
la montagne *mountain,* 4; **à la montagne** *to/in the mountains,* 11
la montée *ascent,* 6
monter *to climb, to rise,* 6
la montre *watch,* 3
montrer *to show,* 9
le monument *monument,* 6
se moquer de *to make fun of,* 9
le moral *morale,* 2
le morceau *piece,* 8; **un morceau de** *a piece of,* 8
le mot *word,* 11; un petit mot *a little note,* 5
le motif *reason, pattern,* 9
la moto(cyclette) *motorcycle,* 12
le moulin *windmill,* 9
la mousseline *chiffon,* 8
la moutarde *mustard,* 8
moyen(ne) *average,* 2; travail moyen *average work,* 2
le Moyen Age *Middle Ages,* 9
la moyenne *average,* 2
le musée *museum,* 6
la musique *music,* 2; **écouter de la musique** *to listen to music,* 1; la musique classique *classical music,* 4
le mystère *mystery,* 5

nager *to swim,* 1
le nain *dwarf,* 6
la naissance *birth,* 7
la natation *swimming,* 4; **faire de la natation** *to swim,* 4
national(e) *national,* 8
naturel(le) *natural,* 3
nautique *nautical;* **faire du ski nautique** *to water-ski,* 4
ne : ne... pas *not,* 1; **ne... pas encore** *not yet,* 9; **ne... jamais** *never,* 4; **ne... ni grand(e) ni petit(e)** *neither tall nor short,* 7; n'est-ce pas? *isn't that so? (tag question added to the end of a declarative phrase to make it a question)*
né(e) (pp. of naître) *born,* 9
la Négritude *movement which asserts the values and spirit of black African civilizations,* 0
la neige *snow,* 4
neige : Il neige. *It's snowing.* 4
le neveu *nephew,* 7
niçois(e) (adj.) *from Nice, France,* 5
la nièce *niece,* 7
le Niger *Niger,* 0
le niveau *level,* 6
le nocturne *late-night opening,* 6
le Noël *Christmas,* 0
noir(e) *black,* 3
la noisette *hazelnut,* 5
la noix *nut,* 5
la noix de coco *coconut,* 8
le nom *name,* 1; nom de famille *last name*
le nombre *number,* 2
nombreux(-euse) *numerous, many,* 9
non *no,* 1; **Moi non plus.** *Neither do I.* 2; **Moi, non.** *I don't.* 2; **Non, c'est...** *No, it's . . . ,* 4; **Non, merci.** *No, thank you.* 8; **Non, pas trop.** *No, not too much.* 2
nos *our,* 7
la note *note;* la note culturelle *culture note,* 1
notre *our,* 7
nouveau (nouvelle) *new,* 7
la Nouvelle-Angleterre *New England,* 0
les nouvelles (f.) *news,* 9
novembre *November,* 4; **en novembre** *in November,* 4
le nuage *cloud,* 12
nul(le) *useless,* 2
le numéro *number,* 0; un numéro de téléphone *telephone number,* 3; les numéros *issues (for magazines, etc.),* 3
nutritionnel(le) *nutritive, having to do with nutrition,* 8

O

l' objet (m.) *object,* 6; objets trouvés *lost and found,* 3
l' observation (f.) *observation,* 2
l' occasion (f.) *occasion,* 10
occupé(e) : C'est occupé. *It's busy.* 9; **Désolé(e), je suis occupé(e).** *Sorry, I'm busy.* 6
s'occuper de *to take care of,* 7
octobre *October,* 4; **en octobre** *in October,* 4
l' odeur (f.) *aroma, smell,* 8
l' œil (m.) *eye,* 12
l' œuf (m.) *egg,* 8
offre (offrir) *to offer;* Le plus grand centre du sport au Canada offre... *The largest sports center in Canada offers . . . ,* 4
l' oignon (m.) *onion,* 8
l' oiseau (m.) *bird,* 12
ombragé(e) (pp. of ombrager) *shaded,* 11
l' omelette (f.) *omelette,* 5
on *one, we, you, they,* 1; Comment dit-on... ? *How do you say . . . ?* 1; On est dans la purée. *We're in trouble.* 8; **On fait du ski?** *How about skiing?* 5; **On joue au base-ball?** *How about playing baseball?* 5; **On peut...** *We can . . . ,*

6; **On va au café?** *Shall we go to the café?* 5; **On...?** *How about . . . ?* 4
l' **oncle** (m.) *uncle,* 7
l' opéra (m.) *opera house,* 10
l' opinion (f.) *opinion,* 7
opposé(e) *opposite,* 12
opulent(e) *rich,* 7
l' or (m.) *gold,* 12
orange (inv.) *orange (color),* 3
l' **orange** (f.) *orange,* 8; **le jus d'orange** *orange juice*
l' **ordinateur** (m.) *computer,* 3
l 'ordre (m.) *order,* 9; l'ordre chronologique (m.) *chronological order,* 3
l' organisation (f.) *organization,* 1
original(e) *original,* 10
l' otarie (f.) *sea lion,* 6
ôter *to cut out,* 8
ou *or,* 1
où *where,* 6; **Où (ça)?** *Where?* 6; **Où est-ce que tu vas aller...?** *Where are you going to go . . . ?* 11; **Tu es allé(e) où?** *Where did you go?* 9
oublier *to forget,* 9; **Je n'ai rien oublié.** *I didn't forget anything.* 11; Oublie-le/-la/-les! *Forget him/her/them!* 9; J'ai oublié. *I forgot.* 3; **N'oublie pas de...** *Don't forget . . . ,* 8; **Tu n'as pas oublié...?** *You didn't forget . . . ?* 11
l' ouest *West,* 8
oui *yes,* 1; **Oui, c'est...** *Yes it's . . . ,* 4; **Oui, s'il te/vous plaît.** *Yes, please.* 8
ouvert(e) *open,* 6
l' ouverture (f.) *opening,* 6
ouvrez : Ouvrez vos livres à la page... *Open your books to page . . . ,* 0

la page *page,* 0
le pagne *a piece of dyed African cloth,* 10
le pain *bread,* 8
la paire *pair,* 5; une paire de genoux *pair of knees, lap,* 7
le palais *palace,* 1; le palais de justice *court, courthouse,* 1
le pamplemousse *grapefruit,* 5
le panier *basket,* 3
le pantalon *pair of pants,* 10
la papaye *papaya,* 8
la papeterie *stationery store,* 12; librairie-papeterie *bookstore/ stationery store,* 3
le papier *paper,* 0; **des feuilles** (f.) **de papier** *sheets of paper,* 3
le paquet *package, box,* 8; **un paquet de** *a package/box of,* 8
par *by,* 12; *per,* 6; par hasard *by chance,* 12; prix par personne *price per person,* 6
le parachute *parachute,* 0
le paragraphe *paragraph,* 7
paraître *to appear; seem,* 12
le parapluie *umbrella,* 11
le parc *park,* 6
parce que *because,* 5; **Je ne peux pas parce que...** *I can't because . . . ,* 5
Pardon. *Pardon me.* 3; **Pardon, madame..., s'il vous plaît?** *Excuse me, ma'am . . . , please?* 12; **Pardon, monsieur. Je cherche..., s'il vous plaît.** *Excuse me, sir. I'm looking for. . . , please.* 12
le parent *parent, relative,* 7
paresseux (-euse) *lazy,* 2
parfait(e) *perfect,* 3; **C'est parfait.** *It's perfect.* 10
parfois *sometimes,* 4
parfumer *to flavor,* 8
la parfumerie *perfumery, perfume shop,* 11
parisien(ne) (adj.) *Parisian,* 5
parlé (pp. of parler) *talked, spoke,* 9; **Nous avons parlé.** *We talked.* 9
parler *to talk,* 1; *to speak,* 9; **(Est-ce que) je peux parler à...?** *Could I speak to. . . ?* 9; **Je peux te parler?** *Can I talk to you?* 9; **parler au téléphone** *to talk on the phone,* 1; Parlons! *Let's talk!* 2
parmi *among,* 9
partagé(e) *split, shared,* 6
le partenaire (la partenaire) *partner,* 7
partir *to leave,* 11; **Tu ne peux pas partir sans...** *You can't leave without . . . ,* 11
pas *not,* 1; **pas bon** *not good,* 5; **Pas ce soir.** *Not tonight.* 7; pas content du tout *not happy at all,* 2; **Il/Elle ne va pas du tout avec...** *It doesn't go at all with . . . ,* 10; **Pas grand-chose.** *Not much.* 6; **Pas mal.** *Not bad.* 1; **pas mauvais** *not bad,* 9; **Pas question!** *Out of the question!* 7; **pas super** *not so hot,* 2; **Pas terrible.** *Not so great.* 1; pas du tout *not at all,* 4
le passeport *passport,* 1
les passe-temps (m. pl.) *pastimes,* 4
passé (pp. of passer) : **Ça s'est bien passé?** *Did it go well?* 11; **Qu'est-ce qui s'est passé?** *What happened?* 9; **Tu as passé un bon week-end?** *Did you have a good weekend?* 9
passer *to pass,* 12; *to go by,* 12; **Tu pourrais passer à...?** *Could you go by . . . ?* 12; **Vous passez...** *You'll pass . . . ,* 12; **passer l'aspirateur** *to vacuum,* 7; **passer un examen** *to take a test,* 9
passerais : je passerais le bac... *I would take the bac . . . ,* 2
passionnant(e) *fascinating,* 2
la pastille *tablet,* 3
la pâte *dough,* 8; la pâte d'arachide *peanut butter,* 8; la pâte de tomates *tomato paste,* 8
le pâté *pâté,* 0
les pâtes (f. pl.) *pasta,* 11
le patin *skating,* 1; **faire du patin à glace** *to ice-skate,* 4
le patin à roulettes *rollerskating,* 4
le patinage *skating,* 4
patiner *to skate,* 4
la patinoire *skating rink,* 6
la pâtisserie *pastry shop, pastry,* 12
le patrimoine *heritage,* 6
patronal(e) *having to do with saints;* la fête patronale *patron saint's holiday,* 12
les pattes d'eph (f. pl.) *bell-bottoms,* 10
pauvre *poor,* 7
le pays *country,* 6
le paysage *landscape,* 11
la pêche *peach,* 8
peindre *to paint,* 9
la peinture *painting,* 6
pendant *during,* 1
pénible *annoying,* 7
penser *to think;* **J'ai pensé à tout.** *I've thought of everything.* 11; Qu'en penses-tu? *What do you think (about it)?* 1
perdre *to lose,* 9
perdu(e) (pp. of perdre) *lost,* 1
le père *father,* 7
permettre *to allow,* 9
le permis de conduire *driver's license,* 12; le permis accompagné *learner's permit (driving),* 12; le permis probatoire *learner's permit (driving),* 12
la permission *permission,* 7
le personnage *individual, character,* 9
la personnalité *personality,* 7
la personne *person,* 7
personnel(le) *personal,* 4
petit(e) *short (height),* 7; *small (size),* 10; petites annonces *classified ads,* 1
le petit copain *boyfriend,* 2
le petit déjeuner *breakfast,* 8
le petit-fils *grandson,* 7
la petite copine *girlfriend,* 2
la petite-fille *granddaughter,* 7
les petits-enfants (m.) *grandchildren,* 7
les petits pois (m.) *peas,* 8
peu *not very,* 2; à peu près *about, approximately,* 9; peu content *not very happy,* 2; un peu *a little,* 6
peut : On peut... *We can . . . ,* 6
peut-être *maybe, perhaps,* 11

peux : Désolé(e), mais je ne peux pas. *Sorry, but I can't.* 4; **Tu peux... ?** *Can you . . . ?* 8
la pharmacie *drugstore,* 12
la philosophie *philosophy,* 2
le phoque *seal,* 6
la photo *picture, photo,* 4; **faire de la photo** *to do photography,* 4; **faire des photos** *to take pictures,* 4
la photographie *photography,* 1
les photographies (f. pl.) *photographs,* 6
la phrase *sentence,* 4
la physique *physics,* 2
physiquement *physically,* 7
la pièce *play,* 6; **voir une pièce** *to see a play,* 6
le pied *foot,* 12; **à pied** *on foot,* 12
la Pierre Levée *name of a megalith in Poitiers, France,* 1
la pince : des pantalons à pinces *pleated pants,* 10
le pinceau *paintbrush,* 3
le pingouin *penguin,* 0
le pique-nique *picnic,* 6; **faire un pique-nique** *to have a picnic,* 6
la piscine *swimming pool,* 6
pittoresque *picturesque,* 8
la pizza *pizza,* 1
la place *place;* Services... de location sur place *On-site rentals,* 4
la plage *beach,* 1
la plaine *plain,* 4
le plaisir *pleasure, enjoyment,* 4; **Oui, avec plaisir.** *Yes, with pleasure.* 8
plaît : Il/Elle me plaît, mais il/elle est cher/chère. *I like it, but it's expensive.* 10; **Il/Elle te/vous plaît?** *Do you like it?* 10; Ça te plaît? *Do you like it?* 2; **s'il vous/te plaît** *please,* 3
la planche *board;* **faire de la planche à voile** *to go windsurfing,* 11
la plaque *plate (of metal or glass);* la plaque d'immatriculation *license plate,* 0
le plat *dish (food),* 5; les plats à emporter (m.) *food to go,* 11
plein(e) de *a lot of,* 8; une ville pleine d'animation *a city full of life,* 8
pleut : Il pleut. *It's raining.* 4
la plongée *diving;* **faire de la plongée** *to go scuba diving,* 11
plus *plus (math),* 2; *(with numbers) higher,* 0; **Je n'en veux plus.** *I don't want any more,* 8; **Moi non plus.** *Neither do I.* 2; **Non, merci. Je n'ai plus faim.** *No thanks. I'm not hungry anymore.* 8
plusieurs (inv.) *several,* 7
la poche *pocket,* 10
le poème *poem,* 0
le point *point,* 10; le point d'intérêt *tourist attraction,* 4
la poire *pear,* 8
le poisson *fish,* 7
la poissonnerie *fish shop,* 12
la poitrine *chest,* 10
le poivre *pepper,* 8
le poivron *green or red pepper,* 5
poliment *politely,* 8
la pollution *pollution,* 1
la pomme *apple,* 8; **jus de pom**me *apple juice, 5*
la pomme de terre *potato,* 8
le pompiste *gas pump attendant,* 11
la population *population,* 4
le porc *pork,* 8
le port *port,* 8
la porte *door,* 0
le portefeuille *wallet,* 3
le porte-monnaie *change purse,* 5
porter *to wear,* 10
le portugais *Portuguese (language),* 2
poser des questions *to ask questions,* 7
possible *possible,* 3
la poste *post office,* 12
le poster *poster,* 0
le pot de colle *container of glue,* 3
la poubelle *trashcan,* 7; **sortir la poubelle** *to take out the trash,* 7
la poudre *powder,* 8
la poule *(animal) chicken,* 8
le poulet *chicken (meat),* 8
pour *for,* 2; **Qu'est-ce qu'il te faut pour...** *What do you need for . . . ? (informal),* 3; **Qu'est-ce que tu fais pour t'amuser?** *What do you do to have fun?* 4
pourquoi *why,* 0; **Pourquoi est-ce que tu ne mets pas... ?** *Why don't you wear . . . ?* 10; **Pourquoi pas?** *Why not?* 6; **Pourquoi tu ne... pas?** *Why don't you . . . ?* 9
pourrais : Tu pourrais passer à ... ? *Could you go by . . . ?* 12
pourtant *yet, nevertheless,* 9
pouvoir *to be able to, can,* 8; **(Est-ce que) je peux... ?** *May I . . . ?* 7; **Tu peux... ?** *Can you . . . ?* 8; **Je ne peux pas maintenant.** *I can't right now.* 8; **Je peux te parler?** *Can I talk to you?,* 9; **Non, je ne peux pas.** *No, I can't.* 12; **On peut...** *We can . . . ,* 6; **Qu'est-ce que je peux faire?** *What can I do?* 9; **(Est-ce que) tu pourrais me rendre un petit service?** *Could you do me a favor?* 12; **Tu pourrais passer à... ?** *Could you go by . . . ?,* 12
pratique *practical,* 3
précieusement *carefully,* 2
précisant : en précisant *specifying,* 1
préféré(e) *favorite,* 4
la préfecture (de police) *police station,* 12
la préférence *preference,* 3
préférer *to prefer,* 1; **Je préfère...** *I prefer . . . ,* 1
premier (-ière) *first,* 1; la première étape *first step,* 1
prendre *to take or to have (food or drink),* 5; **Je vais prendre..., s'il vous plaît.** *I'm going to have . . . , please.* 5; **On peut prendre...** *We can take . . . ,* 12; **Prends...** *Get . . . ,* 8; *Have . . . ,* 5; **Je le/la/les prends.** *I'll take it/them.* 10; **Tu prends... ?** *Will you have . . . ?,* 8; *Are you taking. . . ?,* 11; **Prenez une feuille de papier.** *Take out a sheet of paper.* 0; **Vous prenez... ?** *What are you having?* 5; *Will you have . . . ?,* 8; **Prenez la rue... puis traversez la rue...** *You take . . . Street, then cross . . . Street,* 12; **Vous avez décidé de prendre... ?** *Have you decided to take . . . ?* 10; **Vous le/la/les prenez?** *Are you going to take it/them?* 10
le prénom *first name,* 1
préparer *to prepare (something),* 8; se préparer *to prepare (oneself), to get ready,* 10
près *close,* 12; **près de** *close to,* 12
la présentation *presentation, introduction,* 7
présenter *to introduce;* **Je te (vous) présente...** *I'd like you to meet . . . ,* 7; Présente-toi! *Introduce yourself!* 0
presque *almost,* 12
la presqu'île *peninsula,* 12
prévoir *to anticipate,* 4
prévu(e) (pp. of prévoir) *planned;* **Je n'ai rien de prévu.** *I don't have any plans.* 11
principal(e) *main;* la ville principale *main city,* 12
le printemps *spring,* 4; **au printemps** *in the spring,* 4
pris (pp. of prendre) *took, taken,* 9
le prisonnier *prisoner,* 4
le prix *price,* 6
le problème *problem,* 9; **J'ai un petit problème.** *I've got a little problem.* 9
prochain(e) *next,* 12; **Vous continuez jusqu'au prochain feu rouge.** *You keep going until the next light.* 12
les produits laitiers (m.) *dairy products,* 8
le prof(esseur) *teacher,* 0
les progrès (m.) *progress,* 11
le projet *project,* 6
la promenade *walk,* 6; **faire une promenade** *to go for a walk,* 6
promener *to walk,* 6; **promener le chien** *to walk the dog,* 7; se promener *to take a walk,* 12
promets (promettre) *to promise,* 1
le pronom *pronoun,* 8
prononcer *to pronounce,* 1; ne se

prononcent pas *no response,* 2
la prononciation *pronunciation,* 2
proposé(e) (pp. of proposer) *given, suggested,* 5
proposer *to propose, to suggest,* 5
prospérer *to prosper, to do well,* 9
protéger *to protect,* 9
la protéine *protein,* 8
provençal(e) *Provençal; from the Provence region of France,* 9
la Provence *Provence; region in southeast France on the Mediterranean Sea,* 9
la publicité *advertisment,* 10
le publiphone à cartes *card-operated telephone,* 9
puis *then,* 12; **Prenez la rue... puis traversez la rue...** *Take . . . Street, then cross . . . Street,* 12
le pull(-over) *pullover sweater,* 3
la punition *punishment,* 9
purement *purely,* 12
la pyramide *pyramid,* 11

Q

qu'est-ce que *what,* 1; **Qu'est-ce qu'il te faut pour... ?** *What do you need for . . . ? (informal),* 3; **Qu'est-ce qu'il vous faut pour... ?** *What do you need for . . . ? (formal),* 3; Qu'est-ce qu'il y a dans...? *What's in the . . . ?* 3; Qu'est-ce qu'il y a? *What's wrong?* 2; Qu'est-ce qu'on fait? *What are we/they doing?* 4; **Qu'est-ce que je peux faire?** *What can I do?* 9; **Qu'est-ce que tu as fait... ?** *What did you do . . . ?* 9; **Qu'est-ce que tu fais... ?** *What do you do . . . ?* 4; **Qu'est-ce que tu vas faire... ?** *What are you going to do . . . ?* 6; **Qu'est-ce que vous avez comme boissons?** *What do you have to drink?* 5; **Qu'est-ce qu'il y a à boire?** *What is there to drink?* 5; Qu'est-ce qui manque? *What's missing?* 2
qu'est-ce qui *what* (subj.), 9; **Qu'est-ce qui s'est passé?** *What happened?* 9
quand *when,* 6; **Quand (ça)?** *When?* 6
la quantité *quantity,* 8
quarantième *fortieth,* 7
le quart *quarter,* 6; **et quart** *quarter past,* 6; **moins le quart** *quarter to,* 6
que *that; what,* 1; Que sais-je? *self-check (What do I know?),* 1
le quartier *neighborhood,* 4
le Québec *Quebec,* 0
québécois(e) *from Quebec,* 1
quel(le) *what, which,* 1; Ils ont quels cours? *What classes do they have?* 2; **Tu as quel âge?** *How old are you?* 1; **Tu as quels cours... ?** *What classes do you have . . . ?* 2; **Tu as... à quelle heure?** *At what time do you have . . . ?* 2; **Quelle heure est-il?** *What time is it?* 6; **Quel temps fait-il?** *What's the weather like?* 4
quelque *some,* 10
quelqu'un *someone,* 1
quelque chose *something,* 6; **Je cherche quelque chose pour...** *I'm looking for something for . . . ,* 10
quelquefois *sometimes,* 4
la question *question,* 0
le questionnaire *questionnaire, survey,* 4
qui *who,* 0; **Avec qui?** *With whom?* 6; C'est qui? *Who is it?* 2; Qui suis-je? *Who am I?* 0
la quiche *quiche: a type of custard pie with a filling, such as ham, bacon, cheese, or spinach,* 5
quittez : Ne quittez pas. (telephone) *Hold on.* 9
quoi *what,* 10; **De quoi est-ce que tu as besoin?** *What do you need?* 5; **Je ne sais pas quoi mettre pour...** *I don't know what to wear for/to . . . ,* 10; **Tu as quoi... ?** *What do you have . . . ?* 2 **Tu vas faire quoi?** *What are you going to do?* 6
quotidien(ne) *everyday,* 6

le rabat *flap,* 3
le raccourci *shortcut,* 2
raconter *to tell,* 9
la radio *radio,* 3
le radis *radish,* 8
le raisin *grapes,* 8
la randonnée *hike,* 11; **faire de la randonnée** *to go hiking,* 11
ranger *to arrange, straighten;* **ranger ta chambre** *to pick up your room,* 7
le rap *rap music,* 1
râpé(e) (pp. of râper) *grated,* 8
rapidement *rapidly, quickly,* 7
rappeler *to call back,* 9; **Vous pouvez rappeler plus tard?** *Can you call back later?* 9; Tu te rappelles? *Do you remember?* 3; *to remind,* 12
le rapport *relationship,* 7
rapporter *to bring back,* 8; **Rapporte-moi...** *Bring me back . . . ,* 8; **Tu me rapportes... ?** *Will you bring me . . . ?* 8
rarement *rarely,* 4
rater *to fail,* 9; *to miss,* 9; **rater le bus** *to miss the bus,* 9; **rater une interro** *to fail a quiz,* 9
le rayon *department,* 3; au rayon de musique *in the music department,* 3
la rayonne *rayon,* 10
la réalité *reality,* 11
la recette *recipe,* 8
recevoir *to receive,* 1
reconstruit(e) (pp. of reconstruire) *reconstructed,* 12
la récré(ation) *break,* 2
recueilli (pp. of recueillir) *to take in,* 7
refaire *to redo, remake,* 8
réfléchir *to think about,* 2; *to reflect;* Réfléchissez. *Think about it.* 2
le reflet *reflection,* 10
le refuge *animal shelter,* 7
le réfugié *refugee,* 1
le refus *refusal,* 6
refuser *to refuse,* 7
le regard *look,* 7
regarder *to look,* 10; *to watch,* 1; **Non, merci, je regarde.** *No, thanks, I'm just looking.* 10; **Regarde, voilà...** *Look, here's/there's/it's . . . ,* 12; **regarder la télé** *to watch TV,* 1; **regarder un match** *to watch a game (on TV),* 6; **Regardez la carte!** *Look at the map!* 0
la règle *ruler,* 3
regrette : Je regrette. *Sorry.* 3; **Je regrette, mais je n'ai pas le temps.** *I'm sorry, but I don't have time.* 8
regroupé(e) *rearranged,* 6
rejoint (pp. of rejoindre) *rejoined,* 7
la relation *relation,* 7
relier *to connect,* 9
religieux(-euse) *religious,* 9
relire *to re-read, to read again,* 7
remarquable *remarkable, exceptional,* 3
le remboursement *repayment,* 9
la rencontre *encounter,* 1
rencontrer *to meet,* 9
le rendez-vous *rendez-vous, date, appointment,* 12
rendre *to return something,* 12; rendre un service *to do (someone) a favor,* 12; **Rendez-vous...** *We'll meet . . . ,* 6; pour les rendre plus originales *to make them more original,* 10
le renfort *reinforcement;* renforts aux épaules *reinforced shoulder seams,* 10
les renseignements (m.) *information,* 9
la rentrée *back to school,* 2
rentrer *to go home,* 8
le repas *meal,* 8

le répertoire *index,* 9
répéter *to rehearse, practice,* 9; **Répétez!** *Repeat!* 0
le répondant *respondent,* 4
le répondeur *answering machine,* 9
répondre *to answer,* 9; **Ça ne répond pas.** *There's no answer.* 9
la réponse *response, answer,* 2
reposer *to rest, to relax;* laisser reposer *to let stand,* 8; se reposer *to relax,* 11
représenté(e) (pp. of représenter) *represented,* 7
représenter *to represent,* 8
la république de Côte d'Ivoire *the Republic of Côte d'Ivoire,* 0
la réserve *reserve,* 8
respectueux (-euse) *respectful,* 2
ressemblez : si vous me ressemblez *if you're like me,* 1
la ressource *resource,* 4
le restaurant *restaurant,* 6
la restauration *dining,* 6
rester *to stay, to remain,* 11
le resto *restaurant,* 11
le résultat *result,* 10
retard : en retard *late,* 2
retirer *to take out, to remove;* **retirer de l'argent** *to withdraw money,* 12
le retour *return,* 6
rétro (inv.) *retro,* 10
retrouve : Bon, on se retrouve... *OK, we'll meet . . . ,* 6
retrouver *to find again,* 6
la Réunion *the island of Réunion,* 0
rêvait (imp. of rêver) *to dream,* 7
le rêve *dream,* 11
revenir *to come back,* 5
riche *rich,* 8
ridicule *ridiculous,* 10
rien *nothing,* 6; *anything,* 11; **Ça ne me dit rien.** *I don't feel like it.* 4; **Je n'ai rien oublié.** *I didn't forget anything.* 11; **Rien de spécial.** *Nothing special.* 6
rigoler *to laugh,* 10
le riz *rice,* 8
la robe *dress,* 10
le rocher *rock,* 11
rocheux (-euse) *rocky,* 12
le rock *rock (music),* 4
le rôle *role,* 7
le roller *skating;* **faire du roller en ligne** *to in-line skate,* 4
romain(e) *Roman* (adj.), 9
le roman *novel,* 3
roman(e) *Romanesque; of the style of architecture developed in Europe in the 11th and 12th centuries (characterized by heavy, massive walls and arches, etc.),* 12
rond(e) *round,* 12
le rond-point *traffic circle,* 12
ronronner *to purr,* 7
le rosbif *roast beef,* 5
rose *pink,* 3
la rose *rose,* 0
le rôti *roast,* 5
rouge *red,* 3
le rouleau *roll,* 3; un rouleau protège-livres *a roll of plastic material to protect books,* 3
rouspètent (rouspéter) *to complain,* 9
la routine quotidienne *daily routine,* 11
roux (rousse) *redheaded,* 7
le ruban *ribbon, tape;* ruban adhésif transparent *transparent adhesive tape,* 3
la rue street, 12
la ruine *ruin,* 9
le rythme *rhythm,* 4

s'il te plaît *(informal) please,* 3; **Oui, s'il te plaît.** *Yes, please. (informal),* 8
s'il vous plaît *please,* 3 *(formal);* **Oui, s'il vous plaît.** *Yes, please. (formal),* 8
sa *his, her,* 7
le sac *bag;* **le sac à dos** *backpack,* 3
le sachet *bag, packet,* 3
sage *wise,* 12
sais : Je n'en sais rien. *I have no idea.* 11; **Je ne sais pas.** *I don't know.* 10; Que sais-je? *self-check (What do I know?),* 1
la saison *season,* 4; la basse saison *off season,* 12; la haute saison *tourist season,* 12
la salade *salad,* 8
les salades (f.) *heads of lettuce,* 8
salé(e) *salty, salted,* 5
saler *to salt,* 8
la salle *room,* 2; la salle de classe *classroom,* 2
Salut *Hi!* or *Goodbye!* 1
samedi *Saturday,* 2; **le samedi** *on Saturdays,* 2
les sandales (f.) *sandals,* 10
le sandwich *sandwich,* 5; **un sandwich au fromage** *cheese sandwich,* 5; **un sandwich au jambon** *ham sandwich,* 5; **un sandwich au saucisson** *salami sandwich,* 5
sans *without,* 3; sans doute *probably,* 10
la sauce *sauce,* 5
la sauce arachide *sauce made of peanut butter with beef, chicken, or fish, hot peppers, peanut oil, garlic, onions, tomato paste, tomatoes, and other vegetables,* 8
la sauce pimentée *spicy sauce,* 8
le saucisson *salami,* 5
le saumon *salmon,* 5
sauvage (adj.) *savage,* 9
savais : Savais-tu que... ? *Did you know . . . ?,* 2
savoir *to know,* 1
scellé(e) (pp. of sceller) *sealed,* 9
la science-fiction *science fiction,* 1
les sciences naturelles (f. pl.) *natural science,* 2
scolaire *having to do with school,* 2; la vie scolaire *school life,* 2
la séance *showing (at the movies),* 6
la seconde *second,* 9; **Une seconde, s'il vous plaît.** *One second, please.* 9
le secours *aid, help;* le poste de secours *first-aid station,* 6
secret (secrète) *secret,* 8
le séjour *stay, residence,* 7
le sel *salt,* 8
selon *according to,* 8
la semaine *week,* 4; **une fois par semaine** *once a week,* 4
semblable *similar, the same,* 7
le semestre *semester,* 12
le Sénégal *Senegal,* 0
le sens *sense,* 8; le sens de l'orientation *sense of direction,* 12
sensass (sensationnel) *fantastic,* 10
sept *seven,* 0
septembre *September,* 4; **en septembre** *in September,* 4
sera : ce sera *it will be,* 6
le serpent *snake,* 0
serré(e) *tight,* 10
le serveur (la serveuse) *waiter/waitress,* 5
le service *service,* 3; rendre un service *to do (someone) a favor,* 12; **A votre service.** *At your service; You're welcome,* 3
service compris *tip included,* 5
ses *his, her,* 7
le sésame *sesame,* 8
sévère *severe, harsh,* 0
le short *(pair of) shorts,* 3
si *yes (to contradict a negative question),* 2; **Moi, si.** *I do.* 2; **Oui, si tu veux.** *Yes, if you want to.* 7
sicilien(ne) (adj.) *Sicilian,* 5
le siècle *century,* 6
le signe *sign,* 12
la similarité *similarity,* 2
simple *simple,* 10
simplement *simply,* 6
sinon *otherwise; other than that,* 9
le sirop de fraise (à l'eau) *water with strawberry syrup,* 5
la situation *situation,* 7
situé(e) *situated, located,* 8

le ski *skiing,* 1; **faire du ski** *to ski,* 4; **faire du ski nautique** *to water-ski,* 4
la sœur *sister,* 7
la soie *silk,* 10
la soif *thirst;* **avoir soif** *to be thirsty,* 5
soigné(e) *with attention to detail,* 10
soigneusement *carefully,* 11
le soir *evening; in the evening,* 4; **Pas ce soir.** *Not tonight.* 7
sois (command form of être) : Ne sois pas découragée! *Don't be discouraged!* 9
soit *either;* soit chez moi, ou bien chez eux *whether at my house or at theirs,* 5
les soldes (m.) *sales,* 6
le soleil *sun, sunshine,* 4
le solfège *music theory,* 4
la solution *solution,* 9
le sommet *top, summit,* 6
le son *sound,* 8
son *his, her,* 7
le sondage *poll,* 1
la sonnerie *ringing (of the telephone),* 9
sont : Ce sont... *These/Those are . . . ,* 7; **Ils/Elles sont...** *They are . . . ,* 7; **Ils/Elles sont comment?** *What are they like?* 7
la sorte *kind;* toutes sortes de *all kinds of,* 8
sorti(e) (pp. of sortir) *went out,* 9; **Après, je suis sorti(e).** *Afterwards, I went out.* 9
la sortie *dismissal (when school gets out),* 2
sortir *to go out,* 1; *to take out,* 7; **sortir avec les copains** *to go out with friends,* 1; **sortir la poubelle** *to take out the trash,* 7
souterrain(e) *underground,* 11
le souvenir *souvenir,* 11
souvent *often,* 4
spécial(e) *special,* 6; **Rien de spécial.** *Nothing special.* 6
la spécialité *specialty dish,* 4
le spectacle *show,* 11
le spectateur *spectator, audience member,* 9
le sport *gym,* 2; *sports,* 1; **faire du sport** *to play sports,* 1; **Qu'est-ce que tu fais comme sport?** *What sports do you play?* 4
le sportif (la sportive) *sportsman (sportswoman),* 4
le stade *stadium,* 6
la stalactite *stalactite,* 11
la station-service *service station, gas station,* 11
la statue *statue,* 12
le steak-frites *steak and French fries,* 5
la stratégie *strategy,* 1
le style *style;* **C'est tout à fait ton style.** *It looks great on you!* 10
le stylo *pen,* 0; un stylo plume *fountain pen,* 3
la subvention *subsidy,* 7
le sucre *sugar,* 8
sucré(e) *sweet,* 8
le sud *South,* 9
suggérer *to suggest,* 11
suis : Qui suis-je? *Who am I?* 0; **Désolé(e), je suis occupé(e).** *Sorry, I'm busy.* 6; **Je suis bien chez . . . ?** *Is this . . . . 's house?* 9
suisse *Swiss* (adj.), 1; la Suisse *Switzerland,* 0
suivant(e) *following,* 2
suivre *to follow,* 9
le sujet *subject,* 10
super *super,* 2; **Super!** *Great!* 1; **pas super** *not so hot,* 2
le supermarché *supermarket,* 8
supplémentaire *supplementary, additional,* 1
supportez (supporter) *to put up with,* 2
sur *on;* sur place *on-site,* 4; sur un total de *out of a total of,* 4
le surligneur *highlighting marker,* 3
surtout *especially,* 1
le sweat-shirt *sweatshirt,* 3
sympa (abbrev. of **sympathique**) *nice,* 7

ta *your,* 7
la table *table,* 7; la table de comparaison de tailles *size conversion chart,* 10
le tableau *blackboard,* 0; *painting,* 8
la tache *spot,* 7
la tâche domestique *household chore,* 9
la taille *size,* 10; taille unique *one size fits all,* 10; **en taille...** *in size. . . ,* 10
la taille élastiquée *elastic waist,* 10
le taille-crayon *pencil sharpener,* 3
tant : tant privée que professionelle *private as well as professional,* 9
la tante *aunt,* 7
tard *late;* plus tard *later,* 8
le tarif : tarif réduit *reduced fee,* 6
la tarte *pie,* 8
le tas *pile, heap;* **J'ai des tas de choses à faire.** *I have lots of things to do.* 5
le taux de réussite *rate of success,* 2
le taxi *taxi,* 12; **en taxi** *by taxi,* 12
le Tchad *Chad,* 0
Tchao! *Bye!* 1
la techno *techno music,* 1; La techno me fait délirer. *I'm wild about techno (music),* 1
le tee-shirt *T-shirt,* 3
la télécarte *phone card,* 9
le télécopieur *fax machine,* 9
le téléphone *telephone,* 0; **parler au téléphone** *to talk on the phone,* 1; le téléphone à pièces *coin-operated telephone,* 9; le téléphone sans fil *cordless telephone,* 9
téléphoné (pp. of téléphoner) *called, phoned,* 9; **Vous pouvez lui dire que j'ai téléphoné?** *Can you tell him/her that I called?* 9
téléphoner *to call, to phone,* 9; **Téléphone-lui/-leur!** *Call him/her/them!* 9
téléphonique : la cabine téléphonique *phone booth,* 9
la télévision *television,* 0; **regarder la télé(vision)** *to watch TV,* 1
tellement *so; so much;* **Pas tellement.** *Not too much.* 4
le temps *time,* 4; *weather,* 4; **de temps en temps** *from time to time,* 4; **Je regrette, mais je n'ai pas le temps.** *I'm sorry, but I don't have time.* 8; Quel temps est-ce qu'il fait à... ? *How's the weather in . . . ?* 4; **Quel temps fait-il?** *What's the weather like?* 4
Tenez. *Here you are. (formal, plural),* 10
le tennis *tennis,* 4; **jouer au tennis** *to play tennis,* 4
la tenue *outfit;* une tenue de gymnastique *gym uniform,* 3
la terminale *final year of French high school, usually spent preparing for the* **bac**, 2
termine (terminer) *to finish,* 2
la terrasse *terrace,* 4
terrible *terrible, awful;* **Pas terrible.** *Not so great.* 1
le territoire d'outre-mer *overseas territory,* 12
tes *your,* 7
le test *test,* 10
le théâtre *theater,* 6; **faire du théâtre** *to do drama,* 4
théorique *theoretical,* 12
les thermes (m. pl.) *thermal baths,* 9
le thon *tuna,* 5
Tiens! *Hey!* 3
tient (tenir) *to hold,* 12
le tiers *one third;* un tiers de la population *one third of the population,* 12
le tilleul *lime green,* 10
le timbre *stamp,* 12
timide *shy,* 7
le tissu *cloth, fabric,* 10
toi *you,* 1; **Et toi?** *And you?* 1
le tollé *outcry,* 12
la tomate *tomato,* 8
tomber *to fall,* 10
ton *your,* 7
tondre *to mow,* 7; **tondre le gazon** *to mow the lawn,* 7

le top : le top des radios *the top radio stations,* 3
le total *total,* 10
toujours *still, always,* 9
la tour *tower,* 5
le tour *measurement;* tour de poitrine *chest size,* 10; le tour *turn;* à ton tour *Now it's your turn.* 7
tournez : Vous tournez... *You turn . . . ,* 12
le tournoi *tournament,* 4
tous *all,* 2
tout(e) *all,* 2; **A tout à l'heure!** *See you later!* 1; **J'ai pensé à tout.** *I've thought of everything.* 11; pas du tout *not at all,* 2; **Il/Elle ne va pas du tout avec...** *It doesn't go at all with . . . ,* 10; **C'est tout à fait ton style.** *It looks great on you!* 10; **tout de suite** *right away,* 6; **C'est tout de suite à...** *It's right there on the . . . ,* 12; **J'y vais tout de suite.** *I'll go right away.* 8; **Vous allez tout droit jusqu'à...** *You go straight ahead until you get to . . . ,* 12; tout(e) seul(e) *all alone,* 12
tout le monde (m.s.) *everyone,* 7
la tradition *tradition,* 8
traditionnel(le) *traditional,* 8
le train *train,* 12; **en train** *by train,* 12; **un billet de train** *train ticket,* 11
traité : être traité comme un gosse *to be treated like a kid,* 2
le trajet *route,* 12
la tranche *slice,* 8; **une tranche de** *a slice of,* 8
transparent(e) *transparent,* 3
le travail *work,* 3
le travail scolaire *school work,* 2
travailler *to work,* 9; travailler la pâte *to knead the dough,* 8
les travaux pratiques (m. pl.) *lab,* 2
traverser *to cross,* 12
très *very,* 1; **Très bien.** *Very well.* 1; **Très heureux (heureuse).** *Pleased to meet you.* 7
le trésor *treasure,* 3; chasse au trésor *treasure hunt,* 3
trois *three,* 0
troisième *third,* 9; la troisième étape *third step,* 1
la trompette *trumpet,* 0
trop *too (much),* 10; **Il/Elle est trop cher/chère.** *It's too expensive.* 10; **Non, pas trop.** *No, not too much.* 2
tropical(e) *tropical,* 8
la trousse *pencil case,* 3
trouver *to find,* 9; **Comment tu trouves ça?** *What do you think of that/it?* 2; **Comment tu trouves... ?** *What do you think of . . . ?* 2; **Je le/la/les trouve...** *I think it's/they're . . . ,* 10; Tu trouves? *Do you think so?* 10
le truc *thing,* 5; **J'ai des trucs à faire.** *I have some things to do.* 5
tu *you,* 0; Tu te rappelles? *Do you remember?,* 7
la Tunisie *Tunisia,* 0
typique *typical, characteristic,* 8
typiquement *typically, characteristically,* 8

un (m.) *a, an,* 3
une (f.) *a, an,* 3
l' uniforme (m.) *uniform,* 0
universel(le) *universal,* 12
utiliser *to use,* 10

va : Ça va. *Fine.* 1; **(Comment) ça va?** *How's it going?* 1; **Comment est-ce qu'on y va?** *How can we get there?* 12; **Il/Elle me va?** *Does it suit me?* 10; **Il/Elle ne te/vous va pas du tout.** *It doesn't look good on you at all.* 10; **Il/Elle ne va pas du tout avec...** *It doesn't go at all with . . . ,* 10
les vacances (f. pl.) *vacation,* 1; **Bonnes vacances!** *Have a good vacation!* 11; **en colonie de vacances** *to/at a summer camp,* 11; **en vacances** *on vacation,* 4
vais : Je vais... *I'm going . . . ,* 6; *I'm going (to) . . . ,* 11; **J'y vais tout de suite.** *I'll go right away.* 8
la vaisselle *dishes,* 7; **faire la vaisselle** *to do the dishes,* 7
valable *valid,* 6
la valise *suitcase,* 11
la vanille *vanilla,* 8
vas : Qu'est-ce que tu vas faire? *What are you going to do?* 6
la vedette *celebrity,* 1
végétarien(ne) *vegetarian,* 5
le vélo *biking,* 1; **à vélo** *by bike,* 12; **faire du vélo** *to bike,* 4
le vendeur *salesperson,* 3
la vendeuse *salesperson,* 3
vendre *to sell,* 9
vendredi *Friday,* 2; **le vendredi** *on Fridays,* 2
la vente *sales,* 6
le verbe *verb,* 7
la verdure *vegetation,* 11
véritable *real,* 11; **C'était un véritable cauchemar!** *It was a real nightmare!* 11
le verre *glass,* 6
vers *about,* 6
vert(e) *green,* 3
la veste *suit jacket, blazer,* 10
le vêtement *clothing item,* 10
veux : Je veux bien. *I'd really like to.* 6; **Tu veux... avec moi?** *Do you want to . . . with me?* 6
la viande *meat,* 8
vide *empty,* 12
la vidéo *video,* 4; **faire de la vidéo** *to make videos,* 4; **des jeux vidéo** *video games,* 4
la vidéocassette *videotape,* 3
la vie scolaire *school life,* 2
viennois(e) *Viennese* (adj.), 5
viens : Tu viens? *Will you come?* 6
vietnamien(ne) *Vietnamese* (adj.), 1
vieux (vieille) *old,* 4
le village *town,* 4
la ville *city,* 12
le vinaigre *vinegar,* 8
la violence *violence,* 1
violet(te) *purple,* 3
la virgule *comma,* 3
la visite *visit, tour,* 12
visiter *to visit (a place),* 9
le visiteur *visitor,* 9
vite *fast, quickly,* 2
la vitrine *window (of a shop);* **faire les vitrines** *to window-shop,* 6
vivant(e) *lively, living,* 7
Vive... ! *Hurray for . . . !* 3
vivre *to live,* 2; l'art de vivre *the art of living,* 12
le vocabulaire *vocabulary,* 1
Voici... *Here's . . . ,* 7
Voilà. *Here.* 3; Voilà... *There's . . . ,* 7
la voile *sailing,* 11; **faire de la planche à voile** *to go windsurfing,* 11; **faire de la voile** *to go sailing,* 11
voir *to see,* 6; **voir un film** *to see a movie,* 6; **aller voir un match** *to go see a game,* 6; **voir une pièce** *to see a play,* 6
le voisin (la voisine) *neighbor,* 1
la voiture *car,* 7; **en voiture** *by car,* 12; **laver la voiture** *to wash the car,* 7
la voix *voice,* 3
le volley(-ball) *volleyball,* 4; **jouer au volley(-ball)** *to play volleyball,* 4
volontiers *with pleasure, gladly,* 8
vos *your,* 7
votre *your,* 7
voudrais : Je voudrais... *I'd like . . .* 3
vouloir *to want,* 6; **Je n'en veux plus.** *I don't want anymore.* 8; **Je veux bien.** *I'd really like to.* 6; *Gladly.* 8; **Oui, j'en veux bien.** *Yes, I'd like some.* 8; **Oui, si tu veux.** *Yes, if you want to.* 7; **Tu veux... ?** *Do you want . . . ?*

6; **voulez : Vous voulez... ?** *Do you want . . . ?* 8
vous *you,* 1
le voyage *voyage, trip,* 0
voyager *to travel,* 1; **Bon voyage!** *Have a good trip!* 11
vrai(e) *true,* 2
vraiment *really,* 11; **Non, pas vraiment.** *No, not really.* 11
vu (pp. of voir) *seen, saw,* 9
la vue *view,* 6

le week-end *on weekends,* 4; *weekend,* 6
le western *western (movie),* 0

le xylophone *xylophone,* 0

y *there,* 12; **Allons-y!** *Let's go!* 4; **Comment est-ce qu'on y va?** *How can we get there?* 12; **J'y vais tout de suite.** *I'll go right away.* 8; **On peut y aller...** *We can go there . . . ,* 12

les yaourts (m.) *yogurt,* 8
les yeux (m. pl.) *eyes,* 8
la yole *skiff (a type of boat),* 12
le yo-yo *yo-yo,* 0

le zèbre *zebra,* 0
zéro *a waste of time,* 2; *zero,* 0
le zoo *zoo,* 6
zoologique *zoological, having to do with animals,* 6
le zouk *zouk (style of music and dance),* 12
Zut! *Darn!* 3

English-French Vocabulary

In this vocabulary, the English definitions of all active French words in the book have been listed, followed by their French equivalent. The number after each entry refers to the chapter in which the entry is introduced. It is important to use a French word in its correct context. The use of a word can be checked easily by referring to the chapter where it appears. French words and phrases are presented in the same way as in the French-English vocabulary.

a *un, une,* 3
able: to be able to *pouvoir,* 8
about *vers,* 6
across from *en face de,* 12
adore *adorer,* 1; **I adore . . .** *J'adore...,* 1
advise *conseiller;* **What do you advise me to do?** *Qu'est-ce que tu me conseilles?* 9
aerobics *l'aérobic* (f.), 4; **to do aerobics** *faire de l'aérobic,* 4
after *après,* 9; **And after that, . . .** *Et après ça...,* 9
afternoon *l'après-midi* (m.), 2; **afternoon off** *l'après-midi libre,* 2; **in the afternoon** *l'après-midi,* 2
afterwards *après,* 9; **Afterwards, I went out.** *Après, je suis sorti(e).* 9; **And afterwards?** *Et après?* 9
Agreed. *Entendu.* 6
algebra *l'algèbre* (f.), 2
all *tout(e):* **Not at all.** *Pas du tout.* 4
already *déjà,* 9
also *aussi,* 1
am: I am . . . years old. *J'ai... ans.* 1
an *un, une,* 3
and *et,* 1
annoying *embêtant(e),* 7; *pénible,* 7
answer *répondre,* 9; **There's no answer.** *Ça ne répond pas.* 9
any (of it) *en,* 8; **any more: I don't want any more.** *Je n'en veux plus.* 8
anything: I didn't forget anything. *Je n'ai rien oublié.* 11
apple *la pomme,* 8
apple juice *le jus de pomme,* 5
April *avril,* 4
are: These/those are . . . *Ce sont...,* 7; **They're . . .** *Ils/Elles sont...,* 7
art class *les arts plastiques* (m. pl.), 2
at *à la, au, à l', aux,* 6; **at . . . fifteen** *à... heure(s) quinze,* 2; **at . . . forty-five** *à... heure(s) quarante-cinq,* 2; **at . . . thirty** *à... heure(s) trente,* 2; **at . . . ('s) house** *chez...,* 6; **at the record store** *chez le disquaire,* 12; **At what time?** *A quelle heure?* 6
August *août,* 4
autumn *l'automne* (m.), 4
aunt *la tante,* 7
avocado *l'avocat* (m.), 8

backpack *le sac à dos,* 3
bad *mauvais(e),* 5; **Not bad.** *Pas mal.* 1; **Oh, pas mauvais.** *Oh, not bad.* 9; **Very bad.** *Très mauvais.* 9
bag *le sac,* 3
baggy *large,* 10
bakery *la boulangerie,* 12
banana *la banane,* 8
bank *la banque,* 12
baseball *le base-ball,* 4; **to play baseball** *jouer au base-ball,* 4
basketball *le basket(-ball),* 4; **to play basketball** *jouer au basket (-ball),* 4
bathing suit *le maillot de bain,* 10
be *être,* 7
be able to, can *pouvoir,* 8; **Can you . . . ?** *Tu peux... ?* 12
beach *la plage,* 1
beans *les haricots* (m.), 8; **green beans** *les haricots verts* (m.), 8
because *parce que,* 5
beef *le bœuf,* 8
begin *commencer,* 9
behind *derrière,* 12
belt *la ceinture,* 10
better *mieux,* 9; **It's going to get better!** *Ça va aller mieux!* 9
between *entre,* 12
big *grand(e),* 10
bike *le vélo; faire du vélo,* 4; **by bike** *à vélo,* 12
biking *le vélo,* 1
binder: loose-leaf binder *le classeur,* 3
biology *la biologie,* 2
black *noir(e),* 3
blackboard *le tableau,* 0; **Go to the blackboard!** *Allez au tableau!* 0
blazer *la veste,* 10
blond *blond(e),* 7
blue *bleu(e),* 3
boat *le bateau,* 11; **by boat** *en bateau,* 12; **to go boating** *faire du bateau,* 11
book *le livre,* 0
bookstore *la librairie,* 12
boots *les bottes* (f.), 10
boring *barbant(e),* 2; **It was boring.** *C'était ennuyeux.* 11; *C'était barbant!* 11
borrow *emprunter,* 12
bottle *la bouteille,* 8; **a bottle of** *une bouteille de,* 8
box *le paquet,* 8; **a package/box of** *un paquet de,* 8
boy *le garçon,* 8
bracelet *le bracelet,* 3
bread *le pain,* 8; **long, thin loaf of bread** *la baguette,* 12
break *la récréation,* 2
breakfast *le petit déjeuner,* 8
bring *apporter,* 9; **Bring me back . . .** *Rapporte-moi...,* 8; **Please bring me . . .** *Apportez-moi..., s'il vous plaît.* 5; **Will you bring me . . . ?** *Tu me rapportes... ?* 8
brother *le frère,* 7
brown *marron* (inv.), 3
brunette *brun(e),* 7
bus *le bus,* 12; **by bus** *en bus,* 12; *to miss the bus* **rater le bus,** 9
busy *occupé(e),* 6; **It's busy.** *C'est occupé.* 9; **Sorry, I'm busy.** *Désolé(e), je suis occupé(e).* 6
but *mais,* 1
butter *le beurre,* 8
buy *acheter,* 9; **Buy (me) . . .** *Achète(-moi)...,* 8
Bye! *Tchao!* 1

C

cafeteria *la cantine,* 9; **at the school cafeteria** *à la cantine,* 9
cake *le gâteau,* 8
calculator *la calculatrice,* 3
call *téléphoner,* 9; **Call him/her/them!** *Téléphone-lui/-leur!* 9; **Can you call back later?** *Vous pouvez rappeler plus tard?* 9; **Who's calling?** *Qui est à l'appareil?* 9
camera *l'appareil-photo* (m.), 11
camp *la colonie de vacances,* 11; **to/at a summer camp** *en colonie de vacances,* 11
camping *le camping,* 11; **to go camping** *faire du camping,* 11
can: to be able to, can *pouvoir,* 8; **Can I talk to you?** *Je peux te parler?* 9; **Can you . . . ?** *Est-ce que tu peux... ?* 12; **Can you . . . ?** *Tu peux... ?* 8; **Can I try on . . . ?** *Je peux essayer... ?* 10; **We can . . .** *On peut...,* 6; **What can I do?** *Qu'est-ce que je peux faire?* 9
can *la boîte,* 8; **a can of** *une boîte de,* 8
can't: I can't right now. *Je ne peux pas maintenant.* 8; **No, I can't.** *Non, je ne peux pas.* 12
canary *le canari,* 7
cap *la casquette,* 10
car *la voiture,* 7; **by car** *en voiture,* 12; **to wash the car** *laver la voiture,* 7
cards *les cartes* (f.), 4; **to play cards** *jouer aux cartes,* 4
carrot *la carotte,* 8
cassette tape *la cassette,* 3
cat *le chat,* 7
CD/compact disc *le disque compact/le CD,* 3
Certainly. *Bien sûr.* 9
chair *la chaise,* 0
check *l'addition* (f.), 5; **The check, please.** *L'addition, s'il vous plaît.* 5
cheese *le fromage,* 5; **toasted ham and cheese sandwich** *le croque-monsieur,* 5
chemistry *la chimie,* 2
chic *chic* (inv.), 10
chicken (animal) *la poule,* 8; **chicken meat** *le poulet,* 8
child *l'enfant* (m./f.), 7; **children** *les enfants,* 7
chocolate *le chocolat,* 1; **hot chocolate** *un chocolat,* 5
choir *la chorale,* 2
choose *choisir,* 10; **Have you chosen?** *Vous avez choisi?* 5
class *le cours,* 2; **What classes do you have . . . ?** *Tu as quels cours... ?* 2
clean: to clean the house *faire le ménage,* 7
clear: to clear the table *débarrasser la table,* 7
close: Close the door! *Fermez la porte!* 0
close to *près de,* 12
clothing *les vêtements,* 10
coast *le bord,* 11; **to/on the coast** *au bord de la mer,* 11
coat *le manteau,* 10
coconut *la noix de coco,* 8
coffee *le café,* 5
cola *le coca,* 5
cold *froid(e)* 4; **It's cold.** *Il fait froid.* 4
color *la couleur,* 3; **What color is . . . ?** *De quelle couleur est... ?* 3
come: Will you come? *Tu viens?* 6
compact disc/CD *le disque compact/le CD,* 3
computer *l'ordinateur* (m.), 3
computer science *l'informatique* (f.), 2
concert *le concert,* 1
continue *continuer,* 12
cool *cool,* 2; **It's cool out.** *Il fait frais.* 4; **Very cool (great).** *Très chouette.* 9
corn *le maïs,* 8
corner *le coin,* 12; **on the corner of** *au coin de,* 12
cotton (adj.) *en coton,* 10
could: Could you do me a favor? *(Est-ce que) tu peux me rendre un petit service?* 12; **Could you go by . . . ?** *Tu pourrais passer à... ?* 12
countryside *la campagne,* 11; **to/in the countryside** *à la campagne,* 11
course *le cours,* 2
course: Of course. *Bien sûr.* 3
cousin *le cousin (la cousine),* 7
cross *traverser,* 12
cute *mignon(ne),* 7

D

dairy products *les produits* (m.) *laitiers,* 8
dance *danser,* 1
dance *la danse,* 2
Darn! *Zut!* 3
daughter *la fille,* 7
day *le jour,* 2
December *décembre,* 4; **in December** *en décembre,* 4
decided: Have you decided? *Vous avez choisi?* 5; **Have you decided to take . . . ?** *Vous avez décidé de prendre... ?* 10
delicious *délicieux(-euse),* 5
denim *le jean,* 10; **in denim** *en jean,* 10
deposit *déposer,* 12; **to deposit money** *déposer de l'argent,* 12
dictionary *le dictionnaire,* 3
difficult *difficile,* 2
dinner *le dîner,* 8; **to have dinner** *dîner,* 9
dishes *la vaisselle,* 7; **to do the dishes** *faire la vaisselle,* 7
dismissal (when school gets out) *la sortie,* 2
do *faire,* 4; **Do you play/do . . . ?** *Est-ce que tu fais... ?* 4; **I do.** *Moi, si.* 2; **to do homework** *faire les devoirs,* 7; **to do the dishes** *faire la vaisselle,* 7; **I don't play/do . . .** *Je ne fais pas de...,* 4; **I have errands to do.** *J'ai des courses à faire.* 5; **I play/do . . .** *Je fais...,* 4; **In your opinion, what do I do?** *A ton avis, qu'est-ce que je fais?* 9; **Sorry. I have homework to do.** *Désolé(e). J'ai des devoirs à faire.* 5; **What are you going to do . . . ?** *Qu'est-ce que tu vas faire... ?* 6; *Tu vas faire quoi... ?* 6; **What can I do?** *Qu'est-ce que je peux faire?* 9; **What did you do . . . ?** *Qu'est-ce que tu as fait... ?* 9; **What do you advise me to do?** *Qu'est-ce que tu me conseilles?* 9; **What do you do . . . ?** *Qu'est-ce que tu fais... ?* 4; **What do you do when . . . ?** *Qu'est-ce que tu fais quand... ?* 4
dog *le chien,* 7; **to walk the dog** *promener le chien,* 7
done, made *fait* (pp. of faire), 9
door *la porte,* 0
down: You go down this street to the next light. *Vous continuez jusqu'au prochain feu rouge.* 12
dozen *la douzaine,* 8; **a dozen** *une douzaine de,* 8
drama *le théâtre,* 4; **to do drama** *faire du théâtre,* 4
dress *la robe,* 10
drink *la boisson,* 5; **What do you have to drink?** *Qu'est-ce que vous avez comme boissons?* 5; **What is there to drink?** *Qu'est-ce qu'il y a à boire?* 5
drugstore *la pharmacie,* 12

E

earn *gagner,* 9
earrings *les boucles d'oreilles* (f.), 10
easy *facile,* 2
eat *manger,* 6
egg *l'œuf* (m.), 8
English (language) *l'anglais* (m.), 1
envelope *l'enveloppe* (f.), 12

eraser *la gomme,* 3
errands *les courses* (f.), 7; **I have errands to do.** *J'ai des courses à faire.* 5
especially *surtout,* 1
euro (European Community monetary unit) *l'euro* (m.); *Ça fait... euros./C'est... euros.* It's . . . euros. 5
evening *le soir,* 4; **in the evening** *le soir,* 4
everything *tout,* 11; **I've thought of everything.** *J'ai pensé à tout.* 11
exam *l'examen* (m.), 1
excellent *excellent(e),* 5; **Yes, excellent.** *Oui, excellent.* 9
excuse: Excuse me. *Excusez-moi.* 3; **Excuse me, . . . , please?** *Pardon, ..., s'il vous plaît?* 12; **Excuse me. Where is . . . , please?** *Pardon. Où est..., s'il vous plaît?* 12; **Excuse me. I'm looking for . . . , please.** *Pardon. Je cherche..., s'il vous plaît.* 12
expensive *cher (chère),* 10; **It's too expensive.** *C'est trop cher.* 10

fail *rater,* 9; **to fail a test** *rater un examen,* 9; **to fail a quiz** *rater une interro,* 9
fall *l'automne* (m.), 4; **in the fall** *en automne,* 4
fantastic *sensass (sensationnel),* 10
far from *loin de,* 12
fascinating *passionnant(e),* 2
fat *gros (se),* 7
father *le père,* 7
February *février,* 4; **in February** *en février,* 4
feel: I feel like . . . *J'ai envie de...,* 11; **I don't feel like it.** *Ça ne me dit rien.* 6
finally *enfin,* 9; *finalement,* 9
find *trouver,* 9
Fine. *Ça va.* 1; **Yes, it was fine.** *Oui, ça a été.* 9
first *d'abord,* 7; **OK, if you . . . first.** *D'accord, si tu... d'abord.* 7
fish *le poisson,* 7
flour *la farine,* 8
foot *le pied,* 12; **on foot** *à pied,* 12
football *le football américain,* 4; **to play football** *jouer au football américain,* 4
for *pour,* 3; **What do you need for . . . ?** (informal) *Qu'est qu'il te faut pour... ?* 3
forest *la forêt,* 11; **to/in the forest** *en forêt,* 11
forget *oublier,* 9; **Don't forget . . .** *N'oublie pas de...,* 8; **Forget him/her/them!** *Oublie-le/-la/-les!* 9; **I didn't forget anything.** *Je n'ai rien oublié.* 11; **You didn't forget . . . ?** *Tu n'as pas oublié... ?* 11
franc (former monetary unit of France) *le franc,* 3
French (language) *le français,* 1; **French fries** *les frites* (f.), 1
Friday *vendredi,* 2; **on Fridays** *le vendredi,* 2
friend *l'ami(e)* (m./f.), 1; **to go out with friends** *sortir avec les copains,* 1
from *de,* 0
front: in front of *devant,* 6
fruit *le fruit,* 8
fun: Did you have fun? *Tu t'es bien amusé(e)?* 11; **Have fun!** *Amuse-toi bien!* 11; **What do you do to have fun?** *Qu'est-ce que tu fais pour t'amuser?* 4
funny *amusant(e),* 7

gain: to gain weight *grossir,* 10
game *le match,* 6; *to play video games* **jouer à des jeux vidéo,** 4; **to watch a game (on TV)** *regarder un match,* 6; **to go see a game** *aller voir un match,* 6
geography *la géographie,* 2
geometry *la géométrie,* 2
German (language) *l'allemand* (m.), 2
get: Get . . . *Prends...,* 8; **How can we get there?** *Comment est-ce qu'on y va?* 12
gift *le cadeau,* 11
girl *la fille,* 0
give *donner,* 5; **Please give me . . .** *Donnez-moi..., s'il vous plaît.* 5
Gladly. *Je veux bien.* 8
go *aller,* 6; **Go to the blackboard!** *Allez au tableau!* 0; **I'm going . . .** *Je vais...,* 6; **What are you going to do . . . ?** *Tu vas faire quoi... ?* 6; **It doesn't go at all with . . .** *Il/Elle ne va pas du tout avec...,* 10; **It goes very well with . . .** *Il/Elle va très bien avec...,* 10; **to go out with friends** *sortir avec les copains,* 1; **I'd like . . . to go with . . .** *J'aimerais... pour aller avec...,* 10; **Afterwards, I went out.** *Après, je suis sorti(e).* 9; **Could you go by . . . ?** *Tu pourrais passer à... ?* 12; **Did it go well?** *Ça s'est bien passé?* 11; **I'm going to have . . . , please.** *Je vais prendre..., s'il vous plaît.* 5; **What are you going to do . . . ?** *Qu'est-ce que tu vas faire... ?* 6; **I went . . .** *Je suis allé(e)...,* 9; **I'm going to . . .** *Je vais...,* 11; **Let's go . . .** *Allons...,* 6; **to go for a walk** *faire une promenade,* 6; **We can go there . . .** *On peut y aller...,* 12; **Where are you going to go . . . ?** *Où est-ce que tu vas aller... ?* 11; **Where did you go?** *Tu es allé(e) où?* 9; **You keep going until the next light.** *Vous continuez jusqu'au prochain feu rouge.* 12; **How's it going?** *(Comment) ça va?* 1
golf *le golf,* 4; **to play golf** *jouer au golf,* 4
good *bon(ne),* 5; **Have a good trip!** *Bon voyage!* 11; **Did you have a good . . . ?** *Tu as passé un bon... ?* 11; **It doesn't look good on you at all.** *Il/Elle ne te/vous va pas du tout.* 10; **It's pretty good!** *C'est pas mauvais!* 5; **not good** *pas bon,* 5; **Yes, very good.** *Oui, très bon.* 9
Goodbye! *Au revoir!* 1; *Salut!* 1
got: No, you've got to . . . *Non, tu dois...,* 7
grammar *la grammaire,* 1
grandfather *le grand-père,* 7
grandmother *la grand-mère,* 7
grapes *le raisin,* 8
great *génial(e),* 2; **Great!** *Super!* 1; **It looks great on you!** *C'est tout à fait ton style!* 10; **It was great!** *C'était formidable!* 11; **Not so great.** *Pas terrible,* 1
green *vert(e),* 3
green beans *les *haricots verts* (m.), 8
grey *gris(e),* 3
grocery store (small) *l'épicerie* (f.), 12
gross *dégoûtant(e),* 5
grow *grandir,* 10
guava *la goyave,* 8
gym *le sport,* 2

half *demi(e),* 6; **half past** *et demie,* 6; **half past** (after *midi* and *minuit*) *et demi,* 6
ham *le jambon,* 5; **toasted ham and cheese sandwich** *le croque-monsieur,* 5
hamburger *le hamburger,* 1
hand *la main,* 0
happened: What happened? *Qu'est-ce qui s'est passé?* 9
happy *content(e),* 7
hard *difficile,* 2
hat *le chapeau,* 10
have *avoir,* 2; **At what time do you have . . . ?** *Tu as... à quelle heure?* 2; **Did you have a good**

weekend? *Tu as passé un bon week-end?* 9; **Do you have . . . ?** *Vous avez... ?* 2; *Tu as... ?* 3; **Do you have that in . . . ? (size, fabric, color)** *Vous avez ça en... ?* 10; **Have . . .** *Prends/Prenez...*, 5; **What are you having?** *Vous prenez?* 5; **I don't have . . .** *Je n'ai pas de...*, 3; **I have some things to do.** *J'ai des trucs à faire.* 5; **I have . . .** *J'ai...*, 2; **I'll have . . . , please.** *Je vais prendre..., s'il vous plaît.* 5; **to take or to have (food or drink)** *prendre,* 5; **We have . . .** *Nous avons...,* 2; **What classes do you have . . . ?** *Tu as quels cours... ?* 2; **What do you have . . . ?** *Tu as quoi... ?* 2; **What kind of . . . do you have?** *Qu'est-ce que vous avez comme... ?* 5; **Will you have . . . ?** *Tu prends/Vous prenez... ?* 8
health *le cours de développement personnel et social (DPS),* 2
Hello. *Bonjour.* 1; **Hello? (on the phone)** *Allô?* 9
help: May I help you? *(Est-ce que) je peux vous aider?* 10
her *la,* 9; *son/sa/ses,* 7; **to her** *lui,* 9
Here. *Voilà.* 3; **Here's . . .** *Voici...*, 7
Hi! *Salut!* 1
hiking *la randonnée,* 11; **to go hiking** *faire de la randonnée,* 11
him *le,* 9; **to him** *lui,* 9
his *son/sa/ses,* 7
history *l'histoire* (f.), 2
hockey *le *hockey,* 4; **to play hockey** *jouer au hockey,* 4
Hold on. *Ne quittez pas.* 9
homework *les devoirs* (m.), 2; **I've got homework to do.** *J'ai des devoirs à faire.* 5; **to do homework** *faire les devoirs,* 7
horrible *épouvantable,* 9; **It was horrible.** *C'était épouvantable.* 9
horseback riding *l'équitation* (f.), 1; **to go horseback riding** *faire de l'équitation,* 1
hose (clothing) *le collant,* 10
hot *chaud,* 4; **It's hot.** *Il fait chaud.* 4; **not so hot** *pas super,* 2
hot chocolate *le chocolat,* 5
hot dog *le *hot-dog,* 5
house: at my house *chez moi,* 6; **Is this . . . 's house?** *Je suis bien chez... ?* 9; **to/at . . . 's house** *chez...*, 6
housework *le ménage,* 1; **to do housework** *faire le ménage,* 1
how: How old are you? *Tu as quel âge?* 1; **How about . . . ?** *On... ?* 4; **How do you like it?** *Comment tu trouves ça?* 5; **How much is . . . ?** *C'est combien... ?* 5; **How much is it?** *C'est combien?* 3; **How much is it, please? (total)** *Ça fait combien, s'il vous plaît?* 5; **How's it going?** *(Comment) ça va?* 1
how much *combien,* 3; **How much is . . . ?** *C'est combien,... ?* 3; **How much is it? (total)** *Ça fait combien, s'il vous plaît?* 5
hundred *cent,* 3; **two hundred** *deux cents,* 3
hungry: to be hungry *avoir faim,* 5; **No thanks. I'm not hungry anymore.** *Non, merci. Je n'ai plus faim.* 8
husband *le mari,* 7

I *je,* 1; **I do.** *Moi, si.* 2; **I don't.** *Moi, non.* 2
ice cream *la glace,* 1
ice-skate *faire du patin à glace,* 4
idea *l'idée* (f.), 4; **Good idea.** *Bonne idée.* 4; **I have no idea.** *Je n'en sais rien.* 11
if *si,* 7; **OK, if you . . . first.** *D'accord, si tu... d'abord.* 7
impossible *impossible,* 7; **No, that's impossible.** *Non, c'est impossible.* 7
in *dans,* 6; **in (a city or place)** *à,* 11; **in (before a feminine country)** *en,* 11; **in (before a masculine noun)** *au,* 11; **in (before a plural country)** *aux,* 11; **in front of** *devant,* 6; **in the afternoon** *l'après-midi,* 2; **in the evening** *le soir,* 4; **in the morning** *le matin,* 2
in-line skate *le roller en ligne,* 4; **to in-line skate** *faire du roller en ligne,* 4
indifference: (expression of indifference) *Bof!* 1
intend: I intend to . . . *J'ai l'intention de...*, 11
interest: That doesn't interest me. *Ça ne me dit rien.* 4
interesting *intéressant(e),* 2
is: He is . . . *Il est...*, 7; **It's . . .** *C'est...*, 2; **She is . . .** *Elle est...*, 7; **There's . . .** *Voilà...*, 7; **This is . . .** *C'est... ; Voici...*, 7
it *le, la,* 9
It's . . . *C'est...*, 2; **It's . . .** *Il est...* (time), 6; **It's . . . euros.** *C'est... euros.* 5; *Ça fait... euros.* 5; **No, it's . . .** *Non, c'est...*, 4; **Yes, it's . . .** *Oui, c'est...*, 4

jacket *le blouson,* 10; **suit jacket** *la veste,* 10
jam *la confiture,* 8
January *janvier,* 4; **in January** *en janvier,* 4
jeans *le jean,* 3
jog *faire du jogging,* 4
jogging *le jogging,* 4
juice *le jus,* 5; **orange juice** *le jus d'orange,* 5; **apple juice** *le jus de pomme,* 5
July *juillet,* 4; **in July** *en juillet,* 4
June *juin,* 4; **in june** *en juin,* 4

kilogram *le kilo(kilogramme),* 8; **a kilogram of** *un kilo de,* 8
kind: What kind of . . . do you have? *Qu'est-ce que vous avez comme... ?* 5
know: I don't know. *Je ne sais pas.* 10

lab *les travaux pratiques* (m. pl.), 2
later: Can you call back later? *Vous pouvez rappeler plus tard?* 9; **See you later!** *A tout à l'heure!* 1
Latin (language) *le latin,* 2
lawn *le gazon,* 7; **to mow the lawn** *tondre le gazon,* 7
learn *apprendre,* 0
leather *le cuir,* 10; **in leather** *en cuir,* 10
leave *partir,* 11; **Can I leave a message?** *Je peux laisser un message?* 9; **You can't leave without . . .** *Tu ne peux pas partir sans...*, 11
left *la gauche,* 12; **to the left** *à gauche (de),* 12
lemon *le citron,* 8
lemon soda *la limonade,* 5
lemonade *le citron pressé,* 5
let's: Let's go . . . *Allons...*, 6; **Let's go!** *Allons-y!* 4
letter *la lettre,* 12; **to send letters** envoyer des lettres, 12
lettuce *la salade* (f.), 8
library *la bibliothèque,* 6
like *aimer,* 1; **I'd really like . . .** *Je voudrais bien...*, 11; **Do you**

like . . . ? *Tu aimes... ?* 1; **Do you like it?** *Il/Elle te (vous) plaît?* 10; **How do you like . . . ?** *Comment tu trouves... ?* 10; **How do you like it?** *Comment tu trouves ça?* 5; **I (really) like . . .** *Moi, j'aime (bien)...*, 1; **I don't like . . .** *Je n'aime pas...*, 1; **I like it, but it's expensive.** *Il/Elle me plaît, mais il/elle est cher (chère).* 10; **I'd like . . .** *Je voudrais...*, 3; **I'd like . . . to go with . . .** *J'aimerais... pour aller avec...*, 10; **I'd really like to.** *Je veux bien.* 6; **I'd like to buy . . .** *Je voudrais acheter...*, 3; **What would you like?** *Vous désirez?* 10
like: What are they like? *Ils/Elles sont comment?* 7; **What is he like?** *Il est comment?* 7; **What is she like?** *Elle est comment?* 7
listen *écouter*, 1; **Listen!** *Ecoutez!* 0; **I'm listening.** *Je t'écoute.* 9; **to listen to music** *écouter de la musique*, 1
liter *le litre*, 8; **a liter of** *un litre de*, 8
long *long (ue)*, 10
look: Look at the map! *Regardez la carte!* 0; **It doesn't look good on you at all.** *Il/Elle ne te/vous va pas du tout.* 10; **I'm looking for something for . . .** *Je cherche quelque chose pour...*, 10; **It looks great on you!** *C'est tout à fait ton style!* 10; **Look, here's/there's/it's . . .** *Regarde, voilà...*, 12; **No, thanks, I'm just looking.** *Non, merci, je regarde.* 10; **to look for** *chercher*, 9
look after: to look after . . . *garder...*, 7
looks: It looks great on you! *C'est tout à fait ton style!* 10
loose-leaf binder *le classeur*, 3
lose *perdre*, 9; **to lose weight** *maigrir*, 10
lot: A lot. *Beaucoup.* 4
lots: I have lots of things to do. *J'ai des tas de choses à faire.* 5
lower (number) *moins*, 0
luck *la chance*, 11; **Good luck!** *Bon courage!* 2; *Bonne chance!* 11
lunch *le déjeuner*, 2; **to have lunch** *déjeuner*, 9

ma'am *madame (Mme)*, 1
made *fait* (pp of faire), 9
magazine *le magazine*, 3
make *faire*, 4
mall *le centre commercial*, 6
mango *la mangue*, 8
map *la carte*, 0
March *mars*, 4; **in March** *en mars*, 4
market *le marché*, 8
math *les maths* (f. pl.), *les mathématiques*, 1
May *mai*, 4; **in May** *en mai*, 4
may: May I . . . ? *(Est-ce que) je peux... ?* 7; **May I help you?** *(Est-ce que) je peux vous aider?* 10
me *moi*, 2; **Me, too.** *Moi aussi.* 2; **Not me.** *Pas moi.* 2
mean *méchant(e)*, 7
meat *la viande*, 8
medicine *les médicaments* (m.), 12
meet *retrouver*, 6; *rencontrer*, 9; **I'd like you to meet . . .** *Je te (vous) présente...*, 7; **Pleased to meet you.** *Très heureux (heureuse).* 7; **O.K., we'll meet . . .** *Bon, on se retrouve...*, 6; **We'll meet. . .** *Rendez-vous...*, 6
menu *la carte*, 5; **The menu, please.** *La carte, s'il vous plaît.* 5
message *le message*, 9; **Can I leave a message?** *Je peux laisser un message?* 9
metro *le métro*, 12; **at the . . . metro stop** *au métro...*, 6
midnight *minuit*, 6; **It's midnight.** *Il est minuit.* 6; **It's half past midnight.** *Il est minuit et demi.* 6
milk *le lait*, 8
mineral water *l'eau minérale* (f.), 5
minute *la minute*, 9; **Do you have a minute?** *Tu as une minute?* 9
miss, Miss *mademoiselle (Mlle)*, 1
miss *rater*, 9; **to miss the bus** *rater le bus*, 9
moment *le moment*, 5; **One moment, please.** *Un moment, s'il vous plaît.* 5
Monday *lundi*, 2; **on Mondays** *le lundi*, 2
money *l'argent* (m.), 11
More . . . ? *Encore de... ?* 8; **I don't want any more.** *Je n'en veux plus.* 8
morning *le matin*, 2; **in the morning** *le matin*, 2
mother *la mère*, 7
mountain *la montagne*, 11; **to/in the mountains** *à la montagne*, 11
movie *le film*, 6; **to see a movie** *voir un film*, 6
movie theater *le cinéma*, 6; **the movies** *le cinéma*, 1
mow: to mow the lawn *tondre le gazon*, 7
Mr. *monsieur (M.)*, 1
Mrs. *madame (Mme)*, 1
much: How much is . . . ? *C'est combien,... ?* 5; **How much is it, please?** *Ça fait combien, s'il vous plaît?* 5; **How much is it?** *C'est combien?* 3; **No, not too much.** *Non, pas trop.* 2; **Not much.** *Pas grand-chose.* 6; **Not too much.** *Pas tellement.* 4; **Not very much.** *Pas beaucoup.* 4; **Yes, very much.** *Oui, beaucoup.* 2
museum *le musée*, 6
mushroom *le champignon*, 8
music *la musique*, 2
my *mon/ma/mes*, 7

name: His/Her name is . . . *Il/Elle s'appelle...*, 1; **My name is . . .** *Je m'appelle...*, 0; **What is your name?** *Tu t'appelles comment?* 0
natural science *les sciences naturelles* (f.), 2
need: I need . . . *Il me faut...*, 3; **I need . . .** *J'ai besoin de...*, 8; **What do you need for . . . ?** (formal) *Qu'est-ce qu'il vous faut pour... ?* 3; **What do you need for . . . ?** (informal) *Qu'est-ce qu'il te faut pour... ?* 3; **What do you need?** *De quoi est-ce que tu as besoin?* 8
neither: Neither do I. *Moi non plus.* 2; **neither tall nor short** *ne... ni grand(e) ni petit(e)*, 7
never *ne... jamais*, 4
next *prochain(e)*, 12; **You go down this street to the next light.** *Vous continuez jusqu'au prochain feu.* 12
next to *à côté de*, 12
nice *gentil (gentille)*, 7; *sympa (sympathique)*, 7; **It's nice weather.** *Il fait beau.* 4
nightmare *le cauchemar*, 11; **It was a real nightmare!** *C'était un véritable cauchemar!* 11
no *non*, 1
noon *midi*, 6; **It's noon.** *Il est midi.* 6; **It's half past noon.** *Il est midi et demi.* 6
not: Oh, not bad. *Oh, pas mal/mauvais.* 9; **not yet** *ne... pas encore*, 9; **Not at all.** *Pas du tout.* 4; **Not me.** *Pas moi.* 2; **Not so great.** *Pas terrible.* 1; **not very good** *pas bon*, 5; **No, not really.** *Non, pas vraiment.* 11; **No, not too much.** *Non, pas trop.* 2
notebook *le cahier*, 0, 3
nothing *rien*, 6; **Nothing special.** *Rien de spécial.* 6
novel *le roman*, 3
November *novembre*, 4; **in November** *en novembre*, 4
now *maintenant*, 2; **I can't right now.** *Je ne peux pas maintenant.* 8

O

o'clock *...heures,* 2; **at . . . o'clock** *à... heure(s),* 2

October *octobre,* 4; **in October** *en octobre,* 4

of *de,* 0; **of course** *bien sûr,* 3; **of it** *en,* 8; **of them** *en,* 8

often *souvent,* 4

O.K. *D'accord.* 4; **Is that O.K. with you?** *Tu es d'accord?* 7; **Well, O.K.** *Bon, d'accord.* 8; **Yes, it was O.K.** *Oui, ça a été.*

okra *les gombos* (m.), 8

old: How old are you? *Tu as quel âge?* 1; **I am . . . years old.** *J'ai... ans.* 1; **older** *âgé(e),* 7

omelet *l'omelette* (f.), 5

on: Can I try on . . . ? *Je peux essayer le/la/les... ?* 10; **on foot** *à pied,* 12; **on Fridays** *le vendredi,* 2; **on Mondays** *le lundi,* 2; **on Saturdays** *le samedi,* 2; **on Sundays** *le dimanche,* 2; **on Thursdays** *le jeudi,* 2; **on Tuesdays** *le mardi,* 2; **on Wednesdays** *le mercredi,* 2

once: once a week *une fois par semaine,* 4

onion *l'oignon* (m.), 8

open: Open your books to page . . . *Ouvrez vos livres à la page...*, 0

opinion *l'avis* (m.), 9; **In your opinion, what do I do?** *A ton avis, qu'est-ce que je fais?* 9

or *ou,* 1

orange (color) *orange* (inv.), 3

orange *l'orange* (f.), 8

orange juice *le jus d'orange,* 5;

our *notre/nos,* 7

out: Out of the question! *Pas question!* 7; **out of style,** *démodé(e),*10

package *le paquet,* 8; **a package/box of** *un paquet de,* 8

page *la page,* 0

pancake: a very thin pancake *la crêpe,* 5

pants *le pantalon,* 10

papaya *la papaye,* 8

paper *le papier,* 0; **sheets of paper** *les feuilles de papier* (f.), 3

pardon: Pardon me. *Pardon.* 3

parent *le parent,* 7

park *le parc,* 6

party *la boum,* 6; **to go to a party** *aller à une boum,* 6

pass: You'll pass . . . *Vous passez...,* 12

passport *le passeport,* 11

pastry *la pâtisserie,* 12; **pastry shop** *la pâtisserie,* 12

peach *la pêche,* 8

pear *la poire,* 8

peas *les petits pois* (m.), 8

pen *le stylo,* 0

pencil *le crayon,* 3; **pencil case** *la trousse,* 3; **pencil sharpener** *le taille-crayon,* 3

perfect *parfait(e),* 10; **It's perfect.** *C'est parfait.* 10

phone *le téléphone,* 1; **to talk on the phone** *parler au téléphone,* 1

photography: to do photography *faire de la photo,* 4

physical education *l'éducation physique et sportive (EPS)* (f.), 2

physics *la physique,* 2

pick *choisir,* 10; **to pick up your room** *ranger ta chambre,* 7

picnic *le pique-nique,* 6; **to have a picnic** *faire un pique-nique,* 6

picture *la photo,* 4; **to take pictures** *faire des photos,* 4

pie *la tarte,* 8

piece *le morceau,* 8; **a piece of** *un morceau de,* 8

pineapple *l'ananas* (m.), 8

pink *rose,* 3

pizza *la pizza,* 1

place *l'endroit* (m.), 12

plane *l'avion* (m.), 12; **by plane** *en avion,* 12

plane ticket *le billet d'avion,* 11

plans: I don't have any plans. *Je n'ai rien de prévu.* 11

plate *l'assiette* (f.), 5

play *la pièce,* 6; **to see a play** *voir une pièce,* 6

play *jouer,* 4; *faire,* 4; **I don't play/do . . .** *Je ne fais pas de...,* 4; **I play . . .** *Je joue...,* 4; **I play/do . . .** *Je fais...,* 4; **to play baseball** *jouer au base-ball,* 4; **to play basketball** *jouer au basket (-ball),* 4; **to play football** *jouer au football américain,* 4; **to play golf** *jouer au golf,* 4; **to play hockey** *jouer au hockey,* 4; **to play soccer** *jouer au foot(ball),* 4; **to play sports** *faire du sport,* 1; **to play tennis** *jouer au tennis,* 4; **to play video games** *jouer à des jeux vidéo,* 4; **to play volleyball** *jouer au volley(-ball),* 4; **What sports do you play?** *Qu'est-ce que tu fais comme sport?* 4

please *s'il te/vous plaît,* 3; **Yes, please.** *Oui, s'il te/vous plaît.* 8

pleased: Pleased to meet you. *Très heureux (-euse).* 7

pleasure *le plaisir,* 8; **Yes, with pleasure.** *Oui, avec plaisir.* 8

pork *le porc,* 8

post office *la poste,* 12

poster *le poster,* 0

potato *la pomme de terre,* 8

pound *la livre,* 8; **a pound of** *une livre de,* 8

practice *répéter,* 9

prefer *préférer,* 1; **I prefer . . .** *Je préfère...*, 1; *J'aime mieux...*, 1

problem *le problème,* 9; **I've got a little problem.** *J'ai un petit problème.* 9

pullover (sweater) *le pull-over,* 3

purple *violet(te),* 3

put *mettre,* 10; **to put on** *mettre,*10

quarter *le quart,* 6; **quarter past** *et quart,* 6; **quarter to** *moins le quart,* 6

question: Out of the question! *Pas question!* 7

quiche *la quiche,* 5

quiz *l'interro(gation)* (f.), 9

radio *la radio,* 3

rain: It's raining. *Il pleut.* 4

raise: Raise your hand! *Levez la main!* 0

rarely *rarement,* 4

read *lire,* 1; **read** *lu* (pp. of lire), 9

really *vraiment,* 11; **I (really) like . . .** *Moi, j'aime (bien)...*, 1; **I'd really like . . .** *Je voudrais bien...*, 11; **I'd really like to.** *Je veux bien.* 6; **No, not really.** *Non, pas vraiment.* 11

record store *le disquaire,* 12; **at the record store** *chez le disquaire,* 12

recreation center *la Maison des jeunes et de la culture (MJC),* 6

red *rouge,* 3; **redheaded** *roux (rousse),* 7

rehearse *répéter,* 9

relative *le parent,* 7

Repeat! *Répétez!* 0

restaurant *le restaurant,* 6

retro (style) *rétro* (inv.), 10

return: to return something *rendre,* 12

rice *le riz,* 8

ride: to go horseback riding *faire de l'équitation,* 1

right *la droite,* 12; **to the right** *à droite (de),* 12
right away *tout de suite,* 6; **Yes, right away.** *Oui, tout de suite.* 5; **I'll go right away.** *J'y vais tout de suite.* 8
right now *maintenant,* 8; **I can't right now.** *Je ne peux pas maintenant.* 8
right there: It's right there on the . . . *C'est tout de suite à...,* 12
room *la chambre,* 7; **to pick up your room** *ranger ta chambre,* 7
ruler *la règle,* 3

S

sailing *la voile,* 11; **to go sailing** *faire de la voile,* 11; *faire du bateau,* 11
salad *la salade,* 8
salami *le saucisson,* 5
sandals *les sandales* (f.), 10
sandwich *un sandwich,* 5; **cheese sandwich** *un sandwich au fromage,* 5; **ham sandwich** *un sandwich au jambon,* 5; **salami sandwich** *un sandwich au saucisson,* 5; **toasted ham and cheese sandwich** *le croque-monsieur,* 5
Saturday *samedi,* 2; **on Saturdays** *le samedi,* 2
saw *vu* (pp. of voir), 9
scarf *l'écharpe* (f.), 10
school *l'école* (f.), 1
science class *les sciences naturelles,* 2
scuba diving *la plongée,* 11; **to go scuba diving** *faire de la plongée,* 11
sea *la mer,* 11
second *la seconde,* 9; **One second, please.** *Une seconde, s'il vous plaît.* 9
see *voir,* 6; **See you later!** *A tout à l'heure!* 1; **See you soon.** *A bientôt.* 1; **See you tomorrow.** *A demain.* 1; **to go see a game** *aller voir un match,* 6; **to see a movie** *voir un film,* 6; **to see a play** *voir une pièce,* 6
seen *vu* (pp. of voir), 9
sell *vendre,* 9
send *envoyer,* 12; **to send letters** *envoyer des lettres,* 12
sensational *sensass,* 10
September *septembre,* 4; **in September** *en septembre,* 4
service: At your service; You're welcome. *A votre service.* 3
shall: Shall we go to the café? *On va au café?* 5
sheet *la feuille,* 0; **a sheet of paper** *une feuille de papier,* 0
shirt (man's) *la chemise,* 10; **(woman's)** *le chemisier,* 10
shoes *les chaussures* (f.), 10
shop: to go shopping *faire les magasins,* 1; **to window-shop** *faire les vitrines,* 6; **Can you do the shopping?** *Tu peux aller faire les courses?* 8
shopping *les courses* (f.), 7; **to do the shopping** *faire les courses,* 7
short (height) *petit(e),* 7; (length) *court(e),* 10
shorts: (pair of) shorts *le short,* 3
should: You should . . . *Tu devrais...,* 9; **You should talk to him/her/them.** *Tu devrais lui/leur parler.* 9
show *montrer,* 9
shy *timide,* 7
sing *chanter,* 9
sir *monsieur (M.),* 1
sister *la sœur,* 7
Sit down! *Asseyez-vous!* 0
size *la taille,* 10
skate: to ice-skate *faire du patin à glace,* 4; **to in-line skate** *faire du roller en ligne,* 4
ski *faire du ski,* 4; **How about skiing?** *On fait du ski?* 5; **to water-ski** *faire du ski nautique,* 4; **skiing** *le ski,* 1
skirt *la jupe,* 10
sleep *dormir,* 1
slender *mince,* 7
slice *la tranche,* 8; **a slice of** *une tranche de,* 8
small *petit(e),* 10
smart *intelligent(e),* 7
snack: afternoon snack *le goûter,* 8
snails *les escargots* (m.), 1
sneakers *les baskets* (f. pl.), 3
snow: It's snowing. *Il neige.* 4
so: not so great *pas terrible,* 5
So-so. *Comme ci comme ça.* 1
soccer *le football,* 1; *le foot,* 4; **to play soccer** *jouer au foot(ball),* 4
socks *les chaussettes* (f.), 10
soda: lemon soda *la limonade,* 5
some *des,* 3; **some** *du, de la, de l', des,* 8; **some (of it)** *en,* 8; **Yes, I'd like some.** *Oui, j'en veux bien.* 8
something *quelque chose,* 6; **I'm looking for something for . . . ,** *Je cherche quelque chose pour...,* 10
sometimes *quelquefois,* 4
son *le fils,* 7
soon: See you soon. *A bientôt.* 1
Sorry. *Je regrette.* 3; *Désolé(e).* 5; **Sorry, but I can't.** *Désolé(e), mais je ne peux pas.* 4; **I'm sorry, but I don't have time.** *Je regrette, mais je n'ai pas le temps.* 8; **Sorry, I'm busy.** *Désolé(e), je suis occupé(e).* 6
Spanish (language) *l'espagnol* (m.), 2
speak *parler,* 9; **Could I speak to . . . ?** *(Est-ce que) je peux parler à... ?* 9
special *spécial(e),* 6; **Nothing special.** *Rien de spécial.* 6
sports *le sport,* 1; **to play sports** *faire du sport,* 1; **What sports do you play?** *Qu'est-ce que tu fais comme sport?* 4
spring *le printemps,* 4; **in the spring** *au printemps,* 4
stadium *le stade,* 6
stamp *le timbre,* 12
stand: Stand up! *Levez-vous!* 0
start *commencer,* 9
stationery store *la papeterie,* 12
steak *le bifteck,* 8; **steak and French fries** *le steak-frites,* 5
stop: at the . . . metro stop *au métro...,* 6
store *le magasin,* 1
straight ahead *tout droit,* 12; **You go straight ahead until you get to . . .** *Vous allez tout droit jusqu'à...,* 12
strawberry *la fraise,* 8; **water with strawberry syrup** *le sirop de fraise (à l'eau),* 5
street *la rue,* 12; **Take . . . Street, then cross . . . Street.** *Prenez la rue..., puis traversez la rue...,* 12
strong *fort(e),* 7
student *l'élève* (m./f.), 2
study *étudier,* 1
study hall *l'étude* (f.), 2
style *la mode,* 10; **in style** *à la mode,* 10; **out of style** *démodé(e),* 10
subway *le métro,* 12; **by subway** *en métro,* 12
sugar *le sucre,* 7
suit: Does it suit me? *Il/Elle me va?* 10; **It suits you really well.** *Il/Elle te/vous va très bien.* 10
suit jacket *la veste,* 10
suitcase *la valise,* 11
summer *l'été* (m.), 4; **in the summer** *en été,* 4
summer camp *la colonie de vacances,* 11; **to/at a summer camp** *en colonie de vacances,* 11
Sunday *dimanche,* 2; **on Sundays** *le dimanche,* 2
sunglasses *les lunettes de soleil* (f. pl.), 10
super *super,* 2
supermarket *le supermarché,* 8
sure: I'm not sure. *J'hésite.* 10
sweater *le cardigan,* 10
sweatshirt *le sweat-shirt,* 3
swim *nager,* 1; *faire de la natation,* 4
swimming *la natation,* 4
swimming pool *la piscine,* 6
syrup: water with strawberry syrup *le sirop de fraise (à l'eau),* 5

T

T-shirt *le tee-shirt,* 3
table *la table,* 7; **to clear the table** *débarrasser la table,* 7
tacky *moche,* 10; **I think it's (they're) really tacky.** *Je le/la/les trouve moche(s).* 10
take or have (food or drink) *prendre,* 5; **Are you taking it/them?** *Vous le/la/les prenez?* 10; **Are you taking . . . ?** *Tu prends... ?* 11; **Have you decided to take . . . ?** *Vous avez décidé de prendre... ?* 10; **I'll take it/them.** *Je le/la/les prends.* 10; **to take a test** *passer un examen,* 9; **to take pictures** *faire des photos,* 4; **We can take . . .** *On peut prendre...,* 12; **Take . . . Street, then . . . Street.** *Prenez la rue..., puis la rue...,* 12
take out: Take out a sheet of paper. *Prenez une feuille de papier.* 0; **to take out the trash** *sortir la poubelle,* 7
taken *pris* (pp. of prendre), 9
talk *parler,* 1; **Can I talk to you?** *Je peux te parler?* 9; **to talk on the phone** *parler au téléphone,* 1; **We talked.** *Nous avons parlé.* 9
tall *grand(e),* 7
taxi *le taxi,* 12; **by taxi** *en taxi,* 12
teacher *le professeur,* 0
telephone *le téléphone,* 0
television *la télévision,* 0
tell *dire,* 9; **Can you tell her/him that I called?** *Vous pouvez lui dire que j'ai téléphoné?* 9
tennis *le tennis,* 4; **to play tennis** *jouer au tennis,* 4
terrible *horrible,* 10
test *l'examen* (m.), 1
Thank you. *Merci.* 3; **No thanks. I'm not hungry anymore.** *Non, merci. Je n'ai plus faim.* 8
that *ce, cet, cette,* 3; **This/That is . . .** *Ça, c'est...,* 12
theater *le théâtre,* 6
their *leur/leurs,* 7
them *les,* 9; **to them** *leur,* 9
then *ensuite,* 9
there *-là* (noun suffix), 3; **there** *il y a,* 5; **there** *y, là,* 12; **Is . . . there, please?** *(Est-ce que)... est là, s'il vous plaît?* 9; **There's . . .** *Voilà...,* 7; **There is/There are . . .** *Il y a...,* 5; **What is there to drink?** *Qu'est-ce qu'il y a à boire?* 5
these *ces,* 3; **These/those are . . .** *Ce sont...,* 7
thing *la chose,* 5; *le truc,* 5; **I have lots of things to do.** *J'ai des tas de choses à faire.* 5; **I have some things to do.** *J'ai des trucs à faire.* 5
think *penser,* 11; **I think it's/they're . . .** *Je le/la/les trouve...,* 10; **I've thought of everything.** *J'ai pensé à tout.* 11; **What do you think of . . . ?** *Comment tu trouves... ?* 2; **What do you think of that/it?** *Comment tu trouves ça?* 2
thirsty: to be thirsty *avoir soif,* 5
this *ce, cet, cette,* 3; **This is . . .** *C'est...,* 7; **This is . . .** *Voilà/Voici...,* 7; **This/That is . . .** *Ça, c'est...,* 12
those *ces,* 3; **These/Those are . . .** *Ce sont...,* 7
Thursday *jeudi,* 4; **on Thursdays** *le jeudi,* 2
ticket *le billet,* 11; **plane ticket** *le billet d'avion,* 11; **train ticket** *le billet de train,* 11
tie *la cravate,* 10
tight *serré(e),* 10
time *le temps,* 8; **a waste of time** *zéro,* 2; **at the time of** *à l'heure de,* 1; **At what time do you have . . . ?** *Tu as... à quelle heure?* 2; **At what time?** *A quelle heure?* 6; **from time to time** *de temps en temps,* 4; **I'm sorry, but I don't have time.** *Je regrette, mais je n'ai pas le temps.* 8; *Je suis désolé(e), mais je n'ai pas le temps.* 12; **What time is it?** *Quelle heure est-il?* 6
to *à la, au, à l', aux,* 6; **to (a city or place)** *à,* 11; **to (before a feminine country)** *en,* 11; **to (before a masculine noun)** *au,* 11; **to (before a plural noun)** *aux,* 11; **to her** *lui,* 9; **to him** *lui,* 9; **to them** *leur,* 9; **five to . . .** *moins cinq,* 6
today *aujourd'hui,* 2
tomato *la tomate,* 8
tomorrow *demain,* 2; **See you tomorrow.** *A demain.* 1
tonight *ce soir,* 7; **Not tonight.** *Pas ce soir.* 7
too (much) *trop,* 10; **It's/They're too . . .** *Il/Elle est (Ils/Elles sont) trop...,* 10; **Me too.** *Moi aussi.* 2; **No, it's too expensive.** *Non, c'est trop cher.* 10; **No, not too much.** *Non, pas trop.* 2; **Not too much.** *Pas tellement.* 4
track *l'athlétisme* (m.), 4; **to do track and field** *faire de l'athlétisme,* 4
train *le train,* 12; **by train** *en train,* 12; **train ticket** *le billet de train,* 11
trash(can) *la poubelle,* 7; **to take out the trash** *sortir la poubelle,* 7
travel *voyager,* 1
trip *le voyage,* 11; **Have a good trip!** *Bon voyage!* 11
true *vrai,* 2
try: Can I try on . . . ? *Je peux essayer... ?* 10; **Can I try it (them) on?** *Je peux l'/les essayer?* 10
Tuesday *mardi,* 2; **on Tuesdays** *le mardi,* 2
turn *tourner,* 12; **You turn . . .** *Vous tournez...,* 12
TV *la télé(vision),* 1; **to watch TV** *regarder la télé(vision),* 1

umbrella *le parapluie,* 11
uncle *l'oncle* (m.), 7
uncooked *cru(e),* 5
until *jusqu'à,* 12; **You go straight ahead until you get to . . .** *Vous allez tout droit jusqu'à...,* 12
useless *nul(le),* 2
usually *d'habitude,* 4

vacation *les vacances* (f. pl.), 1; **Have a good vacation!** *Bonnes vacances!* 11; **on vacation** *en vacances,* 4
vacuum (verb) *passer l'aspirateur,* 7
VCR (videocassette recorder) *le magnétoscope,* 0
vegetables *les légumes* (m.), 8
very *très,* 1; **Very well.** *Très bien.* 1; **Yes, very much.** *Oui, beaucoup.* 2
video *la vidéo,* 4; **to make videos** *faire de la vidéo,* 4; **video games** *des jeux vidéo,* 4
videocassette recorder (VCR) *le magnétoscope,* 0
videotape *la vidéocassette,* 3
visit (a place) *visiter,* 9
volleyball *le volley(-ball),* 4; **to play volleyball** *jouer au volley(-ball),* 4

wait for *attendre,* 9
Waiter! *Monsieur!* 5
Waitress! *Madame!* 5; *Mademoiselle!* 5

walk: to go for a walk *faire une promenade,* 6; **to walk the dog** *promener le chien,* 7
wallet *le portefeuille,* 3
want *vouloir,* 6; **Do you want . . . ?** *Tu veux... ?* 6; **Do you want . . . ?** *Vous voulez... ?* 8; **I don't want any more.** *Je n'en veux plus.* 8; **Yes, if you want to.** *Oui, si tu veux.* 7
wash *laver,* 7; **to wash the car** *laver la voiture,* 7
waste: a waste of time *zéro,* 2
watch *la montre,* 3
watch *regarder,* 1; **to watch a game (on TV)** *regarder un match,* 6; **to watch TV** *regarder la télé(vision),* 1
water *l'eau* (f.), 5; **mineral water** *l'eau minérale,* 5; **water with strawberry syrup** *le sirop de fraise (à l'eau),* 5
water ski *le ski nautique,* 4; **to water-ski** *faire du ski nautique,* 4
wear *mettre, porter,* 10; **I don't know what to wear for . . .** *Je ne sais pas quoi mettre pour... ,* 10; **Wear . . .** *Mets... ,* 10; **What shall I wear?** *Qu'est-ce que je mets?* 10; **Why don't you wear . . . ?** *Pourquoi est-ce que tu ne mets pas... ?* 10
weather *le temps,* 4; **What's the weather like?** *Quel temps fait-il?* 4
Wednesday *mercredi,* 2; **on Wednesdays** *le mercredi,* 2
week *la semaine,* 4; **once a week** *une fois par semaine,* 4
weekend *le week-end,* 6; **Did you have a good weekend?** *Tu as passé un bon week-end?* 9; **on weekends** *le week-end,* 4; **this weekend** *ce week-end,* 6
welcome: At your service; You're welcome. *A votre service.* 3
well *bien,* 1; **Did it go well?** *Ça s'est bien passé?* 11; **Very well.** *Très bien.* 1
went: Afterwards, I went out. *Après, je suis sorti(e).* 9; **I went . . .** *Je suis allé(e)... ,* 9
what *comment,* 0; **What is your name?** *Tu t'appelles comment?* 0; **What do you think of . . . ?** *Comment tu trouves... ?* 2; **What do you think of that/it?** *Comment tu trouves ça?* 2; **What's his/her name?** *Il/Elle s'appelle comment?* 1
what *qu'est-ce que,* 1; **What are you going to do . . . ?** *Qu'est-ce que tu vas faire... ?* 6; **What do you do to have fun?** *Qu'est-ce que tu fais pour t'amuser?* 4; **What do you have to drink?** *Qu'est-ce que vous avez comme boissons?* 5; **What do you need for . . . ?** (formal) *Qu'est-ce qu'il vous faut pour... ?* 3; **What happened?** *Qu'est-ce qui s'est passé?* 9; **What kind of . . . do you have?** *Qu'est-ce que vous avez comme... ?* 5
what *quoi,* 2; **I don't know what to wear for . . .** *Je ne sais pas quoi mettre pour... , 10;* **What are you going to do . . . ?** *Tu vas faire quoi... ?* 6; **What do you have . . . ?** *Tu as quoi... ?* 2; **What do you need?** *De quoi est-ce que tu as besoin?* 5
When? *Quand (ça)?* 6
where *où,* 6; **Where?** *Où (ça)?* 6; **Where are you going to go . . . ?** *Où est-ce que tu vas aller... ?* 11; **Where did you go?** *Tu es allé(e) où?* 9
which *quel(le),* 1
white *blanc(he),* 3
who *qui,* 0; **Who's calling?** *Qui est à l'appareil?* 9
whom *qui,* 6; **With whom?** *Avec qui?* 6
why *pourquoi,* 0; **Why don't you . . . ?** *Pourquoi tu ne... pas?* 9; **Why not?** *Pourquoi pas?* 6
wife *la femme,* 7
win *gagner,* 9
window *la fenêtre,* 0; **to window-shop** *faire les vitrines,* 6
windsurfing *la planche à voile,* 11; **to go windsurfing** *faire de la planche à voile,* 11
winter *l'hiver* (m.), 4; **in the winter** *en hiver,* 4
with *avec,* 6; **with me** *avec moi,* 6; **With whom?** *Avec qui?* 6
withdraw *retirer,* 12; **withdraw money** *retirer de l'argent,* 12
without *sans,* 11; **You can't leave without . . .** *Tu ne peux pas partir sans... ,* 11
work *travailler,* 9
worry: Don't worry! *Ne t'en fais pas!* 9
would like: I'd like to buy . . . *Je voudrais acheter... ,* 3

year *l'an* (m.); **I am . . . years old.** *J'ai... ans.* 1
yellow *jaune,* 3
yes *oui,* 1; **Yes, please.** *Oui, s'il te/vous plaît.* 8
yesterday *hier,* 9
yet: not yet *ne... pas encore,* 9
yogurt *les yaourts* (m.), 8
you *tu, vous,* 0; **And you?** *Et toi?* 1
young *jeune,* 7
your *ton/ta/tes,* 7; *votre/vos,* 7

zoo *le zoo,* 6

Grammar Index

Page numbers in boldface type refer to the **Grammaire** and **Note de grammaire** presentations. Other page numbers refer to grammar structures presented in the **Comment dit-on... ?, Tu te rappelles?, Vocabulaire,** and **A la française** sections. Page numbers beginning with **R** refer to the Grammar Summary in this Reference Section.

O

P

Q

Credits

ACKNOWLEDGMENTS

For permission to reprint copyrighted material, grateful acknowledgment is made to the following sources:

Agence Vu: Two photographs from "Je passe ma vie au téléphone" by Anne Vaisman, photographs by Claudine Doury, from *Phosphore,* no. 190, February 1997. Copyright © 1997 by Agence Vu.

Air France: Front of Air France boarding pass, "Carte d'accès à bord."

Bayard Presse International: From "Allez, c'est à vous de choisir," text by Florence Farcouli, illustrations by Olivier Tossan, from *Okapi,* no. 568-9, September 1995. Copyright © 1995 by Bayard Presse International. From "Je passe ma vie au téléphone" by Anne Vaisman from *Phosphore,* no. 190, February 1997. Copyright © 1997 by Bayard Presse International.

C'Rock Radio, Vienne: Logo for C'Rock Radio, 89.5 MHz.

Cacharel: Four adapted photographs with captions of Cacharel products from *Rentrée très classe à prix petits : Nouvelles Galeries Lafayette.*

Canal B, Bruz: Logo for Canal B Radio, 94 MHz.

Cathédrale d'images: Advertisement, "Cathédrale d'images," from *Évasion Plus.*

Comité Français d'Education pour la Santé, 2, rue Auguste Comte-92170 Vanves: From "Les groupes d'aliments" from the brochure *Comment équilibrer votre alimentation,* published and edited by the Comité Français d'Education pour la Santé.

CSA, France: "Sondage: les lycéens ont-ils le moral?" Copyright © 1989 by CSA.

Editions S.A.E.P.: Recipe and photograph for "Croissants au coco et au sésame," recipe and photograph for "Mousseline africaine de petits légumes," "Signification des symboles accompagnant les recettes," and jacket cover from *La Cuisine Africaine* by Pierrette Chalendar. Copyright © 1993 by S.A.E.P.

EF Foundation: From "Le rêve américain devient réalité, en séjour Immersion avec EF: Vivre à l'américaine," photograph, and "Vacances de Printemps" from "Les U.S.A. en cours Principal: le séjour EF idéal" from *EF Voyages Linguistiques: Hiver, Printemps et Eté 1993.*

Femme Actuelle: Text from "En direct des refuges: Poupette, 3 ans" by Nicole Lauroy from *Femme Actuelle,* no. 414, August 31–September 6, 1992. Copyright © 1992 by Femme Actuelle. Text from "En direct des refuges: Jupiter, 7 mois" by Nicole Lauroy from *Femme Actuelle,* no. 436, February 1993. Copyright © 1993 by Femme Actuelle. Text from "En direct des refuges: Flora, 3 ans" by Nicole Lauroy from *Femme Actuelle,* no. 457, July 1993. Copyright © 1993 by Femme Actuelle. Text from "En direct des refuges: Dady, 2 ans" and from "Mayo a trouvé une famille" by Nicole Lauroy from *Femme Actuelle,* no. 466, August 30–September 5, 1993. Copyright © 1993 by Femme Actuelle. Text from "En direct des refuges: Camel, 5 ans" by Nicole Lauroy from *Femme Actuelle,* no. 472, October 11–17, 1993. Copyright © 1993 by Femme Actuelle.

France Miniature: Cover, illustration and adapted text from brochure, *Le Pays France Miniature.*

France Télécom: Front and back of the Télécarte.

Galeries Lafayette: Four adapted photographs with captions of Cacharel products and two photographs with captions of NAF NAF products from *Rentrée très classe à prix petits: Nouvelles Galeries Lafayette.*

Grands Bateaux de Provence: Advertisement, "Bateaux 'Mireio'," from *Evasion Plus.*

Grottes de Thouzon: Advertisement, "Grottes de Thouzon," photograph by M. Crotet, from *Evasion Plus,* Provence, Imprimerie Vincent, 1994.

Groupe Filipacchi: Advertisement, "Casablanca," from *7 à Paris,* no. 534, February 2–18, 1992, p. 43.

Hachette Livre: From "Où dormir?" and "Où manger?" from "Arles (13200)" from *Le Guide du Routard : Provence-Côte d'Azur, 2000/2001.* Copyright by Hachette Livre (Hachette Tourisme).

L'Harmattan: Excerpts from French text and six illustrations from *Cheval de bois/Chouval bwa* by Isabelle and Henri Cadoré, illustrated by Bernadette Coléno. Copyright © 1993 by L'Harmattan.

Loca Center: Advertisement, "Loca Center," from *Guide des Services: La Martinique à domicile.*

Ministère de la Culture: From "Les jeunes aiment sortir" (Retitled: "Les loisirs préférés") from *Francoscopie: Comment vivent les Français, 1997* by Gérard Mermet.

Le Monde: From "Baccalauréat 1996. Les hauts et les bas: Taux de réussite par série" from *Le Monde de l'Education,* no. 240, September 1996. Copyright © 1996 by Le Monde.

Musée de l'Empéri: Adapted advertisement, "Château-Musée de l'Empéri," from *Evasion Plus.*

NAF NAF: Two photographs with captions of NAF NAF products from *Rentrée très classe à prix petits : Nouvelles Galeries Lafayette.*

NRJ, Paris: Adaptation of logo for NRJ Radio, 100.3 MHz.

OUÏ FM, Paris: Logo for OUÏ FM Radio, 102.3 MHz.

Parc Astérix S.A.: Cover of brochure, *Parc Astérix,* 1992. Advertisement for Parc Astérix from *Paris Vision,* 1993, p. 29.

Parc Zoologique de Paris: Cover and map from brochure, *Parc Zoologique de Paris.*

RCV: La Radio Rock, Lille: Logo for RCV: La Radio Rock, 99 MHz.

Village des Sports: Advertisement, "Village des Sports: c'est l'fun, fun, fun!," from *Région de Québec.*

Credits

PHOTOGRAPHY CREDITS

Abbreviations used: (t) top, (b) bottom, (l) left, (r) right, (c) center.

Rencontre culturelle students, HRW Photo/John Langford

Panorama fabric, Copyright © 1992 by Dover Publications, Inc.

All other fabric: HRW Photo.

All globes: Mountain High Maps® Copyright ©1997 Digital Wisdom, Inc.

TABLE OF CONTENTS: vii, HRW Photo/Sam Dudgeon; viii (both), HRW Photo/Marty Granger/Edge Productions; ix (t), © Owen Franken/Stock Boston; ix (b), HRW Photo/Marty Granger/Edge Productions; x, HRW Photo/Marty Granger/Edge Productions; xi (both), HRW Photo/Marty Granger/Edge Productions; xii (t), HRW Photo/Edge Productions; xii (b), © Hilary Wilkes/International Stock Photography; xiii, © Owen Franken/CORBIS; xiv, © Julio Donoso/Woodfin Camp & Associates; xv (both), HRW Photo/Edge Productions; xvi, © Owen Franken/CORBIS; xvii (both), HRW Photo/Marty Granger/Edge Productions; xviii, © Benelux Press/Leo de Wys; xix, HRW Photo/Marty Granger/Edge Productions; xx, Corbis Images; xxi, HRW Photo/Marty Granger/Edge Productions; xxii, HRW Photo/Marty Granger/Edge Productions.

PRELIMINARY CHAPTER: xxvi (t, c), © Joe Viesti/Viesti Collection, Inc.; xxvi (b), © Robert Fried/Stock Boston; 1 (tl), D&P Valenti/H. Armstrong Roberts; 1 (tr), Stone/Tim MacPherson; 1 (c), ©Michael Dwyer/Stock Boston; 1 (bl), © Owen Franken/Stock Boston; 1 (br), Viesti Collection, Inc.; 2 (t, c), Archive Photos; 2 (bl), Stephane Cardinale/People Avenue/Corbis; 2 (br), AP/Wide World Photos; 3 (t), Vedat Acickalin/SIPA PRESS; 3 (c), Gastaud/SIPA Press; 3 (bl), George Lange/CORBIS OUTLINE; 3 (br), Shawn Botterill/Allsport; 4 (tl), Arianespace/SIPA Press; 4 (tc), Nabil Zorkot; 4 (tr), Boisière/SIPA Press; 4 (cl), © Robert Frerck/Odyssey/Chicago; 4 (cr), K. Scholz/H. Armstrong Roberts; 4 (bl), HRW Photo/May Polycarpe; 4 (br), © Telegraph Colour Library/FPG International; 5 (l), Pictor Uniphoto; 5 (r), HRW Photo/John Langford; 6 (row 1, l), Digital imagery® © 2003 PhotoDisc, Inc.; 6 (row 1, cl), © Stockbyte; 6 (row 1, c), Digital imagery® © 2003 PhotoDisc, Inc.; 6 (row 1, cr), HRW Photo/Victoria Smith; 6 (row 1, r), Mountain High Maps® Copyright©1997 Digital Wisdom, Inc.; 6 (row 2, l), David Simson/Stock Boston; 6 (row 2, cl, c), Corbis Images; 6 (row 2, cr), CORBIS/Stuart Westmorland; 6 (row 2, r), Digital imagery® © 2003 PhotoDisc, Inc.; 6 (row 3, l, cl), Digital imagery® © 2003 PhotoDisc, Inc.; 6 (row 3, c), ©1998 Artville, LLC; 6 (row 3, cr), EyeWire, Inc.; 6 (row 3, r), © Stockbyte; 6 (row 4, l), CORBIS/Gunter Marx; 6 (row 4, cl), HRW Photo/Victoria Smith; 6 (row 4, c, cr, r), Digital imagery® © 2003 PhotoDisc, Inc.; 6 (row 5, all), Digital imagery® © 2003 PhotoDisc, Inc.; 6 (row 6), Digital imagery® © 2003 PhotoDisc, Inc.; 7 (tl), Clay Myers/The Wildlife Collection; 7 (tc), Leonard Lee Rue/FPG International; 7 (tr), Tim Laman/The Wildlife Collection; 7 (bl), Jack Swenson/The Wildlife Collection; 7 (bc), Tim Laman/The Wildlife Collection; 7 (br), Martin Harvey/The Wildlife Collection; 9 (tl, tc, tr), HRW Photo/Victoria Smith; 9 (c, cl, bl, bc), HRW Photo/Marty Granger/Edge Productions; 9 (cr), David Frazier Photolibrary; 9 (br), HRW Photo/Louis Boireau; 10, © David Stover/Pictor; 11 (both), HRW Photo/Victoria Smith.

LOCATION: POITIERS: 12-13 (all), HRW Photo/Marty Granger/Edge Productions; 14 (both), Tom Craig/FPG International; 15 (t, c, bl), HRW Photo/Marty Granger/Edge Productions; 15 (br), HRW Photo.

CHAPTER 1 16-17, HRW Photo/Marty Granger/Edge Productions; 18 (tr inset), HRW Photo/Louis Boireau/Edge Productions; 18 (remaining), HRW Photo/Marty Granger/Edge Productions; 19 (all), HRW Photo/Marty Granger/Edge Productions; 20 (all), HRW Photo/Marty Granger/Edge Productions; 21 (tc), HRW Photo/Sam Dudgeon; 21 (br), HRW Photo/Alan Oddie; 21 (remaining), HRW Photo/Marty Granger/Edge Productions; 22 (cl), HBJ Photo/Mark Antman; 22 (c), HRW photo; 22 (cr), HRW photo/John Langford 22; (l), HRW Photo/Marty Granger/Edge Productions; 22 (r), IPA/The Image Works; 23 (all), HRW Photo/Marty Granger/Edge Productions; 24, HRW Photo/Marty Granger/Edge Productions; 25, Toussaint/Sipa Press; 30 (all), HRW Photo/Marty Granger/Edge Productions; 34 (tl), HRW Photo/Sam Dudgeon; 34 (tc), HRW Photo/Marty Granger/Edge Productions; 34 (tr), Robert Brenner/PhotoEdit; 34 (cl), HRW Photo/David Frazier; 34 (c), HBJ Photo/Pierre Capretz; 34 (cr), Marc Antman/The Image Works; 34 (bl), Christine Galida/HRW Photo; 34 (bc), © Stephen Frisch/Stock Boston; 34 (br), © TRIP/ASK Images; 36 (t), Frank Siteman/The Picture Cube; 36 (tc), Richard Hutchings/PhotoEdit; 36 (bc), David C. Bitters/The Picture Cube; 36 (b), R. Lucas/The Image Works; 37 (t), HRW Photo/Russell Dian; 37 (tc), HRW Photo/May Polycarpe; 37 (bc), R. Lucas/The Image Works; 37 (b), © Arthur Tilley/FPG International; 41 (l), HRW Photo/Sam Dudgeon; 41 (r), HRW Photo/David Frazier; 42 (tr), © Telegraph Colour Library/FPG International; 42 (tl, tc, br), HRW Photo/Marty Granger/Edge Productions; 42 (bl), David Young-Wolff/PhotoEdit.

CHAPTER 2 46-47, © Owen Franken/Stock Boston; 48 (all), HRW Photo/Marty Granger/Edge Productions; 49 (br inset), ©1997 Radlund & Associates for Artville; 49 (remaining), HRW Photo/Marty Granger/Edge Productions; 56 (l), HRW Photo/Louis Boireau/Edge

Productions; 56 (remaining), HRW Photo/Marty Granger/Edge Productions.

CHAPTER 3 74-75, HRW Photo/Marty Granger/ Edge Productions; 76 (all), HRW Photo/Edge Productions; 77 (all), HRW Photo/Edge Productions; 79 (all), HRW Photo/Sam Dudgeon; 80, HRW Photo/Sam Dudgeon; 81 (r), HRW Photo/Eric Beggs; 81 (remaining), HRW Photo/Sam Dudgeon; 83 (l,c), HRW Photo/Marty Granger/ Edge Productions; 83 (r), HRW photo/Louis Boireau/Edge Productions; 86 (all), HRW Photo/Sam Dudgeon; 88, © European Communities; 89 (both), © European Communities; 92 (t), Digital imagery® © 2003 PhotoDisc, Inc.; (92 (t inset), Sam Dudgeon; 92 (ctr), HRW Photo; 92 (ctl), Digital imagery® © 2003 PhotoDisc, Inc.; 92 (cbr), Digital imagery® © 2003 PhotoDisc, Inc.; 92 (b), Artville, LLC; 92 (cbl), HRW Photo; 93 (bc), Digital imagery® © 2003 PhotoDisc, Inc.; 93 (remaining), HRW Photo; 95 (both), HRW Photo/Sam Dudgeon; 100 (all), HRW Photo/Sam Dudgeon.

LOCATION: QUEBEC 102-103, J. A. Kraulis/Masterfile; 104 (t, c, bl), HRW Photo/Marty Granger/Edge Productions; 104 (br), Wolfgang Kaehler; 105 (t), HRW Photo/ Marty Granger/Edge Productions; 105 (bl), HRW Photo/Marty Granger/Edge Productions; 105 (br), HRW Photo/Marty Granger/Edge Productions; 105 (cl), Hervey Smyth, Vue de la Prise de Québec, le 13 septembre 1759, Engraving, 35.9 x 47.8 cm, Musée du Québec, 78.375, Photo by Jean-Guy Kérouac.; 105 (cr), HRW Photo/Marty Granger/Edge Productions.

CHAPTER 4 106-107, HRW Photo/Marty Granger/ Edge Productions; 108 (c), HRW Photo/Marty Granger/ Edge Productions; 109 (all), HRW Photo/Marty Granger/Edge Productions; 111 (all), HRW Photo/Marty Granger/Edge Productions; 112 (tl), HRW Photo/ Marty Granger/Edge Productions; 112 (tc), David Young-Wolff/PhotoEdit; 112 (tr), HRW Photo/Sam Dudgeon; 112 (cl), Bill Bachmann/PhotoEdit; 112 (c, cr, bc, HRW Photo/Marty Granger/Edge Productions; 112 (bl), David Lissy/Leo de Wys; 112 (br), HRW Photo; 114 (tl, tc), HRW Photo/Victoria Smith; 114 (tr), © 2000 Robert Fried; 117 (l), Robert Fried Photography; 117 (cl, r), HRW Photo/ Sam Dudgeon; 117 (c), HBJ Photo/May Polycarpe; 117 (cr), HRW Photo/Marty Granger/Edge Productions; 120 (tl), © Telegraph Colour Library/FPG International; 120 (tc), Dean Abramson/Stock Boston; 120 (tr), Corbis Images; 120 (remaining), © Bill Stanton/International Stock Photography; 121 (l), HRW photo/Louis Boireau/ Edge Productions; 121 (c, r), HRW Photo/Marty Granger/ Edge Productions; 128, HRW Photo; 129, HRW Photo/ Marty Granger/Edge Productions; 131, HRW Photo/ Marty Granger/Edge Productions.

LOCATION: PARIS 136-137, Paul Steel/The Stock Market; 138 (all), HRW Photo/Marty Granger/Edge Productions; 139 (tr), Bob Handelman/ STONE; 139 (tl, br), HRW Photo/Marty Granger/Edge Productions; 139 (bl), Peter Menzel/Stock Boston.

CHAPTER 5 140-141, © Hilary Wilkes/International Stock Photography; 142 (all), HRW Photo/Edge Productions; 143 (all), HRW Photo/Edge Productions; 147 (drinks br), Digital imagery® ©2003 PhotoDisc, Inc.; 147 (remaining), HRW Photo/Victoria Smith; 150 (l, c), HRW Photo/Marty Granger/Edge Productions; 150 (r), HRW Photo/Louis Boireau/Edge Productions; 152 (both), HRW Photo/Sam Dudgeon; 154 (cr), HRW Photo/Michelle Bridwell; 154 (remaining), HRW Photo/Sam Dudgeon; 159 (t, b), Pomme de Pain; 159 (c), Steven Mark Needham/ Envision; 160, © Telegraph Colour Library/FPG International.

CHAPTER 6 168-169, © Owen Franken/CORBIS; 170 (cr), Sebastien Raymond/Sipa Press; 170 (remaining), HRW Photo/Marty Granger/Edge Productions; 171 (cr), Corbis Images; 171 (remaining), HRW Photo/Marty Granger/ Edge Productions; 172, Corbis Images; 172 (inset), HRW Photo/Marty Granger/Edge Productions; 175 (tl, tc, tr, br), HRW Photo/Marty Granger/Edge Productions; 175 (bc), David R. Frazier Photolibrary; 175 (bl), HRW Photo/Sam Dudgeon; 176 (tr), Tabuteau/The Image Works; 176 (cl), Maratea/International Stock Photography; 176 (ccl), Greg Meadors/Stock Boston; 176 (bl), Robert Fried/Stock Boston; 176 (bcl), Courtesy Marion Bermondy; 176 (bcr), HBJ Photo/Mark Antman; 176 (br), R. Lucas/The Image Works; 176 (remaining), HRW Photo/Marty Granger/ Edge Productions; 178 (l), HRW Photo/Louis Boireau/ Edge Productions; 178 (c, r), HRW Photo/Marty Granger/ Edge Productions; 182 (tl), Creasource/Series/Picture Quest; 182 (tr), HRW Photo/Marty Granger/Edge Productions; 182 (b), Ulrike Welsch/PhotoEdit; 185, HRW Photo/Marty Granger/Edge Productions; 191 (all), HRW Photo/Marty Granger/Edge Productions; 192, HRW Photo/Dianne Schrader; 194 (tl), HRW Photo/Pierre Capretz; 194 (tr), SuperStock; 194 (b), HRW Photo/ Dianne Schrader.

CHAPTER 7 198-199, © Julio Donoso/Woodfin Camp & Associates; 200 (tl, tc, cl), HRW Photo/Marty Granger/ Edge Productions; 200 (tr), HRW Photo/Marty Granger/ Edge Productions; 200 (cr), HRW Photo/Russell Dian; 200 (b), HRW Photo; 200 (b inset), Digital imagery® ©2003 PhotoDisc, Inc.; 201 (tl, tr, c), HRW Photo; 201 (b), HRW Photo/Marty Granger/Edge Productions; 202 (l, cl), HRW Photo/Russell Dian; 202 (cr, r), HRW Photo; 203, HRW Photo/Russell Dian; 204 (Row 3 cl), HRW Photo/Marty Granger/Edge Productions; 204 (Row 4 cl), Courtesy Marion Bermondy; 204 (Row 4 cr), David Austen/Stock Boston; 204 (Row 4 r), John Lei/Stock Boston; 204 (remaining), HRW Photo; 205 (l), HRW Photo/Daniel Aubry; 205 (cl), David Young-Wolff/PhotoEdit; 205 (c), HRW Photo/May Polycarpe; 205 (cr), Tony Freeman/ PhotoEdit; 205 (r), HRW Photo/Sam Dudgeon; 209 (l),

Firooz Zahedi/The Kobal Collection/Paramount Studios; 209 (r), TM © 20th Century Fox Film Corp., 1992; 212 (all), HRW Photo/Marty Granger/Edge Productions; 216 (t, b), Walter Chandoha; 216 (c), HRW Photo; 217 (t, c), Walter Chandoha; 217 (b), Gerard Lacz/Peter Arnold, Inc.; 220, ©1999 Image Farm Inc.; 220 (inset), HRW Photo/Russell Dian; 221, ©1999 Image Farm Inc.; 221 (inset), HRW Photo/Russell Dian.

LOCATION: ABIDJAN 226-227, Betty Press/Panos Pictures; 228 (t, br), Nabil Zorkot; 228 (b), John Elk III/Bruce Coleman, Inc.; 229 (t), Nabil Zorkot; 229 (bl), M. & E. Bernheim/Woodfin Camp & Associates; 229 (br), Nabil Zorkot.

CHAPTER 8 230-231, HRW Photo/Edge Productions; 232 (all), HRW Photo/Edge Productions; 233 (all), HRW Photo/Edge Productions; 234 (c), HRW Photo/Sam Dudgeon ; 234 (remaining), HRW Photo; 237, Charles & Josette Lenars/CORBIS; 239 (l, r), HRW Photo/Marty Granger/Edge Productions; 239 (c), HRW photo/Edge Productions; 244 (all), HRW Photo; 245 (tl), HRW Photo/Lance Shriner; 245 (tr), HRW Photo; 245 (bl), HRW Photo/Sam Dudgeon; 245 (br), HRW Photo/Eric Beggs;. 252, HRW Photo.

LOCATION: ARLES 260-261, HRW Photo/Marty Granger/Edge Productions; 262 (tl), HRW Photo; 262 (tr), Erich Lessing/Art Resource; 262 (b), © Ruggero Vanni/CORBIS; 263 (br), HRW Photo/Marty Granger/ Edge Productions; 263 (bl), G. Carde/SuperStock; 263 (t), W. Gontscharoff/SuperStock.

CHAPTER 9 264-265, © Owen Franken/CORBIS; 266 (all), HRW Photo/Marty Grange/Edge Productions; 267 (all), HRW Photo/Marty Granger/Edge Productions; 268 (r), Ermakoff/The Image Works; 268 (remaining), HRW Photo/Marty Granger/Edge Productions; 269 (r), © Digital Vision; 269 (l), HRW Photo/John Langford; 270 (l), HRW Photo/Michael Young; 270 (r), HRW Photo/ Victoria Smith; 275 (tl), © Telegraph Colour Library/FPG International; 275 (tcl), HRW Photo/John Langford; 275 (tcr), © Digital Vision; 275 (tr), ©Esbin-Anderson/The Image Works; 275 (bl), Robert Fried; 275 (br), Anthony Redpath/The Stock Market; 278 (all), HRW Photo/Marty Granger/ Edge Productions; 284, © Marcel Scholing/Zefa; 287, HRW Photo/Marty Granger/Edge Productions.

CHAPTER 10 292-293, HRW Photo/Marty Granger/Edge Productions; 294 (all), HRW Photo/Marty Granger/ Edge Productions; 295 (all), HRW Photo/Marty Granger/Edge Productions; 296 (all), HRW Photo/ Marty Granger/Edge Productions; 302, HRW Photo/Michelle Bridwell; 305 (all), HRW Photo/Marty Granger/Edge Productions; 312 (all), HRW Photo/Sam Dudgeon; 313 (all), HRW Photo/Sam Dudgeon; 316, HRW Photo/Marty Granger/Edge Productions; 318, HRW Photo; 320 (both), HRW Photo/Sam Dudgeon.

CHAPTER 11 322-323, © Benelux Press/Leo de Wys; 324 (cl inset), HRW Photo/May Polycarpe; 324 (cr inset), HRW photo/Edge Productions; 324 (bl inset), David Florenz/Option Photo; 324 (remaining), HRW Photo/ Marty Granger/Edge Productions; 325 (all), HRW Photo/Marty Granger/Edge Productions; 326 (all), HRW Photo/Marty Granger/Edge Productions; 329, © Telegraph Colour Library/FPG International; 331 (tl), © Robert Frerck/Woodfin Camp & Associates; 331 (tc), Digital imagery® © 2003 PhotoDisc, Inc.; 331 (tr), CORBIS Images; 331 (bl), © E. Bordis/Leo de Wys, Inc.; 331 (bc), © IFA Bilderteam/Leo de Wys, Inc.; 331 (br), Digital imagery® © 2003 PhotoDisc, Inc.; 332 (l), HRW Photo/Edge Productions; 332 (c, r), HRW Photo/Marty Granger/Edge Productions; 333, © European Communities; 335, Pierre Jaques/FOC photo; 337 (l), HRW Photo/May Polycarpe; 337 (r), HRW Photo/Sam Dudgeon; 337 (bkgd), Digital imagery® © 2003 PhotoDisc, Inc.; 338 (tl), HRW Photo/Marty Granger/ Edge Productions; 338 (tr), Robert Fried/Stock Boston; 338 (bl), Francis De Richem/The Image Works; 338 (bc), Joachim Messer/Leo de Wys; 338 (br), J. Messerschmidt/ Leo de Wys; 342, J. Messerschmidt/Leo de Wys; 345 (l), HRW Photo/Marty Granger/Edge Productions; 345 (r), Corbis Images.

LOCATION: FORT-DE-FRANCE 350-353 (all), HRW Photo/Marty Granger/Edge Productions.

CHAPTER 12 354-355, HRW Photo/Marty Granger/ Edge Productions; 354 (l inset), HRW Photo/Victoria Smith; 356 (all), HRW Photo/Marty Granger/Edge Productions; 357 (all), HRW Photo/Marty Granger/ Edge Productions; 358 (all), HRW Photo/Marty Granger/ Edge Productions; 359 (tl), HRW Photo; 359(tc, tr, bl, br), HRW Photo/Marty Granger/ Edge Productions; 359 (cl), HBJ Photo/Patrick Courtault; 359 (c), HBJ Photo/Pierre Capretz; 359 (cr), IPA/The Image Works; 359 (bc), Robert Fried/Stock Boston; 362 (tl, bc), Chris Huxley/Leo de Wys; 362 (tc, tr, bl), HRW Photo/Marty Granger/Edge Productions; 362 (br), HRW Photo; 365 (tl), HRW Photo/Helen Kolda; 365 (tc), © AFP/CORBIS; 365 (tr), HRW Photo/Sam Dudgeon (by F. Johan and N. Vogel ©Casterman); 365 (bl, br), HRW Photo/Sam Dudgeon; 365 (bc),HRW Photo/Russell Dian; 366 (tl), Elizabeth Zuckerman/PhotoEdit; 366 (tc, cl, cr), HRW Photo/Marty Granger/Edge Productions; 366 (tr), Amy Etra/PhotoEdit; 366 (c), HRW Photo/Louis Boireau; 366 (bl), Robert Rathe/Stock Boston; 366 (bc), Dean Abramson/Stock Boston; 366 (br), Marc Antman/The Image Works; 368 (all), HRW Photo/Marty Granger/Edge Productions; 372 (l), HRW Photo/Marty Granger/Edge Productions; 372 (r), Chris Huxley/Leo de Wys; 376 (bl), David R. Frazier Photolibrary; 376 (remaining), HRW Photo/Marty Granger/Edge Productions; 380 (cr), Chris Huxley/Leo de

Wys; 380 (remaining), HRW Photo/Marty Granger/Edge Productions.

ADDITIONAL VOCABULARY R9 (tl, bl), HRW Photo/Sam Dudgeon; R9 (br, br inset), Digital imagery® ©2003 PhotoDisc, Inc.; R9 (tr 1 and 2), Digital imagery® © 2003 PhotoDisc, Inc.; R9 (tr 3 and 4), HRW Photo/Sam Dudgeon; R10 (cr), HRW Photo/Russell Dian; R10 (remaining), Digital imagery® © 2003 PhotoDisc, Inc.; R11 (tl, bl), Corbis Images; R11 (tr), HRW Photo/Michelle Bridwell; R11 (cl), HRW Photo/Sam Dudgeon; R11 (cr, bc, br), Digital imagery® © 2003 PhotoDisc, Inc.; R12 (t), Corbis Images; R12 (bl, br), Digital imagery® © 2003 PhotoDisc, Inc.; R13 (cr), © Digital Vision; R13 (remaining), Digital imagery® © 2003 PhotoDisc, Inc.; R14 (tl, bl, bc), Digital imagery® © 2003 PhotoDisc, Inc.; R14 (tr), Corbis Images; R14 (br), EyeWire, Inc. Image Club Graphics ©1997 Adobe Systems, Inc.

ILLUSTRATION AND CARTOGRAPHY CREDITS

Abbreviations used: (t) top, (b) bottom, (l) left, (r) right, (c) center.

All art, unless otherwise noted, by Holt, Rinehart & Winston.

PRELIMINARY CHAPTER: Page xxiii, GeoSystems; xxiv, GeoSystems; xxv, GeoSystems; 6, Bruce Roberts; 9, Ellen Beier; 11, Jocelyne Bouchard.

LOCATION: POITIERS

Chapter One: Page 12, MapQuest.com; 22, Vincent Rio; 23, Jocelyne Bouchard; 26, Jocelyne Bouchard; 27, Yves Larvor; 28, Camille Meyer; 29, Yves Larvor; 30, MapQuest.com; 31, Yves Larvor; 33, Vincent Rio; 49, Yves Larvor. **Chapter Two:** Page 51, Yves Larvor; 52 (t), Bruce Roberts; 52 (b), Brian Stevens; 54, Bruce Roberts; 56, Pascal Garnier; 58, Keith Petrus; 59, Guy Maestracci; 60, MapQuest.com; 62, Brian Stevens; 72, Bruce Roberts. **Chapter Three:** Page 79, Yves Larvor; 80, Vincent Rio; 81, Michel Loppé; 82, Brian Stevens; 83, MapQuest.com; 84, Brian Stevens; 87, Vincent Rio; 89, Michel Loppé; 90, Jean-Pierre Foissy; 91, Michel Loppé; 94, Brian Stevens; 100, Bruce Roberts.

LOCATION: QUEBEC

Chapter Four: Page 102, MapQuest.com; 113, Michel Loppé; 115, Yves Larvor; 117, Jocelyne Bouchard; 118, Brian Stevens; 119, Jocelyne Bouchard; 120, MapQuest.com; 134, Jocelyne Bouchard.

LOCATION: PARIS

Chapter Five: Page 136, MapQuest.com; 145, Andrew Bylo; 146, Vincent Rio; 147, Jocelyne Bouchard; 148, Vincent Rio; 149, Camille Meyer; 150, MapQuest.com; 155, Guy Maestracci; 156, Jean-Pierre Foissy; 161, Vincent Rio; 166, Yves Larvor. **Chapter Six:** Page 174, Jocelyne Bouchard; 177 (t), Yves Larvor; 177 (c), Guy Maestracci; 178, MapQuest.com; 179, Jean-Pierre Foissy; 180, Brian Stevens; 181, Jean-Pierre Foissy; 183, Jean-Pierre Foissy; 184, Jocelyne Bouchard; 193, Guy Maestracci; 196 (t), Jocelyne Bouchard, 196 (b), Guy Maestracci. **Chapter Seven:** Page 203, Vincent Rio; 206 (cr), Guy Maestracci; 206 (b), Jocelyne Bouchard; 207, Vincent Rio; 208, Pascal Garnier; 209, Brian Stevens; 210, Jean-Pierre Foissy; 211, Vincent Rio; 212, MapQuest.com; 213 (tr), Pascal Garnier; 213 (br), Guy Maestracci; 214 (t), Vincent Rio; 214 (b), Pascal Garnier; 218, Jocelyn Bouchard; 223, Guy Maestracci; 224, Pascal Garnier.

LOCATION: ABIDJAN

Chapter Eight: Page 226, MapQuest.com; 235, Yves Larvor; 236, Camille Meyer; 237, George Kimani; 239, MapQuest.com; 240, Andrew Bylo; 242, Yves Larvor; 246 (t), Michel Loppé; 246 (b), Jocelyne Bouchard; 247, Michel Loppé; 248 (bl), George Kimani; 248 (tr), Jocelyne Bouchard; 254, George Kimani; 255, Yves Larvor; 258, Yves Larvor.

LOCATION: ARLES

Chapter Nine: Page 260, MapQuest.com; 269, Jean-Pierre Foissy; 271, Camille Meyer; 273, Guy Maestracci; 272, Jocelyne Bouchard; 278, MapQuest.com; 280, Brian Stevens; 285, Vincent Rio; 290, Jocelyne Bouchard. **Chapter Ten:** Page 297, Jocelyne Bouchard; 298 (c), Michel Loppé; 298 (t), Yves Larvor; 299, Vincent Rio; 300, Jean-Pierre Foissy; 305, MapQuest.com; 306, Jean-Pierre Foissy; 268 (t), Brian Stevens; 268 (c), Jocelyne Bouchard; 270, Jean-Pierre Foissy; 307, Michel Loppé; 308, Guy Maestracci; 310, Jean-Pierre Foissy; 320, Yves Larvor. **Chapter Eleven:** Page 327 (c), Brian Stevens; 327 (b), Russell Moore; 328, Guy Maestracci; 332, MapQuest.com; 333, Michel Loppé; 334, Yves Larvor; 336, Jean-Pierre Foissy; 343, Bruce Roberts; 344, Yves Larvor; 354, Yves Larvor.

LOCATION: FORT-DE-FRANCE

Chapter Twelve: Page 350, MapQuest.com; 361, Anne de Masson; 363, Anne de Masson; 364, Jean-Pierre Foissy; 366, Brian Stevens; 367, MapQuest.com; 369, Anne Stanley; 370, Anne de Masson; 371, Anne de Masson; 372, Anne Stanley; 377, Yves Larvor; 379, Anne Stanley; 380, Anne de Masson; 381, Anne de Masson; 382, Anne de Masson.